ECONOMICS

NINTH EDITION

ECONOMICS

PARKIN   POWELL   MATTHEWS

EUROPEAN EDITION   MyEconLab

PEARSON

Harlow, England • London • New York • Boston • San Francisco • Toronto • Sydney • Auckland • Singapore • Hong Kong
Tokyo • Seoul • Taipei • New Delhi • Cape Town • São Paulo • Mexico City • Madrid • Amsterdam • Munich • Paris • Milan

PEARSON EDUCATION LIMITED
Edinburgh Gate
Harlow CM20 2JE
United Kingdom
Tel: +44 (0)1279 623623
Web: www.pearson.com/uk

This edition published by Pearson Education Limited 2014

© Pearson Education Limited 2000, 2003, 2005, 2008, 2012, 2014 (print)
© Pearson Education Limited 2014 (print and electronic)

Pearson Education is not responsible for the content of third-party Internet sites.

The Financial Times. With a worldwide network of highly respected journalists, *The Financial Times* provides global business news, insightful opinion and expert analysis of business, finance and politics. With over 500 journalists reporting from 50 countries worldwide, our in-depth coverage of international news is objectively reported and analysed from an independent, global perspective. To find out more, visit www.ft.com/pearsonoffer.

ISBN: 978-1-292-00945-2 (print)
        978-1-292-00951-3 (PDF)
        978-1-292-00953-7 (eText)

British Library Cataloguing-in-Publication Data
A catalogue record for the print edition is available from the British Library

10 9 8 7 6 5 4 3 2
18 17 16 15 14

Print edition typeset in 10/12.5pt Times LT Std by 35
Print edition printed and bound by L.E.G.O. S.p.A., Italy

NOTE THAT ANY PAGE CROSS REFERENCES REFER TO THE PRINT EDITION

NINTH EDITION

ECONOMICS

PARKIN   POWELL   MATTHEWS

EUROPEAN EDITION

ALWAYS LEARNING

PEARSON

To Our Students

About the Authors

Michael Parkin is Professor Emeritus in the Department of Economics at the University of Western Ontario, Canada, where he teaches the principles course to around 900 students each year. He studied economics at the University of Leicester but received his real training in the subject from an extraordinary group of economists at the University of Essex during the early 1970s. Professor Parkin has held faculty appointments at the Universities of Sheffield, Leicester, Essex and Manchester and visiting appointments at Brown University, Bond University, the Reserve Bank of Australia and the Bank of Japan. He is a past president of the Canadian Economics Association and has served on the editorial boards of the *American Economic Review* and the *Journal of Monetary Economics* and as managing editor of the *Manchester School* and the *Canadian Journal of Economics*. Professor Parkin's economic research has resulted in over 160 publications in journals and edited volumes, including the *American Economic Review*, the *Journal of Political Economy*, the *Review of Economic Studies*, the *Economic Journal*, *Economica*, the *Manchester School*, the *Journal of Monetary Economics* and the *Journal of Money, Credit and Banking*, and edited volumes. He became visible to the public through his work on inflation that discredited the use of prices and incomes policies.

Melanie Powell took her first degree at Kingston University and her MSc in economics at Birkbeck College, University of London. She has been a research fellow in health economics at York University, a principal lecturer in economics at Leeds Metropolitan University, and the director of economic studies and part-time MBAs at the Leeds University Business School. She is now a Reader at the University of Derby, Derbyshire Business School. Her main interests as a microeconomist are in applied welfare economics, and she has many publications in the area of health economics and decision making. Her current research uses the experimental techniques of psychology applied to economic decision making.

Kent Matthews received his training as an economist at the London School of Economics, Birkbeck College University of London and the University of Liverpool. He is currently the Sir Julian Hodge Professor of Banking and Finance at the Cardiff Business School. He has held research appointments at the London School of Economics, the National Institute of Economic and Social Research, the Bank of England and Lombard Street Research Ltd, and faculty positions at the Universities of Liverpool, Western Ontario, Leuven, Liverpool John Moores and Humboldt Berlin. He is the author of eight books and over 60 papers in scholarly journals and edited volumes. His research interest is in applied macroeconomics and the economics of banking.

Brief Contents

Alternative Pathways through the Micro Chapters

Micro Flexibility

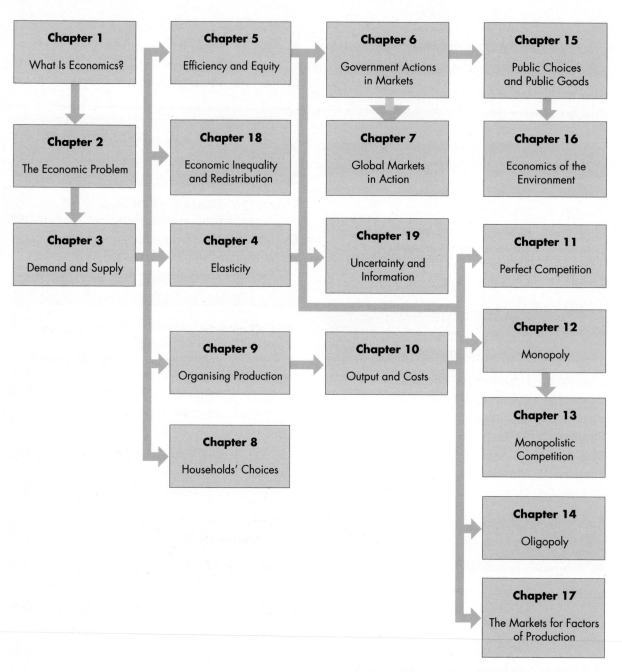

Chapter 1
What Is Economics?

Chapter 5
Efficiency and Equity

Chapter 6
Government Actions in Markets

Chapter 15
Public Choices and Public Goods

Chapter 2
The Economic Problem

Chapter 18
Economic Inequality and Redistribution

Chapter 7
Global Markets in Action

Chapter 16
Economics of the Environment

Chapter 3
Demand and Supply

Chapter 4
Elasticity

Chapter 19
Uncertainty and Information

Chapter 11
Perfect Competition

Chapter 9
Organising Production

Chapter 10
Output and Costs

Chapter 12
Monopoly

Chapter 8
Households' Choices

Chapter 13
Monopolistic Competition

Chapter 14
Oligopoly

Chapter 17
The Markets for Factors of Production

Start here ...

... then jump to any of these ...

... and jump to any of these after doing the pre-requisites indicated

Alternative Pathways through the Macro Chapters

Macro Flexibility

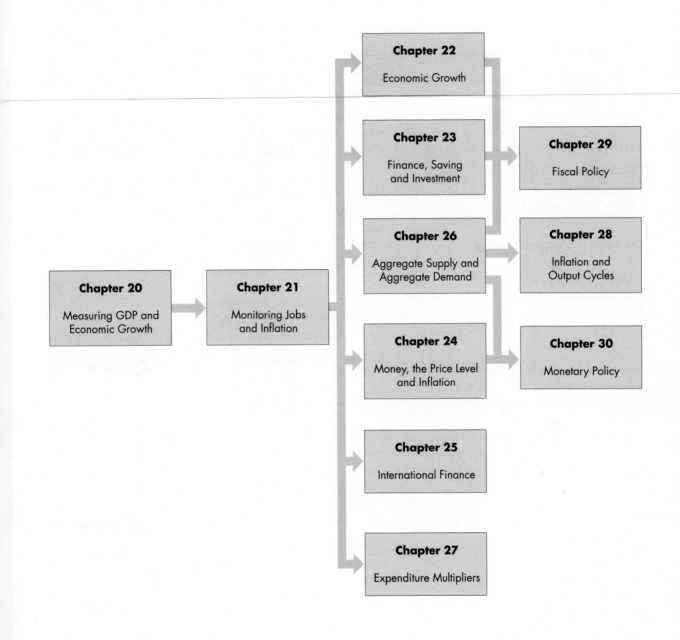

Start here …   … then jump to   … and jump to any of these after
                      any of these …   doing the pre-requisites indicated

Contents

◆ Part 2 How Markets Work

Part 6 Monitoring Macroeconomic Performance

Part 7 Macroeconomic Trends

Part 8 Macroeconomic Fluctuations

Guided Tour for Students

Setting the Scene

Chapter Openers motivate the topic and set the scene. We carry the introductory story into the main body of the chapter and return to it in *Reading Between the Lines* at the end of the chapter.

Objectives enable you to see exactly where the chapter is going and to set your goals before you begin the chapter. We link these goals directly to the chapter's major headings.

1 What Is Economics?

After studying this chapter you will be able to:

◆ Define economics and distinguish between microeconomics and macroeconomics

◆ Explain the big questions of economics

◆ Explain the key ideas that define the economic way of thinking

◆ Describe how economists go about their work as social scientists and policy advisers

Is economics about money: How people make money and spend it? Is economics about business, government, and jobs? Is it about why some people are rich and others are poor? Economics is about all these things, but its core is the study of choices and their consequences.

Your life will be shaped by the choices that you make and the challenges that you face. To face those challenges and seize the opportunities they present, you must understand the powerful forces at play. The economics that you're about to learn will become your most reliable guide. In this chapter, you'll find out about the questions economists ask, the way they think, and the way they search for answers.

1

Using the Study Tools

Highlighted **Key Terms** within the text simplify your task of learning the vocabulary of economics. Each term appears in a list of **Key Terms** at the end of the chapter and in the **Glossary** at the end of the book. The terms are also highlighted in the index and can be found online in the MyEconLab glossary and Flashcards.

Some examples of microeconomic questions are: Why are people downloading more music? How would a tax on downloading music affect the sales of DVDs?

Macroeconomics is the study of the performance of the national economy and the global economy. Some examples of macroeconomic questions are: Why is UK

Cooperative equilibrium The outcome of a game in which the players make and share the monopoly profit. (p. 330)

Cost-push inflation An inflation that results from an initial increase in costs. (p. 670)

Crawling peg An exchange rate that

Key Terms

Benefit, 10
Capital, 4
Economic model, 12
Economics, 2
Efficiency, 5
Entrepreneurship, 4
Factors of production, 3
Goods and services, 3
Human capital, 3
Incentive, 2
Interest, 4

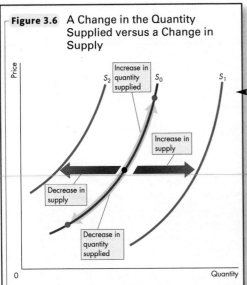

Figure 3.6 A Change in the Quantity Supplied versus a Change in Supply

When the price of the good changes, there is a movement along the supply curve and a change in the quantity supplied, shown by the blue arrows on supply curve S_0.

When any other influence on selling plans changes, there is a shift of the supply curve and a change in supply. An increase in supply shifts the supply curve rightward (from S_0 to S_1), and a decrease in supply shifts the supply curve leftward (from S_0 to S_2).

MyEconLab Animation

Diagrams show where the economic action is! Graphical analysis is the most powerful tool available for teaching and learning economics. We have developed the diagrams with the study and review needs of students in mind. Our diagrams feature:

◆ Original curves consistently shown in blue
◆ Shifted curves consistently shown in red
◆ Colour-blended arrows to suggest movement
◆ Other important features highlighted in red
◆ Graphs often paired with data tables
◆ Graphs labelled with boxed notes
◆ Extended captions that make each diagram and its caption a self-contained object for study and review
◆ Every diagram can be found with a step-by-step animation in MyEconLab.

A **Review Quiz** at the end of every major section is tied to the chapter's learning objectives and enables you to go over the material again to reinforce your understanding of a topic before moving on. These questions with instant feedback, as well as more practice on the topics can be found in the **MyEconLab Study Plan**.

 REVIEW QUIZ

1 What is the equilibrium price of a good or service?
2 Over what range of prices does a shortage arise? What happens to the price when there is a shortage?
3 Over what range of prices does a surplus arise? What happens to the price when there is a surplus?
4 Why is the price at which the quantity demanded equals the quantity supplied the equilibrium price?
5 Why is the equilibrium price the best deal available for both buyers and sellers?

Do these questions in Study Plan 3.4 and get instant feedback.   MyEconLab

Connecting with Reality

***Economics in Action* Boxes** show you the connections between theory and real-world data or events. Tables and figures put the real-world flesh on the bones of the models and help you learn how to apply your newly gained knowledge of economic principles to the economic world around you.

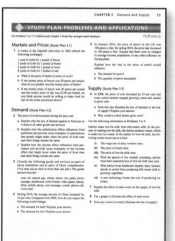

Reading Between the Lines

This Parkin, Powell and Matthews hallmark helps students think like economists by connecting chapter tools and concepts to the world around them. At the end of each chapter in *Reading Between the Lines*, students apply the tools they have just learned by analysing an article from a newspaper or news website. Each article sheds additional light on the questions first raised in the Chapter Opener. Questions about the article also appear with the end-of-chapter problems and applications.

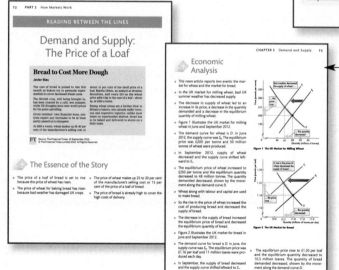

Each chapter closes with a concise **Summary** organised by major topics, a list of **Key Terms** (with page references), **Study Plan Problems and Applications** and **Additional Problems and Applications**. All Study Plan problems are available in MyEconLab with instant feedback. All Additional problems are available in MyEconLab if assigned by your lecturer.

Using MyEconLab

Use the power of MyEconLab to accelerate your learning. You need both an access card and a course ID to access MyEconLab:

1   Is your lecturer using MyEconLab? ***Ask your lecturer*** for your course ID

2   Has an access card been included with the book? ***Check the inside back cover of the book***.

3   If you have a course ID but no access card, ***go to: http://www.myeconlab.com/ to buy access*** to this interactive study programme.

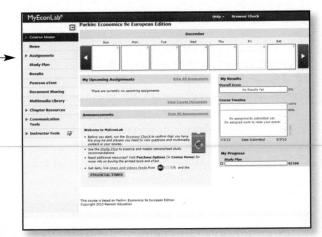

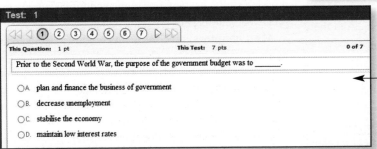

Sample Tests (two for each chapter) are preloaded in MyEconLab and enable you to test your understanding and identify the areas in which you need to do further work. Your lecturer might also create custom tests or quizzes.

MyEconLab creates a personal **Study Plan** for you based on your performance on the sample tests. The Study Plan diagnoses weaknesses and consists of a series of additional exercises with detailed feedback and 'Help Me Solve This' explanations for topics in which you need further help. The Study Plan is also linked to other study tools.

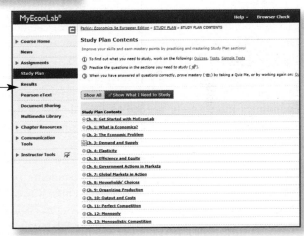

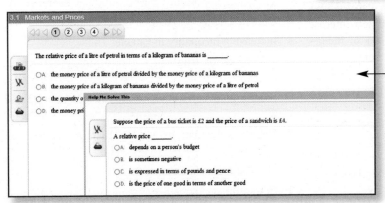

From the Study Plan exercises, you can link to **Help Me Solve This** (step-by-step explanations) and an **electronic version of your textbook** with all the **figures animated**.

Preface

The future is always uncertain. But at some times, and now is one of them, uncertainty is extreme. The major source of extreme uncertainty is economic policy. There is uncertainty about the way international trade policy will evolve as protectionism is returning to the political agenda. There is uncertainty about exchange rate policy as competitive devaluation rears its head. There is extraordinary uncertainty about monetary policy with the central banks having exploded the quantity of bank reserves and continuing to create more money in an attempt to stimulate their fragile economies. And there is uncertainty about fiscal policy as unprecedented deficits interact with ageing healthcare costs.

In the six years since the global financial crisis of August 2007 moved economics from the business report to the front page, justified fear has gripped producers, consumers, financial institutions and governments.

Even the *idea* that the market is an efficient mechanism for allocating scarce resources came into question as some political leaders trumpeted the end of capitalism and the dawn of a new economic order in which tighter regulation reigned in unfettered greed.

Rarely do teachers of economics have such a rich feast on which to draw. And rarely are the principles of economics more surely needed to provide the solid foundation on which to think about economic events and navigate the turbulence of economic life.

Although thinking like an economist can bring a clearer perspective to and deeper understanding of today's events, students don't find the economic way of thinking easy or natural.

Economics seeks to put clarity and understanding in the grasp of the student through its careful and vivid exploration of the tension between self-interest and the social interest, the role and power of incentives – of opportunity cost and marginal benefit – and by demonstrating the possibility that markets supplemented by other mechanisms might allocate resources efficiently.

Students who use this text thoughtfully not only do well in their course and get high marks. They also begin to think about issues the way economists do, and learn how to explore difficult policy problems and make more informed decisions in their own economic lives.

The Ninth Edition Revision

Thoroughly updated, this comprehensive revision builds on the solid foundation of the previous edition and retains its thorough and detailed presentation of the principles of economics, its emphasis on real-world examples and applications, its development of critical thinking skills, its diagrams renowned for pedagogy and precision, and its path-breaking technology.

Most chapters have been thoroughly reworked to achieve even greater clarity and to place greater emphasis on applications to current issues. Some sections of chapters have been removed and other sections added to cover new issues, particularly those that involve current policy problems.

Current issues organise each chapter. News stories about today's major economic events tie each chapter together, from new abbreviated chapter-opening vignettes to *Reading Between the Lines* and end-of-chapter problems and applications and online practice.

A new Economics in the News feature shows students how to use the economic toolkit to understand the events and issues they are confronted with in the media.

A second new At Issue feature shows two sides of a controversial issue and helps students to apply the economic way of thinking to clarify and debate the issues.

Among the many issues covered in one or more of the two new features described above are:

◆ Capitalism and its critics in Chapter 1

◆ The rising opportunity cost of food in Chapter 2

◆ Climate change and carbon tax in Chapter 16

◆ Increasing inequality in Chapter 18

◆ The Bank of England's extraordinary actions in Chapter 30

◆ Fragile recovery from recession in Chapters 22 and 29

◆ Currency fluctuations and the Yuan are covered in Chapter 22

◆ Fiscal stimulus in Chapter 29

◆ Extraordinary monetary stimulus in Chapter 30

Highpoints of the Revision

Most topics are well explained in the previous edition and are hard to improve on. So the highpoints of the current revision are the new *Economics in the News* and *At Issue* features. Nonetheless, three topics have been substantially revised. They are:

◆ Price discrimination

◆ Carbon emissions and climate change externalities

◆ Economic growth and business cycle expansion

Price Discrimination

The key insight we want our students to get about price discrimination is that it converts consumer surplus into producer surplus and economic profit. To strengthen this insight, we now begin with a brief explanation of the relationship between producer surplus and economic profit. We then use a carefully constructed model of two separated markets to show how discrimination between them can increase producer surplus.We build on this model to show how perfect price discrimination, if it were possible, would grab the entire consumer surplus and convert it to producer surplus.We illustrate the attempt to move towards perfect price discrimination with applications to Microsoft's pricing of Windows and Disneyland's pricing of tickets to its theme parks.

Carbon Emissions and Climate Change Externalities

What Nicholas Stern has called the greatest market failure and what some climate-change sceptics see as a problem that markets will eventually solve gets a thoroughly new treatment. We begin by contrasting the success story of local air quality in major cities with the unrelenting rise in atmospheric carbon concentration. We then explain the three methods of coping with environmental externalities: property rights, mandating the use of clean technologies and taxing or pricing emissions. We explore the ability of each method to achieve an efficient outcome. We also explore the special challenge that arises from the global rather than national scope of carbon emission.

Economic Growth and Business Cycle Expansion

In popular discussion, no distinction is made between the trend growth rate and the year-on-year growth rate associated with the phase of the cycle through which the economy is passing. We now introduce the topic of economic growth by explaining this distinction and illustrating it with the production possibilities frontier, expansion being a return to the *PPF* and growth being an outward shift of the *PPF*.

Economics in the News

Complementing *Economics in the News* questions, which have appeared weekly in MyEconLab and in end-of-chapter problems in previous editions, a series of new *Economics in the News* boxes help students to answer news-based questions (see an example below). The topics covered by these boxes are:

◆ The invisible hand and entrepreneurship at work

◆ The fragile global economy in 2013

◆ Rising global food costs

◆ Energy independence, cost and inefficiency

◆ The world markets for wheat and air shipments

◆ UK elasticities of demand for petrol and transport

◆ Trade war in solar panels

◆ The principal–agent problem at JPMorgan Chase

◆ Cost curves at the checkout line

◆ Record stores exit

◆ The falling cost of sequencing DNA

◆ Microsoft monopoly

◆ Airbus versus Boeing

◆ A bright future in the IT sector

◆ Are trades unions in the UK a spent force?

◆ Robots as skilled workers

◆ A massive open market operation (QE)

◆ Taxes and the global location of business

◆ Monetary stimulus not stimulating

ECONOMICS IN THE NEWS

The Opportunity Cost of Food

Cost of Global Food Up Again
The cost of global food has increased by 8 per cent since December 2011. All key food items cost more, except for rice. Asia's strong demand for food imports has contributed to this increase, notwithstanding bumper harvests.

Source: *Food Price Watch*, World Bank, April 2012

The Questions
◆ How does the *PPF* illustrate the effect of Asia's strong demand for food imports on the cost of food?
◆ How does the *PPF* illustrate the effect of a bumper harvest?

The Answers
◆ Figure 1 shows the global *PPF* for food and other goods and services.
◆ Before the bumper harvest, the *PPF* is PPF_0 and before Asia's strong demand for food, the world is producing at point A.
◆ Asia's strong demand for food brings an increase in food production and a decrease in the production of other goods and services, which is illustrated as a movement along the *PPF* from point A to point B.
◆ At point B, the *PPF* slope is steeper than at point A, which means that the opportunity cost of food is higher at point B than at point A.

◆ A bumper harvest increases the production of food at each level of production of other goods and services.
◆ The *PPF* illustrates the effects of a bumper harvest as an outward shift of the *PPF* from PPF_0 to PPF_1.
◆ The bumper harvest lowered the opportunity cost of food, but the news clip says that this effect was not sufficient to offset the rise in opportunity cost resulting from Asia's strong demand.

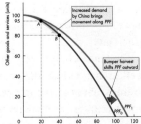

Figure 1 PPF for Food and Other Goods and Services

At Issue

Ten new *At Issue* boxes engage the student in debate and controversy. An At Issue box (see below) introduces an issue and then presents two opposing views. It leaves the matter unsettled so that the student and instructor can continue the argument in tutorials and reach their own conclusions.

The goal of *At Issue* is to motivate the student to think about the opposing arguments and to take a stand on the issues. The ten issues covered by this feature are:

◆ The protest against market capitalism

◆ Do we need a law against price gouging?

◆ Does the minimum wage cause unemployment?

◆ Is outsourcing bad or good for Europe?

◆ Can decentralisation and competition contain costs and maintain a high-quality National Health Service?

◆ Should we be doing more to reduce carbon emissions?

◆ Should GNNP replace GDP?

◆ No more too big to fail?

◆ How, whether and when to balance the goverment's budget

◆ Is the Bank of England's monetary policy stimulus just right, too tight or too loose?

Features to Enhance Teaching and Learning

The new features that we have just described are additions to an already powerful teaching and learning package. Here, we briefly review the features retained from the previous edition.

Reading Between the Lines

This Parkin, Powell and Matthews hallmark helps students think like economists by connecting chapter tools and concepts to the world around them. In *Reading Between the Lines*, which appears at the end of each chapter, students apply the tools they have just learned by analysing an article from a newspaper or news website. Each article sheds additional light on the questions first raised in the Chapter Opener. Questions about the article also appear with the end-of-chapter problems and applications.

READING BETWEEN THE LINES

The Rising Opportunity Cost of Food

The Telegraph, 5 October 2012

Biofuels and the Food That's Going Up in Smoke

Geoffery Lean

The growing use of energy from crops has driven up food prices. . . .

The EU stipulated in 2009 that biofuels should effectively provide 10 per cent of all transport fuels by 2020. . . .

As Lester Brown – president of Washington's Earth Policy Institute – has long pointed out, biofuels pit the hungry against relatively affluent motorists in competition for crops. . . .

Forty per cent of the US corn crop now goes for fuel, not food, while the land used to grow

biofuels for Europe alone could instead be used to feed 127 million people.

The competition drives up food prices. . . . Oxfam reported this week that an area of land eight times the size of the UK had been sold off over the past decade – and that two thirds of the deals appear to have been struck for the growing of biofuels. . . .

Now, finally, the EC is making a move. On October 17 . . . the EC climate commissioner, . . . will propose that biofuels from food crops should be limited to just 5 per cent of transport energy consumption.

Copyright © Telegraph Media Group Limited 2012. Reprinted with permission.

Economic Analysis

◆ Biofuel is made from maize and several other crops, so biofuel and food compete to use the same resources.

◆ Following 2009 EU policy targets, farmers increased the land devoted to growing biofuel crops.

35 After you have studied *Reading Between the Lines* on pp. 46–47, answer the following questions.

 a Why might the EU climate change policy increase EU production of maize?

 b Why would you expect an increase in the quantity of EU maize production to increase the opportunity cost of maize?

 c Why did the cost of producing maize increase in the rest of the world?

 d Is it possible that the increased quantity of maize produced, despite the higher cost of production, moves the EU closer to allocative efficiency?

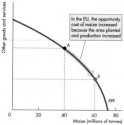

In the EU, the opportunity cost of maize increased because the area planted and production increased

Figure 1 EU PPF

AT ISSUE

Should We Be Doing More to Reduce Carbon Emissions?

Economists agree that tackling the global warming problem requires changes in the incentives that people face. The cost of carbon-emitting activities must rise and the cost of clean-energy technologies must fall.

Disagreement centres on *how* to change incentives. Should more countries set targets for cutting carbon emissions at a faster rate and introduce a carbon tax, emissions charges or cap-and-trade to cut emissions? Should clean energy research and development be subsidised?

Yes: The Stern Review

◆ Confronting emitters with a tax or price on carbon imposes low present costs for high future benefits.

◆ The cost of reducing greenhouse gas emissions to safe levels can be kept to 1 per cent of global income each year.

◆ The future benefits are incomes at least 5 per cent and possibly 20 per cent higher than they will be with inaction every year forever.

◆ Climate change is a global problem that requires an international coordinated response.

◆ Unlike most taxes, which bring deadweight loss, a carbon tax eliminates (or reduces) deadweight loss.

◆ Strong, deliberate policy action is required to change the incentives that emitters face.

◆ Policy actions should include:
1. Emissions limits and emissions trading
2. Increased subsidies for energy research and development, including the development of low-cost clean technology for generating electricity
3. Reduced deforestation and research into new drought and flood resilient crop varieties

No: The Copenhagen Consensus

◆ Confronting emitters with a tax or price on carbon imposes high present costs and low future benefits.

◆ Unless the entire world signs onto an emissions reduction programme, free riders will increase their emissions and carbon leakage will occur.

◆ A global emissions reduction programme and carbon tax would lower living standards in the rich countries and slow the growth rate of living standards in developing countries.

◆ Technology is already advancing and the cost of cleaner energy is falling.

◆ Fracking technology has vastly expanded the natural gas deposits that can be profitably exploited, and replacing coal with gas halves the carbon emissions from electricity generation.

◆ Free-market price signals will allocate resources to the development of new technologies that stop and eventually reverse the upward trend in greenhouse gases.

UK economist Nicholas Stern, principal author of *The Stern Review on the Economics of Climate Change*. Greenhouse gas emission is 'the greatest market failure the world has ever seen.' To avoid the risk of catastrophic climate change, the upward CO_2 trend must be stopped.

Bjørn Lomborg, President of the Copenhagen Consensus and author of *The Skeptical Environmentalist*. 'For little environmental benefit, we could end up sacrificing growth, jobs and opportunities for the big majority, especially in the developing world.'

Diagrams that Show the Action

Through the past eight editions, this book has set new standards of clarity in its diagrams; the ninth edition continues to uphold this tradition. Our goal has always been to show 'where the economic action is'. The diagrams in this book continue to generate an enormously positive response, which confirms our view that graphical analysis is the most powerful tool available for teaching and learning economics.

Because many students find graphs hard to use, we have developed the entire art programme with the study and review needs of the student in mind. The diagrams feature:

◆ Original curves consistently shown in blue
◆ Shifted curves, equilibrium points and other important features highlighted in red
◆ Colour-blended arrows to suggest movement
◆ Graphs paired with data tables
◆ Diagrams labelled with boxed notes
◆ Extended captions that make each diagram and its caption a self-contained object for study and review.

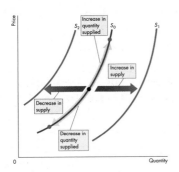

Economics in Action Boxes

This feature uses boxes within the chapter to address current events and economic occurrences that highlight and amplify the topics covered in the chapter. Instead of simply reporting the current events, the material in the boxes applies the event to an economics lesson, enabling students to see how economics plays a part in the world around them as they read through the chapter.

Some of the many issues covered in these boxes include the best affordable choice of recorded music, movies and DVDs, market entry and exit, how Apple doesn't make the iPhone, who in the UK are the rich and the poor, diversity of UK wage rates, loanable funds to kickstart the UK housing market, and the size of the fiscal stimulus multipliers.

Chapter Openers

Each chapter opens with a student-friendly vignette that raises questions to motivate the student and focus the chapter. This chapter-opening story is woven into the main body of the chapter and is explored in the *Reading Between the Lines* feature that ends each chapter.

Key Terms

Highlighted terms simplify the student's task of learning the vocabulary of economics. Each highlighted term appears in an end-of-chapter list with its page number, in an end-of-book glossary with its page number, bold-faced in the index, and in MyEconLab.

In-Text Review Quizzes

A review quiz at the end of each major section enables students to determine whether a topic needs further study before moving on. This feature includes a reference to the appropriate MyEconLab study plan to help students further test their understanding.

ECONOMICS IN ACTION

Best Affordable Choice of Cinema Films and DVD Rentals

Between 2008 and 2012, UK box-office receipts increased by 30 per cent while the average price of a cinema ticket increased by 17 per cent. So most of the rise in box-office receipts is because people went to the cinema more often.

Why is film-going booming? One answer is that some of today's films, such as the 47 3-D films released in 2011, are better viewed on the big screen than at home.

But there is another answer, and at first thought an unlikely one: events in the market for DVD rentals have affected cinema going.

Back in 2008, Blockbuster was booming and charging £4 per DVD film rental. But competition was getting tough. LoveFilm, a new company that had taken over Amazon's UK and German DVD rental business, offered online order and postal return. By 2010, LoveFilm had 1 million subscribers and 20 per cent of the market. LoveFilm now charges just over £1 per rental with monthly membership. You can also stream a film now for just £2. By January 2013, Blockbuster had closed 324 of its 528 stores and was bankrupt.

Figure 1 shows the effects of these events on the share of film revenue for different formats. Revenue from viewing films on TV, in cinemas and by streaming has risen, while revenue from viewing by rental or buying a DVD has fallen.

Easy access to cheap postal DVDs and streamed films transformed the market for film watching, and Figure 2 shows why.

A student has a budget of £40 a month to allocate to films. To keep the story clear, we'll suppose that it cost £8 to go to the cinema in both 2008 and 2012. The price of a DVD rental in 2008 was £4, so the student's budget line is the one that runs from 5 cinema films on the y-axis to 10 DVD rentals on the x-axis. The student's best affordable point is 2 cinema films and 6 rentals a month.

By 2012, the price of a rental falls to £1 a film but the price of a cinema ticket remains at £8. So the budget line

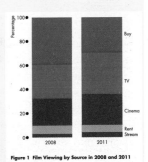

Figure 1 Film Viewing by Source in 2008 and 2011

Source of data: *BFI Statistical Yearbook, 2012*, The British Film Institute.

rotates outward. The student's best affordable point is now at 3 cinema films and 16 rentals a month. Our student is seeing more of both expensive cinema films and cheaper DVD rental films.

Looking ahead, streaming will take the place of rental with a similar effect.

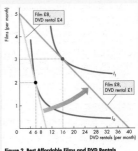

Figure 2 Best Affordable Films and DVD Rentals

REVIEW QUIZ

1 What is the equilibrium price of a good or service?
2 Over what range of prices does a shortage arise? What happens to the price when there is a shortage?
3 Over what range of prices does a surplus arise? What happens to the price when there is a surplus?
4 Why is the price at which the quantity demanded equals the quantity supplied the equilibrium price?
5 Why is the equilibrium price the best deal available for both buyers and sellers?

Do these questions in Study Plan 3.4 and get instant feedback.   MyEconLab

 For the Lecturer

This book enables you to focus on the economic way of thinking and choose your own course structure.

Focus on the Economic Way of Thinking

You know how hard it is to encourage a student to think like an economist, but that is your goal. Consistent with this goal, the text focuses on and repeatedly uses the central ideas: choice; trade-off; opportunity cost; the margin; incentives; the gains from voluntary exchange; the forces of demand, supply and equilibrium; the pursuit of economic rent; the tension between self-interest and the social interest; and the scope and limitations of government actions.

Choose Your Own Course Structure

You want to teach your own course. We have organised this book to enable you to do so. We demonstrate the book's flexibility in the flexibliity charts that show the alternative pathways through the micro and macro chapters on pp. viii–ix. By following the arrows through the charts you can select the path that best fits your preference for course structure. Whether you want to teach a traditional course that blends theory and policy, or one that takes a fast-track through either theory or policy issues, *Economics* gives you the choice.

Lecturer's Support Tools

The Ninth Edition has the following support tools:

◆ Lecturer's manual
◆ Test banks
◆ PowerPoint resources
◆ MyEconLab

Lecturer's Manual

Nicola Lynch and Eugen Michaels of the University of Derby have created a Lecturer's Manual. Each chapter contains an outline, what's new in the Ninth Edition, teaching suggestions, a look at where we have been and where we are going, a description of the electronic supplements and additional discussion questions.

Test Banks

Nicola Lynch and Eugen Michaels of the University of Derby have reviewed and edited all our Test Bank questions and created many new questions to ensure their clarity and consistency with the Ninth Edition.

An electronic Test Bank provides 3,500 multiple-choice questions. This Test Bank is available in Test Generator Software (TestGen with QuizMaster). Fully networkable, it is available for Windows and Macintosh. TestGen's graphical interface enables lecturers to view, edit and add questions; transfer questions to tests; and print different forms of tests. Tests can be formatted with varying fonts and styles, margins and headers and footers, as in any word-processing document. Search and sort features let the lecturer quickly locate questions and arrange them in a preferred order. QuizMaster, working with your university's computer network, automatically marks the exams, stores the results on disk and allows the lecturer to view or print a variety of reports.

A pdf Test Bank provides a further 1,500 true/false and numerical questions.

Both Test Banks are available online to download from **www.myeconlab.com**.

PowerPoint Resources

Robin Bade has developed a Microsoft PowerPoint Lecture Presentation for each chapter that includes all the figures from the text, animated graphs and speaking notes. The lecture notes in the Lecturer's Manual and the slide outlines are correlated, and the speaking notes are based on the Lecturer's Manual Teaching suggestions.

The PowerPoint resources also include a separate set of files that contain large-scale versions of all the text's figures (most of them animated). Use these to make your own presentations. PowerPoint slides are available for Macintosh and Windows.

MyEconLab

MyEconLab works hand-in-hand with *Economics*. Michael Parkin and Robin Bade, assisted by Jeannie Gillmore, Laurel Davies and Sharmistha Nag, have authored and overseen all of the MyEconLab content for *Economics*. Our team has worked hard to ensure that the Parkin, Powell and Matthews MyEconLab is tightly integrated with the book's content and vision.

With comprehensive homework, quiz, test and tutorial options, lecturers can manage all assessment needs in one programme.

- All of the Review Quiz questions and end-of-chapter Problems and Applications are assignable and automatically graded in MyEconLab.

- All the Review Quiz questions and end-of-chapter Study Plan Problems and Applications are available for students to work in Study Plan.

- None of the end-of-chapter Additional Problems and Applications are available to students in MyEconLab unless assigned by the instructor.

- Many of the problems and applications are algorithmic, draw-graph and numerical exercises.

- Test Item File questions are available for assignment as MyEconLab quizzes, tests or homework.

- The Custom Exercise Builder enables instructors to create their own problems for assignment as test or homework questions.

- The powerful Gradebook records each student's performance and time spent on tests, the study plan and homework, and generates reports by student or by chapter.

 # For the Student

Two outstanding support tools for the student are:

- MyEconLab
- PowerPoint Notes

MyEconLab

Optimise your study time with MyEconLab, our online assessment and tutorial system. When you take a sample test online, MyEconLab gives you targeted feedback and a personalised Study Plan to identify the topics that you need to review.

The Study Plan consists of practice problems taken directly from the end-of-chapter Study Plan Problems and Applications and the Review Quiz in the textbook.

The Study Plan gives you unlimited opportunity to practise. And as you work each exercise, instant feedback helps you understand and apply the concepts. Many Study Plan exercises contain algorithmically generated values to ensure that you get as much practice as you need.

Study Plan exercises link to the following learning resources:

1. Step-by-step *Help Me Solve This* help you to break down a problem in much the same way as a lecturer would during a class. These are available for selected problems.

2. Links to the *Pearson e-Text* promote reading of the text when you need to revisit a concept or explanation.

3. *Animated graphs* appeal to a variety of learning styles.

4. A *graphing tool* enables you to build and manipulate graphs to better understand how concepts, numbers and graphs connect.

PowerPoint Notes

Robin Bade has prepared a set of Microsoft PowerPoint Notes for students. These notes contain an outline of each chapter with the textbook figures animated. Students can download these PowerPoint Notes from MyEconLab, print them, bring them to the lecture and use them to create their own set of study notes.

Acknowledgements

We extend our gratitude and thanks to the many people who have contributed to this new edition of our text and to all those who made such important contributions to the previous editions on which this one is based. So many people have provided help and encouragement, either directly or indirectly, that it is impossible to name them all.

We particularly thank our colleagues, present and past, who have helped to shape our understanding of economics and who have provided help in the creation of this new edition. We thank our reviewers who have read and commented on our work and provided countless good ideas that we have eagerly accepted. We also thank our families for their input and patience.

We especially acknowledge and express our deep gratitude to Robin Bade, whose innovative work on the most recent Canadian edition has been invaluable to us. We also thank Robin for her meticulous reading of this edition and for the uncountable, some detailed and some major, improvements she has brought to it.

We thank Richard Parkin for his work on the graphics, both in the text and on MyEconLab.

We thank Nicola Lynch and Eugen Michaels of the University of Derby for their work (with Melanie) on the Lecturer's Manual and the Test Banks.

We thank Jeannie Gillmore, Laurel Davies and Sharmistha Nag for their work on MyEconLab test questions.

We could not have produced this book without the help of the people for whom it is written, our students. We thank the several thousand students we have been privileged to teach over many years. Their comments on previous editions (and on our teaching), whether in complaint or praise, have been invaluable.

Nor could we have produced this book without the help of our publisher. We thank the many outstanding editors, media specialists, and others at Pearson Education who contributed to the concerted publishing effort that brought this edition to completion. They are: Kate Brewin, Publisher; Tim Parker, Production Editor; Sarah Turpie, Assistant Editor; Kevin Ancient, Design Manager; Nicola Woowat, Designer; Kay Holman, Production Editor; Rachel Childs, Media Editor; and Robert Cottee, Media Producer, who managed the development of the online resources.

Finally, we want to thank our reviewers. A good textbook is the distillation of the collective wisdom of a generation of dedicated teachers. We have been privileged to tap into this wisdom. We extend our thanks to Douglas Chalmers, Glasgow Caledonian University; Gary Cook, University of Liverpool; Steve Cook, Swansea University; Adrian Darnell, Durham University; Valerie Dickie, Heriot-Watt University; M. J. McCrostie, University of Buckingham; Maria Gil Molto, Loughborough University; Karen Jackson, University of Bradford; Gorm Jacobsen, Agder University, Norway; Melanie Jones, Swansea University; Chris Reid, University of Portsmouth; Kevin Reilly, Leeds University; Cillian Ryan, University of Birmingham; Jen Snowball, Rhodes University, South Africa; Phil Tomlinson, University of Bath; Gonzolo Varela, University of Sussex; and Robert Wright, Strathclyde University. We also thank other reviewers who have asked to remain anonymous.

As always, the proof of the pudding is in the eating! The value of this book will be decided by its users, and whether you are a student or a teacher, we encourage you to send us your comments and suggestions.

Michael Parkin
University of Western Ontario,
michael.parkin@uwo.ca

Melanie Powell
University of Derby,
m.j.powell@derby.ac.uk

Kent Matthews
Cardiff University,
MatthewsK@Cardiff.ac.uk

1 What Is Economics?

After studying this chapter you will be able to:

- ◆ Define economics and distinguish between microeconomics and macroeconomics
- ◆ Explain the big questions of economics
- ◆ Explain the key ideas that define the economic way of thinking
- ◆ Describe how economists go about their work as social scientists and policy advisers

Is economics about money: How people make money and spend it? Is economics about business, government, and jobs? Is it about why some people and some nations are rich and others are poor? Economics is about all these things, but its core is the *study of choices and their consequences*.

Your life will be shaped by the choices that you make and the challenges that you face. To face those challenges and seize the opportunities they present, you must understand the powerful forces at play. The economics that you're about to learn will become your most reliable guide. In this chapter, you'll find out about the questions economists ask, the way they think, and the way they search for answers.

A Definition of Economics

A fundamental fact dominates our lives: we want more than we can get. Our inability to get everything we want is called scarcity. **Scarcity** is universal. It confronts all living things. Even parrots face scarcity!

Not only do I want a cracker – we all want a cracker!

©Frank Modell/The New Yorker Collection/www.cartoonbank.com

Think about the things that you want and the scarcity that you face. You want to go to a good college or university. You want to live in a well-equipped, spacious and comfortable home. You want the latest smartphone and the fastest Internet connection for your laptop or iPad. You want some sports and recreational gear – perhaps some new running shoes, or a new bike. You want much more time than is available to go to seminars, do your class preparation, play sports and games, read novels, go to the movies, listen to music, travel and go out with your friends. You want to live a long and healthy life.

What you can afford to buy is limited by your income and by the prices you must pay, and your time is limited by the fact that your day has 24 hours. You want some other things that only governments provide.

You want to live in a safe neighbourhood in a peaceful and secure world and enjoy the benefits of clean air, lakes, rivers and oceans.

What governments can afford is limited by the taxes they collect. Taxes lower people's incomes and compete with the other things they want to buy. What everyone can get – what society can get – is limited by the productive resources available. These resources are the gifts of nature, human labour and ingenuity and all the previously produced tools and equipment.

Because we can't get everything we want, we must make *choices*. You can't afford *both* a laptop and an iPhone, so you must *choose* which one to buy. You can't spend tonight *both* studying for your next test *and* going to the cinema, so again, you must *choose* which one to do. Governments can't spend a pound of tax revenue on both national defence and environmental protection, so they must choose how to spend that pound.

Your choices must somehow be made consistent with the choices of *others*. If you choose to buy a laptop, someone else must choose to sell it. Incentives reconcile choices. An **incentive** is a reward that encourages or a penalty that discourages an action. If the price of a laptop is too high, more will be offered for sale than people want to buy. And if the price is too low, fewer will be offered for sale than people want to buy. But there is a price at which choices to buy and sell are consistent.

Economics is the social science that studies the *choices* that individuals, businesses, governments and entire societies make as they cope with *scarcity* and the *incentives* that influence and reconcile those choices.

The subject divides into two main parts:

◆ Microeconomics
◆ Macroeconomics

Microeconomics is the study of the choices that individuals and businesses make, the way these choices interact in markets and the influence of governments. Some examples of microeconomic questions are: Why are people downloading more music? How would a tax on downloading music affect the sales of DVDs?

Macroeconomics is the study of the performance of the national economy and the global economy. Some examples of macroeconomic questions are: Why is UK unemployment so high? Can the Bank of England bring prosperity by keeping interest rates low?

 ## REVIEW QUIZ

1 List some examples of scarcity that you face.
2 Find examples of scarcity in today's headlines.
3 Find an illustration of the distinction between microeconomics and macroeconomics in today's headlines.

Do these questions in Study Plan 1.1 and get instant feedback.   MyEconLab

Two Big Economic Questions

Two big questions summarise the scope of economics:

◆ How do choices end up determining *what*, *how* and *for whom* goods and services get produced?

◆ When do choices made in the pursuit of *self-interest* also promote the *social interest*?

What, How and For Whom?

Goods and services are the objects that people value and produce to satisfy wants. Goods are physical objects such as golf balls. Services are actions performed such as cutting hair and filling teeth. By far the largest part of what people in the rich industrial countries produce today is services such as retail and wholesale services, health services and education. Goods are a small and decreasing part of what we produce.

What?

What we produce changes over time. Every year, new technologies allow us to build better-equipped homes, higher-performance sporting equipment and even deliver a more pleasant experience in the dentist's chair. And technological advance makes us incredibly more productive at producing food and manufacturing goods.

Figure 1.1 shows some trends in what we produce in the UK. It highlights four items that have expanded and four that have shrunk since 2003. What are the forces that bring these changes in what we produce? Why are we producing more services such as health, education, finance and transport? Why are we producing fewer manufactured goods and doing less construction and mining?

How?

Goods and services get produced by using productive resources that economists call **factors of production**. Factors of production are grouped into four categories:

◆ Land
◆ Labour
◆ Capital
◆ Entrepreneurship

Land

The 'gifts of nature' that we use to produce goods and services are called **land**. In economics, land is what in

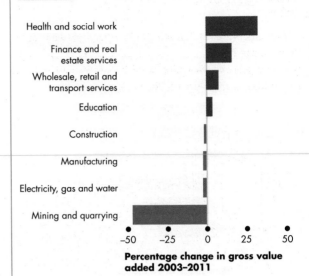

Figure 1.1 Changes in What We Produce

Percentage change in gross value added 2003–2011

The production of many services has expanded, while mining, manufacturing and construction have shrunk.

Source of data: Office for National Statistics, *Change in Gross Value Added by Industry*.

MyEconLab Animation

everyday language we call *natural resources*. It includes land in the everyday sense together with metal ores, oil, gas and coal, water, air, wind and sunshine.

Our land surface and water resources are renewable and some of our mineral resources can be recycled. But the resources that we use to create energy are non-renewable – they can be used only once.

Labour

The work time and work effort that people devote to producing goods and services is called **labour**. Labour includes the physical and the mental efforts of all the people who work on farms and construction sites and in factories, shops and offices.

The *quality* of labour depends on **human capital**, which is the knowledge and skill that people obtain from education, on-the-job training and work experience. You are building your own human capital today as you work on your economics course, and your human capital will continue to grow as you become better at your job.

Human capital expands over time and varies between countries. Figure 1.2 shows the proportion of young people entering post-secondary education and the growth in this measure since 2000 as a measure of human capital in different countries.

Figure 1.2   A Measure of Human Capital

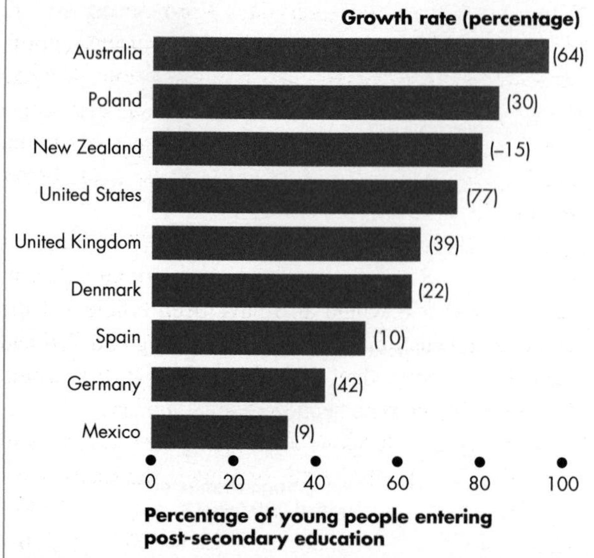

Percentage of young people entering post-secondary education

College and university education is a major source of human capital. The figure shows the percentage of young people entering post-secondary education in nine countries in 2010. Although Australia has the highest entry rate and Mexico the lowest, both countries have growth of human capital. The United States has the fastest growth rate and New Zealand has a falling rate.

Source of data: OECD, *Education at a Glance 2012* Table C2.2.

MyEconLab Animation

Capital

The tools, instruments, machines, buildings and other constructions that businesses now use to produce goods and services are called **capital**.

In everyday language, we talk about money, shares and bonds as being capital. These items are *financial capital*. Financial capital plays an important role in enabling businesses to borrow the funds that they use to buy capital. But financial capital is not used to produce goods and services – it is not a factor of production.

Entrepreneurship

The human resource that organises labour, land and capital is called **entrepreneurship**. Entrepreneurs come up with new ideas about what and how to produce, make business decisions and bear the risks that arise from these decisions.

How are the quantities of factors of production that get used to produce the many different goods and services determined?

For Whom?

Who gets the goods and services that are produced depends on the incomes that people earn. A large income enables a person to buy large quantities of goods and services. A small income leaves a person with few options and small quantities of goods and services.

People earn their incomes by selling the services of the factors of production they own:

1 Land earns **rent**.
2 Labour earns **wages**.
3 Capital earns **interest**.
4 Entrepreneurship earns **profit**.

Which factor of production earns the most income? The answer is labour. Wages and fringe benefits are around 70 per cent of total income. Land, capital and entrepreneurship share the rest. These percentages have been remarkably constant over time.

Knowing how income is shared among the factors of production doesn't tell us how it is shared among individuals. You know of lots of people who earn very large incomes. David Beckham earns £30 million a year in salary and endorsements, and Lady Gaga made £55 million in 2011.

You know of even more people who earn very small incomes. People who serve fast food earn £5 an hour.

Some differences in income are persistent. On average, men earn more than women and whites earn more than ethnic minorities. Europeans earn more on average than Asians, who in turn earn more than Africans. A typical annual income in the poorest countries of the world is just a few hundred pounds, less than the equivalent of a typical weekly wage in the richest countries of the world.

Why is the distribution of income so unequal? Why do women earn less than men? Why do David Beckham and Lady Gaga earn such huge incomes? Why do university graduates earn more than people with only a few GCSEs? Why do Europeans earn more than Africans? Why are the incomes of Asians rising so rapidly?

Economics provides answers to all these questions about what, how and for whom goods and services get produced. And you will discover these answers as you progress with your study of the subject.

The second big question of economics that we'll now examine is a harder question both to appreciate and to answer.

Does the Pursuit of Self-interest Unintentionally Promote the Social Interest?

Every day, you and 465 million other EU citizens, along with 7 billion people in the rest of the world, make economic choices that result in *what*, *how* and *for whom* goods and services get produced.

Self-Interest

A choice is in your **self-interest** if you think that choice is the best one available for you. You make most of your choices in your self-interest. All the choices that people make about how to use their time and other resources are made in the pursuit of self-interest. When you allocate your time or your budget, you might think about how your choices affect other people and take that into account, but it is how *you* feel that influences your choice. You order a home delivery pizza because you're hungry, not because the delivery person needs a job. When the delivery person shows up at your door, he's not doing you a favour. He's pursuing *his* self-interest.

The big question is: Is it possible that all the choices that each one of us makes in the pursuit of self-interest could end up achieving an outcome that is best for everyone?

Social Interest

An outcome is in the **social interest** if it leads to an outcome that is the best for society as a whole. It is easy to see how you decide what is in your self-interest. But how do you decide if something is in the social interest?

To help you answer this question, imagine a scene like the following: Ted, an entrepreneur, creates a new business. He hires a thousand workers and pays them £10 an hour, £1 an hour more than they earned in their old jobs. Ted's business is extremely profitable and his own earnings increase by $1 million per week. You can see that Ted's decision to create the business is in his self-interest – he gains £1 million a week. You can also see that the decisions to work for Ted are in the self-interest of the workers – they gain $1 an hour (say £40 a week). And the decisions of Ted's customers must be in their self-interest otherwise they wouldn't buy from him. But is this outcome in the social interest?

The economist's answer is 'Yes.' It is in the social interest because it makes everyone better off. There are no losers.

Efficiency and the Social Interest

Economists use the everyday word 'efficient' to describe a situation that can't be improved upon. Resource use is **efficient** if it is not possible to make someone better off without making someone else worse off. If it is possible to make someone better off without making anyone worse off, society can be made better off and the situation is not efficient.

In the Ted story everyone is better off, so it improves efficiency and the outcome is in the social interest. But notice that it would also have been efficient if the workers and customers had gained nothing and Ted had gained even more than £1 million a week. But would that efficient outcome be in the social interest?

Many people have trouble seeing the outcome in which Ted is the only winner as being in the social interest. They say that the social interest requires Ted to share some of his gain either with his workers in higher wages or with his customers in lower prices, or with both groups.

Fair Shares and the Social Interest

The idea that the social interest requires 'fair shares' is a deeply held one. Think about what you regard as a fair share. To help you, imagine the following game.

I put £100 on the table and tell someone you don't know and who doesn't know you to propose a share of the money between the two of you. If you accept the proposed share, you each get the agreed shares. If you don't accept the proposed share, you both get nothing.

It would be efficient – you would both be better off – if the proposer offered to take £99 and leave you with £1 and you accepted that offer.

But would you accept the £1? If you are like most people, the idea that the other person gets 99 times as much as you is just too much to stomach. 'No way' you say and the £100 disappears. That outcome is inefficient. You have both given up something.

When this game is played in a classroom experiment, about a half of the players reject offers of below £30.

So fair shares matter. But what is fair? There isn't a crisp definition of fairness to match that of efficiency. Reasonable people have a variety of views about it. Almost everyone agrees that too much inequality is unfair. But how much is too much? And inequality of what: income, wealth or the opportunity to work, earn an income and accumulate wealth?

You will examine efficiency again in Chapter 2 and efficiency and fairness in Chapter 5.

Questions about the social interest are hard ones to answer, and they generate a lot of discussion, debate and disagreement. Let's take a closer look at these questions with four examples:

- ◆ Globalisation
- ◆ The information-age monopolies
- ◆ Climate change
- ◆ Economic instability

Globalisation

The term *globalisation* means the expansion of international trade, borrowing and lending, and investment.

When Nike produces sports shoes, people in Malaysia get work; and when China Airlines buys new aeroplanes, Europeans who work in Airbus Industries build them. While globalisation brings expanded production and job opportunities for some workers, it destroys many European jobs. Workers across the manufacturing industries must learn new skills, take service jobs, which are often lower-paid, or retire earlier than previously planned.

Globalisation is in the self-interest of consumers because they can buy low-cost goods and services pro-duced in other countries. It is also in the self-interest of the multinational firms that produce in low-cost regions and sell in high-price regions. But is globalisation in the self-interest of the low-wage workers in Malaysia who sews your new running shoes and the displaced shoemaker in Northampton? Is it in the social interest?

ECONOMICS IN THE NEWS

The Invisible Hand

From Brewer to Bio-tech Entrepreneur

Kiran Mazumdar-Shaw trained to become a master brewer and learned about enzymes, the stuff from which bio-pharmaceuticals are made. It was impossible for a woman in India to become a master brewer, so the 25-year-old Kiran decided to create a bio-pharmaceutical business.

Kiran's firm, Biocom, employed uneducated workers who loved their jobs and the living conditions made possible by their high wages. But when a trade union entered the scene and unionised the workers, a furious Kiran fired the workers, automated their jobs and hired a smaller number of educated workers. Biocom continued to grow and today, Kiran's wealth exceeds $1 billion.

Kiran has become wealthy by developing and producing bio-pharmaceuticals that improve people's lives. But Kiran is sharing her wealth in creative ways. She has opened a cancer treatment centre to help thousands of patients who are too poor to pay and created a health insurance scheme.

Source of information: Ariel Levy, 'Drug Test' *The New Yorker*, 2 January, 2012

The Questions

- ◆ Whose decisions in the story were taken in self-interest?
- ◆ Whose decisions turned out to be in the social interest?
- ◆ Did any of the decisions harm the social interest?

The Answers

- ◆ All the decisions – Kiran's, the workers', the union's and the firm's customers' – are taken in the pursuit of self-interest.
- ◆ Kiran's decisions serve the social interest: she creates jobs that benefit her workers and products that benefit her customers. And her charitable work brings yet further social benefits.
- ◆ The union's decision might have harmed the social interest because it destroyed the jobs of uneducated workers.

Kiran Mazumdar-Shaw, founder and CEO of Biocom

The Information-Age Monopolies

The technological change of the past 40 years has been called the *Information Revolution*. Gordon Moore, who founded the chip-maker Intel, and Bill Gates, a co-founder of Microsoft, held privileged positions in this revolution. For many years, Intel chips were the only available chips and Windows was the only available operating system for the original IBM PC and its clones. The PC and Apple's Mac competed, but the PC has a huge market share.

An absence of competition gave Intel and Microsoft the power and ability to sell their products at prices far above the cost of production. If the prices of microchips and Windows had been lower, more people would have been able to afford a computer and would have chosen to buy one.

The information revolution has clearly served your self-interest: it has provided your mobile phone, laptop, the latest applications and the Internet. It has also served the self-interest of Bill Gates and Gordon Moore, both of whom have seen their wealth soar.

But did the information revolution best serve the social interest? Did Microsoft produce the best possible Windows operating system and sell it at a price that was in the social interest? Did Intel make the right quality and quantity of microchips and sell them at the right prices? Was the quality too low, and were the prices too high? Would the social interest have been better served if Microsoft and Intel had faced competition?

Climate Change

Climate change is a huge political issue today. Every serious political leader is acutely aware of the problem and of the popularity of having proposals that might lower carbon emissions.

Burning fossil fuels to generate electricity and to power aeroplanes and motor vehicles pours a staggering 28 billion tonnes – 4 tonnes per person – of carbon dioxide into the atmosphere each year.

Two thirds of the world's carbon emissions are produced in the US, China, the EU, Russia and India. The fastest growing emissions are from India and China. The amount of global warming caused by economic activity and its effects are uncertain, but the emissions continue to grow and pose huge risks.

Every day you make self-interested choices to use electricity, petrol and diesel, but you also create carbon emissions; you leave your carbon footprint. You can lessen your carbon footprint by walking, riding a bike, taking a cold shower, or planting a tree. But can we rely upon the self-interested decisions of every individual to make decisions that affect the earth's carbon-dioxide concentration in the social interest? Should governments change the incentives we face so that our self-interested choices are also in the social interest? How can governments change incentives? How can we discourage the use of fossil fuels and encourage the use of alternatives such as wind and solar power?

Economic Instability

The years between 1993 and 2007 were a period of remarkable economic stability, so much so that they've been called the *Great Moderation*. During those years, European and global economies were booming. US incomes increased by 30 per cent and incomes in China tripled. Even the economic shock waves of 9/11 brought only a small dip in the strong pace of US and global economic growth.

Flush with funds and offering record low interest rates, banks went on a lending spree to home buyers. Rapidly rising home prices made home owners feel well off and they were happy to borrow and spend. Home loans were bundled into securities that were sold and resold to banks around the world.

In 2006, as interest rates began to rise and the rate at which home prices were rising slowed, borrowers

AT ISSUE

The Protest against Market Capitalism

Market capitalism is an economic system in which individuals own all the land and capital and are free to buy and sell land, capital and goods and services in markets. Billions of self-interested choices and their coordination in markets determine what, how and for whom goods and services are produced. There is no supreme planner guiding the use of scarce resources and the outcome is unintended and unforeseeable.

Centrally planned socialism is an economic system in which the government owns all the land and capital, directs workers to jobs and decides what, how and for whom to produce. The Soviet Union, several Eastern European countries and China have used this system in the past but have now abandoned it.

Our economy today is a mixed economy, which is market capitalism with government regulation.

The Protest

The protest against market capitalism takes many forms. Historically, **Karl Marx** and other communist and socialist thinkers wanted to replace it with *socialism* and *central planning*. Today, thousands of people who feel let down by the economic system want less market capitalism and more government regulation. The **Occupy Wall Street** movement is a visible example of today's protest. Protesters say:

◆ Big corporations (especially big banks) have too much power and influence on governments.

◆ Democratically elected governments can do a better job of allocating resources and distributing income than uncoordinated markets. More regulation in the social interest is needed – to serve 'human need, not corporate greed'.

◆ In a market, for every winner, there is a loser. Big corporations are the winners. Workers and unemployed people are the losers.

Occupy movement at St Paul's Cathedral

The Economist's Response

Economists agree that market capitalism isn't perfect. But they argue that it is the best system available and, while some government intervention and regulation can help, it is equally likely to harm the social interest. Adam Smith gave the first systematic account of how market capitalism works. He says:

◆ The self-interest of big corporations is *maximum profit*. But an *invisible hand* leads decisions made in pursuit of self-interest to *unintentionally* promote the social interest.

◆ Politicians are ill-equipped to regulate corporations or to intervene in markets, and those who think they can improve on the market outcome are most likely wrong.

◆ In a market, buyers get what they want for less than they would be willing to pay and sellers earn a profit. Both buyers and sellers gain. A market transaction is a 'win-win' event.

'It is not from the benevolence of the butcher, the brewer or the baker that we expect our dinner, but from their regard to their own interest.'

The Wealth of Nations, 1776

Adam Smith

defaulted on their loans. What started as a trickle became a flood. As more people defaulted, banks took losses that totalled billions of dollars by the summer of 2007. Financial markets are global and a bank in France was the first to feel the pain that soon gripped the entire global financial system.

Banks take in deposits from people and businesses and get more funds by borrowing from each other and from other firms. Banks use these funds to make loans. All the banks' choices to borrow and lend and the choices of people and businesses to lend to and borrow from banks are made in self-interest. But does this lending and borrowing

ECONOMICS IN THE NEWS

A Fragile Global Economy

Global Economy Recovering, but Major Risks Remain

In mid-2007, the US mortgage market crashed and triggered a global financial and economic crisis. In mid-2012, the global economy, still recovering from that crisis, remained in a fragile state with more than 1 in 10 people unemployed in Europe. Another global crisis, this time starting in Europe, was feared.

Source: *OECD Press Release*, 22 May 2012

The Data

	Unemployment Rates (percentage of labour force)		
	United States	Euro Area	OECD
2012	8.1	10.8	8.0
2013	7.9	11.1	7.9

The Questions

◆ With the information provided in the news clip and the data table, what caused the financial and economic crisis of 2007?

◆ Has the world fully recovered from that crisis?

◆ Where is the greatest unemployment? Where is unemployment falling and where is it rising?

◆ Why does the existence of persistent high unemployment present a puzzle for economists?

The Answers

◆ Problems in the US mortgage market brought the global economy crashing in 2007.

◆ Even 5 years later in 2012, the recovery was incomplete and a second crisis was feared.

◆ Europe has the greatest unemployment. Unemployment is falling a bit in the United States and the OECD as a whole but is rising in Europe.

◆ Unemployment is a puzzle because it is in no one's self interest. It seems to be a waste of resources and doesn't seem to contribute to overcoming scarcity.

In Spain, 1 in 4 people who want a job can't find one.

serve the social interest? Is there too much borrowing and lending or too little?

When the banks got into trouble, the Bank of England and the European Central Bank bailed them out with big loans backed by the taxpayers. Did the Bank of England's bailout of troubled banks like Lloyds TSB serve the social interest? Did the Bank of England's rescue action just allow banks to repeat their dangerous lending in the future?

Banks weren't the only recipients of public funds. Some European governments supported their motor industries with a 'scrappage' scheme to encourage the purchase of new cars. Government support of the motor industry served the European motor industry self-interest. Did the scheme also serve the social interest?

We've looked at four topics and asked many questions that illustrate the big question: Can choices made in the pursuit of self-interest also promote the social interest? We've asked questions but not answered them because we've not yet explained the economic principles needed to do so.

REVIEW QUIZ

1 Describe the broad facts about *what*, *how* and *for whom* goods and services are produced.

2 Define the four factors of production and give an example of each one. What is the income earned by the people who sell the services of each of these factors of production?

3 Distinguish between self-interest and the social interest.

4 Use headlines from the recent news stories to illustrate the potential for conflict between self-interest and social interest.

Do these questions in Study Plan 1.2 and get instant feedback.   MyEconLab

By working through this book, you will discover the economic principles that help economists figure out when the social interest is being served, when it is not and what might be done when it is not being served. We will return to each of these questions in future chapters.

The Economic Way of Thinking

The questions that economics tries to answer tell us about the scope of economics, but they don't tell us how economists think and go about seeking answers to these questions. You're now going to see how economists go about their work.

We're going to look at six key ideas that define the economic way of thinking. These ideas are:

◆ A choice is a *trade-off*.

◆ People make *rational choices* by comparing benefits and costs.

◆ *Benefit* is what you gain from something.

◆ Cost is what you *must give up* to get something.

◆ Most choices are 'how-much' choices made at the *margin*.

◆ Choices respond to *incentives*.

A Choice Is a Trade-Off

Because we face scarcity, we must make choices. And when we make a choice, we select from the available alternatives. For example, you can spend Saturday night studying for your next economics test or having fun with your friends, but you can't do both of these activities at the same time. You must choose how much time to devote to each. Whatever choice you make, you could have chosen something else.

You can think about your choice as a trade-off. A **trade-off** is an exchange – giving up one thing to get something else. When you choose how to spend your Saturday night, you face a trade-off between studying and hanging out with your friends.

Making a Rational Choice

Economists view the choices that people make as rational. A **rational choice** is one that compares costs and benefits and achieves the greatest benefit over cost for the person making the choice.

Only the wants of the person making a choice are relevant to determine its rationality. For example, you might like your coffee black and strong but your friend prefers his milky and sweet. So it is rational for you to choose espresso and for your friend to choose cappuccino.

The idea of rational choice provides an answer to the first question: What goods and services will be produced and in what quantities? The answer is those that people rationally choose to buy!

But how do people choose rationally? Why do more people choose an iPod rather than a Creative? Why has the UK government chosen to improve the A1 and M1 motorways joining the North and the South rather than build a new rail track? The answers turn on comparing benefits and costs.

Benefit: What You Gain

The **benefit** of something is the gain or pleasure that it brings and is determined by **preferences** – by what a person likes and dislikes and the intensity of those feelings. If you get a huge kick out of updating your Facebook page every day, that activity brings you a large benefit. If you have little interest in listening to a news pod cast, that activity brings you a small benefit.

Some benefits are large and easy to identify, such as the benefit that you get from being at university. A big piece of that benefit is the goods and services that you will be able to enjoy with the boost to your earning power when you graduate. Some benefits are small, such as the benefit you get from a slice of pizza.

Economists measure benefit as the most that a person is willing to give up to get something. You are willing to give up a lot to be at university but you would give up only an iTunes download for a slice of pizza.

Cost: What You *Must* Give Up

The **opportunity cost** of something is the highest-valued alternative that must be given up to get it.

To make the idea of opportunity cost clear, think about your opportunity cost of being at university. It has two components: the things you can't afford to buy and the things you can't do with your time.

Start with the things you can't afford to buy. You've spent all your available income on tuition, residence fees, books and a laptop. If you weren't at university, you would have spent this money on going to clubs and films and all the other things that you enjoy. But that's only the start of your opportunity cost. You've also given up the opportunity to get a job. Suppose that the best job you could get if you weren't at university is working at HSBC as a trainee earning £18,000 a year. Another part of your opportunity cost of being at university is all the things that you could buy with the extra £18,000 you would have.

As you well know, being a student eats up many hours in class time, doing homework assignments, preparing for tests and so on. To do all these school activities, you must give up many hours of what would otherwise be leisure time spent with your friends. So the opportunity cost of being at university is all the good things that you can't afford and don't have the spare time to enjoy. You might want to put a value on that cost or you might just list all the items that make up the opportunity cost.

The examples of opportunity cost that we've just considered are all-or-nothing costs – you're either at university or not at university. Most situations are not like this one. They involve choosing *how much* of an activity to do.

How Much? Choosing at the Margin

You can allocate the next hour between studying and e-mailing your friends. But the choice is not all or nothing. You must decide how many minutes to allocate to each activity. To make this decision, you compare the benefit of a little bit more study time with its cost – you make your choice at the **margin**.

The benefit that arises from an increase in an activity is called **marginal benefit**. For example, your marginal benefit from one more night of study before a test is the boost it gives to your grade. Your marginal benefit doesn't include the grade you're already achieving without that extra night of work.

The *opportunity cost* of an *increase* in an activity is called **marginal cost**. For you, the marginal cost of studying one more night is the cost of not spending that night on your favourite leisure activity.

To make your decisions, you compare marginal benefit against the marginal cost. If the marginal benefit from an extra night of study exceeds its marginal cost, you study the extra night. If the marginal cost exceeds the marginal benefit, you don't study the extra night.

Choices Respond to Incentives

Economists take human nature as given and view people as acting in their self-interest. All people – consumers, producers, politicians and civil servants – pursue their self-interest.

Self-interested actions are not necessarily *selfish* actions. You might decide to use your resources in ways that bring pleasure to others as well as to yourself. But a self-interested act gets the most value for *you* based on *your* view about benefit.

The central idea of economics is that we can predict the self-interested choices that people make by looking at the *incentives* they face. People undertake those activities for which marginal benefit exceeds marginal cost and reject those for which marginal cost exceeds marginal benefit.

For example, your economics lecturer gives you a problem set and tells you these problems will be on the next test. Your marginal benefit from working on these problems is large, so you work hard on them. In contrast, your statistics lecturer gives you a problem set on a topic that she says will never be on a test. You get little marginal benefit from working on these problems, so you decide to skip most of them.

Economists see incentives as the key to reconciling self-interest and social interest. When our choices are not in the social interest, it is because of the incentives we face. One of the challenges for economists is to figure out when the incentives that result in self-interested choices are also in the social interest.

Economists emphasise the crucial role that institutions play in influencing the incentives that people face as they pursue their self-interest. Private property protected by a system of laws and markets that enable voluntary exchange are the fundamental institutions. You will learn as you progress with your study of economics that where these institutions exist, self-interest can indeed promote the social interest.

◆ REVIEW QUIZ

1 Explain the idea of a trade-off and think of three trade-offs that you made today.
2 Explain what economists mean by rational choice and think of three choices that you've made today that are rational.
3 Explain why opportunity cost is the best forgone alternative and provide examples of some opportunity costs that you have faced today.
4 Explain what it means to choose at the margin and illustrate with three choices at the margin that you have made today.
5 Explain why choices respond to incentives and think of three incentives to which you have responded today.

Do these questions in Study Plan 1.3 and get instant feedback.   MyEconLab

Economics as a Social Science and Policy Tool

Economics is a social science and a toolkit for advising on policy decisions.

Economist as Social Scientist

As social scientists, economists seek to discover how the economic world works. In pursuit of this goal, like all scientists, economists distinguish between positive and normative statements.

Positive Statements

A *positive* statement is about what is. It says what is currently believed about the way the world operates. A positive statement might be right or wrong, but we can test it by checking it against the facts. 'Our planet is warming because of the amount of coal that we're burning' is a positive statement. We can test whether it is right or wrong.

A central task of economists is to test positive statements about how the economic world works and to weed out those that are wrong. Economics first got off the ground in the late 1700s, so it is a young science compared with, for example, physics, and much remains to be discovered.

Normative Statements

A normative statement is about *what ought to be*. It depends on values and cannot be tested. Policy goals are normative statements. For example, 'We ought to cut our use of coal by 50 per cent' is a normative policy statement. You may agree or disagree with it, but you can't test it. It doesn't assert a fact that can be checked.

Unscrambling Cause and Effect

Economists are particularly interested in positive statements about cause and effect. Are computers getting cheaper because people are buying them in greater quantities? Or are people buying computers in greater quantities because they are getting cheaper? Or is some third factor causing both the price of a computer to fall and the quantity of computers bought to increase?

To answer such questions, economists create and test economic models. An **economic model** is a description of some aspect of the economic world that includes only those features that are needed for the purpose at hand.

For example, an economic model of a mobile-phone network might include features such as the prices of calls, the number of mobile-phone users and the volume of calls. But the model would ignore mobile-phone colours and ringtones.

A model is tested by comparing its predictions with the facts. However, testing an economic model is difficult because we observe the outcomes of the simultaneous change of many factors. To cope with this problem, economists look for natural experiments (situations in the ordinary course of economic life in which the one factor of interest is different and other things are equal or similar); conduct statistical investigations to find correlations; and perform economic experiments by putting people in decision-making situations and varying the influence of one factor at a time to discover how they respond.

Economist as Policy Adviser

Economics is useful. It is a toolkit for advising governments and businesses and for making personal decisions. Some of the most famous economists work partly as policy advisers.

For example, Sir Alan Budd, who was Provost of The Queen's College, Oxford University until 2008, was the first Chair of the UK government's new Office for Budget Responsibility in 2010. He has also been an economic adviser to the UK Treasury, Barclays Bank and Credit Suisse First Boston as well as many other economic organisations.

All the policy questions on which economists provide advice involve a blend of the positive and the normative. Economics can't help with the normative part – the policy goal. But for a given goal, economics provides a method of evaluating alternative solutions – comparing marginal benefits and marginal costs and finding the solution that makes the best use of available resources.

 REVIEW QUIZ

1   Distinguish between a positive statement and a normative statement and provide examples.
2   What is a model? Can you think of a model that you might use in your everyday life?
3   How do economists try to disentangle cause and effect?
4   How is economics used as a policy tool?

Do these questions in Study Plan 1.4 and get instant feedback.   MyEconLab

SUMMARY

Key Points

A Definition of Economics (p. 2)

◆ All economic questions arise from scarcity – from the fact that wants exceed the resources available to satisfy them.

◆ Economics is the social science that studies the choices people make as they cope with scarcity.

◆ The subject divides into microeconomics and macroeconomics.

Do Problem 1 to give you a better understanding of the definition of economics.

Two Big Economic Questions (pp. 3–9)

◆ Two big questions summarise the scope of economics:

   1 How do choices end up determining what, how and for whom goods and services get produced?

   2 When do choices made in the pursuit of self-interest also promote the social interest?

Do Problems 2 and 3 to give you a better understanding of the two big questions of economics.

The Economic Way of Thinking (pp. 10–11)

◆ Every choice is a trade-off – exchanging more of something for less of something else.

◆ People make rational choices by comparing benefit and cost.

◆ Cost – opportunity cost – is what you must give up to get something.

◆ Most choices are 'how much' choices made at the *margin* by comparing marginal benefit and marginal cost.

◆ Choices respond to incentives.

Do Problems 4 and 5 to give you a better understanding of the economic way of thinking.

Economics as a Social Science and Policy Tool (p. 12)

◆ Economists distinguish between positive statements – what is – and normative statements – what ought to be.

◆ To explain the economic world, economists create and test economic models.

◆ Economics is a tool-kit used to provide advice on government, business and personal economic decisions.

Do Problem 6 to give you a better understanding of economics as a social science and policy tool.

Key Terms

Benefit, 10
Capital, 4
Economic model, 12
Economics, 2
Efficiency, 5
Entrepreneurship, 4
Factors of production, 3
Goods and services, 3
Human capital, 3
Incentive, 2
Interest, 4
Labour, 3
Land, 3
Macroeconomics, 2

Margin, 11
Marginal benefit, 11
Marginal cost, 11
Microeconomics, 2
Opportunity cost, 10
Preferences, 10
Profit, 4
Rational choice, 10
Rent, 4
Scarcity, 2
Self-interest, 5
Social interest, 5
Trade-off, 10
Wages, 4

STUDY PLAN PROBLEMS AND APPLICATIONS

Do Problems 1 to 6 in MyEconLab Chapter 1 Study Plan and get instant feedback.   MyEconLab

A Definition of Economics
(Study Plan 1.1)

1 Apple decides to make iTunes freely available in unlimited quantities.

  a Does Apple's decision change the incentives that
people face?

  b Is Apple's decision an example of a microeconomic or
a macroeconomic issue?

Two Big Economic Questions
(Study Plan 1.2)

2 Which of the following pairs does not match?

  a Labour and wages

  b Land and rent

  c Entreprenuership and profit

  d Capital and profit

3 Explain how the following news headlines concern self-
interest and the social interest:

  a Tesco Expands in Europe

  b McDonald's Moves into Gourmet Coffee

  c Food Must Be Labelled with Nutrition Data

The Economic Way of Thinking
(Study Plan 1.3)

4 The night before an economics exam, you go to the
cinema instead of working your MyEconLab study plan.
You get 50 per cent on your exam compared with the
70 per cent that you normally score.

  a Did you face a trade-off?

  b What was the opportunity cost of your evening at the
cinema?

5 **Costs Soar for London Olympics**

The regeneration of East London, the site of the 2012
Olympic Games, is set to add an extra £1.5 billion to
taxpayers' bill.

          Source: *The Times*, 6 July 2006

Is the cost of regenerating East London an opportunity
cost of hosting the 2012 Olympic Games? Explain.

Economics as a Social Science and Policy Tool (Study Plan 1.4)

6 Which of the following statements is positive, which is
normative and which can be tested?

  a The EU should cut its imports.

  b China is the EU's largest trading partner.

  c If the price of antiretroviral drugs increases, HIV/
AIDS sufferers will consume fewer of the drugs.

ADDITIONAL PROBLEMS AND APPLICATIONS

Do these problems in MyEconLab if assigned by your lecturer.   MyEconLab

A Definition of Economics

7 Hundreds Line up for 5p.m. Ticket Giveaway

By noon, hundreds of Eminem fans had lined up for a
chance to score free tickets to the concert.

        Source: *Detroit Free Press*, 18 May 2009

When Eminem gave away tickets, what was free and
what was scarce? Explain your answer.

Two Big Economic Questions

8 How does the creation of a successful film influence what,
how and for whom goods and services are produced?

9 How does a successful film illustrate self-interested
choices that are also in the social interest?

The Economic Way of Thinking

10 Before starring in *Iron Man*, Robert Downey Jr. had
appeared in 45 films that grossed an average of $5 million

on the opening weekend. In contrast, *Iron Man* grossed
$102 million.

  a How do you expect *Iron Man*'s success to affect the
opportunity cost of hiring Robert Downey Jr.?

  b How have the incentives for a film producer to hire
Robert Downey Jr. changed?

11 What might be an incentive for you to take an extra
university course during the summer break? List some of
the benefits and costs involved in your decision. Would
your choice be rational?

Economics as a Social Science and Policy Tool

12 Look at today's *Financial Times*. What is the leading
economic news story? With which big economic questions does it deal? What trade-offs does it discuss?

13 Give two microeconomic and two macroeconomic statements and classify them as positive or normative.

CHAPTER 1 APPENDIX

Graphs in Economics

After studying this appendix, you will be able to:

◆ Make and interpret a scatter diagram

◆ Identify linear and non-linear relationships and relationships that have a maximum and a minimum

◆ Define and calculate the slope of a line

◆ Graph relationships among more than two variables

Graphing Data

A graph represents a quantity as a distance. Figure A1.1 shows two examples. A distance on the horizontal line represents temperature. A movement from left to right shows an increase in temperature. The point marked 0 represents zero degrees. To the right of 0, the temperature is positive and to the left of 0, it is negative. A distance on the vertical line represents height. The point marked 0 represents sea level. Points above 0 represent metres above sea level. Points below 0 (indicated by a minus sign) represent metres below sea level.

In Figure A1.1, the scale lines are perpendicular to each other and are called *axes*. The vertical line is the *y*-axis and the horizontal line is the *x*-axis. Each axis has a zero point, which is shared by the two axes. This common zero point is called the *origin*.

To show something in a two-variable graph, we need two pieces of information: the value of the *x* variable and the value of the *y* variable. For example, off the coast of Norway on a winter's day, the temperature is 0 degrees – the value of *x*. A fishing boat is located 0 metres above sea level – the value of *y*. This information appears at the origin at point *A* in Figure A1.1. In the heated cabin of the boat, the temperature is a comfortable 24 degrees. Point *B* represents this information. The same 24 degrees in the cabin of an airliner 9,000 metres above sea level is at point *C*.

Finally, the temperature of the ice cube in the drink of the airline passenger is shown by the point marked *D*. This point represents 9,000 metres above sea level at a temperature of 0 degrees.

We can draw two lines, called *coordinates*, from point *C*. One, called the *y*-coordinate, runs from *C* to the horizontal axis. Its length is the same as the

Figure A1.1 Making a Graph

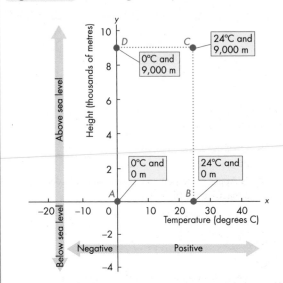

Graphs have axes that measure quantities as distances. Here, the horizontal axis (*x*-axis) measures temperature and the vertical axis (*y*-axis) measures height.

Point *A* represents a fishing boat at sea level (0 on the *y*-axis) on a day when the temperature is 0°C. Point *B* represents inside the cabin of the boat at a temperature of 24°C.

Point *C* represents inside the cabin of an airliner 9,000 metres above sea level at a temperature of 24°C. Point *D* represents an ice cube in an airliner 9,000 metres above sea level.

MyEconLab Animation ─────────────────◆

value marked off on the *y*-axis. The other, called the *x*-coordinate, runs from *C* to the vertical axis. Its length is the same as the value marked off on the *x*-axis. We describe a point in a graph by the values of its *x*-coordinate and its *y*-coordinate. For example, at point *C*, *x* is 24 degrees and *y* is 9,000 metres.

Graphs like that in Figure A1.1 can show any type of quantitative data on two variables. The graph can show just a few points, like Figure A1.1, or many points. Before we look at graphs with many points, let's reinforce what you've just learned by looking at two graphs made with economic data.

Economists measure variables that describe *what*, *how* and *for whom* goods and services are produced. These variables are quantities produced and prices. Figure A1.2 shows two examples of economic graphs.

Figure A1.2(a) is a graph about iTunes song downloads in 2010. The *x*-axis measures the quantity of songs

Figure A1.2 Two Graphs of Economic Data

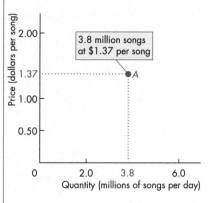

(a) Singles downloads: quantity and price

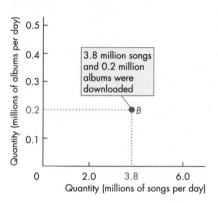

(b) Downloads: singles and albums

The graph in part (a) tells us that in 2010, 3.8 million songs per day were downloaded from the iTunes store at a price of $1.37 a song.

The graph in part (b) tells us that in 2010, 3.8 million songs per day and 0.2 million albums per day were downloaded from the iTunes store.

MyEconLab Animation

---

downloaded per day and the *y*-axis measures the price of a song. Point *A* tells us what the quantity and price were. You can 'read' this graph as telling you that in 2010, 3.8 million songs a day were downloaded at a price of $1.37 per song.

Figure A1.2(b) is a graph about iTunes song and album downloads in 2010. The *x*-axis measures the quantity of songs downloaded per day and the *y*-axis measures the quantity of albums downloaded per day. Point *B* tells us what these quantities were. You can 'read' this graph as telling you that in 2010, 3.8 million songs a day and 0.2 million albums a day were downloaded.

The three graphs that you've just seen tell you how to make a graph and how to read a data point on a graph, but they don't improve on the raw data. Graphs become interesting and revealing when they contain a number of data points because then you can visualise the data.

Economists create graphs based on the principles in Figures A1.1 and A1.2 to reveal, describe and visualise the relationships among variables. We're now going to look at some examples. These graphs are called *scatter diagrams*.

Scatter Diagrams

A **scatter diagram** plots the value of one variable against the value of another variable for a number of different values of each variable. Such a graph reveals whether a relationship exists between two variables and describes their relationship.

The table in Figure A1.3 shows some data on two variables: the number of tickets sold at the box office and the number of DVDs sold for nine of the most popular films in 2011.

What is the relationship between these two variables? Does a big box office success generate a large volume of DVD sales? Or does a box office success mean that fewer DVDs are sold?

We can answer these questions by making a scatter diagram. We do so by graphing the data in the table. Each point in the graph shows the number of box office tickets sold (the *x* variable) and the number of DVDs sold (the *y* variable) of one of the films. With nine films, nine points are 'scattered' within the graph.

The point labelled *A* tells us that *Fast Five* sold 27 million tickets at the box office and 2 million DVDs.

The points in the graph form a pattern, which reveals that larger box office sales are associated with larger DVD sales. But the points also tell us that this association is weak. You can't predict DVD sales with any confidence by knowing only the number of tickets sold at the box office.

Figure A1.4 shows two scatter diagrams of economic variables. Part (a) shows the relationship between expenditure and income on average. Each dot shows expenditure per person and income per person in a given year from 2000 to 2011. The dots are 'scattered' within the graph. The red dot tells us that in 2008, income per person was £14,700 and expenditure per person was £14,900. The dots in this graph form a pattern, which reveals that as income increases, expenditure increases.

Figure A1.3 A Scatter Diagram

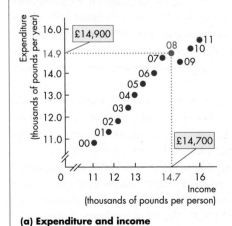

Film	Tickets	DVDs
	(millions)	
Harry Potter and the Deathly Hallows: Part II	48	5.8
Transformers: Death of the Moon	44	2.6
The Hangover: Part 2	32	2.6
Pirates of the Caribbean: On Stranger Tides	30	1.0
Fast Five	**27**	**2.0**
Cars 2	24	4.4
Thor	23	1.2
Rise of the Planet of the Apes	22	1.5
Captain America: The First Avenger	22	1.4

The table lists the number of tickets sold at the box office and the number of DVDs sold for eight popular films.

The scatter diagram reveals the relationship between these two variables. Each point shows the values of the two variables for a specific film. For example, point *A* shows the point for *Fast Five*, which sold 27 million tickets at the box office and 2 million DVDs.

The pattern formed by the points shows that there is a tendency for large box office sales to bring greater DVD sales. But you couldn't predict how many DVDs a film would sell just by knowing its box office sales.

MyEconLab Animation

Figure A1.4(b) shows a scatter diagram of UK unemployment and inflation from 2000 to 2011. The points show no close relationship between the two variables. Movements in the inflation rate are not related to those in the unemployment rate in any simple way.

You can see that a scatter diagram conveys a wealth of information, and it does so in much less space than we have used to describe only some of its features. But you do have to 'read' the graph to obtain all this information.

Figure A1.4 Scatter Diagrams

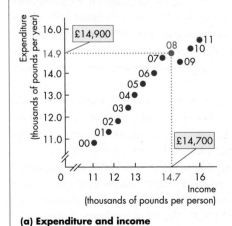

(a) Expenditure and income

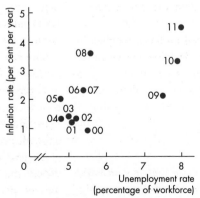

(b) Unemployment and inflation

The scatter diagram in part (a) shows the relationship between income and expenditure from 2000 to 2011. The red dot shows that in 2008, income was £14,700 and expenditure was £14,900. The dots form a pattern that shows that as income increases so too does expenditure.

The scatter diagram in part (b) shows a weak relationship between UK unemployment and inflation during the period since 2000.

MyEconLab Animation

Breaks in the Axes

Figure A1.4(a) and Figure A1.4(b) have breaks in their axes, as shown by the small gaps. The breaks indicate that there are jumps from the origin, 0, to the first values recorded.

In Figure A1.4(a), the breaks are used because the lowest values are £11,000. With no breaks in the axes, there would be a lot of empty space, all the points would be crowded into the top right corner and it would be hard to see the relationship between these two variables. By breaking the axes, we bring the relationship into view.

Putting a break in the axes is like using a zoom lens to bring the relationship into the centre of the graph and magnify it so that it fills the graph.

Misleading Graphs

Breaks can be used to highlight a relationship. But they can also be used to mislead – to make a graph that lies. The most common way of making a graph lie is to use axis breaks and either to stretch or compress a scale. For example, suppose that in Figure A1.4(a), the *y*-axis that measures expenditure ran from zero to £16,000 while the *x*-axis was the same as the one shown, running from £11,000 to £16,000. The graph would now create the impression that despite a huge increase in income, expenditure had barely changed.

To avoid being misled, it is a good idea to get into the habit of looking closely at the values and the labels on the axes of a graph before you start trying to interpret it.

Correlation and Causation

A scatter diagram that shows a clear relationship between two variables, such as Figure A1.4(a), tells us that the two variables have a high correlation. When a high correlation is present, we can predict the value of one variable from the value of the other variable. But correlation does not imply causation.

Sometimes a high correlation is a coincidence, but sometimes it does arise from a causal relationship. It is likely, for example, that rising income causes rising expenditure (Figure A1.4a).

You've now seen how we can use graphs in economics to show economic data and to reveal relationships between variables. Next, we'll learn how economists use graphs to construct and display economic models.

Graphs Used in Economic Models

The graphs used in economics are not always designed to show real-world data. Often they are used to show general relationships among the variables in an economic model.

An *economic model* is a stripped-down, simplified description of an economy or of a component of an economy such as a business or a household. It consists of statements about economic behaviour that can be expressed as equations or as curves in a graph. Economists use models to explore the effects of different policies or other influences on the economy in ways that are similar to the use of model aeroplanes in wind tunnels and models of the climate.

You will encounter many different kinds of graphs in economic models, but there are some repeating patterns. Once you've learned to recognise these patterns, you will instantly understand the meaning of a graph. Here, we'll look at the different types of curves that are used in economic models, and we'll see some everyday examples of each type of curve. The patterns to look for in graphs are the four cases in which:

◆ Variables move in the same direction

◆ Variables move in opposite directions

◆ Variables have a maximum or a minimum

◆ Variables are unrelated

Variables That Move in the Same Direction

A relationship in which two variables move in the same direction is called a **positive relationship** or a **direct relationship**. Figure A1.5 shows some examples of positive relationships. Notice that the line that shows such a relationship slopes upward.

Figure A1.5 shows three types of relationships, one that has a straight line and two that have curved lines. But all the lines in these three graphs are called curves. Any line on a graph – no matter whether it is straight or curved – is called a *curve*.

A relationship shown by a straight line is called a **linear relationship**. Figure A1.5(a) shows a linear relationship between the number of kilometres travelled in 5 hours and speed. For example, point *A* shows that if our speed is 40 kms per hour, we will travel 200

Figure A1.5 Positive (Direct) Relationships

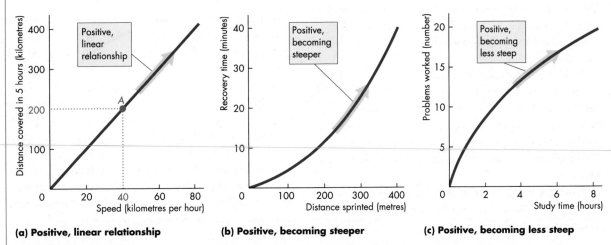

(a) Positive, linear relationship   **(b) Positive, becoming steeper**   **(c) Positive, becoming less steep**

Each part of this figure shows a positive (direct) relationship between two variables. That is, as the value of the variable measured on the x-axis increases, so does the value of the variable measured on the y-axis. Part (a) shows a linear relationship – as the two variables increase together, we move along a straight line.

Part (b) shows a positive relationship such that as the two variables increase together, we move along a curve that becomes steeper.

Part (c) shows a positive relationship such that as the two variables increase together, we move along a curve that becomes less steep.

MyEconLab Animation ◆

kilometres in 5 hours. If we double our speed to 80 kms per hour, we will travel 400 kilometres in 5 hours.

Figure A1.5(b) shows the relationship between distance sprinted and recovery time (the time it takes the heart rate to return to its normal resting rate). This relationship is an upward-sloping one that starts out quite flat but then becomes steeper as we move along the curve away from the origin. The reason why this curve slopes upward and becomes steeper is that the additional recovery time needed from sprinting an additional 100 metres increases. It takes less than 5 minutes to recover from the first 100 metres but more than 10 minutes to recover from the third 100 metres.

Figure A1.5(c) shows the relationship between the number of problems worked by a student and the amount of study time. This relationship is an upward-sloping one that starts out quite steep and becomes flatter as we move away from the origin. Study time becomes less productive as you increase the hours spent studying and become more tired.

Variables That Move in Opposite Directions

A relationship between variables that move in opposite directions is called a **negative relationship** or an **inverse relationship**. Figure A1.6 shows some examples. Figure A1.6(a) shows the relationship between the number of hours available for playing squash and for playing tennis when the total is 5 hours. One extra hour spent playing tennis means one hour less playing squash and vice versa. This relationship is negative and linear.

Figure A1.6(b) shows the relationship between the cost per kilometre travelled and the length of a journey. The longer the journey, the lower is the cost per kilometre. But as the journey length increases, the cost per kilometre decreases, but the fall in the cost is smaller, the longer the journey. This feature of the relationship is shown by the fact that the curve slopes downward, starting out steep at a short journey length and then becoming flatter as the journey length increases. This relationship arises because some of the costs are fixed.

Figure A1.6 Negative (Inverse) Relationships

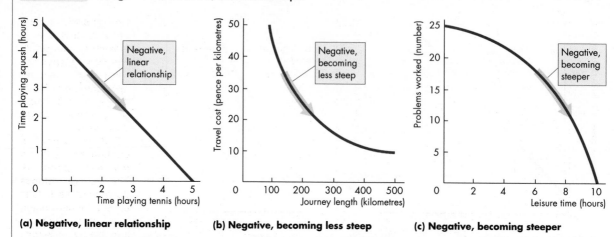

(a) Negative, linear relationship   **(b) Negative, becoming less steep**   **(c) Negative, becoming steeper**

Each part of this figure shows a negative (inverse) relationship between two variables. That is, as the value of the variable measured on the *x*-axis increases, the value of the variable measured on the *y*-axis decreases.

Part (a) shows a linear relationship. The total time spent playing tennis and squash is 5 hours. As the time spent playing tennis increases, the time spent playing squash decreases and we move along a straight line.

Part (b) shows a negative relationship such that as the journey length increases, the travel cost decreases as we move along a curve that becomes less steep.

Part (c) shows a negative relationship such that as leisure time increases, the number of problems worked decreases as we move along a curve that becomes steeper.

MyEconLab Animation ───◆

Figure A1.6(c) shows the relationship between the amount of leisure time and the number of problems worked by a student. Increasing leisure time produces an increasingly large reduction in the number of problems worked. This relationship is a negative one that starts out with a gentle slope at a small number of leisure hours and becomes steeper as the number of leisure hours increases. This relationship is a different view of the idea shown in Figure A1.5(c).

Variables That Have a Maximum or a Minimum

Many relationships in economic models have a maximum or a minimum. For example, firms try to make the largest possible profit and to produce at the lowest possible cost. Figure A1.7 shows relationships that have a maximum or a minimum.

Figure A1.7(a) shows the relationship between rainfall and wheat yield. When there is no rainfall, wheat will not grow, so the yield is zero. As the rainfall increases up to 10 days a month, the wheat yield increases. With 10 rainy days each month, the wheat yield reaches its maximum at 2.0 tonnes per hectare (point *A*). Rain in excess of 10 days a month starts to lower the yield of wheat. If every day is rainy, the wheat suffers from a lack of sunshine and the yield decreases to zero. This relationship is one that starts out sloping upward, reaches a maximum and then slopes downward.

Figure A1.7(b) shows the reverse case – a relationship that begins sloping downward, falls to a minimum and then slopes upward. Most economic costs are like this relationship. An example is the relationship between the travel cost per kilometre and the speed of a car. At low speeds, the car is creeping in a traffic jam. The number of kilometres per litre is low, so the cost per kilometre is high. At high speeds, the car is travelling faster than its efficient speed, using a large quantity of petrol, and again the number of kilometres per litre is low and the cost per kilometre is high. At a speed of 85 kms per hour, the cost per kilometre is at its minimum (point *B*). This relationship is one that starts out sloping downward, reaches a minimum and then slopes upward.

Figure A1.7   Maximum and Minimum Points

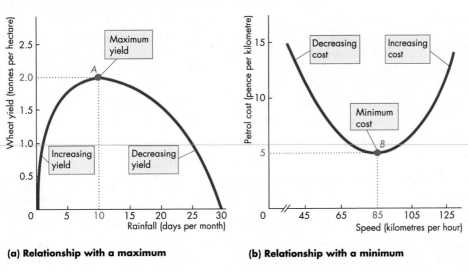

(a) Relationship with a maximum

(b) Relationship with a minimum

Part (a) shows a relationship that has a maximum point, *A*. The curve slopes upward as it rises to its maximum point, is flat at its maximum and then slopes downward.

Part (b) shows a relationship with a minimum point, *B*. The curve slopes downward as it falls to its minimum point, is flat at its minimum and then slopes upward.

MyEconLab Animation

Variables That Are Unrelated

There are many situations in which no matter what happens to the value of one variable, the other variable remains constant. Sometimes we want to show the independence between two variables in a graph. Figure A1.8 shows two ways of achieving this.

In describing the graphs in Figures A1.5 to Figure A1.8, we have talked about curves that slope upward or slope downward and curves that become steeper and less steep. Let's spend a little time discussing exactly what we mean by slope and how we measure the slope of a curve.

Figure A1.8   Variables That Are Unrelated

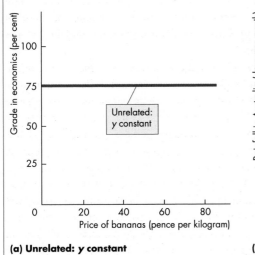

(a) Unrelated: *y* constant

(b) Unrelated: *x* constant

This figure shows how we can graph two variables that are unrelated. In part (a), a student's grade in economics is plotted at 75 per cent on the *y*-axis regardless of the price of bananas on the *x*-axis. The curve is horizontal.

In part (b), the output of the vineyards of France on the *x*-axis does not vary with the rainfall in Australia on the *y*-axis. The curve is vertical.

MyEconLab Animation

The Slope of a Relationship

We can measure the influence of one variable on another by the slope of the relationship. The **slope** of a relationship is the change in the value of the variable measured on the y-axis divided by the change in the value of the variable measured on the x-axis. We use the Greek letter Δ (*delta*) to represent 'change in'. So Δy means the change in the value of the variable measured on the y-axis, and Δx means the change in the value of the variable measured on the x-axis. The slope of the relationship is:

$$\frac{\Delta y}{\Delta x}$$

If a large change in the variable measured on the y-axis (Δy) is associated with a small change in the variable measured on the x-axis (Δx), the slope is large and the curve is steep. If a small change in the variable measured on the y-axis (Δy) is associated with a large change in the variable measured on the x-axis (Δx), the slope is small and the curve is flat.

We can make the idea of slope sharper by doing some calculations.

The Slope of a Straight Line

The slope of a straight line is the same regardless of where on the line you calculate it. The slope of a straight line is constant.

Figure A1.9   The Slope of a Straight Line

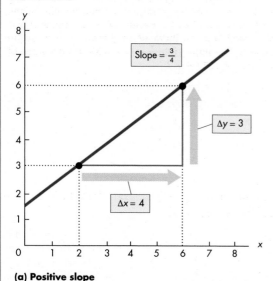

(a) Positive slope

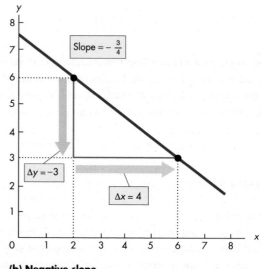

(b) Negative slope

To calculate the slope of a straight line, we divide the change in the value of the variable measured on the y-axis (Δy) by the change in the value of the variable measured on the x-axis (Δx), as we move along the curve.

Part (a) shows the calculation of a positive slope. When x increases from 2 to 6, Δx equals 4. That change in x brings about an increase in y from 3 to 6, so Δy equals 3. The slope (Δy/Δx) equals 3/4.

Part (b) shows the calculation of a negative slope. When x increases from 2 to 6, Δx equals 4. That increase in x brings about a decrease in y from 6 to 3, so Δy equals −3. The slope (Δy/Δx) equals −3/4.

MyEconLab Animation ─────────────────────────────────◆

Let's calculate the slopes of the lines in Figure A1.9. In part (a), when x increases from 2 to 6, y increases from 3 to 6. The change in x is +4: that is, Δx is 4. The change in y is +3: that is, Δy is 3. The slope of that line is:

$$\frac{\Delta y}{\Delta x} = \frac{3}{4}$$

In part (b), when x increases from 2 to 6, y decreases from 6 to 3. The change in y is *minus* 3: that is, Δy is −3. The change in x is *plus* 4: that is, Δx is 4. The slope of the curve is:

$$\frac{\Delta y}{\Delta x} = \frac{-3}{4}$$

Notice that the two slopes have the same magnitude (3/4), but the slope of the line in part (a) is positive (3/4), while the slope in part (b) is negative (−3/4). The slope of a positive relationship is positive; the slope of a negative relationship is negative.

The Slope of a Curved Line

The slope of a curved line is trickier. The slope of a curved line is not constant. Its slope depends on where on the line we calculate it. There are two ways to calculate the slope of a curved line: you can calculate the slope at a point, or you can calculate the slope across an arc of the curve. Let's look at the two alternatives.

Slope at a Point

To calculate the slope at a point on a curve, you need to construct a straight line that has the same slope as the curve at the point in question. Figure A1.10 shows how this is done. Suppose you want to calculate the slope of the curve at point A. Place a ruler on the graph so that it touches point A and no other point on the curve, then draw a straight line along the edge of the ruler. The straight red line is this line, and it is the *tangent* to the curve at point A. If the ruler touches the curve only at point A, then the slope of the curve at point A must be the same as the slope of the edge of the ruler. If the curve and the ruler do not have the same slope, the line along the edge of the ruler will cut the curve instead of just touching it.

Now that you have found a straight line with the same slope as the curve at point A, you can calculate the slope of the curve at point A by calculating the slope of the straight line. Along the straight line, as x increases

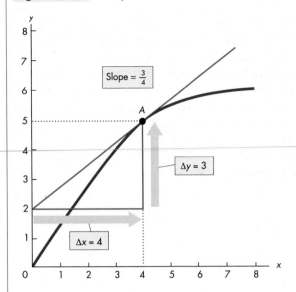

Figure A1.10 Slope at a Point

To calculate the slope of the curve at point A, draw the red line that just touches the curve at A – the tangent. The slope of this straight line is calculated by dividing the change in y by the change in x along the line. When x increases from 0 to 4, Δx equals 4. That change in x is associated with an increase in y from 2 to 5, so Δy equals 3. The slope of the red line is 3/4. So the slope of the curve at point A is 3/4.

MyEconLab Animation ━━━━━━━━━━━━━━◆

from 0 to 4 ($\Delta x = 4$) y increases from 2 to 5 ($\Delta y = 3$). The slope of the line is:

$$\frac{\Delta y}{\Delta x} = \frac{3}{4}$$

So the slope of the curve at point A is 3/4.

Slope Across an Arc

An arc of a curve is a piece of a curve. In Figure A1.11, you are looking at the same curve as in Figure A1.10. But instead of calculating the slope at point A, we are going to calculate the slope across the arc from B to C. You can see that the slope is greater at B than at C. When we calculate the slope across an arc, we are calculating the average slope between two points. As we move along the arc from B to C, x increases from 3 to 5 and y increases from 4 to 5.5. The change in x is 2 ($\Delta x = 2$), and the change in y is 1.5 ($\Delta y = 1.5$).

Figure A1.11   Slope Across an Arc

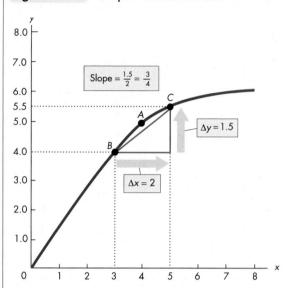

To calculate the average slope of the curve along the arc *BC*, draw a straight line from point *B* to point *C*. The slope of the line *BC* is calculated by dividing the change in *y* by the change in *x*. In moving from *B* to *C*, Δ*x* equals 2 and Δ*y* equals 1.5. The slope of the line *BC* is 1.5 divided by 2, or 3/4. So the slope of the curve across the arc *BC* is 3/4.

MyEconLab Animation ───────────────── ◆

The slope of the red line *BC* is:

$$\frac{\Delta y}{\Delta x} = \frac{1.5}{2} = \frac{3}{4}$$

So the slope of the curve across the arc *BC* is 3/4.

This calculation gives us the slope of the curve between points *B* and *C*. The actual slope calculated is the slope of the straight line from *B* to *C*. This slope approximates the average slope of the curve along the arc *BC*. In this particular example, the slope across the arc *BC* is identical to the slope of the curve at point *A*. But the calculation of the slope of a curve does not always work out so neatly. You might have some fun constructing some more examples and some counter examples.

You now know how to make and interpret a graph. But so far, we've limited our attention to graphs of two variables. We're now going to learn how to graph more than two variables.

Graphing Relationships Among More Than Two Variables

We have seen that we can graph the relationship between two variables as a point formed by the *x*- and *y*-coordinates in a two-dimensional graph. You may be thinking that although a two-dimensional graph is informative, most of the things in which you are likely to be interested involve relationships among many variables, not just two. For example, the amount of ice cream consumed depends on the price of ice cream and the temperature. If ice cream is expensive and the temperature is low, people eat a lot less ice cream than when ice cream is inexpensive and the temperature is high. For any given price of ice cream, the quantity consumed varies with the temperature; and for any given temperature, the quantity of ice cream consumed varies with its price.

Figure A1.12 shows a relationship among three variables. The table shows the number of litres of ice cream consumed each day at various temperatures and ice cream prices. How can we graph these numbers?

To graph a relationship that involves more than two variables, we use the *ceteris paribus* assumption.

Ceteris Paribus

Ceteris paribus (often shortened to *cet. par.*) means 'if all other relevant things remain the same'. To isolate the relationship of interest in a laboratory experiment, a scientist holds everything constant except for the variable whose effect is being studied. Economists use the same method to graph a relationship that has more than two variables.

Figure A1.12(a) shows an example. There, you can see what happens to the quantity of ice cream consumed as the price of ice cream varies when the temperature is held constant.

The curve labelled 20°C shows the relationship between ice cream consumption and the price of a scoop if the temperature remains at 20°C. The numbers used to plot that curve are those in the first two columns of the table. For example, if the temperature is 20°C, 10 litres are consumed when the price is £1.20 a scoop and 6 litres are consumed when the price is £1.60 a scoop.

The curve labelled 25°C shows the relationship between ice cream consumption and the price of a scoop when the temperature remains at 25°C. The numbers used to plot the curve are those in the first and third

Figure A1.12 Graphing a Relationship Among Three Variables

Price (pounds per scoop)	Ice cream consumption (litres per day)	
	20°C	25°C
0.40	52	91
0.80	18	32
1.20	**10**	**17**
1.60	6	10
2.00	5	8
2.40	4	6

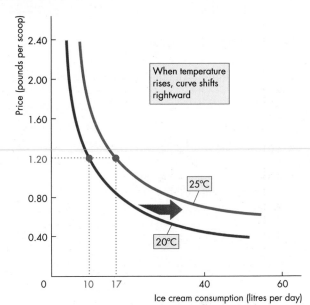

Ice cream consumption depends on its price and the temperature. The table tells us how many litres of ice cream are consumed each day at different prices and two different temperatures. For example, if the price is £1.20 a scoop and the temperature is 20°C, 10 litres of ice cream are consumed.

To graph a relationship among three variables, the value of one variable is held constant. The graph shows the relationship between price and consumption when temperature is held constant. One curve holds temperature at 20°C and the other at 25°C.

A change in the price of ice cream brings a *movement along* one of the curves – along the blue curve at 20°C and along the red curve at 25°C.

When the temperature rises from 20°C to 25°C, the curve that shows the relationship between consumption and price *shifts* rightward from the blue curve to the red curve.

MyEconLab Animation ◆

columns of the table. For example, if the temperature is 25°C, 17 litres of ice cream are consumed when the price is £1.20 a scoop and 32 litres when the price is £0.80 a scoop.

When the price of ice cream changes but the temperature is constant, you can think of what happens in the graph as a movement along one of the curves. At 20°C there is a movement along the blue curve and at 25°C there is a movement along the red curve.

When Other Things Change

The temperature is held constant along each of the curves in Figure A1.12, but in reality the temperature changes. When that event occurs, you can think of what happens in the graph as a shift of the curve.

When the temperature rises from 20°C to 25°C, the curve that shows the relationship between ice cream consumption and the price of ice cream shifts rightward from the blue curve to the red curve.

You will encounter these ideas of movements along and shifts of curves at many points in your study of economics. Think carefully about what you've just learned and make up some examples (with assumed numbers) about other relationships.

With what you have learned about graphs, you can move forward with your study of economics. There are no graphs in this book that are more complicated than those that have been explained in this appendix. Use this appendix as a refresher if you find that you're having difficulty interpreting or making a graph.

MATHEMATICAL NOTE

Equations of Straight Lines

If a straight line in a graph describes the relationship between two variables, we call it a *linear relationship*. Figure 1 shows the linear relationship between Cathy's expenditure and income. Cathy spends £100 a week (by borrowing or spending her past savings) when income is zero. And out of each pound earned, Cathy spends 50 pence (and saves 50 pence).

All linear relationships are described by the same general equation. We call the quantity that is measured on the horizontal (or x-axis) x and we call the quantity that is measured on the vertical (or y-axis) y. In the case of Figure 1, x is income and y is expenditure.

A Linear Equation

The equation that describes a linear relationship between x and y is:

$$y = a + bx$$

In this equation, a and b are fixed numbers and they are called constants. The values of x and y vary so these numbers are called variables. Because the equation describes a straight line, it is called a *linear equation*.

The equation tells us that when the value of x is zero, the value of y is a. We call the constant a the *y-axis intercept*. The reason is that on the graph the straight line hits the y-axis at a value equal to a. Figure 1 illustrates the y-axis intercept.

For positive values of x, the value of y exceeds a. The constant b tells us by how much y increases above a as x increases. The constant b is the slope of the line.

Slope of a Line

As we explain on p. 22, the slope of a relationship is the change in the value of y divided by the change in the value of x. We use the Greek letter Δ (delta) to represent 'change in'. So Δy means the change in the value of the variable measured on the y-axis, and Δx means change in the value of the variable measured on the x-axis. Therefore the slope of the relationship is:

$$\Delta y / \Delta x$$

To see why the slope is b, suppose that initially the value of x is x_1, or £200 in Figure 2. The corresponding value of y is y_1, also £200 in Figure 2. The equation of the line tells us that:

$$y_1 = a + bx_1 \tag{1}$$

Now the value of x increases by Δx to $x_1 + \Delta x$ (or £400 in Figure 2). And the value of y increases by Δy to $y_1 + \Delta y$ (or £300 in Figure 2).

The equation of the line now tells us that:

$$y_1 + \Delta y = a + b(x_1 + \Delta x) \tag{2}$$

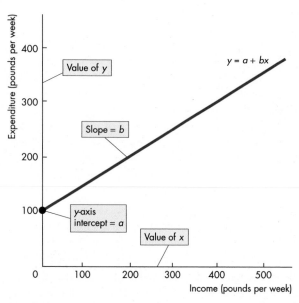

Figure 1 Linear Relationship

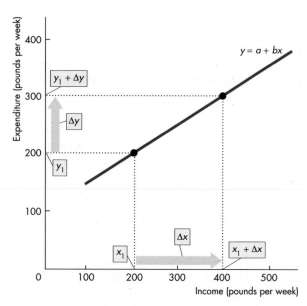

Figure 2 Calculating Slope

To calculate the slope of the line, subtract equation (1) from equation (2) to obtain:

$$\Delta y = b\Delta x \qquad (3)$$

and now divide equation (3) by Δx to obtain:

$$\Delta y/\Delta x = b$$

So the slope of the line is b.

We can calculate the slope of the line in Figure 2. When x increases from 200 to 400, y increases from 200 to 300, so Δx is 200 and Δy is 100. The slope, b, equals:

$$\Delta y/\Delta x = 100/200 = 0.5$$

Position of the Line

The y-axis intercept determines the position of the line on the graph. Figure 3 illustrates the relationship between the y-axis intercept and the position of the line on the graph. In this graph, the y-axis measures saving and the x-axis measures income.

When the y-axis intercept, a, is positive, the line hits the y-axis at a positive value of y – as the blue line does. Its y-axis intercept is 100.

When the y-axis intercept, a, is zero, the line hits the y-axis at the origin – as the purple line does. Its y-axis intercept is 0.

When the y-axis intercept, a, is negative, the line hits the y-axis at a negative value of y – as the red line does. Its y-axis intercept is −100.

As the equations of the three lines show, the value of the y-axis intercept does *not* influence the slope of the line. All three lines have a slope equal to 0.5.

Positive Relationships

Figures 1 and 2 show a positive relationship – the two variables x and y move in the same direction. All positive relationships have a slope that is *positive*. In the equation of the line, the constant b is positive.

In the example in Figure 1, the y-axis intercept, a, is 100. The slope b equals 0.5. The equation of the line is:

$$y = 100 + 0.5x$$

Negative Relationships

Figure 4 shows a negative relationship – the variables x and y move in opposite directions. All negative relationships have a slope that is *negative*. In the equation of the line, the constant b is negative.

In the example in Figure 4, the y-axis intercept, a, is 30. The slope, b, equals $\Delta y/\Delta x$ as we move along the line. When x increases from 0 to 2, y decreases from 30 to 10, so Δx is 2 and Δy is −20. The slope equals $\Delta y/\Delta x$, which is −20/2 or −10. The equation of the line is:

$$y = 30 + (-10)x$$

or

$$y = 30 - 10x$$

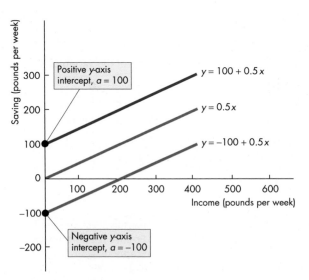

Figure 3 The y-Axis Intercept

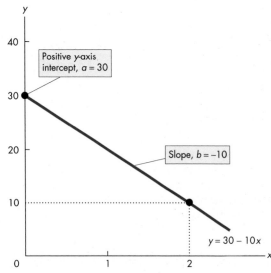

Figure 4 Negative Relationship

REVIEW QUIZ

1 Explain how we 'read' the three graphs in Figures A1.1 and A1.2.
2 Explain what scatter diagrams show and why we use them.
3 Explain how we 'read' the three scatter diagrams in Figure A1.3 and A1.4.
4 Draw a graph to show the relationship between two variables that move in the same direction.
5 Draw a graph to show the relationship between two variables that move in opposite directions.
6 Draw a graph to show the relationship between two variables that have a maximum and a minimum.

7 Which of the relationships in Questions 4 and 5 is a positive relationship and which is a negative relationship?
8 What are the two ways of calculating the slope of a curved line?
9 How do we graph a relationship among more than two variables?
10 Explain what change will bring a movement along a curve.
11 Explain what change will bring a shift of a curve.

Do these questions in Study Plan 1.4 and get instant feedback.   MyEconLab

SUMMARY

Key Points

Graphing Data (pp. 15–18)

◆ A graph is made by plotting the values of two variables x and y at a point that corresponds to their values measured along the x-axis and y-axis.

◆ A scatter diagram is a graph that plots the values of two variables for a number of different values of each.

◆ A scatter diagram shows the relationship between two variables. It shows whether two variables are positively related, negatively related, or unrelated.

Graphs Used in Economic Models (pp. 18–21)

◆ Graphs are used to show relationships among variables in economic models.

◆ Relationships can be positive (an upward-sloping curve), negative (a downward-sloping curve), positive and then negative (have a maximum point), negative and then positive (have a minimum point), or unrelated (a horizontal or vertical curve).

The Slope of a Relationship (pp. 22–24)

◆ The slope of a relationship is calculated as the change in the value of the variable measured on

the y-axis divided by the change in the value of the variable measured on the x-axis, that is, $\Delta y/\Delta x$.

◆ A straight line has a constant slope.

◆ A curved line has a varying slope. To calculate the slope of a curved line, we calculate the slope at a point or across an arc.

Graphing Relationships Among More Than Two Variables (pp. 24–25)

◆ To graph a relationship among more than two variables, we hold constant the values of all the variables except two.

◆ We then plot the value of one of the variables against the value of another.

◆ A *cet. par.* change in the value of a variable on an axis of a graph brings a movement along the curve.

◆ A change in the value of a variable held constant along the curve brings a shift of the curve.

Key Terms

Ceteris paribus, 24
Direct relationship, 18
Inverse relationship, 19
Linear relationship, 18

Negative relationship, 19
Positive relationship, 18
Scatter diagram, 16
Slope, 22

STUDY PLAN PROBLEMS AND AF

Do Problems 1 to 11 in MyEconLab Chapter 1A Study Plan and get instant feedback.

Use this spreadsheet to answer Problems 1 to 3. The spreadsheet gives data on the US economy: column A is the year, column B is the inflation rate, column C is the interest rate, column D is the growth rate and column E is the unemployment rate.

	A	B	C	D	E
1	2001	1.6	3.4	1.1	4.7
2	2002	2.4	1.6	1.8	5.8
3	2003	1.9	1.0	2.5	6.0
4	2004	3.3	1.4	3.5	5.5
5	2005	3.4	3.2	3.1	5.1
6	2006	2.5	4.7	2.7	4.6
7	2007	4.1	4.4	1.9	4.6
8	2008	0.1	1.5	−0.3	5.8
9	2009	2.7	0.2	−3.5	9.3
10	2010	1.5	0.1	3.0	9.6
11	2011	3.0	0.1	1.7	9.0

1 Draw a scatter diagram to show the relationship between the inflation rate and the interest rate. Describe the relationship.

2 Draw a scatter diagram to show the relationship between the growth rate and the unemployment rate. Describe the relationship.

3 Draw a scatter diagram to show the relationship between the interest rate and the unemployment rate. Describe the relationship.

Use the following news clip in Problems 4 to 6.

Avengers **Shatters More Records:**

Film	Cinemas (number)	Revenue (dollars per cinema)
Marvel's The Avengers	4,349	23,696
Dark Shadows	3,755	7,906
Think Like A Man	2,052	2,834
The Last Song	2,531	1,780

Source: boxofficemojo.com,

Data for weekend of 11–12 May 2012

4 Draw a graph of the relationship between the revenue per cinema on the *y*-axis and the number of cinemas on the *x*-axis. Describe the relationship.

5 Calculate the slope of the relationship between 3,755 and 2,052 cinemas.

6 Calculate the slope of the relationship between 2,052 and 2,531 cinemas.

7 Calculate th

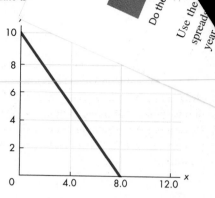

Use the following relationship in Problems 8 and 9.

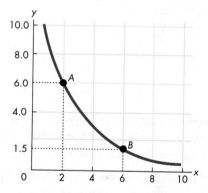

8 Calculate the slope of the relationship at point *A* and at point *B*.

9 Calculate the slope across the arc *AB*.

Use the following table, which gives the price of a balloon ride, the temperature and the number of rides per day, in Problems 10 and 11.

Price (pounds per ride)	Balloon rides (number per day)		
	10°C	20°C	30°C
5.00	32	40	50
10.00	27	32	40
15.00	18	27	32
20.00	10	18	27

10 Draw a graph of the relationships between the price and the number of rides, holding the temperature constant at 20°C.

11 What happens in the graph in Problem 10 if the temperature rises to 30°C?

ODITIONAL PROBLEMS AND APPLICATIONS

ems in MyEconLab if assigned by your lecturer.

following spreadsheet in Problems 12 to 14. The
heet provides data on oil and petrol: column A is the
column B is the price of oil (dollars per barrel), column
s the price of petrol (pence per litre), column D is oil pro-
uction and column E is the quantity of petrol refined (both in
millions of barrels per day).

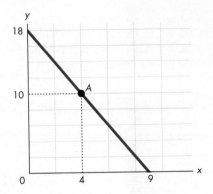

	A	B	C	D	E
1	2001	24	32	5.8	8.3
2	2002	25	31	5.7	8.4
3	2003	29	35	5.7	8.5
4	2004	38	42	5.4	8.7
5	2005	53	51	5.2	8.7
6	2006	64	58	5.1	8.9
7	2007	71	92	5.1	9.0
8	2008	97	95	5.0	8.9
9	2009	62	108	4.9	8.9
10	2010	79	100	4.5	8.6
11	2011	104	117	3.7	8.9

12 Draw a scatter diagram of the price of oil and the quantity
of oil produced. Describe the relationship.

13 Draw a scatter diagram of the price of petrol and the
quantity of petrol refined. Describe the relationship.

14 Draw a scatter diagram of the quantities of oil produced
and petrol refined. Describe the relationship.

Use the following data in Problems 15 to 17.

Draw a graph that shows the relationship between the two
variables x and y:

x	0	1	2	3	4	5
y	25	24	22	18	12	0

15 a Is the relationship positive or negative?

   b Does the slope of the relationship become steeper or
   flatter as the value of x increases?

   c Think of some economic relationships that might be
   similar to this one.

16 Calculate the slope of the relationship between x and y
when x equals 3.

17 Calculate the slope of the relationship across the arc as x
increases from 4 to 5.

18 In the following graph, calculate the slope of the relationship at point A.

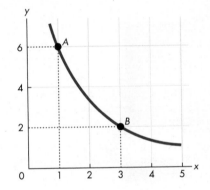

Use the following graph in Problems 19 and 20.

19 Calculate the slope at points A and B.

20 Calculate the slope across the arc AB.

Use the following table, which gives the price of an umbrella,
the amount of rainfall and the number of umbrellas purchased,
in Problems 21 to 23.

Price (pounds per umbrella)	Umbrellas (number purchased per day)		
	0	200	400
		(mm of rainfall)	
5.00	7	8	12
10.00	4	7	8
15.00	2	4	7
20.00	1	2	4

21 Draw a graph of the relationship between the price and
the number of umbrellas purchased, holding the amount
of rainfall constant at 200 mm. Describe the relationship.

22 What happens in the graph in Problem 21 if the price
rises and rainfall is constant?

23 What happens in the graph in Problem 21 if the rainfall
increases from 200 mm to 400 mm?

2

The Economic Problem

After studying this chapter you will be able to:

◆ Define the production possibilities frontier and calculate opportunity cost

◆ Distinguish between production possibilities and preferences and describe an efficient allocation of resources

◆ Explain how current production choices expand future production possibilities

◆ Explain how specialisation and trade expand our production possibilities

◆ Describe the economic institutions that coordinate decisions

Why does food cost much more today than it did a few years ago? How do we know when we are using our resources efficiently? How can we become more productive? Is it really true that both buyers and sellers gain from trade? In this chapter, you will study an economic model that answers these questions.

At the end of the chapter, in *Reading Between the Lines* we'll apply what you've learned to understanding why food costs more today than it did a few years ago and how producing biofuel is one of the sources of higher food costs.

Production Possibilities and Opportunity Cost

Every working day, in mines and factories, shops and offices, on farms and construction sites across the EU, 230 million people produce a vast variety of goods and services valued at €12 billion. But the quantities of goods and services that we can produce are limited by both our available resources and technology. And if we want to increase our production of one good, we must decrease our production of something else – we face a trade-off. You are now going to study the limits to production.

The **production possibilities frontier** (*PPF*) is the boundary between those combinations of goods and services that can be produced and those that cannot. To illustrate the *PPF*, we look at a *model* economy in which everything remains the same (*ceteris paribus*) except for the production of the two goods we are considering.

Let's look at the production possibilities frontier for cola and pizza, which stand for *any* pair of goods or services.

Production Possibilities Frontier

The *production possibilities frontier* for cola and pizza shows the limits to the production of these two goods, given the total resources available to produce them. Figure 2.1 shows this production possibilities frontier. The table lists some combinations of the quantities of pizzas and cola that can be produced in a month given the resources available. The figure graphs these combinations. The *x*-axis shows the quantity of pizzas produced and the *y*-axis shows the quantity of cola produced.

The *PPF* illustrates *scarcity* because points outside the frontier are *unattainable*. These points that describe wants that can't be satisfied.

We can produce at all the points *inside* the *PPF* and *on* the *PPF*. These points are *attainable*. For example, we can produce 4 million pizzas and 5 million cans of cola. Figure 2.1 shows this combination as point *E* and as possibility *E* in the table.

Moving along the *PPF* from point *E* to point *D* (possibility *D* in the table) we produce more cola and less pizza: 9 million cans of cola and 3 million pizzas. Or moving in the opposite direction from point *E* to point *F* (possibility *F* in the table), we produce more pizza and less cola: 5 million pizzas and no cola.

Figure 2.1 The Production Possibilities Frontier

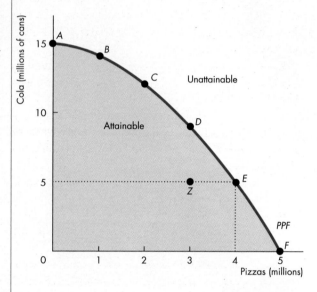

Possibility	Pizzas (millions)		Cola (millions of cans)
A	0	and	15
B	1	and	14
C	2	and	12
D	3	and	9
E	4	and	5
F	5	and	0

The table lists six points on the production possibilities frontier for cola and pizza. Row *A* tells us that if we produce no pizza, the maximum quantity of cola we can produce is 15 million cans. Points *A, B, C, D, E* and *F* in the figure represent the rows of the table. The line passing through these points is the production possibilities frontier (*PPF*).

The *PPF* separates the attainable from the unattainable. Production is possible at any point inside the orange area or on the frontier. Points outside the frontier are unattainable. Points inside the frontier such as point *Z* are inefficient because resources are either wasted or misallocated. At such points, it is possible to use the available resources to produce more of either or both goods.

MyEconLab Animation

Production Efficiency

We achieve **production efficiency** if we produce goods and services at the lowest possible cost. This outcome occurs at all points *on* the *PPF*. At points *inside* the *PPF*, production is *inefficient* because we are giving up more than necessary of one good to produce a given quantity of the other good.

For example, at point *Z* in Figure 2.1, we produce 3 million pizzas and 5 million cans of cola, but we have enough resources to produce 3 million pizzas and 9 million cans of cola. Our pizzas cost more cola than necessary. We can get them for a lower cost. Only when we produce *on* the *PPF* do we incur the lowest possible cost of production.

Production *inside* the *PPF* is inefficient because resources are either unused or misallocated or both.

Resources are *unused* when they are idle but could be working. For example, we might leave some of the factories idle or some workers unemployed.

Resources are *misallocated* when they are assigned to tasks for which they are not the best match. For example, we might assign skilled pizza chefs to work in a cola factory and skilled cola workers to cook pizza in a pizzeria. We could get more pizzas and more cola if we reassigned these workers to the tasks that more closely match their skills.

Trade-Off Along the *PPF*

Every choice *along* the *PPF* involves a *trade-off*. Trade-offs like that between cola and pizza arise in every imaginable real-world situation in which a choice must be made. At any given point in time, we have a fixed amount of labour, land, capital and entrepreneurship. We can employ these resources and technology to produce goods and services, but we are limited in what we can produce.

When doctors say that we must spend more on AIDS and cancer research, they are suggesting a trade-off: more medical research for less of some other things. When a politician says that she wants to spend more on education and healthcare, she is suggesting a trade-off: more education and healthcare for less defence expenditure. When an environmental group argues for less logging in tropical rainforests, it is suggesting a trade-off: greater conservation of endangered wildlife for less hardwood. When you want a higher mark on your next test, you face a trade-off: spend more time studying for less leisure or sleep time.

All trade-offs involve a cost – an opportunity cost.

Opportunity Cost

The **opportunity cost** of an action is the highest-valued alternative forgone. The *PPF* helps us to make this idea precise and enables us to calculate opportunity cost. Along the *PPF*, there are only two goods, so there is only one alternative forgone: some quantity of the other good. To produce more pizzas we must produce less cola. The opportunity cost of an additional pizza is the number of cans of cola we *must* forgo. Similarly, the opportunity cost of an additional can of cola is the quantity of pizzas we *must* forgo.

For example, in Figure 2.1 if we move from point *C* to point *D*, we produce an additional 1 million pizzas but 3 million fewer cans of cola. The additional 1 million pizzas *cost* 3 million cans of cola. Or 1 pizza costs 3 cans of cola.

Opportunity Cost Is a Ratio

Opportunity cost is a ratio. It is the decrease in the quantity produced of one good divided by the increase in the quantity produced of another good as we move along the production possibilities frontier.

Because opportunity cost is a ratio, the opportunity cost of producing an additional can of cola is equal to the *inverse* of the opportunity cost of producing an additional pizza. Check this proposition: Moving along the *PPF* from *C* to *D*, the opportunity cost of a pizza is 3 cans of cola. The inverse of 3 is 1/3, so if we decrease the production of pizzas and increase the production of cola by moving from *D* to *C*, the opportunity cost of a can of cola must be 1/3 of a pizza. That is exactly the number we calculated for the move from *D* to *C*.

Increasing Opportunity Cost

The opportunity cost of a pizza increases as the quantity of pizzas produced increases. The outward-bowed shape of the *PPF* reflects increasing opportunity cost. When we produce a large quantity of cola and a small quantity of pizzas – between points *A* and *B* in Figure 2.1 – the frontier has a gentle slope. An increase in the quantity of pizzas *costs* a small quantity of cola – the opportunity cost of a pizza is a small quantity of cola.

When we produce a large quantity of pizzas and a small quantity of cola – between points *E* and *F* in Figure 2.1 – the frontier is steep. A given increase in the quantity of pizzas *costs* a large decrease in the quantity of cola, so the opportunity cost of a pizza is a large quantity of cola.

ECONOMICS IN THE NEWS

The Opportunity Cost of Food

Cost of Global Food Up Again

The cost of global food has increased by 8 per cent since December 2011. All key food items cost more, except for rice. Asia's strong demand for food imports has contributed to this increase, notwithstanding bumper harvests.

Source: *Food Price Watch*, World Bank, April 2012

The Questions

◆ How does the *PPF* illustrate the effect of Asia's strong demand for food imports on the cost of food?

◆ How does the *PPF* illustrate the effect of a bumper harvest?

The Answers

◆ Figure 1 shows the global *PPF* for food and other goods and services.

◆ Before the bumper harvest, the *PPF* is PPF_0 and before Asia's strong demand for food, the world is producing at point A.

◆ Asia's strong demand for food brings an increase in food production and a decrease in the production of other goods and services, which is illustrated as a movement along the *PPF* from point A to point B.

◆ At point B, the *PPF* slope is steeper than at point A, which means that the opportunity cost of food is higher at point B than at point A.

◆ A bumper harvest increases the production of food at each level of production of other goods and services.

◆ The *PPF* illustrates the effects of a bumper harvest as an outward shift of the *PPF* from PPF_0 to PPF_1.

◆ The bumper harvest lowered the opportunity cost of food, but the news clip says that this effect was not sufficient to offset the rise in opportunity cost resulting from Asia's strong demand.

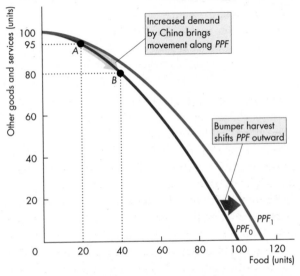

Figure 1 PPF for Food and Other Goods and Services

The *PPF* is bowed outward because resources are not all equally productive in all activities. People with several years of experience working for PepsiCo are good at producing cola but not very good at making pizzas. So if we move some of these people from PepsiCo to Domino's, we get a small increase in the quantity of pizzas but a large decrease in the quantity of cola.

Similarly, people who have spent years working at Domino's are good at producing pizzas, but they have no idea how to produce cola. So if we move some of these people from Domino's to PepsiCo, we get a small increase in the quantity of cola but a large decrease in the quantity of pizzas. The more of either good we try to produce, the less productive are the additional resources we use to produce that good and the larger is the opportunity cost of a unit of that good.

How do we choose among the points on the *PPF*? How do we know which point on the *PPF* is the best one?

REVIEW QUIZ

1   How does the production possibilities frontier illustrate scarcity?

2   How does the production possibilities frontier illustrate production efficiency?

3   How does the production possibilities frontier show that every choice involves a trade-off?

4   How does the production possibilities frontier illustrate opportunity cost?

5   Why is opportunity cost a ratio?

6   Why does the *PPF* for most goods bow outward and what does that imply about the relationship between opportunity cost and the quantity produced?

Do these questions in Study Plan 2.1 and get instant feedback.

MyEconLab

Using Resources Efficiently

We achieve *production efficiency* at every point on the *PPF*, but which point is best? The answer is the point on the *PPF* at which goods and services are produced in the quantities that provide the greatest possible benefit. When goods and services are produced at the lowest possible cost and in the quantities that provide the greatest possible benefit, we have achieved **allocative efficiency**.

The questions that we raised when we reviewed the four big issues in Chapter 1 are questions about allocative efficiency. To answer such questions, we must measure and compare costs and benefits.

The *PPF* and Marginal Cost

Marginal cost is the opportunity cost of producing *one more unit*. We can calculate marginal cost from the slope of the *PPF*. As the quantity of pizzas produced increases, the *PPF* gets steeper and the marginal cost of a pizza increases. Figure 2.2 illustrates the calculation of the marginal cost of a pizza.

Begin by finding the opportunity cost of pizza in blocks of 1 million pizzas. The first million pizzas cost 1 millions of cans of cola, the second million pizzas cost 2 millions of cans of cola, the third million pizzas cost 3 millions of cans of cola, and so on. The bars in part (a) illustrate these calculations.

The bars in part (b) show the cost of an average pizza in each block of the 1 million pizzas. Focus on the third million pizzas – the move from *C* to *D* in part (a). Over this range, because the 1 million pizzas cost 3 millions of cans of cola, one of these pizzas, on average, costs 3 cans of cola – the height of the bar in part (b).

Next, find the opportunity cost of each additional pizza – the marginal cost of a pizza. The marginal cost of a pizza increases as the quantity of pizzas produced increases. The marginal cost at point *C* is less than it is at point *D*. On average over the range from *C* to *D*, the marginal cost of a pizza is 3 cans of cola. But it exactly equals 3 cola only in the middle of the range between *C* and *D*.

The red dot in part (b) indicates that the marginal cost of a pizza is 3 cans of cola when 2.5 million pizzas are produced. Each black dot in part (b) is interpreted in the same way. The red curve that passes through these dots, labelled *MC*, is the marginal cost curve. It shows the marginal cost of a pizza at each quantity of pizza as we move along the *PPF*.

Figure 2.2 The *PPF* and Marginal Cost

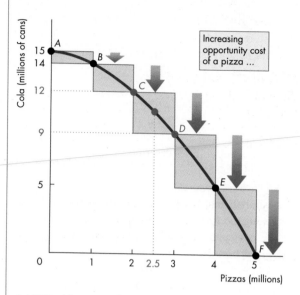

(a) PPF and opportunity cost

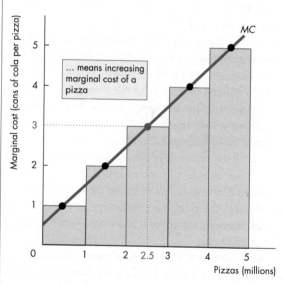

(b) Marginal cost

Marginal cost is calculated from the slope of the *PPF* in part (a). As the quantity of pizzas produced increases, the *PPF* gets steeper and the marginal cost of a pizza increases. The bars in part (a) show the opportunity cost of pizza in blocks of 1 million pizzas. The bars in part (b) show the cost of an average pizza in each of these blocks of 1 million pizzas. The red curve, *MC*, shows the marginal cost of a pizza at each point along the *PPF*. This curve passes through the centre of each of the bars in part (b).

MyEconLab Animation ──────────◆

Preferences and Marginal Benefit

The **marginal benefit** from a good or service is the benefit received from consuming one more unit of it. This benefit is subjective. It depends on people's **preferences** – people's likes and dislikes and the intensity of those feelings.

Marginal benefit and *preferences* stand in sharp contrast to *marginal cost* and *production possibilities*. Preferences describe what people like and want, and the production possibilities describe the limits or constraints on what is feasible.

We need a concrete way of illustrating preferences that parallels the way we illustrate the limits to production using the *PPF*.

The device that we use to illustrate preferences is the **marginal benefit curve**, which is a curve that shows the relationship between the marginal benefit from a good and the quantity consumed of that good. Note that the *marginal benefit curve* is unrelated to the *PPF* and cannot be derived from it.

We measure the marginal benefit from a good or service by the most that people are willing to pay for an additional unit of it. The idea is that you are willing to pay less for a good than it is worth to you but you are not willing to pay more: the most you are willing to pay for something is its marginal benefit.

It is a general principle that the more we have of any good or service, the smaller is its marginal benefit and the less we are willing to pay for another unit of it. This tendency is so widespread and strong that we call it a principle – the *principle of decreasing marginal benefit*.

The basic reason why the marginal benefit of a good or service decreases as we consume more of it is that we like variety. The more we consume of any one good or service, the more we tire of it and would prefer to switch to something else.

Think about your willingness to pay for pizza (or any other item). If pizza is hard to come by and you can buy only a few slices a year, you might be willing to pay a high price to get an additional slice. But if pizza is all you've eaten for the past few days, you are willing to pay almost nothing for another slice.

You've learned to think about cost as opportunity cost, not pounds or euros. You can think about marginal benefit and willingness to pay in the same terms. The marginal benefit, measured by what you are willing to pay for something, is the quantity of other goods and services that you are willing to forgo. Let's continue with the example of cola and pizza and illustrate preferences this way.

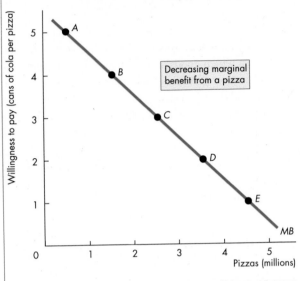

Figure 2.3   Preferences and the Marginal Benefit Curve

Possibility	Pizzas (millions)	Willingness to pay (cans of cola per pizza)
A	0.5	5
B	1.5	4
C	2.5	3
D	3.5	2
E	4.5	1

The smaller the quantity of pizzas produced, the more cola people are willing to give up for an additional pizza. If pizza production is 0.5 million, people are willing to pay 5 cans of cola per pizza. But if pizza production is 4.5 million, people are willing to pay only 1 can of cola per pizza. Willingness to pay measures marginal benefit. A universal feature of people's preferences is that marginal benefit decreases.

MyEconLab Animation ───────────────────◆

Figure 2.3 illustrates preferences as the willingness to pay for pizza in terms of cola. In row *A*, pizza production is 0.5 million, and at that quantity people are willing to pay 5 cans of cola per pizza. As the quantity of pizzas produced increases, the amount that people are willing to pay for a pizza falls. When pizza production is 4.5 million, people are willing to pay only 1 can of cola per pizza.

Let's now use the concepts of marginal cost and marginal benefit to describe allocative efficiency.

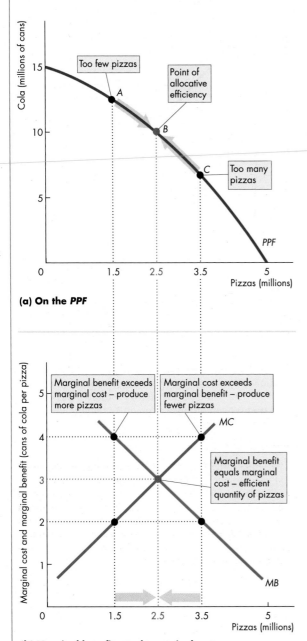

Figure 2.4 Efficient Use of Resources

(a) On the PPF

(b) Marginal benefit equals marginal cost

The greater the quantity of pizzas produced, the smaller is the marginal benefit (*MB*) from pizza – the fewer is the number of cans of cola people are willing to give up to get an additional pizza. But the greater the quantity of pizzas produced, the greater is the marginal cost (*MC*) of pizza – the greater is the number of cans of cola people must give up to get an additional pizza. When marginal benefit equals marginal cost, resources are being used efficiently.

Efficient Use of Resources

At any point on the *PPF*, we cannot produce more of one good without giving up some other good. At the *best* point on the *PPF*, we cannot produce more of one good without giving up some other good that provides greater benefit. We are producing at the point of allocative efficiency – the point on the *PPF* that we prefer above all other points.

Suppose in Figure 2.4, we produce 1.5 million pizzas. The marginal cost of a pizza is 2 cans of cola and the marginal benefit from a pizza is 4 cans of cola. Because someone values an additional pizza more highly than it costs to produce, we can get more value from our resources by moving some of them out of producing cola and into producing pizzas.

Now suppose we produce 3.5 million pizzas. The marginal cost of a pizza is now 4 cans of cola, but the marginal benefit from a pizza is only 2 cans of cola. Because the additional pizza costs more to produce than anyone thinks it is worth, we can get more value from our resources by moving some of them away from producing pizzas and into producing cola.

But suppose we produce 2.5 million pizzas. Marginal cost and marginal benefit are now equal at 3 cans of cola. This allocation of resources between pizzas and cola is efficient. If more pizzas are produced, the forgone cola is worth more than the additional pizzas. If fewer pizzas are produced, the forgone pizzas are worth more than the additional cola.

◆ REVIEW QUIZ

1 What is marginal cost? How is it measured?
2 What is marginal benefit? How is it measured?
3 How does the marginal benefit from a good change as the quantity of that good increases?
4 What is allocative efficiency and how does it relate to the production possibilities frontier?
5 What conditions must be satisfied if resources are used efficiently?

Do these questions in Study Plan 2.2 and get instant feedback.   MyEconLab

You now understand the limits to production and the conditions under which resources are used efficiently. Your next task is to study the expansion of production possibilities.

Economic Growth

During the past 30 years, production per person in the EU has doubled. An expansion of production possibilities is called **economic growth**. Economic growth increases our *standard of living*, but it does not overcome scarcity or avoid opportunity cost. To make our economy grow, we face a trade-off – the faster we make production grow, the greater is the opportunity cost of economic growth.

The Cost of Economic Growth

Economic growth comes from technological change and capital accumulation. **Technological change** is the development of new goods and of better ways of producing goods and services. **Capital accumulation** is the growth of capital resources, which includes *human capital*.

Technological change and capital accumulation have vastly expanded our production possibilities. We can produce automobiles that provide us with more transportation than was available when we had only horses and carriages. We can produce satellites that provide global communications on a much larger scale than that available with the earlier cable technology. And by using technologies, such as fracking (see *Economics in the News* opposite), we can produce vastly more natural gas and other energy products.

But if we use our resources to develop new technologies and produce capital, we must decrease our production of consumption goods and services. New technologies and new capital have an opportunity cost. Let's look at this opportunity cost.

Instead of studying the *PPF* of pizzas and cola, we'll hold the quantity of cola produced constant and examine the *PPF* for pizzas and pizza ovens. Figure 2.5 shows this *PPF* as the blue curve *ABC*. If we devote no resources to producing pizza ovens, we produce at point *A*. If we produce 3 million pizzas, we can produce 6 pizza ovens at point *B*. If we produce no pizzas, we can produce 10 ovens at point *C*.

The amount by which our production possibilities expand depends on the resources we devote to technological change and capital accumulation. If we devote no resources to this activity (point *A*), our *PPF* remains the blue curve PPF_0 in Figure 2.5. If we cut the current production of pizza and produce 6 ovens (point *B*), then in the future, we'll have more capital and our *PPF* will rotate outward to the position shown by the red curve

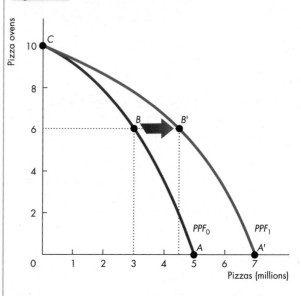

Figure 2.5 Economic Growth

PPF_0 shows the limits to the production of pizza and pizza ovens, with the production of all other goods and services remaining the same. If we allocate no resources to producing pizza ovens and produce 5 million pizzas, our production possibilities will remain the same, PPF_0.

But if we decrease pizza production to 3 million and produce 6 ovens, our production possibilities will expand. After one period, the *PPF* rotates outward to PPF_1 and we can produce at point *B'*, a point outside the original PPF_0.

We can rotate the *PPF* outward, but we cannot avoid opportunity cost. The opportunity cost of producing more pizzas in the future is fewer pizzas today.

MyEconLab Animation ⸻⸻⸻⸻◆

PPF_1. The fewer resources we devote to producing pizza and the more resources we devote to producing ovens, the greater is the future expansion of our production possibilities.

Economic growth brings enormous benefit in the form of increased consumption, but it is not free and does not abolish scarcity.

In Figure 2.5, to make economic growth happen we must use some resources to produce new ovens, which leaves fewer resources to produce pizza. To move to *B'* in the future, we must move from *A* to *B* today. The opportunity cost of more pizzas in the future is fewer pizzas today. Also, on the new *PPF*, we continue to face a trade-off and opportunity cost.

The ideas about economic growth that we have explored in the setting of the pizza industry also apply to nations. Hong Kong and the EU (see *Economics in Action* on p. 40) provide a striking case study.

ECONOMICS IN THE NEWS

Discovery Changes Production Possibilities

Britain Has Shale Gas for 1,500 Years

New fracking technology can tap previously inaccessible seams of shale gas and the British Geological Survey says Britain has enough shale gas to heat every home for 1,500 years – some 200 times the previous estimate. A shale gas revolution in the United States has slashed energy bills. Environmentalists fear that fracking will pollute drinking water sources.

Source: *The Times*, 9 February 2013

The Questions

◆ How does the development of fracking technology change the *PPF* for gas and other goods and services?

◆ How does fracking technology change the opportunity cost of gas?

◆ How does fracking technology change the efficient quantity of gas to produce and consume?

The Answers

◆ Fracking increases production possibilities by making previously inaccessible reserves of gas available. It increases the quantity of gas that can be produced at each quantity of other goods and services.

◆ In Figure 1(a), which shows a *PPF* for gas and other goods and services, the *PPF* shifts from PPF_0 to PPF_1. (This shift is like the one explained in Figure 2.5.)

◆ At any given quantity of gas produced, the opportunity cost of gas falls.

◆ Figure 1(b) shows the change in marginal cost (the opportunity cost of one more unit). The marginal cost curve shifts downward from MC_0 to MC_1.

Fracking near Preston, Lancashire

◆ Fracking increases the efficient quantity of gas produced and consumed.

◆ Before fracking, the efficient quantity of gas was 30 billion cubic feet per week on PPF_0.

◆ After fracking is developed, the efficient quantity of gas increases to 40 billion cubic feet per week.

◆ The efficient quantity of other goods and services also increases.

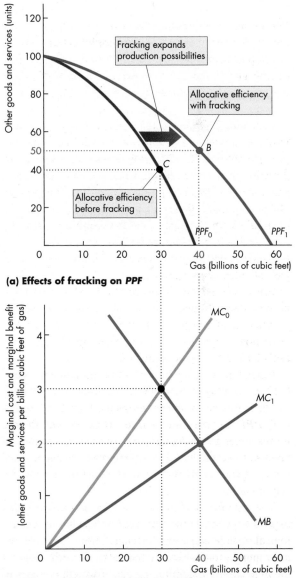

(a) Effects of fracking on PPF

(b) Effects of fracking on MC and efficient quantities

Figure 1 The Economic Effects of Fracking

ECONOMICS IN ACTION

Economic Growth in the EU and Hong Kong

The experiences of the EU and Hong Kong are a striking example of the effects of our choices on the rate of economic growth.

Figure 1 shows that, in 1970, the production possibilities per person in the EU were more than double those in Hong Kong. In 1970, the EU was at point A on its PPF and Hong Kong was at point A on its PPF.

Since 1970, both economies have grown, but Hong Kong has devoted one third of its resources to accumulating capital while the EU has devoted only one fifth.

By 2011, the production possibilities per person in Hong Kong were higher than those in the EU. If Hong Kong continues to devote more resources to accumulating capital (at point B on its 2011 *PPF*) than the EU does (at point C on its 2011 *PPF*), the gap between Hong Kong and the EU will widen further. But if Hong Kong increases consumption and decreases capital accumulation (by moving down along its 2011 *PPF*), then its economic growth rate will slow.

Hong Kong is typical of the fast-growing Asian economies, which include China, South Korea, India, Taiwan and Thailand, which have expanded their production possibilities by between 5 and 10 per cent a year.

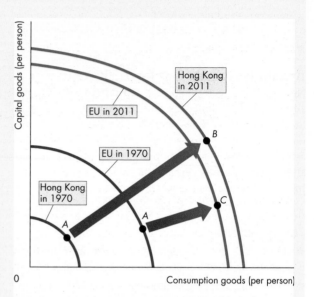

Figure 1   Economic Growth in the EU and Hong Kong

If such high economic growth rates are maintained, these other Asian countries will continue to close the gap between themselves and the EU and possibly overtake the EU as Hong Kong has done.

A Nation's Economic Growth

The experiences of the EU and Hong Kong make a striking example of the effects of our choices about consumption and capital goods on the rate of economic growth.

If a nation devotes all its factors of production to producing consumption goods and services and none to advancing technology and accumulating capital, its production possibilities in the future will be the same as they are today.

To expand production possibilities in the future, a nation must devote fewer resources to producing current consumption goods and services and some resources to accumulating capital and developing new technologies. As production possibilities expand, consumption in the future can increase. The decrease in consumption today is the opportunity cost of an increase in consumption in the future.

 REVIEW QUIZ

1   What are the two key factors that generate economic growth?
2   How does economic growth influence the *PPF*?
3   What is the opportunity cost of economic growth?
4   Why has Hong Kong experienced faster economic growth than the EU?
5   Does economic growth overcome scarcity?

Do these questions in Study Plan 2.3 and get instant feedback.   MyEconLab

We have seen that we can increase our production possibilities by accumulating capital and developing new technology. Next, we'll study another way in which we can expand our production possibilities – the amazing fact that *both* buyers and sellers gain from specialisation and trade.

 # Gains from Trade

People can produce for themselves all the goods and services that they consume, or they can produce one good or a few goods and trade with others. Producing only one good or a few goods is called *specialisation*.

We are going to discover how people gain by specialising in the production of the good in which they have a *comparative advantage* and trading with each other.

Comparative Advantage and Absolute Advantage

A person has a **comparative advantage** in an activity if that person can perform the activity at a lower opportunity cost than anyone else. Differences in opportunity costs arise from differences in individual abilities and from differences in the characteristics of other resources.

No one excels at everything. One person is an outstanding batter but a poor catcher; another person is a brilliant lawyer but a poor teacher. In almost all human endeavours, what one person does easily, someone else finds difficult. The same applies to land and capital. One plot of land is fertile but has no mineral deposits; another plot of land has outstanding views but is infertile. One machine has great precision but is difficult to operate; another is fast but often breaks down.

Although no one excels at everything, some people excel and can outperform others in many activities – perhaps all activities. A person who is more productive than others has an **absolute advantage**.

Absolute advantage involves comparing productivities – production per hour – whereas comparative advantage involves comparing opportunity cost.

A person who has an absolute advantage does not have a *comparative* advantage in every activity. Maria Sharapova can run faster and play tennis better than most people. She has an absolute advantage in these two activities. But compared with other people, she is a better tennis player than a runner, so her *comparative* advantage is in playing tennis.

Because people's abilities and the quality of their resources differ, they have different opportunity costs of producing various goods and services. Such differences give rise to comparative advantage.

To explore the idea of comparative advantage, and its astonishing implications, we'll look at the production process in two smoothie bars: one operated by Erin and the other operated by Jack.

Erin's Smoothie Bar

Erin produces smoothies and salads. In Erin's high-tech bar, she can turn out either a smoothie or a salad every 2 minutes – see Table 2.1.

If Erin spends all her time making smoothies, she can produce 30 an hour. And if she spends all her time making salads, she can also produce 30 an hour. If she splits her time equally between the two, she can produce 15 smoothies and 15 salads an hour. For each additional smoothie Erin produces, she must decrease her production of salads by one, and for each additional salad she produces, she must decrease her production of smoothies by one. So

> **Erin's opportunity cost of producing 1 smoothie is 1 salad,**

and

> **Erin's opportunity cost of producing 1 salad is 1 smoothie.**

Erin's customers buy smoothies and salads in equal quantities, so she splits her time equally between the items and produces 15 smoothies and 15 salads an hour.

Jack's Smoothie Bar

Jack also produces both smoothies and salads. But Jack's bar is smaller than Erin's. Also, Jack has only one blender, and it's a slow old machine. Even if Jack uses all his resources to produce smoothies, he can produce only 6 an hour – see Table 2.2. But Jack is good in the salad department, so if he uses all his resources to make salads, he can produce 30 an hour.

Jack's ability to make smoothies and salads is the same regardless of how he splits an hour between the two tasks. He can make a salad in 2 minutes or a smoothie in 10 minutes. For each additional smoothie Jack produces, he must decrease his production of salads by 5. And for each additional salad he produces, he

---

Table 2.1

Erin's Production Possibilities

Item	Minutes to produce 1	Quantity per hour
Smoothies	2	30
Salads	2	30

Table 2.2

Jack's Production Possibilities

Item	Minutes to produce 1	Quantity per hour
Smoothies	10	6
Salads	2	30

must decrease his production of smoothies by 1/5 of a smoothie. So

Jack's opportunity cost of producing 1 smoothie is 5 salads,

and

Jack's opportunity cost of producing 1 salad is 1/5 of a smoothie.

Jack's customers, like Erin's, buy smoothies and salads in equal quantities. So Jack spends 50 minutes of each hour making smoothies and 10 minutes of each hour making salads. With this division of his time, Jack produces 5 smoothies and 5 salads an hour.

Erin's Comparative Advantage

Comparative advantage is a situation in which one person's opportunity cost of producing a good is less than another person's opportunity cost of producing that *same* good. Erin has a comparative advantage in producing smoothies because her opportunity cost of a smoothie is 1 salad whereas Jack's is 5 salads.

Jack's Comparative Advantage

If Erin has a comparative advantage in producing smoothies, Jack must have a comparative advantage in producing salads. His opportunity cost of a salad is 1/5 of a smoothie, whereas Erin's is 1 smoothie.

Achieving the Gains from Trade

Erin and Jack run into each other one evening in a singles bar. After a few minutes of getting acquainted, Erin tells Jack about her amazing smoothie business. Her only problem, she tells Jack, is that she wishes she could produce more because potential customers leave when the queue gets too long.

Jack is hesitant to risk spoiling his chances by telling Erin about his own struggling business, but he takes the risk. Jack explains to Erin that he spends 50 minutes of every hour making 5 smoothies and 10 minutes making 5 salads. Erin's eyes pop. 'Have I got a deal for you!' she exclaims.

Here's the deal that Erin sketches on a serviette. Jack stops making smoothies and allocates all his time to producing salads. Erin stops making salads and allocates all her time to producing smoothies. That is, they both specialise in producing the good in which they have a comparative advantage. Together they produce 30 smoothies and 30 salads – see Table 2.3(b).

They then trade. Erin sells Jack 10 smoothies and Jack sells Erin 20 salads – the price of a smoothie is 2 salads – see Table 2.3(c).

After the trade, Jack has 10 salads – the 30 he produces minus the 20 he sells to Erin. He also has the 10 smoothies that he buys from Erin. So Jack now has increased the quantities of smoothies and salads that he can sell to his customers – see Table 2.3(d).

Erin has 20 smoothies – the 30 she produces minus the 10 she sells to Jack. She has the 20 salads that she

Table 2.3

Erin and Jack Gain from Trade

(a) Before trade	Erin	Jack
Smoothies	15	5
Salads	15	5

(b) Specialisation	Erin	Jack
Smoothies	30	0
Salads	0	30

(c) Trade	Erin	Jack
Smoothies	sell 10	buy 10
Salads	buy 20	sell 20

(d) After trade	Erin	Jack
Smoothies	20	10
Salads	20	10

(e) Gains from trade	Erin	Jack
Smoothies	+5	+5
Salads	+5	+5

Figure 2.6 The Gains from Trade

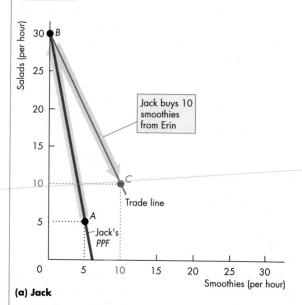

(a) Jack

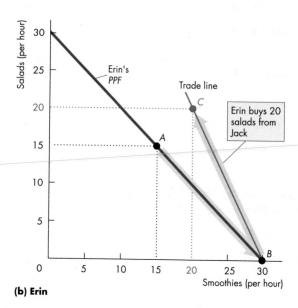

(b) Erin

Jack initially produces at point *A* on his *PPF* in part (a), and Erin initially produces at point *A* on her *PPF* in part (b). Jack has a comparative advantage in producing salads and Erin has a comparative advantage in producing smoothies.

If Jack specialises in salad, he produces 30 salads and no smoothies at point *B* on his *PPF*. If Erin specialises

in making smoothies, she produces 30 smoothies and no salads, she produces at point *B* on her *PPF*.

They exchange salads for smoothies along the red 'Trade line'. Each goes to point *C* – a point outside his or her *PPF*. Both Jack and Erin increase production by 5 smoothies and 5 salads with no change in resources.

MyEconLab Animation

buys from Jack. Erin has increased the quantities of smoothies and salads that she can sell to her customers – see Table 2.3(d). Both Erin and Jack gain 5 smoothies and 5 salads – see Table 2.3(e).

To illustrate her idea, Erin grabs a fresh serviette and draws the graphs in Figure 2.6. The blue *PPF* in part (a) shows Jack's production possibilities. Before trade, he is producing 5 smoothies and 5 salads an hour at point *A*. The blue *PPF* in part (b) shows Erin's production possibilities. Before trade, she is producing 15 smoothies and 15 salads an hour at point *A*.

Erin's proposal is that they each specialise in producing the good in which they have a comparative advantage. Jack produces 30 salads and no smoothies at point *B* on his *PPF*. Erin produces 30 smoothies and no salads at point *B* on her *PPF*.

Erin and Jack then trade smoothies and salads at a price of 2 salads per smoothie or 1/2 of a smoothie per salad. Jack buys smoothies from Erin for 2 salads each, which is less than the 5 salads it costs him to produce a smoothie. Erin buys salads from Jack for 1/2 a smoothie each, which is less than the 1 smoothie that it costs her to produce a salad.

With trade, Jack has 10 smoothies and 10 salads at point *C* – a gain of 5 smoothies and 5 salads. Jack moves to a point *outside* his *PPF*.

With trade, Erin has 20 smoothies and 20 salads at point *C* – a gain of 5 smoothies and 5 salads. Erin moves to a point *outside* her *PPF*.

Despite Erin being more productive than Jack, both Erin and Jack gain from specialising in the production of the good in which each has a comparative advantage and then trading.

◆ REVIEW QUIZ

1 What gives a person a comparative advantage?
2 Distinguish between comparative advantage and absolute advantage.
3 Why do people specialise and trade?
4 What are the gains from specialisation and trade?
5 What is the source of the gains from trade?

Do these questions in Study Plan 2.4 and get instant feedback.   MyEconLab

Economic Coordination

For 7 billion people to specialise and produce millions of different goods and services, individual choices must somehow be coordinated. Two competing coordination systems have been used: central economic planning and markets (see *At Issue*, p. 8).

Central economic planning works badly because economic planners don't know people's production possibilities and preferences, so production ends up inside the *PPF* and the wrong things are produced. Decentralised coordination works best, but to do so it needs four complementary social institutions. They are:

◆ Firms
◆ Markets
◆ Property rights
◆ Money

Firms

A **firm** is an economic unit that employs factors of production and organises them to produce and sell goods and services.

Firms coordinate a huge amount of economic activity. For example, Tesco buys or rent shops across the UK, equips them with shelves and storage space and hires labour. Tesco directs the labour and decides what goods to buy and sell.

But Tesco would not have become Britain's largest retailer if it had produced all the things that it sells. It became the largest UK retailer by specialising in providing retail services and buying the goods it sells from other firms that specialise in producing goods (just like Erin and Jack did). This trade needs markets.

Markets

In ordinary speech, the word *market* means a place where people buy and sell goods such as fish, meat, fruits and vegetables.

In economics, a **market** is any arrangement that enables buyers and sellers to get information and to do business with each other. An example is the world oil market, which is not a place, but a network of oil producers, oil users, wholesalers and brokers who buy and sell oil. In the world oil market, decision makers make deals by using the Internet. Enterprising individuals and firms, each pursuing their own self-interest, have

profited by making markets – by standing ready to buy or sell the items in which they specialise. But markets can work only when property rights exist.

Property Rights

The social arrangements that govern the ownership, use and disposal of anything that people value are called **property rights**. *Real property* includes land and buildings – the things we call property in ordinary speech – and durable goods such as plant and equipment. *Financial property* includes shares and bonds and money in the bank. *Intellectual property* is the intangible product of creative effort. This type of property includes books, music, computer programs and inventions of all kinds and is protected by copyrights and patents.

Where property rights are enforced, people have the incentive to specialise and produce the goods and services in which they have a comparative advantage. Where people can steal the production of others, resources are devoted not to production but to protecting possessions.

Money

Money is any commodity or token that is generally acceptable as a means of payment. Erin and Jack didn't use money; they exchanged salads and smoothies. In principle, trade in markets can exchange any item for any other item. But you can perhaps imagine how complicated life would be if we exchanged goods for other goods. The 'invention' of money makes trading in markets much more efficient.

Circular Flows Through Markets

Trading in markets for goods and services and factors of production creates a circular flow of expenditures and income. Figure 2.7 shows the circular flows. Households specialise and choose the quantities of labour, land, capital and entrepreneurship to sell or rent to firms. Firms choose the quantities of factors of production to hire. These (red) flows go through the *factor markets*. Households choose the quantities of goods and services to buy, and firms choose the quantities to produce. These (red) flows go through the *goods markets*. Households receive incomes from firms and make expenditures on goods and services (the green flows).

How do markets coordinate all these decisions?

Figure 2.7 Circular Flows in the Market Economy

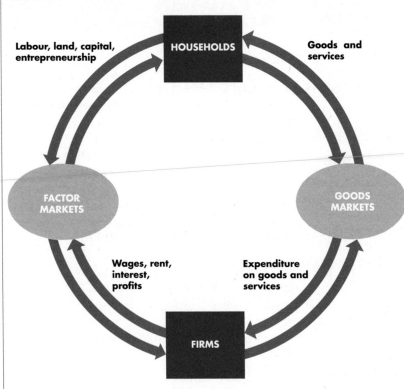

Households and firms make economic choices and markets coordinate these choices.

Households choose the quantities of labour, land, capital and entrepreneurship to sell or rent to firms in exchange for wages, rent, interest and profit. Households also choose how to spend their incomes on the various types of goods and services available.

Firms choose the quantities of factors of production to hire and the quantities of the various goods and services to produce.

Goods markets and factor markets coordinate these choices of households and firms.

The counterclockwise red flows are real flows – the flow of factors of production from households to firms and the flow of goods and services from firms to households.

The clockwise green flows are the payments for the red flows. They are the flow of incomes from firms to households and the flow of expenditure on goods and services from households to firms.

Coordinating Decisions

Markets coordinate decisions through price adjustments. Suppose that some people who want to buy fresh-baked bread are not able to do so. To make the choices of buyers and sellers compatible, buyers must switch to prepackaged bread or more fresh-baked bread must be offered for sale (or both). A rise in the price of fresh-baked bread produces this outcome. A higher price encourages bakers to offer more fresh-baked bread for sale. It also encourages some people to change the bread they buy. Fewer people buy fresh-baked bread, and more buy prepackaged bread. More fresh-baked bread (and more prepackaged bread) are offered for sale.

Alternatively, suppose that more fresh-baked bread is available than people want to buy. In this case, more fresh-baked bread must be bought or less fresh-baked bread must be offered for sale (or both). A fall in the price of fresh-baked bread achieves this outcome. It encourages bakers to produce a smaller quantity of, and encourages people to buy more, fresh-baked bread.

 REVIEW QUIZ

1 Why are social institutions such as firms, markets, property rights and money necessary?
2 What are the main functions of markets?
3 What are the flows in the market economy that go from firms to households and from households to firms?
4 In the circular flows of the market economy, which flows are real flows? Which flows are money flows?

Do these questions in Study Plan 2.5 and get instant feedback.   MyEconLab

You have now begun to see how economists approach economic questions. You can see all around you the lessons you've learned in this chapter.

Reading Between the Lines on pp. 46−47 provides an opportunity to apply the *PPF* model to deepen your understanding of why food costs more today than it did a few years ago.

The Rising Opportunity Cost of Food

The Telegraph, 5 October 2012

Biofuels and the Food That's Going Up in Smoke

Geoffery Lean

The growing use of energy from crops has driven up food prices. . . .

The EU stipulated in 2009 that biofuels should effectively provide 10 per cent of all transport fuels by 2020. . . .

As Lester Brown – president of Washington's Earth Policy Institute – has long pointed out, biofuels pit the hungry against relatively affluent motorists in competition for crops. . . .

Forty per cent of the US corn crop now goes for fuel, not food, while the land used to grow biofuels for Europe alone could instead be used to feed 127 million people.

The competition drives up food prices. . . . Oxfam reported this week that an area of land eight times the size of the UK had been sold off over the past decade – and that two thirds of the deals appear to have been struck for the growing of biofuels. . . .

Now, finally, the EC is making a move. On October 17 . . . the EC climate commissioner, . . . will propose that biofuels from food crops should be limited to just 5 per cent of transport energy consumption.

The Essence of the Story

- ◆ EU climate change policy in 2009 raised the target for biofuels in transport fuel to 10 per cent.

- ◆ EU farmers and farmers around the world have switched from producing crops for food to crops for biofuel.

- ◆ Competition for crops has driven up food prices around the world when land used to grow biofuels could be used to feed 127 million people.

- ◆ The EU will propose that biofuels from food crops be cut to 5 per cent.

Economic Analysis

◆ Biofuel is made from maize and several other crops, so biofuel and food compete to use the same resources.

◆ Following 2009 EU policy targets, farmers increased the land devoted to growing biofuel crops.

◆ Increasing the production of crops for biofuel means decreasing the production of crops for food and decreasing the production of other goods and services.

◆ Figure 1 shows the EU production possibilities frontier, *PPF*, for one of the biofuel crops, maize, and other goods and services.

◆ A movement along the *PPF* in Figure 1 from point *A* to point *B* illustrates the increase in the production of maize and decrease in the production of other goods and services between 2010 and 2012.

◆ In moving from point *A* to point *B*, the EU incurs a higher opportunity cost of producing maize, as the greater slope of the *PPF* at point *B* indicates.

◆ In other regions of the world, despite the fact that more land was devoted to maize production, the amount of maize produced didn't change.

◆ The reason is that bad drought lowered the crop yields in the US and Eastern Europe.

◆ Figure 2 shows the rest of the world's *PPF* for maize and other goods and services in 2010 and 2011.

◆ The increase in the amount of land devoted to producing maize is illustrated by a movement along PPF_{10}.

◆ With a decrease in the crop yield, production possibilities decreased and the *PPF* rotated inward.

◆ The rotation from PPF_{10} to PPF_{12} illustrates this decrease in production possibilities.

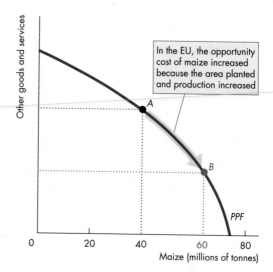

In the EU, the opportunity cost of maize increased because the area planted and production increased

Figure 1   EU *PPF*

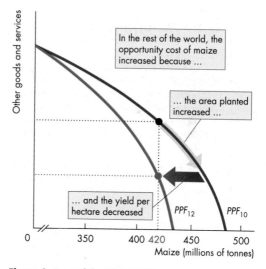

In the rest of the world, the opportunity cost of maize increased because ...

... the area planted increased ...

... and the yield per hectare decreased

Figure 2   Rest of the World *PPF*

◆ The opportunity cost of producing maize in the rest of the world increased for two reasons: the movement along its *PPF* and the inward rotation of the *PPF*.

◆ With a higher opportunity cost of producing maize, the cost of both biofuel and food increases.

SUMMARY

Key Points

Production Possibilities and Opportunity Cost (pp. 32-34)

- The production possibilities frontier is the boundary between production levels that are attainable and those that are unattainable when all available resources are used to their limit.

- Production efficiency occurs at points on the production possibilities frontier.

- Along the production possibilities frontier, the opportunity cost of producing more of one good is the amount of the other good that must be given up.

- The opportunity cost of all goods increases as production of the good increases.

Do Problems 1 to 3 to get a better understanding of production possibilities and opportunity cost.

Using Resources Efficiently (pp. 35-37)

- Allocative efficiency occurs when goods and services are produced at the least possible cost and in the quantities that bring the greatest possible benefit.

- The marginal cost of a good is the opportunity cost of producing one more unit of it.

- The marginal benefit from a good is the benefit received from consuming one more unit of it and is measured by the willingness to pay for it.

- The marginal benefit of a good decreases as the amount of the good available increases.

- Resources are used efficiently when the marginal cost of each good is equal to its marginal benefit.

Do Problems 4 to 10 to get a better understanding of using resources efficiently.

Economic Growth (pp. 38-40)

- Economic growth, which is the expansion of production possibilities, results from capital accumulation and technological change.

- The opportunity cost of economic growth is forgone current consumption.

- The benefit of economic growth is increased future consumption.

Do Problem 11 to get a better understanding of economic growth.

Gains from Trade (pp. 41-43)

- A person has a comparative advantage in producing a good if that person can produce the good at a lower opportunity cost than everyone else.

- People gain by specialising in the activity in which they have a comparative advantage and trading.

Do Problems 12 and 13 to get a better understanding of the gains from trade.

Economic Coordination (pp. 44-45)

- Firms coordinate a large amount of economic activity, but there is a limit to the efficient size of a firm.

- Markets coordinate the economic choices of people and firms.

- Markets can work efficiently only when property rights exist and money makes trading in markets more efficient.

Do Problem 14 to get a better understanding of economic coordination.

Key Terms

Absolute advantage, 41
Allocative efficiency, 35
Capital accumulation, 38
Comparative advantage, 41
Economic growth, 38
Firm, 44
Marginal benefit, 36
Marginal benefit curve, 36
Marginal cost, 35
Market, 44
Money, 44
Opportunity cost, 33
Preferences, 36
Production efficiency, 33
Production possibilities frontier, 32
Property rights, 44
Technological change, 38

STUDY PLAN PROBLEMS AND APPLI

Do Problems 1 to 20 in MyEconLab Chapter 2 Study Plan and get instant feedback.

Production Possibilities and Opportunity Cost (Study Plan 2.1)

Use the following information in Problems 1 to 3.

Brazil produces biofuel from sugar, and the land used to grow sugar can be used to grow food crops. Suppose that Brazil's production possibilities for biofuel and food crops are as follows:

Biofuel (barrels per day)		Food crops (tonnes per day)
70	and	0
64	and	1
54	and	2
40	and	3
22	and	4
0	and	5

1 **a** Draw a graph of Brazil's *PPF* and explain how your graph illustrates scarcity.

b If Brazil produces 40 barrels of biofuel a day, how much food must it produce to achieve production efficiency?

c Why does Brazil face a trade-off on its *PPF*?

2 **a** If Brazil increases its production of biofuel from 40 barrels per day to 54 barrels per day, what is the opportunity cost of the additional biofuel?

b If Brazil increases its production of food crops from 2 tonnes per day to 3 tonnes per day, what is the opportunity cost of the additional food?

c What is the relationship between your answers to parts (a) and (b)?

3 Does Brazil face an increasing opportunity cost of producing biofuel? What feature of Brazil's *PPF* illustrates increasing opportunity cost?

Using Resources Efficiently

(Study Plan 2.2)

Use the table in Problem 1 in Problems 4 and 5.

4 Define marginal cost and calculate Brazil's marginal cost of producing a tonne of food when the quantity produced is 2.5 tonnes per day.

5 Define marginal benefit, explain how it is measured and explain why the data in the table do not enable you to calculate Brazil's marginal benefit from food.

6 Distinguish between *production efficiency* and *allocative efficiency*. Explain why many production possibilities achieve production efficiency but only one achieves allocative efficiency.

Use the following graphs in Pr

Harry enjoys tennis but wants
course. The graphs show his
his *MB* curve for tennis.

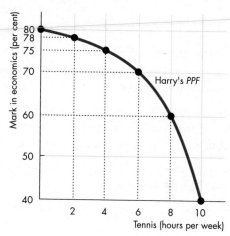

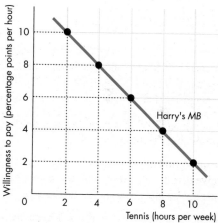

7 What is Harry's marginal cost of tennis if he plays for (i) 3 hours a week, (ii) 5 hours a week and (iii) 7 hours a week?

8 **a** If Harry uses his time to achieve allocative efficiency, what is his economics mark and how many hours of tennis does he play?

b Explain why Harry would be worse off getting a higher mark than your answer in part (a).

9 If Harry becomes a tennis superstar with big earnings from tennis, what happens to his *PPF*, his *MB* curve and his efficient time allocation?

10 If Harry suddenly finds high marks in economics easier to attain, what happens to his *PPF*, his *MB* curve and his efficient time allocation?

... c Growth (Study Plan 2.3)

...rm grows wheat and produces pork. The marginal ...ost of producing each of these products increases as more of it is produced.

  a Make a graph that illustrates the farm's *PPF*.

  b The farm adopts a new technology that allows it to use fewer resources to fatten pigs. On a graph show the impact of the new technology on the farm's *PPF*.

  c With the farm using the new technology described in part (b), has the opportunity cost of producing a tonne of wheat increased, decreased or remained the same? Explain and illustrate your answer.

  d Is the farm more efficient with the new technology than it was with the old one? Why?

Gains from Trade (Study Plan 2.4)

Use the following data in Problems 12 and 13.

In an hour, Sue can produce 40 caps or 4 jackets and Tessa can produce 80 caps or 4 jackets.

12 a Calculate Sue's opportunity cost of producing a cap.

  b Calculate Tessa's opportunity cost of producing a cap.

  c Who has a comparative advantage in producing caps?

  d If Sue and Tessa specialise in producing the good in which each of them has a comparative advantage, and they trade 1 jacket for 15 caps, who gains from the specialisation and trade?

13 Suppose that Tessa buys a new machine for making jackets that enables her to make 20 jackets an hour. (She can still make only 80 caps per hour.)

  a Who now has a comparative advantage in producing jackets?

  b Can Sue and Tessa still gain from trade?

  c Would Sue and Tessa still be willing to trade 1 jacket for 15 caps? Explain your answer.

Economic Coordination (Study Plan 2.5)

14 For 50 years, Cuba has had a centrally planned economy in which the government makes the big decisions on how resources will be allocated.

  a Why would you expect Cuba's production possibilities (per person) to be smaller than those of the EU?

  b What are the social institutions that Cuba might lack that help the EU to achieve allocative efficiency?

Economics in the News (Study Plan 2.N)

Use the following data in Problems 15 to 17.

Brazil produces biofuel from sugar at a cost of 83 cents per gallon. The US produces biofuel from corn at a cost of $1.14 per gallon. Sugar grown on one acre of land produces twice the quantity of biofuel as the corn grown on an acre. The US imports 5 per cent of the biofuel it uses and produces the rest itself. Since 2003, US biofuel production has more than doubled and US corn production has increased by 45 per cent.

15 a Does Brazil or the US have a comparative advantage in producing biofuel?

  b Sketch the *PPF* for biofuel and other goods and services for the US.

  c Sketch the *PPF* for biofuel and other goods and services for Brazil.

16 a Do you expect the opportunity cost of producing biofuel in the US to have increased since 2003? Explain why.

  b Do you think the US has achieved production efficiency in its manufacture of biofuel? Explain why or why not.

  c Do you think the US has achieved allocative efficiency in its manufacture of biofuel? Explain why or why not.

17 Make a graph similar to Figure 2.6 to show how both the US and Brazil gain from specialisation and trade.

Use this news clip in Problems 18 to 20.

Traditional Cuppa Is in Decline

In 21st century Britain, it seems the traditional British cup of tea is in decline. Tea drinking is a ritual and people have it for their comfort, but younger people are not buying into the ritual any more.

Source: *The Guardian*, 8 May 2005

18 a Sketch *PPF*s for the production of tea and other goods and services in India and the UK.

  b Sketch marginal cost curves for the production of tea in India and the UK.

19 a Sketch the marginal benefit curves for tea in the UK before and after younger people stop 'buying into the ritual' of drinking tea.

  b Explain how the quantity of tea that achieves allocative efficiency has changed.

  c Does the change in preferences towards tea affect the opportunity cost of producing tea?

20 Explain why the UK does not produce tea and instead imports it from India.

ADDITIONAL PROBLEMS AND APPLICATIONS

Do these problems in MyEconLab if assigned by your lecturer.

MyEconLab

Production Possibilities and Opportunity Cost

Use the following information in Problems 21 and 22.

Sunland's production possibilities are:

Food (kilograms per month)		Sunscreen (litres per month)
300	and	0
200	and	50
100	and	100
0	and	150

21 **a** Draw a graph of Sunland's *PPF*.

b If Sunland produces 150 kilograms of food, how much sunscreen must it produce if it achieves production efficiency?

c What is Sunland's opportunity cost of producing 1 kilogram of food?

d What is Sunland's opportunity cost of producing 1 litre of sunscreen?

e What is the relationship between your answers to parts (c) and (d)?

22 What feature of a *PPF* illustrates increasing opportunity cost? Explain why Sunland's opportunity cost does or does not increase.

Using Resources Efficiently

23 In Problem 21, what is the marginal cost of a kilogram of food in Sunland when the quantity produced is 150 kilograms per month? What is special about the marginal cost of food in Sunland?

24 The table describes the preferences in Sunland:

Sunscreen (litres per month)		Willingness to pay (kilograms per litre)
25	and	3
75	and	2
125	and	1

a What is the marginal benefit from sunscreen and how is it measured?

b Draw a graph of Sunland's marginal benefit from sunscreen.

Use the following news clip in Problems 25 and 26.

Malaria Eradication Back on the Table

In response to the Gates Malaria Forum in October 2007, countries are debating the pros and cons of eradication. Dr. Arata Kochi of the World Health Organisation believes that with enough money malaria cases could be cut by 90 per cent, but he believes that it would be very expensive to eliminate the remaining 10 per cent of cases. He concluded that countries should not strive to eradicate malaria.

Source: *The New York Times*, 4 March 2008

25 Is Dr. Kochi talking about *production efficiency* or *allocative efficiency* or both?

26 Make a graph with the percentage of malaria cases eliminated on the *x*-axis and the marginal cost and marginal benefit of driving down malaria cases on the *y*-axis. On your graph:

a Draw a marginal cost curve that is consistent with Dr. Kochi's opinion.

b Draw a marginal benefit curve that is consistent with Dr. Kochi's opinion.

c Identify the quantity of malaria eradicated that achieves allocative efficiency.

Economic Growth

27 Capital accumulation and technological change bring economic growth, which means that the *PPF* keeps shifting outward: production that was unattainable yesterday becomes attainable today; production that is unattainable today will become attainable tomorrow. Why doesn't this process of economic growth mean that scarcity is being defeated and will one day be gone?

Gains from Trade

Use the following data in Problems 28 and 29.

Kim can produce 40 pies or 400 cakes an hour. Liam can produce 100 pies or 200 cakes an hour.

28 **a** Calculate Kim's opportunity cost of a pie and Liam's opportunity cost of a pie.

b If each spends 30 minutes of each hour producing pies and 30 minutes producing cakes, how many pies and cakes does each produce?

c Who has a comparative advantage in producing pies? Who has a comparative advantage in producing cakes?

29 a Draw a graph of Kim's *PPF* and Liam's *PPF*.

b On your graph, show the point at which each produces when they spend 30 minutes of each hour producing pies and 30 minutes producing cakes.

c On your graph, show what Kim produces and what Liam produces when they specialise.

d When they specialise and trade, what are the total gains from trade?

e If Kim and Liam share the total gains equally, what trade takes place between them?

Use the following news clip in Problems 30 and 31.

Britain's Music Stores Squeezed off the High Street
Music retailing is changing: Sony Music and Amazon are selling online, supermarkets are selling at low prices, and traditional high street music retailers HMV, Music Zone and Virgin Megastores are all struggling.

Source: *The Economist*, 20 January 2007

30 a Draw the *PPF* curves for high street music retailers and online music retailers before and after the Internet became available.

b Draw the marginal cost and marginal benefit curves for high street music retailers and online music retailers before and after the Internet became available.

31 Explain how changes in production possibilities, preferences or both have changed the way in which recorded music is retailed.

Use the following news clip in Problems 32 and 33.

Pop Star Turned Designer
Victoria Beckham of Spice Girls fame now has a second career as a clothing designer. Figure-flattering, modern-lady-like, cleverly constructed dresses have been the heart of her brand since her first collection.

Source: *The Guardian*, 12 September 2011

32 a Does Victoria Beckham have an absolute advantage in singing and clothing design, and is this the reason for her success in both activities?

b Does Victoria Beckham have a comparative advantage in singing or clothing design or both, and is this the reason for her success in both activities?

33 a Sketch a *PPF* between singing and producing other goods and services for Victoria Beckham and for yourself.

b How do you (and people like you) and Victoria Beckham (and people like her) gain from specialisation and trade?

Economic Coordination

34 Indicate, on a graph of the circular flows in the market economy, the real and money flows in which the following items belong:

a You buy an iPad from the Apple Store.

b Apple Inc. pays the designers of the iPad.

c Apple Inc. decides to expand and rents an adjacent building.

d You buy a new e-book from Amazon.

e Apple Inc. hires a student as an intern during the summer.

Economics in the News

35 After you have studied *Reading Between the Lines* on pp. 46–47, answer the following questions.

a Why might the EU climate change policy increase EU production of maize?

b Why would you expect an increase in the quantity of EU maize production to increase the opportunity cost of maize?

c Why did the cost of producing maize increase in the rest of the world?

d Is it possible that the increased quantity of maize produced, despite the higher cost of production, moves the EU closer to allocative efficiency?

36 Lots of Little Screens
Inexpensive broadband access has created a generation of television producers for whom the Internet is their native medium. As they redirect the focus from TV to computers, mobile phones and iPods, the video market is developing into an open digital network.

Source: *The New York Times*, 2 December 2007

a How has inexpensive broadband changed the production possibilities of video entertainment and other goods and services?

b Sketch a *PPF* for video entertainment and other goods and services before broadband.

c Show how the arrival of inexpensive broadband has changed the *PPF*.

d Sketch a marginal benefit curve for video entertainment.

e Show how the new generation of TV producers for whom the Internet is their native medium might have changed the marginal benefit from video entertainment.

f Explain how the efficient quantity of video entertainment has changed.

3 Demand and Supply

After studying this chapter you will be able to:

◆ Describe a competitive market and think about a price as an opportunity cost

◆ Explain the influences on demand

◆ Explain the influences on supply

◆ Explain how demand and supply determine prices and quantities bought and sold

◆ Use demand and supply to make predictions about changes in prices and quantities

The price of bread rocketed in 2012. Why? Why do some prices rise, some prices fall, and some fluctuate?

This chapter answers these questions. The demand and supply model that you're about to study is the main tool of economics. It explains how prices are determined and how they guide the use of resources to influence *What*, *How* and *For Whom* goods and services are produced.

At the end of the chapter, in *Reading Between the Lines*, we'll apply the model to the market for bread and see why its price rose sharply in 2012.

Markets and Prices

When you want to buy a new pair of running shoes, or a sandwich, or an energy drink, or a bottle of water, or decide to upgrade your CD player, you must find a place where people sell those items. The place in which you find them is a *market*. You learned in Chapter 2 (p. 44) that a market is any arrangement that enables buyers and sellers to get information and to do business with each other.

A market has two sides: buyers and sellers. There are markets for *goods* such as apples and hiking boots, for *services* such as haircuts and tennis lessons, for *resources* such as computer programmers and earth-movers, and for other manufactured *inputs* such as memory chips and car parts. There are also markets for money, such as the euro and the dollar, and for financial securities, such as BP shares and Yahoo! shares. Only our imagination limits what can be traded in markets.

Some markets are physical places where buyers and sellers meet, and where an auctioneer or a broker helps to determine the prices. Examples of this type of market are the London Stock Exchange and the Billingsgate fish market.

Some markets are groups of people spread around the world who never meet and know little about each other but are connected through the Internet or by telephone and fax. Examples are the e-commerce markets and currency markets.

But most markets are unorganised collections of buyers and sellers. You do most of your trading in this type of market. An example is the market for football boots. The buyers in this multi-million pound a year market are the several million people who play football (or who want to make an exotic fashion statement). The sellers are the tens of thousands of retail sports equipment and footwear stores. Each buyer can visit several different stores and each seller knows that the buyer has a choice of stores.

A Competitive Market

Markets vary in the intensity of competition that buyers and sellers face. In this chapter, we're going to study a **competitive market** – a market that has many buyers and many sellers, so no single buyer or seller can influence the price.

Producers offer items for sale only if the price is high enough to cover their opportunity cost. And consumers respond to changing opportunity cost by seeking cheaper alternatives to expensive items.

We are going to study the way people respond to *prices* and the forces that determine prices. But to pursue these tasks, we need to understand the relationship between a price and an opportunity cost.

In everyday life, the *price* of an object is the number of pounds or euros that must be given up in exchange for it. Economists refer to this price as the **money price**.

The *opportunity cost* of an action is the highest-valued alternative forgone. If, when you buy a coffee, the highest-valued thing you forgo is some chocolate, then the opportunity cost of the coffee is the *quantity* of chocolate forgone. We can calculate the quantity of chocolate forgone from the money prices of coffee and chocolate.

If the money price of coffee is £3 a cup and the money price of a chocolate bar is £1, then the opportunity cost of 1 cup of coffee is 3 chocolate bars. To calculate this opportunity cost, we divide the price of a cup of coffee by the price of a chocolate bar and find the *ratio* of one price to the other. The ratio of one price to another is called a **relative price** and a *relative price is an opportunity cost*.

We can express the relative price of coffee in terms of chocolate or any other good. The normal way of expressing a relative price is in terms of a 'basket' of all goods and services. To calculate this relative price, we divide the money price of a good by the money price of a 'basket' of all goods (called a *price index*). The resulting relative price tells us the opportunity cost of the good in terms of how much of the 'basket' we must give up to buy it.

The theory of demand and supply that we are about to study determines *relative prices*, and the word 'price' means *relative* price. When we predict that a price will fall, we do not mean that its *money* price will fall – although it might. We mean that its *relative* price will fall. That is, its price will fall *relative* to the average price of other goods and services.

REVIEW QUIZ

1   What is the distinction between a money price and a relative price?
2   Explain why a relative price is an opportunity cost.
3   Think of examples of goods whose relative price has risen or has fallen by a large amount.

Do these questions in Study Plan 3.1 and get instant feedback.   MyEconLab

Let's begin our study of demand and supply, starting with demand.

 **Demand**

If you demand something, then you

1 Want it,

2 Can afford it and

3 Plan to buy it.

Wants are the unlimited desires or wishes that people have for goods and services. How many times have you thought that you would like something 'if only you could afford it' or 'if it weren't so expensive'? Scarcity guarantees that many – perhaps most – of our wants will never be satisfied. Demand reflects a decision about which wants to satisfy.

The **quantity demanded** of a good or service is the amount that consumers plan to buy during a given time period at a particular price. The quantity demanded is not necessarily the same as the quantity actually bought. Sometimes the quantity demanded exceeds the amount of goods available, so the quantity bought is less than the quantity demanded.

The quantity demanded is measured as an amount per unit of time. For example, suppose that you buy one cup of coffee a day. The quantity of coffee that you demand can be expressed as 1 cup per day, 7 cups per week, or 365 cups per year.

Many factors influence buying plans and one of them is price. We look first at the relationship between the quantity demanded of a good and its price. To study this relationship, we make a *ceteris paribus* assumption. That is, we keep all other influences on buying plans the same and we ask: How, other things remaining the same, does the quantity demanded of a good change as its price changes?

The law of demand provides the answer.

The Law of Demand

The **law of demand** states:

Other things remaining the same, the higher the price of a good, the smaller is the quantity demanded; and the lower the price of a good, the greater is the quantity demanded.

Why does a higher price reduce the quantity demanded? For two reasons:

◆ Substitution effect

◆ Income effect

Substitution Effect

When the price of a good rises, other things remaining the same, its *relative* price – its opportunity cost – rises. Although each good is unique, it has *substitutes* – other goods that can be used in its place. As the opportunity cost of a good rises, people buy less of that good and more of its substitutes.

Income Effect

When the price of a good rises and other influences on buying plans remain unchanged, the price rises relative to incomes. Faced with a higher price and unchanged income, people cannot afford to buy all the things they previously bought. They must decrease the quantities demanded of at least some goods and services, and normally the good whose price has increased will be one of the goods that people buy less of.

To see the substitution effect and the income effect at work, think about the effects of a change in the price of an energy drink. Many goods are substitutes for an energy drink. For example, an energy bar or an energy gel could be consumed in place of an energy drink.

Suppose that an energy drink initially sells for £3 and then its price falls to £1.50. People now substitute energy drinks for energy bars – the substitution effect. And with a budget that now has some slack from the lower price of an energy drink, people buy more energy drinks – the income effect. The quantity of energy drinks demanded increases for these two reasons.

Now suppose that an energy drink sells for £3 and its price rises to £4. People now substitute energy bars for energy drinks – the substitution effect. Faced with tighter budgets, people buy even fewer energy drinks – the income effect. The quantity of energy drinks demanded decreases for these two reasons.

Demand Curve and Demand Schedule

You are now about to study one of the two most used curves in economics: the demand curve. And you are going to encounter one of the most critical distinctions: the distinction between *demand* and *quantity demanded*.

The term **demand** refers to the entire relationship between the price of the good and the quantity demanded of the good. Demand is illustrated by the demand curve and the demand schedule. The term *quantity demanded* refers to a point on a demand curve – the quantity demanded at a particular price.

Figure 3.1 shows the demand curve for energy drinks. A **demand curve** shows the relationship between the quantity demanded of a good and its price when all other influences on consumers' planned purchases remain the same.

The table in Figure 3.1 is the *demand schedule*, which lists the quantity demanded at each price when all the other influences on consumers' planned purchases remain the same. For example, if the price of an energy drink is 50 pence, the quantity demanded is 9 million a week. If the price is £2.50, the quantity demanded is 2 million a week. The other rows of the table show the quantities demanded at prices of £1.00, £1.50 and £2.00.

We graph the demand schedule as a demand curve with the quantity demanded on the *x*-axis and the price on the *y*-axis. The points on the demand curve labelled *A* to *E* correspond to the rows of the demand schedule. For example, point *A* on the graph shows a quantity demanded of 9 million energy drinks a week at a price of 50 pence a drink.

Willingness and Ability to Pay

We can also view a demand curve as a willingness-and-ability-to-pay curve. And the willingness and ability to pay is a measure of *marginal benefit*.

If a small quantity is available, the highest price that someone is willing and able to pay for one more unit is high. As the quantity available increases, the marginal benefit falls and the highest price that someone is willing and able to pay falls along the demand curve.

In Figure 3.1, if only 2 million energy drinks are available each week, the highest price that someone is willing to pay for the 2 millionth drink is £2.50. But if 9 million energy drinks are available each week, someone is willing to pay 50 pence for the last drink bought.

A Change in Demand

When any factor that influences buying plans other than the price of the good changes, there is a **change in demand**. Figure 3.2 illustrates an increase in demand. When demand increases, the demand curve shifts rightward and the quantity demanded is greater at each and every price. For example, at a price of £2.50, on the original (blue) demand curve, the quantity demanded is 2 million energy drinks a week. On the new (red) demand curve, the quantity demanded is 6 million energy drinks a week. Look closely at the numbers in the table in Figure 3.2 and check that the quantity demanded at each price is greater.

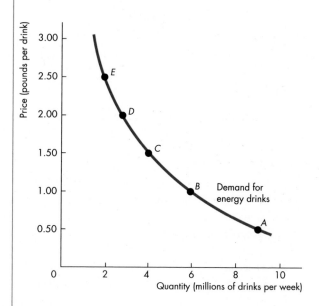

Figure 3.1   The Demand Curve

	Price (pounds per drink)	Quantity demanded (millions of energy drinks per week)
A	0.50	9
B	1.00	6
C	1.50	4
D	2.00	3
E	2.50	2

The table shows a demand schedule for energy drinks. At a price of 50 pence an energy drink, 9 million a week are demanded; at a price of £1.50 an energy drink, 4 million a week are demanded. The demand curve shows the relationship between quantity demanded and price, everything else remaining the same. The demand curve slopes downward: as price decreases, the quantity demanded increases.

The demand curve can be read in two ways. For a given price, the demand curve tells us the quantity that people plan to buy. For example, at a price of £1.50 an energy drink, the quantity demanded is 4 million energy drinks a week. For a given quantity, the demand curve tells us the maximum price that consumers are willing and able to pay for the last energy drink available. For example, the maximum price that consumers will pay for the 6 millionth drink is £1.00.

MyEconLab Animation ————————◆

Figure 3.2 An Increase in Demand

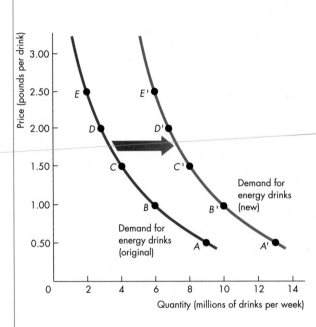

Original demand schedule Original income		New demand schedule New higher income	
Price (pounds per drink)	Quantity demanded (millions of drinks per week)	Price (pounds per drink)	Quantity demanded (millions of drinks per week)
A 0.50	9	A' 0.50	13
B 1.00	6	B' 1.00	10
C 1.50	4	C' 1.50	8
D 2.00	3	D' 2.00	7
E 2.50	2	E' 2.50	6

A change in any influence on buyers' plans other than the price of the good itself results in a new demand schedule and a shift of the demand curve. A change in income changes the demand for energy drinks.

At a price of £1.50 an energy drink, 4 million drinks a week are demanded at the original income (row *C* of the table) and 8 million energy drinks a week are demanded at the new higher income. A rise in income increases the demand for energy drinks. The demand curve shifts *rightward*, as shown by the shift arrow and the resulting red curve.

MyEconLab Animation ———————————◆

Six main factors bring changes in demand. They are changes in:

◆ Prices of related goods
◆ Expected future prices
◆ Income
◆ Expected future income or credit
◆ Population
◆ Preferences

Prices of Related Goods

The quantity of energy drinks that consumers plan to buy depends in part on the prices of its substitutes. A **substitute** is a good that can be used in place of another good. For example, a bus ride is a substitute for a train ride, and an energy bar is a substitute for an energy drink. If the price of an energy bar rises, people buy fewer energy bars and more energy drinks. The demand for energy drinks increases.

The quantity of a good that people plan to buy also depends on the prices of its complements. A **complement** is a good that is used in conjunction with another good. For example, fish and chips are complements, and so are energy drinks and exercise. If the price of an hour at the gym falls, people buy more gym time *and more* energy drinks.

Expected Future Prices

If the expected future price of a good rises and if the good can be stored, the opportunity cost of obtaining the good for future use is lower today than it will be when the price has increased. So people retime their purchases – they substitute over time. They buy more of the good now before its price is expected to rise (and less later), so the demand for the good today increases.

For example, suppose that Spain is hit by a frost that damages the season's orange crop. You expect the price of orange juice to rise in the future, so you fill your freezer with enough frozen juice to get you through the next six months. Your current demand for frozen orange juice has increased and your future demand has decreased.

Similarly, if the expected future price of a good falls, the opportunity cost of buying the good today is high relative to what it is expected to be in the future. So people retime their purchases. They buy less of the good now before its price is expected to fall, so the demand for the good decreases today and increases in the future.

Computer prices are constantly falling, and this fact poses a dilemma. Will you buy a new computer now, in time for the start of the academic year, or will you wait until the price has fallen some more? Because people expect computer prices to keep falling, the current demand for computers is less (the future demand is greater) than it otherwise would be.

Income

Consumers' income influences demand. When income increases, consumers buy more of most goods; and when income decreases, consumers buy less of most goods. Although an increase in income leads to an increase in the demand for *most* goods, it does not lead to an increase in the demand for *all* goods.

A **normal good** is one for which demand increases as income increases. An **inferior good** is one for which demand decreases as income increases. As income increases, the demand for air travel (a normal good) increases and the demand for long-distance bus trips (an inferior good) decreases.

Expected Future Income or Credit

When expected future income increases or credit becomes easier to get, demand for the good might increase now. For example, a sales person gets the news that she will receive a big bonus at the end of the year, so she goes into debt and buys a new car right now, rather than wait until she has received the bonus at the end of the year.

Population

Demand also depends on the size and the age structure of the population. The larger the population, the greater is the demand for all goods and services; the smaller the population, the smaller is the demand for all goods and services.

For example, the demand for parking spaces or cinema seats or energy drinks or just about anything that you can imagine is much greater in London than it is in Leeds.

Also, the larger the proportion of the population in a given age group, the greater is the demand for the goods and services used by that age group. For example, the number of older people is increasing relative to the number of babies. As a result, the demand for walking frames and places in retirement homes is increasing at a faster pace than that at which the demand for prams and places in day-care centres is increasing.

Table 3.1

The Demand for Energy Drinks

The Law of Demand

The quantity of energy drinks demanded

Decreases if:	Increases if:
◆ The price of an energy drink rises	◆ The price of an energy drink falls

Changes in Demand

The demand for energy drinks

Decreases if:	Increases if:
◆ The price of a substitute falls	◆ The price of a substitute rises
◆ The price of a complement rises	◆ The price of a complement falls
◆ The expected future price of an energy drink falls	◆ The expected future price of an energy drink rises
◆ Income falls*	◆ Income rises*
◆ Expected future income falls or credit becomes harder to get*	◆ Expected future income rises or credit becomes easier to get*
◆ The population decreases	◆ The population increases

* An energy drink is a normal good.

Preferences

Demand depends on preferences. *Preferences* are an individual's attitudes towards goods and services. Preferences depend on such things as the weather, information and fashion. For example, greater health and fitness awareness has shifted preferences in favour of energy drinks, so the demand for energy drinks has increased.

Table 3.1 summarises the influences on demand and the direction of those influences.

A Change in the Quantity Demanded versus a Change in Demand

Changes in the factors that influence buyers' plans cause either a change in the quantity demanded or a change in demand. Equivalently, they cause either a movement along the demand curve or a shift of the demand curve. The distinction between a change in the quantity demanded and a change in demand is the same as that between a movement along the demand curve and a shift of the demand curve.

A point on the demand curve shows the quantity demanded at a given price. So a movement along the demand curve shows a **change in the quantity demanded**. The entire demand curve shows demand. So a shift of the demand curve shows a *change in demand*. Figure 3.3 summarises these distinctions.

Movement Along the Demand Curve

If the price of the good changes but no other influence on buying plans changes, we illustrate the effect as a movement along the demand curve.

A fall in the price of a good increases the quantity demanded of it. In Figure 3.3, we illustrate the effect of a fall in price as a movement down along the blue demand curve D_0.

A rise in the price of a good decreases the quantity demanded of it. In Figure 3.3, we illustrate the effect of a rise in price as a movement up along the blue demand curve D_0.

A Shift of the Demand Curve

If the price of a good remains constant but some other influence on buyers' plans changes, there is a change in demand for that good. We illustrate a change in demand as a shift of the demand curve. For example, if more people work out at the gym, consumers buy more energy drinks regardless of the price of a drink. That is what a rightward shift of the demand curve shows – more energy drinks are demanded at each price.

In Figure 3.3, there is a *change in demand* and the demand curve shifts when any influence on buying plans changes, other than the price of the good. Demand *increases* and the demand curve *shifts rightward* (to the red curve D_1) if the price of a substitute rises, the price of a complement falls, the expected future price of the good rises, income increases (for a normal good), expected future income increases, or the population increases.

Demand *decreases* and the demand curve *shifts leftward* (to the red demand curve D_2) if the price of a substitute falls, the price of a complement rises, the expected future price of the good falls, income decreases (for a normal good), expected future income decreases, or the population decreases. (For an inferior good, the effects of changes in income are in the direction opposite to those described above.)

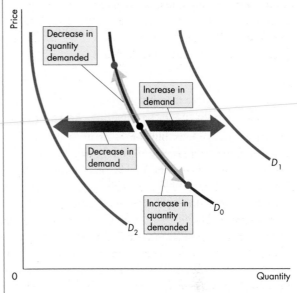

Figure 3.3 A Change in the Quantity Demanded versus a Change in Demand

When the price of the good changes, there is a movement along the demand curve and a change in the quantity demanded, shown by the blue arrows on demand curve D_0.

When any other influence on buyers' plans changes, there is a shift of the demand curve and a change in demand. An increase in demand shifts the demand curve rightward (from D_0 to D_1). A decrease in demand shifts the demand curve leftward (from D_0 to D_2).

MyEconLab Animation ──────────◆

REVIEW QUIZ

1 Define the quantity demanded of a good or service.
2 What is the law of demand, and how do we illustrate it?
3 What does the demand curve tell us about the price that consumers are willing to pay?
4 List all the influences on buying plans that change demand, and for each influence say whether it increases or decreases demand.
5 Distinguish between the quantity demanded of a good and demand for the good.
6 Why does the demand not change when the price of a good changes with no change in the other influences on buying plans?

Do these questions in Study Plan 3.2 and get instant feedback.   MyEconLab

 Supply

If a firm supplies a good or a service, the firm

1   Has the resources and technology to produce it,

2   Can profit from producing it and

3   Plans to produce it and sell it.

A supply is more than just having the *resources* and the *technology* to produce something. *Resources and technology* are the constraints that limit what is possible.

Many useful things can be produced, but they are not produced unless it is profitable to do so. (No one produces electric bed-making machines, for example!) Supply reflects a decision about which technologically feasible items to produce.

The **quantity supplied** of a good or service is the amount that producers plan to sell during a given time period at a particular price. The quantity supplied is not necessarily the same amount as the quantity actually sold. Sometimes the quantity supplied is greater than the quantity demanded, so the quantity sold is less than the quantity supplied.

Like the quantity demanded, the quantity supplied is measured as an amount per unit of time. For example, suppose that Ford produces 1,000 cars a day. The quantity of cars supplied by Ford can be expressed as 1,000 a day, 7,000 a week, or 365,000 a year. Without the time dimension, we cannot tell whether a particular number is large or small.

Many factors influence selling plans and, again, one of them is price. We look first at the relationship between the quantity supplied of a good and its price. And again, as we did when we studied demand, to isolate this relationship we keep all other influences on selling plans the same and we ask: How, other things remaining the same, does the quantity supplied of a good change as its price changes?

The law of supply provides the answer.

The Law of Supply

The **law of supply** states:

> **Other things remaining the same, the higher the price of a good, the greater is the quantity supplied; and the lower the price of a good, the smaller is the quantity supplied.**

Why does a higher price increase the quantity supplied? It is because *marginal cost increases*. As the quantity produced of any good increases, the marginal cost of producing the good increases. (You can refresh your memory of increasing marginal cost in Chapter 2, p. 35.)

It is never worth producing a good if the price received for it does not at least cover the marginal cost of producing it. So when the price of a good rises, other things remaining the same, producers are willing to incur a higher marginal cost and increase production. The higher price brings forth an increase in the quantity supplied.

Let's now illustrate the law of supply with a supply curve and a supply schedule.

Supply Curve and Supply Schedule

You are now going to study the second of the two most used curves in economics: the supply curve. And you're going to learn about the critical distinction between *supply* and *quantity supplied*.

The term **supply** refers to the entire relationship between the quantity supplied and the price of a good. Supply is illustrated by the supply curve and the supply schedule. The term *quantity supplied* refers to a point on a supply curve – the quantity supplied at a particular price.

Figure 3.4 shows the supply curve of energy drinks. A **supply curve** shows the relationship between the quantity supplied of a good and its price when all other influences on producers' planned sales remain the same. The supply curve is a graph of a supply schedule.

The table in Figure 3.4 sets out the supply schedule for energy drinks. A *supply schedule* lists the quantities supplied at each price when all the other influences on producers' planned sales remain the same. For example, if the price of an energy drink is 50 pence, the quantity supplied is zero – in row *A* of the table. If the price of an energy drink is £1.00, the quantity supplied is 3 million drinks a week – in row *B*. The other rows of the table show the quantities supplied at prices of £1.50, £2.00 and £2.50.

To make a supply curve, we graph the quantity supplied on the *x*-axis and the price on the *y*-axis. The points on the supply curve labelled *A* to *E* correspond to the rows of the supply schedule. For example, point *A* on the graph shows a quantity supplied of zero at a price of 50 pence an energy drink. Point *E* shows a quantity supplied of 6 million drinks at £2.50 an energy drink.

Figure 3.4 The Supply Curve

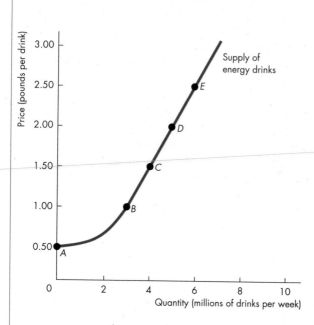

	Price (pounds per energy drink)	Quantity supplied (millions of energy drinks per week)
A	0.50	0
B	1.00	3
C	1.50	4
D	2.00	5
E	2.50	6

The table shows the supply schedule of energy drinks. For example, at a price of £1.00, 3 million energy drinks a week are supplied; at a price of £2.50, 6 million energy drinks a week are supplied. The supply curve shows the relationship between the quantity supplied and price, other things remaining the same. The supply curve usually slopes upward. As the price of a good increases, the quantity supplied increases.

A supply curve can be read in two ways. For a given price, it tells us the quantity that producers plan to sell at that price. For example, at a price of £1.50 a drink, producers are willing to supply 4 million drinks a week. For a given quantity, the supply curve tells us the minimum price at which producers are willing to sell one more drink. For example, if 6 million drinks are produced each week, the lowest price at which someone is willing to sell the 6 millionth drink is £2.50.

Minimum Supply-Price

The supply curve, like the demand curve, has two interpretations. It is the minimum-supply-price curve. It tells us the lowest price at which someone is willing to sell another unit. This lowest price is *marginal cost*.

If a small quantity is produced, the lowest price at which someone is willing to sell one more unit is low. But as the quantity produced increases, the lowest price at which someone is willing to sell one more unit rises along the supply curve.

In Figure 3.4, if 6 million energy drinks are produced each week, the lowest price that a producer is willing to accept for the 6 millionth drink is £2.50. But if only 4 million energy drinks are produced each week, a producer is willing to accept £1.50 for the last drink sold.

A Change in Supply

When any factor that influences selling plans other than the price of the good changes, there is a **change in supply**. Six main factors bring changes in supply. They are changes in:

◆ Prices of factors of production
◆ Prices of related goods produced
◆ Expected future prices
◆ Number of suppliers
◆ Technology
◆ The state of nature

Prices of Factors of Production

The prices of factors of production used to produce a good influence the supply of the good. The easiest way to see this influence is to think about the supply curve as a minimum-supply-price curve. If the price of a factor of production rises, the lowest price a producer is willing to accept rises, so supply decreases. For example, during 2009, as the price of jet fuel increased, the supply of air transportation decreased. Similarly, a rise in the minimum wage decreases the supply of energy drinks.

Prices of Related Goods Produced

The prices of related goods and services that firms produce influence supply. For example, if the price of soft drinks rises, the supply of energy drinks decreases. Energy drinks and soft drinks are *substitutes in production* – goods that can be produced by using the same resources. If the price of beef rises, the supply of leather increases. Beef and leather are *complements in production* – goods that must be produced together.

Expected Future Prices

If the expected future price of a good rises, the return from selling it in the future is higher than it is today. So supply decreases today and increases in the future.

Number of Suppliers

The larger the number of firms that produce a good, the greater is the supply of the good. As firms enter an industry, the supply of the good produced increases. As firms leave an industry, the supply decreases.

Technology

The term 'technology' is used broadly to mean the way that factors of production are used to produce a good. A technology change occurs when a new method is discovered that lowers the cost of producing a good. For example, new methods used in the factories that produce computer chips have lowered the cost and increased the supply of computer chips.

The State of Nature

The state of nature includes all the natural forces that influence production, including the state of the weather. Good weather can increase the supply of many crops and bad weather can decrease their supply. Extreme natural events such as insect plagues also influence supply.

Figure 3.5 illustrates an increase in supply. When supply increases, the supply curve shifts *rightward* and the quantity supplied is larger at each and every price. For example, at a price of £1.00, on the original (blue) supply curve, the quantity supplied is 3 million energy drinks a week. On the new (red) supply curve, the quantity supplied is 6 million energy drinks a week. Look closely at the numbers in the table in Figure 3.5 and check that the quantity supplied at each price is larger.

Table 3.2 summarises the influences on supply and the directions of those influences.

A Change in the Quantity Supplied versus a Change in Supply

Changes in the influences on selling plans bring either a change in the quantity supplied or a change in supply. Equivalently, they bring either a movement along the supply curve or a shift of the supply curve.

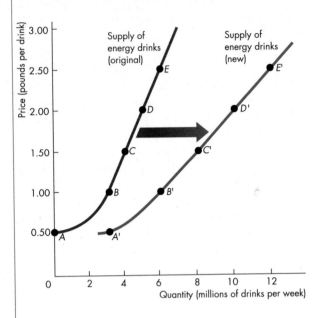

Figure 3.5 An Increase in Supply

Original supply schedule Original technology		New supply schedule New technology	
Price (pounds per drink)	Quantity supplied (millions of drinks per week)	Price (pounds per drink)	Quantity supplied (millions of drinks per week)
A 0.50	0	A' 0.50	3
B 1.00	3	B' 1.00	6
C 1.50	4	C' 1.50	8
D 2.00	5	D' 2.00	10
E 2.50	6	E' 2.50	12

A change in any influence on sellers' plans other than the price of the good itself results in a new supply schedule and a shift of the supply curve. For example, with a new cost-saving technology for producing energy drinks, the supply of energy drinks changes.

At a price of £1.50 a drink, 4 million energy drinks a week are supplied when producers use the old technology (row *C* of the table) and 8 million energy drinks a week are supplied when producers use the new technology. An advance in technology increases the supply of energy drinks. The supply curve shifts rightward, as shown by the shift arrow and the resulting red curve.

MyEconLab Animation

A point on the supply curve shows the quantity supplied at a given price. A movement along the supply curve shows a **change in the quantity supplied**. The entire supply curve shows supply. A shift of the supply curve shows a *change in supply*.

Figure 3.6 illustrates and summarises these distinctions. If the price of a good changes and other things remain the same, there is a *change in the quantity supplied* of the good. If the price of the good falls, the quantity supplied decreases and there is a movement down the supply curve S_0. If the price of a good rises, the quantity supplied increases and there is a movement up the supply curve S_0. When any other influence on selling plans changes, the supply curve shifts and there is a *change in supply*. If the supply curve is S_0 and if production costs fall, supply increases and the supply curve shifts to the red supply curve S_1. If production costs rise, supply decreases and the supply curve shifts to the red supply curve S_2.

Table 3.2

The Supply of Energy Drinks

The Law of Supply

The quantity of energy drinks supplied

Decreases if:	*Increases if:*
◆ The price of an energy drink falls	◆ The price of an energy drink rises

Changes in Supply

The supply of energy drinks

Decreases if:	*Increases if:*
◆ The price of a factor of production used to produce energy drinks rises	◆ The price of a factor of production used to produce energy drinks falls
◆ The price of a substitute in production rises	◆ The price of a substitute in production falls
◆ The price of a complement in production falls	◆ The price of a complement in production rises
◆ The expected future price of an energy drink rises	◆ The expected future price of an energy drink falls
◆ The number of suppliers of energy drinks decreases	◆ The number of suppliers of energy drinks increases
◆ A technology change or natural event decreases energy drink production	◆ A technology change or natural event increases energy drink production

Figure 3.6   A Change in the Quantity Supplied versus a Change in Supply

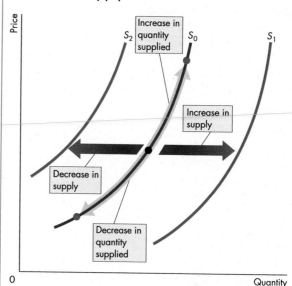

When the price of the good changes, there is a movement along the supply curve and a change in the quantity supplied, shown by the blue arrows on supply curve S_0.

When any other influence on selling plans changes, there is a shift of the supply curve and a change in supply. An increase in supply shifts the supply curve rightward (from S_0 to S_1), and a decrease in supply shifts the supply curve leftward (from S_0 to S_2).

MyEconLab Animation ──────────────◆

◆ REVIEW QUIZ

1   Define the quantity supplied of a good or service.
2   What is the law of supply, and how do we illustrate it?
3   What does the supply curve tell us about the price at which firms will supply a given quantity of a good?
4   List all the influences on selling plans, and for each influence say whether it changes supply.
5   What happens to the quantity of mobile phones supplied and the supply of mobile phones if the price of a mobile phone falls?

Do these questions in Study Plan 3.3 and get instant feedback.   MyEconLab

Your next task is to use what you've learned about demand and supply and see how prices and quantities are determined.

Market Equilibrium

We have seen that when the price of a good rises, the quantity demanded *decreases* and the quantity supplied *increases*. We are now going to see how prices coordinate the plans of buyers and sellers and achieve equilibrium.

Equilibrium is a situation in which opposing forces balance each other. Equilibrium in a market occurs when the price balances the plans of buyers and sellers. The **equilibrium price** is the price at which the quantity demanded equals the quantity supplied. The **equilibrium quantity** is the quantity bought and sold at the equilibrium price. A market moves towards its equilibrium because:

◆ Price regulates buying and selling plans.

◆ Price adjusts when plans don't match.

Price as a Regulator

The price of a good regulates the quantities demanded and supplied. If the price is too high, the quantity supplied exceeds the quantity demanded. If the price is too low, the quantity demanded exceeds the quantity supplied. There is one price at which the quantity demanded equals the quantity supplied. Let's work out what that price is.

Figure 3.7 shows the market for energy drinks. The table shows the demand schedule (from Figure 3.1) and the supply schedule (from Figure 3.4). If the price of an energy drink is 50 pence, the quantity demanded is 9 million drinks a week, but no drinks are supplied. There is a shortage of 9 million drinks a week. This shortage is shown in the final column of the table. At a price of £1.00 a drink, there is still a shortage, but only of 3 million drinks a week. If the price is £2.50 a drink, the quantity supplied is 6 million drinks a week, but the quantity demanded is only 2 million. There is a surplus of 4 million drinks a week. The one price at which there is neither a shortage nor a surplus is £1.50 a drink. At that price, the quantity demanded equals the quantity supplied: 4 million drinks a week. The equilibrium price is £1.50 a drink and the equilibrium quantity is 4 million drinks a week.

Figure 3.7 shows that the demand curve and the supply curve intersect at the equilibrium price of £1.50 a drink. At each price *above* £1.50 a drink, there is a surplus. For example, at £2.00 a drink, the surplus is 2 million drinks a week, as shown by the blue arrow. At each price *below* £1.50 a drink, there is a shortage of drinks.

Figure 3.7 Equilibrium

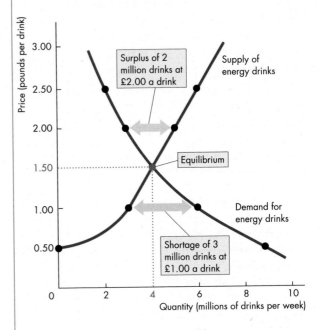

Price (pounds per drink)	Quantity demanded	Quantity supplied	Shortage (−) or surplus (+)
	(millions of drinks per week)		
0.50	9	0	−9
1.00	6	3	−3
1.50	**4**	**4**	**0**
2.00	3	5	+2
2.50	2	6	+4

The table lists the quantities demanded and quantities supplied as well as the shortage or surplus of drinks at each price. If the price is £1.00 an energy drink, 6 million drinks a week are demanded and 3 million are supplied. There is a shortage of 3 million drinks a week and the price rises.

If the price is £2.00 an energy drink, 3 million drinks a week are demanded and 5 million are supplied. There is a surplus of 2 million drinks a week and the price falls.

If the price is £1.50 an energy drink, 4 million drinks a week are demanded and 4 million are supplied. There is neither a shortage nor a surplus. Neither buyers nor sellers have any incentive to change the price. The price at which the quantity demanded equals the quantity supplied is the equilibrium price. The equilibrium quantity is 4 million drinks a week.

MyEconLab Animation ⟶ ◆

For example, at £1.00 a drink, the shortage is 3 million drinks a week, as shown by the red arrow.

Price Adjustments

You've seen that if the price is below equilibrium there is a shortage, and that if the price is above equilibrium there is a surplus. But can we count on the price to change and eliminate a shortage or surplus? We can, because such price changes are beneficial to both buyers and sellers. Let's see why the price changes when there is a shortage or a surplus.

A Shortage Forces the Price Up

Suppose the price of an energy drink is £1. Consumers plan to buy 6 million drinks a week and producers plan to sell 3 million drinks a week. Consumers can't force producers to sell more than they plan, so the quantity that is actually offered for sale is 3 million drinks a week. In this situation, powerful forces operate to increase the price and move it towards the equilibrium price. Some producers, noticing many unsatisfied consumers, raise the price. Some producers increase their output. As producers push the price up, the price rises towards its equilibrium. The rising price reduces the shortage because it decreases the quantity demanded and increases the quantity supplied. When the price has increased to the point at which there is no longer a shortage, the forces moving the price stop operating and the price comes to rest at its equilibrium.

A Surplus Forces the Price Down

Suppose the price is £2 a drink. Producers plan to sell 5 million drinks a week and consumers plan to buy 3 million drinks a week. Producers cannot force consumers to buy more than they plan, so the quantity bought is 3 million drinks a week. In this situation, powerful forces operate to lower the price and move it towards the equilibrium price. Some producers, unable to sell the quantities of drinks they planned to sell, cut their prices. In addition, some producers scale back production. As producers cut the price, the price falls towards its equilibrium. The falling price decreases the surplus because it increases the quantity demanded and decreases the quantity supplied. When the price has fallen to the point at which there is no longer a surplus, the forces moving the price stop operating and the price comes to rest at its equilibrium.

The Best Deal Available for Buyers and Sellers

When the price is below equilibrium, it is forced up towards the equilibrium. Why don't buyers resist the increase and refuse to buy at the higher price? Because they value the good more highly than the current price and they cannot satisfy all their demands at the current price. In some markets – for example, the auction markets that operate on eBay – the buyers might even be the ones who force the price up by offering to pay higher prices.

When the price is above equilibrium, it is bid down towards the equilibrium. Why don't sellers resist this decrease and refuse to sell at the lower price? Because their minimum supply price is below the current price and they cannot sell all they would like to at the current price. Normally, it is the sellers who force the price down by offering lower prices to gain market share.

At the price at which the quantity demanded equals the quantity supplied neither buyers nor sellers can do business at a better price. Buyers pay the highest price they are willing to pay for the last unit bought and sellers receive the lowest price at which they are willing to supply the last unit sold.

When people freely make offers to buy and sell and when buyers try to buy at the lowest possible price and sellers try to sell at the highest possible price, the price at which trade takes place is the equilibrium price – the price at which the quantity demanded equals the quantity supplied. The price coordinates the plans of buyers and sellers, and no one has an incentive to change the price.

REVIEW QUIZ

1   What is the equilibrium price of a good or service?
2   Over what range of prices does a shortage arise? What happens to the price when there is a shortage?
3   Over what range of prices does a surplus arise? What happens to the price when there is a surplus?
4   Why is the price at which the quantity demanded equals the quantity supplied the equilibrium price?
5   Why is the equilibrium price the best deal available for both buyers and sellers?

Do these questions in Study Plan 3.4 and get instant feedback.   MyEconLab

Predicting Changes in Price and Quantity

The demand and supply theory that we have just studied provides us with a powerful way of analysing influences on prices and the quantities bought and sold. According to the theory, a change in price stems from a change in demand, a change in supply, or a change in both demand and supply. Let's look first at the effects of a change in demand.

An Increase in Demand

If more people join health clubs, the demand for energy drinks increases. The table in Figure 3.8 shows the original and new demand schedules for energy drinks (the same as those in Figure 3.2) as well as the supply schedule of energy drinks.

The increase in demand creates a shortage at the original price of £1.50 a drink, and to eliminate the shortage the price must rise.

Figure 3.8 shows what happens. The figure shows the original demand for and supply of energy drinks. The original equilibrium price is £1.50 a drink and the quantity is 4 million drinks a week. When demand increases, the demand curve shifts rightward. The equilibrium price rises to £2.50 a drink and the quantity supplied increases to 6 million drinks a week, as highlighted in the figure. There is an *increase in the quantity supplied* but *no change in supply* – a movement along, but no shift of, the supply curve.

A Decrease in Demand

We can reverse this change in demand. Start at a price of £2.50 a drink with 6 million drinks a week, and then work out what happens if demand decreases to its original level. Such a decrease in demand might arise from a fall in the price of an energy bar (a substitute for energy drinks).

The decrease in demand shifts the demand curve *leftward*. The equilibrium price falls to £1.50 a drink and the equilibrium quantity decreases to 4 million drinks a week.

We can now make our first two predictions:

1 **When demand increases, both the price and the quantity increase.**

2 **When demand decreases, both the price and the quantity decrease.**

Figure 3.8   The Effects of a Change in Demand

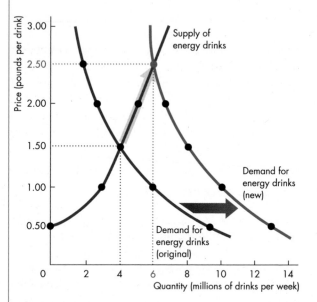

Price (pounds per drink)	Quantity demanded (millions of drinks per week)		Quantity supplied (millions of drinks per week)
	Original	New	
0.50	9	13	0
1.00	6	10	3
1.50	**4**	**8**	**4**
2.00	3	7	5
2.50	**2**	**6**	**6**

Initially, the demand for energy drinks is the blue demand curve. The equilibrium price is £1.50 an energy drink and the equilibrium quantity is 4 million drinks a week. With more health-conscious people doing more exercise, the demand for energy drinks increases and the demand curve shifts rightward to become the red curve.

At £1.50 an energy drink, there is now a shortage of 4 million drinks a week. The price of an energy drink rises to a new equilibrium of £2.50. As the price rises to £2.50, the quantity supplied increases – shown by the blue arrow on the supply curve – to the new equilibrium quantity of 6 million drinks a week. Following an increase in demand, the quantity supplied increases but supply does not change – the supply curve does not shift.

MyEconLab Animation ─────────────────────◆

ECONOMICS IN THE NEWS

The Market for Air Shipments

iPhone 5 Demand Leads to 'Huge' Increase in Air Freight Costs

The launch of Apple's new iPhone 5 in September 2012 posed a huge logistical challenge for DHL and other carriers who struggled to deliver 30 million new phones assembled in China to buyers around the world. The price of air freight jumped.

Source: *The Guardian*, 11 October 2012

The Data

	Price of air shipments from China (dollars per kilogram)	Quantity of iPhones shipped
Quarter 2, 2012 Before iPhone 5 launch	$3.56	26 million iPhone 4s (or 6.5 million kilograms)
Quarter 3, 2012 After iPhone 5 launch	$5.00	56 million iPhones (or 14 million kilograms)

The Questions

◆ What do the data tell us?

◆ Why did the price of iPhone air freight from China rise?

The Answers

◆ The data tell us that both the price of an air shipment from China and the quantity of iPhones shipped increased after the launch of the new iPhone 5 in September 2012.

◆ An increase in the demand brings a rise in the price and an increase in the quantity.

◆ An increase in supply brings a fall in the price and an increase in quantity.

◆ Because both the price (of an air shipment from China) and the quantity (iPhones shipped) have increased, the demand for air shipments must have increased.

◆ Figure 1 shows the market for air shipments from China.

◆ The supply curve of shipments, *S*, slopes upward because the principle of increasing opportunity cost applies to air shipments just as it does to other goods and services.

◆ In Quarter 2, 2012, the demand for shipments from China was D_{Q2}. The equilibrium price was $3.56 per kilogram and 26 million iPhones were shipped.

◆ Between Quarter 2 and Quarter 3, 2012, the new iPhone 5 was successfully launched. iPhone 4s continued to be shipped alongside an extra 30 million iPhone 5s.

◆ The launch of iPhone 5 increased the demand for air shipments from China. The demand curve shifted rightward to D_{Q3}. The equilibrium price increased to $5.00 per kilogram and 56 million iPhones were shipped.

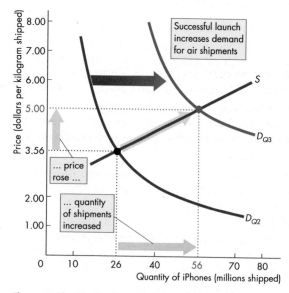

Figure 1 The Market for Air Shipments from China

An Increase in Supply

When the producers of energy drinks switch to new cost-saving technology, the supply of energy drinks increases. The table in Figure 3.9 shows the new supply schedule (the same as that in Figure 3.5). What are the new equilibrium price and quantity? The answer is highlighted in the table: the price falls to £1.00 a drink and the quantity increases to 6 million a week. You can see why by looking at the quantities demanded and supplied at the original price of £1.50 a drink. The quantity supplied at that price is 8 million drinks a week and there is a surplus of drinks. The price falls. Only when the price is £1.00 a drink does the quantity supplied equal the quantity demanded.

Figure 3.9 illustrates the effect of an increase in supply. It shows the demand curve and the original and new supply curves. The initial equilibrium price is £1.50 a drink and the quantity is 4 million drinks a week. When the supply increases, the supply curve shifts rightward. The equilibrium price falls to £1.00 a drink and the quantity demanded increases to 6 million drinks a week, highlighted in the figure. There is an *increase in the quantity demanded* but *no change in demand* – a movement along, but no shift of, the demand curve.

A Decrease in Supply

Start out at a price of £1.00 a drink with 6 million drinks a week being bought and sold. Then suppose that the cost of labour or raw materials rises and the supply of energy drinks decreases. The decrease in supply shifts the supply curve *leftward*. The equilibrium price rises to £1.50 a drink and the quantity demanded decreases. The equilibrium quantity decreases to 4 million drinks a week.

We can now make two more predictions:

1 **When supply increases, the quantity increases and the price falls.**

2 **When supply decreases, the quantity decreases and the price rises.**

You've now seen what happens to the price and the quantity when either demand or supply changes while the other one remains unchanged. In real markets, both demand and supply can change together. When this happens, to predict the changes in price and quantity we must combine the effects that you've just seen. That is your final task in this chapter.

Figure 3.9 The Effects of a Change in Supply

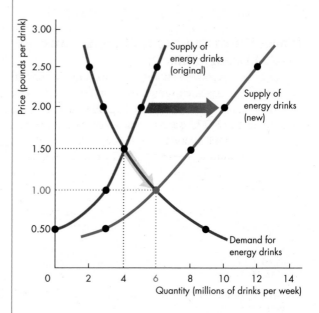

Price (pounds per drink)	Quantity demanded (millions of drinks per week)	Quantity supplied (millions of drinks per week)	
		Original	New
0.50	9	0	3
1.00	6	3	6
1.50	4	4	8
2.00	3	5	10
2.50	2	6	12

Initially, the supply of energy drinks is shown by the blue supply curve. The equilibrium price is £1.50 a drink and the equilibrium quantity is 4 million drinks a week. When the new cost-saving technology is adopted, the supply of energy drinks increases and the supply curve shifts rightward to become the red curve.

At £1.50 a drink, there is now a surplus of 4 million drinks a week. The price of an energy drink falls to a new equilibrium of £1.00 a drink. As the price falls to £1.00 a drink, the quantity demanded increases – shown by the blue arrow on the demand curve – to the new equilibrium quantity of 6 million drinks a week. Following an increase in supply, the quantity demanded increases but demand does not change – the demand curve does not shift.

ECONOMICS IN THE NEWS

The World Market for Wheat

Wheat Prices Rise at Fastest Rate Since 1973 as Drought hits Russia

Wheat prices have seen the biggest one-month jump in more than three decades on the back of a severe drought in Russia. 'This is the fastest wheat price rally we have seen since 1972–73,' said one analyst. The price rise comes as the worst heatwave and drought in more than a century continue to devastate grain crops in Russia, Ukraine and Kazakhstan. To protect the domestic market, Russia banned wheat exports.

Source: *The Financial Times*, 3 August 2010

Drought in Russia and fires in its wheat fields

The Questions

◆ Why did the world wheat price rise rapidly during 2010?

◆ Was the price rise caused by an increase in demand or by a decrease in supply?

The Answers

◆ The price of wheat rose rapidly in 2010 because severe drought in Russia cut production and Russia stopped exporting wheat.

◆ The price rise was caused by a decrease in supply, not by an increase in demand.

◆ The demand for wheat, shown by the demand curve, *D*, in Figure 1 didn't change during June and July 2010. In June, before the Russian fires, wheat stocks were plentiful, fields were full and the price was low at £90 per tonne. The supply of wheat was as shown by the supply curve S_{June} and the equilibrium quantity of wheat was 500 million tonnes.

◆ By July 2010, drought and floods had destroyed crops. The world supply of wheat decreased and the supply curve shifted leftward to S_{July}.

◆ With a shortage of wheat of 50 million tonnes at the June price of £90 per tonne, the price began to rise.

◆ The decrease in supply raised the price and decreased the quantity demanded – a movement along the demand curve.

◆ By July 2010, the equilibrium price hit £150 per tonne and the equilibrium quantity of wheat had decreased to 470 million tonnes per year.

◆ In August 2010, Russia announced its ban on wheat exports.

◆ The world supply of wheat decreased and the supply curve shifted further leftward to S_{August}.

◆ The world price increased to £175 per tonne and the equilibrium quantity decreased to 460 million tonnes.

◆ The events described here explain how a decrease in supply raised the price of wheat with no change in the demand for wheat.

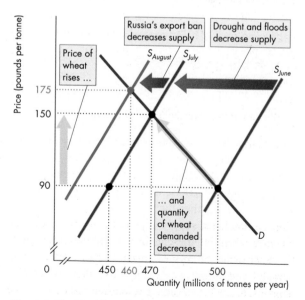

Figure 1 The World Market for Wheat

All the Possible Changes in Demand and Supply

Figure 3.10 brings together and summarises the effects of all the possible changes in demand and supply. With what you've learned about the effects of a change in either demand or supply, you can predict what happens if both demand and supply change together. Let's begin by reviewing what you already know.

Change in Demand with No Change in Supply

The first row of Figure 3.10, parts (a), (b) and (c), summarises the effects of a change in demand with no change in supply. In part (a), with no change in either demand or supply, neither the price nor the quantity changes. With an *increase* in demand and no change in supply in part (b), both the price and the quantity increase. And with a *decrease* in demand and no change in supply in part (c), both the price and the quantity decrease.

Change in Supply with No Change in Demand

The first column of Figure 3.10, parts (a), (d) and (g), summarises the effects of a change in supply with no change in demand. With an *increase* in supply and no change in demand in part (d), the price falls and the quantity increases. And with a *decrease* in supply and no change in demand in part (g), the price rises and the quantity decreases.

Increase in Both Demand and Supply

You've seen that an increase in demand raises the price and increases the quantity. And you've seen that an increase in supply lowers the price and increases the quantity. Figure 3.10(e) combines these two changes. Because either an increase in demand or an increase in supply increases the quantity, the quantity also increases when both demand and supply increase. But the effect on the price is uncertain. An increase in demand raises the price and an increase in supply lowers the price, so we can't say whether the price will rise or fall when both demand and supply increase. We need to know the magnitudes of the changes in demand and supply to predict the effects on price. In the example in Figure 3.10(e), the price does not change. But notice that if demand increases by slightly more than the amount shown in the figure, the price will rise. And if supply increases by slightly more than the amount shown in the figure, the price will fall.

Decrease in Both Demand and Supply

Figure 3.10(i) shows the case in which demand and supply *both decrease*. For the same reasons as those we've just reviewed, when both demand and supply decrease, the quantity decreases and, again, the direction of the price change is uncertain.

Decrease in Demand and Increase in Supply

You've seen that a decrease in demand lowers the price and decreases the quantity. You've also seen that an increase in supply lowers the price and increases the quantity. Figure 3.10(f) combines these two changes. Both the decrease in demand and the increase in supply lower the price. So the price falls. But a decrease in demand decreases the quantity and an increase in supply increases the quantity, so we can't predict the direction in which the quantity will change unless we know the magnitudes of the changes in demand and supply. In Figure 3.10(f), the quantity does not change. But notice that if demand decreases by slightly more than the amount shown in the figure, the quantity will decrease. And if supply increases by slightly more than the amount shown in the figure, the quantity will increase.

Increase in Demand and Decrease in Supply

Figure 3.10(h) shows the case in which demand increases and supply decreases. Now, the price rises and, again, the direction of the quantity change is uncertain.

REVIEW QUIZ

What is the effect on the price and quantity of MP3 players (such as the iPod) if:

1   The price of a PC falls or the price of an MP3 download rises? (Draw the diagrams!)
2   More firms produce MP3 players or electronics workers' wages rise? (Draw the diagrams!)
3   Any two of these events in questions 1 and 2 occur together? (Draw the diagrams!)

Do these questions in Study Plan 3.5 and get instant feedback.   MyEconLab

To complete your study of demand and supply, take a look at *Reading Between the Lines* on pp. 72–73, which explains why the price of bread increased in 2012 and is expected to rise again. Try to get into the habit of using the demand and supply model to understand movements in prices in your everyday life.

Figure 3.10 The Effects of All the Possible Changes in Demand and Supply

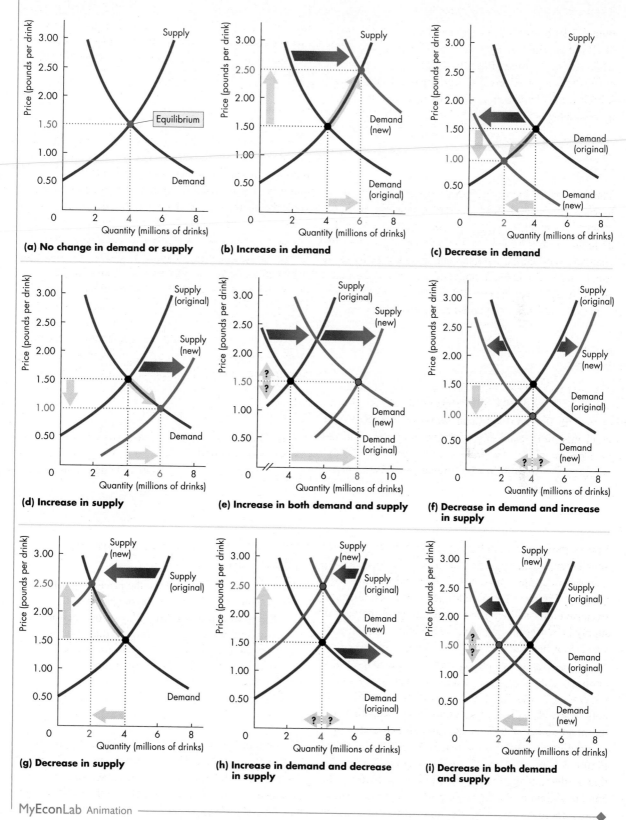

(a) No change in demand or supply

(b) Increase in demand

(c) Decrease in demand

(d) Increase in supply

(e) Increase in both demand and supply

(f) Decrease in demand and increase in supply

(g) Decrease in supply

(h) Increase in demand and decrease in supply

(i) Decrease in both demand and supply

Demand and Supply: The Price of a Loaf

Bread to Cost More Dough

Javier Blas

The cost of bread is poised to rise this month as bakers try to persuade supermarkets to cover increased wheat costs.

The British crop, still being brought in, has been stunted by a cold, wet summer, while US droughts have sent world prices for the grain spiralling.

Given retailers' own financial woes, analysts expect any increases to be at least partly passed on to shoppers.

At £200 a tonne, wheat makes up 25–30 per cent of the manufacturer's selling cost or about 15 per cent of the shelf price of a loaf. Martin Deboo, an analyst at Investec Securities, said every £10 on the wheat price adds 0.8p to the cost of a loaf – about 4p, at £250 a tonne.

Rising wheat prices are a further blow to Britain's bakers, who already suffer tortuous and expensive logistics: unlike most items on supermarket shelves, bread has to be baked and delivered to stores on a daily basis.

 FT *Source*: The Financial Times, 10 September 2012.
© The Financial Times Limited 2012. All Rights Reserved.

 The Essence of the Story

- The price of a loaf of bread is set to rise because the price of wheat has risen.

- The price of wheat for baking bread has risen because bad weather has damaged UK crops.

- The price of wheat makes up 25 to 30 per cent of the manufacturer's selling cost or 15 per cent of the price of a loaf of bread.

- The price of bread is already high to cover the high costs of delivery.

Economic Analysis

- This news article reports two events: the market for wheat and the market for bread.

- In the UK market for milling wheat, bad UK summer weather has decreased supply.

- The decrease in supply of wheat led to an increase in its price, a decrease in the quantity demanded and a decrease in the equilibrium quantity of milling wheat.

- Figure 1 illustrates the UK market for milling wheat in June and September 2012.

- The demand curve for wheat is *D*. In June 2012, the supply curve was S_0. The equilibrium price was £200 per tonne and 50 million tonnes of wheat were produced.

- In September 2012, supply of wheat decreased and the supply curve shifted leftward to S_1.

- The equilibrium price of wheat increased to £250 per tonne and the equilibrium quantity decreased to 48 million tonnes. The quantity demanded decreased, shown by the movement along the demand curve *D*.

- Wheat along with labour and capital are used to make bread.

- So the rise in the price of wheat increased the cost of producing bread and decreased the supply of bread.

- The decrease in the supply of bread increased the equilibrium price of bread and decreased the equilibrium quantity of bread.

- Figure 2 illustrates the UK market for bread in June and September 2012.

- The demand curve for bread is *D*. In June, the supply curve was S_0. The equilibrium price was £1.16 per loaf and 11 million loaves were produced each day.

- In September, the supply of bread decreased and the supply curve shifted leftward to S_1.

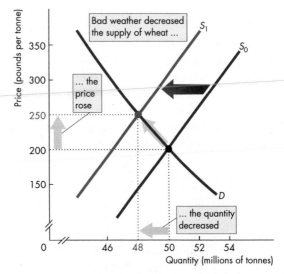

Figure 1 The UK Market for Milling Wheat

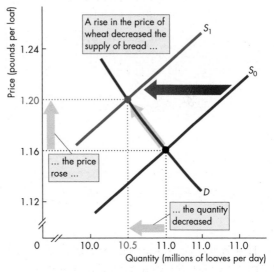

Figure 2 The UK Market for Bread

- The equilibrium price rose to £1.20 per loaf and the equilibrium quantity decreased to 10.5 million loaves. The quantity of bread demanded decreased, shown by the movement along the demand curve *D*.

MATHEMATICAL NOTE

Demand, Supply and Equilibrium

Demand Curve

The law of demand states that as the price of a good or service falls, the quantity demanded of it increases. We illustrate the law of demand by setting out a demand schedule, drawing a graph of the demand curve, or writing down an equation. When the demand curve is a straight line, the following linear equation describes it:

$$P = a - bQ_D$$

where P is the price and Q_D is the quantity demanded. The a and b are positive constants. Figure 1 illustrates this demand curve.

The demand equation tells us three things:

1 The price at which no one is willing to buy the good (Q_D is zero). That is, if the price is a, then the quantity demanded is zero. You can see the price a on Figure 1. It is the price at which the demand curve hits the y-axis – what we call the demand curve's 'intercept on the y-axis'.

2 As the price falls, the quantity demanded increases. If Q_D is a positive number, then the price P must be less than a. And as Q_D gets larger, the price P becomes smaller. That is, as the quantity increases, the maximum price that buyers are willing to pay for the good falls.

3 The constant b tells us how fast the maximum price that someone is willing to pay for the good falls as the quantity increases. That is, the constant b tells us

about the steepness of the demand curve. The equation tells us that the slope of the demand curve is $-b$.

Supply Curve

The law of supply states that as the price of a good or service rises, the quantity supplied of it increases. We illustrate the law of supply by setting out a supply schedule, drawing a graph of the supply curve, or writing down an equation. When the supply curve is a straight line, the following linear equation describes it:

$$P = c + dQ_S$$

where P is the price and Q_S the quantity supplied. The c and d are positive constants. Figure 2 illustrates this supply curve.

The supply equation tells us three things:

1 The price at which no one is willing to sell the good (Q_S is zero). If the price is c, then the quantity supplied is zero. You can see the price c on Figure 2. It is the price at which the supply curve hits the y-axis – what we call the supply curve's 'intercept on the y-axis'.

2 As the price rises, the quantity supplied increases. If Q_S is a positive number, then the price P must be greater than c. And as Q_S increases, the price P gets larger. That is, as the quantity increases, the minimum price that sellers are willing to accept rises.

3 The constant d tells us how fast the minimum price at which someone is willing to sell the good rises as the quantity increases. That is, the constant d tells us about the steepness of the supply curve. The equation tells us that the slope of the supply curve is d.

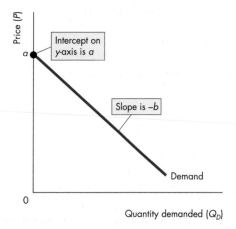

Figure 1 The Demand Curve

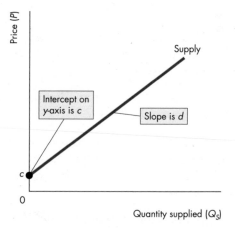

Figure 2 The Supply Curve

Market Equilibrium

Demand and supply determine market equilibrium. Figure 3 shows the equilibrium price (P^*) and equilibrium quantity (Q^*) at the intersection of the demand curve and the supply curve.

We can use the equations to find the equilibrium price and equilibrium quantity. The price of a good will adjust until the quantity demanded equals the quantity supplied. That is:

$$Q_D = Q_S$$

So at the equilibrium price (P^*) and equilibrium quantity (Q^*):

$$Q_D = Q_S = Q^*$$

To find the equilibrium price and equilibrium quantity: first substitute Q^* for Q_D in the demand equation and Q^* for Q_S in the supply equation. Then the price is the equilibrium price (P^*), which gives:

$$P^* = a - bQ^*$$

$$P^* = c + dQ^*$$

Notice that:

$$a - bQ^* = c + dQ^*$$

Now solve for Q^*:

$$a - c = bQ^* + dQ^*$$

$$a - c = (b + d)Q^*$$

$$Q^* = \frac{a - c}{b + d}$$

To find the equilibrium price (P^*) substitute for Q^* in either the demand equation or the supply equation.

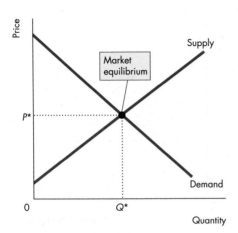

Figure 3 Market Equilibrium

Using the demand equation:

$$P^* = a - b\left(\frac{a - c}{b + d}\right)$$

$$P^* = \frac{a(b + d) - b(a - c)}{b + d}$$

$$P^* = \frac{ad + bc}{b + d}$$

Alternatively, using the supply equation:

$$P^* = c + d\left(\frac{a - c}{b + d}\right)$$

$$P^* = \frac{c(b + d) + d(a - c)}{b + d}$$

$$P^* = \frac{ad + bc}{b + d}$$

An Example

The demand for ice cream is:

$$P = 400 - 2Q_D$$

The supply of ice cream is:

$$P = 100 + 1Q_S$$

The price of an ice cream is expressed in pence and the quantities are expressed in ice creams per day.

To find the equilibrium price (P^*) and equilibrium quantity (Q^*), substitute Q^* for Q_D and Q_S and substitute P^* for P. That is:

$$P^* = 400 - 2Q^*$$

$$P^* = 100 + 1Q^*$$

Now solve for Q^*:

$$400 - 2Q^* = 100 + 1Q^*$$

$$300 = 3Q^*$$

$$Q^* = 100$$

And:

$$P^* = 400 - 2(100) = 200$$

The equilibrium price is £2 an ice cream, and the equilibrium quantity is 100 ice creams per day.

SUMMARY

Key Points

Markets and Prices (p. 54)

◆ A competitive market is one that has so many buyers and sellers that no one can influence the price.

◆ Opportunity cost is a relative price.

◆ Demand and supply determine relative prices.

Do Problem 1 to get a better understanding of markets and prices.

Demand (pp. 55–59)

◆ Demand is the relationship between the quantity demanded of a good and its price when all other influences on buying plans remain the same.

◆ The higher the price of a good, other things remaining the same, the smaller is the quantity demanded – the law of demand.

◆ Demand depends on the prices of related goods (substitutes and complements), expected future prices, income, expected future income and credit, population and preferences.

Do Problems 2 to 5 to get a better understanding of demand.

Supply (pp. 60–63)

◆ Supply is the relationship between the quantity supplied of a good and its price when all other influences on selling plans remain the same.

◆ The higher the price of a good, other things remaining the same, the greater is the quantity supplied – the law of supply.

◆ Supply depends on the prices of factors of production used to produce a good, the prices of related goods produced, expected future prices, the number of suppliers, technology and the state of nature.

Do Problems 6 to 9 to get a better understanding of supply.

Market Equilibrium (pp. 64–65)

◆ At the equilibrium price, the quantity demanded equals the quantity supplied.

◆ At any price above the equilibrium price, there is a surplus and the price falls.

◆ At any price below the equilibrium price, there is a shortage and the price rises.

Do Problems 10 and 11 to get a better understanding of market equilibrium.

Predicting Changes in Price and Quantity (pp. 66–71)

◆ An increase in demand brings a rise in the price and an increase in the quantity supplied. A decrease in demand brings a fall in the price and a decrease in the quantity supplied.

◆ An increase in supply brings a fall in the price and an increase in the quantity demanded. A decrease in supply brings a rise in the price and a decrease in the quantity demanded.

◆ An increase in demand and an increase in supply bring an increased quantity but an uncertain price change. An increase in demand and a decrease in supply bring a higher price but an uncertain change in quantity.

Do Problems 12 and 13 to get a better understanding of predicting changes in price and quantity.

Key Terms

Change in demand, 56
Change in supply, 61
Change in the quantity demanded, 59
Change in the quantity supplied, 63
Competitive market, 54
Complement, 57
Demand, 55
Demand curve, 56
Equilibrium price, 64
Equilibrium quantity, 64
Inferior good, 58
Law of demand, 55
Law of supply, 60
Money price, 54
Normal good, 58
Quantity demanded, 55
Quantity supplied, 60
Relative price, 54
Substitute, 57
Supply, 60
Supply curve, 60

STUDY PLAN PROBLEMS AND APPLICAT

Do Problems 1 to 17 in MyEconLab Chapter 3 Study Plan and get instant feedback.

Markets and Prices (Study Plan 3.1)

1 A notice in the *Edgehill Advertiser* in 1862 offered the following exchanges:

1 yard of cloth for 1 pound of bacon
2 yards of cloth for 1 pound of butter
4 yards of cloth for 1 pound of wool
8 yards of cloth for 1 bushel of salt

a What is the price of butter in terms of wool?

b If the money price of bacon was 20 pence per pound, what do you predict was the money price of butter?

c If the money price of bacon was 20 pence per pound and the money price of salt was £2.00 per bushel, do you think anyone would be willing to trade cloth for salt on the terms advertised above?

Demand (Study Plan 3.2)

2 The price of food increased during the past year.

a Explain why the law of demand applies to food just as it does to all other goods and services.

b Explain how the substitution effect influences food purchases and provide some examples of substitutions that people might make when the price of food rises and other things remain the same.

c Explain how the income effect influences food purchases and provide some examples of the income effect that might occur when the price of food rises and other things remain the same.

3 Classify the following goods and services as pairs of likely substitutes and as pairs of likely complements. (You may use an item in more than one pair.) The goods and services are:

coal, oil, natural gas, wheat, maize, rye, pasta, pizza, sausage, skateboard, roller blades, video game, laptop, iPod, mobile phone, text message, e-mail, phone call, voice mail

4 During 2010, the average income in China increased by 10 per cent. Compared with 2009, how do you expect the following would change:

a The demand for beef? Explain your answer.

b The demand for rice? Explain your answer.

5 In January 2010, the price of petrol 1 ~~was~~ 100 pence a litre. By spring 2010, the price ~~increased~~ to 120 pence a litre. Assume that there were no changes in average income, population, or any other influence on buying plans.

Explain how the rise in the price of petrol would influence

a The demand for petrol.

b The quantity of petrol demanded.

Supply (Study Plan 3.3)

6 In 2008, the price of corn increased by 35 per cent and some cotton farmers stopped growing cotton and started to grow corn.

a Does this fact illustrate the law of demand or the law of supply? Explain your answer.

b Why would a cotton farmer grow corn?

Use the following information in Problems 7 to 9.

Dairies make low-fat milk from full-cream milk. In the process of making low-fat milk, the dairies produce cream, which is made into ice cream. In the market for low-fat milk, the following events occur one at a time:

(i) The wage rate of dairy workers rises.

(ii) The price of cream rises.

(iii) The price of low-fat milk rises.

(iv) With the period of low rainfall extending, dairies raise their expected price of low-fat milk next year.

(v) With advice from healthcare experts, dairy farmers decide to switch from producing full-cream milk to growing vegetables.

(vi) A new technology lowers the cost of producing ice cream.

7 Explain the effect of each event on the supply of low-fat milk.

8 Use a graph to illustrate the effect of each event.

9 Does any event (or events) illustrate the law of supply?

Market Equilibrium (Study Plan 3.4)

10 As more people buy smartphones and tablet computers, the demand for Internet service increases and the price of Internet service decreases. The fall in the price of Internet service decreases the supply of Internet service. Is this statement true or false? Explain your answer.

11 The table sets out the demand and supply schedules for chewing gum.

Price (pence per packet)	Quantity demanded	Quantity supplied
	(millions of packets a week)	
20	180	60
40	140	100
60	100	140
80	60	180
100	20	220

a Draw a graph of the chewing gum market and mark in the equilibrium price and quantity.

b Suppose that chewing gum is 70 pence a packet. Describe the situation in the chewing gum market and explain how the price of chewing gum adjusts.

c Suppose that the price of chewing gum is 30 pence a packet. Describe the situation in the chewing gum market and explain how the price adjusts.

Predicting Changes in Price and Quantity (Study Plan 3.5)

12 The following events occur one at a time:

(i)   The price of crude oil rises.

(ii) The price of a car rises.

(iii) All speed limits on motorways are abolished.

(iv) Robots cut car production costs.

Explain which of these events will increase or decrease (and state which occurs).

a The demand for petrol.

b The supply of petrol.

c The quantity of petrol demanded.

d The quantity of petrol supplied.

13 In Problem 11, a fire destroys some chewing-gum factories and the quantity of chewing gum supplied decreases by 40 million packets a week at each price.

a Explain what happens in the market for chewing gum and draw a graph to illustrate the changes in the chewing gum market.

b If at the time the fire occurs there is an increase in the teenage population, which increases the quantity of chewing gum demanded by 40 million packs a week at each price, what are the new equilibrium price and quantity of chewing gum? Illustrate these changes in your graph.

Economics in the News (Study Plan 3.N)

14 **Airline Fares Soar as Oil Cost Bites**

Fuel bills may lead to higher charges. Ryanair increased its airport check-in charges from £5 to £6 per person return and its baggage charges from £20 to £24 per bag return.

Source: Telegraph.co.uk, 9 February 2008

a According to the news clip, what is the influence on the supply of Ryanair flights?

b Explain how supply changes.

15 **Gambling Grandmothers**

Nevada has plenty of jobs for the over 50s, and its elderly population is growing faster than that in other states.

Source: *The Economist*, 26 July 2006

Explain how grannies have influenced:

a The demand in some Las Vegas markets.

b The supply in other Las Vegas markets.

16 **Frigid Winter is Bad News for Tomato Lovers**

An unusually cold January in Florida destroyed entire fields of tomatoes and forced many farmers to delay their harvest. Florida's growers are shipping only a quarter of their usual 5 million pounds a week. The price has risen from $6.50 for a 25-pound box a year ago to $30 now.

Source: *USA Today*, 3 March 2010

a Make a graph to illustrate the market for tomatoes in January 2009 and January 2010.

b On the graph, show how the events in the news clip influence the market for tomatoes.

c Why is the news 'bad for tomato lovers'?

17 **The Price of Petrol – How Bad Do We Have It?**

The cost of filling up the car is rising as the crude oil price soars and petrol prices continue to rise, hitting a peak of 142 pence a litre in April 2011.

Source: *Significance Magazine*, 11 April 2011

a Does demand for petrol or the supply of petrol or both change when the price of oil soars?

b Use a demand–supply graph to illustrate what happens to the equilibrium price of petrol and the equilibrium quantity of petrol bought when the price of oil soars.

Do these problems in MyEconLab if assigned by your lecturer.   MyEconLab

Markets and Prices

18 What features of the world market for crude oil make it a competitive market?

19 The money price of a mobile phone is £90 and the money price of the Wii game *Super Mario Galaxy* is £45.

  a What is the opportunity cost of a mobile phone in terms of the Wii game?

  b What is the relative price of the Wii game in terms of mobile phones?

Demand

20 The price of petrol has increased during the past year.

  a Explain why the law of demand applies to petrol just as it does to all other goods and services.

  b Explain how the substitution effect influences petrol purchases and provide some examples of substitutions that people might make when the price of petrol rises and other things remain the same.

  c Explain how the income effect influences petrol purchases and provide some examples of the income effects that might occur when the price of petrol rises and other things remain the same.

21 Think about the demand for the three game consoles: Xbox, PS3 and Wii. Explain the effect of the following events on the demand for Xbox games and the quantity of Xbox games demanded, other things remaining the same.

  a The price of an Xbox falls.

  b The prices of a PS3 and a Wii fall.

  c The number of people writing and producing Xbox games increases.

  d Consumers' incomes increase.

  e Programmers who write code for Xbox games become more costly to hire.

  f The expected future price of an Xbox game falls.

  g A new game console that is a close substitute for Xbox comes onto the market.

Supply

22 Classify the following pairs of goods as substitutes in production, complements in production, or neither.

  a Bottled water and health club memberships.

  b Potato crisps and baked potatoes.

  c Leather purses and leather shoes.

  d Hybrids and SUVs.

  e Diet coke and regular coke.

23 As the prices of homes fell across the UK in 2008, the number of homes offered for sale decreased.

  a Does this fact illustrate the law of demand or the law of supply? Explain your answer.

  b Why would home owners decide not to sell?

24 **Ford Shuts 3 European Plants**

Ford plans to cut 18 per cent of its new-car production capacity in Europe and trim 13 per cent of its workforce. The restructuring aims to return Ford's money-losing European operations to profitability.

  Source: *The Wall Street Journal*, 25 October 2012

Explain whether this news clip illustrates a change in the supply of cars or a change in the quantity supplied of cars.

Market Equilibrium

Use the following figure in Problems 25 and 26.

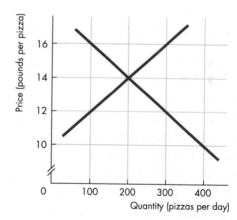

25 a Label the curves. Which curve shows the willingness to pay for pizza?

  b If the price is £16 a pizza, is there a shortage or a surplus of pizza, and does the price rise or fall?

  c Sellers want to receive the highest possible price, so why would they be willing to accept less than £16 a pizza?

26 a If the price of a pizza is £12, is there a shortage or a surplus, and does the price rise or fall?

  b Buyers want to pay the lowest possible price, so why would they be willing to pay more than £12 for a pizza?

27 The table sets out demand and supply schedules for crisps.

Price (pence per bag)	Quantity demanded	Quantity supplied
	(millions of bags per week)	
50	160	130
60	150	140
70	140	150
80	130	160
90	120	170
100	110	180

a Draw a graph of the crisps market and mark in the equilibrium price and quantity.

b Describe the situation in the market for crisps and explain how the price adjusts if crisps are 60 pence a bag.

Predicting Changes in Price and Quantity

28 In Problem 27, a new dip increases the quantity of crisps demanded by 30 million bags per week at each price.

a How does the demand and/or supply of crisps change?

b How do the price and quantity of crisps change?

29 In Problem 27, a virus destroys potato crops and the quantity of crisps supplied decreases by 40 million bags a week at each price. How do the equilibrium price and quantity of crisps change?

30 If the virus in Problem 29 hits just as the new dip comes onto the market in Problem 28, how do the equilibrium price and quantity of crisps change?

31 **'Popcorn Cinema' Experience Gets Pricier**

Cinemas are raising the price of popcorn. Demand for field corn, which is used for animal feed, corn syrup and biofuel, has increased and its price has exploded. That's caused some farmers to shift from growing popcorn to easier-to-grow field corn.

Source: *USA Today*, 24 May 2008

Explain and illustrate graphically the events described in the news clip in the market for (i) popcorn and (ii) cinema tickets.

32 **Eurostar Boosted by *Da Vinci Code***

Eurostar, the train service linking London to Paris, said on Wednesday that first-half year sales rose 6 per cent, boosted by devotees of the blockbuster *The Da Vinci Code*.

Source: CNN, 26 July 2006

a Explain how *Da Vinci Code* fans helped to raise Eurostar's sales.

b CNN commented on the 'fierce competition from budget airlines'. Explain the effect of this competition on Eurostar's sales.

c What markets in Paris do you think these fans influenced? Explain the influence on three markets.

Use the following news clip in Problems 33 and 34.

Sony's Blu-Ray Wins High-Definition War

Toshiba Corp. yesterday withdrew from the race to be the next-generation home movie format, leaving Sony Corp.'s Blu-ray technology the winner. The move could finally jump-start a high-definition home DVD market.

Source: *The Washington Times*, 20 February 2008

33 **a** How would you expect the price of a used Toshiba player on eBay to change? Will the price change result from a change in demand, supply or both, and in which directions?

b How would you expect the price of a Blu-ray player to change?

34 Explain how the market for Blu-ray format films will change.

Economics in the News

35 After you have studied *Reading Between the Lines* on pp. 72–73, answer the following questions.

a What happened to the price of bread in 2012?

b What substitutions do you expect might have been made to decrease the quantity of bread demanded?

c What is the main complement of bread, and what do you predict happened in its market in 2012?

d What is one of the main substitutes in production for wheat, and what do you predict happened in its market in 2012?

e Do you predict that the higher prices of wheat and bread will persist, or will they return to normal after one year?

f Why did the percentage rise in the price of wheat exceed the percentage rise in the price of bread?

36 **Oil Soars to New Record – Over $135 a Barrel**

The price of oil hit a record high, above $135 a barrel, on Thursday – more than twice what it cost a year ago. OPEC has so far blamed price rises on speculators, and says there is no shortage of oil.

Source: BBC News, 22 May 2008

a Explain how the price of oil can rise even though there is no shortage of oil.

b If a shortage of oil does occur, what does that imply about price adjustments and the role of price as a regulator in the market for oil?

c If OPEC is correct, what factors might have changed demand and/or supply and shifted the demand curve and/or the supply curve to cause the price to rise?

4 Elasticity

After studying this chapter you will be able to:

♦ Define, calculate and explain the factors that influence the price elasticity of demand

♦ Define, calculate and explain the factors that influence the cross elasticity of demand and the income elasticity of demand

♦ Define, calculate and explain the factors that influence the elasticity of supply

The UK government wants to discourage wine consumption by raising its price. Will the plan work? Will people buy less wine? Or will they cut out some other items and spend more on wine to maintain their previous consumption levels?

To answer these and similar questions, we use the tool that you study in this chapter: elasticity.

At the end of the chapter, in *Reading Between the Lines*, we use the elasticity tool to answer the questions posed above and assess the effects of the UK government's plan to limit wine consumption.

Price Elasticity of Demand

You know that when supply increases, the equilibrium price falls and the equilibrium quantity increases. But does the price fall by a large amount and the quantity increase by a little? Or does the price barely fall and the quantity increase by a large amount?

The answer depends on the responsiveness of the quantity demanded of a good to a change in its price. If the quantity demanded is not very responsive to a change in the price, the price rises a lot and the equilibrium quantity doesn't change much. If the quantity demanded is very responsive to a change in the price, the price barely rises and the equilibrium quantity changes a lot.

You might think about the responsiveness of the quantity demanded of a good to a change in its price in terms of the slope of the demand curve. If the demand curve is steep, the quantity demanded of the good isn't very responsive to a change in the price. If the demand curve is almost flat, the quantity demanded is very responsive to a change in the price.

But the slope of a demand curve depends on the units in which we measure the price and the quantity – we can make the curve steep or almost flat just by changing the units in which we measure the price and the quantity. Also, we often want to compare the demand for different goods and services, and quantities of these goods are measured in unrelated units. For example, a juice bar operator might want to compare the demand for smoothies with the demand for sandwiches. Which quantity demanded is more responsive to a price change? This question can't be answered by comparing the slopes of two demand curves because smoothies and sandwiches are measured in different units. But the question *can* be answered with a measure of responsiveness that is *independent* of units of measurement. Elasticity is such a measure.

The **price elasticity of demand** is a units-free measure of the responsiveness of the quantity demanded of a good to a change in its price, when all other influences on buyers' plans remain the same.

Calculating Price Elasticity of Demand

We calculate the *price elasticity of demand* by using the formula:

$$\text{Price elasticity of demand} = \frac{\text{Percentage change in quantity demanded}}{\text{Percentage change in price}}$$

To calculate the price elasticity of demand for smoothies, we need to know the quantities demanded at two different prices, when all other influences on buying plans remain the same. Suppose we have the data on prices and quantities demanded of smoothies.

Figure 4.1 zooms in on the demand curve for smoothies and shows how the quantity demanded responds to a small change in price. Initially, the price is £3.10 a smoothie and 9 smoothies an hour are sold – the original point in the figure. The price then falls to £2.90 a smoothie, and the quantity demanded increases to 11 smoothies an hour – the new point in the figure. When the price falls by 20 pence a smoothie, the quantity demanded increases by 2 smoothies an hour.

To calculate the price elasticity of demand, we express the changes in price and quantity as percentages of the *average price* and *average quantity*. By using the average price and average quantity, we calculate the elasticity at a point on the demand curve midway between the original point and the new point.

The original price is £3.10 and the new price is £2.90, so the average price is £3. Call the percentage change in the price, %ΔP, then:

$$\%\Delta P = \Delta P / P_{ave} = (\pounds 0.20 / \pounds 3.00) \times 100 = 6.67\%$$

The original quantity demanded is 9 smoothies and the new quantity demanded is 11 smoothies, so the average quantity demanded is 10 smoothies. Call the percentage change in the quantity demanded, %ΔQ, then:

$$\%\Delta Q = \Delta Q / Q_{ave} = (2/10) \times 100 = 20\%$$

The price elasticity of demand equals the percentage change in the quantity demanded (20 per cent) divided by the percentage change in price (6.67 per cent) and is 3. That is:

$$\text{Price elasticity of demand} = \frac{\%\Delta Q}{\%\Delta P}$$

$$= \frac{20\%}{6.67\%}$$

$$= 3$$

Average Price and Quantity

We use the *average* price and *average* quantity because it gives the most precise measurement of elasticity – midway between the original and new point. If the price falls from £3.10 to £2.90, the 20 pence price change is 6.45 per cent of £3.10. The 2 smoothies change in

Figure 4.1 Calculating the Price Elasticity of Demand

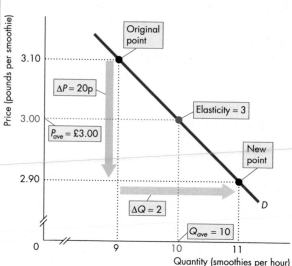

The price elasticity of demand is calculated by using the formula:*

$$\text{Price elasticity of demand} = \frac{\text{Percentage change in quantity demanded}}{\text{Percentage change in price}}$$

$$= \frac{\%\Delta Q}{\%\Delta P} = \frac{\Delta Q/Q_{ave}}{\Delta P/P_{ave}}$$

$$= \frac{2/10}{0.20/3.00}$$

$$= 3$$

This calculation measures the elasticity at an average price of £3.00 a smoothie and an average quantity of 10 smoothies an hour.

* In the formula, the Greek letter delta (Δ) stands for 'change in' and %Δ stands for 'percentage change in'.

MyEconLab Animation ─────────────────◆

quantity is 22.2 per cent of 9 smoothies, the original quantity. So if we use these numbers, the price elasticity of demand is 22.2 divided by 6.45, which equals 3.44. If the price *rises* from £2.90 to £3.10, the 20 pence price change is 6.9 per cent of £2.90. The 2 smoothies change in quantity is 18.2 per cent of 11 smoothies, the original quantity. If we use these numbers, the price elasticity of demand is 18.2 divided by 6.9, which equals 2.64.

By using percentages of the *average* price and *average* quantity, we get the same value for the elasticity regardless of whether the price falls from £3.10 to £2.90 or rises from £2.90 to £3.10.

Percentages and Proportions

When we divide the percentage change in quantity by the percentage change in price, the 100s cancel. A percentage change is a *proportionate* change multiplied by 100. The proportionate change in price is $\Delta P/P_{ave}$, and the proportionate change in quantity demanded is $\Delta Q/Q_{ave}$. So if we divide $\Delta Q/Q_{ave}$ by $\Delta P/P_{ave}$, we get the same answer as we get by using percentage changes.

A Units-Free Measure

Elasticity is a *units-free measure* because the percentage change in each variable is independent of the units in which the variable is measured. And the ratio of the two percentages is a number without units.

Minus Sign and Elasticity

When the price of a good *rises*, the quantity demanded *decreases* along the demand curve. Because a *positive* change in price brings a *negative* change in the quantity demanded, the price elasticity of demand is a negative number. But it is the magnitude, or *absolute value*, of the price elasticity of demand that tells us how responsive – how elastic – demand is. To compare price elasticities of demand, we use the *magnitude* of the elasticity and ignore the minus sign.

Inelastic and Elastic Demand

If the quantity demanded remains constant when the price changes, then the price elasticity of demand is zero and the good is said to have a **perfectly inelastic demand**. One good that has a very low price elasticity of demand (perhaps zero over some price range) is insulin. Insulin is of such importance to some diabetics that if the price rises or falls, they do not change the quantity they buy.

If the percentage change in the quantity demanded equals the percentage change in price, then the price elasticity equals 1 and the good is said to have a **unit elastic demand**.

Between perfectly inelastic demand and unit elastic demand is a general case in which *the percentage change in the quantity demanded is less than the percentage change in price*. In this case, the price elasticity of demand is between zero and 1 and the good is said to have an **inelastic demand**. Food and housing are examples of goods with inelastic demand.

If the quantity demanded changes by an infinitely large percentage in response to a tiny price change, then the price elasticity of demand is infinity and the good is said to have a **perfectly elastic demand**. An example of a good that has a very high elasticity of demand (almost infinite) is a salad from two campus machines located side by side. If the two machines offer the same salads for the same price, some people buy from one machine and some from the other. But if one machine's price is higher than the other's, by even a small amount, no one will buy from the machine with the higher price. Salads from the two machines are perfect substitutes.

Between unit elastic demand and perfectly elastic demand is a general case in which *the percentage change in the quantity demanded exceeds the percentage change in price*. In this case, the price elasticity of demand is greater than 1 and the good is said to have an **elastic demand**. Cars and furniture are examples of goods that have elastic demand.

Figure 4.2 shows three demand curves that cover the entire range of possible elasticities of demand that you've just reviewed. In Figure 4.2(a), the quantity demanded is constant regardless of the price, so this demand is perfectly inelastic. In Figure 4.2(b), the percentage change in the quantity demanded equals the percentage change in price, so this demand is unit elastic. In Figure 4.2(c), the price is constant regardless of the quantity demanded, so this figure illustrates a perfectly elastic demand.

You now know the distinction between elastic and inelastic demand. But what determines whether the demand for a good is elastic or inelastic?

The Factors That Influence the Elasticity of Demand

What makes the demand for some goods elastic and the demand for others inelastic? The magnitude of the elasticity of demand depends on:

◆ Closeness of substitutes
◆ Proportion of income spent on the good
◆ Time elapsed since a price change

Closeness of Substitutes

The closer the substitutes for a good or service, the more elastic is the demand for it. For example, oil has substitutes but none that are currently very close (imagine a steam-driven, coal-fuelled aeroplane). So the demand for oil is inelastic.

The degree of substitutability between two goods also depends on how narrowly (or broadly) we define them. For example, a laptop has no really close substitutes, but a Toshiba laptop is a close substitute for a Dell laptop. So the elasticity of demand for laptop computers is lower than that for a Toshiba or Dell.

In everyday language we call some goods, such as food and housing, *necessities* and other goods, such as cruises, *luxuries*. A necessity is a good that has poor substitutes and is crucial for our well-being, so a necessity has an inelastic demand. A luxury is a good that has many substitutes, so a luxury has an elastic demand.

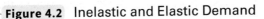

Figure 4.2   Inelastic and Elastic Demand

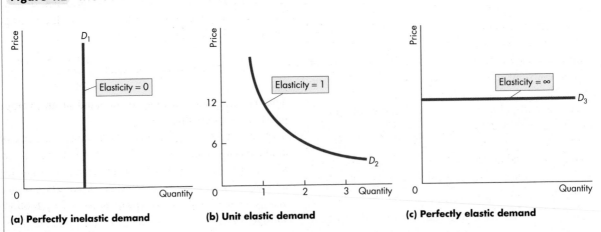

(a) Perfectly inelastic demand   **(b) Unit elastic demand**   **(c) Perfectly elastic demand**

Each demand illustrated here has a constant elasticity. Part (a) illustrates the demand for a good that has a zero price elasticity of demand. Part (b) illustrates the demand for a good with a unit price elasticity of demand. And the Part (c) illustrates the demand for a good with an infinite price elasticity of demand.

Proportion of Income Spent on the Good

Other things remaining the same, the greater the proportion of income spent on a good, the more elastic is the demand for it.

Think about your own demand for toothpaste and housing. If the price of toothpaste doubles, you consume almost as much as before. Your demand for toothpaste is inelastic. If rents doubles, you look for more students to share your accommodation. Your demand for housing is elastic. Why the difference? Housing takes a large proportion of your budget, and toothpaste takes only a tiny proportion. You don't like either price increase, but you hardly notice the higher price of toothpaste, while the higher rent puts your budget under severe strain.

Time Elapsed Since Price Change

The longer the time that has elapsed since a price change, the more elastic is demand. When the price of oil increased by 400 per cent during the 1970s, people barely changed the quantity of oil and petrol they bought. But since then the quantity used gradually decreased as more efficient car and aeroplane engines were developed. The demand for oil has become more elastic as time has elapsed since that huge price hike.

Elasticity Along a Linear Demand Curve

Elasticity of demand is not the same as slope. To understand why, let's look at a demand curve that has a constant slope, but varying elasticity.

The demand curve in Figure 4.3 is linear, which means it has a constant slope – a £1 price rise brings a decrease of 5 smoothies an hour. But the elasticity is not constant. To see why, let's calculate some elasticities.

At the mid-point of the demand curve, the price is £2.50 a smoothie and the quantity is 12.5 smoothies an hour. If the price rises from £2 to £3 a smoothie, the quantity demanded decreases from 15 to 10 smoothies an hour and the average price and average quantity are at the mid-point of the demand curve. So putting these numbers into the elasticity formula:

$$\text{Price elasticity of demand} = \frac{\Delta Q/Q_{ave}}{\Delta P/P_{ave}}$$

$$= \frac{5/12.5}{1/2.5} = 1$$

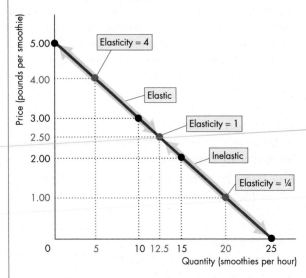

Figure 4.3 Elasticity Along a Linear Demand Curve

On a linear demand curve, demand is unit elastic at the mid-point of the demand curve (elasticity is 1). At prices above the mid-point, demand is elastic; at prices below the mid-point, demand is inelastic.

MyEconLab Animation ————————◆

That is, at the mid-point of a linear demand curve, the price elasticity of demand is 1.

At prices *above* the mid-point, the price elasticity of demand is greater than 1. Demand is elastic. When the price rises from £3 to £5 a smoothie, the quantity demanded decreases from 10 to zero smoothies an hour. The average price is £4 a smoothie, and the average quantity is 5 smoothies. So:

$$\text{Price elasticity of demand} = \frac{10/5}{2/4} = 4$$

That is, the price elasticity of demand at an average price of £4 a smoothie is 4.

At prices *below* the mid-point, the price elasticity of demand is less than 1. Demand is inelastic. For example, if the price rises from zero to £2, the quantity demanded decreases from 25 to 15 smoothies an hour. The average price is now £1 and the average quantity is 20 smoothies an hour. So:

$$\text{Price elasticity of demand} = \frac{10/20}{2/1} = 1/4$$

That is, the price elasticity of demand at an average price of £1 a smoothie is 1/4.

Total Revenue and Elasticity

The **total revenue** from the sale of a good equals the price of the good multiplied by the quantity sold. When a price changes, total revenue also changes. But a rise in the price does not always increase total revenue. The change in total revenue depends on the elasticity of demand in the following way:

◆ If demand is elastic, a 1 per cent price cut increases the quantity sold by more than 1 per cent and total revenue increases.

◆ If demand is inelastic, a 1 per cent price cut increases the quantity sold by less than 1 per cent and total revenue decreases.

◆ If demand is unit elastic, a 1 per cent price cut increases the quantity sold by 1 per cent and so total revenue does not change.

In Figure 4.4(a), over the price range from £5 to £2.50, demand is elastic. Over the price range £2.50 to zero, demand is inelastic. At a price of £2.50, demand is unit elastic.

Figure 4.4(b) shows total revenue. At a price of £5, the quantity sold is zero, so total revenue is zero. At a price of zero, the quantity demanded is 25 smoothies an hour and total revenue is again zero. A price cut in the elastic range brings an increase in total revenue – the percentage increase in the quantity demanded is greater than the percentage decrease in price. A price cut in the inelastic range brings a decrease in total revenue – the percentage increase in the quantity demanded is less than the percentage decrease in price. At unit elasticity, total revenue is at a maximum.

Figure 4.4 shows how we can use this relationship between the price elasticity of demand and total revenue to estimate elasticity using the total revenue test. The **total revenue test** is a method of estimating the price elasticity of demand by observing the change in total revenue that results from a change in the price, when all other influences on the quantity sold remain the same.

◆ If a price cut increases total revenue, demand is elastic.

◆ If a price cut decreases total revenue, demand is inelastic.

◆ If a price cut leaves total revenue unchanged, demand is unit elastic.

Figure 4.4 Elasticity and Total Revenue

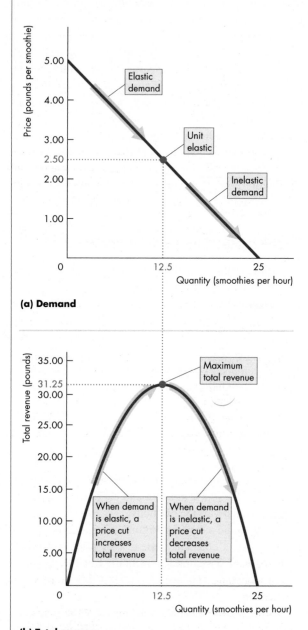

(a) Demand

(b) Total revenue

When demand is elastic, in the price range from £5 to £2.50, a decrease in price in part (a) brings an increase in total revenue in part (b). When demand is inelastic, in the price range from £2.50 to zero, a decrease in price in part (a) brings a decrease in total revenue in part (b). When demand is unit elastic, at a price of £2.50 in part (a), total revenue is at a maximum in part (b).

MyEconLab Animation ⬥

ECONOMICS IN ACTION

Elastic and Inelastic Demand

Table 1 shows some estimates of price elasticities of demand in the UK, which range from 1.3 for tourism to 0.12 for fresh potatoes. Tourists can choose any country to visit so tourism in the UK has many substitutes and its demand is elastic. Fresh potatoes (for fish and chips) have few substitutes and so the demand for fresh potatoes is inelastic. But particular varieties of potato such as Maris Piper or King Edward are close substitutes, so the elasticity of demand for potatoes is smaller than the elasticity of demand for Maris Pipers or the elasticity of demand for King Edward potatoes.

You can see that that the items with elastic demand include luxury goods such as holidays and air travel while items with inelastic demand include necessities such as food, drink and electricity. The demand for cigarettes (duty paid) is elastic because illegally traded cigarettes are close substitutes for legally traded ones on which duty is paid.

Price Elasticity of Demand for Food

Figure 1 shows the proportion of income spent on food and the price elasticity of demand for food in 10 countries. This figure confirms the general tendency that the larger the proportion of income spent on food, the more price elastic is the demand for food.

In a very poor country like Tanzania, where 62 per cent of income is spent on food, the price elasticity of demand for food is 0.77. In contrast, in Germany where 15 per cent of income is spent on food, the elasticity of demand for food is just 0.23.

In a country that spends a large proportion of its income on food, an increase in the price of food forces people to make a bigger adjustment to the quantity of food they buy than in a country in which only a small proportion of income is spent on food.

Table 1

UK Price Elasticities of Demand

Good or service	Elasticity
Elastic demand	
Tourism (visitors to the UK)	1.30
Air travel (short haul)	1.23
Cigarettes (duty paid)	1.02
Inelastic demand	
Fresh meat	0.80
Transport	0.74
Wine	0.67
Beer	0.46
Beverages	0.37
Petrol	0.32
Electricity	0.21
Fresh potatoes	0.12

Sources of data: Bonilla, D. and Foxon, T. (2009), 'Demand for new car fuel economy in the UK, 1970–2005', *Journal of Transport Economics and Policy*, 43(1), 55–83. Collis, J., Grayson, A. and Johal, S. (2010) *Econometric Analysis of Alcohol Consumption in the UK*, HMRC Working Paper No. 10, HMRC. Czubek, M. and Johal, S. (2010), *Econometric Analysis of Cigarette Consumption in the UK*, HMRC Working Paper No. 9, HMRC. Eisenhauer, J and Principe, K. (2009), 'Price Knowledge and Elasticity', *Journal of Empirical Generalisations in Marketing Science*, 12(2), 31–52. Scottish Government Publications (2009), *Food Prices: An Overview of Current Evidence*, www.scotland.gov.uk. *UK Tourism Statistic 2012*, London, Tourism Alliance. Tiffin, R., Balcome, K., Salois, M. and Kehlbacher, A. (2011) *Estimating Food and Drink Elasticities*, Defra, www.defra.gov.uk/statistics.

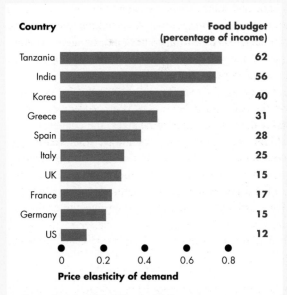

Figure 1 Price Elasticities in 10 Countries

Source of data: Theil, H., Chung, C.-F. and Seale J.L. Jr (1989), *Advances in Econometrics, Supplement 1, International Evidence on Consumption Patterns*. Greenwich, Connecticut, JAI Press Inc.

ECONOMICS IN THE NEWS

The UK Elasticity of Demand for Petrol

Rising Pump Prices Changing Driver Behaviour

When the price of petrol rose in 2012, some people drove slower and some drove less to cut fuel bills. But new on-board technology also cut fuel bills.

Source: *Fleetnews*, 25 April 2012

The Data

Time period	2011 Q2	2012 Q2
Quantity of petrol (billions of litres per quarter)	8.7	8.2
Price of petrol (pence per litre)	136.0	142.2

The Questions

◆ If the data were two points on the demand curve for petrol, what is the price elasticity of demand?

◆ Given the information on p. 87 about the elasticity of demand for petrol, are the data above on the same demand curve?

The Answers

◆ In Figure 1, the price of petrol increases by 6.2 pence with an average price of 139.2 pence, so the price increases by 4.6 per cent.

The quantity decreases by 0.5 billion litres with an average quantity of 8.45 billion litres, so the quantity

decreases by 5.9 per cent. If the points are on *one* demand curve, the price elasticity of demand is $5.9 \div 4.6 = 1.28$.

◆ If the price elasticity of demand for petrol is 0.32 as reported on p. 87, the data represent points on *two* inelastic demand curves. The demand for petrol decreased in 2012 – fuel-saving technology (and other factors) shifted the demand curve leftward.

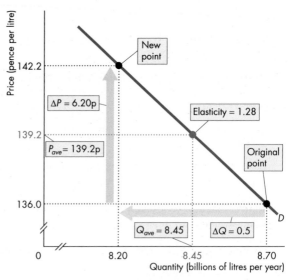

Figure 1 Calculating the Elasticity of Demand for Petrol

Your Expenditure and Your Elasticity

When the price of a good changes, the change in your expenditure on the good depends on *your* elasticity of demand.

◆ If your demand is elastic, a 1 per cent price cut increases the quantity you buy by more than 1 per cent and your expenditure on the item increases.

◆ If your demand is inelastic, a 1 per cent price cut increases the quantity you buy by less than 1 per cent and your expenditure on the item decreases.

◆ If your demand is unit elastic, a 1 per cent price cut increases the quantity you buy by 1 per cent and your expenditure on the item does not change.

So if you spend more on an item when its price falls, your demand for that item is elastic; if you spend the same amount on that item, your demand is unit elastic; and if you spend less on that item, your demand is inelastic.

◆ REVIEW QUIZ

1 Why do we need a units-free measure of the responsiveness of the quantity demanded of a good or service to a change in its price?

2 Define the price elasticity of demand and show how it is calculated.

3 What makes the demand for some goods elastic and the demand for other goods inelastic?

4 Why is the demand for a luxury generally more elastic (or less inelastic) than the demand for a necessity?

5 What is the total revenue test? Explain how it works.

Do these questions in Study Plan 4.1 and get instant feedback.   MyEconLab

You've now completed your study of the *price* elasticity of demand. Two other elasticity concepts tell us about the effects of other influences on demand. Let's look at these other elasticities of demand.

More Elasticities of Demand

Suppose that the economy is expanding and people are enjoying rising incomes. You know that a change in income changes demand. So this increased prosperity brings an increase in the demand for most types of goods and services. But by how much will the increase in income increase the demand for smoothies? The answer depends on the income elasticity of demand.

Income Elasticity of Demand

The **income elasticity of demand** is a measure of the responsiveness of the demand for a good or service to a change in income, other things remaining the same.

The income elasticity of demand is calculated by using the formula:

$$\text{Income elasticity of demand} = \frac{\text{Percentage change in quantity demanded}}{\text{Percentage change in income}}$$

Income elasticities of demand can be positive or negative, and fall into three interesting ranges:

◆ Positive and greater than 1 (*normal* good, income elastic)

◆ Positive and less than 1 (*normal* good, income inelastic)

◆ Negative (*inferior* good)

Income Elastic Demand

Suppose that the price of a smoothie is constant and 9 smoothies an hour are sold. Then incomes rise from £475 to £525 a week and the quantity of smoothies sold increases to 11 an hour. The change in the quantity demanded is 2 smoothies. The average quantity is 10 smoothies, so the quantity demanded increases by 20 per cent. The change in income is £50 and the average income is £500, so incomes increase by 10 per cent. The income elasticity of demand for smoothies is:

$$\frac{20\%}{10\%} = 2$$

Because the income elasticity of demand is greater than 1, the demand for smoothies is income elastic. *When the demand for a good is income elastic, as income increases, the percentage of income spent on that good increases.*

ECONOMICS IN ACTION

Necessities and Luxuries

Table 1 shows estimates of some real-world income elasticities of demand in the UK. The demand for a necessity such as electricity or a green vegetable is income inelastic, while the demand for a luxury good such as fresh meat or wine is income elastic. The demand for some goods such as cigarettes have negative income elasticities, so they are classified as inferior goods.

What is a necessity or a luxury depends on the level of income. For people with low income, food and clothing can be luxuries. So the *level* of income has a big effect on income elasticities of demand. Figure 1 (next page) shows this effect on the income elasticity of demand for food in 10 countries. In countries with low incomes, such as Tanzania and India, the income elasticity of demand for food is high, while in the high-income countries of

Table 1

Some UK Income Elasticities

Good or service	Elasticity
Income elastic demand	
Wine	1.51
Fresh meat	1.14
Petrol	1.10
Income inelastic demand	
Dairy and eggs	0.99
Potatoes	0.96
Vegetables	0.72
Beer	0.55
Electricity	0.27
Inferior goods	
Cigarettes	−0.5

Sources of data: Bonilla, D. and Foxon, T. (2009), 'Demand for new car fuel economy in the UK, 1970–2005', *Journal of Transport Economics and Policy*, 43(1), 55–83. Collis, J., Grayson, A. and Johal, S. (2010) *Econometric Analysis of Alcohol Consumption in the UK*, HMRC Working Paper No. 10, HMRC. Czubek, M. and Johal, S. (2010), *Econometric Analysis of Cigarette Consumption in the UK*, HMRC Working Paper No. 9, HMRC. Eisenhauer, J. and Principe, K. (2009), 'Price knowledge and elasticity', *Journal of Empirical Generalisations in Marketing Science*, 12(2), 31–52. Scottish Government Publications (2009), *Food Prices: An Overview of Current Evidence*, www.scotland.gov.uk. *UK Tourism Statistics 2012*, London, Tourism Alliance. Tiffin, R., Balcome, K., Saois, M. and Kehlbacher, A. (2011), *Estimating Food and Drink Elasticities*, Defra, www.defra.gov.uk/statistics.

Europe and North America, the income elasticity of demand for food is much lower. That is, as income increases, the income elasticity of demand for food decreases. Low income consumers spend a larger percentage of any increase in income on food than do high-income consumers.

The numbers in the figure tell us that a 10 per cent increase in income leads to about a 7.5 per cent increase in demand for food in India, a 3 per cent increase in France, and a less than 2 per cent increase in the US. As countries like India, Korea and Tanzania become richer, the income elasticity of demand for food is likely to fall.

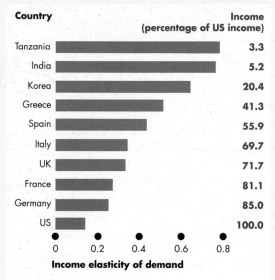

Figure 1 Income Elasticities in 10 Countries

Source of data: Theil, H., Chung, C.-F. and Seale J.L. Jr (1989), *Advances in Econometrics, Supplement 1, International Evidence on Consumption Patterns*, Greenwich, Connecticut, JAI Press Inc.

Income Inelastic Demand

If the percentage increase in the quantity demanded is positive and less than the percentage increase in income, demand is income inelastic. *When the demand for a good is income inelastic, as income increases, the percentage of income spent on that good decreases.*

Inferior Goods

If the quantity demanded decreases as income increases, the income elasticity of demand is negative, and the good is an inferior good. The amount spent on an inferior good decreases as income increases. Goods in this category include small motorcycles, potatoes and rice. Low-income consumers buy most of these goods.

Cross Elasticity of Demand

Andy, who operates a juice bar, wants to know how a rise in the price of coffee at the café next door will affect the demand for his smoothies. He knows that smoothies and coffee are substitutes, and that when the price of coffee rises, the demand for smoothies increases. But by how much?

Andy also wants to know how a rise in the price of his salads will affect the demand for his smoothies. He knows that smoothies and salads are complements, and that when the price of a complement of smoothies rises, the demand for smoothies decreases. But again, by how much?

To answer these questions, Andy uses the cross elasticity of demand. Let's examine this elasticity measure. We measure the influence of a change in the price of a substitute or complement by using the concept of the cross elasticity of demand. The **cross elasticity of demand** is a measure of the responsiveness of the demand for a good to a change in the price of a substitute or complement, other things remaining the same. We calculate the *cross elasticity of demand* by using the formula:

$$\text{Cross elasticity of demand} = \frac{\text{Percentage change in quantity demanded}}{\text{Percentage change in price of substitute or complement}}$$

The cross elasticity of demand can be positive or negative. It is *positive* for a *substitute* and *negative* for a *complement*.

Substitutes

Suppose when the price of a coffee is £1.50, Andy sells 9 smoothies an hour. Now the price of a coffee rises to £2.50. With no change in the price of a smoothie or any other influence on buying plans, the quantity of smoothies sold increases to 11 an hour.

We use the same method that you learned when you studied the price elasticity of demand (pp. 82–83). The change in the quantity demanded is +2 smoothies and the average quantity is 10 smoothies. So the quantity of smoothies demanded changes by 20 per cent. That is:

$$\Delta Q/Q_{ave} = (+2/10) \times 100 = +20\%$$

The change in the price of a coffee, a substitute for a smoothie, is £1 – the new price, £2.50, minus the original price, £1.50. The average price is £2. So the price of a coffee rises by 50 per cent. That is:

$$\Delta P / P_{ave} = (£1/£2) \times 100 = +50\%$$

So the cross elasticity of demand for smoothies with respect to the price of a coffee is:

$$\frac{+20\%}{+50\%} = 0.4$$

Because a *rise* in the price of coffee brings an *increase* in the demand for smoothies, the cross elasticity of demand for smoothies with respect to the price of coffee is *positive*. Both the price of the substitute and the quantity of the good change in the same direction. Figure 4.5 illustrates the cross elasticity of demand. Smoothies and coffees are substitutes. Because they are substitutes, when the price of a coffee *rises*, the demand for smoothies *increases*. The demand curve for smoothies shifts rightward from D_0 to D_1.

Complements

Now suppose that the price of smoothie is constant and 11 smoothies an hour are sold. Then the price of a salad rises from £1.50 to £2.50. No other influence on buying plans changes and the quantity of smoothies sold decreases to 9 an hour.

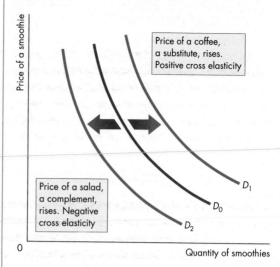

Figure 4.5 Cross Elasticity of Demand

A coffee is a substitute for a smoothie. When the price of a coffee rises, the demand for smoothies increases and the demand curve for smoothies shifts rightward from D_0 to D_1. The cross elasticity of demand is positive.

A salad is a complement of a smoothie. When the price of a salad rises, the demand for smoothies decreases and the demand curve for smoothies shifts leftward from D_0 to D_2. The cross elasticity of demand is negative.

MyEconLab Animation ————————————————◆

ECONOMICS IN THE NEWS

More Elasticities of Demand for Transport

More People Take the Train
During 2011 and 2012, as the price of petrol kept rising, more and more people switched to travelling by train, despite stagnant incomes and a rise in the price of train tickets.

Source: Office of Rail Regulation, NRT Data Portal

The Data

Time period	2011 Q2	2012 Q2
Passengers (billions of kilometres per quarter)	13.7	14.6
Average income (£ per week)	492	488
Price of train travel (pence per kilometre)	12.6	13.0

The Questions

◆ What do the data tell us about changes in the influences on the quantity of train travel demanded and the demand for train travel in 2011 and 2012?

◆ Do the data imply that train travel is a substitute for or a complement of travel by car?

The Answers

◆ The price of train travel increased by 0.4 pence per kilometre to 13 pence. If all other influences had remained the same, the quantity of rail travel demanded would have decreased by an amount determined by the price elasticity of demand.

◆ Average income decreased, and because travel is a normal good, the income elasticity of demand for travel is positive. So the decrease in income decreased the demand for train travel in 2011 and 2012.

◆ The price of petrol increased (see *Economics in the News*, p. 88) and the quantity of train travel increased. This rise in the price of petrol and increase in the quantity of train travel imply that train travel is a substitute for travel by car. The cross elasticity of demand for train travel with respect to the price of petrol is positive – the demand for train travel increased and its demand curve shifted rightward.

The change in the quantity demanded is the opposite of what we've just calculated (again as percentages of the average quantity and average price): the quantity of smoothies demanded decreases by 20 per cent (−20%).

The change in the price of a salad, a complement of smoothie, is the same as the percentage change in the price of a coffee that we've just calculated: the price of a salad rises by 50 per cent (+50%). So the cross elasticity of demand for smoothies with respect to the price of a salad is:

$$\frac{-20\%}{+50\%} = -0.4$$

Because smoothies and salads are complements, when the price of a salad *rises*, the demand for smoothies *decreases*. The demand curve for smoothies shifts leftward from D_0 to D_2. Because a *rise* in the price of a salad brings an *decrease* in the demand for smoothies, the cross elasticity of demand for smoothies with respect to the price of a salad is *negative*. The price and quantity change in *opposite* directions.

The magnitude of the cross elasticity of demand determines how far the demand curve shifts. The larger the cross elasticity (absolute value), the greater is the change in demand and the larger is the shift in the demand curve.

If two items are close substitutes, such as two brands of spring water, the cross elasticity is large. If two items are close complements, such as fish and chips, the cross elasticity is large.

If two items are somewhat unrelated to each other, such as newspapers and smoothies, the cross elasticity is small – perhaps even zero.

REVIEW QUIZ

1 What does the cross elasticity of demand measure?
2 What does the sign (positive versus negative) of the cross elasticity of demand tell us about the relationship between two goods?
3 What does the income elasticity of demand measure?
4 What does the sign (positive versus negative) of the income elasticity of demand tell us about a good?
5 Why does the level of income influence the magnitude of the income elasticity of demand?

Do these questions in Study Plan 4.2 and get instant feedback.   MyEconLab

Elasticity of Supply

You know that when demand increases, the equilibrium price rises and the equilibrium quantity increases. But does the price rise by a large amount and the quantity increase by a little? Or does the price barely rise and the quantity increase by a large amount?

The answer depends on the responsiveness of the quantity supplied to a change in the price. If the quantity supplied is not very responsive to price, then an increase in demand brings a large rise in the price and a small increase in the equilibrium quantity. If the quantity supplied is highly responsive to price, then an increase in demand brings a small rise in the price and a large increase in the equilibrium quantity.

The problems that arise from using the slope of the supply curve to indicate responsiveness are the same as those we considered when discussing the responsiveness of the quantity demanded, so we use a units-free measure – the elasticity of supply.

Calculating the Elasticity of Supply

The **elasticity of supply** measures the responsiveness of the quantity supplied to a change in the price of a good when all other influences on selling plans remain the same. It is calculated by using the formula:

$$\text{Price elasticity of supply} = \frac{\text{Percentage change in quantity supplied}}{\text{Percentage change in price}}$$

We again use the same method that you learned when you studied the price elasticity of demand. (Refer back to pp. 82–83 to check this method.)

Elastic and Inelastic Supply

If the elasticity of supply is greater than 1, we say that supply is elastic, and if the elasticity of supply is less than 1, we say that supply is inelastic.

Suppose that when the price rises from £3 to £5, the quantity supplied increases from 10 to 15 smoothies an hour. The price rise is £2 and the average price is £4, so the price rises by 50 per cent of the average price. The quantity increases by 5 smoothies and the average quantity is 12.5 smoothies an hour, so the quantity increases by 40 per cent. The elasticity of supply is equal to 40 per cent divided by 50 per cent, which equals 0.8. Because the elasticity is less than 1, supply is inelastic.

In contrast, suppose that when the price rises from £3 to £3.20, the quantity increases from 10 to 20 smoothies an hour. The price rise is 20 pence and the average price is £3.10, so the price rises by 6.45 per cent of the average price. The quantity increases from 10 to 20 smoothies an hour, so the increase is 10 smoothies, the average quantity is 15 smoothies, and the quantity increases by 66.67 per cent. The elasticity of supply equals 66.67 per cent divided by 6.45 per cent, which equals 10.34. Now, because the elasticity of supply exceeds 1, supply is elastic.

Figure 4.6 shows the range of elasticities of supply. If the quantity supplied is fixed regardless of the price, the supply curve is vertical and the elasticity of supply is zero. Supply is perfectly inelastic. This case is shown in Figure 4.6(a).

A special intermediate case occurs when the percentage change in price equals the percentage change in quantity. Supply is then unit elastic. This case is shown in Figure 4.6(b). No matter how steep the supply curve is, if it is linear and passes through the origin, supply is unit elastic.

If there is a price at which sellers are willing to offer any quantity for sale, the supply curve is horizontal and the elasticity of supply is infinite. Supply is perfectly elastic. This case is shown in Figure 4.6(c).

The Factors That Influence the Elasticity of Supply

The magnitude of the elasticity of supply depends on:

◆ Resource substitution possibilities
◆ Time frame for the supply decision

Resource Substitution Possibilities

Some goods and services can be produced only by using unique or rare productive resources. These items have a low, perhaps even a zero, elasticity of supply. Other goods and services can be produced by using commonly available resources that could be allocated to a wide variety of alternative tasks. Such items have a high elasticity of supply.

A Van Gogh painting is an example of a good with a vertical supply curve and a zero elasticity of supply. At the other extreme, wheat can be grown on land that is almost equally good for growing corn. So it is just as easy to grow wheat as corn, and the opportunity cost of wheat in terms of forgone corn is almost constant. As a result, the supply curve of wheat is almost horizontal and its elasticity of supply is very large. Similarly, when a good is produced in many different countries (for example, wheat, sugar or beef), the supply of the good is highly elastic.

Figure 4.6 Inelastic and Elastic Supply

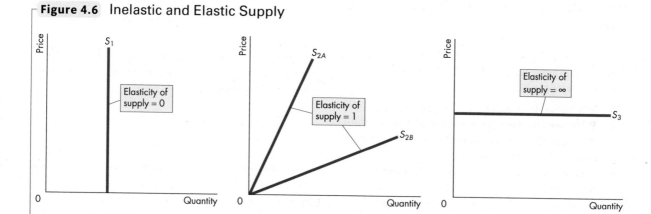

(a) Perfectly inelastic supply (b) Unit elastic supply (c) Perfectly elastic supply

Each supply illustrated here has a constant elasticity. The supply curve in part (a) illustrates the supply of a good that has a zero elasticity of supply. Each supply curve in part (b) illustrates the supply of a good with a unit elasticity of supply. All linear supply curves that pass through the origin illustrate supplies that are unit elastic. The supply curve in part (c) illustrates the supply of a good with an infinite elasticity of supply.

The supply of most goods and services lies between these two extremes. The quantity produced can be increased but only by incurring a higher cost. If a higher price is offered, the quantity supplied increases. Such goods and services have an elasticity of supply between zero and infinity.

Time Frame for Supply Decisions

To study the influence of the length of time elapsed since a price change we distinguish three time frames of supply:

1   Momentary supply
2   Short-run supply
3   Long-run supply

The *momentary supply curve* shows the response of the quantity supplied immediately following a price change.

Some goods, such as fruits and vegetables, have a perfectly inelastic momentary supply – a vertical supply curve. The quantities supplied depend on crop-planting decisions made earlier. In the case of oranges, for example, planting decisions have to be made many years in advance of the crop being available.

The momentary supply curve is vertical because, on a given day, no matter what the price of oranges, producers cannot change their output. They have picked, packed and shipped their crop to market, and the quantity available for that day is fixed.

In contrast, some goods have a perfectly elastic momentary supply. Long-distance phone calls are an example. When many people simultaneously make a call, there is a big surge in the demand for telephone cables, computer switching and satellite time, and the quantity bought increases. But the price remains constant. Long-distance carriers monitor fluctuations in demand and reroute calls to ensure that the quantity supplied equals the quantity demanded without changing the price.

The *short-run supply curve* shows how the quantity supplied responds to a price change when only *some* of the technologically possible adjustments to production have been made. The short-run response to a price change is a sequence of adjustments. The first adjustment that is usually made is in the amount of labour employed. To increase output in the short run, firms work their labour force overtime and perhaps hire additional workers. To decrease their output in the short run, firms either lay off workers or reduce their hours of

work. With the passage of time, firms can make additional adjustments, perhaps training additional workers or buying additional tools and other equipment.

The short-run supply curve slopes upward because producers can take actions quite quickly to change the quantity supplied in response to a price change. For example, if the price of oranges falls, growers can stop picking and leave oranges to rot on the trees. Or if the price rises, they can use more fertiliser and improved irrigation to increase the yields of their existing trees. In the long run, they can plant more trees and increase the quantity supplied even more in response to a given price rise.

The *long-run supply curve* shows the response of the quantity supplied to a change in price after all the technologically possible ways of adjusting supply have been exploited. In the case of oranges, the long run is the time it takes new plantings to grow to full maturity – about 15 years. In some cases, the long-run adjustment occurs only after a completely new production plant has been built and workers have been trained to operate it – typically a process that might take several years.

REVIEW QUIZ

1   Why do we need to measure the responsiveness of the quantity supplied of a good or service to a change in its price?
2   Define and calculate the elasticity of supply.
3   What are the main influences on the elasticity of supply that make the supply of some goods elastic and the supply of other goods inelastic?
4   Provide examples of goods or services whose elasticities of supply are (a) zero, (b) greater than zero but less than infinity, and (c) infinity.
5   How does the time frame over which a supply decision is made influence the elasticity of supply? Explain your answer.

Do these questions in Study Plan 4.3 and get instant feedback.   MyEconLab

You have now learned about the elasticities of demand and supply. Table 4.1 summarises all the elasticities that you've met in this chapter.

In the next chapter, we study the efficiency of competitive markets. But before leaving elasticity, *Reading Between the Lines* on pp. 96–97 uses the concept to look at the effects of a rise in the price of wine on the quantity of wine consumed.

Table 4.1

A Compact Glossary of Elasticities

Price Elasticity of Demand

A relationship is described as	When its magnitude is	Which means that
Perfectly elastic	Infinity	The smallest possible increase in price causes an infinitely large decrease in the quantity demanded*
Elastic	Less than infinity but greater than 1	The percentage decrease in the quantity demanded exceeds the percentage increase in price
Unit elastic	1	The percentage decrease in the quantity demanded equals the percentage increase in price
Inelastic	Greater than zero but less than 1	The percentage decrease in the quantity demanded is less than the percentage increase in price
Perfectly inelastic	Zero	The quantity demanded is the same at all prices

Cross Elasticity of Demand

A relationship is described as	When its magnitude is	Which means that
Close substitutes	Large	The smallest possible increase in the price of one good causes an infinitely large increase in the quantity demanded of the other good*
Substitutes	Positive, less than infinity	If the price of one good increases the quantity demanded of the other good also increases
Unrelated	Zero	The quantity demanded of one good remains constant regardless of the price of the other good
Complements	Less than zero	The quantity demanded of one good decreases when the price of the other good increases

Income Elasticity of Demand

A relationship is described as	When its magnitude is	Which means that
Income elastic (normal good)	Greater than 1	The percentage increase in the quantity demanded is greater than the percentage increase in income*
Income inelastic (normal good)	Less than 1 but greater than zero	The percentage increase in the quantity demanded is less than the percentage increase in income
Negative income elastic (inferior good)	Less than zero	When income increases, quantity demanded decreases

Price Elasticity of Supply

A relationship is described as	When its magnitude is	Which means that
Perfectly elastic	Infinity	The smallest possible increase in price causes an infinitely large increase in the quantity supplied*
Elastic	Less than infinity but greater than 1	The percentage increase in the quantity supplied exceeds the percentage increase in the price
Unit elastic	1	The percentage increase in the quantity supplied equals the percentage increase in price
Inelastic	Greater than zero but less than 1	The percentage increase in the quantity supplied is less than the percentage increase in the price
Perfectly inelastic	Zero	The quantity supplied is the same at all prices

* In each description, the directions of change may be reversed. For example, in this case: the smallest possible decrease in the price causes an infinitely large increase in the quantity demanded.

Elasticity: Demand for Wine

The Telegraph, 16 December 2012

Minimum Alcohol Pricing Will Not Deter Abuse

Ben Martin

Government plans to implement minimum unit pricing are unlikely to stop those more prone to abusing alcohol from buying a drink but would force consumers to spend an additional £659m every year, new research shows.

Proposals to introduce a 45p-per-unit [of alcohol] minimum price are a 'poorly targeted measure,' according to a report from the Centre for Economics and Business Research, which was commissioned by FTSE 100-listed brewer SABMiller.

'A minimum unit alcohol price of 45p has a negligible impact on hazardous and harmful drinking levels among the richest 20 per cent of households in the UK,' CEBR said.

'Yet higher income households exhibit higher levels of combined hazardous and harmful drinking than lower income households.'

The plans are 'highly regressive' and would have a greater impact on the expenditure of the poorest 20pc of households in the country, the report claimed.

'Minimum unit pricing would affect some regions of the UK much harder than others,' the CEBR added. . . .

The Government laid out plans last month that would fix the minimum price for a bottle of wine at £4.20. A can of beer could not be sold for less than 90p.

Jorgen Buhl Rasmussen, chief executive of Carlsberg, said in an interview with the *Sunday Telegraph* at the weekend that the moves are unlikely to stop those who abuse alcohol from buying drinks. . . .

The Essence of the Story

- In December 2012, UK government was considering raising the price of the very cheapest alcohol.

- The proposed minimum price of a drink was related to its alcohol content and was to be at least 45 pence per unit of alcohol.

- The price of a bottle of wine (9.3 units) would have been at least £4.20 and the price of a can of beer (2 units) would have been at least £0.90.

- Producers said the change would be felt most by moderate drinkers on lower incomes.

Economic Analysis

- Table 1 shows some UK wine-market data.

- About 830 million bottles of wine are sold each year, most of which are 12.5 per cent alcohol (9.33 units). About half of these bottles are value wine, sold at an average price of £3.90.

- If the lowest price for a bottle of 12.5 per cent alcohol wine was raised to £4.20, this would affect 410 million bottles a year.

- The table shows the latest estimate of the price elasticity of demand for wine is 0.69. The demand for wine is inelastic.

- If price elasticity of demand for wine is the same for all wine and there is no change in other influences on the demand for wine, we can use the price elasticity to predict the decrease in the quantity demanded and the change in expenditure.

- Figure 1 shows the demand for value wine and the impact of a rise in price from £3.90 to £4.20 a bottle.

- Using the mid-point method, the percentage change in the price equals (£0.30/£4.05) × 100, which equals 7.4 per cent.

- We know the price elasticity of demand (0.69) and the percentage change in the price (7.4), so we can calculate the percentage change in quantity demanded, which is 5.1 per cent. (Check that 5.1/7.4 = 0.69.)

- The 5.1 per cent change in quantity (mid-point method) is a fall of 20 million bottles divided by an average quantity of 400 million bottles.

- The annual revenue (expenditure) from value wine increases from £1,599 million (410 × £3.90) to £1,638 million (390 × £4.20).

- The increase in revenue meets the revenue test: demand is inelastic when a price rise leads to an increase in revenue.

- Households that buy only expensive wines (not affected by the unit price rule) would not change their wine consumption. But low-income households that buy value wine would decrease their wine consumption and increase their expenditure on wine.

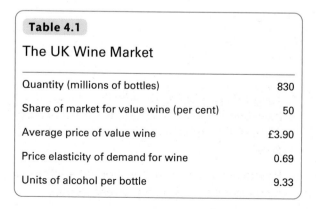

Table 4.1

The UK Wine Market

Quantity (millions of bottles)	830
Share of market for value wine (per cent)	50
Average price of value wine	£3.90
Price elasticity of demand for wine	0.69
Units of alcohol per bottle	9.33

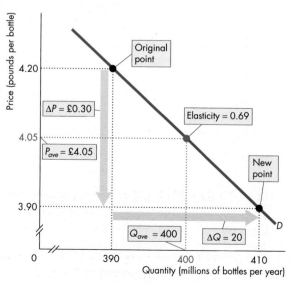

Figure 1 Price Elasticity of Demand for Wine

SUMMARY

Key Points

Price Elasticity of Demand (pp. 82–88)

◆ Elasticity is a measure of the responsiveness of the quantity demanded of a good to a change in its price, other things remaining the same.

◆ Price elasticity of demand equals the percentage change in the quantity demanded divided by the percentage change in price.

◆ The larger the magnitude of the price elasticity of demand, the greater is the responsiveness of the quantity demanded to a given change in price.

◆ If demand is elastic, a fall in the price leads to an increase in total revenue. If demand is unit elastic, a fall in the price leaves total revenue unchanged. If demand is inelastic, a fall in the price leads to a decrease in total revenue.

◆ Price elasticity of demand depends on how easily one good serves as a substitute for another, the proportion of income spent on the good, and the length of time elapsed since the price change

Do Problems 1 to 7 to get a better understanding of the price elasticity of demand.

More Elasticities of Demand
(pp. 89–92)

◆ Income elasticity of demand measures the responsiveness of demand to a change in income, other things remaining the same. For a normal good, the income elasticity of demand is positive. For an inferior good, the income elasticity of demand is negative.

◆ When the income elasticity of demand is greater than 1 (income elastic), the percentage of income spent on the good increases as income increases.

◆ When the income elasticity of demand is less than 1 but greater than zero (income elastic and inferior), the percentage of income spent on the good decreases as income increases.

◆ Cross elasticity of demand measures the responsiveness of demand for one good to a change in the price of a substitute or a complement, other things remaining the same.

◆ The cross elasticity of demand with respect to the price of a substitute is positive. The cross elasticity of demand with respect to the price of a complement is negative.

Do Problems 8 to 16 to get a better understanding of more elasticities of demand.

Elasticity of Supply (pp. 92–95)

◆ Elasticity of supply measures the responsiveness of the quantity supplied of a good to a change in its price.

◆ The elasticity of supply is usually positive, and ranges between zero (vertical supply curve) and infinity (horizontal supply curve).

◆ Supply decisions have three time frames: momentary, short run and long run.

◆ Momentary supply refers to the response of sellers to a price change at the instant that the price changes.

◆ Short-run supply refers to the response of sellers to a price change after some of the technologically feasible adjustments in production have been made

◆ Long-run supply refers to the response of sellers to a price change when all the technologically feasible adjustments in production have been made.

Do Problems 17 to 21 to get a better understanding of the elasticity of supply.

Key Terms

STUDY PLAN PROBLEMS AND APPLICATIONS

Do Problems 1 to 21 in MyEconLab Chapter 4 Study Plan and get instant feedback.

MyEconLab

Price Elasticity of Demand

(Study Plan 4.1)

1 Rain spoils the strawberry crop. As a result, the price rises from £2 to £3 a box and the quantity demanded decreases from 1,000 to 600 boxes a week. Over this price range:

a What is the price elasticity of demand?

b Describe the demand for strawberries.

2 If the quantity of dental services demanded increases by 10 per cent when the price of dental services falls by 10 per cent, is the demand for dental service inelastic, elastic, or unit elastic?

3 The demand schedule for hotel rooms is

Price (euros per room)	Quantity demanded (millions of rooms per year)
200	1,000
250	80
400	50
500	40
800	25

a What happens to total revenue when the price falls from €400 to €250 and from €250 to €200 a night?

b Is the demand for hotel rooms elastic, inelastic or unit elastic?

4 The figure shows the demand for pens.

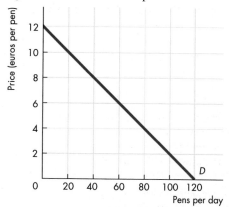

Calculate the elasticity of demand when the price rises from €4 to €6 a pen. Over what price range is the demand for pens elastic?

5 In 2003, when music downloading first took off, Universal Music slashed the average price of a CD from $21 to $15. The company said that it expected the price cut to boost the quantity of CDs sold by 30 per cent.

a What was Universal Music's estimate of the price elasticity of demand for CDs?

b Given your answer to part (a), if you were making the pricing decision at Universal Music, would you cut the price, raise the price, or leave the price unchanged? Explain your decision.

6 The demand for illegal drugs is inelastic. Much of the expenditure on illegal drugs comes from crime. Assuming these statements to be correct:

a How will a successful campaign that decreases the supply of drugs influence the price of illegal drugs and the amount spent on them?

b What will happen to the amount of crime?

c What is the most effective way of decreasing the quantity of illegal drugs bought and decreasing the amount of drug-related crime?

7 **The Grip of Petrol**

Drivers in the US are ranked as the least sensitive to changes in the price of petrol. For example, if the price rose from $3 to $4 per gallon and stayed there for a year US purchases of petrol would fall by only about 5 per cent.

Source: *Slate*, 27 September 2005

a Calculate the US price elasticity of demand for petrol. Is the US demand for petrol elastic, unit elastic or inelastic?

b Explain how the price rise from $3 to $4 a gallon changes the total revenue from petrol sales.

More Elasticities of Demand

(Study Plan 4.2)

8 **Spam Sales Rise as Food Costs Soar**

Sales of Spam are rising as consumers realise that Spam and other lower-cost foods can be substituted for costlier cuts of meat as a way of controlling their already stretched food budgets.

Source: *AOL Money & Finance*, 28 May 2008

a Is Spam a normal good or an inferior good? Explain.

b Would the income elasticity of demand for Spam be negative or positive? Explain.

9 If a 12 per cent rise in the price of orange juice decreases the quantity of orange juice demanded by 22 per cent and increases the quantity of apple juice demanded by 14 per cent, calculate the

a Price elasticity of demand for orange juice.

b Cross elasticity of demand for apple juice with respect to the price of orange juice.

10 When Judy's income increased from €130 to €170 a week, she increased her demand for concert tickets by 15 per cent and decreased her demand for bus rides by 10 per cent. Calculate Judy's income elasticity of demand for (a) concert tickets and (b) bus rides.

11 If a 5 per cent rise in the price of sushi increases the quantity of soy sauce demanded by 2 per cent and decreases the quantity of sushi demanded by 1 per cent, calculate:

a The price elasticity of demand for sushi.

b The cross elasticity of demand for soy sauce with respect to the price of sushi.

12 **Higher Textbook Prices Have Students Saying 'Pass'**

Textbook prices have doubled and risen faster than average prices for the past two decades. Sixty per cent of students do not buy textbooks. Some students hunt for used copies and sell them back at the end of the semester; some buy online, which is often cheaper than the campus store; some use the library copy and wait till it's free; some share the book with a friend.

Source: *The Washington Post*, 23 January 2006

Explain what this news clip implies about:

a The price elasticity of demand for textbooks.

b The income elasticity of demand for textbooks.

c The cross elasticity of demand for textbooks from the local bookstore with respect to the online price of a textbook.

Use the following news clip in Problems 13 to 15.

As Petrol Prices Soar, Buyers Flock to Small Cars

Faced with high petrol prices, Americans are substituting smaller cars for SUVs. In April 2008, Toyota Yaris sales increased by 46 per cent and Ford Focus sales increased by 32 per cent from a year earlier. Sales of SUVs decreased by more than 25 per cent in 2008 and Chevrolet Tahoe sales fell by 35 per cent. Truck sales decreased by more than 15 per cent in 2008 and Ford F-series trucks sales decreased by 27 per cent in April 2008. The effect of a downsized vehicle fleet on fuel consumption is unknown. Petrol consumption decreased by 4 per cent in January 2008 from a year earlier. The price of petrol in January 2008 increased by about 30 per cent from a year earlier.

Source: *The New York Times*, 2 May 2009

13 Calculate the price elasticity of demand for petrol.

14 Calculate the cross elasticity of demand for:

a Toyota Yaris with respect to the price of petrol.

b Ford Focus with respect to the price of petrol.

15 Calculate the cross elasticity of demand for:

a Chevrolet Tahoe with respect to the price of petrol.

b A truck with respect to the price of petrol.

16 In 2008, as petrol and food prices increased and home prices slumped, people had less extra income to spend on home improvements. And the improvements that they made were on small inexpensive types of repairs and not major big-ticket items.

a What does this information imply about the income elasticity of demand for big-ticket home-improvement items?

b Would the income elasticity of demand be greater or less than 1? Explain.

Elasticity of Supply (Study Plan 4.3)

17 The table gives the supply schedule of jeans.

Price (euros per pair)	Quantity supplied (pairs per year)
10	240
20	280
30	320
40	360
50	400

Calculate the elasticity of supply when:

a The price falls from €50 to €30 per pair.

b The average price is €30 a pair.

18 A study ranks Paris number 3 in Europe for the most unaffordable housing market in urban locations, behind London and Berlin, and it is deemed severely unaffordable. With significant constraints on the supply of land for residential development, housing inflation has resulted.

a Would the supply of housing in Paris be elastic or inelastic?

b Explain how the elasticity of supply plays an important role in influencing how rapidly housing prices in Paris rise.

19 If a 10 per cent rise in the price of bread increases the quantity of bread supplied by 20 per cent, calculate the elasticity of supply of bread.

20 The elasticity of supply of blue jeans is 4. If the price of a pair of jeans rises by 5 per cent, what is the percentage change in quantity of jeans supplied?

21 A 10 per cent increase in the price of a good has led to a 1 per cent increase in the quantity supplied of the good after one month and to a 25 per cent increase in the quantity supplied after one year.

a Is the supply of this good elastic, unit elastic or inelastic after one month?

b What is the elasticity of supply after one year? Has the supply of this good become more or less elastic? Why?

ADDITIONAL PROBLEMS AND APPLICATIONS

Do these problems in MyEconLab if assigned by your lecturer.

Price Elasticity of Demand

22 With higher fuel costs, airlines raised their average fare from €0.75 to €1.25 per passenger mile and the number of passenger miles decreased from 2.5 million a day to 1.5 million a day.

    a What is the price elasticity of demand for air travel over this price range?

    b Describe the demand for air travel.

23 The figure shows the demand for DVD rentals.

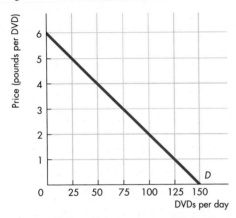

    a Calculate the elasticity of demand when the price of a DVD rental rises from £3 to £5.

    b At what price is the elasticity of demand for DVD rentals equal to 1?

Use the following table in Problems 24 to 26.

The demand schedule for computer chips is

Price (euros per chip)	Quantity demanded (millions of chips per year)
200	50
250	45
300	40
350	35
400	30
450	25
500	20

24 **a** What happens to total revenue if the price falls from €400 to €350 a chip and from €350 to €300 a chip?

    b At what price is total revenue at a maximum?

25 At an average price of €350, is the demand for chips elastic, inelastic, or unit elastic? Use the total revenue test to answer this question.

26 At €250 a chip, is the demand for chips elastic or inelastic? Use the total revenue test to answer this question.

27 Your price elasticity of demand for bananas is 4. If the price of bananas rises by 5 per cent, what is

    a The percentage change in the quantity of bananas you buy?

    b The change in your expenditure on bananas?

28 **As Petrol Prices Soar, Americans Slowly Adapt**

As petrol prices rose in March 2008, Americans drove 11 billion fewer miles than in March 2007. Realising that prices are not going down, Americans are adapting to higher energy costs. Americans spend 3.7 per cent of their disposable income on transportation fuels. How much we spend on petrol depends on the choices we make: what car we drive, where we live, how much time we spend driving, and where we choose to go. For many people, higher energy costs mean fewer restaurant meals, deferred weekend outings, less air travel, and more time closer to home.

Source: *International Herald Tribune*,
23 May 2008

    a List and explain the elasticities of demand that are implicitly referred to in the news clip.

    b Why, according to the news clip, is the demand for petrol inelastic?

More Elasticities of Demand

Use following information in Problems 29 and 30.

This year people are taking fewer exotic holidays by air and instead are visiting local scenic places by car. The global financial crisis has encouraged many people to cut their holiday budgets.

29 Given the prices of the two holidays, is the income elasticity of demand for exotic holidays positive or negative? Are exotic holidays a normal good or an inferior good? Are local holidays a normal good or an inferior good?

30 Are exotic holidays and local holidays substitutes? Explain your answer.

31 When Alex's income was €3,000, he bought 4 cakes and 12 sandwiches a month. Now his income is €5,000 and he buys 8 cakes and 6 sandwiches a month. Calculate Alex's income elasticity of demand for

    a Cakes.

    b Sandwiches.

32 Wal-Mart's Recession-time Pet Project

During the recession, Wal-Mart moved its pet food and supplies to in front of its other fast-growing business, baby products. Retail experts point out that kids and pets tend to be fairly recession-resistant businesses – even in a recession, dogs will be fed and kids will get their toys.

Source: CNN, 13 May 2008

a What does this news clip imply about the income elasticity of demand for pet food and baby products?

b Would the income elasticity of demand be greater or less than 1? Explain.

33 If a 5 per cent fall in the price of chocolate sauce increases the quantity of chocolate sauce demanded by 10 per cent and increases the quantity of ice cream demanded by 15 per cent, calculate the

a Price elasticity of demand for chocolate sauce.

b Cross elasticity of demand for ice cream with respect to the price of chocolate sauce.

34 Netflix to Offer Online Films

Netflix has introduced a feature to allow customers to watch films on their personal computers. Netflix competes with video rental retailer Blockbuster, which has added an online rental service to its in-store rental service.

Source: CNN, 16 January 2007

a How will watching films online influence the price elasticity of demand for in-store DVD rentals?

b Would the cross elasticity of demand for online films and in-store DVD rentals be negative or positive? Explain.

c Would the cross elasticity of demand for online films with respect to high-speed Internet service be negative or positive? Explain.

35 To Love, Honour and Save Money

In a survey of caterers and event planners, nearly half of them said that they were seeing declines in wedding spending in response to the economic slowdown; 12 per cent even reported wedding cancellations because of financial concerns.

Source: *Time*, 2 June 2008

a Based upon this news clip, are wedding events a normal good or inferior good? Explain.

b Are wedding events more a necessity or a luxury? Would the income elasticity of demand be greater than 1, less than 1, or equal to 1? Explain.

Elasticity of Supply

36 The supply schedule for long-distance phone calls is

Price (pence per minute)	Quantity supplied (millions of minutes per day)
10	200
20	400
30	600
40	800

Calculate the elasticity of supply when:

a The price falls from 40 pence to 30 pence a minute.

b The average price is 20 pence a minute.

37 Weak Coal Prices Hit China's Third-largest Coal Miner

The chairman of Yanzhou Coal Mining reported that the recession had decreased the demand for coal, with its sales falling by 11.9 per cent to 7.92 million tons from 8.99 million tons a year earlier, despite a 10.6 per cent cut in the price.

Source: Dow Jones, 27 April 2009

Calculate the price elasticity of supply of coal. Is the supply of coal elastic or inelastic?

Economics in the News

38 After you have studied *Reading Between the Lines* on pp. 96–97, answer the following questions.

a Which demand is more price elastic and why: alcohol in general or wine?

b When the news story says that the higher price 'would force consumers to spend an additional £659m every year', what does it tell you about price elasticity of demand for alcohol and why?

c Why might the price change not affect expenditure and consumption for people on higher incomes as much as those on lower incomes?

d Evidence from *Economics in Action* on p. 89 shows that the income elasticity of wine is 1.51. If the problems of alcohol misuse are related to the amount consumed, will the government's unit price policy work when incomes are rising?

5 Efficiency and Equity

After studying this chapter you will be able to:

- ◆ Describe the alternative methods of allocating scarce resources
- ◆ Explain how marginal benefit and marginal cost determine demand and supply
- ◆ Explain the conditions under which markets are efficient
- ◆ Explain the main ideas about fairness, and evaluate claims that markets result in unfair outcomes

When you order a pizza, your self-interested choice influences how resources are used. A market coordinates your choice with the self-interested choices of a pizza cook and a delivery person to fill your order. Do markets allocate resources between pizza and everything else efficiently?

Markets generate huge inequality. You can afford to buy a pizza but it might be an unaffordable luxury for a very poor person. Is this situation fair?

You're now going to learn how economists approach these questions. At the end of the chapter, in *Reading Between the Lines*, you will apply what you're learned to see how congestion pricing could end the rush-hour crawl and make our motorway use efficient.

Resource Allocation Methods

The goal of this chapter is to evaluate the ability of markets to allocate resources efficiently and fairly. But to see whether the market does a good job, we must compare it with its alternatives. Resources are scarce, so they must be allocated somehow. And trading in markets is just one of several alternative methods.

Resources might be allocated by

◆ Market price
◆ Command
◆ Majority rule
◆ Contest
◆ First-come, first-served
◆ Lottery
◆ Personal characteristics
◆ Force

Let's briefly examine each method.

Market Price

When a market price allocates a scarce resource, the people who are willing and able to pay that price get the resource. Two kinds of people decide not to pay the market price: those who can afford to pay but choose not to buy, and those who are too poor and simply can't afford to buy.

For many goods and services, distinguishing between those who choose not to buy and those who can't afford to buy does not matter. But for some goods and services, it does matter. For example, poor people can't afford to pay school fees, pay for healthcare, or save to provide a pension when they retire. Because poor people can't afford these items that most people consider to be essential, in most societies they are allocated by one of the other methods.

Command

A **command system** allocates resources by the order (command) of someone in authority. A command system is used extensively inside firms, public organisations and government departments. For example, if you have a job, most likely someone tells you what to do. Your labour is allocated to specific tasks by a command.

Command systems work well in organisations in which the lines of authority and responsibility are clear and it is easy to monitor the activities being performed. But a command system works badly when the range of activities to be monitored is large and when these activities are difficult to monitor.

A manager might be able to monitor several employees but a government department cannot monitor every firm in the economy. The system works so badly in North Korea, where it is used in place of markets, that it fails even to deliver an adequate supply of food.

Majority Rule

Majority rule allocates resources in the way that a majority of voters choose. Societies use majority rule to elect representative governments that make some of the biggest decisions. For example, majority rule in each member state of the EU determines the tax rates that eventually allocate scarce resources between private use and public use. Majority rule also determines how tax revenues are allocated among competing uses such as education and healthcare.

Majority rule works well when the decisions being made affect large numbers of people, and self-interest must be suppressed to use resources most effectively.

Contest

A contest allocates resources to a winner (or a group of winners). Sporting events use this method.

Manchester United competes with Chelsea to end up at the top of the Premier League, and the winner gets the biggest payoff. Andy Murray competes to win tennis matches and get the biggest prize. But contests are more general than those in a sports arena, although we don't normally call them contests. For example, there is a contest among Nokia, Motorola and Sony in the mobile phone market. Managers often create contests inside their firms among employees for special bonuses.

Contests work well when the efforts of the 'players' are hard to monitor and reward directly. If everyone is offered the same wage, there is no incentive for anyone to make a special effort. But if a manager offers everyone in the company the opportunity to win a big prize, people are motivated to work hard and try to become the winner. Only a few people win the prize, but many people work harder in the process of trying to win. So total output produced by the workers of the firm is much greater than it would be without the contest.

First-Come, First-Served

A first-come, first-served method allocates resources to those who are first in the queue. Many restaurants won't accept reservations: they use first-come, first-served to allocate their scarce tables. Scarce space on congested motorways is allocated in this way too: the first to arrive on the slip-road gets the road space. If too many vehicles enter the motorway, the speed slows and people wait on the slip-road for space to become available.

First-come, first-served works best when a scarce resource can serve just one user at a time in a sequence. By serving the user who arrives first, this method minimises the time spent waiting for the resource to become available.

Lottery

Lotteries allocate resources to those who pick the winning number, draw the lucky cards, or pick the winning ticket in a gamble. National lotteries throughout Europe reallocate millions of euros' worth of goods and services every year.

But lotteries are more widespread than jackpots and roulette wheels in casinos. Lotteries are used to allocate licensed taxi permits, places in the London marathon, Wimbledon championship tickets, fishing rights, and the electromagnetic spectrum used by mobile phones.

Lotteries work best when there is no effective way to distinguish among potential users of a scarce resource.

Personal Characteristics

When resources are allocated on the basis of personal characteristics, people with the 'right' characteristics get the resources. Some of the resources that matter most to you are allocated in this way. For example, you will choose a marriage partner on the basis of personal characteristics. But this method is also used in unfair ways: for example, allocating the best jobs to white, able-bodied males and discriminating against minorities, older people, people with disabilities and females.

Force

Force plays a crucial role, for both good and ill, in allocating scarce resources. Let's start with the ill.

War, the use of military force by one nation against another, has played an enormous role historically in allocating resources. The economic supremacy of European settlers in the Americas and Australia owes much to the use of this method.

Theft, the taking of the property of others without their consent, also plays a large role. Local crime and international crime throughout Europe allocate billions of euros' worth of resources annually.

But force plays a crucial positive role in allocating resources. It provides the state with an effective method of transferring wealth from the rich to the poor. It also provides the legal framework in which voluntary exchange in markets can take place.

A legal system is the foundation on which our market economy functions. Without courts to enforce contracts, it would not be possible to do business. But the courts could not enforce contracts without the ability to apply force if necessary. The state provides the ultimate force that enables the courts to do their work.

More broadly, the force of the state is essential to uphold the principle of the rule of law. This principle is the bedrock of civilised economic (and social and political) life. With the rule of law upheld, people can go about their daily economic lives with the assurance that their property will be protected – that they can sue for violations against their property (and be sued if they violate the property of others).

Free from the burden of protecting their property, and confident in the knowledge that those with whom they trade will honour their agreements, people can get on with focusing on the activity at which they have a comparative advantage and trading for mutual gain.

REVIEW QUIZ

1 Why do we need methods of allocating scarce resources?
2 Describe the alternative methods of allocating scarce resources.
3 Provide an example of each allocation method that illustrates when it works well.
4 Provide an example of each allocation method that illustrates when it works badly.

Do these questions in Study Plan 5.1 and get instant feedback.   MyEconLab

In the following sections, we're going to see how a market can achieve an efficient use of resources and serve the social interest. We will also examine the obstacles to efficiency and see how an alternative method might sometimes improve on the market. After looking at efficiency, we'll turn our attention to the more difficult issue of fairness.

Benefit, Cost and Surplus

Resources are allocated efficiently and in the *social interest* when they are used in the ways that people value most highly. You saw in Chapter 2 that this outcome occurs when the quantities produced are at the point on the *PPF* at which marginal benefit equals marginal cost (Chapter 2, pp. 35–37). We're now going to see whether competitive markets produce the efficient quantities. We begin on the demand side of a market.

Demand, Willingness to Pay and Value

In everyday life, we talk about 'getting value for money'. When we use this expression, we are distinguishing between *value* and *price*. Value is what we get and the price is what we pay.

The value of one more unit of a good or service is its marginal benefit. We measure marginal benefit by the maximum price that is willingly paid for another unit of the good or service. But willingness to pay determines demand. *A demand curve is a marginal benefit curve.*

In Figure 5.1(a), Lisa is willing to pay €1 for the 30th slice of pizza, and €1 is her marginal benefit from that slice. In Figure 5.1(b), Nick is willing to pay €1 for the 10th slice, and €1 is his marginal benefit from that slice. But for what quantity is the economy willing to pay €1? The answer is provided by the market demand curve.

Individual Demand and Market Demand

The relationship between the price of a good and the quantity demanded by one person is called *individual demand*. And the relationship between the price of a good and the quantity demanded by all buyers is called *market demand*.

> **The market demand curve is the horizontal sum of the individual demand curves and is formed by adding the quantities demanded by all the individuals at each price.**

Figure 5.1(c) illustrates the market demand for pizza if Lisa and Nick are the only people. Lisa's demand curve in part (a) and Nick's demand curve in part (b) sum horizontally to the market demand curve in part (c).

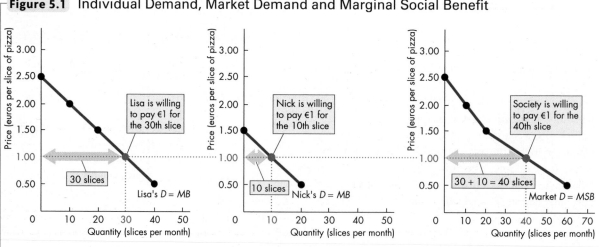

Figure 5.1 Individual Demand, Market Demand and Marginal Social Benefit

(a) Lisa's demand

(b) Nick's demand

(c) Market demand

At a price of €1 a slice, the quantity demanded by Lisa is 30 slices and the quantity demanded by Nick is 10 slices, so the quantity demanded by the market is 40 slices.

Lisa's demand curve in part (a) and Nick's demand curve in part (b) sum horizontally to the market demand curve in part (c).

The market demand curve is also the marginal social benefit curve (*MSB*).

At a price of €1 a slice, Lisa demands 30 slices and Nick demands 10 slices, so the quantity demanded by the market at €1 a slice is 40 slices.

For Lisa and Nick, their demand curves are their marginal benefit curves. For society, the market demand curve is the marginal benefit curve. We call the marginal benefit to the entire society marginal social benefit. So the market demand curve is also the *marginal social benefit curve (MSB)*.

Consumer Surplus

We don't always have to pay what we are willing to pay – we get a bargain. When people buy something for less than it is worth to them, they receive a consumer surplus. A **consumer surplus** is the excess of the benefit received from a good over the amount paid for it. We calculate consumer surplus as the marginal benefit (or value) of a good minus its price, summed over the quantity bought.

Figure 5.2(a) shows Lisa's consumer surplus from pizza when the price is €1 a slice. At this price, she buys 30 slices a month because the 30th slice is worth only €1 to her. But Lisa is willing to pay €2 for the 10th slice,

so her marginal benefit from this slice is €1 more than she pays for it – she receives a *consumer surplus* of €1 on the 10th slice.

Lisa's consumer surplus is the sum of the surpluses on *all of the slices she buys*. This sum is the area of the green triangle – the area below the demand curve and above the market price line. The area of this triangle is equal to its base (30 slices) multiplied by its height (€1.50) divided by 2, which is €22.50. The area of the blue rectangle in Figure 5.2(a) shows what Lisa pays for 30 slices of pizza.

Figure 5.2(b) shows Nick's consumer surplus. Part (c) shows the consumer surplus for the economy, which is the sum of the consumer surpluses of Lisa and Nick.

All goods and services, like pizza, have decreasing marginal benefit, so people receive more benefit from consumption than the amount they pay.

Supply and Marginal Cost

Your next task is to see how market supply reflects marginal cost. The connection between supply and cost closely parallels the related ideas about demand and benefit that you've just studied. Firms are in business to

Figure 5.2 Demand and Consumer Surplus

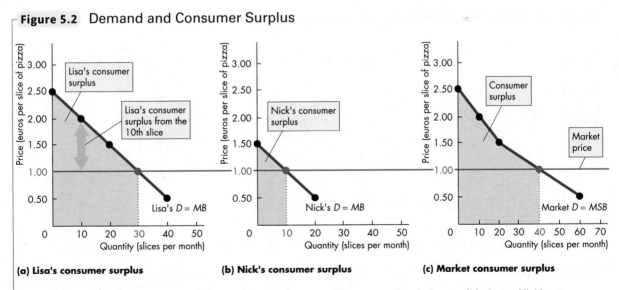

(a) Lisa's consumer surplus   **(b) Nick's consumer surplus**   **(c) Market consumer surplus**

Lisa is willing to pay €2.00 for her 10th slice of pizza (part a). At a market price of €1 a slice, Lisa receives a consumer surplus of €1 on the 10th slice. The green triangle shows her consumer surplus on the 30 slices she buys at €1 a slice.

The green triangle in part (b) shows Nick's consumer surplus on the 10 slices he buys at €1 a slice. The green area in part (c) shows the consumer surplus for the economy. The blue rectangles show the amounts spent on pizza.

make a profit. To do so, they must sell their output for a price that exceeds the cost of production. Let's investigate the relationship between cost and price.

Supply, Cost and Minimum Supply-Price

Firms make a profit when they receive more from the sale of a good than the cost of producing it. Just as consumers distinguish between value and price, so producers distinguish between *cost* and *price*. Cost is what a producer gives up, and price is what a producer receives.

The cost of producing one more unit of a good or service is its marginal cost. Marginal cost is the minimum price that producers must receive to induce them to offer to sell another unit of the good or service. But the minimum supply-price determines supply. *A supply curve is a marginal cost curve.*

In Figure 5.3(a), Maria is willing to produce the 100th pizza for €15, her marginal cost of that pizza. In Figure 5.3(b), Mario is willing to produce the 50th pizza for €15, his marginal cost of that pizza. But what quantity is the economy willing to produce for €15 a pizza? The answer is provided by the *market supply curve*.

Individual Supply and Market Supply

The relationship between the price of a good and the quantity supplied by one producer is called *individual supply*. And the relationship between the price of a good and the quantity supplied by all producers is called *market supply*.

> **The market supply curve is the horizontal sum of the individual supply curves and is formed by adding the quantities supplied by all the producers at each price.**

Figure 5.3(c) illustrates the market supply if Maria and Mario are the only producers. Maria's supply curve in part (a) and Mario's supply curve in part (b) sum horizontally to the market supply curve in part (c).

At a price of €15 a pizza, Maria supplies 100 pizzas and Mario supplies 50 pizzas, so the quantity supplied by the market at €15 a pizza is 150 pizzas.

For Maria and Mario, their supply curves are their marginal cost curves. For society, the market supply curve is the society's marginal cost curve. We call the society's marginal cost the *marginal social cost*. So the market supply curve is also the *marginal social cost curve (MSC)*.

Figure 5.3 Individual Supply, Market Supply and Marginal Social Cost

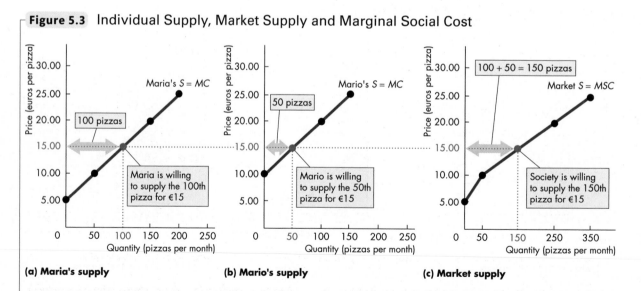

(a) Maria's supply   **(b) Mario's supply**   **(c) Market supply**

At a price of €15 a pizza, the quantity supplied by Maria is 100 pizzas and the quantity supplied by Mario is 50 pizzas, so the quantity supplied by the market is 150 pizzas.

Maria's supply curve in part (a) and Mario's supply curve in part (b) sum horizontally to the market supply curve in part (c). The market supply curve is also the marginal social cost curve (*MSC*).

Producer Surplus

When price exceeds marginal cost, the firm receives a producer surplus. A **producer surplus** is the excess of the amount received from the sale of a good or service over the cost of producing it. Producer surplus is calculated as the price received for a good minus its minimum supply-price (or marginal cost), summed over the quantity sold.

Figure 5.4(a) shows Maria's producer surplus from pizzas when the price is €15 a pizza. At this price, she sells 100 pizzas a month because the 100th pizza costs her €15 to produce. But Maria is willing to produce the 50th pizza for her marginal cost, which is €10. So she receives a *producer surplus* of €5 on this pizza.

Maria's producer surplus is the sum of the surpluses on each pizza she sells. This sum is the area of the blue triangle – the area below the market price and above the supply curve. The area of this triangle is equal to its base (100) multiplied by its height (€10) divided by 2, which is €500. The red area in Figure 5.4(a) below the supply curve shows what it costs Maria to produce 100 pizzas.

The area of the blue triangle in Figure 5.4(b) shows Mario's producer surplus, and the blue area in

Figure 5.4(c) shows the producer surplus for the market. The producer surplus for the market is the sum of the producer surpluses of Maria and Mario.

Consumer surplus and producer surplus can be used to measure the efficiency of a market. Let's see how we can use these concepts to study the efficiency of a competitive market.

REVIEW QUIZ

1   What is the relationship between the marginal benefit, value and demand?
2   What is the relationship between individual demand and market demand?
3   What is consumer surplus? How is it measured?
4   What is the relationship between the marginal cost, minimum supply-price and supply?
5   What is the relationship between individual supply and market supply?
6   What is producer surplus? How is it measured?

Do these questions in Study Plan 5.2 and get instant feedback.   MyEconLab

---

Figure 5.4   Supply and Producer Surplus

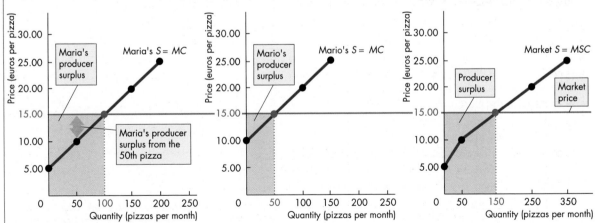

(a) Maria's producer surplus   **(b) Mario's producer surplus**   **(c) Market producer surplus**

Maria is willing to produce the 50th pizza for €10 in part (a). At a market price of €15 a pizza, Maria gets a producer surplus of €5 on the 50th pizza. The blue triangle shows her producer surplus on the 100 pizzas that she sells at €15 each.

The blue triangle in part (b) shows Mario's producer surplus on the 50 pizzas that he sells at €15 each. The blue area in part (c) shows the producer surplus for the market. The red areas show the costs of producing the pizzas sold.

MyEconLab Animation

Is the Competitive Market Efficient?

Figure 5.5(a) shows the market for pizza. The market forces that you studied in Chapter 3 (pp. 64–65) will pull the pizza market to its equilibrium price of €15 a pizza and equilibrium quantity of 10,000 pizzas a day. Buyers enjoy a consumer surplus (green area) and sellers enjoy a producer surplus (blue area). But is this competitive equilibrium efficient?

Efficiency of Competitive Equilibrium

You've seen that the market demand curve for a good or service tells us the marginal social benefit from it. You've also seen that the market supply of a good or service tells us the marginal social cost of producing it.

Equilibrium in a competitive market occurs when the quantity demanded equals the quantity supplied at the intersection of the demand curve and the supply curve. At this intersection point, marginal social benefit on the demand curve equals marginal social cost on the supply curve. This equality is the condition for allocative efficiency. So, in equilibrium, a competitive market achieves allocative efficiency.

Figure 5.5 illustrates the efficiency of the competitive equilibrium. The demand curve and the supply curve intersect in part (a) and marginal social benefit equals marginal social cost in part (b). This condition delivers an efficient use of resources for the society.

If production is less than 10,000 pizzas a day, the marginal pizza is valued more highly than it costs to produce it. If production exceeds 10,000 pizzas a day, it costs more to produce the marginal pizza than the value consumers place on it. Only when 10,000 pizzas a day are produced is the marginal pizza worth what it costs to produce.

The competitive market pushes the quantity of pizzas produced to its efficient level of 10,000 a day. If production is less than 10,000 pizzas a day, a shortage raises the price of a pizza, which increases production. If production exceeds 10,000 pizzas a day, a surplus lowers the price of a pizza, which decreases production. So a competitive pizza market is efficient.

Figure 5.5(a) also shows the consumer surplus and the producer surplus. The sum of consumer surplus and producer surplus is called **total surplus**. When the efficient quantity is produced, total surplus is maximised. Buyers and sellers acting in their self-interest end up promoting the social interest.

Figure 5.5 An Efficient Market for Pizza

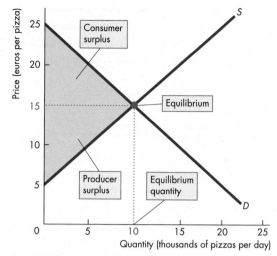

(a) Equilibrium and surpluses

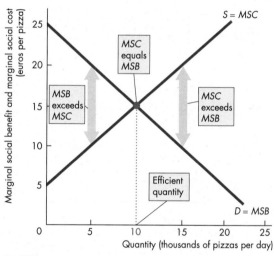

(b) Efficiency

Competitive equilibrium in part (a) occurs when the quantity demanded equals the quantity supplied. Resources are used efficiently in part (b) when marginal social benefit, *MSB*, equals marginal social cost, *MSC*. Total surplus, which is the sum of consumer surplus (green triangle) and producer surplus (blue triangle) is maximised.

The efficient quantity in part (b) is the same as the equilibrium quantity in part (a). The competitive pizza market produces the efficient quantity of pizza.

MyEconLab Animation ──────────────◆

ECONOMICS IN ACTION

The Invisible Hand

Writing in his book *The Wealth of Nations* in 1776, Adam Smith was the first to suggest that competitive markets send resources to the uses in which they have the highest value. Smith believed that each participant in a competitive market is 'led by an invisible hand to promote an end [the efficient use of resources] which was no part of his intention'.

You can see the invisible hand at work in the cartoon and in the world today.

Umbrella for Sale

The cold drinks vendor has both cold drinks and shade, and he has a marginal cost and a minimum supply-price of each. The reader on the park bench has a marginal benefit and a willingness to pay for each.

The reader's marginal benefit from shade exceeds the vendor's marginal cost; but the vendor's marginal cost of a cold drink exceeds the reader's marginal benefit. They trade the umbrella. The vendor gets a producer surplus from selling the shade for more than its marginal cost, and the reader gets a consumer surplus from buying the shade for less than its marginal benefit. Both are better off, and the umbrella has moved to its highest-valued use.

The Invisible Hand at Work Today

The market economy relentlessly performs the activity illustrated in the cartoon to achieve an efficient allocation of resources.

A European frost cuts the supply of grapes. With fewer grapes available, the marginal social benefit increases. A shortage of grapes raises their price, so the market allocates the smaller quantity available to the people who value them most highly.

A new technology cuts the cost of producing a laptop. With a lower production cost, the supply of laptops increases and the price falls. The lower price encourages an increase in the quantity demanded. The marginal social benefit from a laptop is brought to equality with its marginal social cost.

© Mike Twohy/The New Yorker Collection/
www.cartoonbank.com

Market Failure

Markets do not always achieve an efficient outcome. We call a situation in which a market delivers an inefficient outcome one of **market failure**. Market failure can occur because too little of a good or service is produced (underproduction) or too much is produced (overproduction). We'll describe these two market failure outcomes and then see why they arise.

Underproduction

Figure 5.6(a) shows that the quantity of pizzas produced is 5,000 a day. At this quantity, consumers are willing to pay €20 for a pizza that costs only €10 to produce. The total surplus from pizza is smaller than its maximum possible. The quantity produced is inefficient – there is underproduction.

We measure the scale of inefficiency by **deadweight loss**, which is the decrease in total surplus that results

Figure 5.6 Underproduction and Overproduction

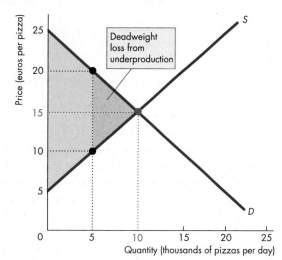

(a) Underproduction

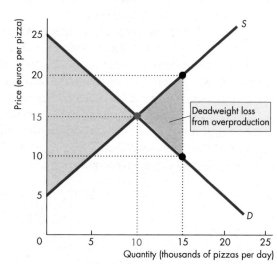

(b) Overproduction

If pizza production is cut to only 5,000 a day, a deadweight loss (the grey triangle) arises in part (a). Consumer surplus and producer surplus (the green and blue areas) are reduced. At 5,000 pizzas, the benefit of one more pizza exceeds its cost. The same is true for all levels of production up to 10,000 pizzas a day.

If production increases to 15,000 pizzas a day, a deadweight loss arises in part (b). At 15,000 pizzas a day, the cost of the 15,000th pizza exceeds its benefit. The cost of each pizza above 10,000 exceeds its benefit. Consumer surplus plus producer surplus equals the sum of the green and blue areas minus the deadweight loss triangle.

MyEconLab Animation ━━━━━━━━━━━━━━━━━◆

from an inefficient level of production. The grey triangle in Figure 5.6(a) shows the deadweight loss.

Overproduction

In Figure 5.6(b), the quantity of pizzas produced is 15,000 a day. At this quantity, consumers are willing to pay only €10 for a pizza that costs €20 to produce. By producing the 15,000th pizza, €10 of resources are wasted. Again, the grey triangle shows the deadweight loss, which reduces the total surplus to less than its maximum. Inefficient production creates a deadweight loss that is borne by the entire society: it is a *social* loss.

Sources of Market Failure

Obstacles to efficiency that bring market failure and create deadweight loss are:

◆ Price and quantity regulations
◆ Taxes and subsidies
◆ Externalities
◆ Public goods and common resources
◆ Monopoly
◆ High transactions costs

Price and Quantity Regulations

Price regulations that put a cap on the rent a landlord can charge and laws that require employers to pay a minimum wage sometimes block the price adjustments that balance the quantity demanded and the quantity supplied. Price regulations lead to underproduction. *Quantity regulations* that limit the amount that a farm is permitted to produce also lead to underproduction.

Taxes and Subsidies

Taxes increase the prices paid by buyers and lower the prices received by sellers. So taxes decrease the quantity produced and lead to underproduction. *Subsidies*, which are payments by the government to producers, decrease the prices paid by buyers and increase the prices received by sellers. So subsidies increase the quantity produced and lead to overproduction.

Externalities

An *externality* is a cost or a benefit that affects someone other than the seller or the buyer of a good or service.

An electric power utility creates an external cost by burning coal that brings acid rain and crop damage. The utility doesn't consider the cost of pollution when it decides how much power to produce. The result is overproduction. An apartment owner would provide an *external benefit* if she installed a smoke detector. But she doesn't consider her neighbour's marginal benefit when she is deciding whether to install a smoke detector. There is underproduction.

Public Goods and Common Resources

A *public good* is a good or service that is consumed simultaneously by everyone even if they don't pay for it. Examples are national defence and law enforcement. Competitive markets would underproduce a public good because of the *free-rider problem*: it is in each person's interest to free ride on everyone else and avoid paying for her or his share of a public good.

A *common resource* is owned by no one but used by everyone. Atlantic cod is an example. It is in everyone's self-interest to ignore the costs of their own use of a common resource that fall on others (called the *tragedy of the commons*), which leads to overproduction.

Monopoly

A *monopoly* is a firm that is the sole provider of a good or service. Local water supply and cable television are supplied by firms that are monopolies. The self-interest of a monopoly is to maximise its profit. The monopoly has no competitors, so it can set the price to achieve its self-interested goal. To achieve its goal, a monopoly produces too little and charges too high a price. It leads to underproduction.

High Transactions Costs

Retail markets employ enormous quantities of scarce labour and capital resources. It is costly to operate any market. Economists call the opportunity costs of making trades in a market **transactions costs**.

To use market price to allocate scarce resources, it must be worth bearing the opportunity cost of establishing a market. Some markets are just too costly to operate. For example, when you want to play tennis on your local 'free' court, you don't pay a market price for use of the court. You wait until the court becomes vacant and you 'pay' with your waiting time. When transactions costs are high, the market might underproduce.

You now know the conditions under which resource allocation is efficient. You've seen how a competitive market can be efficient, and you've seen some impediments to efficiency.

Alternatives to the Market

When a market is inefficient, can one of the alternative non-market methods that we described at the beginning of this chapter do a better job? Sometimes it can.

Often, majority rule might be used, but majority rule has its own shortcomings. A group that pursues the self-interest of its members can become the majority. For example, a price or quantity regulation that creates a deadweight loss is almost always the result of a self-interested group becoming the majority and imposing costs on the minority. Also, with majority rule, votes must be translated into actions by bureaucrats who have their own agendas based on their self-interest.

Managers in firms issue commands and avoid the transactions costs that would arise if they went to a market every time they needed a job done.

First-come, first-served saves a lot of hassle. A queue could have markets in which people trade their place in the queue – but someone would have to enforce the agreements. Can you imagine the hassle at a busy ATM if you had to buy your spot at the head of the queue?

There is no one efficient mechanism for allocating resources efficiently. But markets, when supplemented by majority rule, command systems inside firms and occasionally by first-come, first-served work well.

◆ REVIEW QUIZ

1   Do competitive markets use resources efficiently? Explain why or why not.
2   What is deadweight loss and under what conditions does it occur?
3   What are the obstacles to achieving an efficient allocation of resources in the market economy?

Do these questions in Study Plan 5.3 and get instant feedback.   MyEconLab

Is an efficient allocation of resources also a fair allocation? Does the competitive market provide people with fair incomes, and do people always pay a fair price? Don't we need the government to step into some competitive markets to prevent the price from falling too low or rising too high? Let's now study these questions.

Is the Competitive Market Fair?

When a natural disaster strikes, such as a severe winter storm or a major flood, the prices of many essential items jump. The reason why the prices jump is that some people have a greater demand and greater willingness to pay when the items are in limited supply. So the higher prices achieve an efficient allocation of scarce resources. News reports of these price hikes almost never talk about efficiency. Instead, they talk about equity or fairness. The claim often made is that it is unfair for profit-seeking dealers to cheat the victims of natural disaster.

Similarly, when low-skilled people work for a wage that is below what most would regard as a 'living wage', the media and politicians talk of employers taking unfair advantage of their workers.

How do we decide whether something is fair or unfair? You know when *you* think something is unfair. But how do you know? What are the *principles* of fairness?

Philosophers have tried for centuries to answer this question. Economists have offered their answers too. But before we look at the proposed answers, you should know that there is no universally agreed-upon answer.

Economists agree about efficiency. That is, they agree that it makes sense to make the economic pie as large as possible and to bake it at the lowest possible cost. But they do not agree about equity. That is, they do not agree about what are fair shares of the economic pie for all the people who make it. The reason is that ideas about fairness are not exclusively economic ideas. They touch on politics, ethics and religion. Nevertheless, economists have thought about these issues and have a contribution to make. So let's examine the views of economists on this topic.

To think about fairness, think of economic life as a game – a serious game. All ideas about fairness can be divided into two broad groups. They are:

◆ It's not fair if the *result* isn't fair.
◆ It's not fair if the *rules* aren't fair.

It's Not Fair if the *Result* Isn't Fair

The earliest efforts to establish a principle of fairness were based on the view that the result is what matters. The general idea was that it is unfair if people's incomes are too unequal. It is unfair that bank presidents earn millions of pounds a year while bank tellers earn only thousands of pounds a year. It is unfair that a shop owner enjoys a large profit and her customers pay higher prices in the aftermath of a flood.

There was a lot of excitement during the nineteenth century when economists thought they had made the incredible discovery that efficiency requires equality of incomes. To make the economic pie as large as possible, it must be cut into equal pieces, one for each person. This idea turns out to be wrong, but there is a lesson in the reason why it is wrong. So this nineteenth century idea is worth a closer look.

Utilitarianism

The nineteenth-century idea that only equality brings efficiency is called *utilitarianism*. **Utilitarianism** is a principle that states that we should strive to achieve 'the greatest happiness for the greatest number'. The people who developed this idea were known as utilitarians. They included some famous thinkers, such as Jeremy Bentham and John Stuart Mill.

Utilitarianism argues that to achieve 'the greatest happiness for the greatest number', income must be transferred from the rich to the poor up to the point of complete equality – to the point at which there are no rich and no poor.

They reasoned in the following way: first, everyone has the same basic wants and are similar in their capacity to enjoy life. Second, the greater a person's income, the smaller is the marginal benefit of a pound. The millionth pound spent by a rich person brings a smaller marginal benefit to that person than the marginal benefit of the thousandth pound spent by a poorer person. So by transferring a pound from the millionaire to the poorer person, more is gained than is lost, and the two people added together are better off.

Figure 5.7 illustrates this utilitarian idea. Tom and Jerry have the same marginal benefit curve, *MB*. (Marginal benefit is measured on the same scale of 1 to 3 for both Tom and Jerry.) Tom is at point *A*. He earns €5,000 a year and his marginal benefit of a euro is 3. Jerry is at point *B*. He earns €45,000 a year and his marginal benefit of a euro is 1. If a euro is transferred from Jerry to Tom, Jerry loses 1 unit of marginal benefit and Tom gains 3 units. So together, Tom and Jerry are better off. They are sharing the economic pie more efficiently. If a second euro is transferred, the same thing happens: Tom gains more than Jerry loses. And the same is true for every euro transferred until they both reach point *C*. At point *C*, Tom and Jerry have €25,000 each, and each has a marginal benefit of 2 units. Now they are sharing the economic pie in the most efficient way. It is bringing the greatest attainable happiness to Tom and Jerry.

Figure 5.7 Utilitarian Fairness

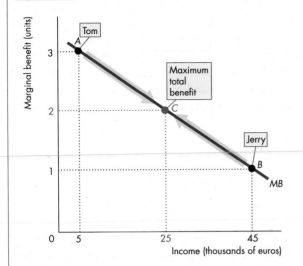

Tom earns €5,000 and has 3 units of marginal benefit at point *A*. Jerry earns €45,000 and has 1 unit of marginal benefit at point *B*. If income is transferred from Jerry to Tom, Jerry's loss is less than Tom's gain. Only when they have €25,000 each and 2 units of marginal benefit (at point *C*) can the sum of their total benefits increase no further.

MyEconLab Animation ────────────────────◆

The Big Trade-Off

One big problem with the utilitarian ideal of complete equality is that it ignores the costs of making income transfers. The economist Arthur Okun, in his book *Equality and Efficiency: The Big Tradeoff*, says the process of redistributing income is like trying to transfer water from one barrel to another with a leaky bucket. The more we try to increase equity by redistributing income, the more we reduce efficiency. Recognising the cost of making income transfers leads to what is called the **big trade-off** – a trade-off between efficiency and fairness.

The big trade-off is based on the following facts. Income can be transferred from people with high incomes to people with low incomes only by taxing the high incomes. Taxing people's income from employment makes them work less. It results in the quantity of labour being less than the efficient quantity. Taxing people's income from capital makes them save less. It results in the quantity of capital being less than the efficient quantity. With smaller quantities of both labour and capital, the quantity of goods and services produced is less than the efficient quantity. The economic pie shrinks.

The trade-off is between the size of the economy and the degree of equality with which its produce is shared. The greater the amount of income redistribution through income taxes, the greater the inefficiency – the smaller is the economic pie.

A second source of inefficiency arises because a euro taken from a rich person does not end up as a euro in the hands of a poorer person. Some of it is spent on administration of the tax and transfer system. The cost of the tax-collection agency, HM Revenue & Customs, and the welfare-administering agency, Department for Work and Pensions, must be paid with some of the taxes collected.

Also, taxpayers hire accountants, auditors and lawyers to help ensure that they pay the correct amount of taxes. These activities use skilled labour and capital resources that could otherwise be used to produce goods and services that people value.

You can see that when all these costs are taken into account, taking a euro from a rich person does not give a euro to a poor person. It is even possible that, with high taxes, those with low incomes end up being worse off. Suppose, for example, that highly taxed entrepreneurs decide to work less hard and shut down some of their businesses. Low-income workers get fired and must seek other, perhaps even lower-paid, work.

Because of the big trade-off, those who say that fairness is equality propose a modified version of utilitarianism.

Make the Poorest as Well Off as Possible

A Harvard philosopher, John Rawls, proposed a modified version of utilitarianism in a classic book entitled *A Theory of Justice*, published in 1971. Rawls says that, taking all the costs of income transfers into account, the fair distribution of the economic pie is the one that makes the poorest person as well off as possible.

The incomes of rich people should be taxed, and after paying the costs of administering the tax and transfer system, what is left should be transferred to the poor. But the taxes must not be so high that they make the economic pie shrink to the point at which the poorest person ends up with a smaller piece. A bigger share of a smaller pie can be less than a smaller share of a bigger pie. The goal is to make the piece enjoyed by the poorest person as big as possible. Most likely this piece will not be an equal share.

The 'fair results' idea requires a change in the results after the game is over. Some economists say these changes are themselves unfair, and they propose a different way of thinking about fairness.

It's Not Fair if the *Rules* Aren't Fair

The idea that it's not fair if the rules aren't fair is based on a fundamental principle that seems to be hard-wired into the human brain. It is the symmetry principle. The **symmetry principle** is the requirement that people in similar situations be treated similarly. It is the moral principle that lies at the centre of all the big religions. It says, in some form or other, 'behave towards others in the way you expect them to behave towards you'.

In economic life, this principle translates into *equality of opportunity*. But equality of opportunity to do what? This question is answered by the Harvard philosopher Robert Nozick, in a book entitled *Anarchy, State and Utopia*, published in 1974. Nozick argues that the idea of fairness as an outcome or result cannot work, and that fairness must be based on the fairness of the rules. He suggests that fairness obeys two rules:

1 The state must enforce laws that establish and protect private property.

2 Private property may be transferred from one person to another only by voluntary exchange.

The first rule says that everything that is valuable must be owned by individuals, and that the state must ensure that theft is prevented. The second rule says that the only legitimate way a person can acquire property is to buy it in exchange for something else that the person owns. If these rules, which are fair rules, are followed, then the result is fair. It doesn't matter how unequally the economic pie is shared, provided that the pie is baked by people, each one of whom voluntarily provides services in exchange for a share of the pie offered in compensation.

These rules satisfy the symmetry principle. And if these rules are not followed, the symmetry principle is broken. You can see these facts by imagining a world in which the laws are not followed.

First, suppose that some resources or goods are not owned. They are common property. Then everyone is free to participate in a grab to use these resources or goods. The strongest will prevail. But when the strongest prevails, the strongest effectively *owns* the resources or goods in question and prevents others from enjoying them.

Second, suppose that we do not insist on voluntary exchange for transferring ownership of resources from one person to another. The alternative is *involuntary* transfer. In simple language, the alternative is theft.

Both of these situations violate the symmetry principle. Only the strong get to acquire what they want. The weak end up with only the resources and goods that the strong don't want.

In a majority-rule political system, the strong are those in the majority or those with enough resources to influence opinion and achieve a majority.

In contrast, if the two rules of fairness are followed, everyone, strong and weak, is treated in a similar way. All individuals are free to use their resources and human skills to create things that are valued by themselves and others and to exchange the fruits of their efforts with all others. This set of arrangements is the only one that obeys the symmetry principle.

Fair Rules and Efficiency

If private property rights are enforced and if voluntary exchange takes place in a competitive market with none of the obstacles described above (pp. 112–113), resources will be allocated efficiently.

According to the Nozick fair rules view, no matter how unequal is the resulting distribution of income and wealth, it will be fair.

It would be better if everyone were as well off as those with the highest incomes, but scarcity prevents that outcome, and the best attainable outcome is the efficient one.

Case Study: A Shortage of Hotel Rooms in a Natural Disaster

The ash cloud from Iceland's volcanic eruption in 2010 shut down airports, stranded travellers, and increased the local demand for hotel rooms. What is the fair way to allocate the available hotel rooms?

If the market price is used, the outcome is efficient. Sellers and buyers are better off and no one is worse off. People who own hotels make a larger profit, and the rooms go to those who can afford them and want the rooms most. Is that fair?

On the Nozick rules view, the outcome is fair. On the fair outcome view, the outcome might be considered unfair. But what are the alternatives? They are command, majority rule, contest, first-come-first-served, lottery, personal characteristics, and force. None of these methods delivers an allocation of rooms that is either fair or efficient except by chance. It is unfair in the rules view because the distribution involves involuntary transfers of resources among citizens. It is unfair in the results view because the poorest don't end up being made as well off as possible.

AT ISSUE

Price Gouging

Price gouging is the practice of offering an essential item for sale following a natural disaster at a price much higher than its normal price. In the aftermath of the Icelandic volcano eruption, news stories reported that the price of an overnight room near Europe's stricken airports increased from €460 to €800 in one afternoon. Hotels, B&Bs and local households opened up rooms not usually used. Many stranded travellers who could not afford the prices had to sleep in the airports. Some suggested there should be a law against this type of price gouging.

In Favour of a Law Against Price Gouging

Supporters of laws against price gouging say:

◆ It unfairly exploits vulnerable needy buyers.

◆ It unfairly rewards unscrupulous sellers.

◆ In situations of extraordinary shortage, prices should be regulated to prevent these abuses and scarce resources should be allocated by one of the non-market mechanisms such as majority vote or equal shares for all.

Should the price that hotels and B&B renters may charge during a natural disaster be regulated?

The Economist's Response

Economists say that preventing a voluntary market transaction leads to inefficiency – makes some people worse off without making anyone better off.

◆ In Figure 1, when the demand for hotel rooms increases from D_0 to D_1, the equilibrium price rises from €460 to €800 per room.

◆ Calling the price rise 'gouging' and blocking it with a law prevents additional rooms from being made available and creates a deadweight loss.

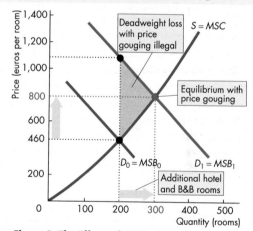

Figure 1 The Effects of a Price-Gouging Law

REVIEW QUIZ

1 What are the two big approaches to thinking about fairness?
2 Explain the utilitarian idea of fairness and what is wrong with it.
3 Explain the big trade-off. What idea of fairness has been developed to deal with it?
4 What is the main idea of fairness based on fair rules? Explain your answer.

Do these questions in Study Plan 5.4 and get instant feedback.   MyEconLab

You've now studied efficiency and equity, or fairness, the two biggest issues that run right through the whole of economics. *Reading Between the Lines* on pp. 118–119 looks at an example of an efficient market in our economy today. At many points throughout this book – and in your life – you will return to and use the ideas about efficiency and fairness that you've learned in this chapter. In the next chapter, we study some sources of *in*efficiency and *un*fairness.

Making Traffic Flow Efficiently

The Independent, 15 May 2012

Charge Motorists Per Mile, says IFS

Nigel Morris

Motorists should be charged for every mile they drive as a way of cutting petrol prices and reducing traffic jams, an influential think tank says in a report today.

The Institute for Fiscal Studies (IFS) argues there is a compelling case for making a switch from motoring taxes to a system of national road pricing. Such a shift would be highly controversial, but it could be used to encourage drivers to avoid the busiest times and routes by varying the amount they are charged for making journeys. . . .

The think tank says . . . road use would be a more sustainable way of raising tax as the total distance driven in Britain annually is forecast to increase from 321 billion miles in 2010 to 396 billion miles by 2030.

'Such a move would generate substantial economic efficiency gains from reduced congestion, reduce the tax levied on the majority of miles driven, leave many [particularly rural] motorists better off, and provide a stable long-term footing for motoring taxes without necessarily raising net additional revenue from drivers,' it says.

 ## The Essence of the Story

- The Institute for Fiscal Studies says motorists should pay to use roads by the mile to reduce road congestion.

- Road pricing could replace current motoring taxes such as tax per car and fuel duties.

- The total distance driven in Britain is forecast to rise, increasing congestion costs.

- Road pricing could create large economic efficiency gains.

Economic Analysis

- When an additional vehicle enters an uncongested road, it imposes no cost on other road users. But when an additional vehicle enters a congested road, the traffic slows, and time and fuel costs increase for all road users.

- The UK Department of Transport estimates that on average the congestion cost for each extra kilometre driven is £0.13, and on a heavily congested road, it can be as high as £2.50.

- Figures 1 and 2 show the marginal social cost curve (*MSC*) for a motorway that can carry 15,000 vehicles per hour with no congestion. Up to 15,000 vehicles per hour, *MSC* = 0. Above 15,000 vehicles per hour congestion occurs and *MSC* increases as more vehicles enter the motorway.

- During the night and at off-peak parts of the day, the marginal social benefit (*MSB*) and demand for road space are low and there is no congestion.

- Figure 1 illustrates off-peak road use. The demand and marginal benefit curve is $D_O = MSB_O$; the marginal cost curve is *MSC*; and the equilibrium and efficient outcome occurs at a zero price for road use.

- Figure 2 illustrates road use at a peak congestion time. The demand and marginal benefit curve is $D_P = MSB_P$, and with a zero price for road use, 40,000 vehicles per hour enter the

Electronic Road Pricing (ERP) avoids congestion and keeps vehicles moving in Singapore.

motorway. There is a deadweight loss (of time and fuel) shown by the grey triangle.

- Imposing a congestion charge of £2 per mile brings an equilibrium at 25,000 vehicles per hour, which is the efficient quantity. In this situation, total surplus, the sum of consumer surplus (green) plus producer surplus (blue), is maximised.

- Singapore has the world's most sophisticated congestion pricing, with the price displayed on gantries (see photo), and the price rises as congestion increases and falls as congestion eases.

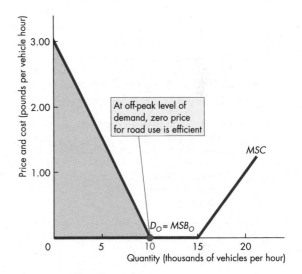

Figure 1 Off-Peak Road Use

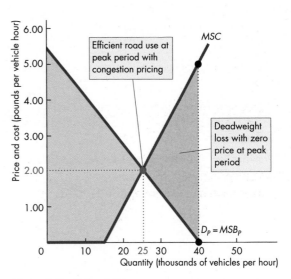

Figure 2 Peak Road Use

SUMMARY

Key Points

Resource Allocation Methods

(pp. 104–105)

◆ Because resources are scarce, some mechanism must allocate them.

◆ The alternative allocation methods are market price; command; majority rule; contest; first-come, first-served; lottery; personal characteristics; and force.

Do Problems 1 and 2 to get a better understanding of resource allocation methods.

Benefit, Cost and Surplus

(pp. 106–109)

◆ The maximum price willingly paid is marginal benefit, so a demand curve is a marginal benefit curve.

◆ The market demand curve is the horizontal sum of the individual demand curves and is the marginal social benefit curve.

◆ Value is what people are *willing to* pay; price is what people *must* pay.

◆ Consumer surplus is the excess of the benefit received from a good or service over the amount paid for it.

◆ The minimum supply-price is the marginal cost, so a supply curve is also a marginal cost curve.

◆ The market supply curve is the horizontal sum of the individual supply curves and is the marginal social cost curve.

◆ Cost is what producers pay; price is what producers receive.

◆ Producer surplus is the excess of the amount received from the sale of a good or service over the cost of producing it.

Do Problems 3 to 10 to get a better understanding of benefit, cost and surplus.

Is the Competitive Market Efficient?

(pp. 110–113)

◆ In a competitive equilibrium, marginal social benefit equals marginal social cost and resource allocation is efficient.

◆ Buyers and sellers acting in their self-interest end up promoting the social interest.

◆ The sum of consumer surplus and producer surplus is maximised. Producing less than or more than the efficient quantity creates deadweight loss.

◆ Price and quantity regulations; taxes and subsidies; externalities; public goods and common resources; monopoly; and high transactions costs can create inefficiency and deadweight loss.

Do Problems 11 to 13 to get a better understanding of the efficiency of competitive markets.

Is the Competitive Market Fair?

(pp. 114–117)

◆ Ideas about fairness divide into two groups: fair results and fair rules.

◆ Fair-results ideas require income transfers from the rich to the poor.

◆ Fair-rules ideas require property rights and voluntary exchange.

Do Problems 14 and 15 to get a better understanding of the fairness of competitive markets.

Key Terms

Big trade-off, 115
Command system, 104
Consumer surplus, 107
Deadweight loss, 111
Market failure, 111
Producer surplus, 109
Symmetry principle, 116
Total surplus, 110
Transactions costs, 113
Utilitarianism, 114

STUDY PLAN PROBLEMS AND APPLICATIONS

Do Problems 1 to 17 in MyEconLab Chapter 5 Study Plan and get instant feedback.   MyEconLab

Resource Allocation Methods
(Study Plan 5.1)

Use the following information in Problems 1 and 2.

At Fifteen, the Jamie Oliver restaurant in London, reservations are essential. At Square, a restaurant in Leeds, reservations are recommended. At Maddisons, a restaurant in York, reservations are not accepted.

1 a Describe the method of allocating scarce table resources at these three restaurants.

   b Why do you think restaurants have different reservations policies?

2 Why do you think restaurants don't use the market price to allocate their tables?

Benefit, Cost and Surplus (Study Plan 5.2)

Use the following table in Problems 3 to 5.

The table gives the demand schedules for train travel for the only buyers in the market: Ann, Beth and Cathy.

Price (euros per kilometre)	Quantity demanded (kilometres)		
	Ann	**Beth**	**Cathy**
3	30	25	20
4	25	20	15
5	20	15	10
6	15	10	5
7	10	5	0
8	5	0	0
9	0	0	0

3 Construct the market demand schedule. What is the maximum price that Ann, Beth and Cathy are willing to pay to travel 20 kilometres? Why?

4 When the total distance travelled is 60 kilometres,

   a What is the marginal social benefit? Why?

   b What is the marginal private benefit for each person and how many kilometres does each person travel?

5 When the price is €4 a kilometre,

   a What is each traveller's consumer surplus?

   b What is the market consumer surplus?

Use the following news clip in Problems 6 and 7.

eBay Saves Billions for Bidders

If you think you would save money by bidding on eBay auctions, you would probably be right. Two Maryland researchers calculated the difference between the actual purchase price paid for auction items and the top price bidders stated they were willing to pay. They found that the difference averaged at least €4 per auction.

Source: *Information Week*, 28 January 2008

6 What method is used to allocate goods on eBay? How does the allocation method used by eBay auctions influence consumer surplus?

7 a Can an eBay auction give the seller a surplus?

   b On a graph show the consumer surplus and producer surplus from an eBay auction.

Use the following table in Problems 8 to 10.

The table gives the supply schedules of hot air balloon rides for the only sellers in the market: Xavier, Yasmin and Zack.

Price (euros per ride)	Quantity supplied (rides)		
	Xavier	**Yasmin**	**Zack**
100	30	25	20
90	25	20	15
80	20	15	10
70	15	10	5
60	10	5	0
50	5	0	0
40	0	0	0

8 Construct the market supply schedule. What are the minimum prices that Xavier, Yasmin and Zack are willing to accept to supply 20 rides? Why?

9 When the total number of rides is 30,

   a What is the marginal social cost of a ride?

   b What is the marginal cost for each supplier and how many rides does each of the firms supply?

10 When the price is €70 a ride,

   a What is each firm's producer surplus?

   b What is the market producer surplus?

Is the Competitive Market Efficient?
(Study Plan 5.3)

11 The figure shows the demand for and supply of mobile phones.

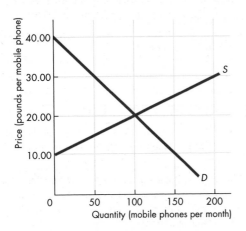

a What are the equilibrium price and equilibrium quantity of mobile phones?

b Shade in and label the consumer surplus at the competitive equilibrium.

c Shade in and label the producer surplus at the competitive equilibrium.

d Calculate the total surplus at the competitive equilibrium.

e Is the competitive market for mobile phones efficient?

12 The table gives the demand and supply schedules of sunscreen.

Price (euros per bottle)	Quantity demanded	Quantity supplied
	(bottles per day)	
0	400	0
5	300	100
10	200	200
15	100	300
20	0	400

Factories producing sunscreen are required to limit production to 100 bottles per day.

a What is the maximum price that consumers are willing to pay for the 100th bottle?

b What is the minimum price that producers are willing to accept for the 100th bottle?

c Describe the situation in the market for sunscreen.

13 Explain why each restaurant in Problem 1 might be using an efficient allocation method.

Is the Competitive Market Fair?
(Study Plan 5.4)

14 Explain why the allocation method used by each restaurant in Problem 1 is fair or not fair.

15 In Problem 12, how can the 100 bottles available be allocated to beach-goers? Which possible methods would be fair and which would be unfair?

Economics in the News (Study Plan 5.N)

16 **The World's Largest Tulip and Flower Market**

Every day 20 million tulips, roses and other cut flowers are auctioned at the Dutch market called the Bloemenveiling. Each day 55,000 Dutch auctions take place, matching buyers and sellers.

Source: Tulip-Bulbs.com

A Dutch auction is one in which the auctioneer starts by announcing the highest price. If no one offers to buy the flowers, the auctioneer lowers the price until a buyer is found.

a What method is used to allocate flowers at the Bloemenveiling?

b How does a Dutch flower auction influence consumer surplus and producer surplus?

c Are the flower auctions at the Bloemenveiling efficient?

17 **Wii Sells Out Across Japan**

After a two-month TV-ad blitz for Wii in Japan, demand was expected to be much higher than supply. Yodobashi Camera was selling Wii games on a first-come, first-served basis. Eager customers showed up early so as not to miss out on their favourite titles. Those who tried to join the queue after 6 or 7 a.m. were turned away – many could be spotted rushing off to the smaller Akihabara stores that were holding raffles to decide who got a Wii.

Source: *Gamespot News*, 1 December 2006

a Why was the quantity demanded of Wii expected to exceed the quantity supplied?

b Did Nintendo produce the efficient quantity of Wii? Explain.

c Can you think of reasons why Nintendo might want to underproduce and leave the market with fewer Wii than people want to buy?

d What are the two methods of resource allocation described in the news clip? Is either method of allocating Wii efficient?

e What do you think some of the people who managed to buy a Wii did with it?

f Explain which is the fairer method of allocating the Wii: the market price or the two methods described in the news clip.

ADDITIONAL PROBLEMS AND APPLICATIONS

Do these problems in MyEconLab if assigned by your lecturer.

Resource Allocation Methods

18 At McDonald's, no reservations are accepted; at the Rex Whistler Restaurant at Tate Britain, reservations are accepted; at Zaffrano in Knightsbridge, reservations are essential. Describe the method of allocating table resources in these three restaurants. Why do you think restaurants have different reservations policies?

Benefit, Cost and Surplus

Use the following table in Problems 19 to 22.

The table gives the demand schedules for jet-ski rides by the only suppliers: Rick, Sam and Tom.

Price (euros per ride)	Quantity demanded (rides per day)		
	Rick	**Sam**	**Tom**
10.00	0	0	0
12.50	5	0	0
15.00	10	5	0
17.50	15	10	5
20.00	20	15	10

19 What is each owner's minimum supply-price of 10 rides a day?

20 Which owner has the largest producer surplus when the price of a ride is €17.50? Explain why.

21 What is the marginal social cost of producing 45 rides a day?

22 Construct the market supply schedule of jet-ski rides.

23 The table gives the demand and supply schedules of sandwiches.

Price (pounds per sandwich)	Quantity demanded	Quantity supplied
	(sandwiches per hour)	
0	300	0
1	250	50
2	200	100
3	150	150
4	100	200
5	50	250
6	0	300

a What is the maximum price that consumers are willing to pay for the 200th sandwich?

b What is the minimum price that producers are willing to accept for the 200th sandwich?

c Are 200 sandwiches a day less than or greater than the efficient quantity?

Is the Competitive Market Efficient?

24 Use the data in the table in Problem 23.

a If the sandwich market is efficient, calculate the consumer surplus, the producer surplus and the total surplus.

b If the demand for sandwiches increases and the sandwich makers continue to produce the efficient quantity, describe the change in producer surplus and the deadweight loss.

Use the following news clip in Problems 25 to 27.

The Right Price for Digital Music

Apple's $1.29-for-the-latest-songs model isn't perfect, and isn't it too much to pay for music that appeals to just a few people? What we need is a system that will be profitable but yet fair to music lovers. The solution: price song downloads according to demand. The more people who download a particular song, the higher will be the price of that song; the fewer people who buy a particular song, the lower will be the price of that song. That is a free-market solution – the market would determine the price.

Source: *Slate*, 5 December 2005

Assume that the marginal social cost of downloading a song from the iTunes Store is zero. (This assumption means that the cost of operating the iTunes Store doesn't change if people download more songs.)

25 a Draw a graph of the market for downloadable music with a price of $1.29 for all the latest songs. On your graph, show consumer surplus and producer surplus.

b With a price of $1.29 for all the latest songs, is the market efficient or inefficient? If it is inefficient, show the deadweight loss on your graph.

26 If the pricing scheme described in the news clip were adopted, how would consumer surplus, producer surplus and the deadweight loss change?

27 a If the pricing scheme described in the news clip were adopted, would the market be efficient or inefficient? Explain.

b Is the pricing scheme described in the news clip a 'free-market solution'? Explain.

28 Only 1 per cent of the world supply of water is fit for human consumption. Some places have more water than they can use; some could use much more than they have. The 1 per cent available would be sufficient if only it were in the right place.

    a What is the major problem in achieving an efficient use of the world's water?

    b If there were a global market in water, like there is in oil, how do you think the market would be organised?

    c Would a free world market in water achieve an efficient use of the world's water resources? Explain why or why not.

Is the Competitive Market Fair?

29 Use the information in Problem 28. Would a free world market in water achieve a fair use of the world's water resources? Explain why or why not, and be clear about the concept of fairness that you are using.

30 The winner of the men's and women's tennis singles at the US Open is paid twice as much as the runner-up, but it takes two players to have a singles final. Is the compensation arrangement fair?

31 **The Scandal of Phone Call Price Gouging by Prisons**

In most states, the phone company guarantees the prison a commission of a percentage on every call. The average commission is 42% of the cost of the call, but in some states it is 60%. So 60% of what families pay to receive a collect call from their imprisoned relative has nothing to do with the cost of the phone service. Also, the phone company that offers the highest commission is often the company to get the prison contract.

    Source: *The Guardian*, 23 May 2012

    a Who is practising price gouging: the prison, the phone company, or both? Explain.

    b Evaluate the 'fairness' of the prison's commission.

Use the following information in Problems 32 and 33.

A winter storm cuts the power supply and isolates a small town in the mountains. The people rush to buy candles from the town store, which is the only source of candles. The store owner decides to ration the candles to one per family but to keep the price of a candle unchanged.

32 Who gets to use the candles? Who receives the consumer surplus and who receives the producer surplus on candles?

33 Is the allocation efficient? Is the allocation fair?

Economics in the News

34 After you have studied *Reading Between the Lines* on pp. 118–119, answer the following questions.

    a What is the method used to allocate motorway space in the UK and what is the method used in Singapore?

    b Who benefits from the UK method of motorway resource allocation? Explain your answer using the ideas of marginal social benefit, marginal social cost, consumer surplus and producer surplus.

    c Who benefits from the Singaporean method of road use resource allocation? Explain your answer using the ideas of marginal social benefit, marginal social cost, consumer surplus and producer surplus.

    d If road use were rationed by limiting drivers with even-date birthdays to drive only on even days (and odd-date birthdays to drive only on odd days), would motorway use be more efficient? Explain your answer.

35 **Tennis Fans Getting Ripped Off for Australian Open Tickets**

Scalpers on eBay are flogging Australian Open tickets for up to $1,250 each, more than triple the face value. Tennis Australia takes scalping seriously and will pursue those persons seeking to profiteer from the Australian Open.

    Source: *Herald Sun*, 14 October 2011

    a What is 'ticket scalping'? Is ticket scalping in the social interest or self-interest?

    b Explain the effect of 'scalping' on consumer surplus and producer surplus.

    c How might Tennis Australia allocate tickets to the Australian Open final that would be fair and efficient?

    d Is it fair that Tennis Australia prevents holders of Australian Open tickets from selling them to others?

36 **Hotels Ramp up Rates to Cash in on Rugby Touristss**

Major hotels in Sydney are charging as much as double the normal rate for rooms on the night of the Sydney Test. 30,000 British and Irish fans are expected to visit Australia for the Lions rugby tour, 10,000 more fans than the number who visited when the Lions last toured.

    Source: *The Sydney Morning Herald*, 9 June 2013

    a What is price gouging?

    b Is the doubling of the price of a hotel room during the Lions tour an example of price gouging?

    c Does the rise in the price of a hotel room mean that the market for hotel rooms is inefficient?

    d If hotel rooms are not allocated by the market price, what other mechanisms could have been used? Would any of these other mechanisms be fair?

6 Government Actions in Markets

After studying this chapter you will be able to:

- Explain how a rent ceiling creates a housing shortage
- Explain how a minimum wage law creates unemployment
- Explain the effects of a tax
- Explain the effects of production quotas, subsidies and price supports
- Explain how markets for illegal goods work

London rents are shooting up. Can government cap them to make housing more affordable? Would a rise in the minimum wage help young people find a good job? Who really pays the tax on petrol: motorists or petrol station owners? Do farm subsidies make agricultural markets more efficient? How do markets work in the 'underground economy' where people trade illegal goods? These are the questions you study in this chapter.

In *Reading Between the Lines* at the end of the chapter, we apply what we have learned and see why government support payments to farmers have fallen in recent years but still create inefficiency.

A Housing Market with a Rent Ceiling

We spend more of our income on housing than on any other good or service, so it isn't surprising that rents can be a political issue. When rents are high, or when they jump by a large amount, renters might lobby the government for limits on rents.

A government regulation that makes it illegal to charge a price higher than a specified level is called a **price ceiling** or **price cap**.

The effects of a price ceiling on a market depend crucially on whether the ceiling is imposed at a level that is above or below the equilibrium price.

A price ceiling set *above the equilibrium price* has no effect. The reason is that the price ceiling does not constrain the market forces. The force of the law and the market forces are not in conflict.

But a price ceiling *below the equilibrium price* has powerful effects on a market. The reason is that the price ceiling attempts to prevent the price from regulating the quantities demanded and supplied. The force of the law and the market forces are in conflict.

When a price ceiling is applied to a housing market, it is called a **rent ceiling** – the maximum rent that may be legally charged.

A rent ceiling set below the equilibrium rent creates:

◆ A housing shortage
◆ Increased search activity
◆ A black market

A Housing Shortage

At the equilibrium price, the quantity demanded equals the quantity supplied. In a housing market, when the rent is at the equilibrium level, the quantity of housing supplied equals the quantity of housing demanded and there is neither a shortage nor a surplus of housing.

But at a rent set below the equilibrium rent, the quantity of housing demanded exceeds the quantity of housing supplied – there is a shortage. So if a rent ceiling is set below the equilibrium rent, there will be a shortage of housing.

When there is a shortage, the quantity available is the quantity supplied, and when there is no price ceiling the price would rise. But when there is a price ceiling, the quantity supplied must somehow be allocated among the frustrated demanders. One way in which this allocation occurs is through increased search activity.

Increased Search Activity

The time spent looking for someone with whom to do business is called **search activity**. We spend some time in search activity almost every time we make a purchase. When you're shopping for the latest hot new mobile phone and you know four stores that stock it, how do you find which store has the best deal? You spend a few minutes on the Internet, checking out the various prices. In some markets, such as the housing market, people spend a lot of time checking the alternatives available before making a choice.

When a price is regulated and there is a shortage, search activity increases. In the case of a rent-controlled housing market, frustrated would-be renters scan the newspapers, not only for housing adverts but also for death notices! Any information about newly available housing is useful, and apartment seekers race to be first on the scene when news of a possible supplier breaks.

The *opportunity cost* of a good is equal not only to its price but also to the value of the search time spent finding the good. So the opportunity cost of housing is equal to the rent (a regulated price) plus the time and other resources spent searching for the restricted quantity available. Search activity is costly. It uses time and other resources, such as phone calls and car journeys that could have been used in other productive ways.

A rent ceiling controls only the rent portion of the cost of housing. The cost of increased search activity might end up making the full cost of housing higher than it would be without a rent ceiling.

Black Market

A rent ceiling also encourages illegal trading in a **black market**, an illegal market in which the equilibrium price exceeds the price ceiling. Black markets occur in rent-controlled housing markets. They also occur in the market for tickets to big sporting events and rock concerts, where 'ticket touts' (or 'scalpers') operate.

When a rent ceiling is in force, frustrated renters and landlords constantly seek ways of increasing rents. One common way is for a new tenant to pay a high price for worthless fittings, such as charging €2,000 for threadbare curtains. Another is for the tenant to pay an exorbitant price for new locks and keys, called 'key money'.

The level of a black market rent depends on how tightly the rent ceiling is enforced. With loose enforcement, the black market rent is close to the unregulated rent. But with strict enforcement, the black market rent is equal to the maximum price that a renter is willing to pay.

Figure 6.1 illustrates the effects of a rent ceiling. The demand curve for housing is D and the supply curve is S. A rent ceiling is imposed at €1,000 a month. Rents that exceed €1,000 a month are in the grey-shaded illegal region in the figure. You can see that the equilibrium rent, where the demand and supply curves intersect, is in the illegal region.

At a rent of €1,000 a month, the quantity of housing supplied is 4,400 units and the quantity demanded is 10,000 units. So with a rent of €1,000 a month, there is a shortage of 5,600 units.

To rent the 4,400th unit, someone is willing to pay €1,200 a month. They might pay this amount by incurring search costs that bring the total cost of housing to €1,200 a month, or they might pay a black market price of €1,200 a month. Either way, the renter ends up incurring a cost that exceeds what the equilibrium rent would be in an unregulated market.

Inefficiency of Rent Ceilings

A rent ceiling set below the equilibrium rent results in an inefficient underproduction of housing services. The *marginal social benefit* of housing exceeds its *marginal social cost*, and a deadweight loss shrinks the producer surplus and consumer surplus (see Chapter 5, pp. 107–109).

Figure 6.2 shows this inefficiency. The rent ceiling (€1,000 per month) is below the equilibrium rent (€1,100 per month), and the quantity of housing supplied (4,400 units) is less than the efficient quantity (7,400 units).

Because the quantity of housing supplied (the quantity available) is less than the efficient quantity, there is a deadweight loss, shown by the grey triangle. Producer surplus shrinks to the blue triangle and consumer surplus shrinks to the green triangle. The red rectangle represents the potential loss from increased search activity. This loss is borne by consumers, and the full loss from the rent ceiling is the sum of the deadweight loss and the increased cost of search.

Figure 6.1 A Rent Ceiling

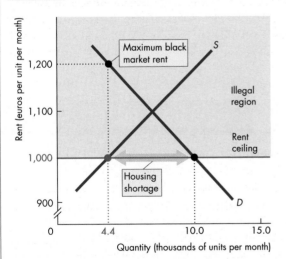

A rent above the rent ceiling of €1,000 a month is illegal (in the grey-shaded region). At a rent of €1,000 a month, the quantity of housing supplied is 4,400 units and the quantity demanded is 10,000 units. There is a housing shortage of 5,600 units.

Frustrated renters spend time searching for housing, and they make deals with landlords in a black market. Someone is willing to pay €1,200 a month for the 4,400th unit. This is the maximum black market rent.

Figure 6.2 The Inefficiency of a Rent Ceiling

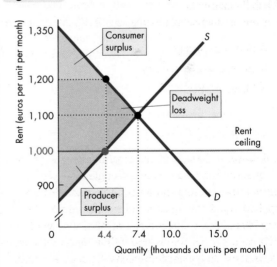

Without a rent ceiling, the market produces an efficient 7,400 units of housing at a rent of €1,100 a month. A rent ceiling of €1,000 a month decreases the quantity of housing supplied to 4,400 units. Producer surplus and consumer surplus shrink, and a deadweight loss arises. The red rectangle represents the cost of resources used in increased search activity. The full loss from the rent ceiling equals the sum of the red rectangle and the grey triangle.

MyEconLab Animation ─────────────◆   MyEconLab Animation ─────────────◆

Are Rent Ceilings Fair?

Rent ceilings might be inefficient, but don't they achieve a fairer allocation of scarce housing? Let's explore this question.

The Two Views of Fairness

Chapter 5 (pp. 114–117) reviews two key ideas about fairness. According to the *fair rules* view, anything that blocks voluntary exchange is unfair, so rent ceilings are unfair. But according to the *fair result* view, a fair outcome is one that benefits the less well off. So according to this view, the fairest outcome is the one that allocates scarce housing to the poorest. To see whether rent ceilings help to achieve a fairer outcome in this sense, we need to consider how the market allocates scarce housing resources in the face of a rent ceiling.

Allocating Housing Among Demanders

Blocking rent adjustments doesn't eliminate scarcity. Rather, because it decreases the quantity of housing available, it creates an even bigger challenge for the housing market. Somehow, the market must ration a smaller quantity of housing and allocate that housing among the people who demand it. When the rent is not permitted to allocate scarce housing, what other mechanisms are available and are they fair? Three possible mechanisms are:

◆ A lottery

◆ First-come, first-served

◆ Discrimination

A lottery allocates housing to those who are lucky, not to those who are poor. First-come, first-served allocated housing in England after the Second World War to those with the foresight to get their names on a list first, not to the poorest. Discrimination allocates scarce housing based on the views and self-interest of owners. Discrimination based on friendship, family ties and criteria such as race, ethnicity or sex is more likely to enter the equation. We might make such discrimination illegal, but we cannot prevent it from occurring.

In principle, self-interested owners and bureaucrats could allocate housing to satisfy some criterion of fairness, but they are not likely to do so. It is hard, then, to make a case for rent ceilings on the basis of fairness. Non-price methods of allocation do not produce a fair outcome.

 ECONOMICS IN ACTION

Rent Ceilings: A Political Winner?

The economic case against rent ceilings is now widely accepted, but they still attract political support.

A Chartered Institute of Housing Report[1] in August 2010 argued that UK housing policy needs to target lower paid workers who cannot afford home ownership or private rented property but who will not be offered local authority housing. They argue that housing associations should offer housing at below market rent (housing with a rent ceiling) to this group.

There are still about 100,000 rent-controlled apartments in the UK. Anyone still in a tenancy that started before January 1989 is protected by a 'fair rent' clause limiting rent rises to the rate of inflation. This means that the same small London apartment with a market rent of £1,500 a month could be rented out at a 'fair rent' of £350 a month. Everyone wants a 'fair rent' apartment.

Because more people support rent ceilings than oppose them, politicians are sometimes willing to support them too. Local authority spending on housing is being cut in the UK, and so local and central government politicians are likely to support charitable groups such as housing associations introducing rent ceilings.

Fair rent sounds good, but the outcome is inefficient because scarce housing resources don't get allocated to the people who value them most highly.

[1] guardian.co.uk/society/2010/aug/15/renting-buying-home

 REVIEW QUIZ

1   What is a rent ceiling and what are its effects if it is set above the equilibrium rent?

2   What are the effects of a rent ceiling that is set below the equilibrium rent?

3   How are scarce housing resources allocated when a rent ceiling is in place?

4   Why does a rent ceiling create an inefficient and unfair outcome in the housing market?

Do these questions in Study Plan 6.1 and get instant feedback.   MyEconLab

You now know how a price ceiling (rent ceiling) works. Next, we'll learn about the effects of a price floor by studying a minimum wage in a labour market.

A Labour Market with a Minimum Wage

For each of us, the labour market is the market that influences the jobs we get and the wages we earn. Firms decide how much labour to demand, and the lower the wage rate, the greater is the quantity of labour demanded. Households decide how much labour to supply, and the higher the wage rate, the greater is the quantity of labour supplied. The wage rate adjusts to make the quantity of labour demanded equal to the quantity supplied.

When wage rates fail to keep up with rising prices, labour unions might lobby the government for a higher wage rate. A government-imposed regulation that makes it illegal to charge a price lower than a specified level is called a **price floor**.

The effects of a price floor on a market depend crucially on whether the floor is imposed at a level that is above or below the equilibrium price.

A price floor set *below the equilibrium price* has no effect. The reason is that the price floor does not constrain the market forces. The force of the law and the market forces are not in conflict. But a price floor *above the equilibrium price* has powerful effects on a market. The reason is that the price floor attempts to prevent the price from regulating the quantities demanded and supplied. The force of the law and the market forces are in conflict.

When a price floor is applied to a labour market, it is called a **minimum wage**. A minimum wage imposed at a level that is above the equilibrium wage creates unemployment. Let's look at the effects of a minimum wage.

Minimum Wage Brings Unemployment

At the equilibrium price, the quantity demanded equals the quantity supplied. In a labour market, when the wage rate is at the equilibrium level, the quantity of labour supplied equals the quantity of labour demanded. But at a wage rate above the equilibrium wage, the quantity of labour supplied exceeds the quantity of labour demanded – there is a surplus of labour. So when a minimum wage is set above the equilibrium wage, there is a surplus of labour. The demand for labour determines the level of employment, and the surplus of labour is unemployed.

Figure 6.3 illustrates the effect of the minimum wage on unemployment in a European economy. The demand

Figure 6.3 Minimum Wage and Unemployment

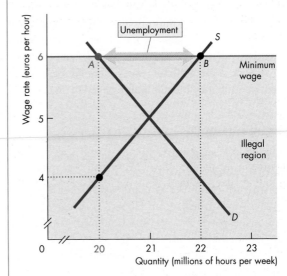

The minimum wage is €6 an hour. Any wage below €6 an hour is illegal (in the grey-shaded illegal region). At a minimum wage of €6 an hour, 20 million hours are hired but 22 million hours are available. Unemployment – *AB* – of 2 million hours a week is created. With only 20 million hours demanded, someone is willing to supply the 20 millionth hour for €4.

MyEconLab Animation ———————————◆

for labour curve is *D* and the supply of labour curve is *S*. The horizontal red line shows the minimum wage set at €6 an hour. A wage rate below this level is illegal, in the grey-shaded illegal region of the figure. At the minimum wage rate, 20 million hours of labour are demanded (point *A*) and 22 million hours of labour are supplied (point *B*), so 2 million hours of available labour are unemployed.

With only 20 million hours demanded, someone is willing to supply that 20 millionth hour for €4. Frustrated unemployed workers spend time and other resources searching for hard-to-find jobs.

Is the Minimum Wage Fair?

The minimum wage is unfair on both views of fairness. It delivers an unfair *result* and it imposes unfair *rules*.

The *result* is unfair because only those people who have jobs and keep them benefit from the minimum wage. The unemployed end up worse off than they would be with no minimum wage. Some of them who search for jobs and find them end up worse off because of the increased cost of job search they incur. In addition, those who find jobs are not always the least well off.

When the wage rate doesn't allocate labour, other mechanisms determine who finds a job. One such mechanism is discrimination, which is another source of unfairness.

The minimum wage imposes an unfair *rule* because it blocks voluntary exchange. Firms looking for workers are willing to hire more labour and people who are looking for work or are willing to work more hours, but they are not permitted by the minimum wage law to do so.

Inefficiency of a Minimum Wage

In the labour market, the supply curve measures the marginal social cost of labour to workers. This cost is leisure forgone. The demand curve measures the marginal social benefit from labour. This benefit is the value of the goods and services produced. An unregulated labour market allocates the economy's scarce labour resources to the jobs in which they are valued most highly. The market is efficient.

The minimum wage frustrates the market mechanism and results in unemployment and increased job search. At the quantity of labour employed, the marginal social benefit of labour exceeds its marginal social cost, and a deadweight loss shrinks the firms' surplus and the workers' surplus.

Figure 6.4 shows this inefficiency. The minimum wage (€6 an hour) is above the equilibrium wage (€5 an hour) and the quantity of labour demanded and employed (20 million hours) is less than the efficient quantity (21 million hours).

Because the quantity of labour employed is less than the efficient quantity, a deadweight loss shown by the grey triangle arises. The firms' surplus shrinks to the blue triangle and the workers' surplus shrinks to the green triangle. The red rectangle shows the potential loss from increased job search, which is borne by workers. The full loss from the minimum wage is the sum of the deadweight loss and the increased cost of job search.

AT ISSUE

Does the Minimum Wage Cause Unemployment?

In Europe, minimum wages policies are widespread but rates vary. They are highest in France at 60 per cent of the median wage and lowest in the Czech Republic at 34 per cent. The UK minimum wage for those aged over 21 is £6.19, or 45 per cent of the median wage.

Does the minimum wage result in unemployment, and if so, how much unemployment does it create?

No, It Doesn't

David Card of the University of California at Berkeley and Alan Krueger of Princeton University say:

◆ An increase in the minimum wage *increases* teenage *employment* and *decreases unemployment*.

◆ Their US study of minimum wages in California, New Jersey and Texas found that the employment rate of low-income workers increased following an increase in the minimum wage.

◆ A higher wage *increases* employment by making workers more conscientious and productive as well as less likely to quit, which lowers unproductive labour turnover.

◆ A higher wage rate makes managers seek ways to increase labour productivity.

Yes, It Does

Most economists are skeptical about Card and Krueger's conclusion.

◆ The consensus view is that a 10 per cent rise in the minimum wage *decreases teenage employment* by between 1 and 3 per cent.

◆ Chris Pissarides, a Nobel Prize Laureate and Professor at the London School of Economics, agrees that a minimum wage above 40 per cent of the median wage causes youth unemployment.

◆ Firms freely pay wage rates above the equilibrium wage to encourage more productive work habits.

◆ Daniel Hamermesh of the University of Texas at Austin says that firms anticipate the rise and cut employment *before* the minimum wage goes up.

Figure 6.4 The Inefficiency of a Minimum Wage

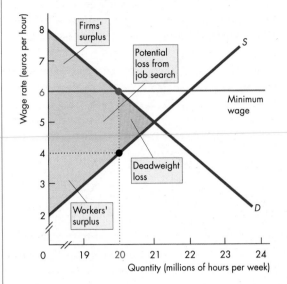

A minimum wage decreases employment. Firms' surplus (blue) and workers' surplus (green) shrink, and a deadweight loss (grey area) arises. Job search increases and the red area shows the loss from this activity.

MyEconLab Animation ──────────────◆

REVIEW QUIZ

1 What is a minimum wage and what are its effects if it is set above the equilibrium wage?
2 What are the effects of a minimum wage set below the equilibrium wage?
3 Explain how scarce jobs are allocated when a minimum wage is in place.
4 Explain why a minimum wage creates an inefficient allocation of labour resources.
5 Explain why a minimum wage is unfair.

Do these questions in Study Plan 6.2 and get instant feedback. MyEconLab

Next we're going to study a more widespread government action in markets: taxes. We'll see how taxes change the prices and quantities of the things taxed. You will discover the surprising fact that while the government can impose a tax, it cannot decide who will pay the tax! You will also see that a tax is inefficient and creates a deadweight loss.

Taxes

Everything you earn and almost everything you buy is taxed. The income tax and a National Insurance contribution are deducted from your earnings. The prices of most of the things you buy include VAT, and the prices of a few goods such as cigarettes, alcoholic drinks and petrol include a heavy excise tax. Firms also pay some taxes, one of which is a National Insurance contribution for every person they employ.

Who *really* pays these taxes? Because the income tax and National Insurance contribution are deducted from your pay, isn't it obvious that *you* pay these taxes? And isn't it equally obvious that you pay the VAT, that smokers pay the tax on cigarettes, and that your employer pays the employer's National Insurance contribution?

You're going to discover that it isn't obvious who *really* pays a tax, and that lawmakers don't make that decision. We begin with a definition of tax incidence.

Tax Incidence

Tax incidence is the division of the burden of a tax between buyers and sellers. When the government imposes a tax on the sale of a good,[1] the price paid by buyers might rise by the full amount of the tax, by a lesser amount, or not at all. If the price paid by buyers rises by the full amount of the tax, then the burden of the tax falls entirely on buyers – buyers pay the tax. If the price paid by buyers rises by a lesser amount than the tax, then the burden of the tax falls partly on buyers and partly on sellers. And if the price paid by buyers doesn't change at all, then the burden of the tax falls entirely on sellers.

Tax incidence does not depend on the tax law. The law might impose a tax on sellers or on buyers, but the outcome is the same in either case. To see why, let's look at the tax on cigarettes.

A Tax on Sellers

The government of France increased the tax on the sale of cigarettes three times during 2003. We'll assume the tax was €1.50 a pack. To work out the effects of this tax on the sellers of cigarettes, we begin by examining the effects on demand and supply in the market for cigarettes.

---

[1] These propositions also apply to services and factors of production (land, labour and capital).

In Figure 6.5, the demand curve is *D*, and the supply curve is *S*. With no tax, the equilibrium price is €3 per pack and 350 million packs a year are bought and sold.

A tax on sellers is like an increase in cost, so it decreases supply. To determine the position of the new supply curve, we add the tax to the minimum price that sellers are willing to accept for each quantity sold. You can see that without the tax, sellers are willing to offer 350 million packs a year for €3 a pack. So with a €1.50 tax, they will offer 350 million packs a year only if the price is €4.50 a pack. The supply curve shifts to the red curve labelled *S + tax on sellers*.

Equilibrium occurs where the new supply curve intersects the demand curve at 325 million packs a year. The price paid by buyers rises by €1 to €4 a pack. The price received by sellers falls by 50 cents to €2.50 a pack. So buyers pay €1 of the tax and sellers pay the other 50 cents.

A Tax on Buyers

Suppose that instead of taxing sellers, the French government taxes cigarette buyers €1.50 a pack.

A tax on buyers lowers the amount they are willing to pay sellers, so it decreases demand and shifts the demand curve leftward. To determine the position of this new demand curve, we subtract the tax from the maximum price that buyers are willing to pay for each quantity bought.

You can see in Figure 6.6 that with no tax, buyers are willing to buy 350 million packs a year for €3 a pack. So with a €1.50 tax, they will buy 350 packs a year only if the price including the tax is €3 a pack, which means that they're willing to pay sellers only €1.50 a pack. The demand curve shifts to become the red curve labelled *D – tax on buyers*.

Equilibrium occurs where the new demand curve intersects the supply curve at a quantity of 325 million packs a year. The price received by sellers is €2.50 a pack, and the price paid by buyers is €4.

Equivalence of Tax on Buyers and Sellers

You can see that the tax on buyers in Figure 6.6 has the same effects as the tax on sellers in Figure 6.5. The quantity decreases to 325 million packs a year, the price paid by buyers rises to €4 a pack, and the price received by sellers falls to €2.50 a pack. Buyers pay €1 of the €1.50 tax. Sellers pay the other 50 cents of the tax.

Figure 6.5 A Tax on Sellers

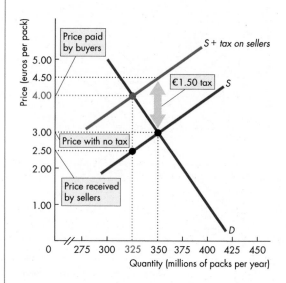

With no tax, 350 million packs a year are bought and sold at €3 a pack. A tax on sellers of €1.50 a pack decreases the supply of cigarettes and shifts the supply curve leftward to *S + tax on sellers*. The equilibrium quantity decreases to 325 million packs a year, the price paid by buyers rises to €4 a pack, and the price received by sellers falls to €2.50 a pack. The tax raises the price paid by buyers by less than the tax and lowers the price received by sellers, so buyers and sellers share the burden of the tax.

MyEconLab Animation ━━━━━━━━━━━━━━◆

Can We Share the Burden Equally?

Suppose that the government wants the burden of the cigarette tax to fall equally on buyers and sellers and declares that a 75 cents tax be imposed on each. Is the burden of the tax then shared equally?

You can see that it is not. The tax is still €1.50 a pack. You've seen that the tax has the same effect regardless of whether it is imposed on sellers on buyers. So imposing half the tax on one and half on the other is like an average of the two cases you've examined. In this case, the demand curve shifts downward by 75 cents and the supply curve shifts upward by 75 cents. The equilibrium quantity is still 325 million packs. Buyers pay €4 a pack, of which €1 is tax. Sellers receive €2.50 a pack (€3 from buyers minus the 50 cents tax).

When a transaction is taxed, there are two prices: the price paid by buyers, which includes the tax; and the price received by sellers, which excludes the tax. Buyers respond only to the price that includes the tax because

Figure 6.6 A Tax on Buyers

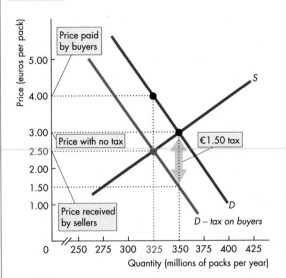

With no tax, 350 million packs a year are bought and sold at €3 a pack. A tax on buyers of €1.50 a pack decreases the demand for cigarettes and shifts the demand curve leftward to *D – tax on buyers*. The equilibrium quantity decreases to 325 million packs a year. The price paid by buyers rises to €4 a pack and the price received by sellers falls to €2.50 a pack. The tax raises the price paid by buyers by less than the tax and lowers the price received by sellers, so buyers and sellers share the burden of the tax.

MyEconLab Animation ——————————◆

that is the price they pay. Sellers respond only to the price that excludes the tax because that is the price they receive.

A tax is like a wedge between the price buyers pay and the price sellers receive. The size of the wedge determines the effects of the tax, not the side of the market – demand side or supply side – on which the government imposes the tax.

Payroll Taxes

Some governments impose payroll taxes and share the tax equally between employers (buyers) and workers (sellers). But the principles you've just learned apply to this tax too. The market for labour, not the government, determines how the burden of the tax is divided between firms and workers.

In the cigarette tax example, buyers pay twice as much of the tax as sellers pay. In general, the division of the tax between buyers and sellers depends on the elasticities of demand and supply, as you will now see.

Tax Incidence and Elasticity of Demand

The division of the tax between buyers and sellers depends partly on the elasticity of demand. There are two extreme cases:

◆ Perfectly inelastic demand – buyers pay
◆ Perfectly elastic demand – sellers pay

Perfectly Inelastic Demand

Figure 6.7 shows the UK market for insulin. Demand is perfectly inelastic at 100,000 bottles a day, regardless of the price, as shown by the vertical curve *D*. That is, a diabetic would sacrifice all other goods and services rather than not consume the quantity of insulin that provides good health. The supply curve of insulin is *S*. With no tax, the price is £2 a bottle and the quantity is 100,000 bottles a day.

If insulin is taxed at 20 pence a bottle, we must add the tax to the minimum price at which drug companies are willing to sell insulin. The result is the new supply curve *S + tax*. The price rises to £2.20 a bottle, but the quantity does not change. Buyers pay the entire tax of 20 pence a bottle.

Figure 6.7 Tax with Perfectly Inelastic Demand

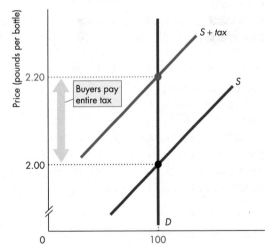

In the market for insulin, demand is perfectly inelastic. With no tax, the price is £2 a bottle and the quantity is 100,000 bottles a day. A tax of 20 pence a bottle decreases supply and shifts the supply curve to *S + tax*. The price rises to £2.20 a bottle, but the quantity bought does not change. Buyers pay the entire tax.

MyEconLab Animation ——————————◆

Perfectly Elastic Demand

Figure 6.8 shows the UK market for pink marker pens. Demand is perfectly elastic at £1 a pen, as shown by the horizontal curve *D*. If pink markers are less expensive than the other pens, everyone uses pink. If pink pens are more expensive than the others, no one uses pink. The supply curve is *S*. With no tax, the price of a pink marker pen is £1 and the quantity is 4,000 a week.

Suppose that the government imposes a tax of 20 pence on pink marker pens but not on other colours. The new supply curve is *S + tax*. The price remains at £1 a pen and the quantity decreases to 1,000 a week. The tax leaves the price paid by buyers unchanged but lowers the amount received by sellers by the full amount of the tax. Sellers pay the entire tax of 20 pence a pink pen.

We've seen that when demand is perfectly inelastic, buyers pay the entire tax and, when demand is perfectly elastic, sellers pay the entire tax. In the usual case, demand is neither perfectly inelastic nor perfectly elastic and the tax is split between buyers and sellers. But the division depends on the elasticity of demand: the more inelastic the demand for a good, the larger is the amount of the tax paid by buyers.

Figure 6.8   Tax with Perfectly Elastic Demand

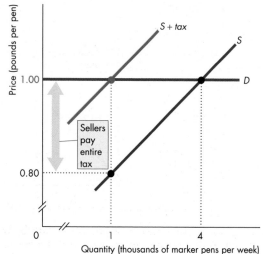

In this market for pink marker pens, demand is perfectly elastic. With no tax, the price of a pen is £1 and the quantity is 4,000 pens a week. A tax of 20 pence a pink pen decreases supply and shifts the supply curve to *S + tax*. The price remains at £1 a pen, and the quantity of pink pens sold decreases to 1,000 a week. Sellers pay the entire tax.

MyEconLab Animation ⎯⎯⎯⎯⎯⎯⎯⎯⎯⎯➤

Tax Incidence and Elasticity of Supply

The division of the tax between buyers and sellers depends, in part, on the elasticity of supply. There are two extreme cases:

◆ Perfectly inelastic supply – sellers pay
◆ Perfectly elastic supply – buyers pay

Perfectly Inelastic Supply

Figure 6.9(a) shows the UK market for water from a spring which flows at a constant rate that can't be controlled. The quantity supplied is 100,000 bottles a week, as shown by the supply curve *S*. The demand curve for the water from this spring is *D*. With no tax, the price is 50 pence a bottle and the quantity is 100,000 bottles.

Suppose this spring water is taxed at 5 pence a bottle. The supply curve does not change because the spring owners still produce 100,000 bottles a week even though the price has fallen. But buyers are willing to buy the 100,000 bottles only if the price is 50 pence a bottle. So the price remains at 50 pence a bottle. The tax reduces the price received by sellers to 45 pence a bottle and sellers pay the entire tax.

Perfectly Elastic Supply

Figure 6.9(b) illustrates the UK market for sand from which computer-chip makers extract silicon. The supply of sand is perfectly elastic at 10 pence a kilogram. The supply curve is *S*. The demand curve is *D*. With no tax, the price is 10 pence a kilogram and 5,000 kilograms a week are bought.

If sand is taxed at 1 penny a kilogram, we add the tax to the minimum supply-price. Sellers are now willing to offer any quantity at 11 pence a kilogram along the curve *S + tax*. The price rises to 11 pence a kilogram and 3,000 kilograms a week are bought. The price paid by buyers increases by the full amount of the tax. Buyers pay the entire tax.

We've seen that when supply is perfectly inelastic, sellers pay the entire tax, and when supply is perfectly elastic, buyers pay the entire tax. In the usual case, supply is neither perfectly inelastic nor perfectly elastic and the tax is split between sellers and buyers. But how the tax is split depends on the elasticity of supply. The more elastic the supply, the larger is the amount of the tax paid by buyers.

Figure 6.9 Tax and the Elasticity of Supply

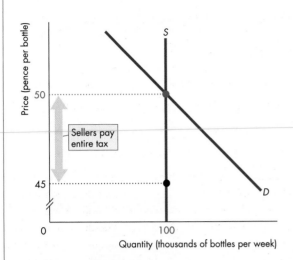

(a) Inelastic supply

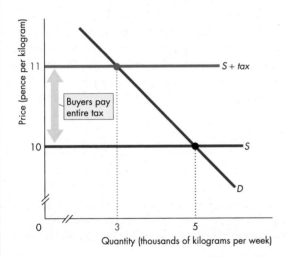

(b) Elastic supply

Part (a) shows the market for water from a mineral spring. Supply is perfectly inelastic. With no tax, the price is 50 pence a bottle. With a tax of 5 pence a bottle, the price remains at 50 pence a bottle. The number of bottles bought remains the same, but the price received by sellers decreases to 45 pence a bottle. Sellers pay the entire tax.

Part (b) shows the market for sand. Supply is perfectly elastic. With no tax, the price of sand is 10 pence a kilogram. A tax of 1 penny a kilogram increases the minimum supply-price to 11 pence a kilogram. The supply curve shifts to *S + tax*. The price increases to 11 pence a kilogram. Buyers pay the entire tax.

Taxes and Efficiency

A tax drives a wedge between the price buyers pay and the price sellers receive and results in inefficient under-production. The price buyers pay is also the buyers' willingness to pay or *marginal social benefit*. The price sellers receive is also the sellers' minimum supply price, which equals *marginal social cost*.

Figure 6.10 shows the inefficiency of a tax on MP3 players. The demand curve, *D*, shows marginal social benefit, and the supply curve, *S*, shows marginal social cost. With no tax on MP3 players, the market produces the efficient quantity (5,000 MP3 players a week).

With a tax, the sellers' minimum supply-price rises by the amount of the tax, and the supply curve shifts to *S + tax*. This supply curve does not show marginal social cost. The tax component isn't a social cost of production. It is a transfer of resources to the government.

At the new equilibrium quantity (4,000 MP3s a week), both consumer surplus and producer surplus

Figure 6.10 Taxes and Efficiency

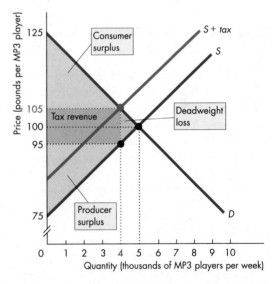

With no tax on MP3 players, 5,000 MP3 players are produced. With a tax on MP3 players of £10 a player, the buyers' price rises to £105 a player, the sellers' price falls to £95 a player, and the quantity decreases to 4,000 MP3 players a week. Consumer surplus shrinks to the green area, and the producer surplus shrinks to the blue area. Part of the loss of consumer surplus and producer surplus goes to the government as tax revenue (the purple area) and part becomes a deadweight loss (the grey area).

shrink. Part of each surplus goes to the government in tax revenue – the purple area; part becomes a dead-weight loss – the grey area.

Only in the extreme cases of perfectly inelastic demand and perfectly inelastic supply does a tax not change the quantity bought and sold so that no dead-weight loss arises.

Taxes and Fairness

We've examined the incidence and the efficiency of taxes, but when political leaders debate tax issues, it is fairness, not incidence and efficiency, that gets the most attention. Some politicians complain that tax cuts are unfair because they give the benefits of lower taxes to the rich. Others say it is fair that the rich get most of the tax cuts because they pay most of the taxes. No easy answers are available to questions about the fairness of taxes.

Economists have proposed two conflicting principles of fairness to apply to a tax system:

◆   The benefits principle

◆   The ability-to-pay principle

The Benefits Principle

The *benefits principle* is the proposition that people should pay taxes equal to the benefits they receive from the services provided by government. This arrangement is fair because it means that those who benefit most pay most taxes. It makes tax payments and the consumption of government-provided services similar to private con-sumption expenditures.

The benefits principle can justify high petrol taxes to pay for motorways, high taxes on alcoholic beverages and tobacco products to pay for public healthcare ser-vices, and high income tax rates on high incomes to pay for the benefits from law and order and living in a secure environment, from which the rich might benefit more than the poor.

The Ability-to-Pay Principle

The *ability-to-pay principle* is the proposition that people should pay taxes according to how easily they can bear the burden of the tax. A rich person can more easily bear the burden than a poor person can, so the ability-to-pay principle can reinforce the benefits principle to jus-tify high rates of income tax on high incomes.

 ECONOMICS IN ACTION

Workers and Consumers Pay Most Tax

A low elasticity of supply of labour and a high elasticity of demand for labour mean that workers pay most of the income taxes and most of the National Insurance taxes. Because the elasticities of demand for alcohol, tobacco and petrol are low and the elasticities of supply are high, the burden of these (excise) taxes falls more on buyers than on sellers.

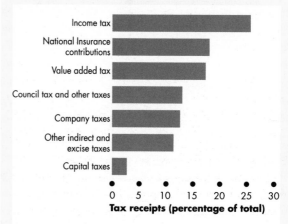

Figure 1   UK Taxes

Source of data: James Browne and Barra Roantree, *A survey of the UK tax system*, IFS Briefing Note BN09, Economic and Social Research Council, 2012

◆ REVIEW QUIZ

1   How does the elasticity of demand influence the incidence of a tax, the tax revenue and the deadweight loss?
2   How does the elasticity of supply influence the incidence of a tax, the tax revenue and the deadweight loss?
3   Why is a tax inefficient?
4   When would a tax be efficient?
5   What are the two principles of fairness that are applied to a tax system?

Do these questions in Study Plan 6.3 and get instant feedback.   MyEconLab

Next, we look at agricultural markets and see how gov-ernments intervene in these markets to try to stabilise and boost farm revenues.

Production Quotas and Subsidies and Price Supports

Fluctuations in the weather bring fluctuations in farm output and prices and sometimes leave farmers with low incomes. To help farmers avoid low prices and low incomes, governments intervene in the markets for farm products. The three main methods of intervention in the markets for farm products are:

◆ Production quotas
◆ Production subsidies
◆ Price supports

Production Quotas

The markets for sugar beet, milk and cotton (among others) have, from time to time, been regulated with production quotas. A **production quota** is an upper limit to the quantity of a good that may be produced in a specified period. To discover the effects of a production quota, we'll look at the market for sugar beet.

Suppose that the sugar beet growers want to limit total production to get a higher price. They persuade the government to introduce a production quota on sugar beet.

The effect of a production quota depends on whether it is set below or above the equilibrium quantity. If the government introduced a production quota above the equilibrium quantity, nothing would change because sugar beet growers are already producing less than the quota. But a production quota *below the equilibrium quantity* has big effects, which are:

◆ A decrease in supply
◆ A rise in the price
◆ A decrease in marginal cost
◆ Inefficient underproduction
◆ An incentive to cheat and overproduce

Figure 6.11 illustrates these effects.

A Decrease in Supply

A production quota on sugar beet decreases the supply of sugar beet. Each grower is assigned a production limit that is less than the amount that would be produced – and supplied – without the quota. The total of the growers' limits equals the quota, and any production in excess of the quota is illegal.

The quantity supplied becomes the amount permitted by the production quota, and this quantity is fixed. The

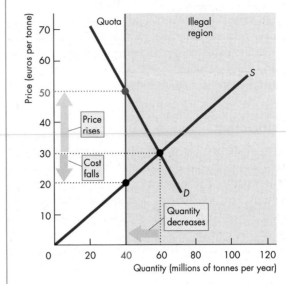

Figure 6.11 The Effects of a Production Quota

With no quota, 60 million tonnes a year are produced at €30 a tonne. A quota of 40 million tonnes a year restricts total production to that amount. The equilibrium quantity decreases to 40 million tonnes a year, the price rises to €50 a tonne, and the farmers' marginal cost falls to €20 a tonne. In the new equilibrium, marginal social cost (on the supply curve) is less than marginal social benefit (on the demand curve) and a deadweight loss arises from underproduction.

MyEconLab Animation ──────────────◆

supply of sugar beet becomes perfectly inelastic at the quantity permitted under the quota.

In Figure 6.11, with no quota, growers would produce 60 million tonnes of sugar beet a year – the market equilibrium quantity. With a production quota set at 40 million tonnes a year, the grey shaded area shows the illegal region. As in the case of price ceilings and price floors, market forces and political forces are in conflict in this illegal region. The vertical red line labelled 'Quota' becomes the supply curve of sugar beet at prices above €20 a tonne.

A Rise in Price

The production quota raises the price of sugar beet. When the government sets a production quota, it leaves market forces free to determine the price. Because the quota decreases the supply of sugar beet, it raises the price. In Figure 6.11, with no quota, the price is €30 a tonne. With a quota of 40 million tonnes, the price rises to €50 a tonne.

A Decrease in Marginal Cost

The production quota lowers the marginal cost of growing sugar beet. Marginal cost decreases because growers produce less and stop using the resources with the highest marginal cost. Sugar beet growers slide down their supply (and marginal cost) curves. In Figure 6.11, marginal cost decreases to €20 a tonne.

Inefficiency

The production quota results in inefficient underproduction. Marginal social benefit at the quantity produced is equal to the market price, which has increased. Marginal social cost at the quantity produced has decreased and is less than the market price. So marginal social benefit exceeds marginal social cost and a deadweight loss arises.

An Incentive to Cheat and Overproduce

The production quota creates an incentive for growers to cheat and produce more than their individual production limit. With the quota, the price exceeds marginal cost, so the grower can get a larger profit by producing one more unit. But if all growers produce more than their assigned limit, the production quota becomes ineffective, and the price falls to the equilibrium (no quota) price.

To make the production quota effective, growers must set up a monitoring system to ensure that no one cheats and overproduces. But it is costly to set up and operate a monitoring system and it is difficult to detect and punish producers who violate their quotas. Because of the difficulty of operating a quota, producers often lobby governments to establish a quota and provide the monitoring and punishment systems that make it work.

Production Subsidies

A **production subsidy** is a payment made by the government to a producer for each unit produced. The effects of a production subsidy are opposite to the effects of a tax and they are:

◆ An increase in supply
◆ A fall in the price and an increase in quantity
◆ An increase in marginal cost
◆ Payments by government to farmers
◆ Inefficient overproduction

An Increase in Supply

In Figure 6.12, with no subsidy, the price of sugar beet is €40 a tonne and the quantity is 40 million tonnes a year. Suppose that the government introduces a subsidy to sugar beet farmers of €20 a tonne . A subsidy is like a negative tax or a decrease in cost, so the subsidy brings an increase in supply. To determine the new supply curve, we subtract the subsidy from the farmers' minimum supply-price. With no subsidy, farmers are willing to offer 40 million tonnes a year at a price of €40 a tonne. With a production subsidy of €20 a tonne, farmers will offer 40 million tonnes a year at €20 a tonne. The new supply curve is labelled *S – subsidy*.

A Fall in Price and an Increase in Quantity

The subsidy lowers the price of sugar beet and increases the quantity produced. In Figure 6.12, equilibrium occurs where the new supply curve intersects the demand curve at a price of €30 a tonne and a quantity of 60 million tonnes a year.

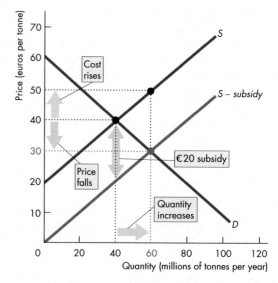

Figure 6.12 The Effects of a Production Subsidy

With no subsidy, 40 million tonnes a year are produced at €40 a tonne. With a subsidy of €20 a tonne, the new supply curve is *S – subsidy*. The equilibrium quantity increases to 60 million tonnes a year, the price falls to €30 a tonne, and the price plus subsidy received by farmers rises to €50 a tonne. In the new equilibrium, marginal social cost (on the blue supply curve) exceeds marginal social benefit (on the demand curve) and a deadweight loss arises from overproduction.

MyEconLab Animation ─────────────────◆

An Increase in Marginal Cost

The subsidy lowers the price paid by consumers but increases the marginal cost of producing sugar beet. Marginal cost increases because to grow more sugar beet farmers use some resources that are less ideal for growing sugar beet. Farmers slide up their supply curve *S*. In Figure 6.12, marginal cost increases to €50 a tonne.

Payments by Government to Farmers

The government pays a subsidy to sugar beet farmers on each tonne produced. In this example, farmers increase production to 60 million tonnes a year and receive a subsidy of €20 a tonne. So sugar beet farmers receive a subsidy payment from the government that totals €1,200 million a year.

Inefficient Overproduction

The production subsidy results in inefficient overproduction. At the quantity produced with the subsidy, marginal social benefit is equal to the market price, which has fallen. Marginal social cost has increased and it exceeds the market price. Because marginal social cost exceeds marginal social benefit, the increased production brings inefficiency.

Subsidies spill over to the rest of the world. Because a subsidy lowers the domestic market price, subsidised farmers will offer some of their output for sale on the world market. The increase in supply on the world market lowers the price in the rest of the world. Faced with lower prices, farmers in other countries decrease production and receive smaller revenues.

Price Supports

A **price support** is a government-guaranteed minimum price for a good. The EU Common Agricultural Policy (CAP) is the world's most extensive farm support programme. Every year, the EU sets the target price *above the equilibrium price* for many agricultural products. The main effects of a price support are:

◆ A rise in the price
◆ An increase in marginal cost
◆ Payments by government to farmers
◆ Inefficient overproduction

Figure 6.13 illustrates the effects of a price support in the market for wheat.

A Rise in the Price

Without price support, the competitive equilibrium price of wheat is €130 a tonne and 4 million tonnes are produced. If the EU sets a target price of €135 a tonne, the market price increases to €135 a tonne and the quantity demanded decreases to 2 million tonnes.

An Increase in Marginal Cost

A higher price encourages farmers to increase the quantity supplied to 6 million tonnes. But as they grow more wheat, they use more resources that are less suited to growing wheat. The marginal cost of production increases.

Payments by Government to Farmers

At the guaranteed price there is a surplus of 4 million tonnes, which the EU must buy to avoid the price falling below the target price. In Figure 6.13, this payment to farmers is €540 million a year.

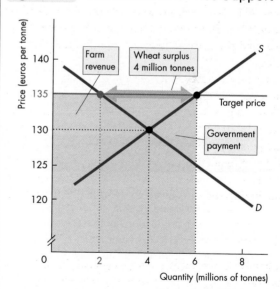

Figure 6.13   The Effects of a Price Support

With no price support, 4 million tonnes are produced at €130 a tonne. A price support of €135 a tonne raises the price to €135 a tonne, increases the quantity produced to 6 million tonnes, decreases the quantity sold to 2 million tonnes, and creates a surplus of 4 million tonnes. To maintain the price support, the government buys the surplus for €540 million a year. If the government does not buy the surplus, the price will return to €130 a tonne.

MyEconLab Animation ──────────◆

Inefficient Overproduction

The EU price support system is inefficient because marginal social cost exceeds marginal social benefit. The overproduction or surpluses must be bought and stored at high cost to maintain the target price.

In 2009, the EU spent €55 billion under the CAP to buy and store surplus agricultural produce and more than €120 billion in support payments to farmers.

ECONOMICS IN ACTION

Rich High-Cost Farmers the Winners

OECD countries spend €182 billion on subsidies to farmers, which is a major obstacle to achieving an efficient use of resources in the global markets. The EU and the US pay their farmers the biggest subsidies, which create inefficient overproduction of food in these rich economies.

At the same time, EU and US subsidies make it more difficult for farmers in the developing nations to compete in global food markets. Farmers, in developing countries can often produce at a lower opportunity cost than the EU and US farmers.

Two rich countries, Australia and New Zealand, have stopped subsidising farmers, with the result that efficiency of farming has improved. The EU plans to cut its expenditure on farm subsidies over the next five years.

International opposition to EU and US farm subsidies is strong, but so is the domestic pro-farm lobby, so don't expect an early end to these subsidies.

REVIEW QUIZ

1 Summarise the effects of a production quota on the market price and quantity produced.
2 Explain why a production quota is inefficient.
3 Summarise the effects of a production subsidy on the market price and the quantity produced.
4 Explain why a production subsidy is inefficient.
5 Summarise the effects of a price support on the market price and the quantity produced.
6 Explain why a price support is inefficient.

Do these questions in Study Plan 6.4 and get instant feedback.   MyEconLab

Governments intervene in some markets by making it illegal to trade in a good. Let's see how these markets work.

Markets for Illegal Goods

Figure 6.14 shows a market for a drug. With demand curve D and supply curve S, if drugs are not illegal, the quantity bought and sold is Q_C and the price is P_C.

When a good is illegal, the cost of trading in it increases. By how much the cost increases and on whom the cost falls depend on the penalties for breaking the law and the effectiveness with which the law is enforced. The larger the penalties and the more effective the policing, the higher are the costs of trading the drug. Penalties might be imposed on sellers or buyers, or on both sellers and buyers.

If selling drugs is illegal, sellers will face fines and prison sentences if their activities are detected. Penalties for selling illegal drugs are part of the cost of supplying those drugs. These penalties lead to a decrease in supply and shift the supply curve of the drug leftward. To determine the new supply curve, we add the cost of breaking the law to the minimum price that drug dealers are willing to accept. In Figure 6.14, the cost of breaking the law by selling drugs (CBL) is added to the minimum price that dealers will accept and the supply curve shifts leftward to $S + CBL$. If penalties are imposed only on sellers, the market moves from point E to point F. The price rises and the quantity bought decreases.

If buying drugs is illegal, buyers face fines and prison sentences if their activities are detected. Penalties for buying the illegal drugs fall on buyers, and the cost of breaking the law must be subtracted from the value of the good to determine the maximum price that buyers are willing to pay. Demand decreases and the demand curve shifts leftward. In Figure 6.14, the demand curve shifts to $D - CBL$. If penalties are imposed only on buyers, the market moves from point E to point G. The market price falls and the quantity bought decreases.

If penalties are imposed on sellers *and* buyers, both supply and demand decrease. In Figure 6.14, the costs of breaking the law are the same for both buyers and sellers, so the demand and supply curves shift leftward by the same amounts. The market moves to point H. The market price remains at the competitive market price, but the quantity bought decreases to Q_P. Buyers pay P_C plus the cost of breaking the law, which is P_B. And sellers receive P_C minus the cost of breaking the law, which is P_S.

The larger the penalty and the greater the degree of law enforcement, the larger is the decrease in demand and/or supply and the greater is the shift of the demand and/or supply curve. If the penalties are heavier on

Figure 6.14   A Market for an Illegal Good

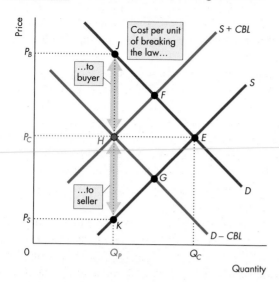

The demand curve for drugs is D and the supply curve is S. If drugs are not illegal, the quantity bought and sold is Q_C at a price of P_C at point E.

If selling drugs is illegal, the cost of breaking the law by selling drugs (*CBL*) is added to the minimum supply-price and supply decreases to $S + CBL$. The market moves to point F. If buying drugs is illegal, the cost of breaking the law is subtracted from the maximum price that buyers are willing to pay and demand decreases to $D - CBL$. The market moves to point G.

With both buying and selling illegal, the supply curve and the demand curve shift and the market moves to point H. The market price remains at P_C, but the market price plus the penalty for buying rises to P_B (point J) and the market price minus the penalty for sellers falls to P_S (point K).

MyEconLab Animation ━━━━━━━━━━━━━◆

sellers, the supply curve shifts further than the demand curve and the market price rises above P_C. If the penalties are heavier on buyers, the demand curve shifts further than the supply curve and the price falls below P_C. In many European countries, the penalties on sellers of illegal drugs are larger than those on buyers. As a result, the decrease in supply is much larger than the decrease in demand. The quantity of drugs traded decreases and the price is higher than in a free market.

With high enough penalties and effective law enforcement, it is possible to reduce the quantity bought to zero. But in reality such an outcome is unusual as law enforcement is too costly.

Because of this situation, some people suggest that drugs and other illegal goods should be legalised and sold openly, but that they should also be taxed at a high rate in the same way that legal drugs such as alcohol are taxed. How would such an arrangement work?

From your study of the effects of taxes, you can see that the quantity of drugs bought would decrease if they were taxed. A sufficiently high tax could be imposed to decrease supply, raise the price and achieve the same decrease in the quantity bought as with a prohibition on drugs. The government would collect tax revenue. Such a debate in the UK concerning cannabis led the government to reduce penalties on the illegal trade in 2003 but not to legalise the trade.

It is likely that a very high tax rate would be needed to cut the quantity of drugs bought to the level prevailing with a prohibition. It is also likely that many drug dealers and consumers would try to cover up their activities to evade the tax. If they did act in this way, they would face the cost of breaking the law – the tax law. If the penalty for tax law violation is as severe and as effectively policed as drug-dealing laws, the analysis we've already conducted applies also to this case. The quantity of drugs bought would depend on the penalties for law breaking and on the way in which the penalties are assigned to buyers and sellers.

Which is more effective: prohibition or taxes? In favour of taxes and against prohibition is the fact that the tax revenue can be used to make law enforcement more effective. It can also be used to run a more effective education campaign against illegal drug use. In favour of prohibition and against taxes is the fact that prohibition sends a signal that might influence preferences, decreasing the demand for illegal drugs. Also, some people intensely dislike the idea of the government profiting from trade in harmful substances.

REVIEW QUIZ

1   How does a penalty on sellers of an illegal good influence demand, supply, price and the quantity consumed?
2   How does a penalty on buyers of an illegal good influence demand, supply, price and the quantity consumed?
3   How does a penalty on both sellers and buyers of an illegal good influence demand, supply, price and the quantity consumed?
4   What is the case for legalising drugs?

Do these questions in Study Plan 6.4 and get instant feedback.   MyEconLab

Reading Between the Lines on pp. 142–143 looks at why farm subsidies decreased in 2010.

Inefficient Farm Subsidies

Farm Subsidies Plunge to a 30-Year Low

Javier Blas

The rise in agricultural commodities prices has led to the lowest support by rich countries to their farmers in nearly three decades, according to new figures released by the Organisation for Economic Cooperation and Development.

The share of farm income derived of subsidies fell in 2010 to 8 per cent in OECD countries, down from 22 per cent in 2009. 'This is the lowest level observed since the mid-1980s and confirms a long-term declining trend,' the OECD said. . . .

But the OECD, which advised rich countries on economic policy and has argued for long that subsidies should be reduced, warned that the drop was due to rising agricultural commodities prices, rather than a re-orientation of agricultural policy. . . .

The Paris-based organisation urged governments to use the current period of high agricultural prices to reform their agricultural policies. 'High prices today . . . undermine the stated rationale for traditional price and output support policies,' it said.

The rise in agricultural commodities prices is due to a combination of factors, including higher consumption in emerging countries [and] the use of crops to produce biofuels . . .

The Essence of the Story

- In 2010, the share of farm revenue derived from subsidies fell to its lowest level since the 1980s.

- The Organisation for Economic Cooperation and Development (OECD) says the lower share from subsidies resulted from a rise in in the prices of farm products, not from lower subsidy rates.

- The OECD says governments in rich countries should cut the subsidy rate and lower subsidies even further.

Economic Analysis

♦ The news article reports that farm subsidy payments fell from 22 per cent of total revenue in 2009 to 18 per cent in 2010.

♦ Subsidy payments as a percentage of total revenue decreased because the prices of farm products increased, not because the subsidy per unit produced decreased.

♦ Figure 1 shows the effect of government production subsidies on wheat in 2009. (The numbers are assumed.) The demand curve is D_{09} and the supply curve is S. With no subsidy, the price would be £200 per tonne and the quantity produced would be 20 million tonnes a year.

♦ With a production subsidy of £50 per tonne, the supply curve is $S - subsidy$. The market price is £175 a tonne, farmers receive £225 per tonne, and the quantity produced is 22 million tonnes a year.

♦ Farm total revenue equals the subsidy payment of £1,100 million (the red area) plus £3,850 revenue from the market (the blue area), which equals £4,950 million. The £1,100 million subsidy payment is 22 per cent of total revenue of £4,950 million.

♦ Figure 2 shows the effect of an increase in demand in 2010, with no change in the subsidy of £50 per tonne. The demand curve shifts rightward to D_{10}. The market price rises to £225 a tonne, farmers receive £275 per tonne, and the quantity produced increases to 26 million tonnes a year.

♦ Farm total revenue equals the subsidy payment of £1,300 million (the red area) plus £5,850 revenue from the market (the total blue area), which equals £7,150 million. The £1,300 million subsidy payment is 18 per cent of total revenue of £7,150 million.

♦ The subsidy payment as a percentage of total revenue decreased because the market price increased while the subsidy per unit produced remained the same.

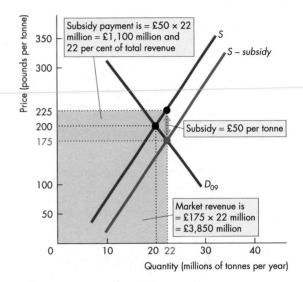

Figure 1 **The Market for Wheat in 2009**

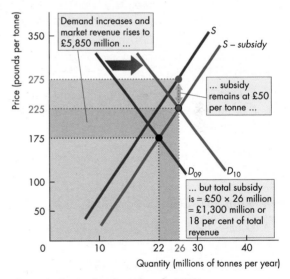

Figure 2 **The Market for Wheat in 2010**

♦ Even though the share of farm income derived from subsidies fell, inefficient overproduction remained.

♦ The OECD says that governments should cut subsidy per unit produced, which would reduce overproduction and make the markets for farm products more efficient.

SUMMARY

Key Points

A Housing Market with a Rent Ceiling (pp. 126–128)

◆ A rent ceiling set above the equilibrium rent has no effect.

◆ If a rent ceiling is set below the equilibrium rent it creates a housing shortage, increases search activity, and creates a black market.

◆ A rent ceiling that is set below the equilibrium rent is inefficient and unfair.

Do Problems 1 to 6 to get a better understanding of a housing market with a rent ceiling.

A Labour Market with a Minimum Wage (pp. 129–131)

◆ A minimum wage set below the equilibrium price has no effect.

◆ A minimum wage set above the equilibrium wage rate creates unemployment and increases search activity.

◆ A minimum wage set above the equilibrium wage rate is inefficient, is unfair, and hits low-skilled young people hardest.

Do Problems 7 to 12 to get a better understanding of a labour market with a minimum wage.

Taxes (pp. 131–136)

◆ A tax raises the price paid by buyers but usually by less than the tax.

◆ The elasticity of demand and the elasticity of supply determine the share of tax paid by buyers and sellers.

◆ The less elastic the demand and the more elastic the supply, the larger is the portion of the tax paid by buyers.

◆ If demand is perfectly elastic or supply is perfectly inelastic, sellers pay the entire tax. And if demand is perfectly inelastic or supply is perfectly elastic, buyers pay the entire tax.

Do Problems 13 to 15 to get a better understanding of taxes.

Production Quotas and Subsidies and Price Supports (pp. 137–140)

◆ A production quota leads to inefficient underproduction, which raises price.

◆ A production subsidy is like a negative tax. It lowers the price and leads to inefficient overproduction.

◆ A price support leads to inefficient overproduction.

◆ The Common Agricultural Policy uses costly price supports.

Do Problems 16 to 18 to get a better understanding of production quotas, subsidies and price supports.

Markets for Illegal Goods (pp. 140–141)

◆ Penalties on sellers increase the cost of selling of an illegal good and decrease its supply.

◆ Penalties on buyers decrease their willingness to pay for an illegal good and decrease the demand for it.

◆ The higher the penalties and the more effective the law enforcement, the smaller is the quantity bought.

◆ Legalising and taxing can achieve the same outcome as penalities on buyers and sellers.

Do Problem 19 to get a better understanding of markets for illegal goods.

Key Terms

Black market, 126
Minimum wage, 129
Price cap, 126
Price ceiling, 126
Price floor, 129
Price support, 139
Production quota, 137
Production subsidy, 138
Rent ceiling, 126
Search activity, 126
Tax incidence, 131

STUDY PLAN PROBLEMS AND APPLICATIONS

Do Problems 1 to 19 in MyEconLab Chapter 6 Study Plan and get instant feedback.

MyEconLab

A Housing Market with a Rent Ceiling (Study Plan 6.1)

Use the following graph of the market for rental housing in Townsville in Problems 1 and 2.

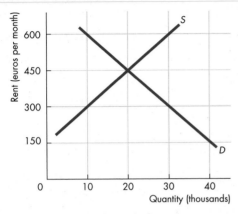

1 a What are the equilibrium rent and equilibrium quantity of rented housing?

b If a rent ceiling is set at €600 a month, what is the quantity of housing rented and what is the shortage of housing?

2 If a rent ceiling is set at €300 a month, calculate the quantity of housing rented, the shortage of housing and the maximum price that someone is willing to pay for the last unit available.

Use the following news clip in Problems 3 to 6.

Capping Petrol Prices

As petrol prices rise, many people are calling for price caps, but price caps generate a distorted reflection of reality, which leads buyers and suppliers to act in ways inconsistent with the price cap. By masking reality, price caps only make matters worse.

Source: *Pittsburgh Tribune-Review*,
12 September 2005

Suppose that a price ceiling is set below the equilibrium price.

3 How does the price cap influence the quantity of petrol supplied and the quantity demanded?

4 How does the price cap influence:

a The quantity of petrol sold and the shortage or surplus of petrol?

b The maximum price that someone is willing to pay for the last litre of petrol available on a black market?

5 Draw a graph to illustrate the effects of a price ceiling set below the equilibrium price in the market for petrol.

6 Explain the various ways in which a price ceiling on petrol that is set below the equilibrium price would make buyers and sellers of petrol better off or worse off. What would happen to total surplus and deadweight loss in this market?

A Labour Market with a Minimum Wage (Study Plan 6.2)

Use the following data in Problems 7 to 9.

The table gives the demand and supply schedules of teenage labour.

Wage rate (pounds per hour)	Quantity demanded	Quantity supplied
	(hours per month)	
4	3,000	1,000
5	2,500	1,500
6	2,000	2,000
7	1,500	2,500
8	1,000	3,000

7 Calculate the equilibrium wage rate, the number of hours worked and the quantity of unemployment.

8 If a minimum wage for teenagers is £5 an hour, how many hours do they work and how many hours of teenage labour are unemployed?

9 If a minimum wage for teenagers is £7 an hour,

a How many hours do teenagers work and how many hours are unemployed?

b Demand for teenage labour increases by 500 hours a month. What is the wage rate paid to teenagers and how many hours of teenage labour are unemployed?

Use the following news clip in Problems 10 to 12.

India Steps Up Pressure for Minimum Wage for Its Workers in the Gulf

Oil-rich countries in the Persian Gulf, already confronted by strong labour protests, are facing renewed pressure from India to pay minimum wages for unskilled workers. With five million immigrant workers in the region, India is trying to win better conditions for its citizens.

Source: *International Herald Tribune*,
27 March 2008

Suppose that the Gulf countries paid a minimum wage above the equilibrium wage to Indian workers.

10 How would the market for labour be affected in the Gulf countries? Draw a supply and demand graph to illustrate your answer.

11 How would the market for labour be affected in India? Draw a supply and demand graph to illustrate your answer. [Be careful: the minimum wage is in the Gulf countries, not in India.]

12 Would migrant Indian workers be better off or worse off or unaffected by this minimum wage?

Taxes (Study Plan 6.3)

13 The table shows the demand and supply schedules for chocolate brownies in the UK.

Price (pence per brownie)	Quantity demanded (millions per day)	Quantity supplied
50	5	3
60	4	4
70	3	5
80	2	6
90	1	7

a If brownies are not taxed, what is the price of a brownie and how many are consumed?

b If sellers are taxed at 20 pence a brownie, what is the price and how many brownies are sold? Who pays the tax?

c If buyers are taxed at 20 pence a brownie, what is the price and how many brownies are bought? Who pays the tax?

14 Will Cuts on China's Luxury Goods Tax Prevent Chinese from Buying Abroad?

Last year Chinese tourists bought almost two thirds of luxury goods sold in Europe. If you look at China's luxury goods tax, it is easy to see why shopping overseas is so popular. According to the Chinese Ministry of Commerce, prices for luxury goods in China are 45% higher than in Hong Kong, 51% higher than the United States and 72% higher than France.

Source: PRLog, 21 March 2012

a Explain why it is 'easy to see why shopping overseas is so popular' with wealthy Chinese shoppers.

b Who pays most of the Chinese luxury tax: sellers or buyers? Explain your answer.

c Explain how a cut in China's luxury tax rate would change the quantity of luxury goods purchased in China.

15 Suppose the tax on petrol is reduced by 18 pence a litre during August. Despite the cut in tax, high petrol prices are predicted to keep UK residents at home this summer.

Would the price of petrol that UK consumers pay fall by 18 pence a litre? How would consumer surplus change? Explain your answers.

Production Quotas and Subsidies and Price Supports (Study Plan 6.4)

Use the following data in Problems 16 to 18.

The demand and supply schedules for rice are:

Price (pounds per box)	Quantity demanded (boxes per week)	Quantity supplied
1.00	3,500	500
1.10	3,250	1,000
1.20	3,000	1,500
1.30	2,750	2,000
1.40	2,500	2,500
1.50	2,250	3,000
1.60	2,000	3,500

16 Calculate the price, the marginal cost of producing rice and the quantity produced if the government sets a production quota of 2,000 boxes a week.

17 Calculate the price, the marginal cost of producing rice and the quantity produced if the government introduces a production subsidy of £0.30 a box.

18 Calculate the price, the marginal cost of producing rice and the quantity produced if the government introduces a price support of £1.50 a box.

Markets for Illegal Goods (Study Plan 6.5)

19 The figure shows the market for a banned substance.

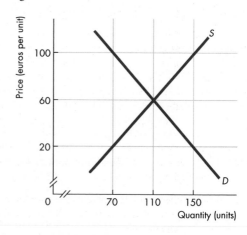

What are the equilibrium price and quantity if a penalty of €20 a unit is imposed on:

a Sellers only?

b Buyers only?

c Both sellers and buyers?

ADDITIONAL PROBLEMS AND APPLICATIONS

Do these problems in MyEconLab if assigned by your lecturer.

MyEconLab

A Housing Market with a Rent Ceiling

Use the following news clip in Problems 20 and 21.

Why Rent Control Won't Go Away

Once in place, rent control usually proves extremely difficult to undo. London and Paris still have rent controls adopted as temporary measures during the First World War. 'Nelson's Third Law' – the contention by the late economist Arthur Nelson that the worse a government regulation is, the more difficult it is to get rid of – seems to apply here.

Source: William Tucker, Heartland Institute, 1 September 1997

20 a Who are the people who gain from rent controls?

b Why are rent controls inefficient?

21 a Are the rent controls in London that remain from the First World War fair?

b Explain 'Nelson's Third Law'. Why does it seem to apply to the rental market in London?

A Labour Market with a Minimum Wage

Use the following news clip in Problems 22 and 23.

Malaysia Passes Its First Minimum Wage Law

About 3.2 million low-income workers across Malaysia are expected to benefit from the country's first minimum wage, which the government says will transform Malaysia into a high-income nation. Employer groups argue that paying the minimum wage, which is not based on productivity or performance, would raise their costs and reduce business profits.

Source: *The New York Times*, 1 May 2012

22 On a graph of the market for low-skilled labour, show the effect of the introduction of a minimum wage on the quantity of labour employed.

23 Explain the effects of the minimum wage on the workers' surplus, the firms' surplus and the efficiency of the market for low-skilled workers.

Taxes

24 Use the news clip in Problem 22. If the Malaysian government cut the tax on business profits, would it offset the effect of the minimum wage on employment? Explain.

25 The demand and supply schedules for roses are:

Price (pounds per bunch)	Quantity demanded	Quantity supplied
		(bunches per week)
10	100	40
12	90	60
14	80	80
16	70	100
18	60	120

a If there is no tax on roses, what is the price and how many bunches of roses are bought?

b If roses are taxed at £6 a bunch, what is the price and quantity bought? Who pays the tax?

26 Cigarette Smuggling Ring Smashed

Customs officers have cracked a multimillion-euro cigarette smuggling operation. About 28 million illegally imported cigarettes – worth 11.8 million euros – were seized. The potential loss to the exchequer is 9.4 million euros.

Source: *Belfast Telegraph*, 23 February 2010

a How has the market for cigarettes in the UK responded to the high tax on cigarettes?

b What effect does the emergence of a black market have on the elasticity of demand in the legal market for cigarettes?

c Why might an increase in the tax rate actually cause a decrease in the tax revenue?

Production Quotas and Subsidies and Price Supports

27 French Farmers Man the Blockades in Brussels

Farmers want the dairy industry to guarantee a minimum milk price of €300 per tonne – against €210 per tonne this month. Max Bottier, a dairy farmer in Normandy said that he needed €300 per tonne to break even.

Source: *The Times*, 26 May 2009

If a support price for milk is introduced and set at €300 per tonne, how will such a support price change the quantity of milk produced and the quantity bought by consumers? Who buys the excess supply? Will the European milk market be more or less efficient than it is today?

Use the following figure in Problems 28 to 30.

The figure shows the market for tomatoes. The government introduces a price support for tomatoes at €8 per pound.

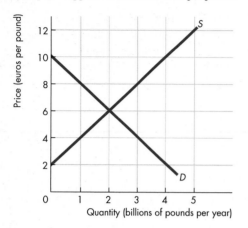

28 Before the price support is introduced, what are the equilibrium price and quantity of tomatoes? Is the market for tomatoes efficient?

29 After the government introduces a price support, what are the quantity of tomatoes produced, the quantity demanded and the payment received by tomato farmers?

30 With the price support, is the market for tomatoes efficient? Who gains and who loses from the price support and is it efficient? Could the price support be regarded as being fair?

Markets for Illegal Goods

31 The table sets out the demand and supply schedules for an illegal drug.

Price (euros per unit)	Quantity demanded	Quantity supplied
	(units per day)	
50	500	300
60	400	400
70	300	500
80	200	600
90	100	700

a If there are no penalties on buying or selling the drug, what is the price and how many units a day are consumed?

b If the penalty on sellers is €20 per unit, what are the price and the quantity consumed?

c If the penalty on buyers is €20 per unit, what are the price and the quantity consumed?

Economics in the News

32 After you have studied *Reading Between the Lines* on pp. 142–143, answer the following questions.

   a With a given production subsidy per unit produced, how would a decrease in demand change the percentage of farm income received from the government?

   b Draw a graph to illustrate the effects of a decrease in demand with the production subsidy.

   c Given that the demand for farm products is inelastic, how would a rise in farm costs with the production subsidy change the percentage of farm income received from the government?

   d Draw a graph to illustrate the effects of a rise in farm costs with a production subsidy.

33 **Hollywood: Organised Crime Hits the Movies**

The Mexican army seized 1,180 disc burners and 3.14 million copies of movies and TV shows from 23 warehouses in a move to fight piracy that costs Hollywood about $590 million a year.

Source: *Businessweek*, 7 April 2011

Assume that the marginal cost of producing a DVD (legal or illegal) is a constant $3, and that legal DVDs bear an additional marginal cost of $5 each in royalty payments to film studios.

   a Draw a graph of the market for counterfeit DVDs, assuming that there are no effective penalties on either buyers or sellers for breaking the law.

   b How do the events reported in the news clip change the market outcome? Show the effects in your graph.

   c With no penalty on buyers, if a penalty for breaking the law is imposed on sellers at more than $5 a disc, how does the market work? What is the market price?

   d With no penalty on sellers, if a penalty for breaking the law is imposed on buyers at more than $5 a disc, how does the market work? What is the market price?

   e What is the marginal benefit of an illegal DVD in the situations described in parts (c) and (d)?

   f Given your answer to part (e), why does law enforcement usually focus on sellers rather than on buyers?

34 **Motorway Protest Over Rising Fuel Prices**

After fuel prices have soared to an all-time high, hundreds of bikers and motorists are expected to stage a go-slow protest along one of the North of England's main motorways. The AA said a two-car family had seen its monthly fuel costs rise from £233.32 to £254.60.

Source: *The Yorkshire Post*, 27 September 2010

Explain to protesting drivers why a cap on the price of fuel would hurt families more than the high price of fuel.

7 Global Markets in Action

After studying this chapter you will be able to:

◆ Explain how markets work with international trade

◆ Explain the gains from international trade, and identify its winners and losers

◆ Explain the effects of international trade barriers

◆ Explain and assess the arguments used to justify international trade barriers

Cargo jets and container ships carry billions of euros worth of cheap fashion goods, iPhones, Wii games and a host of other items around the globe. Why do we go to such lengths to trade with others in far away places?

Globalisation is having a profound effect on our lives. The impact of globalisation is controversial and under debate. Can EU companies compete with Asian companies where wages are much lower? Shouldn't governments restrict international trade and protect local producers?

In *Reading Between the Lines* at the end of the chapter you can apply what you have learned and see why EU car makers want to keep tariffs on South Korean cars and why Korean vintners want to keep tariffs on French wine.

How Global Markets Work

Because we trade with people in other countries, the goods and services that we can buy and consume are not limited by what we can produce. The goods and services that we buy from other countries are our **imports**; and the goods and services that we sell to people in other countries are our **exports**.

International Trade Today

Global trade today is vast. In 2011, global exports and imports were over $22 trillion, which is one third of the value of global production. The US is by far the world's largest international trader, with Germany ranked second and China ranked third.

The EU of 27 member states is the world's main exporting region. EU trade with countries outside the member states is 20 per cent of global trade. EU countries trade both goods and services with the rest of the world. About 70 per cent of UK international trade is trade in goods such as cars and chemicals and 30 per cent is trade in services such as tourism and finance.

Some EU member states, such as Germany, Finland and the Netherlands, export more in value than they import, whereas others, such as the UK, Ireland and Spain, import more than they export.

What Drives International Trade?

Comparative advantage is the fundamental force that drives international trade. Comparative advantage (see Chapter 2, p. 41) is a situation in which a person can perform an activity or produce a good or service at a lower opportunity cost than anyone else. This same idea applies to nations. We can define *national comparative advantage* as a situation in which a nation can perform an activity or produce a good or service at a lower opportunity cost than any other nation.

The opportunity cost of producing a car is lower in Japan than in the UK, so Japan has a comparative advantage in producing cars. The opportunity cost of producing chemicals is lower in the UK than in Japan, so the UK has a comparative advantage in producing chemicals.

You saw in Chapter 2 how Erin and Jack reap gains from trade by specialising in the production of the good at which they have a comparative advantage and then trading with each other. Both are better off.

ECONOMICS IN ACTION

EU Trade Focus

Figure 1 shows the four main areas of EU exports and EU imports. The EU exported goods and services worth €1,531,358 million and imported €1,658,398 million in 2011. Manufactured goods made up 56.2 per cent of imports but 80 per cent of exports. The second main import was fuel. Agricultural goods and others (including services) each are about 7 per cent of imports and exports.

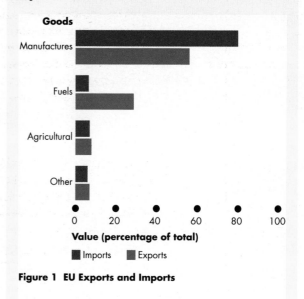

Figure 1 EU Exports and Imports

Source of data: Europa.

This same principle applies to trade among nations. Because Japan has a comparative advantage at producing cars and the UK has a comparative advantage at producing chemicals, the people of both countries can gain from specialisation and trade. Japan can buy chemicals from the UK at a lower opportunity cost than that at which Japanese firms can produce them. People in the UK can buy cars from Japan for a lower opportunity cost than that at which UK firms can produce them. Also, through international trade, Japanese producers can get higher prices for their cars and Blue Circle can sell cement powder for a higher price. Both countries gain from international trade.

Let's now illustrate the gains from trade that we've just described by studying demand and supply in the global markets for cars and chemicals.

Why the UK Imports Cars

The UK imports cars because the rest of the world has a comparative advantage in producing cars. Figure 7.1 illustrates how this comparative advantage generates international trade and how trade influences the price of a car and the quantities produced and bought.

The demand curve D_{UK} and the supply curve S_{UK} show the demand and supply in the UK domestic market with no international trade. The demand curve tells us the quantity of cars that UK consumers are willing to buy at various prices. The supply curve tells us the quantity of cars that UK car makers are willing to sell at various prices – that is, the quantity supplied at each price when all cars sold in the UK are produced in the UK.

Figure 7.1(a) shows what the UK car market would be like with no international trade. The price of a car

would be £20,000 and 1 million cars a year would be produced by UK car makers and bought by UK consumers.

Figure 7.1(b) shows the market for cars with international trade. Now the price of a car is determined in the world market, not the UK domestic market. The world price is less than £20,000 a car, which means that the rest of the world has a comparative advantage in producing cars. The world price line shows the world price at £15,000 a car.

The UK demand curve, D_{UK}, tells us that at £15,000 a car, UK consumers buy 1.4 million cars a year. The UK supply curve, S_{UK}, tells us that at £15,000 a car, UK car makers produce 0.4 million cars a year. To buy 1.4 million cars when only 0.4 million are produced in the UK, we must import cars from the rest of the world. The quantity of cars imported is 1 million a year.

Figure 7.1 A Market with Imports

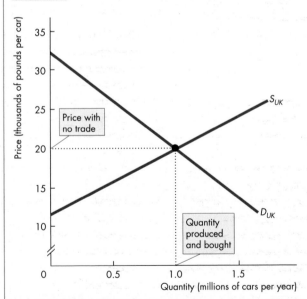

(a) Equilibrium without international trade

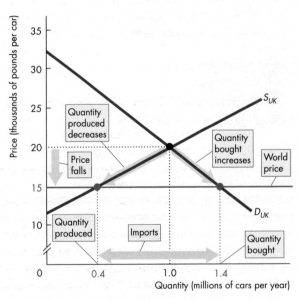

(b) Equilibrium in a market with imports

The supply of cars produced by UK car makers is S_{UK} and the demand for cars by UK consumers is D_{UK}. With no international trade, in part (a), the equilibrium price of a car in the UK is £20,000 and 1 million cars a year are produced and bought.

In part (b), the world price of a car is £15,000 and the rest of the world has a comparative advantage in

producing cars. With international trade, the price of a car in the UK falls to the world price.

The quantity of cars bought in the UK increases to 1.4 million a year and the quantity produced in the UK decreases to 0.4 million a year. The quantity imported equals the quantity bought minus the quantity produced in the UK, which is 1 million cars a year.

Figure 7.2   A Market with Exports

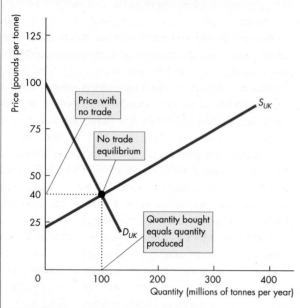

(a) Equilibrium without international trade

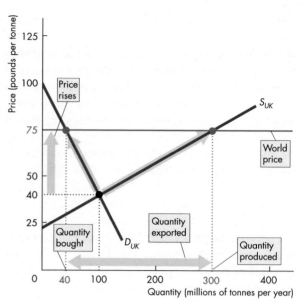

(b) Equilibrium in a market with exports

In part (a), the UK market with no international trade, the UK domestic demand curve D_{UK} and the UK domestic supply curve S_{UK} determine the price at £40 a tonne and 100 million tonnes a year are produced and bought.

In part (b), the UK market with international trade, world demand and world supply determine the world

price, which is £75 a tonne. The price in the UK market rises. UK chemical production increases to 300 million tonnes a year, UK purchases of chemicals decrease to 40 million tonnes a year, and the UK exports 260 million tonnes of chemicals a year.

MyEconLab Animation

Why the UK Exports Chemicals

Figure 7.2 illustrates international trade in chemicals. The demand curve D_{UK} and the supply curve S_{UK} show the demand and supply in the UK domestic market only. The demand curve tells us the quantity of chemicals that UK buyers are willing to buy at various prices. The supply curve tells us the quantity of chemicals that UK chemical makers are willing to sell at various prices.

Figure 7.2(a) shows what the UK chemicals market would be like with no international trade. The price would be £40 per tonne and 100 million tonnes of chemicals a year would be produced by UK makers and bought by UK buyers.

Figure 7.2(b) shows the UK chemicals market with international trade. Now the price of chemicals is determined in the world market and the world price is higher than £40 per tonne, which means that the UK has a comparative advantage in producing chemicals. The world price line shows the world price at £75 a tonne.

The UK demand curve, D_{UK}, tells us that at £75 a tonne 40 million tonnes of chemicals are bought by UK buyers a year. The UK supply curve, S_{UK}, tells us that at £75 a tonne UK chemical makers produce 300 million tonnes a year. The quantity produced in the UK (300 million tonnes a year) minus the quantity purchased by UK buyers (40 million tonnes a year) is the quantity of chemicals exported, which is 260 million tonnes a year.

◆ REVIEW QUIZ

1   Describe the situation in the market for a good or service that the UK imports.
2   Describe the situation in the market for a good or service that the UK exports.

Do these questions in Study Plan 7.1 and get instant feedback.   MyEconLab

Winners, Losers and the Net Gain from Trade

In Chapter 1 (see p. 6), we asked whether globalisation is in the self-interest of low-wage worker in India who sews the sequins on your low-cost top or a displaced clothing worker in London – whether it is in the social interest. We're now going to answer these questions. You will learn why producers complain about cheap foreign imports and why consumers of imported goods and services never complain.

Gains and Losses from Imports

We measure the gains and losses from imports by examining their effect on consumer surplus, producer surplus and total surplus. In the importing country the winners are those whose surplus increases and the losers are those whose surplus decreases.

Figure 7.3(a) shows what consumer surplus and producer surplus would be with no international trade in cars. UK domestic demand, D_{UK}, and UK domestic supply, S_{UK}, determine the price in the UK and the quantity of cars produced in the UK. The green area shows consumer surplus and the blue area shows producer surplus. Total surplus is the sum of consumer surplus and producer surplus.

Figure 7.3(b) shows how consumer surplus, producer surplus and total surplus change when the UK market opens to international trade. The UK price falls to the world price. The quantity bought in the UK increases to the quantity demanded at the world price, and consumer surplus expands from area A to the larger green area $A + B + D$. The quantity produced in the UK decreases to the quantity supplied at the world price, and producer surplus shrinks to the smaller blue area C.

Part of the gain in consumer surplus, the area B, is a loss of producer surplus – a redistribution of total surplus. But the other part of the increase in consumer surplus, the area D, is a net gain from imports. This increase in total surplus results from the lower price of a car and increased purchases of cars and is the gain from international trade in cars.

Figure 7.3 Gains and Losses in a Market with Imports

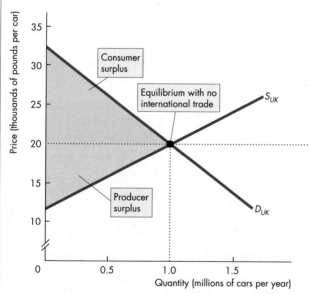

(a) Consumer and producer surplus without international trade

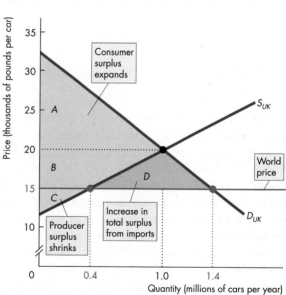

(b) The gains and losses from imports

In part (a), with no international trade, the green area shows the consumer surplus and the blue area shows the producer surplus.

In part (b), with international trade, the price of a car falls to the world price of £15,000. Consumer surplus expands to area $A + B + D$. Producer surplus shrinks to the area C. Area B is a transfer of surplus from producers to consumers. Area D is an increase in total surplus.

MyEconLab Animation ◆

Figure 7.4 Gains and Losses in a Market with Exports

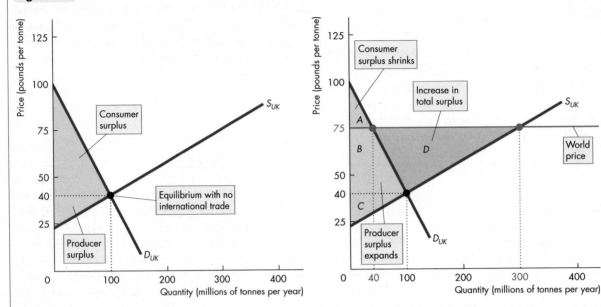

(a) Consumer and producer surplus without international trade

(b) The gains and losses from exports

In part (a), the UK market with no international trade, the green area shows the consumer surplus and the blue area shows the producer surplus. In part (b), the UK market with international trade, the price rises to the world price.

Consumer surplus shrinks to area *A*. Producer surplus expands to area *B* + *C* + *D*. Area *B* is a transfer of surplus from consumers to producers. Area *D* is an increase in total surplus – the gains from exports.

MyEconLab Animation ◆

Gains and Losses from Exports

We measure the gains and losses from exports just like we measured those from imports, by their effect on consumer surplus, producer surplus and total surplus.

Figure 7.4(a) shows the situation with no international trade. The UK demand, D_{UK}, and UK supply, S_{UK}, determine the price and quantity. The green area shows the consumer surplus and the blue area shows the producer surplus. The two surpluses sum to the total surplus.

Figure 7.4(b) shows how the consumer surplus and producer surplus change when the good is exported. The price rises to the world price. The quantity bought decreases to the quantity demanded at the world price and the consumer surplus shrinks to the green area *A*. The quantity produced increases to the quantity supplied at the world price and the producer surplus expands to the blue area *B* + *C* + *D*.

Part of the gain in producer surplus, the area *B*, is a loss in consumer surplus – a redistribution of the total surplus. But the other part of the increase in producer surplus, the area *D*, is a net gain. This increase in total surplus results from the higher price and increased production and is the gain from exports.

Gains for All

You've seen that both imports and exports bring gains. Because one country's exports are other countries' imports, international trade brings gain for all countries. International trade is a win–win game.

REVIEW QUIZ

1 How are the gains from imports distributed between consumers and domestic producers?
2 How are the gains from exports distributed between consumers and domestic producers?
3 Why is the net gain from international trade positive?

Do these questions in Study Plan 7.2 and get instant feedback.

MyEconLab

International Trade Restrictions

Governments use four main tools to restrict international trade and to protect domestic industries from foreign competition. They are:

◆ Tariffs
◆ Import quotas
◆ Export subsidies
◆ Other import barriers

Tariffs

A **tariff** is a tax that is imposed by the importing country when an imported good crosses its international boundary. For example, the EU imposed a new tariff of 20 per cent at its border on imported leather shoes from China in 2006. So when an EU citizen imports a pair of Chinese leather shoes costing €50, the EU administration collects an import duty of €10.

Tariffs raise revenue for governments and serve the self-interest of people who earn their incomes in import-competing industries. But as you will see, restrictions on free international trade decrease the gains from trade and are not in the social interest.

The Effects of a Tariff

To see the effects of a tariff, let's return to the example in which the UK imports cars. With free trade, cars are imported and sold at the world price. Then under pressure from UK car producers, the UK government imposes a tariff on imported cars. Buyers of cars must now pay the world price plus the tariff. Several consequences follow and Figure 7.5 illustrates them.

In Figure 7.5(a) with no international trade, the world price is £15,000 per car, UK car makers produce 0.4 million cars per year and the UK imports 1 million cars a year. Figure 7.5(b) shows what happens with a tariff set at £4,000 per car.

Figure 7.5 The Effects of a Tariff

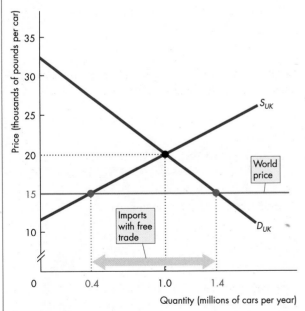

(a) Free trade

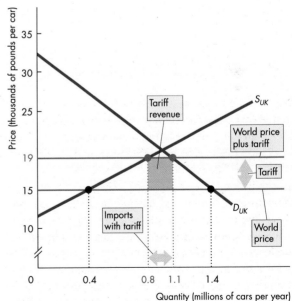

(b) Market with tariff

The world price of a car is £15,000. With free international trade in part (a), 1.4 million cars a year are bought by UK citizens. UK car makers produce 0.4 million cars a year and the UK imports 1 million cars a year.

With a tariff of £4,000 a car in part (b), the price in the UK rises to £19,000 a car. UK production increases, UK purchases decrease and UK imports decrease. The UK government collects a tariff revenue of £4,000 on each car imported (the purple rectangle).

The following changes occur in the UK car market:

♦ The price of a car rises

♦ The quantity of cars bought decreases

♦ The quantity of cars produced increases

♦ The quantity of cars imported decreases

♦ The UK government collects a tariff revenue

The Price of a Car Rises

To buy a car, UK citizens must pay the world price plus the tariff, so the price of a car rises by the £4,000 tariff to £19,000. Figure 7.5(b) shows the new domestic price line, which lies £4,000 above the world price line. The price rises by the full amount of the tariff. The buyer pays the entire tariff because supply from the rest of the world is perfectly elastic (see Chapter 6, pp. 134–135).

The Quantity of Cars Bought Decreases

The higher price of a car brings a decrease in the quantity demanded along the demand curve. Figure 7.5(b) shows the decrease from 1.4 million cars a year at £15,000 a car to 1.1 million a year at £19,000 a car.

The Quantity of Cars Produced Increases

The higher price of a car stimulates domestic production, and UK car makers increase the quantity supplied along the supply curve. Figure 7.5(b) shows the increase from 0.4 million cars at £15,000 a car to 0.8 million a year at £19,000 a car.

The Quantity of Cars Imported Decreases

UK imports of cars decrease by 0.7 million, from 1 million to 0.3 million a year. Both the decrease in UK purchases and the increase in UK production contribute to this decrease in UK imports.

Tariff Revenue

The government's tariff revenue is £1,200 million – £4,000 per car on 0.3 million imported cars – and is shown by the purple rectangle of Figure 7.5(b).

Winners, Losers and the Social Loss from a Tariff

A tariff on an imported good creates winners and losers and a social loss. When the UK government imposes a tariff on an imported good,

♦ UK consumers of the good lose

♦ UK producers of the good gain

♦ UK consumers lose more than UK producers gain

♦ Society loses: a deadweight loss arises

 ECONOMICS IN ACTION

Free Trade and EU Tariffs

The EU Single European Market has created the largest tariff-free area in the world. The EU has also cut other non-tariff barriers to internal trade and created some free trade areas with non-EU countries.

EU buyers of agricultural products face prices that are on the average 40 per cent above world prices. These higher prices result from the Common Agricultural Policy price support programme for farmers (see Chapter 6, p. 139). To keep EU prices higher than world prices, the EU imposes tariffs on non-EU imports of agricultural products. The higher the price support for farm income, the higher are the tariffs on imports.

Figure 1 shows how EU support to farmers has changed their income over the past 30 years. As the level of EU price support has fallen, so too has the average level of tariffs on non-EU imported agricultural products.

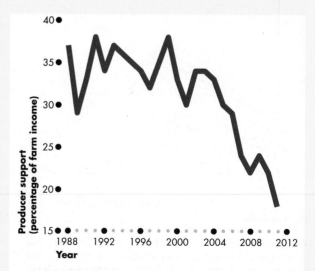

Figure 1 EU Agricultural Support

Source of data: OECD.

UK Consumers of the Good Lose

Because the UK price of a car rises, the quantity of cars demanded decreases. The combination of a higher price and smaller quantity bought decreases consumer surplus – the loss to UK consumers that arises from a tariff.

UK Producers of the Good Gain

Because the price of an imported car rises by the amount of the tariff, UK car makers are now able to sell their cars for the world price plus the tariff. At the higher price, the quantity of cars supplied by UK car makers increases. The combination of a higher price and larger quantity produced increases producer surplus – the gain to UK producers from the tariff.

UK Consumers Lose More than UK Producers Gain

Consumer surplus decreases for four reasons: some becomes producer surplus, some is lost in a higher cost of production (UK production costs are higher than foreign costs), some is lost because imports decrease, and some goes to the UK government as tariff revenue.

Figure 7.6 shows these sources of lost consumer surplus. Part (a) shows the consumer surplus and producer surplus with free international trade in cars. Part (b) shows these surpluses with a £4,000 tariff on imported cars. By comparing the two parts of the figure, you can see how a tariff changes the surpluses.

Consumer surplus – the green area – shrinks for the four reasons just discussed. First, the higher price transfers surplus from consumers to producers. The blue area *B* represents this transfer. Second, UK production costs are higher than foreign production costs. The supply curve S_{UK} shows the higher cost and the grey area *E* shows this loss. Third, some of the consumer surplus is transferred to the government as tariff revenue. The purple area *D* shows this transfer. Fourth, some consumer surplus is lost because imports decrease. The grey area *F* shows this loss.

Society Loses: a Deadweight Loss Arises

Some of the loss of consumer surplus is transferred to producers and some to the government and spent on government programmes that people value. But the increase in production cost and the loss from decreased imports are transferred to no one: they are a social loss – a deadweight loss. The grey areas labelled *E* and *F* represent this deadweight loss. Total surplus decreases by the area $E + F$.

Figure 7.6 The Effects of a Tariff

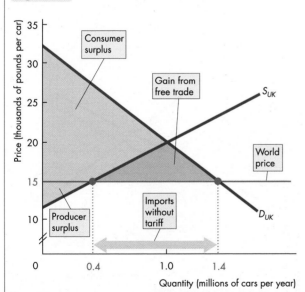

(a) Free trade

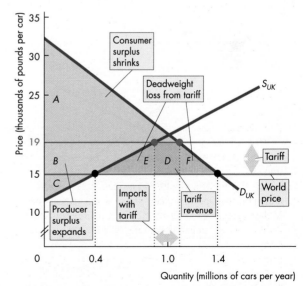

(b) Market with tariff

The world price of a car is £15,000. In part (a), with free trade, the UK imports 1 million cars a year. Consumer surplus, producer surplus and the gains from free trade are as large as possible.

In part (b), a tariff of £4,000 a car raises the UK price to £19,000 per car. The quantity imported decreases. Consumer surplus shrinks by the areas *B, E, D* and *F*. Producer surplus increases by the area *B*. The government's tariff revenue is area *D* and the tariff creates a deadweight loss equal to the area $E + F$.

MyEconLab Animation ──────────────────────────────◆

Import Quotas

We now look at the second tool for restricting international trade: import quotas. An **import quota** is a restriction that limits the maximum quantity of a good that may be imported in a given period.

Many countries impose import quotas on a wide range of goods. The UK imposed them on Japanese cars during the 1990s. The EU had import quotas on textiles and clothing until 2009. The US has import quotas on many manufactured goods including EU steel.

Import quotas enable the government to satisfy the self-interest of the people who earn their incomes in the import-competing industries. But you will discover that, like a tariff, an import quota decreases the gains from trade and is not in the social interest.

The Effects of an Import Quota

The effects of an import quota are similar to those of a tariff. When the UK imposes a quota on imported cars,

the UK price rises, the quantity bought decreases, and the quantity produced in the UK increases. Figure 7.7 illustrates the effects.

Figure 7.7(a) shows the situation with free international trade. Figure 7.7(b) shows what happens with an import quota of 0.3 million cars a year. The UK supply curve of cars becomes the domestic supply curve, S_{UK}, plus the import quota. So the supply curve becomes $S_{UK} + quota$. The price of a car rises to £19,000, the quantity of cars bought in the UK decreases to 1.1 million a year, the quantity of cars produced in the UK increases to 0.8 million a year, and the quantity of cars imported decreases to the quota quantity of 0.3 million a year. All the effects of this quota are identical to those of a £4,000 per car tariff, as you can check in Figure 7.5(b).

Winners, Losers and the Social Loss from an Import Quota

An import quota creates winners and losers that are similar to those of a tariff but with an interesting difference.

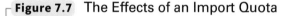

Figure 7.7 The Effects of an Import Quota

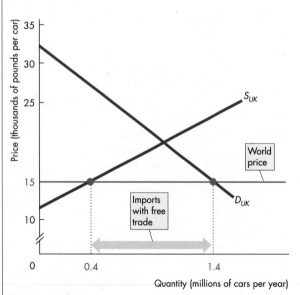

(a) Free trade

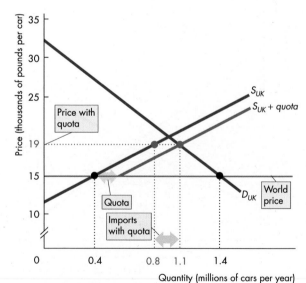

(b) Market with import quota

With free international trade, in part (a), UK citizens buy 1.4 million cars a year at the world price of £15,000 a car. The UK produces 0.4 million cars a year and imports 1 million cars.

With an import quota set at 0.3 million cars a year, in part (b), the supply of cars in the UK is shown by curve $S_{UK} + quota$. The price in the UK rises to £19,000 a car, UK production increases, UK purchases decrease and the quantity of cars imported decreases.

When the UK government imposes an import quota:

◆ UK consumers of the good lose.

◆ UK producers of the good gain.

◆ UK consumers lose more than UK producers gain.

◆ Society loses: a deadweight loss arises.

Figure 7.8 shows the gains and losses from the import quota. By comparing Figure 7.8(b) with a quota and Figure 7.8(a) with free trade, you can see how an import quota of 0.3 million cars a year changes the consumer and producer surpluses.

Consumer surplus – the green area – shrinks. This decrease is the loss to consumers from the import quota. The decrease in consumer surplus is made up of four parts. First, some of the consumer surplus is transferred to producers. The blue area *B* represents this loss of consumer surplus (and gain of producer surplus). Second, part of the consumer surplus is lost because the domes-tic cost of production is higher than the world price. The grey area *C* represents this loss. Third, part of the consumer surplus is transferred to importers who buy cars for £15,000 (the world price) and sell them for £19,000 (the UK domestic price). The two purple areas *D* represent this loss of consumer surplus and profit for importers. Fourth, part of the consumer surplus is lost because the quantity of cars imported decreases. The grey area *E* represents this loss of consumer surplus.

The loss of consumer surplus from the higher cost of production and the decrease in imports is a social loss – a deadweight loss. The grey areas labelled *C* and *E* represent this deadweight loss. Total surplus decreases by the area *C* + *E*.

You can now see the one difference between an import quota and a tariff. A tariff brings in revenue for the government whereas an import quota brings a profit for the importers. All the other effects are the same, provided the import quota is set at the same quantity of imports that results from the tariff.

Figure 7.8 Winners and Loser from an Import Quota

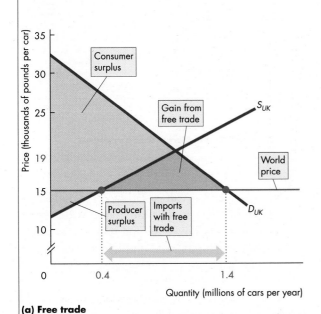

(a) Free trade

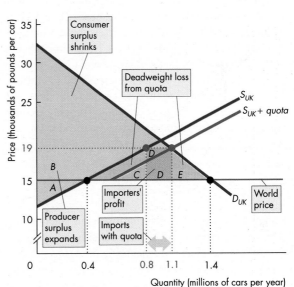

(b) Market with import quota

The world price of a car is £15,000. In part (a), with free trade, the UK produces 0.4 million cars and imports 1 million cars a year. Consumer surplus, producer surplus and the gain from free international trade (darker green area) are as large as possible.

In part (b), consumer surplus shrinks by the areas *B*, *C*, *D* and *E*. Producer surplus expands by area *B*. Importers' profit is the two areas *D*, and the quota creates a deadweight loss equal to area *C* + *E*.

ECONOMICS IN THE NEWS

Trade War in Solar Panels

EU Faces up to China in 'Mother of all Trade Wars'

EU solar panel makers say that Chinese firms receive illegal subsidies and are dumping solar panels in Europe. The EU could retaliate with a tariff.

Source: *The Financial Times*, 31 January 2013

The Question

Why do EU solar panel makers complain? Would Europeans be better off with a tariff on solar panel imports from China? Is a subsidy to China's solar panel makers in China's self-interest?

The Answers

◆ European solar panel makers complain because the low price decreases their producer surplus (see Figure 7.6(a) on p. 157).

◆ Europeans would be worse off with a tariff (see Figure 7.6(b) on p. 157).

◆ A subsidy to China's solar panel makers is not in China's self-interest. Figure 1 illustrates. D_C and S_C are demand and supply in China. P_W is the world price. With no subsidy, China exports 10 million panels a year. A subsidy shifts the supply curve to $S_C - subsidy$ (see pp. 138–139). Exports increase to 14 million, but the additional 4 million cost more to produce than the price for which they are sold. The grey triangle shows the deadweight loss from overproduction.

Chinese workers examine a solar panel before packing it for export to Europe.

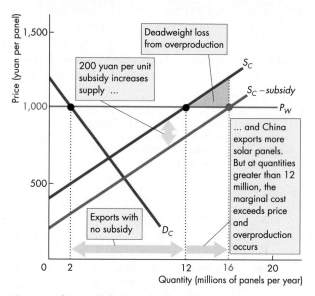

Figure 1 China's Global Market for Solar Panels

Export Subsidies

We now look at the third tool for restricting international trade: export subsidy. An **export subsidy** is a payment made by a government to a domestic producer of an exported good. Examples of subsidies are payments made by the EU to sugar producers. You saw in Chapter 6 (pp. 138–139) that a subsidy shifts the domestic supply curve rightward, lowers the domestic price and increases the quantity bought and produced. But when the item that receives a subsidy is an export or an import, the subsidy also changes the amount of international trade. We can illustrate the effects of agricultural subsidies using the example of the market for sugar and African farmers.

Figure 7.9 shows the African market for sugar. Demand for sugar in Africa is D_A and the supply of

sugar in Africa is S_A. With no EU or US subsidies, the world price of sugar is €4 a kilogram. At this price, African consumers buy 1 million tonnes a year and African farmers produce 14 million tonnes a year. African sugar exports are 13 million tonnes a year.

The subsidies reduce the cost of producing sugar in the EU and the US and increase the supply of sugar. The world supply increases and the world price falls.

In Figure 7.9 the world price falls to €2 a kilogram. The quantity bought by Africans increases to 3 million tonnes a year, but the quantity produced by African farmers decreases to 6 million tonnes a year. Exports fall from 13 million tonnes to 3 million tonnes a year.

A subsidy on an exported good creates winners and losers and a social loss. Figure 7.9 shows the gains and losses from an export subsidy. Consumer surplus in

Figure 7.9   The Effects of EU and US Export Subsidies

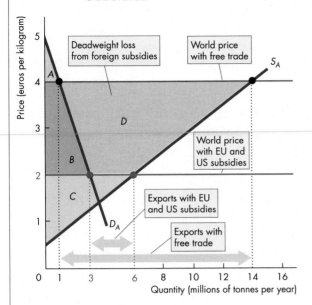

With EU and US subsidies, the world price falls from €4 to €2 per kilogram. In an African economy, people buy more sugar, farmers produce less sugar and exports decrease. Consumer surplus expands from A to A + B, producer surplus shrinks from B + C + D to C, and a deadweight loss D arises.

MyEconLab Animation ————————————◆

Africa increases from the green area *A* to the area *A + B* as Africans purchase more sugar at the lower world price. Producer surplus shrinks from the area *B + C + D* to the area *C*. Part of the loss, area *D*, arises because Africans produce less sugar and receive a lower price for it. Part of the loss of producer surplus, area *B*, is transferred to African consumers.

The total loss to producers, area *D + B*, exceeds the gains to consumers, area *B*. Total surplus decreases by the grey area *D*. The deadweight losses created by EU and US farm subsidies is a social loss for Africa.

Other Import Barriers

Two sets of policies that influence imports are health, safety and regulation barriers and voluntary export restraints. Thousands of detailed health, safety and other regulations restrict international trade. For example, the EU bans imports of most genetically modified foods such as US-produced soya beans. Although such regulations are not designed to limit international trade, they have that effect.

A voluntary export restraint is like a quota allocated to a foreign exporter of a good. This type of trade barrier isn't common, but was used in Japan in the 1980s.

ECONOMICS IN ACTION

Self-Interest Beats the Social Interest

The **World Trade Organisation (WTO)** is an international body established by the world's major trading nations for the purpose of supervising international trade and lowering the barriers to trade.

In 2001, at a meeting of trade ministers from all the WTO member-countries held in Doha, Qatar, an agreement was made to begin negotiations to lower tariff barriers and quotas that restrict international trade in farm products and services. These negotiations are called the **Doha Development Agenda** or the **Doha Round**.

In the period since 2001, thousands of hours of conferences in Cancún in 2003, Geneva in 2004 and Hong Kong in 2005, and ongoing meetings at WTO headquarters in Geneva, costing millions of taxpayers' dollars, have made disappointing progress.

Rich nations, led by the EU, US and Japan, want greater access to the markets of developing nations in exchange for allowing those nations greater access to the markets of the rich world, especially those for farm products.

Developing nations, led by Brazil, China, India and South Africa, want access to the markets of farm products of the rich world, but they also want to protect their infant industries.

With two incompatible positions, these negotiations are stalled and show no signs of a breakthrough. The self-interests of rich nations and developing nations are preventing the achievement of the social interest.

REVIEW QUIZ

1   What are the tools that a country can use to restrict international trade?
2   Explain the effects of tariffs on domestic production, the quantity bought and the price.
3   Explain who gains and who loses from a tariff and why the losses exceed the gains.
4   Explain the effects of an import quota on domestic production, consumption and price.
5   Explain who gains and who loses from an import quota and why the losses exceed the gains.

Do these questions in Study Plan 7.3 and get instant feedback.   MyEconLab

Let's now look at some commonly heard arguments for restricting international trade and see why they are never correct.

The Case Against Protection

You've seen that free trade promotes prosperity and protection is inefficient. Yet trade is restricted with tariffs, quotas and other barriers. Why? Seven arguments for trade restrictions are that protecting domestic industries from foreign competition:

◆ Helps an infant industry grow

◆ Counteracts dumping

◆ Saves domestic jobs

◆ Allows us to compete with cheap foreign labour

◆ Penalises lax environmental standards

◆ Prevents rich countries from exploiting developing countries

◆ Reduces offshore outsourcing that sends good UK jobs abroad

Helps an Infant Industry Grow

Comparative advantages change with on-the-job experience – *earning-by-doing*. When a new industry or a new product is born – an *infant industry* – it is not as productive as it will become with experience. It is argued that such an industry should be protected from international competition until it can stand alone and compete.

It is true that learning-by-doing can change comparative advantage, but this fact doesn't justify protecting an infant industry. Firms anticipate and benefit from learning-by-doing without protection from foreign competition.

When Rolls-Royce started to build jet engines in Derby, productivity was at first low. But after a period of learning-by-doing, huge productivity gains followed. Rolls-Royce didn't need a tariff to achieve these productivity gains.

Counteracts Dumping

Dumping occurs when a foreign firm sells its exports at a lower price than its cost of production. Dumping might be used by a firm that wants to gain a global monopoly. In this case, the foreign firm sells its output at a price below its cost to drive domestic firms out of business. When the domestic firms have gone, the foreign firm takes advantage of its monopoly position and charges a higher price for its product. Dumping is illegal

under the rules of the World Trade Organisation and is usually regarded as a justification for temporary tariffs, which are called *countervailing duties*.

But it is virtually impossible to detect dumping because it is hard to determine a firm's costs. As a result, the test for dumping is whether a firm's export price is below its domestic price. But this test is weak because it is rational for a firm to charge a low price in a market in which the quantity demanded is highly sensitive to price and a higher price in a market in which demand is less price-sensitive.

Saves Domestic Jobs

First, free trade does destroy some jobs, but it also creates other jobs. It brings about a global rationalisation of labour and allocates labour resources to their highest-valued activities. International trade in textiles has cost thousands of jobs as UK textile mills and other factories closed. But thousands of jobs have been created in other countries as textile mills opened. And thousands of UK workers have better-paying jobs than as textile workers because UK export industries have expanded and created new jobs. More jobs have been created than destroyed.

Imports don't only destroy jobs. They create jobs for retailers that sell imported goods and for firms that service those goods. Imports also create jobs by creating income in the rest of the world, some of which is spent on UK-made goods and services.

Allows Us to Compete with Cheap Foreign Labour

The relatively high wages in the UK and other EU member states don't imply that the EU cannot compete.

Wages are higher, other things remaining the same, the higher is the productivity of labour. EU workers are more productive, on average, than lower-paid workers in China or India. For example, the productivity of EU labour is higher in financial services, biotechnology products and business computer systems than in assembling cars or televisions. These activities are ones in which the EU has a comparative advantage.

By engaging in free trade, the EU can increase production and exports of the goods in which it has a comparative advantage and increase the imports of goods in which our trading partners have a comparative advantage.

Penalises Lax Environmental Standards

Another argument for protection is that it provides an incentive to poor countries to raise their environmental standards – free trade with the richer and 'greener' countries is a reward for improved environmental standards.

This argument for protection is weak. First, a poor country cannot afford to be as concerned about its environmental standard as a rich country can. Today, some of the worst pollution of air and water is found in China, Mexico and the former communist countries of Eastern Europe. But only a few decades ago, London and Los Angeles topped the pollution league chart. The best hope for cleaner air in Beijing and Mexico City is rapid income growth, which free trade promotes. As incomes in developing countries grow, they have the *means* to match their desires to improve their environment.

Second, a poor country may have a comparative advantage at doing 'dirty' work, which helps it to raise its income and at the same time enables the global economy to achieve higher environmental standards than would otherwise be possible.

Prevents Rich Countries from Exploiting Developing Countries

Another argument for protection is that international trade must be restricted to prevent the people of the rich industrial world from exploiting the poorer people of the developing countries and forcing them to work for slave wages.

Child labour and near-slave labour are serious problems. But by trading with poor countries, we increase the demand for the goods that these countries produce and increase the demand for their labour. When the demand for labour in developing countries increases, the wage rate rises. So, rather than exploiting people in developing countries, international trade can improve their opportunities and increase their incomes.

Reduces Offshore Outsourcing that Sends Good UK Jobs Abroad

Offshore outsourcing – buying goods, components, or services from firms in other countries – brings gains from trade identical to those of any other type of trade. We could easily change the names of the items traded

from cars and chemicals (the examples in the previous sections of this chapter) to banking services and call centre services (or any other pair of services). A UK bank might export banking services to Indian firms, and Indians might provide call centre services to UK firms. This type of trade would benefit both the UK citizens and Indians, provided the UK has a comparative advantage in banking services and India has a comparative advantage in call centre services.

Despite the gain from specialisation and trade that offshore outsourcing brings, many people believe that it also brings costs that eat up the gains. Why?

A major reason is that it seems to send good UK jobs to other countries. Offshore outsourcing has been the main reason why UK manufacturing has declined as a percentage of UK output in the twentieth century. But as UK manufacturing jobs have declined, new UK service jobs have been created to take their place. London's financial sector and the UK university sector grew rapidly during this time.

Since the 1990s, however, some UK service sector jobs started going overseas as well. The fear is that there will not be enough new service sector jobs to replace those going overseas. But this fear is misplaced.

The UK imports call centre services, but it exports education, tourism, legal, financial, and a host of other types of services. The number of jobs in these sectors is expanding and will continue to expand.

The exact number of jobs that have moved to lower-cost offshore locations is not known, and estimates vary. But even the highest estimate is small compared with the normal rate of job creation and labour turnover.

Gains from trade do not bring gains for every single person. UK citizens, on average, gain from offshore outsourcing, but some people lose. The losers are those who have invested in the human capital to do a specific job that has now gone offshore.

Unemployment benefits provide short-term temporary relief for these displaced workers. But the long-term solution requires retraining and the acquisition of new skills.

Beyond bringing short-term relief through unemployment benefits, government has a larger role to play. By providing education and training, it can enable the labour force of the twenty-first century to engage in the ongoing learning and sometimes rapid retooling that jobs we can't foresee today will demand.

Schools, colleges and universities will expand and become better at doing their job of producing a more highly educated and flexible labour force.

Is Offshore Outsourcing Bad or Good for Europe?

Barclays, Rolls-Royce, Dyson and Tesco engage in offshore outsourcing when they buy finished goods, components or services from firms in other countries. Buying goods and components has been going on for centuries, but buying *services*, such as customer support call centre services, is new and is made possible by the development of low-cost telephone and Internet services.

Should this type of offshore outsourcing be discouraged and penalised with taxes and regulations?

Bad

♦ When the UK's Birmingham City Council announced it would shift 70–100 IT services jobs to India to save money in 2011, the employee trade union, Unite, protested. Similarly, Amicus, the trade union for the financial services sector, has argued that all UK financial jobs are at risk.

♦ Estimates suggest that 2–3 per cent of UK service sector jobs could be outsourced by 2015 and public opinion is mainly against this because of fears of rising unemployment.

Have these Indian call-centre workers destroyed UK jobs? Or does their work benefit UK workers?

Good

♦ Economist N. Gregory Mankiw said, 'I think outsourcing . . . is probably a plus for the economy in the long run.'

♦ Greg Mankiw says that the economic analysis of the gains from international trade – exactly the same as what you have studied on pp. 153–154 above – applies to all types of international trade including offshore outsourcing.

♦ In the UK, the Confederation of British Industry and the Institute of Directors say that offshore outsourcing can mean UK job losses in the short run but more growth in the longer run.

♦ A McKinsey Global Institute report suggests that every $1 of offshore outsourcing in India can raise $1.12 in the domestic economy and $0.33 in India – everyone gains.

Avoiding Trade Wars

We have reviewed the arguments commonly heard in favour of protection and the counter-arguments against it. But one counter-argument to protection that is general and quite overwhelming is that protection invites retaliation and can trigger a trade war.

A trade war is a contest in which when one country raises its import tariffs, other countries retaliate with increases of their own, which trigger yet further increases from the first country. A trade war occurred during the Great Depression of the 1930s when the US introduced the Smoot-Hawley tariff. Country after country retaliated with its own tariff, and in a short period world trade had almost disappeared. The costs to all countries were large and led to a renewed international resolve to avoid such self-defeating moves in the future. The costs also led to attempts to liberalise trade following the Second World War.

Why Is International Trade Restricted?

Why, despite all the arguments against protection, is trade restricted? There are two key reasons:

♦ Tariff revenue

♦ Rent seeking

Tariff Revenue

Government revenue is costly to collect. In developed countries such as the UK, a well-organised tax collection system is in place that can generate billions of pounds of income tax and VAT revenues.

But governments in developing countries have a difficult time collecting taxes from their citizens. Much economic activity takes place in an informal economy with few financial records. The one area in which economic transactions are well recorded is international trade. So tariffs on international trade are a convenient source of revenue in these countries.

Rent Seeking

Rent seeking is the major reason why international trade is restricted. **Rent seeking** is lobbying for special treatment by the government to create economic profit or to divert consumer surplus or producer surplus away from others. Free trade increases consumption possibilities, on average, but not everyone shares in the gain and some people even lose. Free trade brings benefits to some and imposes costs on others, with total benefits exceeding total costs. The uneven distribution of costs and benefits is the principal obstacle to achieving more liberal international trade.

Returning to the example of trade in cars and chemicals, the benefits from free trade accrue to all the producers of chemicals and to those producers of cars that do not bear the costs of adjusting to a smaller car industry. These costs are transition costs, not permanent costs. The costs of moving to free trade are borne by the car producers and their employees who must become producers of other goods and services in which the UK has a comparative advantage.

The number of winners from free trade is large, but because the gains are spread thinly over a large number of people, the gain per person is small. The winners could organise and become a political force lobbying for free trade. But political activity is costly. It uses time and other scarce resources, and the gains per person are too small to make the cost of political activity worth bearing.

In contrast, the number of losers from free trade is small, but the loss per person is large. Because the loss per person is large, the people who lose are willing to incur considerable expense to lobby against free trade.

Both the winners and losers weigh benefits and costs. Those who gain from free trade weigh the benefits it brings against the cost of achieving it. Those who lose from free trade and gain from protection weigh the benefit of protection against the cost of maintaining it. The protectionists undertake a larger quantity of political lobbying than the free traders.

Compensating Losers

If, in total, the gains from free international trade exceed the losses, why don't those who gain compensate those who lose so that everyone is in favour of free trade?

Some compensation does take place. The losers from international trade are compensated directly through unemployment compensation arrangements. But only limited attempts are made to compensate those who lose.

The main reason why full compensation is not attempted is that the cost of identifying the losers from free trade and of estimating the value of their losses would be enormous.

Also, it would never be clear whether a person who has fallen on hard times is suffering because of free trade or for other reasons, perhaps reasons that are largely under the control of the individual.

Furthermore, some people who look like losers at one point in time may, in fact, end up gaining. The young car worker who loses his job and becomes a webmaster resents the loss of work and the need to move. But a year or two later, looking back on events, he counts himself fortunate. He's made a move that has increased his income and given him greater job security.

Because we do not explicitly compensate the losers from free international trade, protectionism remains a popular and permanent feature of our national economic and political life.

REVIEW QUIZ

1   What are the infant-industry and dumping arguments for protection? Are they correct?
2   Can protection save domestic jobs and the environment and prevent workers in developing countries from being exploited?
3   What is offshore outsourcing? Who benefits from it and who loses?
4   What are the main reasons for imposing a tariff?
5   Why don't the winners from free trade win the political argument?

Do these questions in Study Plan 7.4 and get instant feedback.   MyEconLab

You've now seen how free international trade enables people to gain from increased specialisation and trade, and how barriers to international trade bring gains for some, but greater losses for all.

Reading Between the Lines on pp. 166–167 shows why car makers in France and vintners in Korea oppose a new EU agreement with Korea to cut tariffs.

READING BETWEEN THE LINES

EU–Korea Free Trade Deal

Koreans Question Benefit of EU Trade Deal

Simon Mundy and Song Jung-a

South Korea's trade agreement with the EU may have sparked unrest in France, but officials in Seoul are battling to explain to their public why it has not given a bigger boost to their economy. Exports to the EU have fallen heavily this year amid the turmoil of the sovereign debt crisis. . . .

Yet export data suggest that the decline in exports to Europe would have been more severe without the agreement. Although the overall figure fell 3.6 per cent between July 2011, when the FTA agreement came into force, and March 2012, exports benefiting from reduced tariffs increased

16.5 per cent, says Myung Jin-ho, a researcher at the Korea International Trade Association. . . .

But while South Korea bridles at the complaints of French carmakers, some of its own industries are also fretting about the impact of the trade agreement. . . . Producers of beef, liquor and dairy products are also protesting about the influx of goods from . . . the EU.

'People are buying less of our products as foreign wines are sold more cheaply because of FTAs,' says Chung Nam-sup, a wine producer in the southern county of Sunchang.

FT   *Source*: FT.com, 12 September 2012.
© The Financial Times Limited 2012. All Rights Reserved.

 The Essence of the Story

- ◆ A new trade deal reducing tariffs on trade between the European Union and South Korea came into force in July 2011.

- ◆ Overall, South Korea's exports to Europe fell by 3.6 per cent in the 12 months after the trade deal due to the poor economic climate.

- ◆ But South Korea's exports of goods with reduced tariffs (including cars) increased by 16.5 per cent.

- ◆ French car-makers complain about increased imports of South Korean cars and South Korean wine makers complain about increased imports of French wines.

Economic Analysis

◆ To enjoy the gains from trade, a country must expand the production of items in which it has a comparative advantage and shrink the production of items in which other countries have a comparative advantage.

◆ The markets for cars and wine in France and Korea illustrate the adjustments that must be made to enjoy the gains from free trade.

◆ Figure 1 shows the market for cars in France. The demand for cars is D_F and the supply of cars – cars produced in France – is S_F. Cars can be imported at the world price P_W (€10,000). Before the trade deal with Korea, the French price was €11,000 – the world price plus a 10 per cent tariff.

◆ In Figure 1, with the tariff, France produced 7 million cars a year, imported 3 million, and French consumers bought 10 million a year.

◆ With the tariff removed, France cuts car production to 5 million cars a year, expands imports to 7 million, and French consumers enjoy 12 million cars a year, which they buy at the lower price of €10,000.

◆ Figure 2 shows the market for wine in Korea. The demand for wine is D_K and the supply of wine produced in Korea is S_K. Wine can be imported at the world price P_W (14,000 won* per bottle). Before the trade deal, the Korean price was 15,400 won – the world price plus a 10 per cent tariff.

◆ In Figure 2, with the tariff, Korea produced 30 million bottles a year, imported 70 million, and Korean consumers bought 100 million bottles a year.

◆ With the tariff removed, Korea cuts wine production to 10 million bottles a year, expands imports to 110 million bottles and Korean consumers enjoy 120 million bottles a year, which they buy at the lower price of 14,000 won per bottle.

* The won is Korea's money. €1 = 1,400 won (approximately).

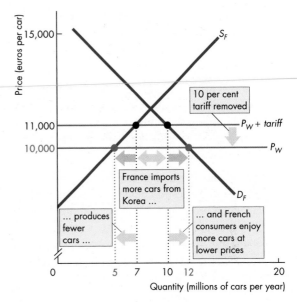

Figure 1 The Market for Cars in France

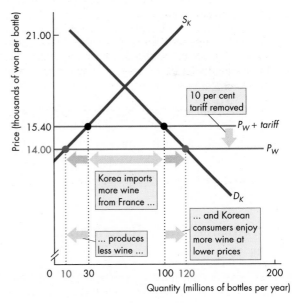

Figure 2 The Market for Wine in Korea

◆ The data show that EU exports to Korea in the first 9 months after the trade deal increased by €6.7 billion, and EU consumers benefited from €350 billion lower tariff payments.

◆ The benefits to South Korea will be even larger when the EU economy picks up.

SUMMARY

Key Points

How Global Markets Work

(pp. 150–152)

◆ Comparative advantage drives international trade.

◆ If the world price of a good is lower than the domestic price, the rest of the world has a comparative advantage in producing that good, and the domestic country gains by producing less, consuming more and importing the good.

◆ If the world price of a good is higher than the domestic price, the domestic country has a comparative advantage in producing that good, and the domestic country gains by producing more, consuming less and exporting the good.

Do Problems 1 to 6 to get a better understanding of how global markets work.

Winners, Losers and the Net Gain from Trade (pp. 153–154)

◆ Compared with a no-trade situation, in a market with imports, consumer surplus is larger, producer surplus is smaller and total surplus is larger with free international trade.

◆ Compared with a no-trade situation, in a market with exports, consumer surplus is smaller, producer surplus is larger and total surplus is larger with free international trade

Do Problems 7 and 8 to get a better understanding of winners, losers and the net gains from trade.

International Trade Restrictions

(pp. 155–161)

◆ Countries restrict international trade by imposing tariffs, import quotas, export subsidies or other import barriers.

◆ Trade restrictions raise the domestic price, decrease the quantity imported, decrease consumer surplus, increase producer surplus and create a deadweight loss.

Do Problems 9 to 20 to get a better under-standing of international trade restrictions.

The Case Against Protection

(pp. 162–165)

◆ Arguments that protection helps the infant industry to grow and counteracts dumping are weak.

◆ Arguments that protection saves domestic jobs, allows us to compete with cheap foreign labour, penalises lax environmental standards, and prevents exploitation of developing countries are flawed.

◆ Offshore outsourcing is just a new way of reaping gains from trade and does not justify protection.

◆ Trade restrictions are popular because protection brings a small loss per person to a large number of people and a large gain per person to a small number of people. Those who gain have a stronger political voice than those who lose, and it is too costly to identify and compensate losers.

Do Problem 21 to get a better understanding of the case against protection.

Key Terms

Doha Developing Agenda (Doha Round), 161
Dumping, 162
Export subsidy, 160
Exports, 150
Import quota, 158
Imports, 150
Offshore outsourcing, 163
Rent seeking, 165
Tariff, 155
World Trade Organisation (WTO), 161

STUDY PLAN PROBLEMS AND APPLICATIONS

Do Problems 1 to 21 in MyEconLab Chapter 6 Study Plan and get instant feedback.

MyEconLab

How Global Markets Work

(Study Plan 7.1)

Use the following information in Problems 1 to 3.

Wholesalers of roses (the firms that supply your local flower shop with roses for Valentine's Day) buy and sell roses in containers that hold 120 stems. The table provides information about the wholesale market for roses in the UK. The demand schedule is the wholesalers' demand and the supply schedule is the UK rose growers' supply.

Price (pounds per container)	Quantity demanded	Quantity supplied
	(millions of containers per year)	
100	15	0
125	12	2
150	9	4
175	6	6
200	3	8
225	0	10

Wholesalers can buy roses at auction in Aalsmeer, Holland, for £125 per container.

1 a Without international trade, what would be the price of a container of roses and how many containers of roses a year would be bought and sold in the UK?

b At the price in your answer to part (a), does the UK or the rest of the world have a comparative advantage in producing roses?

2 If UK wholesalers buy roses at the lowest possible price, how many do they buy from UK growers and how many do they import?

3 Draw a graph to illustrate the UK wholesale market for roses. Show the equilibrium in that market with no international trade and the equilibrium with free trade. Mark the quantity of roses produced in the UK, the quantity imported and the total quantity bought.

Use the following news clip in Problems 4 and 5.

Underwater Oil Discovery to Transform Brazil into a Major Exporter

A huge underwater oil field discovered late last year has the potential to transform Brazil into a sizable exporter. Fifty years ago, Petrobras was formed as a trading company to import oil to support Brazil's growing economy. Two years ago, Brazil reached its long-sought goal of energy self-sufficiency.

Source: *International Herald Tribune*, 11 January 2008

4 Describe Brazil's comparative advantage in producing oil and explain why it has changed.

5 a Draw a graph to illustrate the Brazilian market for oil and explain why Brazil was an importer of oil until a few years ago.

b Draw a graph to illustrate the Brazilian market for oil and explain why Brazil may become an exporter of oil in the near future.

6 The End of Cheap Chinese Goods

Beginning in the 1990s, as China emerged as a major exporter, the prices of many goods fell. For example, clothing prices fell through 2007 when they bottomed out. But as China's labour costs started to rise, clothing production moved from China to other countries.

Source: *The New York Times*, 21 October 2011

a Explain why China emerged as a major exporter of clothing through 2007.

b Explain why China no longer exports cheap clothing.

Winners, Losers and the Net Gain from Trade **(Study Plan 7.2)**

7 In the news clip in Problem 6, who will gain and who will lose from the trade in clothing as it is moved from China to other countries?

8 Use the information on the UK wholesale market for roses in Problem 1 to:

a Explain who gains and who loses from free international trade in roses compared with a situation in which UK citizens buy only roses grown in the UK.

b Draw a graph to illustrate the gains and losses from free trade.

c Calculate the gain from international trade.

International Trade Restrictions

(Study Plan 7.3)

Use the following news clip in Problems 9 and 10.

Steel Tariffs Appear to Have Backfired on Bush

President Bush set aside his free-trade principles last year and imposed heavy tariffs on imported steel to help out struggling mills in Pennsylvania and West Virginia. Some economists say the tariffs may have cost more jobs than they saved, by driving up costs for car makers and other steel users.

Source: *The Washington Post*, 19 September 2003

9 a Explain how a high tariff on steel imports can help US domestic steel producers.

b Explain how a high tariff on steel imports can harm steel users.

10 Draw a graph of the US market for steel to show how a high tariff on steel imports helps US steel producers, harms US steel users and creates a deadweight loss.

Use the information on the UK wholesale market for roses in Problem 1 in Problems 11 to 16.

11 If the UK puts a tariff of £25 per container on imports of roses, what happens to the UK price of roses, the quantity of roses bought, the quantity produced in the UK and the quantity imported?

12 Who gains and who loses from this tariff?

13 Draw a graph to illustrate the gains and losses from the tariff, and on the graph identify the gains and losses, the tariff revenue and the deadweight loss.

14 If the UK puts an import quota on roses of 5 million containers, what happens to the UK price of roses, the quantity of roses bought, and the quantity produced in the UK and the quantity imported?

15 Who gains and who loses from this quota?

16 Draw a graph to illustrate the gains and losses from the import quota, and on the graph identify the gains and losses, the importers' profit and the deadweight loss created.

Use the following news clip in Problems 17 and 18.

Car Sales Go Up as Prices Tumble

Car affordability in Australia is now at its best in 20 years, fuelling a surge in sales as prices tumble. In 2000, Australia cut the tariff to 15 per cent and on 1 January 2005, it cut the tariff to 10 per cent.

Source: *The Courier Mail*, 26 February 2005

17 Explain who gains and who loses from the lower tariff on imported cars.

18 Draw a graph to show how the price of a car, the quantity of cars bought, the quantity of cars produced in Australia and the quantity of cars imported into Australia changed.

Use the following news clip in Problems 19 and 20.

A New Food Crisis Is on Our Plates

Over the past year, the price of corn has risen 52 per cent, wheat 49 per cent, and soybeans 28 per cent. Alarmed at spiking food prices, a score of countries, including Russia and Ukraine, have banned food exports to make sure they can feed their own people first.

Source: *The Sydney Morning Herald*, 22 February 2011

19 a What are the benefits to a country from importing food?

b What costs might arise from relying on imported food?

20 If a country restricts food exports, what effect does this restriction have in that country on the price of food, the quantity of food it produces, the quantity of food it consumes and the quantity of food it exports?

The Case Against Protection
(Study Plan 7.4)

21 Chinese Tyre Maker Rejects US Charge of Defects

US regulators ordered the recall of more than 450,000 faulty tyres. The Chinese producer of the tyres disputed the allegations and hinted that the recall might be an effort by foreign competitors to hamper Chinese exports to the US. Mounting scrutiny of Chinese-made goods has become a source of new trade frictions between the US and China and fuelled worries among regulators, corporations and consumers about the risks associated with many products imported from China.

Source: *International Herald Tribune*, 26 June 2007

a What does the information in the news clip imply about the comparative advantage of producing tyres in the US and China?

b Could product quality be a valid argument against free trade?

c How would the product-quality argument against free trade be open to abuse by domestic producers of the imported good?

Economics in the News (Study Plan 7.N)

22 In a recent report, Global Trade Alert say that recessions bring about protectionist policies and the debt crisis in Europe has led countries to protect local firms. Their data shows between 2008 and 2011, the number of protectionist policies in African countries increased by 89 compared to an increase of 259 in the EU27 group.

Source: African Development Bank Group, 2013

a What does the report suggest is the main reason why protectionist policies have risen in Europe?

b How would African countries justify their increase in protectionist policies?

c What arguments would African countries put forward against the increase in EU protectionist policies?

ADDITIONAL PROBLEMS AND APPLICATIONS

Do these problems in MyEconLab if assigned by your lecturer.

MyEconLab

How Global Markets Work

23 Suppose that the world price of sugar is 10 pence a pound, the UK does not trade internationally, and the equilibrium price of sugar in the UK is 20 pence a pound. The UK then begins to trade internationally.

a How does the price of sugar in the UK change?

b Do UK consumers buy more or less sugar?

c Do UK sugar growers produce more or less sugar?

d Does the UK export or import sugar and why?

24 Suppose that the world price of steel is $100 a tonne, India does not trade internationally and the equilibrium price of steel in India is $60 a tonne. India then begins to trade internationally.

a How does the price of steel in India change?

b How does the quantity of steel produced in India change?

c How does the quantity of steel bought by India change?

d Does India export or import steel and why?

25 A semiconductor is a key component in your laptop, mobile phone and iPod. The table provides information about the market for semiconductors in the EU.

Price (euros per unit)	Quantity demanded	Quantity supplied
	(billions of units per year)	
10	25	0
12	20	20
14	15	40
16	10	60
18	5	80
20	0	100

Producers of semiconductors get €18 a unit on the world market.

a With no international trade, what would be the price of a semiconductor and how many semiconductors a year would be bought and sold in the EU?

b Does the EU have a comparative advantage in producing semiconductors?

26 Act Now, Eat Later

The hunger crisis in poor countries has its roots in EU and US policies of subsidising the diversion of food crops such as soya beans to produce biofuels such as ethanol. That is, doling out subsidies to put the world's dinner into the petrol tank.

Source: *Time*, 5 May 2008

a What is the effect on the world price of soya beans of the increased use of soya beans to produce ethanol in the EU and US?

b How does the change in the world price of soya beans affect the quantity of soya beans produced in a poor developing country with a comparative advantage in producing soya beans, the quantity the poor country consumes, and the quantity that it either exports or imports?

Winners, Losers and the Net Gain from Trade

27 Use the news clip in Problem 26. Draw a graph of the market for soya beans in a poor developing country to show the changes in consumer surplus, producer surplus and deadweight loss.

Use the following news clip in Problems 28 and 29.

South Korea to Resume US Beef Imports

South Korea will reopen its market to most US beef. South Korea banned imports of US beef in 2003 amid concerns over a case of mad cow disease in the US. The ban closed what was then the third-largest market for US beef exporters.

Source: CNN, 29 May 2008

28 a Explain how South Korea's import ban on US beef affected beef producers and consumers in South Korea.

b Draw a graph of the market for beef in South Korea to illustrate your answer to part (a). Identify the changes in consumer surplus, producer surplus and deadweight loss.

29 a Assuming that South Korea is the only importer of US beef, explain how South Korea's import ban on US beef affected beef producers and consumers in the US.

b Draw a graph of the market for beef in the US to illustrate your answer to part (a). Identify the changes in consumer surplus, producer surplus and deadweight loss.

International Trade Restrictions

Use the following information in Problems 30 to 32.

Before 1995, trade between the US and Mexico was subject to tariffs. In 1995, Mexico joined NAFTA and all US and Mexican tariffs have gradually been removed.

30 Explain how the price that US consumers pay for goods from Mexico and the quantity of US imports from Mexico have changed. Who are the winners and who are the losers from this free trade?

31 Explain how the quantity of US exports to Mexico and the US government's tariff revenue from trade with Mexico have changed.

32 Suppose that in 2008, tomato growers in Florida lobby the US government to impose an import quota on Mexican tomatoes. Explain who in the US would gain and who would lose from such a quota.

Use the following information in Problems 33 and 34.

Suppose that in response to huge job losses in the EU textile industry, the EU imposes a 100 per cent tariff on imports of textiles from China.

33 Explain how the tariff on textiles will change the price that EU buyers pay for textiles, the quantity of textiles imported, and the quantity of textiles produced in the EU.

34 Explain how the EU and Chinese gains from trade will change. Who in the EU will lose and who will gain?

Use the following information in Problems 35 and 36.

With free trade between Australia and the US, Australia would export beef to the US. But the US imposes an import quota on Australian beef.

35 Explain how this quota influences the price that US consumers pay for beef, the quantity of beef produced in the US, and the US and the Australian gains from trade.

36 Explain who in the US gains from the quota on beef imports and who loses.

The Case Against Protection

37 **Trading Up**

Higher prices from tariffs cost US consumers $826,000 a year to save a single job in the sugar industry, $685,000 a year to save a job in the dairy industry, and $263,000 a year to save a job in manufacturing handbags.

Source: *The New York Times*, 26 June 2006

a What are the arguments for saving the jobs mentioned in this news clip?

b Explain why these arguments are faulty.

c Is there any case for saving these jobs?

Economics in the News

38 After you have studied *Reading Between the Lines* on pp. 166–167, answer the following questions.

a What is a free trade agreement and what is its aim?

b Explain how removing the 10 per cent tariff on EU car imports changes consumer surplus, producer surplus and deadweight loss.

c Illustrate your answer to part (b) with an appropriate graphical analysis.

d Explain how removing the 10 per cent tariff on Korean wine imports changes consumer surplus, producer surplus and deadweight loss.

e Illustrate your answer to part (d) with an appropriate graphical analysis.

f Explain why EU car producers and Korean wine producers oppose the tariff cuts.

39 **Gulf Louvre Deal Riles French Art World**

The Louvre in Paris will benefit from the deal, officials insist, but a storm is raging in France over the government's decision to build a branch of the Louvre in Abu Dhabi – the first-ever foreign annex of the world-famous art gallery. The controversy is not over public spending on culture but on the fact that France stands to make money from the deal.

Source: BBC News, 6 March 2007

Who will gain and who will lose from the deal?

40 **EU Trade with Latin America**

The EU plans to boost trade with Argentina, Brazil, Paraguay and Uruguay by negotiating a free trade deal. EU farmers say any deal will hurt them. The French Agriculture Minister Bruno Le Maire voiced opposition to a relaunch of negotiations, saying: 'I don't see why agriculture always has to be the bargaining chip in Europe's trade negotiations . . . especially when some South American countries, notably Argentina, are putting new protectionist tariffs on food imports.'

Source: BBC News, 17 May 2010

a Explain how a free trade deal with Argentina, Brazil, Paraguay and Uruguay will boost trade.

b Explain why French farmers say any trade deal will hurt them.

c Illustrate your answer to part (b) with an appropriate graphical analysis.

d Explain why Argentina is putting protectionist tariffs on food imports.

8 Households' Choices

After studying this chapter you will be able to:

◆ Describe a household's budget line and show how it changes when a price or income changes

◆ Use indifference curves to map preferences and explain the principle of diminishing marginal rate of substitution

◆ Predict the effects of changes in prices and income on consumption choices

◆ Describe some new ways of explaining households' choices

Beef prices, from prime cuts to value steak, are rising, and we are buying more value steak. Why?

The price of a DVD rental and streaming video has fallen and we are watching more films at home, but we're also going to the cinema more often. Why?

What determines our choices, what makes our choices change, and how do we make the best affordable choice?

In this chapter we study a model of choice that helps answer these questions. In *Reading Between the Lines* at the end of the chapter we use the model to explain why, even at a higher price, value steak has become more popular.

Consumption Possibilities

Consumption choices are limited by income and by the prices of goods and services. A household has a given amount of income to spend and cannot influence the prices of the goods and services it buys. It takes the prices as given. A household's **budget line** describes the limits to its consumption choices.

The Budget Line

Let's look at Lisa's budget line. Lisa is the only person in her household and she has £30 a month to spend. She buys two goods: films and cola. The price to see a film is £6 and the price of cola is £3 for a pack of 6 cans.

Figure 8.1 shows the alternative affordable ways for Lisa to see films and buy cola. In Row A she buys 10 packs of cola and sees no films. In Row F she sees 5 films and drinks no cola. Both of these combinations of films and packs of cola exhaust Lisa's income of £30 a month. Check that each of the other rows also exhausts Lisa's £30. The rows of the table define Lisa's consumption possibilities, given her income (£30 a month), and the prices of cola (£3 a pack) and a cinema ticket (£6).

Divisible and Indivisible Goods

Some goods – called divisible goods – can be bought in any quantity desired. Examples are petrol and electricity. We can best understand the household choice we're about to study if we assume that all goods and services are divisible. For example, Lisa can see half a film a month *on average* by seeing one film every two months. When we think of goods as being divisible, the consumption possibilities are not just the points A to F shown in Figure 8.1 but all the points that form the line from A to F. This line is Lisa's budget line.

Affordable and Unaffordable Quantities

Lisa's budget line is a constraint on her choices. It marks the boundary between what she can afford and what she cannot afford. Lisa can afford any point on the line and inside it. She cannot afford any point outside the budget line. The constraint on her consumption depends on the prices of the two goods (cinema tickets and packs of cola) and her income. This constraint changes when either price or her income changes. Let's see how by studying an equation that describes her consumption possibilities.

Figure 8.1 The Budget Line

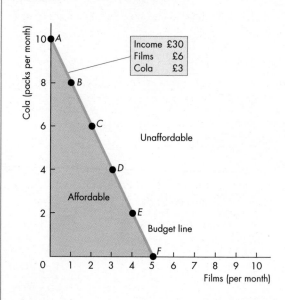

Consumption possibility	Films (per month)	Cola (packs per month)
A	0	10
B	1	8
C	2	6
D	3	4
E	4	2
F	5	0

Lisa's budget line is the boundary between what she can and cannot afford. The rows of the table are Lisa's affordable combinations of films and cola when her income is £30, the price of a cinema ticket is £6 and the price of cola is £3 a pack. For example, row A tells us that Lisa spends her £30 income when she buys 10 packs of cola and sees no films.

The graph shows Lisa's budget line. Points A to F on the graph represent the rows of the table. For divisible goods, the budget line is the continuous line AF.

To calculate the equation of Lisa's budget line, start from the fact that expenditure equals income. If the quantity of films that Lisa sees is Q_F and the quantity of cola she buys is Q_C, then:

$$£3Q_C + £6Q_F = £30$$

Divide by £3 to obtain:

$$Q_C + 2Q_F = 10$$

Subtract $2Q_F$ from both sides to obtain:

$$Q_C = 10 - 2Q_F$$

MyEconLab Animation

The Budget Equation

We can describe the budget line by using a *budget equation*. The budget equation starts with the fact that:

Expenditure = Income

Expenditure is equal to the sum of the price of each good multiplied by the quantity bought. For Lisa:

Expenditure = (Price of cola × Quantity of cola)
+ (Price to see a film × Quantity of films)

Call the price of cola P_C, the quantity of cola Q_C, the price to see a film P_F, the quantity of films Q_F and income Y. We can write Lisa's budget equation as:

$$P_C Q_C + P_F Q_F = Y$$

Using the prices Lisa faces, £3 a pack for cola and £6 to see a film, and Lisa's income, £30, we get:

$$£3Q_C + £6Q_F = £30$$

Lisa can choose any quantities of cola (Q_C) and films (Q_F) that satisfy this equation. To find the relationship between these quantities, divide both sides of the equation by the price of cola (P_C) to get:

$$Q_C + \frac{P_F}{P_C} \times Q_F = \frac{Y}{P_C}$$

Now subtract the term $(P_F/P_C) \times Q_F$ from both sides of this equation to give:

$$Q_C = \frac{Y}{P_C} - \frac{P_F}{P_C} \times Q_F$$

For Lisa, income (Y) is £30, P_F is £6 to see a film and P_C is £3 a pack. So Lisa must choose the quantities of films and cola to satisfy the equation:

$$Q_C = \frac{£30}{£3} - \frac{£6}{£3} \times Q_F$$

or

$$Q_C = 10 - 2Q_F$$

To interpret the equation, look at the budget line in Figure 8.1 and check that the equation delivers that budget line. First, set Q_F equal to zero. The budget equation tells us that Q_C, the quantity of cola, equals Y/P_C, which is 10 packs. This combination of Q_F and Q_C is the one in row A of the table in Figure 8.1. Next, set Q_F equal to 5. Now Q_C equals zero (the combination in row F). Check that you can derive the other rows.

The budget equation contains two variables chosen by the household (Q_F and Q_C) and two variables (Y/P_C and P_F/P_C) that the household takes as given. Let's look more closely at these variables.

Real Income

A household's **real income** is its income expressed as the quantity of goods that the household can afford to buy. Lisa's real income in terms of cola is Y/P_C. This quantity is the maximum number of packs that Lisa can buy. It is equal to her money income divided by the price of cola. Lisa's income is £30 and the price of cola is £3 a pack, so her real income is 10 packs of cola. In Figure 8.1, real income is the point at which the budget line intersects the y-axis.

Relative Price

A **relative price** is the price of one good divided by the price of another good. In Lisa's budget equation, the variable (P_F/P_C) is the relative price of a film in terms of cola. For Lisa, P_F is £6 a film and P_C is £3 a pack of cola, so P_F/P_C is equal to 2 packs per film. That is, to see one more film, Lisa must give up 2 packs of cola.

You've just calculated Lisa's opportunity cost of seeing a film. Recall that the opportunity cost of an action is the best alternative forgone. For Lisa to see 1 more film a month, she must forgo 2 packs of cola. You've also calculated Lisa's opportunity cost of cola. For Lisa to buy 2 more packs a month, she must give up seeing 1 film. So her opportunity cost of 2 packs of cola is 1 film.

The relative price of a film in terms of cola is the magnitude of the slope of Lisa's budget line. To calculate the slope of the budget line, recall the formula (see the Chapter 1 Appendix): slope equals the change in the variable measured on the y-axis divided by the change in the variable measured on the x-axis as we move along the line. In Lisa's case (Figure 8.1), the variable measured on the y-axis is the quantity of cola and the variable measured on the x-axis is the quantity of films. Along Lisa's budget line, as cola decreases from 10 to 0 packs, films increase from 0 to 5. So the slope of the budget line is 10 packs divided by 5 films, or 2 packs per film. The magnitude of this slope is the same as the relative price of a film we've just calculated. It is also the opportunity cost of a film.

A Change in Prices

When prices change, so does the budget line. The lower the price of the good measured on the x-axis, other things remaining the same, the flatter is the budget

Figure 8.2 Changes in Prices and Income

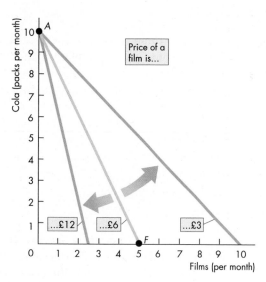

(a) A change in price

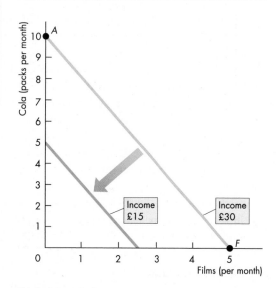

(b) A change in income

In part (a), the price to see a film changes. A fall in the price from £6 to £3 increases the number of films that Lisa can see for £30, so her budget line rotates outward and becomes flatter. A rise in the price from £6 to £12 rotates the budget line inward and makes it steeper.

In part (b), income falls from £30 to £15 while the prices of cola and seeing a film remain constant. The budget line shifts leftward but its slope does not change.

line. For example, if the price to see a film falls from £6 to £3, real income in terms of cola does not change but the relative price to see a film falls. The budget line rotates *outward* and becomes flatter, as shown in Figure 8.2(a). The higher the price of the good measured on the *x*-axis, other things remaining the same, the steeper is the budget line. For example, if the price to see a film rises from £6 to £12, the relative price to see a film increases. The budget line rotates *inward* and becomes steeper, as shown in Figure 8.2(a).

A Change in Income

A change in *money* income changes real income but does not change the relative price. The budget line shifts, but its slope does not change. An increase in money income increases real income and shifts the budget line rightward. A decrease in money income decreases real income and shifts the budget line leftward.

Figure 8.2(b) shows the effect of a change in income on Lisa's budget line. The initial budget line when Lisa's income is £30 is the same one that we began with in Figure 8.1. The new budget line shows what Lisa can consume if her income falls to £15 a month. The two budget lines have the same slope because the relative price is the same. The new budget line is closer to the origin than the initial one because Lisa's real income has decreased.

REVIEW QUIZ

1 What does a household's budget line show?
2 Explain how the relative price and a household's real income influence its budget line.
3 If a European household has an income of €40 and buys only bus rides at €2 each and magazines at €4 each, what is the equation that describes the household's budget line?
4 If the price of one good changes, what happens to the relative price and what happens to the slope of the household's budget line?
5 If a household's money income changes and prices do not change, what happens to the household's real income and budget line?

Do these questions in Study Plan 8.1 and get instant feedback.　　　MyEconLab

We've studied the limits to what a household can consume. Let's now learn how we can describe the household's preferences and make a map that contains a lot of information about a household's preferences.

Preferences and Indifference Curves

Preferences are your likes and dislikes. You are going to discover a neat idea: that of drawing a map of a person's preferences. A preference map is based on the intuitively appealing assumption that people can sort all the possible combinations of goods they might consume into three groups: preferred, not preferred and indifferent. To make this idea more concrete, we asked Lisa to rank various combinations of films and cola.

Figure 8.3(a) shows part of Lisa's answer. She tells us that she currently sees 2 films and drinks 6 packs of cola a month at point C. She then lists all the combinations of films and cola that she thinks are just as good as her current combination. When we plot these combinations of films and cola, we get the green curve shown in Figure 8.3(a). This curve is the key element in a map of preferences and is called an indifference curve.

An **indifference curve** is a line that shows combinations of goods among which a consumer is *indifferent*. The indifference curve in Figure 8.3(a) tells us that Lisa is just as happy to see 2 films and drink 6 packs of cola a month at point C as she is to have the combination of films and cola at point G or at any other point along the curve.

Lisa also says she prefers any of the combinations of films and cola above the indifference curve in Figure 8.3(a) – the yellow area – to any combination on the indifference curve. And she prefers any combination on the indifference curve to any combination in the grey area below the indifference curve.

The indifference curve in Figure 8.3(a) is just one of a family of such curves. This indifference curve appears again in Figure 8.3(b). It is labelled I_1 and it passes through points C and G. The curves labelled I_0 and I_2 are two other indifference curves. Lisa prefers any point on indifference curve I_2 to any point on indifference curve I_1 and she prefers any point on I_1 to any point on I_0. We refer to I_2 as being a higher indifference curve than I_1 and I_1 as being higher than I_0. Because Lisa prefers I_2 to I_1 and I_1 to I_0, indifference curves do not intersect.

A *preference map* is a series of indifference curves that look like the contour lines on a map. By looking at a map, we can draw some conclusions about the terrain. Similarly, by looking at the shape of the indifference curves, we can draw conclusions about a person's preferences.

Let's see how to 'read' a preference map.

Figure 8.3 A Preference Map

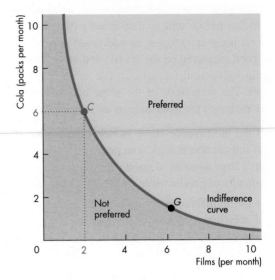

(a) An indifference curve

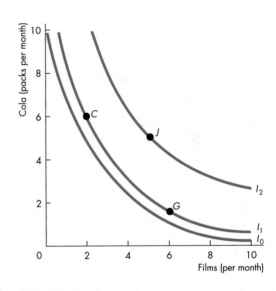

(b) Lisa's preference map

In part (a), Lisa consumes 6 packs of cola and sees 2 films a month at point C. She is indifferent between all the points on the green indifference curve such as C and G. She prefers any point above the indifference curve (yellow area) to any point on it, and she prefers any point on the indifference curve to any point below it (grey area).

Part (b) shows three indifference curves – I_0, I_1 and I_2 – that are part of Lisa's preference map. She prefers point J to point C or G, so she prefers any point on I_2 to any point on I_1.

MyEconLab Animation ──────────────◆

Marginal Rate of Substitution

The **marginal rate of substitution** (or *MRS*) is the rate at which a person will give up good *y* (the good measured on the *y*-axis) to get an additional unit of good *x* (the good measured on the *x*-axis) and at the same time remain indifferent (remain on the same indifference curve). The magnitude of the slope of an indifference curve measures the marginal rate of substitution.

1   If the indifference curve is *steep*, the marginal rate of substitution is *high*. The person is willing to give up a large quantity of good *y* in exchange for a small quantity of good *x* while remaining indifferent

2   If the indifference curve is *flat*, the marginal rate of substitution is *low*. The person is willing to give up only a small amount of good *y* in exchange for a large amount of good *x* to remain indifferent

Figure 8.4 shows you how to calculate the marginal rate of substitution. Suppose that Lisa drinks 6 packs of cola and sees 2 films at point *C* on indifference curve *I₁*. To calculate her marginal rate of substitution, we measure the magnitude of the slope of the indifference curve at point *C*. To measure this magnitude, place a straight line against, or tangent to, the indifference curve at point *C*. Along that line, as the quantity of cola decreases by 10 packs, the number of films increases by 5 – an average of 2 packs per film. So at point *C*, Lisa is willing to give up cola for films at the rate of 2 packs per film – a marginal rate of substitution of 2.

Now, suppose that Lisa sees 6 films and drinks 1.5 packs of cola at point *G* on indifference curve *I₁* in Figure 8.4. Her marginal rate of substitution is now measured by the magnitude of the slope of the indifference curve at point *G*. That slope is the same as the slope of the tangent to the indifference curve at point *G*. Here, as cola consumption decreases by 4.5 packs, film consumption increases by 9 – an average of 1/2 packs per film. So at point *G*, Lisa is willing to give up cola for films at the rate of 1/2 packs per film – a marginal rate of substitution of 1/2.

As Lisa sees more films and drinks less cola, her marginal rate of substitution diminishes. Diminishing marginal rate of substitution is the key assumption of consumer theory. The assumption of **diminishing marginal rate of substitution** is a general tendency for a person to be willing to give up less of good *y* to get one more unit of good *x*, while at the same time remaining indifferent as the quantity of *x* increases. In Lisa's case, she is less willing to give up cola to see one more film as the number of films she sees increases.

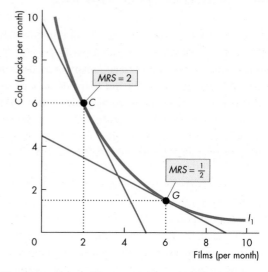

Figure 8.4 The Marginal Rate of Substitution

The magnitude of the slope of an indifference curve is called the marginal rate of substitution (*MRS*). The red line at point *C* tells us that Lisa is willing to give up 10 packs to see 5 films. Her marginal rate of substitution at point *C* is 10 divided by 5, which equals 2. The red line at point *G* tells us that Lisa is willing to give up 4.5 packs to see 9 films. Her marginal rate of substitution at point *G* is 4.5 divided by 9, which equals 1/2.

MyEconLab Animation ──────────────◆

Your Own Diminishing Marginal Rate of Substitution

Think about your own diminishing marginal rate of substitution. Suppose that in one month you drink 10 packs of cola and see no films. You would probably be happy to give up lots of cola just to see one film. But now suppose that in a month you see 6 films and drink only 1 pack of cola. Most likely, you will probably not now be willing to give up much cola to see a seventh film. As a general rule, the greater the number of films you see, the smaller is the quantity of cola you are willing to give up to see an additional film.

The shape of the indifference curves incorporates the principle of the diminishing marginal rate of substitution because the curves are bowed towards the origin. The tightness of the bend of an indifference curve tells us how willing a person is to substitute one good for another while remaining indifferent. The examples that follow will make this point clear.

Degree of Substitutability

Most of us would not regard films and cola as being *close* substitutes for each other. Substitutes are goods that can be used in place of each other. But to some degree, we are willing to substitute between these two goods. No matter how enthusiastic you are about cola, there is surely some increase in the number of films you can see that will compensate you for being deprived of a can of cola. Similarly, no matter how addicted you are to films, surely some amount of cola will compensate you for being deprived of seeing one film. A person's indifference curves for films and cola might look something like those shown in Figure 8.5(a).

Close Substitutes

Some goods substitute so easily for each other that most of us do not even notice which we are consuming. There are different brands of marker pens and roller-ball pens. Most of us don't care whether we use a marker pen from the university bookshop or from the local supermarket. When two goods are perfect substitutes, their

indifference curves are straight lines that slope downward, as Figure 8.5(b) illustrates. The marginal rate of substitution between perfect substitutes is constant.

Complements

Some goods cannot substitute for each other at all. Instead, they are complements. The complements in Figure 8.5(c) are left and right running shoes. Indifference curves of perfect complements are L-shaped. For most of us, one left running shoe and one right running shoe are as good as one left running shoe and two right ones. Having two of each is preferred to having one of each, but two of one and one of the other is no better than one of each.

The extreme cases of perfect substitutes and perfect complements shown here don't often happen in reality. But they do illustrate that the shape of the indifference curve shows the degree of substitutability between two goods. The more perfectly substitutable the two goods, the more nearly are their indifference curves straight lines and the less quickly does the marginal rate of substitution diminish. Poor substitutes for each other

Figure 8.5 The Degree of Substitutability

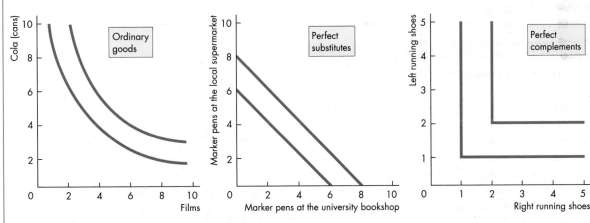

(a) Ordinary goods   **(b) Perfect substitutes**   **(c) Perfect complements**

The shape of the indifference curves reveals the degree of substitutability between two goods. Part (a) shows the indifference curves for two ordinary goods: films and cola. To consume less cola and remain indifferent, one must see more films. The number of films that compensates for a reduction in cola increases as less cola is consumed.

Part (b) shows the indifference curves for two perfect substitutes. For the consumer to remain indifferent, one

additional marker pen from the local supermarket must be replaced by giving up one marker pen from the university bookshop.

Part (c) shows two perfect complements – goods that cannot be substituted for each other at all. One left running shoe with two right running shoes is no better than one of each. But having two of each is preferred to having one of each.

**'With the pork I'd recommend
an Alsatian white or a Coke.'**

© Robert Weber/The New Yorker Collection/
www.cartoonbank.com

have tightly curved indifference curves, approaching the shape of those shown in Figure 8.5(c).

As you can see in the cartoon, according to the waiter's preferences, Alsatian white and Coke are perfect substitutes and each is a complement to pork. We hope the customers agree with him.

REVIEW QUIZ

1   What is an indifference curve and how does an indifference map show preferences?
2   Why does an indifference curve slope downward, and why is it bowed towards the origin?
3   What do we call the magnitude of the slope of an indifference curve?
4   What is the key assumption about a consumer's marginal rate of substitution?

Do these questions in Study Plan 8.2 and
get instant feedback.   MyEconLab

The two components of the model of household choice are now in place: the budget line and the preference map. We will use these components to work out the consumer's choice and to predict how choices change when prices and income change.

 ## Predicting Consumer Behaviour

We are now going to develop a model to predict the quantities of films and cola that Lisa chooses to buy. We're also going to see how these quantities change when a price changes or when Lisa's income changes. Finally, we're going to see how the *substitution effect* and the *income effect*, two ideas that you met in Chapter 3 (see p. 55), guarantee that for a normal good the demand curve slopes downward.

Best Affordable Choice

When Lisa makes her best affordable choice of films and cola, she spends all her income and is on her highest attainable indifference curve. Figure 8.6 illustrates this choice: the budget line is from Figure 8.1 and her indifference curves are from Figure 8.3(b). Lisa's best affordable choice is 2 films and 6 packs of cola at point *C* – the *best affordable point*.

Figure 8.6   The Best Affordable Point

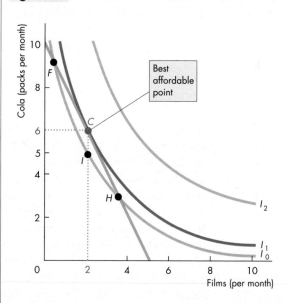

Lisa's best affordable choice is at point *C*, the point on her budget line and on her highest attainable indifference curve. At point *C*, Lisa's marginal rate of substitution between films and cola (the magnitude of the slope of the indifference curve I_1) equals the relative price of films and cola (the slope of the budget line).

MyEconLab Animation ──────────────────◆

On the Budget Line

The best affordable point is on the budget line. For every point inside the budget line such as point *I*, there are points on the budget line that Lisa prefers. For example, she prefers all the points on the budget line between *F* and *H* to point *I*. So she chooses a point *on* the budget line.

On the Highest Attainable Indifference Curve

Every point on the budget line lies on an indifference curve. For example, points *F* and *H* lie on the indifference curve I_0. By moving along her budget line from either *F* or *H* towards *C*, Lisa reaches points on ever higher indifference curves that she prefers to points *F* or *H*. When Lisa gets to point *C*, she is on the highest attainable indifference curve.

Marginal Rate of Substitution Equals Relative Price

At point *C*, Lisa's marginal rate of substitution between films and cola (the magnitude of the slope of the indifference curve) is equal to the relative price of films and cola (the magnitude of the slope of the budget line). Lisa's willingness to pay for a film equals her opportunity cost of a film.

Let's now see how Lisa's choices change when a price changes.

A Change in Price

The effect of a change in the price of a good on the quantity of the good consumed is called the **price effect**. We'll use Figure 8.7(a) to work out the price effect of a fall in the price of seeing a film. We start with the price at £6, the price of cola at £3 a pack and with Lisa's income at £30 a month. In this situation, Lisa chooses 6 packs of cola and sees 2 films a month at point *C*.

Now suppose that the price of a film falls to £3. With a lower price of film, the budget line rotates outward and becomes flatter. The new budget line is the darker orange line in Figure 8.7(a). To check how a price change affects the budget line, see Figure 8.2(a).

Lisa's best affordable point is now *J*, where she sees 5 films and buys 5 packs of cola. When the price of a film falls and the price of cola and her income remain constant, Lisa cuts her cola purchases from 6 to 5 packs and increases the number of films she sees from 2 to 5 a month. Lisa substitutes films for cola.

Figure 8.7 Price Effect and Demand Curve

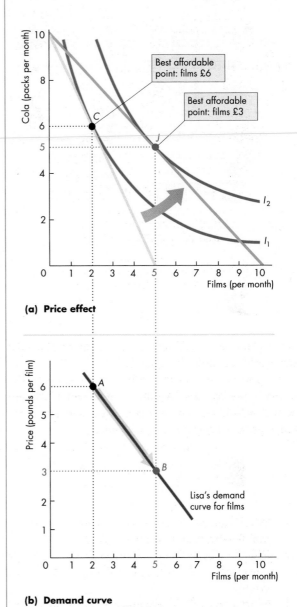

(a) Price effect

(b) Demand curve

Initially, Lisa consumes at point *C* in part (a). If the price to see a film falls from £6 to £3, Lisa chooses point *J*. Lisa increases the number of films she sees from 2 to 5 a month and decreases the cola she drinks from 6 to 5 packs. The move from point *C* to point *J* is the price effect.

At a price of £6 a film, Lisa sees 2 films a month at point *A* in part (b). At a price of £3 a film, Lisa sees 5 films a month at point *B* in part (b). Lisa's demand curve for films passes through points *A* and *B* and traces out her best affordable quantity of films as the price of a film varies.

MyEconLab Animation ───────────◆

ECONOMICS IN ACTION

Best Affordable Choice of Cinema Films and DVD Rentals

Between 2008 and 2012, UK box-office receipts increased by 30 per cent while the average price of a cinema ticket increased by 17 per cent. So most of the rise in box-office receipts is because people went to the cinema more often.

Why is film-going booming? One answer is that some of today's films, such as the 47 3-D films released in 2011, are better viewed on the big screen than at home.

But there is another answer, and at first thought an unlikely one: events in the market for DVD rentals have affected cinema going.

Back in 2008, Blockbuster was booming and charging £4 per DVD film rental. But competition was getting tough. LoveFilm, a new company that had taken over Amazon's UK and German DVD rental business, offered online order and postal return. By 2010, LoveFilm had 1 million subscribers and 20 per cent of the market. LoveFilm now charges just over £1 per rental with monthly membership. You can also stream a film now for just £2. By January 2013, Blockbuster had closed 324 of its 528 stores and was bankrupt.

Figure 1 shows the effects of these events on the share of film revenue for different formats. Revenue from viewing films on TV, in cinemas and by streaming has risen, while revenue from viewing by rental or buying a DVD has fallen.

Easy access to cheap postal DVDs and streamed films transformed the market for film watching, and Figure 2 shows why.

A student has a budget of £40 a month to allocate to films. To keep the story clear, we'll suppose that it cost £8 to go to the cinema in both 2008 and 2012. The price of a DVD rental in 2008 was £4, so the student's budget line is the one that runs from 5 cinema films on the y-axis to 10 DVD rentals on the x-axis. The student's best affordable point is 2 cinema films and 6 rentals a month.

By 2012, the price of a rental falls to £1 a film but the price of a cinema ticket remains at £8. So the budget line

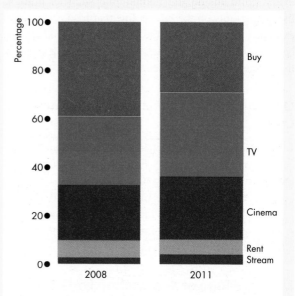

Figure 1 Film Viewing by Source in 2008 and 2011

Source of data: *BFI Statistical Yearbook, 2012,* The British Film Institute.

rotates outward. The student's best affordable point is now at 3 cinema films and 16 rentals a month. Our student is seeing more of both expensive cinema films and cheaper DVD rental films.

Looking ahead, streaming will take the place of rental with a similar effect.

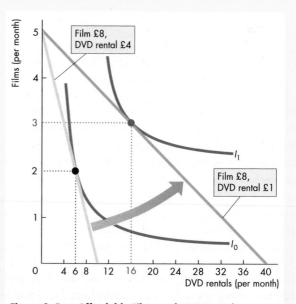

Figure 2 Best Affordable Films and DVD Rentals

The Demand Curve

In Chapter 3, we asserted that the demand curve slopes downward and that it shifts when the consumer's income changes or when the price of another good changes. We can now derive a demand curve from a consumer's budget line and indifference curves. By doing so, we can see that the law of demand and the downward-sloping demand curve are consequences of the consumer choosing his or her best affordable combination of goods.

To derive Lisa's demand curve for films, we lower the price to see a film and find her best affordable point at different prices, holding all other things constant. We've just done this for two film prices in Figure 8.7(a). Figure 8.7(b) highlights these two prices and two points that lie on Lisa's demand curve for films. When the price to see a film is £6, Lisa sees 2 films a month at point A. When the price falls to £3, she increases the number of films she sees to 5 films a month at point B. Lisa's demand curve for films is made up of these two points plus all the other points of Lisa's best affordable consumption of films at each film price, provided the price of cola and Lisa's income remain the same. As you can see, Lisa's demand curve for films slopes downward – the lower the price to see a film, the more films she sees each month. This is the law of demand.

Next, let's see how Lisa adjusts her purchases of films and cola when her income changes.

A Change in Income

The effect of a change in income on buying plans is called the **income effect**. Figure 8.8(a) shows the income effect when Lisa's income falls. With an income of £30, the price of a film £3 and the price of cola £3 a pack, Lisa's best affordable point is J – she sees 5 films and buys 5 packs of cola a month. If her income falls to £21, her best affordable point is K – she sees 4 films and buys 3 packs of cola a month. When Lisa's income falls, she buys less of both goods. Films and cola are normal goods.

The Demand Curve and the Income Effect

A change in income leads to a shift in the demand curve, as shown in Figure 8.8(b). With an income of £30, Lisa's demand curve is D_0, the same as in Figure 8.7. But when her income falls to £21, she plans to see fewer films at each price, so her demand curve for films shifts leftward to D_1.

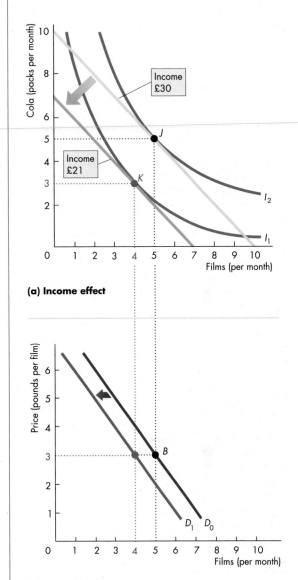

Figure 8.8 Income Effect and Change in Demand

(a) Income effect

(b) Demand curve

A change in income shifts the budget line, changes the best affordable point and shifts the demand curve.

When Lisa's income is £30, the price of a film is £3 and the price of cola is £3 a pack, her best affordable point is J in part (a). When her income decreases from £30 to £21, her best affordable point is K. She sees fewer films and buys less cola.

When Lisa's income is £30, her demand curve for films is D_0 in part (b). When her income decreases to £21, her demand curve for films shifts leftward to D_1. For Lisa, seeing films is a normal good. Her demand for films decreases because she now sees fewer films at each price.

MyEconLab Animation ─────────────◆

Substitution Effect and Income Effect

For a normal good, a fall in price *always* increases the quantity bought. We can prove this assertion by dividing the price effect into two parts:

◆ The substitution effect
◆ The income effect

Figure 8.9(a) shows the price effect and Figures 8.9(b) and 8.9(c) divide the price effect into its two parts.

Substitution Effect

The **substitution effect** is the effect of a change in price on the quantities bought when the consumer (hypothetically) remains indifferent between the original and the new combinations of goods consumed. To work out Lisa's substitution effect, when the price of a film falls, we cut her income by enough to leave her on the same indifference curve as before.

Figure 8.9(a) shows the price effect of a fall in the price of seeing a film from £6 to £3. The number of films increases from 2 to 5 a month. When the price falls, suppose (hypothetically) that we cut Lisa's income to £21. What's special about £21? It is the income that is just enough, at the new price of seeing a film, to keep Lisa's best affordable point on the same indifference curve as her original consumption point *C*. Lisa's budget line is now the medium orange line in Figure 8.9(b). With the lower price of a film and less income, Lisa's best affordable point is *K* on indifference curve I_1. The move from *C* to *K* is the substitution effect of the price change. The substitution effect of the fall in the price of a film is an increase in the films she sees from 2 to 4 a month. The direction of the substitution effect never varies: when the relative price of a good falls, the consumer substitutes more of that good for the other good.

Income Effect

To calculate the substitution effect, we gave Lisa a £9 pay cut. To calculate the income effect, we give Lisa back her £9. The £9 increase in income shifts Lisa's budget line outward, as shown in Figure 8.9(c). The

---

Figure 8.9   Substitution Effect and Income Effect

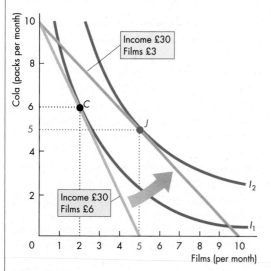

(a) Price effect

When the price of a film falls from £6 to £3, Lisa moves from point *C* to point *J* in part (a). The price effect is an increase in the number of films from 2 to 5 a month. This price effect is separated into a substitution effect in part (b) and an income effect in part (c).

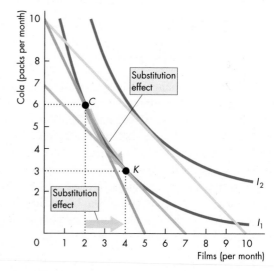

(b) Substitution effect

To isolate the substitution effect, we confront Lisa with the new price of films but keep her on her original indifference curve, I_1. The substitution effect is the move from *C* to *K* along indifference curve I_1 – an increase from 2 to 4 films a month.

slope of the budget line does not change because both prices remain constant. This change in Lisa's budget line is similar to the one illustrated in Figure 8.8. As Lisa's budget line shifts outward, her consumption possibilities expand and her best affordable point becomes J on indifference curve I_2 in Figure 8.9(c). The move from K to J is the income effect of the price change.

As Lisa's income increases, she sees more films. For Lisa, films are a normal good. For a normal good, the income effect *reinforces* the substitution effect. Because the two effects work in the same direction, we can be sure that the demand curve slopes downward. But some goods are inferior goods. What can we say about the demand for an inferior good?

Inferior Goods

Recall that an inferior good is a good for which *demand decreases* when *income increases*. For an inferior good, the income effect is negative, which means that a lower price does not inevitably lead to an increase in the quantity demanded. The substitution effect of a fall in the price increases the quantity demanded, but the negative

income effect works in the opposite direction and offsets the substitution effect to some degree. The key question is to what degree?

If the negative income effect *equals* the positive substitution effect, a fall in the price leaves the quantity bought the same. When a fall in the price leaves the quantity demanded unchanged, the demand curve is vertical and demand is perfectly inelastic.

If the negative income effect *is smaller than* the positive substitution effect, a fall in the price increases the quantity bought and the demand curve slopes downward like that for a normal good. But demand for an inferior good might be less elastic than that for a normal good.

If the negative income effect *exceeds* the positive substitution effect, a fall in the price *decreases* the quantity bought and the demand curve *slopes upward*. This case does not appear to occur in the real world.

You can apply the indifference curve model to explain the changes in the way we buy recorded music, see films, and make all our other consumption choices. We allocate our budgets to make our best affordable choices. Changes in prices and incomes change our best affordable choices and change consumption patterns.

(c) Income effect

To isolate the income effect, we confront Lisa with the new price of films but increase her income so that she can move from the original indifference curve, I_1, to the new one, I_2. The income effect is the move from K to J – an increase from 4 to 5 films a month.

Do these questions in Study Plan 8.3 and get instant feedback. MyEconLab

REVIEW QUIZ

1 When a consumer chooses the combination of goods and services to buy, what is she or he trying to achieve?
2 Explain the conditions that are met when a consumer has found the best affordable combination of goods and services to buy. (Use the terms *budget line*, *marginal rate of substitution* and *relative price* in your explanation.)
3 If the price of a normal good falls, what happens to the quantity demanded of that good?
4 Into what two effects can we divide the effect of a price change?
5 For a normal good, does the income effect reinforce the substitution effect or does it partly offset the substitution effect?

We're going to end this chapter by looking at some new ways of studying individual economic choices and consumer behaviour.

New Ways of Explaining Households' Choices

When William Stanley Jevons developed a theory in the 1860s, he would have loved to look inside people's brains and 'see' what he called 'utility'. But he believed that the human brain was the ultimate black box that could never be observed directly. For Jevons, and for most economists today, the purpose of consumer choice theory is to explain our *actions*, not what goes on inside our brains.

Economics has developed over the past 150 years with little help from and paying little attention to advances being made in psychology. Both economics and psychology seek to explain human behaviour, but they have developed different ways of attacking the challenge.

A few researchers *have* paid attention to the potential payoff from exploring economic problems by using the tools of psychology. These researchers, some economists and some psychologists, think that consumer theory is based on a view of how people make choices that attributes too much to reason and rationality. They propose an alternative approach based on the methods of psychology.

Other researchers, some economists and some neuroscientists, are using new tools to look inside the human brain and open up Jevons' 'black box'.

This section provides a very brief introduction to these new and exciting areas of economics. We'll explore the two related research agendas:

◆ Behavioural economics
◆ Neuroeconomics

Behavioural Economics

Behavioural economics studies the ways in which limits on the human brain's ability to compute and implement rational decisions influence economic behaviour – both the decisions that people make and the consequences of those decisions for the way markets work.

Behavioural economics starts with observed behaviour. It looks for anomalies – choices that do not seem to be rational. It then tries to account for the anomalies by using ideas developed by psychologists that emphasise features of the human brain that limit rational choice.

In behavioural economics, instead of being rational, people are assumed to have three impediments that prevent rational choice: bounded rationality, bounded willpower and bounded self-interest.

Bounded Rationality

Bounded rationality is rationality that is limited by the computing power of the human brain. We can't always work out the rational choice.

For Lisa, choosing between films and cola, it seems unlikely that she would have much trouble figuring out what to buy. But toss Lisa some uncertainty and the task becomes harder. She's read the reviews of *Skyfall* on Fandango, but does she really want to see that film? How much marginal utility will it give her? Faced with uncertainty, people might use rules of thumb, listen to the views of others, and make decisions based on gut instinct rather than on rational calculation.

Bounded Willpower

Bounded willpower is the less than perfect willpower that prevents us from making a decision that we know, at the time of implementing the decision, we will later regret.

Lisa might be feeling particularly thirsty when she passes a cola vending machine. Under Lisa's rational best affordable buying plan, she buys her cola at the discount shop, where she gets it for the lowest possible price. Lisa has already bought her cola for this month, but it is at home. Spending 50 pence on a can now means giving up a film later this month.

Lisa's rational choice is to ignore the temporary thirst and stick to her plan. But she might not possess the willpower to do so – sometimes she will and sometimes she won't.

Bounded Self-Interest

Bounded self-interest is the limited self-interest that results in sometimes suppressing our own interests to help others.

A winter storm hits Wales and Lisa, feeling sorry for the victims, donates £10 to a fund-raiser. She now has only £20 to spend on films and cola this month. The quantities that she buys are not, according to her indifference curve, the ones at her best affordable point.

The main applications of behavioural economics are in two areas: finance, where uncertainty is a key factor in decision making; and savings, where the future is a key factor.

But one behaviour observed by behavioural economists is more general and might affect your choices. It is called the endowment effect.

The Endowment Effect

The *endowment effect* is the tendency for people to value something more highly simply because they own it. If you are at your best affordable point, then the price you would be willing to accept to give up something that you own (for example, your coffee mug) should be the same as the price you are willing to pay for an identical one.

In experiments, students seem to display the endowment effect: the price they are willing to pay for a coffee mug that is identical to the one they own is *less* than the price they would be willing to accept to give up the coffee mug that they own. Behavioural economists say that this behaviour contradicts consumer theory.

Neuroeconomics

Neuroeconomics is the study of the activity of the human brain when a person makes an economic decision. The discipline uses the observational tools and ideas of neuroscience to obtain a better understanding of economic decisions.

Neuroeconomics is an experimental discipline. In an experiment, a person makes an economic decision and the electrical or chemical activity of the person's brain is observed and recorded using the same type of equipment that neurosurgeons use to diagnose brain disorders.

The observations provide information about which regions of the brain are active at different points in the process of making an economic decision.

Observations show that some economic decisions generate activity in the area of the brain (called the prefrontal cortex) where we store memories, analyse data and anticipate the consequences of our actions. If people make rational decisions, it is in this region of the brain that the decision occurs.

But observations also show that some economic decisions generate activity in the region of the brain (called the hippocampus) where we store memories of anxiety and fear. Decisions that are influenced by activity in this part of the brain might not be rational and be driven by fear or panic.

Neuroeconomists are also able to observe the amount of a brain hormone (called dopamine), the quantity of which increases in response to pleasurable events and decreases in response to disappointing events. These observations might one day enable neuroeconomists to actually measure 'utility' and shine a bright light inside what was once believed to be the ultimate black box.

Controversy

The new ways of studying consumer choice that we've briefly described here are being used more widely to study business decisions and decisions in financial markets, and this type of research is surely going to become more popular.

But behavioural economics and neuroeconomics generate controversy. Most economists hold the view of Jevons that the goal of economics is to explain the decisions that we observe people making and not to explain what goes on inside people's heads.

Most economists would prefer to probe apparent anomalies more deeply and figure out why they are not anomalies after all.

REVIEW QUIZ

1   Define behavioural economics.
2   What are the three limitations on human rationality that behavioural economics emphasises?
3   Define neuroeconomics.
4   What do behavioural economics and neuroeconomics seek to achieve?

Do these questions in Study Plan 8.4 and get instant feedback.   MyEconLab

You have now completed your study of households' choices and some new ideas about how people make economic choices.

Reading Between the Lines on pp. 188–189 shows you how the theory of households' choices explains why even though its price has risen people are buying larger quantities of value steak.

In the chapters that follow, we study the choices that firms make in their pursuit of profit and how those choices determine the supply of goods and services and the demand for productive resources.

Prime Beef versus Value Steak

The Telegraph, 17 December 2012

Blow for Families as Supermarket Own Brand Product Prices 'Rise by Nearly Half'

Andrew Hough

The prices of items in major supermarkets' own-brand budget ranges, . . . have risen sharply in the past year. . . .

Millions of families have been forced to tighten their belts in the downturn by switching to the cheaper value ranges launched by High Street supermarket giants. . . . But figures today showed some range of 'cheaper' products are now costing nearly double, among Britain's major supermarket chains. . . .

Experts today blamed the rises on higher costs and food inflation. . . . Researchers found 153 from 353 . . . value products available last week cost more than their equivalent value lines cost in 2011.

Price rises were recorded on produce including frying steak, up from £2.96 to £5.49 per kg and a 500g bag of grated cheese, up from £2.18 to £3. . . .

Rising prices will take the annual food bill for the average family to over £4,000 within a decade, up from £2,766 last year, heaping further pressure on already-stretched households.

Both Tesco and Sainsbury's insisted to *The Grocer*, the trade magazine which reported the research, that their budget ranges were as popular as ever.

 ## The Essence of the Story

- Supermarkets have expanded their value range of low-priced products.

- Shoppers are facing tighter budgets in the downturn and are switching to value products from premium brands.

- Supermarkets have increased the prices of many value brands, with some nearly doubling in price.

- Even with rising prices, supermarkets say shoppers still want value products.

Economic Analysis

- Prime steak (the premium cuts) and value steak (the cheaper cuts and mince) are substitutes for shoppers on tight budgets.

- Richard is one such shopper. He has a budget for steak of £24 a month. He buys two types of beef, prime steak at £12 per kilogram and value steak at £4 per kilogram.

- With this budget and these prices, Richard can afford 2 kilograms of prime steak if he buys no value steak, or 6 kilograms of value steak if he buys no prime steak.

- Figure 1 shows Richard's consumption possibilities as the light orange budget line.

- Figure 1 also shows Richard's indifference curves – the green curves – and the black dot at point C is his best affordable choice on indifference curve – I_2. He buys 1 kilogram of price steak and 3 kilograms of value steak each month.

- Now the price of value steak rises by 50 per cent to £6 per kilogram. The price of prime steak and Richard's steak budget remain unchanged.

- Richard's budget line rotates inward to become the dark orange line in Figure 1.

- Richard's best affordable point now become point J on indifference curve I_1. He continues to buy 3 kilograms of value steak but cuts his prime steak to 500 grams.

- Figure 2 explains Richard's choice by breaking it into a substitution effect and an income effect.

- The substitution effect (explained in Figure 8.9) is the move from C to K. With a rise in the price of value steak and no change in real income, Richard buys less value steak and more premium steak.

- The income effect is the move from K to J. When Richard's real income *falls*, he buys *more* value steak. Value steak is an inferior good.

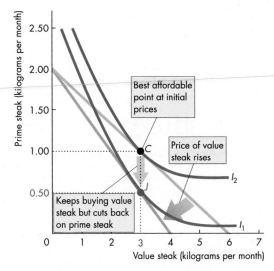

Figure 1 Price Effect

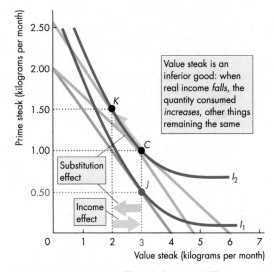

Figure 2 Substitution Effect and Income Effect

- In the example in Figure 2, the income effect exactly offsets the substitution effect. More likely, the income effect would be smaller than the substitution effect.

- Because value steak is an inferior good, supermarkets are saying it is still popular even though its price has risen relative to the price of prime steak.

SUMMARY

Key Points

Consumption Possibilities

(pp. 174–176)

◆ The budget line is the boundary between what a household can and cannot afford, given its income and the prices of goods.

◆ The point at which the budget line intersects the *y*-axis is the household's real income in terms of the good measured on that axis.

◆ The magnitude of the slope of the budget line is the relative price of good *x* (on the *x*-axis) in terms of good *y* (on the *y*-axis).

◆ A change in price changes the slope of the budget line. A change in income shifts the budget line but does not change its slope.

Do Problems 1 to 10 to get a better understanding of consumption possibilities.

Preferences and Indifference Curves

(pp. 177–180)

◆ A consumer's preferences can be represented by indifference curves. An indifference curve joins all the combinations of goods among which the consumer is indifferent.

◆ A consumer prefers any point above an indifference curve to any point on it and any point on an indifference curve to any point below it.

◆ The magnitude of the slope of an indifference curve is called the marginal rate of substitution.

◆ The marginal rate of substitution diminishes as consumption of the good measured on the *y*-axis decreases and consumption of the good measured on the *x*-axis increases.

Do Problems 11 to 15 to get a better understanding of preferences and indifference curves.

Predicting Consumer Behaviour

(pp. 180–185)

◆ A household consumes at its best affordable point. This point is on the budget line and on the highest attainable indifference curve, and has a marginal rate of substitution equal to the relative price.

◆ The effect of a price change (the price effect) can be divided into a substitution effect and an income effect.

◆ The change in quantity when the price changes but the consumer (hypothetically) remains on the initial indifference curve is the substitution effect.

◆ The substitution always results in an increase in consumption of the good whose relative price has decreased.

◆ The income effect is the effect of a change in income on consumption.

◆ For a normal good, the income effect reinforces the substitution effect. For an inferior good, the income effect works in the opposite direction to the substitution effect.

Do Problems 16 to 21 to get a better understanding of predicting consumer behaviour.

New Ways of Explaining Households' Choices (pp. 186–187)

◆ Behavioural economics studies limits on the ability of the human brain to compute and implement rational decisions.

◆ Bounded rationality, bounded willpower and bounded self-interest are believed to explain some choices.

◆ Neuroeconomics uses the ideas and tools of neuroscience to study the effects of economic events and choices inside the human brain.

Do Problems 22 and 23 to get a better understanding of the new ways of explaining households' choices.

Key Terms

Budget line, 174
Diminishing marginal rate of substitution, 178
Income effect, 183
Indifference curve, 177
Marginal rate of substitution, 178
Price effect, 181
Real income, 175
Relative price, 175
Substitution effect, 184

STUDY PLAN PROBLEMS AND APPLICATIONS

You can work Problems 1 to 21 in MyEconLab Chapter 6 Study Plan and get instant feedback.   MyEconLab

Consumption Possibilities
(Study Plan 8.1)

Use the following information in Problems 1 to 4.

Sara has an income of £12 a week. The price of popcorn is £3 a bag, and the price of a smoothie is £3.

1 Calculate Sara's real income in terms of smoothies. Calculate her real income in terms of popcorn.

2 What is the relative price of smoothies in terms of popcorn? What is the opportunity cost of a smoothie?

3 Calculate the equation for Sara's budget line (with bags of popcorn on the left side).

4 Draw a graph of Sara's budget line with the quantity of smoothies on the x-axis. What is the slope of Sara's budget line? What determines its value?

Use the following information in Problems 5 to 8.

Sara's income falls from £12 to £9 a week, while the price of popcorn is unchanged at £3 a bag and the price of a smoothie is unchanged at £3.

5 What is the effect of the fall in Sara's income on her real income in terms of smoothies?

6 What is the effect of the fall in Sara's income on her real income in terms of popcorn?

7 What is the effect of the fall in Sara's income on the relative price of a smoothie in terms of popcorn?

8 What is the slope of Sara's new budget line if it is drawn with smoothies on the x-axis?

Use the following information in Problems 9 and 10.

Sara's income is £12 a week. The price of popcorn rises from £3 to £6 a bag, and the price of a smoothie is unchanged at £3.

9 How does a rise in the price of popcorn affect Sara's real income in terms of smoothies and her real income in terms of popcorn?

10 How does a rise in the price of popcorn affect the relative price of a smoothie in terms of popcorn? What is the slope of Sara's new budget line if it is drawn with smoothies on the x-axis?

Preferences and Indifference Curves
(Study Plan 8.2)

11 Draw figures that show your indifference curves for the following pairs of goods. For each pair, explain whether the goods are perfect substitutes, perfect complements or unrelated. The pairs of goods are:

a Right gloves and left gloves

b Coca-Cola and Pepsi

c Neurofen and ibuprofen (the generic form of Neurofen)

d Desktop computers and laptop computers

e Strawberries and cream

12 Discuss the shape of the indifference curve for each of the following pairs of goods. Explain the relationship between the shape of the indifference curve and the marginal rate of substitution as the quantities of the two goods change. The pairs of goods are:

a Orange juice and smoothies

b Cricket balls and cricket bats

c Left shoe and right shoe

d Ice cream and fudge sauce

e Eye glasses and contact lenses

Use the following news clip in Problems 13 and 14.

The Year in Medicine

Sudafed, used by allergy sufferers, contains as the active ingredient pseudoephedrine, which is widely used to make home-made methamphetamine. Allergy sufferers looking to buy Sudafed must now show photo ID, and sign a logbook. The most common alternative, phenylephrine, isn't as effective as pseudoephedrine.

Source: *Time*, 4 December 2006

13 Sketch an indifference curve for Sudafed and phenylephrine that is consistent with this news clip. On your graph, identify combinations that allergy sufferers prefer, do not prefer, and are indifferent among.

14 Explain how the marginal rate of substitution changes as an allergy sufferer increases the consumption of Sudafed.

Use the following information in Problems 15 and 16.

With high petrol prices, 12 per cent of the people surveyed say that they have cancelled their Bank Holiday car trip and 11 per cent will take a shorter trip near home. That may save consumers some money, but it will also probably hurt service centres, which will sell less petrol and fewer snacks, and hurt hotels, which will have fewer rooms used and serve fewer casual meals.

15 Describe the degree of substitutability between Bank Holiday trips and other trip-related goods and services, and sketch a consumer's preference map that illustrates your description.

Predicting Consumer Behaviour
(Study Plan 8.3)

16 a Sketch a consumer's preference map between Bank Holiday trips and other goods and services. Draw a consumer's budget line prior to the rise in the price of petrol and mark the consumer's best affordable point.

   b On your graph, show how the best affordable point changes when the price of petrol rises.

Use the following information in Problems 17 and 18.

Pam has chosen her best affordable combination of biscuits and cereal bars. She spends all of her weekly income on 30 biscuits at £1 each and 5 cereal bars at £2 each. Next week, people expect the price of a biscuit to fall to 50p and the price of a cereal bar to rise to £5.

17 a Will Pam be able to buy and want to buy 30 biscuits and 5 cereal bars next week?

   b Which situation does Pam prefer: biscuits at £1 and cereal bars at £2 or biscuits at 50p and cereal bars at £5?

18 a If Pam changes how she spends her weekly income, will she buy more or fewer biscuits and more or fewer cereal bars?

   b When the prices change next week, will there be an income effect, a substitution effect or both at work?

19 **Shoppers Turn Scrooge as Cost-of-Living Pressures Bite into Retail Spending**

Extravagant shopping sprees on credit are being replaced with thrifty gifts and worries about being able to afford a decent Christmas lunch for the family, an exclusive online survey of more than 1,000 of its readers found.

      Source: *Daily Telegraph*, 15 November 2011

Draw a graph to show the effect of increased thriftiness on sales of Christmas gifts and food for the Christmas lunch.

Use the following news clip in Problems 20 and 21.

Boom Time For Charity Shops

High street retailers are feeling the squeeze in the economic downturn whilst charity shops open new shops. Charity shop sales are up 34 per cent on last year, hitting an all time high of £1 billion. More than 1 million more middle income families are now buying clothes and household goods second hand because their incomes are falling. Existing customers say they are making more frequent visits.

      Source: *The Telegraph*, 14 May 2012

20 a According to the news clip, is used clothing a normal good or an inferior good?

   b If the price of used clothing falls and income remains the same, explain how the quantity of used clothing bought changes.

   c If the price of used clothing falls and income remains the same, describe the substitution effect and the income effect that occur.

21 a Use a graph to illustrate a family's indifference curves for used clothing and other goods and services.

   b In your graph in part (a), draw two budget lines to show the effect of a fall in income on the quantity of used clothing purchased.

New Ways of Explaining Households' Choices (Study Plan 8.4)

Use the following news clip in Problems 22 and 23.

Eating Away the Innings in Baseball's Cheap Seats

Baseball and gluttony, two of America's favourite pastimes, are merging and taking hold at Major League Baseball stadiums: all-you-can-eat seats. Some fans try to 'set personal records' during their first game in the section, but by their second or third time in such seats they eat normally, just as they would at a game.

      Source: *USA Today*, 6 March 2008

22 a What conflict might exist between the best affordable point and setting 'personal records' for eating?

   b What does the fact that fans eat less at subsequent games indicate about the shape of the consumer's indifference curves as the quantity of food consumed increases?

23 a How can setting personal records for eating be reconciled with consumer theory?

   b Which ideas of behavioural economics are consistent with the information in the news clip?

ADDITIONAL PROBLEMS AND APPLICATIONS

Do these problems in MyEconLab if assigned by your lecturer.

MyEconLab

Consumption Possibilities

Use the following information in Problems 24 to 27.

Marc has a budget of £20 a month to spend on pizza and DVDs. The price of a pizza is £5, and the price of a DVD is £10.

24 What is the relative price of pizza in terms of DVDs and what is the opportunity cost of a pizza?

25 Calculate Marc's real income in terms of pizza. Calculate his real income in terms of DVDs.

26 Calculate the equation for Marc's budget line (with the quantity of pizza on the left side).

27 Draw a graph of Marc's budget line with the quantity of DVDs on the *x*-axis. What is the slope of Marc's budget line? What determines its value?

Use the following information in Problems 28 to 31.

Amy has £20 a week to spend on coffee and cake. The price of coffee is £4 a cup, and the price of cake is £2 a slice.

28 Calculate the relative price of cake in terms of coffee.

29 Calculate the equation for Amy's budget line (with cups of coffee on the left side).

30 If Amy's income increases to £24 a week and the prices of coffee and cake remain unchanged, describe the change in her budget line.

31 If the price of a cake slice doubles while the price of coffee remains at £4 a cup and Amy's income remains at £20, describe the change in her budget line.

Use the following news clip in Problems 32 and 33.

Petrol Prices Straining Budgets

Tesco's reports the lowest sales on non-essential goods for 20 years. Higher fuel and food prices are making customers cut back on electrical and entertainment goods. Higher fuel prices make it difficult for customers to cope on tight budgets.

Source: *The Guardian*, 5 October 2011

32 a Sketch a budget line for a household that spends its income on only two goods: petrol and entearnment goods, such as games. Identify the combinations of petrol and games that are affordable and those that are unaffordable.

b Sketch a second budget line to show how a rise in the price of petrol changes the affordable and unafford-able combinations of petrol and games. Describe how the household's consumption possibilities change.

33 How does a rise in the price of petrol change the relative price of a restaurant meal? How does a rise in the price of petrol change real income in terms of restaurant meals?

Preferences and Indifference Curves

Use the following information in Problems 34 and 35.

Rashid buys only books and DVDs and the figure shows his preference map.

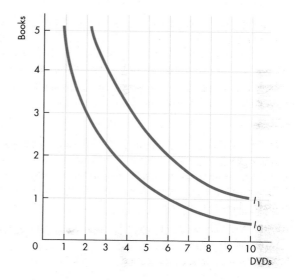

34 a If Rashid chooses 3 books and 2 DVDs, what is his marginal rate of substitution?

b If Rashid chooses 2 books and 6 DVDs, what is his marginal rate of substitution?

35 Do Rashid's indifference curves display diminishing marginal rate of substitution? Explain why or why not.

36 You May Be Paid More (or Less) Than You Think

It's so hard to put a price on happiness, isn't it? But if you've ever had to choose between a job you like and a better-paying one that you like less, you probably wished some economist would tell you how much job satisfac-tion is worth. Trust in management is by far the biggest component to consider. Say you get a new boss and your trust in management goes up a bit (say, up 1 point on a 10-point scale). That's like getting a 36 per cent pay raise. In other words, that increased level of trust will boost your level of overall satisfaction in life by about the same amount as a 36 per cent raise would.

Source: CNN, 29 March 2006

a Measure trust in management on a 10-point scale, measure pay on the same 10-point scale, and think of them as two goods. Sketch an indifference curve (with trust on the *x*-axis) that is consistent with the news clip.

b What is the marginal rate of substitution between trust in management and pay according to this news clip?

c What does the news clip imply about the principle of diminishing marginal rate of substitution? Is that implication likely to be correct?

Predicting Consumer Behaviour

Use the following information in Problems 37 and 38.

Jim has made his best affordable choice of muffins and coffee. He spends all of his income on 10 muffins at £1 each and 20 cups of coffee at £2 each. Now the price of a muffin rises to £1.50 and the price of coffee falls to £1.75 a cup.

37 a Will Jim now be able and want to buy 10 muffins and 20 coffees?

b Which situation does Jim prefer: muffins at £1 and coffee at £2 a cup or muffins at £1.50 and coffee at £1.75 a cup?

38 a If Jim changes the quantities that he buys, will he buy more or fewer muffins and more or less coffee?

b When the prices change, will there be an income effect, a substitution effect, or both at work?

Use the following information in Problems 39 to 41.

Sara's income is £12 a week. The price of popcorn is £3 a bag, and the price of cola is £1.50 a can. The figure shows Sara's preference map for popcorn and cola.

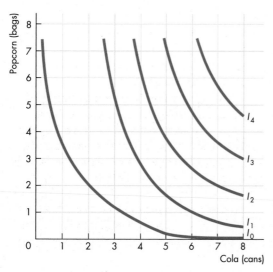

39 What quantities of popcorn and cola does Sara buy? What is Sara's marginal rate of substitution at the point at which she consumes?

40 Suppose that the price of cola rises to £3.00 a can and the price of popcorn and Sara's income remain the same. What quantities of cola and popcorn does Sara now buy? What are two points on Sara's demand curve for cola? Draw Sara's demand curve.

41 Suppose that the price of cola rises to £3.00 a can and the price of popcorn and Sara's income remain the same.

a What is the substitution effect of this price change and what is the income effect of the price change?

b Is cola a normal good or an inferior good? Explain.

New Ways of Explaining Consumer Choices

Use the following news clip in Problems 42 to 44.

Putting a Price on Human Life

Researchers at Stanford and the University of Pennsylvania estimated that a healthy human life is worth about $129,000. Using government records on treatment costs for kidney dialysis as a benchmark, the authors tried to pinpoint the threshold beyond which ensuring another 'quality' year of life was no longer financially worthwhile. The study comes amid debate over whether the government should start rationing healthcare on the basis of cost effectiveness.

Source: *Time*, 9 June 2008

42 Why might the government ration healthcare according to treatment that is 'financially worthwhile' as opposed to providing as much treatment as is needed by a patient, regardless of costs?

43 What conflict might exist between a person's valuation of his or her own life and the rest of society's valuation of that person's life?

44 How does the potential conflict between self-interest and the social interest complicate setting a financial threshold for healthcare treatments?

Economics in the News

45 After you have studied *Reading Between the Lines* on pp. 188–189, answer the following questions.

a Explain what affects your choice for premium cheese and value cheese.

b Sketch your budget line for premium cheese and value cheese and your indifference curves, and show your best affordable choice.

c If supermarkets double the price of value cheese but don't alter the price of premium cheese, how does this affect your choice?

d Explain whether value cheese is a normal good or an inferior good to you.

9 Organising Production

After studying this chapter you will be able to:

- Explain the economic problems that all firms face
- Distinguish between technological efficiency and economic efficiency
- Define and explain the principal–agent problem
- Distinguish between the different types of markets
- Explain why firms coordinate some economic activities and markets coordinate others

When Tim Berners-Lee invented the World Wide Web in 1990, he paved the way for the creation of thousands of profitable businesses such as Apple, Facebook, Google and Twitter. The Internet has also created new ways for businesses to organise, trade, advertise and monitor the actions of their employees. How do businesses operate efficiently?

In this chapter, you're going to learn about firms and the choices they make. In *Reading Between the Lines* at the end of the chapter, we'll look at the battle for Internet advertising revenue between Facebook and Google.

The Firm and Its Economic Problem

The 20 million or so firms in the EU differ in their size and in the scope of what they do. But they all perform the same basic economic functions. Each **firm** is an institution that hires factors of production and organises those factors to produce and sell goods and services. Our goal is to predict how firms behave. To do so, we need to know a firm's goals and the constraints it faces. We begin with the goals.

The Firm's Goal

When economists ask entrepreneurs what they are trying to achieve, they get many different answers. Some talk about making a high-quality product, others about business growth, others about market share, others about the job satisfaction of their workforce, and an increasing number today talk about social and environmental responsibility. All of these goals are pursued by firms, but they are not the fundamental goal. They are the means to that goal.

A firm's goal is to *maximise profit*. A firm that does not seek to maximise profit will either go out of business or be bought by a firm that does seek to maximise profit.

What is the profit that a firm seeks to maximise? To answer this question, we're going to look at Fashion First, a small firm that makes knitted jumpers. It is owned and operated by Norma.

Accounting Profit

In 2012, Fashion First received £400,000 a year for the jumpers sold and paid out £80,000 for wool, £20,000 for utilities, £120,000 for wages, £5,000 for lease of a computer from Dell, Inc. and £5,000 in interest on a bank loan. These expenses total £230,000, so the firm had a cash surplus of £170,000.

To measure the profit made by Fashion First, Norma's accountant subtracted £20,000 for depreciation of the firm's buildings and knitting machines from the £170,000 cash surplus. Depreciation is the fall in the value of the firm's capital. To calculate depreciation, accountants use standard rules set by accounting professionals. Using these rules, Norma's accountant calculated that Fashion First made a profit of £150,000 in 2012.

Economic Accounting

Accountants measure a firm's profit to ensure that a firm pays the correct amount of income tax and to show the bank how its loan has been used.

Economists measure a firm's profit to enable them to predict the firm's decisions, and the goal of these decisions is to maximise *economic profit*. **Economic profit** is equal to total revenue minus total cost, with total cost measured as the *opportunity cost of production*.

Opportunity Cost of Production

The *opportunity cost* of any action is the highest-valued alternative forgone. The *opportunity cost of production* is the value of the best alternative use of the resources that a firm uses in production.

A firm's opportunity cost of production is the value of *real* alternatives forgone. We express opportunity cost in money units so that we can compare and add up the value of the alternatives forgone. A firm's opportunity cost of production is the sum of the cost of using resources that are:

◆ Bought in the market

◆ Owned by the firm

◆ Supplied by the firm's owner

Resources Bought in the Market

A firm incurs an opportunity cost when it buys resources in the market. The amount spent on these resources is an opportunity cost of production because the firm could have bought different resources to produce some other good or service. For Fashion First, the resources bought in the market are wool, utilities, labour, a leased computer and a bank loan. The £230,000 spent on these items in 2012 could have been spent on other things, so it is an opportunity cost of producing jumpers.

Resources Owned by the Firm

A firm incurs an opportunity cost when it uses its own capital. The cost of using capital owned by the firm is an opportunity cost of production because the firm could sell the capital that it owns and rent capital from another firm. When a firm uses its own capital, it implicitly rents it from itself. In this case, the firm's opportunity cost of using the capital it owns is called the **implicit rental rate** of capital. The implicit rental rate has two components: economic depreciation and forgone interest.

Economic Depreciation

Accountants measure depreciation, the fall in the value of a firm's capital, using formulas that are unrelated to the change in the market value of capital. **Economic depreciation** is the fall in the *market value* of a firm's capital over a given period. It equals the market price of the capital at the beginning of the period minus the market price of the capital at the end of the period.

Suppose that Fashion First could have sold its buildings and knitting machines on 1 January 2012 for £400,000 and that it can sell the same capital on 31 December 2012 for £375,000. The firm's economic depreciation during 2012 is £25,000 (£400,000 − £375,000). This forgone £25,000 is an opportunity cost of production.

Forgone Interest

The funds used to buy capital could have been used for some other purpose, and in their next best use they would have earned interest. This forgone interest is an opportunity cost of production. Suppose that Fashion First used £300,000 of its own funds to buy capital. If the firm invested its £300,000 in bonds instead of a knitting factory (and rented the capital it needs to produce jumpers), it would have earned £15,000 a year in interest. This forgone interest is an opportunity cost of production.

Resources Supplied by the Firm's Owner

A firm's owner might supply *both* entrepreneurship and labour. The factor of production that organises a firm and makes its business decisions might be supplied by the firm's owner or by a hired entrepreneur. The return to entrepreneurship is profit, and the return that an entrepreneur can expect to receive *on average* is called **normal profit**. Normal profit is the cost of entrepreneurship and is an opportunity cost of production.

If Norma supplies entrepreneurial services herself, and if the normal profit she can earn on these services is £45,000 a year, this amount is an opportunity cost of production at Fashion First.

In addition to supplying entrepreneurship, the owner of a firm might supply labour but not take a wage. The opportunity cost of the owner's labour is the wage income that the owner forgoes by not taking the best alternative job. If Norma supplies labour to Fashion First, and if the wage she can earn on this labour at another firm is £55,000 a year, this amount of wages forgone is an opportunity cost of production at Fashion First.

Economic Accounting: A Summary

Table 9.1 summarises economic accounting. Fashion First's total revenue is £400,000, its opportunity cost of production is £370,000 and its economic profit is £30,000.

Norma's personal income is the £30,000 of economic profit plus the £100,000 that she earns by supplying resources to Fashion First.

The Firm's Decisions

To achieve the objective of maximum economic profit, a firm must make five basic decisions:

1. What to produce and in what quantities.
2. How to produce.
3. How to organise and compensate its managers and workers.
4. How to market and price its products.
5. What to produce itself and what to buy from others.

In all these decisions, a firm's actions are limited by the constraints that it faces. Our next task is to learn about these constraints.

Table 9.1

Economic Accounting

Item	Amount (pounds)	Total (pounds)
Total revenue		**400,000**
Cost of resources bought in the market		
Wool	80,000	
Utilities	20,000	
Wages paid	120,000	
Computer lease	5,000	
Bank interest paid	5,000	230,000
Cost of resources owned by firm		
Forgone interest	15,000	
Economic depreciation	25,000	40,000
Cost of resources supplied by owner		
Normal profit	45,000	
Norma's forgone wages	55,000	100,000
Opportunity cost of production		**370,000**
Economic profit		**30,000**

The Firm's Constraints

Three features of a firm's environment limit the maximum profit it can make. They are:

◆ Technology constraints

◆ Information constraints

◆ Market constraints

Technology Constraints

Economists define technology broadly. A **technology** is any method of producing a good or service. Technology includes the detailed designs of machines. It also includes the layout of the workplace and the organisation of the firm. For example, the shopping centre is a technology for producing retail services. It is a different technology from catalogue shopping, which in turn is different from the high street stores.

It might seem surprising that a firm's profits are limited by technology. Every year we learn about the latest technological advances that will revolutionise future production and consumption. Technology is advancing, but to produce more output and gain more revenue with current technology, a firm must hire more resources and incur greater costs. At any point in time, the increase in profit that the firm can achieve is limited by the technology currently available. For example, using its current plant and workforce, BMW can produce some maximum number of cars per day. To produce more cars per day, BMW must hire more resources, which increases BMW's costs and limits the increase in profit that BMW can make by selling the additional cars.

Information Constraints

A business manager can never possess all the information needed to make decisions. Businesses lack information about the present and the future – uncertainty. For example, suppose you plan to buy a new computer for your business. When should you buy it? The answer depends on how the price is going to change in the future. Where should you buy it? The answer depends on the prices at many different suppliers. To get the best deal, you must compare the quality and price in all the different shops. The opportunity cost of actually getting all this information and making all these comparisons will exceed the cost of the computer!

Similarly, a firm is constrained by limited information about the quality and effort of its workforce, the current and future plans of its customers, and the plans of its competitors. Workers may slacken off while managers believe they are working hard. Customers may switch to competing suppliers. Firms must face competition from new firms and the new products and services they offer.

Firms try to create incentive systems for workers to ensure they work hard even when no one is monitoring their efforts. Firms also spend billions every year on market research and product development. But none of these efforts and expenditures eliminates the problems of incomplete information and uncertainty. Again, the cost of coping with limited information and uncertainty itself limits profit.

Market Constraints

What each firm can sell and the price it can obtain are constrained by the willingness of customers to pay and by the prices and marketing efforts of other firms. Similarly, the resources that each firm can buy and the prices it must pay are limited by the willingness of people to work for and invest in the firm. Firms spend billions every year marketing and selling their products. Some of the most creative minds strive to find the right message that will produce a knockout television advertisement. Market constraints and the expenditures firms make to overcome them limit the profit a firm can make.

 REVIEW QUIZ

1   What is a firm's fundamental goal and what happens if the firm does not pursue this goal?

2   Why do accountants and economists calculate a firm's cost and profit in different ways?

3   What are the items that make opportunity cost different from the accountants' measure of cost?

4   Why is normal profit an opportunity cost?

5   What are the constraints that each firm faces? How does each constraint limit the firm's profit?

Do these questions in Study Plan 9.1 and get instant feedback.   MyEconLab

In the rest of this chapter and in Chapters 10 to 13, we study the decisions that firms make. You will learn how to predict a firm's behaviour as the response to both the constraints that it faces and the changes in those constraints. We begin by taking a closer look at the technology constraints that firms face.

Technological and Economic Efficiency

Microsoft employs a large workforce, and most Microsoft workers possess a large amount of human capital. But the firm also uses a small amount of physical capital. In contrast, an oil extraction company employs a huge amount of drilling equipment (physical capital) and relatively little labour. Why? The answer lies in the concept of efficiency. There are two concepts of production efficiency: technological efficiency and economic efficiency. **Technological efficiency** occurs when the firm produces a given output by using the least amount of inputs. **Economic efficiency** occurs when the firm produces a given output at least cost. Let's explore the two concepts of efficiency by studying an example.

Suppose that there are four alternative techniques for making TV sets:

A *Robot production.* One person monitors the entire computer-driven process.

B *Production line.* Workers specialise in a small part of the job as the emerging TV set passes them on a production line.

C *Hand-tool production.* A single worker uses a few hand tools to make a TV set.

D *Bench production.* Workers specialise in a small part of the job but walk from bench to bench to perform their tasks.

Table 9.2 sets out the amounts of labour and capital required by each of these four methods to make 10 TV sets a day.

Which of these alternative methods are technologically efficient?

Technological Efficiency

Recall that *technological efficiency* occurs when the firm produces a given output by using the least amount of inputs. Inspect the numbers in Table 9.2 and notice that method A uses the most capital but the least labour. Method C uses the most labour but the least capital. Method B and method D use less capital but more labour than method A and less labour but more capital than method C.

Compare methods B and D. Method D requires 100 workers and 10 units of capital to produce 10 TV sets.

Table 9.2

Four Ways of Making 10 TV Sets a Day

	Quantities of inputs	
Method	Labour	Capital
A Robot production	1	1,000
B Production line	10	10
C Hand-tool production	1,000	1
D Bench production	100	10

Those same 10 TV sets can be produced by method B with 10 workers and the same 10 units of capital. Because method D uses the same amount of capital but more labour than method B, method D is not technologically efficient.

Are any of the other methods not technologically efficient? The answer is no. Each of the other three methods is technologically efficient. Method A uses more capital but less labour than method B, and method C uses more labour but less capital than method B.

Which of these methods are economically efficient?

Economic Efficiency

Recall that *economic efficiency* occurs when the firm produces a given output at least cost. Method D, which is technologically inefficient, is also economically inefficient. It uses the same amount of capital as method B but 10 times as much labour, so it costs more. A technologically inefficient method is never economically efficient.

One of the three technologically efficient methods is economically efficient. But which method is economically efficient depends on factor prices.

In Table 9.3(a), the wage rate is £75 per day and the rental rate of capital is £250 per day. By studying Table 9.3(a), you can see that method B has the lowest cost and is the economically efficient method.

In Table 9.3(b), the wage rate is £150 per day and the rental rate of capital is £1 per day. Looking at Table 9.3(b), you can see that method A has the lowest cost and is the economically efficient method. In this case, capital is cheap relative to labour, so the method that uses the most capital is the economically efficient method.

Table 9.3

The Costs of Different Ways of Making 10 TV Sets a Day

(a) Wage rate £75 per day. Capital rental rate £250 per day

Method	Inputs Labour	Capital	Labour cost (£75 per day)		Capital cost (£250 per day)		Total cost
A	1	1,000	£75	+	£250,000	=	£250,075
B	10	10	750	+	2,500	=	3,250
C	1,000	1	75,000	+	2,500	=	75,250

(b) Wage rate £150 per day. Capital rental rate £1 per day

Method	Inputs Labour	Capital	Labour cost (£150 per day)		Capital cost (£1 per day)		Total cost
A	1	1,000	£150	+	£1,000	=	£1,150
B	10	10	1,500	+	10	=	1,510
C	1,000	1	150,000	+	1	=	150,001

(c) Wage rate £1 per day. Capital rental rate £1,000 per day

Method	Inputs Labour	Capital	Labour cost (£1 per day)		Capital cost (£1,000 per day)		Total cost
A	1	1,000	1	+	£1,000,000	=	£1,000,001
B	10	10	10	+	10,000	=	10,010
C	1,000	1	1,000	+	1,000	=	2,000

In Table 9.3(c), the wage rate is £1 per day and the rental rate of capital is £1,000 per day. You can see that method *C* has the lowest cost and is economically efficient. In this case, labour is so cheap relative to capital that the method that uses the most labour is the economically efficient method.

From these examples, you can see that while technological efficiency depends only on what is feasible, economic efficiency depends on the relative costs of resources. The economically efficient method is the one that uses the smaller amount of a more expensive resource and a larger amount of a less expensive resource.

A firm that is not economically efficient does not maximise profit. Natural selection favours efficient firms, and inefficient firms disappear. Inefficient firms go out of business or are taken over by firms that produce with lower costs.

 REVIEW QUIZ

1   Is a firm technologically efficient if it uses the latest technology? Why or why not?
2   Is a firm economically inefficient if it can cut costs by producing less? Why or why not?
3   Explain the key distinction between technological efficiency and economic efficiency.
4   Why do some firms use lots of capital and not much labour, while others use very little capital and lots of labour?

Do these questions in Study Plan 9.2 and get instant feedback.   MyEconLab

---

Next we'll study information constraints that firms face and the diversity of organisational structures that these constraints generate.

 # Information and Organisation

Each firm organises the production of goods and services by combining and coordinating the factors of production it hires. But there is variety across firms in how they organise production. Firms use a mixture of two systems:

◆ Command systems
◆ Incentive systems

Command Systems

A **command system** is a method of organising production that uses a managerial hierarchy. Commands pass downward through the managerial hierarchy and information passes upward. Managers collect and process information about the performance of the people under their control, make decisions about commands to issue, and report to their own superiors.

The military uses the purest form of command system. Command systems in firms are less rigid than those in the military but share similar features. A chief executive officer (CEO) sits at the top of a firm's command system. Executives report to and receive commands from the CEO and pass their own commands down to middle managers, who in turn supervise the day-to-day operations of the business.

Small-scale firms have one or two layers of managers while large-scale firms have several layers. As production processes have become ever more complex, management ranks have swollen. Managers always have incomplete information about the efforts of those for whom they are responsible. It is for this reason that firms use incentive systems.

Incentive Systems

An **incentive system** is a method of organising production that uses a market-like mechanism inside the firm. Instead of issuing commands, managers create compensation schemes that induce workers to perform in ways that maximise the firm's profit.

Incentive systems operate at all levels in a firm. CEOs share in the firm's profit, factory floor workers receive wages based on the quantity they produce, and sales representatives, who spend most of their working time alone and unsupervised, are induced to work hard by being paid a small salary and a large performance-related bonus.

The Principal–Agent Problem

The **principal–agent problem** is the problem of devising compensation rules that induce an *agent* to act in the best interest of a *principal*. The principal might be the firm's shareholders, in which case the managers are the *agents*. The shareholders (the principals) want to induce the managers (the agents) to act in the shareholders' interest. Or the principals might be the managers, in which case the agents are the workers below the managers. There is a chain of principal–agent relationships throughout a firm.

Agents pursue their own goals and often impose costs on a principal. For example, the goal of a shareholder of the HSBC Bank (a principal) is to maximise the bank's profit. But the bank's profit depends on the actions of its managers (agents), who have their own goals. A manager might want to expand the size of her workforce to gain status when this action is inefficient.

Issuing commands does not solve the principal–agent problem. In most firms, the shareholders can't monitor the managers and often the managers can't monitor workers. Each principal must create incentives that induce each agent to work in the interests of the principal.

Coping with the Principal–Agent Problem

Three ways of coping with the principal–agent problem are:

◆ Ownership
◆ Incentive pay
◆ Long-term contracts

Ownership

By assigning ownership (or part-ownership) of a business to managers or workers, it is sometimes possible to induce a job performance that increases the firm's profits. Part-ownership is quite common for senior managers but less common for workers. In the UK, the John Lewis partnership is an example of a business where all employees own part of the company.

Incentive Pay

Incentive pay schemes – pay related to performance – are very common. Incentives are based on a variety of performance criteria such as profits, production or sales targets. Promoting an employee for good performance is another example of the use of incentive pay.

Long-Term Contracts

Long-term contracts tie the long-term fortunes of managers and workers (agents) to the success of the principal(s) – the owner(s) of the firm. For example, a multi-year employment contract for a CEO encourages that person to take a long-term view and devise strategies that achieve maximum profit over a sustained period.

These three ways of coping with the principal–agent problem give rise to different types of business organisation.

Types of Business Organisations

The three main types of business organisations are:

◆ Proprietorship
◆ Partnership
◆ Company

Proprietorship

A *proprietorship* is a firm with a single owner who has unlimited liability. *Unlimited liability* is the legal

ECONOMICS IN THE NEWS

Principals and Agents Get it Wrong

JPMorgan Pay May be Clawed Back

In May 2012, JPMorgan Chase announced that traders in London had incurred losses of $2 billion. CEO Jamie Dimon said the losses arose from a 'flawed, complex, poorly reviewed, poorly executed, and poorly monitored' trading strategy. JPMorgan Chase's share price fell on the news. One top executive took early retirement.

JPMorgan executives and traders are compensated by results with bonus payments in cash and share options. Dimon said 'It's likely that there will be clawbacks' of compensation.

Sources: *AP, Bloomberg* and *Reuters*, May/June 2012

The Questions

◆ Who are the principals and who are the agents?
◆ How did JPMorgan try to cope with its principal–agent problem?
◆ How, on the occasion reported here, did JPMorgan get it wrong?
◆ What role did JPMorgan's share price play?

The Answers

◆ The JPMorgan shareholders are principals and Jamie Dimon is their agent.
◆ Jamie Dimon, as CEO, is a principal and the top executives are agents.
◆ JPMorgan top executives are principals, and the traders who incurred the losses are agents.
◆ JPMorgan tried to cope with the principal–agent problem by compensating agents with performance bonuses, profit shares through share options, and the possibility of clawbacks for poor performance.

◆ We don't know the details, but based on what Jamie Dimon said, it seems that the specific trading activities that incurred a $2 billion loss were complex and not properly understood either by the traders (the agents at the end of the line) or by the managers who designed the trading activities.

◆ The fall in JPMorgan's share price (shown in Figure 1) not only lowered the wealth of shareholders but also lowered the compensation of Jamie Dimon and the other executives compensated with share options.

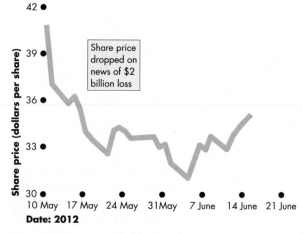

Figure 1 JPMorgan Share Price

responsibility for all the debts of a firm up to an amount equal to the entire wealth of the owner including the personal property of the owner. The proprietor makes management decisions, receives the firm's profits and is responsible for its losses. Profits are taxed at the same rate as other sources of the proprietor's income.

Partnership

A *partnership* is a firm with two or more owners who have unlimited liability. Partners must agree on an appropriate management structure and on how to divide the firm's profits among themselves. The profits of a partnership are taxed as the personal income of the owners. But each partner is legally liable for all the debts of the partnership (limited only by the wealth of an individual partner). Liability for the full debts of the partnership is called *joint unlimited liability*.

Company

A *company* is a firm owned by one or more limited liability shareholders. *Limited liability* means that the owners have legal liability only for the value of their initial investment. This limitation of liability means that if the company becomes bankrupt, its owners are not required to use their personal wealth to pay the company's debts.

Company profits are taxed independently of shareholders' incomes. Because shareholders pay taxes on the income they receive as dividends on shares, corporate profits are taxed twice. Shareholders also pay capital gains tax when they sell a share for a higher price than they paid for it. Company shares generate capital gains when a company retains some of its profit and reinvests it in profitable activities. So even retained earnings are taxed twice because of the capital gains they generate.

Pros and Cons of Different Types of Firms

The different types of business organisation arise from firms trying to cope with the principal–agent problem. Each type of business has advantages in particular situations and because of its special advantages, each type continues to exist. Each type of business organisation also has its disadvantages. Table 9.4 summarises these and other pros and cons of the different types of firms.

Table 9.4

The Pros and Cons of Different Types of Firms

Type of firm	Pros	Cons
Proprietorship	◆ Easy to set up ◆ Simple decision making ◆ Profits taxed only once as owner's income	◆ Bad decisions not checked by need for consensus ◆ Owner's entire wealth at risk ◆ Firm dies with owner ◆ Capital is expensive ◆ Labour is expensive
Partnership	◆ Easy to set up ◆ Diversified decision making ◆ Can survive withdrawal of partner ◆ Profits taxed only once as owners' incomes	◆ Achieving consensus may be slow and expensive ◆ Owners' entire wealth at risk ◆ Withdrawal of a partner may create capital shortage ◆ Capital is expensive
Company	◆ Owners have limited liability ◆ Large-scale, low-cost capital available ◆ Professional management not restricted by ability of owners ◆ Perpetual life ◆ Long-term labour contracts cut labour costs	◆ Complex management structure can make decisions slow and expensive ◆ Profits taxed twice as company profit and as shareholders' income

ECONOMICS IN ACTION

Types of Firms in the UK Economy

Companies Most Common

At the start of 2012, about 4.8 million UK firms employed 23.9 million people and made £3.1 billion of revenue. Figure 1 shows that 23 per cent of the firms were proprietorships, 12 per cent were partnerships and 65 per cent were companies.

Small Firms Dominate

Figure 1 also shows that 76 per cent of UK firms employ fewer than 5 people. Another 19 per cent employ from 5 to 19 people. And only 5 per cent of UK firms have 20 employees or more. Not visible in the figure, less than half of 1 per cent of UK firms employ 250 people or more.

Variety Across Industries

Figure 2 shows how firm types differ across industries. Proprietorships and partnerships, mainly small firms with no

limited liability, dominate in agriculture, forestry and fishing, and are important in transport and storage, health, and hotel and food services. Companies, larger firms with limited liability, dominate in finance, property, manufacturing, education and construction and are important in all sectors of the economy except agriculture.

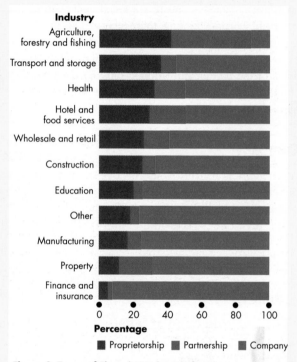

Figure 2 Types of Firms in Various Industries

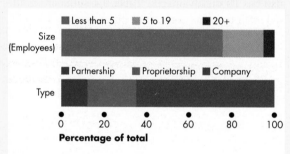

Figure 1 Size and Types of Firms

Source of data: UK Business Activity, Size and Location, 2012, Tables B2 and B5.2a, b and c. Office for National Statistics.

REVIEW QUIZ

1 Explain the distinction between a command system and an incentive system.
2 What is the principal–agent problem? What are three ways in which firms try to cope with it?
3 What are the three types of firms? Explain the advantages and disadvantages of each type.

Do these questions in Study Plan 9.3 and get instant feedback.   MyEconLab

You've now seen how technological constraints and information constraints influence the way firms operate. You've seen why some firms operate with a large amount of labour and human capital and a small amount of physical capital. You've also seen how firms use a mixture of command and incentive systems and employ different types of business organisation to cope with the principal–agent problem.

Your next task is to look at the variety of market situations in which firms operate and to classify the different market environments in which firms do business.

Markets and the Competitive Environment

The markets in which firms operate vary a great deal. Some markets are highly competitive and profits are hard to come by. Some appear to be almost free from competition, and firms in these markets make large profits. Some markets are dominated by fierce advertising campaigns in which each firm seeks to persuade buyers that it has the best products. Some markets display a war-like character.

Economists identify four market types:

◆ Perfect competition
◆ Monopolistic competition
◆ Oligopoly
◆ Monopoly

Perfect Competition

Perfect competition arises when there are many firms that sell an identical product, many buyers, and no restrictions on the entry of new firms into the industry. The many firms and buyers are all well informed about the prices of the products of each firm in the industry. The worldwide markets for wheat, rice and other grain crops are examples of perfect competition.

Monopolistic Competition

Monopolistic competition is a market structure in which a large number of firms compete by making similar but slightly different products. Making a product slightly different from the product of a competing firm is called **product differentiation**.

Firms in monopolistic competition are in fierce competition with each other. But product differentiation gives each monopolistically competitive firm an element of monopoly power. The firm is the sole producer of the particular version of the good in question.

For example, in the market for running shoes, Nike, Adidas, Fila, Asics and many other firms compete, but all make their own version of the perfect shoe. Each of these firms is the sole producer of a particular brand and so has a monopoly on that particular brand of shoe.

Differentiated products need not be different products. What matters is that consumers perceive the products to be different. For example, different brands of ibuprofen tablets are chemically identical and differ only in their packaging.

Oligopoly

Oligopoly is a market structure in which a small number of firms compete. Aeroplane manufacture, international air transport and computer software are examples of oligopolistic industries. Oligopolies might produce

almost identical products, such as the colas produced by Coca-Cola and PepsiCo; or they might produce differentiated products such as the Airbus A380 and the Boeing 747.

Monopoly

Monopoly arises when there is one firm that produces a good or service for which no close substitute exists and in which the firm is protected from competition by a barrier preventing the entry of new firms. In some places, the phone, gas, electricity and water suppliers are local monopolies – monopolies restricted to a given location. Microsoft, the software developer that created Windows, the operating system used by the vast majority of PCs, is an example of a global monopoly.

Perfect competition is the most extreme form of competition. Monopoly is the most extreme absence of competition. The other two market types fall between these extremes.

We've described the four types of markets, but how do we recognise them? You would probably have little difficulty recognising the difference between a perfectly competitive market and a monopoly market. But how would you distinguish between monopolistic competition and oligopoly?

Identifying a Market Structure

Many factors must be taken into account to determine which market structure describes a particular real-world market. One of these factors is the extent to which the market is dominated by a small number of firms. To measure this feature of markets, economists use indexes called measures of concentration.

Measures of Concentration

The most common measure of concentration uses total revenue and puts five firms in the group of largest firms. The result is the **five-firm concentration ratio**, which is the percentage of total revenue (or the value of sales) in an industry accounted for by the five firms with the largest value of sales. The range of the concentration ratio is from almost zero for perfect competition to 100 for monopoly.

Table 9.5 shows two hypothetical calculations of the five-firm concentration ratio, one for shoe manufacturing and one for egg farming. In this example, there are 15 firms in the shoe manufacturing industry. The largest five firms have 81 per cent of total industry sales, so the five-firm concentration ratio for that industry is 81 per cent. In the egg-producing industry, with 1,005 firms,

---

Table 9.5

Concentration Ratio Calculations

Shoemakers		Egg farmers	
Firm	Sales (millions of pounds)	Firm	Sales (millions of pounds)
Lace-up plc	250	Bills's	0.9
Finefoot plc	200	Sue's	0.7
Easyfit plc	180	Jane's	0.5
Comfy plc	120	Tom's	0.4
Loafers plc	70	Jill's	0.3
Top 5 sales	820	Top 5 sales	2.8
Other 10 firms	190	Other 1,000 firms	349.2
Industry sales	1,010	Industry sales	352.0

Five-firm concentration ratios:

Shoemakers: $\dfrac{820}{1,010} = 81$ per cent

Egg farmers: $\dfrac{2.8}{352} = 0.8$ per cent

the top five firms account for only 0.8 per cent of total industry sales. In this case, the five-firm concentration ratio is 0.8 per cent.

The five-firm concentration ratio helps us measure the degree of competitiveness of a market. A low concentration ratio indicates a high degree of competition, and a high concentration ratio indicates an absence of competition. In the extreme case of monopoly, the concentration ratio is 100 per cent because the largest (and only) firm makes the entire industry sales. Between these extremes, the five-firm concentration ratio is regarded as being a useful indicator of the likelihood of collusion among firms in an oligopoly. If the concentration ratio exceeds 60 per cent, it is likely that firms have a high degree of market power and may collude and behave like a monopoly.

If the concentration ratio is less than 40 per cent, the industry is regarded as competitive. A concentration ratio between 40 and 60 per cent indicates that the market structure is oligopoly.

 ## ECONOMICS IN ACTION

Concentration in Europe

Concentration ratios for Europe are calculated from the revenue data of individual firms and cover most public and private firms. The five-firm concentration ratio is calculated as the total revenue of the top five revenue earners in an industry divided by the total revenue in the industry. Figure 1 shows some of these five-firm concentration ratios as a percentage. Plastic, furniture and paint making all have low concentration ratios, which indicate that they are relatively competitive. Iron mining, pharmaceuticals, tobacco and satellite communications all have relatively high concentration ratios, which indicate a high degree of market power. Paper making, travel agents and hotels have low to intermediate levels of concentration, which indicate some but limited market power.

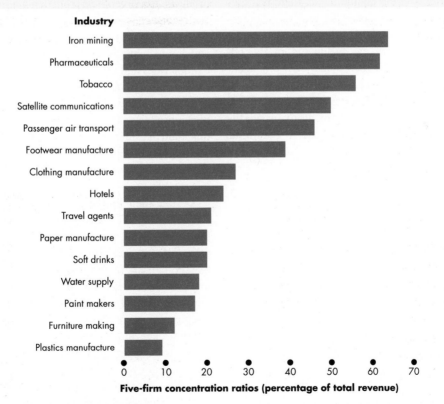

Figure 1 Concentration Ratios

Source of data: Amadeus Database 2012. The data are for 2011.

Limitations of Concentration Measures

Concentration ratios are useful, but they have some limitations. They must be supplemented by other information to determine the market structure of an industry and the degree of market power of firms in that industry. The three key problems are:

◆ The geographical scope of the market

◆ Barriers to entry and firm turnover

◆ Market and industry correspondence

Geographical Scope of the Market

Concentration ratio data are based on a *national* view of the market. Many goods are sold in a national market, and the concentration measures for them are useful.

But some goods are sold in a *regional* market. There are many national firms but few firms in each regional market. In this type of market, the national concentration ratios underestimate the true degree of concentration. The brewing industry is an example of a good in which the local market is more relevant than the national market. So although the national concentration ratio for brewers is in the middle range, there is a high degree of concentration in most regions.

Other industries operate in a *global* market. So although the largest five car producers in the UK account for 80 per cent of all cars sold by UK producers, they account for a smaller percentage of the total UK car market, which includes imports. In the global market for cars, UK producers account for an even smaller percentage of total sales. In this case, the national concentration ratios overestimate the true degree of concentration.

Barriers to Entry and Firm Turnover

Measures of concentration do not measure the severity of barriers to entry in a market. Some industries are highly concentrated but their markets have virtually free entry and a high turnover of firms. For example, many small towns have few restaurants, but there are few restrictions on opening a restaurant. Many firms enter and exit with great regularity.

Even if the turnover of firms in a market is limited, an industry might be competitive because of *potential entry* – because a few firms in the market face competition from many firms that can easily enter the market and will do so if economic profits are available.

Market and Industry Correspondence

The classifications used to calculate concentration ratios allocate every firm in the economy to a particular industry. But markets for particular goods do not usually correspond to these industries, for three reasons.

First, markets are often narrower than industries. For example, the pharmaceutical industry, which has a low concentration ratio, operates in many separate markets for individual products – for example, measles vaccine and AIDS-fighting drugs. These drugs do not compete with each other, so this industry, which looks competitive, includes firms that are monopolies (or near monopolies) in markets for individual drugs.

Second, most firms make many products. For example, the tobacco firms also operate in the food and insurance industries. The privatised water companies operate hotels and printing works. The value of sales for each firm show up in the industry to which the firm has been assigned. So their contribution to the industry to which they have been assigned might be overestimated.

Third, firms switch from one market to another depending on profit opportunities. Virgin, which today produces air transport services, train services and other products, has diversified from being a retail record shop and recording studio. Virgin no longer produces albums. Today, the Virgin group's products include credit cards and home loans, soft drinks, mobile phones, wines, balloon rides and more.

Publishers of newspapers, magazines and textbooks are today rapidly diversifying into Internet and multimedia products. These switches among industries show that there is much scope for entering and exiting an industry, and so measures of concentration have limited usefulness in describing the true degree of competition in a market.

Despite their limitations, concentration measures do provide a basis for determining the degree of competition in a market, provided they are supplemented with other information about the geographical scope of a market, barriers to entry, and the extent to which large, multi-product firms straddle a variety of markets. The less concentrated an industry and the lower its barriers to entry, the more closely it approximates perfect competition. The more concentrated an industry and the higher the barriers to entry, the more it approximates oligopoly or even monopoly.

Table 9.6 summarises the characteristics of different market structures and their concentration ratios.

Table 9.6

Market Structure

Characteristics	Perfect competition	Monopolistic competition	Oligopoly	Monopoly
Number of firms in industry	Many	Many	Few	One
Product	Identical	Differentiated	Either identical or differentiated	No close substitutes
Barriers to entry	None	None	Moderate	High
Firm's control over price	None	Some	Considerable	Considerable or regulated
Concentration ratio	0	Low	High	100
Examples	Agricultural products	Cosmetics, bread, clothing	Washing powders, cereals	Local water utility, postal letter service

UK Market Structures

The majority of markets for goods and services in Europe are highly competitive, and only a few markets are monopolies. For example, more than 70 per cent by value of goods and services bought and sold in the UK are traded in highly competitive markets. Where monopoly does arise, it is usually in the public services, although with privatisation public services have become more competitive.

But market power can still be strong in markets where privatisation attracts few new entrants, such as in the telecommunications industry. Less than 6 per cent of goods and services traded in the UK markets are essentially uncompetitive. Oligopoly is more common in manufacturing than in the services sector, but more than 55 per cent of UK manufacturing industries have a concentration ratio of less than 40 per cent.

The overall level of concentration in an economy can be measured by the proportion of total output accounted for by the largest 100 firms. The UK aggregate concentration ratio in manufacturing increased in the post-war period, indicating an increase in market power, but it levelled off in the 1970s and 1980s and has fallen in recent years. The increase in concentration resulted from several waves of merger activity and the growth of transnational companies serving new global markets. But given the growth in world trade and advances in telecommunications and low-cost transport, many UK firms operate in global markets, which are highly competitive.

 REVIEW QUIZ

1 What are the four market types? Explain the distinguishing characteristics of each.
2 Describe the five-firm concentration ratio.
3 Under what conditions do measures of concentration give a good indication of the degree of competition in the market?
4 Is our economy competitive? Is it becoming more competitive or less competitive?

Do these questions in Study Plan 9.4 and get instant feedback.   MyEconLab

You now know the variety of market types and the way we classify firms and industries into the different market types. Our final question in this chapter is: what determines which items firms decide to buy from other firms rather than produce for themselves?

Produce or Outsource? Firms and Markets

To produce a good or service, even a simple one such as a shirt, factors of production must be hired and their activities coordinated. To produce a good as complicated as an iPhone, an enormous range of specialist factors of production must be coordinated.

Factors of production can be coordinated either by firms or by markets. We'll describe these two ways of organising production and then see why firms play a crucial role in achieving an efficient use of resources.

Firm Coordination

Firms hire labour, capital and land, and by using a mixture of command systems and incentive systems (see p. 201) organise and coordinate their activities to produce goods and services.

Firm coordination occurs when you take your car to the garage for an oil change, brake check and service. The garage owner hires a mechanic and tools and coordinates all the activities that get your car serviced. Firms also coordinate the production of cornflakes, golf clubs and a host of other items.

Market Coordination

Markets coordinate production by adjusting prices and making the decisions of buyers and sellers of factors of production and components consistent. Markets can coordinate production.

Market coordination occurs to produce a rock concert. A promoter books a stadium, rents some stage equipment, hires some audio and video recording engineers and technicians, engages some rock groups, a superstar, a publicity agent and a ticket agent. The promoter sells tickets to thousands of rock fans, audio rights to a recording company, and video and broadcasting rights to a television network. All these transactions take place in markets that coordinate this huge variety of factors of production.

Outsourcing, buying parts or products from other firms, is another example of market coordination. Car makers outsource the production of windshields, windows, transmission systems, engines, tyres and many other auto parts. Apple outsources the entire production of iPods and iPhones.

What determines whether a firm or a market coordinates a particular set of activities?

Why Firms?

How does a firm decide whether to buy an item from another firm or manufacture it itself? The answer is cost. Taking account of the opportunity cost of time as well as the costs of the other inputs, a firm uses the method that costs least. In other words, it uses the economically efficient method.

If a task can be performed at a lower cost by markets than by a firm, markets will do the job and any attempt to set up a firm to replace such market activity will be doomed to failure.

Firms coordinate economic activity when a task can be performed more efficiently by a firm than by markets. Firms are often more efficient than markets as coordinators of economic activity because they can achieve:

◆ Lower transactions costs
◆ Economies of scale
◆ Economies of scope
◆ Economies of team production

Lower Transactions Costs

Firms eliminate transactions costs. **Transactions costs** are the costs arising from finding someone with whom to do business, of reaching an agreement about the price and other aspects of the exchange, and of ensuring that the terms of the agreement are fulfilled. *Market* transactions require buyers and sellers to get together and to negotiate the terms and conditions of their trading. Sometimes lawyers have to be hired to draw up contracts. A broken contract leads to still more expenses. A *firm* can lower such transactions costs by reducing the number of individual transactions undertaken.

Imagine getting your car fixed using market coordination. You hire a mechanic to diagnose the problems and make a list of the parts and tools needed to fix them. You buy the parts from several dealers, rent the tools, hire a car mechanic, return the tools and pay your bills. You can avoid all these transactions and the time they cost you by letting your local garage fix the car.

Economies of Scale

When the cost of producing a unit of a good falls as its output rate increases, **economies of scale** exist. A car maker experiences economies of scale because as the scale of production increases, the firm can use cost-saving equipment and highly specialised labour. A car

ECONOMICS IN ACTION

Apple Doesn't Make the iPhone

Apple designed the iPhone and markets it, but Apple doesn't manufacture it. Why? Apple wants to produce the iPhone at the lowest possible cost. Apple achieves its goal by assigning the production task to more than 30 firms, some of which are listed in the table opposite. These 30 firms produce the components in Asia, Europe and North America, and then the components are assembled in the familiar case by Foxconn and Quanta in Taiwan. Most electronic products – TV sets, DVD players, iPods and iPads and personal computers – are produced in a similar way to the iPhone with a combination of firm and market coordination. Hundreds of little-known firms compete fiercely to get their components into well-known consumer products.

Altus-Tech	Taiwan
Balda	Germany
Broadcom	US
Cambridge Silicon Radio	UK
Catcher	Taiwan
Cyntec	Taiwan
Delta Electronics	Taiwan
Epson	Japan
Foxconn	Taiwan
Infineon Technology	Germany
Intel	US
Largan Precision	Taiwan
Lite On	Taiwan
Marvell	US
Micron	US
Novatek	Taiwan
Primax	Taiwan
Quanta	Taiwan
Samsung	Korea
Sanyo	Japan
Sharp	Japan
Taiwan Semiconductor	Taiwan
TMD	Japan

maker that produces only a few cars a year must use hand-tool methods that are costly. Economies of scale arise from specialisation and the division of labour. Firm coordination can reap these economies of scale more effectively than can market coordination.

Economies of Scope

A firm experiences **economies of scope** when it uses its specialised and often expensive resources to produce a *range of goods and services*. For example, Toshiba uses its designers and specialised equipment to make the hard drive for the iPod. But it makes many different types of hard drives and other related products. As a result, Toshiba produces the iPod hard drive at a lower cost than a firm that makes only the iPod hard drive could achieve.

Economies of Team Production

A production process in which the individuals in a group specialise in mutually supportive tasks is *team production*. Sports provide the best examples of team activity. In football, some team members specialise in defence and others in striking. The production of goods and services offers many examples of team activity. For example, production lines in a car plant work most efficiently when individual activity is organised in teams,

with each worker specialising in a few tasks. You can also think of an entire firm as being a team. The team has buyers of raw materials and other inputs, production workers and salespeople. Each individual member of the team specialises, but the value of the output of the team and the profit that it earns depend on the co-ordinated activities of all the team's members.

Because firms can economise on transactions costs, reap economies of scale and economies of scope, and organise efficient team production, it is firms rather than markets that coordinate most economic activity.

REVIEW QUIZ

1 Describe the two ways in which economic activity can be coordinated.
2 What determines whether a firm or markets coordinate production?
3 What are the main reasons why firms can often coordinate production at lower cost than markets?

Do these questions in Study Plan 9.5 and get instant feedback.   MyEconLab

Reading Between the Lines on pp. 212–213 explores the market for Internet advertising. In the next four chapters, we continue to study firms and their decisions.

Competition in Markets for Internet Advertising

The Telegraph, 13 September 2012

Facebook Launches Real-Time Bidding for Advertisers

Katherine Rushton

Facebook has stepped up its assault on the advertising market by taking on Google with so-called 'real-time bidding' for advertising space on its website.

The social network has been trialling a sophisticated system which makes it much easier for customers to focus their advertising spend on ads that are relevant to users. . . .

The move is expected to boost Facebook, . . . since its troubled $104m flotation in May amid concerns that it is not able to make enough money from advertising. . . .

Facebook Exchange allows companies to specify who they want to reach in a more calculated way.

It enables them to enter an ongoing, automatic auction for advertising space, and bid to place their adverts, depending on who is looking at Facebook at that particular time.

Advertisers are also able to set limits on what they want to spend, ensuring even small businesses can enter the race for advertising slots. Google uses a similar system to power its very successful Google AdWords service.

© Katherine Rushton, Telegraph.co.uk 2012.

 ## The Essence of the Story

- Facebook is under pressure to generate advertising revenue.

- Facebook Exchange is a real-time bidding system that allows advertisers to focus their advertising spend by monitoring Facebook users' browsing activity.

- Advertisers will bid to get their ads in front of the right Facebook users at the right time.

- Both Facebook and Google are getting better at capturing user activity for targeting advertising.

Economic Analysis

- Like all firms, Facebook and Google aim to maximise profit in the face of constraints imposed by the market and technology.

- Facebook competes with 200 firms in the market for social networking, and Google competes with more than another 100 firms in the market for Internet search.

- The equilibrium price of social networking services and of Internet search services is zero, and the equilibrium quantity of each is the quantity demanded at a zero price.

- Social network and Internet search providers enjoy economies of scope: they produce advertising services as well as other services.

- Unlike social networking and search, Internet advertising generates big revenue and profit.

- Social networking and search providers know a lot about their users, so they can offer advertisers access to potential customers and charge a high price for this precision.

- Google has been successful at delivering advertising based on a user's search activity, and its revenue has grown from almost zero in 2001 to $38 billion in 2011 (see Figure 1). Google's profit in 2011 was almost $12 billion (see Figure 2).

- Facebook is still learning how to tap its advertising potential, and the news article describes its plans in 2012 to develop real-time bidding for advertising based on a user's browsing.

- Facebook's revenue is beginning to grow, but by 2011 it had reached only $4 billion (see Figure 1).

- Providing a social networking service or search service doesn't guarantee success in generating advertising revenue and profit.

- Yahoo! is an example of a firm that hasn't performed as well as its owners would wish. Its revenue peaked in 2008 and has been falling

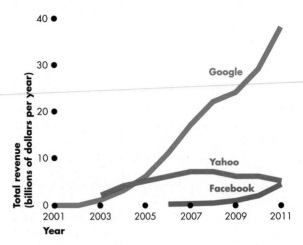

Figure 1 Total Revenue Comparison

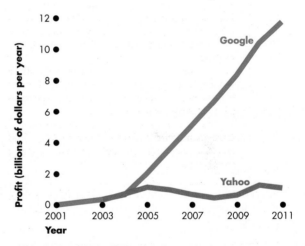

Figure 2 Profit Comparison

while Google's and Facebook's have grown (Figure 1).

- Yahoo's profit has been flat while Google's has soared (Figure 2). We don't know how much profit Facebook has made.

- The data shown in Figures 1 and 2 suggest that so far, Internet search is a more effective tool for generating revenue and profit than social networking. Perhaps Facebook's new revenue model will change that.

SUMMARY

Key Points

The Firm and Its Economic Problem
(pp. 196–198)

◆ Firms hire and organise factors of production to produce and sell goods and services.

◆ A firm's goal is to maximise economic profit, which is total revenue minus total cost measured as the opportunity cost of production.

◆ A firm's opportunity cost of production is the sum of the cost of the resources bought in the market, owned by the firm and supplied by the firm's owner.

◆ Normal profit is the opportunity cost of entrepreneurship and is part of the firm's opportunity cost.

◆ Technology, information and markets limit the economic profit that the firm can make.

Do Problems 1 and 2 to get a better understanding of the firm and its economic problem.

Technological and Economic Efficiency (pp. 199–200)

◆ A method of production is technologically efficient when a firm produces a given output by using the least amount of resources.

◆ A method of production is economically efficient when the cost of producing a given output is as low as possible.

Do Problems 3 and 4 to get a better understanding of technological and economic efficiency.

Information and Organisation
(pp. 201–204)

◆ Firms use a combination of command systems and incentive systems to organise production.

◆ Faced with incomplete information and uncertainty, firms induce managers and workers to perform in ways that are consistent with the firm's goals.

◆ Proprietorships, partnerships and companies use ownership, incentives and long-term contracts to cope with the principal–agent problem.

Do Problems 5 to 8 to get a better understanding of information and organisation.

Markets and the Competitive Environment (pp. 205–209)

◆ In perfect competition, many sellers offer an identical product to many buyers.

◆ In monopolistic competition, many sellers offer slightly different products to many buyers, and entry is free.

◆ In oligopoly, a small number of firms compete.

◆ In monopoly, one firm produces a good or service that has no close substitutes, and the firm is protected by a barrier that prevents the entry of competitors.

Do Problems 9 and 10 to get a better understanding of markets and the competitive environment.

Produce or Outsource? Firms and Markets (pp. 210–211)

◆ Firms coordinate economic activities when they can perform a task more efficiently – at lower cost – than markets can.

◆ Firms economise on transactions costs and achieve the benefits of economies of scale, economies of scope and team production.

Do Problems 11 and 12 to get a better understanding of firms and markets.

Key Terms

STUDY PLAN PROBLEMS AND APPLICATIONS

Do Problems 1 to 13 in MyEconLab Chapter 9 Study Plan and get instant feedback.

MyEconLab

The Firm and Its Economic Problem
(Study Plan 9.1)

1 One year ago, Jack and Jill set up a vinegar-bottling firm (called JJVB). Use the following information to calculate JJVB's opportunity cost of production during its first year of operation:

◆ Jack and Jill put €50,000 of their own money into the firm.

◆ They bought equipment for €30,000.

◆ They hired one employee to help them for an annual wage of €20,000.

◆ Jack gave up his previous job, at which he earned €30,000 and spent all his time working for JJVB.

◆ Jill kept her old job, which paid €30 an hour, but gave up 10 hours of leisure each week (for 50 weeks) to work for JJVB.

◆ JJVB bought €10,000 of goods and services from other firms.

◆ The market value of the equipment at the end of the year was €28,000.

◆ Jack and Jill have a €100,000 home loan on which they pay an interest rate of 6 per cent a year.

2 Joe, who has no skills, no job experience and no alternative employment, runs a shoeshine stand at the airport. Operators of other shoeshine stands earn €10,000 a year. Joe pays rent to the airport of €2,000 a year, and his total revenue from shining shoes is €15,000 a year. Joe spent €1,000 on a chair, polish and brushes, using his credit card to buy them. The interest on a credit card balance is 20 per cent a year. At the end of the year, Joe was offered €500 for his business and all its equipment. Calculate Joe's opportunity cost of production and his economic profit.

Technological and Economic Efficiency (Study Plan 9.2)

3 Alternative ways of laundering 100 shirts are:

Method	Labour (hours)	Capital (machines)
A	1	10
B	5	8
C	20	4
D	50	1

a Which methods are technologically efficient?

b Which method is economically efficient if the hourly wage rate and the implicit rental rate of capital are:
  (i) Wage rate €1, rental rate €100?
  (ii) Wage rate €5, rental rate €50?
  (iii) Wage rate €50, rental rate €5?

4 **John Deere's Farm Team**

Deere opened up the Pune [India] centre in 2001. Deere's move was unexpected: Deere is known for its heavy-duty farm equipment and big construction gear whereas many of India's 300 million farmers still use oxen-pulled ploughs.

Source: *Fortune*, 14 April 2008

a Why do many Indian farmers still use oxen-pulled ploughs? Are they efficient or inefficient? Explain.

b How might making John Deere farm equipment available to Indian farmers change the technology constraint they face?

Information and Organisation
(Study Plan 9.3)

5 **Here It Is. Now, You Design It!**

The idea is that the most successful companies no longer invent new products and services on their own. They create them along with their customers, and they do it in a way that produces a unique experience for each customer. The important corollary is that no company owns enough resources – or can possibly own enough – to furnish unique experiences for each customer, so companies must organise a constantly shifting global web of suppliers and partners to do the job.

Source: *Fortune*, 26 May 2008

a To organise and coordinate production, do successful companies use a command system or an incentive system?

b How does this method of organising and coordinating production help firms achieve lower costs?

6 **Rewarding Failure**

Over the past 25 years CEO pay has risen faster than company profits, economic growth or average wages. A more sensible alternative to the current compensation system would require CEOs to own a lot of company shares. If shares are given to the boss, his or her salary and bonus should be docked to reflect its value. As for bonuses, they should be based on improving a company's cash earnings relative to its cost of capital, not to more easily manipulated earnings per share. Bonuses should not be capped, but they should be unavailable to the CEO for some period of years.

Source: *Fortune*, 28 April 2008

a What is the economic problem that CEO compensation schemes are designed to solve?

b How do the proposed changes to CEO compensation outlined in the news clip address the problem you described in part (a)?

Use the following news clip in Problems 7 and 8.

Steps to Creating a Super Startup

Starting a business is a complicated and risky task. Just two thirds of new small businesses survive at least two years, and only 44 per cent survive at least four years. Most entrepreneurs start their businesses by dipping into their savings, borrowing from the family and using the founder's credit cards. Getting a bank loan is tough unless you have assets – and that often means using your home as security.

Source: CNN, 18 October 2007

7 When starting a business, what are the risks and potential rewards identified in the news clip that are associated with a proprietorship?

8 How might (i) a partnership and (ii) a company help to overcome the risks identified in the news clip?

Markets and the Competitive Environment (Study Plan 9.4)

9 Sales of the firms in the tattoo industry are:

Firm	Sales (euros)
Bright Spots plc	450
Freckles plc	325
Love Galore plc	250
Native Birds plc	200
Tiny Tattoo plc	175
Other 15 firms	800

a Calculate the five-firm concentration ratio.

b What is the structure of the tattoo industry on the basis of just the concentration ratio data?

c What other information would you need to determine whether the tattoo industry is competitive?

10 **GameStop Racks Up the Points**

No retailer has more cachet among gamers than GameStop. For now, only Wal-Mart has a larger market share – 21.3 per cent last year. GameStop's share was 21.1 per cent last year, and may well overtake Wal-Mart this year. But if new women gamers prefer shopping at Target to GameStop, Wal-Mart and Target might erode GameStop's market share.

Source: *Fortune*, 9 June 2008

a According to the news clip, what is the structure of the US retail video-game market?

b Estimate a range for a five-firm concentration ratio based on the information provided in this news clip.

Produce or Outsource? Firms and Markets (Study Plan 9.5)

11 Car makers buy parts from independent suppliers rather than produce the parts themselves. In the 1980s, Chrysler got about 70 per cent of its parts from independent suppliers, while Ford got about 60 per cent and General Motors got 25 per cent. A decade earlier, the proportions were 50 per cent at Chrysler, 5 per cent at Ford and 20 per cent at General Motors.

Source: The Cato Institute Policy Analysis, 1987

a Why did car makers decide to outsource most of their parts production?

b Explain why independent producers of car parts are more efficient than the car makers.

12 Federal Express enters into contracts with independent truck operators who offer FedEx service and who are rewarded by the volume of packages they carry. Why doesn't FedEx buy more trucks and hire more drivers? What incentive problems might arise from this arrangement?

Economics in the News (Study Plan 9.N)

13 Lego, the Danish toymaker, incurred economic losses in 2003 and 2004. Lego faced competition from low-cost copiers of its products and a fall in demand. In 2004, to restore profits, Lego fired 3,500 of its 8,000 workers; closed factories in Switzerland and the US; opened factories in Eastern Europe and Mexico; and introduced performance-based pay for its managers. Lego returned to profit in 2005.

Source: *The Economist*, 28 October 2006

a Describe the problems that Lego faced in 2003 and 2004, using the concepts of the three types of constraints that all firms face.

b Which of the actions that Lego took to restore profits addressed an inefficiency? How did Lego seek to achieve economic efficiency?

c Which of Lego's actions addressed an information and organisation problem? How did Lego change the way in which it coped with the principal–agent problem?

d In what type of market does Lego operate?

ADDITIONAL PROBLEMS AND APPLICATIONS

Do these problems in MyEconLab if assigned by your lecturer.

MyEconLab

The Firm and Its Economic Problem

Use the following data in Problems 14 and 15.

Lee is a computer programmer who earned £35,000 in 2011. But on 1 January 2012, Lee opened a body board manufacturing business. At the end of the first year of operation, he submitted the following information to his accountant:

♦ He stopped renting out his cottage for £3,500 a year and used it as his factory. The market value of the cottage increased from £70,000 to £71,000.

♦ He spent £50,000 on materials, phone, etc.

♦ He leased machines for £10,000 a year.

♦ He paid £15,000 in wages.

♦ He used £10,000 from his savings account, which earns 5 per cent a year interest.

♦ He borrowed £40,000 at 10 per cent a year.

♦ He sold £160,000 worth of body boards.

♦ Normal profit is £25,000 a year.

14 Calculate Lee's opportunity cost of production and his economic profit.

15 Lee's accountant recorded the depreciation on his cottage during 2012 as £7,000. According to the accountant, what profit did Lee make?

16 In 2011, Toni taught music and earned £20,000. She also earned £4,000 by renting out her basement. On 1 January 2012, she quit teaching, stopped renting out her basement and began to use it as the office for her new website design business. She took £2,000 from her savings account to buy a computer. During 2012, she paid £1,500 for the lease of a Web server and £1,750 for a high-speed Internet service. She received a total revenue from website designing of £45,000 and earned interest at 5 per cent a year on her savings account balance. Normal profit is £55,000 a year. At the end of 2012, Toni could have sold her computer for £500. Calculate Toni's opportunity cost of production and her economic profit in 2012.

17 **The Colvin Interview: Chrysler**

The key driver of profitability will be that the focus of the company isn't on profitability. Our focus is on the customer. If we can find a way to give customers what they want better than anybody else, then what can stop us?

Source: *Fortune*, 14 April 2008

a In spite of what Chrysler's vice chairman and co-president claims, why is Chrysler's focus actually on profitability?

b What would happen to Chrysler if it didn't focus on maximising profit, but instead focused its production and pricing decisions to 'give customers what they want'?

18 **Must Watches**

Shares too volatile? Bonds too boring? Then try an alternative investment – one you can wear on your wrist. The typical return on a watch over five to ten years is roughly 10 per cent. One could do better in an index fund, but what other investment is so wearable?

Source: *Fortune*, 14 April 2008

a What is the cost of buying a watch?

b What is the opportunity cost of owning a watch?

c Does owning a watch create an economic profit opportunity?

Technological and Economic Efficiency

Use the following data in Problems 19 and 20.

Four methods of completing a tax return are: a personal computer (PC), a pocket calculator, a pocket calculator with pencil and paper, a pencil and paper. With a PC, the job takes an hour; with a pocket calculator, it takes 12 hours; with a pocket calculator and pencil and paper, it takes 12 hours; and with a pencil and paper, it takes 16 hours. The PC and its software cost €1,000, the pocket calculator costs €10 and the pencil and paper cost €1.

19 Which, if any, of the methods is technologically efficient?

20 Which method is economically efficient if the wage rate is

(i) €5 an hour?

(ii) €50 an hour?

(iii) €500 an hour?

21 A Medical Sensation

Hospitals are buying da Vinci surgical robots. Surgeons, sitting comfortably at a da Vinci console, can use various robotic attachments to perform even the most complex procedures.

Source: *Fortune*, 28 April 2008

a Assume that performing surgery with a surgical robot requires fewer surgeons and nurses. Is using the surgical robot technologically efficient?

b What additional information would you need to be able to say that switching to surgical robots is economically efficient for a hospital?

Information and Organisation

22 Tesco plc has more than 2,700 stores, more than a quarter of a million employees, and total revenues of about £40 million a year. Sarah runs the family-owned Frey Farms and supplies Tesco plc with mushrooms and other fresh produce.

a How do you think Tesco plc coordinates its activities? Is it likely to use mainly a command system or also to use incentive systems?

b How do you think Sarah coordinates the activities of Frey Farms? Is she likely to use mainly a command system or also to use incentive systems? Why?

c Describe, compare and contrast the principal–agent problems faced by Tesco plc and Frey Farms. How might each firm cope with its principal–agent problems?

23 Public sector workers in all areas are now subject to appraisal and bonus payments based on performance rather than their years on the job and coursework completed. In the education sector, some argue that improving teacher instruction and paying bonuses for raising student achievement encourage efforts to raise teaching quality. How could 'merit pay' attempt to cope with the principal–agent problem in education?

24 Where Does Google Go Next?

Google gives its engineers one day a week to work on whatever project they want. A couple of colleagues did what many of the young geniuses do at Google: they came up with a cool idea. At Google, you often end up with a laissez-faire mess instead of resource allocation.

Source: *Fortune*, 26 May 2008

a Describe Google's method of organising production with its software engineers.

b What are the potential gains and opportunity costs associated with this method?

Markets and the Competitive Environment

25 Market shares of chocolate makers are:

Firm	Market share (per cent)
Truffles plc	25
Magic plc	20
Mayfair plc	15
All Natural plc	15
Gold plc	15
Bond plc	10

Calculate the five-firm concentration ratio. What is the structure of the chocolate industry?

Produce or Outsource? Firms and Markets

Use the following information in Problems 26 to 28.

Two leading design firms, Astro Studios of San Francisco and Hers Experimental Design Laboratory, Inc. of Osaka, Japan, worked with Microsoft to design the Xbox 360 video game console. IBM, ATI and SiS designed the Xbox 360's hardware. Two firms, Flextronics & Wistron and Celestica, manufacture the Xbox 360 at their plants in China and Taiwan.

26 Describe the roles of market coordination and coordination by firms in the design, manufacture and marketing of the Xbox 360.

27 Why do you think Microsoft works with a large number of other firms rather than performing all the tasks required to bring the Xbox to market at its headquarters in Seattle?

28 What are the roles of transactions costs, economies of scale, economies of scope and economies of team production in the design, manufacture and marketing of the Xbox?

Economics in the News

29 After you have studied *Reading Between the Lines* on pp. 212–213, answer the following questions.

a What products do Facebook and Google sell?

b In what types of markets do Facebook and Google compete?

c How do social networks and Internet search providers generate revenue?

d What is special about social networking sites that makes them attractive to advertisers?

e What is special about Internet search providers that makes them attractive to advertisers?

f What technological changes might increase the profit of social networks compared with Internet search providers?

10 Output and Costs

After studying this chapter you will be able to:

◆ Distinguish between the short run and the long run

◆ Explain the relationship between a firm's output and labour employed in the short run

◆ Explain the relationship between a firm's output and costs in the short run and derive a firm's short-run cost curves

◆ Explain the relationship between a firm's output and costs in the long run and derive a firm's long-run average cost curve

What do the car-maker Jaguar Land Rover and a small-scale (fictional) producer of knitwear that we study in this chapter have in common? They must decide how much to produce, how many people to employ and how much and what type of capital equipment to use. How do firms make these decisions?

We are going to answer these questions in this chapter. We'll apply what you learn to the cost of operating a supermarket checkout lane and in *Reading Between the Lines* at the end of the chapter, we'll look at some recent production decisions at Jaguar Land Rover.

Time Frames for Decisions

People who operate firms make many decisions. All of these decisions are aimed at one overriding objective: maximum attainable profit. But the decisions are not all equally critical. Some of the decisions are big ones. Once made, they are costly (or impossible) to reverse. If such a decision turns out to be incorrect, it might lead to the failure of the firm. Some of the decisions are small ones. They are easily changed. If one of these decisions turns out to be incorrect, the firm can change its actions and survive.

The biggest decision that an entrepreneur makes is in what industry to establish a firm. For most entrepreneurs, their background knowledge and interests drive this decision. But the decision also depends on profit prospects – on the expectation that total revenue will exceed total cost.

Norma has decided to set up Fashion First to produce jumpers. She has also decided the most effective method of organisation. But she has not decided the quantity to produce, the quantities of factors of production to hire, or the price to charge for jumpers.

Decisions about the quantity to produce and the price to charge depend on the type of market in which the firm operates. Perfect competition, monopolistic competition, oligopoly and monopoly all confront the firm with *different* problems.

But decisions about *how* to produce a given output do not depend on the type of market in which the firm operates. These decisions are similar for *all* types of firms in *all* types of markets.

The actions that a firm can take to influence the relationship between output and cost depend on how soon the firm wants to act. A firm that plans to change its output rate tomorrow has fewer options than one that plans to change its output rate six months from now.

To study the relationship between a firm's output decision and its costs, we distinguish between two decision time frames:

◆ The short run
◆ The long run

The Short Run

The **short run** is a time frame in which the quantity of at least one factor of production is fixed. For most firms, capital, land and entrepreneurship are fixed factors of production, and labour is the variable factor of production. We call the fixed factors of production the firm's

plant. So in the short run, a firm's plant is fixed. Fashion First's fixed plant is its factory building and its knitting machines. For an electric power utility, the fixed plant is its buildings, generators, computers and control systems.

To increase output in the short run, a firm must increase the quantity of a variable factor of production, which is usually labour. So to produce more output, Fashion First must hire more labour and operate its knitting machines for more hours per day. Similarly, an electric power utility must hire more labour and operate its generators for more hours per day.

Short-run decisions are easily reversed. The firm can increase or decrease output in the short run by increasing or decreasing the labour it hires.

The Long Run

The **long run** is a time frame in which the quantities of *all* factors of production can be varied. That is, the long run is a period in which the firm can change its *plant*.

To increase output in the long run, a firm is able to choose whether to change its plant as well as whether to increase the quantity of labour it hires. Fashion First can decide whether to install some additional knitting machines, use a new type of machine, reorganise its management or hire more labour. An electric power utility can decide whether to install more generators. And an airport can decide whether to build more runways, terminals and traffic-control facilities.

Long-run decisions are *not* easily reversed. Once a plant decision is made, the firm must live with it for some time. To emphasise this fact, we call the *past* expenditure on a plant that has no resale value a **sunk cost**. A sunk cost is irrelevant to the firm's current decisions. The only costs that influence its current decisions are the short-run cost of changing the quantity of labour and the long-run cost of changing its plant.

REVIEW QUIZ

1 Distinguish between the short run and the long run.
2 Why is a sunk cost irrelevant to a firm's current decisions?

Do these questions in Study Plan 10.1 and get instant feedback.   MyEconLab

We're going to study costs in the short run and the long run. We begin with the short run and describe the technology constraint the firm faces.

Short-Run Technology Constraint

To increase output in the short run, a firm must increase the quantity of labour employed. We describe the relationship between output and the quantity of labour employed by using three related concepts:

1 Total product
2 Marginal product
3 Average product

These product concepts can be illustrated either by product schedules or by product curves. We'll look first at the product schedules.

Product Schedules

Table 10.1 shows some data that describe Fashion First's total product, marginal product and average product. The numbers tell us how Fashion First's production changes as more workers are employed, for a fixed level of plant and machines. They also tell us about the productivity of Fashion First's workforce.

Look first at the columns headed 'Labour' and 'Total product'. **Total product** is the maximum output that a given quantity of labour can produce. The table shows how total product increases as Fashion First employs more labour. For example, when Fashion First employs 1 worker, total product is 4 jumpers a day, and when Fashion First employs 2 workers, total product is 10 jumpers a day. Each increase in employment brings an increase in total product.

The **marginal product** of labour is the increase in total product resulting from a one-unit increase in the quantity of labour employed with all other inputs remaining the same. For example, in Table 10.1, when Fashion First increases employment from 2 to 3 workers and does not change its capital, the marginal product of the third worker is 3 jumpers – total product increases from 10 to 13 jumpers.

The **average product** tells how productive workers are on the average. The average product of labour is equal to total product divided by the quantity of labour employed. For example, in Table 10.1, 3 workers can knit 13 jumpers a day, so the average product of labour is 13 divided by 3, which is 4.33 jumpers per worker.

If you look closely at the numbers in Table 10.1, you can see some patterns. For example, as Fashion First employs more workers, marginal product at first increases and then begins to decrease. For example,

Table 10.1

Total Product, Marginal Product and Average Product

Labour (workers per day)	Total product (jumpers per day)	Marginal product (jumpers per worker)	Average product (jumpers per worker)
A 0	0		
		·········· 4	
B 1	4		4.00
		·········· 6	
C 2	10		5.00
		·········· 3	
D 3	13		4.33
		·········· 2	
E 4	15		3.75
		·········· 1	
F 5	16		3.20

Total product is the total amount produced. Marginal product is the change in total product resulting from a one-unit increase in labour. For example, when labour increases from 2 to 3 workers a day (row *C* to row *D*), total product increases from 10 to 13 jumpers a day. The marginal product of going from 2 to 3 workers is 3 jumpers. (Marginal product is shown between the rows because it is the result of a change in the quantity of labour.) Average product of labour is total product divided by the quantity of labour employed. For example, 3 workers produce 13 jumpers a day, so the average product of 3 workers is 4.33 jumpers per worker.

marginal product increases from 4 jumpers a day for the first worker to 6 jumpers a day for the second worker and then decreases to 3 jumpers a day for the third worker. Also average product at first increases and then decreases. You can see the relationships between the number of workers employed and the three product concepts more clearly by looking at the product curves.

Product Curves

The product curves are graphs of the relationships between employment and the three product concepts that you've just studied. They show how total product, marginal product and average product change as employment changes. They also show the relationships among the three concepts. Let's look at the three product curves.

Total Product Curve

Figure 10.1 shows Fashion First's total product curve, *TP*. As employment increases, so does the number of jumpers knitted. Points *A* to *F* on the curve correspond to the same rows in Table 10.1. These points show total product at various quantities of labour per day. But labour is divisible into hours and even minutes. By varying the amount of labour in the smallest units possible, we can draw the total product curve shown in Figure 10.1.

Look carefully at the shape of the total product curve. As employment increases from zero to 1 worker a day, the curve becomes steeper. Then, as employment continues to increase to 3, 4 and 5 workers per day, the curve becomes less steep.

The total product curve is similar to the *production possibilities frontier* (explained in Chapter 2). It separates the attainable output levels from those that are unattainable. All the points that lie above the curve are unattainable. Points that lie below the curve, in the orange area, are attainable. But they are inefficient – they use more labour than is necessary to produce a given output. Only the points *on* the total product curve are technologically efficient.

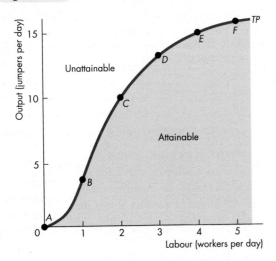

Figure 10.1 Total Product Curve

The total product curve (*TP*) is based on the data in Table 10.1. The total product curve shows how the quantity of jumpers changes as the quantity of labour employed changes. For example, using 1 knitting machine, 2 workers can produce 10 jumpers a day (row *C*). Points *A* to *F* on the curve correspond to the rows of Table 10.1. The total product curve separates the attainable output from the unattainable output. Points on the *TP* curve are efficient.

MyEconLab Animation ————————————◆

Marginal Product Curve

Figure 10.2 shows Fashion First's marginal product of labour with 1 knitting machine. Part (a) reproduces the total product curve from Figure 10.1. Part (b) shows the marginal product curve, *MP*.

In Figure 10.2(a), the orange bars illustrate the marginal product of labour. The height of each bar measures marginal product. Marginal product is also measured by the slope of the total product curve. Recall that the slope of a curve is the change in the value of the variable measured on the *y*-axis – output – divided by the change in the variable measured on the *x*-axis – labour – as we move along the curve. A one-unit increase in labour, from 2 to 3 workers, increases output from 10 to 13 jumpers, so the slope from point *C* to point *D* is 3 jumpers per worker, the same as the marginal product that we've just calculated.

By varying the amount of labour in the smallest imaginable units, we can draw the marginal product curve shown in Figure 10.2(b). The *height* of this curve measures the *slope* of the total product curve at a point. The total product curve in part (a) shows that an increase in employment from 2 to 3 workers increases output from 10 to 13 jumpers (an increase of 3). The increase in output of 3 jumpers appears on the *y*-axis of part (b) as the marginal product of going from 2 to 3 workers. We plot that marginal product at the mid-point between 2 and 3 workers. Notice that marginal product in Figure 10.2(b) reaches a peak at 1.5 workers and at that point marginal product is 6 jumpers. The peak occurs at 1.5 workers because the total product curve is steepest when employment increases from 1 to 2 workers.

The total product and marginal product curves differ across firms and types of goods. An airline's product curves are different from those of your local supermarket, which in turn are different from those of Fashion First. But the shapes of the product curves are similar because almost every production process has two features:

◆ Increasing marginal returns initially

◆ Diminishing marginal returns eventually

Increasing Marginal Returns

Increasing marginal returns occur when the marginal product of an additional worker exceeds the marginal product of the previous worker. Increasing marginal returns arise from increased specialisation and division of labour in the production process.

Figure 10.2 Total Product and Marginal Product

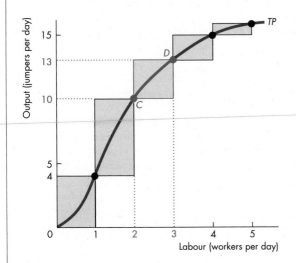

(a) Total product

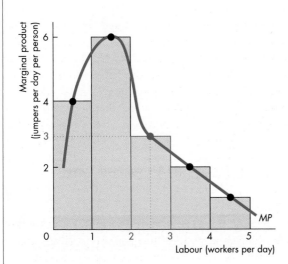

(b) Marginal product

Marginal product is illustrated in both parts of the figure by the orange bars. For example, when labour increases from 2 to 3 workers a day, marginal product is the orange bar whose height is 3 jumpers. (Marginal product is shown midway between the quantities of labour to emphasise that it is the result of changing the quantity of labour.)

The steeper the slope of the total product curve (*TP*) in part (a), the larger is marginal product (*MP*) in part (b). Marginal product increases to a maximum (in this example when the second worker is employed) and then declines – diminishing marginal product.

MyEconLab Animation ──────────────◆

For example, if Fashion First employs just 1 worker, that person has to learn all the different aspects of jumper production: running the knitting machines, fixing breakdowns, packaging and mailing jumpers and buying and checking the type and colour of the wool. All of these tasks have to be done by that one person.

If Fashion First employs a second person, the 2 workers can specialise in different parts of the production process. As a result, 2 workers produce more than twice as much as 1. The marginal product of the second worker is greater than the marginal product of the first worker. Marginal returns are increasing.

Diminishing Marginal Returns

Most product processes experience increasing marginal returns initially, but all production processes eventually reach a point of diminishing marginal returns. **Diminishing marginal returns** occur when the marginal product of an additional worker is less than the marginal product of the previous worker.

Diminishing marginal returns arise from the fact that more and more workers are using the same capital and working in the same space. As more workers are added, there is less and less for the additional workers to do that is productive. For example, if Fashion First employs a third worker, output increases but not by as much as it did when it added the second worker. In this case, after two workers are employed, all the gains from specialisation and the division of labour have been exhausted. By employing a third worker, the factory produces more jumpers, but the equipment is being operated closer to its limits. There are even times when the third worker has nothing to do because the machine is running without the need for further attention. Adding more and more workers continues to increase output but by successively smaller amounts. Marginal returns are diminishing. This phenomenon is such a pervasive one that it is called 'the law of diminishing returns'.

The **law of diminishing returns** states that:

> **As a firm uses more of a variable factor of production, with a given quantity of the fixed factor of production, the marginal product of the variable factor eventually diminishes.**

You will return to the law of diminishing returns when we study a firm's costs. But before we do, let's look at average product and the average product curve.

Average Product Curve

Figure 10.3 illustrates Fashion First's average product of labour, *AP*, and the relationship between the average and marginal product. Points *B* to *F* on the average product curve correspond to those same rows in Table 10.1.

Average product increases from 1 to 2 workers (its maximum value is at point *C*) but then decreases as yet more workers are employed. Also, average product is largest when average product and marginal product are equal. That is, the marginal product curve cuts the average product curve at the point of maximum average product. For the number of workers at which the marginal product exceeds average product, average product is *increasing*. For the number of workers at which marginal product is less than average product, average product is *decreasing*.

The relationship between the average product and marginal product curves is a general feature of the relationship between the average and marginal values of any variable. Let's look at a familiar example.

Figure 10.3 Average Product

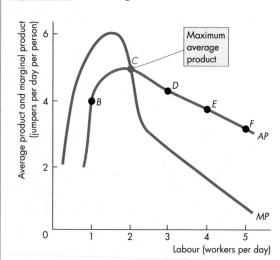

The figure shows the average product of labour and the connection between the average product and marginal product. With 1 worker a day, marginal product exceeds average product, so average product is increasing. With 2 workers a day, marginal product equals average product, so average product is at its maximum. With more than 2 workers a day, marginal product is less than average product, so average product is decreasing.

MyEconLab Animation

How to Pull Up Your Average

Do you want to pull up your average mark? Then make sure that your mark on this test is better than your current average! This test is your marginal test. If your marginal mark exceeds your average mark (like the second test in the graph), your average will rise. If your marginal mark equals your average mark (like the third test in the graph), your average won't change. If your marginal mark is below your average mark (like the fourth test in the figure), your average will fall.

The relationship between your marginal and average grades is exactly the same as that between marginal product and average product.

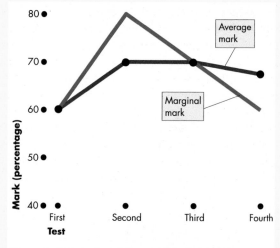

Figure 1 **Marginal and Average Mark Curves**

◆ **REVIEW QUIZ**

1. Explain how the marginal product and the average product change as the labour employed increases (a) initially and (b) eventually.
2. What is the law of diminishing returns? Why does marginal product eventually diminish?
3. Explain the relationship between marginal product and average product.

Do these questions in Study Plan 10.2 and get instant feedback.   MyEconLab

Norma, the owner of Fashion First, cares about Fashion First's product curves because they influence its costs. Let's look at Fashion First's costs.

Short-Run Cost

To produce more output in the short run, a firm must employ more labour, which means it must increase its costs. We describe the relationship between output and costs by using three concepts:

◆ Total cost

◆ Marginal cost

◆ Average cost

Total Cost

A firm's **total cost** (*TC*) is the cost of *all* the factors of production it uses. We separate total cost into total *fixed* cost and total *variable* cost.

Total fixed cost (*TFC*) is the cost of the firm's fixed factors. For Fashion First, total fixed cost includes the cost of renting knitting machines and *normal profit*, which is the opportunity cost of Norma's entrepreneurship (see Chapter 9, p. 197). The quantities of a fixed factor don't change as output changes, so total fixed cost is the same at all outputs.

Total variable cost (*TVC*) is the cost of the firm's variable inputs. For Fashion First, labour is the variable factor, so this component of cost is its wage bill. Total variable cost changes as total product changes.

Total cost is the sum of total fixed cost and total variable cost. That is:

$$TC = TFC + TVC$$

The table in Figure 10.4 shows Fashion First's total costs. With one knitting machine that Fashion First rents for £25 a day, *TFC* is £25 a day. To produce jumpers, Fashion First hires labour, which costs £25 a day. *TVC* is the number of workers multiplied by £25. For example, to produce 13 jumpers a day, Fashion First hires 3 workers and its *TVC* is £75. *TC* is the sum of *TFC* and *TVC*, so to produce 13 jumpers a day, Fashion First's total cost, *TC*, is £100. Check the calculation in each row of the table.

Figure 10.4 shows Fashion First's total cost curves, which graph total cost against output. The green total fixed cost curve (*TFC*) is horizontal because total fixed cost is constant at £25. It does not change when output changes. The purple total variable cost curve (*TVC*) and the blue total cost curve (*TC*) both slope upward because total variable cost increases as output increases. The arrows highlight total fixed cost as the vertical distance between the *TVC* and *TC* curves.

Figure 10.4 Short-run Total Cost

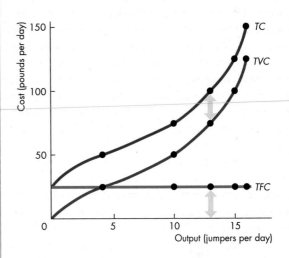

	Labour (workers per day)	Output (jumpers per day)	Total fixed cost (*TFC*)	Total variable cost (*TVC*)	Total cost (*TC*)
				(pounds per day)	
A	0	0	25	0	25
B	1	4	25	25	50
C	2	10	25	50	75
D	3	13	25	75	100
E	4	15	25	100	125
F	5	16	25	125	150

Fashion First rents a knitting machine for £25 a day. This amount is Fashion First's total fixed cost. Fashion First hires workers at a wage rate of £25 a day, and this cost is Fashion First's total variable cost. For example, if Fashion First employs 3 workers, its total variable cost is (3 × £25), which equals £75.

Total cost is the sum of total fixed cost and total variable cost. For example, when Fashion First employs 3 workers, its total cost is £100: total fixed cost of £25 plus total variable cost of £75. The graph shows Fashion First's total cost curves.

Total fixed cost (*TFC*) is constant – it graphs as a horizontal line – and total variable cost (*TVC*) increases as output increases. Total cost (*TC*) also increases as output increases. The vertical distance between the total cost curve and the total variable cost curve is total fixed cost, as illustrated by the two arrows.

MyEconLab Animation ─────────────────◆

Marginal Cost

In Figure 10.4, total variable cost and total cost increase at a decreasing rate at small outputs and begin to increase at an increasing rate as output increases. To understand these patterns in the changes in total cost, we need to use the concept of *marginal cost.*

A firm's **marginal cost** is the change in total cost resulting from a one-unit increase in output. Marginal cost (MC) is calculated as the change in total cost (ΔTC) divided by the change in output (ΔQ). That is:

$$MC = \frac{\Delta TC}{\Delta Q}$$

The table in Figure 10.5 shows this calculation. For example, an increase in output from 10 to 13 jumpers increases total cost from £75 to £100. The change in output is 3 jumpers, and the change in total cost is £25. The marginal cost of one of those 3 jumpers is (£25 ÷ 3), which equals £8.33.

Figure 10.5 graphs the marginal cost as the red marginal cost curve, MC. This curve is U-shaped because when Fashion First hires a second worker, marginal cost decreases, but when it hires a third, a fourth and a fifth worker, marginal cost successively increases.

Marginal cost decreases at low outputs because of economies from greater specialisation. It eventually increases because of *the law of diminishing returns.* The law of diminishing returns means that each additional worker produces a successively smaller addition to output. So to get an additional unit of output, ever more workers are required. Because more workers are required to produce one additional unit of output, the cost of the additional output – marginal cost – must eventually increase.

Marginal cost tells us how total cost changes as output changes. The final cost concept tells us what it costs, on the average, to produce a unit of output. Let's now look at Fashion First's average costs.

Average Cost

Average cost is cost per unit of output. There are three average costs:

1 Average fixed cost
2 Average variable cost
3 Average total cost

Average fixed cost (AFC) is total fixed cost per unit of output. **Average variable cost** (AVC) is total variable cost per unit of output. **Average total cost** (ATC) is total cost per unit of output. The average cost concepts are calculated from the total cost concepts as follows:

$$TC = TFC + TVC$$

Divide each total cost term by the quantity produced, Q, to give:

$$\frac{TC}{Q} = \frac{TFC}{Q} + \frac{TVC}{Q}$$

or:

$$ATC = AFC + AVC$$

The table in Figure 10.5 shows the calculation of average total costs. For example, in the third row when output is 10 jumpers, average fixed cost is (£25 ÷ 10), which equals £2.50, average variable cost is (£50 ÷ 10), which equals £5.00, and average total cost is (£75 ÷ 10), which equals £7.50. Note average total cost is equal to average fixed cost (£2.50) plus average variable cost (£5.00).

Figure 10.5 shows the average cost curves. The green average fixed cost curve (AFC) slopes downward. As output increases, the same constant fixed cost is spread over a larger output. The blue average total cost curve (ATC) and the purple average variable cost curve (AVC) are U-shaped. The vertical distance between the average total cost and average variable cost curves is equal to average fixed cost – as indicated by the arrows. The vertical distance between the ATC and AVC curves shrinks as output increases because average fixed cost decreases as output increases.

Marginal Cost and Average Cost

The red marginal cost curve (MC) intersects the average variable cost curve and the average total cost curve *at their minimum point.* When marginal cost is less than average cost, average cost is decreasing, and when marginal cost exceeds average cost, average cost is increasing. This relationship holds for both the ATC and the AVC curves and is another example of the relationship you saw in Figure 10.3 between average product and marginal product and your marginal and average test marks.

Why the Average Total Cost Curve Is U-Shaped

Average total cost, ATC, is the sum of average fixed cost, AFC, and average variable cost, AVC. So the shape

Figure 10.5 Marginal Cost and Average Costs

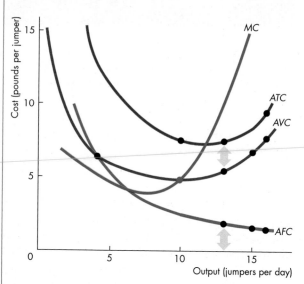

Marginal cost is calculated as the change in total cost divided by the change in output. When output increases from 4 to 10, an increase of 6, total cost increases by £25 and marginal cost is £25 ÷ 6, which equals £4.17. Each average cost concept is calculated by dividing the related total cost by output. When 10 jumpers are produced, *AFC* is £2.50 (£25 ÷ 10), *AVC* is £5 (£50 ÷ 10) and *ATC* is £7.50 (£75 ÷ 10).

The graph shows the marginal cost curve and the average cost curves. The marginal cost curve (*MC*) is U-shaped and intersects the average variable cost curve and the average total cost curve at their minimum points. Average fixed cost (*AFC*) decreases as output increases. The average total cost curve (*ATC*) and average variable cost curve (*AVC*) are U-shaped. The vertical distance between these two curves is equal to average fixed cost, as illustrated by the two arrows.

Labour (workers per day)	Output (jumpers per day)	Total fixed cost (*TFC*)	Total variable cost (*TVC*)	Total cost (*TC*)	Marginal cost (*MC*)	Average fixed cost (*AFC*)	Average variable cost (*AVC*)	Average total cost (*ATC*)
		(pounds per day)				(pounds per jumper)		
0	0	25		25				
					.... 6.25			
1	4	25	25	50		6.25	6.25	12.50
					.... 4.17			
2	10	25	50	75		2.50	5.00	7.50
					.... 8.33			
3	13	25	75	100		1.92	5.77	7.69
					.... 12.50			
4	15	25	100	125		1.67	6.67	8.33
					.... 25.00			
5	16	25	125	150		1.56	7.81	9.38

MyEconLab Animation

of the *ATC* curve combines the shapes of the *AFC* and *AVC* curves. The U-shape of the average total cost curve arises from the influence of two opposing forces:

1 Spreading fixed cost over a larger output

2 Eventually diminishing returns

When output increases, the firm spreads its total fixed costs over a larger output and its average fixed cost decreases – its *AFC* curve slopes downward.

Diminishing returns mean that as output increases, ever-larger amounts of labour are needed to produce an additional unit of output. So as output increases, average variable cost decreases initially, but eventually

it increases and the firm's *AVC* curve eventually slopes upward. The *AVC* curve is U-shaped.

The shape of the *ATC* curve combines these two effects. Initially, as output increases, both average fixed cost and average variable cost decrease, so average total cost decreases and the *ATC* curve slopes downward.

But as output increases further and diminishing returns set in, average variable cost begins to increase. With average fixed cost decreasing more quickly than average variable cost is increasing, the *ATC* curve continues to slope downward. Eventually, average variable cost increases more quickly than average fixed cost decreases, so average total cost increases and the *ATC* curve slopes upward.

Cost Curves and Product Curves

The technology that a firm uses determines its costs. And a firm's cost curves come directly from its product curves. You've used this link in the tables in which we have calculated total cost from the total product schedule and information about the prices of the factors of production. We're now going to get a clearer view of the link between the product curves and the cost curves. We'll look first at the link between total cost and total product and then at the links between the average and marginal product and cost curves.

Total Product and Total Cost

Figure 10.6 shows the links between the firm's total product curve, *TP*, and its total variable cost curve, *TVC*. The graph is a bit unusual in two ways. First, it measures two variables on the *x*-axis – labour and cost. Second, it graphs the *TVC* curve but with cost on the *x*-axis and output on the *y*-axis. The graph can show labour and cost on the *x*-axis because variable cost is proportional to labour. One worker-day costs £25. Graphing output against labour gives the *TP* curve and graphing variable cost against output gives the *TVC* curve.

Figure 10.6　Total Product and Total Variable Cost

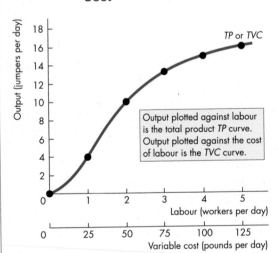

Output plotted against labour is the total product *TP* curve. Output plotted against the cost of labour is the *TVC* curve.

The figure shows the total product curve, *TP*, as a graph of output (jumpers per day) plotted against labour (workers per day). It also shows the total variable cost curve, *TVC*, as a graph of cost (pounds per day) against output. The only difference between the *TVC* curve here and that in Figure 10.4 is that we've switched the *x*-axis and *y*-axis.

ECONOMICS IN

Checkout Cost Curves

Self-Service Checkouts are Expanding

Up to 70 per cent of lanes in larger UK supermarkets are now self-service allowing 40 million customers a week to checkout their own shopping, avoid queues and releasing staff to work on other activities.

Source: *RetailWeek*, 26 September 2012

Data and Assumptions

A grocery store paid £10,000 to install 5 worker-operated checkout lanes. With a life of 5 years and operating for 10 hours a day, these machines have an *implicit rental rate* of £1 an hour. Checkout clerks can be hired for £6 an hour. This store's *TP* schedule (checkouts per hour) is:

Checkout clerks	1	2	3	4	5
Checkouts per hour	12	22	30	36	40

Another store has converted to all self-checkout. It paid £50,000 to install a 5-lane self-operated system. With a 5-year life and operating for 10 hours a day, the system has an *implicit rental rate* of £3.50 an hour. It hires checkout assistants to help customers at £6 an hour – the same wage as paid to checkout clerks. This store's *TP* schedule is:

Checkout assistants	1	1	1	2
Checkouts per hour	12	22	30	36

That is, one checkout assistant can help shoppers check out up to a rate of 30 an hour and a second assistant can boost output to 36 an hour. (Shoppers using self-checkout aren't as quick as clerks, so the fastest rate at which this store can check out customers is 36 an hour.)

The Problem

Which checkout system has the lower *ATC*? Sketch the *ATC* and *MC* curves for the two systems.

The Solution

◆ Start with the worker-operated checkout system. Fixed cost is £0.50 per hour and variable cost is £6.00 per clerk. So the total cost schedule is:

Checkout clerks	1	2	3	4	5
Checkouts per hour	12	22	30	36	40
Total cost (*TC*) per hour	7	13	19	25	31

THE NEWS

◆ Calculate *MC* as the change in *TC* divided by the change in output (change in number of checkouts) and calculate *ATC* as *TC* divided by output to get:

Checkouts per hour	12	22	30	36	40
Marginal cost (*MC*)	0.50	0.60	0.75	1.00	1.50
Average total cost (A*TC*)	0.58	0.59	0.63	0.69	0.78

◆ Figure 1 graphs the *MC* and *ATC* values at each output rate.

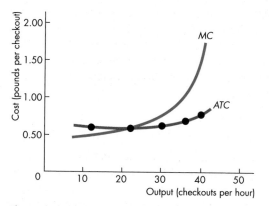

Figure 1 Operator Checkout

◆ Now do similar calculations for the self-checkout system. Fixed cost is £3.50 per hour and variable cost is £6.00 per clerk hour. So the total cost schedule is:

Checkout assistants	1	1	1	2
Checkouts per hour	12	22	30	36
Total cost (*TC*) per hour	9.50	9.50	9.50	15.50

◆ Calculate *MC* and *ATC* in the same way as before to get:

Checkouts per hour	12	22	30	36
Marginal cost (*MC*)	0.50	0	0	1.00
Average total cost (A*TC*)	0.79	0.43	0.32	0.43

◆ Figure 2 graphs the *MC* and *ATC* values at each output rate.

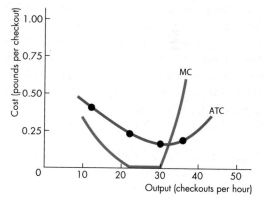

Figure 2 Self-Checkout

◆ Figure 3 compares the *ATC* of the two systems. You can see that the self-checkout system has higher *ATC* at low output rates and lower *ATC* at higher output rates. The reason is that self-checkout has a higher fixed cost and lower variable cost than the worker operated system.

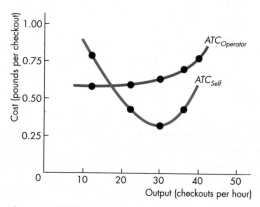

Figure 3 *ATC* Compared

Average and Marginal Product and Cost

Figure 10.7 shows the links between the firm's average and marginal product curves and its average and marginal cost curves. The upper graph shows the average product curve, *AP*, and the marginal product curve, *MP* – like those in Figure 10.3. The lower graph shows the average variable cost curve, *AVC*, and the marginal cost curve, *MC* – like those in Figure 10.5.

As labour increases up to 1.5 workers a day (upper graph), output increases to 6.5 jumpers a day (lower graph). Marginal product and average product rise and marginal cost and average variable cost fall. At the point of maximum marginal product, marginal cost is at a minimum.

As labour increases from 1.5 workers to 2 workers a day (upper graph), output increases from 6.5 jumpers to 10 jumpers a day (lower graph). Marginal product falls and marginal cost rises, but average product continues to rise and average variable cost continues to fall. At the point of maximum average product, average variable cost is at a minimum. As labour increases further, output increases. Average product diminishes and average variable cost increases.

Shifts in the Cost Curves

The position of a firm's short-run cost curves depends on two factors:

◆ Technology
◆ Prices of factors of production

Technology

A technological change that increases productivity shifts the total product curve upward. It also shifts the marginal product curve and the average product curve upward. With better technology, the same factors of production can produce more output. So technological change lowers cost and shifts the cost curves downward.

For example, advances in robotic production techniques have increased productivity in the car industry. As a result, the product curves of BMW, Renault and Volvo have shifted upward and their cost curves have shifted downward. But the relationships between their product curves and cost curves have not changed. The curves are still linked in the way shown in Figure 10.6.

Often, a technological advance results in a firm using more capital (a fixed factor) and less labour (a variable factor). For example, today the telephone companies use

Figure 10.7 Product Curves and Cost Curves

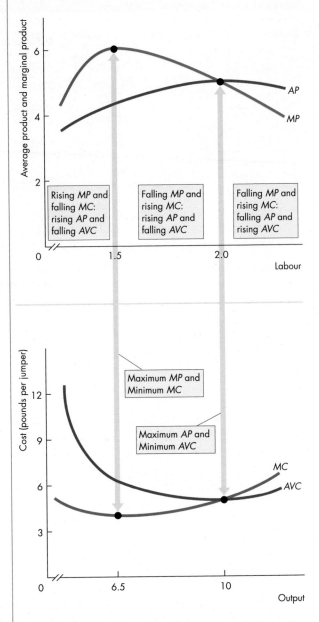

A firm's *MP* curve is linked to its *MC* curve. If, as the firm increases its labour from 0 to 1.5 workers a day, the firm's marginal product rises, its marginal cost falls. If marginal product is at a maximum, marginal cost is at a minimum. If, as the firm hires more labour, its marginal product diminishes, its marginal cost rises.

A firm's *AP* curve is linked to its *AVC* curve. If, as the firm increases its labour to 2 workers a day, its average product rises, its average variable cost falls. If average product is at a maximum, average variable cost is at a minimum. If, as the firm hires more labour, its average product diminishes, its average variable cost rises.

Table 10.2

A Compact Glossary of Costs

Term	Symbol	Definition	Equation
Fixed cost		Cost that is independent of the output level; cost of a fixed factor of production	
Variable cost		Cost that varies with the output level; cost of a variable factor of production	
Total fixed cost	TFC	Cost of the fixed factors of production (equals their number times their unit price)	
Total variable cost	TVC	Cost of the variable factors of production (equals their number times their unit price)	
Total cost	TC	Cost of all factors of production	$TC = TFC + TVC$
Total product (output)	TP	Total quantity produced (Q)	
Marginal cost	MC	Change in total cost resulting from a one-unit increase in total product	$MC = \Delta TC \div \Delta Q$
Average fixed cost	AFC	Total fixed cost per unit of output	$AFC = TFC \div Q$
Average variable cost	AVC	Total variable cost per unit of output	$AVC = TVC \div Q$
Average total cost	ATC	Total cost per unit of output	$ATC = AFC + AVC$

computers to provide directory assistance in place of the human operators they used in the 1980s. When such a technological change occurs, total cost decreases, but fixed costs increase and variable costs decrease. This change in the mix of fixed cost and variable cost means that at low output levels, average total cost might increase, while at high output levels, average total cost decreases.

Prices of Factors of Production

An increase in the price of a factor of production increases costs and shifts the cost curves. But the way the curves shift depends on which factor price changes. An increase in rent or some other component of *fixed* cost shifts the fixed cost curves (*TFC* and *AFC*) upward and the total cost curve (*TC*) upward, but leaves the variable cost curves (*AVC* and *TVC*) and the marginal cost curve (*MC*) unchanged. An increase in the wage rate or some other component of *variable* cost shifts the variable curves (*TVC* and *AVC*) upward, the total cost curve (*TC*) and the marginal cost curve (*MC*) upward, but leaves the fixed cost curves (*AFC* and *TFC*) unchanged. So for example, if the wage rate of lorry

drivers increases, the variable cost and marginal cost of transportation services increase. If the interest expense paid by a trucking company increases, the fixed cost of transportation services increases.

You've now completed your study of short-run costs. All the concepts that you've met are summarised in a compact glossary in Table 10.2.

REVIEW QUIZ

1   What relationships do a firm's short-run cost curves show?
2   How does marginal cost change as output increases (a) initially, and (b) eventually?
3   What does the law of diminishing returns imply for the shape of the marginal cost curve?
4   What is the shape of the *AFC* curve and why?
5   What are the shapes of the *AVC* curve and *ATC* curve and why?

Do these questions in Study Plan 10.3 and get instant feedback.   MyEconLab

Long-Run Cost

In the short run, a firm can vary the quantity of labour but the quantity of capital is fixed. So the firm has variable costs of labour and fixed costs of capital. In the long run, a firm can vary both the quantity of labour and the quantity of capital. So in the long run, all the firm's costs are variable. We are now going to study the firm's costs in the long run, when *all* costs are variable costs and when the quantity of labour and capital vary.

The behaviour of long-run costs depends on the firm's production function. The *production function* is the relationship between the maximum output attainable and the quantities of both labour and capital.

The Production Function

Table 10.3 shows Fashion First's production function. The table lists the total product for four different quantities of capital. The quantity of capital is defined as the plant size. Plant 1 represents a factory with 1 knitting machine – the case we have just studied. The other three plants have 2, 3 and 4 knitting machines. If Fashion First doubles its plant size from 1 to 2 knitting machines, the various amounts of labour can produce the outputs shown in the column under Plant 2 of the table. The next two columns show the outputs of yet larger plants. Each column in the table could be graphed as a total product curve for each plant size.

Diminishing Returns

Diminishing returns occur in each of the four plants as the quantity of labour increases. You can check that fact by calculating the marginal product of labour in plants with 2, 3 and 4 knitting machines. At each plant size, as the quantity of labour increases, the marginal product of labour (eventually) decreases.

Diminishing Marginal Product of Capital

Diminishing returns also occur as the quantity of capital increases. You can check that fact by calculating the marginal product of capital at a given quantity of labour. The *marginal product of capital* is the change in total product divided by the change in capital employed when the amount of labour employed is constant. It is the change in output resulting from a one-unit increase in the quantity of capital employed.

Table 10.3

The Production Function

Labour (workers per day)	Output (jumpers per day)			
	Plant 1	Plant 2	Plant 3	Plant 4
1	4	10	13	15
2	10	15	18	20
3	13	18	22	24
4	15	20	24	26
5	16	21	25	27
Knitting machines (number)	1	2	3	4

The table shows the total product data for four quantities of capital – four plant sizes. The bigger the plant size, the larger is the total product for any given amount of labour employed. But for a given plant size, the marginal product of labour diminishes as more labour is employed. For a given quantity of labour, the marginal product of capital diminishes as the quantity of capital used increases.

For example, if Fashion First employs 3 workers and increases its capital from 1 machine to 2 machines, output increases from 13 to 18 jumpers a day. The marginal product of capital is 5 jumpers a day. If with 3 workers, Fashion First increases its capital from 2 machines to 3 machines, output increases from 18 to 22 jumpers a day. The marginal product of the third machine is 4 jumpers a day, down from 5 jumpers a day for the second machine.

We can now see what the production function implies for long-run costs.

Short-Run Cost and Long-Run Cost

Continue to assume that labour costs £25 per worker per day and capital costs £25 per machine per day. Using these factor prices and the data in Table 10.3, we can calculate and graph the average total cost curves for factories with 1, 2, 3 and 4 knitting machines. We've already studied the costs of a factory with 1 knitting machine in Figures 10.5 and 10.6. In Figure 10.8, the average total cost curve for that case is ATC_1. Figure 10.8 also shows the average total cost curves for a factory with 2 machines, ATC_2, with 3 machines, ATC_3, and with 4 machines, ATC_4.

Figure 10.8 Short-Run Costs of Four Different Plants

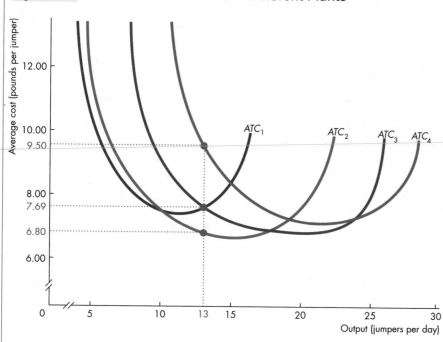

The figure shows short-run average total cost curves for four different quantities of capital.

Fashion First can produce 13 jumpers a day with 1 knitting machine on ATC_1, or with 3 knitting machines on ATC_3 for an average cost of £7.69 per jumper. Fashion First can produce the same number of jumpers by using 2 knitting machines on ATC_2 for £6.80 per jumper or with 4 machines on ATC_4 for £9.50 per jumper.

If Fashion First produces 13 jumpers a day, the least-cost method of production (the long-run method) is to use 2 machines on ATC_2.

MyEconLab Animation

You can see, in Figure 10.8, that plant size has a big effect on the firm's average total cost. Two things stand out:

1 Each short-run *ATC* curve is U-shaped.

2 For each short-run *ATC* curve, the larger the plant, the greater is the output at which average total cost is a minimum.

Each short-run average total cost curve is U-shaped because, as the quantity of labour increases, its marginal product at first increases and then diminishes. This pattern in the marginal product of labour, which we examined in some detail for the plant with 1 knitting machine on pp. 222–223, occurs at all plant sizes.

The minimum average total cost for a larger plant occurs at a greater output than it does for a smaller plant because the larger plant has a higher fixed cost and therefore, for any given output level, a higher average fixed cost.

Which short-run average cost curves Fashion First operates on depends on its plant size. But in the long run, Fashion First chooses its plant size. Its choice of plant size depends on the output that it plans to produce. The reason is that the average total cost of producing a given output depends on the plant size.

To see why, suppose that Fashion First plans to produce 13 jumpers a day. With 1 machine, the average total cost curve is ATC_1 (in Figure 10.8) and the average total cost of 13 jumpers a day is £7.69 per jumper. With 2 machines, on ATC_2, average total cost is £6.80 per jumper. With 3 machines on ATC_3, average total cost is £7.69 per jumper, the same as with 1 machine. Finally, with 4 machines, on ATC_4, average total cost is £9.50 per jumper.

The economically efficient plant size for producing a given output is the one that has the lowest average total cost. For Fashion First, the economically efficient plant to use to produce 13 jumpers a day is the one with 2 machines. In the long run, Fashion First chooses the plant size that minimises average total cost. When a firm is producing a given output at the least possible cost, it is operating on its *long-run average cost curve*.

The **long-run average cost curve** is the relationship between the lowest attainable average total cost and output when both the plant size and labour are varied. The long-run average cost curve is a planning curve. It tells the firm the plant size and the quantity of labour to use at each output to minimise cost. Once the plant size is chosen, the firm operates on the short-run cost curves that apply to that plant size.

The Long-Run Average Cost Curve

Figure 10.9 shows how the long-run average cost curve is derived. The long-run average cost curve *LRAC* consists of pieces of the four short-run *ATC* curves. For output up to 10 jumpers a day, the average total cost is lowest on ATC_1. For output rates between 10 and 18 jumpers a day, average total cost is lowest on ATC_2. For output rates between 18 and 24 jumpers a day, average total cost is lowest on ATC_3. For output rates in excess of 24 jumpers a day, average total cost is lowest on ATC_4. The piece of each *ATC* curve with the lowest average total cost is shown as dark blue in Figure 10.8. The dark blue scallop-shaped curve made up of the four pieces is Fashion First's *LRAC* curve.

Economies and Diseconomies of Scale

Economies of scale are features of a firm's technology that make average total cost *fall* as output increases. When economies of scale are present, the *LRAC* curve slopes downward. The *LRAC* in Figure 10.8 shows that Fashion First experiences economies of scale for outputs up to 15 jumpers a day.

Greater specialisation of both labour and capital is the main source of economies of scale. For example, if

BMW produces only 100 cars a week, each worker must be capable of performing many different tasks and the capital must be general-purpose machines and tools. But if BMW produces 10,000 cars a week, each worker specialises in a small number of tasks, uses task-specific tools and becomes highly proficient.

Diseconomies of scale are features of a firm's technology that make average total cost *rise* as output increases. When diseconomies of scale are present, the *LRAC* curve slopes upward. In Figure 10.9, Fashion First experiences diseconomies of scale at outputs greater than 15 jumpers a day.

The challenge of managing a large enterprise is the main source of diseconomies of scale.

Constant returns to scale are features of a firm's technology that keep average total costs constant as output increases. When constant returns to scale are present, the *LRAC* curve is horizontal.

The economies of scale and diseconomies of scale at Fashion First arise from the firm's production function in Table 10.3. With 1 worker and 1 machine, the firm produces 4 jumpers a day. With 2 workers and 2 machines, total cost doubles but output more than doubles to 15 jumpers a day, so average total cost decreases and Fashion First experiences economies of scale.

Figure 10.9 The Long-Run Average Cost Curve

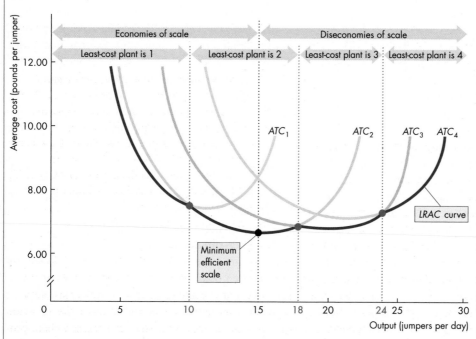

The long-run average cost curve traces the lowest attainable *ATC* when both labour and capital change. The green arrows highlight the output range over which each plant achieves the lowest *ATC*. Within each range, to change the quantity produced, the firm changes the quantity of labour it employs.

Along the *LRAC* curve economies of scale occur if average cost falls as output increases and diseconomies of scale occur if average cost rises as output increases.

Minimum efficient scale is the output at which average cost is lowest, 15 jumpers a day.

ECONOMICS IN ACTION

Produce More to Cut Cost

Why do BMW, Citroen and other car makers have expensive equipment lying around that isn't fully used? You can now answer this question with what you have learned in this chapter.

The basic answer is that car production faces economies of scale. A larger output rate brings a lower long-run average cost – the firm's *LRAC* curve slopes downward.

A car producer's average total cost curves look like those in Figure 1. To produce 20 vehicles an hour, the firm installs the plant with the short-run average total cost curve ATC_1. The average cost of producing a vehicle is €20,000.

Producing 20 vehicles an hour doesn't use the plant at its lowest possible average total cost. If the firm could sell

enough cars for it to produce 40 vehicles an hour, the firm could use its current plant and produce at an average cost of €15,000 a vehicle.

But if the firm planned to produce 40 vehicles an hour, it would not use its current plant. The firm would install a bigger plant with the short-run average total cost curve ATC_2, and produce 40 vehicles an hour for €10,000 a car.

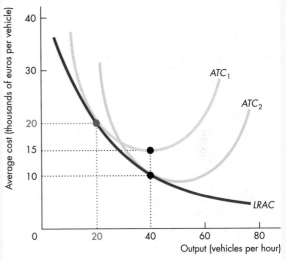

Figure 1 Car Plant's Average Cost Curves

With 4 workers and 4 machines, total cost doubles again, but output less than doubles to 26 jumpers a day, so average total cost increases and Fashion First experiences diseconomies of scale.

Minimum Efficient Scale

A firm's **minimum efficient scale** is the *smallest* quantity of output at which long-run average cost reaches its lowest level. At Fashion First, the minimum efficient scale is 15 jumpers per day.

The minimum efficient scale plays a role in determining market structure. In a market in which the minimum efficient scale is small relative to the market demand, the market has room for many firms. The market is competitive. In a market in which the minimum efficient scale is large relative to market demand, only a small number of firms, and sometimes only one firm, can make a profit. The market is an oligopoly or monopoly. We'll look at these ideas in the next three chapters.

REVIEW QUIZ

1 What does a firm's production function show and how is it related to a total product curve?
2 Does the law of diminishing returns apply to capital as well as labour? Explain why or why not.
3 What does a firm's *LRAC* curve show? How is it related to the firm's short-run *ATC* curve?
4 What are economies and diseconomies of scale? How do they arise? What do they imply for the shape of the *LRAC* curve?
5 What is a firm's minimum efficient scale?

Do these questions in Study Plan 10.4 and get instant feedback.   MyEconLab

You have now studied how a firm's costs vary as it changes its output. *Reading Between the Lines* on pp. 236–237 applies what you have learned about production costs to cost curves at Jaguar Land Rover. The Appendix presents an alternative analysis of costs.

READING BETWEEN THE LINES

JLR Expanding Engine Plant Capacity

Jaguar Land Rover to Create 700 Jobs

Peter Marsh

Some 700 additional jobs are to be created in the Midlands through an additional £150m investment in a new engine factory in Wolverhampton from Jaguar Land Rover.

The company – part of India's Tata industrial group – has authorised the extra investment to cover the possibility of a large expansion in output in its UK car plants in the next few years. . . . The new commitment brings the total investment to £500m and the total workforce when fully operational to 1,400. . . .

JLR managers and the company's Indian owners have become more confident about expansion. Last year JLR, which currently has all its vehicle production in Britain, built 350,000 cars with 80 per cent of them exported to more than 170 countries. . . .

By 2016 observers believe the group could be selling 600,000 cars a year: all from its three UK plants. . . . While almost all JLR vehicles at present have engines made by Ford of the US, by 2016 most will be produced by the Wolverhampton facility.

JLR managers need to plan for the possibility of the new plant having a capacity to make at least 500,000 engines a year – well above the number envisaged two years ago. . . .

 Source: FT.com, 5 March 2013.

 ## The Essence of the Story

- Jaguar Land Rover (JLR) is increasing the output capacity of its planned new engine factory in the UK.

- The extra £150 million investment will add a further 700 new jobs.

- JLR believes its UK car plants will be making and selling nearly double the number of cars in three year's time.

- Currently JLR buys in US engines, but by 2016 most engines will come from its new UK plant.

Economic Analysis

♦ Jaguar Land Rover (JLR) is increasing the planned output of its new engine plant to be built in Wolverhampton.

♦ A firm can increase output with its existing plant by hiring more labour, or it can increase its plant size without hiring more labour, or it can increase plant size and hire more labour.

♦ JLR is comparing technology constraints and costs and working out how to minimise cost in the long run by increasing the planned plant size and the number of workers hired.

♦ Figure 1 shows the total product curve TP_0 (assumed) for the original planned plant size. With this TP curve, if JLR hires 700 workers, it can produce 5,000 engines a week (enough for most of its cars) at point A.

♦ This plant can produce 8,000 engines a week at point B on TP_0 if JLR hires 1,400 workers.

♦ To make 500,000 engines a year (10,000 per week), JLR must increase the planned plant size to TP_1 in Figure 1.

♦ With 700 workers on TP_1, JLR would produce more engines, but not enough more to meet its target of 10,000 engines a week.

♦ To increase production to 10,000 engines per week, JLR must increase the number of workers to 1,400 and produce at point C.

♦ With the larger plant, JLR can buy in components more cheaply, install more robotic equipment, save on shipping cost, and produce more engines with fewer workers.

♦ With the larger plant, fixed cost increases, so at low output levels, average total cost of an engine also increases. But at higher output levels average total cost decreases.

♦ Figure 2 shows JLR's average total cost curves: ATC_0 for the original planned plant size and the new ATC_1 for the larger plant size.

♦ If JLR hires more workers with the original plant, it moves along ATC_0 from point A to

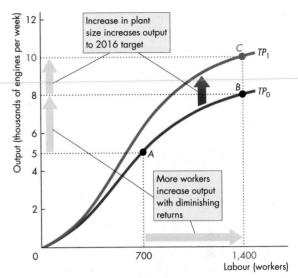

Figure 1 JLR Long-Run Plant Size Decision

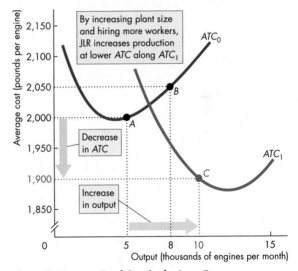

Figure 2 Average Total Cost in the Long Run

point B and faces a rising average total cost of an engine.

♦ By increasing its plant and hiring more workers, JLR moves along ATC_1 to point C and increases output at a lower average total cost.

♦ JLR benefits from economies of scale.

SUMMARY

Key Points

Time Frames for Decisions (p. 220)

◆ In the short run, the quantity of at least one factor of production is fixed and the quantities of the other factors can be varied.

◆ In the long run, the quantities of all factors of production can be varied.

Do Problems 1 and 2 to get a better understanding of a firm's decision time frames.

Short-Run Technology Constraint (pp. 221–224)

◆ A total product curve shows the quantity of output that a firm can produce using a given quantity of capital and different quantities of labour.

◆ Initially, the marginal product of labour increases as the quantity of labour increases because of increased specialisation and the division of labour.

◆ Eventually, marginal product diminishes because an increased quantity of labour must share a fixed quantity of capital – the law of diminishing marginal returns.

◆ Initially, average product increases as the quantity of labour increases, but eventually average product diminishes.

Do Problems 3 to 8 to get a better understanding of a firm's short-run technology constraint.

Short-Run Cost (pp. 225–231)

◆ As output increases, total fixed cost is constant, and total variable cost and total cost increase.

◆ As output increases, average variable cost, average total cost and marginal cost decrease at small outputs and increase at large outputs. These cost curves are U-shaped.

Do Problems 9 to 14 to get a better understanding of a firm's short-run cost.

Long-Run Cost (pp. 232–235)

◆ Long-run cost is the cost of production when all factors of production – labour and plant – have been adjusted to their economically efficient levels.

◆ The firm has a set of short-run cost curves for each different plant. For each output, the firm has one least-cost plant. The larger the output, the larger is the plant that will minimise average total cost.

◆ The long-run average cost curve traces the relationship between the lowest attainable average total cost and output when both capital and labour can be varied.

◆ With economies of scale, the long-run average cost curve slopes downward. With diseconomies of scale, the long-run average cost curve slopes upward.

Do Problems 15 to 20 to get a better understanding of a firm's long-run cost.

Key Terms

Average fixed cost, 226
Average product, 221
Average total cost, 226
Average variable cost, 226
Constant returns to scale, 234
Diminishing marginal returns, 223
Diseconomies of scale, 234
Economies of scale, 234
Law of diminishing returns, 223
Long run, 220
Long-run average cost curve, 233
Marginal cost, 226
Marginal product, 221
Minimum efficient scale, 235
Short run, 220
Sunk cost, 220
Total cost, 225
Total fixed cost, 225
Total product, 221
Total variable cost, 225

STUDY PLAN PROBLEMS AND APPLICATIONS

Do Problems 1 to 21 in MyEconLab Chapter 10 Study Plan and get instant feedback.

MyEconLab

Decision Time Frames (Study Plan 10.1)

1 Which of the following news items involve a short-run decision and which involve a long-run decision? Explain.

18 April 2009: By next March, Tesco plans to open more than 100 shops in the UK, selling mobile and land-line packages in its largest stores.

6 October 2009: Tesco said that it would 'mothball' 13 stores in Nevada, Arizona and California – by boarding them up or subletting them, with a plan to reopen them in four to five years once the US economy recovers.

22 August 2010: Tesco is lauching its first drive-through supermarket this week. Customers order online and at the supermarket drive-through staff pack the shopping into the boot.

1 September 2010: Tesco plans to open 80 vast shopping malls in China by 2016.

2 Farmers Turn from Tobacco to Flowers

US tobacco farmers will be subsidised if they switch from growing tobacco to growing crops such as flowers and organic vegetables.

Source: *The New York Times*, 25 February 2001

a How does offering farmers a payment to exit tobacco growing influence the opportunity cost of growing tobacco?

b What is the opportunity cost of using the equipment owned by a tobacco farmer?

Short-Run Technology Constraint
(Study Plan 10.2)

Use the following table in Problems 3 to 7.

The table sets out Sue's Snowboards' total product schedule:

Labour (workers per week)	Output (snowboards per week)
1	30
2	70
3	120
4	160
5	190
6	210
7	220

3 Draw the total product curve.

4 Calculate the average product of labour and draw the average product curve.

5 Calculate the marginal product of labour and draw the marginal product curve.

6 a Over what output range does the firm enjoy the benefits of increased specialisation and division of labour?

b Over what output range does the firm experience diminishing marginal product of labour?

c Over what range of output does the firm experience an increasing average product of labour but a diminishing marginal product of labour?

7 Explain how it is possible for a firm to experience simultaneously an increasing *average* product but a diminishing *marginal* product.

8 Sales at a footwear company rose from €160,000 in 2006 to €2.3 million in 2007, but in 2008 sales dipped to €1.5 million. Priscilla, the owner, blames the decline partly on a flood that damaged the firm's office and sapped morale. Assume that the prices of footwear didn't change.

a Explain the effect of the flood on the company's total product curve and marginal product curve.

b Draw a graph to show the effect of the flood on the company's total product curve and marginal product curve.

Short-Run Cost (Study Plan 10.3)

Use the following data in Problems 9 to 13.

Sue's Snowboards in Problem 3 employs workers at €500 a week and its total fixed cost is €1,000 a week.

9 Calculate total cost, total variable cost and total fixed cost for each output and draw the short-run total cost curves.

10 Calculate average total cost, average fixed cost, average variable cost and marginal cost at each output and draw the short-run average and marginal cost curves.

11 Illustrate the connection between Sue's *AP*, *MP*, *AVC* and *MC* curves like those in Figure 10.7.

12 Sue's Snowboards rents a factory building. If the rent is increased by €200 a week and other things remain the same, how do Sue's Snowboards' short-run average cost curves and marginal cost curve change?

13 Workers at Sue's Snowboards negotiate a wage increase of €100 a week for each worker. If other things remain the same, explain how Sue's Snowboards' short-run average cost curves and marginal cost curve change.

14 Grain Prices Go the Way of the Oil Price

Every morning millions of people confront the latest trend in commodities markets at their kitchen table. Rising prices for crops have begun to drive up the cost of breakfast cereals.

Source: *The Economist*, 21 July 2007

Explain how the rising price of crops affects the average total cost and marginal cost of producing breakfast cereals.

Long-Run Cost (Study Plan 10.4)

Use the table in Problem 3 and the following information in Problems 15 and 16.

Sue's Snowboards buys a second plant and the output produced by each worker increases by 50 per cent. The total fixed cost of operating each plant is €1,000 a week. Each worker is paid €500 a week.

15 Calculate the average total cost of producing 180 and 240 snowboards a week when Sue's Snowboards operates two plants. Graph these points and sketch the *ATC* curve.

16 a To produce 180 snowboards a week, is it efficient to operate one or two plants?

   b To produce 160 snowboards a week, is it efficient for Sue's to operate one or two plants?

Use the following table in Problems 17 to 20.

The table shows the production function of Jackie's Canoe Rides.

Labour (workers per day)	Output (rides per day)			
	Plant 1	Plant 2	Plant 3	Plant 4
10	20	40	55	65
20	40	60	75	85
30	65	75	90	100
40	75	85	100	110
Canoes (number)	10	20	30	40

Jackie pays €100 a day for each canoe she rents and €50 a day for each canoe operator she hires.

17 Graph the *ATC* curves for Plant 1 and Plant 2. Explain why these *ATC* curves differ from each other.

18 Graph the *ATC* curves for Plant 3 and Plant 4. Explain why these *ATC* curves differ from each other.

19 a On Jackie's *LRAC* curve, what is the average cost of producing 40, 75 and 85 rides a week?

   b What is Jackie's minimum efficient scale?

20 a Explain how Jackie's uses her *LRAC* curve to decide how many canoes to rent.

   b Does Jackie's production function feature economies of scale or diseconomies of scale?

Economics in the News (Study Plan 10.N)

21 Airlines Seek Out New Ways to Save on Fuel as Costs Soar

The financial pain of higher fuel prices is particularly acute for airlines because it is their single biggest expense. Airlines pump about 7,000 gallons into a Boeing 737 and about 60,000 gallons into the bigger 747 jet. Each generation of aircraft is more efficient: an Airbus A330 long-range jet uses 38 per cent less fuel than the DC-10 it replaced, while the Airbus A319 medium-range jet is 27 per cent more efficient than the DC-9 it replaced.

Source: *The New York Times*, 11 June 2008

a Is the price of fuel a fixed cost or a variable cost for an airline?

b Explain how an increase in the price of fuel changes an airline's total costs, average costs and marginal cost.

c Draw a graph to show the effects of an increase in the price of fuel on an airline's *TFC*, *TVC*, *AFC*, *AVC* and *MC* curves.

d Explain how a technological advance that makes an airplane engine more fuel efficient changes an airline's total product, marginal product and average product curves.

e Draw a graph to illustrate the effects of a more fuel-efficient aircraft on an airline's *TP*, *MP* and *AP* curves.

f Explain how a technological advance that makes an airplane engine more fuel efficient changes an airline's average variable cost, marginal cost and average total cost.

g Draw a graph to illustrate how a technological advance that makes an airplane engine more fuel efficient changes an airline's *AVC*, *MC* and *ATC* curves.

ADDITIONAL PROBLEMS AND APPLICATIONS

Do these problems in MyEconLab if assigned by your lecturer.

MyEconLab

Decision Time Frames

22 A Bakery on the Rise

Some 500 customers a day line up to buy Avalon's breads, scones, muffins and coffee. Staffing and management are worries. Avalon now employs 35 and plans to hire 15 more. Its payroll will climb by 30 per cent to 40 per cent. The new CEO has executed an ambitious agenda that includes the move to a larger space, which will increase the rent from $3,500 to $10,000 a month.

Source: CNN, 24 March 2008

a Which of Avalon's decisions described in the news clip is a short-run decision and which is a long-run decision?

b Why is Avalon's long-run decision riskier than its short-run decision?

23 The Sunk-Cost Fallacy

You have good tickets to a football game an hour's drive away. There's a storm raging outside, and the game is being televised. You can sit warm and safe at home and watch it on TV, or you can bundle up and go to the game. What do you do?

Source: *Slate*, 9 September 2005

a What type of cost is your expenditure on tickets?

b Why is the cost of the ticket irrelevant to your current decision about whether to stay at home or go to the game?

Short-Run Technology Constraint

24 Terri runs a rose farm. One worker produces 1,000 roses a week; hiring a second worker doubles her total product; hiring a third worker doubles her output again; hiring a fourth worker increases her total product but by only 1,000 roses. Construct Terri's marginal product and average product schedules. Over what range of workers do marginal returns increase?

Short-Run Cost

25 Use the events described in the news clip in Problem 22. By how much will Avalon's short-run decision increase its total variable cost? By how much will Avalon's long-run decision increase its monthly total fixed cost? Sketch Avalon's short-run *ATC* curve before and after the events described in the news clip.

26 Coffee King Starbucks Raises Its Prices

Starbucks is raising its prices because the wholesale price of milk has risen 70 per cent and there's a lot of milk in Starbucks' lattes.

Source: *USA Today*, 24 July 2007

Is milk a fixed factor of production or a variable factor of production? Describe how the increase in the price of milk changes Starbucks' short-run cost curves.

27 Bill's Bakery has a fire and Bill loses some of his cost data. The bits of paper that he recovers after the fire provide the data in the following table (all the cost numbers are euros).

TP	AFC	AVC	ATC	MC
10	120	100	220	
				80
20	A	B	150	
				90
30	40	90	130	
				130
40	30	C	D	
				E
50	24	108	132	

Bill asks you to come to his rescue and provide the missing data in the five spaces identified as *A*, *B*, *C*, *D* and *E*.

Use the following table in Problems 28 and 29.

ProPainters hires students at €250 a week to paint houses. It leases equipment at €500 a week. The table sets out its total product schedule.

Labour (workers per week)	Output (houses painted per week)
1	2
2	5
3	9
4	12
5	14
6	15

28 If ProPainters paints 12 houses a week, calculate its total cost, average total cost and marginal cost. At what output is average total cost a minimum?

29 Explain why the gap between ProPainters' total cost and total variable cost is the same no matter how many houses are painted.

Long-Run Cost

Use the table in Problem 28 and the following information in Problems 30 and 31.

If ProPainters doubles the number of students it hires and doubles the amount of equipment it leases, it experiences dis-economies of scale.

30 Explain how the *ATC* curve with one unit of equipment differs from that when ProPainters uses double the amount of equipment.

31 Explain what might be the source of the diseconomies of scale that ProPainters experiences.

Use the following information in Problems 32 and 33.

The table shows the production function of Bonnie's Balloon Rides. Bonnie's pays $500 a day for each balloon it rents and $25 a day for each balloon operator it hires.

Labour (workers per day)	Output (rides per day)			
	Plant 1	**Plant 2**	**Plant 3**	**Plant 4**
1	6	10	13	15
2	10	15	18	21
3	13	18	22	24
4	15	20	24	26
5	16	21	25	27
Balloons (number)	**1**	**2**	**3**	**4**

32 Graph the *ATC* curves for Plant 1 and Plant 2. Explain why these *ATC* curves differ.

33 Graph the *ATC* curves for Plant 3 and Plant 4. Explain why these *ATC* curves differ.

34 **a** On Bonnie's *LRAC* curve, what is the average cost of producing 18 rides and 15 rides a day?

  b Explain how Bonnie's uses its long-run average cost curve to decide how many balloons to rent.

Use the following news clip in Problems 35 and 36.

Gap Will Focus on Smaller Scale Stores

Gap has too many stores that are 12,500 square feet. The target store size is 6,000 square feet to 10,000 square feet, so Gap plans to combine previously separate concept stores. Some Gap body, adult, maternity, baby and kids stores will be combined in one store.

Source: CNN, 10 June 2008

35 Thinking of a Gap store as a production plant, explain why Gap is making a decision to reduce the size of its stores. Is Gap's decision a long-run decision or a short-run decision?

36 How might combining Gap's concept stores into one store help better take advantage of economies of scale?

Economics in the News

37 After you have studied *Reading Between the Lines* on pp. 236–237, answer the following questions.

  a Explain the distinction between the short run and the long run for JLR, using Figure 1 from p. 237.

  b Explain under what circumstances might it be efficient for JLR to hire more workers but not expand the plant size.

  c Explain economies of scale. Would it be worth JLR expanding capacity if its average total cost had not fallen at ouputs greater than 8,000 cars a week?

38 **Self-serve Espresso Bars**

Automated, self-service espresso kiosks are now being introduced in some stores. The machines can grind beans and deliver latte and espresso coffee and take credit and debit cards and cash. The kiosks cost €40,000 per unit, but must be installed and maintained. Self-service kiosks remove the labour costs for service. The kiosks must be refilled by store staff with coffee beans and milk.

Source: MSNBC, 1 June 2008

  a What is the total fixed cost of operating one self-service kiosk?

  b What are the variable costs of providing coffee at a self-service kiosk?

  c Assume that a coffee machine in a traditional service cafe costs less than €40,000. Explain how the fixed costs, variable costs and total costs of traditionally served and self-served coffee differ.

  d Sketch the marginal cost and average cost curves implied by your answer to part (c).

39 The cost of producing electricity using hydro power is about one-third of the cost of using coal, oil or nuclear power plants and is less than one-quarter the cost of using gas turbine plants. Most of the cost differences come from differences in fuel costs. But part of the cost difference comes from differences in plant costs. It costs less to build a hydroelectric plant than a coal, oil or nuclear plant. Gas turbine plants cost the least to build but are the most expensive to operate.

(Based on *Projected Costs of Generating Electricity*, International Energy Agency, 2005)

  a Use the above information to sketch the *AFC*, *AVC* and *ATC* curves for electricity production using three technologies: (i) hydro, (ii) coal, oil or nuclear and (iii) gas turbine.

  b Use the above information to sketch the marginal cost curves for electricity production using three technologies: (i) hydro, (ii) coal, oil or nuclear and (iii) gas turbine.

  c Given the cost differences among the three methods of generating electricity, why do we use more than one?

CHAPTER 10 APPENDIX

Producing at Least Cost

After studying this Appendix, you will be able to:

◆ Make an isoquant map and explain the law of diminishing marginal rate of substitution

◆ Describe an isocost line and explain how a change in factor price shifts it

◆ Calculate the least-cost technique of production

Isoquants and Factor Substitution

A firm's long-run production function describes all the technically feasible combinations of labour and capital that can produce given output levels. Whatever goods it produces, a firm can choose between labour-intensive or capital-intensive production techniques. To move from one technique to another, a firm must change the combination of labour and capital it uses – a change called factor substitution.

In this Appendix, you are going to use a new model to find the best combination of factors.

Figure A10.1 shows Fashion First's production function. The figure shows that in the long run, Fashion First can use three different combinations of labour and capital to produce 15 jumpers a day, and two different combinations to produce 10 and 21 jumpers a day. So to maximise profit, Fashion First uses the least-cost combination of labour and capital that minimises its total cost.

An Isoquant Map

An **isoquant** is a curve that shows the different combinations of labour and capital required to produce a given quantity of output. The word isoquant means 'equal quantity'. There is an isoquant for each output level. A series of isoquants is called an **isoquant map**. Figure A10.2 shows an isoquant map for Fashion First with three isoquants: one for 10 jumpers a day, one for 15 jumpers a day and one for 21 jumpers a day. Each isoquant shown is based on the production function in Figure A10.1.

Although all goods and services can be produced using a variety of alternative production techniques,

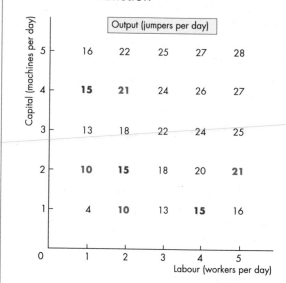

Figure A10.1   Fashion First's Production Function

The figure shows how many jumpers can be produced each day using different combinations of labour and capital. For example, Fashion First can produce 15 jumpers a day using 1 worker and 4 machines, or 2 workers and 2 machines, or 4 workers and 1 machine.

MyEconLab Animation ──────────────────◆

the ease with which labour and capital can be substituted for each other varies from industry to industry. The production function reflects the ease of factor substitution and can be used to calculate the degree of substitutability between factors. This calculation involves the marginal rate of substitution of labour for capital. The **marginal rate of substitution of labour for capital** is the increase in labour needed per unit decrease in capital to allow output to remain constant. Let's look at this in more detail.

The Marginal Rate of Substitution

The marginal rate of substitution is the magnitude of the slope of an isoquant. Figure A10.3 shows the isoquant for 13 jumpers a day. Pick any point on this isoquant and imagine decreasing capital by the smallest conceivable amount and increasing labour by the amount necessary to keep output constant at 13 jumpers. As we decrease the quantity of capital and increase the quantity of labour to keep output constant at 13 jumpers a day, we travel down along the isoquant.

Figure A10.2 An Isoquant Map

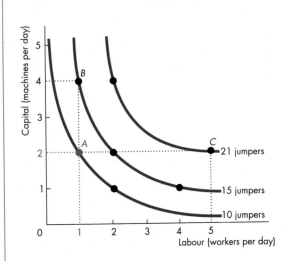

The figure shows three isoquants that are part of Fashion First's isoquant map. Along each isoquant, the output produced by labour and capital is constant. These isoquants correspond to the production function for 10, 15 and 21 jumpers a day in Figure A10.1.

If Fashion First uses 2 machines and 1 worker (at point A), it produces 10 jumpers a day. If Fashion First uses 4 machines and 1 worker (at point B), it produces 15 jumpers a day. If Fashion First uses 2 machines and 5 workers (at point C), it produces 21 jumpers a day.

MyEconLab Animation ─────────────────◆

Figure A10.3 The Marginal Rate of Substitution

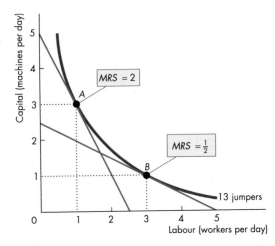

The marginal rate of substitution is measured by the magnitude of the slope of the isoquant. For example, to find the slope of the isoquant at point A, calculate the slope of the red line tangential to the isoquant at point A. The magnitude of the slope at point A is 2 (5 ÷ 2.5), so the marginal rate of substitution of labour for capital at point A is 2. Similarly, the magnitude of the marginal rate of substitution at point B equals the magnitude of the slope of the red tangential line at point B and is 1/2. So the marginal rate of substitution of labour for capital at point B is 1/2.

MyEconLab Animation ─────────────────◆

In Figure A10.3, the marginal rate of substitution at point A is the magnitude of the slope of the red line tangential to the isoquant at point A. The slope of the isoquant at point A equals the slope of the line. To calculate the slope, move along the red line from 5 knitting machines and no workers to 2.5 workers and no knitting machines. Capital decreases by 5 knitting machines and labour increases by 2.5 workers. The magnitude of the slope is 5 divided by 2.5, which equals 2. So when using technique A to produce 13 jumpers a day, the marginal rate of substitution of labour for capital is 2.

The marginal rate of substitution at point B is the magnitude of the slope of the red line tangential to the isoquant at point B. Along this red line, if capital decreases by 2.5 knitting machines, labour increases by 5 workers. The magnitude of the slope is 2.5 knitting machines divided by 5, which equals 1/2. So when using technique B to produce 13 jumpers a day, the marginal rate of substitution of labour for capital is 1/2.

The marginal rates of substitution we have just calculated obey the **law of diminishing marginal rate of substitution** which states that:

The marginal rate of substitution of labour for capital diminishes as the amount of labour increases and the amount of capital decreases.

The law of diminishing marginal rate of substitution determines the shape of the isoquant. When the quantity of capital is large and the quantity of labour is small, the isoquant is steep and the marginal rate of substitution of labour for capital is large. As the quantity of capital decreases and the quantity of labour increases, the isoquant becomes flatter and the marginal rate of substitution of labour for capital diminishes. Isoquants bow towards the origin.

We are going to use Fashion First's isoquant map to work out the firm's least-cost technique of production, but first we must add the firm's costs to the model.

Isocost Lines

An **isocost line** shows the combinations of labour and capital that can be bought for a given total cost and given factor prices. Suppose that a knitting-machine worker can be hired for £25 a day and that a knitting machine can be rented for £25 a day. Figure A10.4 shows five possible combinations of labour and capital (A, B, C, D and E) that Fashion First can employ for a total cost of £100 a day. For example, point B shows that Fashion First can use 3 machines (for a cost of £75) and 1 worker (for a cost of £25). If Fashion First can employ workers and machines for fractions of a day, then any combination along the line AE will cost Fashion First £100 a day. This line is Fashion First's isocost line for a total cost of £100.

The Isocost Equation

An isocost equation describes an isocost line. The variables that affect a firm's total cost (TC) are the price of labour (P_L), the price of capital (P_K), the quantity of labour (L) and the quantity of capital (K).

The cost of the labour is ($P_L \infty L$). The cost of capital is ($P_K \infty K$). Total cost is the sum of these two costs.

Equation 1 shows a firm's total cost:

$$P_L L + P_K K = TC \qquad (1)$$

Equation 2 shows the total cost for Fashion First using the numbers in our example. The wage rate is £25 a day and the capital rental rate is also £25 a day, so Fashion First's total cost is:

$$£25L + £25K = £100 \qquad (2)$$

Now rearrange equation (1) by dividing by the price of capital and then subtract (P_L/P_K)L from both sides of the equation. The resulting equation is the equation of the isocost line:

$$K = \frac{TC}{P_K} - \frac{P_L}{P_K} \times L \qquad (3)$$

Equation 3 tells us how the firm can vary the quantity of capital as it changes the quantity of labour, holding total cost constant. Fashion First's isocost line is:

$$K = 4 - L \qquad (4)$$

Equation 4 corresponds to the isocost line in Figure A10.4.

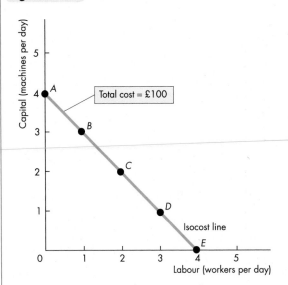

Figure A10.4 An Isocost Line

If labour is £25 a day and a knitting machine rents for £25 a day, Fashion First can employ the combinations of labour and capital shown by points A to E for a total cost of £100. The line through these points is an isocost line. It shows all possible combinations of labour and capital that Fashion First can hire for a total cost of £100 when labour is £25 a day and capital can be rented for £25 a day.

MyEconLab Animation ⎯⎯⎯⎯⎯⎯⎯◆

The Isocost Map

An **isocost map** is a series of isocost lines, each one of which represents a different total cost but for given prices of labour and capital.

The larger the total cost, the greater are the quantities of labour and capital that can be employed. Figure A10.5 shows an isocost map. The middle isocost is the one you've seen before for a total cost of £100, when labour and capital cost £25 a day each. The other two isocost lines are for a total cost of £125 and £75, holding constant the factor prices at £25 a day each. The larger the total cost, the further is the isocost line from the origin.

The Effect of Factor Prices

The magnitude of the slope of the isocost lines shown in Figure A10.5 is 1. The slope tells us that 1 unit of labour costs 1 unit of capital. To decrease its capital by 1 unit and keep its total cost at £100 a day, Fashion First must increase the quantity of labour by 1 unit.

Figure A10.5 An Isocost Map

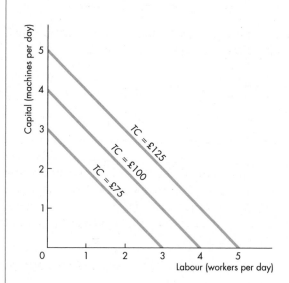

An isocost map shows the set of isocost lines, each for a different total cost. This isocost map shows three isocost lines, one for a total cost of £75 a day, one for £100 a day and one for £125 a day. Along the isocost lines, the prices of labour and capital are constant. For each isocost line shown here, the prices of labour and capital are £25 a day. The slope of an isocost line is equal to the relative price of labour to capital. The larger the total cost, the farther is the isocost line from the origin.

MyEconLab Animation ————————◆

Figure A10.6 Factor Prices and the Isocost Line

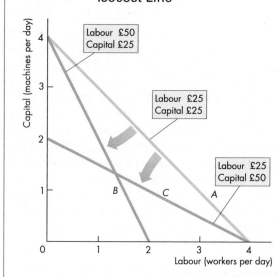

The slope of the isocost line depends on the relative factor price. Each of the isocost lines shown here has a total cost of £100 a day. If the prices of labour and capital are £25 a day, the isocost line is the line labelled *A*. If the price of labour rises to £50 a day but the price of capital remains at £25 a day, the isocost line becomes steeper and is the line labelled *B*. If the price of capital rises to £50 a day and the price of labour remains at £25 a day, the isocost line becomes flatter and is the line labelled *C*.

MyEconLab Animation ————————◆

If factor prices change, the slope of the isocost line changes. To see the effect of factor prices on the slope of the isocost line, start with the isocost equation:

$$K = \frac{TC}{P_K} - \frac{P_L}{P_K} \times L \qquad (3)$$

If the wage rate rises to £50 a day and the rental rate of a machine remains at £25 a day, then 1 unit of labour costs 2 units of capital. The relative price of labour to capital is £50 ÷ £25, which is 2. The isocost line becomes the steeper line *B* in Figure A10.6.

If the capital rental rate rises to £50 a day and the wage rate remains at £25 a day, then 1 unit of capital costs 2 units of labour. The relative price of labour to capital becomes £25 ÷ £50, which is 0.5. The isocost line becomes the flatter line *C* in Figure A10.6.

The higher the relative price of labour, the steeper is the isocost line. The magnitude of the slope of the isocost line measures the relative price of labour in terms of capital – the price of labour divided by the price of capital.

The Least-Cost Technique

The **least-cost technique** is the combination of labour and capital that minimises the total cost of producing a given level of output.

Suppose Fashion First plans to produce 15 jumpers a day, given the prices of capital and labour at £25 a day. What is the least-cost technique that Fashion First can use? Figure A10.7 shows the isoquant for an output of 15 jumpers and two isocost lines. One isocost is for a total cost of £125 a day and the other for £100 a day.

At point *A* in Figure A10.7, Fashion First can produce 15 jumpers using 1 worker and 4 machines. With this technique, the total cost is £125 a day. Point *C*, which uses 4 workers and 1 machine, is another technique that produces 15 jumpers for the same cost of £125 a day. At point *B*, Fashion First can use 2 machines and 2 workers to produce 15 jumpers, but the cost is £100 a day. So point *B* is the least-cost technique or the economically efficient technique for producing 15 jumpers, when machines and workers cost £25 a day each.

Figure A10.7 The Least-Cost Technique of Production

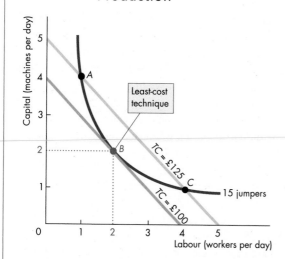

Fashion First can produce 15 jumpers a day by using 4 machines and 1 worker at point *A* or 1 machine and 4 workers at point *C*. The total cost using either of these techniques is £125 a day.

Fashion First can also use 2 machines and 2 workers at point *B* to produce 15 jumpers a day. The total cost using this technique is £100 a day. Point *B* is the least-cost technique of producing 15 jumpers.

At point B, the isoquant for 15 jumpers is tangential to the isocost line. The slope of the isoquant (the marginal rate of substitution) and the slope of the isocost line (the relative price of the factors) are the same.

MyEconLab Animation ─────────────◆

Figure A10.7 shows that there is only one way for Fashion First to produce 15 jumpers for £100 a day, but several ways to produce 15 jumpers for more than £100 a day. Techniques shown by points *A*, *B* and *C* are just examples. The points between *A*, *B* and *C* are also possible ways of producing 15 jumpers but for a total cost between £100 and £125 a day. Isocost lines exist between those shown which cut the isoquant for 15 jumpers at points between *A*, *B* and *C*. Fashion First could also produce 15 jumpers for a total cost of more than £125 a day by moving to a point on the isoquant outside the isocost line shown.

The least-cost technique for producing 15 jumpers a day is at point *B* in Figure A10.7. Fashion First cannot produce 15 jumpers for less than £100 a day. An isocost line for a total cost of less than £100 a day would not touch the isoquant for 15 jumpers because at the given prices of capital and labour, the total cost will not buy the factors needed to produce 15 jumpers.

Marginal Rate of Substitution and Marginal Products

The marginal rate of substitution and the marginal products are linked by an interesting formula:

The marginal rate of substitution of labour for capital equals the marginal product of labour divided by the marginal product of capital.

A few steps of reasoning are needed to establish this proposition.

First, we know that output changes when a firm changes the quantities of labour and capital employed. The change in output that results from a change in one of the factors is determined by the marginal product of the factor. So:

$$\text{Change in output} = (MP_L \times \Delta L) + (MP_K \times \Delta K) \quad (4)$$

Equation 4 shows a change in output equals the marginal product of labour, MP_L, multiplied by the change in labour, ΔL, plus the marginal product of capital, MP_K, multiplied by the change in capital, ΔK.

Suppose that Fashion First wants to change the quantities of labour and capital but continue to produce the same number of jumpers. That is, Fashion First wants to stay on the same isoquant, so the change in output must be zero. We can make the change in output zero in equation (4) to give equation (5):

$$MP_L \times \Delta L = -(MP_K \times \Delta K) \quad (5)$$

To stay on an isoquant when labour increases, capital must decrease. That is, when labour increases by ΔL, capital must decrease by:

$$MP_L \times \Delta L = MP_K \times -\Delta K \quad (6)$$

Equation 6 states that the marginal product of labour multiplied by the increase in labour equals the marginal product of capital multiplied by the decrease in capital. Dividing both sides of equation 6 by the increase in labour, ΔL, and then dividing both sides by the marginal product of capital, MP_K, gives equation 7:

$$\frac{MP_L}{MP_K} = \frac{\Delta K}{\Delta L} \quad (7)$$

Equation 7 shows that when Fashion First remains on an isoquant, the decrease in its capital, $-\Delta K$, divided by the increase in its labour, ΔL, is equal to the marginal product of labour, MP_L, divided by the marginal product of capital, MP_K.

The decrease in capital divided by the increase in labour when the firm remains on a given isoquant is the *marginal rate of substitution of labour for capital*. What we have shown is that the marginal rate of substitution of labour for capital equals the ratio of the marginal product of labour to the marginal product of capital.

Marginal Cost

We can use the fact that the marginal rate of substitution of labour for capital equals the ratio of the marginal product of labour to the marginal product of capital to examine marginal cost.

We know that when the least-cost technique is used, the slope of the isoquant and the isocost line are equal as shown in equation 8:

$$\frac{MP_L}{MP_K} = \frac{P_L}{P_K} \qquad (8)$$

We can now show that the total cost is minimised when the marginal product of labour per pound spent on labour equals the marginal product of capital per pound spent on capital.

Rearrange equation 8 by multiplying both sides by the marginal product of capital and then dividing both sides by the price of labour, to get equation 9:

$$\frac{MP_L}{P_L} = \frac{MP_K}{P_K} \qquad (9)$$

Equation 9 says that the marginal product of labour per pound spent on labour is equal to the marginal product of capital per pound spent on capital. In other words, the extra output produced by the last pound spent on labour equals the extra output produced by the last pound spent on capital.

If the extra output produced by the last pound spent on labour exceeds the extra output produced by the last pound spent on capital, it pays a firm to use less capital and more labour. The firm can produce the same output at a lower total cost. Conversely, if the extra output produced by the last pound spent on capital exceeds the extra output produced by the last pound spent on labour, the firm can lower its cost of producing a given output by using less labour and more capital. A firm achieves the least-cost technique of production only when the extra output produced by the last pound spent on all the factors of production is the same.

Finally, we can show that the marginal cost of producing a unit of output with fixed capital and variable labour equals the marginal cost with fixed labour and variable capital. To see why, invert equation 9 to give:

$$\frac{P_L}{MP_L} = \frac{P_K}{MP_K} \qquad (10)$$

Equation 10 shows that the price of labour divided by its marginal product equals the price of capital divided by its marginal product. The price of labour divided by the marginal product of labour is marginal cost of producing a unit of output when the quantity of capital is constant. Remember that marginal cost is the change in total cost resulting from a unit increase in output.

If output increases when one more unit of labour is employed, total output increases by the marginal product of labour. So marginal cost is the price of labour divided by the marginal product of labour. For example, if labour costs £25 a day and the marginal product of labour is 2 jumpers, then the marginal cost of a jumper is £12.50 (£25 ÷ 2).

The price of capital divided by the marginal product of capital has a similar interpretation. The price of capital divided by the marginal product of capital is marginal cost when the quantity of labour is constant.

You can see from equation 10 that with the least-cost technique, the marginal cost of producing a unit of output is the same regardless of whether the quantity of capital is constant and more labour is used or the quantity of labour is constant and more capital is used.

Making Connections

You're probably thinking that what you've learned in this Appendix looks a lot like what you learned in Chapter 8 about a consumer's decision. You are right. In a graph, an isoquant is like an indifference curve; an isocost line is like a budget line; and the least-cost production technique is like the consumer's best affordable point.

But there is an important difference between the two models. The consumer's goal is to get to the *highest* attainable indifference curve with a given budget. The firm's goal is to get to the *lowest* attainable isocost line for a given output. Nonetheless, the two models share similar techniques of analysis.

Key Terms

Isocost line, 245
Isocost map, 245
Isoquant, 243
Isoquant map, 243
Law of diminishing marginal rate of substitution, 244
Least-cost technique, 246
Marginal rate of substitution of labour for capital, 243

11 Perfect Competition

After studying this chapter you will be able to:

◆ Define perfect competition

◆ Explain how a firm makes its output decision

◆ Explain how price and output are determined in perfect competition

◆ Explain why firms enter and exit a market

◆ Predict the effects of technological change in a competitive market

◆ Explain why perfect competition is efficient

A million 'apps' have been created for smartphones and tablets, most of them the work of individuals in intense competition with each other. No single app writer can influence the price of an app, but each can and must decide how much to work and how many apps to produce.

In this chapter, we study producers who, like small app developers, are in intense competition – in *perfect competition*.

At the end of the chapter, in *Reading Between the Lines*, we apply the perfect competition model to the highly competitive market in apps.

What Is Perfect Competition?

The firms that you study in this chapter face the force of raw competition. This type of extreme competition is called perfect competition. **Perfect competition** is a market in which:

◆ Many firms sell identical products to many buyers.

◆ There are no restrictions on entry into the market.

◆ Established firms have no advantage over new ones.

◆ Sellers and buyers are well informed about prices.

Farming, fishing, paper milling, the manufacture of paper cups, grocery retailing, plumbing and dry cleaning are examples of highly competitive industries.

How Perfect Competition Arises

Perfect competition arises if the firm's minimum efficient scale is small relative to the market demand for the good. In this situation, there is room for many firms in the industry. A firm's *minimum efficient scale* is the smallest quantity of output at which long-run average cost reaches its lowest level. (See Chapter 10, p. 235.)

In perfect competition, each firm produces a good or service that has no unique characteristics, so consumers don't care which firm's good they buy.

Price Takers

Firms in perfect competition are price takers. A **price taker** is a firm that cannot influence the market price because its production is an insignificant part of the total market.

Imagine you are a wheat farmer with a hundred hectares under cultivation, which sounds like a lot. But when compared to the millions of hectares in Ukraine, Canada, Australia, Argentina and the US, your hundred hectares is a drop in the ocean. Nothing makes your wheat any better than any other farmer's, and all the buyers of wheat know the price at which they can do business.

If the market price of wheat is £85 a tonne and you ask £90 a tonne, no one will buy from you. People can go to the next farmer and the next and the one after that and buy all they need for £85 a tonne. If you set your price at £84 a tonne, you'll have lots of buyers. But you can sell all your output for £85 a tonne, so you're just giving away £1 a tonne. You can do no better than sell for the market price – you are a *price taker*.

Economic Profit and Revenue

A firm's goal is to maximise *economic profit*, which is equal to total revenue minus total cost. Total cost is the *opportunity cost* of production, which includes *normal profits* (see Chapter 9, p. 197).

A firm's **total revenue** equals the price of its output multiplied by the quantity sold (price × quantity). **Marginal revenue** is the change in total revenue that results from a one-unit increase in the quantity sold. Marginal revenue is calculated by dividing the change in total revenue by the change in the quantity sold.

Figure 11.1 illustrates these concepts in the market for jumpers. In part (a), the market demand curve, *D*, and the market supply curve, *S*, determine the market price. The market price is £25 a jumper. Fashion First is just one of many producers of jumpers, so the best that it can do is to sell its jumpers for £25 each.

Total Revenue

Total revenue is equal to the price multiplied by the quantity sold. In the table in Figure 11.1, if Fashion First sells 9 jumpers, the firm's total revenue is 9 × £25, which equals £225.

Figure 11.1(b) shows the firm's total revenue curve (*TR*), which graphs the relationship between total revenue and quantity sold. At point *A* on the *TR* curve, Fashion First sells 9 jumpers and has total revenue of £225. Because each additional jumper sold brings in a constant amount – £25 – the total revenue curve is an upward-sloping straight line.

Marginal Revenue

Marginal revenue is the change in total revenue that results from a one-unit increase in quantity sold. In the table in Figure 11.1, when the quantity sold increases from 8 to 9 jumpers, total revenue increases from £200 to £225, so marginal revenue is £25 a jumper.

Because the firm in perfect competition is a price taker, the change in total revenue that results from a one-unit increase in the quantity sold equals market price. In *perfect competition, the firm's marginal revenue equals the market price.* Figure 11.1(c) shows Fashion First's marginal revenue curve (*MR*), which is a horizontal line at the market price.

Demand for the Firm's Product

The firm can sell any quantity it chooses at the market price. So the demand curve for the firm's product is a

Figure 11.1   Demand, Price and Revenue in Perfect Competition

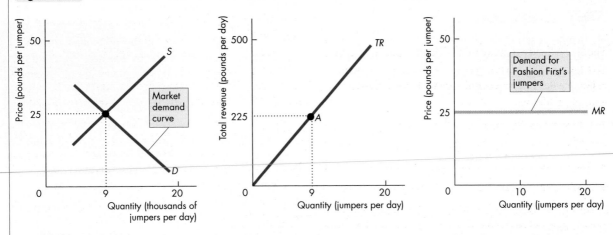

(a) Jumper industry

(b) Fashion First's total revenue

(c) Fashion First's marginal revenue

Quantity sold (Q) (jumpers per day)	Price (P) (pounds per jumper)	Total revenue (TR = P × Q) (pounds)	Marginal revenue (MR = ΔTR/ΔQ) (pounds per jumper)
8	25	200	
			25
9	25	225	
			25
10	25	250	

In part (a), market demand and market supply determine the market price (and quantity). Part (b) shows Fashion First's total revenue curve (*TR*). Point *A* corresponds to the second row of the table – Fashion First sells 9 jumpers at £25 a jumper, so total revenue is £225. Part (c) shows Fashion First's marginal revenue curve (*MR*). This curve is the demand curve for jumpers produced by Fashion First. Fashion First faces a perfectly elastic demand for its jumpers at the market price of £25 a jumper.

 MyEconLab Animation

---

horizontal line at the market price, the same as the firm's marginal revenue curve.

A horizontal demand curve illustrates a perfectly elastic demand, so the demand for the firm's output is perfectly elastic. One of Fashion First's jumpers is a *perfect substitute* for jumpers from the factory next door, or from any other factory. But the *market* demand for jumpers is *not* perfectly elastic. Its elasticity depends on the substitutability of jumpers for other goods and services.

The Firm's Decisions

The goal of the competitive firm is to maximise economic profit, given the constraints it faces. To achieve its goal, a firm must decide:

◆ How to produce at minimum cost

◆ What quantity to produce

◆ Whether to enter or exit a market

You've already seen how a firm makes the first decision. It does so by operating with the plant that minimises long-run average cost – by being on its long-run average cost curve. We'll now see how the firm makes the other two decisions. We start by looking at the firm's output decision.

REVIEW QUIZ

1 Why is a firm in perfect competition a price taker?
2 In perfect competition, what is the relationship between the demand for the firm's output and the market demand?
3 In perfect competition, why is a firm's marginal revenue curve also the demand curve for the firm's output?
4 What decisions must a firm make to maximise profit?

Do these questions in Study Plan 11.1 and get instant feedback.   MyEconLab

The Firm's Output Decision

A firm's cost curves (total cost, average cost and marginal cost) describe the relationship between its output and costs (see Chapter 10, pp. 225–229). And a firm's revenue curves (total revenue and marginal revenue) describe the relationship between its output and its revenue (p. 251). From the firm's cost curves and revenue curves, we can find the output that maximises the firm's economic profit.

Figure 11.2 shows you how to do this for Fashion First. The table lists Fashion First's total revenue and total cost at different outputs, and part (a) of the figure shows its total revenue curve (*TR*) and total cost curve

(*TC*). These curves are graphs of the numbers shown in the first three columns of the table.

Economic profit equals total revenue minus total cost. The fourth column of the table in Figure 11.2 shows economic profit made by Fashion First, and part (b) of the figure graphs these numbers as its economic profit curve (*EP*).

Fashion First maximises economic profit by producing 9 jumpers a day. Total revenue is £225, total cost is £183 and economic profit is £42. No other output rate achieves a larger profit. At outputs of less than 4 jumpers and more than 12 jumpers a day, Fashion First would incur an economic loss. At either 4 or 12 jumpers a day, Fashion First would make zero economic profit, called a *break-even* point.

Figure 11.2   Total Revenue, Total Cost and Economic Profit

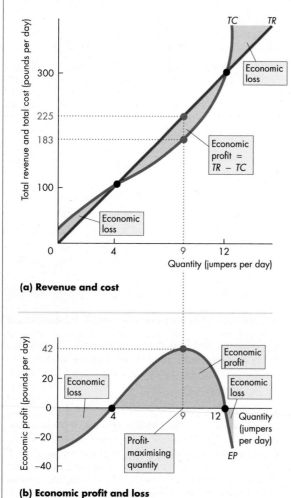

(a) Revenue and cost

(b) Economic profit and loss

Quantity (Q) (jumpers per day)	Total revenue (TR) (pounds)	Total cost (TC) (pounds)	Economic profit (TR – TC) (pounds)
0	0	22	–22
1	25	45	–20
2	50	66	–16
3	75	85	–10
4	100	100	0
5	125	114	11
6	150	126	24
7	175	141	34
8	200	160	40
9	**225**	**183**	**42**
10	250	210	40
11	275	245	30
12	300	300	0
13	325	360	–35

The table lists Fashion First's total revenue, total cost and economic profit. Part (a) graphs the total revenue and total cost curves, and part (b) graphs economic profit. Fashion First makes maximum economic profit, £42 a day (£225 – £183), when it produces 9 jumpers. At outputs of 4 jumpers a day and 12 jumpers a day, Fashion First makes zero economic profit – these are break-even points. At outputs less than 4 and greater than 12 jumpers a day, Fashion First incurs an economic loss.

Marginal Analysis

Another way of finding the profit-maximising output is to use *marginal analysis*, by comparing marginal revenue, *MR*, with marginal cost, *MC*. As output increases, marginal revenue remains constant but marginal cost changes. At low output levels, marginal cost decreases as output increases, but eventually marginal cost increases.

If marginal revenue exceeds marginal cost (if *MR > MC*), then the extra revenue from selling one more unit exceeds the extra cost incurred to produce it. The firm makes an economic profit on the marginal unit, so economic profit increases if output *increases*.

If marginal revenue is less than marginal cost (if *MR < MC*), then the extra revenue from selling one more unit is less than the extra cost incurred to produce it. The firm incurs an economic loss on the marginal unit, so its economic profit decreases if output increases and its economic profit increases if output *decreases*.

If marginal revenue equals marginal cost (*MR = MC*), the firm makes maximum economic profit. The rule *MR = MC* is an example of marginal analysis.

Figure 11.3 illustrates these propositions. If Fashion First increases output from 8 jumpers to 9 jumpers, marginal revenue (£25) exceeds marginal cost (£23), so by producing the ninth jumper economic profit increases by £2 from £40 to £42 a day. The blue area in the figure shows the increase in economic profit when the firm increases production from 8 to 9 jumpers a day.

If Fashion First increases output from 9 jumpers to 10 jumpers, marginal revenue (£25) is less than marginal cost (£27), so by producing the tenth jumper, economic profit decreases. The red area in the figure shows the economic loss that arises from increasing production from 9 to 10 jumpers a day.

Fashion First maximises economic profit by producing 9 jumpers a day, the quantity at which marginal revenue equals marginal cost.

A firm's profit-maximising output is its quantity supplied at the market price. The quantity supplied at a price of £25 a jumper is 9 jumpers a day. If the price were higher than £25 a jumper, the firm would increase production. If the price were lower than £25 a jumper, the firm would decrease production. These profit-maximising responses to different market prices are the foundation of the law of supply:

Other things remaining the same, the higher the market price of a good, the greater is the quantity supplied of that good.

Figure 11.3 Profit-Maximising Output

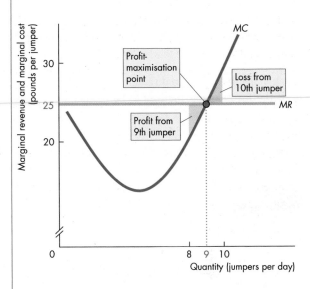

Quantity (Q) (jumpers per day)	Total revenue (TR) (pounds)	Marginal revenue (MR) (pounds per jumper)	Total cost (TC) (pounds)	Marginal cost (MC) (pounds per jumper)	Economic profit (TR − TC) (pounds)
7	175		141		34
		 25		 19	
8	200		160		40
		 25		 23	
9	225		183		42
		 25		 27	
10	250		210		40
		 25		 35	
11	275		245		30

Another way of finding the profit-maximising output is to determine the output at which marginal revenue equals marginal cost. The table and figure show that marginal cost and marginal revenue are equal when Fashion First produces 9 jumpers a day. The table shows that if output increases from 8 to 9 jumpers, marginal cost is £23, which is less than the marginal revenue of £25. If output increases from 9 to 10 jumpers, marginal cost is £27, which exceeds the marginal revenue of £25. If marginal revenue exceeds marginal cost, an increase in output increases economic profit. If marginal revenue is less than marginal cost, an increase in output decreases economic profit. If marginal revenue equals marginal cost, economic profit is maximised.

MyEconLab Animation ──────────────◆

Temporary Shutdown Decision

You've seen that a firm maximises profit by producing the quantity at which marginal revenue (price) equals marginal cost. But suppose that at this quantity, price is less than average total cost. In this case, the firm incurs an economic loss. Maximum profit is a loss (a minimum loss). What does the firm do?

If the firm expects the loss to be permanent, it goes out of business. But if it expects the loss to be temporary, the firm must decide whether to shut down temporarily and produce no output, or to keep producing. To make this decision, the firm compares the loss from shutting down with the loss from producing and takes the action that minimises its loss.

Loss Comparisons

A firm's economic loss equals total fixed cost, TFC, plus total variable cost minus total revenue. Total variable cost equals average variable cost, AVC, multiplied by the quantity produced, Q, and total revenue equals price, P, multiplied by the quantity Q. So

$$\text{Economic loss} = TFC + (AVC - P) \times Q$$

If the firm shuts down, it produces no output ($Q = 0$). The firm has no variable costs and no revenue, but it must pay its fixed costs, so its economic loss equals total fixed cost.

If the firm produces, then in addition to its fixed costs, it incurs variable costs. But it also receives revenue. Its economic loss equals total fixed cost – the loss when shut down – plus total variable cost minus total revenue. If total variable cost exceeds total revenue, this loss exceeds total fixed cost and the firm shuts down. Equivalently, if average variable cost *exceeds* price, this loss exceeds total fixed cost and the firm *shuts down*.

The Shutdown Point

A firm's **shutdown point** is the price and quantity at which it is indifferent between producing and shutting down. The shutdown point occurs at the price and the quantity at which average variable cost is a minimum. At the shutdown point, the firm is minimising its loss, and its loss equals total fixed cost. If the price falls below minimum average variable cost, the firm shuts down temporarily and incurs a loss equal to total fixed cost. At prices above minimum average variable cost but below average total cost, the firm produces the loss-minimising output and incurs a loss that is less than total fixed cost.

Figure 11.4 illustrates the firm's shutdown decision and the shutdown point that we've just described for Fashion First.

The firm's average variable cost curve is AVC and the marginal cost curve is MC. Average variable cost has a minimum of £17 a jumper when output is 7 jumpers a day. The MC curve intersects the AVC curve at its minimum. (We explained this relationship between marginal cost and average cost in Chapter 10; see p. 226.)

The figure shows the marginal revenue curve MR when the price is £17 a jumper, a price equal to minimum average variable cost.

Marginal revenue equals marginal cost at 7 jumpers a day, so this quantity maximises economic profit (minimises economic loss). The ATC curve shows that the firm's average total cost of producing 7 jumpers a day is £20.14 a jumper. The firm incurs a loss equal to £3.14 a jumper on 7 jumpers a day, so its loss is £22 a day, which equals total fixed cost.

Figure 11.4   The Shutdown Decision

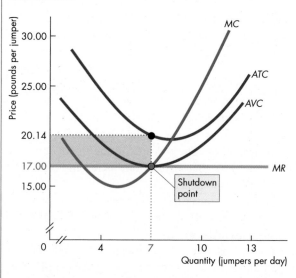

The shutdown point is at minimum average variable cost. At a price below minimum average variable cost, the firm shuts down and produces no output. At a price equal to minimum average variable cost, the firm is indifferent between shutting down and producing no output or producing the output at minimum average variable cost. Either way, the firm minimises its economic loss. The area of the red rectangle shows that at the shutdown point the economic loss equals total fixed cost.

MyEconLab Animation ━━━━━━━━━━━━━━━━◆

Figure 11.5 A Firm's Supply Curve

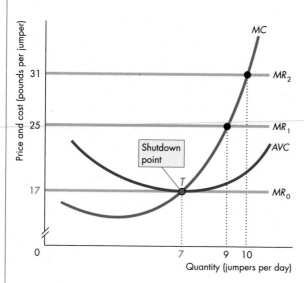

(a) Marginal cost and average variable cost

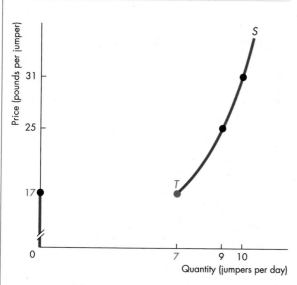

(b) Fashion First's supply curve

Part (a) shows Fashion First's profit-maximising output at each market price. At £25 a jumper, Fashion First produces 9 jumpers. At £17 a jumper, Fashion First produces 7 jumpers. At any price below £17 a jumper, Fashion First produces nothing. Fashion First's shutdown point is *T*.

Part (b) shows Fashion First's supply curve – the quantity of jumpers it will produce at each price. It is made up of the marginal cost curve at all points above minimum average variable cost and the *y*-axis at all prices below minimum average variable cost.

MyEconLab Animation ——————————— ◆

The Firm's Short-Run Supply Curve

A perfectly competitive firm's supply curve shows how its profit-maximising output varies as the market price varies, other things remaining the same. The supply curve is derived from the firm's marginal cost curve and average variable cost curves. Figure 11.5 illustrates the derivation of the supply curve.

When the price *exceeds* minimum average variable cost (more than £17), the firm maximises profit by producing the output at which marginal cost equals price. If the price rises, the firm increases its output – it moves up along its marginal cost curve.

When the price is *less* than minimum average variable cost (less than £17 a jumper), the firm maximises profit by temporarily shutting down and producing no output. The firm produces zero output at all prices below minimum average variable cost.

When the price *equals* minimum average variable cost, the firm maximises profit either by temporarily shutting down and producing no output or by producing the output at which average variable cost is a minimum – the shutdown point, *T*. The firm never produces a quantity between zero and the quantity at the shutdown point *T* (a quantity greater than zero and less than 7 jumpers a day).

The firm's supply curve in Figure 11.5(b) runs along the *y*-axis from a price of zero to a price equal to minimum average variable cost, jumps to point *T*, and then, as the price rises above minimum average variable cost, follows the marginal cost curve.

REVIEW QUIZ

1 Why does a firm in perfect competition produce the quantity at which marginal cost equals price?
2 What is the lowest price at which a firm produces an output? Explain why.
3 What is the relationship between a firm's supply curve, its marginal cost curve and its average variable cost curve?

Do these questions in Study Plan 11.2 and get instant feedback.   MyEconLab

So far, we've studied a single firm in isolation. We've seen that the firm's profit-maximising decision depends on the market price, which it takes as given. How is the market price determined? Let's find out.

Output, Price and Profit in the Short Run

To determine the price and quantity in a perfectly competitive market, we need to know how market demand and market supply interact. We start by studying a perfectly competitive market in the short run. The short run is a situation in which the number of firms is fixed.

Market Supply in the Short Run

The **short-run market supply curve** shows the quantity supplied by all the firms in the market at each price when each firm's plant and the number of firms in the market remain the same.

You've seen how an individual firm's supply curve is determined. The market supply curve is derived from the supply curves of all the individual firms. The quantity supplied by the market at a given price is the sum of the quantities supplied by all the firms in the market at that price.

Figure 11.6 shows the supply curve for the competitive jumper industry. In this example, the industry consists of 1,000 firms exactly like Fashion First. At each price, the quantity supplied by the industry is 1,000 times the quantity supplied by a single firm.

The table in Figure 11.6 shows Fashion First's and the market's supply schedules. It also shows how the market supply curve is constructed. At prices below £17 a jumper, every firm in the market shuts down and produces nothing. The quantity supplied by the market is zero. At a price of £17 a jumper, each firm is indifferent between shutting down and producing nothing or producing 7 jumpers a day. Some firms will shut down and others will produce 7 jumpers a day. The quantity supplied by each firm is *either* 0 or 7 jumpers, but the quantity supplied by the market is *between* 0 (all firms shut down) and 7,000 (all firms produce 7 jumpers a day each).

The market supply curve is a graph of the market supply schedule, and the points *A* to *D* on the supply curve represent the rows of the table.

To construct the market supply curve, we sum the quantities supplied by all firms at each price. Each of the 1,000 firms in the market has a supply schedule like Fashion First's.

At prices below £17 a jumper, the market supply curve runs along the *y*-axis. At a price of £17 a jumper, the market supply curve is horizontal – supply is perfectly elastic. As the price rises above £17 a jumper, each firm increases its quantity supplied and the quantity supplied by the market increases by 1,000 times that of an individual firm. Figure 11.6 shows the market supply curve S_M.

Figure 11.6   Short-Run Market Supply Curve

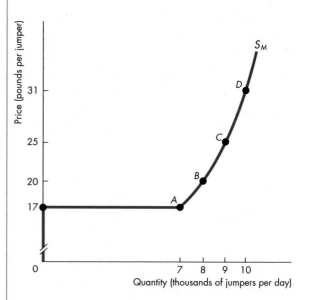

	Price (pounds per jumper)	Quantity supplied by Fashion First (jumpers per day)	Quantity supplied by market (jumpers per day)
A	17	0 or 7	0 to 7,000
B	20	8	8,000
C	25	9	9,000
D	31	10	10,000

The market supply schedule is the sum of the supply schedules of all individual firms. A market that consists of 1,000 identical firms has a supply schedule similar to that of the individual firm, but the quantity supplied by the market is 1,000 times as large as that of the individual firm (see the table).

The market supply curve is S_M. Points *A*, *B*, *C* and *D* correspond to the rows of the table. At the shutdown price of £17, each firm produces either 0 or 7 jumpers per day. The market produces between 0 and 7,000 jumpers a day. The market supply is perfectly elastic at the shutdown price.

MyEconLab Animation ━━━━━━━━━━━━━━━━━━◆

Short-Run Equilibrium

Market demand and market supply determine market price and market output. Figure 11.7 shows the short-run equilibrium. The short-run supply curve, S, is the same as S_M in Figure 11.6. If the market demand curve is D_1, the equilibrium price is £20 a jumper. Each firm takes this price as given and produces its profit-maximising output, which is 8 jumpers a day. Because the market has 1,000 firms, the market output is 8,000 jumpers a day.

A Change in Demand

Changes in market demand bring changes to short-run market equilibrium. Figure 11.7(b) shows these changes.

If the market demand increases and the demand curve shifts rightward to D_2, the price rises to £25 a jumper. At this price, each firm maximises profit by increasing its output. The new output is 9 jumpers a day for each firm and 9,000 jumpers a day for the industry.

If demand decreases and the demand curve shifts leftward to D_3, the price falls to £17. At this price, each firm maximises profit by decreasing its output. If each firm produces 7 jumpers a day, the market output decreases to 7,000 jumpers a day.

If the demand curve shifts further leftward than D_3, the market price remains constant at £17 because the market supply curve is horizontal at that price. Some firms continue to produce 7 jumpers a day and others temporarily shut down. Firms are indifferent between these two activities, and whichever they choose, they incur an economic loss equal to total fixed cost. The number of firms continuing to produce is just enough to satisfy the market demand at a price of £17 a jumper.

Profits and Losses in the Short Run

In short-run equilibrium, although the firm produces the profit-maximising output, it does not necessarily end up making an economic profit. It might do so, but it might alternatively break even (make zero economic profit) or incur an economic loss.

Figure 11.7 Short-Run Equilibrium

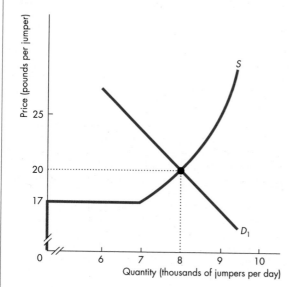

(a) Equilibrium

In part (a), the market supply curve is S, the market demand curve is D_1 and the market price is £20 a jumper. At this price, each firm produces 8 jumpers a day and the market produces 8,000 jumpers a day.

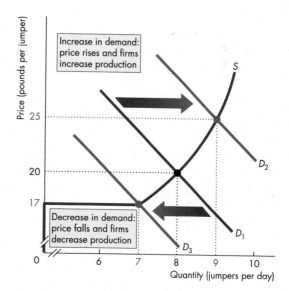

(b) Change in equilibrium

In part (b), when the market demand increases to D_2, the price rises to £25. Each firm increases its output to 9 jumpers a day and the market output is 9,000 jumpers a day. If demand decreases to D_3, the price falls to £17 and each firm decreases its output to 7 jumpers a day. The market output is 7,000 jumpers a day.

Economic profit (or loss) per jumper is price, P, minus average total cost, ATC. So the firm's economic profit (loss) is $(P - ATC) \times Q$. If price equals average total cost, a firm breaks even – makes zero economic profit. The entrepreneur makes normal profit. If price exceeds average total cost, a firm makes an economic profit. If price is less than average total cost, the firm incurs an economic loss. Figure 11.8 shows these three possible short-run profit outcomes for Fashion First. These outcomes correspond to the three levels of market demand that we've just examined.

Three Possible Short-Run Outcomes

Figure 11.8(a) corresponds to the situation in Figure 11.7(b) where the market demand is D_1. The equilibrium price of a jumper is £20 and Fashion First produces 8 jumpers a day. Average total cost is £20 a jumper. Price equals average total cost (ATC), so Fashion First breaks even (makes zero economic profit).

Figure 11.8(b) corresponds to the situation in Figure 11.7(b) where the market demand is D_2. The equilibrium price of a jumper is £25. Fashion First maximises profit by producing 9 jumpers a day. Here, price exceeds average total cost, so Fashion First makes an economic profit. Economic profit is £42 a day. It is made up of

£4.67 a jumper (£25.00 – £20.33), multiplied by 9, the profit-maximising number of jumpers produced. The blue rectangle shows this economic profit. The height of the rectangle is profit per jumper, £4.67, and the length is the quantity of jumpers produced, 9 a day, so the area of the rectangle measures Fashion First's economic profit of £42 a day.

Figure 11.8(c) corresponds to the situation in Figure 11.7(b) where the market demand is D_3. The equilibrium price of a jumper is £17. Here, price is less than average total cost and Fashion First incurs an economic loss. Price and marginal revenue are £17 a jumper, and the profit-maximising (in this case, loss-minimising) output is 7 jumpers a day. Total revenue is £119 a day (7 × £17). Fashion First's average total cost is £20.14 a jumper, so its economic loss per jumper is £3.14 (£20.14 – £17.00). Fashion First's economic loss equals this loss per jumper multiplied by the number of jumpers (£3.14 × 7), which equals £22 a day. The red rectangle shows this economic loss. The height of that rectangle is economic loss per jumper, £3.14, and the length is the quantity of jumpers produced, 7 a day, so the area of the rectangle is Fashion First's economic loss of £22 a day. If the price dips below £17 a jumper, the firm temporarily shuts down and incurs an economic loss equal to total fixed cost.

Figure 11.8 Three Short-Run Outcomes for the Firm

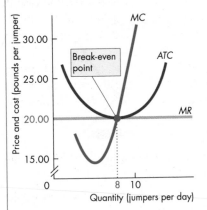

(a) Break-even

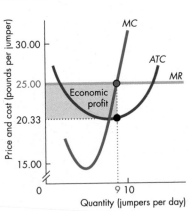

(b) Economic profit

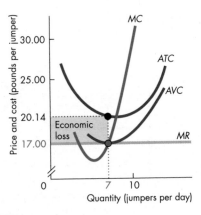

(c) Economic loss

In the short run, the firm might break even (make zero economic profit), make an economic profit or incur an economic loss. In part (a), the price equals minimum average total cost. At the profit-maximising output, the firm breaks even and makes zero economic profit. In part (b), the market price is £25 a jumper. At the profit-maximising output, the price exceeds the average total cost and the firm makes an economic profit equal to the area of the blue rectangle. In part (c), the market price is £17 a jumper. At the profit-maximising output, the price is below minimum average total cost and the firm incurs an economic loss equal to the area of the red rectangle.

ECONOMICS IN ACTION

Production Cutback and Temporary Shutdown

After 2008, the high price of petrol and anxiety about unemployment and future incomes brought a decrease in the demand for luxury goods, including large luxury cars made by Honda in the UK.

Honda's profit-maximising response to the decrease in demand was to cut production and lay off workers. Some of the production cuts and layoffs were temporary and some were permanent.

Honda's UK production plant in Swindon was temporarily shut down for four months in 2009 because total revenue was insufficient to cover total variable cost.

The firm also cut its workforce by 1,300 people. This cut was like that at Fashion First when the market demand for jumpers decreased from D_1 to D_3 in Figure 11.7(b).

REVIEW QUIZ

1 How do we derive the short-run market supply curve in perfect competition?
2 In perfect competition, when market demand increases, explain how the price of the good and the output and profit of each firm change in the short run.
3 In perfect competition, when market demand decreases, explain how the price of the good and the output and profit of each firm change in the short run.

Do these questions in Study Plan 11.3 and get instant feedback.   MyEconLab

Output, Price and Profit in the Long Run

In short-run equilibrium, a firm might make an economic profit, incur an economic loss or break even. Although each of these three situations is a short-run equilibrium, only one of them is a long-run equilibrium. To see why, we need to examine the forces at work in a competitive market in the long run. The reason is that in the long run, firms can enter or exit the market.

Entry and Exit

Entry occurs in a market when new firms come into the market and the number of firms increases. Exit occurs when existing firms leave a market and the number of firms decreases.

Firms respond to economic profit and economic loss by either entering or exiting a market. New firms enter a market in which existing firms are making an economic profit. Firms exit a market in which they are incurring an economic loss. Temporary economic profit and temporary economic loss don't trigger entry and exit. It's the prospect of persistent economic profit or loss that triggers entry and exit.

Entry and exit change the market supply, which influences the market price, the quantity produced by each firm, and its economic profit (or loss).

If firms enter a market, supply increases and the market supply curve shifts rightward. The increase in supply lowers the market price and eventually eliminates economic profit. When economic profit reaches zero, entry stops.

If firms exit a market, supply decreases and the market supply curve shifts leftward. The market price rises and economic loss decreases. Eventually, economic loss is eliminated and exit stops.

To summarise:

◆ New firms enter a market in which existing firms are making an economic profit.

◆ As new firms enter a market, the market price falls and the economic profit of each firm decreases.

◆ Firms exit a market in which they are incurring an economic loss.

◆ As firms exit a market, the market price rises and the economic loss incurred by the remaining firms decreases.

◆ Entry and exit stop when firms make zero economic profit.

A Closer Look at Entry

The jumper market has 800 firms with cost curves like those in Figure 11.9(a). The market demand curve is D, the market supply curve is S_1, and the price is £25 a jumper in Figure 11.9(b). Each firm produces 9 jumpers a day and makes an economic profit.

This economic profit is a signal for new firms to enter the market. As entry takes place, supply increases and the market supply curve shifts rightward towards S^*. As supply increases with no change in demand, the market price gradually falls from £25 to £20 a jumper. At this lower price, each firm makes zero economic profit and entry stops.

Entry results in an increase in market output, but each firm's output decreases. Because the price falls, each firm moves down its supply curve and produces less. Because the number of firms increases, the market produces more.

A Closer Look at Exit

The jumper market has 1,200 firms with cost curves like those in Figure 11.9(a). The market demand curve is D, the market supply curve is S_2, and the price is £17 a jumper in Figure 11.9(b). Each firm produces 7 jumpers a day and incurs an economic loss.

This economic loss is a signal for firms to exit the market. As exit takes place, supply decreases and the market supply curve shifts leftward towards S^*. As supply decreases with no change in demand, the market price gradually rises from £17 to £20 a jumper. At this higher price, losses are eliminated, each firm makes zero economic profit and exit stops.

Exit results in a decrease in market output, but each firm's output increases. Because the price rises, each firm moves up its supply curve and produces more. Because the number of firms decreases, the market produces less.

Figure 11.9 Entry, Exit and Long-Run Equilibrium

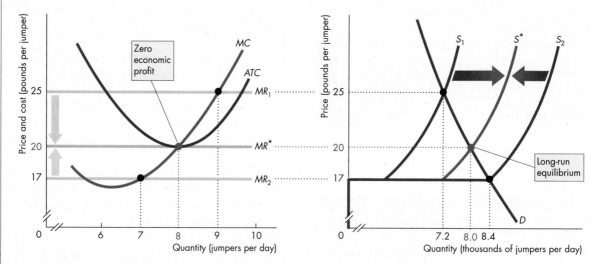

(a) Fashion First

(b) The jumper market

Each firm has cost curves like those of Fashion First in part (a). The market demand curve is D in part (b).

When the market supply curve in part (b) is S_1, the price is £25 a jumper. In part (a), each firm produces 9 jumpers a day and makes an economic profit. Profit triggers the entry of new firms, and as new firms enter, the market supply curve shifts rightward, from S_1 towards S^*. The price falls from £25 to £20 a jumper, and the quantity produced increases from 7,200 to 8,000 jumpers.

Each firm's output decreases to 8 jumpers a day and economic profit falls to zero.

When the market supply curve is S_2, the price is £17 a jumper. In part (a), each firm produces 7 jumpers a day and incurs an economic loss. Loss triggers exit, and as firms exit, the market supply curve shifts leftward, from S_2 towards S^*. The price rises from £17 to £20 a jumper, and the quantity produced decreases from 8,400 to 8,000 jumpers. Each firm's output increases from 7 to 8 jumpers a day and economic profit rises to zero.

MyEconLab Animation ◆

ECONOMICS IN ACTION

Entry and Exit

An example of entry and falling prices occurred during the 1980s and 1990s in the personal computer market. When IBM introduced its first PC in 1981, IBM had little competition. The price was $7,000 (about $16,850 in today's money) and IBM made a large economic profit selling the new machine.

Observing IBM's huge success, new firms such as Gateway, NEC, Dell and a host of others entered the market with machines that were technologically identical to IBM's. In fact, they were so similar that they came to be called 'clones'. The massive wave of entry into the personal computer market increased the market supply and lowered the price. The economic profit for all firms decreased.

Today, a £300 computer is vastly more powerful than its 1981 ancestor that cost 42 times as much. The same PC market that saw entry during the 1980s and 1990s has experienced some exit more recently.

In 2001, IBM, the firm that first launched the PC, announced that it was exiting the market. The intense competition from Gateway, NEC, Dell and others that entered the market following IBM's lead has lowered the price and eliminated the economic profit. So IBM now concentrates on servers and other parts of the computer market.

IBM exited the PC market because it was incurring economic losses. Its exit decreased market supply and made it possible for the remaining firms in the market to make zero economic profit.

Whitbread, which built the first mass brewery in the UK in 1750, is another example of exit. For 250 years, people associated the name Whitbread with brewing beer. But the brewing market became globally competitive, and UK brewing firms suffered economic losses. Whitbread Group plc doesn't make beer any more. After years of shrinking revenues, Whitbread got out of the brewing and pub business in 2001 and is now a profitable hotel and restaurant business with a global coffee brand, Costa Coffee. Whitbread's expansion into its other new business areas increased its profits.

Whitbread exited brewing because it was facing an economic loss. Its exit decreased supply and made it possible for the remaining brewing firms in the market to break even.

Long-Run Equilibrium

You've now seen how economic profit induces entry, which in turn eliminates the profit. You've also seen how economic loss induces exit, which in turn eliminates the loss.

When economic profit and economic loss have been eliminated and entry and exit have stopped, a competitive market is in *long-run equilibrium*.

You've seen how a competitive market adjusts towards its long-run equilibrium. But a competitive market is rarely *in* a state of long-run equilibrium. Instead, it is constantly and restlessly evolving *towards* long-run equilibrium. The reason is that the market is constantly bombarded with events that change the constraints that firms face.

Markets are constantly adjusting to keep up with changes in tastes, which change demand, and changes in technology, which change costs.

In the next sections, we're going to see how a competitive market reacts to changing tastes and technology and how it guides resources to their highest-valued use.

REVIEW QUIZ

1 What triggers entry in a competitive market? Describe the process that ends further entry.
2 What triggers exit in a competitive market? Describe the process that ends further exit.

Do these questions in Study Plan 11.4 and get instant feedback.   MyEconLab

Changes in Demand and Supply as Technology Advances

The arrival of high-speed Internet service increased the demand for personal computers and the demand for music and movie downloads. At the same time, the arrival of these technologies decreased the demand for the retail services of record stores. What happens in a competitive market when the demand for its product changes? The perfect competition model can answer this question.

An Increase in Demand

Producers of computer components are in long-run equilibrium making zero economic profit when the arrival of the high-speed Internet brings an increase in the demand for computers and their components. The equilibrium price of a component rises and producers make economic profits. New firms start to enter the mar-

ket. Supply increases and the price stops rising and then begins to fall. Eventually, enough firms have entered for the supply and the increased demand to be in balance at a price that enables the firms in the market to return to zero economic profit – long-run equilibrium.

Figure 11.10 illustrates. In the market in part (a) the demand curve is D_0, the supply curve is S_0, the price is P_0 and market output is Q_0. At the firm in part (b), profit is maximised with marginal revenue MR_1 equal to marginal cost, MC, at output q_0. Economic profit is zero.

Market demand increases and the demand curve shifts rightward to D_1, in Figure 11.10(a). The price ries to P_1 and the quantity supplied by the market increases from Q_0 to Q_1 as the market moves up along its short-run supply curve S_0. In Figure 11.10(b), the firm maximises profit by producing q_1, where marginal revenue MR_1 equals marginal cost MC, and in short-run equilibrium, each firm makes an economic profit.

The economic profit brings entry and short-run market supply increases. The supply curve shifts rightward. The increase in supply lowers the price – as shown by the arrows along the market demand curve D_1 in Figure 11.10(a).

Figure 11.10 An Increase in Demand

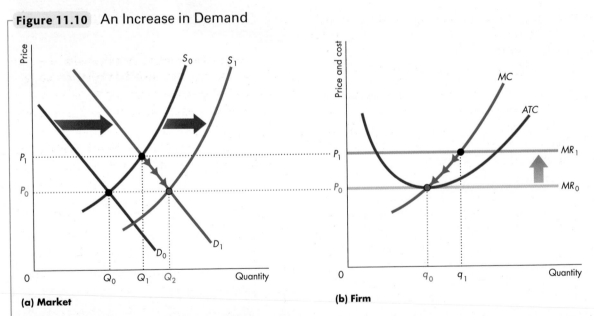

(a) Market

(b) Firm

A market starts in long-run competitive equilibrium. Part (a) shows the market demand curve D_0, the market supply curve S_0, the equilibrium quantity Q_0 and the market price P_0. Each firm sells at the price P_0, so its marginal revenue curve is MR_0 in part (b). Each firm produces q_0 and makes zero economic profit.

Market demand increases from D_0 to D_1 in part (a). The market price rises to P_1, each firm increases its output to q_1 in part (b) and the market output increases to Q_1 in part (a).

Firms now make economic profits. New firms enter the market, and as they do so, the market supply curve gradually shifts rightward, from S_0 towards S_1. This shift gradually lowers the market price from P_1 back to P_0. While the price is above P_0, firms continue to make economic profits and more firms enter the market. Once the price has returned to P_0, each firm makes zero economic profit and there is no incentive to enter the market. Each firm produces q_0 and market output is Q_2.

Eventually, entry shifts the supply curve to S_1 in Figure 11.10(a). The price has returned to its original level, P_0. At this price, each firm produces q_0, the same as the quantity produced before demand increased. Market output is Q_2 in a long-run equilibrium.

The difference between the initial long-run equilibrium and the new long-run equilibrium is the number of firms in the market. An increase in demand has increased the number of firms. In the process of moving from the initial equilibrium to the new one, each firm makes an economic profit.

A Decrease in Demand

A *decrease* in demand triggers a response similar to the one you've just seen for an increase in demand, but in the opposite direction. A decrease in demand brings a lower market price, firms incur economic losses, and some firms exit. Exit decreases the market supply, which raises the market price and increases economic profit. Eventually, firms' losses decrease until in a new long-run equilibrium firms make zero economic profit. *Economics in the News* below looks at an example.

ECONOMICS IN THE NEWS

Record Stores Exit

Record Shop 'Borderline' to Close

Dublin record shop Borderline opened twenty years ago is closing down. Borderline is not alone. The high street retailer HMV also closed stores. The demand for records has fallen.

Source: comeheretome.com, 9 July 2011

The Problem

Provide a graphical analysis to explain why Borderline exited the market and the effects of exit on the market for record store services.

The Solution

◆ With demand D_0 and supply S_0, Q_0 customers are served at a price P_0 in part (a) of Figure 1.

◆ With marginal revenue MR_0 and marginal cost MC, a record store serves q_0 customers in long-run equilibrium in part (b) of Figure 1.

◆ Demand decreases to D_1, the price falls to P_1, and marginal revenue falls to MR_1. Customers decrease to q_1 (and Q_1) and stores incur economic losses.

◆ Faced with economic loss, Borderline and other stores exit and the market supply decreases to S_1.

◆ The decrease in supply raises the price and the firms remaining return to zero economic profit.

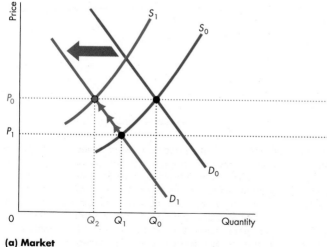

(a) Market

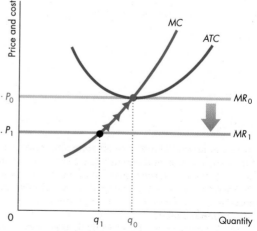

(b) Individual record store

Figure 1 The Market for Record Store Services

Technological Advances Change Supply

We've studied the effects of technological change on demand, and to isolate those effects we've kept the individual firm's cost curves unchanged. But new technologies also lower production costs. We now study those effects of advancing technology.

Starting from a long-run equilibrium, when a new technology becomes available that lowers production costs, the first firms to use it make economic profit. But as more firms begin to use the new technology, market supply increases and the price falls. At first, new-technology firms continue to make positive economic profits, so more enter. But firms that continue to use the old technology incur economic losses. Why? Initially they were making zero economic profit and now with the lower price they incur economic losses. So old-technology firms exit.

Eventually, all the old-technology firms have exited and enough new-technology firms have entered to increase the market supply to a level that lowers the price to equal the minimum average total cost using the new technology. In this situation, all the firms, all

of which are now new-technology firms, are making zero economic profit.

Figure 11.11 illustrates the process that we've just described. Part (a) shows the market demand and supply curves and market equilibrium. Part (b) shows the cost and revenue curves for a firm using the original old technology. Initially these are the only firms. Part (c) shows the cost and revenue curves for a firm that uses a new technology after it becomes available.

In part (a), the demand curve is D and initially, the supply curve is S_0, so the price is P_0 and the equilibrium quantity is Q_0.

In part (b), marginal revenue is MR_0 and each firm produces q_0 where MR_0 equals MC_{Old}. Economic profit is zero and firms are producing at minimum average total cost on the curve ATC_{Old}.

When a new technology becomes available, average total cost and marginal cost of production fall, and firms that use the new technology produce with the average total cost curve ATC_{New} and marginal cost curve MC_{New} in part (c).

When one firm adopts the new technology, it is too small to influence supply, so the price remains at P_0 and the firm makes an economic profit. But economic profit

Figure 11.11 A Technological Advance Lowers Production Costs

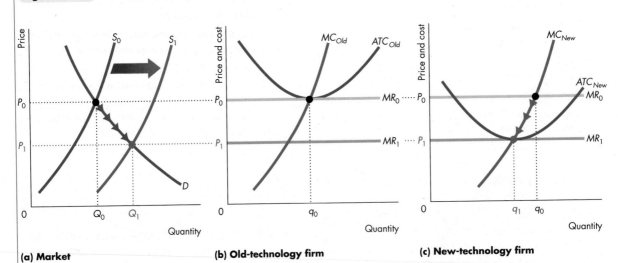

In part (a), the demand curve is D, and initially the supply curve is S_0. The price is P_0 and the equilibrium quantity is Q_0. In part (b), marginal revenue is MR_0 and each firm produces q_0 where MR_0 equals MC_{Old}. Economic profit is zero.

A new technology becomes available with lower costs of ATC_{New} and MC_{New} in part (c). A firm that uses this technology produces q_0 where MR_0 equals MC_{New}.

As more firms use this technology, market supply

increases and the price falls. With price below P_0 and above P_1, old-technology firms incur economic losses and exit while new-technology firms make economic profits and new firms enter the market.

In the new long-run equilibrium, the old-technology firms have gone. New-technology firms increase the market supply to S_1. The price falls to P_1, marginal revenue is MR_1, and each firm produces q_1 where MR_1 equals MC_{New}.

ECONOMICS IN THE NEWS

Falling Cost of Sequencing DNA

Oxford Nanopore Unveils Mini-DNA Reader

A small British company announced its entry into the gene-sequencing market this week with a DNA sequencer the size of a USB stick. It reads DNA more quickly and more cheaply than existing technology and will bring the cost of sequencing below $1,000.

Source: *The Financial Times*, 17 February, 2012

Some Data

Figure 1 shows how the cost of sequencing a person's entire genome has fallen. Oxford Nanopore (in the news clip) is one of around 40 firms competing to develop a machine that can lower that cost from the current $5,000 to $1,000 or less. Many dozens of firms operate DNA-sequencing machines and sell their services in a competitive market.

The Questions

◆ What are the competitive markets in the news clip?

◆ Are any of these markets in long-run equilibrium?

◆ Are any firms in these markets likely to be making an economic profit?

◆ Are any of the firms in these markets likely to be incurring an economic loss?

◆ Are these markets likely to be experiencing entry, exit or both? If both, which is likely to be greater?

◆ Who gains from the advances in DNA-sequencing technology in the short run and in the long run: producers, consumers or both?

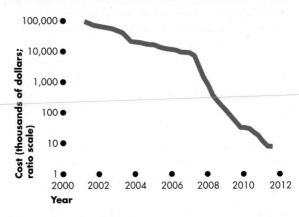

Figure 1 Cost per Genome

Source of data: National Human Genome Research Institute.

The Answers

◆ The markets are for DNA-sequencing machines and for DNA sequencing services.

◆ With massive ongoing technological change, neither market is likely to be in long-run equilibrium.

◆ Firms using the latest technology are likely to be making economic profit.

◆ Firms using the older technology are likely to be incurring economic loss.

◆ New-technology firms are entering and old-technology firms are exiting, but with falling prices there is more entry than exit.

◆ In the short run, firms gain from higher profit and consumers gain from the lower price. In the long run, economic profit will be zero but consumers will continue to gain from the low price.

brings entry of new-technology firms. Market supply increases and the price falls.

With price below P_0, old-technology firms in Figure 11.11(b) incur economic loss and some exit. With price above P_1, new-technology firms make an economic profit and new firms enter. When the new long-run equilibrium is achieved, all the old-technology firms have gone. The new-technology firms that have entered have shifted the supply curve to S_1. The price is P_1, marginal revenue is MR_1, and each firm in Figure 11.11(c) produces q_1 using the new technology where MR_1 equals MC_{New}.

Technological change brings only temporary gains to producers. But the lower prices and better products that technological advances bring are permanent gains for consumers.

REVIEW QUIZ

Describe what happens to output, market price and economic profit in the short run and in the long run in a competitive market following:

1 An increase in market demand.
2 A decrease in market demand.
3 The adoption of a new technology that lowers production costs.

Do these questions in Study Plan 11.5 and get instant feedback.   MyEconLab

We've seen how a competitive market works in the short run and the long run. But does a competitive market achieve an efficient use of resources?

Competition and Efficiency

A competitive market can achieve an efficient use of resources. You first studied efficiency in Chapter 2. Then in Chapter 5, using only the concepts of demand, supply, consumer surplus and producer surplus, you saw how a competitive market achieves efficiency. Now that you have learned what lies behind demand and supply curves in a competitive market, you can gain a deeper understanding of the efficiency of a competitive market.

Efficient Use of Resources

Resource use is efficient when we produce the goods and services that people value most highly (see Chapter 2, pp. 35–37 and Chapter 5, p. 110). If someone can become better off without anyone else becoming worse off, resources are *not* being used efficiently. For example, suppose we produce a computer that no one wants and no one will ever use and, at the same time, some people are clamouring for more video games. If we produce one less computer and reallocate the unused resources to produce more video games, some people will become better off and no one will be worse off. So the initial resource allocation was inefficient.

We can test whether resources are allocated efficiently by computing marginal social benefit and marginal social cost. In the computer and video games example, the marginal social benefit of a video game exceeds its marginal social cost. And the marginal social cost of a computer exceeds its marginal social benefit. So by producing fewer computers and more video games, we move resources towards a higher-valued use.

Choices, Equilibrium and Efficiency

We can use what you have learned about the decisions made by consumers and competitive firms and market equilibrium to describe an efficient use of resources.

Choices

Consumers allocate their budgets to get the most value possible out of them. We derive a consumer's demand curve by finding how the best budget allocation changes as the price of a good changes. So consumers get the most value out of their resources at all points along their demand curves. If the people who consume a good or service are the only ones who benefit from it, then the market demand curve measures the benefit to the entire society and is the marginal social benefit curve.

Competitive firms produce the quantity that maximises profit. We derive the firm's supply curve by finding the profit-maximising quantity at each price. So firms get the most value out of their resources at all points along their supply curves. If the firms that produce a good or service bear all the costs of producing it, then the market supply curve measures the marginal cost to the entire society, and the market supply curve is the marginal social cost curve.

Equilibrium and Efficiency

Resources are used efficiently when marginal social benefit equals marginal social cost. Competitive equilibrium achieves this efficient outcome because, with no externalities, price equals marginal social benefit for consumers, and price equals marginal social cost for producers.

The gains from trade are the consumer surplus plus the producer surplus. The gains from trade for consumers are measured by *consumer surplus*, which is the area below the demand curve and above the price paid (see Chapter 5, p. 107). The gains from trade for producers are measured by *producer surplus*, which is the area above the supply curve and below the price received (see Chapter 5, p. 109). The total gains from trade are the sum of consumer surplus and producer surplus. When the market for a good or service is in equilibrium, the gains from trade are maximised.

Efficiency in the Jumper Market

Figure 11.12 illustrates an efficient allocation in perfect competition in long-run equilibrium. Part (a) shows the market and part (b) shows our firm, Fashion First.

In part (a), consumers get the most value out of their resources at all points on the market demand curve, $D = MSB$. Producers get the most value out of their resources at all points on the market supply curve, $S = MSC$. At the equilibrium quantity and price, marginal social benefit equals marginal social cost, so resources are allocated efficiently. Consumer surplus is the green area, producer surplus is the blue area, and total surplus (the sum of producer surplus and consumer surplus) is maximised.

In part (b), at the equilibrium price, Fashion First (and every other firm) makes zero economic profit and each firm has the plant that enables it to produce at the lowest possible average total cost. Consumers are

Figure 11.12 Efficiency of Perfect Competition

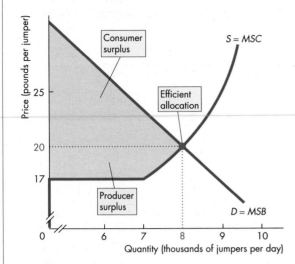

(a) The jumper market

(b) Fashion First

In part (a), market demand, *D*, and market supply, *S*, determine the equilibrium price and quantity. Consumers have made the best available choices on the demand curve, and firms are producing at least cost on the supply curve.

Marginal social benefit, *MSB*, equals marginal social cost, *MSC*, so resources are used efficiently. In part (b), Fashion First produces at the lowest possible long-run average total cost and makes zero economic profit.

MyEconLab Real-time data

as well off as possible because the good cannot be produced at a lower cost and the price equals that least-possible cost.

When firms in perfect competition are away from long-run equilibrium, either entry into the market or exit from the market is taking place and the market is moving towards the situation depicted in Figure 11.12. During this process the competitive market is still efficient because marginal social benefit (on the market demand curve) equals marginal social cost (on the market supply curve). But it is only in long-run equilibrium that profit is driven to zero and consumers pay the lowest possible price.

You've now completed your study of perfect competition. *Reading Between the Lines* on pp. 268–269 gives you an opportunity to use what you have learned to understand the market for smartphones and tablet computer 'apps'.

Although many markets approximate the model of perfect competition, many do not. In Chapter 12, we study markets at the opposite extreme of market power: monopoly. Then we study markets that lie between per-

fect competition and monopoly. In Chapter 13, we study monopolistic competition and in Chapter 14, we study oligopoly. When you have completed this study, you'll have a toolkit that will enable you to understand the variety of real-world markets.

◈ **REVIEW QUIZ**

1 State the conditions that must be met for resources to be allocated efficiently.
2 Describe the choices that consumers make and explain why consumers are efficient on the market demand curve.
3 Describe the choices that producers make and explain why producers are efficient on the market supply curve.
4 Explain why resources are used efficiently in a competitive market.

Do these questions in Study Plan 11.6 and get instant feedback.   MyEconLab

Perfect Competition in iPhone 'Apps'

GigaOm, 29 June 2012

Because of the iPhone, There Is an App for That

. . . The iPhone only offered web apps when it debuted in 2007. But the powerful hardware and unique user interface lit a fire of demand among developers for a software development kit. Apple obliged a year later and also introduced the App Store, kicking off the modern mobile app era. That market is now worth $8.5 billion and is expected to grow to $46 billion in 2016.

As we celebrate the five-year anniversary of the iPhone's launch on Friday, the true impact of the device can't be measured without talking about the era of mobile apps it spawned, creating success stories like Instagram, Angry Birds, Foursquare and many others. Suddenly, 'apps' became an easy way of understanding software, opening up opportunities to thousands of eager developers who could sell directly to a fast growing base of users. And that has in turn changed the way people compute, weaning them off of PCs to smaller devices: first smartphones, and now tablets. . . .

Apple's App Store now boasts 650,000 apps, including 225,000 for the iPad. Apple users have downloaded 30 billion apps from the App Store, generating $5 billion in revenue for developers after Apple's 30 per cent cut. To be sure, there were mobile apps prior to the iPhone, but they were either found on third party app stores or they were controlled by carriers, which chose which apps got to appear on phones sold for their networks.

 ## The Essence of the Story

- The iPhone has created opportunities for thousands of 'apps' developers who can sell directly to a fast growing base of users.

- The mobile app market had total revenue of $8.5 billion in 2012 and is expected to grow to $46 billion in 2016.

- Apple's App Store offers 650,000 apps, including 225,000 for the iPad.

- Apple users have downloaded 30 billion apps from the App Store, generating $5 billion in revenue for developers after Apple's 30 per cent cut.

Economic Analysis

- The iPhone, iPad and Android smartphones and tablet computers have created a large demand for apps.

- Although apps are not like corn or jumpers and come in thousands of varieties, the market for apps is highly competitive and we can use the perfect competition model to explain what is happening in that market.

- In 2007, the market for apps didn't exist. The market began to operate in 2008, when the first app developers got to work using a software development kit made available by Apple.

- From 2009 to 2012, the number of iPhones and Android smartphones increased dramatically. By 2012, 218 million iPhones and 400 million Android phones had been sold.

- The increase in the number of devices in use increased the demand for apps.

- Thousands of developers, most of them individuals, saw a profit opportunity and got to work creating apps. Their entry into the market increased the supply of apps.

- But the demand for apps kept growing, and despite the entry of more developers, profit opportunities remained.

- Figure 1 illustrates the market for apps. In 2011, the demand for apps was D_0 and the supply was S_0. The equilibrium price was P_0 and the quantity was Q_0.

- Figure 2 shows that the individual developer maximises profit by producing an app that sells q_0 units and makes an economic profit.

- Economic profit brings entry, so in Figure 1, supply increases to S_1. But the demand for apps keeps increasing, and in 2012 the demand curve is D_1.

- The equilibrium quantity increases to Q_1, and this quantity is produced by an increased number of developers – each producing q_0 units and each continuing to make an economic profit.

- In Figure 2, the developer's cost curves are unchanged, but as development tools improve, development costs will fall and the cost curves will shift downward, which will further increase the market supply.

- At some future date, market supply will increase by enough to eliminate economic profit, and the market for apps will be in long-run equilibrium. That date is likely to be a long way off.

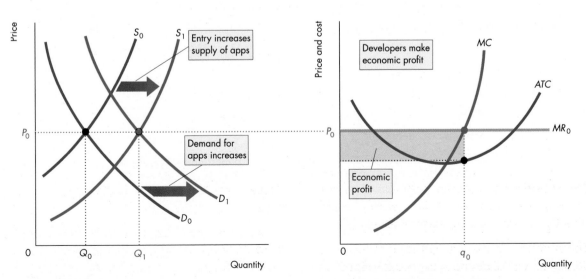

Figure 1 The Market for Apps

Figure 2 An Individual App Developer

SUMMARY

Key Points

What Is Perfect Competition?
(pp. 250–251)

◆ In perfect competition, many firms sell identical products to many buyers; there are no restrictions on entry; sellers and buyers are well informed about prices.

◆ A perfectly competitive firm is a price taker.

◆ A perfectly competitive firm's marginal revenue always equals the market price.

Do Problems 1 to 3 to get a better understanding of perfect competition.

The Firm's Output Decision (pp. 252–255)

◆ The firm produces the output at which marginal revenue (price) equals marginal cost.

◆ In short-run equilibrium, a firm can make an economic profit, incur an economic loss, or break even.

◆ If price is less than minimum average variable cost, the firm temporarily shuts down.

◆ At prices below minimum average variable cost, a firm's supply curve runs along the y-axis; at prices above minimum average variable cost, a firm's supply curve is its marginal cost curve.

Do Problems 4 to 6 to get a better understanding of a firm's output decision.

Output, Price and Profit in the Short Run (pp. 256–259)

◆ A market supply curve shows the sum of the quantities supplied by each firm at each price.

◆ Market demand and market supply determine price.

◆ A firm might make a positive economic profit, incur an economic loss or break even.

Do Problems 7 to 9 to get a better understanding of output, price and profit in the short run.

Output, Price and Profit in the Long Run (pp. 259–261)

◆ Economic profit induces entry and economic loss induces exit.

◆ Entry increases supply and lowers the market price and economic profit. Exit decreases supply and raises the market price and economic profit.

◆ In long-run equilibrium, economic profit is zero. There is no entry or exit.

Do Problems 10 and 11 to get a better understanding of output, price and profit in the long run.

Changes in Demand and Supply as Technology Advances (pp. 262–265)

◆ A permanent increase in demand leads to a larger market output and a larger number of firms. A permanent decrease in demand leads to a smaller market output and a smaller number of firms.

◆ New technologies lower the cost of production, increase supply and in the long run lower the price and increase the quantity.

Do Problems 12 to 16 to get a better understanding of changing tastes and advancing technologies.

Competition and Efficiency
(pp. 266–267)

◆ Resources are used efficiently when we produce goods and services in the quantities that everyone values most highly.

◆ Perfect competition achieves an efficient allocation. In long-run equilibrium, consumers pay the lowest possible price and marginal social benefit equals marginal social cost.

Do Problems 17 and 18 to get a better understanding of competition and efficiency.

Key Terms

Marginal revenue, 250
Perfect competition, 250
Price taker, 250
Short-run market supply curve, 256
Shutdown point, 254
Total revenue, 250

STUDY PLAN PROBLEMS AND APPLICATIONS

Do Problems 1 to 18 in MyEconLab Chapter 11 Study Plan and get instant feedback.

MyEconLab

What Is Perfect Competition?
(Study Plan 11.1)

Use the following information in Problems 1 to 3.

Leo's makes amaretto biscuits that are identical to those made by dozens of other firms, and there is free entry in the amaretto biscuit market. Buyers and sellers are well informed about prices.

1 In what type of market does Leo's operate? What determines the price of amaretto biscuits and what determines Leo's marginal revenue?

2 a If amaretto biscuits sell for €10 a box and Leo offers his biscuits for sale at €10.50 a box, how many boxes does he sell?

   b If amaretto biscuits sell for €10 a box and Leo offers his biscuits for sale at €9.50 a box, how many boxes does he sell?

3 What is the elasticity of demand for Leo's amaretto biscuits and how does it differ from the elasticity of the market demand for amaretto biscuits?

The Firm's Output Decision
(Study Plan 11.2)

Use the following information in Problems 4 to 6.

Pat's Pizza Restaurant is a price taker and its costs are:

Output (pizzas per hour)	Total cost (euros per hour)
0	10
1	21
2	30
3	41
4	54
5	69

4 What is Pat's profit-maximising output and economic profit if the market price is (i) €14 a pizza, (ii) €12 a pizza and (iii) €10 a pizza?

5 What is Pat's shutdown point and what is its economic profit if it shuts down temporarily?

6 Derive Pat's supply curve.

Output, Price and Profit in the Short Run (Study Plan 11.3)

Use the following data in Problems 7 and 8.

The market for paper is perfectly competitive and there are 1,000 firms that produce paper. The market demand schedule for paper is:

Price (euros per box)	Quantity demanded (thousands of boxes per week)
3.65	500
5.20	450
6.80	400
8.40	350
10.00	300
11.60	250
13.20	200

Each paper producer has the same costs when it uses its least-cost plant. The following table sets out those costs:

Output (boxes per week)	Marginal cost	Average variable cost	Average total cost
		(euros per box)	
200	4.60	7.80	11.80
250	7.00	7.00	11.00
300	7.65	7.10	10.43
350	8.40	7.20	10.06
400	10.00	7.50	10.00
450	12.40	8.00	10.22
500	20.70	9.00	11.00

7 a What are the market price and the market's output?

   b What is the output produced by each firm?

   c What is the economic profit made or economic loss incurred by each firm?

8 As more documents are read online rather than by printing them, the market demand schedule for paper becomes:

Price (euros per box)	Quantity demanded (thousands of boxes per week)
2.95	500
4.13	450
5.30	400
6.48	350
7.65	300
8.83	250
10.00	200
11.18	150

What are the market price and the economic profit made or economic loss incurred of each firm in the short run?

9 British Airways Ups Fuel Surcharges

British Airways announced it would increase the fuel surcharge on all its flights starting on June 3, the third hike since the start of the year. On long-haul flights of more than 9 hours the fuel surcharge will rise by £30 to £109 per flight, whereas on short-haul flights it will increase by £3 to £16.

Source: Forbes.com, 29 May 2008

a Explain how an increase in fuel prices might cause an airline to change its output (number of flights) in the short run.

b Draw a graph to show the increase in fuel prices on an airline's output in the short run.

c Explain why an airline might incur an economic loss in the short run as fuel prices rise.

Output, Price and Profit in the Long Run (Study Plan 11.4)

10 The pizza market is perfectly competitive, and all pizza producers have the same costs as Pat's Pizza Restaurant in Problem 4.

a At what price will some firms exit the pizza market in the long run?

b At what price will firms enter the pizza market in the long run?

11 In Problem 7, in the long run,

a Do firms have an incentive to enter or exit the paper market?

b If firms do enter or exit the market, explain how the economic profit or loss of the remaining paper producers will change.

c What are the long-run equilibrium market price and the quantity of paper produced? What is the number of firms in the market?

Changes in Demand and Supply as Technology Advances (Study Plan 11.5)

12 If in the long run, the market demand for paper remains the same as in Problem 8, what are the long-run equilibrium price of paper, the market output and the economic profit or loss of each firm?

13 Explain and illustrate graphically how the growing world population is influencing the world market for wheat and a representative individual wheat farmer.

14 Explain and illustrate graphically how the market for holiday travel has been affected by the introduction of low-cost budget airlines.

Use the following news clip in Problems 15 and 16.

Coors Brewing Expanding Plant

Coors Brewing Company will expand its Virginia packaging plant at a cost of $24 million. The addition will accommodate a new production line, which will bottle beer faster. Coors Brewing employs 470 people at its Virginia plant. The expanded packaging line will add another eight jobs.

Source: *Denver Business Journal*, 6 January 2006

15 a How will Coors' expansion change its marginal cost curve and short-run supply curve?

b What does this expansion decision imply about the point on Coors' *LRAC* curve at which the firm was before the expansion?

16 a If other breweries follow the lead of Coors, what will happen to the market price of beer?

b How will the adjustment that you have described in part (a) influence the economic profit of Coors and other beer producers?

Competition and Efficiency (Study Plan 11.6)

17 In a perfectly competitive market in long-run equilibrium, can consumer surplus be increased? Can producer surplus be increased? Can a consumer become better off by making a substitution away from this market?

18 Never Pay Retail Again

Not only has scouring the Web for the best possible price become standard protocol before buying a big-ticket item, but more consumers are employing creative strategies for scoring hot deals. Comparison shopping and haggling are all becoming mainstream marks of savvy shoppers. Online shoppers can check a comparison service like Price Grabber before making a purchase.

Source: CNN, 30 May 2008

a Explain the effect of the Internet on the degree of competition in the market.

b Explain how the Internet influences market efficiency.

ADDITIONAL PROBLEMS AND APPLICATIONS

Do these problems in MyEconLab if assigned by your lecturer.

MyEconLab

What Is Perfect Competition?

Use the following information in Problems 19 to 21.

Two service stations stand on opposite sides of the road: ABC and XYZ. The owner of ABC doesn't even have to look across the road to know when XYZ changes its petrol price. When the owner of XYZ raises the price, ABC's pumps are busy. When XYZ lowers its prices, there's not a car in sight. Both service stations survive, but each has no control over the price.

19 In what type of market do these service stations operate? What determines the price of petrol and what determines the marginal revenue from petrol?

20 Describe the elasticity of demand for petrol that each of these service stations faces.

21 Why does each of these service stations have so little control over the price of the petrol it sells?

The Firm's Output Decision

22 The figure shows the costs of Quick Copy, one of the many copy shops in London.

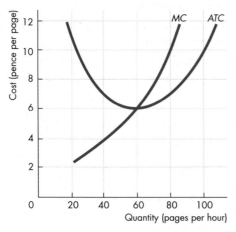

If the market price of copying one page is 10 pence, calculate Quick Copy's

a Profit-maximising output.

b Economic profit.

Output, Price and Profit in the Short Run

23 The market for smoothies is perfectly competitive, and the table sets out the market demand for smoothies.

Price (euros per smoothie)	Quantity demanded (smoothies per hour)
1.90	1,000
2.00	950
2.20	800
2.91	700
4.25	550
5.25	400
5.50	300

Each of the 100 producers of smoothies has the following costs when it uses its least-cost plant.

Output (smoothies per hour)	Marginal cost	Average variable cost	Average total cost
	(euros per smoothie)		
3	2.50	4.00	7.33
4	2.20	3.53	6.03
5	1.90	3.24	5.24
6	2.00	3.00	4.67
7	2.91	2.91	4.34
8	4.25	3.00	4.25
9	8.00	3.33	4.44

a What are the market price and the market output?

b How many smoothies does each firm sell?

c What is the economic profit made or economic loss incurred by each firm?

Use the following news clip in Problems 24 and 25.

Honda Workers Return after Four Month Shutdown

Honda shut down its UK Swindon car plant for four months in 2009, cutting annual production by 50 per cent to 11,300 vehicles and shedding 1,300 workers through voluntary redundancies. Workers were paid 2 months' full pay and 2 months on 60 per cent of pay during the shutdown.

Source: Independent online, 17 February 2009

24 Explain how the shutdown decision will affect the company's *TFC*, *TVC* and *TC*.

25 Under what conditions:

  a Would this shutdown decision maximise the company's economic profit (or minimise its loss)?

  b Did Honda start producing again?

26 Wheat Prices Down 40 per cent from Peak

Wheat prices in April have fallen more than 40 per cent from their peak in February. Farmers planted more wheat as prices increased and this year's harvest may be a record crop.

Source: BBC online, 25 April 2008

Why did wheat prices fall in 2008? Draw a graph to show that short-run effect on an individual farmer's economic profit.

Output, Price and Profit in the Long Run

27 In Problem 23, do firms enter or exit the market in the long run? What is the market price and the equilibrium quantity in the long run?

28 In Problem 24, under what conditions will Honda exit the car market?

29 Exxon Mobil Selling All Its Retail Outlets

Exxon Mobil is not alone among Big Oil exiting the retail business, a market where profits have gotten tougher as crude oil prices have risen. Owners say they're struggling to turn a profit because while wholesale petrol prices have risen sharply, they've been unable to raise pump prices fast enough to keep pace.

Source: *Houston Chronicle*, June 12, 2008

  a Is Exxon Mobil making a shutdown or exit decision in the retail petrol market?

  b Under what conditions will this decision maximise Exxon Mobil's economic profit?

  c How might Exxon Mobil's decision affect the economic profit of other petrol retailers?

Changes in Demand and Supply as Technology Advances

30 Another DVD Format, but It's Cheaper

New Medium Enterprises claims the quality of its new system, HD VMD, is equal to Blu-ray's but it costs only $199 – cheaper than the $300 cost of a Blu-ray player. Chairman of the Blu-ray Disc Association says New Medium will fail because it believes that Blu-ray technology will always be more expensive. But mass production will cut the cost of a Blu-ray player to $90.

Source: *The New York Times*, 10 March 2008

  a Explain how technological change in Blu-ray production might lead to lower prices in the long run. Illustrate your explanation with a graph.

  b Even if Blu-ray prices do drop to $90 in the long run, why might the HD VMD still end up being less expensive at that time?

Competition and Efficiency

31 In a perfectly competitive market, each firm maximises its profit by choosing only the quantity to produce. Regardless of whether the firm makes an economic profit or incurs an economic loss, the short-run equilibrium is efficient. Is the statement true? Explain why or why not.

Economics in the News

32 After you have studied *Reading Between the Lines* on pp. 268–269, answer the following questions.

  a What are the features of the market for apps that make it competitive?

  b Does the information provided in the news article suggest that the app market is in long-run equilibrium? Explain why or why not.

  c How would an advance in development technology that lowered a developer's costs change the market supply and the developer's marginal revenue, marginal cost, average total cost and economic profit?

  d llustrate your answer to part (c) with an appropriate graphical analysis.

33 Mobile Phone Sales Hit 1 Billion Mark

More than 1.15 billion mobile phones were sold worldwide in 2007, a 16 per cent increase in a year. Emerging markets, especially China and India, provided much of the growth as many people bought their first phone. In mature markets, such as Japan and Western Europe, consumers' appetite for feature-laden phones was met with new models packed with TV tuners, touch screens and cameras.

Source: CNET News, 27 February 2008

  a Explain the effects of the increase in global demand for mobile phones on the market for mobile phones and on an individual mobile phone producer in the short run.

  b Draw a graph to illustrate your answer in part (a).

  c Explain the long-run effects of the increase in global demand for mobile phones on the market for mobile phones.

  d What factors will determine whether the price of a mobile phone will rise, fall or stay the same in the new long-run equilibrium?

12 Monopoly

After studying this chapter you will be able to:

◆ Explain how monopoly arises, and distinguish between single-price and price-discriminating monopolies

◆ Explain how a single-price monopoly determines its output and price

◆ Compare the performance and efficiency of single-price monopoly and competition

◆ Explain how a price-discriminating monopoly increases profit

◆ Explain the effects of monopoly regulation

Google is a big player in the market for Web search and advertising, a market that is obviously not perfectly competitive.

In this chapter, we study markets dominated by one big firm. We call such a market *monopoly*. We study the performance and the efficiency of monopoly and compare it with perfect competition.

In *Reading Between the Lines* at the end of the chapter, we look at the remarkable success of Google and ask whether Google is serving the social interest or has abused its market power and violated Europe's competition laws.

Monopoly and How It Arises

A **monopoly** is a market with a single firm that produces a good or service with no close substitute and that is protected by a barrier that prevents other firms from selling that good or service.

How Monopoly Arises

Monopoly has two key features:

◆ No close substitute
◆ Barriers to entry

No Close Substitute

If a good has a close substitute, even though only one firm produces it, that firm effectively faces competition from the producer of the substitute. A monopoly sells a good or service that has no good close substitute. Water supplied by a local water board and bottled spring water are close substitutes for drinking, but not for showering or washing a car. A local water board is a monopoly.

Barriers to Entry

A constraint that protects a firm from potential competitors is called a **barrier to entry**. Three types of barrier to entry are:

◆ Natural
◆ Ownership
◆ Legal

Natural Barriers to Entry

Natural barriers to entry create **natural monopoly**, a market in which economies of scale enable one firm to supply the entire market at the lowest possible cost.

In Figure 12.1, the market demand curve for electric power is *D*, and the long-run average cost curve is *LRAC*. Economies of scale prevail over the entire length of the *LRAC* curve.

One firm can produce 4 million kilowatt-hours at 5 pence a kilowatt-hour. At this price, the quantity demanded is 4 million kilowatt-hours. So if the price were 5 pence, one firm could supply the entire market. If two firms shared the market, it would cost each of them 10 pence a kilowatt-hour to produce a total of 4 million kilowatt-hours. In conditions like those shown in Figure 12.1, one firm can supply the entire market at

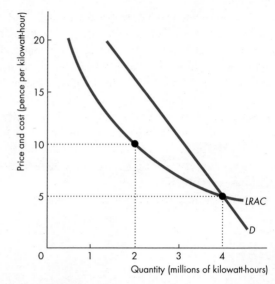

Figure 12.1 Natural Monopoly

The market demand curve for electric power is *D*, and the long-run average cost curve is *LRAC*. Economies of scale exist over the entire *LRAC* curve. One firm can distribute 4 million kilowatt-hours at a cost of 5 pence a kilowatt-hour. This same total output costs 10 pence a kilowatt-hour with two firms. So one firm can meet the market demand at a lower cost than two or more firms can, and the market is a natural monopoly.

MyEconLab Animation ———————————◆

a lower cost than two or more firms can. The market is a natural monopoly.

Ownership Barriers to Entry

An ownership barrier to entry occurs if one firm owns a significant portion of a resource. An example of this type of monopoly occurred during the last century when De Beers controlled up to 90 per cent of the world's supply of diamonds. (Today, its share is only 65 per cent.)

Legal Barriers to Entry

Legal barriers to entry create legal monopoly. A **legal monopoly** is a market in which competition and entry are restricted by the granting of a monopoly franchise, a government licence, a patent or a copyright.

A *monopoly franchise* is an exclusive right granted to a firm to supply a good or service. An example in the UK is the Royal Mail, which has the exclusive right to carry first-class mail.

A *government licence* controls entry into particular occupations and professions. This type of barrier to entry occurs in medicine, law, dentistry and many other professional services. A government licence doesn't always create a monopoly, but it does restrict competition.

A *patent* is an exclusive right granted to the inventor of a product or service. A *copyright* is an exclusive right granted to the author or composer of a literary, musical, dramatic or artistic work. Patents and copyrights are valid for a limited time period. In the UK, a patent is valid for 20 years. Patents encourage the *invention* of new products and production methods. Patents also stimulate *innovation* – the use of new inventions – by encouraging inventors to publicise their discoveries and offer them for use under licence. Patents have stimulated innovations in areas as diverse as tomato seeds, pharmaceuticals, memory chips and video games.

 ECONOMICS IN ACTION

Information-Age Monopolies

Information-age technologies have created four natural monopolies – firms with large plant costs but almost zero marginal cost, so they experience economies of scale.

These firms are: Microsoft, with 92 per cent of personal computers using a version of Windows; Google, which performs 83 per cent of Internet searches; Facebook, with 64 per cent of the social media market; and eBay, with 62 per cent of the Internet auction market.

These same information-age technologies also destroyed monopoly. Cloud computing is weakening Microsoft's monopoly and couriers and email have weakened the monopolies of national postal services such as the Royal Mail.

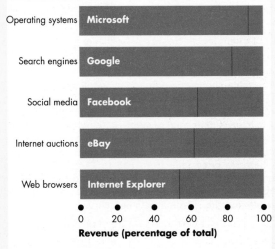

Figure 1 Market Shares

Monopoly Price-Setting Strategies

A major difference between monopoly and competition is that a monopoly sets its own price. In doing so, the monopoly faces a market constraint: to sell a larger quantity, the monopoly must charge a lower price. But there are two monopoly situations that create two pricing strategies:

◆ Single price
◆ Price discrimination

Single Price

A **single-price monopoly** is a monopoly that must sell each unit of its output for the same price to all its customers. De Beers sells diamonds (of a given size and quality) for the same price to all its customers. If it tried to sell at a lower price to some customers and at a higher price to others, only the low-price customers would buy from De Beers. Others would buy from De Beers' low-price customers. De Beers is a *single-price* monopoly.

Price Discrimination

When a firm practises **price discrimination**, it sells different units of a good or service for different prices. Many firms price discriminate. Microsoft sells Windows and Office software at different prices to different buyers. Computer manufacturers who install the software on new machines, students, teachers, governments and businesses all pay different prices. Airlines offer a dizzying array of different prices for the same trip. Pizza producers often charge one price for a single pizza and almost give away a second pizza. These are all examples of *price discrimination*.

When a firm price discriminates, it looks as though it is doing its customers a favour. In fact, it is charging the highest possible price for each unit that it sells and making the largest possible profit.

◆ **REVIEW QUIZ**

1 How does monopoly arise?
2 How does a natural monopoly differ from a legal monopoly?
3 Distinguish between a price-discriminating monopoly and a single-price monopoly.

Do these questions in Study Plan 12.1 and get instant feedback. MyEconLab

A Single-Price Monopoly's Output and Price Decision

To understand how a single-price monopoly makes its output and price decision, we must first study the link between price and marginal revenue.

Price and Marginal Revenue

Because in a monopoly there is only one firm, the demand curve facing the firm is the market demand curve. Let's look at Gina's Cut and Dry, the only hairdressing salon within a 15 mile radius of a North Yorkshire town. The table in Figure 12.2 shows the market demand schedule. At a price of £20, she sells no haircuts. The lower the price, the more haircuts per hour Gina can sell. For example, at £12, consumers demand 4 haircuts per hour (row *E*).

Total revenue (*TR*) is the price (*P*) multiplied by the quantity sold (*Q*). For example, in row *D*, Gina sells 3 haircuts at £14 each, so total revenue is £42. *Marginal revenue* (*MR*) is the change in total revenue (*ΔTR*) resulting from a one-unit increase in the quantity sold. For example, if the price falls from £16 (row *C*) to £14 (row *D*), the quantity sold increases from 2 to 3 haircuts. Total revenue rises from £32 to £42, so the change in total revenue is £10. Because the quantity sold increases by 1 haircut, marginal revenue equals the change in total revenue and is £10. Marginal revenue is placed between the two rows to emphasise that marginal revenue relates to the *change* in the quantity sold.

Figure 12.2 shows the market demand curve and marginal revenue curve (*MR*) and also illustrates the calculation we've just made. Notice that at each level of output, marginal revenue is less than price – the marginal revenue curve lies below the demand curve.

Why is marginal revenue *less* than price? It is because when the price is lowered to sell one more unit, two opposing forces affect total revenue. The lower price results in a revenue loss and the increased quantity sold results in a revenue gain. For example, at a price of £16, Gina sells 2 haircuts (point *C*). If she lowers the price to £14, she sells 3 haircuts (point *D*) and has a revenue gain of £14 on the third haircut. But she now receives only £14 on the first two – £2 less than before. She loses £4 of revenue on the first 2 haircuts. To calculate marginal revenue, she must deduct this amount from the revenue gain of £14. So her marginal revenue is £10, which is less than the price.

Figure 12.2   Demand and Marginal Revenue

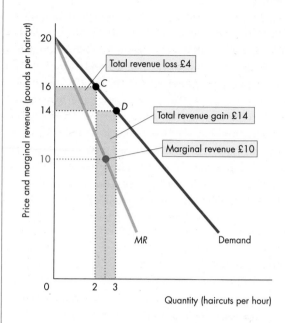

	Price (*P*) (pounds per haircut)	Quantity demanded (*Q*) (haircuts per hour)	Total revenue (*TR* = *P* × *Q*) (pounds)	Marginal revenue (*MR* = *ΔTR*/*ΔQ*) (pounds per haircut)
A	20	0	0	
				 18
B	18	1	18	
				 14
C	16	2	32	
				 10
D	14	3	42	
				 6
E	12	4	48	
				 2
F	10	5	50	

The table shows the demand schedule. Total revenue (*TR*) is price multiplied by quantity sold. For example, in row *C*, the price is £16 a haircut. Cut and Dry sells 2 haircuts and its total revenue is £32. Marginal revenue (*MR*) is the change in total revenue that results from a one-unit increase in the quantity sold. For example, when the price falls from £16 to £14 a haircut, the quantity sold increases by 1 haircut and total revenue increases by £10. Marginal revenue is £10. The demand curve and the marginal revenue curve, *MR*, are based on the numbers in the table and illustrate the calculation of marginal revenue when the price falls from £16 to £14 a haircut.

MyEconLab Animation ◆

Marginal Revenue and Elasticity

A single-price monopoly's marginal revenue is related to the *elasticity of demand* for its good. The demand for a good can be *elastic* (the elasticity of demand is greater than 1), *inelastic* (the elasticity of demand is less than 1), or *unit elastic* (the elasticity of demand is equal to 1). Demand is *elastic* if a 1 per cent fall in the price brings a greater than 1 per cent increase in the quantity demanded. Demand is *inelastic* if a 1 per cent fall in the price brings a less than 1 per cent increase in the quantity demanded. And demand is *unit elastic* if a 1 per cent fall in the price brings a 1 per cent increase in the quantity demanded. (See Chapter 4, pp. 83–84.)

If demand is elastic, a fall in price brings an increase in total revenue – the increase in revenue from the increase in quantity sold outweighs the decrease in revenue from the lower price – and marginal revenue is *positive*. If demand is inelastic, a fall in the price brings a decrease in total revenue – the increase in revenue from the increase in quantity sold is outweighed by the decrease in revenue from the lower price – and marginal revenue is *negative*. If demand is unit elastic, total revenue does not change – the increase in revenue from the increase in quantity sold offsets the decrease in revenue from the lower price – and marginal revenue is *zero*. (The relationship between total revenue and elasticity is explained in Chapter 4, p. 86.)

Figure 12.3 illustrates the relationship between marginal revenue, total revenue and elasticity. As the price of a haircut gradually falls from £20 to £10, the quantity of haircuts demanded increases from 0 to 5 an hour, marginal revenue is positive in part (a), total revenue increases in part (b), and the demand for haircuts is elastic. As the price falls from £10 to £0, the quantity of haircuts demanded increases from 5 to 10 an hour, marginal revenue is negative in part (a), total revenue decreases in part (b), and the demand for haircuts is inelastic. When the price is £10 a haircut, marginal revenue is zero in part (a), total revenue is a maximum in part (b), and the demand for haircuts is unit elastic.

In Monopoly, Demand Is Always Elastic

The relationship between marginal revenue and elasticity that you've just discovered implies that a profit-maximising monopoly never produces an output in the inelastic range of its demand curve. If it did so, it could produce a smaller quantity, charge a higher price and increase its economic profit. Let's now look at a monopoly's price and output decision.

Figure 12.3   Marginal Revenue and Elasticity

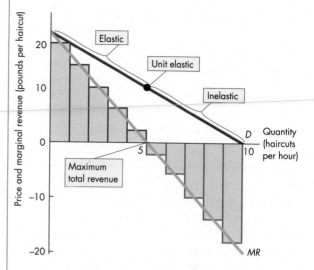

(a) Demand and marginal revenue curves

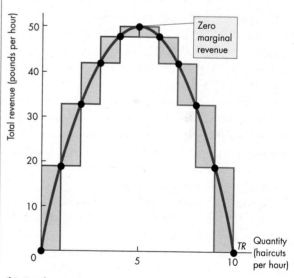

(b) Total revenue curve

In part (a), the demand curve is *D* and the marginal revenue curve is *MR*. In part (b), the total revenue curve is *TR*. Over the range from 0 to 5 haircuts an hour, a price cut increases total revenue, so marginal revenue is positive – as shown by the blue bars. Demand is elastic. Over the range from 5 to 10 haircuts an hour, a price cut decreases total revenue, so marginal revenue is negative – as shown by the red bars. Demand is inelastic. At 5 haircuts an hour, total revenue is maximised and marginal revenue is zero. Demand is unit elastic.

MyEconLab Animation ——————————————◆

Price and Output Decision

A monopoly sets its price and output at the levels that maximise economic profit. To determine this price and output level, we need to study the behaviour of both cost and revenue as output varies. A monopoly faces the same types of technology and cost constraints as a competitive firm, so its costs (total cost, average cost and marginal cost) behave just like those of a firm in perfect competition. And a monopoly's revenues (total revenue, price and marginal revenue) behave in the way we've just described.

Let's see how Cut and Dry maximises its profit.

Maximising Economic Profit

You can see in Table 12.1 and Figure 12.4(a) that total cost (*TC*) and total revenue (*TR*) both rise as output increases, but *TC* rises at an increasing rate and *TR* rises at a decreasing rate.

Economic profit, which equals *TR* minus *TC*, increases at small output levels, reaches a maximum and then decreases. The maximum profit (£12) occurs when Cut and Dry sells 3 haircuts for £14 each. If it sells 2 haircuts for £16 each or 4 haircuts for £12 each, Cut and Dry's economic profit will be only £8.

Marginal Revenue Equals Marginal Cost

You can see Cut and Dry's marginal revenue (*MR*) and marginal cost (*MC*) in Table 12.1 and Figure 12.4(b). When Cut and Dry increases output from 2 to 3 haircuts, *MR* is £10 and *MC* is £6. *MR* exceeds *MC* by £4 and Cut and Dry's profit increases by that amount. If Cut and Dry increases output yet further, from 3 to 4 haircuts, *MR* is £6 and *MC* is £10. In this case, *MC* exceeds *MR* by £4, so Cut and Dry's profit decreases by that amount.

When *MR* exceeds *MC*, profit increases if output increases. When *MC* exceeds *MR*, profit increases if output *decreases*. When *MC* equals *MR*, profit is maximised.

Figure 12.4(b) shows the maximum profit as price (on the demand curve *D*) minus average total cost (on the *ATC* curve) multiplied by the quantity produced – the blue rectangle.

Maximum Price the Market Will Bear

Unlike a firm in perfect competition, a monopoly influences the price of what it sells. But a monopoly doesn't set the price at the maximum *possible* price. At the maximum possible price, the firm would be able to sell only one unit of output, which in general is less than the profit-maximising quantity. Rather, a monopoly

---

Table 12.1

A Monopoly's Output and Price Decision

Price (P) (pounds per haircut)	Quantity demanded (Q) (haircuts per hour)	Total revenue (TR = P × Q) (pounds)	Marginal revenue (MR = ΔTR/ΔQ) (pounds per haircut)	Total cost (TC) (pounds)	Marginal cost (MC = ΔTC/ΔQ) (pounds per haircut)	Profit (TR − TC) (pounds)
20	0	0		20		−20
			18		1	
18	1	18		21		−3
			14		3	
16	2	32		24		8
			10		6	
14	**3**	**42**		**30**		**+12**
			6		10	
12	4	48		40		+8
			2		15	
10	5	50		55		−5

Total revenue (*TR*) equals price (*P*) multiplied by the quantity sold (*Q*). Profit equals total revenue minus total cost (*TC*). Profit is maximised when the price is £14 a haircut and 3 haircuts are sold. Total revenue is £42 an hour, total cost is £30 an hour and economic profit is £12 an hour.

Figure 12.4 A Monopoly's Output and Price

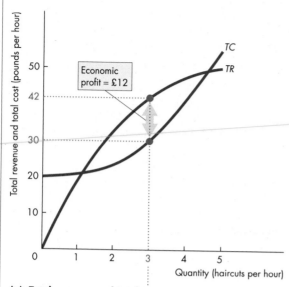

(a) Total revenue and total cost curves

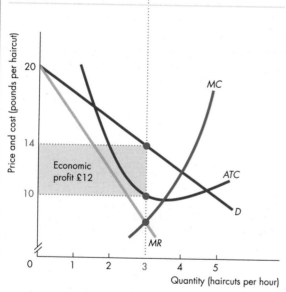

(b) Demand and marginal revenue and cost curves

In part (a), economic profit is the vertical distance equal to total revenue (*TR*) minus total cost (*TC*), and it is maximised at 3 haircuts an hour.

In part (b), economic profit is maximised when marginal cost (*MC*) equals marginal revenue (*MR*). The profit-maximising output is 3 haircuts an hour. The price is determined by the demand curve (*D*) and is £14 a haircut. The average total cost is £10 a haircut, so economic profit, the blue rectangle, is £12, which equals the profit per haircut (£4) multiplied by 3 haircuts.

produces the profit-maximising quantity and sells that quantity for the highest price it can get.

All firms maximise profit by producing the output at which marginal revenue equals marginal cost. For a competitive firm, price equals marginal revenue, so price also equals marginal cost. For a monopoly, price exceeds marginal revenue, so price also exceeds marginal cost.

A monopoly charges a price that exceeds marginal cost, but does it always make an economic profit? In Figure 12.4(b), Cut and Dry produces 3 haircuts an hour. Its average total cost is £10 (read from the *ATC* curve) and its price is £14 (read from the *D* curve). It makes a profit of £4 a haircut (£14 minus £10). Cut and Dry's economic profit is shown by the blue rectangle, which equals the profit per haircut (£4) multiplied by the number of haircuts (3), for a total of £12 an hour.

If firms in a perfectly competitive market make a positive economic profit, new firms enter. That does *not* happen in monopoly. Barriers to entry prevent new firms from entering a market in which there is a monopoly. So a monopoly can make a positive economic profit and might continue to do so indefinitely. Sometimes that profit is large, as in the international diamond business.

Cut and Dry makes a positive economic profit. But suppose that the owner of the shop that Gina rents increases Cut and Dry's rent. If Cut and Dry pays an additional £12 an hour, its fixed cost increases by £12 an hour. Its marginal cost and marginal revenue don't change, so its profit-maximising output remains at 3 haircuts an hour. Economic profit decreases by £12 an hour to zero. If Cut and Dry pays more than an additional £12 an hour for its shop rent, it incurs an economic loss. If this situation were permanent, Cut and Dry would go out of business.

REVIEW QUIZ

1 What is the relationship between marginal cost and marginal revenue when a single-price monopoly maximises profit?

2 How does a single-price monopoly determine the price it will charge its customers?

3 What is the relationship between price, marginal revenue and marginal cost when a single-price monopoly is maximising profit?

4 Why can a monopoly make a positive economic profit even in the long run?

Do these questions in Study Plan 12.2 and get instant feedback.

MyEconLab

Single-Price Monopoly and Competition Compared

Imagine a market that is made up of many small firms operating in perfect competition. Then imagine that a single firm buys out all these small firms and creates a monopoly.

What will happen in this market? Will the price rise or fall? Will the quantity produced increase or decrease? Will economic profit increase or decrease? Will either the original competitive situation or the new monopoly situation be efficient?

These are the questions we're now going to answer. First, we look at the effects of monopoly on the price and quantity produced. Then we turn to the questions about efficiency.

Comparing Price and Output

Figure 12.5 shows the market we'll study. The market demand curve is D. The demand curve is the same regardless of how the market is organised. But the supply side and the equilibrium are different in monopoly and competition. First, let's look at the case of perfect competition.

Perfect Competition

Initially, with many small, perfectly competitive firms in the market, the market supply curve is S. This supply curve is obtained by summing the supply curves of all the individual firms in the market.

In perfect competition, equilibrium occurs where the market supply curve and market demand curve intersect. The quantity produced is Q_C and the price is P_C. Each firm takes the price P_C and maximises its profit by producing the output at which its own marginal cost equals the price. Because each firm is a small part of the total market, there is no incentive for any firm to try to manipulate the price by varying its output.

Monopoly

Now suppose that this market is taken over by a single firm. Consumers do not change, so the market demand curve remains the same as in the case of perfect competition. But now the monopoly recognises this demand curve as a constraint on the price at which it can sell its output. The monopoly's marginal revenue curve is MR.

The monopoly maximises profit by producing the quantity at which marginal revenue equals marginal cost. To find the monopoly's marginal cost curve, first recall that in perfect competition the market supply curve is the sum of the supply curves of the firms in the market. Also recall that each firm's supply curve is its marginal cost curve (see Chapter 11, p. 255). So when the market is taken over by a single firm, the competitive market's supply curve becomes the monopoly's marginal cost curve. To remind you of this fact, the supply curve is also labelled MC.

The output at which marginal revenue equals marginal cost is Q_M. This output is smaller than the competitive output Q_C. And the monopoly charges the price P_M, which is higher than P_C. We have established that:

Compared with a perfectly competitive market, a single-price monopoly produces a smaller output and charges a higher price.

We've seen how the output and price of a monopoly compare with those in a competitive market. Let's now compare the efficiency of the two types of market.

Figure 12.5   Monopoly's Smaller Output and Higher Price

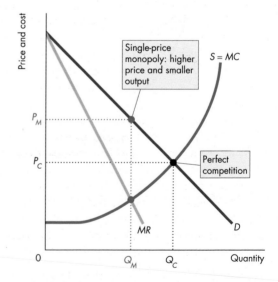

A competitive market produces the quantity Q_C at price P_C. A single-price monopoly produces the quantity Q_M at which marginal revenue equals marginal cost and sells that quantity for the price P_M. Compared with perfect competition, a single-price monopoly produces a smaller output and charges a higher price.

MyEconLab Animation ━━━━━━━━━━━━━━━◆

Efficiency Comparison

Perfect competition (with no external costs and benefits) is efficient. Figure 12.6(a) illustrates the efficiency of perfect competition and serves as a benchmark against which to measure the inefficiency of monopoly.

Along the demand curve and marginal social benefit curve ($D = MSB$), consumers are efficient. Along the supply curve and marginal social cost curve ($S = MSC$), producers are efficient. In competitive equilibrium, the price is P_C, the quantity is Q_C, and marginal social benefit equals marginal social cost.

Consumer surplus is the green triangle under the demand curve and above the equilibrium price (see Chapter 5, p. 107). *Producer surplus* is the blue area above the supply curve and below the equilibrium price (see Chapter 5, p. 109). Total surplus (the sum of the consumer surplus and producer surplus) is maximised.

Also, in long-run competitive equilibrium, entry and exit ensure that each firm produces its output at the minimum possible long-run average cost.

To summarise: at the competitive equilibrium, marginal social benefit equals marginal social cost; total surplus is maximised; firms produce at the lowest possible long-run average cost; and resource use is efficient.

Figure 12.6(b) illustrates the inefficiency of monopoly and the sources of that inefficiency. A monopoly produces Q_M and charges P_M. The smaller output and higher price drive a wedge between marginal social benefit and marginal social cost and create a *deadweight loss*. The grey area shows the deadweight loss, and its magnitude is a measure of the inefficiency of monopoly.

Consumer surplus shrinks for two reasons. First, consumers lose by having to pay more for the good. This loss to consumers is a gain for the monopoly and increases the the monopoly's producer surplus. Second, consumers lose by getting less of the good, and this loss is part of the deadweight loss created by monopoly.

Although the monopoly gains from a higher price, it loses some producer surplus because it produces a smaller output. That loss is another part of the deadweight loss created by monopoly.

A monopoly produces a smaller output than perfect competition and faces no competition, so it does not produce at the lowest possible long-run average cost. As a result, monopoly damages the consumer interest in three ways: a monopoly produces less, it increases the cost of production, and it raises the price to above the increased cost of production.

Figure 12.6 Inefficiency of Monopoly

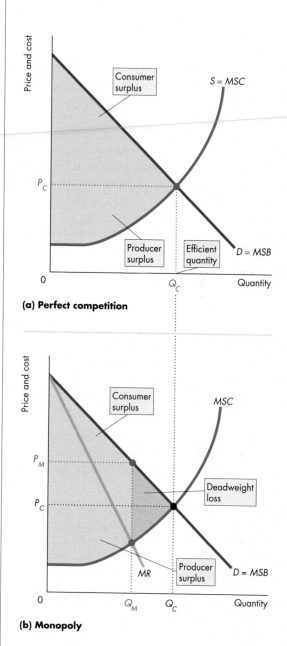

(a) Perfect competition

(b) Monopoly

In perfect competition in part (a), output is Q_C and the price is P_C. Marginal social benefit (*MSB*) equals marginal social cost (*MSC*); total surplus, the sum of consumer surplus (the green triangle) and producer surplus (the blue area), is maximised; and in the long run, firms produce at the lowest possible average cost.

The monopoly in part (b) restricts output to Q_M and raises the price to P_M. Consumer surplus shrinks, the monopoly gains and a deadweight loss (the grey area) arises.

MyEconLab Animation ——————————◆

Redistribution of Surpluses

You've seen that monopoly is inefficient because marginal social benefit exceeds marginal social cost and there is deadweight loss – a social loss. But monopoly also brings a *redistribution* of surpluses.

Some of the lost consumer surplus goes to the monopoly. In Figure 12.6(b), the monopoly gets the difference between the higher price, P_M, and the competitive price, P_C, on the quantity sold, Q_M. So the monopoly takes part of the consumer surplus. This portion of the loss of consumer surplus is not a loss to society. It is a redistribution from consumers to the monopoly producer.

Rent Seeking

You've seen that monopoly creates a deadweight loss and is inefficient. But the social cost of monopoly can exceed the deadweight loss because of an activity called rent seeking. Any surplus – consumer surplus, producer surplus or economic profit – is called **economic rent**. And **rent seeking** is the pursuit of wealth by capturing economic rent.

You've seen that a monopoly makes its economic profit by diverting part of consumer surplus to itself – by converting consumer surplus into economic profit. So the pursuit of economic profit by a monopoly is rent seeking. It is the attempt to capture consumer surplus.

Rent seekers pursue their goals in two main ways. They might:

◆ Buy a monopoly
◆ Create a monopoly

Buy a Monopoly

To rent seek by buying a monopoly, a person searches for a monopoly that is for sale at a lower price than the monopoly's economic profit. Trading of taxi licences is an example of this type of rent seeking. In some cities, taxis are regulated. The city restricts both the fares and the number of taxis that can operate so that operating a taxi results in economic profit or rent. A person who wants to operate a taxi must buy a licence from someone who already has one. People rationally devote time and effort to seeking out profitable monopoly businesses to buy. In the process, they use up scarce resources that could otherwise have been used to produce goods and services. The value of this lost production is part of the social cost of monopoly. The amount paid for a

monopoly is not a social cost because the payment is just a transfer of an existing producer surplus from the buyer to the seller.

Create a Monopoly

Rent seeking by creating a monopoly is mainly a political activity. It takes the form of lobbying and seeking to influence the political process. Such influence is sometimes sought by making political contributions in exchange for legislative support, or by indirectly seeking to influence political outcomes through publicity in the media or via more direct contacts with politicians and bureaucrats. An example of this type of rent seeking would be the donations that alcohol and tobacco companies make to political parties in an attempt to avoid a tightening of legislation on activities such as advertising and licensing, which might affect their profits.

This type of rent seeking is a costly activity that uses up scarce resources. In aggregate, firms spend millions of pounds lobbying Parliament in the pursuit of licences and laws that create barriers to entry and establish a monopoly. Everyone has an incentive to rent seek, and because there are no barriers to entry into rent seeking, there is a great deal of competition in this activity. The winners of the competition become monopolies.

Rent-Seeking Equilibrium

How much will a person be willing to give up to acquire a monopoly right? The answer is the entire value of a monopoly's economic profit. Barriers to entry create monopoly. But there is no barrier to entry into rent seeking. Rent seeking is like perfect competition. If an economic profit is available, a new rent seeker will try to get some of it. And competition among rent seekers pushes up the price that must be paid for a monopoly to the point at which the rent seeker makes zero economic profit by operating the monopoly.

Figure 12.7 shows a rent-seeking equilibrium. The cost of rent seeking is a fixed cost that must be added to a monopoly's other costs. Rent seeking and rent-seeking costs increase to the point at which no economic profit is made. The average total cost curve, which includes the fixed cost of rent seeking, shifts upward until it just touches the demand curve. Economic profit is zero. It has been lost in rent seeking.

Consumer surplus is unaffected. But the deadweight loss of monopoly now includes the original deadweight loss plus the lost producer surplus, shown by the enlarged grey area in Figure 12.7.

Figure 12.7   Rent-Seeking Equilibrium

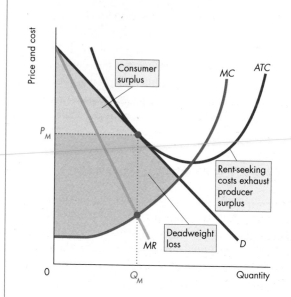

With competitive rent seeking, a monopoly uses all its economic profit to prevent another firm from taking its economic rent. The firm's rent-seeking costs are fixed costs. They add to total fixed cost and to average total cost, and the *ATC* curve shifts upward. Rent seeking will continue until the *ATC* curve has shifted up by so much that at the profit-maximising price, the firm breaks even. The grey area shows the deadweight loss.

MyEconLab Animation ————————◆

So far, we've considered only a single-price monopoly. But many monopolies do not operate with a single price. Instead, they price discriminate. Let's now see how price-discriminating monopoly works.

Price Discrimination

You encounter *price discrimination* – selling a good or service at a number of different prices – when you travel, go to the cinema, go shopping or go out to eat. These are all firms with market power, setting the prices of an identical good or service at different levels for different customers.

Not all price *differences* are price *discrimination*: they reflect differences in production costs. For example, the cost of producing electricity depends on the time of day. If an electric power company charges a higher price during the peak consumption periods from 7:00 to 9:00 in the morning and from 4:00 to 7:00 in the evening than it does at other times of the day, it is not price discriminating.

At first sight, price discrimination appears to be inconsistent with profit maximisation. Why would a railway company give a student discount? Why would a hairdresser charge students and senior citizens less? Aren't these firms losing profit by being so generous to their customers? The answer, as you are about to discover, is that price discrimination is profitable: it increases economic profit.

But to be able to price discriminate, the firm must sell a product that cannot be resold and it must be possible to identify and separate different buyer types.

Two Ways of Price Discriminating

Firms price discriminate in two broad ways. They discriminate:

◆ Among groups of buyers
◆ Among units of a good

Discriminating Among Groups of Buyers

People differ in the value they place on a good – their marginal benefit and willingness to pay. Some of these differences are correlated with features such as age, employment status and other easily distinguished characteristics. When such a correlation is present, firms can profit by price discriminating among the different groups of buyers.

For example, a face-to-face sales meeting with a customer might bring a large and profitable order. So for salespeople and other business travellers, the marginal benefit from a trip is large and the price that such a traveller is willing to pay for a trip is high. In contrast, for a holiday traveller, any of several different trips and even no holiday trip are options. So for holiday travellers the marginal benefit of a trip is small, and the price that such a traveller is willing to pay for a trip is low. Because the price that business travellers are willing to pay exceeds what holiday travellers are willing to pay, it is possible for an airline to discriminate between these two groups and increase its profit. We'll return to this example of price discrimination below.

Discriminating Among Units of a Good

Everyone experiences diminishing marginal benefit and has a downward-sloping demand curve. For this reason, if all the units of the good are sold for a single price, buyers end up with a consumer surplus equal to the value they get from each unit of the good minus the price paid for it.

A firm that price discriminates by charging a buyer one price for a single item and a lower price for a second or third item can capture some of the consumer surplus. Buy one pizza and get a second one free (or for a low price) is an example of this type of price discrimination.

Increase Profit and Producer Surplus

By getting buyers to pay a price as close as possible to their maximum willingness to pay, a monopoly captures the consumer surplus and converts it into producer surplus. More producer surplus means more economic profit.

To see why more producer surplus means more economic profit, recall some definitions. With total revenue TR and total cost TC,

$$\text{Economic profit} = TR - TC$$

Producer surplus is total revenue minus the area under the marginal cost curve. But the area under the marginal cost curve is total variable cost, TVC. So:

$$\text{Producer surplus} = TR - TVC$$

You can see that the difference between economic profit and producer surplus is the same as the difference between TC and TVC. But TC minus TVC equals total fixed cost, TFC. So:

$$\text{Economic profit} = \text{Producer surplus} - TFC$$

For a given total fixed cost, anything that increases producer surplus also increases economic profit.

Let's now see how price discrimination works by looking at a price-discriminating airline.

Profiting by Price Discriminating

Inter-City Airlines has a monopoly on passenger flights between two cities. Figure 12.8 shows the market demand curve, D, for travel on this route. It also shows Inter-City Airline's marginal revenue curve, MR, and marginal cost curve, MC. Inter-City's marginal cost is a constant €40 per trip. (It is easier to see how price discrimination works for a firm with constant marginal cost.)

Single Price Profit-Maximisation

As a single-price monopoly, Inter-City maximises profit by producing the quantity of trips at which MR equals MC, which is 8,000 trips a week, and charging €120 a trip. With a marginal cost of €40 a trip, producer surplus is €80 a trip, and Inter-City's producer surplus is €640,000 a week, shown by the area of the blue rectangle. Inter-City's customers enjoy a consumer surplus shown by the area of the green triangle.

Figure 12.8   A Single Price of Air Travel

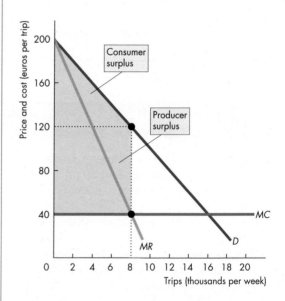

Inter-City Airlines has a monopoly on an air route with a market demand curve D. Inter-City's marginal cost, MC, is €40 per trip. As a single-price monopoly, Inter-City's marginal revenue curve is MR. Profit is maximised by selling 8,000 trips a week at €120 a trip. Producer surplus is €640,000 a week – the blue rectangle – and Inter-City's customers enjoy a consumer surplus – the green triangle.

MyEconLab Animation ─────────────◆

Discriminating Between Two Types of Travellers

Inter-City surveys its customers and discovers that they are all business travellers. It also surveys people who are not its customers and discovers that they are mainly people who travel for leisure. These people travel by bus or car, but would travel by air if the fare was low enough. Inter-City would like to attract some of these travellers and knows that to do so it must offer a fare below the current €120 a trip. How can it do that?

Inter-City digs more deeply into its survey results and discovers that its current customers always plan their travel less than two weeks before departure. In contrast, the people who travel by bus or car know their travel plans at least two weeks ahead of time.

Inter-City sees that it can use what it has discovered about its current and potential new customers to separate the two types of travellers into two markets: one market for business travel and another for leisure travel.

Figure 12.9 shows Inter-City's two markets. Part (a), the market for business travel, is the same as Figure 12.8. Part (b) shows the market for leisure travel. No leisure traveller is willing to pay the business fare of €120 a trip, so at that price the quantity demanded in part (b) is zero. The demand curve D_L is the demand for travel on this route after satisfying the demand of business travellers. Inter-City's marginal cost remains at €40 a trip, so its marginal revenue curve is MR_L. Inter-City maximises profit by setting the leisure fare at €80 a trip and attracting 4,000 leisure travellers a week. Inter-City's producer surplus increases by €160,000 a week – the area of the blue rectangle in Figure 12.9(b) and leisure travellers enjoy a consumer surplus – the area of the green triangle.

Inter-City announces its new fare schedule: no restrictions €120 and 14-day advance purchase $80. Inter-City increases its passenger count by 50 per cent and increases its producer surplus by €160,000.

Figure 12.9 Price Discrimination

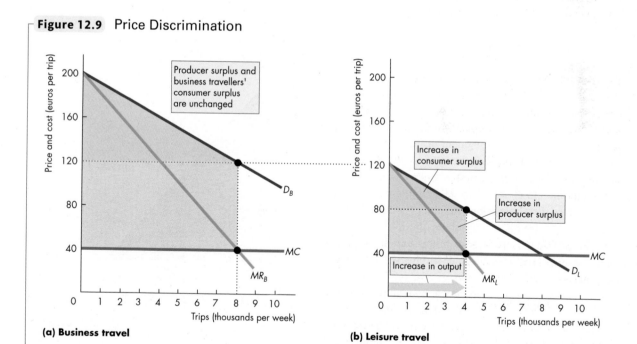

(a) Business travel

(b) Leisure travel

Inter-City separates its market into two types of travel: business travel with no restrictions in part (a) and leisure travel which requires a 14-day advance purchase in part (b). For business travel, the profit-maximising price is €120 a trip with 8,000 trips a week. For leisure travel, the profit-maximising price is €80 a trip with 4,000 trips a week.

Inter-City continues to make the same producer surplus on business travel as it did with a single price, and business travellers continue to enjoy the same consumer surplus. But in part (b), Inter-City sells 4,000 trips to leisure travellers, which increases its producer surplus – the blue rectangle – and increases consumer surplus – the green triangle.

MyEconLab Animation

Discriminating Among Several Types of Travellers

Pleased with the success of its price discrimination between business and leisure travellers, Inter-City sees that it might be able to profit even more by dividing its customers into a larger number of types. So it does another customer survey, which reveals that some business travellers are willing to pay €160 for a fully refundable, unrestricted ticket while others are willing to pay only €120 for a non-refundable ticket. So applying the same principles as it used to discriminate between business and leisure travellers, Inter-City now discriminates between business travellers who want a refundable ticket and those who want a non-refundable ticket.

Another survey of leisure travellers reveals that they fall into two groups: those who are able to plan 14 days ahead and others who can plan 21 days ahead. So Inter-City discriminates between these two groups with two fares: an €80 and a €60 fare.

By offering travellers four different fares, the airline increases its producer surplus and increases its economic profit. But why only four fares? Why not keep looking for more traveller types and offer more fares?

Perfect Price Discrimination

Firms try to capture an ever larger part of consumer surplus by devising a host of special conditions, each one of which appeals to a tiny segment of the market but at the same time excludes others from taking advantage of a lower price. The more consumer surplus a firm is able to capture, the closer it gets to the extreme case called **perfect price discrimination**, which occurs if a firm is able to sell each unit of output for the highest price someone is willing to pay for it. In this extreme (hypothetical) case, the entire consumer surplus is eliminated and captured as producer surplus.

With perfect price discrimination, something special happens to marginal revenue – the market demand curve becomes the firm's marginal revenue curve. The reason is that when the price is cut to sell a larger quantity, the firm sells only the marginal unit at the lower price. All the other units continue to be sold for the highest price that each buyer is willing to pay. So for the perfect price discriminator, marginal revenue *equals* price and the demand curve becomes the firm's marginal revenue curve.

With marginal revenue equal to price, Inter-City can obtain even greater producer surplus by increasing

output up to the point at which price (and marginal revenue) is equal to marginal cost.

So Inter-City now seeks additional travellers who will not pay as much as €60 a trip but who will pay more than €40, its marginal cost. Inter-City offers a variety of holiday specials at different low fares that appeal only to new travellers. Existing customers continue to pay the higher fares and some, with further perks and frills that have no effect on cost, are induced to pay fares that go all the way up to €200 a trip.

With all these fares and specials, Inter-City increases its output to the quantity demanded at marginal cost, extracts the entire consumer surplus on that quantity, and maximises economic profit.

Figure 12.10 shows the outcome with perfect price discrimination and compares it with the single-price monopoly outcome. The range of business class fares extract the entire consumer surplus from this group. The new holiday-class fares going down to €40 a trip attract an additional 8,000 travellers and take the entire consumer surplus of leisure travellers. Inter-City makes the maximum economic profit.

Figure 12.10 Perfect Price Discrimination

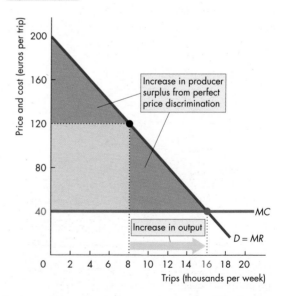

Dozens of fares discriminate among many different types of business travellers and many new low fares with restrictions appeal to leisure travellers. With perfect price discrimination, the market demand curve becomes Inter-City's marginal revenue curve. Producer surplus is maximised when the lowest price equals marginal cost. Inter-City sells 16,000 trips and makes the maximum possible economic profit.

MyEconLab Animation ───────────────◆

Efficiency and Rent Seeking with Price Discrimination

Because perfect price discrimination achieves an output at which price equals marginal cost, the same quantity as perfect competition, it creates no deadweight loss and is efficient.

The more perfectly a monopoly can price discriminate, the closer its output is to the competitive output and the more efficient is the outcome.

But the outcomes of perfect competition and perfect price discrimination differ. First, the distribution of the total surplus is not the same. In perfect competition, total surplus is shared by consumers and producers whereas with perfect price discrimination, the monopoly takes it all.

Second, because the monopoly takes the entire total surplus, rent seeking becomes more profitable, and more resources get used in pursuing rents. With free entry into rent seeking, in long-run equilibrium rent seekers use up the entire producer surplus.

Real-world firms don't achieve perfect price discrimination, but they are just as creative as Inter-City Airlines, as you can see in the cartoon! Disney Corporation is creative too in extracting consumer surplus, as *Economics in Action* shows.

We next study some monopoly policy issues.

Would it bother you to hear how little I paid for this flight?

From William Hamilton, *Voodoo Economics*, 1992, Chronicle Books, p. 3. Reprinted with permission from William Hamilton.

ECONOMICS IN ACTION

Attempting Perfect Price Discrimination

If you want to spend a day at the two Disneyland Paris parks, it will cost you £63. You can spend a second consecutive day for £55 and a third day for £26. You would pay £25 for each of the fourth and fifth consecutive days.

The Disney Corporation hopes that it has read your willingness to pay correctly and not left you with too much consumer surplus.

Notice that the third, fourth and fifth days cost almost the same and £25 is the lowest price. If Disney is doing a good job at maximising profit, its marginal cost must be £25 per person-day.

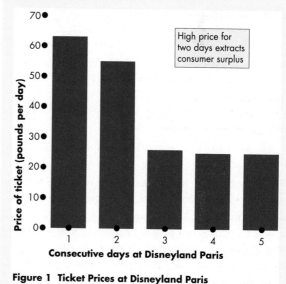

Figure 1 Ticket Prices at Disneyland Paris

REVIEW QUIZ

1 What is price discrimination and how is it used to increase a monopoly's profit?
2 Explain how consumer surplus changes when a monopoly price discriminates.
3 Explain how consumer surplus, economic profit and output change when a monopoly perfectly price discriminates.
4 What are some of the ways that real-world airlines use to price discriminate?

Do these questions in Study Plan 12.4 and get instant feedback.   MyEconLab

ECONOMICS IN THE NEWS

Microsoft Monopoly

Microsoft Windows 8 to Go on Sale in October

Microsoft announced that its Windows 8 operating system will be released in October 2012, three years after Windows 7 went public. Windows 8 will be available in 109 languages across 231 markets worldwide.

Source: AFP, 9 July 2012

Some Data

Microsoft Windows 7 Versions and Eurozone Prices

Version	Price (euros)
Full from Microsoft	233.99
Upgrade from Microsoft	177.99
Full from Amazon	106.48
Full from Mission Softs (OEM)	60.45
Student from Microsoft	50.66

Microsoft sold 240 million Windows 7 licences per year and at different prices in different national markets.

The Questions

◆ Is Microsoft a monopoly?

◆ Is Microsoft a natural monopoly or a legal monopoly?

◆ Does Microsoft price discriminate or do the different prices of Windows reflect cost differences?

◆ Sketch a demand curve for Windows, Microsoft's marginal cost curve, and the division of total surplus between consumer surplus and Microsoft's producer surplus.

The Answers

◆ Microsoft controls 92 per cent of the market for computer operating systems, and almost 100 per cent of the non-Apple market, which makes it an effective monopoly.

◆ Microsoft is a natural monopoly. It has large fixed costs and almost zero marginal cost, so its long-run average cost curve (*LRAC*) slopes downward and economies of scale are achieved when the *LRAC* curve intersects the demand curve.

◆ Microsoft sells Windows for a number of different prices to different market segments, and the marginal cost of a Windows licence is the same for all market segments, so Microsoft is a price-discriminating monopoly.

◆ Figure 1 illustrates the demand curve, *D*, and marginal cost curve, *MC*, for Windows licences.

◆ Using only the Eurozone prices in the data table, the figure sketches how Microsoft converts consumer surplus into producer surplus by price discriminating.

◆ Because Microsoft also price discriminates among its different national markets, it gains even more producer surplus than the figure illustrates.

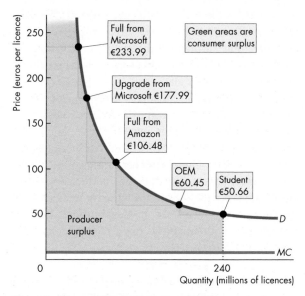

Figure 1 Microsoft Grabs Consumer Surplus

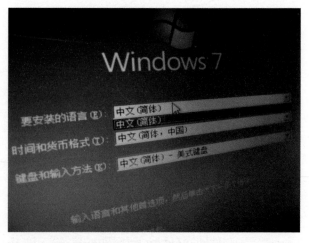

Windows 8 will have many more foreign language versions than Windows 7 and greater scope for price discrimination.

Monopoly Regulation

Natural monopoly presents a dilemma. With economies of scale, it produces at the lowest possible cost. But with market power, it has an incentive to raise the price above the competitive price and produce too little – to operate in the self-interest of the monopoly and not in the social interest.

Regulation – rules administered by a government agency to influence prices, quantities, entry and other aspects of economic activity in a firm or industry – is a possible solution to this dilemma.

To implement regulation, the government establishes agencies to oversee and enforce the rules. For example, in the UK, Ofgem regulates prices for electricity and gas supply, and Ofwat regulates water prices. By the 1970s, almost a quarter of the nation's output was produced by regulated industries (far more than just natural monopolies) and a process of deregulation began.

Deregulation is the process of removing regulation of prices, quantities, entry and other aspects of economic activity in a firm or industry. During the past 30 years, deregulation has occurred in UK domestic airlines, telephone service, electricity, water and gas supply, national rail services, and banking and financial services among other things. While deregulation is progressing in other EU countries, it is not as widespread as in the UK.

Regulation is a possible solution to the dilemma presented by natural monopoly but not a guaranteed solution. There are two theories about how regulation actually works:

1 Social interest theory
2 Capture theory

The **social interest theory** is that the political and regulatory process relentlessly seeks out inefficiency and introduces regulation that eliminates deadweight loss and allocates resources efficiently.

The **capture theory** is that regulation serves the self-interest of the producer, who captures the regulator and maximises economic profit. Regulation that benefits the producer but creates a deadweight loss gets adopted because the producer's gain is large and visible while each individual consumer's loss is small and invisible. No individual consumer has an incentive to oppose the regulation but the producer has a big incentive to lobby for it.

We're going to examine efficient regulation that serves the social interest and see why it is not a simple matter to design and implement such regulation.

Efficient Regulation of a Natural Monopoly

A gas distribution company is a natural monopoly – it can supply the entire market at a lower price than two or more competing firms can. Centrica is the current name for a private gas supplier that was a UK government monopoly called British Gas. The firm has invested heavily in household meters, pipes, regional storage facilities and other equipment. These fixed costs are part of the firm's average total cost. Its average total cost decreases as the number of customers supplied increases because the fixed cost is spread over a larger number of households.

Unregulated, and acting as a monopoly after privatisation, Centrica produces the quantity that maximises profit. Like all single-price monopolies, the profit-maximising quantity is less than the efficient quantity, and underproduction results in a deadweight loss.

How can Centrica be regulated to produce the efficient quantity of gas? The answer is by being regulated to set its price equal to marginal cost, known as the **marginal cost pricing rule**. The quantity demanded at a price equal to marginal cost is the efficient quantity – the quantity at which marginal social benefit equals marginal social cost.

Figure 12.11 illustrates the marginal cost pricing rule. The demand curve for gas is *D*. Centrica's marginal cost curve is *MC*, which is assumed to be constant at 10 pence per cubic metre. That is, the cost of supplying each additional household with gas is 10 pence per cubic metre. The efficient outcome occurs if the price is regulated at 10 pence per cubic metre with 4 million cubic metres a day produced.

But there is a problem: at the efficient output, because price equals marginal cost, the price is below average total cost. Average total cost minus the price is the loss per unit produced. It's pretty obvious that if Centrica is required to use a marginal cost pricing rule it will not stay in business for long. How can a company cover its costs and, at the same time, obey a marginal cost pricing rule?

There are two possible ways of enabling the firm to cover its costs: price discrimination and a two-part price (called a *two-part tariff*). For example, a mobile phone company offers plans at a fixed monthly price that give access to the phone network and unlimited free calls. The price of a call (zero) equals the marginal cost of a call. Similarly, a gas supplier can charge a one-time connection fee that covers its fixed cost and then charge a monthly fee equal to marginal cost.

Figure 12.11 Regulating a Natural Monopoly

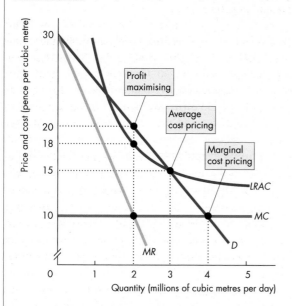

A natural monopoly gas producer faces the market demand curve *D*. The firm's marginal cost is constant at 10 pence per cubic metre, as shown by the curve labelled *MC*. The long-run average cost curve is *LRAC*.

Unregulated, as a profit maximiser, the firm produces 2 million cubic metres a day and charges a price of 20 pence per cubic metre. An efficient marginal cost pricing rule sets the price at 10 pence per cubic metre. The monopoly produces 4 million cubic metres per day and incurs an economic loss. A second-best average cost pricing rule sets the price at 15 pence per cubic metre. The monopoly produces 3 million cubic metres per day and makes zero economic profit.

MyEconLab Animation ────────────── ◆

Second-Best Regulation of a Natural Monopoly

A natural monopoly cannot always be regulated to achieve an efficient outcome. Two possible ways of enabling a regulated monopoly to avoid an economic loss are:

◆ Average cost pricing
◆ Government subsidy

Average Cost Pricing

An **average cost pricing rule** sets the price equal to average total cost. With this rule the firm produces the quantity at which the long-run average cost curve cuts the demand curve. This rule results in the firm making

zero economic profit – breaking even. But because for a natural monopoly average cost exceeds marginal cost, the quantity produced is less than the efficient quantity and a deadweight loss arises.

Figure 12.11 illustrates the average cost pricing rule. The price is 15 pence a cubic metre and 3 million cubic metres a day are produced.

Government Subsidy

A government subsidy is a direct payment to the firm equal to its economic loss. To pay a subsidy, the government must raise the revenue by taxing some other activity. You saw in Chapter 6 that taxes themselves generate deadweight loss.

And the Second Best Is . . .

Which is the better option, average cost pricing or marginal cost pricing with a government subsidy? The answer depends on the relative magnitudes of the two deadweight losses. Average cost pricing generates a deadweight loss in the market served by the natural monopoly. A subsidy generates deadweight losses in the markets for the items that are taxed to pay for the subsidy. The smaller deadweight loss is the second-best solution to regulating a natural monopoly. Making this calculation in practice is too difficult and average cost pricing is generally preferred to a subsidy.

Implementing average cost pricing presents the regulator with a challenge because it is not possible to be sure what a firm's costs are. So regulators use one of two practical rules:

◆ Rate of return regulation
◆ Price cap regulation

Rate of Return Regulation

Under **rate of return regulation**, a firm must justify its price by showing that its return on capital doesn't exceed a specified target rate. This type of regulation can end up serving the self-interest of the firm rather than the social interest. The firm's managers have an incentive to inflate costs by spending on items such as private jets, free football tickets (disguised as public relations expenses), and lavish entertainment. Managers also have an incentive to use more capital than the efficient amount. The rate of return on capital is regulated but not the total return on capital, and the greater the amount of capital, the greater is the total return.

Price Cap Regulation

For the reason that we've just examined, rate of return regulation is increasingly being replaced by price cap regulation. **Price cap regulation** is a price ceiling – a rule that specifies the highest price the firm is permitted to set. This type of regulation gives a firm an incentive to operate efficiently and keep costs under control. Price cap regulation has become common for the electricity and telecommunications industries and is replacing rate of return regulation.

To see how a price cap works, let's suppose that the gas distribution company is subject to this type of regulation. Figure 12.12 shows that without regulation, the firm maximises profit by producing 2 million cubic metres a day and charging a price of 20 pence a cubic metre. If a price cap is set at 15 pence a cubic metre, the

firm is permitted to sell any quantity it chooses at that price or at a lower price.

At 2 million cubic metres a day, the firm now incurs an economic loss. It can decrease the loss by increasing output to 3 million cubic metres a day. To increase output above 3 million cubic metres a day, the firm would have to lower the price and again it would incur an economic loss. So the profit-maximising quantity is 3 million cubic metres a day – the same as with average cost pricing.

Notice that a price cap lowers the price and increases output. This outcome is in sharp contrast to the effect of a price ceiling in a competitive market that you studied in Chapter 6 (pp. 126–128). The reason is that in a monopoly, the unregulated equilibrium output is less than the competitive equilibrium output, and the price cap regulation replicates the conditions of a competitive market.

In Figure 12.12, the price cap delivers average cost pricing. In practice, the regulator might set the cap too high. For this reason, price cap regulation is often combined with *earnings sharing regulation* – a regulation that requires firms to make refunds to customers when profits rise above a target level.

Figure 12.12 Price Cap Regulation

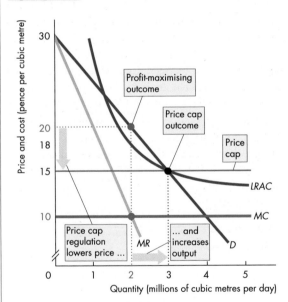

A natural monopoly gas producer faces the market demand curve D. The firm's marginal cost is constant at 10 pence per cubic metre – shown by the curve labelled MC. The long-run average total cost curve is LRAC. Unregulated, the firm produces 2 million cubic metres a day and charges a price of 20 pence per cubic metre.

A price cap is set at 15 pence a cubic metre. The maximum price that the firm can charge is 15 pence a cubic metre, so the firm has an incentive to minimise cost and produce the quantity demanded at the price cap. The price cap regulation lowers the price to 15 pence a cubic metre and the firm increases the quantity to 3 million cubic metres a day.

MyEconLab Animation

REVIEW QUIZ

1 What is the pricing rule that achieves an efficient outcome for a regulated monopoly? What is the problem with this rule?
2 What is the average cost pricing rule? Why is it not an efficient way of regulating a natural monopoly?
3 What is a price cap? Why might it be a more effective way of regulating monopoly than rate of return regulation?
4 Compare the consumer surplus, producer surplus and deadweight loss that arise from average cost pricing with those that arise from profit-maximisation pricing and marginal cost pricing.

Do these questions in Study Plan 12.5 and get instant feedback. MyEconLab

You've now completed your study of monopoly. *Reading Between the Lines* on pp. 294–295 looks at Google's dominant position in the market for Internet search advertising.

In the next chapter, we study markets that lie between the extremes of perfect competition and monopoly and which blend elements of the two.

READING BETWEEN THE LINES

Is Google Misusing Monopoly Power?

The Telegraph, 4 January 2013

EU: Google Antitrust Case Not Affected by US FTC Ruling

Matt Warman

In a boost for rivals such as Microsoft, the European Commissions has said . . . 'We have taken note of the FTC (Federal Trade Commission) decision, but we don't see that it has any direct implications for our investigation, for our discussions with Google, which are ongoing,' Michael Jennings, a spokesman for the European Commission, told Reuters.

Google was accused of manipulating its search results to disadvantage competitors. . . . The FTC decided yesterday that there was no evidence of the manipulation of search results other than to give the best performance. . . .

European investigators, however, face greater legal pressure than their US counterparts because they could be sued by complainants such as Microsoft. . . .

The European Commission has for the past two years been investigating complaints against Google, including the claims rejected by the FTC that it unfairly favoured its own services in its search results.

Google presented informal settlement proposals to the Commission in July. On December 18 the Commission gave the company a month to come up with detailed proposals to resolve the investigation. If it fails to address the complaints and is found guilty, Google could eventually be fined up to 10 per cent of its revenue – a fine of up to $4 billion.

 ## The Essence of the Story

- The European Commission and US Federal Trade Commission (FTC) are investigating claims that Google manipulated search results to favour its own services.

- The FTC has declared it found no evidence of Google's manipulation of search results other than for quality reasons.

- The European Commission is facing pressure from Google's competitors and says it will continue to investigate Google despite the FTC decision.

- Google has to offer the EU detailed proposals for changing its strategy, or it could face fines up to $4 billion.

Economic Analysis

- Google gained its dominant position in the search market by selling advertisements associated with search keywords within its innovative search engine.

- Google sells keywords based on a combination of willingness-to-pay and the number of clicks an advertisement receives.

- Google has steadily improved its search engine and its interface with both searchers and advertisers to make searches more powerful and advertising more effective.

- Figure 1 shows Google's extraordinary success in terms of its revenue, cost and profit.

- Google could have provided a basic search engine without innovation.

- If Google had followed this strategy, people would use competitor search engines and advertisers would have been willing to pay low prices for Google ads.

- Google would have faced the market described in Figure 2 and made a small economic profit.

- Instead, Google improved its search engine and the effectiveness of advertising. The demand for Google search and ads increased.

- By selling keywords to the highest bidder it achieves perfect price discrimination.

- Figure 3 shows shows how, with perfect price discrimination, Google's producer surplus is maximised. The FTC believes Google produces the efficient quantity of search and advertising by accepting ads as long as price exceeds marginal cost.

- Google has a dominant position and if the EU decide it is creating a barrier to entry and acting against the EU social interest it will impose heavy fines.

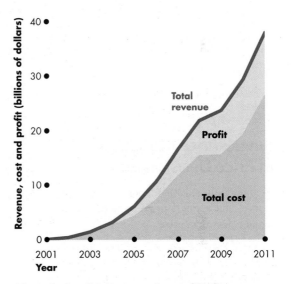

Figure 1 Google's Revenue, Cost and Profit

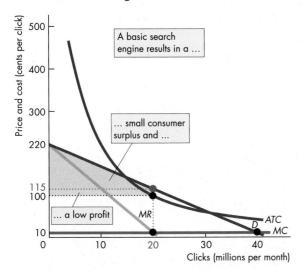

Figure 2 Basic Search Engine

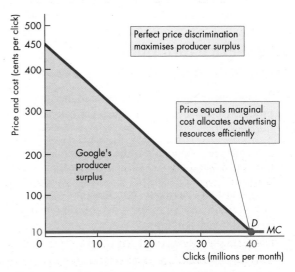

Figure 3 Google with Keywords and Other Features

SUMMARY

Key Points

Monopoly and How It Arises
(pp. 276–277)

◆ A monopoly is a market with a single supplier of a good or service with no close substitutes and in which barriers to entry prevent competition.

◆ Barriers to entry may be legal (monopoly franchise, licence, patent or copyright), ownership (one firm controls a resource) or natural (created by economies of scale).

◆ A monopoly might be able to price discriminate when there is no resale possibility.

◆ Where resale is possible, a firm charges one price.

Do Problems 1 to 4 to get a better understanding of monopoly and how it arises.

A Single-Price Monopoly's Output and Price Decision (pp. 278–281)

◆ A monopoly's demand curve is the market demand curve, and a single-price monopoly's marginal revenue is less than price.

◆ A monopoly maximises profit by producing the output at which marginal revenue equals marginal cost and by charging the maximum price that consumers are willing to pay for that output.

Do Problems 5 to 9 to get a better understanding of a single-price monopoly's output and price.

Single-Price Monopoly and Competition Compared (pp. 282–285)

◆ A single-price monopoly charges a higher price and produces a smaller quantity than a perfectly competitive market.

◆ A single-price monopoly restricts output and creates a deadweight loss.

◆ The total loss that arises from monopoly equals the deadweight loss plus the cost of the resources devoted to rent seeking.

Do Problems 10 to 12 to get a better understanding of the comparison of single-price monopoly and perfect competition.

Price Discrimination (pp. 285–290)

◆ Price discrimination is an attempt by the monopoly to convert consumer surplus into economic profit.

◆ Perfect price discrimination extracts the entire consumer surplus; each unit is sold for the maximum price that each customer is willing to pay; the quantity produced is efficient.

◆ Rent seeking with perfect price discrimination might eliminate the entire consumer surplus and producer surplus.

Do Problems 13 to 16 to get a better understanding of price discrimination.

Monopoly Regulation (pp. 291–293)

◆ Monopoly regulation might serve the social interest or the interest of the monopoly (monopoly captures the regulator).

◆ Price equal to marginal cost achieves efficiency but results in economic loss.

◆ Price equal to average cost enables the firm to cover its costs but is inefficient.

◆ Rate of return regulation creates incentives for inefficient production and inflated cost.

◆ Price cap regulation with earnings sharing regulation can achieve a more efficient outcome than rate of return regulation.

Do Problems 17 to 19 to get a better understanding of monopoly regulation.

Key Terms

Average cost pricing rule, 292
Barrier to entry, 276
Capture theory, 291
Deregulation, 291
Economic rent, 284
Legal monopoly, 276
Marginal cost pricing rule, 291
Monopoly, 276
Natural monopoly, 276
Perfect price discrimination, 288
Price cap regulation, 293
Price discrimination, 277
Rate of return regulation, 292
Regulation, 291
Rent seeking, 284
Single-price monopoly, 277
Social interest theory, 291

STUDY PLAN PROBLEMS AND APPLICATIONS

Do Problems 1 to 19 in MyEconLab Chapter 12 Study Plan and get instant feedback.

MyEconLab

Monopoly and How It Arises
(Study Plan 12.1)

Use the following information in Problems 1 to 3.

The Royal Mail has a monopoly on first class mail and the exclusive right to put mail in private mailboxes. Pfizer Inc. makes LIPITOR, a prescription drug that lowers cholesterol. Yorkshire Water is the sole supplier of drinking water in parts of northern England.

1 a What are the substitutes, if any, for the goods and services described above?

   b What are the barriers to entry, if any, that protect these three firms from competition?

2 Which of these three firms, if any, is a natural monopoly? Explain your answer and illustrate it by drawing an appropriate figure.

3 a Which of these three firms, if any, is a legal monopoly? Explain your answer.

   b Which of these three firms is most likely to be able to profit from price discrimination and which is most likely to sell its good or service for a single price?

4 Barbie's Revenge: Brawl over Doll Is Heading to Trial

Four years ago, Mattel Inc. exhorted its executives to help save Barbie from a new doll clique called the Bratz. With its market share dropping at a 'chilling rate,' Barbie needed to be more 'aggressive, revolutionary, and ruthless.' Mattel has gone to court and is trying to seize ownership of the Bratz line, which Mattel accuses of stealing the idea for the pouty-lipped dolls with the big heads.

Source: *The Wall Street Journal*, 23 May 2008

a Before Bratz entered the market, what type of monopoly did Mattel Inc. possess in the market for 'the pouty-lipped dolls with the big heads'?

b What is the barrier to entry that Mattel might argue should protect it from competition in the market for Barbie dolls?

c Explain how the entry of Bratz dolls might be expected to change the demand for Barbie dolls.

A Single-Price Monopoly's Output and Price Decision (Study Plan 12.2)

Use the following table in Problems 5 to 8.

Minnie's Mineral Springs, a single-price monopoly, faces the market demand schedule:

Price (euros per bottle)	Quantity demanded (bottles)
10	0
8	1
6	2
4	3
2	4
0	5

5 a Calculate the total revenue schedule for Minnie's Mineral Springs.

   b Calculate the marginal revenue schedule.

6 a Draw a graph of the market demand curve and Minnie's marginal revenue curve.

   b Why is Minnie's marginal revenue less than the price?

7 a At what price is Minnie's total revenue maximised?

   b Over what range of prices is the demand for water from Minnie's Mineral Springs elastic?

8 Why will Minnie not produce a quantity at which the market demand for water is inelastic?

9 Minnie's Mineral Springs faces the demand schedule in Problem 5 and has the following total cost schedule:

Quantity produced (bottles)	Total cost (euros)
0	1
1	3
2	7
3	13
4	21
5	31

a Calculate Minnie's profit-maximising output and price.

b Calculate economic profit.

Single-Price Monopoly and Competition Compared (Study Plan 12.3)

Use the following news clip in Problems 10 to 12.

Zoloft Faces Patent Expiration

Pfizer's antidepressant Zoloft, with $3.3 billion in 2005 sales, loses patent protection on June 30. When a brand name drug loses its patent, both the price of the drug and the dollar value of its sales each tend to drop 80 per cent over the next year, as competition opens to a host of generic drugmakers. The real winners are the patients and the insurers, who pay much lower prices. The Food and Drug Administration insists that generics work identically to brand-names.

Source: CNN, 15 June 2006

10 a Assume that Pfizer has a monopoly in the antidepressant market and that Pfizer cannot price discriminate. Use a graph to illustrate the market price and quantity of Zoloft sold.

    b On your graph, identify consumer surplus, producer surplus and deadweight loss.

11 How might you justify protecting Pfizer from competition with a legal barrier to entry?

12 a Explain how the market for an antidepressant drug changes when a patent expires.

    b Draw a graph to illustrate how the expiration of the Zoloft patent will change the price and quantity in the market for antidepressants.

    c Explain how consumer surplus, producer surplus and deadweight loss change with the expiration of the Zoloft patent.

Price Discrimination (Study Plan 12.4)

Use the following news clip in Problems 13 and 14.

The Saturday-Night Stay Requirement Is on Its Final Approach

The Saturday-night stay – the requirement that airlines instituted to ensure that a business traveller pays an outrageous airfare if he or she wants to go home for the weekend – has gone the way of the dodo bird. Experts agree that low-fare carriers are the primary reason major airlines are adopting more consumer-friendly fare structures, which include the elimination of the Saturday-night stay, the introduction of one-way and standby fares, and the general restructuring of fares.

Source: *Los Angeles Times*, 15 August 2004

13 Explain why the opportunity for price discrimination exists for air travel. How does an airline profit from price discrimination?

14 Describe the change in price discrimination in the market for air travel when discount airlines entered the market and explain the effect of discount airlines on the price and the quantity of air travel.

Use the following information in Problems 15 and 16.

La Bella Pizza can produce a pizza for a marginal cost of €2. Its standard price is €15 per pizza. It offers a second pizza for €5. It also distributes coupons that give a €5 rebate on a standard price pizza.

15 How can La Bella Pizza make a larger economic profit with this range of prices than it could if it sold every pizza for €14.99? Draw a figure that illustrates your answer.

16 How might La Bella Pizza make even more economic profit? Would La Bella Pizza then be more efficient than if it charged €15 for each pizza?

Monopoly Regulation (Study Plan 12.5)

Use the following information in Problems 17 to 19.

The figure shows a situation similar to that facing Milford Haven pipelines owned by National Grid, a firm that operates a natural gas distribution system in the UK. The gas distributor is a natural monopoly that cannot price discriminate.

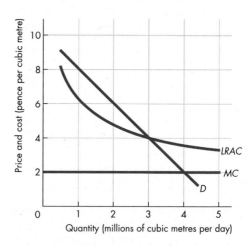

What quantity will the gas distributor produce, what price will it charge, what is total surplus and what is the deadweight loss if it is:

17 An unregulated profit-maximising firm?

18 Regulated to make zero economic profit?

19 Regulated to be efficient?

ADDITIONAL PROBLEMS AND APPLICATIONS

Do these problems in MyEconLab if assigned by your lecturer.

MyEconLab

Monopoly and How It Arises

Use the following list, which gives some information about seven firms, in Problems 20 and 21.

◆ Coca-Cola cuts its price below that of Pepsi-Cola in an attempt to increase its market share.

◆ A single firm, protected by a barrier to entry, produces a personal service that has no close substitutes.

◆ A barrier to entry exists, but the good has some close substitutes.

◆ A firm offers discounts to students and seniors.

◆ A firm can sell any quantity it chooses at the going price.

◆ The government issues Nike an exclusive licence to produce footballs.

◆ A firm experiences economies of scale even when it produces the quantity that meets the entire market demand.

20 In which of the seven cases might monopoly arise?

21 Which of the seven cases are natural monopolies and which are legal monopolies? Which can price discriminate, which cannot, and why?

A Single-Price Monopoly's Output and Price Decision

Use the following information in Problems 22 to 26.

Hot Air Balloon Rides is a single-price monopoly. Columns 1 and 2 of the table set out the market demand schedule and columns 2 and 3 set out the total cost schedule:

Price (pounds per ride)	Quantity demanded (rides per month)	Total cost (pounds per month)
220	0	80
200	1	160
180	2	260
160	3	380
140	4	520
120	5	680

22 Construct Hot Air's total revenue and marginal revenue schedules.

23 Draw a graph of the market demand curve and Hot Air's marginal revenue curve.

24 Find Hot Air's profit-maximising output and price and calculate the firm's economic profit.

25 If the government imposes a tax on Hot Air's profit, how do its output and price change?

26 If instead of taxing Hot Air's profit the government imposes a sales tax on balloon rides of £30 a ride, what are the new profit-maximising quantity, price and economic profit?

27 The figure illustrates the situation facing the publisher of the only newspaper containing local news in an isolated community.

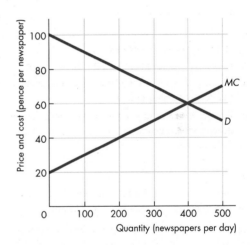

a On the graph, mark the profit-maximising quantity and price.

b What is the publisher's daily total revenue?

Single-Price Monopoly and Competition Compared

28 Show on the graph in Problem 27 the consumer surplus and the deadweight loss created by the monopoly. Explain why this market might encourage rent seeking.

29 If the newspaper market in Problem 27 were perfectly competitive, what would be the quantity, price, consumer surplus and producer surplus? Mark each on the graph.

30 Telecoms Look to Grow by Acquisition

Multibillion-dollar telecommunications mergers show how global cellular powerhouses are scouting for growth in emerging economies while consolidating in their own, crowded backyards. France Télécom offered to buy TeliaSonera, a Swedish–Finnish telecommunications operator, but within hours, TeliaSonera rejected the offer as too low. Analysts said higher bids – either from France Télécom or others – could persuade TeliaSonera to accept a deal. In the United States, Verizon Wireless agreed to buy Alltel for $28.1 billion – a deal that would make the company the biggest mobile phone operator in the United States. A combination of France Télécom and TeliaSonera would create the world's fourth-largest mobile operator, smaller only than China Mobile, Vodafone and Telefónica of Spain.

Source: *International Herald Tribune*, 5 June 2008

a Explain the rent-seeking behaviour of global telecommunications companies.

b Explain how mergers may affect the efficiency of the telecommunications market.

Price Discrimination

31 AT&T Moves Away from Unlimited-Data Pricing

AT&T said it will eliminate its $30 unlimited data plan as the crush of data use from the iPhone has hurt call quality. AT&T is introducing new plans costing $15 a month for 200 megabytes of data traffic or $25 a month for 2 gigabytes. AT&T says those who exceed 2 gigabytes of usage will pay $10 a month for each additional gigabyte. AT&T hopes that these plans will attract more customers.

Source: *The Wall Street Journal*, 2 June 2010

a Explain why AT&T's new plans might be price discrimination.

b Draw a graph to illustrate the original plan and the new plans.

Monopoly Regulation

32 Sky High Prices

Ofcom may force Sky to put a cap on its wholesale prices to rivals like BT Vision. Ofcom said that a cap on the prices Sky charged rivals to show sports and film channels was the 'most appropriate way to ensure fair and effective competition'. BT is ready to undercut Sky's prices for sports channels if prices are capped.

Source: BBC News, 30 March 2010

a What is the effect of Sky's monopoly of UK satellite television provision on the prices charged to access the satellite network?

b Explain why Ofcom thinks a price cap is the 'most appropriate way to ensure fair and effective competition'.

Use the following news clip in Problems 33 and 34.

Google vs eBay

Google is the most popular search engine and 75 per cent of referrals to websites originate from its searches. Some bankers estimate Google's value at $15 billion or more. It is almost impossible for Google to stay permanently ahead of other search-engine technologies because it takes only a bright idea by another set of programmers to lose its lead. Google does not have the natural-monopoly advantages that have made eBay dominant – network effect of buyers and sellers knowing they do best by all trading in one place.

Source: *The Economist*, 30 October 2002

33 **a** Why is eBay a monopoly but Google not a monopoly?

b Under what circumstances would eBay's monopoly be illegal? Explain why.

34 **a** How would you regulate the Internet auction business to ensure that resources are used efficiently?

b 'Anyone is free to buy shares in eBay, so everyone could benefit from eBay's economic profit, and the bigger that economic profit, the better for all.' Evaluate this statement.

Economics in the News

35 After you have studied *Reading Between the Lines* on pp. 294–295, answer the following questions.

a Why do the companies that complained about Google say that it needs to be investigated? Do you agree? Explain why or why not.

b Explain why it would be inefficient to regulate Google to make it charge the same price per keyword click to all advertisers.

c Explain why selling keywords to the highest bidder can lead to an efficient allocation of advertising resources.

13 Monopolistic Competition

After studying this chapter you will be able to:

◆ Define and identify monopolistic competition

◆ Explain how price and output are determined in a monopolistically competitive industry

◆ Explain why advertising and branding costs are high in monopolistic competition

The online fashion hub Asos.com lists women's designer shoes made by 60 producers in 11 categories. Designer shoe producers compete, but each has a monopoly on its own special style of shoe – the market is an example of monopolistic competition.

The model of monopolistic competition helps us to understand the competition that we see every day in the markets for fashion shoes and many other goods. And in *Reading Between the Lines* at the end of the chapter, we apply the monopolistic competition model to the market for smartphones as new entrants take market share from the Apple iPhone.

What Is Monopolistic Competition?

You have studied perfect competition, in which a large number of firms produce at the lowest possible cost, make zero economic profit and are efficient. You've also studied monopoly, in which a single firm restricts output, produces at a higher cost and price than in perfect competition and is inefficient.

Most real-world markets are competitive, but not perfectly competitive because firms in these markets have some power to set their prices as monopolies do. We call this type of market *monopolistic competition*.

Monopolistic competition is a market structure in which:

◆ A large number of firms compete.

◆ Each firm produces a differentiated product.

◆ Firms compete on product quality, price and marketing.

◆ Firms are free to enter and exit.

Large Number of Firms

In monopolistic competition, as in perfect competition, the industry consists of a large number of firms. The presence of a large number of firms has three implications for the firms in the industry.

Small Market Share

In monopolistic competition, each firm supplies a small part of the total industry output. Consequently, each firm has only limited market power to influence the price of its product. Each firm's price can deviate from the average market price by a relatively small amount.

Ignore Other Firms

A firm in monopolistic competition must be sensitive to the average market price of the product, but each firm does not pay attention to any one individual competitor. Because all the firms are relatively small and each firm has only a small share of the total market, no one firm can dictate market conditions. So no one firm's actions directly affect the actions of the other firms.

Collusion Impossible

Firms in monopolistic competition would like to be able to conspire to fix a higher price – called collusion. But because there are many firms, collusion is not possible.

Product Differentiation

A firm practises **product differentiation** if it makes a product that is slightly different from the products of competing firms. A differentiated product is one that is a close substitute but not a perfect substitute for the products of the other firms. Some people are willing to pay more for one variety of the product, so when its price rises, the quantity demanded decreases but it does not (necessarily) fall to zero. For example, Adidas, Asics, Diadora, Etonic, Fila, New Balance, Nike, Puma and Reebok all make differentiated running shoes. Other things remaining the same, if the price of Adidas running shoes rises and the prices of the other shoes remain constant, Adidas sells fewer shoes and the other producers sell more. But Adidas shoes don't disappear unless the price rises by a large enough amount.

Competing on Quality, Price and Marketing

Product differentiation enables a firm to compete with other firms in three areas: product quality, price and marketing.

Quality

The quality of a product is the physical attributes that make it different from the products of other firms. Quality includes design, reliability, the service provided to the buyer and the buyer's ease of access to the product. Quality lies on a spectrum that runs from high to low. Some firms – such as Dell Computer Corp. – offer high-quality products. They are well designed and reliable, and the customer receives quick and efficient service. Other firms offer a lower-quality product that is less well designed, which might not work perfectly and which the buyer must travel some distance to obtain.

Price

Because of product differentiation, a firm in monopolistic competition faces a downward-sloping demand curve. So, like a monopoly, the firm can set both its price and its output. But there is a trade-off between the product's quality and price. A firm that makes a high-quality product can charge a higher price than a firm that makes a low-quality product.

ECONOMICS IN ACTION

Monopolistic Competition in Europe Today

These 10 industries operate in monopolistic competition. The red bar shows the percentage of industry output produced by the 5 largest firms and the blue bar shows the percentage of industry output produced by the next 5 largest European firms. So the entire length of the bar shows the percentage of industry output produced by the largest 10 firms.

The industries shown have many firms that produce differentiated products and compete on quality, price and marketing.

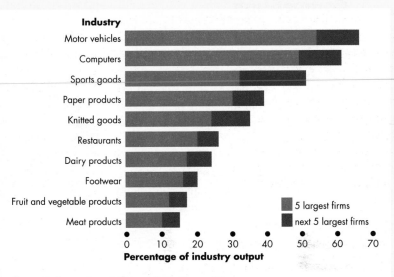

Figure 1 Examples of Monopolistic Competition

Source of data: Amadeus Financial Database, 2012.

Marketing

Because of product differentiation, a firm in monopolistic competition must market its product. Marketing takes two main forms: advertising and packaging. A firm that produces a high-quality product wants to sell it for a suitably high price. To be able to sell a high-quality product for a high price, a firm must advertise and package its product in a way that convinces buyers that they are getting the higher quality for which they are paying. For example, pharmaceutical companies advertise and package their brand-name drugs to persuade buyers that these items are superior to lower-priced generic alternatives. Similarly, a low-quality producer uses advertising and packaging to persuade buyers that although the quality is low, the low price more than compensates for this fact.

Entry and Exit

In monopolistic competition, there is free entry and free exit. Consequently, a firm cannot make an economic profit in the long run. When existing firms make economic profits, new firms enter the industry. This entry lowers prices and eventually eliminates economic profit. When firms incur economic losses, some firms leave the industry. This exit increases prices and eventually eliminates economic loss. In long-run equilibrium, firms neither enter nor leave the industry and the firms in the industry make zero economic profit.

Examples of Monopolistic Competition

Figure 1 in *Economics in Action* above shows 10 examples of industries in Europe in which firms operate in monopolistic competition. These industries have a large number of firms, they produce differentiated products, and they compete on quality, price and marketing. In the most concentrated of these industries, motor vehicles, the largest 5 firms produce 54 per cent of industry output and the largest 10 firms produce 66 per cent of industry output. In the least concentrated of these industries, meat products, the largest 5 firms produce only 10 per cent of industry output and the largest 10 firms produce 5 per cent of industry output.

REVIEW QUIZ

1 What are the distinguishing characteristics of monopolistic competition?
2 How do firms in monopolistic competition compete?
3 Provide some examples of industries near your university that operate in monopolistic competition (excluding those in the figure above).

Do these questions in Study Plan 13.1 and get instant feedback.   MyEconLab

Price and Output in Monopolistic Competition

Suppose you've been employed by French Connection to manage the production and marketing of jackets. Think about the decisions that you must make at French Connection. First, you must decide on the design and quality of jackets and on your marketing plan. Second, you must decide on the quantity of jackets to produce and the price at which to sell them.

We'll suppose that French Connection has already made its decisions about design, quality and marketing, and now we'll concentrate on the output and pricing decision. We'll study quality and marketing decisions in the next section.

For a given quality of jackets and marketing activity, French Connection faces given costs and market conditions. How, given its costs and the demand for its jackets, does French Connection decide the quantity of jackets to produce and the price at which to sell them?

The Firm's Short-Run Output and Price Decision

In the short run, a firm in monopolistic competition makes its output and price decision just like a monopoly firm does. Figure 13.1 illustrates this decision for French Connection jackets.

The demand curve for French Connection jackets is *D*. This demand curve tells us the quantity of French Connection jackets demanded at each price, given the prices of other jackets. It is not the demand curve for jackets in general.

The *MR* curve shows the marginal revenue curve associated with the demand curve for French Connection jackets. It is derived just like the marginal revenue curve of a single-price monopoly that you studied in Chapter 12.

The *ATC* curve and the *MC* curve show the average total cost and the marginal cost of producing French Connection jackets.

French Connection's goal is to maximise its economic profit. To do so, it will produce the output at which marginal revenue equals marginal cost. In Figure 13.1, this output is 125 jackets a day. French Connection charges the price that buyers are willing to pay for this quantity, which is determined by the demand curve. This price is £75 per jacket. When it produces 125 jackets a day, French Connection's average

Figure 13.1 Economic Profit in the Short Run

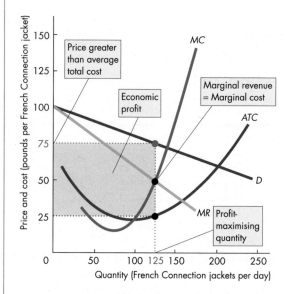

Profit is maximised where marginal revenue equals marginal cost. The profit-maximising quantity is 125 jackets a day. The price of £75 a jacket exceeds the average total cost of £25 a jacket, so the firm makes an economic profit of £50 a jacket. The blue rectangle illustrates economic profit, which equals £6,250 a day (£50 a jacket multiplied by 125 jackets a day).

MyEconLab Animation ───────────────────◆

total cost is £25 per jacket and it makes an economic profit of £6,250 a day (£50 per jacket multiplied by 125 jackets a day). The blue rectangle shows French Connection's economic profit.

Profit Maximising Might Be Loss Minimising

Figure 13.1 shows that French Connection is making a healthy economic profit. But such an outcome is not inevitable. A firm might face a level of demand for its product that is too low for it to make an economic profit.

Excite@Home was such a firm. Offering high-speed Internet service, Excite@Home hoped to capture a large share of the Internet portal market in competition with AOL, MSN, Yahoo! and a host of other providers.

Figure 13.2 illustrates the situation facing Excite@Home in 2001. The demand curve for its portal service is *D*, the marginal revenue curve is *MR*, the average total cost curve is *ATC* and the marginal

◆ Apple s
its powe

◆ By creat
uct, App
interest

◆ In the f
average

◆ But App
other s
operatir

◆ To rema
more p
the con
better tc

◆ The mor
what is h

◆ Figure 1
iPhone.

◆ Because
other sn
value, th
enue cur
opportu

◆ Apple m
ducing t
which in
quarter.

◆ This qua
equivale
shows A|

◆ Because
place. Sa
and Nok

◆ Figure 2
demand
ket is sha

◆ Apple's p
falls, and
eliminate

Figure 13.2 Economic Loss in the Short Run

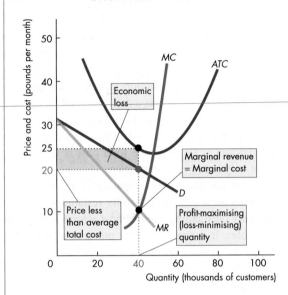

Profit is maximised where marginal revenue equals marginal cost. The loss-minimising quantity is 40,000 customers. The price of £20 a month is less than the average total cost of £25 a month, so the firm incurs an economic loss of £5 a customer. The red rectangle illustrates economic loss, which equals £200,000 a month (£5 a customer multiplied by 40,000 customers).

MyEconLab Animation ─────────────── ◆

cost curve is *MC*. Excite@Home maximised profit – equivalently, it minimised its loss – by producing the output at which marginal revenue equals marginal cost. In Figure 13.2, this output is 40,000 customers.

Excite@Home charged the price that buyers were willing to pay for this quantity, which was determined by the demand curve and which was £20 a month. With 40,000 customers, Excite@Home's average total cost was £25 per customer, so it incurred an economic loss of £200,000 a month (£5 a customer multiplied by 40,000 customers). The red rectangle shows Excite@Home's economic loss.

So far, the firm in monopolistic competition looks like a single-price monopoly. It produces the quantity at which marginal revenue equals marginal cost and then charges the price that buyers are willing to pay for that quantity, determined by the demand curve. The key difference between monopoly and monopolistic competition lies in what happens next when firms either make an economic profit or incur an economic loss.

Long Run: Zero Economic Profit

A firm like Excite@Home is not going to incur an economic loss for long. Eventually, it goes out of business. Also, there is no restriction on entry in monopolistic competition, so if firms in an industry are making an economic profit, other firms have an incentive to enter that industry.

As Burberry, Gap and other firms start to make jackets similar to those made by French Connection, the demand for French Connection jackets decreases. The demand curve for French Connection jackets and the marginal revenue curve shift leftward. And as these curves shift leftward, the profit-maximising quantity and price fall.

Figure 13.3 shows the long-run equilibrium. The demand curve for French Connection jackets and the marginal revenue curve have shifted leftward. The firm produces 75 jackets a day and sells them for £50 each. At this output level, average total cost is also £50 per jacket.

Figure 13.3 Output and Price in the Long Run

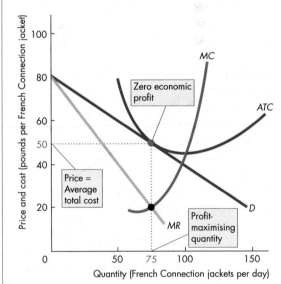

Economic profit encourages entry, which decreases the demand for each firm's product. When the demand curve touches the *ATC* curve at the quantity at which *MR* equals *MC*, the market is in long-run equilibrium. The output that maximises profit is 75 jackets a day and the price is £50 per jacket. Average total cost is also £50 per jacket, so economic profit is zero.

MyEconLab Animation ─────────────── ◆

a Explain how Starbucks' past attempts to maximise profits ended up eroding product differentiation.

b Explain how Starbucks' new plan intends to increase economic profit.

12   The Shoe That Won't Quit

Amy finally decided to take the plunge and buy a pair of Uggs, but when she got around to shopping for her Uggs, the style that she wanted was sold out. The scarcity factor was not a glitch in the supply chain, but rather a carefully calibrated strategy by Ugg's parent Deckers Outdoor that is one of the big reasons behind the brand's success. Deckers tightly controls distribution to ensure that supply does not outstrip demand. If Deckers ever opened up the supply of Uggs to meet demand, sales would shoot up like a rocket, but they'd come back down just as fast.

Source: *Fortune*, 5 June 2008

a Explain why Deckers intentionally restricts the quantity of Uggs that the firm sells.

b Draw a graph to illustrate how Deckers maximises the economic profit from Uggs.

Product Development and Marketing (Study Plan 13.3)

Use the following information in Problems 13 to 16.

Suppose that Tommy Hilfiger's marginal cost of a jacket is a constant £100 and the total fixed cost at one of its stores is £2,000 a day. This store sells 20 jackets a day, which is its profit-maximising number of jackets. Then, the stores nearby start to advertise their jackets. The Tommy Hilfiger store now spends £2,000 a day advertising its jackets and its profit-maximising number of jackets sold jumps to 50 a day.

13   a What is this store's average total cost of a jacket sold before the advertising begins?

b What is this store's average total cost of a jacket sold after the advertising begins?

14   a Can you say what happens to the price of a Tommy Hilfiger jacket? Why or why not?

b Can you say what happens to Tommy's markup? Why or why not?

c Can you say what happens to Tommy's economic profit? Why or why not?

15 How might Tommy Hilfiger use advertising as a signal? How is a signal sent and how does it work?

16 How does having a brand name help Tommy Hilfiger to increase its economic profit?

Use the following news clip in Problems 17 and 18.

Food's Next Billion-Dollar Brand?

While it's not the biggest brand in margarine, Smart Balance has an edge on its rivals in that it's made with a patented blend of vegetable and fruit oils that has been shown to help improve consumers' cholesterol levels. Smart Balance sales have sky-rocketed while overall sales for margarine have stagnated. It remains to be seen if Smart Balance's healthy message and high price will resound with consumers.

Source: *Fortune*, 4 June 2008

17 How do you expect advertising and the Smart Balance brand name will affect Smart Balance's ability to make a positive economic profit?

18 Are long-run economic profits a possibility for Smart Balance? In long-run equilibrium, will Smart Balance have excess capacity or a markup?

Economics in the News

(Study Plan 13.N)

19   Computer Makers Prepare to Stake Bigger Claim in Phones

Apple's success with its iPhone has encouraged other PC makers and chip companies to enter the mobile phone business, promising new palm-held devices with the power of a standard computer – devices that handle the Internet, power two-way video conferences and stream high-definition movies to your TV. It is a development that spells serious competition for established mobile phone makers and phone companies.

Source: *The New York Times*, 15 March 2009

a Draw a graph of the cost curves and revenue curves of a mobile phone company that makes a positive economic profit in the short run.

b If mobile phone companies start to include the popular features introduced by PC makers, explain how this decision will affect their profit in the short run.

c What do you expect to happen to a mobile phone company's economic profit in the long run, given the information in the news clip?

d Draw a graph to illustrate your answer to part (c).

Economic Analysis

◆ Apple sold its first iPhone in 2007 and brought its powerful 4S version to market in 2011.

◆ By creating a substantially differentiated product, Apple was able to generate a great deal of interest in smartphones throughout the world.

◆ In the first year and a quarter, Apple sold an average of 1 million iPhones per quarter.

◆ But Apple soon had competitors as a host of other smartphones using Google's Android operating system hit the market.

◆ To remain competitive, Apple introduced ever more powerful versions of the iPhone. And the competitors' smartphones kept getting better too.

◆ The monopolistic competition model explains what is happening in the smartphone market.

◆ Figure 1 shows the market for Apple's first iPhone. (The numbers are assumptions.)

◆ Because the Apple iPhone is different from other smartphones and has features that users value, the demand curve, *D*, and marginal revenue curve, *MR*, create a large short-run profit opportunity.

◆ Apple maximises its economic profit by producing the quantity at which *MR* equals *MC*, which in this example is 1 million iPhones per quarter.

◆ This quantity of iPhones can be sold for the equivalent of $400 each. The blue rectangle shows Apple's economic profit.

◆ Because this market is profitable, entry takes place. Samsung and others (such as HTC, LG and Nokia) enter the smartphone market.

◆ Figure 2 shows the consequence of entry. The demand for the iPhone decreases as the market is shared with other phones.

◆ Apple's profit-maximising price for the iPhone falls, and in the long run, economic profit is eliminated.

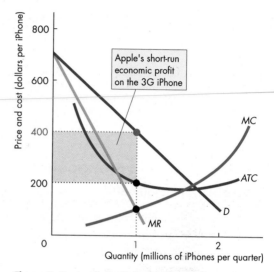

Figure 1 **Economic Profit in the Short Run**

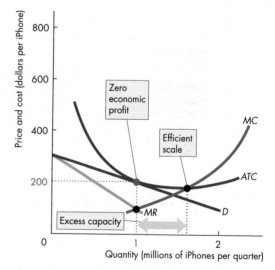

Figure 2 **Zero Economic Profit in the Long Run**

◆ With zero economic profit, Apple has an incentive to develop another new differentiated product and start the cycle of innovation described here again, making an economic profit with a new phone in the short run.

◆ The iPhone 4S launched in 2011 and the iPhone 5 launched in 2012 are examples of Apple's response to the competition from Samsung (and others) described in the news article.

SUMMARY

Key Points

What Is Monopolistic Competition?
(pp. 302–303)

◆ In monopolistic competition, a large number of firms compete on product quality, price and marketing.

Do Problems 1 and 2 to get a better understanding of what monopolistic competition is.

Price and Output in Monopolistic Competition (pp. 304–307)

◆ Each firm in monopolistic competition faces a downward-sloping demand curve and produces the profit-maximising quantity.

◆ Entry and exit result in zero economic profit and excess capacity in long-run equilibrium.

Do Problems 3 to 12 to get a better understanding of price and output in monopolistic competition.

Product Development and Marketing (pp. 308–311)

◆ Firms innovate and develop new products.

◆ Advertising expenditures increase total cost, but average total cost might fall if the quantity sold increases by enough.

◆ Advertising expenditures might increase or decrease the demand for a firm's product.

◆ Whether monopolistic competition is inefficient depends on the value we place on product variety.

Do Problems 13 to 18 to get a better understanding of product development and marketing.

Key Terms

Efficient scale, 306
Excess capacity, 306
Markup, 307
Monopolistic competition, 302
Product differentiation, 302
Signal, 310

STUDY PLAN PROBLEMS AND APPLICATIONS

Do Problems 1 to 19 in MyEconLab Chapter 13 Study Plan and get instant feedback.   MyEconLab

What Is Monopolistic Competition?
(Study Plan 13.1)

1 Which of the following items are sold by firms in monopolistic competition? Explain your selections.

 ◆ Satellite television service
 ◆ Wheat
 ◆ Athletic shoes
 ◆ Fizzy drinks
 ◆ Toothbrushes
 ◆ Ready-mix concrete

2 The five-firm concentration ratio for audio equipment makers is 30 and for electric lamp makers it is 89. Which of these markets is an example of monopolistic competition?

Price and Output in Monopolistic Competition (Study Plan 13.2)

Use the following information in Problems 3 and 4.

Sara is a dot.com entrepreneur who has established a website at which people can design and buy sweatshirts. Sara pays £1,000 a week for her Web server and Internet connection. The sweatshirts that her customers design are made to order by another firm, and Sara pays this firm £20 a sweatshirt. Sara has no other costs. The table sets out the demand schedule for Sara's sweatshirts.

Price (pounds per sweatshirt)	Quantity demanded (sweatshirts per week)
0	100
20	80
40	60
60	40
80	20
100	0

3 Calculate Sara's profit-maximising output, price and economic profit.

4 a Do you expect other firms to enter the Web sweatshirt business and compete with Sara?

  b What happens to the demand for Sara's sweatshirts in the long run? What happens to Sara's economic profit in the long run?

Use the following figure, which shows the situation facing a producer of running shoes, in Problems 5 to 10.

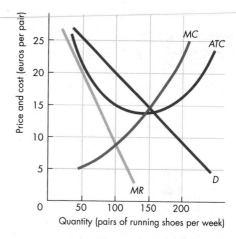

5 What quantity does the firm produce, what price does it charge and what is its economic profit or economic loss?

6 In the long run, how does the number of firms producing running shoes change?

7 In the long run, how does the price of running shoes and the quantity the firm produces change? What happens to the market output?

8 Does the firm have excess capacity in the long run? If the firm has excess capacity in the long run, why doesn't it decrease its capacity?

9 In the long run, compare the price of a pair of running shoes and the marginal cost of producing the pair.

10 Is the market for running shoes efficient or inefficient in the long run?

11 **Wake Up and Smell the Coffee**

Every change that Starbucks made over the past few years – automated espresso machines, pre-ground coffee, fewer soft chairs and less carpeting – was made for a reason: to smooth operations or boost sales. Those may have been the right choices at the time, but together they ultimately diluted the coffee-centric experience. By 2008, Starbucks experienced a drop in traffic as customers complained that in pursuing rapid growth, the company has strayed too far from its roots. Starbucks will once again grind beans in its stores for espresso coffee, give free espresso refills and provide two hours of wi-fi. The company will roll out its new sleek, low-rise espresso machine that makes the coffee server more visible.

Source: *Time*, 7 April 2008

a Explain how Starbucks' past attempts to maximise profits ended up eroding product differentiation.

b Explain how Starbucks' new plan intends to increase economic profit.

12 The Shoe That Won't Quit

Amy finally decided to take the plunge and buy a pair of Uggs, but when she got around to shopping for her Uggs, the style that she wanted was sold out. The scarcity factor was not a glitch in the supply chain, but rather a carefully calibrated strategy by Ugg's parent Deckers Outdoor that is one of the big reasons behind the brand's success. Deckers tightly controls distribution to ensure that supply does not outstrip demand. If Deckers ever opened up the supply of Uggs to meet demand, sales would shoot up like a rocket, but they'd come back down just as fast.

Source: *Fortune*, 5 June 2008

a Explain why Deckers intentionally restricts the quantity of Uggs that the firm sells.

b Draw a graph to illustrate how Deckers maximises the economic profit from Uggs.

Product Development and Marketing (Study Plan 13.3)

Use the following information in Problems 13 to 16.

Suppose that Tommy Hilfiger's marginal cost of a jacket is a constant £100 and the total fixed cost at one of its stores is £2,000 a day. This store sells 20 jackets a day, which is its profit-maximising number of jackets. Then, the stores nearby start to advertise their jackets. The Tommy Hilfiger store now spends £2,000 a day advertising its jackets and its profit-maximising number of jackets sold jumps to 50 a day.

13 a What is this store's average total cost of a jacket sold before the advertising begins?

b What is this store's average total cost of a jacket sold after the advertising begins?

14 a Can you say what happens to the price of a Tommy Hilfiger jacket? Why or why not?

b Can you say what happens to Tommy's markup? Why or why not?

c Can you say what happens to Tommy's economic profit? Why or why not?

15 How might Tommy Hilfiger use advertising as a signal? How is a signal sent and how does it work?

16 How does having a brand name help Tommy Hilfiger to increase its economic profit?

Use the following news clip in Problems 17 and 18.

Food's Next Billion-Dollar Brand?

While it's not the biggest brand in margarine, Smart Balance has an edge on its rivals in that it's made with a patented blend of vegetable and fruit oils that has been shown to help improve consumers' cholesterol levels. Smart Balance sales have skyrocketed while overall sales for margarine have stagnated. It remains to be seen if Smart Balance's healthy message and high price will resound with consumers.

Source: *Fortune*, 4 June 2008

17 How do you expect advertising and the Smart Balance brand name will affect Smart Balance's ability to make a positive economic profit?

18 Are long-run economic profits a possibility for Smart Balance? In long-run equilibrium, will Smart Balance have excess capacity or a markup?

Economics in the News

(Study Plan 13.N)

19 Computer Makers Prepare to Stake Bigger Claim in Phones

Apple's success with its iPhone has encouraged other PC makers and chip companies to enter the mobile phone business, promising new palm-held devices with the power of a standard computer – devices that handle the Internet, power two-way video conferences and stream high-definition movies to your TV. It is a development that spells serious competition for established mobile phone makers and phone companies.

Source: *The New York Times*, 15 March 2009

a Draw a graph of the cost curves and revenue curves of a mobile phone company that makes a positive economic profit in the short run.

b If mobile phone companies start to include the popular features introduced by PC makers, explain how this decision will affect their profit in the short run.

c What do you expect to happen to a mobile phone company's economic profit in the long run, given the information in the news clip?

d Draw a graph to illustrate your answer to part (c).

ADDITIONAL PROBLEMS AND APPLICATIONS

Do these problems in MyEconLab if assigned by your lecturer.

What Is Monopolistic Competition?

20 Which of the following items are sold by firms in monopolistic competition? Explain your selections.

♦ Orange juice

♦ Canned soup

♦ PCs

♦ Chewing gum

♦ Breakfast cereals

♦ Corn

21 The five-firm concentration ratio for man-made fibre makers is 79 and for knitted goods makers it is 45. Which of these markets is an example of monopolistic competition?

Price and Output in Monopolistic Competition

Use the following information in Problems 22 and 23.

Lorie teaches singing. Her fixed costs are £1,000 a month and it costs her £50 of labour to give one class. The table shows the demand schedule for Lorie's singing lessons.

Price (pounds per lesson)	Quantity demanded (lessons per week)
0	250
50	200
100	150
150	100
200	50
250	0

22 Calculate Lorie's profit-maximising output, price and economic profit.

23 a Do you expect other firms to enter the singing lesson business and compete with Lorie?

b What happens to the demand for Lorie's lessons in the long run? What happens to Lorie's economic profit in the long run?

Use the figure in the next column, which shows the situation facing Mike's Bikes, a producer of mountain bikes, in Problems 24 to 28. The demand and costs of other bike producers are similar to those of Mike's Bikes.

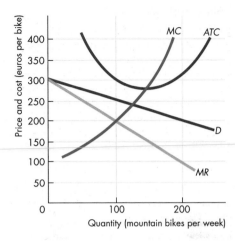

24 What quantity does the firm produce and what price does it charge? Calculate the firm's economic profit or economic loss.

25 What will happen to the number of firms producing mountain bikes in the long run?

26 How will the price of a mountain bike and the number of bikes produced by Mike's Bikes change in the long run?

27 Is there any way for Mike's Bikes to avoid having excess capacity in the long run?

28 Is the market for mountain bikes efficient or inefficient in the long run? Explain your answer.

Use the following news clip in Problems 29 and 30.

Groceries for the Gourmet Palate

No food, it seems, is safe from being repackaged to look like an upscale product. Samuel Adams' $120 Utopias, in a ridiculous copper-covered 24-oz. bottle meant to resemble an old-fashioned brew kettle, is barely beer. It's not carbonated like most beers, but aged in oak barrels like scotch. It has a vintage year, like a Bordeaux, is light, complex and free of any alcohol sting, despite having six times as much alcohol content as a regular can of brew.

Source: *Time*, 14 April 2008

29 a Explain how Samuel Adams has differentiated its Utopias to compete with other beer brands in terms of quality, price and marketing.

b Predict whether Samuel Adams produces at, above or below the efficient scale in the short run.

30 a Predict whether the $120 price tag on the Utopias is at, above or below marginal cost:

   (i) In the short run.

   (ii) In the long run.

b Do you think that Samuel Adams Utopias makes the market for beer inefficient?

Use the following news clip in Problems 31 and 32.

Swinging for Female Golfers

One of the hottest areas of innovation is in clubs for women, who now make up nearly a quarter of the 24 million golfers in the US. Callaway and Nike, two of the leading golf-equipment manufacturers, recently released new clubs designed specifically for women.

Source: *Time*, 21 April 2008

31 a How are Callaway and Nike attempting to maintain economic profit?

b Draw a graph to illustrate the cost curves and revenue curves of Callaway or Nike in the market for golf clubs for women.

c Show on your graph in part (b) the short-run economic profit.

32 a Explain why the economic profit that Callaway and Nike make on golf clubs for women is likely to be temporary.

b Draw a graph to illustrate the cost curves and revenue curves of Callaway or Nike in the market for golf clubs for women in the long run. Mark the firm's excess capacity.

Product Development and Marketing

Use the following information in Problems 33 to 35.

Bianca bakes delicious cookies. Her total fixed cost is £40 a day and her average variable cost is £1 a bag. Few people know about Bianca's Cookies and she is maximising her profit by selling 10 bags a day for £5 a bag. Bianca thinks that if she spends £50 a day on advertising, she can increase her market share and sell 25 bags a day for £5 a bag.

33 If Bianca's advertising works as she expects, can she increase her economic profit by advertising?

34 If Bianca advertises, will her average total cost increase or decrease at the quantity produced?

35 If Bianca advertises, will she continue to sell her cookies for £5 a bag or will she change her price?

Use the following news clip in Problems 36 and 37.

A Thirst for More Champagne

Champagne exports have tripled in the past 20 years. That poses a problem for northern France, where the bubbly hails from – not enough grapes. So French authorities have unveiled a plan to extend the official Champagne grape-growing zone to cover 40 new villages. This revision has provoked debate. The change will take several years to become effective. In the meantime the vineyard owners whose land values will jump markedly if the changes are finalised certainly have reason to raise a glass.

Source: *Fortune*, 12 May 2008

36 a Why is France so strict about designating the vineyards that can use the Champagne label?

b Explain who most likely opposes this plan.

37 Assuming that vineyards in these 40 villages are producing the same quality of grapes with or without this plan, why will their land values 'jump markedly' if this plan is approved?

38 Under Armour's Big Step Up

Under Armour, the red-hot brand of athletic apparel, has joined Nike, Adidas and New Balance as a major player in the market for athletic footwear. Under Armour plans to revive the long-dead cross-training category. But will young athletes really spend $100 for a cross-training shoe to lift weights in?

Source: *Time*, 26 May 2008

What factors influence Under Armour's ability to make an economic profit in the cross-training shoe market?

Economics in the News

39 After you have studied *Reading Between the Line*s on pp. 312–313, answer the following questions.

a Describe the cost curves (*MC* and *ATC*) and the marginal revenue and demand curves for the iPhone when Apple first introduced it.

b How do you think the creation of the iPhone influenced the demand for older generation mobile phones?

c Explain the effects of the introduction of the iPhone 5 on Samsung and other firms in the market for smartphones.

d Draw a graph to illustrate your answer to part (c).

e Explain the effect on Apple of the decisions by Samsung and others to bring their own smartphones to market.

f Draw a graph to illustrate your answer to part (e).

g Do you think the market for smartphones is efficient? Explain your answer.

h Do you predict that producers of smartphones have excess capacity? Explain your answer.

14 Oligopoly

After studying this chapter you will be able to:

- ◆ Define and identify oligopoly
- ◆ Use game theory to explain how price and output are determined in oligopoly
- ◆ Use game theory to explain other strategic decisions
- ◆ Describe the antitrust law that regulates oligopoly

The chip in your laptop was made by Intel or AMD; the battery in your TV remote was made by Duracell or Energizer; and the aeroplane that takes you on a long-distance trip was made by the European firm Airbus or the US firm Boeing.

How does a market work when only two or a handful of firms compete? To answer this question we use the model of oligopoly.

At the end of the chapter in *Reading Between the Lines*, we'll look at the oligopoly market for soap powder in France and see how four producers battled for profit.

What Is Oligopoly?

Oligopoly, like monopolistic competition, lies between perfect competition and monopoly. The firms in oligopoly might produce an identical product and compete only on price, or they might produce a differentiated product and compete on price, product quality and marketing. **Oligopoly** is a market structure in which:

◆ Natural or legal barriers prevent the entry of new firms.

◆ A small number of firms compete.

Barriers to Entry

Either natural or legal barriers to entry can create oligopoly. You saw in Chapter 12 how economies of scale and demand form a natural barrier to entry that can create a *natural monopoly*. These same factors can create a *natural oligopoly*.

Figure 14.1 illustrates two natural oligopolies. The demand curve, *D* (in both parts of the figure), shows the market demand for taxi rides in a town. If the average total cost curve of a taxi company is ATC_1 in part (a), the market is a natural **duopoly** – an oligopoly with two firms. You can probably see some examples of duopoly where you live. Some cities have only two suppliers of milk, two local newspapers, two taxi companies, two car rental firms, two copy centres or two bookshops.

The lowest price at which the firm would remain in business is £10 a ride. At that price, the quantity of rides demanded is 60 a day, the quantity that can be provided by just two firms. There is no room in this market for three firms. But if there were only one firm, it would make an economic profit, and a second firm would enter to take some of the business and economic profit.

If the average total cost curve of a taxi company is ATC_2 in part (b), the efficient scale of one firm is 20 rides a day. This market is large enough for three firms.

A legal oligopoly arises when a legal barrier to entry protects the small number of firms in a market. A city might license two taxi firms or two bus companies, for example, even though the combination of market demand and economies of scale leaves room for more than two firms.

Figure 14.1 Natural Oligoply

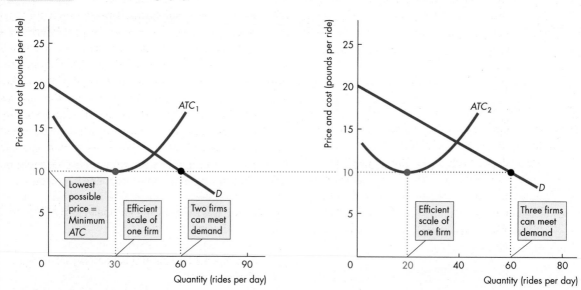

(a) Natural duopoly

The lowest possible price is £10 a ride, which is the minimum average total cost. When a firm produces 30 rides a day, the efficient scale, two firms can satisfy the market demand. This natural oligopoly has two firms – a natural duopoly.

(b) Natural oligopoly with three firms

When the efficient scale of one firm is 20 rides per day, three firms can satisfy the market demand at the lowest possible price. This natural oligopoly has three firms.

ECONOMICS IN ACTION

Oligopoly in Europe

These 10 markets are oligopolies. The red bar shows the percentage of industry output produced by the five largest firms and the blue bar shows the percentage of industry output produced by the next 10 largest firms. So the entire length of the bar shows the percentage of industry output produced by the largest 15 firms.

These European markets have a few interdependent firms and the most concentrated markets are those with a five-firm concentration ratio above 60 per cent.

Source of data: Amadeus Financial Database 2012.

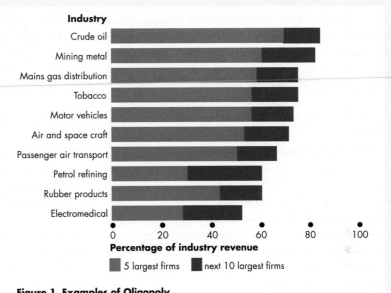

Figure 1 Examples of Oligopoly

Small Number of Firms

Because barriers to entry exist, oligopoly consists of a small number of firms, each of which has a large share of the market. Such firms are interdependent, but they face a temptation to cooperate to increase their joint economic profit.

Interdependence

With a small number of firms in a market, each firm's actions influence the profits of all the other firms. When Starbucks opened in Meadowhall Shopping Centre all the other coffee shops took a hit. Within days, Café Moda began to attract Starbucks' customers with enticing offers and lower prices. Eventually, Café Moda survived but others went out of business. The coffee shops in Meadowhall are interdependent.

Temptation to Cooperate

When a small number of firms share a market, they can increase their profits by forming a cartel and acting like a monopoly. A **cartel** is a group of firms acting together – colluding – to limit output, raise price and increase economic profit. Cartels are illegal, but they do operate in some markets. But for reasons you'll discover in this chapter, cartels tend to break down.

Examples of Oligopoly

The *Economics in Action* above shows some examples of oligopoly. The dividing line between oligopoly and monopolistic competition is hard to pin down. As a practical matter, we try to identify oligopoly by looking at the five-firm concentration ratio qualified with other information about the geographical scope of the market and barriers to entry. A concentration ratio that divides oligopoly from monopolistic competition is generally taken to be 60 per cent. A market in which the concentration ratio exceeds 60 per cent is usually an example of oligopoly and a market in which the concentration ratio is below 60 per cent is monopolistic competition.

 ### REVIEW QUIZ

1 What are the two distinguishing characteristics of oligopoly?
2 Why are firms in oligopoly interdependent?
3 Why do firms in oligopoly face the temptation to collude?
4 Give some examples of oligopolies that you buy from.

Do these questions in Study Plan 14.1 and get instant feedback.   MyEconLab

Oligopoly Games

Economists think about oligopoly as a game, and to study oligopoly markets they use a set of tools called game theory. **Game theory** is a set of tools for studying *strategic behaviour* – behaviour that takes into account the expected behaviour of others and the recognition of mutual interdependence. Game theory was invented by John von Neumann in 1937 and extended by von Neumann and Oskar Morgenstern in 1944. Today, it is one of the major research fields in economics.

Game theory seeks to understand oligopoly as well as all other forms of economic, political, social and even biological rivalries, by using a method of analysis specifically designed to understand games of all types, including the familiar games of everyday life. We will begin our study of game theory and its application to the behaviour of firms by thinking about familiar games.

What Is a Game?

What is a game? At first thought, the question seems silly. After all, there are many different games – ball games and parlour games, games of chance and games of skill. But what is it about all these different activities that make them games? What do they have in common? All games share four features:

◆ Rules
◆ Strategies
◆ Payoffs
◆ Outcome

We're going to look at these features of a game by playing the 'prisoners' dilemma' game. This game captures some of the essential features of many games, including oligopoly, and it gives a good illustration of how game theory works and generates predictions.

The Prisoners' Dilemma

Art and Bob have been caught red-handed, stealing a car. Facing airtight cases, they will receive a 2-year sentence each for their crime. During his interviews with the two prisoners, the police sergeant begins to suspect that he has stumbled on the two people who were responsible for a multimillion-pound bank robbery some months earlier. But this is just a suspicion. The police sergeant has no evidence on which he can convict them of the greater crime unless he can get them to

confess. But how can he extract a confession? He makes the prisoners play a game, which we now describe.

Rules

Each prisoner (player) is placed in a separate room and cannot communicate with the other prisoner. Each is told that he is suspected of having carried out the bank robbery and that:

> **If both of them confess to the larger crime, each will receive a sentence of 3 years for both crimes.**

> **If he alone confesses and his accomplice does not, he will receive an even shorter sentence of 1 year whereas his accomplice will receive a 10-year sentence.**

Strategies

In game theory, **strategies** are all the possible actions of each player. Art and Bob each have two possible actions:

1   Confess to the bank robbery
2   Deny having committed the bank robbery

Because there are two players, each with two strategies, there are four possible outcomes:

1   Both confess
2   Both deny
3   Art confesses and Bob denies
4   Bob confesses and Art denies

Payoffs

Each prisoner can work out his *payoff* in each of these four situations. We can tabulate the four possible payoffs for each of the prisoners in what is called a payoff matrix for the game. A **payoff matrix** is a table that shows the payoffs for every possible action by each player for every possible action by each other player.

Table 14.1 shows a payoff matrix for Art and Bob. The squares show the payoffs for each prisoner – the red triangle in each square shows Art's and the blue triangle shows Bob's. If both confess (top left), each gets a 3-year sentence. If Bob confesses but Art denies (top right), Art gets a 10-year sentence and Bob gets a 1-year sentence. If Art confesses and Bob denies (bottom left), Art gets a 1-year sentence and Bob gets a 10-year sentence. Finally, if both of them deny (bottom right), neither can be convicted of the bank robbery charge but both are sentenced for the car theft – a 2-year sentence.

Table 14.1

Prisoners' Dilemma Payoff Matrix

Art's strategies

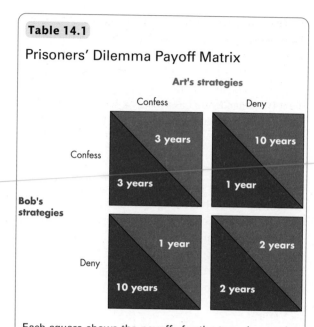

Each square shows the payoffs for the two players, Art and Bob, for each possible pair of actions. In each square, the red triangle shows Art's payoff and the blue triangle shows Bob's. For example, if both confess, the payoffs are in the top left square. The equilibrium of the game is for both players to confess and each gets a 3-year sentence.

Outcome

The choices of both players determine the outcome of the game. To predict that outcome, we use an equilibrium idea proposed by John Nash of Princeton University (who received the Nobel Prize in Economic Sciences in 1994 and was the subject of the 2001 film *A Beautiful Mind*). In a **Nash equilibrium**, player *A* takes the best possible action given the action of player *B* and player *B* takes the best possible action given the action of player *A*.

In the case of the prisoners' dilemma, the Nash equilibrium occurs when Art makes his best choice given Bob's choice and when Bob makes his best choice given Art's choice.

To find the Nash equilibrium, we compare all the possible outcomes associated with each choice and eliminate those that are dominated – that are not as good as some other choice. Let's find the Nash equilibrium for the prisoners' dilemma game.

Finding the Nash Equilibrium

Look at the situation from Art's point of view. If Bob confesses, Art's best action is to confess because in that case he is sentenced to 3 years rather than 10 years. If Bob does not confess, Art's best action is still to confess because in that case he receives 1 year rather than 2 years. So Art's best action is to confess.

Now look at the situation from Bob's point of view. If Art confesses, Bob's best action is to confess because in that case he is sentenced to 3 years rather than 10 years. If Art does not confess, Bob's best action is still to confess because in that case he receives 1 year rather than 2 years. So Bob's best action is to confess.

Because each player's best action is to confess, each does confess, each gets a 3-year prison term, and the police sergeant has solved the bank robbery. This is the Nash equilibrium of the game.

The Nash equilibrium for the prisoners' dilemma is called a **dominant-strategy equilibrium**, which is an equilibrium in which the best strategy for each player is to confess *regardless of the strategy of the other player*.

The Dilemma

The dilemma arises as each prisoner contemplates the consequences of denying. Each prisoner knows that if both of them deny, they will receive only a 2-year sentence for stealing the car. But neither has any way of knowing that his accomplice will deny. But each also knows that if he denies it is in the best interest of the other to confess. So each considers whether to deny and rely on his accomplice to deny or to confess hoping that his accomplice denies but expecting him to confess. The dilemma leads to the equilibrium of the game.

A Bad Outcome

For the prisoners, the equilibrium of the game, with each confessing, is not the best outcome. If neither of them confesses, each gets only 2 years for the lesser crime. Isn't there some way in which this better outcome can be achieved? It seems that there is not, because the players cannot communicate with each other. Each player can put himself in the other player's place, and so each player can figure out that there is a best strategy for each of them. The prisoners are indeed in a dilemma. Each knows that he can serve 2 years *only* if he can trust the other to deny. But each prisoner also knows that it is *not* in the best interest of the other to deny. So each prisoner knows that he must confess, thereby delivering a bad outcome for both.

The firms in an oligopoly are in a similar situation to Art and Bob in the prisoners' dilemma game. Let's see how we can use this game to understand oligopoly.

An Oligopoly Price-Fixing Game

We can use game theory and a game like the prisoners' dilemma to understand price fixing, price wars and other aspects of the behaviour of firms in oligopoly.

We'll begin with a price-fixing game. To understand price fixing, we're going to study the special case of duopoly – an oligopoly with two firms. Duopoly is easier to study than oligopoly with three or more firms, and it captures the essence of all oligopoly situations. Somehow, the two firms must share the market. And how they share it depends on the actions of each. We're going to describe the costs of the two firms and the market demand for the item they produce. We're then going to see how game theory helps us to predict the prices charged and the quantities produced by the two firms in a duopoly.

Cost and Demand Conditions

Two firms, Trick and Gear, produce switchgears. They have identical costs. Figure 14.2(a) shows their average total cost curve (ATC) and marginal cost curve (MC). Figure 14.2(b) shows the market demand curve for switchgears (D).

The two firms produce identical switchgears, so one firm's switchgear is a perfect substitute for the other's. So the market price of each firm's product is identical. The quantity demanded depends on that price – the higher the price, the smaller is the quantity demanded.

This industry is a natural duopoly. Two firms can produce this good at a lower cost than either one firm or three firms can. For each firm, average total cost is at its minimum when production is 3,000 units a week. And when price equals minimum average total cost, the total quantity demanded is 6,000 units a week. So two firms can just produce that quantity.

Collusion

We'll suppose that Trick and Gear enter into a collusive agreement. A **collusive agreement** is an agreement between two (or more) producers to form a cartel to restrict output, raise the price and increase profits. Because such an agreement is illegal in the European Union, it is undertaken in secret. The strategies that firms in a cartel can pursue are to:

1 Comply

2 Cheat

A firm that complies carries out the agreement. A firm that cheats breaks the agreement to its own benefit and to the cost of the other firm.

Because each firm has two strategies, there are four possible combinations of actions for the firms:

1 Both firms comply

2 Both firms cheat

3 Trick complies and Gear cheats

4 Gear complies and Trick cheats

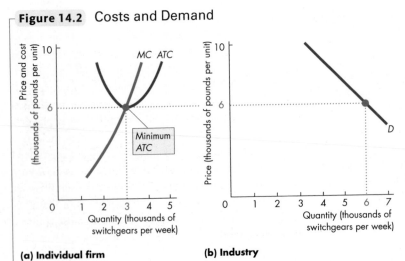

Figure 14.2 Costs and Demand

(a) Individual firm

(b) Industry

The average total cost curve for each firm is ATC and the marginal cost curve is MC in part (a). Minimum average total cost is £6,000 a unit, and it occurs at a production of 3,000 units a week.

Part (b) shows the market demand curve. At a price of £6,000, the quantity demanded is 6,000 units per week. The two firms can produce this output at the lowest possible average cost. If the market had one firm, it would be profitable for another to enter. If the market had three firms, one would exit. There is room for only two firms in this industry. It is a natural duopoly.

Colluding to Maximise Profits

Let's work out the payoffs to the two firms if they collude to make the maximum profit for the cartel by acting like a monopoly. The calculations that the two firms perform are the same calculations that a monopoly performs. (You can refresh your memory of these calculations by looking at Chapter 12, pp. 280–281.)

The only thing that the duopolists must do beyond what a monopolist does is to agree on how much of the total output each of them will produce.

Figure 14.3 shows the price and quantity that maximise industry profit for the duopolists. Part (a) shows the situation for each firm and part (b) shows the situation for the industry as a whole. The curve labelled *MR* is the industry marginal revenue curve. This marginal revenue curve is like that of a single price monopoly (Chapter 12, p. 278). The curve labelled MC_I is the industry marginal cost curve if each firm produces the same level of output. That curve is constructed by adding together the outputs of the two firms at each level of marginal cost. That is, at each level of marginal cost, industry output is twice the output of each individual firm. So the curve MC_I in part (b) is twice as far to the right as the curve *MC* in part (a).

To maximise industry profit, the duopolists agree to restrict output to the rate that makes the industry marginal cost and marginal revenue equal. That output

rate, as shown in part (b), is 4,000 units a week. The demand curve shows that the highest price for which the 4,000 switchgears can be sold is £9,000 each. Trick and Gear agree to charge this price.

To hold the price at £9,000 a unit, production must not exceed 4,000 units a week. So Trick and Gear must agree on production levels for each of them that total 4,000 units a week. Let's suppose that they agree to split the market equally so that each firm produces 2,000 switchgears a week. Because the firms are identical, this division is the most likely.

The average total cost of producing 2,000 switchgears a week is £8,000, so the profit per unit is £1,000 and economic profit is £2 million (2,000 units × £1,000 per unit). The economic profit of each firm is represented by the blue rectangle in Figure 14.3(a).

We have just described one possible outcome for a duopoly game: the two firms collude to produce the monopoly profit-maximising output and divide that output equally between them. From the industry point of view, this solution is identical to a monopoly. A duopoly that operates in this way is indistinguishable from a monopoly. The economic profit that is made by a monopoly is the maximum total profit that can be made by the duopoly when the firms collude.

But with price greater than marginal cost, either firm might think of trying to increase its profit by cheating on the agreement and producing more than the agreed amount. Let's see what happens if one of the firms does cheat in this way.

Figure 14.3 Colluding to Make Monopoly Profits

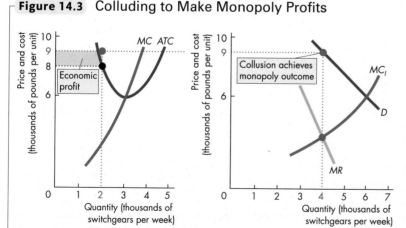

(a) Individual firm

(b) Industry

The industry marginal cost curve, MC_I in part (b), is the horizontal sum of the two firms' marginal cost curves, *MC* in part (a). The industry marginal revenue curve is *MR*. To maximise profit, the firms produce 4,000 units a week (the quantity at which marginal revenue equals marginal cost). They sell that output for £9,000 a unit. Each firm produces 2,000 units a week. Average total cost is £8,000 a unit, so each firm makes an economic profit of £2 million (blue rectangle) – 2,000 units multiplied by £1,000 profit a unit.

One Firm Cheats on a Collusive Agreement

To set the stage for cheating on their agreement, Trick convinces Gear that demand has decreased and that it cannot sell 2,000 units a week. Trick tells Gear that it plans to cut its price in order to sell the agreed 2,000 units each week. Because the two firms produce an identical product, Gear matches Trick's price cut but still produces only 2,000 units a week.

In fact, there has been no decrease in demand. Trick plans to increase output, which it knows will lower the price, and Trick wants to ensure that Gear's output remains at the agreed level.

Figure 14.4 illustrates the consequences of Trick's cheating. Part (a) shows Gear (the complier); part (b) shows Trick (the cheat); and part (c) shows the industry as a whole. Suppose that Trick increases output to 3,000 units a week. If Gear sticks to the agreement to produce only 2,000 units a week, total output is 5,000 a week, and given demand in part (c), the price falls to £7,500 a unit.

Gear continues to produce 2,000 units a week at a cost of £8,000 a unit and incurs a loss of £500 a unit, or £1 million a week. This economic loss is represented by the shaded rectangle in part (a). Trick produces 3,000 units a week at a cost of £6,000 a unit.

With a price of £7,500, Trick makes a profit of £1,500 a unit and therefore an economic profit of £4.5 million. This economic profit is the blue rectangle in part (b).

We've now described a second possible outcome for the duopoly game: one of the firms cheats on the collusive agreement. In this case, the industry output is larger than the monopoly output and the industry price is lower than the monopoly price. The total economic profit made by the industry is also smaller than the monopoly's economic profit. Trick (the cheat) makes an economic profit of £4.5 million and Gear (the complier) incurs an economic loss of £1 million. The industry makes an economic profit of £3.5 million. The industry profit is £0.5 million less than the economic profit a monopoly would make, but the profit is distributed unevenly. Trick makes a bigger economic profit than it would under the collusive agreement, while Gear incurs an economic loss.

A similar outcome would arise if Gear cheated and Trick complied with the agreement. The industry profit and price would be the same, but in this case, Gear (the cheat) would make an economic profit of £4.5 million and Trick (the complier) would incur an economic loss of £1 million.

Let's next see what happens if both firms cheat.

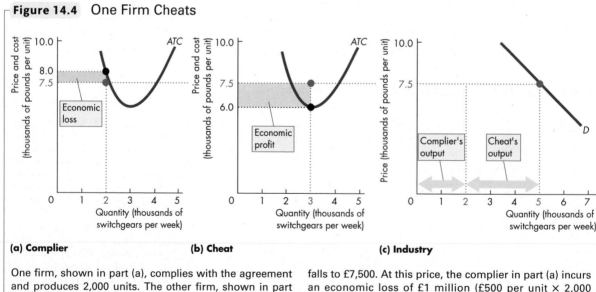

Figure 14.4 **One Firm Cheats**

(a) Complier   (b) Cheat   (c) Industry

One firm, shown in part (a), complies with the agreement and produces 2,000 units. The other firm, shown in part (b), cheats on the agreement and increases its output to 3,000 units. Given the market demand curve in part (c) and with a total production of 5,000 units a week, the price falls to £7,500. At this price, the complier in part (a) incurs an economic loss of £1 million (£500 per unit × 2,000 units), shown by the shaded rectangle. In part (b), the cheat makes an economic profit of £4.5 million (£1,500 per unit × 3,000 units), shown by the blue rectangle.

Both Firms Cheat

Suppose that both firms cheat and that each firm behaves like the cheating firm that we have just analysed. Each tells the other that it is unable to sell its output at the going price and that it plans to cut its price. But because both firms cheat, each will propose a successively lower price. As long as price exceeds marginal cost, each firm has an incentive to increase its production – to cheat. Only when price equals marginal cost is there no further incentive to cheat. This situation arises when the price has reached £6,000. At this price, marginal cost equals price. Also, price equals minimum average total cost. At a price less than £6,000, each firm incurs an economic loss. At a price of £6,000, each firm covers all its costs and makes zero economic profit (makes normal profit). Also, at a price of £6,000, each firm wants to produce 3,000 units a week, so the industry output is 6,000 units a week. Given the demand conditions, 6,000 units can be sold at a price of £6,000 each.

Figure 14.5 illustrates the situation just described. Each firm, in part (a), produces 3,000 units a week, and its average total cost is a minimum (£6,000 per unit). The market as a whole, in part (b), operates at the point at which the market demand curve (D) intersects the industry marginal cost curve (MC_I). Each firm has lowered its price and increased its output to try to gain an advantage over the other firm. Each has pushed this process as far as it can without incurring an economic loss.

We have now described a third possible outcome of this duopoly game: both firms cheat. If both firms cheat on the collusive agreement, the output of each firm is 3,000 units a week and the price is £6,000. Each firm makes zero economic profit.

The Payoff Matrix

Now that we have described the strategies and payoffs in the duopoly game, we can summarise the strategies and the payoffs in the form of the game's payoff matrix. Then we can find the Nash equilibrium.

Table 14.2 sets out the payoff matrix for this game. It is constructed in the same way as the payoff matrix for the prisoners' dilemma in Table 14.1. The squares show the payoffs for the two firms – Gear and Trick. In this case, the payoffs are profits. (For the prisoners' dilemma, the payoffs were losses.)

The table shows that if both firms cheat (top left), they achieve the perfectly competitive outcome – each firm makes zero economic profit. If both firms comply (bottom right), the industry makes the monopoly profit and each firm makes an economic profit of £2 million. The top right and bottom left squares show what happens if one firm cheats while the other complies. The firm that cheats makes an economic profit of £4.5 million, and the one that complies incurs a loss of £1 million.

Nash Equilibrium in the Duopolists' Dilemma

The duopolists have a dilemma like the prisoners' dilemma. Do they comply or cheat? To answer this question, we must find the Nash equilibrium.

Figure 14.5   Both Firms Cheat

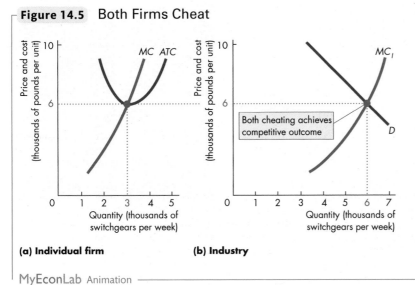

(a) Individual firm

(b) Industry

If both firms cheat by increasing production, the collusive agreement collapses. The limit to the collapse is the competitive equilibrium. Neither firm will cut the price below £6,000 (minimum average total cost) because to do so will result in losses.

In part (a), each firm produces 3,000 units a week at an average total cost of £6,000. In part (b), with a total production of 6,000 units, the price falls to £6,000. Each firm now makes zero economic profit. This output and price are the ones that would prevail in a competitive industry.

Table 14.2

Duopoly Payoff Matrix

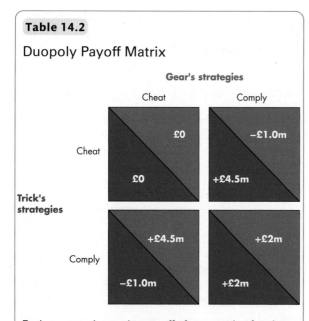

Gear's strategies

Each square shows the payoffs from a pair of actions. For example, if both firms comply with the collusive agreement, the payoffs are recorded in the bottom right square. The red triangle shows Gear's payoff, and the blue triangle shows Trick's. In the Nash equilibrium, both firms cheat.

Look at things from Gear's point of view. Gear reasons as follows. Suppose that Trick cheats. If I comply, I will incur an economic loss of £1 million. If I also cheat, I will make zero economic profit. Zero is better than *minus* £1 million, so I'm better off if I cheat. Now suppose Trick complies. If I cheat, I will make an economic profit of £4.5 million, and if I comply, I will make an economic profit of £2 million. A £4.5 million profit is better than a £2 million profit, so I'm better off if I cheat. So regardless of whether Trick cheats or complies, it pays Gear to cheat. Cheating is Gear's best strategy.

Trick comes to the same conclusion as Gear because the two firms face an identical situation. So both firms cheat. The Nash equilibrium of the duopoly game is that both firms cheat. And, although the industry has only two firms, they charge the same price and produce the same quantity as those in a competitive industry. Also, as in perfect competition, each firm makes zero economic profit.

Economics in Action (opposite) and *Economics in the News* (p. 331) look at some other prisoners' dilemma games. But not all games are prisoners' dilemmas, as you'll now see.

 ECONOMICS IN ACTION

A Game in Supermarket Retailing

Supermarkets didn't start retailing laptops to help you sort out your problems accessing Facebook. Tesco introduced electronic products to its grocery business as part of a costly store development game with its main market rival, Asda.

The table below illustrates the game (with hypothetical numbers). Each firm can spend either £10 million developing additional floor space in existing stores to sell electronic goods or nothing on store development. If neither firm spends on additional floor space, both firms see profit rise by 8 per cent (bottom right). If each firm spends on store development and investment, both Tesco and Asda see a rise in profit of 4 per cent (top left).

The other parts of the matrix show the rise in economic profits for each when one spends on development and the other doesn't.

Confronted with these payoffs, Tesco sees that it gets a bigger profit if it spends on store development regardless of what Asda does. Asda reaches the same conclusion. It, too, gets a bigger profit by spending on store development regardless of what Tesco does.

Because development is the best strategy for both players, it is the Nash equilibrium – a dominant-strategy Nash equilibrium.

The outcome of this game is that both firms spend on store development. They make less profit than they would if they could collude to achieve the cooperative outcome, but you get to try the latest laptop.

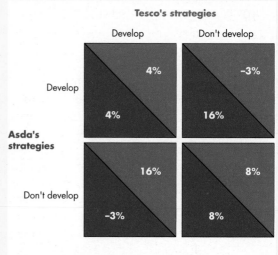

Table 1 A Strategic Game

A Game of Chicken

The Nash equilibrium for the prisoners' dilemma is unique: both players cheat (confess). Not all games have a unique equilibrium, and one that doesn't is a game called 'chicken'.

An Example of a Game of Chicken

A graphic, if disturbing, version of 'chicken' has two cars racing towards each other. The first driver to swerve and avoid a crash is the 'chicken'. The payoffs are a big loss for both if no one 'chickens out', zero for both if both 'chicken out', and a gain for the player who stays the course. If player 1 swerves, player 2's best strategy is to stay the course. And if player 1 stays the course, player 2's best strategy is to swerve.

An Economic Example of Chicken

An economic game of chicken can arise when research and development (R&D) creates a new technology that cannot be kept secret or patented, so both firms benefit from the R&D of either firm. The chicken in this case is the firm that does the R&D.

Suppose, for example, that either Apple or Nokia spends £9 million developing a new touch-screen technology that both would end up being able to use regardless of which of them developed it.

Table 14.3 illustrates a payoff matrix for the game that Apple and Nokia play. Each firm has two strategies: do the R&D ('chicken out') or do not do the R&D. Each entry shows the additional profit (the profit from the new technology minus the cost of the research), given the strategies adopted.

If neither firm does the R&D, each makes zero additional profit. If both firms conduct the R&D, each firm makes an additional £5 million. If one of the firms does the R&D ('chickens out'), it makes £1 million and the other firm makes £10 million. Confronted with these payoffs the two firms calculate their best strategies. Nokia is better off doing R&D if Apple does no R&D. Apple is better off doing R&D if Nokia does no R&D. There are two Nash equilibrium outcomes: only one of them does the R&D, but we can't predict which one.

You can see that an outcome with no firm doing R&D isn't a Nash equilibrium because one firm would be better off doing it. Also, both firms doing R&D isn't a Nash equilibrium because one firm would be better off *not* doing it. To decide *which* firm does the R&D, the firms might toss a coin, called a mixed strategy.

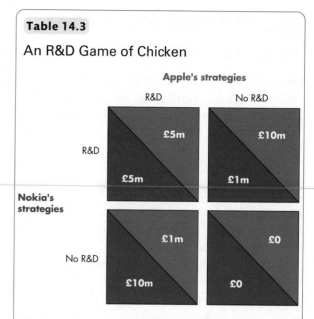

Table 14.3

An R&D Game of Chicken

If neither firm does the R&D, their payoffs are in the bottom right square. When one firm 'chickens out' and does the R&D while the other does no R&D, their payoffs are in the top right and bottom left squares. When both 'chicken out' and do the R&D, the payoffs are in the top left square. The red triangle shows Apple's payoff, and the blue triangle shows Nokia's. The equilibrium for this R&D game of chicken is for only one firm to undertake the R&D. We cannot tell which firm will do the R&D and which will not.

REVIEW QUIZ

1 What are the common features of all games?
2 Describe the prisoners' dilemma game and explain why the Nash equilibrium delivers a bad outcome for both players.
3 Why does a collusive agreement to restrict output and raise price create a game like the prisoners' dilemma?
4 What creates an incentive for firms in a collusive agreement to cheat and increase production?
5 What is the equilibrium strategy for each firm in a duopolists' dilemma and why do the firms not succeed in colluding to raise the price and profits?
6 Describe two structures of payoffs for an R&D game and contrast the prisoners' dilemma and chicken game.

Do these questions in Study Plan 14.2 and get instant feedback.   MyEconLab

Repeated Games and Sequential Games

The games that we've studied are played just once. In contrast, many real-world games are played repeatedly. This feature of games turns out to enable real-world duopolists to cooperate, collude and make a monopoly profit.

Another feature of the game that we've studied is that the players move simultaneously. But in many real-world situations one player moves first and then the other moves – the play is sequential rather than simultaneous. This feature of real-world games creates a large number of possible outcomes.

We're now going to examine these two aspects of strategic decision making.

A Repeated Duopoly Game

If two firms play a game repeatedly, one firm has the opportunity to penalise the other for previous 'bad' behaviour. If Gear cheats this week, perhaps Trick will cheat next week. Before Gear cheats this week, won't it consider the possibility that Trick will cheat next week? What is the equilibrium of this game?

Actually, there is more than one possibility. One is the Nash equilibrium that we have just analysed. Both players cheat, and each makes zero economic profit forever. In such a situation, it never pays one of the players to start complying unilaterally because to do so will result in a loss for that player and a profit for the other. But a **cooperative equilibrium** in which the players make and share the monopoly profit is possible.

A cooperative equilibrium might occur if cheating is punished. There are two extremes of punishment. The smallest penalty is called 'tit for tat'. A *tit-for-tat strategy* is one in which a player cooperates in the current period if the other player cooperated in the previous period but cheats in the current period if the other player cheated in the previous period. The most severe form of punishment is called a trigger strategy. A *trigger strategy* is one in which a player cooperates if the other player cooperates but plays the Nash equilibrium strategy forever thereafter if the other player cheats.

In the duopoly game between Gear and Trick, a tit-for-tat strategy keeps both players cooperating and making monopoly profits. Let's see why with an example.

Table 14.4 shows the economic profit that Trick and Gear will make over a number of periods under two alternative sequences of events: colluding, and cheating with a tit-for-tat response by the other firm.

If both firms stick to the collusive agreement in period 1, each makes an economic profit of £2 million. Suppose that Trick contemplates cheating in period 1. The cheating produces a quick £4.5 million economic profit and inflicts a £1 million economic loss on Gear.

But a cheat by Trick in period 1 produces a response from Gear in period 2. If Trick wants to get back into a profit-making situation, it must return to the agreement in period 2 even though it knows that Gear will punish it for cheating in period 1. So in period 2, Gear punishes Trick and Trick cooperates. Gear now makes an economic profit of £4.5 million, and Trick incurs an economic loss of £1 million.

Adding up the profits over two periods of play, Trick would have made more profit by cooperating – £4 million compared with £3.5 million.

What is true for Trick is also true for Gear. Because each firm makes a larger profit by sticking with the collusive agreement, both firms do so and the monopoly price, quantity and profit prevail.

In reality, whether a cartel works like a one-play game or a repeated game depends primarily on the number of players and the ease of detecting and punishing

---

Table 14.4

Cheating with Punishment

Period of play	Collude		Cheat with tit-for-tat	
	Trick's profit (millions of pounds)	Gear's profit (millions of pounds)	Trick's profit (millions of pounds)	Gear's profit (millions of pounds)
1	2	2	4.5	–1.0
2	2	2	–1.0	4.5
3	2	2	2.0	2.0
4	•	•	•	•

If duopolists repeatedly collude, each makes an economic profit of £2 million per period of play. If one player cheats in period 1, the other player plays a tit-for-tat strategy and cheats in period 2. The profit from cheating can be made for only one period and must be paid for in the next period by incurring a loss. Over two periods of play, the best that a duopolist can achieve by cheating is an economic profit of £3.5 million, compared with an economic profit of £4 million by colluding.

ECONOMICS IN THE NEWS

Airbus Versus Boeing

Boeing Strikes Back in Single-Aisle Market

Airbus and Boeing are in fierce competition in the narrow-body passenger jet market. Airbus got moving first with its A320 Neo for which it has 1,400 orders. Boeing responded with the 737 Max for which it had 549 orders in mid-2012 and an aim for 1,000 orders by the end of 2012.

Boeing rejected suggestions that it was in a price war with Airbus over the A320 Neo and 737 Max but confirmed it would woo some airline customers of its European rival.

Source: *The Financial Times*, 9 July 2012

Some Data

Aircraft	List price
Airbus Neo	$96.7 million
Boeing Max	$96.0 million

Assumptions

◆ The performance and operating costs of the Neo and the Max are identical.

◆ At list prices, Airbus and Boeing can get another 200 orders each and make $3 billion each in economic profit.

◆ At discounted prices, Airbus and Boeing can get another 225 orders each and make $1 billion each in economic profit.

◆ If one of them holds the list price and the other discounts, the discounter can get 450 new orders and makes $2 billion and the other will get no new orders.

The Questions

◆ In what type of market are Airbus and Boeing competing?

◆ How did moving first benefit Airbus?

◆ Given the assumptions above, will the aeroplane producers discount their prices or stick to the list prices? To answer this question, set out the payoff matrix for the game that Airbus and Boeing are playing and find the Nash equilibrium.

◆ If the game could be played repeatedly, how might the strategies and equilibrium change?

The Answers

◆ Airbus and Boeing are a duopoly.

◆ By moving first, Airbus had a temporary monopoly and was able to grab a large market share.

◆ The table illustrates the payoff matrix for the game between Airbus and Boeing.

◆ The outcome is a dominant-strategy Nash equilibrium. Both firms discount their prices and get 225 new orders each. If one firm held the list price, the other would discount and take the 450 new orders.

◆ If the game could be played repeatedly, the discounter could be punished and a cooperative equilibrium would arise in which neither discounts.

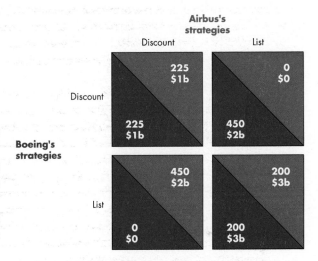

Table 1 Duopoly Game: Market for Airplanes

Are the Neo and Max in a price war?

cheating. The larger the number of players, the harder it is to maintain a cartel.

Games and Price Wars

A repeated duopoly game can help us understand real-world behaviour and, in particular, price wars. Some price wars can be interpreted as the implementation of a tit-for-tat strategy. But the game is a bit more complicated than the one we've looked at because the players are uncertain about the demand for the product.

Playing a tit-for-tat strategy, firms have an incentive to stick to the monopoly price. But fluctuations in demand lead to fluctuations in the monopoly price, and sometimes, when the price changes, it might seem to one of the firms that the price has fallen because the other has cheated. In this case, a price war will break out. The price war will end only when each firm is satisfied that the other is ready to cooperate again. There will be cycles of price wars and the restoration of collusive agreements. Fluctuations in the world price of oil might be interpreted in this way.

Some price wars arise from the entry of a small number of firms into an industry that had previously been a monopoly. Although the industry has a small number of firms, the firms are in a prisoners' dilemma and they cannot impose effective penalties for price cutting.

A Computer Chip Price War

The prices of computer chips during 1995 and 1996 can be explained by the game you've just examined. Until 1995, the market for chips for IBM-compatible computers was dominated by Intel Corporation. Intel was able to make maximum economic profit by producing the quantity of chips at which marginal cost equalled marginal revenue. The price of Intel's chips was set to ensure that the quantity demanded equalled the quantity produced. Then in 1995 and 1996, with the entry of a small number of new firms, the industry became an oligopoly. If the firms had maintained Intel's price and shared the market, together they could have made economic profits equal to Intel's profit. But the firms were in a prisoners' dilemma, so prices fell towards the competitive level.

Let's now study a sequential game. There are many such games, and the one we'll examine is among the simplest. It has an interesting implication and it will give you the flavour of this type of game. We'll study an entry game in a contestable market.

A Sequential Entry Game in a Contestable Market

If two firms play a sequential game, one firm makes a decision at the first stage of the game and the other makes a decision at the second stage.

We're going to study a sequential game in a **contestable market** – a market in which firms can enter and leave so easily that firms in the market face competition from *potential* entrants. Examples of contestable markets are routes served by airlines and by barge companies that operate on Europe's major waterways. These markets are contestable because firms could enter if an opportunity for economic profit arose and could exit with no penalty if the opportunity for economic profit disappeared.

If the five-firm concentration ratio (see Chapter 9, p. 206) is used to determine the degree of competition, a contestable market appears to be uncompetitive. But a contestable market can behave as if it were perfectly competitive. To see why, let's look at an entry game for a contestable air route.

A Contestable Air Route

Agile Air is the only firm operating on a particular route. Demand and cost conditions are such that there is room for only one airline to operate. Wanabe plc is another airline that could offer services on the route.

We describe the structure of a sequential game by using a *game tree* like that in Figure 14.6. At the first stage, Agile Air must set a price. Once the price is set and advertised, Agile can't change it. That is, once set, Agile's price is fixed and Agile can't react to Wanabe's entry decision. Agile can set its price at either the monopoly level or the competitive level.

At the second stage, Wanabe must decide whether to enter or to stay out. Customers have no loyalty (there are no frequent flyer programmes) and they buy from the lowest-price firm. So if Wanabe enters, it sets a price just below Agile's and takes all the business.

Figure 14.6 shows the payoffs from the various decisions (Agile's in the red triangles and Wanabe's in the blue triangles).

To decide on its price, Agile's CEO reasons as follows. Suppose that Agile sets the monopoly price. If Wanabe enters, it earns 90 (think of all payoff numbers as thousands of pounds). If Wanabe stays out, it earns nothing. So Wanabe will enter. In this case Agile will lose 50.

Figure 14.6   Agile versus Wanabe: A Sequential Entry Game in a Contestable Market

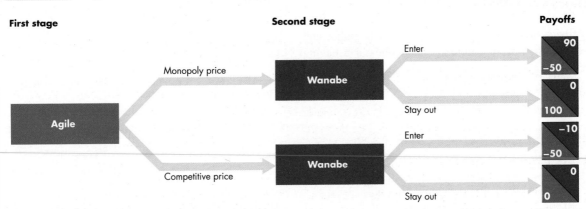

If Agile sets the monopoly price, Wanabe makes 90 (thousand pounds) by entering and earns nothing by staying out. So if Agile sets the monopoly price, Wanabe enters.

If Agile sets the competitive price, Wanabe earns nothing if it stays out and incurs a loss if it enters. So if Agile sets the competitive price, Wanabe stays out.

MyEconLab Animation

Now suppose that Agile sets the competitive price. If Wanabe stays out, it earns nothing, and if it enters, it loses 10, so Wanabe will stay out. In this case, Agile will make zero economic profit.

Agile's best strategy is to set its price at the competitive level and make zero economic profit. The option of earning 100 by setting the monopoly price with Wanabe staying out is not available to Agile. If Agile sets the monopoly price, Wanabe enters, undercuts Agile, and takes all the business.

In this example, Agile sets its price at the competitive level and makes zero economic profit. A less costly strategy, called **limit pricing**, sets the price at the highest level that inflicts a loss on the entrant. Any loss is big enough to deter entry, so it is not always necessary to set the price as low as the competitive price. In the example of Agile and Wanabe, at the competitive price Wanabe incurs a loss of 10 if it enters. A smaller loss would still keep Wanabe out.

This game is interesting because it points to the possibility of a monopoly behaving like a competitive industry and serving the consumer interest without regulation. But the result is not general and depends on one crucial feature of the setup of the game: at the second stage, Agile is locked into the price set at the first stage.

If Agile could change its price in the second stage, it would want to set the monopoly price if Wanabe stayed out – 100 with the monopoly price exceeds zero with the competitive price. But Wanabe can figure out what Agile would do, so the price set at the first stage has no effect on Wanabe. Agile sets the monopoly price and Wanabe might either stay out or enter.

We've looked at two of the many possible repeated and sequential games, and you've seen how these types of game can provide insights into the complex forces that determine prices and profits.

◆◆ **REVIEW QUIZ**

1   If a prisoners' dilemma game is played repeatedly, what punishment strategies might the players employ and how does playing the game repeatedly change the equilibrium?
2   If a market is contestable, how does the equilibrium differ from that of a monopoly?

Do these questions in Study Plan 14.3 and get instant feedback.   MyEconLab

So far, we've studied oligopoly with unregulated market power. Firms like Trick and Gear are free to collude to maximise their profit with no concern for the consumer or the law.

But when firms collude to achieve the monopoly outcome, they also have the same effects on efficiency and the social interest as monopoly. Profit is made at the expense of consumer surplus, and a deadweight loss arises. We now look at how UK and EU competition and anti-monopoly law limits market power.

Antitrust Law

Antitrust law is any law that regulates oligopolies and prevents them from becoming monopolies or behaving like monopolies. The term 'antitrust law' is American, but is now widely used in Europe to describe what was previously called 'competition and monopoly law'.

UK and EU Antitrust Laws

In the UK, the two main sources of antitrust law are:

1 UK competition and monopoly laws
2 EU competition and monopoly laws

Antitrust law in the UK began in 1948 when the Monopolies and Restrictive Practices Act created a regulatory agency called the Monopolies and Mergers Commission to monitor and control monopolies that act against the social interest, as defined by the political leadership.

Several subsequent Acts have adapted and developed UK law, which is now defined under the Competition Act of 1998 and the Enterprise Act of 2002. The UK regulatory agency was renamed the Competition Commission under the 1988 Act because the focus of regulation switched from monopoly to anti-competitive practice. Under UK law, the Office of Fair Trading can investigate abuse of dominant market power (an entity having more than a 25 per cent share of the market) and a variety of anti-competitive practices, and refer companies to the Competition Commission.

Table 14.5 summarises the main focus of the two main UK antitrust laws. Both laws prohibit anti-competitive agreements between companies – in particular, any agreements that fix prices, directly or indirectly, that cut production or supply to raise prices, or that share market customers or rig bids for contracts. Examples of indirect price fixing include agreements about relative price levels, rebates, discounts, transport charges and quotas.

EU law has focused on anti-competitive behaviour from the outset when the Treaty of Rome was signed in 1957. Since then, several new Treaties and Regulations have updated the law as the EU was formed and expanded. Table 14.6 sets out the main regulations. Since May 2004, all national competition authorities are empowered to apply EU law as well as national law. The European Commission has diverse powers to impose stringent fines, break up cartels and impose legally binding requirements on firms. It can also reduce or eliminate fines under leniency rules for companies that confess.

Table 14.5

UK Antitrust Laws

Law	Main Regulation
Competition Act 1988	Prohibits agreements that restrict competition by: ◆ Fixing prices or trade terms ◆ Limiting production ◆ Sharing markets Prohibits abuse of dominant market position
Enterprise Act 2002	Prohibits cartels and merger agreements that: ◆ Fix prices ◆ Limit production or supply ◆ Share markets ◆ Engage in bid rigging Prohibits agreements whether carried out or not

The driving force of EU regulation is the criterion of abuse of a dominant position. Since Regulation 130 in 2004, this criterion applies to duopolies and oligopolies and all anti-competitive effects of mergers on oligopolistic markets. The European Commission can investigate any agreements that distort competition and any alleged cartel, duopoly or oligopoly or merger that might lead to a dominant position where the companies concerned have a Community dimension. The Community dimension is determined by a threshold of turnover worldwide and within the EU borders.

Price Fixing Always Illegal

Colluding with competitors to fix the price is always a violation of UK and EU antitrust law. If the Competition agency can prove the existence of a price-fixing cartel, also called a horizontal price-fixing agreement, defendants can offer no acceptable excuse.

The predictions of the effects of price fixing that you saw in the previous sections of this chapter provide the reasons for the unqualified attitude towards price fixing. A duopoly cartel can maximise profit and behave like a monopoly. To achieve the monopoly outcome, the cartel restricts production and fixes the price at the monopoly level. The consumer suffers because consumer surplus shrinks, and the outcome is inefficient because a deadweight loss arises.

Table 14.6

EU Antitrust Laws

Law	Main Regulation
Treaty of Rome 1957; Article 81, now Article 101 of the Treaty on the Functioning of the EU	Prohibits cartels Prohibits agreements between firms that distort competition within the Single Market including any form of price fixing, tying agreements, or limitations on supply in contracts.
Treaty of Rome 1957, Article 82, now Article 102 of the Treaty on the Functioning of the EU.	Prohibits the abuse of a dominant market position, for example in the form of predatory pricing to eliminate competitors or actions to raise barriers to entry
European Union Merger Regulation 1989 (updated in Council Regulation 13/9/2004)	Identifies the 'dominant position' principle for examining mergers where a merger creates the economic power to influence the terms of competition, prices, production, product quality, marketing and innovation, and restricts competition appreciably.

It is for these reasons that the law declares that all price fixing is illegal. No excuse can justify the practice.

Other antitrust practices are more controversial and generate debate among lawyers and economists. We'll examine three of these practices.

Three Antitrust Policy Debates

The three practices that we'll examine are:

◆ Resale price maintenance
◆ Tying arrangements
◆ Predatory pricing

Resale Price Maintenance

Resale price maintenance is a distributor's agreement with a manufacturer to resell a product *at or above a specified minimum price*.

The Restrictive Trade Practices Act of 1956 and the Resale Prices Act of 1965 made resale price maintenance agreements in the UK illegal, unless proved otherwise under EU law. However, setting a minimum retail price is not illegal in the UK unless proved so on a case-by-case basis.

The UK Net Book Agreement was an allowed agreement on the minimum price at which books would be sold to the public. It was allowed because it helped publishers to produce less widely read but socially valuable books. However, the Net Book Agreement ended in 1997 after a second legal review found it illegal. Since 1997, book prices have fallen as supermarkets and international book sellers have entered the popular book market and many small specialist bookshops have closed.

Does resale price maintenance create an inefficient or efficient use of resources? Economists can be found on both sides of this question.

Inefficient Resale Price Maintenance

Resale price maintenance is inefficient if it enables dealers to charge the monopoly price. By setting and enforcing the resale price, the manufacturer might be able to achieve the monopoly price.

Efficient Resale Price Maintenance

Resale price maintenance might be efficient if it enables a manufacturer to induce dealers to provide the efficient standard of service. Suppose that SilkySkin wants shops to demonstrate the use of its new, unbelievable moisturising cream in an inviting space. With resale price maintenance, SilkySkin can offer all the retailers the same incentive and compensation. Without resale price maintenance, a cut-price supermarket might offer SilkySkin products at a low price. Buyers would then have an incentive to visit a high-price shop for a product demonstration and then buy from the low-price shop. The low-price shop would be a free rider (like the consumer of a public good in Chapter 15, p. 351), and an inefficient level of service would be provided.

SilkySkin could pay a fee to retailers that provide good service and leave the resale price to be determined by the competitive forces of supply and demand. But it might be too costly for SilkySkin to monitor shops and ensure that they provide the desired level of service.

Tying Arrangements

A **tying arrangement** is an agreement to sell one product only if the buyer agrees to buy another, different product. With tying, the only way the buyer can get the one product is to also buy the other product. Microsoft has been accused of tying Internet Explorer and Windows. Textbook publishers sometimes tie a website and a textbook and force students to buy both. (You can't buy the book you're now reading, new, without the website. But you can buy the website access without the book, so these products are not tied.)

Could textbook publishers make more money by tying a book and access to a website? The answer is sometimes but not always. Suppose that you and other students are willing to pay £50 for a book and £10 for access to a website. The publisher can sell these items separately for these prices or bundled for £60. The publisher does not gain from bundling.

But now suppose that you and only half of the students are willing to pay £50 for a book and £10 for a website, and the other half of the students are willing to pay £50 for a website and £10 for a book. Now if the two items are sold separately, the publisher can charge £50 for the book and £50 for the website. Half the students buy the book but not the website, and the other half buy the website but not the book. But if the book and website are bundled for £60, everyone buys the bundle and the publisher makes an extra £10 per student. In this case, bundling has enabled the publisher to price discriminate.

There is no simple, clear-cut test of whether a firm is engaging in tying or whether, by doing so, it has increased its market power and profit and created inefficiency.

Predatory Pricing

Predatory pricing is setting a low price to drive competitors out of business with the intention of setting a

ECONOMICS IN ACTION

The EU versus Microsoft

In 1998, Sun Microsystems complained to the European Commission that Microsoft would not give it the information needed to run Microsoft's operating system. In 2001, after the release of Windows 2000, complaints were made that Microsoft had engaged in anti-competitive tying of its Windows Media Player with its Windows PC operating system. In 2008, the European Commission began to investigate Microsoft for abusing its dominant position in the market for client PC operating systems by tying its browser, Internet Explorer, to the Windows operating system.

The Case Against Microsoft

The claims against Microsoft were that it

◆ Possessed monopoly power

◆ Used predatory pricing and tying arrangements

◆ Used other anti-competitive practices

Microsoft had 80 per cent of the market for PC operating systems, a dominant position. This dominant position arose from two barriers to entry: economies of scale and network economies. Microsoft's average total cost falls as production increases (economies of scale) because the fixed cost of developing an operating system such as Windows is large while the marginal cost of producing one copy of Windows is small. Further, as the number of Windows users increases, the range of Windows applications expands (network economies), so a potential competitor would need

to produce not only a competing operating system but also an entire range of supporting applications as well.

When Microsoft entered the Web browser market with its Internet Explorer and the media market with Media Player, it offered the software for a zero price. Microsoft integrated the software with Windows so that anyone using Windows would not need a competing media package or browser. Microsoft's competitors claimed that this practice was an illegal tying arrangement.

Microsoft's Response

Microsoft challenged all these claims. It said that Windows was vulnerable to competition from other operating systems such as Linux and Apple's Mac OS, and that there was a permanent threat of competition from new entrants. Microsoft claimed that integrating software like Internet Explorer with Windows provided a single, unified product of greater consumer value.

The Outcome

The European Commission agreed in 2004 that Microsoft's refusal to supply information limited competition and ordered Microsoft to disclose the information. It also agreed that tying Media Player to the operating system harmed competition and ordered Microsoft to provide a version of Windows without Media Player. Finally, in 2009, the Commission did not identify abuse of power. Microsoft offered to provide a Choice Screen so that the 100 million EU users could choose a different browser. The Commission made this offer legally binding from March 2010.

monopoly price when the competition has gone. Predatory pricing is an attempt to create a monopoly, and as such it is illegal under Article 102 of the European Treaty.

It is easy to see that predatory pricing is an idea, not a reality. Economists are skeptical that predatory pricing occurs. They point out that a firm that cuts its price below the profit-maximising level loses during the low-price period. Even if it succeeds in driving its competitors out of business, new competitors will enter as soon as the price is increased, so any potential gain from a monopoly position is temporary. A high and certain loss is a poor exchange for a temporary and uncertain gain. No case of predatory pricing has been definitively found.

Mergers and Acquisitions

Mergers, which occur when two or more firms agree to combine to create one larger firm, and *acquisitions*, which occur when one firm buys another firm, are common events. Mergers occurred when Chrysler and the German auto producer Daimler-Benz combined to form DaimlerChrysler and when the Belgian beer producer InBev bought the US brewing giant Anheuser-Busch and created a new combined company, Anheuser-Busch InBev. An acquisition occurred when Rupert Murdoch's News Corp bought Myspace.

The mergers and acquisitions that occur don't usually create a monopoly. But two (or more) firms might be tempted to try to merge so that they can gain market power and operate like a monopoly. If such a situation arises, the UK Office of Fair Trading and the European Commission take an interest in the move and can block the merger.

Before taking action, the European Commission must establish a *Community dimension* to the takeover. To do this, the European Commission uses two turnover rules from Articles 1(2) and 1(3) of the Merger Regulation. These are a combined worldwide turnover:

1 Above €5 billion and at least two firms having an EU turnover of at least €50 million or

2 Of €2.5 billion and above €100 million in at least three member states; and in those states, the turnover of at least two firms is above €25 million and the EU-wide turnover of at least two firms exceeds €100 million, unless each firm has more than two-thirds of its EU turnover in one member state.

The EU rarely blocks mergers or acquisitions, but it will if a monopoly position is likely to result. You can see such an example in *Economics in Action*.

ECONOMICS IN ACTION

The EU Blocks No Frills Takeover

In 2006, Ryanair made a €1.48-billion aggressive takeover bid for its Irish rival, Aer Lingus. The bid was investigated by the European Commission and blocked under the EU competition rules in 2007. Ryanair contested the Commission ruling and applied to the European General Court to overrule the block. The basis for determining a Community dimension was contested. The European General Court decided in July 2010 that the Commission was right to block the takeover because it would have created a near monopoly on 22 of 35 routes to and from Dublin, Cork and Shannon airports.

The case did not have a Community dimension under the first EU rule and parts of the second EU rule, but the Community dimension was contested. How is turnover measured in each EU member state? Is turnover allocated by country of customer origin or destination, or simply where the ticket sale occurred? The Commission measured both and found evidence that turnover met the rules for Community dimension.

REVIEW QUIZ

1 What are the main antitrust laws affecting the UK and when were they enacted?
2 What is the main focus of EU antitrust law?
3 What are resale price maintenance, tying arrangements and predatory pricing?
4 Under what circumstances is an EU merger unlikely to be approved?

Do these questions in Study Plan 14.4 and get instant feedback.   MyEconLab

Oligopoly is a market structure that you encounter in your daily life. *Reading Between the Lines* on pp. 338–339 looks at the market for soap powders in France.

Collusion in Soap Powder

The Wall Street Journal, 9 December 2011

Dirty Secrets In Soap Prices

M. Colchester and C. Passariello

The Autorité de la Concurrence slapped fines totaling €361 million . . . on (Proctor & Gamble) P&G, Henkel AG and Colgate-Palmolive Co. for colluding to set the price of soaps in France between 1997 and 2004. . . .

The French regulator detailed what it called a long running scheme that pushed up prices for consumers before finally falling apart when the group's interests diverged. . . . Unilever PLC. . . . wasn't fined, as it was the first to cooperate with the investigation. . . .

Managers from several of the companies met as far back as the 1980s to share price information. . . . According to a statement . . . to the commission, the detergent makers wanted 'to limit the intensity of the competition between them and clean up the market'. Nevertheless, by the early 1990s, a price war had broken out among them. . . .

According to one anonymous Unilever employee . . . 'They were aware that there had already been [price] wars and they didn't want to revive them'. Yet while fixing prices proved relatively simple, monitoring . . . was proving complex. . . .

By 2004, the scheme began to crumble. . . . Unilever was the first to break the accord, launching a June 'D-Day' deal of 10% off. At the end of the year, P&G responded by slashing the price. . . .

After its own investigation, the European Commission fined P&G €211.2 million and Unilever €104.0 million in April.

© The Wall Street Journal.

 The Essence of the Story

- The French antitrust authority fined three of four detergent producers a total of €361 million in December 2011 for colluding to set prices.

- Proctor and Gamble, Unilever, Henkel and Colgate-Palmolive had colluded to set a monopoly price for powdered soap between 1997 and 2004.

- But during the period, each company tried to beat the agreement by cutting prices and starting a price war.

- After each price war, the companies agreed to try again until Unilever broke the agreement and confessed to the French authorities to avoid a fine.

Economic Analysis

- Proctor and Gamble (P&G), Unilever, Henkel and Colgate-Palmolive compete in the French soap powder market, which is an oligopoly.

- Figure 1 shows the shares in this market. You can see that P&G and Unilever each have a bit more than a third of the market.

- From 1997 to 2004, the companies colluded to set the monopoly profit-maximising price. In 2004, the collusive agreement ended and a price war began.

- We can interpret the price-fixing agreement as the cooperative equilibrium outcome of a repeated prisoners' dilemma game.

- Table 1 shows the payoffs (millions of euros of profit) for Unilever and P&G over a number of periods from 1997 if they cooperate and set the monopoly profit-maximising price, and if they cheat on the agreement with tit-for-tat punishment. (The numbers are hypothetical.)

- Table 1 and its interpretation is similar to Table 14.4 on page 330.

- If both firms stick to the collusive agreement, they make the monopoly profit of €5 million a year each.

- If P&G cheats in 1997–1998, it makes a profit of €10 million and Unilever incurs a loss of €2 million.

- If P&G wants to regain monopoly profit in the future, it must go back to the agreement in 1999–2000. But Unilever must cheat to punish P&G, so Unilever gets €10 million profit and P&G incurs a €2 million loss.

- By adding the profit over these two periods with the 'tit-for-tat' strategy, both P&G and Unilever make more profit by colluding (€10 million each compared with €8 million).

- If the cartel agreement ends in 2001–2003, the price falls and both firms have a profit of €2 million.

- The equilibrium of this game is to cooperate and collude, and that is what the firms did.

- But between 2001 and 2004, fears mounted that the agreement would be found out.

- Under the EU leniency rule, no fine is imposed on the first firm that confesses to being in a cartel. So there is an incentive to confess and be the first to do so.

- Unilever responded to this incentive. It ended the collusive agreement in 2004, started a price war, and reported the agreement to the competition authority.

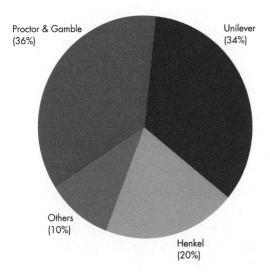

Proctor & Gamble (36%)

Unilever (34%)

Others (10%)

Henkel (20%)

Figure 1 Soap Powder Market Shares in France

Table 1				
Repeated Soap Powder Game				
	Collude		**Cheat with tit-for-tat**	
Period of play	P&G's profit	Unilever's profit	P&G's profit	Unilever's profit
	(millions of euros)		(millions of euros)	
1997–1998	5	5	10	−2
1999–2000	5	5	−2	10
2001–2003	5	5	2	2

SUMMARY

Key Points

What Is Oligopoly? (pp. 320–321)

◆ Oligopoly is a market in which a small number of firms compete.

Do Problems 1 to 3 to get a better understanding of what oligopoly is.

Oligopoly Games (pp. 322–329)

◆ Oligopoly is studied by using game theory, which is a method of analysing strategic behaviour.

◆ In a prisoners' dilemma game, two prisoners acting in their own self-interest harm their joint interest.

◆ An oligopoly (duopoly) price-fixing game is a prisoners' dilemma in which the firms might collude or cheat.

◆ In Nash equilibrium, both firms cheat and output and price are the same as in perfect competition.

◆ Firms' decisions about advertising and R&D can be studied by using game theory.

Do Problems 4 to 7 to get a better understanding of oligopoly games.

Repeated Games and Sequential Games (pp. 330–333)

◆ In a repeated game, a punishment strategy can produce a cooperative equilibrium in which price and output are the same as in monopoly.

◆ In a sequential contestable market game, a small number of firms can behave like firms in perfect competition.

Do Problem 8 to get a better understanding of repeated games and sequential games.

Antitrust Law (pp. 334–337)

◆ The UK antitrust regulations are based on European Union Treaty rules and United Kingdom Acts of Parliament.

◆ All price-fixing agreements are violations of EU and UK laws.

◆ Resale price maintenance might be efficient if it enables a producer to ensure the efficient level of service by distributors.

◆ Tying arrangements can enable a monopoly to price discriminate and increase profit, but in many cases tying would not increase profit.

◆ Predatory pricing is unlikely to occur because it brings losses and only temporary potential gains.

◆ The European Commission uses market turnover guidelines to determine whether there is a Community dimension on mergers to investigate and possibly block.

Do Problems 9 to 11 to get a better understanding of antitrust law.

Key Terms

Antitrust law, 334
Cartel, 321
Collusive agreement, 324
Contestable market, 332
Cooperative equilibrium, 330
Dominant-strategy equilibrium, 323
Duopoly, 320
Game theory, 322
Limit pricing, 333
Nash equilibrium, 323
Oligopoly, 320
Payoff matrix, 322
Predatory pricing, 336
Resale price maintenance, 335
Strategies, 322
Tying arrangement, 335

STUDY PLAN PROBLEMS AND APPLICATIONS

Do Problems 1 to 12 in MyEconLab Chapter 14 Study Plan and get instant feedback.

MyEconLab

What is Oligopoly? (Study Plan 14.1)

1 Two firms make most of the chips that power a PC: Intel and Advanced Micro Devices. What makes the market for PC chips a duopoly? Sketch the market demand curve and cost curves which describe the situation in this market and that prevent other firms from entering.

2 Sparks Fly for Energizer

Energizer is gaining market share against competitor Duracell and its profit is rising despite the sharp rise in the price of zinc, a key battery ingredient.

Source: www.businessweek.com, August 2007

In what type of market are batteries sold? Explain your answer.

3 Oil City

In the late 1990s, Reliance spent $6 billion to build a world-class oil refinery at Jamnagar, India. Now Reliance is more than doubling the size of the facility, which will make it the world's biggest producer of petrol – 1.2 million gallons of petrol per day, or about 5% of global capacity. Reliance plans to sell the petrol in Europe and in the US where it's too expensive and politically difficult to build new refineries. The bulked-up Jamnagar will be able to move the market and Singapore traders expect a drop in fuel prices as soon as it's going at full steam.

Source: *Fortune*, 28 April 2008

a Explain why the news clip claims that the global market for petrol is not perfectly competitive.

b What barriers to entry might limit competition in this market and give a firm like Reliance the power to influence the market price?

Oligopoly Games (Study Plan 14.2)

4 Consider a game with two players and in which each player is asked a question. The players can answer the question honestly or lie. If both answer honestly, each receives €100. If one answers honestly and the other lies, the liar receives €500 and the honest player gets nothing. If both lie, then each receives €50.

a Describe strategies and payoffs of this game.

b Construct the payoff matrix.

c What is the equilibrium of this game?

d Compare this game with the prisoners' dilemma. Are the two games similar or different? Explain your answer.

Use the following information in Problems 5 and 6.

Two firms, Soapy plc and Suddsies plc, are the only producers of soap powder. They collude and agree to share the market equally. If neither firm cheats on the agreement, each makes €1 million economic profit. If either firm cheats, the cheat makes an economic profit of €1.5 million while the complier incurs an economic loss of €0.5 million. If both cheat, they break even. Neither firm can monitor the other's actions.

5 a What are the strategies in this game?

b Construct the payoff matrix.

6 a What is the equilibrium if the game is played only once?

b Is the equilibrium a dominant-strategy equilibrium? Explain.

7 The World's Largest Airline

On 3 May 2010, United Airlines and Continental Airlines announced a $3 billion merger that would create the world's biggest airline. The deal was completed in a remarkably short three weeks, and would give the airlines the muscle to fend off low-cost rivals at home and to take on foreign carriers abroad. For consumers, the merger could eventually result in higher US prices although the new company does not intend to raise fares. One of the rationales for airline mergers is to cut capacity.

Source: *The New York Times*, 7 June 2010

a Explain how this airline merger might increase US air travel prices.

b Explain how this airline merger might lower air travel production costs.

c Explain how cost savings arising from a cut in capacity might get passed on to travellers and might boost producers' profits. Which do you predict will happen from this airline merger and why?

Repeated Games and Sequential Games (Study Plan 14.3)

8 If Soapy plc and Suddies plc repeatedly play the duopoly game that has the payoffs described in Problem 5, on each round of play:

   a What now are the strategies that each firm might adopt?

   b Can the firms adopt a strategy that gives the game a cooperative equilibrium?

   c Would one firm still be tempted to cheat in a cooperative equilibrium? Explain your answer.

Antitrust Law (Study Plan 14.4)

9 **Intel Fined €1.06 billion for Abuse of Dominant Position**

The European Commission has fined Intel €1.6 billion for abuse of a dominant market position (70% share). It used anti-competitive practices to exclude competitors from the computer chip market. The Commission found Intel gave hidden rebates to computer manufacturers who bought their chip exclusively, and made payments to retailers who only stocked computers with their chips. Intel also paid manufacturers to limit production of computers with their chips. The European Commission forced Intel to stop these payments and said it had limited competition and innovation and harmed EU consumers. The European market has a 30% share of the €22 billion world market for computer chips.

   Source: Europa Press Release, 13 May 2009

   a How do Intel's actions reduce competition in the European computer chip market?

   b Which aspects of EU antitrust laws have been breached?

10 **Animal Feed Producers Fined for Price Fixing and Market Sharing**.

The Commission fined producers of animal feed phosphates €175 million for creating a cartel operating for 30 years. The case began in 2003 when one firm applied for leniency. The cartel covered most of Europe and allocated market shares, sales quotas and shared customers as well as coordinated prices and sales conditions. It is a serious violation of Article 101 of the Treaty.

   Source: Europa Press Release, 20 July 2010

   a What types of anti-competitive practice did the cartel use?

   b What is the purpose of the leniency rule?

11 **Commission Agrees Acquisition of Arriva by Deutsche Bahn with Conditions**

The European Commission has allowed the incumbent German rail and bus operator Deutsche Bahn to buy the UK rail and bus operator Arriva plc. Arriva operates services across Europe and is one of the few competitors for Deutsche Bahn in the German market. The Commission is concerned that the acquisition will increase existing barriers to entry in the German market and has said that Deutsche Bahn must sell Arriva's German operations for the acquisition to go ahead.

   Source: Europa Press Release, 11 August 2010

   a Explain the guidelines for establishing a Community dimension for a merger or acquisition.

   b Why has the Commission imposed a condition on the merger?

Economics in the News (Study Plan 14.N)

12 **Commission Fines Wanadoo**

The Commission fined Wanadoo Interactive, a subsidiary of France Télécom, €10.4 million for predatory pricing in the market for ADSL-based Internet access services. Up to 2002, Wanadoo's retail prices were below cost to restrict market entry by competitors. Wanadoo deliberately suffered losses to increase its market share from 46 to 72 per cent in 2002 to get the biggest share of the booming market. One competitor went out of business and all others saw their shares fall to 10 per cent or less.

   Source: Europa Press Release, 16 July 2003

   a Explain how Wanadoo violated EU antitrust laws.

   b Explain why few firms use predatory pricing to permanently drive out competition.

   c What is the crucial evidence that Wanadoo engaged in predatory pricing?

   d Sketch a graph that shows the situation facing Wanadoo's competitor when it went out of business.

ADDITIONAL PROBLEMS AND APPLICATIONS

Do these problems in MyEconLab if assigned by your lecturer.

What is Oligopoly?

13 An Energy Drink with a Monster of a Stock

The $5.7 billion energy-drink category, in which Monster holds the No. 2 position behind industry leader Red Bull, has slowed down as copycat brands jostle for shelf space. Over the past five years Red Bull's market share in dollar terms has gone from 91 per cent to well under 50 per cent and much of that loss has been Monster's gain.

Source: *Fortune*, 25 December 2006

a Describe the structure of the energy-drink market. How has that structure changed over the past few years?

b If Monster and Red Bull formed a cartel, how would the price charged for energy drinks and the profits made change?

Oligopoly Games

Use the following information in Problems 14 and 15.

Black and Green are the only two producers of aniseed beer, a New Age product designed to displace ginger beer. Black and Green are trying to figure out how much of this new beer to produce. They know the following:

(i) If they both limit production to 10,000 litres a day, they will make the maximum attainable joint profit of £200,000 a day – £100,000 a day each.

(ii) If either firm produces 20,000 litres a day while the other produces 10,000 a day, the one that produces 20,000 litres will make an economic profit of £150,000 and the other one will incur an economic loss of £50,000.

(iii) If both increase production to 20,000 litres a day, each firm will make zero economic profit.

14 Construct a payoff matrix for the game that Black and Green must play.

15 Find the Nash equilibrium of the game that Black and Green play.

16 Asian Rice Exporters to Discuss Cartel

The rice-exporting nations Thailand, Cambodia, Laos, and Myanmar planned to discuss a proposal by Thailand, the world's largest rice exporter, that they form a cartel. Ahead of the meeting, the countries said that the purpose of the rice cartel would be to contribute to ensuring food stability, not just in an individual country but also to address food shortages in the region and the world. The cartel will not hoard rice and raise prices when there are shortages. The Philippines says that it is a bad idea. It will create an oligopoly, and the cartel could price the grain out of reach for millions of people.

Source: CNN, 6 May 2008

a Assuming the rice-exporting nations become a profit-maximising colluding oligopoly, explain how they would influence the global market for rice and the world price of rice.

b Assuming the rice-exporting nations become a profit-maximising colluding oligopoly, draw a graph to illustrate their influence on the global market for rice.

c Even in the absence of international antitrust laws, why might it be difficult for this cartel to collude successfully? Use the ideas of game theory to explain.

17 Suppose that Mozilla and Microsoft each develop their own versions of an amazing new Web browser that allows advertisers to target consumers with great precision. Also, the new browser is easier and more fun to use than existing browsers. Each firm is trying to decide whether to sell the browser or give it away. What are the likely benefits from each action? Which action is likely to occur?

18 Why do Coca-Cola and PepsiCo spend huge amounts on advertising? Do they benefit? Does the consumer benefit? Explain your answer by constructing a game to illustrate the choices Coca-Cola and PepsiCo make.

Use the following information in Problems 19 and 20.

Microsoft with Xbox 360, Nintendo with Wii, and Sony with PlayStation 3 are slugging it out in the market for the latest generation of video game consoles. Xbox 360 was the first to market; Wii has the lowest price; PS3 uses the most advanced technology and has the highest price.

19 a Thinking of the competition among these firms in the market for consoles as a game, describe the firms' strategies concerning design, marketing and price.

b What, based on the information provided, turned out to be the equilibrium of the game?

20 Can you think of reasons why the three consoles are so different?

Repeated Games and Sequential Games (Study Plan 14.3)

21 If Black and Green in Problem 15 play the game repeatedly, what is the equilibrium of the game?

22 Agile Airlines' profit on a route on which it has a monopoly is £10 million a year. Wanabe Airlines is considering entering the market and operating on this route. Agile warns Wanabe to stay out and threatens to cut the price so that if Wanabe enters it will make no profit. Wanabe determines that the payoff matrix for the game in which it is engaged with Agile is as shown in the table.

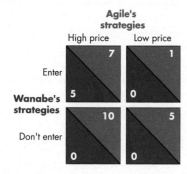

Does Wanabe believe Agile's assertion? Does Wanabe enter or not? Explain.

23 Oil Trading Probe May Uncover Manipulation

Amid soaring oil prices the Commodity Futures Trade Commission (CFTC) is looking into manipulation of the oil market – withholding oil in an attempt to drive prices higher. The CFTC has found such evidence in the past and it's likely it will find evidence again. But it is unlikely that a single player acting alone would be able to run the price up from $90 to $135.

Source: CNN, 30 May 2008

What type of market does the news clip imply best describes the US oil market?

Antitrust Law

Use the following news clip in Problems 24 and 25.

Commission Investigates IBM

The European Commission opened antitrust investigations against IBM Corporation for alleged breaches of EU antitrust rules related to the abuse of a dominant market position for mainframe computers. The mainframe market is worth €8.5 billion worldwide and €3 billion in Europe. Software developers complained that IBM ties mainframes to its operating system to limit competition by emulation software companies that could let users run critical applications on non-IBM hardware. The Commission also suspects IBM has engaged in discriminatory behaviour against mainframe maintenance companies, by limiting access to spare parts when IBM is the only source.

Source: Europa Press Release, 26 July 2010

24 **a** Describe the anti-competitive practice IBM is alleged to engage in.

b Which parts of EU antitrust law might IBM infringe and why?

25 What is meant by abuse of a dominant market position?

Economics in the News

26 After you have studied *Reading Between the Lines* on pp. 338–339, answer the following questions.

a Why is the decision for P&G and Unilever not like a prisoners' dilemma game with Nash equilibrium where both companies cheat?

b What is the incentive for P&G to start a price war after an initial agreement?

c What is the incentive for P&G to go back to the agreement after the price war is settled?

d Why do you think both P&G and Unilever settled for the monopoly agreement between 2000 and 2003 without another price war?

e Why did Unilever decide to break the agreement forever in 2004?

f What is the consequence for customers of a decision by soap powder manufacturers to act like a monopoly?

g What is the purpose of the EU leniency rule?

27 Boeing and Airbus Predict Asian Sales Surge

Airlines in the Asia-Pacific region are emerging as the biggest customers for aircraft makers Boeing and Airbus. The two firms predict that over the next 20 years, more than 8,000 planes worth up to $1.2 trillion will be sold there.

Source: BBC News, 3 February 2010

a In what type of market are big aeroplanes sold?

b Thinking of competition between Boeing and Airbus as a game, what are the strategies and the payoffs?

c Set out a hypothetical payoff matrix for the game you've described in part (b). What is the equilibrium of the game?

d Do you think the market for big aeroplanes is efficient? Explain and illustrate your answer.

15 Public Choices and Public Goods

After studying this chapter you will be able to:

◆ Explain why some choices are *public* choices and how these choices are made in the political marketplace

◆ Explain how the free-rider problem arises and how the quantity of public goods is determined

◆ Explain why goods with external benefits lead to inefficient underproduction and how public choices can achieve allocative efficiency

Flood rescue service, healthcare services and university research and education: governments are involved in all these activities. But why? Why don't we leave it to private firms to provide these items? Is government provision efficient, or is a public–private mix better?

These are the questions that we study in this chapter. In *Reading Between the Lines* at the end of the chapter, we compare the provision of healthcare services in the UK and US and discover some surprising numbers.

Public Choices

All economic choices are made by individuals, but some choices are *private* and some are *public*. A *private choice* is a decision that has consequences only for the person making it. Decisions to buy (demand) or to sell (supply) goods and services in competitive markets are examples of private choices. At the market equilibrium price these choices are consistent, and one person's decision to buy or sell a little bit more or a little bit less has an imperceptible effect on the outcome.

A **public choice** is a decision that has consequences for many people and perhaps for an entire society. Decisions by political leaders and senior public servants about price and quantity regulations, taxes, international trade policy and government spending are examples of public choices.

You studied the consequences of some public choices in Chapter 6, where you saw how price ceilings and price floors prevent voluntary exchanges even though marginal social benefit exceeds marginal social cost; you also saw how taxes drive a wedge between marginal social benefit and marginal social cost. In Chapter 7, you saw how tariffs and import quotas restrict international trade. All of these public choices result in scarce resources being used inefficiently – they create deadweight loss.

Why do governments do things that create inefficiency? Aren't they supposed to make things better? If governments make things worse, why do they exist? Why aren't the successful societies those that have no government? The economic theory of government explains both why governments exist and why they do a less-than-perfect job.

Why Governments Exist

Governments exist for three major reasons. First, they establish and maintain property rights. Second, they provide non-market mechanisms for allocating scarce resources. Third, they implement arrangements that redistribute income and wealth.

Property rights are the fundamental foundation of the market economy. By establishing property rights and the legal system that enforces them, governments enable markets to function. In many situations, markets function well and allocate scarce resources efficiently. But sometimes the market results in inefficiency – market failure (see Chapter 5, pp. 111–112).

When market failure occurs, too many of some things and too few of some other things are produced. Choices made in the pursuit of self-interest have not served the social interest. By reallocating resources, it is possible to make some people better off while making no one worse off.

The market economy also delivers a distribution of income and wealth that most people regard as unfair. Equity requires some redistribution.

Replacing markets with government resource-allocation decisions is no simple matter. Just as there can be market failure, there can also be government failure. **Government failure** is a situation in which government actions lead to inefficiency – to either underprovision or overprovision.

Government failure can arise because government is made up of many individuals, each with their own economic objectives. Public choices are the outcome of the choices made by these individuals. To analyse these choices, economists have developed a public choice theory of the political marketplace.

Public Choice and the Political Marketplace

Four groups of decision makers, shown in Figure 15.1, interact in the political marketplace. They are:

◆ Voters

◆ Firms

◆ Politicians

◆ Bureaucrats

Voters

Voters evaluate politicians' policy proposals, benefit from public goods and services, and pay some of the taxes. In the economic model of public choice, voters support the politicians whose policy proposals make them better off, and express their demand for public goods and services by voting, helping in political campaigns, lobbying and making campaign contributions.

Firms

Firms also evaluate politicians' policy proposals, benefit from public goods and services, and pay some of the taxes. Although firms don't vote, they do make campaign contributions and are a major source of funds for political parties. Firms also engage in lobbying to persuade politicians to propose policies that benefit them.

Politicians

Politicians are the elected persons in the EU, national and local governments – from the President of the EU parliament to your local council. Politicians at all levels

Figure 15.1 The Political Marketplace

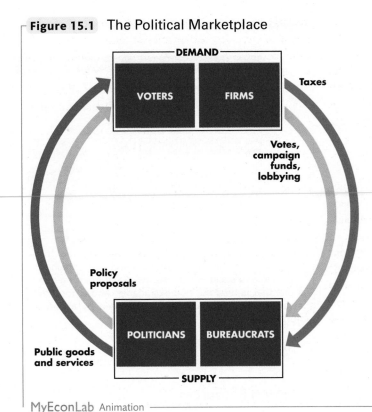

Voters express their demand for policies with their votes.

Voters and firms express their demand for policies with campaign contributions and by lobbying.

Politicians express their supply of policies with proposals that they hope will attract enough votes to get them elected and keep them in office. Politicians also set the taxes paid by voters and firms.

Bureaucrats provide public goods and services and try to get the largest possible budget for their departments.

A political equilibrium balances all these public choices.

MyEconLab Animation

---

form coalitions – political parties – to develop policy proposals, which they present to voters in the hope of attracting majority support. Politicians also direct bureaucrats in the delivery of public goods and services and other policy actions. The goal of a politician is to get elected and to remain in office. Votes, to a politician, are like profit to a firm.

Bureaucrats

Bureaucrats are the public servants who work in government departments. They administer tax collection, the delivery of public goods and services, and the administration of rules and regulations.

The self-interest of a bureaucrat is best served when the budget of her or his department is maximised. The bigger the budget of a department, the greater is the prestige of its chief and the greater are the opportunities for promotion for people further down the bureaucratic ladder. So all the members of a department have an interest in maximising the department's budget. This economic assumption does not imply that bureaucrats do a poor job. Rather it implies that, in doing what they perceive to be a good job, they take care of their own self-interest too.

Political Equilibrium

Voters, firms, politicians and bureaucrats make their economic choices to achieve their own self-interest. Public choices, like private choices, are constrained by what is feasible. Each person's public choices are also constrained by the public choices of others.

The balance of forces in the political marketplace determines the outcome of all the public choices that people make. In a **political equilibrium** the choices of voters, firms, politicians and bureaucrats are all compatible, and no group can see a way of improving its position by making a different choice.

Ideally, the political equilibrium will achieve allocative efficiency and serve the social interest, but such an outcome is not guaranteed, as you'll see later in this chapter.

We make public choices because some situations just don't permit private choices. The core of the reason why we can't always make private choices is that some goods and services (and some factors of production) have a public nature – they are *public* goods and services.

Your next task is to see exactly what we mean by a *public* good or service.

What is a Public Good?

To see what makes a good a *public* good, we distinguish two features of all goods: the extent to which people can be *excluded* from consuming them and the extent to which one person's consumption *rivals* someone else's consumption.

Excludable

A good is **excludable** if it is possible to prevent someone from enjoying its benefits. Brink's security services, Peterhead Seafood's fish and a U2 concert are examples. You must pay to benefit from them.

A good is **non-excludable** if everyone benefits from it regardless of whether they pay for it. The services of the London Metropolitan Police, fish in the North Sea and a concert on network television are examples. When police enforce the speed limit, everyone on the road benefits; anyone with a boat can fish in the ocean; and anyone with a TV can watch a network broadcast.

Rival

A good is **rival** if one person's use decreases the quantity available for someone else. A Brink's truck can't deliver cash to two banks at the same time. A fish can be consumed only once. And one seat at a concert can hold only one person at a time. These items are rival.

A good is **non-rival** if one person's use does not decrease the quantity available for someone else. The services of the police and a concert on network television are non-rival.

A Fourfold Classification

Figure 15.2 classifies goods, services and resources into four types.

Private Goods

A **private good** is both rival and excludable. A can of cola and a fish on Peterhead Seafood's farm are examples of private goods.

Public Goods

A **public good** is both non-rival and non-excludable. A public good simultaneously benefits everyone, and no one can be excluded from enjoying its benefits. National defence is the best example of a public good.

Figure 15.2   Fourfold Classification of Goods

	Private goods	Common resources
Rival	Food and drink Car House	Fish in ocean Atmosphere City parks
	Natural monopoly goods	**Public goods**
Non-rival	Internet Cable television Bridge or tunnel	National defence The law Air traffic control
	Excludable	**Non-excludable**

A private good is one that is rival and excludable. A public good is one that is non-rival and from which it is impossible to exclude a consumer. A common resource is one that is rival but non-excludable. And a good that is non-rival but excludable is produced by a natural monopoly.

MyEconLab Animation ────────────────◆

Common Resources

A **common resource** is rival and non-excludable. A unit of a common resource can be used only once, but no one can be prevented from using what is available. Ocean fish are a common resource. They are rival because a fish taken by one person isn't available for anyone else, and they are non-excludable because it is difficult to prevent people from catching them.

Natural Monopoly Goods

A **natural monopoly good** is non-rival and excludable. When buyers can be excluded if they don't pay but the good is non-rival, marginal cost is zero. The fixed cost of producing such a good is usually high, so economies of scale exist over the entire range of output for which there is a demand (see Chapter 12, p. 276). An iTunes song and satellite television are examples.

Mixed Goods

Some goods don't fit neatly into the above four-fold classification. They are mixed goods. A **mixed good** is a private good the production or consumption of which creates an externality. An **externality** is a cost (external cost) or a benefit (external benefit) that arises from the production or consumption of a private good and which falls on someone other than its producer or consumer.

ECONOMICS IN ACTION

Is a Lighthouse a Public Good?

This lighthouse, built on Flamborough Head in 1806, protects ships from hitting the rocks off the North Yorkshire coast.

For two centuries, economists considered the lighthouse to be an example of a public good. No one can be prevented from seeing its warning light – *non-excludable* – and one person seeing its light doesn't prevent someone else from seeing it too – *non-rival*.

Ronald Coase, who won the 1991 Nobel Prize in economic sciences for ideas he first developed when he was an undergraduate at the London School of Economics, discovered that before the nineteenth century, lighthouses in England were built and operated by private companies that earned profits by charging tolls on ships docking at nearby ports. A ship that refused to pay the lighthouse toll was *excluded* from the port.

So the benefit arising from the services of a lighthouse is *excludable*. Because the services provided by a lighthouse are non-rival but excludable, a lighthouse is an example of a natural monopoly good and not a public good.

Mixed Goods with External Benefits

Two of the things that have the greatest impact on your welfare, your education and healthcare, are mixed goods with external benefits.

Think about a childhood measles vaccination. It is *excludable* because it would be possible to sell vaccinations and exclude those not willing to pay from benefiting from them. A measles vaccination is also *rival* because providing one person with a vaccination means one fewer available for everyone else. A vaccination is a private good, but it creates an externality.

If a parent decides to vaccinate a child, the child benefits from a lower risk of infection from a dangerous disease. But if the child does not get infected, other children who didn't get vaccinated have a better chance of avoiding measles too. A vaccination brings a benefit to others, so it is a *mixed good* with an external benefit.

The external benefit of a measles vaccination is like a public good. It is non-excludable because everyone with whom your child comes into contact can benefit. You can't selectively benefit only your friends! And it is non-rival – protecting one child from measles does not diminish the protection for others.

Education is another example of a mixed good with external benefits. If all education was organised by private schools and universities, those not willing or able to pay would be excluded, and one person's place in a class would rival another's. So education is a private good.

Your education brings benefits to others. It brings benefits to your friends who enjoy your sharp, educated wit, and it brings benefits to the community in which you live because well-educated people with a strong sense of community and responsibility towards others make good neighbours. These external benefits are like a public good. You can't selectively decide who benefits from your good community spirit, and one person's enjoyment of your good behaviour doesn't rival someone else's. So education is a mixed good with an external benefit.

Mixed Goods with External Costs

Mixed goods with external costs have become a huge political issue in recent years. The main ones are electricity and transport (road, rail and air) produced by burning hydrocarbon fuels – coal, oil and natural gas.

Electricity and transport are excludable and rival – they are private goods. But when you use electricity or travel by car, bus, train or aeroplane, carbon dioxide and other chemicals pour into the atmosphere. This consequence of consuming a private good creates an external cost and is a public bad. (A 'bad' is the opposite of a good.) No one can be excluded from bearing the external cost, and one person's discomfort doesn't rival another's. Electricity and transport are mixed goods with external costs.

Other private goods that generate external costs include logging and the clearing of forests, which destroy the habitat of wildlife and influence the amount of carbon dioxide in the atmosphere; smoking cigarettes in a confined space, which imposes a health risk on others; and driving under the influence of alcohol, which increases the risk of accident and injury for others.

Inefficiencies that Require Public Choices

Public goods, mixed goods, common resources and natural monopoly goods all create inefficiency problems that require public choices. Public choices must be made to:

◆ Provide public goods and mixed goods

◆ Conserve common resources

◆ Regulate natural monopoly

Provide Public Goods and Mixed Goods

Because no one can be excluded from enjoying the benefits of a public good, no one has an incentive to pay for their share of it. Even people with a social conscience have no incentive to pay because one person's enjoyment of a public good doesn't lower the enjoyment of others – it is non-rival.

If private firms tried to produce and sell public goods to consumers, they wouldn't remain in business for very long. The market economy would fail to deliver the efficient quantity of those goods. For example, there would be too little national defence, police services and law enforcement, courts and judges, storm-water and sewage disposal services.

Mixed goods pose a less extreme problem. The market economy would underprovide mixed goods with external benefits because their producers and consumers don't take the external benefits into account when they make their own choices. The market economy would overprovide mixed goods with external costs because

their producers and consumers don't take the external costs into account when they make their own choices.

Conserve Common Resources

Because no one can be excluded from enjoying the benefits of a common resource, no one has an incentive to pay for their share of it or to conserve the common resource for future enjoyment.

If boat owners are left to catch as much cod as they wish, the stock will deplete and eventually the species will vanish. The market economy would overproduce cod for sale while stocks lasted and then underproduce as stocks ran out.

This problem, called the *tragedy of the commons*, requires public choices to limit the overuse and eventual destruction of common resources.

Regulate Natural Monopoly

When people can be excluded from enjoying the benefits of a good if they don't pay for it, and when the good is non-rival, the marginal cost of producing it is zero. A natural monopoly can produce such a good at the lowest cost. But as Chapter 12 explains, when one firm serves a market, that firm maximises profit by producing too little of the good.

 REVIEW QUIZ

1　List three main reasons why governments exist.
2　Describe the political marketplace. Who demands, who supplies and what is the political equilibrium?
3　Distinguish among public goods, private goods, common resources, natural monopoly goods and mixed goods.
4　What are the problems that arise from public goods, common resources, natural monopoly goods and mixed goods?

Do these questions in Study Plan 15.1 and get instant feedback.　　MyEconLab

You studied the regulation of natural monopoly in Chapter 12. This chapter and the next one study the other two public choices that must be made. In this chapter, we'll focus on the underprovision of public goods and mixed goods with external benefits. Chapter 16 studies mixed goods with external costs and conserving common resources.

Providing Public Goods

Why do governments provide flood rescue services? Why don't the people of Cornwall buy flood rescue services from a private firm – Flashflood – that competes for our pounds and euros in the marketplace in the same way that Costa Coffee does? The answer is that flood rescue is a public good. It is non-excludable and non-rival, and it has a free-rider problem.

The Free-Rider Problem

A free rider enjoys the benefits of a good or service without paying for it. Because a public good is provided for everyone to use and no one can be excluded from its benefits, no one has an incentive to pay his or her share of the cost. Everyone has an incentive to free-ride. The **free-rider problem** is that the economy would provide an inefficiently small quantity of a public good. Marginal social benefit from the public good would exceed its marginal social cost and a deadweight loss would arise.

Let's look at the marginal social benefit and marginal social cost of a public good.

Marginal Social Benefit from a Public Good

Lisa and Max (the only people in a society) value flood rescue helicopters. Figures 15.3(a) and 15.3(b) graph their marginal benefits from the helicopters as MB_L for Lisa and MB_M for Max. The marginal benefit from a public good (like that from a private good) diminishes as the quantity of the good increases.

Figure 15.3(c) shows the marginal *social* benefit curve, *MSB*. Because everyone gets the same quantity of a public good, its marginal social benefit curve is the sum of the marginal benefits of all the individuals at each *quantity* – it is the *vertical* sum of the individual marginal benefit curves. So the curve *MSB* is the marginal social benefit curve for the economy made up of Lisa and Max. For each helicopter, Lisa's marginal benefit is added to Max's marginal benefit to calculate the marginal social benefit from that helicopter.

Contrast the *MSB* curve for a public good with that of a private good. To obtain the economy's *MSB* curve for a private good, we sum the *quantities demanded* by all the individuals in the economy at each price – we sum the individual marginal benefit curves *horizontally* (see Chapter 5, pp. 106–107).

Figure 15.3   Benefits of a Public Good

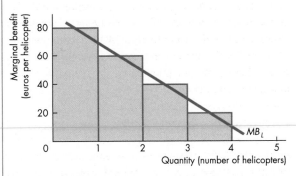

(a) Lisa's marginal benefit

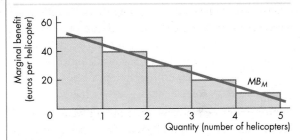

(b) Max's marginal benefit

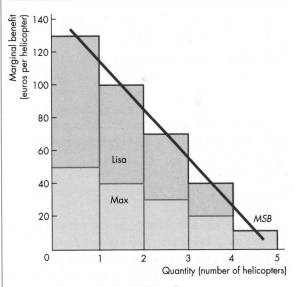

(c) Economy's marginal social benefit

The marginal social benefit at each quantity of the public good is the sum of the marginal benefits of all individuals in the economy. The marginal benefit curves are MB_L for Lisa and MB_M for Max. The economy's marginal social benefit curve is *MSB*.

MyEconLab Animation ———————————◆

Marginal Social Cost of a Public Good

The marginal social cost of a public good is determined in exactly the same way as that of a private good – see Chapter 5, p. 108. The principle of increasing marginal cost applies to the marginal cost of a public good, so the marginal social cost increases as the quantity of the public good increases.

Efficient Quantity of a Public Good

To determine the efficient quantity of a public good, we use the principles that you learned in Chapter 5. The efficient quantity is that at which marginal social benefit equals marginal social cost. Figure 15.4 shows the marginal social benefit curve, *MSB*, and the marginal social cost curve, *MSC*, for flood rescue helicopters. (We'll now think of society as consisting of Lisa and Max and the other 360 million Europeans.)

If marginal social benefit exceeds marginal social cost, as it does with 2 helicopters, resources can be used more efficiently by increasing the number of helicopters. The extra benefit exceeds the extra cost. If marginal social cost exceeds marginal social benefit, as it does with 4 helicopters, resources can be used more efficiently by decreasing the number of helicopters. The cost saving exceeds the loss of benefit.

If marginal social benefit equals marginal social cost, as it does with 3 helicopters, resources are allocated efficiently. Resources cannot be used more efficiently because to provide more than 3 helicopters increases cost by more than the extra benefit, and to provide fewer than 3 helicopters lowers the benefit by more than the cost saving.

Inefficient Private Provision

Could a private firm – Flashflood – deliver the efficient quantity of flood rescue helicopters? Most likely it couldn't, because no one would have an incentive to buy his or her share of the helicopters. Everyone would reason as follows: the number of helicopters provided by Flashflood is not affected by my decision to pay my share or not. But my own private consumption will be greater if I free-ride and do not pay my share of the cost of the helicopters. If I don't pay, I enjoy the same level of flood rescue and I can buy more private goods. I will spend my money on private goods and free-ride on flood rescue. Such reasoning is the free-rider problem. If everyone reasons the same way, Flashflood has no

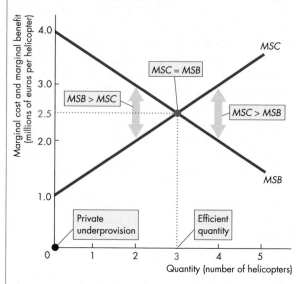

Figure 15.4 The Efficient Quantity of a Public Good

With fewer than 3 helicopters, marginal social benefit, *MSB*, exceeds marginal social cost, *MSC*. With more than 3 helicopters, *MSC* exceeds *MSB*. Only with 3 helicopters is *MSC* equal to *MSB* and the number of helicopters is efficient.

MyEconLab Animation ——————————————————◆

revenue and so provides no helicopters. Because the efficient number of helicopters is 3, private provision is inefficient.

Efficient Public Provision

The outcome of the political process might be efficient or inefficient. We look first at an efficient outcome. There are two political parties: Fears and Hopes. They agree on all issues except the number of flood rescue helicopters: the Fears want 4, and the Hopes want 2. Both parties want to get elected, so they run a voter survey and discover the marginal social benefit curve of Figure 15.5. They also consult with helicopter producers to establish their marginal cost and the marginal social cost curve. The parties then do a 'what-if' analysis. If the Fears propose 4 helicopters and the Hopes propose 2, the voters will be equally unhappy with both parties. Compared with the efficient quantity, the Hopes want an underprovision of 1 helicopter and the Fears want an overprovision of 1 helicopter. The deadweight losses are equal, and the election would be too close to call.

Contemplating this outcome, the Fears realise that they are too fearful to get elected. They figure that, if they scale back to 3 helicopters, they will win the election if the Hopes stick with 2. The Hopes reason in a similar way and figure that, if they increase the number of helicopters to 3, they can win the election if the Fears propose 4.

So they both propose 3 helicopters. The voters are indifferent between the parties, and each party receives 50 per cent of the vote. But regardless of which party wins the election, 3 helicopters are provided, and this quantity is efficient. Competition in the political place results in the efficient provision of a public good.

The Principle of Minimum Differentiation

The **principle of minimum differentiation** is the tendency for competitors to make themselves similar to appeal to the maximum number of clients or voters. This principle not only describes the behaviour of political parties, but also explains why fast-food restaurants cluster in the same block. For example, if Dominos' opens a new pizza outlet, it is likely that Pizza Express will soon open nearby.

Figure 15.5 An Efficient Political Outcome

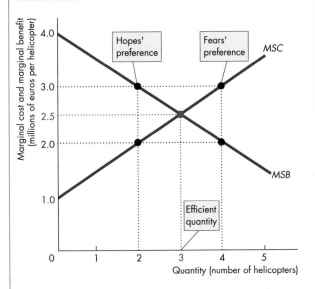

The Hopes would like to provide 2 helicopters and the Fears would like to provide 4 helicopters. The political outcome is 3 helicopters because unless each party proposes 3 helicopters, the other party will beat it in an election.

MyEconLab Animation ───────────── ◆

 ECONOMICS IN ACTION

Public Provision Without Public Production: Private Prison Services

Prisons are an example of a public good. Their benefits are enjoyed by all citizens (*non-excludable*), and one person's enjoyment of living in a safer society doesn't detract from the enjoyment of others (*non-rival*).

The cost of the UK prison system is large. In 2009, keeping a population of 85,000 people in prison cost £3.98 billion, or almost £47,000 per prisoner.

As a public good, the UK's prisons are provided by government and paid for with tax revenues. And traditionally, government ran the prisons. But while governments must *provide* and pay for prison services, they don't have to *produce* those services.

Today in the UK, many prisons are private. The first private prisons run by three firms, Sodexo, Serco and G4S, opened in 1990.

Sodexo, Serco and G4S employ and train prison staff and produce prison services to maximise profit. And that is the benefit of private production. To maximise profit, these firms must produce prison services at the lowest possible cost.

If Sodexo tried to sell its services to each individual home, it wouldn't get enough revenue to remain in business. There would be a free-rider problem. The free-rider problem is avoided because the UK government buys the prison services from private producers – government is the *provider* of this public good and Sodexo and others are the *producers*.

For the political process to deliver the efficient outcome, voters must be well informed, evaluate the alternatives and vote in the election. Political parties must be well informed about voter preferences. As the next section shows, we can't expect to achieve this outcome.

Inefficient Public Overprovision

If competition between two political parties is to deliver the efficient quantity of a public good, bureaucrats must cooperate and help to achieve this outcome. But bureaucrats might have a different idea and end up frustrating rather than facilitating an efficient outcome. Their actions might bring government failure.

Objective of Bureaucrats

Bureaucrats want to maximise their department's budget because a bigger budget brings greater status and more power. So the Emergency Services Department's objective is to maximise the budget for flood rescue helicopters. Figure 15.6 shows the outcome if the bureaucrats are successful in the pursuit of their goal. They might try to persuade the politicians that 3 helicopters cost more than the originally budgeted amount; or they might press their position more strongly and argue for more than 3 helicopters.

In Figure 15.6, the Emergency Services Department persuades the politicians to provide 4 helicopters. Why don't the politicians block the bureaucrats? Won't overprovision of helicopters cost future votes? It will if voters are well informed and know what is best for them. But voters might not be well informed, and well-informed interest groups might enable the bureaucrats to achieve their objective and overcome the objections of the politicians.

Rational Ignorance

A principle of the economic analysis of public choices is that it is rational for a voter to be ignorant about an issue unless that issue has a perceptible effect on the voter's economic welfare. Each voter knows that he or she can make virtually no difference to the flood rescue policy of the UK government and that it would take an enormous amount of time and effort to become even moderately well informed about alternative flood rescue technologies. Rationally uninformed voters enable bureaucrats and special interest groups to overprovide public goods.

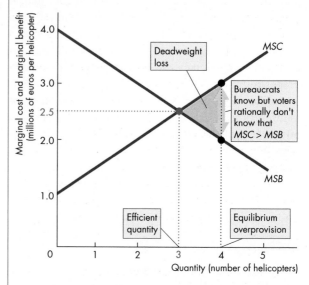

Figure 15.6   Bureaucratic Overprovision

Well-informed bureaucrats want to maximise their budget, and rationally ignorant voters enable the bureaucrats to go some way towards achieving their goal. A public good might be inefficiently overprovided with a deadweight loss.

MyEconLab Animation ──────────────◆

REVIEW QUIZ

1   What is the free-rider problem? Why do free riders make the private provision of a public good inefficient?
2   Under what conditions will competition among politicians for votes result in an efficient quantity of a public good?
3   How do rationally ignorant voters and budget-maximising bureaucrats prevent competition in the political marketplace from delivering the efficient quantity of a public good?
4   Explain why public choices might lead to the overprovision rather than the underprovision of a public good.

Do these questions in Study Plan 15.2 and get instant feedback.   MyEconLab

You've seen how the political marketplace provides public goods and why it might overprovide them. Your next task is to see how the political marketplace provides mixed goods that bring external benefits.

Positive Externalities: Education and Healthcare

Most of the goods and services provided by governments are *mixed* goods, not *public* goods. Two of the largest mixed goods are education and healthcare. These goods have *external benefits*. We're going to see how governments operate in such markets. We're also going to examine suggested improvements on the current arrangements in these markets.

To keep our explanation clear, we'll focus first on the market for university education. We'll then apply the lessons we learn to the market for healthcare.

We begin our study of the provision of mixed goods by defining positive externalities.

Positive Externalities

A **positive externality** arises when the social benefit exceeds the private benefit.

A *private benefit* is a benefit that the consumer of a good or service receives. For example, expanded job opportunities and a higher income are private benefits of a university education. *Marginal benefit* is the benefit from an additional unit of a good or service.

So **marginal private benefit** (*MB*) is the benefit that the consumer of a good or service receives from an additional unit of it. When one additional student attends university, the benefit that student receives is the marginal private benefit from university education.

The *external benefit* from a good or service is the benefit that someone other than the consumer of the good or service receives. University graduates generate many external benefits. On average, they are better citizens, have lower crime rates, and are more tolerant of the views of others. They enable the success of high-quality newspapers and television channels, music, theatre and other organised social activities that bring benefits to many other people.

A **marginal external benefit** is the benefit from an additional unit of a good or service that people *other than its consumer* enjoy. The benefit that your friends and neighbours get from your university education is the marginal external benefit of your university education.

Marginal social benefit (*MSB*) is the marginal benefit enjoyed by society – by the consumer of a good or service (marginal private benefit) and by others (the marginal external benefit). That is,

$$MSB = MB + \text{Marginal external benefit}$$

Figure 15.7 shows an example of the relationship between marginal private benefit, marginal external benefit and marginal social benefit. The marginal benefit curve, *MB*, describes the marginal private benefit enjoyed by the people who receive a university education. Marginal private benefit decreases as the number of students attending university increases.

In the example in Figure 15.7, when 15 million students attend university, the marginal external benefit is €15,000 per student per year. The marginal social benefit curve, *MSB*, is the sum of marginal private benefit and marginal external benefit at each number of students. For example, when 15 million students a year attend university, the marginal private benefit is €10,000 per student and the marginal external benefit is €15,000 per student, so the marginal social benefit is €25,000 per student.

When people make schooling decisions, they ignore its external benefits and consider only its private benefits. So if education were provided by private profit-maximising firms that charged full-cost tuition, there would be too few university graduates.

Figure 15.7 An External Benefit

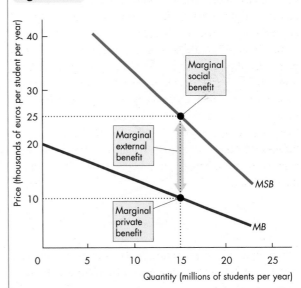

The *MB* curve shows the marginal private benefit enjoyed by the people who receive a university education. The *MSB* curve shows the sum of marginal private benefit and marginal external benefit. When 15 million students attend university, the marginal private benefit is €10,000 per student, the marginal external benefit is €15,000 per student, and the marginal social benefit is €25,000 per student.

MyEconLab Animation ——————————◆

Figure 15.8 illustrates this private underprovision. The supply curve is the marginal social cost curve, $S = MSC$. The demand curve is the marginal private benefit curve, $D = MB$. Market equilibrium occurs at a tuition of €15,000 per student per year and 7.5 million students per year. At this equilibrium, the marginal social benefit of €38,000 per student exceeds the marginal social cost by €23,000 per student. Too few students attend university. The efficient number of students is 15 million per year, where marginal social benefit equals marginal social cost. The grey triangle shows the deadweight loss created.

To get closer to producing the efficient quantity of a mixed good with an external benefit, we make public choices.

Public Choices

To encourage more students to attend university – to achieve an efficient quantity of university education –

students must be confronted with a lower price, and taxpayers must somehow pay for the costs not covered by what the student pays.

Figure 15.9 illustrates an efficient outcome. With the marginal social cost curve MSC and the marginal social benefit curve MSB, the efficient number of university students is 15 million per year. The marginal *private* benefit curve MB tells us that 15 million students will attend university only if the price is €10,000 per year. But the marginal social cost of 15 million students is €25,000 per year. To enable the marginal social cost to be paid, taxpayers must pay the balance of €15,000 per student per year.

Three devices that governments can use to achieve a more efficient allocation of resources in the presence of external benefits are:

◆ Public production

◆ Private subsidies

◆ Vouchers

Figure 15.8 Inefficiency with an External Benefit

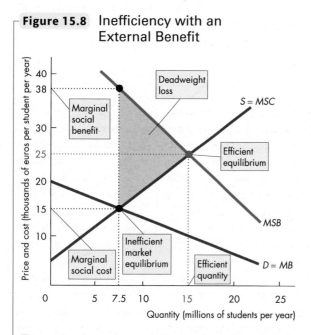

The market demand curve is the marginal private benefit curve, $D = MB$. The supply curve is the marginal social cost curve, $S = MSC$. Market equilibrium at a price of €15,000 a year and 7.5 million students is inefficient because marginal social benefit exceeds marginal social cost. The efficient quantity is 15 million students. A deadweight loss arises (grey triangle) because too few students attend university.

Figure 15.9 An Efficient Outcome with an External Benefit

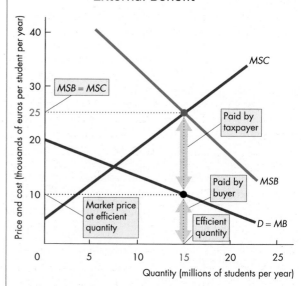

The efficient number of university students is 15 million per year, where marginal social benefit equals marginal social cost. With the demand and marginal private benefit curve, $D = MB$, the price at which the efficient number will attend is €10,000 per year. If students pay this price, the taxpayer must somehow pay the rest, which equals the marginal external cost at the efficient quantity – €15,000 per student per year.

Public Production

With **public production**, a good or service is produced by a public authority that receives its revenue from the government. The education services produced by state universities and state schools are examples of public production.

In the example in Figure 15.9, efficient public production occurs if state universities receive funds from government equal to €15,000 per student per year, charge €10,000 per student per year, and 15 million students attend university.

Private Subsidies

A **subsidy** is a payment that the government makes to private producers. By making the subsidy depend on the level of output, the government can induce private decision-makers to consider external benefits when they make their choices.

In the example in Figure 15.9, efficient private provision would occur if private universities received a government subsidy of €15,000 per student per year. This subsidy reduces the universities' costs and would make their marginal cost equal to €10,000 per student at the efficient quantity. A price of €10,000 per year would cover this cost, and the subsidy of €15,000 per student would cover the balance of the cost.

Vouchers

A **voucher** is a token that the government provides to households, which they can use to buy specified goods or services. Food stamps are examples of vouchers. The vouchers (food stamps) can be spent only on food and are designed to improve the diet and health of extremely poor families.

School vouchers are used in Sweden and have been advocated as a means of improving the quality of the UK secondary school system. A school voucher allows parents to choose the school their children will attend and use the voucher to pay part of the cost. The school cashes the vouchers to pay its bills. A voucher could be provided to a university student in a similar way, and although technically not a voucher, UK local authority fee payments for university students have a similar effect.

Because vouchers can be spent only on a specified item, they increase the willingness to pay for that item and so increase the demand for it.

Efficient provision of university education occurs if the government provides a voucher to each student with a value equal to the marginal external benefit at the efficient number of students. In the example in Figure 15.9, the efficient number of students is 15 million per year and the voucher is valued at €15,000 per student. Each student pays €10,000 and gives the university a €15,000 voucher. The universities receive €25,000 per student, which equals their marginal cost.

Bureaucratic Inefficiency and Government Failure

You've seen three government actions that achieve an efficient provision of a mixed good with an external benefit. In each case, if the government estimates the marginal external benefit correctly and makes marginal social benefit equal to marginal social cost, the outcome is efficient.

Does the comparison that we've just made mean that public provision, subsidised private provision and vouchers are equivalent? It does not. The reason lies in something that you've already encountered in your study of public goods earlier in this chapter – the behaviour of bureaucrats combined with rational ignorance that leads to government failure.

The Problem with Public Production

State universities (and schools) are operated by a bureaucracy and are subject to the same problems as the provision of public goods. If bureaucrats seek to maximise their budgets, the outcome might be inefficient. But *overprovision* of universities (and schools) doesn't seem to be a problem. Just the opposite: people complain about *underprovision* – about inadequate university places and schools. One reason is that there is another type of bureaucratic budget maximisation: budget padding and waste.

Bureaucrats often incur costs that exceed the minimum efficient cost. They might hire more assistants than the number needed to do their work efficiently; give themselves sumptuous offices; get generous expense allowances; or build schools in the wrong places where land costs are too high.

Economists have studied the possibility that bureaucrats pad their budgets by comparing the production costs of private and US state universities and schools. They have found that the costs per student of US state schools are of the order of *three times* the costs of comparable private schools.

Problems with Private Subsidies

Subsidising private producers might overcome some of the problems created by public production. A private producer has an incentive to produce at minimum cost and avoid the budget padding of a bureaucratic producer. But two problems arise with private subsidies.

First, it is in the self-interest of the bureaucrats who administer the subsidies to maximise their own budget, a problem similar to that of public production. Second, it is in the self-interest of subsidised producers to lobby for a subsidy that brings overprovision.

So subsidised private provision is likely to be inefficient. What about the third method: vouchers?

Are Education Vouchers the Solution?

Education vouchers have three advantages over the other two approaches. First, they can be used with public production, private provision or competition between the two. Second, governments can set the total voucher budget to overcome bureaucratic overprovision and budget padding. Third, vouchers force producers to compete and provide a high standard of service at the lowest attainable cost.

For these reasons, vouchers are popular with economists, but they are controversial and opposed by most education administrators and teachers. Vouchers have been used in the UK for nursery education, and currently there is debate about introducing vouchers for secondary education.

Healthcare Services

Healthcare is another mixed good with external benefits. These external benefits include avoiding infectious diseases; living and working with healthy neighbours; and living in a society that cares for the sick and the poor and provides them with affordable healthcare.

Because of the external benefits that healthcare brings, no country leaves its delivery entirely to the private market economy. Most countries have both private and public healthcare providers.

Private healthcare is delivered in two sets of markets: one for health insurance and one for healthcare services. People buy health insurance from private insurance companies and healthcare services from private doctors, nurses and hospitals. They pay for these services and get some reimbursement from their health insurer.

In the public healthcare sector, services are provided at a zero price, and doctors, nurses and hospitals receive their incomes from the government.

 ECONOMICS IN ACTION

Vouchers for Glasses

When the UK National Health Service (NHS) began in 1948 it provided (among other things) free eye testing and glasses. But NHS glasses were not the latest fashion statement, and they became a mark of low income.

To resolve this problem, vouchers for glasses were introduced. Children, pensioners and low-income adults receive vouchers for glasses with a free eye test. In 2009, 21 per cent of adults were eligible for vouchers ranging in value from £36 to £182.

The voucher system removed the stigma associated with NHS glasses and allowed the growth of competitive low-cost optician services. In 2009 consumers spent £2.65 billion on optical services. Private opticians accounted for 41 per cent of the market and vouchers paid for 31 per cent of all glasses dispensed.

Source of data: Optical Goods and Eye Care 2010, Mintel.

Which is more efficient and which provides the best quality of care: public or private? And does spending more and encouraging competition among healthcare providers bring improved quality?

Economics in Action (above) suggests that public healthcare can be both efficient and of high quality. And *At Issue* (opposite) notes some evidence that competition *within* the public sector can be efficient.

REVIEW QUIZ

1 What is special about education and healthcare that makes them mixed goods with external benefits?

2 Why would the market economy produce too little education and healthcare?

3 How might public production, private subsidies and vouchers achieve an efficient provision of a mixed good with external benefits?

4 What are the key differences among public production, private subsidies and vouchers?

You can work these questions in Study Plan 15.3 and get instant feedback.   MyEconLab

Reading Between the Lines on pp. 360–361 compares healthcare in the UK and the US and reinforces the conclusion that public choices improve health outcomes.

AT ISSUE

Can Decentralisation and Competition Contain Costs and Maintain a High-Quality National Health Service?

Healthcare costs are rising faster than the average of other prices and are taking an ever-increasing percentage of government expenditure. With an ageing population and an ongoing expansion of the range of conditions that can be successfully treated, no end to this process is in sight. Are decentralisation and competition the solution?

The UK Government: Yes

◆ The UK government thinks the solution lies in fixing the budget, placing its administration at arm's length from government, decentralising budgets and spending decisions and encouraging.

◆ The Health and Social Care Act 2012 seeks to impement these ideas in the following ways:

Groups of GPs and other medical professionals forming 240 clinical commissioning groups get fixed budgets to spend on the healthcare of their local communities.

The aggregate healthcare budget is managed by a new, politically independent national board.

A watchdog guards against 'anti-competitive' practices that raise prices and costs.

Health and Wellbeing Boards integrate health and social services for the elderly to better target spending.

Competition is encouraged among public providers and between public and private providers.

The Doctors: No

◆ A survey found that the vast majority of members of the Royal College of Physicians oppose the 2012 Act.

◆ Doctors who oppose the new arrangements say:

They are bad for the country's health and healthcare.

They will result in greater inequalities in access to quality care.

They will increase NHS waiting times and force more patients into private care.

The Economists: It's More Complicated

◆ Economists agree that hard budget constraints are essential, but economists like to examine evidence, and they emphasise the effects of incentives and substitution possibilities.

◆ A team at the London School of Economics* say that average length of stay (LOS) for patients undergoing elective surgery is a good measure of hospital efficiency.

◆ They looked at the effects of reforms from 2006 onwards that forced competition among public hospitals and between private public hospitals, and they discovered that for patients undergoing elective surgery competition among public providers decreases pre-surgery and post-surgery LOS, but competition with private hospitals sends harder-to-treat patients to public hospitals (a substitution effect), which increases post-surgical LOS in public hospitals and so increases NHS costs.

◆ Economists say that healthcare reform is complex and needs much more *economic* research.

*'Does Competition Improve Public Hospitals' Efficiency? Evidence from a Quasi-Experiment in the English National Health Service' by Zack Cooper, Stephen Gibbons, Simon Jones and Alistair McGuire, Discussion Paper No 1125, February 2012, London School of Economics Centre for Economic Performance.

Healthcare in the UK and US

The Telegraph, 30 June 2010

US Government Spends More on Health than the NHS

Edmund Conway

It may surprise you that . . . that the US government now spends more on provision of healthcare than does Britain's. . . . The costs of running various US health programmes – Medicare and Medicaid most significantly – is, at 7.4 per cent of gross domestic product, greater than the 7.2 per cent of GDP the UK government spends on the NHS. . . . The US must just have overtaken Britain this year on this basis (the latest figures date from 2008), having risen worryingly fast in recent years. . . .

Obviously the first striking thing is just how much the US spends as a whole – at 16 per cent of GDP it is almost double Britain's 8.7 per cent.

Is this disproportionate amount of healthcare spending justified? . . . Based on two key measures of healthcare effectiveness – infant mortality and life expectancy – the US actually has worse outcomes than Britain. . . .

However, an area which is rather less flattering for the UK is the equipment provided by hospitals. . . . Britain has fewer CT scanners per head than Turkey or Poland, and fewer MRI units than the Slovak Republic. And yet despite these third-world levels of investment, the NHS still manages to provide a service of true developed world standards. . . .

 The Essence of the Story

- The US government spends more on healthcare as a percentage of income than the UK government does on the National Health Service (NHS).

- Including public and private healthcare, the US spends nearly double what the UK spends.

- Despite higher expenditure, two major measures of health outcomes are worse in the US than in the UK: infant mortality and life expectancy.

- The UK has poor levels of specialist equipment per person when compared with other developed economies.

Economic Analysis

◆ Table 1 compares UK and US health spending and efficiency in 2009 (a year later than in the news story).

◆ The UK is ranked as more efficient than the US, which means that the US wastes more resources and creates a larger deadweight loss than the UK.

◆ Figures 1 and 2 compare the US and UK healthcare markets. In each figure, the marginal social cost curve is *MSC*, the marginal private benefit curve is *MB*, and the marginal social benefit curve is *MSB*. The numbers are assumptions.

◆ Figure 1 illustrates the US system. For most people, private healthcare is the only option and the *MB* curve is MB_1. In a year, 8 million of these people pay $18,000 per patient.

◆ Public healthcare is provided to the aged and the poor at a zero price and a further 12 million people (8 + 12 = 20 million total) receive healthcare services that cost $30,000 per patient per year to deliver. Large overprovision creates a deadweight loss.

◆ Figure 2 illustrates the UK system. Because everyone has access to the NHS, the willingness-to-pay is lower and the *MB* curve (MB_2) is below that in the US.

◆ The new Health and Social Care Act 2012 plans to reduce the underprovision in Figure 2 by increasing the total capacity of the NHS without increasing expenditure.

◆ Under the Act, clinicians rather than managers allocate NHS resources to avoid waste and new Health and Wellbeing Boards better integrate local authority services with health provision in an ageing population.

◆ If successful, the reorganisation will allocate limited resources more efficiently between the NHS and local authority care for the elderly, raising the capacity of both services.

Table 1

Healthcare in the UK and US in 2009

Item	UK	US
Expenditure (% of income)	9.8	17.4
Public healthcare (% of total)	84	48
Expenditure per person	3,487	7,960
Efficiency ranking	1	7

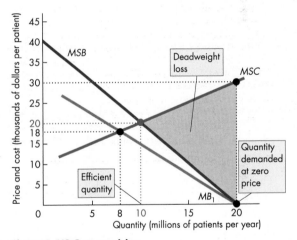

Figure 1 US Overprovision

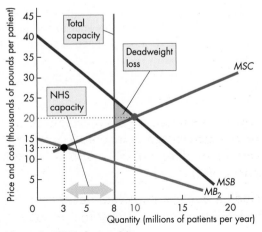

Figure 2 UK Underprovision

SUMMARY

Key Points

Public Choices (pp. 346–350)

◆ Governments establish and maintain property rights, provide non-market mechanisms for allocating scarce resources, and redistribute income and wealth.

◆ Public choice theory explains how voters, firms, politicians and bureaucrats interact in the political marketplace and why government failure might occur.

◆ A private good is a good or service that is rival and excludable.

◆ A public good is a good or service that is non-rival and non-excludable.

◆ A mixed good is a private good that creates an external benefit or external cost.

Do Problems 1 to 6 to get a better understanding of public choices.

Providing Public Goods (pp. 351–354)

◆ Because a public good is a good or service that is *non-rival* and *non-excludable*, it creates a *free-rider* problem: no one has an incentive to pay their share of the cost of providing a public good.

◆ The efficient level of provision of a public good is that at which marginal social benefit equals marginal social cost.

◆ Competition between political parties can lead to the efficient scale of provision of a public good.

◆ Bureaucrats who maximise their budgets and voters who are rationally ignorant can lead to the inefficient overprovision of a public good – government failure.

Do Problems 7 to 15 to get a better understanding of providing public goods.

Positive Externalities: Education and Healthcare (pp. 355–359)

◆ Mixed goods provide external benefits – benefits that are received by people other than the consumer of a good or service.

◆ Marginal social benefit equals marginal private benefit plus marginal external benefit.

◆ External benefits arise from education and healthcare.

◆ Vouchers provided to households can achieve a more efficient provision of education and healthcare than public production or subsidies to private producers.

Do Problems 16 to 20 to get a better understanding of providing mixed goods with external benefits.

Key Terms

Common resource, 348
Excludable, 348
Externality, 348
Free-rider problem, 351
Government failure, 346
Marginal external benefit, 355
Marginal private benefit, 355
Marginal social benefit, 355
Mixed good, 348
Natural monopoly good, 348
Non-excludable, 348
Non-rival, 348
Political equilibrium, 347
Positive externality, 355
Principle of minimum differentiation, 353
Private good, 348
Public choice, 346
Public good, 348
Public production, 357
Rival, 348
Subsidy, 357
Voucher, 357

STUDY PLAN PROBLEMS AND APPLICATIONS

Do Problems 1 to 20 in MyEconLab Chapter 15 Study Plan and get instant feedback.

MyEconLab

Public Choices (Study Plan 15.1)

1 Classify each of the following items as excludable, non-excludable, rival or non-rival.

- A Big Mac
- The Humber Bridge
- A view of the Eiffel Tower

2 Classify each of the following items as a public good, a private good, a natural monopoly good or a common resource.

- Police patrol service
- City pavements
- Royal Mail
- FedEx courier service

3 Classify the following services for computer owners with an Internet connection as rival, non-rival, excludable or non-excludable:

- eBay
- A mouse
- A Twitter page
- MyEconLab website

4 Classify each of the following items as a public good, a private good, a mixed good or a common resource:

- Firefighting service
- A courtside seat at the Wimbledon (tennis) Club
- A well-stocked buffet that promises all you can eat for £10
- The Danube River

5 Explain which of the following events creates an external benefit or an external cost:

- A huge noisy crowd gathers outside the lecture room.
- Your neighbour grows beautiful flowers on his apartment patio.
- A fire alarm goes off accidentally during a lecture.
- Your tutor offers a free tutorial after class.

6 **Wind Farm Clears Hurdle**

The nation's first offshore wind farm with 130 turbines will be built five miles off the coast. Wind turbines are noisy, stand 440 feet tall, can be seen from the coast and will produce power for 75 per cent of nearby homes.

Source: *The New York Times*, 16 January 2009

List the externalities created by this wind farm.

Providing Public Goods (Study Plan 15.2)

7 For each of the following goods, explain whether there is a free-rider problem. If there is no such problem, how is it avoided?

- November 5th fireworks display
- M1 motorway in Britain
- Wireless Internet access in hotels
- The public library in your city

8 The table sets out the marginal benefits that Terri and Sue receive from police officers on duty on the university campus:

Police officers on duty (number per night)	Marginal benefit	
	Terri	Sue
	(pounds per police officer)	
1	18	22
2	14	18
3	10	14
4	6	10
5	2	6

a If the police officers are provided by the government, is the presence of the police on campus a private good or a public good?

b Suppose that Terri and Sue are the only students on the campus at night. Draw a graph to show the marginal social benefit from on-campus police officers on duty at night.

9 For each of the following goods and services, explain whether there is a free-rider problem. If there is no such problem, how is it avoided?

- National gale warning system
- Ambulance service
- Road safety signs
- A national coastguard

10 **Vaccination Dodgers**

Doctors struggle to eradicate polio worldwide, but one of the biggest problems is persuading parents to vaccinate their children. Since the discovery of the vaccine, polio has been eliminated from Europe and the law requires everyone to be vaccinated. People who refuse to be vaccinated are 'free riders'.

Source: *USA Today*, 12 March 2008

Explain why someone who has not opted out on medical or religious grounds and refuses to be vaccinated is a 'free rider'.

Use the following figure in Problems 11 to 13.

The figure provides information about a waste disposal system that a city of 1 million people is considering installing.

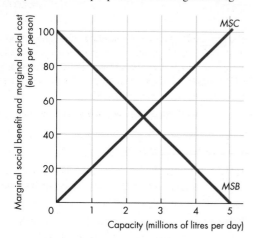

11 What is the efficient capacity of the waste disposal system? How much will each person have to pay in taxes for the city to install the efficient capacity?

12 What is the political equilibrium if voters are well informed?

13 What is the political equilibrium if voters are rationally ignorant and bureaucrats achieve the highest attainable budget?

Use the data on a mosquito control programme in the following table in Problems 14 and 15.

Quantity (square miles sprayed per day)	Marginal social cost	Marginal social benefit
	(thousands of pounds per day)	
1	2	10
2	4	8
3	6	6
4	8	4
5	10	2

14 What quantity of spraying would a private mosquito control programme provide? What is the efficient quantity of spraying? In a single-issue election on the quantity of spraying, what quantity would the winner of the election provide?

15 If the government sets up a Department of Mosquito Control and appoints a bureaucrat to run it, would mosquito spraying most likely be underprovided, overprovided or provided at the efficient quantity?

Positive Externalities: Education and Healthcare (Study Plan 15.3)

Use the following figure, which shows the marginal private benefit from university education, in Problems 16 to 19.

The marginal cost of a university education is a constant €6,000 per student per year. The marginal external benefit from a university education is a constant €4,000 per student per year.

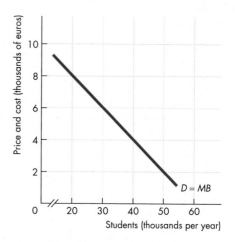

16 What is the efficient number of students? If all universities are private, how many people enrol in university and what is the tuition fee?

17 If the government provides public universities, what tuition fee will these universities charge to achieve the efficient enrolment? How much will taxpayers have to pay?

18 If the government subsidises private universities, what subsidy will achieve the efficient enrolment?

19 If the government offers vouchers and no subsidy to those who attend university, what is the value of the voucher that will achieve the efficient enrolment?

20 **University Fees Rise as Support Cut**

Teaching subsidies to universities will be cut for the first time by £315 million this year. Some universities want tuition fees to rise from £3,225 to £7,000 a year alongside cuts in subsidies for student loans and grants.

Source: *The Times online*, 28 January 2010

If government cuts the subsidy to universities, why will tuition fees rise and the number of enrolled students decrease? Why might it be a better policy for government to maintain the subsidy to universities?

ADDITIONAL PROBLEMS AND APPLICATIONS

Do these problems in MyEconLab if assigned by your lecturer.

MyEconLab

Public Choices

21 Classify each of the following items as excludable, non-excludable, rival or non-rival.

◆ Firefighting service
◆ A Starbucks coffee
◆ A view of Big Ben
◆ The Pennine Way
◆ Lake Windermere

22 Classify each of the following items as a public good, a private good, a natural monopoly good, a common resource or a mixed good.

◆ Measles vaccination
◆ Tuna in the Mediterranean Sea
◆ Air service in the UK
◆ Local flood-water protection system

23 Consider each of the following activities or events and say for each one whether it creates an externality. If so, say whether it creates an external benefit or external cost, and whether the externality arises from production or consumption.

◆ Aeroplanes taking off from Heathrow during the tennis tournament taking place at nearby Wimbledon
◆ A sunset over the Mediterranean Sea
◆ An increase in the number of people who are studying for graduate degrees
◆ A person wearing strong perfume in your tutorial class

24 Classify each of the following items as a public good, a private good or a mixed good, and say whether it creates an external benefit, external cost or neither.

◆ Chewing gum
◆ The London M25 motorway at peak travel time
◆ The London Underground
◆ A skateboard
◆ A beach in the South of France

Providing Public Goods

Use the following news clip in Problems 25 and 26.

Private versus State Education

UK parents must choose between moderate-quality state secondary schools financed entirely by taxes or high-quality private schools financed entirely by fees. If quality is related to cost, a private school that was just a bit better than a state school would get no students, so only high-quality private schools exist. Most parents choose state schools because they can't afford high quality. Most would prefer to contribute to the cost to raise the quality at state schools, but they are not allowed to. Instead people spend money on moving house or buying educational toys, which is inefficient.

Source: *The Independent*, 14 January 2010

25 Explain why government state education services can create a free-rider problem.

26 Explain why the allocation of funds between UK state schools and private schools is inefficient. How might a school voucher system achieve efficiency?

27 The table sets out the marginal benefits that Sam and Nick receive from the town's street lighting:

Number of street lights	Marginal benefit	
	Sam	Nick
	(pounds per street light)	
1	10	12
2	8	9
3	6	6
4	4	3
5	2	0

a Is the town's street lighting a private good or a public good?

b Suppose that Sam and Nick are the only residents of the town. Draw a graph to show the marginal social benefit from the town's street lighting.

28 What is the principle of diminishing marginal benefit? In Problem 27, does Sam's, Nick's or the society's marginal benefit diminish faster?

Use the following news clip for Problems 29 and 30.

A Bridge Too Far Gone

Petrol taxes paid for much of America's post-war motorway system. Now motorists pay about one-third in petrol taxes to drive a mile as they did in the 1960s. Yet raising such taxes is politically tricky. This would matter less if private cash was flooding into infrastructure or new ways were being found to control demand. Neither is happening, and private companies building toll roads brings howls of outrage.

Source: *The Economist*, 9 August 2007

29 Why is it 'politically tricky' to raise petrol taxes to finance infrastructure?

30 What in this news clip points to a distinction between public *production* of a public good and public *provision*? Give examples of three public goods that are produced by private firms but provided by government and paid for with taxes.

Positive Externalities: Education and Healthcare

Use the following information and figure in Problems 31 to 34.

The marginal cost of educating a student is a constant £4,000 a year and the figure shows the students' marginal benefit curve. Suppose that university education creates an external benefit of a constant £2,000 per student per year.

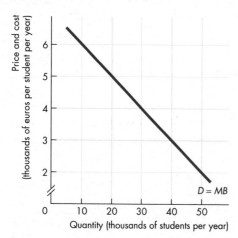

31 If all universities are private and the market for education is competitive, how many students enrol, what is the tuition fee and what is the deadweight loss created?

32 If the government decides to provide public universities, what tuition fees will these universities charge to achieve the efficient number of students? How much will taxpayers have to pay?

33 If the government decides to subsidise private universities, what subsidy will achieve the efficient number of university students?

34 If the government offers vouchers to those who enrol at a university and no subsidy, what is the value of the voucher that will achieve the efficient number of students?

35 My Child, My Choice

Fully vaccinating all US children born in a given year saves 33,000 lives, prevents 14 million infections and saves $10 billion in medical costs. Part of the reason is that vaccinations protect not only the kids that receive the shots but also those who can't receive them – such as newborns and cancer patients with suppressed immune systems.

Source: *Time*, 2 June 2008

a Describe the private benefits and external benefits of vaccinations and explain why a private market for vaccinations would produce an inefficient outcome.

b Draw a graph to illustrate a private market for vaccinations and show the deadweight loss.

c Explain how government intervention could achieve an efficient quantity of vaccinations and draw a graph to illustrate this outcome.

Economics in the News

36 After you have studied *Reading Between the Lines* on pp. 360–361, answer the following questions.

a What are the main differences in healthcare expenditures and health outcomes in the UK and US?

b Compare the main features of the UK public health system with the US public health system.

c Which of the two systems achieves the more efficient outcome and why?

d How does the UK public healthcare system limit overprovision?

e How could healthcare vouchers improve the UK and US healthcare systems?

37 Who's Hiding under Our Umbrella?

Students of the Cold War learn that, to deter possible Soviet aggression, the US placed a 'strategic umbrella' over NATO Europe and Japan, with the US providing most of their national security. Under President Ronald Reagan, the US spent 6 per cent of GDP on defence, whereas the Europeans spent only 2 to 3 per cent and the Japanese spent only 1 per cent, although all faced a common enemy. Thus the US taxpayer paid a disproportionate share of the overall defence spending, whereas NATO Europe and Japan spent more on consumer goods or saved.

Source: *International Herald Tribune*, 30 January 2008

a Explain the free-rider problem described in this news clip.

b Does the free-rider problem in international defence mean that the world has too little defence against aggression?

c How do nations try to overcome the free-rider problem among nations?

16 Economics of the Environment

After studying this chapter you will be able to:

◆ Explain why external costs bring market failure and too much pollution, and how property rights and public choices might achieve an efficient outcome

◆ Explain the tragedy of the commons and its possible solutions

How can we cut our carbon emissions to reduce global warming and climate change? How can we conserve the ocean's fish stocks and save some species from extinction?

Questions like these arise because some of our choices impose costs on others that we don't fully consider when we make these choices. How can we be made to take these costs into account? You will find out in this chapter.

In *Reading Between the Lines* at the end of the chapter, we look at the EU market for trading carbon emissions as a way of limiting global warming and climate change.

Negative Externalities: Pollution

Generating electric power from coal and oil, transporting goods and people by road, rail and air, and producing steel, chemicals, paint and plastic create air pollution in our cities and emissions of carbon dioxide (CO_2) and other greenhouse gases that contribute to global warming and climate change. So, every time we use electricity, travel by bus, train, car or aeroplane, or buy something online that is delivered to our door, we contribute to our local air pollution and we add to our carbon footprint.

Air pollution and carbon emission are examples of a broader class of pollution problems that arise from economic activity. Industrial processes, fertilisers and rubbish disposal all pollute the air, rivers, lakes and land, and these individual areas of pollution interact through the ecosystem.

The effects of pollution mean that production and consumption decisions impose costs that are not taken fully into account when those decisions are made. You are now going to see how economists analyse these decisions and solve pollution problems.

The challenge that pollution brings is to get consumers and producers to make decisions in the social interest. The incentives that we face must direct our self-interested choices to be in the social interest.

How can governments change incentives? How can we encourage the use of technologies that improve air quality and lessen climate change?

The principles that you learn in this chapter apply to all types of pollution and, more broadly, to all economic activities that bring negative externalities. We focus on air quality and climate change as examples and because they are important issues. We'll begin by defining and explaining how we measure negative externalities.

ECONOMICS IN ACTION

Opposing Trends: Success and Failure

Two distinct air pollution problems present their own different challenges. They are the problem of *national* air quality and the *global* problem of climate change.

National Air Quality

National air quality is influenced by more than 180 airborne substances that, in sufficiently large concentrations, can damage human health. The five most important ones are carbon dioxide, lead, nitrogen oxide, particulates and sulphur dioxide. The trend in these pollutants is downward in the advanced industrial countries.

Figure 1 shows the downward trends in the UK between 1990 and 2010. The concentration of all these pollutants (shown here as percentages of 1990 levels) has decreased.

UK legislation has introduced regulations that cut emissions of carbon monoxide, nitrogen oxide, particulates, sulphur

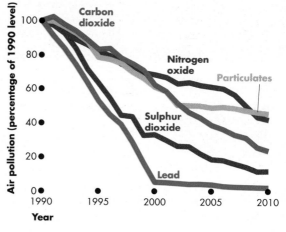

Figure 1 Trends in Air Pollution

Source of data: National Atmospheric Emissions Inventory.

Despite improvements in air quality, London still has some smoggy days . . .

. . . and Berlin some smoggy sunsets.

Negative Externalities

A **negative externality** arises when the *social cost* of production exceeds the *private cost*.

A *private cost* of production is a cost that is borne by the producer. *Marginal cost* is the cost of producing an *additional unit* of a good or service. So **marginal private cost** (*MC*) is the cost of producing an additional unit of a good or service that is borne by its producer.

An *external cost* is a cost of producing a good or service that is *not* borne by the producer but borne by other people. A **marginal external cost** is the cost of producing an additional unit of a good or service that falls on people other than the producer.

Marginal social cost (*MSC*) is the sum of marginal private cost and marginal external cost. That is,

$$MSC = MC + \text{Marginal external cost}$$

Valuing an External Cost

We express costs using money units – pounds – but we must always remember that the cost of a good or service is its opportunity cost – something real, such as clean air or a clean river, that is given up to get it.

Whenever possible, economists use market prices to put a money value on the cost of pollution. For example, suppose that there are two similar rivers, one polluted and the other clean. Ten identical homes are built along the side of each river. The homes on the clean river rent for £2,500 a month while those on the polluted river rent for £1,500 a month. If the pollution is the only detectable difference between the two locations, the rent difference of £1,000 per month is the pollution cost per home. With 10 homes, the pollution cost is £10,000 a month. The opportunity cost of the clean river is equivalent to £10,000 of other goods and services.

---

dioxide and lead to less than 45 per cent of their 1990 levels. Some economic actions that you will learn about in this chapter have almost eliminated lead from motor vehicles and industrial processes. Even the more stubborn problems of particulates and nitrogen dioxide have been more than halved.

These reductions in air pollution are even more impressive seen against the trends in economic activity. Between 1990 and 2010, total production in the UK increased by 50 per cent, vehicle miles travelled increased by 24 per cent, and the population increased by 8 per cent.

Global Air Quality: Greenhouse Gas Emissions

Global temperature is influenced by human emissions of greenhouse gases, of which the most important is carbon dioxide (CO_2). Less important greenhouse gases include methane and nitrous oxide.

China and the US each account for about one-quarter of the CO_2 poured into the global atmosphere in a year. Some of this additional CO_2 is taken up by the oceans or by vegetation on land, so the amount in the atmosphere changes by the emissions minus the net amount removed. But more CO_2 is emitted than removed, and so the amount in the atmosphere is rising.

Figure 2 shows the upward global trends in carbon dioxide (CO_2) concentration and temperature. CO_2 concentration has increased by almost 40 per cent since 1880, and global temperature has been rising for more than 100 years.

Scientists agree that the scale on which we burn fossil fuels is the major source of the rising CO_2 trend. There is more uncertainty about the effect of the increase in CO_2 on global temperature, but the consensus is that the effect is significant.

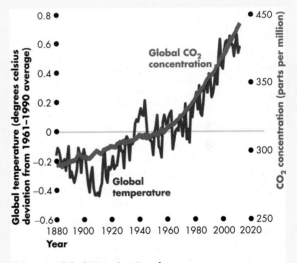

Figure 2 Global Warming Trends

Sources of data: National Climate Data Center and Scripps Institution of Oceanography.

Stopping the rising CO_2 trend requires joint action by the governments of every nation. While the UK and members of the EU signed the Kyoto Protocol, a binding agreement among nations to reduce greenhouse gas emissions, that agreement excluded the major developing countries and the US refused to ratify it.

You will see in this chapter why global warming is a much harder problem to solve than reducing air pollution.

External Cost and Output

Figure 16.1 shows an example of the relationship between output and cost in a chemical industry that pollutes. The marginal cost curve, *MC*, describes the marginal private cost borne by the firms that produce the chemical. Marginal cost increases as the quantity of chemical produced increases.

If firms pollute a river, they impose an external cost on other users of the river. Pollution and its marginal external cost increase.

The marginal social cost curve, *MSC*, is found by adding the marginal external cost to the marginal private cost. So a point on the *MSC* curve shows the sum of the marginal cost of producing a given quantity of output and the marginal external cost created.

For example, when output is 4,000 tonnes of chemical per month, marginal private cost of producing the chemical is £100 a tonne, marginal external cost created is £125 a tonne and marginal social cost is £225 a tonne.

Let's now see how much chemical gets produced and how much pollution is created.

Equilibrium and Amount of Pollution

Equilibrium in the market for the chemical determines the amount of pollution. Figure 16.2 has the same *MC* and *MSC* curves as in Figure 16.1 and a market demand curve and marginal social benefit curve *D* = *MSB*. Equilibrium occurs at a price of £100 a tonne and a quantity of 4,000 tonnes of chemical a month. This equilibrium is one with *inefficient overproduction* (Chapter 5, p. 112) because marginal social cost at £225 a tonne exceeds marginal social benefit at £100 a tonne. The efficient equilibrium occurs where marginal social benefit *equals* marginal social cost at 2,000 tonnes a month. Too much chemical is produced, too much pollution is created, and the area of the deadweight loss triangle measures the society's loss.

If some method can be found to get the factories to create less pollution and eliminate the deadweight loss, everyone – the owners of the chemical factories and the residents of the riverside homes – can gain.

Figure 16.2 Inefficiency with an External Cost

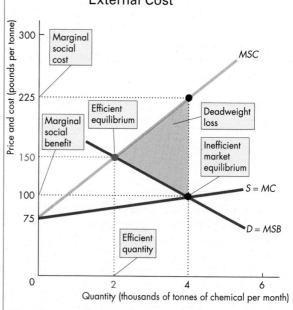

The market supply curve is the marginal private cost curve, *S* = *MC*. The demand curve is the marginal social benefit curve, *D* = *MSB*. Market equilibrium occurs at a price of £100 a tonne and 4,000 tonnes of chemical a month. This market outcome is inefficient because the marginal social cost exceeds marginal social benefit. The efficient quantity of chemical is 2,000 tonnes a month. The grey triangle shows the deadweight loss created by the pollution.

Figure 16.1 An External Cost

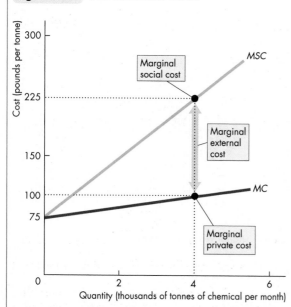

The *MC* curve shows the marginal private cost borne by the factories that produce a chemical. The *MSC* curve shows the sum of marginal private cost and marginal external cost. When output of the chemical is 4,000 tonnes a month, marginal private cost is £100 a tonne, marginal external cost is £125 a tonne and marginal social cost is £225 a tonne.

So what can be done to fix the inefficiency that arises from an external cost? Three available approaches are:

◆ Establish property rights
◆ Mandate clean technology
◆ Tax or price pollution

Establish Property Rights

Property rights are legally established titles to the ownership, use and disposal of factors of production and goods and services that are enforceable in the courts. Establishing property rights where they do not exist can confront producers with the costs of their actions and provide incentives that allocate resources efficiently.

Suppose that the factories have property rights on the river and the homes alongside it – they *own* the river and the homes. The rental income that the factories are able to make on the homes depends on the amount of pollution they create. Using the earlier example, people are willing to pay £2,500 a month to live alongside a pollution-free river but only £1,500 a month to live with the pollution created by 4,000 tonnes of chemical a month.

The forgone income from the homes alongside a polluted river is an opportunity cost of producing the chemical. The factories must now decide how to respond to this cost. There are two possible responses:

◆ Use abatement technology
◆ Produce less and pollute less

Use an Abatement Technology

An **abatement technology** is a production technology that reduces or prevents pollution. The catalytic converter in every car is an example of an abatement technology. Its widespread adoption (with lead-free petrol) has dramatically reduced pollution from vehicles and helped to achieve the trends in air quality on p. 368.

Abatement technologies exist to eliminate or reduce pollution from electricity generation and many industrial processes, including chemical production.

Produce Less and Pollute Less

An alternative to incurring the cost of using an abatement technology is to use the polluting technology but cut production, reduce pollution and get a higher income from renting homes by the river. The decision turns on cost. Firms will choose the least-cost alternative.

Efficient Market Equilibrium

Figure 16.3 illustrates the outcome by using the same example as in Figure 16.2. With property rights in place, the *MC* curve no longer measures all the costs that the factories face in producing the chemical. It excludes the pollution costs that they must now bear. The *MSC* curve now becomes the marginal private cost curve *MC*. The factories bear *all* the costs, so the market supply curve is based on all the marginal costs and is the curve labelled $S = MC = MSC$.

Market equilibrium now occurs at a price of £150 a tonne of chemical and a quantity of 2,000 tonnes of chemical a month. This outcome is efficient. The factories still produce some pollution, but it is the efficient quantity.

If the forgone rent is less than the abatement cost, the factories will still create some pollution, but it will be the efficient quantity. If the abatement cost is lower than the forgone rent, the factories will stop polluting. But they will produce the efficient quantity because marginal cost includes the abatement cost.

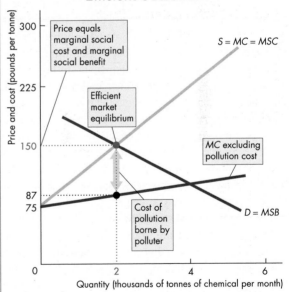

Figure 16.3 Property Rights Achieve an Efficient Outcome

With property rights, the marginal cost curve that excludes pollution and abatement costs shows only part of the producers' marginal cost. The marginal cost of producing the chemical now includes the cost of pollution (the external cost) or the abatement cost, so the market supply curve is $S = MC = MSC$. Market equilibrium now occurs at £150 a tonne and 2,000 tonnes of chemical a month. Marginal social cost equals marginal social benefit, so the outcome is efficient.

MyEconLab Animation ──────────────────◆

The Coase Theorem

Does it matter whether the polluter or the victim of the pollution owns the resource that might be polluted? Until 1960, everyone thought that it did matter. But in 1960, Ronald Coase had a remarkable insight, now called the Coase theorem.

The **Coase theorem** is the proposition that if property rights exist and the transactions costs of enforcing them are low, then private transactions are efficient and it doesn't matter who has the property rights.

Application of the Coase Theorem

Suppose that instead of the factories owning the river and the homes, the residents own their homes and the river. Now the factories must pay a fee to the homeowners for the right to dump their waste. The greater the quantity of waste dumped into the river, the more the factories must pay. So, again, the factories face the opportunity cost of the pollution they create. The quantity of chemical produced and the amount of waste dumped are the same whoever owns the homes and the river. If the factories own them, they bear the cost of pollution because they receive a lower income from home rents. And if the residents own the homes and the river, the factories bear the cost of pollution because they must pay a fee to the homeowners. In both cases, the factories bear the cost of their pollution and dump the efficient amount of waste into the river.

The Coase solution works only when transactions costs are low. **Transactions costs** are the opportunity costs of conducting a transaction. For example, when you buy a house, you pay an agent to help you find the best place and a lawyer to check that the seller owns the property and that after you've paid for it, the ownership has been properly transferred to you.

In our example, the transactions costs that are incurred by a small number of chemical factories and a few homeowners might be low enough to enable them to negotiate the deals that produce an efficient outcome. But in many situations, transactions costs are so high that it would be inefficient to incur them. In these situations, the Coase solution is not available.

Mandate Clean Technology

When property rights are too difficult to define and enforce, public choices are made. Regulation is a government's most likely response.

Most countries regulate what may be dumped in rivers and lakes and emitted into the atmosphere. The environmental resources of the UK and the EU are heavily regulated.

Examples of environmental regulation are the UK Clean Air Act of 1993 and the Pollution Prevention and Control Act of 1999 and later amendments, which give the Department for Environment, Food and Rural Affairs (Defra) the authority to issue regulations to limit emissions and achieve defined air quality standards.

In addition, the European Commission has issued thousands of regulations that make chemical plants, utilities and steel mills adopt best-practice pollution abatement technologies and limit their emissions of specified air pollutants.

Other regulations have been issued that govern road vehicle emission limits, which must be met by the vehicle manufacturers.

In 2008, the UK Climate Change Act set the world's first legal target to reduce greenhouse gas emissions by 80 per cent by 2050. Although direct regulation can and has reduced emissions and improved air quality, economists are generally skeptical about this approach. Abatement is not always the least-cost solution. Also, government agencies are not well placed to find the cost-minimising solution to a pollution problem. Individual firms seeking to minimise cost and maximise profit and responding to price signals are more likely to achieve an efficient outcome. We'll now examine these other approaches to pollution.

Tax or Cap and Price Pollution

Governments use two main methods of confronting polluters with the costs of their decisions:

◆ Taxes
◆ Cap-and-trade

Taxes

Governments can use taxes as an incentive for producers to cut back on pollution. Taxes used in this way are called **Pigovian taxes**, in honour of Arthur Cecil Pigou, the British economist who first worked out this method of dealing with externalities during the 1920s.

By setting the tax rate equal to the marginal external cost, firms can be made to behave in the same way as they would if they bore the cost of the externality directly.

To see how government actions can change market outcomes in the face of externalities, let's return to the example of the chemical factories and the river. Assume that the government has assessed the marginal external cost accurately and imposes a tax on the factories that exactly equals this marginal external cost. Figure 16.4 illustrates the effects of this tax.

Figure 16.4 illustrates the effects of a Pigovian tax on chemical factory pollution. The demand curve and marginal social benefit curve is $D = MSB$, and the firms' marginal private cost curve is MC. The pollution tax equals the marginal external cost of the pollution. We add this tax to the marginal private cost to find the market supply curve. This curve is the one labelled $S = MC + tax = MSC$. This curve is the market supply curve because it tells us the quantity of chemical supplied at each price, given the factories' marginal private cost and the tax they must pay. This curve is also the marginal social cost curve because the pollution tax has been set equal to the marginal external cost.

Demand and supply now determine the market equilibrium price at £150 a tonne and the equilibrium quantity at 2,000 tonnes of chemical a month. At this quantity of chemical production the marginal social cost is £150 a tonne and the marginal social benefit is £150 a tonne, so the outcome is efficient. The factories incur a marginal private cost of £88 a tonne and pay a pollution tax of £62 a tonne. The government collects tax revenue of £124,000 a month (the purple rectangle).

Cap-and-Trade

A cap is an upper limit – a quota. A government that uses this method must first estimate the efficient quantity of pollution and set the overall cap at that level.

Just like a production quota or an import quota, a pollution quota or cap must somehow be allocated to individual firms (and possibly even households). In an efficient allocation of pollution quotas, each firm has the same marginal social cost. So to make an efficient allocation of the cap across firms, the government would need to know each firm's marginal production cost and marginal abatement cost.

A Pigovian tax achieves an efficient allocation of pollution across firms because each firm chooses how much to produce and pollute, taking the tax into account, and produces the quantity at which marginal social cost equals price. Because all firms face the same market price, they also incur the same marginal social cost.

The government solves the allocation problem by making an initial distribution of the cap across firms and

Figure 16.4 A Pollution Tax to Achieve an Efficient Outcome

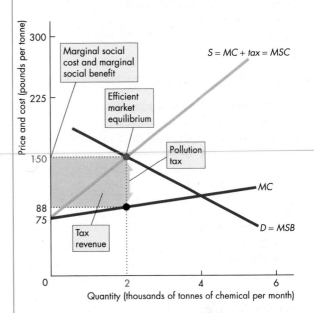

When the government imposes a pollution tax equal to the marginal external cost of pollution, the market supply curve becomes the marginal private cost curve, MC, plus the tax – the curve $S = MC + tax$. Market equilibrium occurs at a price of £150 a tonne and a quantity of 2,000 tonnes of chemical a month. This equilibrium is efficient because marginal social cost equals marginal social benefit. The purple rectangle shows the government's tax revenue.

MyEconLab Animation ──────────────◆

allowing them to trade in a market for pollution permits. Firms that have a low marginal abatement cost sell permits and make big cuts in pollution. Firms that have a high marginal abatement cost buy permits and make smaller cuts or perhaps even no cuts in pollution.

The market in permits determines the equilibrium price of pollution, and each firm, confronted with that price, maximises profit by setting its marginal pollution cost or marginal abatement cost, whichever is lower, equal to the market price of a permit. By confronting polluters with a price of pollution, trade in pollution permits can achieve the same efficient outcome as a Pigovian tax.

Following the Kyoto Protocol, the EU set up a cap-and-trade system for carbon in 2005. The system has been criticised for issuing too many permits in the cap, and as business slowed after the financial crash, the carbon price crashed in 2013.

ECONOMICS IN ACTION

Taxing Carbon Emissions

The Canadian province of British Columbia, Australia and the UK are making their carbon footprints smaller.

British Columbia's Carbon Tax

Introduced in 2008 at $10 per tonne of carbon emitted, British Columbia's tax increased each year to its final rate of $30 per tonne in 2012. The tax applies to all forms of carbon emission from coal, oil and natural gas. The tax is revenue-neutral, which means that other taxes, personal and corporate income taxes, are cut by the amount raised by the carbon tax. Between 2008 and 2010, carbon emissions fell by almost 5 per cent.

Australia's Carbon Tax

Introduced in 2012 at $23 per tonne of carbon emitted, Australia's carbon tax is set to rise through 2015 and then become a market-determined price. Australia has excluded petrol from the carbon tax, but the petrol price in Australia is higher than in British Columbia because of a high excise tax.

UK Tax on Petrol

The UK doesn't call its petrol tax a carbon tax, but it has the same effect on drivers. Figure 1 shows the UK price of petrol compared with that in three other countries. The enormous differences arise almost entirely from tax differences.

An effect of these price differences is that cars in the UK get an average of 38 miles per gallon whereas in the US, the average is 23 miles per gallon. A high petrol tax cuts carbon emissions by inducing people to drive smaller cars and to drive less.

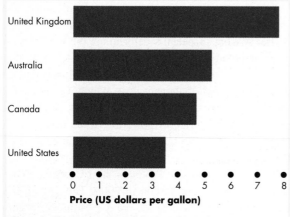

Figure 1 The Price of Petrol in Four Countries

Coping with Global Emissions

The UK has made its own air cleaner by adopting the measures you've just seen. But one country, or even all 27 European Union countries with a large share of global production, can't solve the problem of global warming and climate change alone. Coping with this problem requires public choices at a *global* level, which are much harder to make.

A lower CO_2 concentration in the world's atmosphere is a global *public good*. Like all public goods, it brings a *free-rider problem* (see Chapter 15, p. 351). Without a mechanism to compel participation in a global carbon reduction programme, countries have an incentive to leave the task to others.

Not only is carbon reduction hampered by free riders, but it also faces *carbon leakage* – a tendency for non-participants in carbon reduction to increase emissions.

The only major attempt at international coordination of carbon reduction is the Kyoto Protocol, signed in 1997 by only 37 countries, but not ratified by the US and renounced by Canada. This agreement ended in December 2012.

However, some governments have introduced a carbon tax, including Australia and the Canadian province of British Columbia. The UK has high petrol taxes, which are a partial carbon tax (see *Economics in Action*). The proposed EU carbon tax on international air flights has been postponed until 2014.

At Issue on the opposite page summarises two views about what needs to happen next to limit carbon emissions.

REVIEW QUIZ

1   What is the distinction between private cost and social cost?
2   How do external costs prevent a competitive market from allocating resources efficiently?
3   How can external costs be eliminated by assigning property rights?
4   How do taxes, pollution charges and cap-and-trade work to reduce emissions?

Do these questions in Study Plan 16.1 and get instant feedback.   MyEconLab

Your next task is to study common resources and the government actions that can result in their efficient use.

AT ISSUE

Should We Be Doing More to Reduce Carbon Emissions?

Economists agree that tackling the global warming problem requires changes in the incentives that people face. The cost of carbon-emitting activities must rise and the cost of clean-energy technologies must fall.

Disagreement centres on *how* to change incentives. Should more countries set targets for cutting carbon emissions at a faster rate and introduce a carbon tax, emissions charges or cap-and-trade to cut emissions? Should clean energy research and development be subsidised?

Yes: *The Stern Review*	No: The Copenhagen Consensus

Yes: *The Stern Review*

◆ Confronting emitters with a tax or price on carbon imposes low present costs for high future benefits.

◆ The cost of reducing greenhouse gas emissions to safe levels can be kept to 1 per cent of global income each year.

◆ The future benefits are incomes at least 5 per cent and possibly 20 per cent higher than they will be with inaction every year forever.

◆ Climate change is a global problem that requires an international coordinated response.

◆ Unlike most taxes, which bring deadweight loss, a carbon tax eliminates (or reduces) deadweight loss.

◆ Strong, deliberate policy action is required to change the incentives that emitters face.

◆ Policy actions should include:

1. Emissions limits and emissions trading

2. Increased subsidies for energy research and development, including the development of low-cost clean technology for generating electricity

3. Reduced deforestation and research into new drought and flood resilient crop varieties

No: The Copenhagen Consensus

◆ Confronting emitters with a tax or price on carbon imposes high present costs and low future benefits.

◆ Unless the entire world signs onto an emissions reduction programme, free riders will increase their emissions and carbon leakage will occur.

◆ A global emissions reduction programme and carbon tax would lower living standards in the rich countries and slow the growth rate of living standards in developing countries.

◆ Technology is already advancing and the cost of cleaner energy is falling.

◆ Fracking technology has vastly expanded the natural gas deposits that can be profitably exploited, and replacing coal with gas halves the carbon emissions from electricity generation.

◆ Free-market price signals will allocate resources to the development of new technologies that stop and eventually reverse the upward trend in greenhouse gases.

UK economist Nicholas Stern, principal author of *The Stern Review on the Economics of Climate Change.*
Greenhouse gas emission is 'the greatest market failure the world has ever seen.'
To avoid the risk of catastrophic climate change, the upward CO_2 trend must be stopped.

Bjørn Lomborg, President of the Copenhagen Consensus and author of *The Skeptical Environmentalist.*
'For little environmental benefit, we could end up sacrificing growth, jobs and opportunities for the big majority, especially in the developing world.'

The Tragedy of the Commons

Overgrazing the pastures around a village in Middle Ages England and overfishing the cod stocks of the North Sea and the North Atlantic Ocean during the recent past are tragedies of the commons. Other tragedies are the destruction of tropical rainforests in Africa and the Amazon basin of South America.

The **tragedy of the commons** is the overuse of a common resource that arises when its users have no incentive to conserve it and use it sustainably.

To study the tragedy of the commons and its possible remedies, we'll focus on the recent and current tragedy – overfishing and depleting the stock of Atlantic cod. You're about to discover that there are two problems that give rise to the tragedy of the commons:

◆ Unsustainable use of a common resource
◆ Inefficient use of a common resource

Unsustainable Use of a Common Resource

Many common resources are renewable – they replenish themselves by the birth and growth of new members of the population. Fish, trees and the fertile soil are all examples of this type of resource. At any given time, there is a stock of the resource and a rate at which it is being used.

A common resource is being used *unsustainably* if its rate of use persistently decreases its stock. A common resource is being used *sustainably* if its rate of use is less than or equal to its rate of renewal so that the stock available either grows or remains constant.

Focusing on the example of fish, a species is being used unsustainably if the catch persistently decreases the stock, and it is being used sustainably if the catch is less than or equal to the rate of renewal of the fish population.

The sustainable catch depends on the stock and in the way illustrated in Figure 16.5 by the sustainable catch curve, *SCC*. Along the *SCC* curve, with a small stock of fish the quantity of new fish born is also small, so the sustainable catch is small.

With a large stock of fish many fish are born but they must compete with each other for food, so only a few survive to reproduce and to grow large enough to catch. Again the sustainable catch is small.

Figure 16.5 Sustainable Catch

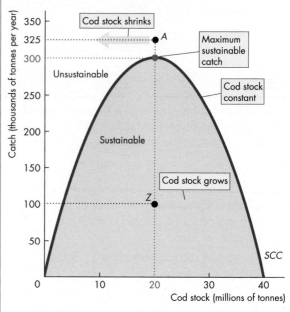

As the fish stock (on the *x*-axis) increases, the sustainable catch (on the *y*-axis) increases to a maximum. At the stock increases further, the fish must compete for food and the sustainable catch falls. If the catch exceeds the sustainable catch, such as at point *A*, the fish stock diminishes. If the catch is less than the sustainable catch, such as at point *Z*, the fish stock increases.

MyEconLab Animation ──────────────◆

Between a small and a large stock is a quantity of fish stock that maximises the sustainable catch. In Figure 16.5, this fish stock is 3 million tonnes and the sustainable catch is 300,000 tonnes a year.

The maximum sustainable catch arises from a balancing of the birth of new fish from the stock and the availability of food to sustain the fish population. If the quantity of fish caught is less than the sustainable catch, at a point such as Z, the fish stock grows; if the quantity caught exceeds the sustainable catch, the fish stock shrinks; and if the quantity caught equals the sustainable catch, at any point on the *SCC* curve, the fish stock remains constant and is available for future generations of fishers in the same quantity that is available today.

But if the quantity caught exceeds the sustainable catch, at a point such as *A*, the fish stock shrinks and unchecked will eventually fall to zero.

You now understand the problem of using a common renewable natural resource sustainably. But another problem is using it efficiently.

ECONOMICS IN ACTION

The Original Tragedy of the Commons

The term 'tragedy of the commons' comes from fourteenth-century England, where areas of rough grassland surrounding villages were overgrazed, and the number of cows and sheep that the commons could feed kept falling.

During the sixteenth century, the price of wool increased and England became a wool exporter to the world. Sheep farming became profitable, and sheep owners wanted to gain more effective control of the land they used. So the commons were gradually privatised and enclosed. Overgrazing ended, and land use became more efficient.

One of Today's Tragedies of the Commons

Before 1970, Atlantic cod was abundant. It was fished for many centuries and was a major food source for the first European settlers in North America. During the sixteenth century, hundreds of European ships caught large quantities of cod in the north-west Atlantic off the coast of what is now New England and Newfoundland, Canada. By 1620, there were more than 1,000 fishing boats in the waters off Newfoundland, and in 1812 about 1,600 boats. During these years, cod were huge fish, typically weighing in at more than 220 pounds and measuring 3–6 feet in length.

Most of the fishing during these years was done using lines and productivity was low. But low productivity limited the catch and enabled cod to be caught sustainably over hundreds of years.

The situation changed dramatically during the 1960s with the introduction of high-efficiency nets (called trawls, seines and gill nets), sonar technology to find fish concentrations, and large ships with efficient processing and storage facilities. Figure 1 shows that these technological advances brought soaring cod harvests. In less than a decade, cod landings increased from less than 300,000 tonnes a year to 800,000 tonnes.

This volume of cod could not be taken without a serious collapse in the remaining stock and by the 1980s it became vital to regulate cod fishing. But regulation was of limited success and stocks continued to fall.

In 1992, a total ban on cod fishing in the North Atlantic stabilized the population but at a very low level. Two decades of ban have enabled the species to repopulate, and it is now hoped that one day cod fishing will return but at a low and sustainable rate.

By 2000, North Sea cod stocks were also on the brink of extinction at 30,000 tonnes, well below the sustainable minimum stock, reckoned to be 150,000 tonnes. The EU stopped all fishing of cod in nursery areas and agreed to recovery measures for a 10-year period. These measures fell short of a ban on cod fishing as member states could not agree. Instead, catch quotas were cut by 45 per cent. By 2009, North Sea cod stocks had recovered to 53,000 tonnes but were still short of the 150,000 tonnes needed for a sustainable stock.

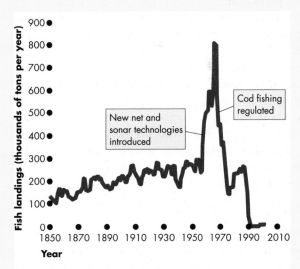

Figure 1 The Atlantic Cod Catch: 1850–2005

Source of data for graph: Millenium Ecosystem Assessment.

Source of information: Codfishes – Atlantic cod and its fishery, http://science.jrank.org/

Inefficient Use of a Common Resource

In an unregulated market, even if the catch is sustainable, it will be bigger than the efficient catch: overfishing occurs. And, most likely, the catch will not be sustainable. Why does overfishing occur? The answer is that fishers face only their own private cost and don't face the cost they impose on others – external cost. The *social* cost of fishing combines the *private* cost and *external* cost.

Let's examine the costs of catching fish to see how the presence of external cost brings overfishing.

Marginal Private Cost

You can think of the *marginal private cost* of catching fish as the additional cost incurred by keeping a boat and crew at sea for long enough to increase the catch by one tonne. Keeping a fishing boat at sea for an additional amount of time eventually runs into *diminishing marginal returns* (see Chapter 10, p. 244). As the crew gets tired, the storage facilities get overfull and the boat's speed is cut to conserve fuel, the catch per hour decreases. The cost of keeping the boat at sea for an additional hour is constant, so the marginal cost of catching fish increases as the quantity caught increases.

You've just seen that the *principle of increasing marginal cost* applies to catching fish just as it applies to other production activities: marginal private cost increases as the quantity of fish caught increases.

The marginal private cost of catching fish determines an individual fisher's supply of fish. A profit-maximising fisher is willing to supply the quantity at which the market price of fish covers the marginal private cost. The market supply is the sum of the quantities supplied by each individual fisher.

Marginal External Cost

The *marginal external cost* of catching fish is the cost per additional tonne that one fisher's catch imposes on all other fishers. This additional cost arises because one fisher's catch decreases the remaining stock, which in turn decreases the renewal rate of the stock and makes it harder for other fishers to find and catch fish.

Marginal external cost also increases as the quantity of fish caught increases. If the quantity of fish caught is so large that it drives the species to near extinction, the marginal external cost becomes infinitely large.

Marginal Social Cost

The *marginal social cost* of catching fish is the marginal private cost plus the marginal external cost. Because both of its components increase as the quantity caught increases, marginal social cost also increases with the quantity of fish caught.

Marginal Social Benefit and Demand

The marginal social benefit from fish is the price that consumers are willing to pay for an additional kilogram of fish. Marginal social benefit decreases as the quantity of fish consumed increases, so the demand curve (also the marginal social benefit curve) slopes downward.

Overfishing Equilibrium

Figure 16.6 illustrates overfishing and how it arises. The market demand curve for fish is the marginal social benefit curve, *MSB*. The market supply curve is the

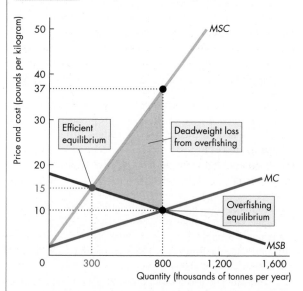

Figure 16.6 Why Overfishing Occurs

The market supply curve is the marginal private cost curve, *MC*. The market demand curve is the marginal social benefit curve, *MSB*. Market equilibrium occurs at a quantity of 800,000 tonnes and a price of £10 per kilogram. The marginal social cost curve is *MSC* and at the market equilibrium there is overfishing – marginal social cost exceeds marginal social benefit. The quantity at which *MSC* equals *MSB* is the efficient quantity, 300,000 tonnes per year. The grey triangle shows the deadweight loss from overfishing.

MyEconLab Animation ━━━━━━━━━━━━━━━◆

marginal private cost curve, *MC*. Market equilibrium occurs at the intersection point of these two curves. The equilibrium quantity is 800,000 tonnes per year and the equilibrium price is £10 per kilogram.

At this market equilibrium, overfishing is running down the fish stock. At the market equilibrium quantity, marginal social benefit (and willingness to pay) is £10 per kilogram, but the marginal social cost exceeds this amount. The marginal external cost is the cost of running down the fish stock.

Efficient Equilibrium

The efficient use of a common resource is to use the quantity that makes the marginal social benefit from the resource equal to the marginal social cost. In Figure 16.6 the efficient quantity of fish is 300,000 tonnes per year – the quantity that makes marginal social cost (on the *MSC* curve) equal to marginal social benefit (on the *MSB* curve). At this quantity, the marginal catch of each individual fisher costs society what people are willing to pay for it.

Deadweight Loss from Overfishing

Deadweight loss measures the cost of overfishing. It is the marginal social cost minus the marginal social benefit from all the fish caught in excess of the efficient quantity – the area of the grey triangle in Figure 16.6 .

Achieving an Efficient Outcome

Defining the conditions under which a common resource is used efficiently is easier than delivering those conditions. To use a common resource efficiently, it is necessary to design an incentive mechanism that confronts the users of the resource with the marginal social consequences of their actions. The same principles apply to common resources as those that you met earlier in this chapter when you studied the external cost of pollution. The three main methods that might be used to achieve the efficient use of a common resource are

◆ Property rights
◆ Production quotas
◆ Individual transferable quotas (ITQs)

Property Rights

A common resource that no one owns and which anyone is free to use contrasts with *private property*, which is a

resource that someone owns and has an incentive to use in the way that maximises its value. One way of overcoming the tragedy of the commons is to convert a common resource to private property. By assigning private property rights to the resource, its owner faces the same conditions as society faces. It doesn't matter who owns the resource. The users of the resource will be confronted with the full cost of using it because they either own it or pay a fee to the owner for permission to use it.

When private property rights over a resource are established and enforced, the *MSC* curve becomes the marginal private cost curve, and the use of the resource is efficient.

Figure 16.7 illustrates an efficient outcome with property rights. The supply curve *S = MC = MSC* and the demand curve *D = MSB* determine the equilibrium price and quantity. The price equals both marginal social benefit and marginal social cost and the quantity is efficient.

Figure 16.7 Property Rights Achieve an Efficient Outcome

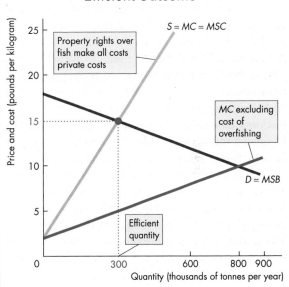

With private property rights, fishers pay the owner of the fish stock for permission to fish and face the full social cost of their actions. The marginal cost curve includes the external cost, so the supply curve is the marginal private cost curve and the marginal social cost curve, *S = MC = MSC*.

Market equilibrium occurs at £15 per kilogram and at that price, the quantity is 300,000 tonnes per year. At this quantity, marginal social cost equals marginal social benefit, and the catch is efficient. The property rights convert the fish stock from a common resource to a private resource and it is used efficiently.

MyEconLab Animation ────────────────◆

The private property solution to the tragedy of the commons is available in some cases. It was the solution to the original tragedy of the commons in England's Middle Ages. It is also a solution that has been used to prevent overuse of the airwaves that carry mobile-phone services. The right to use this space (called the frequency spectrum) has been auctioned by governments to the highest bidders. The owner of each part of the spectrum is the only one permitted to use it (or license someone else to use it).

But assigning private property rights is not always feasible. It would be difficult, for example, to assign private property rights to the oceans. It would not be impossible, but the cost of enforcing private property rights over thousands of square kilometres of ocean would be high. It would be even more difficult to assign and protect private property rights to the atmosphere.

In some cases, there is an emotional objection to assigning private property rights to a resource that is regarded as public. In the absence of property rights, some form of government intervention is used, one of which is a production quota.

Production Quotas

A *production quota* is an upper limit to the quantity of a good that may be produced in a specified period. The quota is allocated to individual producers, so each producer has its own quota.

You studied the effects of a production quota in Chapter 6 (pp. 137–138) and learned that a quota can drive a wedge between marginal social benefit and marginal social cost and create deadweight loss. In that earlier example, the market was efficient without a quota. But in the case of common resources, the market overuses the resource and produces an inefficient quantity. A production quota in this market brings a move towards a more efficient outcome.

Figure 16.8 shows a quota that achieves an efficient outcome. The quota limits the catch (production) to 300,000 tonnes, the efficient quantity at which marginal social benefit, *MSB*, equals marginal social cost, *MSC*. If everyone sticks to their own quota, the outcome is efficient. But implementing a production quota has two problems.

First, it is in every fisher's self-interest to catch more fish than the quantity permitted under the quota. The reason is that price exceeds marginal private cost, so by catching more fish, a fisher gets a higher income. If enough fishers break the quota, overfishing and the tragedy of the commons remain.

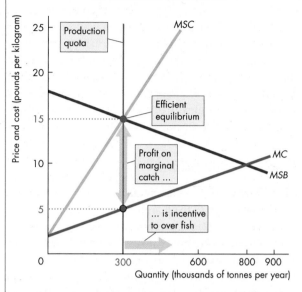

Figure 16.8 A Production Quota to Achieve an Efficient Outcome

A quota of 300,000 tonnes limits production to this quantity, raises the price to £15 per kilogram and lowers marginal cost to £5 per kilogram. A fisher who cheats and produces more than the allotted quota increases his profit by £10 per kilogram. If all (or most) fishers cheat, production exceeds the quota and there is a return to overfishing.

MyEconLab Animation ────────────◆

Second, marginal cost is not, in general, the same for all producers – as we're assuming here. Efficiency requires that the quota be allocated to the producers with the lowest marginal cost. But bureaucrats who allocate quotas do not have information about the marginal cost of individual producers. Even if they tried to get this information, producers would have an incentive to lie about their costs so as to get a bigger quota.

So where producers are difficult, or very costly, to monitor or where marginal cost varies across producers, a production quota cannot achieve an efficient outcome.

Individual Transferable Quotas

Where producers are difficult to monitor or where marginal cost varies across producers, a more sophisticated quota system can be effective. It is an **individual transferable quota (ITQ)**, which is a production limit assigned to an individual who is then free to transfer (sell) the quota to someone else. A market in ITQs emerges and ITQs are traded at their market price. (Cap-and-trade to limit pollution is an ITQ for pollution.)

The market price of an ITQ is the highest price that someone is willing to pay for one. That price is marginal social benefit minus marginal cost. The price of an ITQ will rise to this level because fishers who don't have a quota would be willing to pay this amount to get one.

A fisher with an ITQ could sell it for the market price, so by not selling the ITQ the fisher incurs an opportunity cost. The marginal cost of fishing, which now includes the opportunity cost of the ITQ, equals the marginal social benefit from the efficient quantity.

Figure 16.9 illustrates how ITQs work. Each fisher receives an allocation of ITQs such that the total catch permitted by the ITQs is 300,000 tonnes per year. Fishers trade ITQs: those with low marginal cost buy ITQs from those with high marginal cost and the market price of an ITQ settles at £10 per kilogram of fish. The marginal private cost is now equal to the marginal private cost, *MC*, plus the price of the ITQ. The marginal private cost curve shifts upwards to become *MC* + price of ITQ, and each fisher is confronted with the marginal social cost of fishing. No one has an incentive to exceed the quota and the outcome is efficient.

ECONOMICS IN ACTION

ITQs Work

Iceland introduced the first ITQs in 1984 to conserve its lobster stocks. In 1986, New Zealand and a bit later Australia introduced ITQs to conserve fish stocks in the South Pacific and Southern Oceans. The evidence from these countries suggests that ITQs work well.

ITQs help maintain fish stocks, but they also reduce the size of the fishing industry. This consequence of ITQs puts them against the self-interest of fishers. In all countries the fishing industry opposes restrictions on its activities, but in Australia and New Zealand the opposition is not strong enough to block ITQs.

In the US the opposition has been harder to overcome and in 1996 the US Congress passed the Sustainable Fishing Act, which put a moratorium on ITQs. This moratorium was lifted in 2004, and since then ITQs have been applied to 28 fisheries from the Gulf of Alaska to the Gulf of Mexico.

Economists have studied the effects of ITQs extensively and agree that they work. ITQs offer an effective tool for achieving an efficient use of the stock of ocean fish.

Figure 16.9 ITQs to Achieve an Efficient Outcome

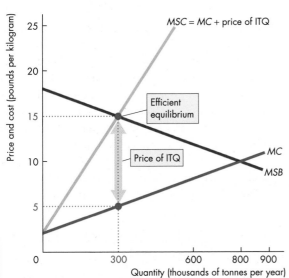

ITQs are issued to keep the total catch at the efficient level. The market price of an ITQ equals the marginal social benefit minus marginal cost. Because each fisher faces the opportunity cost of using the resource, self-interest achieves the social interest.

MyEconLab Animation ━━━━━━━━━━━━━━━━━━━◆

REVIEW QUIZ

1 What is the tragedy of the commons? Give two examples including one from your area.
2 Describe the conditions under which a common resource is used efficiently.
3 Review three methods that might achieve the efficient use of a common resource and explain the obstacles to efficiency.

Do these questions in Study Plan 16.2 and get instant feedback.   MyEconLab

Reading Between the Lines on pp. 382–383 looks at the EU cap-and-trade system to lower carbon emissions.

The next two chapters examine the third big question of economics: for whom are goods and services produced? We examine the markets for factors of production and discover how factor incomes and the distribution of income are determined.

READING BETWEEN THE LINES

Cap-and-Trade in the EU

UK Businesses Warn on Emissions Tax

Pilita Clark, Environment Correspondent

UK businesses will face sharply higher energy costs than continental peers if the European Parliament refuses to prop up the EU carbon market. . . . A contentious new UK carbon floor price . . . is likely to keep British carbon prices much higher than those in the EU market, where they have crashed to record lows. . . .

The EU emissions trading market has been hit by weak economic conditions that have lowered demand for the carbon allowances that let companies emit CO_2. This has driven down prices that had already been affected by a glut of allowances. . . .

The plan, known as backloading, is staunchly supported by the UK govern-ment, which does not want the EU carbon price to be sharply lower than Britain's national carbon floor. . . . The UK carbon floor price will require power generators to pay just over £18 a tonne of carbon emitted by 2015.

EU carbon prices fell to less than €3 earlier this year, having been as high as almost €30 in 2008. The low price does little to encourage companies to reduce emissions, so the European Commission has proposed the backloading measure to withdraw 900m permits from the system temporarily and push up prices.

FT   *Source*: FT.com, 31 March 2013.
© The Financial Times Limited 2013. All Rights Reserved.

 The Essence of the Story

- The EU carbon price was almost €30 per tonne of carbon emitted in 2008.

- A glut of permits and a fall in demand lowered the EU carbon price to less than €3 a tonne in 2013.

- The price is too low to reduce emissions.

- A UK carbon floor price will be just over £18 (€25) per tonne by 2015.

- The UK wants a higher EU price.

- The European Commission proposes with-drawing 900 million permits to raise the EU price.

Economic Analysis

- To confront electric power utilities with the external cost of their carbon emissions, they must buy emission permits at a price determined in the European carbon market.

- Figure 1 shows how this system works in the UK market for electricity. The demand curve and marginal social benefit curve is $D = MSB$. The supply curve and private marginal cost curve is $S = MC$.

- Power stations produce 400 million MWh of electricity a year at a price of 8 pence per kWh where MC equals MSB.

- Electricity production creates carbon, an external cost, which is part of the marginal social cost, MSC.

- The efficient outcome is where MSB equals MSC. With no regulation, a deadweight loss (the grey area) arises.

- To achieve the efficient outcome, the EU issues enough carbon permits to confront electric utilities with the marginal external cost.

- Using the numbers assumed here, the efficient outcome would be achieved by issuing carbon permits to generate 300 million MWh per year, and allowing the permits to be traded.

- Figure 2 shows how this scheme has broken and why the UK has introduced a carbon floor price.

- The demand curve for permits is D_1. If the efficient quantity of permits, S_1, is issued, the price of a permit is €35 (equivalent to 3 pence per kWh). Confronted with this price, utilities reduce production to the efficient quantity shown in Figure 1.

- The EU has issued too many permits at S_2, and at the same time the demand for permits has slumped to D_2. The price has fallen to €3 per permit.

- At a permit price of €3, utilities overproduce, so the UK has introduced a carbon floor price of £18 (or €25) per permit as in Figure 2.

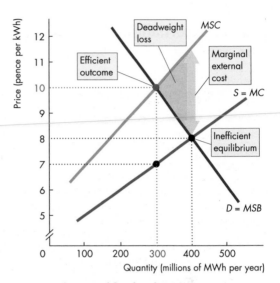

Figure 1 **The UK Market for Electricity**

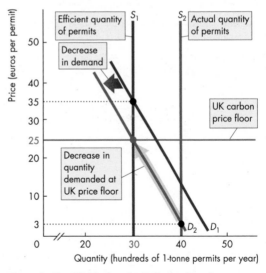

Figure 2 **The UK Market for Pollution Permits**

- The UK price floor is high enough to make UK utilities cut production to the efficient level. But other EU utilities continue to produce more than the efficient quantity of electricity.

- The EU proposal to cut the supply of permits will lead to the efficient level of production if it shifts supply back from S_2 to S_1 in Figure 2.

SUMMARY

Key Points

Negative Externalities: Pollution
(pp. 368–375)

◆ A competitive market would produce too much of a good that has external production costs.

◆ External costs are costs of production that fall on people other than the producer of a good or service. Marginal social cost equals marginal private cost plus marginal external cost.

◆ Producers take account only of marginal private cost and produce more than the efficient quantity when there is a marginal external cost.

◆ Sometimes it is possible to overcome a negative externality by assigning a property right.

◆ When property rights cannot be assigned, governments might overcome externalities by using taxes, emission charges or marketable permits.

Do Problems 1 to 15 to get a better understanding of the external costs of pollution.

The Tragedy of the Commons
(pp. 376–381)

◆ Common resources create a problem that is called the tragedy of the commons – no one has a private incentive to conserve the resources and use them at an efficient rate.

◆ A common resource is used to the point at which the marginal social benefit equals the marginal private cost.

◆ A common resource might be used efficiently by creating a private property right, setting a quota, or issuing individual transferable quotas.

Do Problems 16 to 22 to get a better understanding of the tragedy of the commons.

Key Terms

Abatement technology, 371
Coase theorem, 372
Individual transferable quota (ITQ), 380
Marginal external cost, 369
Marginal private cost, 369
Marginal social cost, 369
Negative externality, 369
Pigovian taxes, 372
Property rights, 371
Tragedy of the commons, 376
Transactions costs, 372

STUDY PLAN PROBLEMS AND APPLICATIONS

Do Problems 1 to 22 in MyEconLab Chapter 16 Study Plan and get instant feedback.

MyEconLab

Negative Externalities: Pollution

(Study Plan 16.1)

Use the following figure in Problems 1 to 5.

The figure illustrates the market for European cotton. Consider a small town surrounded by a large cotton farm. Suppose that the cotton grower sprays the plants with chemicals to control insects and that the chemical waste flows into the river passing through the town. The marginal external cost of the chemical waste is equal to the marginal private cost of producing the cotton (that is, the marginal social cost of producing the cotton is double the marginal private cost).

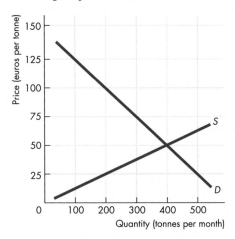

1 If no one owns the river and the town takes no action to control the waste, what is the quantity of cotton, and the deadweight loss created?

2 a Suppose that the town owns the river and makes the cotton grower pay the cost of pollution. How much cotton is produced and what does the grower pay the town per tonne of cotton produced?

b Suppose that the cotton grower owns the river and rents it to the town. How much cotton is produced and how is the rent paid by the town to the grower (per tonne of cotton produced) influenced by cotton growing?

c Compare the quantities of cotton produced in parts (a) and (b), and explain the relationship between these quantities.

3 Suppose that no one owns the river and that the city introduces a pollution tax. What is the tax per tonne of cotton produced that achieves an efficient outcome?

4 Compare the outcomes when property rights exist and when the pollution tax achieves the efficient amount of waste.

5 Suppose that no one owns the river and that the government issues two marketable pollution permits: one to the cotton grower and one to the city. Each permit allows the same amount of pollution of the river, and the total pollution created is the efficient amount.

What is the quantity of cotton produced and what is the market price of a pollution permit? Who buys and who sells a permit?

Use the following news clip in Problems 6 to 8.

As the developing countries turn to the mining industry to secure their economic futures, indigenous peoples and peasant farmers in Panama are trying to stop the development of a gold mine and the world's last major copper reserve, which would strip thousands of hectares of rainforest, deplete and contaminate water supplies and displace communities that have lived in the area for centuries.

Source: NPR, 14 June 2012

6 List the negative externalites mentioned in the news clip.

7 How would the outcome be changed if the indigenous communities had property rights over the resources?

8 Which of the public choice methods might be used to achieve an efficient allocation of resources in this situation?

Use the following news clip to work Problems 9 to 11.

Bag Revolution

Thin plastic carrier bags aren't biodegradable and often end up in the ocean or in the environment. In the UK we use about 10 billion bags a year, many from supermarkets. Supermarkets have agreed to take action to reduce carrier bag use to avoid governments forcing them to charge for bags.

Source: *The Independent*, 26 August 2010

9 a Describe the externality that arises from plastic bags.

b Draw a graph to illustrate how plastic bags create deadweight loss.

10 a With the majority of plastic bags coming from super-markets and grocery stores, the Irish government introduced a tax of 12p a bag in 2002, which has cut carrier bag use by 90 per cent. Explain the effects of the Irish policy on the use of plastic bags.

b Draw a graph to illustrate the Irish policy, and show the change in the deadweight loss that arises from this policy.

11 The Italian government banned the use of non-biodegradable carrier bags from 2011. Explain why a complete ban on plastic bags might be inefficient.

Use the following news clip in Problems 12 to 14.

The Year in Medicine: Mobile Phones

Talking on a hands-free mobile phone while driving might seem safe, but think again. People who used hands-free mobile phones in simulation trials exhibited slower reaction times and took longer to hit the brakes than drivers who weren't otherwise distracted. Data from real-life driving tests show that mobile-phone use rivals drowsy driving as a major cause of accidents.

Source: *Time*, 4 December 2006

12 a Explain the external costs that arise from using a mobile phone while driving.

b Explain why the market for mobile phone service creates a deadweight loss.

13 Draw a graph to illustrate how a deadweight loss arises from the use of mobile phones.

14 Explain how government intervention might improve the efficiency of mobile phone use.

15 Pollution Rules Squeeze Strawberry Crop

Last year, Ventura County farmers harvested nearly 12,000 acres of strawberries valued at more than $323 million. To comply with the federal Clean Air Act, growers must use 50 per cent less pesticide. It is estimated that strawberry output will fall by 60 per cent.

Source: *USA Today*, 29 February 2008

Explain how a limit on pesticide will change the efficiency of the strawberry industry. Would a cap-and-trade scheme be more efficient?

The Tragedy of the Commons

(Study Plan 16.2)

Use the following figure in Problems 16 to 18.

The figure shows the market for North Atlantic tuna.

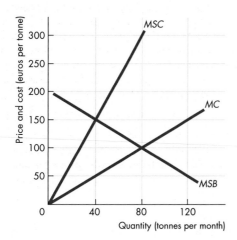

16 a What is the quantity of tuna that fishing boats catch and the price of tuna? Is the tuna stock being used efficiently? Explain why or why not.

b What would be the price of tuna if the stock of tuna is used efficiently?

17 a With a quota of 40 tonnes a month for the tuna fishing industry, what is the equilibrium price of tuna and the quantity of tuna that fishers catch?

b Is the equilibrium an overfishing equilibrium?

18 If the government issues ITQs to individual fishing boats that limit the total catch to the efficient quantity, what is the market price of an ITQ?

19 Whaling 'Hurts Tourist Industry'

Leah Garces, the director of programmes at the World Society for the Protection of Animals, reported that whale watching is more economically significant and sustainable to people and communities than whaling. The global whale watching industry is estimated to be a $1.25 billion business enjoyed by over 10 million people in more than 90 countries each year.

Source: BBC, 2 June 2009

Describe the trade-off facing communities that live near whaling areas. How might a thriving whale watching industry avoid the tragedy of the commons?

Use the following information in Problems 20 and 21.

A natural spring runs under land owned by 10 people. Each person has the right to sink a well and can take water from the spring at a constant marginal cost of £0.05 a litre. The table sets out the external cost and the social benefit of water.

Quantity of water (litres per day)	Marginal external cost	Marginal social benefit
	(pence per litre)	
10	1	10
20	2	9
30	3	8
40	4	7
50	5	6
60	6	5
70	7	4

20 Draw a graph to illustrate the market equilibrium. On your graph, show the efficient quantity of water taken.

21 If the government sets a quota on the total amount of water such that the spring is used efficiently, what would that quota be?

22 If the government issues ITQs to landowners that limit the total amount of water taken to the efficient quantity, what is the market price of an ITQ?

ADDITIONAL PROBLEMS AND APPLICATIONS

Do these problems in MyEconLab if assigned by your instructor.   MyEconLab

Negative Externalities: Pollution

23 Betty and Anna work at the same office in Brussels. They both must attend a meeting in Paris, so they decide to drive to the meeting together. Betty is a cigarette smoker, and her marginal benefit from smoking a package of cigarettes a day is €40. Cigarettes are €6 a packet. Anna dislikes cigarette smoke, and her marginal benefit from a smoke-free environment is €50 a day. What is the outcome if:

   a Betty drives her car with Anna as a passenger?

   b Anna drives her car with Betty as a passenger?

Use the following information and the figure, which illustrates the market for a pesticide with no government intervention, in Problems 24 to 27.

When factories produce pesticide, they also create waste, which they dump into a lake on the outskirts of the town. The marginal external cost of the waste is equal to the marginal private cost of producing the pesticide (that is, the marginal social cost of producing the pesticide is double the marginal private cost).

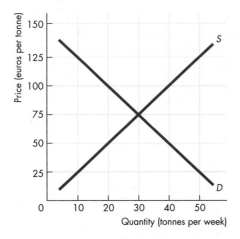

24 What is the quantity of pesticide produced if no one owns the lake and what is the efficient quantity of pesticide?

25 If the residents of the town own the lake, what is the quantity of pesticide produced and how much do residents of the town charge the factories to dump waste?

26 If the pesticide factories own the lake, how much pesticide is produced?

27 If no one owns the lake and the government levies a pollution tax, what is the tax that achieves the efficient outcome?

Use the following table in Problems 28 to 30.

The first two columns of the table show the demand schedule for electricity from a European coal-burning utility; the second and third columns show the utility's cost of producing electricity. The marginal external cost of the pollution created is equal to the marginal cost.

Price (cents per kilowatt)	Quantity (kilowatts per day)	Marginal cost (cents per kilowatt)
4	500	10
8	400	8
12	300	6
16	200	4
20	100	2

28 With no government action to control pollution, what is the quantity of electricity produced, the price of electricity and the marginal external cost of the pollution generated?

29 With no government action to control pollution, what is the marginal social cost of the electricity generated and the deadweight loss created?

30 Suppose that the government levies a pollution tax, such that the utility produces the efficient quantity. What is the price of electricity? What is the tax levied, and the government's tax revenue per day?

31 **EPA Pushes to have Companies Track Greenhouse Gases**

The US government plans to make large polluters, such as oil refiners and automobile manufacturers, and makers of cement, aluminium, glass and paper, start tracking their emissions next year. The EPA's climate change division noted that this is an important step. A cap-and-trade scheme will be introduced for factories that emit 90 per cent of US greenhouse gases.

Source: *USA Today*, 11 March 2009

The monitoring cost of the scheme is expected to be about $127 million a year. Who will benefit from the scheme? Who will bear the burden of this scheme?

The Tragedy of the Commons

32 If hikers and other visitors were required to pay a fee to use the Pennine Way,

    a Would the use of this common resource be more efficient?

    b Would it be even more efficient if the most popular spots along the way had the highest prices?

    c Why do you think we don't see more market solutions to the tragedy of the commons?

Use the following information in Problems 33 to 35.

A spring runs under a village. Everyone can sink a well on their own land and take water from the spring. The following figure shows the marginal social benefit from and the marginal cost of taking water.

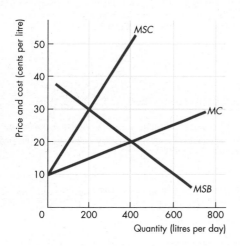

33 What is the quantity of water taken and what is the private cost of the water taken?

34 What is the efficient quantity of water taken and the marginal social cost at the efficient quantity?

35 If the village council sets a quota on the total amount of water such that the spring is used efficiently, what would be the quota and the market value of the water taken per day?

36 Polar Ice Cap Shrinks Further and Thins

With the warming of the planet, the polar ice cap is shrinking and the Arctic Sea is expanding. As the ice cap shrinks further, more and more underwater mineral resources will become accessible. Many countries are staking out territorial claims to parts of the polar region.

    Source: *The Wall Street Journal*, 7 April 2009

Explain how ownership of these mineral resources will influence the amount of damage done to the Arctic Sea and its wildlife.

Economics in the News

37 After you have studied *Reading Between the Lines* on pp. 382–383, answer the following questions.

    a Why do carbon dioxide emissions make the marginal social cost of electricity production exceed the marginal private cost?

    b Why is a carbon cap-and-trade system superior to either a carbon tax or a fixed pollution quota as a way of reducing carbon dioxide emissions?

    c What is the main problem with the EU cap-and-trade system for pollution permits and how can auctions of new permits improve the efficiency of the market for pollution permits?

Use the following information in Problems 38 and 39.

Where the Tuna Roam

To the first settlers, the Great Plains of North America posed the same problem as the oceans today: a vast, open area where there seemed to be no way to protect animals. But animals thrived once the settlers divvied up the land and devised ways to protect their livestock. Today, the oceans are much like an open range. Fishermen catch as much as they can this year, even if they are overfishing. They figure any fish they don't take for themselves will just be taken by someone else.

    Source: *The New York Times*, 4 November 2006

38 **a** What are the similarities between the problems faced by the earliest American settlers and today's fishers?

    b Can the tragedy of the commons in the oceans be eliminated in the same manner used by the early settlers on the plains?

39 How can ITQs change the short-term outlook of fishers to a long-term outlook?

40 Cleaning the Sewer: A High Tech revival for Europe's Foulest River

The Emscher river is in the heart of Germany's old industrial zone and for 100 years, steel mills, coal mines and slaughter houses have been pumping waste into the river, used as an open sewer. The mines have closed and now a new sewage plant, water elevators and cleaning robots are bringing the river back to life as a social amenity. Fish have been spotted in the upper region already.

    Source: *Der Speigel*, 12 November 2012

    a Describe the externalities in the Emscher river, and draw a graph to illustrate the inefficiency arising from them.

    b Which methods for achieving an efficient use of resources in the face of pollution were used for the clean-up?

    c Draw a graph to explain and illustrate the Emscher river situation when allocative efficiency is achieved.

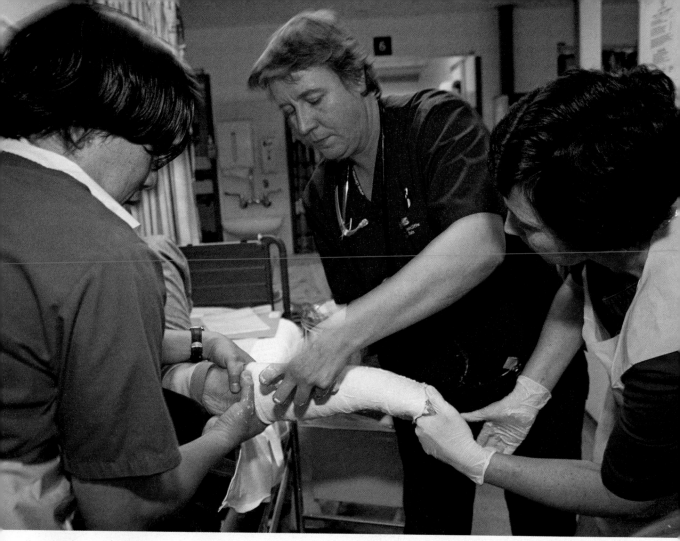

17 The Markets for Factors of Production

After studying this chapter you will be able to:

- Describe the anatomy of factor markets
- Explain how the value of marginal product determines the demand for a factor of production
- Explain how wage rates and employment are determined and how trades unions influence labour markets
- Explain how capital and land rental rates and natural resource prices are determined

Nurses do vital work but earn much less than premier league footballers. Why? What determines the wages that people earn? And what determines the jobs available. Why are manufacturing jobs disappearing, and what new jobs are being created?

In this chapter, we study labour markets as well as the markets for capital and natural resources. In *Reading Between the Lines* at the end of the chapter, we look at the market for skilled nuclear engineers.

The Anatomy of Factor Markets

The four factors of production are:

◆ Labour
◆ Capital
◆ Land (natural resources)
◆ Entrepreneurship

Let's take a brief look at the anatomy of the markets in which these factors of production are traded.

Markets for Labour Services

Labour services are the physical and mental work effort that people supply to produce goods and services. A labour market is a collection of people and firms who trade labour services. The price of labour services is the wage rate.

Some labour services are traded day by day. These services are called *casual labour*. People who pick fruit and vegetables often just show up at a farm and take whatever work is available that day. But most labour services are traded on a contract, called a **job**.

Most labour markets have many buyers and many sellers and are competitive. In these labour markets, the wage rate is determined by supply and demand, just as the price is determined in any other competitive market.

In some labour markets, a trades union organises labour, which introduces an element of monopoly on the supply-side of the labour market. In this type of labour market, a bargaining process between the trades union and the employer determines the wage rate.

We'll study both competitive labour markets and trades unions in this chapter.

Markets for Capital Services

Capital consists of the tools, instruments, machines, buildings and other constructions that have been produced in the past and which businesses now use to produce goods and services. These physical objects are themselves goods – capital goods. Capital goods are traded in goods markets, just as bottled water and toothpaste are. The price of a dump truck, a capital good, is determined by supply and demand in the market for dump trucks. This market is not a market for capital services.

A market for *capital services* is a rental market – a market in which the services of capital are hired.

An example of a market for capital services is the vehicle rental market in which Avis, Budget, Hertz, U-Haul and many other firms offer automobiles and trucks for hire. The price in a capital services market is a *rental rate*.

Most capital services are not traded in a market. Instead, a firm buys capital and uses it itself. The services of the capital that a firm owns and operates have an implicit price that arises from depreciation and interest costs (see Chapter 9, pp. 196–197). You can think of this price as the implicit rental rate of capital. Firms that buy capital and use it themselves are *implicitly* renting the capital to themselves.

Markets for Land Services and Natural Resources

Land consists of all the gifts of nature – natural resources. The market for land as a factor of production is the market for the services of land – the use of land. The price of the services of land is a rental rate.

Most natural resources, such as farmland, can be used repeatedly. But a few natural resources are non-renewable. **Non-renewable natural resources** are resources that can be used only once. Examples are oil, natural gas and coal. The prices of non-renewable natural resources are determined in global commodity markets and are called *commodity prices*.

Entrepreneurship

Entrepreneurial services are not traded in markets. Entrepreneurs receive the profit or bear the loss that results from their business decisions.

REVIEW QUIZ

1 What are the factors of production and their prices?
2 What is the distinction between capital and the services of capital?
3 What is the distinction between the price of capital equipment and the rental rate of capital?

Do these questions in Study Plan 17.1 and get instant feedback.   MyEconLab

In the rest of this chapter, we explore the influences on the demand for and supply of factors of production. We begin by studying the demand for a factor of production.

The Demand for a Factor of Production

The demand for a factor of production is a **derived demand** – it is derived from the demand for the goods and services that the labour produces. You've seen, in Chapters 9 to 14, how a firm determines its profit-maximising output. The quantities of factors of production demanded are a consequence of the firm's output decision. A firm hires the quantities of factors of production that produce the firm's profit-maximising output.

To decide the quantity of a factor of production to hire, a firm compares the cost of hiring an additional unit of the factor with its value to the firm. The cost of hiring an additional unit of a factor of production is the factor price. The value to the firm of hiring one more unit of a factor of production is called the factor's **value of marginal product**. We calculate the value of marginal product as the price of a unit of output multiplied by the marginal product of the factor of production.

To study the demand for a factor of production, we'll use labour as the example. But what you learn here about the demand for labour applies to the demand for all factors of production.

Value of Marginal Product

Table 17.1 shows you how to calculate the value of marginal product of labour at Angelo's Bakery. The first two columns show Angelo's total product schedule – the number of loaves per hour that each quantity of labour can produce. The third column shows the marginal product of labour – the change in total product that results from a one-unit increase in the quantity of labour employed. (See Chapter 10, pp. 221–224 for a refresher on product schedules.)

Angelo can sell bread at the going market price of £2 a loaf. Given this information, we can calculate the value of marginal product (fourth column). It equals price multiplied by marginal product. For example, the marginal product of the second worker is 6 loaves. Each loaf sold brings in £2, so the value of marginal product of the second worker is £12 (6 loaves at £2 each).

A Firm's Demand for Labour

The value of marginal product of labour tells us what an additional worker is worth to a firm. It tells us the revenue that the firm makes by hiring one more worker. The wage rate tells us what an additional worker costs a firm.

The value of marginal product of labour and the wage rate together determine the quantity of labour demanded by a firm. Because the value of marginal product decreases as the quantity of labour employed increases, there is a simple rule for maximising profit: hire the quantity of labour at which the value of marginal product equals the wage rate.

If the value of marginal product of labour exceeds the wage rate, a firm can increase its profit by hiring one more worker. If the wage rate exceeds the value of

Table 17.1

Value of Marginal Product at Angelo's Bakery

	Quantity of labour (L) (workers)	Total product (TP) (loaves per hour)	Marginal product (MP = ΔTP/ΔL) (loaves per worker)	Value of marginal product (VMP = MP × P) (pounds per worker)
A	0	0		
			7	14
B	1	7		
			6	**12**
C	**2**	13		
			5	10
D	3	18		
			4	8
E	4	22		
			3	6
F	5	25		

The value of marginal product of labour equals the price of the product produced multiplied by marginal product of labour. If Angelo's hires 2 workers, the marginal product of the second worker is 6 loaves (in the third column). The price of a loaf is £2, so the value of marginal product of the second worker is £2 a loaf multiplied by 6 loaves, which is £12 (in the fourth column).

marginal product of labour, a firm can increase its profit by firing one worker. But if the wage rate equals the value of marginal product of labour, the firm cannot increase its profit by changing the number of workers it employs. The firm is making the maximum possible profit. So

> **The quantity of labour demanded by a firm is the quantity at which the value of marginal product of labour equals the wage rate.**

A Firm's Demand for Labour Curve

A firm's demand for labour curve is derived from its value of marginal product curve. Figure 17.1 shows these two curves. Figure 17.1(a) shows the value of marginal product curve at Angelo's Bakery. The blue bars graph the numbers in Table 17.1. The curve labelled *VMP* is Angelo's value of marginal product curve.

If the wage rate falls and other things remain the same, a firm hires more workers. Figure 17.1(b) shows Angelo's demand for labour curve.

Suppose the wage rate is £10 an hour. You can see in Figure17.1(a) that if Angelo hires 2 workers, the value of marginal product of labour is £12 an hour. At a wage rate of £10 an hour, Angelo makes a profit of £2 an hour on the second worker. If Angelo hires a third worker, the value of marginal product of that worker is £10 an hour. So on this third worker, Angelo breaks even.

If Angelo hired 4 workers, his profit would fall. The fourth worker generates a value of marginal product of only £8 an hour but costs £10 an hour, so Angelo does not hire the fourth worker. When the wage rate is £10 an hour, the quantity of labour demanded by Angelo is 3 workers.

Figure 17.1(b) shows Angelo's demand for labour curve, *D*. At £10 an hour, the quantity of labour demanded by Angelo is 3 workers. If the wage rate increased to £12 an hour, Angelo would decrease the quantity of labour demanded to 2 workers. If the wage rate decreased to £8 an hour, Angelo would increase the quantity of labour demanded to 4 workers.

A change in the wage rate brings a change in the quantity of labour demanded and a movement along the demand for labour curve.

A change in any other influence on a firm's labour hiring plans changes the demand for labour and shifts the demand for labour curve.

Figure 17.1 The Demand for Labour at Angelo's Bakery

(a) Value of marginal product

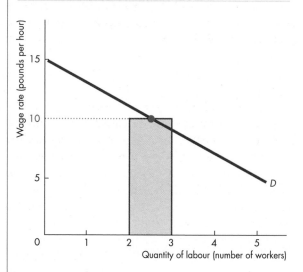

(b) Demand for labour

Angelo's Bakery can sell any quantity of bread at £2 a loaf. The blue bars in part (a) represent the firm's value of marginal product of labour (based on Table 17.1). The line labelled *VMP* is the firm's value of marginal product curve. Part (b) shows Angelo's demand for labour curve. Angelo hires the quantity of labour that makes the value of marginal product equal to the wage rate. The demand for labour curve slopes downward because the value of marginal product diminishes as the quantity of labour employed increases.

MyEconLab Animation ━━━━━━━━━━━━━◆

Changes in the Demand for Labour

A firm's demand for labour depends on:

◆ The price of the firm's output
◆ Other factor prices
◆ Technology

The Price of the Firm's Output

The higher the price of a firm's output, the greater is the firm's demand for labour. The price of output affects the demand for labour through its influence on the value of marginal product of labour. A higher price for the firm's output increases the value of marginal product of labour. A change in the price of a firm's output leads to a shift in the firm's demand for labour curve. If the price of the firm's output increases, the demand for labour curve shifts rightward.

For example, if the price of bread increased to £3 a loaf, the value of marginal product of Angelo's fourth worker would increase from £8 an hour to £12 an hour. At a wage rate of £10 an hour, Angelo would now hire 4 workers instead of 3.

Other Factor Prices

If the price of using capital decreases relative to the wage rate, a firm substitutes capital for labour and increases the quantity of capital it uses. Usually, the demand for labour will decrease when the price of using capital falls. For example, if the price of a breadmaking machine falls, Angelo might decide to install one machine and lay off a worker. But the demand for labour could increase if the lower price of capital led to a sufficiently large increase in the scale of production.

For example, with cheaper machines available, Angelo might install a machine and hire more labour to operate it. This type of factor substitution occurs in the long run when the firm can change the size of its plant.

Technology

New technologies decrease the demand for some types of labour and increase the demand for other types. For example, if a new automated breadmaking machine becomes available, Angelo might install one of these machines and fire most of his workforce – a decrease in the demand for bakery workers. But the firms that manufacture and service automated breadmaking machines hire more labour, so there is an increase in the demand for this type of labour. An event similar to this one occurred during the 1990s when the introduction of electronic telephone exchanges decreased the demand for telephone operators and increased the demand for computer programmers and electronics engineers.

Table 17.2 summarises the influences on a firm's demand for labour.

Table 17.2

A Firm's Demand for Labour

The Law of Demand

(Movements along the demand for labour curve)

The quantity of labour demanded by a firm

Decreases if:	*Increases if:*
◆ The wage rate increases	◆ The wage rate decreases

Changes in Demand

(Shifts in the demand for labour curve)

A firm's demand for labour

Decreases if:	*Increases if:*
◆ The price of the firm's output decreases	◆ The price of the firm's output increases
◆ The price of a substitute for labour falls	◆ The price of a substitute for labour rises
◆ The price of a complement of labour rises	◆ The price of a complement of labour falls
◆ A new technology decreases the marginal product of labour	◆ A new technology increases the marginal product of labour

---

◆ REVIEW QUIZ

1 What is the value of marginal product of labour?
2 What is the relationship between the value of marginal product of labour and the marginal product of labour?
3 How is the demand for labour derived from the value of marginal product of labour?
4 What are the influences on the demand for labour?

Do these questions in Study Plan 17.2 and get instant feedback.   MyEconLab

Labour Markets

Labour services are traded in many different labour markets. Examples are markets for bakery workers, van drivers, train drivers, computer support specialists, air traffic controllers, dentists and economists. Some of these markets, such as the market for bakery workers, are local. They operate in a given urban area. Some labour markets, such as the market for air traffic controllers, are national. Firms and workers search across the nation for the right match of worker and job. And some labour markets are global, such as the market for superstar footballers and basketball players.

We'll look at a local market for bakery workers as an example. First, we'll look at a competitive labour market. Then, we'll see how monopoly elements can influence a labour market.

A Competitive Labour Market

A competitive labour market is one in which many firms demand labour and many households supply labour.

Market Demand for Labour

Earlier in the chapter, you saw how an individual firm decides how much labour to hire. The market demand for labour is derived from the demand for labour by individual firms. We determine the market demand for labour by adding together the quantities of labour demanded by all the firms in the market at each wage rate. (The market demand for a good or service is derived in a similar way – see Chapter 5, p. 106.)

Because each firm's demand for labour curve slopes downward, the market demand for labour curve also slopes downward.

The Market Supply of Labour

The market supply of labour is derived from the supply of labour decisions made by individual households.

Individual's Labour Supply Decision

People can allocate their time to two broad activities: labour supply and leisure. (Leisure is a catch-all term. It includes all activities other than supplying labour.) For most people, leisure is more fun than work, so to induce them to work they must be offered a wage. Think about the labour supply decision of Jill, one of the workers at Angelo's Bakery. Let's see how the wage rate influences the quantity of labour she is willing to supply.

Reservation Wage Rate

Jill enjoys her leisure time, and she would be pleased if she didn't have to spend her time working at Angelo's Bakery. But Jill wants to earn an income, and as long as she can earn a wage rate of at least £5 an hour, she's willing to work. This wage is called her *reservation wage*. At any wage rate above her reservation wage, Jill supplies some labour.

The wage rate at Angelo's is £10 an hour, and at that wage rate, Jill chooses to work 30 hours a week. At a wage rate of £10 an hour, Jill regards this use of her time as the best available. Figure 17.2 illustrates.

Backward-Bending Labour Supply Curve

If Jill were offered a wage rate between £5 and £10 an hour, she would want to work fewer hours. If she were offered a wage rate above £10 an hour, she would want to work more hours, but only up to a point. If Jill could earn £25 an hour, she would be willing to work 40 hours a week (and earn £1,000 a week). But at a wage rate above £25 an hour, with the goods and services that Jill

Figure 17.2 Jill's Labour Supply Curve

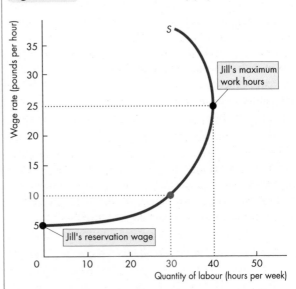

Jill's labour supply curve is *S*. Jill supplies no labour at wage rates below her reservation wage of £5 an hour. As the wage rate rises above £5 an hour, the quantity of labour that Jill supplies increases to a maximum of 40 hours a week at a wage rate of £25 an hour. As the wage rate rises above £25 an hour, Jill supplies a decreasing quantity of labour: her labour supply curve bends backward. The income effect on the demand for leisure dominates the substitution effect.

MyEconLab Animation

can buy for £1,000, her priority would be a bit more leisure time. So if the wage rate increased above £25 an hour, Jill would cut back on her work hours and take more leisure. Jill's labour supply curve eventually bends backward.

Jill's labour supply decisions are influenced by a substitution effect and an income effect.

Substitution Effect

Other things remaining the same, the higher the wage rate Jill is offered, at least over a range, the greater is the quantity of labour that she supplies. The reason is that Jill's wage rate is her *opportunity cost of leisure*. If she takes an hour off work to go shopping, the cost of that extra hour of leisure is the wage forgone. The higher the wage rate, the less willing is Jill to forgo the income and take the extra leisure time. This tendency for a higher wage rate to induce Jill to work longer hours is a *substitution effect*.

But there is also an *income effect* that works in the opposite direction to the substitution effect.

Income Effect

The higher Jill's wage rate, the higher is her income. A higher income, other things remaining the same, induces Jill to increase her demand for most goods. Leisure is one of these goods. Because an increase in income creates an increase in the demand for leisure, it also creates a decrease in the quantity of labour supplied.

Market Supply Curve

Jill's supply curve shows the quantity of labour supplied by Jill as her wage rate varies. Most people behave like Jill and have a backward-bending labour supply curve, but their reservation wage rates and wage rates at which their labour supply curves bend backward are different.

A market supply curve shows the quantity of labour supplied by all households in a given job market. It is found by adding together the quantities of labour supplied by all households to that market at each wage rate.

Also, along a supply curve in a particular job market the wage rates available in other job markets remain the same. For example, along the supply curve of bakery workers, the wage rates of chefs, van drivers and all other labour are constant.

Despite the fact that an individual's labour supply curve eventually bends backward, the market supply curve of labour slopes upward. The higher the wage rate for bakery workers, the greater is the quantity of labour supplied in that labour market.

Let's now look at labour market equilibrium.

Competitive Labour Market Equilibrium

Labour market equilibrium determines the wage rate and employment. In Figure 17.3, the market demand curve for bakery workers is *D* and the market supply curve of bakery workers is *S*. The equilibrium wage rate is £10 an hour, and the equilibrium quantity is 300 bakery workers.

At a wage rate above £10 an hour, there is a surplus of bakery workers. More people are looking for jobs in bakeries than firms are willing to hire. In such a situation, the wage rate will fall because firms find it easy to hire people at a lower wage rate. At a wage rate below £10 an hour, there is a shortage of bakery workers. Firms are not able to fill all the positions they have available. In this situation, the wage rate will rise because firms find it necessary to offer a higher wage rate to attract labour. Only at a wage rate of £10 an hour are there no forces operating to change the wage rate.

Figure 17.3 The Market for Bakery Workers

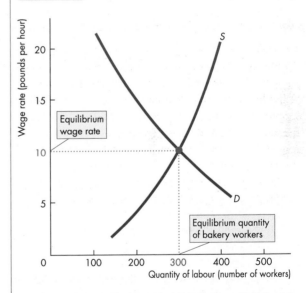

A competitive labour market coordinates firms' and households' plans. The market is in equilibrium – the quantity of labour demanded equals the quantity supplied at a wage rate of £10 an hour when 300 workers are employed.

At a wage rate above £10 an hour, the quantity of labour supplied exceeds the quantity demanded and the wage rate will fall.

At a wage rate below £10 an hour, the quantity of labour demanded exceeds the quantity supplied and the wage rate will rise.

MyEconLab Animation ———————————◆

Differences and Trends in Wage Rates

You can use what you've learned about labour markets to explain the difference in wage rates across occupations and the trends in wage rates.

Wage rates are unequal, and *Economics in Action* shows a sample of the inequality in wages in 2011. The differences in wage rates across occupations are driven by differences in demand and supply in labour markets. The highest wage rates are earned in occupations where the value of marginal product is highest and where few people have the ability and training to perform the job.

Rising Wage Rates

Wage rates increase over time and trend upward. The reason is that the value of marginal product of labour trends upward. Technological change and the new types of capital that it brings make workers more productive. With greater labour productivity, the demand for labour increases and so does the average wage rate. Even for jobs in which productivity doesn't increase, experience can increase the *value* of marginal product. Childcare is an example. A childcare worker can't care for an increasing number of children, but an increasing number of parents who earn high wage rates are willing to hire childcare workers. The *value* of marginal product of these workers increases, so the demand for their services increases and so does the wage rate.

Increasing Wage Inequality

Wage rates are unequal, and in recent years they have become increasingly unequal. High wage rates have increased rapidly while low wage rates have stagnated or even fallen. The reasons are complex and not fully understood, but the best explanation is that there is an interaction between technology and education.

The new technologies of the 1990s and 2000s made well-educated, skilled workers more productive and raised their wage rates. For example, the computer created the jobs and increased the wage rates of computer programmers and electronic engineers.

These same technologies destroyed some low-skilled jobs. Examples are the ATM, which took the jobs of bank clerks and lowered their wage rate, and automatic telephones took the jobs of telephone operators.

Another reason is that globalisation has brought increased competition for domestic low-skilled workers from workers in other countries and at the same time opened global markets for high-skilled workers.

 ECONOMICS IN ACTION

The Diversity of UK Wage Rates

Figure 1 shows the average hourly wage rate for 20 jobs selected from the 430 jobs in the Government's *Annual Survey of Hours of Earnings*.

The lowest-paid workers, a group that includes bar workers, hairdressers and barbers, earned less than £8 an hour – less than half the average wage rate. At the other extreme, company chief executives and finance managers earned between £34 and £51 an hour. Remember these numbers are averages. Some earn a lot more than the average and some earn less.

Many more occupations earn a wage rate below the national average than above it. Most of the occupations that earn more than the national average require a university degree and postgraduate training.

Earning differences are explained by differences in the value of marginal product of the skills in the various occupations and by differences in market power.

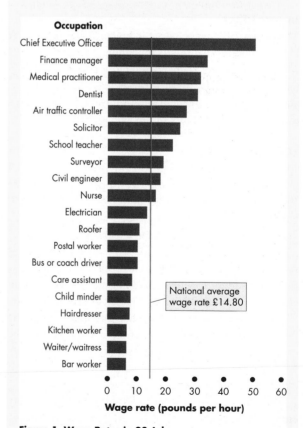

Figure 1 Wage Rates in 20 Jobs

Source of data: Office for National Statistics, *Annual Survey of Hours of Earnings 2012*.

ECONOMICS IN THE NEWS

A Bright Future in the IT Sector

The Most Valuable University Degree

Which university degree will give you the best salary now and in the future? IT tops the list of surveys.

Cloud computing and the proliferation of smartphones and tablets have brought a large increase in the demand for software and mobile applications designers. While IT salaries were flat for several years following a global recession in 2008, they have now started to rise and were up 9.1 per cent in 2011, a year in which job adverts doubled. Salaries will rise more as business employers demand these new IT skills. More companies are hiring and the supply of these specialist talents is very low.

Source: *Computer World UK*, 3 December 2011

The Questions

◆ Why is the number of jobs for specialist IT graduates increasing?

◆ What determines the demand for software designers and why might it be increasing?

◆ What determines the supply of software designers and why might it be increasing?

◆ What determines whether the wage rate of software designers will rise?

◆ Provide a graphical illustration of the market for software designers in 2012 and 2020.

The Answers

◆ The number of jobs for software designers is growing because *both* demand for and supply of specialist software designers are increasing.

◆ The demand for software designers is *derived* from the demand for new electronic products. The demand for smartphones and cloud computing services is increasing because technological advances are creating new and improved products.

◆ The supply of software designers is determined by the working-age population and the number of people who decide to get degrees in the subject. The supply is increasing because the working-age population is increasing and good job prospects are attracting a larger percentage of people to study software design.

◆ The wage rate of software designers will rise if the demand for their services increases faster than the supply.

◆ Figure 1 illustrates the market for software designers in 2012 and in 2020.

◆ Demand is expected to increase from D_{12} to D_{20}.

◆ Supply is expected to increase from S_{12} to S_{20}.

◆ The increase in demand is much greater than the increase in supply.

◆ The equilibrium number of jobs increases from 20,000 in 2012 to 30,000 in 2020.

◆ Because demand increases by more than supply, the equilibrium wage rate rises. (The 2020 wage rate is an assumption.)

A software designer at work planning a new business application.

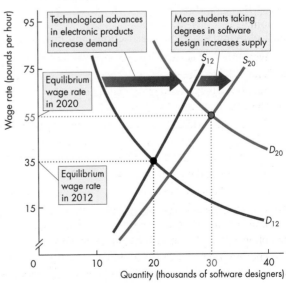

Figure 1 The Market for Software Designers in 2012 and 2020

A Labour Market with a Union

A **trades union** is an organised group of workers that aims to increase the wage rate and influence other job conditions. Let's see what happens when a union enters a competitive labour market.

Influences on Labour Supply

One way of raising the wage rate is to decrease the supply of labour. In some labour markets, a union can restrict supply by controlling entry into apprenticeship programmes or by influencing job qualification standards. Markets for skilled workers, doctors, dentists and lawyers are the easiest ones to control in this way.

If there is an abundant supply of non-union labour, a union can't decrease supply. For example, in the market for farm labour in south-east England, the flow of non-union labour from the EU makes it difficult for a union to control the supply. On the demand side of the labour market, the union faces a tradeoff: the demand for labour curve slopes downward, so restricting supply to raise the wage rate costs jobs. For this reason, unions also try to influence the demand for union labour.

Influences on Labour Demand

A union tries to increase the demand for the labour of its members in four main ways:

♦ Increasing the value of marginal product of its members by organising and sponsoring training schemes and apprenticeship programmes, and by professional certification.

♦ Lobbying for import restrictions and encouraging people to buy goods made by unionised workers.

♦ Supporting minimum wage laws, which increase the cost of employing low-skilled labour and lead firms to substitute high-skilled union labour for low-skilled non-union labour.

♦ Lobbying for restrictive immigration laws to decrease the supply of foreign workers.

Labour Market Equilibrium with a Union

Figure 17.4 illustrates what happens to the wage rate and employment when a union successfully enters a competitive labour market. With no union, the demand curve is D_C, the supply curve is S_C, the wage rate is £10 an hour, and 300 workers have jobs. Now a union enters

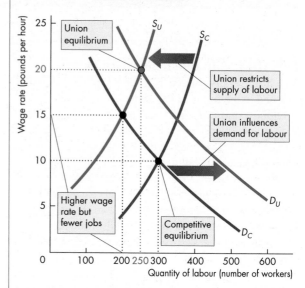

Figure 17.4 A Union Enters a Competitive Labour Market

In a competitive labour market, the demand curve is D_C and the supply curve is S_C. Competitive equilibrium occurs at a wage rate of £10 an hour and 300 workers are employed. If a union decreases the supply of labour and the supply of labour curve shifts to S_U, the wage rate rises to £15 an hour and employment decreases to 200 workers. If the union can also increase the demand for labour and shift the demand for labour curve to D_U, the wage rate rises to £20 an hour and 250 workers are employed.

MyEconLab Animation ─────────────────◆

this labour market. First, look at what happens if the union has sufficient control over the supply of labour to be able to restrict supply below its competitive level – to S_U. If that is all the union is able to do, employment falls to 200 workers and the wage rate rises to £15 an hour.

Suppose now that the union is also able to increase the demand for labour to D_U. The union can get an even bigger increase in the wage rate and with a smaller fall in employment. By maintaining the restricted labour supply at S_U, the union increases the wage rate to £20 an hour and achieves an employment level of 250 workers.

Because a union restricts the supply of labour in the market in which it operates, the union's actions spill over into non-union markets. Workers who can't get union jobs must look elsewhere for work. This action increases the supply of labour in non-union markets and lowers the wage rate in those markets. This spillover effect further widens the gap between union and non-union wages.

Monopsony in the Labour Market

Not all labour markets in which unions operate are competitive. Rather, some are labour markets in which the employer possesses market power and the union enters to try to counteract that power.

A market in which there is a single buyer is called a **monopsony**. A monopsony labour market has one employer. With the growth of large-scale production over the last century, large manufacturing plants such as coal mines, steel and textile mills and car production plants became the major employer in some regions, and in some places a single firm employed almost all the labour. Today, in some regions, managed healthcare organisations are the major employer of healthcare professionals. These firms have market power.

A monopsony acts on the buying side of a market in a similar way to a monopoly on the selling side. The firm maximises profit by hiring the quantity of labour that makes the marginal cost of labour equal to the value of marginal product of labour and by paying the lowest wage rate at which it can attract this quantity of labour.

Figure 17.5 illustrates a monopsony labour market. Like all firms, a monopsony faces a downward-sloping value of marginal product curve, *VMP*, which is its demand for labour curve, *D* – the curve labelled *VMP = D* in the figure.

What is special about monopsony is the marginal cost of labour. For a firm in a competitive labour market, the marginal cost of labour is the wage rate. For a monopsony, the marginal cost of labour exceeds the wage rate. The reason is that being the only buyer in the market, the firm faces an upward-sloping supply of labour curve – the curve *S* in the figure.

To attract one more worker, the monopsony must offer a higher wage rate. But it must pay this higher wage rate to all its workers, so the marginal cost of a worker is the wage rate plus the increased wage bill that arises from paying all the workers the higher wage rate.

The supply curve is now the average cost of labour curve and the relationship between the supply curve and the marginal cost of labour curve, *MCL*, is similar to that between a monopoly's demand curve and marginal revenue curve (see Chapter 12, p. 278). The relationship between the supply curve and the *MCL* curve is also similar to that between a firm's average total cost curve and marginal cost curve (see Chapter 10, pp. 226–227).

To find the profit-maximising quantity of labour, the monopsony sets the marginal cost of labour equal to the value of marginal product of labour. In Figure 17.5, this outcome occurs when the firm employs 100 workers.

To hire 100 workers, the firm must pay £10 an hour (on the supply of labour curve). Each worker is paid £10 an hour, but the value of marginal product of labour is £20 an hour, so the firm makes an economic profit of £10 an hour on the marginal worker.

If the labour market in Figure 17.5 were competitive, the equilibrium wage rate and employment would be determined by the demand and supply curves. The wage rate would be £15 an hour, and 150 workers would be employed. So compared with a competitive labour market, a monopsony pays a lower wage rate and employs fewer workers.

A Union and a Monopsony

A union is like a monopoly. If the union (monopoly seller) faces a monopsony buyer, the situation is called **bilateral monopoly**. An example of bilateral monopoly is the Communications Workers Union, which represents postal workers, and the Royal Mail.

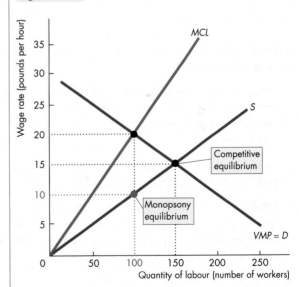

Figure 17.5 A Monopsony Labour Market

A monopsony is a market structure in which there is a single buyer. A monopsony in the labour market has a value of marginal product curve *VMP* and faces a labour supply curve *S*. The marginal cost of labour curve is *MCL*. The monopsony maximises profit by making the marginal cost of labour equal to the value of marginal product. The monopsony employs 100 workers and pays the lowest wage for which that quantity of labour will work, which is £10 an hour.

MyEconLab Animation ──────────── ◆

ECONOMICS IN THE NEWS

Are Trades Unions in the UK a Spent Force?

Trades Unions: Not Dead Yet

The BBC reported that over two million public sector workers joined the national strike in November 2011 to protest against changes to pension benefits as part of government expenditure cuts. A similar strike took place at Unilever over the decision to end final-salary pension schemes. The government made concessions to the public sector workers as a result of the strike, suggesting that union power is not dead yet.

Source: BBCNews, 25 January 2012

Public sector workers march through Westminster in protest against changes to pension plans and retirement policies June 2011.

Data

Union membership	1995	2000	2011
Total (millions)	6.9	6.8	6.2
% in private sector	21.5	18.5	14.0
% in public sector	61.0	60.3	56.5
Union wage premium			
Private sector (%)	15.3	5.6	8.0
Public sector (%)	30.4	26.5	18.0

Source: Trades union statistics updated 20 April 2012

The Questions

◆ Are trades unions in decline in the UK?

◆ Which unions are in the greater decline, public sector or private sector?

◆ Can UK trades unions still influence workers' wage rates?

◆ Why might public sector trades unions be stronger than those in the private sector?

The Answers

◆ Trades unions are in decline. Their membership was more than 9.5 million workers during the 1950s and it fell to 8.7 million workers in 1989.

By 1995 membership numbers were just under 7 million, but the rate of decline slowed in the decade after 2000.

Fewer than 1 in 10 employees are now members of a trades union.

◆ Private sector membership of a trades union has declined much more than public sector membership.

More than 50 per cent of public sector workers are still members of a trades union compared with just 14 per cent in the private sector.

So almost all of the decline has been in the private sector.

◆ UK trades unions can still influence workers' wage rates. The table shows the trades union wage premium, which measures the percentage difference between union and non-union wage rates in the same job.

The data shows that union membership is associated with higher wage rates in both the private and the public sector, but the power of the unions to raise wage rates has declined since the 1990s.

◆ Trades unions in the public sector might be stronger than those in the private sector because the public sector unions have a higher proportion of skilled and professional workers who are more difficult to replace.

The greater strength of public sector unions is also reflected in a much higher trades union wage premium. Even now, public sector workers' wage rates are 18 per cent higher than those of non-union public sector workers.

Every few years, the Communications Workers Union and the Royal Mail negotiate a pay deal.

In bilateral monopoly, the outcome is determined by bargaining, which depends on the costs that each party can inflict on the other. The firm can shut down temporarily and lock out its workers, and the workers can shut down the firm by striking. Each party estimates the other's strength and what it will lose if it does not agree to the other's demands.

Usually, an agreement is reached without a strike or a lockout. The threat is usually enough to bring the bargaining parties to an agreement. When a strike or lockout does occur, it is because one party has misjudged the costs each party can inflict on the other. Such an event occurred in November 2007 when the writers and entertainment producers failed to agree on a compensation deal. A 100-day strike followed that ended up costing the entertainment industry an estimated £2 billion.

In the example in Figure 17.5, if the union and employer are equally strong, and each party knows the strength of the other, they will agree to split the gap between £10 (the wage rate on the supply curve) and £20 (the wage rate on the demand curve) and agree to a wage rate of £15 an hour.

You've now seen that in a monopsony, a union can bargain for a higher wage rate without sacrificing jobs. A similar outcome can arise in a monopsony labour market when a minimum wage law is enforced. Let's look at the effect of a minimum wage.

Monopsony and the Minimum Wage

In a competitive labour market, a minimum wage that exceeds the equilibrium wage decreases employment (see Chapter 6, pp. 129–130). But this outcome does not occur in all types of labour markets. In particular, it does not occur in monopsony. In a monopsony labour market, a minimum wage can end up increasing both the wage rate and employment. Let's see how.

Figure 17.6 shows a monopsony labour market in which the wage rate is £10 an hour and 100 workers are employed.

A minimum wage law is passed that requires employers to pay at least £15 an hour. The monopsony now faces a perfectly elastic supply of labour at £15 an hour up to 150 workers. To hire more than 150 workers, a wage rate above £15 an hour must be paid (along the supply of labour curve). Because the wage rate is £15 an hour up to 150 workers, so is the marginal cost of labour £15 up to 150 workers. To maximise profit, the monopsony sets the marginal cost of labour equal to the value of

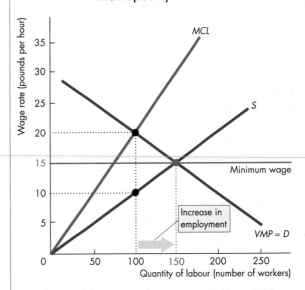

Figure 17.6 Minimum Wage Law in Monopsony

In a monopsony labour market, the wage rate is £10 an hour and 100 workers are hired. If a minimum wage law increases the wage rate to £15 an hour, the wage rate rises to this level and employment increases to 150 workers.

MyEconLab Animation ◆

marginal product of labour (on the demand curve). The monopsony employs 150 workers at £15 an hour. The minimum wage law has succeeded in raising the wage rate by £5 an hour and increasing the number of workers employed.

REVIEW QUIZ

1 What determines the amount of labour that households plan to supply?
2 How are the wage rate and employment determined in a competitive labour market?
3 How do unions influence wage rates?
4 What is a monopsony and why is a monopsony able to pay a lower wage rate than a firm in a competitive labour market?
5 How is the wage rate determined when a union faces a monopsony?
6 What is the effect of a minimum wage law in a monopsony labour market?

Do these questions in Study Plan 17.3 and get instant feedback.   MyEconLab

Capital and Natural Resource Markets

The markets for capital and land can be understood by using the same basic ideas that you've seen when studying a competitive labour market. But markets for non-renewable natural resources are different. We'll now examine three groups of factor markets:

◆ Capital rental markets

◆ Land rental markets

◆ Non-renewable natural resource markets

Capital Rental Markets

The demand for capital is derived from the *value of marginal product of capital*. Profit-maximising firms hire the quantity of capital services that makes the value of marginal product of capital equal to the *rental rate of capital*. The *lower* the rental rate of capital, other things remaining the same, the *greater* is the quantity of capital demanded. The supply of capital responds in the opposite way to the rental rate. The *higher* the rental rate, other things remaining the same, the *greater* is the quantity of capital supplied. The equilibrium rental rate makes the quantity of capital demanded equal to the quantity supplied.

Figure 17.7 illustrates the rental market for tower cranes – capital used to construct high-rise buildings. The value of marginal product and the demand curve is $VMP = D$. The supply curve is S. The equilibrium rental rate is £1,000 per day and 100 tower cranes are rented.

Rent-versus-Buy Decision

Some capital services are obtained in a rental market like the market for tower cranes. And as for tower cranes, many of the world's large airlines rent their aeroplanes. But not all capital services are obtained in a rental market. Instead, firms buy the capital equipment that they use. You saw in Chapter 9 (pp. 196–197) that the cost of the services from the capital that a firm owns and operates is an implicit rental rate that arises from depreciation and interest costs. Firms that buy capital *implicitly* rent the capital to themselves.

The decision to obtain capital services in a rental market rather than buy capital and rent it implicitly is made to minimise cost. The firm compares the cost of explicitly renting the capital and the cost of buying and implicitly renting it. This decision is the same as the one

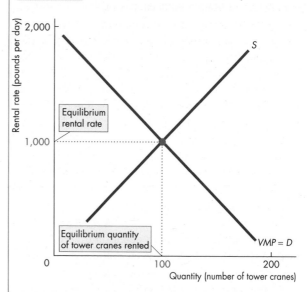

Figure 17.7 A Rental Market for Capital

The value of marginal product of tower cranes, *VMP*, determines the demand, *D*, for tower cranes. With the supply curve, *S*, the equilibrium rental rate is £1,000 a day and 100 cranes are rented.

MyEconLab Animation ━━━━━━━━━━━━━━━━━━◆

that a household makes in deciding whether to rent or buy a home.

To make a rent-versus-buy decision, a firm must compare a cost incurred in the *present* with a stream of rental costs incurred over some *future* period. The Mathematical Note (pp. 408–409) explains how to make this comparison by calculating the *present value* of a future amount of money. If the *present value* of the future rental payments of an item of capital equipment exceeds the cost of buying the capital, the firm will buy the equipment. If the *present value* of the future rental payments of an item of capital equipment is less than the cost of buying the capital, the firm will rent (or lease) the equipment.

Land Rental Markets

The demand for land is based on the same factors as the demand for labour and the demand for capital – the *value of marginal product of land*. Profit-maximising firms rent the quantity of land at which the value of marginal product of land is equal to the *rental rate of land*. The *lower* the rental rate, other things remaining the same, the *greater* is the quantity of land demanded.

But the supply of land is special: its quantity is fixed, so the quantity supplied cannot be changed by people's decisions. The supply of each particular block of land is perfectly inelastic.

The equilibrium rental rate makes the quantity of land demanded equal to the quantity available. Figure 17.8 illustrates the market for a plot of 10 hectares of land in Chelsea, London. The quantity supplied is fixed and the supply of land curve is *S*. The value of marginal product and the demand for land curve is *VMP = D*. The equilibrium rental rate is £1,000 a hectare per day.

The rental rate of land is high in Chelsea, London because the willingness to pay for the services produced by that land is high, which in turn makes the *VMP* of land high. A haircut costs more at a salon in Chelsea than in Liverpool, but not because the rental rate of land is higher in Chelsea.

The rental rate of land is higher in Chelsea because of the greater willingness to pay for a haircut (and other goods and services) in Chelsea than in Liverpool.

Non-renewable Natural Resource Markets

The non-renewable natural resources are oil, gas and coal. Burning one of these fuels converts it to energy and other by-products, and the used resource cannot be re-used. The natural resources that we use to make metals are also non-renewable, but they can be used again, at some cost, by recycling them.

Oil, gas, and coal are traded in global commodity markets. The price of a given grade of crude oil is the same in New York, London and Singapore. Traders, linked by telephone and the Internet, operate these markets around the clock every day of the year.

Demand and supply determine the prices and the quantities traded in these commodity markets. We'll look at the influences on demand and supply by considering the global market for crude oil.

The Demand for Oil

The two key influences on the demand for oil are:

◆   The value of marginal product of oil
◆   The expected future price of oil

The value of marginal product of oil is the *fundamental* influence on demand. It works in exactly the same way for a non-renewable resource as it does for any other factor of production. The greater the quantity of oil used, the smaller is the value of marginal product of oil. Diminishing value of marginal product makes the demand curve for oil slope downward. The lower the price, the greater is the quantity of oil demanded.

The higher the expected future price of oil, the greater is the present demand for oil. The expected future price is a *speculative* influence on demand. Oil in the ground and oil in storage tanks are inventories that can be held or sold. A trader might plan to buy oil to hold now and to sell it later for a profit. Instead of buying oil to hold and sell later, the trader could buy a bond and earn interest. The *interest forgone* is the opportunity cost of holding the oil. If the price of oil is expected to rise by a bigger percentage than the interest rate, a trader will hold oil and incur the opportunity cost – the return from holding oil exceeds the return from holding bonds.

The Supply of Oil

The three key influences on the supply of oil are:

◆   The known oil reserves
◆   The scale of current oil production facilities
◆   The expected future price of oil

Figure 17.8   A Rental Market for Land

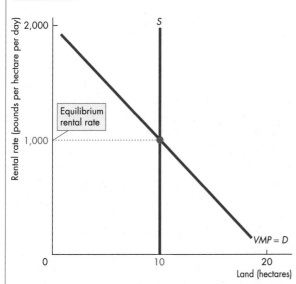

The value of marginal product of a 10-hectare block of land, *VMP*, determines the rental demand, *D*, for this land. With the supply curve, *S*, this block rents for £10,000 a day.

Known oil reserves are the oil that has been discovered and can be extracted with today's technology. This quantity increases over time because advances in technology enable ever-less accessible sources to be discovered. The greater the size of known reserves, the greater is the supply of oil. But this influence on supply is small and indirect. It operates by changing the expected distant future price of oil. Even a major new discovery of oil would have a negligible effect on the current supply of oil.

The scale of current oil production facilities is the *fundamental* influence on the supply of oil. Producing oil is like any production activity: it is subject to increasing marginal cost. The increasing marginal cost of extracting oil means that the supply curve of oil slopes upward. The higher the price of oil, the greater is the quantity of oil supplied. When new oil wells are sunk or when new faster pumps are installed, the supply of oil increases and the supply of oil curve shifts rightward. When existing wells run dry, the supply of oil decreases and the supply of oil curve shifts leftward. Over time, the factors that increase supply are more powerful than those that decrease supply, so changes in the fundamental influence on the supply of oil increase it.

Speculative forces based on expectations about the future price also influence the supply of oil. The *higher* the expected future price of oil, the *smaller* is the present supply of oil. A trader with an oil inventory might plan to sell now or to hold and sell later. You've seen that interest forgone is the opportunity cost of holding the oil. If the price of oil is expected to rise by a bigger percentage than the interest rate, it is profitable to incur the opportunity cost of holding oil rather than sell it immediately.

The Equilibrium Price of Oil

The demand for oil and the supply of oil determine the equilibrium price and quantity of oil traded. Figure 17.9 illustrates the market equilibrium.

The value of marginal product of oil, *VMP*, is the fundamental determinant of the demand for oil, and the marginal cost of extraction, *MC*, is the fundamental determinant of the supply of oil. Together, they determine the market fundamentals price.

If expectations about the future price are also based on fundamentals, the equilibrium price is the market fundamentals price. But if expectations about the future price of oil depart from what the market fundamentals imply, speculation can drive a wedge between the equilibrium price and the market fundamentals price.

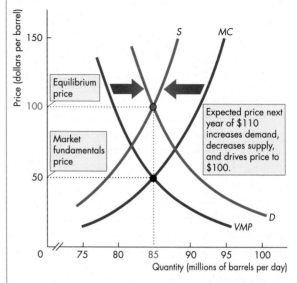

Figure 17.9 A Non-renewable Natural Resource Market

The value of marginal product of a non-renewable natural resource, *VMP*, and the marginal cost of extraction, *MC*, determine the market fundamentals price. Demand, *D*, and supply, *S*, which determine the equilibrium price, are influenced by the expected future price. Speculation can bring a gap between the market fundamentals price and the equilibrium price.

MyEconLab Animation ⸻⸻⸻⸻◆

The Hotelling Principle

Harold Hotelling, an economist at Columbia University, had an incredible idea: traders expect the price of a non-renewable natural resource to rise at a rate equal to the interest rate. We call this idea the **Hotelling Principle**. Let's see why it is correct.

You've seen that the interest rate is the opportunity cost of holding an oil inventory. If the price of oil is expected to rise at a rate that exceeds the interest rate, it is profitable to hold a bigger inventory. Demand increases, supply decreases and the price rises. If the interest rate exceeds the rate at which the price of oil is expected to rise, it is not profitable to hold an oil inventory. Demand decreases, supply increases and the price falls. But if the price of oil is expected to rise at a rate equal to the interest rate, holding an inventory of oil is just as good as holding bonds. Demand and supply don't change and the price does not change. Only when the price of oil is expected to rise at a rate equal to the interest rate is the price at its equilibrium.

ECONOMICS IN ACTION

The World and EU Markets for Oil

The world produced about 87 billion barrels of oil in 2011 and the price shot upward from $70 in 2010 to $100 in 2011. The high price and foreign dependence became major political issues.

Although the EU imports most of its oil from other countries, much of it comes from close to home. Figure 1 provides the details: only 20 per cent of the EU oil supply comes from the Middle East, 2 per cent comes from the US, 44 per cent comes from Russia and 19 per cent comes from Africa.

Even if the EU produced all its own oil, it would still face a fluctuating global price. EU producers, such as Norway, would not willingly sell to EU buyers for a price below the world price. So energy independence doesn't mean an independent oil price.

The Hotelling Principle tells us that we must expect the price of oil to rise at a rate equal to the interest rate. But expecting the price to rise at a rate equal to the interest rate doesn't mean that the price will rise at this rate. As you can see in Figure 2, the price of oil over the past 50 or so years has not followed the path predicted by the Hotelling Principle.

The forces that influence expectations are not well understood. The expected future price of oil depends on its expected future rate of use and the rate of discovery of new sources of supply. One person's expectation about a future price also depends on guesses about other people's expectations. These guesses can change abruptly and become self-

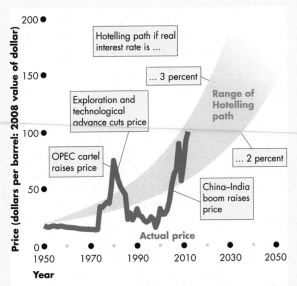

Figure 2 The Price of Oil and Its Hotelling Path

Source of data: Energy Information Administration.

reinforcing. When the expected future price of oil changes for whatever reason, demand and supply change, and so does the price. Prices in speculative markets are always volatile.

REVIEW QUIZ

1 What determines demand and supply in rental markets for capital and land?
2 What determines the demand for a non-renewable natural resource?
3 What determines the supply of a non-renewable natural resource?
4 What is the market fundamentals price and how might it differ from the equilibrium price?
5 Explain the Hotelling Principle.

Do these questions in Study Plan 17.4 and get instant feedback.   MyEconLab

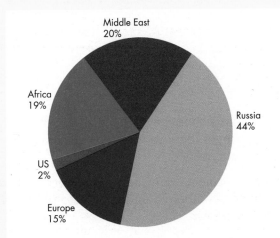

Figure 1 Diverse Sources of the EU's Oil

Source of data: http://ec.europa.eu/energy/observatory/oil/.

Reading Between the Lines on pp. 406–407 focuses on the rising wages of nuclear engineers needed for a new 14-year project to clean up the ageing nuclear power stations in the UK.

The next chapter looks at how the market economy distributes income and how government policy is used to redistribute income and modify the market outcome.

READING BETWEEN THE LINES

A Job Market in Action

The Telegraph, 21 April 2013

Salaries 'Rise 10pc' for Scarce Nuclear Clean-up Engineers

Emily Gosden

Salaries in the nuclear industry rose by 10pc last year amid fierce competition for engineers to carry out a £7bn decommissioning programme at 12 sites around Britain. . . .

The clean-up programme will be worth £4bn–£5bn over the first seven years and almost £2bn over the following seven years.

Project Resource said basic salaries for qualified nuclear engineers rose 10pc to £45,000 last year, with salaries for senior planners rising to £50,000. . . .

Simon Griffiths, regional manager at Project Resource, said: 'Attracting staff to work in some of the most remote locations within the UK, such as Dounreay in the far north of Scotland, is challenging, particularly when these staff are in short supply.'

'Unlike in other business sectors, nuclear decommissioning contractors cannot respond to a limited supply of engineering staff by importing candidates from other countries,' the agency said. 'This is partly because of strict security requirements . . .'.

The Essence of the Story

- Salaries for nuclear engineers rose 10 per cent in 2012 to £45,000.

- More nuclear engineers are needed for a new £7 billion clean-up programme for UK power stations, running over 14 years.

- There is a shortage of engineers and it is difficult to get them to move to the areas where they are needed.

- The project contractor cannot employ staff from other countries because of security restrictions.

Economic Analysis

- Skilled nuclear engineers are a factor of production and their services are traded in a competitive market.

- The demand for nuclear engineers is derived from the value of marginal product (*VMP*) of their labour.

- If the annual wage increased by 10 per cent to £45,000, and other things remained the same, firms would cut employment to the level at which the *VMP* equalled £45,000.

- But in 2012, vacancies increased and the number of nuclear engineers seeking jobs increased, so the *VMP* and demand for skilled workers must have increased.

- The *VMP* and demand for nuclear engineers increased because Britain's nuclear power stations are being decommissioned over 14 years. The project increased the UK demand for nuclear engineering services, which increased the price of those services.

- Figure 1 illustrates the market for nuclear engineers in 2011 and 2012 in Britain. In 2011, the demand curve was D_{11} and the supply curve was S_{11}. The equilibrium wage rate was £41,000 a year and the equilibrium number of workers was 300.

- In 2012, the demand for nuclear engineers increased to D_{12}. At the 2011 wage rate, there was a shortage of 200 workers. The shortage made the wage rate rise to £45,000 a year and an increase in the quantity of workers supplied increased employment to 400.

- In 2012, a small number of new UK graduates with the right qualifications entered the market. These new entrants increased the supply of nuclear engineers.

- Figure 2 illustrates the effect of this increase in supply. Supply increased a little from S_{11} to S_{12}, but demand remained at D_{12}. The wage rate fell slightly and the number of nuclear engineers employed increased.

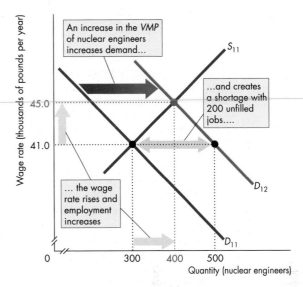

Figure 1 An Increase in Demand for UK Nuclear Engineers

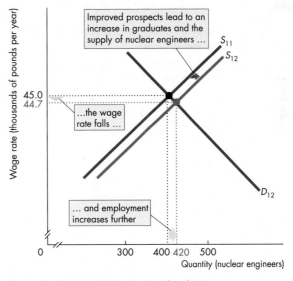

Figure 2 An Increase in the Supply of UK Nuclear Engineers

- If the project could have employed non-UK nuclear engineers in 2012, the supply would have increased more and the wage rate would have fallen further. As new UK graduates enter the market over the coming years, supply will increase further, and if demand does not change, the wage rate will continue to fall.

MATHEMATICAL NOTE

Present Value and Discounting

Rent-versus-Buy Decision

To decide whether to rent an item of capital equipment or to buy the capital equipment and implicitly rent it, a firm must compare the present expenditure on the capital equipment with its future rental cost.

Comparing Current and Future Amounts of Money

To compare a present expenditure with a future expenditure, we convert the future expenditure to its 'present value'. The **present value** of a future amount of money is the amount that, if invested today, will grow to be as large as that future amount when the interest it will earn is taken into account.

So the present value of a future amount of money is smaller than the future amount. The calculation that we use to convert the future amount of money to a present value is called **discounting**.

The easiest way to understand discounting and present value is to consider how a present value grows to a future amount of money because of *compound interest*.

Compound Interest

Compound interest is the interest on an initial investment plus the interest on the interest that the investment has previously earned. Because of compound interest, a present amount of money (a present value) grows into a larger future amount. The future amount is equal to the present amount (present value) plus the interest it will earn in the future. That is:

Future amount = Present value + Interest income

The interest income in the first year is equal to the present value multiplied by the interest rate, r, so:

Amount after 1 year = Present value +
($r \times$ Present value)

Amount after 1 year = Present value $\times (1 + r)$

If you invest £100 today and the interest rate is 10 per cent a year ($r = 0.1$), one year from today you will have £110 – the original £100 plus £10 interest. Check that the above formula delivers that answer:

$$£100 \times 1.1 = £110$$

If you leave this £110 invested to earn 10 per cent during a second year, at the end of that year, you will have

Amount after 2 years = Present value $\times (1 + r)^2$

With the numbers of the previous example, you invest £100 today at an interest rate of 10 per cent a year ($r = 0.1$). After one year you have £110 – the original £100 plus £10 interest. And after the second year, you have £121. In the second year, you earned £10 on your initial £100 plus £1 on the £10 interest that you earned in the first year.

Check that the above formula delivers that answer:

$$£100 \times (1.1)^2 = £100 \times 1.21 = £121$$

If you have £100 invested for n years, it will grow to:

Amount after n years = Present value $\times (1 + r)^n$

With an interest rate of 10 per cent a year, your £100 will be £195 after 7 years ($n = 7$) – almost double the present value of £100.

Discounting a Future Amount

We have just calculated future values one year, two years and n years in the future, knowing the present amount and the interest rate. To calculate the present value of these future amounts, one year, two years and n years in the future, we just work backwards.

To find the present value of an amount one year in the future, we divide the future amount by $(1 + r)$.

That is:

$$\text{Present value} = \frac{\text{Amount of money 1 year in the future}}{(1 + r)}$$

Let's check that we can use the present value formula by calculating the present value of £110 one year from now when the interest rate is 10 per cent a year. You'll be able to guess that the answer is £100 because we just calculated that £100 invested today at 10 per cent a year becomes £110 in one year. So the present value of £110 one year from today is £100. But let's use the formula. Putting the numbers into the above formula, we have:

$$\text{Present value} = \frac{£110}{(1 + 0.1)}$$

$$= \frac{£110}{1.1} = £100$$

To calculate the present value of an amount of money two years in the future, we use the formula:

$$\text{Present value} = \frac{\begin{array}{c}\text{Amount of money}\\ \text{2 years in future}\end{array}}{(1 + r)^2}$$

Use this formula to calculate the present value of £121 two years from now at an interest rate of 10 per cent a year. With these numbers the formula gives:

$$\text{Present value} = \frac{£121}{(1 + 0.1)^2}$$

$$= \frac{£121}{(1.1)^2}$$

$$= \frac{£121}{1.21} = £100$$

We can calculate the present value of an amount of money n years in the future by using the general formula:

$$\text{Present value} = \frac{\begin{array}{c}\text{Amount of money}\\ n \text{ years in the future}\end{array}}{(1 + r)^n}$$

For example, if the interest rate is 10 per cent a year, £100 to be received 10 years from now has a present value of £38.55. That is, if £38.55 is invested today at an interest rate of 10 per cent a year, it will accumulate to £100 in 10 years.

Present Value of a Sequence of Future Amounts

You've seen how to calculate the present value of an amount of money one year, two years and n years in the future. Most practical applications of present value calculate the present value of a sequence of future amounts of money that spread over several years. An airline's rent for lease of aeroplanes is an example.

To calculate the present value of a sequence of amounts over several years, we use the formula you have learned and apply it to each year. We then sum the present values for each year to find the present value of the sequence of amounts.

For example, suppose that a firm expects to pay £100 a year for each of the next five years. And suppose that the interest rate is 10 per cent per year ($r = 0.1$). The present value of these five payments of £100 each is calculated by using the following formula:

$$PV = \frac{£100}{1.1} + \frac{£100}{1.1^2} + \frac{£100}{1.1^3} + \frac{£100}{1.1^4} + \frac{£100}{1.1^5}$$

which equals:

$$PV = £90.91 + £82.64 + £75.13 + £68.30 + £62.09$$
$$= £379.07$$

You can see that the firm pays £500 over five years. But because the money is paid in the future, it is not worth £500 today. Its present value is only £379.07. And the further in the future it is paid, the smaller is its present value. The £100 paid one year in the future is worth £90.91 today. And the £100 paid five years in the future is worth only £62.09 today.

The Decision

If this firm could lease a machine for five years at £100 a year or buy the machine for £500, it would jump at leasing. Only if the firm could buy the machine for less than £379.07 would it want to buy.

Many personal and business decisions turn on calculations like the one we've just made. A decision to rent or buy a flat, to lease or buy a car, to pay off a student loan or let the loan run another year can all be made using the above calculations.

SUMMARY

Key Points

The Anatomy of Factor Markets
(p. 390)

◆ The factor markets are: job markets for labour; rental markets (often implicit rental markets) for capital and land; and global commodity markets for non-renewable natural resources.

◆ The services of entrepreneurs are not traded in a factor market.

Do Problem 1 to get a better understanding of the anatomy of factor markets.

The Demand for a Factor of Production (pp. 391–393)

◆ The value of marginal product determines the demand for a factor of production.

◆ The value of marginal product decreases as the quantity of the factor employed increases.

◆ The firm employs the quantity of each factor of production that makes the value of marginal product equal to the factor price.

Do Problems 2 to 8 to get a better understanding of the demand for a factor of production.

Labour Markets (pp. 394–401)

◆ The value of marginal product of labour determines the demand for labour. A rise in the wage rate brings a decrease in the quantity demanded.

◆ The quantity of labour supplied depends on the wage rate. At low wage rates, a rise in the wage rate increases the quantity supplied. Beyond a high enough wage rate, a rise in the wage rate decreases the quantity supplied – the supply curve eventually bends backward.

◆ Demand and supply determine the wage rate in a competitive labour market.

◆ A trades union can raise the wage rate by restricting the supply of or increasing the demand for labour.

◆ A monopsony can lower the wage rate below the competitive level.

◆ A union or a minimum wage in a monopsony labour market can raise the wage rate without a fall in employment.

Do Problems 9 to 11 to get a better understanding of labour markets.

Capital and Natural Resource Markets (pp. 402–405)

◆ The value of marginal product of capital (and land) determines the demand for capital (and land).

◆ Firms make a rent-versus-buy decision by choosing the option that minimises cost.

◆ The supply of land is inelastic and the demand for land determines the rental rate.

◆ The demand for a non-renewable natural resource depends on the value of marginal product and on the expected future price.

◆ The supply of a non-renewable natural resource depends on the known reserves, the cost of extraction and the expected future price.

◆ The price of a non-renewable natural resource can differ from the market fundamentals price because of speculation based on expectations about the future price.

◆ The price of a non-renewable natural resource is expected to rise at a rate equal to the interest rate.

Do Problems 12 to 17 to get a better understanding of capital and natural resource markets.

Key Terms

Bilateral monopoly, 399
Compound interest, 408
Derived demand, 391
Discounting, 408
Hotelling Principle, 404
Job, 390
Monopsony, 399
Non-renewable natural resources, 390
Present value, 408
Trades union, 398
Value of marginal product, 391

STUDY PLAN PROBLEMS AND APPLICATIONS

Do Problems 1 to 19 in MyEconLab Chapter 17 Study Plan and get instant feedback.

MyEconLab

The Anatomy of Factor Markets
(Study Plan 17.1)

1 Tim is opening a new online store from Berlin. He plans to hire two people to key in the data at €10 an hour. Tim is also considering buying or leasing some new computers. The purchase price of a computer is €900 and after three years it is worthless. The annual cost of leasing a computer is €450.

a In which factor markets does Tim operate?

b What is the price of the capital equipment and the rental rate of capital?

The Demand for a Factor of Production (Study Plan 17.2)

Use the following data in Problems 2 to 7.

Wanda owns a fish shop in Barcelona. She employs students to sort and pack the fish. Students can pack the following amounts of fish in an hour:

Number of students	Quantity of fish (kilograms)
1	20
2	50
3	90
4	120
5	145
6	165
7	180
8	190

The fish market is competitive. The market price of fish is 50¢ a kilogram and the wage rate of packers is €7.50 an hour.

2 Calculate the marginal product of the students and draw the marginal product curve.

3 Calculate the value of marginal product of labour and draw the value of marginal product curve.

4 a Find Wanda's demand for labour curve.

b How many students does Wanda employ?

Use the following additional information in Problems 5 and 6.

The market price of fish falls to 33¢ a kilogram, but the packers' wage rate remains at €7.50 an hour.

5 a How does the students' marginal product change?

b How does the value of marginal product of labour change?

6 a How does Wanda's demand for labour change?

b What happens to the number of students that Wanda employs?

7 At Wanda's fish shop, packers' wages increase to €10 an hour, but the price of fish remains at 50¢ a kilogram.

a What happens to the value of marginal product of labour?

b What happens to Wanda's demand for labour curve?

c How many students does Wanda employ?

8 British Construction Activity Falls

Construction activity in Britain declined in June at the fastest rate in 11 years. A major home builder was unable to raise more capital – both signs of worsening conditions in the battered housing industry. Employment of construction labour declined in June after 23 months of growth. Average house prices fell 0.9 per cent in June, the eighth consecutive month of decline, leaving the average 6.3 per cent below June 2007.

Source: *Forbes*, 2 July 2008

a Explain how a fall in house prices influences the market for construction labour.

b On a graph illustrate the effect of falling house prices in the market for construction labour.

Labour Markets (Study Plan 17.3)

Use the following news clip in Problems 9 to 11.

In Modern Rarity, Workers Form Union at Small Chain

In New York's low-income areas, trades unions have virtually no presence. But after a year-long struggle, 95 workers at a chain of 10 sports shoe stores have formed a union. After months of negotiations, the two sides signed a three-year contract that sets the wage rate at $7.25 an hour.

Source: *The New York Times*, 5 February 2006

9 Why are trades unions scarce in New York's low-income areas?

10 Who wins from this union contract? Who loses?

11 How can this union try to change the demand for labour?

Capital and Natural Resource Markets (Study Plan 17.4)

12 Classify the following items as a non-renewable natural resource, a renewable natural resource or not a natural resource. Explain your answers.

   a Canary Wharf
   b Lake Garda
   c Coal in a Polish coal mine
   d The Internet
   e The Lake District
   f Power generated by wind turbines

13 **Most Expensive Property in the World**

   Property developers are turning a 1930s building in St. James Square, London into 6 exclusive flats in the centre of the financial sector. One flat will cost £115 million and is now the most expensive flat in the world. The building is situated close to Buckingham Palace and Downing Street. Top market property prices have continued to rise despite the recession.

   Source: *The Times online*, 16 March 2008

   a Why has the price of land in St. James Square continued to increase despite the recession? In your answer include a discussion of the demand for and supply of land.
   b Use a graph to show why the price of land in St. James Square increased over the past few years.
   c Is the supply of land in St. James's Square perfectly inelastic?

14 In the news clip in Problem 8,

   a Explain how a fall in house prices influences the market for construction equipment leases.
   b Draw a graph to illustrate the effect of a fall in house prices on the market for construction equipment leases.

Use the following news clip in Problems 15 and 16.

Intensive Farming

According to the European Commission, global agricultural production needs to be doubled by 2050 to feed the world. But at the same time, it says this will have to be done with less water and fewer pesticides and greenhouse gas emissions, amid growing competition for land.

   Source: *euractiv.com*, 16 August 2011

15 **a** Is farmland a renewable or non-renewable resource?
   b Explain how the growing demand for farm products will affect the market for land and draw a graph to illustrate your answer.

16 How might farmers meet the growing demand for farm products without having to use a greater quantity of farmland?

17 **Copter Crisis**

   Helicopters are in short supply these days. You could blame a rise in military spending, a jump in disaster relief, even crowded airports pushing executives into private travel. But the fastest growth is coming from the offshore oil-and-gas industry, where helicopters are the only way to ferry crews to and from rigs and platforms. Hundred-dollar oil has pushed producers to work existing fields harder and to open new deep-sea wells in Brazil, India and Alaska. The number of rigs and platforms has grown by 13 per cent over the past decade. Oil companies are facing a two-year backlog in orders for the Sikorsky S92, a favourite of the oil industry, and a 40 per cent rise in prices for used models.

   Source: *Fortune*, 12 May 2008

   a Explain how high oil prices influence the market for helicopter leases and services (such as the Sikorsky S92).
   b What happens to the value of marginal product of a helicopter as a firm leases or buys additional helicopters?

Mathematical Note (Study Plan 17.MN)

18 Keshia is opening a book-keeping service in Brussels. She is considering buying or leasing some new laptop computers. The purchase price of a laptop is €1,500 and after three years it is worthless. The annual lease rate is €550 per laptop. The value of marginal product of one laptop is €700 a year. The value of marginal product of a second laptop is €625 a year. The value of marginal product of a third laptop is €575 a year. And the value of marginal product of a fourth laptop is €500 a year.

   a How many laptops will Keshia lease or buy?
   b If the interest rate is 4 per cent a year, will Keshia lease or buy her laptops?
   c If the interest rate is 6 per cent a year, will Keshia lease or buy her laptops?

Economics in the News

19 **Baronet to the Rescue of Parkland under Threat**

   Residents in Salford who are campaigning to block a proposed housing development discovered that the plot was once a farm owned by the ancestors of Sir Peter Heywood, the 6th Baronet of Claremont, and that they had sold it to the council in 1902 on the condition that it be used only for recreation. Council officials had claimed that there was little chance of tracking down descendants but now the council may be forced to rethink its plan to sell the land for £1.5 million.

   Source: *The Times*, 4 April 2007

   Explain why the plot of land in Salford would be worth £1.5 million.

ADDITIONAL PROBLEMS AND APPLICATIONS

Do these problems in MyEconLab if assigned by your lecturer.

MyEconLab

The Anatomy of Factor Markets

20 Venus is opening a tennis school in France. She plans to hire a marketing graduate to promote the school and an administrator at €20 an hour. Venus is also considering buying or leasing a new tennis ball machine. The purchase price of the machine is €1,000 and after three years it is worthless. The annual cost of leasing the machine is €500.

a In which factor markets does Venus operate?

b What is the price of the capital equipment and the rental rate of capital?

The Demand for a Factor of Production

Use the following data in Problems 21 to 24.

Kaiser's Smoothie Bar in Bonn hires workers to produce smoothies. The market for smoothies is perfectly competitive, and the price of a smoothie is €4. The labour market is competitive, and the wage rate is €40 a day. The table shows the workers' total product schedule:

Number of workers	Quantity produced (smoothies per day)
1	7
2	21
3	33
4	43
5	51
6	55

21 Calculate the marginal product of hiring the fourth worker and the fourth worker's value of marginal product.

22 How many workers will Kaiser's hire to maximise its profit and how many smoothies a day will Kaiser's produce?

23 If the price rises to €5 a smoothie, how many workers will Kaiser's hire?

24 Kaiser's installs a new machine that increases the productivity of workers by 50 per cent. If the price of a smoothie remains at €4 and the wage rate rises to €48 a day, how many workers does Kaiser's hire?

25 **Detroit Oil Refinery Expansion Approved**

Marathon Oil Saturday started work on a $1.9 billion expansion of its petrol refinery in Detroit. Marathon will employ 800 construction workers and add 135 permanent jobs to the existing 480 workers at the refinery.

Source: *United Press International*, 21 June 2008

a Explain how rising petrol prices influence the market for refinery labour.

b Draw a graph to illustrate the effects of rising petrol prices on the market for refinery labour.

Labour Markets

Use the following news clip in Problems 26 to 29.

Miner Sacks 17,000 Workers Over Pay Dispute

Impala Platinum has sacked 17,000 South African miners at its Rustenburg mine because they took part in an illegal strike. The miners refused to have their union negotiate in the two-week pay dispute with the world's second largest platinum producer. Mining provides a quarter of all jobs in Rustenburg.

Source: abc.com.au, 3 February 2012

26 How would the wage rate and employment for the Rustenburg miners be determined in a competitive market?

27 **a** Explain how it is possible that the mine workers were being paid less than the wage that would be paid in a competitive labour market.

b What would be the effect of a minimum wage law in the market for miners?

28 **a** Explain how a miners' union would attempt to counteract Impala Platinum's wage offers.

b Is it possible that the union officials might be acting in their own interest and not in the interest of the miners?

29 If the market for labour in mining is competitive, explain the potential effect of a union on the wage rate. Draw a graph to illustrate your answer

Use the following news clip in Problems 30 to 33.

The New War over Wal-Mart

Today, Wal-Mart employs more people – 1.7 million – than any other private employer in the world. With size comes power: Wal-Mart's prices are lower and United Food and Commercial Workers International Union argues that Wal-Mart's wages are also lower than its competitors. Last year, the workers at a Canadian outlet joined the union and Wal-Mart immediately closed the outlet. But does Wal-Mart behave any worse than its competitors? When it comes to payroll, Wal-Mart's median hourly wage tracks the national median wage for general merchandise retail jobs.

Source: *The Atlantic*, June 2006

30 a Assuming that Wal-Mart has market power in a labour market, explain how the firm could use that market power in setting wages.

b Draw a graph to illustrate how Wal-Mart might use labour market power to set wages.

31 a Explain how a union of Wal-Mart's employees would attempt to counteract Wal-Mart's wage offers (a bilateral monopoly).

b Explain the response by the Canadian Wal-Mart to the unionisation of employees.

32 Based upon evidence presented in this article, does Wal-Mart function as a monopsony in labour markets, or is the market for retail labour more competitive? Explain.

33 If the market for retail labour is competitive, explain the potential effect of a union on the wage rates. Draw a graph to illustrate your answer.

Capital and Natural Resource Markets

Use the following news clip in Problems 34 and 35.

Natural Gas Prices Create Land Rush

There is a land rush going on across Pennsylvania, but buyers aren't interested in the land itself. Buyers are interested in what lies beneath the earth's surface – mineral rights to natural gas deposits. Record high natural gas prices have already pushed up drilling activity across the state, but drilling companies have discovered a new technology that will enable deep gas-bearing shale to be exploited. Development companies, drilling companies and speculators have been crisscrossing the state, trying to lease mineral rights from landowners. The new drilling techniques might recover about 10 per cent of those reserves, and that would ring up at a value of $1 trillion.

Source: *Erie Times-News*, 15 June 2008

34 a Is natural gas a renewable or non-renewable resource? Explain.

b Explain why the demand for land in Pennsylvania has increased.

35 a If companies are responding to the higher prices for natural gas by drilling right now wherever they can, what does that imply about their assumptions about the future price of natural gas in relation to current interest rates?

b What could cause the price of natural gas to fall in the future?

36 New technology has allowed oil to be pumped from much deeper offshore oil fields than before. For example, 28 deep ocean rigs operate in the deep waters of the Gulf of Mexico.

a What effect do you think deep ocean sources have had on the world oil price?

b Who will benefit from drilling for oil in the Gulf of Mexico? Explain your answer.

37 Water is a natural resource that is plentiful in Yorkshire but not plentiful in London or the South East of England.

a If Yorkshire Water started to export bulk water to London and the South East, what do you predict would be the effect on the price of bulk water?

b Will Yorkshire eventually run out of water?

c Do you think the Hotelling Principle applies to Yorkshire's water? Explain why or why not.

Economics in the News

38 After you have studied *Reading Between the Lines* on pp. 406– 407, answer the following questions.

a Name some jobs for which you think future employment will expand and some for which it will shrink.

b What are the influences on the demand for labour that bring an increase in demand, and what are the influences that bring a decrease in demand?

c In the past, computerisation and nuclear physics have had a major impact on the power generation industry. How has technology affected the demand for skilled workers in the power generation industry?

d Why might an increase in the demand for skilled nuclear engineers increase the supply of skilled nuclear engineers and what would be the effect on wages?

e Changes in technology are likely to reduce the demand for low-skilled factory workers over the next 10 years. Draw a graph of the market for factory workers in 2013 and 2021. Show the effects of a decrease in the demand for factory workers with no change in the supply on the employment and wage rate of factory workers.

f If the outcome you've shown in part (e) occurred, explain how the incentives faced by young workers just entering the labour force would be affected.

Mathematical Note

39 Terry is opening a new online bookshop in Leeds. He is considering buying or leasing some computers. The purchase price of a computer is £1,600 and after three years a computer is worthless. The annual lease is £550 per computer. The value of marginal product of one computer is £700 a year. The value of marginal product of a second computer is £650 a year. The value of marginal product of a third computer is £500 a year. And the value of marginal product of a fourth computer is £300 a year.

a How many computers will Terry lease or buy?

b If the interest rate is 4 per cent a year, will Terry lease or buy his computers?

c If the interest rate is 6 per cent a year, will Terry lease or buy his computers?

18 Economic Inequality and Redistribution

After studying this chapter you will be able to:

◆ Describe the distributions of income and wealth and the trends in economic inequality in the UK

◆ Describe the distribution of income and the trends in inequality in selected countries and the world

◆ Explain the sources of economic inequality and its trends

◆ Describe the scale of government income redistribution in the UK

Extreme poverty and extreme wealth exist side by side in every major city in the UK, in Europe and in most parts of the world. How does the distribution of income in the UK compare with that in other countries? Are the rich getting richer and the poor getting poorer?

In this chapter, we study economic inequality – its extent, its sources, and the things governments do to make it less extreme. And *Reading Between the Lines* at the end of the chapter takes a close look at the problem of increasing inequality of wealth in the UK.

Economic Inequality in the UK

The most commonly used measure of economic inequality is the distribution of annual disposable income. **Disposable income** is defined as *original income* plus cash benefits from government minus income taxes. **Original income** is wages, interest, rent and profit earned in factor markets, *before* paying income taxes. Original income plus government cash benefits is called *gross income*. Individual incomes are estimated from household income survey data.

The Distribution of Income

Figure 18.1 shows the distribution of *disposable income* across the 63 million individuals in the UK in 2009. Note that the *x*-axis measures individual income and the *y*-axis is percentage of individuals.

The most common income in 2009, called the *mode income*, was received by the 6.2 per cent of the population whose incomes fell between £300 and £350 a week. The value of £325 marked on Figure 18.1 is the middle of that range.

The middle level of income in 2009, called the *median income*, was £407 a week. One half of the UK population had incomes greater than this amount, and the other half had incomes less than this amount.

The average weekly income in 2009, called the *mean income*, was £507 a week.

You can see in Figure 18.1 that the mode income is less than the median income and the median income is less than the mean income. This feature of the distribution of income tells us that there are more individuals with low incomes than with high incomes. But some individuals have high incomes that are off the scale, over £1,000 a week.

The income distribution in Figure 18.1 is called a *positively skewed* distribution, which means that it has a long tail of high values. This distribution contrasts with a bell-shaped distribution such as the distribution of people's heights. In a bell-shaped distribution, the mean, median and mode are all equal.

Another way of looking at the distribution of income is to measure the percentage of total income received by each given percentage of households. Data are reported for five groups – called quintiles or fifth shares – each consisting of 20 per cent of households.

Figure 18.2 shows the distribution based on these shares in 2010. The 20 per cent of households with the lowest incomes received 8 per cent of total income; the second 20 per cent received 12 per cent of total income; the middle 20 per cent received 16 per cent of total income; the next highest 20 per cent received 22 per cent of total income; and the highest 20 per cent received 42 per cent of total income.

The distribution of income in Figure 18.1 and the quintile shares in Figure 18.2 tell us that disposable income is distributed unequally. But we need a way of comparing the distribution of income in different periods and using different measures. A neat graphical tool called the *Lorenz curve* enables us to make such comparisons.

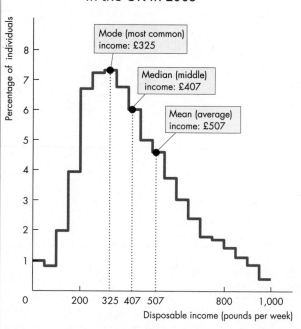

Figure 18.1 The Distribution of Income in the UK in 2009

The distribution of disposable income is positively skewed. The mode (most common) income is less than the median (middle) income, which in turn is less than the mean (average) income. The percentage of individuals with an income above £1,000 a week (not shown) falls off slowly and the highest incomes are more than £100,000 a week.

Source of data: Office for National Statistics.

MyEconLab Animation ————————————————◆

Figure 18.2 UK Quintile Shares in 2010

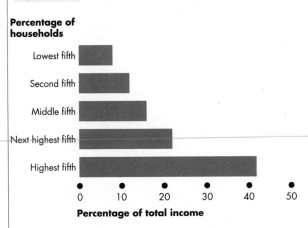

In 2010, the 20 per cent of households with the lowest incomes received 8 per cent of total income; the second 20 per cent received 12 per cent of total income; the middle 20 per cent received 16 per cent; the next highest 20 per cent received 22 per cent; and the highest 20 per cent received 42 per cent.

Households (percentage)	Income (percentage of total income)
Lowest 20	8
Second 20	12
Middle 20	16
Next highest 20	22
Highest 20	42

Source of data: Office for National Statistics.

MyEconLab Animation ⬧

Figure 18.3 The Income Lorenz Curve in 2010

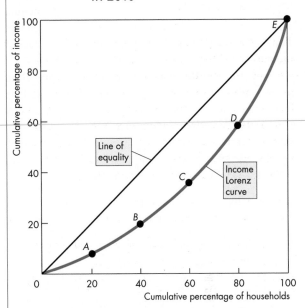

	Households		Income	
	Percentage	**Cumulative percentage**	**Percentage**	**Cumulative percentage**
A	Lowest 20	20	8	8
B	Second 20	40	12	20
C	Middle 20	60	16	36
D	Next highest 20	80	22	58
E	Highest 20	100	42	100

The cumulative percentage of income is graphed against the cumulative percentage of households. Points A to E on the Lorenz curve correspond to the rows of the table.

If incomes were distributed equally, each 20 per cent of households would receive 20 per cent of total income and the Lorenz curve would fall along the line of equality. The Lorenz curve shows that income is unequally distributed.

Source of data: Office for National Statistics.

MyEconLab Animation ⬧

The Income Lorenz Curve

The income **Lorenz curve** graphs the cumulative percentage of income against the cumulative percentage of households. Figure 18.3 shows the income Lorenz curve using the quintile shares from Figure 18.2. The table shows the percentage of disposable income of each quintile group. For example, row A tells us that the lowest quintile of households receives 8 per cent of total income. The table also shows the cumulative percentages of households and income. For example, row B tells us that the lowest two quintiles (lowest 40 per cent) of households receive 20 per cent of total income – 8 per cent for the lowest quintile and 12 per cent for the next lowest.

The Lorenz curve provides a direct visual clue about the degree of income inequality by comparing it with the line of equality. This line, identified in Figure 18.3, shows what the Lorenz curve would be if everyone had the same level of income.

If income were distributed equally across all the households, each quintile would receive 20 per cent of total income and the cumulative percentages of income received by the cumulative percentages of households would fall along the straight line labelled 'Line of equality'.

The actual distribution of income is shown by the curve labelled 'Income Lorenz curve'. The closer the Lorenz curve is to the line of equality, the more equal is the distribution.

The Distribution of Wealth

The distribution of wealth provides another way of measuring economic inequality. A household's **wealth** is the value of the things that it owns at a *point in time*. In contrast, income is the amount that the household receives over a given *period of time*.

Figure 18.4 shows the Lorenz curve for wealth in the UK in 2008–2010. During this period, average household wealth was £237,500. But the variation around this value is enormous. Wealth is extremely unequally distributed, and for this reason the data are grouped by five unequal groups of households. The poorest 50 per cent of households own only 10 per cent of total wealth (row A' in the table in Figure 18.4). The next 20 per cent of households own 16 per cent of total wealth (row B' in the table). So the poorest 70 per cent of households own only 26 per cent of total wealth and the richest 30 per cent of households own 74 per cent of total wealth. Because this group owns such a large percentage of total wealth, we break it into smaller bits in rows C' to E'. The richest 10 per cent of households own 44 per cent of total wealth (row E').

Figure 18.4 shows the income Lorenz curve (from Figure 18.3) alongside the wealth Lorenz curve. You can see that the Lorenz curve for wealth is much farther away from the line of equality than is the Lorenz curve for income, which means that the distribution of wealth is much more unequal than the distribution of income.

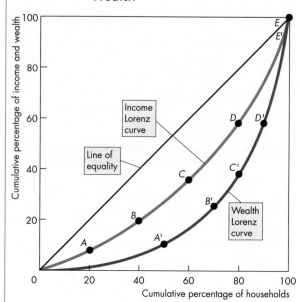

Figure 18.4 Lorenz Curves for Income and Wealth

	Households		Wealth	
	Percentage	Cumulative percentage	Percentage	Cumulative percentage
A'	Lowest 50	50	10	10
B'	Next 20	70	16	26
C'	Next 10	90	12	38
D'	Next 10	99	18	56
E'	Highest 10	100	44	100

The cumulative percentage of wealth is graphed against the cumulative percentage of households. Points A' to E' on the Lorenz curve for wealth correspond to the rows of the table. By comparing the Lorenz curves for income and wealth, we can see that wealth is distributed much more unequally than income.

Source of data: Office for National Statistics.

MyEconLab Animation ───────────◆

Wealth or Income?

We've seen that wealth is much more unequally distributed than income. Which distribution provides the better description of the degree of inequality? To answer this question, we need to think about the connection between wealth and income.

Wealth is a stock of assets and *income* is the flow of earnings that results from the stock of wealth. Suppose

that a person owns assets worth £1 million – has a wealth of £1 million. If the rate of return on assets is 5 per cent a year, then this person receives an income of £50,000 a year from those assets. We can describe this person's economic condition by using either the wealth of £1 million or the income of £50,000. When the rate of return is 5 per cent a year, £1 million of wealth equals

£50,000 of income in perpetuity. Wealth and income are just different ways of looking at the same thing.

But in Figure 18.4, the distribution of wealth is more unequal than the distribution of income. Why? It is because the wealth data do not include the value of human capital, while the income data measure income from all wealth, including human capital.

Think about Lee and Peter, two people with equal income and equal wealth. Lee's wealth is human capital, and his entire income is from employment. Peter's wealth is in the form of investments in stocks and bonds, and his entire income is from these investments.

When Lee and Peter are surveyed by the Office for National Statistics in a national wealth and income survey, their incomes are recorded as being equal, but Lee's wealth is recorded as being zero, while Peter's wealth is recorded as the value of his investments. Peter looks vastly more wealthy than Lee in the survey data.

Because the national survey of wealth excludes human capital, the income distribution is a more accurate measure of economic inequality than the wealth distribution.

Annual or Lifetime Income and Wealth?

A typical household's income changes over its life cycle. Income starts out low, grows to a peak when the household's workers reach retirement age and then falls after retirement. Also, a typical household's wealth changes over time. Like income, wealth starts out low, grows to a peak at the point of retirement and then falls.

Suppose we look at three households that have identical lifetime incomes: one household is young, one is middle-aged and one is retired. The middle-aged household has the highest income and wealth, the retired household has the lowest and the young household falls in the middle. The distributions of annual income and wealth in a given year are unequal, but the distributions of lifetime income and wealth are equal.

Although some of the inequality in annual income arises because different households are at different stages in the life cycle, after allowing for this factor a substantial amount of inequality remains.

So far, we have examined the extent of inequality in income and wealth in a few recent years. What are the trends in inequality? Is the distribution of income becoming less equal or more equal? We can see trends in the income distribution by looking at a number of years.

Trends in Inequality

To see trends in the income distribution, we need a measure that enables us to rank distributions on the scale of more equal and less equal. No perfect scale exists, but one that is much used is called the Gini coefficient.

The **Gini coefficient** is based on the Lorenz curve and equals the area between the line of equality and the Lorenz curve as a percentage of the entire area beneath the line of equality. The larger the Gini coefficient, the greater is the degree of income inequality. If income is equally distributed, the Lorenz curve is the same as the line of equality, so the Gini coefficient is zero. If one person has all the income and everyone else has none, the Gini coefficient is 100 per cent.

Figure 18.5 shows the UK Gini coefficient from 1983 to 2011. The Gini coefficient has increased over the period, which means that, on this measure, incomes have become more unequal. The major increase in inequality occurred during the 1980s. Since 1990, the Gini coefficient has fluctuated around a very slightly falling trend.

Figure 18.5 The UK Gini Coefficient: 1983–2011

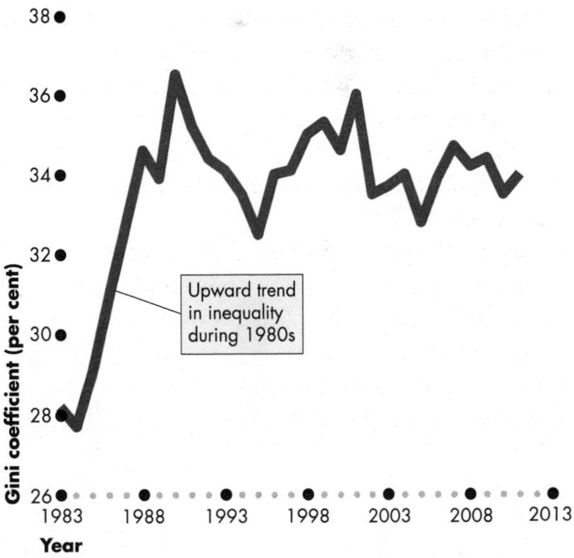

Measured by the Gini coefficient, the distribution of income in the UK became more unequal between 1983 and 1990. Since 1990, the Gini coefficient has fluctuated around a very slightly falling trend.

Source of data: Office for National Statistics.

MyEconLab Animation

ECONOMICS IN ACTION

Who in the UK Are the Rich and the Poor?

So who are the richest and the poorest people in the UK? Are there some economic and demographic characteristics that make people more likely to be rich or poor? We can find out from the UK government Family Spending Survey, which provides data on incomes organised by six characteristics shown in the figure below. They are:

♦ Economic status
♦ Occupation
♦ Age of householder
♦ Household composition
♦ Tenure
♦ Region

Economic Status

Economic status – whether an employer or employee or an unemployed person – is one of the most important influences on income. People are most likely to be rich if they are an employer and most likely to be poor if they are unemployed.

Occupation

A person's occupation is the second most important influence on income. Professional workers and managers earn, on average, twice the income of lower-skilled routine workers.

Age of Householder

The households with the highest incomes are those in which the householder is in mid- and late-career. The households with the lowest incomes are those in which the householder is young or old. The young are still acquiring skills and the oldest are usually not employed.

Household Composition

The highest-income household is likely to be one with two professionals aged between 30 and 49 with one child. Single people are most likely to be poor, young or old.

Tenure

People who own their homes have incomes, on average, twice the level of those who live in social housing or local council housing. Private renters fall between these two groups.

Region

Regional differences in income are not large but, on average, people who live in England have higher incomes than those who live in Northern Ireland, Wales or Scotland.

Figure 1 shows that the highest-income households are professional couples, both working, in mid- to late-career, living in their own home in England. The lowest-income households are unemployed singles, young or old, living in social housing in Northern Ireland, Wales or Scotland.

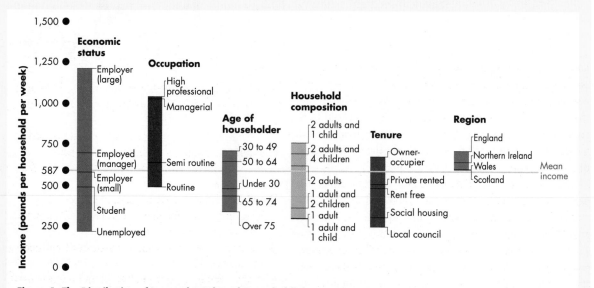

Figure 1 The Distribution of Income by Selected Household Characteristics

Source of data: Office for National Statistics, *Family Spending 2009: A Report on Living Costs and Food Survey* 2011.

ECONOMICS IN ACTION

Poverty in the EU

The *poverty line* is defined within Europe as 60 per cent of median EU income, and poverty rates vary throughout the EU. The *poverty rate* is the percentage of people who fall below the *poverty line*.

Figure 1 shows that five of the early members, including the UK, have poverty rates that exceed the 2011 EU average. The accession of new low-income member states such as Bulgaria and Latvia in 2006 lowered EU median income and increased the number of member states with relatively high poverty rates.

Problems with debt and recession have raised poverty rates in most EU countries since 2009 as incomes have fallen. Despite a lower median income in the 27 countries of the EU, the UK has a relatively high poverty rate on the EU definition. Even if we define the poverty line as 60 per cent of median UK income, 16.1 per cent of UK households lived in poverty in 2011. Using this UK-based measure, UK poverty rates were at their highest in 1991 at 22 per cent and lowest in 1977 when just 10 per cent of UK households lived in poverty.

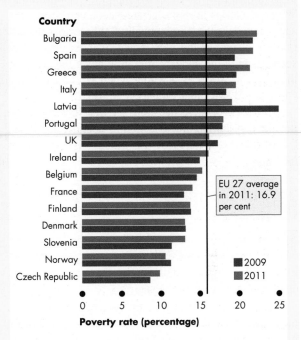

Figure 1 Poverty Rates in the EU

Sources of data: Eurostat, *At Risk of Poverty* tables.

Poverty

The poorest households are considered to be living in **poverty**, a state in which a household's income is too low to be able to buy the quantities of food, shelter and clothing that are deemed necessary. This concept of poverty is relative: the *poverty line* is a benchmark defined as 60 per cent of the median income. A person with an income below the poverty line is defined to be living in poverty. The *poverty rate* is the percentage of people who are living below the poverty line.

Because measures of poverty are relative, they don't provide information about the *absolute* level of poverty and how it is changing. People who are living in poverty in the UK would be considered well off in the black townships of South Africa. And people living in poverty in Ireland today would have been considered reasonably well off compared with the people of rural Ireland 40 years ago.

REVIEW QUIZ

1 Which is distributed more unequally: income or wealth? Why? Which is the better measure of inequality?

2 What does a Lorenz curve show and how do we use it to gauge the degree of inequality?

3 What is the Gini coefficient and how is it used to measure inequality?

4 Has the distribution of income in the UK become more unequal or less unequal? When did the largest changes occur?

5 What are the main characteristics of low-income households?

6 What is the poverty line? Explain how it is used.

Do these questions in Study Plan 18.1 and get instant feedback.   MyEconLab

Inequality in the World Economy

Which countries have the greatest economic inequality and which have the least inequality? Where does the UK rank? Is it one of the most equal or most unequal or somewhere in the middle? And how much inequality is there in the world as a whole when we consider the entire world as a single global economy?

We'll answer these questions by first looking at the income distribution in a selection of countries and then by examining features of the global distribution of income.

Income Distributions in Selected Countries

By inspecting the income distribution data for every country, we can compare the degree of income inequality and identify the countries with the most inequality and those with the least inequality.

Figure 18.6 summarises some extremes and compares them with the largest economy, the US, that falls between the extremes.

Look first at the numbers in the table. They tell us that in Brazil and South Africa the poorest 20 per cent of households receive only 2 per cent of total income while the highest 20 per cent receive 65 per cent of total income. An average person in the highest quintile receives 32.5 times the income of an average person in the lowest quintile.

Contrast these numbers with those for Finland and Sweden. In these countries the poorest 20 per cent receive 8 per cent of total income and the highest 20 per cent receive 35 per cent. So an average person in the highest quintile receives 4.4 times the income of an average person in the lowest quintile.

The numbers for the US lie between these extremes, with an average person in the highest quintile receiving just under 10 times the amount received by an average person in the lowest quintile.

Brazil and South Africa are extremes not matched in any other major country or region. Inequality is large in these countries because they have a relatively small but rich European population and a large and relatively poor indigenous population.

Finland and Sweden are extremes, but they are not unusual. Income distributions similar to these are found in many European countries in which governments pursue aggressive income redistribution policies.

We look next at the global income distribution.

Figure 18.6 Lorenz Curves Compared

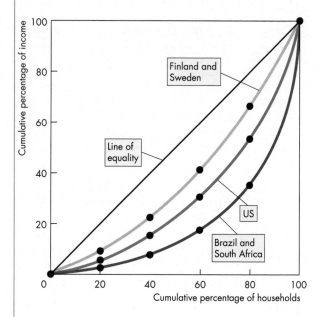

	Percentage of total income		
Households	**Brazil and South Africa**	**US**	**Finland and Sweden**
Lowest 20 per cent	2	5	8
Second 20 per cent	5	10	14
Middle 20 per cent	10	16	20
Next highest 20 per cent	18	22	23
Highest 20 per cent	65	47	35

The table shows the percentages of total income received by each quintile. The figure shows the cumulative percentage of income graphed against the cumulative percentage of households. The data and the Lorenz curves show that income is distributed most unequally in Brazil and South Africa and least unequally in Finland and Sweden. The degree of income inequality in the US lies between these extremes.

Sources of data: Brazil, South Africa, Finland and Sweden: Klaus W. Deininger and Lyn Squire, Measuring Income Inequality Database, World Bank, http://go.worldbank.org/. UK: National Office for Statistics.

MyEconLab Animation ⎯⎯⎯⎯⎯⎯⎯⎯⎯⎯◆

Global Inequality and Its Trends

The global distribution of income is much more unequal than the distribution within any one country. The reason is that many countries, especially in Africa and Asia, are in a pre-industrial stage of economic development and are poor, while industrial countries such as the US and the UK are rich. When we look at the distribution of income across the entire world – from the low income of the poorest African to the high income of the richest European – we see a very large degree of inequality.

To put some raw numbers on this inequality, start with the poorest. Measured in the value of the US dollar in 2005, a total of 3 billion people or 50 per cent of the world population live on $2.50 a day or less. Another 2 billion people or 30 per cent of the world population live on more than $2.50 but less than $10 a day. So 5 billion people or 80 per cent of the world's population live on $10 a day or less.

In contrast, in the rich world of the US, the *average* person has an income of $115 per day and an average person in the highest income quintile has an income of $460 a day. So the average American earns 46 times ($115/$2.50) the income of one of the world's 3 billion poorest people and more than 11.5 times ($115/$10) the income of 80 per cent of the people who live in developing economies. An American with an average income in the highest quintile earns about 180 times that of the world's poorest people but only 15 times that of an average American in the lowest quintile.

World Gini Coefficient

We can compare world inequality with UK inequality by comparing Gini coefficients. The world Gini coefficient is about 61 per cent. The UK Gini coefficient for original income – before government benefits and taxes – was 52.1 per cent in 2009. Recalling the interpretation of the Gini coefficient in terms of the Lorenz curve, the world Lorenz curve lies much farther from the line of equality than the UK Lorenz curve.

World Trend

You saw (in Figure 18.5) that incomes became more unequal in the UK during the 1980s – the Gini coefficient increased. Similar changes are found in most economies. Increased income inequality is a big issue in two of the world's largest and poorer nations, China and India. In these two economies, urban middle classes are getting richer at a faster pace than the rural farmers.

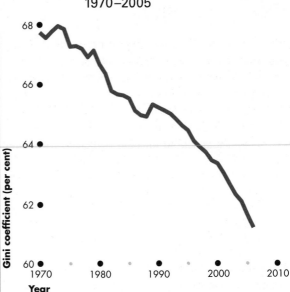

Figure 18.7 The World Gini Coefficient: 1970–2005

Measured by the Gini coefficient, the distribution of income in the entire world became more equal during the period 1970 to 2000.

Source of data: Xavier Sala-i-Martin and Maxim Pinkovskiy, 'Parametric estimations of the world distribution of income', 22 January 2010. http://www.voxeu.org/article/parametric-estimations-world-distribution-income.

MyEconLab Animation ———————————◆

Despite greater inequality within countries, the world is becoming less unequal. Figure 18.7 shows the world Gini coefficient over time. How can the world income distribution become less unequal while individual countries become more unequal? The answer is that average incomes in poorer countries are rising much faster than average incomes in rich countries. While the gap between rich and poor is widening within countries, it is narrowing across countries.

◆ REVIEW QUIZ

1   In which countries are incomes distributed most unequally and least unequally?
2   Which income distribution is more unequal and why: the income distribution in the US or in the entire world?
3   How can incomes become more unequally distributed within countries and less unequally distributed across countries?

Do these questions in Study Plan 18.2 and get instant feedback.   MyEconLab

The Sources of Economic Inequality

We've described economic inequality in the UK. Our task now is to explain it. We began this task in Chapter 17 by learning about the forces that influence demand and supply in the markets for labour, capital and land. We're now going to deepen our understanding of these forces.

Economic inequality arises from unequal labour market outcomes and from unequal ownership of capital. We'll begin by looking at labour markets, and three features of them that contribute to differences in income:

◆ Human capital

◆ Discrimination

◆ Contests among superstars

Human Capital

A clerk in a legal firm earns less than a tenth of the amount earned by the barrister he assists. An operating room nurse earns less than a tenth of the amount earned by the surgeon with whom she works. A bank teller earns less than a tenth of the amount earned by the bank's CEO. Some of the differences in these earnings arise from differences in human capital.

To see the influence of human capital on labour incomes, consider the example of a legal clerk and the barrister he assists. (The same reasoning can be applied to an operating room nurse and surgeon, or a bank teller and bank CEO.)

Demand, Supply and Wage Rates

A barrister performs many tasks that a legal clerk cannot perform. Imagine an untrained legal clerk cross-examining a witness in a complicated trial. The tasks that the barrister performs are valued highly by her clients, who willingly pay for her services. Using a term that you learned in Chapter 17, a barrister has a high value of marginal product, and a higher value of marginal product than her legal clerk. But you also learned in Chapter 17 that the value of marginal product of labour determines (is the same as) the demand for labour. So, because a barrister has a high value of marginal product, the demand for her services is also high.

To become a barrister, a person must acquire human capital. But human capital is costly to acquire. This cost – an opportunity cost – includes expenditures on tuition and textbooks. It also includes forgone earnings during the years spent in university and law school. It might also include low earnings doing on-the-job training in a law office during the summer.

Because the human capital needed to supply barrister services is costly to acquire, a person's willingness to supply these services reflects this cost. The supply of barrister services is smaller than the supply of legal-clerk services.

The demand for and supply of each type of labour determine the wage rate that each type of labour earns. Barristers earn a higher wage rate than legal clerks because the demand for barristers is greater and the supply of barristers is smaller. The gap between the wage rates reflects the higher value of marginal product of a barrister (demand) and the cost of acquiring human capital (supply).

Do Education and Training Pay?

You know that a barrister earns much more than a legal clerk, but does human capital add more to earning power generally and on average? The answer is that it does. Rates of return on university education have been estimated to be 35 per cent for women and 17.5 per cent for men, which suggests that a university degree is a better investment than almost any other that a person can undertake.

Human capital differences help to explain much of the inequality that we observe. High-income households tend to be better educated, professional, middle-aged couples (*Economics in Action* on p. 420). Human capital differences are correlated with these household characteristics. Education contributes directly to human capital. Age contributes indirectly to human capital because older workers have more experience than younger workers. But a larger proportion of younger workers than older workers have a university education. Human capital differences also explain a small part of the inequality associated with sex. A larger proportion of men than women have a university degree. The difference in education levels between the sexes is becoming smaller, but it has not been eliminated.

Career interruptions can decrease human capital. A person (most often a woman) who interrupts a career to raise young children usually returns to the labour force with a lower earning capacity than a similar person who has kept working. Likewise, a person who has suffered a spell of unemployment often finds a new job at a lower wage rate than that of a similar person who has not been unemployed.

Trends in Inequality Explained by Technological Change and Globalisation

You've seen that high-income households have earned an increasing share of total income while low-income households have earned a decreasing share: the distribution of income in the UK has become more unequal. Technological change and globalisation are two possible sources of this increased inequality.

Technological Change

Information technologies such as computers and laser scanners are *substitutes* for low-skilled labour: they perform tasks that previously were performed by low-skilled labour. The introduction of these technologies has lowered the marginal product and the demand for low-skilled labour. These same technologies require high-skilled labour to design, program and run them. High-skilled labour and the information technologies are *complements*. So the introduction of these technologies has increased the marginal product and increased the demand for high-skilled labour.

Figure 18.8 illustrates the effects on wages and employment. The supply curves of low-skilled labour in part (a) and of high-skilled labour in part (b) are S, and initially, the demand curve in each market is D_0. The low-skill wage rate is £5 an hour, and the high-skill wage rate is £10 an hour. The demand for low-skilled labour decreases to D_1 in part (a) and the demand for high-skilled labour increases to D_1 in part (b). The low-skill wage rate falls to £4 an hour and the high-skill wage rate rises to £15 an hour.

Globalisation

The entry of China and other developing countries into the global economy has lowered the prices of many manufactured goods. Lower prices for the firm's output reduce the value of marginal product of the firm's workers and decrease the demand for their labour. A situation like that in Figure 18.8(a) occurs. The wage rate falls and employment shrinks.

At the same time, the growing global economy increases the demand for services that employ high-skilled workers, and the value of marginal product and the demand for high-skilled labour increases. A situation like that in Figure 18.8(b) occurs. The wage rate rises, and employment opportunities for high-skilled workers expand.

Figure 18.8 Explaining the Trend in Income Distribution

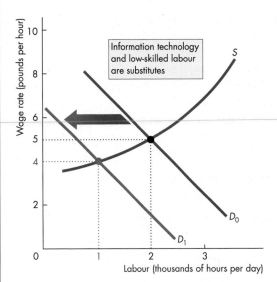

(a) A decrease in demand for low-skilled labour

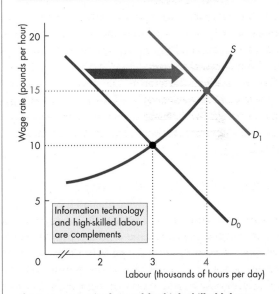

(b) An increase in demand for high-skilled labour

Low-skilled labour in part (a) and information technologies are substitutes. When these technologies were introduced, the demand for low-skilled labour decreased and the quantity of this type of labour employed and its wage rate decreased. High-skilled labour in part (b) and information technologies are complements. When these technologies were introduced, the demand for high-skilled labour increased and the quantity of this type of labour employed and its wage rate increased.

MyEconLab Animation ——————◆

Discrimination

Human capital differences can explain some of the economic inequality that we observe. But it can't explain all of it. Discrimination is another possible source of inequality.

An Example of Discrimination

Suppose that women and men have identical abilities as investment advisers. Figure 18.9 shows the supply curves of women, S_W in part (a), and of men, S_M in part (b). The value of marginal product of investment advisers shown by the two curves labelled *VMP* is the same for both groups.

If everyone is free of sex prejudice, the market determines a wage rate of £40,000 a year for investment advisers. But if the customers are prejudiced against women, this prejudice is reflected in the wage rate and employment. Suppose that the perceived value of marginal product of the women, when discriminated against, is VMP_{DA}. Suppose that the perceived value of marginal product of men, the group discriminated in favour of, is VMP_{DF}. With these *VMP* curves, women earn £20,000 a year and only 1,000 women work as investment advisers. Men earn £60,000 a year, and 3,000 of them work as investment advisers.

Counteracting Forces

Economists disagree about whether prejudice actually causes wage differentials, and one line of reasoning implies that it does not. In the example you've just studied, customers who buy from men pay a higher service charge for investment advice than do the customers who buy from women. This price difference acts as an incentive to encourage people who are prejudiced to buy from the people against whom they are prejudiced.

This force could be strong enough to eliminate the effects of discrimination altogether. Suppose, as is true in manufacturing, that a firm's customers never meet its workers. If such a firm discriminates against women, it can't compete with firms that hire women because its costs are higher than those of the non-prejudiced firms. Only firms that do not discriminate survive in a competitive industry.

Whether because of discrimination or from some other source, women do earn lower incomes than men. Another possible source of lower wage rates of women arises from differences in the relative degree of specialisation of women and men.

Figure 18.9 Discrimination

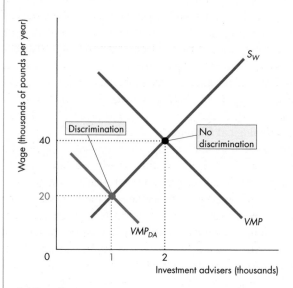

(a) Females

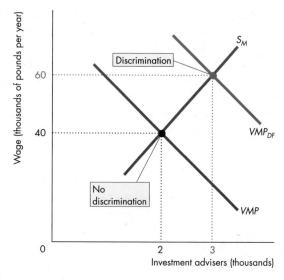

(b) Males

With no discrimination, the wage rate is £40,000 a year and 2,000 of each group are employed. With discrimination against women, the value of marginal product curve in part (a) is VMP_{DA}.

With discrimination in favour of men, the value of marginal product curve in part (b) is VMP_{DF}. The wage rate for women falls to £20,000 a year, and only 1,000 are employed. The wage rate for men rises to £60,000 a year, and 3,000 are employed.

MyEconLab Animation ─────────────◆

Differences in the Degree of Specialisation

Couples must choose how to allocate their time between working for a wage and doing jobs in the home, such as cooking, cleaning, shopping, organising holidays and, most important, bearing and rearing children. Let's look at the choices of Bob and Sue.

Bob might specialise in earning an income and Sue in taking care of the home. Or Sue might specialise in earning an income and Bob in taking care of the home. Or both of them might earn an income and share home production jobs.

The allocation they choose depends on their preferences and on the earning potential of each of them. The choice of an increasing number of households is for each person to diversify between earning an income and doing some home chores. But in most households, Bob will specialise in earning an income and Sue will both earn an income and bear a larger share of the task of running the home. With this allocation, Bob will probably earn more than Sue. If Sue devotes time and effort to ensuring Bob's mental and physical well-being, the quality of Bob's market labour will be higher than it would be if he were diversified. If the roles were reversed, Sue would be able to supply market labour that earns more than Bob.

To test whether the degree of specialisation accounts for earnings differences between the sexes, economists have compared the incomes of never-married men and women. They have found that, on average, with equal amounts of human capital, the wages of these two groups are the same.

Contests Among Superstars

The differences in income that arise from differences in human capital affect a large proportion of the population, but human capital differences can't account for some of the really large income differences.

The super rich – those in the top 1 per cent of the income distribution whose income share has been rising – earn vastly more than can be explained by human capital differences. What makes a person super rich?

A clue to the answer is provided by thinking about the super rich in tennis and golf. What makes tennis players and golfers special is that their earnings depend on where they finish in a tournament. When Roger Federer won the Wimbledon Championship in 2012, he received £1,150,000. The runner-up in this event, Andy Murray, received £575,000. So Roger earned double the amount earned by Andy. And he earned 88 times the amount received by the players who lost in the first round of the tournament.

It is true that Roger Federer has a lot of human capital. He practises hard and long and is a remarkable athlete. But anyone who is good enough to get into a tennis Grand Slam tournament is similarly well equipped with human capital and has spent a similar number of long hours in training and practice. It isn't human capital that explains the differences in earnings. It is the tournament and the prize differences that account for the large differences in earnings.

But three questions jump out. First, why do we reward superstar tennis players (and golfers) with prizes for winning a contest? Second, why are the prizes so different? And third, do the principles that apply on the tennis court (and golf course) apply more generally?

Why Prizes for a Contest?

The answer to this question (which was noted in Chapter 5, see p. 104) is that contests with prizes do a good job of allocating scarce resources efficiently when the efforts of the participants are hard to monitor and reward directly. There is only one winner, but many people work hard in an attempt to be that person. So a great deal of diligent effort is induced by a contest.

Why Are Prizes So Different?

The prizes need to be substantially different to induce enough effort. If the winner received 10 per cent more than the runner up, the gain from being the winner would be insufficient to encourage anyone to work hard enough. Someone would win but no one would put in much effort. Tennis matches would be boring, golf scores would be high, and no one would be willing to pay to see these sports. Big differences are necessary to induce a big enough effort to generate the quality of performance that people are willing to pay to see.

Does the Principle Apply More Generally?

Winner-takes-all isn't confined to tennis and golf. Film stars, football superstars and top corporate executives can all be viewed as participants in contests that decide the winners. The winner's prize is an income at least double that of the runner up and many multiples of the incomes of those who drop out earlier in the tournament.

Do Contests Among Superstars Explain the Trend?

Contests among superstars can explain large differences in incomes. But can contests explain the trend toward greater inequality with an increasing share of total income going to the super rich?

An idea first suggested by University of Chicago economist Sherwin Rosen suggests that a winner-takes-all contest can explain the trend. The key is that globalisation has increased the market reach of the winner and increased the spread between the winner and the runners-up.

Global television audiences now watch all the world's major sporting events, and the total revenue generated by advertising spots during these events has increased. Competition among terrestrial and cable and satellite television distributors has increased the fees that event organisers receive. To attract the top star performers, prize money has increased and the winner gets the biggest share of the prize pot.

So the prizes in sports have become bigger and the share of income going to the 'winner' has increased.

A similar story can be told about superstars and the super rich in business. As the cost of doing business on a global scale has fallen, more and more businesses have become global in their reach. Not only are large multinational corporations sourcing their inputs from far afield and selling in every country, they are also recruiting their top executives from a global talent pool. With a larger source of talent, and greater total revenue, firms must make the 'prize'– the reward for the top job – more attractive to compete for the best managers.

We've examined some sources of inequality in the labour market. Let's now look at the way inequality arises from unequal ownership of capital.

Unequal Wealth

You've seen that inequality in wealth (excluding human capital) is much greater than inequality in income. This inequality arises from saving and transfers of wealth from one generation to the next.

The higher a household's income, the more that household tends to save and pass on to the next generation. Saving is not always a source of increased inequality. If a household's saving redistributes an uneven income over the household's life, consumption will fluctuate less than its income and saving decreases inequality. If a lucky generation that has a high income saves a large part of that income and leaves capital to a succeeding generation that is unlucky, this act of saving also decreases the degree of inequality. But two features of intergenerational transfers of wealth lead to increased inequality: people can't inherit debts, and marriage tends to concentrate wealth.

Intergenerational Transfers

Some households inherit wealth from the previous generation. Some save more than enough on which to live during retirement and transfer wealth to the next generation. But these intergenerational transfers of wealth do not always increase wealth inequality. If a generation that has a high income saves a large part of that income and leaves wealth to a succeeding generation that has a lower income, this transfer decreases the degree of inequality. But one feature of intergenerational transfers of wealth leads to increased inequality: wealth concentration through marriage.

Marriage and Wealth Concentration

People tend to marry within their own socioeconomic class – a phenomenon called *assortative mating*. In everyday language, 'like attracts like'. Although there is a good deal of folklore that 'opposites attract', perhaps such Cinderella tales appeal to us because they are so rare in reality. Wealthy people seek wealthy partners.

Because of assortative mating, wealth becomes more concentrated in a small number of families and the distribution of wealth becomes more unequal.

◆ REVIEW QUIZ

1 What role does human capital play in accounting for income inequality?
2 What role might discrimination play in accounting for income inequality?
3 What role might contests among superstars play in accounting for income inequality?
4 How might technological change and globalisation explain trends in the distribution of income?
5 Does inherited wealth make the distribution of income less equal or more equal?

Do these questions in Study Plan 18.3 and get instant feedback.   MyEconLab

Next we're going to see how taxes and government policies redistribute income and wealth and decrease the degree of economic inequality.

Income Redistribution

Governments use three main types of policies to redistribute income. They are:

◆ Income taxes
◆ Benefit payments
◆ Subsidised welfare services

Income Taxes

Income taxes may be progressive, regressive or proportional. A **progressive income tax** is one that taxes income at an average rate that increases as income increases. A **regressive income tax** is one that taxes income at an average rate that decreases as income increases. A **proportional income tax** (also called a *flat-rate income tax*) is one that taxes income at a constant average rate regardless of the level of income.

Income taxes are progressive in all EU member states. For example, in 2012/13 in the UK, people who earned £8,105 a year or less paid no income tax. A tax of 20 per cent was paid on the first £34,370 above £8,105. Any income up to £150,000 was taxed at 40 per cent and a tax of 50 per cent was imposed on incomes over £150,000.

Benefit Payments

Benefit payments redistribute income by making direct payments to people with low incomes. In 2011/12, the UK government paid £159 billion in benefit payments. The main types of benefit payments are:

◆ Income support payments
◆ Tax credits
◆ State pensions

Income Support Payments

Governments use a wide range of payments to raise household incomes and reduce poverty, including income support, unemployment and incapacity payments and child benefit. For example, in the UK, the Job Seekers' Allowance is paid for a limited period to individuals who have lost their jobs involuntarily and have no other main source of income. This allowance was £67.50 a week for people over 25 years of age in 2011/12 compared with the incapacity benefit, which was £92.25 a week.

Tax Credits

Tax credits are a method of helping low-income employed households. A tax credit increases a household's disposable income by reducing their tax bill. In 2011/12, the Working Tax Credit for a single person caring for one child was a maximum of £175 a week. An additional child tax credit was also available to couples who had joint incomes of up to £60,000.

State Pensions

State pensions for the elderly are the main component of government benefit payments in all EU member states. These pensions are paid out of current taxes, so they result in redistribution from people currently working to those retired. In the UK in 2011/12, more than 7 million people received a state pension of up to £137.00 a week for a single person (more for a couple).

Subsidised Welfare Services

A great deal of redistribution takes place in most European countries through the subsidised provision of welfare goods and services. These are the goods and services provided by the government at prices below marginal cost. Taxpayers who consume these goods and services receive a transfer in kind from taxpayers who do not consume them. The two main areas in which this form of redistribution takes place are education – from nursery care through to university – and healthcare.

In the UK, 50 per cent of government expenditure is on benefits in kind: 18 per cent on the National Health Service, 13 per cent on education and the remainder on other services. The National Health Service provides almost all healthcare services free at the point of demand. Primary and secondary education is provided free for all children in the UK.

In the EU, the extent and method of subsidising education and healthcare services vary greatly across member states. For example, in some countries healthcare is free at the point of demand, and in other countries healthcare is privately provided and the government reimburses patients' costs. In some countries, people are required to pay into compulsory health insurance systems.

Whatever the method, subsidised provision of services improves access to good-quality healthcare and education and reduces inequality in health status and basic human capital.

ECONOMICS IN ACTION

Redistribution in the EU

EU governments use both progressive income taxes and benefit payments to redistribute income.

The role of income tax varies a great deal. Income taxes constitute just 14 per cent of all tax revenue in the UK and Portugal, 10 per cent in Spain and Slovakia and 19 per cent in Sweden and Denmark.

Benefit payments also vary. Figure 1 compares EU member state spending on benefit payments as a percentage of total income in 2010.

EU benefit spending as a percentage of income is much higher in the richer northern countries than in the UK, the poorer southern countries and the new member states from central Europe. EU poverty rates shown in *Economics in Action* on p. 421 are affected by the level of benefits and the level of taxes.

Figure 2 shows the combined impact of taxes and benefits in the UK in 2012 for the five quintile income groups, from lowest fifth to highest fifth.

On average, the fifth with the lowest incomes received £7,040 in cash benefits each year, whereas the fifth with the highest incomes received only £2,115. (The group with the highest incomes receives benefits because some benefits, such as pensions, are universally available.) The effect of cash benefits and tax credits is limited because many who are entitled to benefits fail to claim them.

Benefits in kind – mainly health benefits provided by the National Health Service and free or heavily subsidised education – are strongly progressive and represent 50 per cent of post-tax income for the fifth with the lowest incomes but only 6 per cent for the fifth with the highest incomes.

Income taxes have a strong effect on the distribution of income. The fifth with the highest incomes pay £19,727 in income taxes each year and the fifth with the lowest incomes pay £1,271 each year.

Expenditure taxes such as VAT have a smaller effect because the groups with low incomes spend a larger percentage of income on goods and services.

Overall, the net impact of UK taxes and benefits is a redistribution of income from the 40 per cent of households with the highest incomes to the 40 per cent with the lowest incomes, with a small net gain to the middle 20 per cent of households.

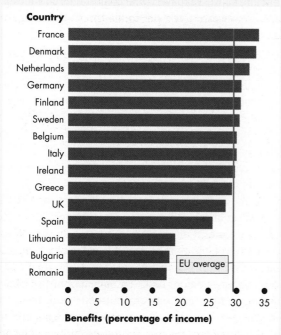

Figure 1 Benefits in the EU

Source of data: Eurostat Yearbook 2012.

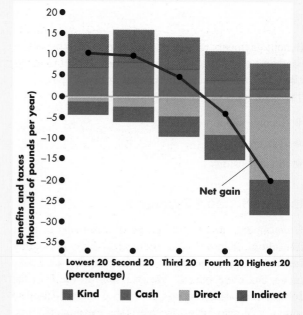

Figure 2 The Effects of Benefits and Taxes on the Distribution of Income

Source of data: Office for National Statistics, *Social Trends*, 2012.

The Big Trade-Off

All income redistribution creates what has been called the **big trade-off**, a trade-off between efficiency and fairness – see Chapter 5, p. 115. To achieve greater equity, we redistribute from the rich to the poor by imposing taxes on the rich and paying benefits to the poor. The big trade-off arises because redistribution uses scarce resources and weakens incentives. Both taxes and benefits bring inefficiency, which is the cost that must be borne to achieve greater equity.

Inefficient Taxes

Taxes are inefficient because they drive a wedge between marginal social cost and marginal social benefit and create deadweight loss. (Pigovian taxes that correct an externality are an exception – see Chapter 16, p. 372.) When a 40 per cent income tax is imposed on a high-income person, the marginal product of that person is 40 per cent greater than the marginal cost to that person of working. A potentially large deadweight loss arises. The taxes on the rich reduce their incentive to work and save. And the weaker incentive to save spills over to the poor because it means less capital is accumulated and fewer jobs are created.

Inefficient Benefits

Benefits for the poor are also inefficient. They lower the incentive of low-skilled people to work. More seriously, benefits lower the incentive to acquire human capital and move into a higher income group.

The inefficiencies arising from taxes and benefits result in less output and consumption for everybody – rich and poor. The disincentive effect of the benefits system is so severe that it gives rise to what is called a *benefit trap*.

The Benefit Trap

A *benefit trap* arises if a person who receives benefits takes a job or works longer hours and the loss of benefits exceeds the income earned. If a person loses £1 of benefit for every extra £1 earned – a *withdrawal rate* of 100 per cent – there is no gain from working. The person in effect faces a tax rate of 100 per cent!

There are two main types of benefit trap – the unemployment trap and the poverty trap. In the unemployment trap, people make decisions based on the expected wage they might earn compared with the benefit pay-

ments they will lose if they take a job. If the expected wage is only slightly higher than the unemployment benefit, the rational choice is to remain unemployed.

In the poverty trap, people are in low-paid work but are receiving benefit payments. They may want to work longer hours to earn an extra £10, but they may pay tax on the extra £10 and lose up to £10 of benefit payments. Again, the rational choice is not to work more hours.

Benefit Reform

In 2010, the UK government announced a radical simplification of the welfare benefit system with changes aimed at reducing poverty and unemployment traps. The government will merge five of the main income support benefits into one universal credit in 2013 and withdraw the benefits more slowly for part-time workers who earn more. Under the current system, some people in part-time work keep just 4 pence of every extra pound they earn as benefits are withdrawn and extra tax is paid. Under the new system, taxpayers will keep 24 pence of every extra pound earned and non-taxpayers will keep 35 pence.

The changes to the UK benefit system are not cost free. The cost before 2013 was £2 billion, which must come from higher taxes on the rich. The inefficiency created by redistribution in a tax and benefit system results in less output and consumption for everybody – rich and poor – but this must be weighed against increased equality.

◆ REVIEW QUIZ

1　How do EU governments redistribute income?
2　Describe the scale of redistribution in the UK.
3　What is the benefit trap and how does the UK government plan to tackle it?

Do these questions in Study Plan 18.4 and get instant feedback.　　　MyEconLab

We've examined economic inequality in the UK. We've seen how inequality arises and that inequality is increasing. *Reading Between the Lines* on pp. 432–433 looks at the stubborn persistence of the inequality of wealth in the UK.

The next chapter studies some problems for the market economy that arise from uncertainty and incomplete information. But unlike the cases we studied in Chapters 15 and 16, the market does a good job of coping with the problems.

READING BETWEEN THE LINES

Wealth: Rising Inequality in the UK

The Independent, 8 April 2013

Rise in Household Wealth Masks Huge Inequalities

Simon Read

Household wealth in the UK has soared past the £7 trillion mark for the first time, according to research from a bank.

It suggests that total household wealth . . . is up £2.71 trillion over the last decade, or £86,000 per household.

The rise in the nation's wealth has far out-stripped incomes and inflation. The consumer price index has climbed 29 per cent in a decade. . . . In comparison the value of household wealth since 2002 has grown by 62 per cent. However, most of the increase came prior to 2007, when the economy grew rapidly.

The research . . . suggests that the average household is now worth £255,502. But it con-cedes that there is a massive divide between the wealthy and the rest. Nitesh Patel, economist at Lloyds TSB Private Banking, said: 'While wealth has soared in the past decade, there is a large divide in where it has accumulated. The wealthiest 10 per cent of households hold 22 times more wealth, on average, than those in the bottom half.' . . .

 The Essence of the Story

- Recent research shows that UK household wealth is more than £7 trillion.

- The average household is £86,000 richer than 10 years ago.

- Wealth has risen faster than inflation but most of the increase in wealth occurred before 2007.

- The average household is worth £255,502.

- Wealth is distributed extremely unevenly.

- The top 10 per cent of UK households have 22 times more wealth than the bottom 50 per cent.

Economic Analysis

♦ The news article reports that total household wealth in the UK exceeds £7 trillion and the average household has £86,000 more wealth than in 2000.

♦ The wealth reported is private wealth, not total wealth: it ignores wealth arising from government redistribution.

♦ The value of household private wealth is the sum of the value of different types of assets that households own.

♦ Figure 1 shows the components of UK household private wealth, which is mainly property values and pension funds but also financial wealth such as bank accounts and physical wealth such as cars.

♦ Figure 1 also shows how the components of UK household wealth have changed since 2006–2008. The proportion of assets held in property has increased and the proportion of assets held in pension funds has decreased.

♦ Figure 2 shows the UK Gini coefficient for wealth from 1980 to 2005. An increase in the Gini coefficient means that the distribution of UK wealth has become more unequal.

♦ The news article's focus on aggregate private wealth misses two important features of wealth: a gender bias in its distribution and the effect of government policy on true wealth.

♦ Women, on average, own much less than men. The median private wealth held by women in 2010 was £8,800 compared with £64,300 held by men. The wealth of the top 10 per cent of men was £375,000 compared with just £156,000 for women.

♦ The impact of government policy to reduce the wealth gap makes a big difference to the amount of wealth inequality. At current levels of state pension and life expectancy, the state pension translates into wealth at age 65 of

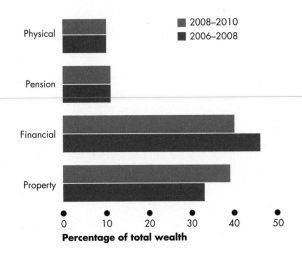

Figure 1 **Changes in Forms of Wealth**

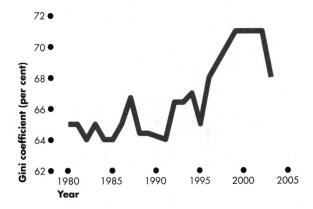

Figure 2 **Gini Coefficient for Wealth**

£86,000. This number is the present value of the 2011 pension rate over the future retirement years.

♦ Adjusting the wealth data to add this £86,000 to each person's wealth makes a big reduction in inequality.

♦ Ignoring the government pension, the top 10 per cent own 22 times the wealth of the bottom 50 per cent. Taking the government pension into account lowers this ratio from 22 to 11 per cent. Inequality is still large, but not as large as the private wealth data suggest.

SUMMARY

Key Points

Economic Inequality in the UK
(pp. 416–421)

◆ In 2009, the mode disposable income was £325 a week, the median disposable income was £407, and the mean disposable income was £507.

◆ The income distribution is positively skewed.

◆ In 2010, the 20 per cent of households with the lowest incomes received 8 per cent of total income and the 20 per cent with the highest incomes received 42 per cent of total income.

◆ Wealth is distributed more unequally than income because the wealth data exclude the value of human capital.

◆ The distribution of income became more unequal between 1983 and 1990, but since then it has become slightly less unequal.

◆ Occupation, economic status, type and region of household, age of householder and tenure all affect household income.

Do Problems 1 to 7 to get a better understanding of economic inequality in the UK.

Inequality in the World Economy
(pp. 422–423)

◆ Incomes are distributed most unequally in Brazil and South Africa and least unequally in Finland, Sweden, and some other European economies.

◆ The US income distribution lies between the extremes.

◆ The distribution of income across individuals in the global economy is more unequal than in the US.

◆ The global income distribution has been getting less unequal as rapid income growth in China and India has lifted millions from poverty.

Do Problems 8 to 11 to get a better understanding of inequality in the world.

The Sources of Economic Inequality
(pp. 424–428)

◆ Inequality arises from differences in human capital and from contests among superstars.

◆ Trends in the distribution of human capital and the rewards to superstars that arise from technological change and globalisation can explain some of the increased trend in inequality.

◆ Inequality might arise from discrimination.

◆ Inequality between men and women might arise from differences in the degree of specialisation.

◆ Intergenerational transfers of wealth lead to increased inequality because people can't inherit debts, and assortative mating tends to concentrate wealth.

Do Problems 12 to 15 to get a better understanding of the sources of economic inequality.

Income Redistribution (pp. 429–431)

◆ Governments redistribute income through progressive income taxes and the payment of cash benefits and benefits in kind.

◆ Redistribution in the UK transfers income from the richest 40 per cent of households to the poorest 40 per cent and has little effect on the middle 20 per cent.

◆ Because the redistribution of income weakens incentives, it creates a trade-off between equity and efficiency.

◆ Major UK benefit reform aims to lessen the severity of the benefit trap.

Do Problems 16 and 17 to get a better understanding of income redistribution.

Key Terms

Big trade-off, 431
Disposable income, 416
Gini coefficient, 419
Lorenz curve, 417
Original income, 416
Poverty, 421
Progressive income tax, 429
Proportional income tax, 429
Regressive income tax, 429
Wealth, 418

STUDY PLAN PROBLEMS AND APPLICATIONS

Do Problems 1 to 17 in MyEconLab Chapter 18 Study Plan and get instant feedback. MyEconLab

Economic Inequality in the UK
(Study Plan 18.1)

1 What is disposable income? Describe the distribution of disposable income in the UK in 2009.

2 The table shows shares of US income in 1967 and 2007.

	Gross income	
	1967	2007
Households	(percentage of total)	
Lowest 20 per cent	4.0	3.4
Second 20 per cent	10.8	8.6
Middle 20 per cent	17.3	14.6
Next highest 20 per cent	24.2	23.2
Highest 20 per cent	43.7	50.2

a Draw the US Lorenz curve for the gross income in 1967 and compare it with the Lorenz curve in 2007.

b Was US gross income distributed more equally or less equally in 2007 than it was in 1967?

Use the following news clip in Problems 3 to 6.

Only Work Ends Poverty

According to Jim Murphy, the employment and welfare minister, work is the only route out of poverty. The welfare state will never pay enough in benefits to lift people out of poverty. His remarks were greeted with consternation by anti-poverty campaigners. 'The more successful they are in getting people off benefit and into work, the more important it is that those who are left behind, and who cannot work, still have a decent standard of living.'

Source: FT.com, 26 March 2007

3 How is poverty measured? Explain the difference between a relative measure of poverty based on income and an absolute level of poverty.

4 What does the minister mean when he says that the welfare state will never pay enough in benefits to lift people out of poverty?

5 Why are the anti-poverty campaigners aghast? Explain your answer.

6 How will the minister's suggestion help those who cannot work to have a decent standard of living?

7 **Census: Income Fell Sharply Last Year**

The US Census Bureau reported that in 2008 the median household income fell 3.6%. The share of people living in poverty rose to 13.2% in 2008 from 12.5% in 2007. Only households led by people aged 65 or older enjoyed income gains – a 1.2% increase.

Source: *USA Today*, 11 September 2009

a What does the information in this news report tell you about changes in the distribution of US income in 2008?

b What additional information would you need to describe how the US Lorenz curve changed?

Inequality in the World Economy
(Study Plan 18.2)

8 Incomes in China and India are a small fraction of incomes in the US. But incomes in China and India are growing at more than twice the rate of those in the US.

a Explain how economic inequality in China and India is changing relative to that in the US.

b How are the world Lorenz curve and world Gini coefficient changing?

Use the following table in Problems 9 to 11.

The table shows shares of disposable income in Canada and the UK.

	Canadian income	UK income
Households	(percentage of total)	
Lowest 20 per cent	5	7
Second 20 per cent	11	11
Middle 20 per cent	16	15
Next highest 20 per cent	24	19
Highest 20 per cent	44	48

9 Create a table that shows the cumulative distribution of Canadian and UK incomes. Is the distribution of income more unequal in Canada or in the UK?

10 Draw a Lorenz curve for Canada and compare it with the Lorenz curve for the US in 2007. (Use the US data in Problem 2.) In which country is income less equally distributed?

11 Draw a Lorenz curve for the UK and compare it with the Lorenz curve for the US in 2007. (Use the US data in Problem 2.) In which country is income less equally distributed?

The Sources of Economic Inequality

(Study Plan 18.3)

12 The following figure shows the market for low-skilled labour in Europe.

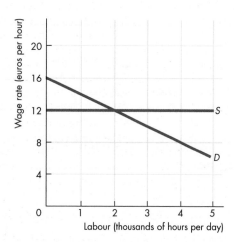

The value of marginal product of high-skilled workers is €16 an hour greater than that of low-skilled workers at each quantity of labour. The cost of acquiring human capital adds €12 an hour to the wage that must be offered to attract high-skilled labour.

Compare the equilibrium wage rates of low-skilled labour and high-skilled labour. Explain why the difference between these wage rates equals the cost of acquiring human capital.

Use the following information in Problems 13 and 14.

In 2000, 30 million Americans had full-time professional jobs that paid about $800 a week while 10 million Americans had full-time sales jobs that paid about $530 a week.

13 Explain why US professionals are paid more than salespeople and why, despite the higher weekly wage, more people are employed as professionals than as salespeople.

14 If the online shopping trend continues, how do you think the market for salespeople will change in coming years?

15 The following figure shows the European market for a group of workers who are discriminated against. Suppose that other workers in the same industry are not discriminated against and their value of marginal product is perceived to be twice that of the workers who are discriminated against. Suppose also that the supply of these other workers is 2,000 hours per day less at each wage rate.

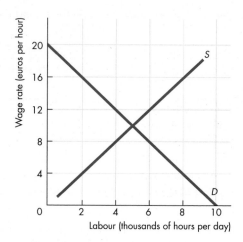

a What is the wage rate of the workers who are discriminated against?

b What is the quantity of workers employed who are discriminated against?

c What is the wage rate of the workers who do not face discrimination?

d What is the quantity of workers employed who do not face discrimination?

Income Redistribution (Study Plan 18.4)

Use the following table in Problems 16 and 17.

The table shows three European redistribution schemes.

Before-tax income (euros)	Plan A tax (euros)	Plan B tax (euros)	Plan C tax (euros)
10,000	1,000	1,000	2,000
20,000	2,000	4,000	2,000
30,000	3,000	9,000	2,000

16 Which scheme has a proportional tax? Which scheme has a regressive tax? Which scheme has a progressive tax?

17 Which scheme will increase economic inequality? Which scheme will reduce economic inequality? Which scheme will have no effect on economic inequality?

ADDITIONAL PROBLEMS AND APPLICATIONS

Do these problems in MyEconLab if assigned by your lecturer.

MyEconLab

Economic Inequality in the UK

Use the following table in Problems 18 and 19.

The table shows distribution of US original income in 2007.

Households	Original income (percentage of total)
Lowest 20 per cent	1.1
Second 20 per cent	7.1
Middle 20 per cent	13.9
Next highest 20 per cent	22.8
Highest 20 per cent	55.1

18 **a** What is the definition of original income?

   b Draw the Lorenz curve for the distribution of original income.

19 Compare the distribution of original income in 2007 with the distribution of gross income in 2007 shown in Problem 2. Which distribution is more unequal and why?

Inequality in the World Economy

Use the following table in Problems 20 to 22.

The table shows shares of income in Australia.

Households	Income share (percentage of total)
Lowest 20 per cent	7
Second 20 per cent	13
Middle 20 per cent	18
Next highest 20 per cent	25
Highest 20 per cent	37

20 Draw the Lorenz curve for the income distribution in Australia and in Brazil and South Africa (use the data in Figure 18.7 on p. 423). Is income distributed more equally or less equally in Brazil and South Africa than in Australia?

21 Is the Gini coefficient for Australia larger or smaller than that for Brazil and South Africa? Explain your answer.

22 What are some reasons for the differences in the distribution of income in Australia and in Brazil and South Africa?

The Sources of Economic Inequality

Use the following news clip in Problems 23 to 26.

Bernanke Links Education and Equality

Ben Bernanke, the chairman of the US central bank, said that increased education opportunities would help reduce the increased economic inequality that has occurred over the last 30 years. He also said that globalisation and the advent of new technologies, the two main causes of income inequality, will lead to economic growth, but inhibiting them will do far more harm than good in the long run. Instead, Bernanke said that the best method to improve economic opportunities is to focus on raising the level of and access to education. Workers will become more skilful, and firms will undertake more innovation. It is time to recognise that education should be lifelong and can come in many forms: early childhood education, community colleges, vocational schools, on-the-job training, online courses, adult education. With increased skills, lifetime earning power will increase.

Source: *International Herald Tribune*, 5 June 2008

23 Explain how the two main causes of increased income inequality in the US identified by Mr Bernanke work.

24 Draw a graph to illustrate how the two main causes of increased income inequality generate this outcome.

25 What are the short-term costs and long-term benefits associated with these two causes of inequality?

26 Explain Bernanke's solutions to help address growing income inequality.

27 **Where Women's Pay Trumps Men's**

Men work more than women on the job, at least in terms of overall hours. That's just one reason why in most fields, men's earnings exceed women's earnings. But Warren Farrell found 39 occupations in which women's median earnings exceeded men's earnings by at least 5 per cent and in some cases by as much as 43 per cent. In fields like engineering, a company may get one woman and seven men applying for a job. If the company wants to hire the woman, it might have to pay a premium to get her. Also, where women can combine technical expertise with people skills – such as those required in sales and where customers prefer dealing with a woman – that's likely to contribute to a premium in pay.

Source: CNN, 2 March 2006

a Draw a graph to illustrate why discrimination could result in female workers getting paid more than male workers for some jobs.

b Explain how market competition could potentially eliminate this wage differential.

c If customers 'prefer dealing with a woman' in some markets, how might that lead to a persistent wage differential between men and women?

Income Redistribution

28 Use the information provided in Figure 18.2 on p. 417 and the following table.

Households (percentage)	Original income (percentage of total income)
Lowest 20	4
Second 20	8
Middle 20	14
Next highest 20	22
Highest 20	52

a What is the percentage of total income that is redistributed from the highest income group?

b What percentages of total income are redistributed to the lower income groups?

29 Describe the effects of increasing the amount of income redistribution in the UK to the point at which the lowest income group receives 15 per cent of total income and the highest income group receives 30 per cent of total income.

Use the following news clip in Problems 30 and 31.

The Tax Debate Americans Should be Having

A shrinking number of Americans are bearing an even bigger share of the nation's income tax burden. In 2005, the bottom 40 per cent of Americans by income had, in the aggregate, an effective tax rate that's negative: Their households received more money through the income tax system, largely from the earned income tax credit, than they paid. The top 50% of taxpayers pay 97% of total income tax and the top 10% of taxpayers pay 70%. The top 1% paid almost 40% of all income tax, a proportion that has jumped dramatically since 1986. Given the US tax system, any tax cut must benefit the rich, but in terms of the change in effective tax rates: the bottom 50% got a much bigger tax cut under the Bush tax cut than the top 1%. Did the dollar value of Bush's tax cuts go mostly to the wealthy? Absolutely.

Source: *Fortune*, 14 April 2008

30 Explain why tax cuts in a progressive income tax system are consistently criticised for favouring the wealthy.

31 How might the benefits of tax cuts 'trickle down' to others whose taxes are not cut?

Economics in the News

32 After you have studied *Reading Between the Lines* on pp. 432–433, answer the following questions.

a What are the broad facts reported in the news article about the inequality of wealth in the UK?

b Why might men have higher levels of wealth than women?

c What is the distinction between private wealth and total wealth?

d Can you think of other respects in which the survey reported in the news article omits the effects of UK government actions on economic inequality?

33 **The Best and Worst Degrees by Salary**

Business is always a strong contender for honours degrees at the most popular universities. This is no surprise since students think business is the way to make big salaries. But is business really as lucrative as students and their parents believe? No. In a new survey by PayScale, Inc. of salaries by degree type, business didn't even break into the list of the top 10 or 20 most lucrative degrees. A variety of engineering degrees claim eight of the top 10 salary spots with chemical engineering ($65,700) winning best for starting salaries. Out of 75 undergraduate degrees, business ($42,900) came in 35th, behind such degrees as occupational therapy ($61,300), information technology ($49,400), and economics ($48,800).

Source: moneywatch.com, 21 July 2009

a Why do university graduates with different degrees have drastically different starting salaries?

b Draw a graph of the labour markets for economics degrees and business degrees to illustrate your explanation of the differences in the starting salaries of these two groups.

19 Uncertainty and Information

After studying this chapter you will be able to:

- Explain how people make decisions when they are uncertain about the consequences

- Explain how markets enable people to buy and sell risk

- Explain how markets cope with private information

- Explain how uncertainty and incomplete information influence efficiency

When you buy a second-hand car, you could get stuck with a lemon. Should you buy a warranty with the car? How can you make this decision when you don't know what its consequences will be?

Although markets do a good job of allocating resources efficiently, they face some obstacles. Can markets lead to an efficient outcome when there is uncertainty and incomplete information? You'll find the answers to these questions in this chapter.

In *Reading Between the Lines* at the end of the chapter, find out why you don't want to be in a course where everyone gets an A!

Decisions in the Face of Uncertainty

Tania, a student, is trying to decide which of two summer jobs to take. She can work as a house painter and earn enough for her to save £2,000 by the end of the summer. There is no uncertainty about the income from this job. If Tania takes it, she will definitely have £2,000 in her bank account at the end of the summer.

The other job, working as a telemarketer selling subscriptions to a magazine, is risky. If Tania takes this job, her bank balance at the end of the summer will depend on her success at selling. She will earn enough to save £5,000 if she is successful but only £1,000 if she turns out to be a poor salesperson. Tania has never tried selling, so she doesn't know how successful she'll be. But some of her friends have done this job, and 50 per cent of them do well and 50 per cent do poorly. Basing her expectations on this experience, Tania thinks there is a 50 per cent chance that she will earn £5,000 and a 50 per cent chance that she will earn £1,000.

Tania is equally as happy to paint as she is to make phone calls. She cares only about the money. Which job does she prefer: the one that provides her with £2,000 for sure or the one that offers her a 50 per cent chance of making only £1,000?

To answer this question, we need a way of comparing the two outcomes. One comparison is the expected wealth that each job creates.

Expected Wealth

Expected wealth is the money value of what a person expects to own at a given point in time. An expectation is an average calculated by using a formula that weights each possible outcome with the probability (chance) that it will occur.

For Tania, the probability that she will have £5,000 is 0.5 (a 50 per cent chance) and the probability that she will have £1,000 is also 0.5. Notice that the probabilities sum to 1. Using these numbers, we calculate Tania's expected wealth, *EW*, as:

$$EW = (£5,000 \times 0.5) + (£1,000 \times 0.5) = £3,000$$

Notice that expected wealth decreases if the risk of a poor outcome increases. For example, if Tania has a 20 per cent chance of success (and an 80 per cent chance of failure), her expected wealth falls to:

$$EW = (£5,000 \times 0.2) + (£1,000 \times 0.8) = £1,800$$

Tania can now compare the expected wealth from each job – £3,000 for the risky job and £2,000 for the non-risky job.

So does Tania prefer the risky job because it gives her a greater expected wealth? The answer is we don't know because we don't know how much Tania dislikes risk.

Risk Aversion

Risk aversion is the dislike of risk. Almost everyone is risk averse but some more than others. In rugby, running is less risky than passing. In international rugby, a team coach who favours a cautious running game is risk averse. A team coach who favours a risky passing game is less risk averse. But almost everyone is risk averse to some degree.

We can measure the degree of risk aversion by the compensation needed to make a given amount of risk acceptable. Returning to Tania: if she needs to be paid more than £1,000 to take on the risk arising from the telemarketing job, she will choose the safe painting job and take the £2,000 non-risky income.

But if she thinks that the extra £1,000 of expected income is enough to compensate her for the risk, she will take the risky job.

To make this idea concrete, we need a way of thinking about how a person values different levels of wealth. The concept that we use is *utility*. We apply the same idea that explains how people make expenditure decisions to explain risk aversion and decisions in the face of risk.

Utility of Wealth

Wealth (money in the bank and other assets of value) is like all good things. It yields utility. The more wealth a person has, the greater is that person's *total utility*. But each additional pound of wealth brings a diminishing increment in total utility – the *marginal utility* of wealth diminishes as wealth increases.

Diminishing marginal utility of wealth means that the gain in utility from an increase in wealth is smaller than the loss in utility from an equal decrease in wealth. Stated differently, *the pain from a loss is greater than the pleasure from a gain of equal size*.

Figure 19.1 illustrates Tania's utility of wealth. Each point *A* to *F* on Tania's utility of wealth curve corresponds to the value identified by the same letter in the table. For example, at point *C*, Tania's wealth is £2,000, and her total utility is 70 units. As Tania's wealth increases, her total utility increases and her marginal utility decreases. Her marginal utility is 25 units when wealth increases from £1,000 to £2,000, but only 13 units when wealth increases from £2,000 to £3,000.

We can use a person's utility of wealth curve to calculate expected utility and the cost of risk.

Expected Utility

Expected utility is the utility value of what a person expects to own at a given point in time. Like expected wealth, it is calculated by using a formula that weights each possible outcome with the probability that it will occur. But it is the utility outcome, not the money outcome, that is used to calculate expected utility.

Figure 19.2 illustrates the calculation for Tania. Wealth of £5,000 gives 95 units of utility and wealth of £1,000 gives 45 units of utility. Each outcome has a probability of 0.5 (a 50 per cent chance). Using these numbers, we can calculate Tania's expected utility, EU, which is:

$$EU = (95 \times 0.5) + (45 \times 0.5) = 70$$

Figure 19.1 The Utility of Wealth

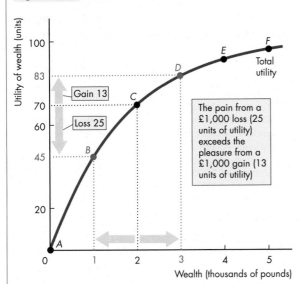

	Wealth (pounds)	Total utility (units)	Marginal utility (units)
A	0	0	
			45
B	1,000	45	
			25
C	2,000	70	
			13
D	3,000	83	
			8
E	4,000	91	
			4
F	5,000	95	

The table shows Tania's utility of wealth schedule, and the figure shows her utility of wealth curve. Utility increases as wealth increases, but the marginal utility of wealth diminishes.

Figure 19.2 Expected Utility

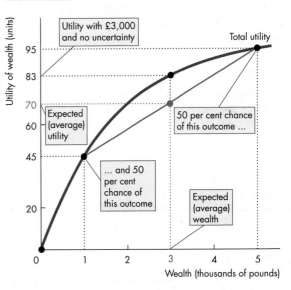

Tania has a 50 per cent chance of having £5,000 of wealth and a total utility of 95 units. She also has a 50 per cent chance of having £1,000 of wealth and a total utility of 45 units.

Tania's expected wealth is £3,000 (the average of £5,000 and £1,000) and her expected utility is 70 units (the average of 95 and 45).

With a wealth of £3,000 and no uncertainty, Tania's total utility is 83 units. For a given expected wealth, the greater the range of uncertainty, the smaller is expected utility.

Expected utility decreases if the risk of a poor outcome increases. For example, if Tania has a 20 per cent chance of success (and an 80 per cent chance of failure), her expected utility is 55 units:

$$(95 \times 0.2) + (45 \times 0.8) = 55$$

Notice how the range of uncertainty affects expected utility. Figure 19.2 shows that with £3,000 of wealth and no uncertainty, total utility is 83 units. But with the same expected wealth and Tania's uncertainty – a 50 per cent chance of having £5,000 and a 50 per cent chance of having £1,000 – expected utility is only 70 units. Tania's uncertainty lowers her expected utility by 13 units.

Expected utility combines expected wealth and risk into a single index.

Making a Choice with Uncertainty

Faced with uncertainty, a person chooses the action that maximises expected utility. To select the job that gives her the maximum expected utility, Tania must:

◆ Calculate the expected utility from the risky telemarketing job

◆ Calculate the expected utility from the safe painting job

◆ Compare the two expected utilities

Figure 19.3 illustrates the calculations. You've just seen that the risky telemarketing job gives Tania an expected utility of 70 units. The safe painting job also gives Tania a utility of 70 units. That is, the total utility of £2,000 with no risk is 70 units. So with either job, Tania has an expected utility of 70 units. She is indifferent between these two jobs.

If Tania had only a 20 per cent chance of success and an 80 per cent chance of failure in the telemarketing job, her expected utility would be 55 (calculated above). In this case, she would take the painting job and get 70 units of utility. But if the probabilities were reversed and she had an 80 per cent chance of success and only a 20 per cent chance of failure in the telemarketing job, her expected utility would be 85 units:

$$(95 \times 0.8) + (45 \times 0.2) = 85$$

In this case, Tania would take the risky telemarketing job. We can calculate the cost of risk by comparing the expected wealth in a given risky situation with the wealth that gives the same total utility but no risk.

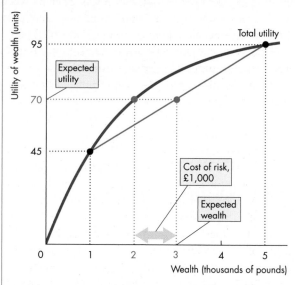

Figure 19.3 Choice under Uncertainty

With a 50 per cent chance of having £5,000 of wealth and a 50 per cent chance of having £1,000 of wealth, Tania's expected wealth is £3,000 and her expected utility is 70 units. Tania would have the same 70 units of total utility with wealth of £2,000 and no risk, so her cost of bearing this risk is £1,000. Tania is indifferent between the job that pays £2,000 with no risk and the job that offers an equal chance of £5,000 and £1,000.

MyEconLab Animation ──────────────────◆

Using this principle, we can find Tania's cost of bearing the risk that arises from the telemarketing job. That cost, highlighted in Figure 19.3, is £1,000.

REVIEW QUIZ

1 What is the distinction between expected wealth and expected utility?

2 How does the concept of the utility of wealth capture the idea that the pain of loss exceeds the pleasure of gain?

3 What do people try to achieve when they make a decision under uncertainty?

4 How is the cost of risk calculated when making a decision under uncertainty?

Do these questions in Study Plan 19.1 and get instant feedback. MyEconLab

You've now seen how a person makes a risky decision. In the next section, we'll see how markets enable people to reduce the risks they face.

Buying and Selling Risk

You've seen at many points in your study of markets how both buyers and sellers gain from trade. Buyers gain because they value what they buy more highly than the price they must pay – they receive a *consumer surplus*. And sellers gain because they face costs that are less than the price at which they can sell – they receive a *producer surplus*.

Just as buyers and sellers gain from trading goods and services, so they can also gain by trading risk. But risk is a bad, not a good. The good that is traded is risk avoidance. A buyer of risk avoidance can gain because the value of avoiding risk is greater than the price that must be paid to someone else to get them to bear the risk. The seller of risk avoidance faces a lower cost of risk than the price that people are willing to pay to avoid the risk.

We're going to put some flesh on the bare bones of this brief account of how people can gain from trading risk by looking at insurance markets.

Insurance Markets

Insurance plays a huge role in our economic lives. We'll explain:

◆ How insurance reduces risk

◆ Why people buy insurance

◆ How insurance companies earn a profit

How Insurance Reduces Risk

Insurance reduces the risk that people face by sharing or pooling the risks. When people buy insurance against the risk of an unwanted event, they pay an insurance company a *premium*. If the unwanted event occurs, the insurance company pays out the amount of the insured loss.

Think about car collision insurance. The probability that any one person will have a serious car accident is small. But a person who does have a car accident incurs a large loss. For a large population, the probability of one person having an accident is the proportion of the population that has an accident. But this proportion is known, so the probability of an accident occurring and the total cost of accidents can be predicted. An insurance company can pool the risks of a large population and enable everyone to share the costs. It does so by collecting premiums from everyone and paying out benefits to those who suffer a loss. An insurance com-

pany that remains in business collects at least as much in premiums as it pays out in benefits.

Why People Buy Insurance

People buy insurance and insurance companies earn a profit by selling insurance because people are risk averse. To see why people buy insurance and why it is profitable, let's consider an example. Dan owns a car worth £10,000, and that is his only wealth. There is a 10 per cent chance that Dan will have a serious accident that makes his car worth nothing. So there is a 90 per cent chance that Dan's wealth will remain at £10,000 and a 10 per cent chance that his wealth will be zero.

Dan's expected wealth is £9,000:

$$(£10,000 \times 0.9) + (£0 \times 0.1)$$

Dan is risk averse (just like Tania in the previous example). Because Dan is risk averse, he will be better off by buying insurance to avoid the risk that he faces, if the insurance premium isn't too high.

Without knowing some details about just how risk averse Dan is, we don't know the most that he would be willing to pay to avoid this risk. But we do know that he would pay more than £1,000. If Dan did pay £1,000 to avoid the risk, he would have £9,000 of wealth and face no uncertainty about his wealth. If he does not have an accident, his wealth is the £10,000 value of his car minus the £1,000 he pays the insurance company. If he does lose his car, the insurance company pays him £10,000, so he still has £9,000. Being risk averse, Dan's expected utility from £9,000 with no risk is greater than his expected utility from an expected £9,000 with risk. So Dan would be willing to pay more than £1,000 to avoid this risk.

How Insurance Companies Earn a Profit

For the insurance company, £1,000 is the minimum amount at which it would be willing to insure Dan and other people like him. With say 50,000 customers all like Dan, 5,000 customers (50,000 × 0.1) lose their cars and 45,000 don't. Premiums of £1,000 give the insurance company a total revenue of £50,000,000. With 5,000 claims of £10,000, the insurance company pays out £50,000,000. So a premium of £1,000 enables the insurance company to break even (make zero economic profit) on this business.

But Dan (and everyone else) is willing to pay more than £1,000, so insurance is a profitable business and there is a gain from trading risk.

The gain from trading risk is shared by Dan (and the other people who buy insurance) and the insurance company. The exact share of the gain depends on the state of competition in the market for insurance.

If the insurance market is a monopoly, the insurance company can take all the gains from trading risk. But if the insurance market is competitive, economic profit will induce entry and profits will be competed away. In this case, Dan (and the other buyers of insurance) get the gain.

A Graphical Analysis of Insurance

We can illustrate the gains from insurance by using a graph of Dan's utility of wealth curve. We begin, in Figure 19.4, with the situation if Dan doesn't buy insurance and decides to bear the risk he faces.

Risk-Taking Without Insurance

With no accident, Dan's wealth is £10,000 and his total utility is 100 units. If Dan has an accident, his car is worthless, he has no wealth and no utility. Because the chance of an accident is 10 per cent (or 0.1), the chance of not having an accident is 90 per cent (or 0.9). Dan's expected wealth is £9,000: (£10,000 × 0.9) + (£0 × 0.1). And his expected utility is 90 units: (100 × 0.9) + (0 × 0.1).

You've just seen that without insurance, Dan gets 90 units of utility. But Dan also gets 90 units of utility if he faces no uncertainty with a smaller amount of wealth.

We're now going to see how much Dan will pay to avoid uncertainty.

The Value and Cost of Insurance

Figure 19.5 shows the situation when Dan buys insurance. You can see that for Dan, having £7,000 with no risk is just as good as facing a 90 per cent chance of having £10,000 and a 10 per cent chance of having no wealth. So if Dan pays £3,000 for insurance, he has £7,000 of wealth, faces no uncertainty, and gets 90 units of utility. The amount of £3,000 is the maximum that Dan is willing to pay for insurance. It is the value of insurance to Dan.

Figure 19.5 also shows the cost of insurance. With a large number of customers each of whom has a 10 per cent chance of making a £10,000 claim for the loss of a vehicle, the insurance company can provide insurance at a cost of £1,000 (10 per cent of £10,000). If Dan pays

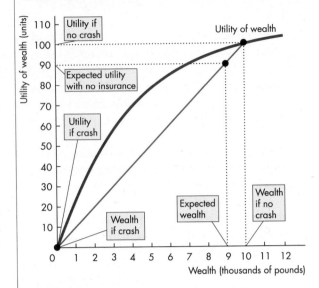

Figure 19.4 Taking a Risk Without Insurance

Dan's wealth (the value of his car) is £10,000, which gives him 100 units of utility.

With no insurance, if Dan has a crash, he has no wealth and no utility.

With a 10 per cent chance of a crash, Dan's expected wealth is £9,000 and his expected utility is 90 units.

MyEconLab Animation ─────────────◆

only £1,000 for insurance, his wealth is £9,000 (the £10,000 value of his car minus the £1,000 he pays for insurance), and his utility from £9,000 of wealth with no uncertainty is about 98 units.

Gains from Trade

Because Dan is willing to pay up to £3,000 for insurance that costs the insurance company £1,000, there is a gain from trading risk of £2,000 per insured person. How the gains are shared depends on the nature of the market.

If the insurance market is competitive, entry will increase supply of insurance and lower the price to £1,000 (plus zero economic profit and operating costs). Dan (and the other buyers of insurance) enjoys a consumer surplus. If the insurance market is a monopoly, the insurance company takes the £2,000 per insured person as economic profit.

Figure 19.5 The Gains from Insurance

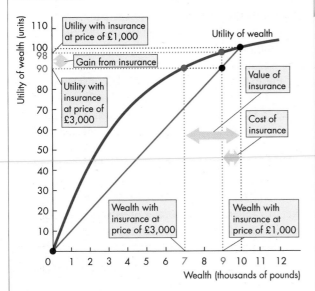

If Dan pays £3,000 for insurance, his wealth is £7,000 and his utility is 90 units – the same utility as with no insurance – so £3,000 is the value of insurance for Dan.

If Dan pays £1,000 for insurance, which is the insurance company's cost of providing insurance, his wealth is £9,000 and his utility is about 98 units.

Dan and the insurance company share the gain from insurance.

MyEconLab Animation ──────────◆

Risk That Can't Be Insured

The gains from car collision insurance that we've studied here apply to all types of insurance. Examples are property and casualty insurance, life insurance and healthcare insurance. One person's risks associated with driving, life and health are independent of other persons. That's why insurance is possible. The risks are spread across a population.

But not all risks can be insured. To be insurable, risks must be independent. If an event causes everyone to be a loser, it isn't possible to spread and pool the risks. For example, flood insurance is often not available for people who live on a floodplain because if one person incurs a loss, most likely all do.

Also, to be insurable, a risky event must be observable to both the buyer and seller of insurance. But much of the uncertainty that we face arises because we know less (or more) than others with whom we do business. In the next section, we look at the way markets cope when buyers and sellers have different information.

ECONOMICS IN ACTION

Insurance in the UK

We spend close to 12 per cent of our income on private insurance. That's as much as we spend on housing and more than we spend on cars and food. In addition, we buy insurance through our taxes in the form of National Insurance and unemployment insurance. Figure 1 shows UK household spending on insurance premiums in 2010. Average annual spending is highest on pension, medical and life insurance, but less than 20 percent of households are covered. In contrast, more than 70 percent of households spend £250 on average on property insurance and £500 on motor insurance.

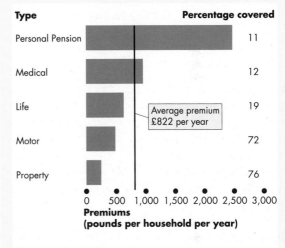

Figure 1 The UK Insurance Industry

Source of data: Association of British Insurers. UK Insurance: Key Facts, 2012.

REVIEW QUIZ

1 How does insurance reduce risk?
2 How do we determine the value (willingness to pay) of insurance?
3 How can an insurance company offer people a deal worth taking? Why do both the buyers and sellers of insurance gain?
4 What kinds of risks can't be insured?

Do these questions in Study Plan 19.2 and get instant feedback.

MyEconLab

Private Information

In all the markets that you've studied so far, the buyers and the sellers are well informed about the good, service or factor of production being traded. But in some markets, either the buyers or the sellers – usually the sellers – are better informed about the value of the item being traded than the person on the other side of the market. Information about the value of the item being traded that is possessed by only buyers or sellers is called **private information**. And a market in which the buyers or sellers have private information has **asymmetric information**.

Asymmetric Information: Examples and Problems

Asymmetric information affects many of your own economic transactions. One example is your knowledge about your driving skills and temperament. You know much more than your car insurance company does about how carefully and defensively you drive – about your personal risk of having an accident that would cause the insurance company to pay a claim. Another example is your knowledge about your work effort. You know more than your employer about how hard you are willing to work. Yet another example is your knowledge about the quality of your car. You know whether it's a lemon, but the person to whom you are about to sell it does not know and can't find out until after he or she has bought it.

Asymmetric information creates two problems:

◆ Adverse selection
◆ Moral hazard

Adverse Selection

Adverse selection is the tendency for people to *enter into agreements* in which they can use their private information to their own advantage and to the disadvantage of the less-informed party.

For example, if Jackie offers salespeople a fixed wage, she will attract lazy salespeople. Hardworking salespeople will prefer not to work for Jackie because they can earn more by working for someone who pays by results. The fixed-wage contract adversely selects those with private information (knowledge about their work habits) who can use that knowledge to their own advantage and to the disadvantage of the other party.

Moral Hazard

Moral hazard is the tendency for people with private information, *after entering into an agreement*, to use that information for their own benefit and at the cost of the less-informed party.

For example, Jackie hires Mitch as a salesperson and pays him a fixed wage regardless of his sales. Mitch faces a moral hazard. He has an incentive to put in the least possible effort, benefiting himself and lowering Jackie's profits. For this reason, salespeople are usually paid by a formula that makes their income higher the greater is the volume (or value) of their sales.

A variety of devices have evolved that enable markets to function in the face of adverse selection and moral hazard. We've just seen one, the use of incentive payments for salespeople. We're going to look at how three markets cope with adverse selection and moral hazard. They are:

◆ The market for used cars
◆ The market for loans
◆ The market for insurance

The Market for Used Cars

When a person buys a car, it might turn out to be a lemon. If the car is a lemon, it is worth less to the buyer and to everyone else than if it has no defects. Does the used car market have two prices reflecting these two values – a low price for lemons and a higher price for cars without defects? It turns out that it does. But it needs some help to do so and to overcome what is called the **lemons problem** – the problem that in a market in which it is not possible to distinguish reliable products from lemons, there are too many lemons and too few reliable products traded.

To see how the used car market overcomes the lemons problem, we'll first look at a used car market that has a lemons problem.

The Lemons Problem in a Used Car Market

To explain the lemons problem as clearly as possible, we'll assume that there are only two kinds of cars: defective cars – lemons – and cars without defects that we'll call good cars. Whether or not a car is a lemon is private information that is available only to the current owner. The buyer of a used car can't tell whether he is buying a lemon until after he has bought the car and learned as much about it as its current owner knows.

Some people with low incomes and the time and ability to fix cars are willing to buy lemons as long as they know what they're buying and pay an appropriately low price. Suppose that a lemon is worth £5,000 to a buyer. More people want to buy a good car and we'll assume that a good car is worth £25,000 to a buyer.

But the buyer can't tell the difference between a lemon and a good car. Only the seller has this information, and telling the buyer that a car is not a lemon does not help. So the most that the buyer knows is the probability of buying a lemon. If half of the used cars sold turn out to be lemons, the buyer knows that he has a 50 per cent chance of getting a good car and a 50 per cent chance of getting a lemon.

The price that a buyer is willing to pay for a car of unknown quality is more than the value of a lemon because the car might be a good one. But the price is less than the value of a good car because it might turn out to be a lemon.

Now think about the sellers of used cars, who know the quality of their cars. Someone who owns a good car is going to be offered a price that is less than the value of that car to the buyer. Many owners will be reluctant to sell for such a low price. So the quantity of good used cars supplied will not be as large as it would be if people paid the price they are worth.

In contrast, someone who owns a lemon is going to be offered a price that is greater than the value of that car to the buyer. So owners of lemons will be eager to sell, and the quantity of lemons supplied will be greater than it would be if people paid the price that a lemon is worth.

Figure 19.6 illustrates the used car market that we've just described. Part (a) shows the demand for used cars, D, and the supply of used cars, S. Equilibrium occurs at a price of £10,000 per car with 400 cars traded each month.

Some cars are good ones and some are lemons, but buyers can't tell the difference until it is too late to influence their decision to buy. But buyers do know what a good car and a lemon are worth to them, and sellers know the quality of the cars they are offering for sale. Figure 19.6(b) shows the demand curve for good cars, D_G, and the supply curve of good cars, S_G. Figure 19.6(c) shows the demand curve for lemons, D_L, and the supply curve of lemons, S_L.

Figure 19.6 The Lemons Problem

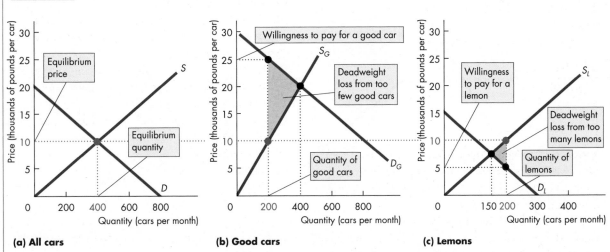

(a) All cars   **(b) Good cars**   **(c) Lemons**

Buyers can't tell a good used car from a lemon. Demand and supply determine the price and quantity of used cars traded in part (a). In part (b), D_G is the demand curve for good used cars and S_G is the supply curve. At the market price, too few good cars are available, which brings a deadweight loss. In part (c), D_L is the demand curve for lemons and S_L is the supply curve. At the market price, too many lemons are available, which brings a deadweight loss.

At the market price of £10,000, owners of good cars, in Figure 19.6(b), supply 200 cars a month for sale. Owners of lemons, in Figure 19.6(c), supply 200 cars a month for sale. The used car market is inefficient because too many lemons and not enough good cars are for sale. Figure 19.6 shows this inefficiency by using the concept of deadweight loss (Chapter 5, pp. 111–112).

At the quantity of good cars supplied, buyers are willing to pay £25,000 for a good car. They are willing to pay more than a good car is worth to its current owner for all good cars up to 400 cars a month. The grey triangle shows the deadweight loss that results from there being too few good used cars.

At the quantity of lemons supplied, buyers are willing to pay £5,000 for a lemon, but that is less than a lemon is worth to its current owner for all lemons above 150 cars a month. The grey triangle shows the deadweight loss that results from there being too many lemons.

You can see *adverse selection* in this used car market because there is a greater incentive to offer a lemon for sale. You can also see *moral hazard* because the owner of a lemon has little incentive to take good care of the car, so it is likely to become an even worse lemon. The market for used cars is not working well. Too many lemons and too few good used cars are traded.

A Used Car Market with Dealers' Warranties

How can used car dealers convince buyers that a car isn't a lemon? The answer is by giving a guarantee in the form of a warranty. By providing warranties only on good cars, dealers signal which cars are good ones and which are lemons.

Signalling occurs when an informed person takes actions that send information to uninformed persons. The grades and degrees that a university awards students are signals. They inform potential (uninformed) employers about the ability of the people they are considering hiring.

In the used car market, dealers send signals by giving warranties on the used cars they offer for sale. The message in the signal is that the dealer agrees to pay the costs of repairing the car if it turns out to have a defect.

Buyers believe the signal because the cost of sending a false signal is high. A dealer who gives a warranty on a lemon ends up bearing a high cost of repairs – and gains a bad reputation. A dealer who gives a warranty only on good cars has no repair costs and a reputation that gets better and better. It pays dealers to send an accurate signal, and it is rational for buyers to believe the signal.

Figure 19.7 Warranties Make the Used Car Market Efficient

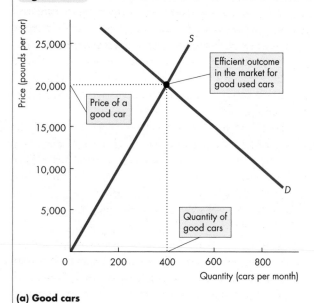

(a) Good cars

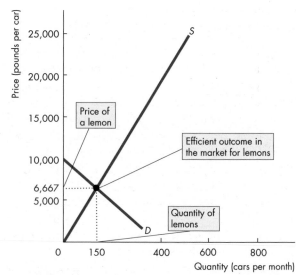

(b) Lemons

With dealers' warranties as signals, the equilibrium price of a good used car is £20,000 and 400 cars are traded. The market for good used cars is efficient. Because the signal enables buyers to spot a lemon, the price of a lemon is £6,667 and 150 lemons are traded. The market for lemons is efficient.

So a car with a warranty is a good car; a car without a warranty is a lemon. Warranties solve the lemon problem and enable the used car market to function efficiently with two prices: one for lemons and one for good cars.

Figure 19.7 illustrates this outcome. In part (a) the demand for and supply of good cars determine the price of a good car. In part (b), the demand for and supply of lemons determine the price of a lemon. Both markets are efficient.

Pooling Equilibrium and Separating Equilibrium

You've seen two outcomes in the market for used cars. Without warranties, there is only one message visible to the buyer: all cars look the same. So there is one price regardless of whether the car is a good car or a lemon. We call the equilibrium in a market when only one message is available and an uninformed person cannot determine quality a **pooling equilibrium**.

But in a used car market with warranties, there are two messages. Good cars have warranties and lemons don't. So there are two car prices for the two types of cars. We call the equilibrium in a market when signalling provides full information to a previously uninformed person a **separating equilibrium**.

The Market for Loans

When you buy a tank of petrol and swipe your credit card, you are taking a loan from the bank that issued your card. You demand and your bank supplies a loan. Have you noticed the interest rate on an unpaid credit card balance? It ranges between 12 per cent a year and 20 per cent a year. Why are these interest rates so high? And why is there such a huge range?

The answer is that when banks make loans, they face the risk that the loan will not be repaid. The risk that a borrower, also known as a creditor, might not repay a loan is called **credit risk** or **default risk**. For credit card borrowing, the credit risk is high and it varies among borrowers. The borrowers with the highest risk for default pay the highest interest rate.

Interest rates and the price of credit risk are determined in the market for loans. The lower the interest rate, the greater is the quantity of loans demanded, and for a given level of credit risk, the higher the interest rate, the greater is the quantity of loans supplied. Demand and supply determine the interest rate and the price of credit risk.

If lenders were unable to charge different interest rates to reflect different degrees of credit risk, there would be a pooling equilibrium and an inefficient loans market.

Inefficient Pooling Equilibrium

To see why a pooling equilibrium would be inefficient, suppose that banks can't identify the individual credit risk of their borrowers: they have no way of knowing how likely it is that a given loan will be repaid. In this situation, every borrower pays the same interest rate and the market is in a pooling equilibrium.

If all borrowers pay the same interest rate, the market for loans has the same problem as the used car market. Low-risk customers borrow less than they would if they were offered the low interest rate appropriate for their low credit risk. High-risk customers borrow more than they would if they faced the high interest rate appropriate for their high credit risk. So banks face an *adverse selection* problem. Too many borrowers are high risk and too few are low risk.

Signalling and Screening in the Market for Loans

Lenders don't know how likely it is that a given loan will be repaid, but the borrower does know. Low-risk borrowers have an incentive to signal their risk by providing lenders with relevant information. Signals might include information about the length of time a person has been in the current job or has lived at the current address, home ownership, marital status, age and business records.

High-risk borrowers might be identified simply as those who have failed to signal low risk. These borrowers have an incentive to mislead lenders; and lenders have an incentive to induce high-risk borrowers to reveal their risk level. Inducing an informed party to reveal private information is called **screening**.

By not lending to people who refuse to reveal relevant information, banks are able to screen as well as receive signals that help them to separate their borrowers into a number of credit-risk categories. If lenders succeed, the market for loans comes to a separating equilibrium with a high interest rate for high-risk borrowers and a low interest rate for low-risk borrowers. Signalling and screening work like warranties in the used car market and avoid the deadweight loss of a pooling equilibrium.

ECONOMICS IN ACTION

The Sub-Prime Credit Crisis

A sub-prime mortgage is a loan to a homebuyer who has a high risk of default. Figure 1 shows that between 2001 and 2005, the price of risk was low. Figure 2 shows why: the supply of credit, S_0, was large and so was the amount of risk taking. In 2007, the supply of credit decreased to S_1. The price of risk jumped and, faced with a higher interest rate, many sub-prime borrowers defaulted. Defaults in the sub-prime mortgage market spread to other markets that supplied the funds that financed mortgages.

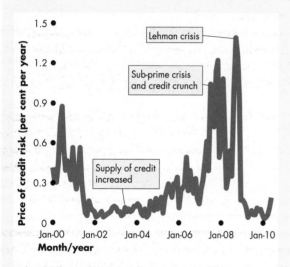

Figure 1 The Price of Commercial Credit Risk

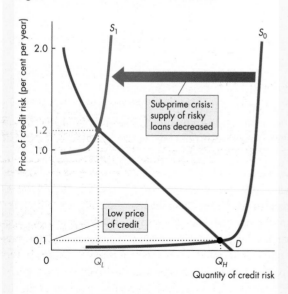

Figure 2 The Market for Risky Loans

The Market for Insurance

People who buy insurance face moral hazard, and insurance companies face adverse selection. Moral hazard arises because a person with insurance against a loss has less incentive than an uninsured person to avoid the loss. For example, a business with fire insurance has less incentive to install a fire alarm or sprinkler system than a business with no fire insurance does. Adverse selection arises because people who create greater risks are more likely to buy insurance. For example, a person with a family history of serious illness is more likely to buy health insurance than is a person with a family history of good health.

Insurance companies have an incentive to find ways around the moral hazard and adverse selection problems. By doing so, they can lower premiums for low-risk people and raise premiums for high-risk people.

One device that car insurance companies use is the *no-claim bonus*. A driver accumulates a no-claim bonus by driving safely and avoiding accidents and claims. The greater the bonus, the greater is the incentive to drive carefully.

Car insurance companies also use an excess as a signal. An *excess* is the amount of a loss that the insured person agrees to bear. The premium is smaller the greater is the excess, and the decrease in the premium is more than proportionate to the increase in the excess. By offering insurance with full coverage – no excess – on terms that are attractive only to the highest-risk people and by offering coverage with an excess on more favourable terms that are attractive to other people, insurance companies can do profitable business with everyone. High-risk people choose policies with low excesses and high premiums; low-risk people choose policies with high excesses and low premiums.

REVIEW QUIZ

1   How does private information create moral hazard and adverse selection?
2   How do markets for cars use warranties to cope with private information?
3   How do markets for loans use signalling and screening to cope with private information?
4   How do markets for insurance use no-claim bonuses to cope with private information?

Do these questions in Study Plan 19.3 and get instant feedback.

MyEconLab

Uncertainty, Information and the Invisible Hand

A recurring theme throughout microeconomics is the big question: When do choices made in the pursuit of self-interest also promote the social interest? When does the invisible hand work well and when does it fail us? You've learned about the concept of efficiency, a major component of what we mean by the social interest. And you've seen that while competitive markets generally do a good job in helping to achieve efficiency, impediments such as monopoly and the absence of well-defined property rights can prevent the attainment of an efficient use of resources.

How do uncertainty and incomplete information affect the ability of self-interested choices to lead to a social interest outcome? Are these features of economic life another reason why markets fail and why some type of government intervention is required to achieve efficiency?

These are hard questions, and there are no definitive answers. But there are some useful things that we can say about the effects of uncertainty and a lack of complete information on the efficiency of resource use. We'll begin our brief review of this issue by thinking about information as just another good.

Information as a Good

More information is generally useful. And less uncertainty about the future is generally useful. Think about information as one of the goods of which we always want more.

The most basic lesson about efficiency that you learned in Chapter 2 can be applied to information. Along our production possibilities frontier, we face a trade-off between information and all other goods and services. Information, like everything else, can be produced at an increasing opportunity cost – an increasing marginal cost. For example, we could get more accurate weather forecasts, but only at increasing marginal cost, as we increased the amount of information that we gather from the atmosphere and the amount of money that we spend on super-computers to process the data.

The principle of decreasing marginal benefit also applies to information. More information is valuable, but the more you know, the less you value another increment in information. For example, knowing that it will rain tomorrow is valuable information. Knowing the amount of rain to within an inch is even more useful. But knowing the amount of rain to within a couple of millimetres probably isn't worth much more.

Because the marginal cost of information is increasing and the marginal benefit from information is decreasing, there is an efficient amount of information. It would be inefficient to be overinformed.

In principle, competitive markets in information might deliver this efficient quantity. Whether they actually do so is hard to determine.

Monopoly in Markets That Cope with Uncertainty

There are probably large economies of scale in providing services that cope with uncertainty and incomplete information. The banking and insurance industries, for example, are highly concentrated and have very large economies of scale. Where monopoly elements exist, exactly the same inefficiency issues arise as they do in markets where uncertainty and incomplete information are not big issues. So it is likely that in some information markets, including the markets for loans and insurance, there is underproduction arising from the attempt to maximise monopoly profit.

 REVIEW QUIZ

1 Thinking about information as a good, what determines the information that people are willing to pay for?
2 Why is it inefficient to be overinformed?
3 Why are some of the markets that provide information likely to be dominated by monopolies?

Do these questions in Study Plan 19.4 and get instant feedback.   MyEconLab

You've seen how people make decisions when faced with uncertainty and how markets work when there is asymmetric information. *Reading Between the Lines* on pages 452–453 looks at the way markets in human capital and labour use university grades as signals that sort students by ability so that employers can hire the type of labour they seek. You'll discover that grade deflation can be efficient and grade inflation is inefficient. Discriminating grades are in the social interest and in the self-interest of universities and students.

Grades as Signals

The Telegraph, 12 January 2012

Warning over 'Grade Inflation' as First-class Degrees Double

Graeme Paton

The number of students leaving university with first-class honours degrees has more than doubled in a decade, figures show, prompting fresh warnings over 'grade inflation'. A record 53,215 undergraduates – one-in-six – finished courses last summer with top degrees, it was revealed.

Figures published by the Higher Education Statistics Agency show numbers have increased by 14 per cent in just 12 months and 125 per cent in a decade. The rise dramatically outstrips the overall increase in the student population over the same period, raising fears that some academics are coming under pressure to mark up students' work to boost universities' positions in league tables. . . .

Alan Smithers, professor of education at Buckingham University, said grades had been inflated. . . . Employers said that so many people were leaving university with top degrees that companies had been forced to introduce increasingly sophisticated systems to screen job applicants.

Carl Gilleard, chief executive of the Association of Graduate Recruiters, said: 'Over the past decade, employers have become less confident that the degree class in itself tells them what they need to know.'

The Essence of the Story

- The number of students leaving British universities with first-class awards has risen by 125 per cent in ten years since 2002.

- The rise in first-class award numbers is faster than the rise in the student population. 15 per cent now gain a first-class award compared with 9 per cent ten years ago.

- Universities have been accused of grade inflation.

- Employers have noticed the inflation in rates and no longer trust that degree results measure job potential.

Economic Analysis

◆ Accurate grades provide valuable information to students and potential employers about a student's ability.

◆ Universities try to provide accurate grades but face pressures to grade more softly to attract more research income.

◆ Figure 1 shows a labour market for university graduates when there is grade inflation.

◆ Students with high ability are not distinguished from other students, and the supply curve represents the supply of students of all ability levels.

◆ The demand curve shows the employers' willingness to hire new workers without knowledge of their ability.

◆ All graduates get jobs at the same low wage rate.

◆ Figures 2 and 3 show the outcome with accurate grading. In Figure 2 students with high grades get high-wage jobs, and in Figure 3 students with low grades get low-wage jobs.

◆ Even with grade inflation, employers discover ability from on-the-job performance and eventually, even with grade inflation, earnings reflect ability.

◆ But accurate grades are valuable because they enable employers and graduates to avoid the costly process of discovering and revealing true ability on the job and to get people into the right jobs at the time of graduation.

◆ Continued grade inflation leads employers to distrust the degree result as a signal of student ability.

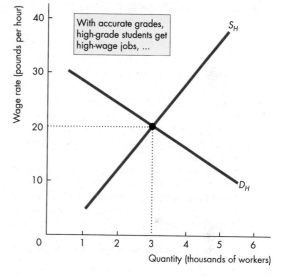

Figure 2 The Market for A Students

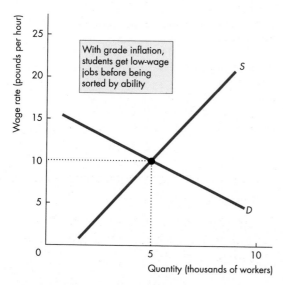

Figure 1 Market with Grade Inflation

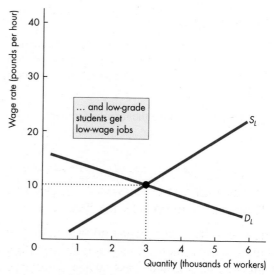

Figure 3 The Market for D Students

SUMMARY

Key Points

Decisions in the Face of Uncertainty
(pp. 440–442)

◆ To make a rational choice under uncertainty, people choose the action that maximises the expected utility of wealth.

◆ A decreasing marginal utility of wealth makes people risk averse. A sure outcome with a given expected wealth is preferred to a risky outcome with the same expected wealth – risk is costly.

◆ The cost of risk is found by comparing the expected wealth in a given risky situation with the wealth that gives the same utility but with no risk.

Do Problems 1 to 3 to get a better understanding of decisions in the face of uncertainty.

Buying and Selling Risk (pp. 443–445)

◆ People trade risk in markets for insurance.

◆ By pooling risks, insurance companies can reduce the risks people face (from insured activities) at a lower cost than the value placed on the lower risk.

Do Problems 4 to 6 to get a better understanding of buying and selling risk.

Private Information (pp. 446–450)

◆ Asymmetric information creates adverse selection and moral hazard problems.

◆ When it is not possible to distinguish good-quality products from lemons, too many lemons and too few good-quality products are traded in a pooling equilibrium.

◆ Signalling can overcome the lemons problem.

◆ In the market for used cars, warranties signal good cars and enable an efficient separating equilibrium.

◆ Private information about credit risk is overcome by using signals and screening based on personal characteristics.

◆ Private information about risk in insurance markets is overcome by using the no-claim bonus and excesses.

Do Problems 7 to 11 to get a better understanding of private information.

Uncertainty, Information and the Invisible Hand (p. 451)

◆ Less uncertainty and more information can be viewed as a good that has increasing marginal cost and decreasing marginal benefit.

◆ Competitive information markets might be efficient, but economies of scale might bring inefficient under-production of information and insurance.

Do Problems 12 and 13 to get a better understanding of uncertainty, information and the invisible hand.

Key Terms

Adverse selection, 446
Asymmetric information, 446
Credit risk or default risk, 449
Expected utility, 441
Expected wealth, 440
Lemons problem, 446
Moral hazard, 446
Pooling equilibrium, 449
Private information, 446
Risk aversion, 440
Screening, 449
Separating equilibrium, 449
Signalling, 448

STUDY PLAN PROBLEMS AND APPLICATIONS

Do Problems 1 to 15 in MyEconLab Chapter 19 Study Plan and get instant feedback.

MyEconLab

Decisions in the Face of Uncertainty
(Study Plan 19.1)

1 The figure shows Lee's utility of wealth curve.

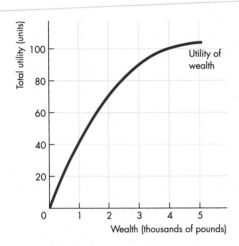

Lee is offered a job as a salesperson in which there is a 50 per cent chance that she will make £4,000 a month and a 50 per cent chance that she will make nothing.

a What is Lee's expected income from taking this job?

b What is Lee's expected utility from taking this job?

c How much would another firm have to offer Lee with certainty to persuade her not to take the risky sales job?

d What is Lee's cost of risk?

Use the following news clip in Problems 2 and 3.

Larry Page on How to Change the World

As president of Google, Larry Page said that the risks that Google has taken have led to hot new applications like Gmail and Google Maps. In 2004, Page set out Google's risk strategy: Google would do some things that would have only a 10 per cent chance of making $1 billion over the long term, but not many people will work on those things; 90 per cent work on everything else. So that's not a big risk. Many of Google's new features come from the riskier investments. Before we began, we thought that Google might fail and we almost didn't do it. The reason we started Google was probably Stanford's decision that we could go back and finish our Ph.D.s if we didn't succeed.

Source: *Fortune*, 12 May 2008

2 If much of Google's success has come from 'riskier investments', explain why Google doesn't dedicate all of their resources towards these riskier innovations.

3 In spite of the many risks that Larry Page has taken with Google, what evidence does this news clip provide that he is risk averse?

Buying and Selling Risk (Study Plan 19.2)

4 Lee in Problem 1 has built a small weekend shack on a steep, unstable hillside. She spent all her wealth, which is £5,000, on this project. There is a 75 per cent chance that the house will be washed down the hill and be worthless. How much is Lee willing to pay for an insurance policy that pays her £5,000 if the house is washed away?

Use the following information in Problems 5 and 6.

Larry lives in a neighbourhood in which 20 per cent of the cars are stolen every year. Larry's only wealth is his car, which he parks on the street overnight. His car is worth £20,000. The table shows Larry's utility of wealth schedule.

Wealth (pounds)	Utility (units)
20,000	400
16,000	350
12,000	280
8,000	200
4,000	110
0	0

5 If Larry cannot buy car theft insurance, what is his expected wealth and his expected utility?

6 High-Crime Car Theft, an insurance company, offers to sell Larry insurance at £8,000 a year and promises to provide Larry with a replacement car worth £20,000 if his car is stolen. Is Larry willing to buy this insurance? If not, is he willing to pay £4,000 a year for such insurance?

Private Information (Study Plan 19.3)

Use the following information in Problems 7 and 8.

Zaneb is a high-school teacher and is well known in her community for her honesty and integrity. She is shopping for a new car and plans to borrow the money to pay for it from her local bank.

7 **a** Does Zaneb create any moral hazard or adverse selection problems for either the bank or the car dealer? Explain your answer.

  b Do the bank or the car dealer create any moral hazard or adverse selection problems for Zaneb? Explain your answer.

8 What arrangements is Zaneb likely to encounter that are designed to help cope with the moral hazard and adverse selection problems she encounters in her car buying and bank loan transactions?

9 Suppose that there are three national football leagues: the Time League, the Goal Difference League and the Bonus for Win League. The leagues are of equal quality, but the players in each league are paid differently. In the Time League, they are paid by the hour for time spent practising and time spent playing. In the Goal Difference league, they are paid an amount that depends on the number of goals that the team scores minus the number of goals scored against it. In the Bonus for Win League, the players are paid one wage for a loss, a higher wage for a tie and the highest wage of all for a win.

  a Briefly describe the predicted differences in the quality of the games played by each of these leagues.

  b Which league will be the most attractive to players?

  c Which league will generate the largest profits?

10 **We All Pay for the Uninsured**

  When buying private healthcare, most of us don't behave like regular consumers: 70 per cent of what we spend is somebody else's money, and we don't have very good information about doctors or hospitals. You can go online and find out your treatment fees before you make an appointment. That's helpful for a routine service, but when you have a serious condition, you really want to know about the quality of care. Now, with the collaboration of doctors, to agree on quality standards and all health plans willing to pool their data, consumers can look at a set of performance indicators and be able to judge the quality of their healthcare.

  Source: *Fortune*, 12 May 2008

  a Explain how the adverse selection problem applies to private healthcare.

  b How does the moral hazard problem apply to healthcare insurance?

11 You can't buy insurance against the risk of being sold a lemon. Why isn't there a market in insurance against being sold a lemon? How does the market provide a buyer with some protection against being sold a lemon? What are the main ways in which markets overcome the lemons problem?

Uncertainty, Information and the Invisible Hand (Study Plan 19.4)

12 In Problem 10, what role can better information play in the healthcare market? Is it possible for there to be too much information in this market?

13 **Show Us Our Money**

  I have no clue what my colleagues make and I consider my salary my own business. It turns out that could be a huge mistake. What if employers made all employee salaries known? If you think about it, who is served by all the secrecy? Knowing what other workers make might be more ammunition to gun for a raise.

  Source: *Time Magazine*, 12 May 2008

  Explain why a worker might be willing to pay for the salary information of other workers.

Economics in the News (Study Plan 19.N)

14 **Making the Grade**

  Grade inflation is unfair to students who truly deserve exceptional marks. It also is unfair to graduate applicants who come from universities that don't inflate grades.

  Source: NJ.com, 25 September 2007

  a What economic role do accurate grades play?

  b Who benefits from grade inflation: students, professors, universities or future employers?

  c Who bears the cost of grade inflation? How do you think grade inflation might be controlled?

  d Is grade inflation efficient?

15 **Manchester United Star Wayne Rooney has £30m 'Break Clause' in New Contract**

  Wayne Rooney has signed a new five-year contract with Manchester United that will pay him about £160,000 a week. It is believed that his contract includes a 'break clause' which would allow Rooney to leave for £30 million if yearly targets set for the club are not met.

  Source: goal.com, 24 October 2010

  a Provide some examples of private information that Wayne Rooney possesses.

  b Does a football player present a moral hazard to his team?

  c Does a football player present adverse selection problems to his team?

  d How does Manchester United get the best possible performance out of Wayne Rooney?

ADDITIONAL PROBLEMS AND APPLICATIONS

Do these problems in MyEconLab if assigned by your lecturer.

MyEconLab

Decisions in the Face of Uncertainty

Use the following table in Problems 16 to 18.

The table sets out Jimmy's and Zenda's utility of wealth schedules:

Wealth	Jimmy's utility	Zenda's utility
0	0	0
100	200	512
200	300	640
300	350	672
400	375	678
500	387	681
600	393	683
700	396	684

16 What are Jimmy's and Zenda's expected utilities from a bet that gives them a 50 per cent chance of having a wealth of £600 and a 50 per cent chance of having nothing?

17 **a** Calculate Jimmy's and Zenda's marginal utility of wealth schedules.

   b Who is more risk averse, Jimmy or Zenda? How do you know?

18 Suppose that Jimmy and Zenda have £400 each and that each sees a business project that involves committing the entire £400 to the project. They reckon that the project could return £600 (a profit of £200) with a probability of 0.85 or £200 (a loss of £200) with a probability of 0.15. Who goes for the project and who hangs on to the initial £400?

Use the following information in Problems 19 to 21.

Two students, Jim and Kim, are offered summer jobs managing a student house-painting business. There is a 50 per cent chance that either of them will be successful and end up with £21,000 of wealth to get them through the next college year. But there is also a 50 per cent chance that either will end up with only £3,000 of wealth. Each could take a completely safe but back-breaking job picking fruit that would leave them with a guaranteed £9,000 at the end of the summer.

The table in the next column shows Jim's and Kim's utility of wealth schedules.

Wealth	Jim's utility	Kim's utility
0	0	0
3,000	100	200
6,000	200	350
9,000	298	475
12,000	391	560
15,000	491	620
18,000	586	660
21,000	680	680

19 Does anyone take the painting job? If so, who takes it and why? Does anyone take the fruit-picking job? If so, who takes it and why?

20 What is each student's maximised expected utility? Who has the larger expected wealth? Who ends up with the larger wealth at the end of the summer?

21 If one of the students takes the risky job, how much more would the fruit-picking job have needed to pay to attract that student?

Buying and Selling Risk

Use the following table, which shows Chris's utility of wealth schedule, in Problems 22 and 23.

Chris's wealth is £5,000 and it consists entirely of her share in a risky ice cream business. If the summer is cold, the business will fail, and she will have no wealth. Where Chris lives there is a 50 per cent chance each year that the summer will be cold.

Wealth (pounds)	Utility (units)
5,000	150
4,000	140
3,000	120
2,000	90
1,000	50
0	0

22 If Chris cannot buy cold summer insurance, what is her expected wealth and what is her expected utility?

23 Business Loss Recovery, an insurance company, is willing to sell Chris cold summer insurance at a price of £3,000 a year and promises to pay her £5,000 if the summer is cold and the business fails. Is Chris willing to buy this loss insurance? If she is, is she willing to pay £4,000 a year for it?

Private Information

Use the following information in Problems 24 to 26.

Larry has a good car that he wants to sell; Harry has a lemon that he wants to sell. Each knows what type of car he is selling. You are looking at used cars and plan to buy one.

24 If both Larry and Harry are offering their cars for sale at the same price, from whom would you most want to buy, Larry or Harry, and why?

25 If you made an offer of the same price to Larry and Harry, who would sell to you and why? Describe the adverse selection problem that arises if you offer the same price to Larry and Harry.

26 How can Larry signal that he is selling a good car so that you are willing to pay Larry the price that he knows his car is worth, and a higher price than what you are willing to offer Harry?

27 Pam is a safe driver and Fran is a reckless driver. Each knows what type of driver she is, but no one else knows. What might a car insurance company do to get Pam to signal that she is a safe driver so that it can offer her insurance at a lower premium than it offers to Fran?

28 Why do you think it is not possible to buy insurance against having to put up with a low-paying, miserable job? Explain why a market in insurance of this type would be valuable to workers but unprofitable for an insurance provider and so would not work.

Uncertainty, Information and the Invisible Hand

Use the following news clip in Problems 29 and 30.

Why We Worry About the Things We Shouldn't . . . and Ignore the Things We Should

We pride ourselves on being the only species that understands the concept of risk, yet we have a confounding habit of worrying about mere possibilities while ignoring probabilities, building barricades against perceived dangers while leaving ourselves exposed to real ones: 20 per cent of all adults still smoke; nearly 20 per cent of drivers and more than 30 per cent of backseat passengers don't use seat belts; two-thirds of us are overweight or obese. We dash across the street against the light and build our homes in flood prone areas – and when they're demolished by a storm, we rebuild in the same spot.

Source: *Time Magazine*, 4 December 2006

29 Explain how 'worrying about mere possibilities while ignoring probabilities' can result in people making decisions that not only fail to satisfy social interest, but also fail to satisfy self-interest.

30 How can information be used to improve people's decision making?

Economics in the News

31 After you have studied *Reading Between the Lines* on pp. 452–453, answer the following questions:

  a What information do accurate grades provide that grade inflation hides?

  b If grade inflation became widespread in secondary schools and universities, what new arrangements do you predict would emerge to provide better information about student ability?

  c Do you think grade inflation is in anyone's self-interest? Explain who benefits and how they benefit from grade inflation.

  d How do you think grade inflation might be controlled?

32 **Are You Paid What You're Worth?**

How do you know if your pay adequately reflects your contributions to your employer's profits? In many instances, you don't. Your employer has more and better information than you do about how your salary and bonus compare to others in your field, to others in your office, and relative to the company's profits in any given year. You can narrow the information gap a bit if you're willing to buy salary reports from compensation sources. For example, at $200, a quick-call salary report from the US Economic Research Institute will offer you compensation data for your position based on your years of experience, your industry and the place where your company is located.

Source: CNN, 3 April 2006

  a Explain the role that asymmetric information can play in worker wages.

  b What adverse selection problem exists if a firm offers lower wages to existing workers?

  c What will determine how much a worker should actually pay for a detailed salary report?

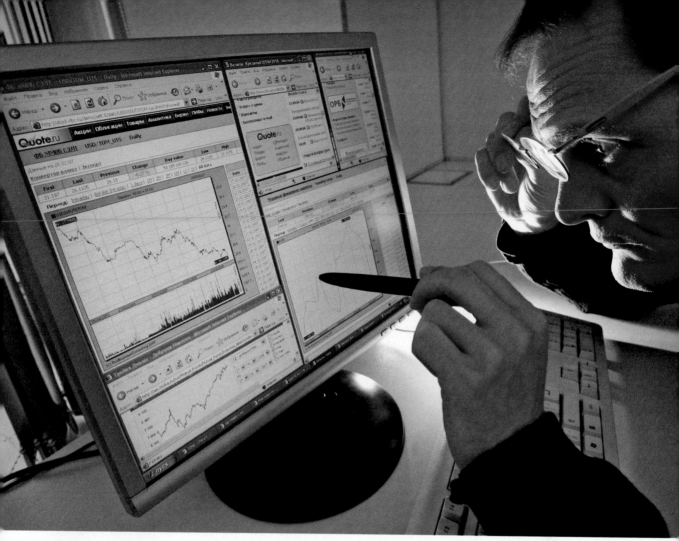

20 Measuring GDP and Economic Growth

After studying this chapter you will be able to:

◆ Define GDP and explain why it equals aggregate expenditure and aggregate income

◆ Explain how the Office for National Statistics measures UK GDP and real GDP

◆ Explain the uses and limitations of real GDP as a measure of economic well-being

Is the UK economy heading towards a triple dip recession? When firms like BP and BT make big decisions about investment and expansion, they want the answer to this question. In search of an answer, they make forecasts of GDP and its growth rate. What exactly is GDP and what does it tell us about the state of the economy?

In this chapter, you will find out how economic statisticians at the Office for National Statistics measure GDP and the economic growth rate; and in *Reading Between the Lines* at the end of the chapter, you will look at an attempt to improve on GDP and create alternative measures of economic performance.

Gross Domestic Product

What exactly is GDP, how is it calculated, what does it mean, and why do we care about it? You are going to discover the answers to these questions in this chapter. First, what is GDP?

GDP Defined

GDP or **gross domestic product** is the market value of all the final goods and services produced within a country in a given time period – usually a year. This definition has four parts:

◆ Market value
◆ Final goods and services
◆ Produced within a country
◆ In a given time period

We examine each in turn.

Market Value

To measure total production, we must add together the production of apples and oranges, computers and popcorn. Just counting the items doesn't get us very far. For example, which is the greater total production: 100 apples and 50 oranges, or 50 apples and 100 oranges?

GDP answers this question by valuing items at their *market values* – the prices at which items are traded in markets. If the price of an apple is 10 pence, the market value of 50 apples is £5. If the price of an orange is 20 pence, the market value of 100 oranges is £20. By valuing production at market prices, we can add the apples and oranges together. The market value of 50 apples and 100 oranges is £5 plus £20, or £25.

Final Goods and Services

To calculate GDP, we value the *final goods and services* produced. A **final good** (or service) is an item that is bought by its final user during a specified time period. It contrasts with an **intermediate good** (or service), which is an item that is produced by one firm, bought by another firm and used as a component of a final good or service.

For example, a Ford Focus is a final good, but a tyre on the Ford Focus is an intermediate good. A Dell computer is a final good, but an Intel Core i7 chip inside it is an intermediate good.

If we were to add the value of intermediate goods and services produced to the value of final goods and services, we would count the same thing many times – a problem called *double counting*. The value of a Ford Fiesta already includes the value of the tyres, and the value of a Dell PC already includes the value of the Core i7 chip inside it.

Some goods can be an intermediate good in some situations and a final good in other situations. For example, the ice cream that you buy on a hot summer day is a final good, but the ice cream that a café buys and uses to make sundaes is an intermediate good. The sundae is the final good. So whether a good is an intermediate good or a final good depends on what it is used for, not on what it is.

Some items that people buy are neither final goods nor intermediate goods and they are not part of GDP. Examples of such items include financial assets – stocks and bonds – and secondhand goods – used cars or existing homes. A secondhand good was part of GDP in the year in which it was produced, but not of GDP this year.

Produced Within a Country

Only goods and services that are produced *within a country* count as part of that country's GDP. When Burberry, an iconic British fashion brand, produces clothes in China, the market value of that clothing is part of China's GDP, not part of the UK's GDP. Nissan, a Japanese firm, produces cars in Tyneside, North East England, and the value of this production is part of UK GDP, not part of Japan's GDP.

In a Given Time Period

GDP measures the value of production *in a given time period* – normally either a quarter of a year (called the quarterly GDP data) or a year (called the annual GDP data).

GDP measures not only the value of total production but also total income and total expenditure. The equality between the value of total production and total income is important because it shows the direct link between productivity and living standards. Our standard of living rises when our incomes rise and we can afford to buy more goods and services. But we must produce more goods and services if we are to be able to buy more goods and services.

Rising incomes and a rising value of production go together. They are two aspects of the same phenomenon: increasing production. To see why, we study the circular flow of expenditure and income.

GDP and the Circular Flow of Expenditure and Income

Figure 20.1 illustrates the circular flow of expenditure and income. The economy consists of households, firms, governments and the rest of the world (the rectangles), which trade in factor markets and goods (and services) markets. Let's focus first on households and firms.

Households and Firms

Households sell and firms buy the services of labour, capital and land in factor markets. For these factor services, firms pay income to households: wages for labour services, interest for the use of capital and rent for the use of land. A fourth factor of production, entrepreneurship, receives profit.

Firms' retained earnings – profits that are not distributed to households – are also part of the household sector's income. You can think of retained earnings as being income that households save and lend back to firms. Figure 20.1 shows the *aggregate income* received by all households, including retained earnings, as the blue flow labelled Y.

Households buy and firms sell consumption goods and services – such as beer, pizzas and dry cleaning services – in goods markets. Total payment for these goods and services is **consumption expenditure**, shown by the red flow labelled C.

Firms buy and sell new capital equipment – such as computer systems, aeroplanes, trucks, trains and assembly line equipment – in goods markets.

Some of what firms produce is not sold but is added to their stocks (or inventories). For example, if Ford produces 1,000 cars and sells 950 of them, the other 50 cars remain unsold and the firm's stock of cars increases by 50. When a firm adds unsold output to its stocks, we can think of the firm as buying goods from itself. The purchase of new plant, equipment and buildings, and the additions to stocks, are **investment**, shown by the red flow labelled I.

Figure 20.1 The Circular Flow of Expenditure and Income

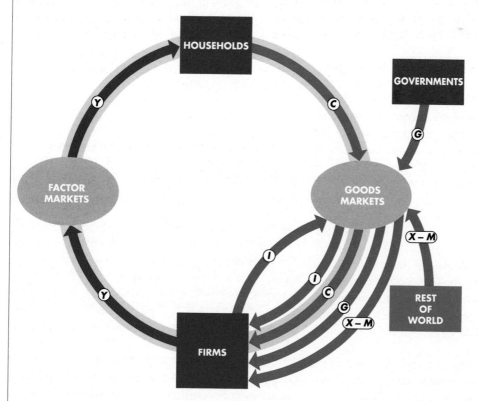

Households make consumption expenditures (C); firms make investments (I); the government purchases goods and services (G); the rest of the world buys net exports ($X - M$). Firms pay incomes (Y) to households.

Aggregate income (blue flow) equals aggregate expenditure (red flows).

Billions of pounds in 2012

$C =$	1,029
$I =$	229
$G =$	341
$X - M =$	−37
$Y =$	1,562

Governments

Governments buy goods and services from firms, and their expenditure on goods and services is called **government expenditure**. In Figure 20.1, government expenditure on goods and services is shown as the red flow G.

Governments finance their expenditure with taxes, but taxes are not part of the circular flow of expenditure and income. Governments also make financial transfers to households, such as unemployment benefits, and subsidies to firms. These financial transfers, like taxes, are not part of the circular flow of expenditure and income. Financial transfers and taxes are neither expenditures on goods and services nor income from the services of factors of production.

Rest of World

Firms in the UK sell goods and services to the rest of the world, **exports**, and buy goods and services from the rest of the world, **imports**. The value of exports (X) minus the value of imports (M) is called **net exports**. Figure 20.1 shows net exports by the red flow X − M.

If net exports are positive, the net flow of goods and services is from UK firms to the rest of the world. If net exports are negative, the net flow of goods and services is from the rest of the world to UK firms.

GDP Equals Expenditure Equals Income

GDP can be measured in two ways: by the total expenditure on goods and services (called the expenditure approach) or by the total income earned by producing goods and services (called the income approach).

The total expenditure – *aggregate expenditure* – is the sum of the red flows in Figure 20.1. Aggregate expenditure equals consumption expenditure plus investment plus government expenditure plus net exports.

Aggregate income earned by producing goods and services is equal to the total amount paid for the factors used – wages, interest, rent and profit. The blue flow in Figure 20.1 shows aggregate income. Because firms pay out as incomes (including retained profits) everything they receive from the sale of their output, aggregate income (the blue flow) equals aggregate expenditure (the sum of the red flows). That is:

$$Y = C + I + G + X - M$$

The table in Figure 20.1 shows the UK numbers for 2012. You can see that the sum of the expenditures is £1,562 billion, which also equals aggregate income.

Because aggregate expenditure equals aggregate income, these two methods of valuing GDP give the same answer. So:

GDP equals aggregate expenditure and equals aggregate income.

The circular flow model is the foundation on which the national economic accounts are built.

Why Is Domestic Product 'Gross'?

What does the 'gross' in GDP mean? *Gross* means before deducting the depreciation of capital. The opposite of 'gross' is net, which means after deducting the depreciation of capital.

Depreciation is the decrease in the value of a firm's capital that results from wear and tear and obsolescence. The total amount spent on purchases of new capital and on replacing depreciated capital is called **gross investment**. The amount by which the value of the firm's capital increases is called **net investment**.

Net investment = Gross investment − Depreciation

For example, if easyJet buys 5 new aeroplanes and retires 2 old aeroplanes from service, its gross investment is the value of the 5 new aeroplanes, depreciation is the value of the 2 old aeroplanes retired, and net investment is the value of 3 new aeroplanes.

Gross investment is one of the expenditures included in the expenditure approach to measuring GDP. So the resulting value of total product is a gross measure.

Gross profit, which is a firm's profit before subtracting depreciation, is one of the incomes included in the income approach to measuring GDP. So again, the resulting value of total product is a gross measure.

◆ REVIEW QUIZ

1. Define GDP and distinguish between a final good and an intermediate good. Provide examples.
2. Why does GDP equal aggregate income and also equal aggregate expenditure?
3. What is the distinction between gross and net?

Do these questions in Study Plan 20.1 and get instant feedback.   MyEconLab

Let's now see how the ideas that you have just studied can be used in practice. We'll see how GDP and its components are measured in the UK today.

Measuring UK GDP

The Office for National Statistics uses the concepts in the circular flow model to measure GDP, which it publishes in the *United Kingdom National Accounts – The Blue Book*. Because the value of aggregate output equals aggregate expenditure and aggregate income, two ways of measuring GDP are available, and both are used. They are:

◆ The expenditure approach

◆ The income approach

The Expenditure Approach

The *expenditure approach* measures GDP as the sum of consumption expenditure (*C*), investment (*I*), government expenditure on goods and services (*G*) and net exports of goods and services (*X − M*), corresponding to the red flows in the circular flow model in Figure 20.2. Table 20.1 shows the results of this approach for 2012. The table also shows the terms used in the *Blue Book*.

Consumption expenditure is the expenditure by households on goods and services produced in the UK and the rest of the world. It includes goods such as cars and services such as healthcare, but it does *not* include the purchase of new houses; they are counted as part of investment.

Investment is expenditure on capital equipment and buildings and the additions to inventories by firms. It also includes expenditure on new homes by households.

Figure 20.2 Aggregate Expenditure

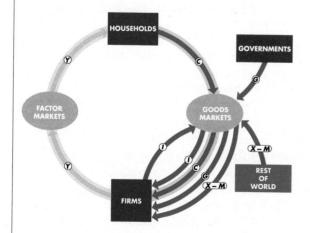

Aggregate expenditure is the sum of the red flows.

MyEconLab Animation ──────────────◆

Table 20.1

GDP: The Expenditure Approach

Item	Symbol	Amount in 2012 (billions of pounds)	Percentage of GDP
Consumption expenditure (Final consumption expenditure: personal)	C	1,029	65.9
Investment (Gross capital formation)	I	229	14.7
Government expenditure (Final consumption expenditure: governments)	G	341	21.8
Net exports (External balance of goods and services)	X − M	−37	−2.4
Gross domestic product	Y	1,562	100.0

The expenditure approach measures GDP as the sum of consumption expenditure (*C*), investment (*I*), government expenditure (*G*) and net exports (*X − M*). In 2012, GDP as measured by the expenditure approach was £1,562 billion. Almost two-thirds of aggregate expenditure is consumption expenditure.

Source of data: Office for National Statistics, *Statistical Bulletin*, 31 July 2013.

Government expenditure is the purchase by all levels of government of items such as national defence, law and order, street lighting and refuse collection. It does *not* include unemployment benefits because they are not expenditure on goods or services.

Net exports are the value of UK exports minus the value of UK imports.

Table 20.1 shows the relative magnitudes of the four items of aggregate expenditure.

The Income Approach

The *income approach* measures GDP by summing the incomes paid by firms to households for the services of the factors of production they hire – wages for labour, interest for capital, rent for land and profit for entrepreneurship. The *Blue Book* incomes are grouped into three components:

1 Compensation of employees

2 Gross operating surplus

3 Mixed income

Compensation of employees is the total payments by firms for labour services. This item includes gross wages and benefits such as pension contributions, and is shown by the blue flow *W* in Figure 20.3.

Gross operating surplus is the total profit made by companies and the surpluses generated by publicly owned enterprises. Some of the profits are paid to households as dividends, and some are retained by companies as undistributed profits, but they are all income and are shown by the blue flow *P* in Figure 20.3.

Mixed income is a combination of rental income and income from self-employment. Rental income is the payment for the use of land and other rented inputs including rented housing and imputed rent for owner-occupied housing. (Imputed rent is an estimate of what homeowners would pay to rent the housing they own and use themselves. By including this item in the national accounts, we measure the total value of housing services, whether they are owned or rented.) Income from self-employment is a mixture of all the factor incomes. The small business owner supplies labour and capital to the business. Mixed income is shown by the blue flow *M* in Figure 20.3.

Table 20.2 shows these three components of aggregate income and their relative magnitudes.

The sum of the incomes is called *gross domestic income at factor cost*. The term *factor cost* is used because it is the cost of the *factors of production* used to produce final goods and services. When we sum all the expenditures on final goods and services, we arrive at a total called *domestic product at market prices*. Market

---

Table 20.2

GDP: The Income Approach

Item	Amount in 2012 (billions of pounds)	Percentage of GDP
Compensation of employees	842	53.9
Gross operating surplus	309	19.8
Mixed income	209	13.4
Gross domestic income at factor cost	1,360	87.1
Indirect taxes less subsidies	199	12.7
GDP (income approach)	1,559	99.8
Statistical discrepancy	3	0.2
GDP (expenditure approach)	1,562	100.0

The sum of all factor incomes equals gross domestic income at factor cost. GDP equals net domestic income at factor cost plus indirect taxes less subsidies. In 2012, GDP measured by the factor incomes approach was £1,559 billion. The amount is $3 billion less than GDP measured by the expenditure approach – a statistical discrepancy of $3 billion or 0.2 per cent. Compensation of employees – labour income – was by far the largest part of total factor income.

Source of data: Office for National Statistics, *Statistical Bulletin*, 31 July 2013.

---

prices and factor cost would be the same except for indirect taxes and subsidies.

An *indirect tax* is a tax paid by consumers when they buy goods and services, such as VAT. An indirect tax makes the market price exceed the factor cost. A *subsidy* is a payment by the government to a producer. With a subsidy, the factor cost exceeds the market price. To get from factor cost to market price, we add indirect taxes and subtract subsidies.

We've now arrived at GDP using the income approach. This number is not exactly the same as GDP using the expenditure approach. For example, a waiter might not report all his tips as income but your credit card slip shows them as an expenditure, so measured income and expenditure are not the same.

The gap between the expenditure and income measure of GDP is called the *statistical discrepancy* and it is calculated as the GDP expenditure total minus the GDP income total. The discrepancy is usually not large, and in 2012 it was 0.2 per cent of GDP.

Figure 20.3   Aggregate Income

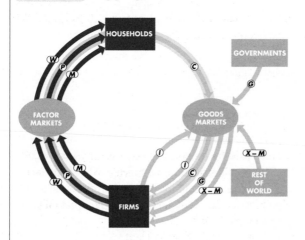

Aggregate income is the sum of the components of the blue flows.

MyEconLab Animation ———————————◆

Nominal GDP and Real GDP

You've just seen that in 2012, GDP was £1,562 billion. Three years earlier, in 2009, it was £1,402 billion. How much of the £160 billion or 10 per cent increase in GDP comes from an increase in production and how much from a rise in prices? To answer this question and isolate the increase in production from the rise in prices, we distinguish between *real* GDP and *nominal* GDP.

Real GDP is the value of final goods and services produced in a given year when valued at the *prices of a reference base year*. By comparing the value of production in the two years at the same prices, we reveal the change in production.

Currently, the reference base year is 2010 and we describe real GDP as measured in 2010 pounds – in terms of what the pound would buy in 2010.

Nominal GDP is the value of final goods and services produced in a given year when valued at the prices of that year. Nominal GDP is just a more precise name for GDP.

Economic statisticians at the Office for National Statistics calculate real GDP using the method described in the Mathematical Note on pp. 474–475. Here, we'll explain the basic idea but not the technical details.

Calculating Real GDP

We'll calculate real GDP for an economy that produces one consumption good, one capital good and one government service. Net exports are zero.

Table 20.3 shows the quantities produced and the prices in 2010 (the base year) and in 2013. In part (a), we calculate nominal GDP in 2010. For each item, we multiply the quantity produced in 2010 by its price in 2010 to find the total expenditure on the item. We sum the expenditures to find nominal GDP, which in 2010 is £100 million. Because 2010 is the base year, both real GDP and nominal GDP equal £100 million.

In Table 20.3(b), we calculate nominal GDP in 2013, which is £300 million. Nominal GDP in 2013 is three times its value in 2010. But by how much has production increased? Real GDP will tell us.

In Table 20.3(c), we calculate real GDP in 2013. The quantities of the goods and services produced are those of 2013, as in part (b). The prices are those in the reference base year – 2010, as in part (a).

For each item, we multiply the quantity produced in 2013 by its price in 2010. We then sum these expenditures to find real GDP in 2013, which is £160 million. This number is what total expenditure would have been

in 2013 if prices had remained the same as they were in 2010.

Nominal GDP in 2013 is three times its value in 2010, but real GDP in 2013 is only 1.6 times its 2010 value – a 60 per cent increase in production.

Table 20.3

Calculating Nominal GDP and Real GDP

Item	Quantity (millions)	Price (pounds)	Expenditure (millions of pounds)
(a) In 2010			
C Shirts	10	5	50
I Computer chips	3	10	30
G Security services	1	20	20
Y Real and nominal GDP in 2010			100
(b) In 2013			
C Shirts	4	5	20
I Computer chips	2	20	40
G Security services	6	40	240
Y Nominal GDP in 2013			300
(c) Quantities of 2013 valued at prices of 2010			
C Shirts	4	5	20
I Computer chips	2	10	20
G Security services	6	20	120
Y Real GDP in 2013			160

In 2010, the reference base year, real GDP equals nominal GDP and was £100 million. In 2013, nominal GDP increased to £300 million. But real GDP in 2013 in part (c), which is calculated by using the quantities of 2013 in part (b) and the prices of 2010 in part (a), was only £160 million – a 60 per cent increase from 2010.

REVIEW QUIZ

1 What is the expenditure approach to measuring GDP?
2 What is the income approach to measuring GDP?
3 What adjustment must be made to total income to make it equal to GDP?
4 What is the distinction between nominal GDP and real GDP?
5 How is real GDP calculated?

Do these questions in Study Plan 20.2 and get instant feedback.   MyEconLab

The Uses and Limitations of Real GDP

We use estimates of real GDP for two main purposes. They are:

♦ To compare the standard of living over time
♦ To compare the standard of living across countries

The Standard of Living Over Time

One method of comparing the standard of living over time is to calculate real GDP per person in different years. **Real GDP per person** is real GDP divided by the population. Real GDP per person tells us the value of goods and services that the average person can enjoy. By using *real* GDP, we remove any influence that rising prices and a rising cost of living might have had on our comparison.

We're interested in both the long-term trends and the shorter-term cycles in the standard of living.

Long-term Trend

A handy way of comparing real GDP per person over time is to express it as a ratio of some reference year. For example, in 1962 real GDP per person was £8,175 and in 2012 it was £23,631. So real GDP per person in 2012 was 2.9 times its 1962 level – that is, £23,631 divided by £8,175. To the extent that real GDP per person measures the standard of living, people were 2.9 times as well off in 2012 as their grandparents had been in 1962.

Figure 20.4 shows the path of UK real GDP per person for the 50 years from 1962 to 2012 and highlights two features of our expanding living standard:

♦ The growth of potential GDP per person
♦ Fluctuations of real GDP per person

The Growth of Potential GDP

Potential GDP is the value of production when all the economy's labour, capital, land and entrepreneurial ability are fully employed. Potential GDP per person, the smoother black line in Figure 20.4, grows at a steady pace because the quantities of the factors of production and their productivities grow at a steady pace.

But potential GDP per person doesn't grow at a constant pace. During the 1960s, it grew at 2.5 per cent per year but slowed to only 2.0 per cent per year during the

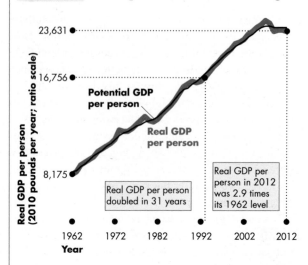

Figure 20.4 Rising UK Standard of Living

Real GDP per person in the UK doubled between 1962 and 1993. In 2012, real GDP per person was 2.9 times its 1962 level. Real GDP per person, the red line, fluctuates around potential GDP per person, the black line. The *y*-axis is a ratio scale – see the Appendix, pp. 481–482.)

Sources of data: Authors'assumptions and calculations based on data from the Office for National Statistics, the IMF and OECD.

MyEconLab Animation ──────────────────◆

1970s. This slowdown might seem small, but it had big consequences, as you'll soon see.

Fluctuations of Real GDP

You can see that real GDP per person, shown by the red line in Figure 20.4, fluctuates around potential GDP per person, and sometimes real GDP per person shrinks.

Let's take a closer look at the two features of our expanding living standard that we've just outlined.

Productivity Growth Slowdown

How costly was the slowdown in productivity growth after 1970? The answer is provided by the *Lucas wedge*, which is the pound value of the accumulated gap between what real GDP per person would have been if the 1960s growth rate had persisted and what real GDP per person turned out to be. (Nobel Laureate Robert E. Lucas Jr drew attention to this gap.)

Figure 20.5 illustrates the Lucas wedge. The wedge started out small during the 1970s, but by 2012 real GDP per person was £7,653 per year lower than it would have been with no growth slowdown and the accumulated gap was £75,000 per person.

Figure 20.5 The Cost of Slower Growth

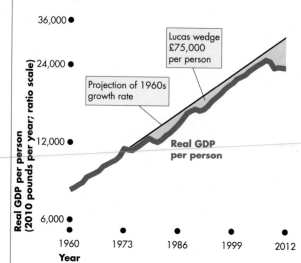

The black line projects the 1960s growth rate of real GDP per person to 2012. The Lucas wedge arises from the slowdown of productivity growth that began during the 1970s. The cost of the slowdown is £75,000 per person.

Source of data: Office for National Statistics. Lucas wedge based on authors' assumptions about the 1960s growth trend.

MyEconLab Animation ───────────────◆

Real GDP Fluctuations – The Business Cycle

We call the fluctuations in the pace of expansion of real GDP the business cycle. The **business cycle** is a periodic but irregular up-and-down movement of total production and other measures of economic activity. The business cycle isn't a regular predictable cycle like the phases of the moon, but every cycle has two phases:

1 Expansion

2 Recession

and two turning points:

1 Peak

2 Trough

Figure 20.6 shows these features of the two most recent UK business cycles.

An **expansion** is a period during which real GDP increases. In the early stage of an expansion, real GDP returns to potential GDP, and as the expansion progresses, potential GDP grows and real GDP eventually exceeds potential GDP.

A common definition of **recession** is a period during which real GDP decreases – its growth rate is negative –

for at least two successive quarters. Another definition, and the one used by the National Bureau of Economic Research, which dates US business cycle phases and turning points, is 'a period of significant decline in total output, income, employment and trade, usually lasting from six months to a year, and marked by contractions in many sectors of the economy'.

An expansion ends and a recession begins at a business cycle peak, which is the highest level that real GDP has attained up to that time. A recession ends at a trough, when real GDP reaches a temporary low point and from which the next expansion begins.

In the second quarter of 2008, the UK economy went into recession. From a long way below potential GDP, a recovery began at the end of 2009. The recovery looked strong in 2010 and at the beginning of 2011, but by the fourth quarter of 2011 real GDP was falling again, and a second – *double-dip* – recession occurred, which reached a trough in mid-2012. A new but brief recovery began bringing the fear of a *triple-dip* recession in 2013.

Figure 20.6 The Most Recent UK Business Cycles

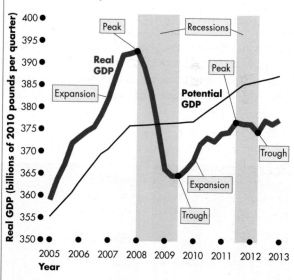

A business cycle expansion, which began in the fourth quarter of 2001, ended at a peak in the second quarter of 2008. A deep and long recession followed the 2008 peak and ended in a trough at the end of 2009 when an expansion began. A second (double-dip) recession began in the fourth quarter of 2011 and ended in mid-2012.

Sources of data: Authors' assumptions and calculations based on data from the Office for National Statistics, the IMF and OECD.

MyEconLab Animation ───────────────◆

The Standard of Living Across Countries

Two problems arise in using real GDP to compare living standards across countries. First, the real GDP of one country must be converted into the same currency units as the real GDP of the other country. Second, the goods and services in both countries must be valued at the same prices. Comparing the US and China provides a striking example of these two problems.

China and the US in US Dollars

In 2012, nominal GDP per person in the US was $49,600 and in China it was 38,750 yuan. The yuan is the currency of China, and the price at which the dollar and the yuan exchanged, the market exchange rate, was 6.6 yuan per US dollar. Using this exchange rate, 38,750 yuan converts to $5,871. On these numbers, GDP per person in the US in 2012 was 8.4 times that in China.

The red line in Figure 20.7 shows real GDP per person in China from 1980 to 2012 when the market exchange rate is used to convert yuan to US dollars.

China and the US at PPP

Figure 20.7 shows a second estimate of China's real GDP per person that values China's production on the same terms as US production. It uses *purchasing power parity* or *PPP* prices, which are the *same prices* for both countries.

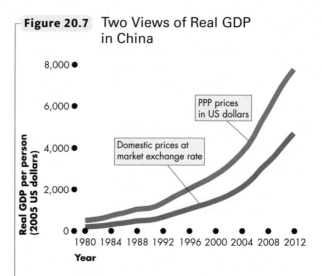

Figure 20.7 Two Views of Real GDP in China

Real GDP per person in China has grown rapidly. But how rapidly it has grown and to what level depends on how real GDP is valued. When GDP in 2012 is valued at the market exchange rate, US income per person is 8.4 times that in China. China looks like a poor developing country. But the comparison is misleading. When GDP is valued at purchasing power parity prices, US income per person is only 5.6 times that in China.

Source of data: International Monetary Fund, *World Economic Outlook* database, October 2012.

MyEconLab Animation ————————————◆

The price of a Big Mac is $3.75 in Chicago and 13.25 yuan or $1.62 in Shanghai. To compare real GDP in China and the US, we must value China's Big Macs at the $3.75 US price – the PPP price.

The prices of some goods are higher in the US than in China, so these items get a smaller weight in China's real GDP than they get in US real GDP. An example is a Big Mac, which costs $3.75 in Chicago. In Shanghai, a Big Mac costs 13.25 yuan, which is the equivalent of $2.00. So in China's real GDP, a Big Mac gets about half the weight that it gets in US real GDP.

Some prices in China are higher than in the US but more prices are lower, so Chinese prices put a lower value on China's production than do US prices.

According to the PPP comparisons, real GDP per person in the US in 2012 was 5.6 times that of China, not 8.4 times.

You've seen how real GDP is used to make standard of living comparisons over time and across countries. But real GDP isn't a perfect measure of the standard of living and we'll now examine its limitations.

Limitations of Real GDP

Real GDP measures the value of goods and services that are bought in markets. Some of the factors that influence the standard of living and which are not part of GDP are:

◆ Household production
◆ Underground economic activity
◆ Leisure time
◆ Environmental quality

Household Production

An enormous amount of production takes place every day in our homes. Changing a light bulb, mowing the lawn, washing the car and growing vegetables are all examples of household production. Because these productive activities are not traded in markets, they are not included in GDP.

The omission of household production from GDP means that GDP *underestimates* total production. But it also means that the growth rate of GDP *overestimates* the growth rate of total production. The reason is that some of the growth of market production (included in GDP) is a replacement for home production. So part of the increase in GDP arises from a decrease in home production.

Underground Economic Activity

The *underground economy* is the part of the economy purposely hidden from the view of the government to avoid taxes and regulations or because the goods and services they are producing are illegal. Because underground economic activity is unreported, it is omitted from GDP. Estimates of the underground economy in the UK range between 3.5 and 13.5 per cent of GDP (£51 billion to £195 billion).

Leisure Time

Leisure time is an economic good that adds to our standard of living. Other things remaining the same, the more leisure we have, the better off we are. Our time spent working is valued as part of GDP, but our leisure time is not. Yet that leisure time must be at least as valuable to us as the wage that we earn for the last hour worked. If it were not, we would work instead of taking the leisure. Over the years, leisure time has steadily increased. The working week has become shorter and the number and length of holidays have increased. These improvements in economic well-being are not reflected in GDP.

Environmental Quality

Economic activity directly influences the quality of the environment. The burning of hydrocarbon fuels brings global warming and climate change. The depletion of non-renewable resources, the mass clearing of forests, and the pollution of lakes and rivers are other major environmental consequences of industrial production.

Resources used to protect the environment are valued as part of GDP. For example, the value of catalytic converters that help to protect the atmosphere from vehicle emissions is part of GDP. But the cost of pollution is not subtracted from GDP.

An industrial society possibly produces more atmospheric pollution than does an agricultural society. But pollution does not always increase as we become wealthier. Wealthy people value a clean environment and are willing to pay for one. Compare the pollution in China today with pollution in the UK. China, a poor country, pollutes its rivers, lakes and atmosphere in a way that is unimaginable in the UK.

Whose production is more valuable: the chef's whose work gets counted in GDP . . .

. . . or the busy mother's whose dinner preparations and child minding don't get counted?

AT ISSUE

Should GNNP Replace GDP?

The standard view of economists is that despite its limitations, GDP is a useful measure of the value of production and the overall level of economic activity in a country or region.

But a prominent economist, Joseph Stiglitz, has argued that GDP is dangerously misleading and needs to be replaced by a measure that he calls Green Net National Product (or GNNP).

Let's look at both sides of this issue.

Joe Stiglitz says . . .

- ◆ GDP has passed its use-by date.
- ◆ A *gross* measure is wrong because it ignores the depreciation of assets.
- ◆ A *domestic* measure is wrong because it ignores the incomes paid to foreigners who exploit a nation's resources.
- ◆ A *green* measure is needed to take account of the environmental damage that arises from production.
- ◆ GNNP subtracts from GDP incomes paid to foreigners, depreciation, the value of depleted natural resources and the cost of a degraded environment.
- ◆ The existence of a market price for carbon emissions makes it possible to measure the cost of these emissions and subtract them from GDP.
- ◆ A bad accounting framework is likely to lead to bad decisions.
- ◆ America's 'drain America first' energy policy is an example of a bad decision. It increases GDP but decreases GNNP and makes us poorer.

The Mainstream View

- ◆ As a measure of the value of market production in an economy, GDP does a good job.
- ◆ GDP is used to track the ups and downs of economic activity and it is a useful indicator for making macroeconomic stabilisation policy decisions.
- ◆ GDP is *not* used to measure net national economic well-being nor to guide microeconomic resource allocation decisions.
- ◆ There is no disagreement that a *net national* measure is appropriate for measuring national economic well-being.
- ◆ There is no disagreement that 'negative externalities' arising from carbon emissions and other pollution detract from economic well-being.
- ◆ The omissions from GDP of household production and underground production are *bigger* problems than those emphasised by Stiglitz.
- ◆ It isn't clear that depleting oil and coal resources is costly and misguided because advances in green energy technology will eventually make oil and coal of little value. The stone age didn't end because we ran out of stone, and the carbon age won't end because we run out of oil and coal!

Bad accounting frameworks are likely to lead to bad decisions. A government focused on GDP might be encouraged to give away mining or oil concessions; a focus on green NNP might make it realise that the country risks being worse off.
Joseph Stiglitz, 'Good Numbers Gone Bad,' *Fortune,* September 25, 2006

When Anglo-Australian company BHP Billiton mines copper in Papua New Guinea, the country's GDP rises, but profits go abroad and 40,000 who live by a polluted river lose their means of earning a living. GNNP measures that loss.

ECONOMICS IN ACTION

A Broader Indicator of Economic Well-Being

The limitations of real GDP reviewed in this chapter affect the standard of living and general well-being of every country. So to make international comparisons of the general state of economic well-being, we must look at real GDP and other indicators.

The United Nations has constructed a broader measure called the Human Development Index (HDI), which combines real income, life expectancy, health and education. The dots in the figure show the relationship between real GDP per person (using a PPP measure) and the HDI.

In 2012, Norway had the highest HDI and the highest real GDP per person. Australia had the second highest HDI but ranked tenth on real GDP per person. The US ranked second on real GDP and third on the HDI. The US HDI is lower than that of Australia and Norway because the people of those countries live longer and have better access to healthcare and education than Americans.

The UK ranks 21 on GDP and 28 on the HDI.

Several African nations have the lowest levels of economic well-being as measured by both GDP and the HDI.

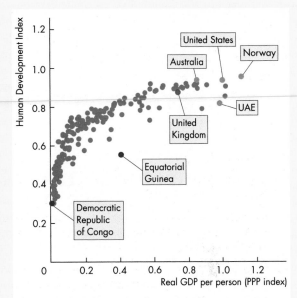

Figure 1   The Human Development Index

Sources of data: United Nations, hdr.undp.org/en/statistics/hdi and International Monetary Fund *World Economic Outlook database*, October 2012.

The Bottom Line

Do we get the wrong message about the growth in economic welfare by looking at the growth of real GDP? The influences that are omitted from real GDP are probably important and could be large. Developing countries have more household production and a larger underground economy than do developed countries, so the gap between their living standards is exaggerated. Also, as real GDP grows, part of the measured growth might reflect a switch from home production to market production and from underground to regular production. This measurement error overstates the growth in economic well-being and the improvement in the standard of living.

It is possible to construct broader measures that combine the many influences that contribute to human happiness. The United Nation's Human Development Index or HDI (above) and Green Net National Product or GNNP (previous page) are two examples of dozens of other measures that have been proposed.

Despite all the alternatives, real GDP per person remains the most widely used indicator of economic well-being and the standard of living.

Reading Between the Lines on pp. 472–473 looks more closely at European real GDP and HDI measures and also looks at yet another alternative to GDP calculated by the Office for National Statistics.

REVIEW QUIZ

1   Distinguish between real GDP and potential GDP and describe how each grows over time.
2   How does the growth rate of real GDP contribute to an improved standard of living?
3   What is a business cycle and what are its phases and turning points?
4   What is PPP and how does it help us to make valid international comparisons of real GDP?
5   Explain why real GDP might be an unreliable indicator of the standard of living.

Do these questions in Study Plan 20.3 and get instant feedback.   MyEconLab

READING BETWEEN THE LINES

Alternative Measures of the State of the UK Economy

Are Squeezed Households Happier?

Claire Jones and Kate Allen

Money doesn't make you happy – but it helps. The traditional gauge of economic progress has long been gross domestic product. . . . But the Office for National Statistics' (ONS) first report into the nation's well-being shows that using GDP as a measure of economic contentment suggests people got happier as the economy shrank. . . .

Another measure . . . used in the ONS . . . real household actual income (RHAI) – accounts for the effect of policies such as the Bank of England's ultra-low interest rates and the rise in benefits and decrease in tax revenue that occur automatically when the economy contracts. It also attempts to quantify the impact of free healthcare and education on well-being.

RHAI continued to rise during the 2008–09 recession, along with levels of life satisfaction.

The ONS data, which go back to 2002 – covering only one downturn – are far from conclusive on

how to measure economic well-being. But they add weight to the view increasingly shared among economists that GDP is a poor gauge of the relationship between happiness and wealth.

Internationally, economists are devoting more resources to alternative measures of well-being. Lord O'Donnell the former head of the civil service said: 'We're at the start of this process, but it will end up being pretty transformational on the way in which we conduct public policy.'

Economists have already put forward a variety of alternatives, some of which are controversial due to their crunching together of indicators. The most commonly used international comparison is the UN Human Development Index. This assesses countries' development based on life expectancy, educational achievement and income levels. On these measures, the UK languishes in 28th place.

The Essence of the Story

◆ Real GDP is the traditional measure of the state of the economy.

◆ Real Household Actual Income or RHAI is a new alternative measure.

◆ The RHAI includes an assessment of the effects of interest rates, welfare payments and taxes

as well as the impact of education and healthcare services provided by government.

◆ A variety of alternative measures have been proposed, the most commonly used of which is the UN Human Development Index (HDI).

Economic Analysis

◆ In 2012, the Office for National Statistics (ONS) published the first annual *Measuring National Well-Being* report, which aims to provide a rich picture of 'how society is doing'.

◆ Real household actual income (RHAI) is one component of the ONS report. RHAI subtracts taxes from income but adds welfare and other benefits and also adds a measure of the value of services provided by the state such as healthcare and education.

◆ Figure 1 shows RHAI since 2005 (rebased to 2010 pounds) and compares it with real GDP. RHAI is *countercyclical* – when real GDP falls, RHAI rises, and when real GDP rises, RHAI falls. This inverse relationship is not exact but it is visible in the figure.

◆ According to the ONS measures, the value of government services increased when real GDP shrank and decreased when real GDP expanded.

◆ One reason for this outcome might be that families used public education and healthcare more frequently and private education and healthcare less frequently when real GDP and incomes decreased.

◆ RHAI looks at the UK over time. To make international comparisons, we must use other measures, such as the HDI.

◆ Figure 2 looks at the HDI and real GDP per person in Europe. (Figure 1 on p. 471 shows the same data for the entire world.)

◆ The HDI ranks the UK towards the bottom end of the distribution behind Norway, Germany, France, Spain and Italy.

◆ But on GDP per person (on a PPP basis), the UK is below Norway and Germany but above France, Spain and Italy.

◆ While real GDP is an imperfect measure of economic well-being, Figure 2 shows the same clear positive relationship between the

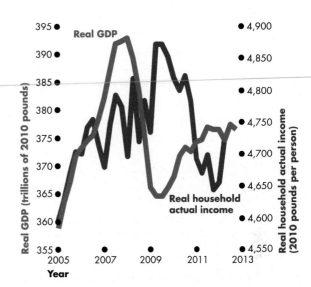

Figure 1 Real GDP and Real Household Actual Income

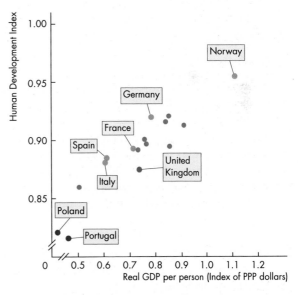

Figure 2 Real GDP and Human Development in Europe

HDI and real GDP per person as that for the world as a whole in *Economics in Action* on p. 471.

◆ Alternative measures of economic well-being have alternative limitations. Real GDP is an objective and widely used measure that may well be the least imperfect measure.

MATHEMATICAL NOTE

Chain Volume Measure of Real GDP

In the real GDP calculation on p. 465, real GDP in 2013 is 1.6 times its value in 2010. But suppose that we use 2013 as the reference base year and value real GDP in 2010 at 2013 prices. If you do the mathematics, you will see that real GDP in 2010 is £150 million at 2013 prices. GDP in 2013 is £300 million (in 2013 prices), so now the numbers say that real GDP has doubled. Which is correct? Did real GDP increase 1.6 times or double? Should we use the prices of 2010 or 2013? The answer is that we need to use both sets of prices.

The Office for National Statistics uses a measure of real GDP called the **chain volume measure** of real GDP. Three steps are needed to calculate this measure:

◆ Value production in the prices of adjacent years
◆ Find the average of two percentage changes
◆ Link (chain) back to the reference base year

Value Production in Prices of Adjacent Years

The first step is to value production in adjacent years at the prices of both years. We'll make these calculations for 2013 and its preceding year, 2012.

Table 1 shows the quantities produced and prices in the two years. Part (a) shows the nominal GDP calculation for 2012 – the quantities produced in 2012 valued at the prices of 2012. Nominal GDP in 2012 is £145 million. Part (b) shows the nominal GDP calculation for 2013 – the quantities produced in 2013 valued at the prices of 2013. Nominal GDP in 2013 is £300 million. Part (c) shows the value of the quantities produced in 2013 at the prices of 2012 – a total of £160 million. And part (d) shows the value of the quantities produced in 2012 at the prices of 2013 – a total of £275 million.

Find the Average of Two Percentage Changes

The second step is to find the percentage change in the value of production based on the prices in the two adjacent years. Table 2 summarises these calculations.

Part (a) shows that, valued at the prices of 2012, production increased from £145 million in 2012 to

---

Table 1

Real GDP Calculation Step 1: Value Production in Adjacent Years at Prices in Both Years

Item	Quantity (millions)	Price (pounds)	Expenditure (millions of pounds)
(a) In 2012			
C Shirts	3	5	15
I Computer chips	3	10	30
G Security services	5	20	100
Y Real and nominal GDP in 2012			**145**
(b) In 2013			
C Shirts	4	5	20
I Computer chips	2	20	40
G Security services	6	40	240
Y Nominal GDP in 2013			**300**
(c) Quantities of 2013 valued at prices of 2012			
C Shirts	4	5	20
I Computer chips	2	10	20
G Security services	6	20	120
Y 2013 production at 2012 prices			**160**
(d) Quantities of 2012 valued at prices of 2013			
C Shirts	3	5	15
I Computer chips	3	20	60
G Security services	5	40	200
Y 2012 production at 2013 prices			**275**

Step 1 is to value the production of adjacent years at the prices of both years. Here, we value the production of 2012 and 2010 at the prices of both 2012 and 2013. The value of 2012 production at 2012 prices, in part (a), is nominal GDP in 2012. The value of 2013 production at 2013 prices, in part (b), is nominal GDP in 2013. Part (c) calculates the value of 2013 production at 2012 prices and part (d) calculates the value of 2012 production at 2013 prices. We use these numbers in Step 2.

£160 million in 2013, an increase of 10.3 per cent. Part (b) shows that, valued at the prices of 2013, production increased from £275 million in 2012 to £300 million in 2013, an increase of 9.1 per cent. Part (c) shows that the average of these two percentage changes in the value of production is 9.7. That is, $(10.3 + 9.1) \div 2 = 9.7$.

This average percentage change is the *growth rate* of real GDP in 2013. This growth rate depends only on production and prices in 2012 and 2013.

The final step is to find the *level* of real GDP.

Table 2

Real GDP Calculation Step 2: Find Average of Two Percentage Changes

Value of production	Millions of pounds
(a) At 2012 prices	
Nominal GDP in 2012	145
2013 production at 2012 prices	160
Percentage change in production at 2012 prices	**10.3**
(b) At 2013 prices	
2012 production at 2013 prices	275
Nominal GDP in 2013	300
Percentage change in production at 2013 prices	**9.1**
(c) Average percentage change in 2013	**9.7**

Using the numbers in Step 1, the percentage change in production from 2012 to 2013 valued at 2012 prices is 10.3 per cent, in part (a). The percentage change in production from 2012 to 2013 valued at 2013 prices is 9.1 per cent, in part (b). The average of these two percentage changes is 9.7 per cent, in part (c).

Link (Chain) to the Base Year

The *level* of real GDP depends on the choice of a base year. To see how, we'll first suppose that the base year is 2012. Then we'll change the base year to the current one of 2010.

By definition, real GDP and nominal GDP are equal in the base year. So real GDP in 2012 (in 2012 pounds) is £145 million (in Table 1).

In 2013, real GDP grew by 9.7 per cent, so real GDP in 2013 (in 2012 pounds) is 9.7 per cent greater than £145 million, which equals £159 million. (Check the calculation: Real GDP increased by £14 million, which is 9.7 per cent of £145 million.)

Today, the base year is 2010, and to find the level of real GDP three years later in 2013 more calculations are needed.

The ONS must calculate the percentage change or growth rate in real GDP for each pair of years from the base year (2010) to the most recent year. And to find real GDP for years before the base year, the ONS must calculate the growth rates for each pair of years from the base year back to the earliest one for which it has data.

Finally, using the percentage changes it has calculated, the ONS finds the levels of real GDP in 2010

prices by linking the percentage changes to the level of GDP in 2010.

To illustrate this third step, we'll assume that the ONS has used the method we've described to calculate the percentage changes of real GDP for the years 2008 through to 2013.

Figure 1 illustrates the chain-link calculations and the growth rates (assumed) that the ONS has calculated.

In the reference base year, 2010, real GDP equals nominal GDP, which we'll assume is £143 million. The growth rate of real GDP was 6 per cent in 2010, so real GDP in 2010 was 6 per cent higher than it was in 2009, which means that real GDP in 2009 was £135 million (135 × 1.06 = 143).

The growth rate of real GDP was 7 per cent in 2011, so real GDP in 2011 was 7 per cent higher than it was in 2010, which means that real GDP in 2011 was £153 million (143 × 1.07 = 153).

By repeating these calculations for each year, we obtain the chained volume measure of real GDP in 2010 pounds for each year. In 2012, the chained volume measure of real GDP in 2010 pounds was £165 million. So the 9.7 per cent growth rate in 2013 that we calculated in Table 2 means that real GDP in 2013 was £181 million.

Notice that although the level of real GDP depends on the choice of the base year, the growth rates of real GDP are independent of the reference base year. So a change in the reference base year does not change the growth rates of real GDP.

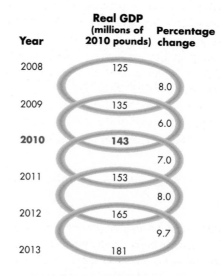

Year	Real GDP (millions of 2010 pounds)	Percentage change
2008	125	
		8.0
2009	135	
		6.0
2010	**143**	
		7.0
2011	153	
		8.0
2012	165	
		9.7
2013	181	

Figure 1 Real GDP Calculation Step 3: Link (Chain) Back to Base Year

SUMMARY

Key Points

Gross Domestic Product (pp. 460–462)

◆ GDP, or gross domestic product, is the market value of all the final goods and services produced in a country during a given period.

◆ A final good is an item that is bought by its final user and it contrasts with an intermediate good, which is a component of a final good.

◆ GDP is calculated by using the expenditure or income totals in the circular flow model of expenditure and income.

◆ Aggregate expenditure on goods and services equals aggregate income and GDP.

Do Problems 1 to 7 to get a better understanding of gross domestic product.

Measuring UK GDP (pp. 463–465)

◆ Because aggregate expenditure, aggregate income and the value of aggregate output are equal, we can measure GDP by either the expenditure approach or the income approach.

◆ The expenditure approach adds together consumption expenditure, investment, government expenditure on goods and services and net exports.

◆ The income approach adds together the incomes paid to the factors of production – wages, interest, rent and profit – and indirect taxes less subsidies.

◆ Real GDP is measured using a common set of prices to remove the effects of inflation from GDP.

Do Problems 8 to 15 to get a better understanding of measuring UK GDP.

The Uses and Limitations of Real GDP (pp. 466–471)

◆ Real GDP is used to compare the standard of living over time and across countries.

◆ Real GDP per person grows and fluctuates around the more smoothly growing potential GDP.

◆ A slowing of the growth rate of real GDP per person during the 1970s has lowered incomes by a large amount.

◆ International real GDP comparisons use PPP prices.

◆ Real GDP is not a perfect measure of economic welfare because it excludes household production, the underground economy, leisure time and environmental quality.

Do Problems 16 and 17 to get a better understanding of the uses and limitations of real GDP.

Key Terms

STUDY PLAN PROBLEMS AND APPLICATIONS

Do Problems 1 to 19 in MyEconLab Chapter 20 Study Plan and get instant feedback.   MyEconLab

Gross Domestic Product (Study Plan 20.1)

1 Classify each of the following items as a final good or service or an intermediate good or service and identify which is a component of consumption expenditure, investment, or government expenditure on goods and services:

- ◆ Banking services bought by a student
- ◆ New cars bought by Hertz, the car rental firm
- ◆ Newsprint bought by *The Times* newspaper
- ◆ The purchase of a new limo for the prime minister
- ◆ A new house bought by Wayne Rooney

2 The firm that printed this textbook bought the paper from XYZ Paper Mills. Was this purchase of paper part of GDP? If not, how does the value of the paper get counted in GDP?

Use the following figure, which illustrates the circular flow model, in Problems 3 and 4.

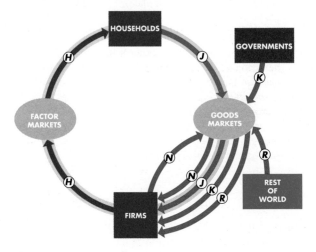

3 During 2011, in an economy:

- ◆ Flow *J* was £90 billion.
- ◆ Flow *K* was £20 billion.
- ◆ Flow *N* was £30 billion.
- ◆ Flow *R* was –£7 billion.

Name the flows and calculate the value of:

a Aggregate income.

b GDP.

4 During 2012, flow *H* was £130 billion, flow *J* was £91 billion, flow *N* was £33 billion, and flow *R* was –£8 billion.

Calculate the 2012 values of:

a GDP

b Government expenditure

5 Use the following data to calculate aggregate expenditure and imports of goods and services.

- ◆ Government expenditure: £20 billion
- ◆ Aggregate income: £100 billion
- ◆ Consumption expenditure: £67 billion
- ◆ Investment: £21 billion
- ◆ Exports of goods and services: £30 billion

6 US Economy Expands

GDP increased 2.4 per cent as businesses raised investment by 4.6 per cent, consumers raised spending by 1.8 per cent, purchases of new houses increased 13.4 per cent and exports increased 5.4 per cent.

Source: Bureau of Economic Analysis, 31 July 2013

Use the letters on the figure in Problem 3 to indicate the flow in which each item in the news clip occurs. How can GDP have risen by only 2.4 per cent with the big expenditure increases reported?

7 A market research firm deconstructed an Apple iPod and studied the manufacturers' costs and profits of each of the parts and components. The final results are:

- ◆ An Apple iPod sells in the US for $299.
- ◆ A Japanese firm, Toshiba, makes the hard disk and display screen, which cost $93.
- ◆ Other components produced in South Korea cost $25.
- ◆ Other components produced in the US cost $21.
- ◆ The iPod is assembled in China at a cost of $5.
- ◆ The costs and profits of retailers, advertisers and transportation firms in the US are $75.

a What is Apple's profit?

b Where in the national accounts of the US, Japan, South Korea and China are these transactions recorded?

c What contribution does one iPod make to world GDP?

Measuring UK GDP (Study Plan 20.2)

Use the following table, which lists some macroeconomic data for the UK, in Problems 8 and 9.

Item	Billions of pounds
Compensation of employees	750
Consumption expenditure	900
Gross operating surplus	300
Investment	250
Government expenditure	300
Net exports	–40
Mixed income	150

8 Calculate UK GDP.

9 Given the data supplied, which approach (expenditure or income) to measuring GDP can you use to calculate UK GDP? Explain your answer.

Use the following data in Problems 10 and 11.

The national accounts of Parchment Paradise are kept on (you guessed it) parchment. A fire destroys the statistics office. The accounts are now incomplete, but they contain the following data:

◆ Consumption expenditure: £2,000

◆ Indirect taxes less subsidies: £100

◆ Gross operating surplus: £500

◆ Investment: £800

◆ Government expenditure: £400

◆ Compensation of employees: £2,000

◆ Net exports: –£200

10 Calculate GDP.

11 Calculate gross domestic income at factor cost.

Use the following data in Problems 12 and 13.

Tropical Republic produces only bananas and coconuts. The base year is 2012. The table gives the quantities produced and the prices.

Quantities	2012	2013
Bananas	800 kilograms	900 kilograms
Coconuts	400	500

Prices	2012	2013
Bananas	£2 per kilogram	£4 per kilogram
Coconuts	£10 each	£5 each

12 Calculate nominal GDP in 2012 and 2013.

13 Calculate real GDP in 2013 expressed in base-year prices.

Use the following news clip in Problems 14 and 15.

Foreign Carmakers Ship More US-Made Cars Overseas

After building its one millionth automobile in the US for export, Honda is on the verge of becoming a net exporter of vehicles from North America. Within two years, the company says it will be exporting more North American-built vehicles than it imports into the US from Japan.

Source: *Forbes*, 6 December 2012

14 Explain how Honda's activities influence US GDP and the components of aggregate expenditure.

15 Explain how Honda's activity influences the factor incomes that make up US GDP.

The Uses and Limitations of Real GDP (Study Plan 20.3)

16 Based on the following data, in which years did the UK standard of living (a) increase and (b) decrease. Explain your answer.

Year	Real GDP	Population
2008	£1,541.0 billion	61.4 million
2009	£1,461.4 billion	61.8 million
2010	£1,485.6 billion	62.3 million
2011	£1,502.2 billion	63.2 million
2012	£1,504.8 billion	63.7 million

17 In 2013, Jackie stopped working at Barclays and stayed at home to take care of her new baby girl. She started to do her own laundry instead of buying laundry service. She also started to bake her own bread and cakes. But she increased the volume of music and movies that she downloaded almost every day. Explain how Jackie's new lifestyle shows up in real GDP. What changes are misleading and not changes in production?

Mathematical Note (Study Plan 20.MN)

Use the following table on the economy of Maritime Republic in Problems 18 and 19.

Maritime Republic produces only fish and crabs.

Quantities	2012	2013
Fish	1,000 tonnes	1,100 tonnes
Crabs	500 tonnes	525 tonnes

Prices	2012	2013
Fish	£20 per tonne	£30 per tonne
Crabs	£10 per tonne	£8 per tonne

18 Calculate nominal GDP in 2012 and 2013.

19 Calculate Maritime Republic's chain volume measure of real GDP in 2013 expressed in 2012 pounds.

ADDITIONAL PROBLEMS AND APPLICATIONS

Do these problems in MyEconLab if assigned by your lecturer.

MyEconLab

Gross Domestic Product

20 Classify each of the following items as a final good or service or an intermediate good or service and identify which is a component of consumption expenditure, investment, or government expenditure on goods and services:

- Banking services bought by Google
- Security system bought by Barclays
- Coffee beans bought by Starbucks
- New coffee grinders bought by Starbucks
- Starbuck's grande mocha frappuccino bought by a student
- An aircraft carrier bought by the Royal Navy

Use the figure in Problem 3 on p. 477 in Problems 21 and 22.

21 In 2012, flow *H* was £1,000 billion, flow *K* was £250 billion, flow *J* was £650 billion, and flow *R* was £50 billion. Calculate investment.

22 In 2013, flow *N* was £2 trillion, flow *R* was –£1 trillion, flow *H* was £10 trillion, and flow *K* was £4 trillion. Calculate consumption expenditure.

Use the following information in Problems 23 and 24.

Tata, an Indian company, builds Range Rovers and Jaguar cars in England, some of which are sold in England and some of which are exported to India.

23 Explain where these activities appear in the UK national accounts.

24 Explain where these activities appear in the Indian national accounts.

Use the following news clip in Problems 25 and 26 and use the circular flow model to illustrate your answers.

Blades of Glory

With production facilities in the US, UK, Germany, Norway and Sweden, GKN and Rolls Royce are cooperating to produce composite fan blades for the next generation of lightweight, fuel-efficient airplane engines.

> Source: *Royal Aeronautical Society,* February 2012

25 Explain how GKN's and Rolls Royce's activities and their transactions affect GDP in the countries mentioned in the news clip.

26 Explain how transactions with the airlines that buy the engines from Rolls Royce affect UK GDP.

Measuring UK GDP

Use the following data in Problems 27 and 28.

The table lists some macroeconomic data for the UK.

Item	Billions of pounds
Compensation of employees	770
Consumption expenditure	900
Gross operating surplus	300
Investment	200
Government expenditure	2,900
Net exports	–30

27 Calculate UK GDP.

28 Given the data supplied, which approach (expenditure or income) to measuring GDP can you use to calculate UK GDP? Explain your answer.

Use the following data in Problems 29 and 30.

An economy produces only apples and oranges. The base year is 2012 and the table gives the quantities produced and the prices.

Quantities	2012	2013
Apples	60	160
Oranges	80	220

Prices	2012	2013
Apples	£0.50 each	£1 each
Oranges	£0.25 each	£2 each

29 Calculate nominal GDP in 2012 and 2013.

30 Calculate real GDP in 2012 and 2013 expressed in base-year prices.

31 **China's GDP growth slows in 2nd quarter of 2013**

Gross domestic product growth slowed to 7.5 per cent in the second quarter of 2013, down from 7.7 per cent in the first quarter, data from the National Bureau of Statistics showed. Lu Zhengwei, chief economist with Industrial Bank, said the slower growth was mainly caused by the industrial sector, which faces overcapacity and weakening foreign demand.

> Source: *The China Daily,* 15 July 2013

Use the expenditure approach for measuring China's GDP to explain why 'weakening foreign demand' might slow the country's real GDP growth rate.

The Uses and Limitations of Real GDP

32 The United Nations' Human Development Index (HDI) is based on real GDP per person, life expectancy at birth and indicators of the quality and quantity of education.

   a Explain why the HDI might be better than real GDP as a measure of economic welfare.

   b Which items in the HDI are part of real GDP and which items are not in real GDP?

   c Do you think the HDI should be expanded to include items such as pollution, resource depletion and political freedom? Explain.

   d What other influences on economic welfare should be included in a comprehensive measure?

33 **UK Living Standards Outstrip US**

   Oxford analysts report that living standards in Britain are set to rise above those in America for the first time since the nineteenth century. Real GDP per person in Britain will be £23,500 this year, compared with £23,250 in America, reflecting not only the strength of the pound against the dollar but also the UK economy's record run of growth since 2001. But the Oxford analysts also point out that Americans benefit from lower prices than those in Britain.

   Source: *The Sunday Times*, 6 January 2008

   If real GDP per person is more in the UK than in the US but Americans benefit from lower prices, does this comparison of real GDP per person really tell us which country has the higher standard of living?

34 Use the news clip in Problem 31.

   a Why might China's recent GDP growth rates overstate the actual increase in the level of production taking place in China?

   b Explain the complications involved with attempting to compare economic welfare in China and the US by using the GDP for each country.

35 **Poor India Makes Millionaires at Fastest Pace**

   India, with the world's largest population of poor people, created millionaires at the fastest pace in the world in 2007. India added another 23,000 more millionaires in 2007 to its 2006 tally of 100,000 millionaires measured in euros. That is 1 millionaire for about 7,000 people living on less than 2 euros a day.

   Source: *The Times of India*, 25 June 2008

   a Why might real GDP per person misrepresent the standard of living of the average Indian?

   b Why might 2 euros day underestimate the standard of living of the poorest Indians?

Economics in the News

36 After you have studied *Reading Between the Lines* on pp. 472–473, answer the following questions.

   a What does Real Household Actual Income (RHAI) seek to measure and what are some of its components that distinguish it from real GDP?

   b How does RHIA fluctuate over the business cycle and what are some of the reasons for its different behaviour from real GDP?

   c What does the UN Human Development Index (HDI) seek to measure and what are some of its components that distinguish it from real GDP?

   d Why might the UK rank lower on the HDI than it does on real GDP among its European neighbours?

37 **Totally Gross**

   GDP has proved useful in tracking both short-term fluctuations and long-run growth. Which isn't to say GDP doesn't miss some things. Amartya Sen, at Harvard, helped create the UN Human Development Index, which combines health and education data with per capita GDP to give a better measure of the wealth of nations. Joseph Stiglitz, at Columbia, advocates a 'green net national product' that takes into account the depletion of natural resources. Others want to include happiness in the measure. These alternative benchmarks have merit but can they be measured with anything like the frequency, reliability and impartiality of GDP?

   Source: *Time*, 21 April 2008

   a Explain the factors that the news clip identifies as limiting the usefulness of GDP as a measure of economic welfare.

   b What are the challenges involved in trying to incorporate measurements of those factors in an effort to better measure economic welfare?

   c What does the ranking of the UK in the Human Development Index imply about the levels of health and education relative to other nations?

Mathematical Note

38 Use the information in Problem 29 to calculate the chain volume measure of real GDP in 2013 expressed in 2012 pounds.

39 Explain why the growth rate of the chain volume measure of real GDP is independent of the base year while the level of the chain volume measure depends on the base year. Illustrate your answer with a numerical example.

CHAPTER 20 APPENDIX

Graphs in Macroeconomics

After studying this appendix, you will be able to:

◆ Make and interpret a time-series graph

◆ Make and interpret a graph that uses a ratio scale

The Time-Series Graph

In macroeconomics we study the fluctuations and trends in the key variables that describe macroeconomic performance and policy. These variables include GDP and its expenditure and income components that you've learned about in this chapter. They also include variables that describe the labour market and consumer prices that you study in Chapter 21.

Regardless of the variable of interest, we want to be able to compare its value today with that in the past; and we want to describe how the variable has changed over time. The most effective way to do these things is to make a time-series graph.

Making a Time-Series Graph

A **time-series graph** measures time (for example, years, quarters or months) on the x-axis and the variable or variables in which we are interested on the y-axis. Figure A20.1 is an example of a time-series graph. It provides some information about unemployment in the UK from 1982 to 2012. In this figure, we measure time in years starting in 1982. We measure the unemployment rate (the variable we're interested in) on the y-axis.

A time-series graph enables us to visualise how a variable has changed over time and how its value in one period relates to its value in another period. It conveys an enormous amount of information quickly and easily.

Let's see how to 'read' a time-series graph.

Reading a Time-Series Graph

To practise reading a time-series graph, take a close look at Figure A20.1. The graph shows the level, change and speed of change of the variable.

Figure A20.1 A Time-Series Graph

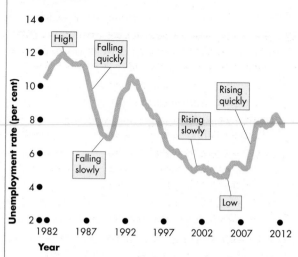

A time-series graph plots the level of a variable on the y-axis against time (here measured in years) on the x-axis. This graph shows the unemployment rate each year from 1982 to 2012. It shows when unemployment was high, when it was low, when it increased, when it decreased and when it changed quickly and when it changed slowly.

MyEconLab Animation ————————————➤

◆ The *level* of the variable: it tells us when unemployment is high and low. When the line is a long distance above the x-axis, the unemployment rate is high, as it was, for example, in 1983 and again in 2011. When the line is close to the x-axis, the unemployment rate is low, as it was, for example, in 2005.

◆ The *change* in the variable: it tells us how unemployment changes – whether it increases or decreases. When the line slopes upward, as it did in 2008 and 2009, the unemployment rate is rising. When the line slopes downward, as it did in 1984 and 1997, the unemployment rate is falling.

◆ The *speed* of change in the variable: it tells us whether the unemployment rate is rising or falling quickly or slowly. If the line is very steep, then the unemployment rate increases or decreases quickly. If the line is not steep, the unemployment rate increases or decreases slowly. For example, the unemployment rate rose quickly in 2008 and slowly in 2003 and it fell quickly in 1987 and slowly in 1989.

Ratio Scale Reveals Trend

A time-series graph also reveals whether a variable has a **cycle**, which is a tendency for a variable to alternate between upward and downward movements, or a **trend**, which is a tendency for a variable to move in one general direction.

The unemployment rate in Figure A20.1 has a cycle but no strongly visible trend. When a trend is present, a special kind of time-series graph, one that uses a ratio scale on the *y*-axis, reveals the trend.

A Time-Series with a Trend

Many macroeconomics variables, among them GDP and the average level of prices, have an upward trend. Figure A20.2 shows an example of such a variable: the average prices paid by consumers.

In Figure A20.2(a), consumer prices since 1972 are graphed on a normal scale. In 1972, the level is 100. In other years, the average level of prices is measured as a percentage of the 1972 level.

The graph clearly shows the upward trend of prices. But it doesn't tell us when prices were rising fastest or whether there was any change in the trend. Just looking at the upward-sloping line in Figure A20.2(a) gives the impression that the pace of growth of consumer prices was constant.

Using a Ratio Scale

On a graph axis with a normal scale, the gap between 1 and 2 is the same as that between 3 and 4. On a graph axis with a ratio scale, the gap between 1 and 2 is the same as that between 2 and 4. The ratio 2 to 1 equals the ratio 4 to 2. By using a ratio scale, we can 'see' when the growth rate (the percentage change per unit of time) changes.

Figure A20.2(b) shows an example of a ratio scale. Notice that the values on the *y*-axis get closer together but the gap between 400 and 200 equals the gap between 200 and 100. The ratio gaps are equal.

Graphing the data on a ratio scale reveals the trends. In the case of consumer prices, the trend is much steeper during the 1970s and early 1980s than in the later years. The steeper the line in the ratio-scale graph in part (b), the faster are prices rising. Prices rose rapidly during the 1970s and early 1980s and more slowly in the later 1980s and 1990s. The ratio-scale graph reveals this fact. We use ratio-scale graphs extensively in macroeconomics.

Figure A20.2 Ratio Scale Reveals Trend

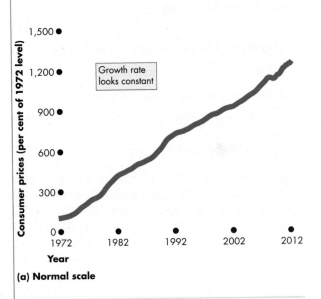

(a) Normal scale

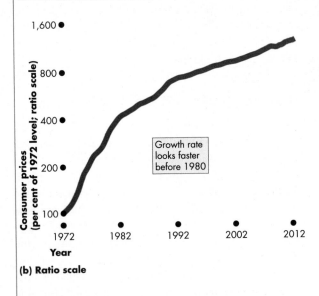

(b) Ratio scale

The graph shows the average of consumer prices from 1972 to 2012. The level is 100 in 1972 and the value in other years is a percentage of the 1972 level. Consumer prices normally rise each year, so the line slopes upward. In part (a), where the *y*-axis scale is normal, the rate of increase appears to be constant.

In part (b), where the *y*-axis is a ratio scale (the ratio of 400 to 200 equals the ratio 200 to 100), prices rose faster in the 1970s and early 1980s and slower in the later years. The ratio scale reveals this trend.

MyEconLab Animation

21

Monitoring Jobs and Inflation

After studying this chapter you will be able to:

- ◆ Explain why unemployment is a problem and how we measure the unemployment rate and other labour market indicators

- ◆ Explain why unemployment occurs and why it is present even at full employment

- ◆ Explain why inflation is a problem and how we measure it

Each month, we chart the course of unemployment as a sign of economic health. How do we measure unemployment? And is it a reliable vital sign?

Having a good job that pays a decent wage is only one half of the equation that determines the standard of living. The other half is the cost of living, which we measure using the CPI or RPI. How are these measures constructed and do they provide a good guide to changes in the cost of living?

These are the questions we study in this chapter. And in *Reading Between the Lines* at the end of the chapter, we ask why unemployment in Europe is so stubbornly high and much higher than UK unemployment.

Employment and Unemployment

The state of the labour market has a big impact on our incomes and our lives. In a few years you will be entering the labour market. What kind of market will you enter? Will there be plenty of good jobs to choose among, or will jobs be so hard to find that you end up taking one that doesn't use your education and pays a low wage? The answer depends, to a large degree, on the total number of jobs available and on the number of people competing for them.

Those leaving university in 2012 had a tough time in the jobs market. In January 2013, three and a half years after the recession bottomed out, 2.5 million people in the UK who wanted a job couldn't find one and registered as unemployed. In a normal year, the UK economy is an incredible job-creating machine. Even in July 2009 at the depths of recession, 27.4 million people had jobs – 900,000 more than in 1999 and 1.5 million more than in 1989. But in recent years, population growth has outstripped jobs growth, so unemployment has become a major problem.

Why Unemployment is a Problem

Unemployment is a serious personal, social and economic problem for two main reasons. It results in:

◆ Lost incomes and production
◆ Lost human capital

Lost Incomes and Production

The loss of a job brings with it a loss of income and lost production. These losses are devastating for the people who have to bear them. Unemployment benefits create a safety net and cushion the blow of loss of earnings, but they do not replace lost earnings.

Lost production means lower income and lower consumption. It also means lower investment in capital, which lowers the standard of living both in the present and in the future.

Lost Human Capital

Prolonged unemployment permanently damages a person's job prospects by destroying human capital.

ECONOMICS IN ACTION

What Kept John Maynard Keynes Awake at Night

In 1921, the UK unemployment rate shot up to 15 per cent. It remained between 10 and 15 per cent until the early 1930s when it jumped yet higher to almost 25 per cent. Unemployment wouldn't return to below 5 per cent until the first years of Second World War in the 1940s.

Puzzled by persistently high unemployment, economist John Maynard Keynes set to work trying to understand how it could happen and what might be done about it. He published his answers in 1936 in the *General Theory of Employment, Interest, and Money*, a book that created what we now call macroeconomics.

Many economists have studied this period of economic history and a shorter yet equally severe Great Depression that occurred in the US and many other economies. Among them are the current chairman of the US Federal Reserve System, Ben Bernanke.

A key reason why the Federal Reserve and the Bank of England were so aggressive in cutting interest rates and injecting money to save banks like Bear Stearns in the US and Northern Rock and the Royal Bank of Scotland in the

UK during the recent recession is that economists today are keenly aware of the horrors of total economic collapse. Both the Federal Reserve and the Bank of England were determined to avoid what they see as the mistakes of the 1920s and 1930s that brought Britain's interwar depression and the Great Depression in the US.

Think about a manager who loses his job when his employer downsizes. He takes work as a taxi driver. After a year he finds out that he can't compete with fresh graduates. Eventually he gets a management job but in a small firm at a lower salary than he was earning before. He has lost some of his human capital.

The cost of unemployment is spread unequally and is one of the most important causes of poverty and social deprivation.

Governments try to measure unemployment accurately and adopt policies to ease its pain. Let's see how the UK government measures unemployment.

Labour Force Survey

Every working day, interviewers of the Social and Vital Statistics Division of the Office for National Statistics (the ONS) contact close to 1,000 households (60,000 in a three-month period) and ask them questions about the age and labour market status of the household's members. This survey is called the Labour Force Survey. The ONS uses the information obtained to describe the changing anatomy of the labour market.

Figure 21.1 shows the population categories used by the ONS and the relationships among them. The population divides into two groups: the working-age population and others. The **working-age population** is the total number of people aged 16 to 64 who are not in prison, hospital or some other form of institutional care.

Members of the working-age population are either economically active or economically inactive. The **economically active** – also called the **workforce** – are people who have a job or are willing and able to take a job. The **economically inactive** are people who don't want a job. Most of the economically inactive are in full-time education or have retired.

The economically active are either employed or unemployed. To be counted as employed, a person must have either a full-time job or a part-time job. A student who does part-time work is counted as employed. To be counted as *un*employed, people must be available for work within the two weeks following their interview and must be in one of three categories:

1 Without work, but having made specific efforts to find a job within the previous four weeks.

2 Waiting to be called back to a job from which they have been laid off.

3 Waiting to start a new job within 30 days.

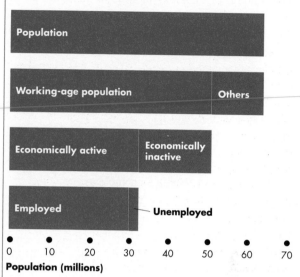

Figure 21.1 Population Workforce Categories

The population is divided into the working-age population and others (the young, the retired and the institutionalised). The working-age population is divided into those who are economically active (in the workforce) and those who are economically inactive. The economically active are either employed or unemployed.

Source of data: Office for National Statistics.

MyEconLab Animation

People in the working-age population who are neither employed nor unemployed are classified as economically inactive.

In 2012, the population of the UK was 63.7 million. There were 13.0 million below or above working age or living in institutions. So the working-age population in 2012 was 50.7 million. Of this number, 18.4 million were economically inactive (not in the workforce). The remaining 32.3 million were economically active. Of the economically active, 29.8 million were employed and 2.5 million were unemployed.

Three Labour Market Indicators

The Office for National Statistics calculates three indicators of the state of the labour market. They are:

◆ The unemployment rate

◆ The employment rate

◆ The economic activity rate

The Unemployment Rate

The amount of unemployment is an indicator of the extent to which people who want jobs can't find them. The **unemployment rate** is the percentage of economically active people who are unemployed.

$$\text{Unemployment rate} = \frac{\text{Number of people unemployed}}{\text{Workforce}} \times 100$$

and

$$\text{Workforce} = \text{Number employed} + \text{Number unemployed}$$

In January 2013, the number of people employed in the UK was 29.7 million and the number unemployed was 2.5 million. By using the above equations, the workforce was 32.2 million (29.7 million plus 2.5 million) and the unemployment rate was 7.8 per cent (2.5 million divided by 32.2 million, multiplied by 100).

Figure 21.2 shows the unemployment rate between 1980 and 2012. The average unemployment rate was 10 per cent during the 1980s and 8.1 per cent during the 1990s, but during the 2000s it was 5.5 per cent and 8 per cent again in the 2010s. The unemployment rate fluctuates and reached peak values at the end of recessions in 1980–1982 and 1990–1992. It looks as if unemployment reached a peak in 2011, but it is too early to say.

The Employment Rate

The number of people of working age who have jobs is an indicator of the availability of jobs and the degree of match between people's skills and jobs. The **employment rate** is the percentage of the people of working age who have jobs. That is:

$$\text{Employment rate} = \frac{\text{Number of people employed}}{\text{Working-age population}} \times 100$$

In the UK in January 2013, the number of people employed was 29.7 million and the working-age population was 50.7 million. By using the above equation, the employment rate was 58.6 per cent (29.7 million divided by 50.7 million, multiplied by 100).

Figure 21.3 shows the UK employment rate. It has followed a gently rising trend through the period since 1980. This upward trend means that the economy has created jobs at a faster rate than the working-age population has grown.

Figure 21.2   The Unemployment Rate: 1980–2012

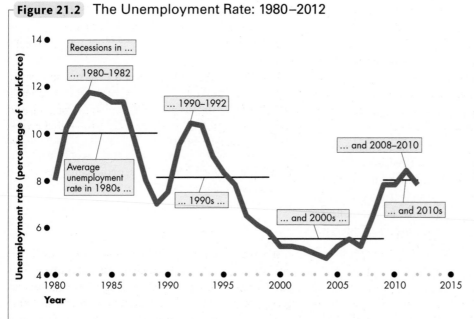

The average unemployment rate was 10 per cent during the 1980s, 8.1 per cent during the 1990s, and 5.5 per cent during the 2000s, but during the early 2010s it increased to 8 per cent.

The unemployment rate increases in recessions and decreases in expansions.

Source of data: Office for National Statistics.

MyEconLab Animation ◆

Figure 21.3 Economic Activity Rate and Employment Rate: 1980–2012

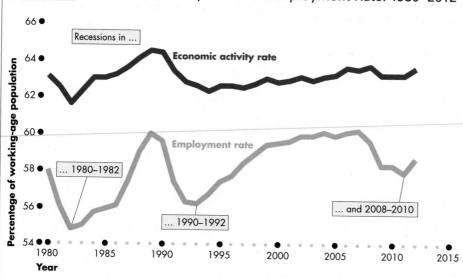

The employment rate decreases in recessions and increases in expansions. It has a slight upward trend over the period 1980 to 2012. The economic activity rate has no trend.

The employment rate fluctuates more than the economic activity rate and reflects cyclical fluctuations in the unemployment rate. Fluctuations in the economic activity rate arise from fluctuations in the number of workers who want a job.

Source of data: Office for National Statistics.

MyEconLab Animation

This labour market indicator also fluctuates over the business cycle. It reached a trough of 65.9 per cent in 1983, and its fluctuations coincide with, but are opposite to, those in the unemployment rate.

The Economic Activity Rate

The number of people in the workforce is an indicator of the willingness of the people of working age to take jobs. The **economic activity rate** is the percentage of the working-age population who are economically active. They are the members of the workforce.

$$\text{Economic activity rate} = \frac{\text{Workforce}}{\text{Working-age population}} \times 100$$

In January 2013, the workforce was 32.2 million and the working-age population was 50.7 million. By using the above equation, you can calculate the economic activity rate. It was 63.5 per cent (32.2 million divided by 50.7 million, multiplied by 100).

Figure 21.3 shows the economic activity rate. It rose slightly from 63.1 per cent in 1980 to 63.6 per cent in 2012. It also had some mild fluctuations, which result from unsuccessful job seekers leaving the workforce during a recession and re-entering during an expansion.

Other Definitions of Economic Inactivity and Unemployment

Do fluctuations in the economic activity rate over the business cycle mean that people who leave the workforce during a recession should be counted as unemployed? Or are they correctly counted as economically inactive?

The ONS believes that the official unemployment definition gives the best measure of the unemployment rate. But the ONS provides data on the reasons for economic inactivity. These data provide information on two relevant groups of people:

◆ Discouraged workers

◆ Others who want a job

Discouraged Workers

A **discouraged worker** is someone who is available and willing to work but who has stopped looking for a job because of repeated failure to find one. A discouraged worker is like an unemployed person in being available and willing to work. The only difference is that an unemployed person has looked for a job while a discouraged worker has stopped looking.

Others Who Want a Job

Others who want a job are people who are economically inactive and are willing to work but who have stopped actively looking for a job and who are not available to start a job in the next two weeks.

The official unemployment measure excludes economically inactive people because they haven't made specific efforts to find a job within the past four weeks and they are not available for work in the next two weeks. In other respects, they are unemployed.

Most Costly Unemployment

All unemployment is costly, but the most costly is long-term unemployment that results from job loss. People who are unemployed for a few weeks and then find another job bear some costs of unemployment. But these costs are low compared with the costs borne by people who remain unemployed for many weeks.

Also, people who are unemployed because they voluntarily leave their jobs to find better ones or because they have just entered or re-entered the labour market bear some costs of unemployment. But these costs are lower than those borne by people who lose their job and are forced back into the job market.

The official unemployment measure doesn't distinguish among these categories of the unemployed. If most of the unemployed are long-term and job losers, the situation is much worse than if most are short-term and voluntary job searchers.

Other Measures of Unemployment

The ONS reports data (starting in 1993) on the aspects of unemployment that we've just discussed, and we have used the data to calculate the alternative unemployment rates shown in Figure 21.4.

The 'Want a job' rate is based on the sum of the unemployed (official measure), discouraged workers and others who want a job. This broadest measure is much larger than the official unemployment rate. On average it is 1.6 times the official rate, and in a state of low unemployment it is double the official rate.

The 'Unemployed + discouraged' measure is only slightly higher than the official measure, but it fluctuates more than the official measure. In recessions, the discouraged worker category becomes more important.

The long-term unemployment rate (one year or longer) follows the cycle of the official measure and becomes important in recessions.

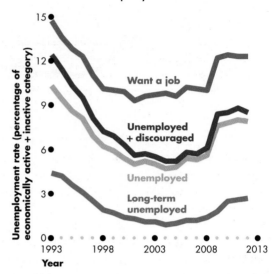

Figure 21.4 Alternative Measures of Unemployment: 1993–2012

'Unemployed' is the official measure. Fluctuations in all the alternative unemployment measures are similar to those in the official measure. The broadest 'Want a job' measure fluctuates less than the official measure but is larger than the official rate. 'Unemployed + discouraged workers' fluctuates more than the official measure but discouraged workers are a small part of the wider measure. Long-term unemployment (a year or more) increases in recessions.

Source of data: Office for National Statistics. Alternative unemployment rates calculated by the authors.

MyEconLab Animation ————————————◆

REVIEW QUIZ

1   What determines if a person is economically active?
2   What distinguishes an unemployed person from one who is economically inactive?
3   Describe the trends and fluctuations in the UK unemployment rate from 1980 to 2012.
4   Describe the trends and fluctuations in the UK employment rate and economic activity rate from 1980 to 2012.
5   Describe the types of economic inactivity that might be considered to be unemployed labour resources.

Do these questions in Study Plan 21.1 and get instant feedback.   MyEconLab

You've now seen how we measure employment and unemployment. Your next task is to see what we mean by full employment and how unemployment and real GDP fluctuate over the business cycle.

Unemployment and Full Employment

There is always someone without a job who is searching for one, so there is always some unemployment. The key reason is that the economy is always changing and experiences frictions, structural change and cycles.

Frictional Unemployment

The unemployment that arises from people entering and leaving the workforce and from an ongoing process of job creation and job destruction is called **frictional unemployment**.

There is an unending flow of people into and out of the workforce as people move through the stages of life – from being at university to finding a job, to working, perhaps to becoming unhappy with a job and looking for a new one and, finally, to retiring from full-time work.

There is also an unending process of job creation and job destruction as new firms are born, firms expand or contract and some firms fail and go out of business.

The flows into and out of the workforce and the processes of job creation and job destruction create the need for people to search for jobs and for businesses to search for workers. By this process of search, people can match their own skills and interests with the available jobs and find a satisfying job and a good income.

The frictional unemployment rate of younger workers is much higher than that of older workers and for two main reasons. First, every young worker must enter the labour market and search for a first job. Second, if a firm shrinks, it is more likely to fire its recently hired younger workers than its older ones. So a large percentage of unemployed jobseekers are younger workers.

Structural Unemployment

The unemployment that arises when changes in technology or international competition change the skills needed to perform jobs or change the location of jobs is called **structural unemployment**. Structural unemployment usually lasts longer than frictional unemployment because workers must usually retrain and possibly relocate to find a job.

An example of structural unemployment occurred when 600 shipyard jobs disappeared in Scotland and 750 new jobs at a computer chip company in Wales were created. The unemployed former shipyard workers remained unemployed for several months until they moved home, retrained and got one of the new jobs created in other parts of the country.

Structural unemployment is painful, especially for older workers for whom the best available option might be to retire early or to take a lower-skilled, lower-paid job.

Cyclical Unemployment

The higher than normal unemployment at a business cycle trough and the lower than normal unemployment at a business cycle peak is called **cyclical unemployment**. A worker who is laid off because the economy is in a recession and who gets rehired some months later when the expansion begins has experienced cyclical unemployment.

'Natural' Unemployment

Natural unemployment is the unemployment that arises from frictions and structural change when there is no cyclical unemployment – when all the unemployment is frictional and structural. Natural unemployment as a percentage of the workforce is called the **natural unemployment rate**.

Full employment is defined as a situation in which the unemployment rate equals the natural unemployment rate.

What determines the natural unemployment rate? Is it constant or does it change over time?

The natural unemployment rate is influenced by many factors, but the most important ones are:

◆ The age distribution of the population
◆ The scale of structural change
◆ The real wage rate
◆ Unemployment benefits

The Age Distribution of the Population

An economy with a young population has a large number of new job seekers every year and has a high level of frictional unemployment. An economy with an ageing population has fewer new job seekers and a low level of frictional unemployment.

The Scale of Structural Change

The scale of structural change is sometimes small. The same jobs using the same machines remain in place for many years. But sometimes there is a technological upheaval. The old ways are swept aside: millions of jobs are lost and the skill to perform them loses value. The amount of structural unemployment fluctuates with the pace and volume of technological change and the change driven by fierce international competition, especially from fast-changing Asian economies. A high level of structural unemployment is present in many parts of the UK today.

The Real Wage Rate

The natural unemployment rate is influenced by the level of the real wage rate. Real wages rates that bring unemployment are a minimum wage and an efficiency wage. Chapter 6 (see pp. 129–130) explains how the minimum wage creates unemployment. An *efficiency wage* is a wage set above the going market wage to enable firms to attract the most productive workers, get them to work hard and discourage them from leaving.

Unemployment Benefits

Unemployment benefits increase the natural unemployment rate by lowering the opportunity cost of job search. European countries have more generous unemployment benefits and higher natural unemployment rates than those in the US. Extending unemployment benefits increases the natural unemployment rate.

There is no controversy about the existence of a natural unemployment rate. Nor is there disagreement that the natural unemployment rate changes. But economists don't know its exact size or the extent to which it fluctuates.

There is no official estimate of the natural unemployment rate for the UK. The one in Figure 21.5 is our own estimate. Our estimate of the natural unemployment rate in 2012 is 7.2 per cent.

Real GDP and Unemployment Over the Business Cycle

The quantity of real GDP at full employment is potential GDP (Chapter 20, p. 466). Over the business cycle, real GDP fluctuates around potential GDP. The gap between real GDP and potential GDP is called the **output gap**. As the output gap fluctuates over the business cycle, the unemployment rate fluctuates around the natural unemployment rate.

Figure 21.5 The Output Gap and the Unemployment Rate

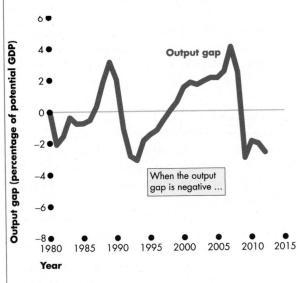

(a) Output gap

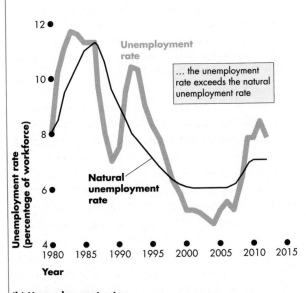

(b) Unemployment rate

As real GDP fluctuates around potential GDP in part (a), the unemployment rate fluctuates around the natural unemployment rate in part (b). During the recession in the early 1990s, the output gap became negative and the unemployment rate increased to 10 per cent. During the 1980s, the natural unemployment rate fell but rose again as the ouput gap became negative after 2008.

Sources of data: Office for National Statistics; and authors' assumptions and calculations.

MyEconLab Animation ◆

ECONOMICS IN ACTION

Jobs in Recession and Recovery

You've seen in Figure 21.5 how fluctuations in the output gap line up with fluctuations in the unemployment rate around the natural unemployment rate.

Here, we are looking at the relationship between real GDP and employment. When real GDP falls during a recession, employment falls too; when real GDP rises in an expansion, employment rises. But there is a delay in the response of employment that is visible in high-frequency quarterly data.

The figure shows the changes in real GDP and employment during the recession and expansion during 2008 to 2012. Real GDP shrank until the second quarter of 2009 and then started to expand. Total employment shrank with real GDP, but kept on shrinking until the first quarter of 2010. Only in the second quarter of 2010 did total employment begin to increase, and by the second quarter of 2012 it had returned to its level before the recession began.

There is an interesting difference in the way that part-time and full-time employment change during recession and expansion. Part-time employment increases through the recession and into the expansion. Full-time employment falls until the expansion has been running for six months. In the fourth quarter of 2012, full-time employment was still below its level in the first quarter of 2008.

In a recession, firms are reluctant to take on new full-time workers. Hiring part-time workers gives them greater flexibility to respond in either direction to changes in production.

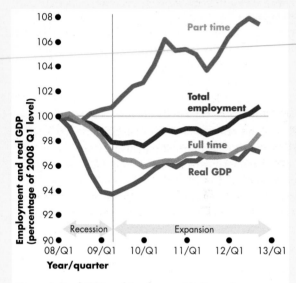

Figure 1 Real GDP and Employment in Recession and Recovery

Source of data: Office for National Statistics.

Figure 21.5 illustrates these fluctuations in the UK between 1980 and 2012 – the output gap in part (a) and the unemployment rate and natural unemployment rate in part (b).

When the economy is at full employment, the unemployment rate equals the natural unemployment rate and real GDP equals potential GDP so the output gap is zero. When the unemployment rate is less than the natural unemployment rate, real GDP is greater than potential GDP and the output gap is positive. And when the unemployment rate is greater than the natural unemployment rate, real GDP is less than potential GDP and the output gap is negative.

Figure 22.5(b) shows an estimate of the natural unemployment rate that is consistent with the estimate of the output gap in part (a). While we have a good estimate of real GDP and unemployment, we must use assumptions to estimate potential GDP, the output gap and the natural unemployment rate. So the picture presented in the figure is just one estimate. In the figure, the natural unemployment rate is high during the 1980s but falls steadily through the 1980s and 1990s to around 6 per cent by 2006 and rises to 7.2 per cent in 2012. This

estimate of the natural unemployment rate in the UK is one that many, but not all, economists would accept.

REVIEW QUIZ

1   Define frictional, structural and cyclical unemployment and provide an example of each type of unemployment.
2   What is the natural unemployment rate?
3   What factors might make the natural unemployment rate change?
4   How does the unemployment rate fluctuate over the business cycle?

Do these questions in Study Plan 21.2 and get instant feedback.   MyEconLab

Your final task in this chapter is to learn about two more vital signs that get monitored every month, the Retail Prices Index (RPI) and the Consumer Prices Index (CPI). What are the RPI and CPI, how do we measure them and what do they mean?

The Price Level, Inflation and Deflation

What will it *really* cost you to pay off your student loan? What will your parents' life savings buy when they retire? The answers depend on what happens to the **price level**, the average level of prices and the value of money. A persistently rising price level is called **inflation**; a persistently falling price level is called **deflation**.

We are interested in the price level, inflation and deflation for two main reasons. First, we want to measure the price level and the inflation rate or deflation rate. Second, we want to distinguish between the money values and real values of economic variables such as your student loan and your parents' savings.

We begin by explaining why inflation and deflation are problems, then we look at how we measure the price level and the inflation rate, and finally, we return to the task of distinguishing real values from money values.

Why Inflation and Deflation are Problems

Low, steady and anticipated inflation or deflation isn't a problem, but an unexpected burst of inflation or period of deflation brings four big problems and costs. It:

◆ Redistributes income
◆ Redistributes wealth
◆ Lowers real GDP and employment
◆ Diverts resources from production

Redistributes Income

Workers and employers sign wage contracts that last for a year or more. An unexpected burst of inflation raises prices but doesn't immediately raise wages. Workers are worse off because their wages buy less than they bargained for and employers are better off because their profits rise.

An unexpected deflation has the opposite effect. With a fall in prices, workers are better off because their fixed wages buy more than they bargained for and employers are worse off with lower profits.

Redistributes Wealth

People enter into loan contracts that are fixed in money terms and which pay an interest rate agreed as a percentage of the money borrowed and lent. With an unexpected burst of inflation, the money that the borrower repays to the lender buys less than the money originally loaned. The borrower wins and the lender loses. The interest paid on the loan doesn't compensate the lender for the loss in the value of the money loaned. With an unexpected deflation, the money that the borrower repays to the lender buys more than the money originally loaned. The borrower loses and the lender wins.

Lowers Real GDP and Employment

Unexpected inflation that raises firms' profits brings a rise in investment and a boom in production and employment. Real GDP rises above potential GDP and the unemployment rate falls below the natural rate. But this situation is temporary. Profitable investment dries up, spending falls, real GDP falls below potential GDP and the unemployment rate rises. Avoiding these swings in production and jobs means avoiding unexpected swings in the inflation rate.

An unexpected deflation has even greater consequences for real GDP and jobs. Businesses and households that are in debt (borrowers) are worse off and they cut their spending. A fall in total spending brings a recession and rising unemployment.

Diverts Resources from Production

Unpredictable inflation or deflation turns the economy into a casino and diverts resources from productive activities to forecasting inflation. It can become more profitable to forecast the inflation rate or deflation rate correctly than to invent a new product. Doctors, lawyers, accountants, farmers – just about everyone – can make themselves better off, not by specialising in the profession for which they have been trained but by spending more of their time dabbling as amateur economists and inflation forecasters and managing their investments.

From a social perspective, the diversion of talent that results from unpredictable inflation is like throwing scarce resources into a landfill. This waste of resources is a cost of inflation.

At its worst, inflation becomes **hyperinflation** – an inflation rate of 50 per cent a month or higher that grinds the economy to a halt and society to a collapse. Hyperinflation is rare, but Zimbabwe experienced it in recent years.

The ONS monitors the price level every month and devotes considerable resources to measuring it accurately. You're now going to see how the ONS does this.

The Price Indexes

The ONS calculates two price indexes every month. They are the **Retail Prices Index (RPI)** and the **Consumer Prices Index (CPI)** and both measure an average of the prices paid by consumers for a fixed 'basket' of goods and services. What you learn in this section will help you to interpret the RPI and the CPI and see how they tell you what has happened to the value of your money.

Reading the RPI and CPI

The RPI is defined to equal 100 for a period called the **reference base period**. Currently, the reference base period is January 1987. That is, for January 1987, the RPI equals 100. In January 2013, the RPI was 245.8. This number tells us that the average of the prices paid by households for a particular basket of consumer goods and services was 145.8 per cent higher in January 2013 than it was in January 1987.

The reference base period for the CPI is June 2005, and in June 2012, the CPI was 122.3. We read the CPI and calculate the percentage change since the base period in the same way as you've just seen for the RPI. The CPI in June 2012 was 22.3 per cent higher than it was in June 2005.

Constructing the RPI and CPI

Constructing the RPI and the CPI is a huge operation that costs millions of pounds and involves three stages:

◆ Selecting the basket

◆ Conducting a monthly price survey

◆ Calculating the price index

Selecting the Basket

The first stage in constructing a price index is to select the 'basket' of goods and services that the index will cover. The RPI basket contains the goods and services bought by an average household in the UK. The idea is to make the relative importance of the items in the RPI basket the same as that in the budget of an average household. For example, because people spend more on housing than on bus rides, the RPI places more weight on the price of housing than on the price of a bus ride.

The CPI basket is a bit different from the RPI basket and covers expenditure in the UK by private households, residents of institutions and tourists on the consumer goods and services in the CPI basket.

To determine the spending patterns of households and to select the RPI and CPI baskets, the ONS conducts periodic expenditure surveys. These surveys are costly and so are undertaken infrequently. Figure 21.6 shows the RPI and CPI baskets in 2012.

Figure 21.6 The RPI and CPI Baskets

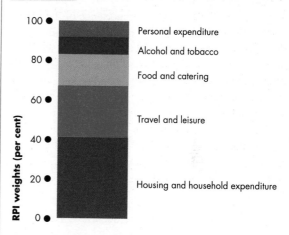

(a) The RPI basket

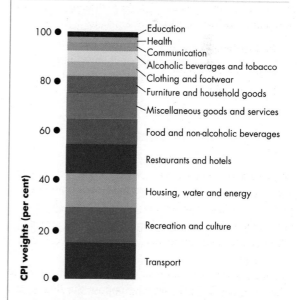

(b) The CPI basket

The RPI basket contains items that the average UK household buys. The CPI basket is broader and contains the goods and services bought by private households, residents of institutions and tourists in the UK.

Source of data: Office for National Statistics.

MyEconLab Animation ————————◆

For the RPI, there are five major categories of which by far the largest is housing and household expenditure. Travel and leisure comes next and is larger than food, alcoholic drinks and tobacco combined.

The ONS breaks down each of these categories into ever smaller ones, right down to distinguishing between packaged and loose new potatoes!

The CPI basket contains 12 major categories of which transport and recreation and culture are the largest.

As you look at the relative importance of the items in the RPI and CPI baskets, remember that they apply to an *average* household. *Individual* households are spread around the average. Think about your own expenditure and compare the basket of goods and services you buy with the RPI and CPI baskets.

Conducting a Monthly Price Survey

Each month, ONS employees check 180,000 prices of more than 700 types of goods and services. They visit shops in about 150 places throughout the UK to see the goods and the prices to ensure accuracy. Because the RPI and CPI aim to measure price *changes*, it is important that the prices recorded each month refer to exactly the same item. For example, suppose the price of a packet of biscuits has decreased but a packet now contains fewer biscuits. Has the price of biscuits decreased, remained the same or increased? The ONS price checker must record the details of changes in quality or packaging so that price changes can be isolated from other changes.

Calculating the Price Index

The RPI and CPI calculations have three steps:

1   Find the cost of the basket at base-period prices.
2   Find the cost of the basket at current-period prices.
3   Calculate the index for the base period and the current period.

We'll work through these three steps for a simple example of an RPI calculation. Suppose the RPI basket contains only two goods and services: oranges and haircuts. We'll construct an annual price index rather than a monthly index with the reference base period 2012 and the current period 2013.

Table 21.1 shows the quantities in the RPI basket and the prices in the base period and current period. Part (a) contains the data for the base period. In that period, consumers bought 10 oranges at £1 each and 5 haircuts at

---

Table 21.1

The RPI: A Simplified Calculation

(a) The cost of the RPI basket at base-period prices: 2012

RPI basket

Item	Quantity	Price	Cost of basket
Oranges	10	£1	£10
Haircuts	5	£8	£40
Cost of the RPI basket at base-period prices			£50

(b) The cost of the RPI basket at current-period prices: 2013

RPI basket

Item	Quantity	Price	Cost of basket
Oranges	10	£2	£20
Haircuts	5	£10	£50
Cost of the RPI basket at current-period prices			£70

£8 each. To find the cost of the RPI basket in the base-period prices, multiply the quantities in the basket by the base-period prices. The cost of oranges is £10 (10 at £1 each), and the cost of haircuts is £40 (5 at £8 each). So total cost of the RPI basket in the base period is £50 (£10 + £40).

Part (b) contains the price data for the current period. The price of an orange increased from £1 to £2, which is a 100 per cent increase (£1 ÷ £1 × 100 = 100). The price of a haircut increased from £8 to £10, which is a 25 per cent increase (£2 ÷ £8 × 100 = 25).

A price index provides a way of averaging these price increases by comparing the cost of the basket rather than the price of each item. To find the cost of the RPI basket in the current period, 2013, multiply the quantities in the basket by their 2013 prices. The cost of oranges is £20 (10 at £2 each), and the cost of haircuts is £50 (5 at £10 each). So the total cost of the basket at current-period prices is £70 (£20 + £50).

You've now taken the first two steps towards calculating a RPI: calculating the cost of the RPI basket in the base period and the current period. The third step uses the numbers you've just calculated to find the value of the RPI in 2012 and 2013.

To calculate the RPI, we use the formula:

$$RPI = \frac{\text{Cost of basket at current-period prices}}{\text{Cost of basket at base-period prices}} \times 100$$

In Table 21.1 you have established that in 2012 the cost of the RPI basket was £50 and in 2013 it was £70. You also know that the base period is 2012. So the cost of the RPI basket at base-period prices is £50. If we use these numbers in the formula above, we can find the RPI for 2012 and 2013. For 2010:

$$\text{RPI in 2012} = \frac{£50}{£50} \times 100 = 100$$

For 2013:

$$\text{RPI in 2013} = \frac{£70}{£50} \times 100 = 140$$

The principles that you've applied in this simplified RPI calculation apply to the more complex calculations performed every month by the ONS.

Measuring the Inflation Rate

A major purpose of the RPI is to measure *changes* in the cost of living and in the value of money. To measure these changes, we calculate the **inflation rate**, which is the percentage change in the price level from one year to the next. To calculate the inflation rate, we use the formula:

$$\text{Inflation rate} = \frac{(\text{RPI this year} - \text{RPI last year})}{\text{RPI last year}} \times 100$$

We can use this formula to calculate the inflation rate in 2012. The RPI in January 2013 was 245.8, and the RPI in January 2012 was 238.0. So the inflation rate during 2012 was:

$$\text{Inflation rate} = \frac{(245.8 - 238.0)}{238.0} \times 100$$

$$= 3.3 \text{ per cent}$$

Distinguishing High Inflation from a High Price Level

Figure 21.7 shows the RPI and the inflation rate from 1970 to 2012. The two parts of the figure are related and emphasise the distinction between high inflation and high prices.

Figure 21.7 The RPI and the Inflation Rate

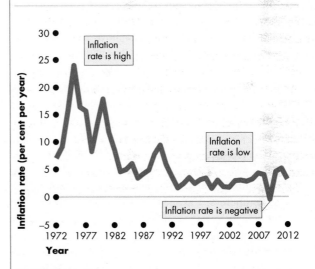

(a) RPI

(b) Inflation rate

During the 1970s and early 1980s, the price level in part (a) increased rapidly and the inflation rate in part (b) was high. After 1985, the price level increased more slowly and the inflation rate was lower. In 2009, the price level fell and inflation was negative – there was deflation.

Source of data: Office for National Statistics.

MyEconLab Animation ◆

When the price *level* in part (a) *rises rapidly*, the inflation rate in part (b) is *high*. When the price level in part (a) *rises slowly*, the inflation rate in part (b) is *low*.

A high inflation rate means that the price level is rising rapidly, while a high price level means that there has been a sustained period of inflation.

When the price level in part (a) falls, as it did in 2009, the inflation rate in part (b) is negative – *deflation*.

The RPI is not a perfect measure of the price level, and changes in the RPI can overstate the inflation rate. Let's look at the sources of bias in price indexes such as the RPI and CPI against which the ONS must guard.

Biased Price Indexes

The main sources of bias in a price index are:

◆ New goods bias
◆ Quality change bias
◆ Substitution bias

New Goods Bias

New goods keep replacing old goods. For example, CDs have replaced LP records and PCs have replaced typewriters. If you want to compare the price level in 2005 with that in 1975, you somehow have to compare the price of a CD and a computer today with that of an LP and typewriter in 1975. Because CDs and PCs are more expensive today than LPs and typewriters, the arrival of these new goods puts an upward bias into the estimate of the price level.

Quality Change Bias

Most goods undergo constant quality improvement. Cars, computers, CD players and even textbooks get better year after year. Quality improvements often increase the price, but such price increases are not inflation. For example, suppose that a 1999 car is 5 per cent better and costs 5 per cent more than a 1995 car. Adjusted for the quality change, the price of the car has not changed. But in calculating the RPI, the price of the car will have increased by 5 per cent.

Estimates have been made of the quality change bias, especially for obvious changes such as those in cars and computers. Allowing for quality improvements changes the inflation picture by 1 percentage point a year, on average, according to some economists. That is, correctly measured, the inflation rate might be as much as 1 percentage point a year less than the published numbers.

Substitution Bias

A change in the price index measures the percentage change in the price of a *fixed* basket of goods and services. But changes in relative prices lead consumers to seek less costly items. For example, by shopping more frequently at discount shops and less frequently at corner shops, consumers can cut the prices they pay. By using discount fares on airlines, they can cut the cost of travel. This kind of substitution of cheaper items for more costly items is not picked up by the price index. Because consumers make such substitutions, a price index based on a fixed basket overstates the effects of a given price change on the inflation rate.

Some Consequences of Bias in the RPI and CPI

The RPI is also used to calculate increases in pensions and other government outlays. So a bias in the RPI could end up swelling government expenditure (and taxes). The CPI is used by the Bank of England to determine whether the interest rate needs to be raised or lowered. So a bias in the CPI could lead to an inappropriate policy decision.

Mindful of these potentially harmful effects, our price indexes are constructed with the greatest possible care to minimise the biases we've just examined.

An Alternative Price Index: The GDP Deflator

The RPI and the CPI are just two of many alternative price level index numbers. Because of the bias in the price indexes, other measures are used for some purposes. One of these alternative price indexes is the **GDP deflator**, which is an index of the prices of all the items in GDP. So the GDP deflator is an index of the prices of the items in consumption expenditure, investment, government expenditure and net exports.

The RPI and CPI measure only the prices of consumption goods and services, so they cover a narrower range of items than does the GDP deflator.

The GDP deflator is calculated using two numbers that you have already met: GDP and real GDP. The formula for the GDP deflator is:

GDP deflator = (Nominal GDP ÷ Real GDP) × 100

This broader price index is appropriate for macroeconomics because it is a comprehensive measure of the cost of the real GDP basket of goods and services.

Another difference between the GDP deflator and the other two indexes is the dating of the expenditure basket. Because real GDP is a *chained volume measure* (see Chapter 20, pp. 474–475), it is based on expenditures in the two adjacent years that are being compared and then 'chained' back to the reference base year. This procedure means that the weights in the GDP deflator are current weights so they avoid some of the sources of bias that we described above.

The main disadvantage of the GDP deflator is that it is calculated only every quarter and with a time lag and is subject to ongoing revisions. These features make it unsuitable for timely and firm estimation of the inflation rate. But it is a good measure for macroeconomic analysis and our efforts to understand economic performance.

The Alternatives Compared

No matter whether we calculate the inflation rate using the RPI, the CPI or the GDP deflator, the number bounces around a good deal from quarter to quarter. How do the alternative measures compare? How different are the inflation stories they tell?

The three measures give different average inflation rates and different inflation fluctuations. From 2000 to 2012, the RPI increased at an average rate of 3.0 per cent per year, the CPI at an average rate of 2.2 per cent per year and the GDP deflator at 2.2 per cent per year.

Figure 21.8 shows the path of each measure of inflation. You can see that the RPI is much more variable than the other two measures and it is the only one to show deflation in 2009. The CPI and the RPI have a mild upward trend while the GDP deflator has no trend.

The key conclusion is that there is no unique measure of inflation and we must carefully determine which measure is most useful for the purpose at hand.

Real Variables in Macroeconomics

You saw in Chapter 20 how we measure real GDP. And you've seen in this chapter how we can use nominal GDP and real GDP to provide another measure of the price level – the GDP deflator. But viewing real GDP as nominal GDP deflated opens up the idea of other real variables. By using the GDP deflator, we can deflate other nominal variables. For example, the *real wage rate* is the nominal wage rate divided by the GDP deflator.

There is one variable that is a bit different – an interest rate. A real interest rate is not a nominal interest rate divided by the price level. You'll learn how to adjust the nominal interest rate for inflation to find the real interest rate in Chapter 23. But all the other real variables of macroeconomics are calculated by dividing a nominal variable by the price level.

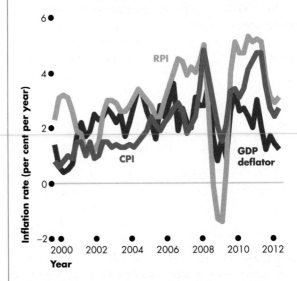

Figure 21.8 Comparing Three Measures of Inflation

The three measures of the inflation rate give different average rates and different fluctuations. The RPI and CPI measures tend to increase and decrease together, but the RPI measure fluctuates more. The GDP deflator measure of inflation is the least volatile.

Source of data: Office for National Statistics.

MyEconLab Animation ———————————◆

REVIEW QUIZ

1 What is the price level?
2 What are the RPI and CPI and how are they calculated?
3 How do we calculate the inflation rate and what is the relationship between the price index and the inflation rate?
4 How might a price index be biased?
5 What problems arise from the biased RPI and CPI?
6 What is the GDP deflator and what are its advantages and disadvantages?

Do these questions in Study Plan 21.3 and get instant feedback. MyEconLab

You've now completed your study of the measurement of macroeconomic performance. Your task in the following chapters is to learn what determines that performance. But first, take a look at the state of the labour market in the euro area in *Reading Between the Lines* on pp. 498–499.

READING BETWEEN THE LINES

Euro Area Unemployment

Eurozone Joblessness Stays at Record High

James Fontanella-Kahn

Joblessness in the euro area stayed at 12 per cent in February, but rose significantly from a year earlier when the unemployment rate was 10.9 per cent, according to Eurostat, the EU's statistical office.

Tough austerity measures, combined with worsening business sentiment and slowing consumer demand, left 33,000 more people out of a job in February compared with January, pushing the overall number of jobless to 19.07m. Compared with a year earlier, an additional 1.78m people are without work. . . .

Youth unemployment – joblessness among under-25s – continued to grow, up to 23.5 per cent from 22.5 per cent during the same period a year ago, an indication that the eurozone debt crisis is hitting future generations the most. . . .

The unemployment figures come as manufacturing output data showed a further contraction in production in March compared with February, a negative change that suggests unemployment could deteriorate further. . . .

The countries with the worst unemployment rates are Greece and Spain, where joblessness is above 26 per cent. But among the member states that suffered the highest annual increase was Cyprus, where unemployment rose from 10.2 per cent to 14 per cent, a rise that highlights the devastating impact of the debt crisis on the small island that was bailed out by international creditors late in March. . . .

FT *Source*: FT.com, 2 April 2013.
© The Financial Times Limited 2013. All Rights Reserved.

 ## The Essence of the Story

◆ The Eurozone unemployment rate was constant at 12 per cent in February 2013, up from 10.9 per cent a year earlier, but the number unemployed increased by 1.78 million to 19.07 million.

◆ The unemployment rate of under-25s was 23.5 per cent, up from 22.5 per cent a year earlier.

◆ Greece and Spain have the highest unemployment rates, which are above 26 per cent.

◆ Cyprus had the largest increase in unemployment, from 10.2 per cent to 14 per cent.

◆ The rise in unemployment was caused by austerity measures, worsening business sentiment, slowing consumer demand and a contraction in manufacturing production.

Economic Analysis

♦ Unemployment in the 17 euro area countries (the EU members that use the euro) is higher than in the UK.

♦ In February 2013, when the UK unemployment rate was 7.8 per cent, the euro area average rate was 12 per cent.

♦ Eurozone unemployment rates have been persistently higher than the UK rate.

♦ Figure 1 shows the history of euro area and UK unemployment since 1992.

♦ In 1992 and 1993, UK unemployment exceeded that of the euro area countries but not by much: unemployment was high everywhere in the recession.

♦ Throughout the 1990s, and until 2004, UK unemployment fell and it bottomed at 4.7 per cent in 2004.

♦ During these same years, euro area unemployment remained high. It rose to 10.8 per cent in 1997, fell for four years to 2001 and then started to rise again.

♦ Why is the euro area unemployment rate so high? Is it because its natural unemployment rate is higher or is it because it has higher cyclical unemployment?

♦ The news article says that the rise in unemployment over 2012 was caused by 'austerity measures, worsening business sentiment, slowing consumer demand and a contraction in manufacturing production'. These forces are cyclical.

♦ The news article also says that Greece and Spain have extremely high unemployment rates. Youth unemployment is also extremely high. These forces are structural and contribute to a high natural unemployment rate.

♦ Figure 2, which graphs the output gaps of the euro area and UK, helps to disentangle the cyclical and natural forces at play in creating unemployment.

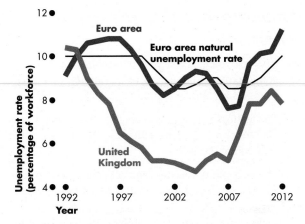

Figure 1   Unemployment Rates in the Euro Area and United Kingdom

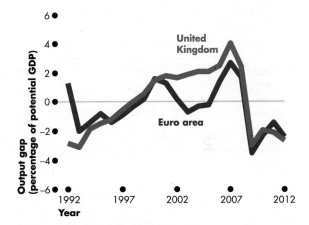

Figure 2   Output Gaps in the Euro Area and United Kingdom

♦ When the output gap is positive (real GDP is greater than potential GDP), cyclical unemployment is negative. And when the output gap is negative (real GDP is less than potential GDP), cyclical unemployment is positive.

♦ Figure 1 contains our estimate of euro area natural unemployment rate, which is consistent with the output gap data in Figure 2.

♦ Most of the euro area's unemployment problem is structural and natural. It does have cyclical unemployment too, but its main challenge is to lower its natural unemployment rate.

SUMMARY

Key Points

Employment and Unemployment
(pp. 484–488)

◆ Unemployment is a serious personal, social and economic problem because it results in lost output and income and human capital.

◆ The unemployment rate averaged 10 per cent during the 1980s, 8.1 per cent during the 1990s and 5.5 per cent during the 2000s.

◆ The unemployment rate, the economic activity rate and the employment rate fluctuate with the business cycle.

◆ Broader measures of unemployment and a narrower measure of long-term unemployment fluctuate in a similar way to the official unemployment rate.

Do Problems 1 to 7 to get a better understanding of employment and unemployment.

Unemployment and Full Employment (pp. 489–491)

◆ People are constantly entering and leaving the state of unemployment.

◆ Three types of unemployment are frictional, structural and cyclical.

◆ When all the unemployment is frictional and structural, the unemployment rate equals the natural unemployment rate, the economy is at full employment and real GDP equals potential GDP.

◆ Over the business cycle, real GDP fluctuates around potential GDP and the unemployment rate fluctuates around the natural unemployment rate.

Do Problems 8 to 13 to get a better understanding of unemployment and full employment.

The Price Level, Inflation and Deflation (pp. 492–497)

◆ Inflation and deflation that are unexpected redistribute income and wealth and divert resources from production.

◆ The Retail Prices Index (RPI) and the Consumer Prices Index (CPI) measure the average prices paid by consumers for a specified basket of goods and services.

◆ The inflation rate is the percentage change in the RPI (or CPI) from one year to the next.

◆ Changes in the RPI and CPI probably overstate the inflation rate because of the bias that arises from new goods, quality changes and substitutions between goods and services.

◆ The RPI bias increases government outlays and the CPI bias might lead to inappropriate interest rate policy.

◆ The GDP deflator is an alternative price level measure that avoids the bias of the RPI and CPI but does not make a large difference to the measured inflation rate.

◆ Real economic variables are calculated by dividing nominal variables by the price level.

Do Problems 14 to 27 to get a better understanding of the price level, inflation and deflation.

Key Terms

Consumer Prices Index (CPI), 493
Cyclical unemployment, 489
Deflation, 492
Discouraged worker, 487
Economic activity rate, 487
Economically active, 485
Economically inactive, 485
Employment rate, 486
Frictional unemployment, 489
Full employment, 489
GDP deflator, 496
Hyperinflation, 492
Inflation, 492
Inflation rate, 495
Natural unemployment rate, 489
Output gap, 490
Price level, 492
Reference base period, 493
Retail Prices Index (RPI), 493
Structural unemployment, 489
Unemployment rate, 486
Workforce, 485
Working-age population, 485

STUDY PLAN PROBLEMS AND APPLICATIONS

Do Problems 1 to 27 in MyEconLab Chapter 21 Study Plan and get instant feedback.   MyEconLab

Employment and Unemployment
(Study Plan 21.1)

1 In 2012, the Labour Force Survey measured the economically active at 32,067,000, employment at 29,519,000 and the working-age population at 50,419,800. Calculate for 2012:

   a The unemployment rate.

   b The economic activity rate.

   c The employment rate.

2 During 2012, the working-age population increased by 187,000, employment increased by 353,000 and the number of economically active people increased by 337,000. Use this information along with the data in Problem 1 to calculate the change in unemployment during 2012.

Use the following information in Problems 3 and 4.

In July 2012, in the economy of Sandy Island, 10,000 people were employed, 1,000 were unemployed and 5,000 were economically inactive.

3 Calculate the unemployment rate and the employment rate in July 2012.

4 During August 2012, 80 people lost their jobs and didn't look for new ones, 20 people quit their jobs and retired, 150 unemployed people were hired, 50 people quit the workforce and became economically inactive and 40 people entered the workforce to look for work.

   Calculate the number of people unemployed, the number of people employed and the unemployment rate at the end of August 2012.

Use the following information in Problems 5 and 6.

The UK unemployment rate was 8.4 per cent in 2011 and 7.8 per cent in 2012.

5 Predict what happened to unemployment between 2011 and 2012 if the economically-active population remained the same.

6 Predict what happened to the economically active population if the number of people unemployed remained the same.

7 **Eight Million People 'Economically Inactive'**

   The number of people who are neither in work nor seeking employment reached 8.08 million in the last three months of last year, the highest on record. In all, 21.3 per cent of working-age adults are now 'economically inactive' and 78,000 of the inactive were recorded as 'discouraged' workers.

   Source: *The Telegraph*, 17 February 2010

What is a discouraged worker? Explain how an increase in discouraged workers influences the official unemployment rate.

Unemployment and Full Employment (Study Plan 21.2)

Use the following news clip in Problems 8 to 10.

UK Employment Increases by 154,000

For October to December 2012, compared with the previous three months, the number of people in employment increased and the number of people unemployed decreased. The rise in the number of people in work was 154,000 comparing October to December 2012 to the previous three months. Overall there were 29.73 million people employed of which 73 per cent were people working full-time and 27 per cent people working part-time.

   Source: Office for National Statistics, 20 February 2013

8 With the demand for full-time and part-time workers rising, explain which type of unemployment is most likely to fall if the recovery continues.

9 As the economic recovery gains momentum, explain which type of unemployment might decrease.

10 Would you expect the increase in employment to lower the natural unemployment rate in the UK?

Use the following news clip in Problems 11 to 13.

UK Unemployment Total Hits Highest in 17 Years

Over June to August 2011, 2.57 million people were out of work. Economist Alan Clarke of Scotia Capital said 'The economy is growing at half the pace it needs to in order to keep unemployment stable and it is probably going to get worse.' As the total number of unemployed people rose by 114,000 during the quarter, the unemployment rate reached 8.1 per cent, its highest since the autumn of 1996.

   Source: *The Guardian*, 12 October 2011

11 Based on information in the news clip, how does the UK unemployment rate in mid-2011 compare with that in earlier recessions?

12 Why does Alan Clarke say the unemployment rate will increase further?

13 Given the information in the news clip, does the jump in the UK unemployment rate in mid-2011 look like an increase in the natural unemployment rate or an increase in the cyclical unemployment rate? What information would you need on the output gap to confirm your answer?

The Price Level, Inflation and Deflation (Study Plan 21.3)

Use the following information in Problems 14 and 15.

The people on Coral Island buy only juice and cloth. The RPI basket contains the quantities bought in 2012. The average household spent €60 on juice and €30 on cloth in 2012 when the price of juice was €2 a bottle and the price of cloth was €5 a metre. In the current year, 2013, juice is €4 a bottle and cloth is €6 a metre.

14 Calculate the RPI basket and the percentage of the household's budget spent on juice in 2012.

15 Calculate the RPI and the inflation rate in 2013.

Use the following data in Problems 16 to 18.

The Office for National Statistics reported the following RPI data:

> June 2011: 235.2
>
> June 2012: 241.8
>
> June 2013: 249.7

16 Calculate the inflation rates for the years ended June 2012 and June 2013. How did the inflation rate change in 2013?

17 Why might these RPI numbers be biased?

18 Does the GDP deflator help to avoid some of the bias in the RPI numbers?

19 Inflation Can Act as a Safety Valve

Workers will more readily accept a real wage cut that arises from an increase in the price level than a cut in their nominal wage rate.

Source: *FT.com*, 28 May 2009

How does inflation influence the real wage rate?

20 The IMF *World Economic Outlook* reports the following price level data:

Region	2011	2012	2013
US	224.9	229.6	233.8
Eurozone	102.7	105.3	107.1
Japan	99.7	99.7	99.7

a In which region was inflation the highest in 2012 and 2013?

b Describe the path of the price level in Japan.

21 We are Heading Back to Massive Inflation

Inflation is an arbitrary tax that falls hardest on those who have done the right thing: it penalises thrift, disadvantages businesses and weakens competitiveness.

Source: *The Telegraph*, 13 January 2011

a Explain why unexpected inflation 'penalises thrift'.

b Explain why unexpected inflation 'disadvantages businesses'.

c Explain why unexpected inflation 'weakens competitiveness'.

Use the following data in Problems 22 to 24.

The Office for National Statistics reported that the annual CPI inflation rate in June 2013 was 2.9 per cent and the annual RPI inflation rate was 3.3 per cent.

Food and non-alcoholic drink prices fell by 0.5 per cent compared with a fall of 0.1 per cent a year earlier, bread and cereal prices fell by 0.4 per cent and meat prices rose by 0.7 per cent.

Clothing and footwear prices fell by 1.9 per cent, compared with a fall of 4.2 per cent a year earlier, while furniture and household equipment rose 1.9 per cent.

Air fares fell by 2.8 per cent, compared with a rise of 7.4 per cent a year earlier. Fuel prices didn't change but fell by 0.4 per cent a year earlier. Recreation and culture prices fell by 0.2 per cent this year but rose by 0.1 per cent a year earlier.

22 Which components of the CPI basket experienced price increases (a) faster and (b) slower than the average?

23 The change in which price contributed most to the 2.9 per cent increase in the CPI?

24 Distinguish between the CPI and RPI. Why might the RPI inflation rate be higher than the CPI inflation rate?

25 What is the GDP deflator and what are the main differences between it and the RPI and CPI?

26 Why might the GDP deflator provide a more reliable indicator of the inflation rate than the CPI and RPI?

27 If the GDP deflator does provide a more reliable indicator of the inflation rate than the CPI and RPI, why might we nevertheless use the CPI and RPI?

ADDITIONAL PROBLEMS AND APPLICATIONS

Do these problems in MyEconLab if assigned by your lecturer.

MyEconLab

Employment and Unemployment

28 What is the unemployment rate supposed to measure and why is it an imperfect measure?

29 The Office for National Statistics reported the following data for 2012:

Economic activity rate: 63.6 per cent

Working-age population: 50.34 million

Employment rate: 58.7 per cent

Calculate the:

a Workforce.

b Number of people employed.

c Unemployment rate.

30 In 2009, the Labour Force Survey measured the economically active at 30.6 million, employment at 28.2 million and the working-age population at 39.8 million. Calculate for 2009:

a The unemployment rate.

b The economic activity rate.

c The employment rate.

31 The Office for National Statistics reported the following reasons for economic inactivity in August to October 2010 (the numbers are thousands):

Students	2,209
Looking after family at home	2,265
Temporarily sick	175
Long-term sick	2,216
Discouraged workers	67
Retired	1,530
Other	823
Do not want a job	6,969
Want a job	2,367

a Which of the above categories were counted in the official unemployment rate? Explain your answer.

b Which of the above categories of reasons for economic inactivity would you expect to fluctuate with real GDP over the business cycle?

c What are the implications of your answer to part (b) for the mismeasurement of the unemployment rate?

32 A high unemployment rate tells us that a large percentage of the workforce is unemployed, but it doesn't tell us why the unemployment rate is high. What other information would be useful to tell us why the unemployment rate is high?

33 Why might the official unemployment rate underestimate the underutilisation of labour resources?

34 Some Firms Struggle to Hire Despite High Unemployment

With about 15 million Americans looking for work, some employers are swamped with job applicants, but many employers can't hire enough workers. During the recession, millions of middle-skill, middle-wage jobs disappeared. Now with the recovery, these people can't find the skilled jobs that they seek and have a hard time adjusting to lower-skilled work with less pay.

Source: *The Wall Street Journal*, 9 August 2010

a What has changed in the jobs market?

b If the government decided to extend the period over which a worker can claim unemployment benefits, how would the cost of unemployment change?

Unemployment and Full Employment

Use the following data in Problems 35 to 37.

The IMF *World Economic Outlook* reports the following unemployment rates:

Region	2012	2013
US	8.1	7.7
Eurozone	11.4	12.3
Japan	4.4	4.1

35 What do these numbers tell us about the phase of the business cycle in the three regions in 2013?

36 What do these numbers tell us about the relative size of the natural unemployment rates in the three regions?

37 Do these numbers tell us anything about the relative size of the economic activity rate and the employment rate in the three regions?

38 UK Has Lost Two Million Jobs Since Recession

A report by the Institute for Public Policy Research calculates that between 1.5 million and 2 million jobs need to be generated to return the UK from its current employment rate of 70.7 per cent to its pre-recession employment rate of 73 per cent.

Source: *The Telegraph*, 14 September 2011

a Based on the news clip, what might be the main source of increased unemployment?

b Based on the news clip, what might be the main type of unemployment that increased?

c What is the employment rate referred to in the news clip and how does the unemployment rate affect it?

The Price Level, Inflation and Deflation

39 Explain how inflation can redistribute income. Why does an unexpected rise in the inflation rate make workers worse off? Who is made better off? Why does correctly anticipated inflation not have these distributional effects?

40 Explain how inflation can redistribute wealth. Why does an unexpected rise in the inflation rate make lenders worse off? Who is made better off? Why does correctly anticipated inflation not have these distributional effects?

41 Explain how inflation can create jobs. Does inflation always create jobs and deflation always destroy them? Provide reasons for your answer.

42 A French tourist who visits the UK every year complains to her UK friend that prices have increased by a large amount since her previous visit. Her UK friend expresses surprise. She thinks prices have risen but not by much. Explain to these two people why both of them could be correct. Also explain which price index has most likely increased by more, the RPI or the CPI.

43 A typical family on Sandy Island consumes only juice and cloth. Last year, which was the reference base year, the family spent €40 on juice and €25 on cloth. Last year, juice was €4 a bottle and cloth was €5 a metre. This year, juice is €4 a bottle and cloth is €6 a metre. Calculate:

  a The RPI basket.

  b The RPI in the current year.

  c The inflation rate in the current year.

44 Smartphones get ever smarter, and because of competition among their makers they get ever cheaper. Because the prices of smartphones are falling and the quality of smartphones is improving, does the measured inflation rate equal the true inflation rate, or is there a bias? If there is a bias, what is its direction?

45 Amazon.com agreed to pay its workers $20 an hour in 1999 and $22 an hour in 2001. The price level for these years was 166 in 1999 and 180 in 2001. Calculate the real wage rate in each year. Did these workers really get a pay raise between 1999 and 2001?

46 In the third quarter of 2010, UK real GDP was £331.2 billion and nominal GDP was £365.9 billion. In the third quarter of 2009, real GDP was £322.7 billion and nominal GDP was £348.1 billion. Calculate the GDP deflator in these two quarters and the inflation rate over the year.

Economics in the News

47 After you have studied *Reading Between the Lines* on pp. 498–499, answer the following questions.

  a Compare the natural unemployment rate in the euro area with that in the UK shown in Figure 21.5(b) on p. 490.

  b What happened to the unemployment rate in Cyprus in February 2013? Would that be a change in cyclical unemployment or natural unemployment?

  c Why is the unemployment rate of younger people so much higher than that of older people?

  d If the euro area can end its recession and bring about a strong expansion, how low would you expect its unemployment rate to go? Why?

48 Out of a Job and Out of Luck at 54

Too young to retire, too old to get a new job. That's how many older workers feel after getting the sack and spending time on the unemployment line. Many lack the skills to craft resumes and search online, experts say. Older workers took an average of 21.1 weeks to get a new job in 2007, about 5 weeks longer than younger people. 'Older workers will be more adversely affected because of the time it takes to transition into another job', said Deborah Russell, AARP's director of workforce issues.

Source: CNN, 21 May 2008

  a What type of unemployment might older workers be more prone to experience?

  b Explain how the unemployment rate of older workers is influenced by the business cycle.

  c Why might older unemployed workers become discouraged workers during a recession?

49 Jaguar Land Rover Job Applications 'Overwhelm' Halewood

More than 14,000 people applied for 1,500 new jobs at a new Jaguar Land Rover car plant at Halewood on Merseyside. The jobs have been created by the decision to produce a new Range Rover at this plant.

Source: BBC, 15 January 2010

  a What does this news clip suggest about unemployment on Merseyside?

  b How will this new car plant change the economic activity rate, the employment rate and the working-age population on Merseyside?

  c How will this new car plant change the natural unemployment rate and the cyclical unemployment rate on Merseyside?

22 Economic Growth

After studying this chapter you will be able to:

◆ Define and calculate the growth rate of real GDP and explain the implications of sustained growth

◆ Describe the economic growth trends in the UK and other countries and regions

◆ Explain what makes potential GDP grow

◆ Explain the sources of labour productivity growth

◆ Explain the theories of economic growth and policies to increase its rate

The BRICS nations – Brazil, Russia, India, China and South Africa – are home to 43 per cent of the world's population and produce 27 per cent of the world's real GDP. But their real GDP is growing at a rapid 7 per cent a year, more than double the real GDP growth rate in the rest of the world.

In this chapter, we study the forces that make real GDP grow. And in *Reading Between the Lines* at the end of the chapter, we look at the growth challenge faced by South Africa and the lessons it can learn from its tiny neighbour, Botswana.

The Basics of Economic Growth

Economic growth is a sustained expansion of production possibilities measured as the increase in real GDP over a given period.

Even slow economic growth maintained over many centuries brings great wealth. That is the story of human economic growth up to the Industrial Revolution that began around 1760.

Rapid economic growth maintained over only a small number of years can transform a poor nation into a rich one. That has been the story of Hong Kong, South Korea and Taiwan, and it is the story of China, India and some other Asian economies today.

The absence of growth can condemn a nation to devastating poverty. Such has been the fate of Sierra Leone, Somalia, Zambia and much of the rest of Africa.

The goal of this chapter is to help you to understand why some economies expand rapidly and others stagnate. We'll begin by learning how to calculate the economic growth rate and by discovering the magic of sustained growth.

Calculating Growth Rates

We express the **growth rate** as the annual percentage change of real GDP. To calculate this growth rate, we use the formula:

$$\text{Real GDP growth rate} = \frac{\text{Real GDP in current year} - \text{Real GDP in previous year}}{\text{Real GDP in previous year}} \times 100$$

For example, if real GDP in the current year is £1,320 billion and if real GDP in the previous year was £1,200 billion, then the economic growth rate is 10 per cent.

The growth rate of real GDP tells us how rapidly the *total* economy is expanding. This measure is useful for telling us about potential changes in the balance of economic power among nations. But it does not tell us about changes in the standard of living.

The standard of living depends on **real GDP per person** (also called *per capita* real GDP), which is real GDP divided by the population. So the contribution of real GDP growth to the change in the standard of living depends on the growth rate of real GDP per person. We use the above formula to calculate this growth rate, replacing real GDP with real GDP per person.

Suppose, for example, that in the current year, when real GDP is £1,320 billion, the population is 60.6 million. Then real GDP per person is £1,320 billion divided by 60.6 million, which equals £21,782. And suppose that in the previous year, when real GDP was £1,200 billion, the population was 60 million. Then real GDP per person in that year was £1,200 billion divided by 60 million, which equals £20,000. Use these two real GDP per person values with the growth formula above to calculate the growth rate of real GDP per person. That is,

$$\text{Real GDP per person growth rate} = \frac{£21,782 - £20,000}{£20,000} \times 100 = 8.9 \text{ per cent}$$

The growth rate of real GDP per person can also be calculated (approximately) by subtracting the population growth rate from the real GDP growth rate. In the example you've just worked through, the growth rate of real GDP is 10 per cent. The population changes from 60 million to 60.6 million, so the population growth rate is 1 per cent. The growth rate of real GDP per person is approximately equal to 10 per cent minus 1 per cent, which equals 9 per cent.

Real GDP per person grows only if real GDP grows faster than the population grows. If the growth rate of the population exceeds the growth of real GDP, real GDP per person falls.

Economic Growth versus Business Cycle Expansion

Real GDP can increase for two distinct reasons: the economy might be returning to full employment in an expansion phase of the business cycle, or potential GDP might be increasing.

The return to full employment in an expansion phase of the business cycle isn't economic growth. It is just taking up the slack that resulted from the previous recession. The expansion of potential GDP is economic growth.

Figure 22.1 illustrates this distinction using the production possibilities frontier (the *PPF* that you studied in Chapter 2). A return to full employment in a business cycle expansion is a movement from inside the *PPF* at a point such as *A* to a point on the *PPF* such as *B*.

Economic growth is the expansion of production possibilities. It is an outward movement of the *PPF* such as the shift from *PPF*$_0$ to *PPF*$_1$ and the movement from point *B* on *PPF*$_0$ to point *C* on *PPF*$_1$.

The growth rate of potential GDP measures the pace of expansion of production possibilities and smooths

Figure 22.1 Economic Growth and the Business Cycle

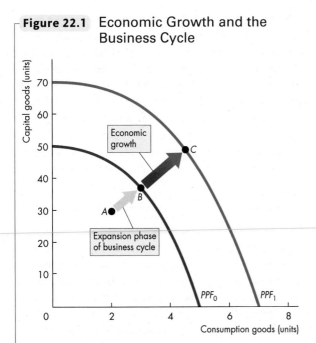

The increase in aggregate production in the move from point A inside PPF_0 to point B on PPF_0 is an expansion phase of the business cycle and it occurs with no change in production possibilities. Such an expansion is not economic growth. The increase in aggregate production in the move from point B on PPF_0 to point C on PPF_1 is economic growth – an expansion of production possibilities shown by an outward shift of the PPF.

MyEconLab Animation ————————◆

Figure 22.2 Growth Rates of Real GDP and Potential GDP

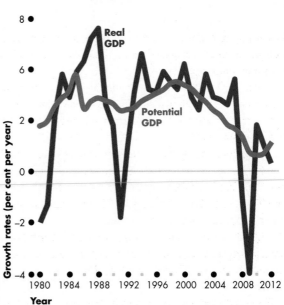

The annual growth rate of real GDP fluctuates widely over the business cycle and masks changes in the underlying trend growth rate. The annual growth rate of potential GDP provides information about changes in the trend growth rate. Both the growth rate of potential GDP and the trend growth rate of real GDP have fallen since 2000.

Sources of data: Office for National Statistics and OECD.

MyEconLab Animation ————————◆

out the business cycle fluctuations in the growth rate of real GDP.

Figure 22.2 shows how the growth rate of potential GDP (red curve) smooths the more erratic fluctuations in the growth rate of real GDP. Business cycle fluctuations in the real GDP growth rate mask the underlying *trend* growth rate revealed by the growth rate of *potential* GDP.

The Magic of Sustained Growth

Sustained growth of real GDP per person can transform a poor society into a wealthy one. The reason is that economic growth is like compound interest.

Compound Interest

Suppose that you put £100 in the bank and earn 5 per cent a year interest on it. After one year, you have £105.

If you leave that £105 in the bank for another year, you earn 5 per cent interest on the original £100 and on the £5 interest that you earned last year. You are now earning interest on interest! The next year, things get even better. Then you earn 5 per cent on the original £100 and on the interest earned in the first year and the second year. You are even earning interest on the interest that you earned on the interest of the first year.

Your money in the bank is growing at a rate of 5 per cent a year. Before too many years have passed, your initial deposit of £100 will have grown to £200. But after how many years?

The answer is provided by a formula called the **Rule of 70**, which states that the number of years it takes for the level of any variable to double is approximately 70 divided by the annual percentage growth rate of the variable. Using the Rule of 70, you can now calculate how many years it takes your £100 to become £200. It is 70 divided by 5, which is 14 years.

Figure 22.3 The Rule of 70

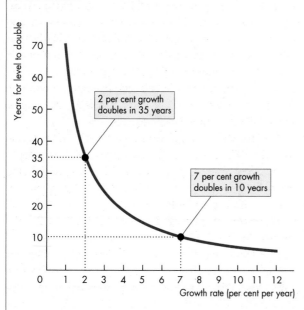

Growth rate (per cent per year)	Years for level to double
1	70.0
2	35.0
3	23.3
4	17.5
5	14.0
6	11.7
7	10.0
8	8.8
9	7.8
10	7.0
11	6.4
12	5.8

The number of years it takes for the level of a variable to double is approximately 70 divided by the annual percentage growth rate.

Applying the Rule of 70

The Rule of 70 applies to any variable, so it applies to real GDP per person. Figure 22.3 shows the doubling time for growth rates of 1 per cent per year to 12 per cent per year.

You can see that real GDP per person doubles in 70 years (70 divided by 1) – an average human lifespan – if the growth rate is 1 per cent a year. It doubles in 35 years if the growth rate is 2 per cent a year and in just 10 years if the growth rate is 7 per cent a year.

We can use the Rule of 70 to answer other questions about economic growth. For example, in 2010, US real GDP per person was approximately 4 times that of China. China's recent growth rate of real GDP per person was 10 per cent a year. If this growth rate were maintained, how long would it take China's real GDP per person to reach that of the US in 2010?

The answer, provided by the Rule of 70, is 14 years. China's real GDP per person doubles in 7 (70 divided by 10) years. It doubles again to 4 times its current level in another 7 years. So after 14 years of growth at 10 per cent a year, China's real GDP per person will be 4 times its current level and equal that of the US in 2010. Of course, after 14 years, US real GDP per person would have increased, so China would still not have caught up to the US. But at the current growth rates, China's real GDP per person will equal that of the US by 2026.

 REVIEW QUIZ

1   What is economic growth and how do we calculate its rate?
2   What is the relationship between the growth rate of real GDP and the growth rate of real GDP per person?
3   Use the Rule of 70 to calculate the growth rate that leads to a doubling of real GDP per person in 20 years.

Do these questions in Study Plan 22.1 and get instant feedback.   MyEconLab

You now know the basics of economic growth. Let's next review the trends in economic growth in the UK and around the world.

Long-Term Growth Trends

You've seen the power of economic growth to increase incomes. At a 1 per cent growth rate, it takes a human life span to double the standard of living. But at a 7 per cent growth rate, the standard of living doubles every decade. How fast is our economy growing? How fast are other economies growing? Are poor countries catching up to rich ones, or do the gaps between the rich and poor persist or even widen? Let's answer these questions.

Long-Term Growth in the UK Economy

Figure 22.4 shows real GDP per person in the UK for the 100 years from 1912 to 2012. The red line is the path of real GDP and the black line is potential GDP. The trend in potential GDP per person tells us about economic growth. Fluctuations around potential GDP tell us about the business cycle.

Some extraordinary events dominate the first 50 years in this graph: two world wars and two periods, the 1920s and the 1930s, of extreme recession and depression. The recession of 2008–2009 is clearly visible in the graph as a serious event, but it is not on the scale of severity of those interwar depressions.

For the century as a whole, the average growth rate was 1.6 per cent a year, which represents a doubling of real GDP per person every 44 years.

But the economic growth rate has varied. During the years to 1952, it was 1.2 per cent per year – too slow to double real GDP per person in the 50-year period. In the 50 years to 2012, the growth rate was 2.1 per cent per year – doubling the level in 33 years.

Growth was most rapid during the 1960s at 2.2 per cent per year and the 1980s at 2.8 per cent per year.

A major goal of this chapter is to explain why our economy grows and why the long-term growth rate varies. Another goal is to explain variations in the economic growth rate across countries. Let's look at some facts about other countries' growth rates.

Figure 22.4 One Hundred Years of Economic Growth in the UK

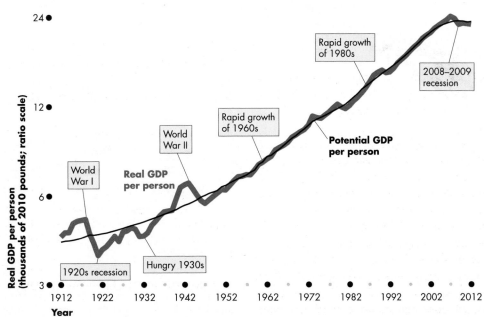

During the 100 years from 1912 to 2012, real GDP per person in the UK grew by 1.6 per cent a year, on average. The growth rate was slower during the first 50 years, at 1.2 per cent (58 years to double) than in the second 50 years at 2.1 per cent (33 years to double). Growth was fastest during the 1960s and the 1980s.

Sources of data: Charles Feinstein, *National Income Expenditure and Output of the United Kingdom 1855–1965*, Cambridge, Cambridge University Press, 1972; Office for National Statistics; and OECD.

MyEconLab Animation ◆

Real GDP Growth in the World Economy

Figure 22.5 shows real GDP per person in the US and in other countries between 1960 and 2010. Part (a) looks at the seven richest countries – known as the G7 nations. Among these nations, the US has the highest real GDP per person. In 2010, Canada had the second-highest real GDP per person, ahead of Japan and France, Germany, Italy and the UK (collectively the Europe Big 4).

During the 50 years shown here, the gaps between the US, Canada and the Europe Big 4 have been almost constant. But starting from a long way below, Japan grew fastest. It caught up to Europe in 1982 and to Canada in 1990. But during the 1990s, Japan's economy stagnated.

Many other countries are growing more slowly than, and falling farther behind, the US. Figure 22.5(b) looks at some of these countries.

Real GDP per person in Central and South America was 28 per cent of the US level in 1960 and reached 30 per cent of the US level by 1980, but then growth slowed, and by 2010 real GDP per person in these countries was 23 per cent of the US level.

In Eastern Europe, real GDP per person has grown more slowly than anywhere except Africa, and fell from 32 per cent of the US level in 1980 to 19 per cent in 2003 and then increased again to 22 per cent in 2010.

Real GDP per person in Africa, the world's poorest continent, fell from 10 per cent of the US level in 1960 to 5 per cent in 2007 and then increased slightly to 6 per cent in 2010.

Figure 22.5   Economic Growth Around the World: Catch-Up or Not?

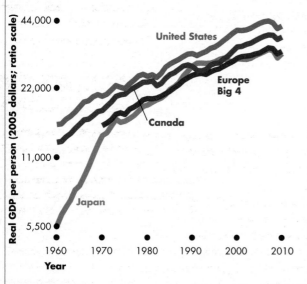

(a) Catch-up?

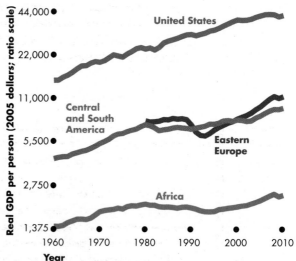

(b) No catch-up?

Real GDP per person has grown throughout the world. Among the rich industrial countries in part (a), real GDP per person has grown slightly faster in the US than in Canada and the four big countries of Europe (France, Germany, Italy and the UK). Japan had the fastest growth rate before 1973, but then growth slowed and Japan's economy stagnated during the 1990s.

Among a wider range of countries shown in part (b), growth rates have been lower than that of the US. The gaps between the real GDP per person in the US and in these countries have widened. The gap between the real GDP per person in the US and Africa has widened by a large amount.

Source of data: Alan Heston, Robert Summers and Bettina Aten, Penn World Table Version 7.1, Center for International Comparisons at the University of Pennsylvania, July 2012.

ECONOMICS IN ACTION

Fast Trains on the Same Track

Five Asian economies, Hong Kong, Korea, Singapore, Taiwan and China, have experienced spectacular growth, which you can see in Figure 1. During the 1960s, real GDP per person in these economies ranged from 3 to 28 per cent of that in the US. But by 2010, real GDP per person in Singapore and Hong Kong had surpassed that of the US.

The figure also shows that China is catching up rapidly but from a long way behind. China's real GDP per person increased from 3 per cent of the US level in 1960 to 26 per cent in 2010.

The Asian economies shown here are like fast trains running on the same track at similar speeds and with a roughly constant gap between them. Singapore and Hong Kong are hooked together as the lead train, which runs about 20 years in front of Taiwan and Korea and about 40 years in front of China.

Real GDP per person in Korea in 2010 was similar to that in Hong Kong in 1988, and real GDP in China in 2010 was similar to that of Hong Kong in 1976. Between 1976 and 2010, Hong Kong transformed itself from a poor developing economy into one of the richest economies in the world.

The rest of China is now doing what Hong Kong has done. China has a population 200 times that of Hong Kong and more than 4 times that of the US. So if China continues its rapid growth, the world economy will change dramatically.

As these fast-growing Asian economies catch up with the US, we can expect their growth rates to slow. But it will be surprising if China's growth rate slows much before it has closed the gap on the US.

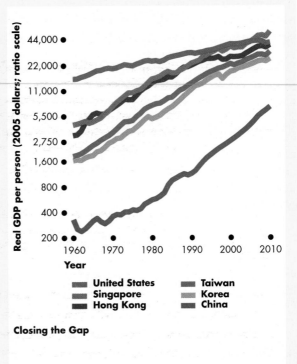

Closing the Gap

Source of data: Alan Heston, Robert Summers and Bettina Aten, Penn World Table Version 7.1, Center for International Comparisons at the University of Pennsylvania, July 2012.

Even modest differences in economic growth rates sustained over a number of years bring enormous differences in the standard of living. So the facts about economic growth in the UK and around the world raise some big questions.

What are the preconditions for economic growth and what sustains it? How can we identify the sources of economic growth and measure the contribution that each source makes? What can we do to increase the sustainable rate of economic growth?

We're now going to address these questions. We start by seeing how potential GDP is determined and what makes it grow. You will see that labour productivity growth is the key to rising living standards, and go on to explore the sources of this growth.

REVIEW QUIZ

1 What has been the average growth rate in the UK over the past 100 years? In which period was growth most rapid and in which was it slowest?

2 Describe the gaps between the levels of real GDP per person in the US and other countries. For which countries are the gaps narrowing? For which countries are the gaps widening? For which countries are the gaps remaining unchanged?

3 Compare the growth rates and levels of real GDP per person in Hong Kong, South Korea, Singapore, Taiwan, China and the US. How far is China behind the other Asian economies?

Do these questions in Study Plan 22.2 and get instant feedback.

MyEconLab

How Potential GDP Grows

Economic growth occurs when real GDP increases. But a one-shot rise in real GDP or a recovery from recession isn't economic growth. Economic growth is a sustained, year-after-year increase in potential GDP.

So what determines potential GDP and what are the forces that make it grow?

What Determines Potential GDP?

Labour, capital, land and entrepreneurship produce real GDP, and the productivity of the factors of production determines the quantity of real GDP that can be produced.

The quantity of land is fixed, and on any given day the quantities of entrepreneurial ability and capital are also fixed and their productivities are given. The quantity of labour employed is the only variable factor of production. Potential GDP is the level of real GDP when the quantity of labour employed is the full-employment quantity.

To determine potential GDP, we use a model with two components:

◆ An aggregate production function
◆ An aggregate labour market

Aggregate Production Function

When you studied the limits to production in Chapter 2 (see p. 32), you learned that the production possibilities frontier is the boundary between the combinations of goods and services that can be produced and those that cannot. We're now going to think about the production possibilities frontier for two special 'goods': real GDP and the quantity of leisure time.

Think of real GDP as a number of big shopping carts. Each cart contains some of each kind of different goods and services produced, and one cartload of items costs £1 billion. To say that real GDP is £1.5 trillion (or £1,500 billion) means that it is 1,500 very big shopping carts of goods and services.

The quantity of leisure time is the number of hours spent not working. Each leisure hour could be spent working. If we spent all our time taking leisure, we would do no work and produce nothing. Real GDP would be zero. The more leisure we forgo, the greater is the quantity of labour we supply and the greater is the quantity of real GDP produced.

But labour hours are not all equally productive. We use our most productive hours first, and as more hours are worked, less and less productive hours are used. So for each additional hour of leisure forgone (each additional hour of labour), real GDP increases by successively smaller amounts.

The **aggregate production function** is the relationship that tells us how real GDP changes as the quantity of labour changes when all other influences on production remain the same. Figure 22.6 shows this relationship – the curve labelled *PF*. An increase in the quantity of labour (and a corresponding decrease in leisure hours) brings a movement along the production function and an increase in real GDP.

Aggregate Labour Market

In macroeconomics, we pretend that there is one large labour market that determines the quantity of labour employed and the quantity of real GDP produced. To see how this aggregate labour market works, we study the demand for labour, the supply of labour and labour market equilibrium.

The Demand for Labour
The demand for labour is the relationship between the quantity of labour demanded and the real wage rate. The

Figure 22.6 The Aggregate Production Function

An increase in labour hours brings an increase in real GDP

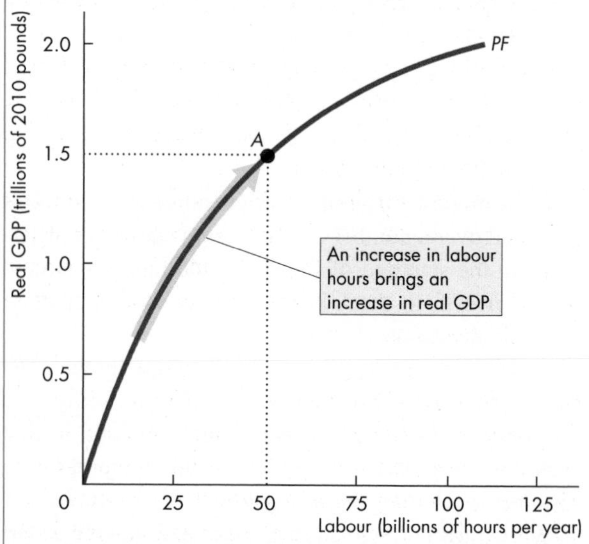

At point *A* on the aggregate production function *PF*, 50 billion hours of labour produce £1.5 trillion of real GDP.

MyEconLab Animation ────────────────────◆

quantity of labour demanded is the number of labour hours hired by all the firms in the economy during a given period. This quantity depends on the price of labour, which is the real wage rate.

The **real wage rate** is the quantity of goods and services that an hour of labour earns. It contrasts with the money wage rate, which is the number of pounds that an hour of labour earns. The real wage rate is calculated by dividing the money wage rate by the price level.

The *real* wage rate influences the quantity of labour demanded because what matters to firms is not the number of pounds they pay (money wage rate) but how much output they must sell to earn those pounds.

The quantity of labour demanded *increases* as the real wage rate *decreases* – the demand for labour curve slopes downward. Why? The answer lies in the shape of the production function.

You've seen that along the production function, each additional hour of labour increases real GDP by successively smaller amounts. This tendency has a name: *the law of diminishing returns*. Because of diminishing returns, firms will hire more labour only if the real wage rate falls to match the fall in the extra output produced by that labour.

The Supply of Labour

The *supply of labour* is the relationship between the quantity of labour supplied and the real wage rate. The quantity of labour supplied is the number of labour hours that all the households in the economy plan to work during a given period. This quantity depends on the real wage rate.

The *real* wage rate influences the quantity of labour supplied because what matters to households is not the number of pounds they earn (money wage rate) but what they can buy with those pounds.

The quantity of labour supplied *increases* as the real wage rate *increases* – the supply of labour curve slopes upward. At a higher real wage rate, more people choose to work, and more people choose to work longer hours if they can earn more per hour.

Labour Market Equilibrium

The price of labour is the real wage rate. The forces of supply and demand operate in labour markets to eliminate a shortage or a surplus, but a shortage or a surplus of labour brings only a gradual change in the real wage rate. If there is a shortage of labour, the real wage rate rises to eliminate it; and if there is a surplus of labour, the real wage rate eventually falls to eliminate it. When there is neither a shortage nor a surplus, the

labour market is in equilibrium – a full-employment equilibrium.

Figure 22.7 illustrates labour market equilibrium. The demand for labour curve is *LD* and the supply of labour curve is *LS*. This labour market is in equilibrium at a real wage rate of £20 an hour, and 50 billion hours a year are employed.

If the real wage rate exceeds £20 an hour, the quantity of labour supplied exceeds the quantity demanded and there is a surplus of labour. When there is a surplus of labour, the real wage rate falls towards the equilibrium real wage rate where the surplus is eliminated.

If the real wage rate is less than £20 an hour, the quantity of labour demanded exceeds the quantity supplied and there is a shortage of labour. When there is a shortage of labour, the real wage rate rises towards the equilibrium real wage rate where the shortage is eliminated.

If the real wage rate is £20 an hour, the quantity of labour demanded equals the quantity supplied and there is neither a shortage nor a surplus of labour. In this

Figure 22.7 Labour Market Equilibrium

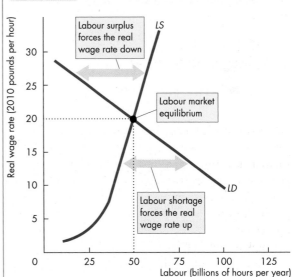

Labour market equilibrium occurs when the quantity of labour demanded equals the quantity of labour supplied. The equilibrium real wage rate is £20 per hour and equilibrium employment is 50 billion hours per year.

At a wage rate above £20 an hour, there is a surplus of labour and the real wage rate falls to eliminate the surplus. At a wage rate below £20 an hour, there is a shortage of labour and the real wage rate rises to eliminate the shortage.

MyEconLab Animation ───────────────◆

situation, there is no pressure in either direction on the real wage rate. So the real wage rate remains constant and the market is in equilibrium. At this equilibrium real wage rate and level of employment, the economy is at full employment.

Potential GDP

You've seen that the production function tells us the quantity of real GDP that a given amount of labour can produce – see Figure 22.8. The quantity of real GDP produced increases as the quantity of labour increases. At the equilibrium quantity of labour, the economy is at full employment and the quantity of real GDP at full employment is potential GDP. So the full-employment quantity of labour produces potential GDP.

Figure 22.8 illustrates the determination of potential GDP. Part (a) shows the labour market. At the equilibrium real wage rate, equilibrium employment is 50 billion hours. Part (b) shows the production function. With 50 billion hours of labour, the economy can produce a real GDP of £1.5 trillion. This amount is potential GDP.

What Makes Potential GDP Grow?

We can divide all the forces that make potential GDP grow into two categories:

◆ Growth of the supply of labour
◆ Growth of labour productivity

Growth of the Supply of Labour

When the supply of labour grows, the supply of labour curve shifts rightward. The quantity of labour at a given real wage rate increases.

The quantity of labour is the number of workers employed multiplied by average hours per worker; and the number employed equals the employment rate multiplied by the working-age population (see Chapter 21, pp. 486–487). So the quantity of labour changes as a result of changes in

1 Average hours per worker
2 The employment rate
3 The working-age population

Average hours per worker have decreased as the work-week has become shorter, and the employment rate has increased as more women have entered the labour force. The combined effects of these factors have kept average hours per working-age person (approximately) constant.

Figure 22.8   The Labour Market and Potential GDP

(a) The labour market

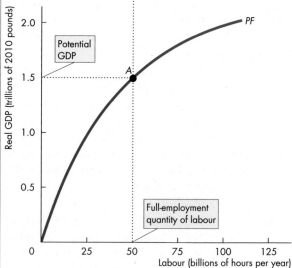

(b) Potential GDP

The economy is at full employment when the quantity of labour demanded equals the quantity of labour supplied, in part (a). The real wage rate is £20 an hour and employment is 50 billion hours per year. In part (b), potential GDP is determined by the production function and the full-employment quantity of labour.

MyEconLab Animation ──────────────◆

Growth in the supply of labour has come from growth in the working-age population. In the long run, the working-age population grows at the same rate as the total population.

The Effects of Population Growth

Population growth brings growth in the supply of labour, but it does not change the demand for labour or the production function. The economy can produce more output by using more labour, but there is no change in the quantity of real GDP that a given quantity of labour can produce.

With an increase in the supply of labour and no change in the demand for labour, the real wage rate falls and the equilibrium quantity of labour increases. The increased quantity of labour produces more output and potential GDP increases.

Illustrating the Effects of Population Growth

Figure 22.9 illustrates the effects of an increase in the population. In Figure 22.9(a), the demand for labour curve is *LD* and initially the supply of labour curve is *LS*$_0$. The equilibrium real wage rate is £20 an hour and the quantity of labour is 50 billion hours a year. In Figure 22.9(b), the production function, *PF*, shows that with 50 billion hours of labour employed, potential GDP is £1.5 trillion at point *A*.

An increase in the population increases the supply of labour, and the supply of labour curve shifts rightward to *LS*$_1$. At a real wage rate of £20 an hour, there is now a surplus of labour. So the real wage rate falls. In this example, the real wage rate will fall until it reaches £15 an hour. At £15 an hour, the quantity of labour demanded equals the quantity of labour supplied. The equilibrium quantity of labour increases to 75 billion hours a year.

Figure 22.9(b) shows the effect on real GDP. As the equilibrium quantity of labour increases from 50 billion to 75 billion hours, potential GDP increases along the production function from £1.5 trillion to £1.8 trillion at point *B*.

So an increase in the population increases the full-employment quantity of labour, increases potential GDP and lowers the real wage rate. But the population increase decreases potential GDP per hour of labour. Initially, it was £30 (£1.5 trillion divided by 50 billion). With the population increase, potential GDP per hour of labour is £24 (£1.8 trillion divided by 75 billion).

Diminishing returns are the source of the decrease in potential GDP per hour of labour.

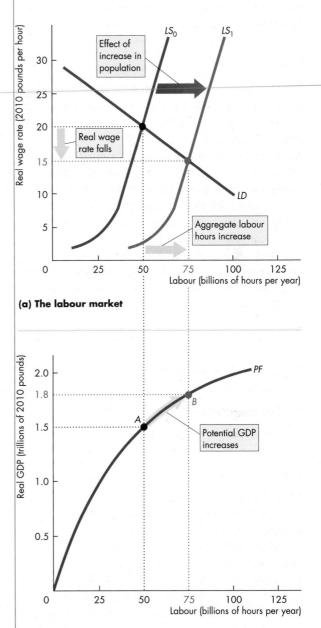

Figure 22.9 The Effects of an Increase in Population

(a) The labour market

(b) Potential GDP

In part (a) an increase in the population increases the supply of labour and shifts the supply of labour curve rightward. The real wage rate falls and the full-employment quantity of labour increases. In part (b), the increase in aggregate labour hours brings an increase in potential GDP. But diminishing returns bring a decrease in potential GDP per hour of labour.

MyEconLab Animation

Growth of Labour Productivity

Labour productivity is the quantity of real GDP produced by an hour of labour. It is calculated by dividing real GDP by aggregate labour hours. For example, if real GDP is £1.5 trillion and aggregate hours are 50 billion, labour productivity is £30 per hour.

When labour productivity grows, real GDP per person grows and brings a rising standard of living. Let's see how an increase in labour productivity changes potential GDP.

Effects of an Increase in Labour Productivity

If labour productivity increases, production possibilities expand. The quantity of real GDP that any given quantity of labour can produce increases. If labour is more productive, firms are willing to pay more for a given number of hours of labour, so the demand for labour also increases.

With an increase in the demand for labour and *no change in the supply of labour*, the real wage rate rises and the quantity of labour supplied increases. The equilibrium quantity of labour also increases.

So an increase in labour productivity increases potential GDP for two reasons: labour is more productive and more labour is employed.

Illustrating the Effects of an Increase in Labour Productivity

Figure 22.10 illustrates an increase in labour productivity. In part (a), the production function initially is PF_0. With 50 billion hours of labour employed, potential GDP is £1.5 trillion at point A. In part (b), the demand for labour curve is LD_0 and the supply of labour curve is LS. The real wage rate is £20 an hour and the equilibrium quantity of labour is 50 billion hours a year.

Now labour productivity increases. In Figure 22.10(a), the increase in labour productivity shifts the production function upward to PF_1. At each quantity of labour, more real GDP can be produced. For example, at 50 billion hours, the economy can now produce £2.0 trillion of real GDP at point B.

In Figure 22.10(b), the increase in labour productivity increases the demand for labour and the demand for labour curve shifts rightward to LD_1. At the initial real wage rate of £20 an hour, there is now a shortage of labour. The real wage rate rises. In this example, the real wage rate will rise until it reaches £25 an hour. At £25 an hour, the quantity of labour demanded equals the quantity of labour supplied and the equilibrium quantity of labour is 55 billion hours a year.

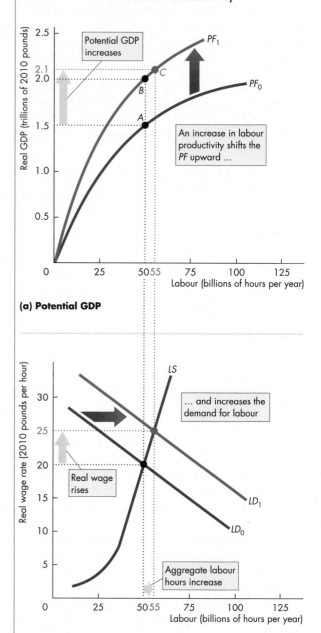

Figure 22.10 The Effects of an Increase in Labour Productivity

(a) Potential GDP

(b) The labour market

An increase in labour productivity shifts the production function upward from PF_0 to PF_1 in part (a) and shifts the demand for labour curve rightward from LD_0 to LD_1 in part (b). The real wage rate rises to £25 an hour, and aggregate labour hours increase from 50 billion to 55 billion. Potential GDP increases from £1.5 trillion to £2.1 trillion.

MyEconLab Animation ────────────◆

Figure 22.10(a) shows the effects of the increase in labour productivity on potential GDP. There are two effects. At the initial quantity of labour, real GDP increases to point *B* on the new production function. But as the equilibrium quantity of labour increases from 50 billion to 55 billion hours, potential GDP increases to £2.1 trillion at point *C*.

Potential GDP per hour of labour also increases. Initially, it was £30 (£1.5 trillion divided by 50 billion). With the increase in labour productivity, potential GDP per hour of labour is £38.18 (£2.1 trillion divided by 55 billion).

The increase in aggregate labour hours that you have just seen is a consequence of an increase in labour productivity. This increase in aggregate labour hours and labour productivity is an example of the interaction effects that economists seek to identify in their search for the ultimate causes of economic growth.

In the case that we've just studied, aggregate labour hours increase, but that increase is a *consequence*, not a *cause*, of the growth of potential GDP. The source of the increase in potential GDP is an increase in labour productivity.

REVIEW QUIZ

1 What is the aggregate production function?
2 What determines the demand for labour, the supply of labour, and labour market equilibrium?
3 What determines potential GDP?
4 What are the two broad sources of potential GDP growth?
5 What are the effects of an increase in the population on potential GDP, the quantity of labour employed, the real wage rate and potential GDP per hour of labour?
6 What are the effects of an increase in labour productivity on potential GDP, the quantity of labour employed, the real wage rate and potential GDP per hour of labour?

Do these questions in Study Plan 22.3 and get instant feedback.   MyEconLab

Labour productivity is the key to increasing output per hour of labour and rising living standards. But what brings an increase in labour productivity? The next section answers this question.

Why Labour Productivity Grows

You've seen that labour productivity growth makes potential GDP grow; and you've seen that labour productivity growth is essential if real GDP per person and the standard of living are to grow. But why does labour productivity grow? What are the preconditions that make labour productivity growth possible and what are the forces that make it grow? Why does labour productivity grow faster at some times and in some places than others?

Preconditions for Labour Productivity Growth

The fundamental precondition for labour productivity growth is the *incentive* system created by firms, markets, property rights and money. These four social institutions are the same as those described in Chapter 2 (see pp. 44–45) that enable people to gain by specialising and trading.

It was the presence of secure property rights in Britain in the middle 1700s that got the Industrial Revolution going (see *Economics in Action* on p. 519). And it is their absence in some parts of Africa today that is keeping labour productivity stagnant.

With the preconditions for labour productivity growth in place, three things influence its pace:

◆ Physical capital growth
◆ Human capital growth
◆ Technological advances

Physical Capital Growth

As the amount of capital per worker increases, labour productivity also increases. Production processes that use hand tools can create beautiful objects, but production methods that use large amounts of capital per worker are much more productive. The accumulation of capital on farms, in textile factories, in iron foundries and steel mills, in coal mines, on building sites, in chemical plants, in car plants, in banks and insurance companies and in shopping centres has added incredibly to our labour productivity.

The next time you see a movie set in historical times, look carefully at the small amount of capital around. Try to imagine how productive you would be in such circumstances compared with your productivity today.

ECONOMICS IN ACTION

Women Are the Better Borrowers

Economic growth is driven by the decisions made by billions of individuals to save and invest, and to borrow and lend. But most people in developing countries are poor, have no credit history and can't borrow from a bank.

But low-income people in developing countries can start a business, employ a few people and earn an income with the help of a microloan. And many of the most successful microloan borrowers are women.

Microloans originated in Bangladesh and have spread throughout the developing world. Kiva.org and MicroPlace.com (owned by eBay) are websites that enable people to lend money that is used to make microloans in developing economies.

Microloans are helping women to feed and clothe their families and to grow their businesses, often in agriculture. As the incomes of microloan borrowers rise, they pay off their loans and accumulate capital. A million microloans pack a macro punch.

Human Capital Growth

Human capital – the accumulated skill and knowledge of human beings – is the fundamental source of labour productivity growth. Human capital grows when a new discovery is made and it grows as more and more people learn how to use past discoveries.

The development of one of the most basic human skills – writing – was the source of some of the earliest major gains in productivity. The ability to keep written records made it possible to reap ever-larger gains from specialisation and trade. Imagine how hard it would be to do any kind of business if all the accounts, invoices and agreements existed only in people's memories.

Later, the development of mathematics laid the foundation for the eventual extension of knowledge about physical forces and chemical and biological processes. This base of scientific knowledge was the foundation for the technological advances of the Industrial Revolution and of today's information revolution.

But a lot of human capital that is extremely productive is much more humble. It takes the form of millions of individuals learning and becoming remarkably more productive by repetitively doing simple production tasks. One much-studied example of this type of human capital growth occurred in the Second World War. With no change in physical capital, thousands of workers and managers in US shipyards learned from experience and accumulated human capital that more than doubled their productivity in less than two years.

Technological Advances

The accumulation of physical capital and human capital has made a large contribution to labour productivity growth. But technological change – the discovery and the application of new technologies – has made an even greater contribution.

Labour is many times more productive today than it was a hundred years ago, but not because we have more steam engines and more horse-drawn carriages per person. Rather, it is because we have transport equipment that uses technologies that were unknown a hundred years ago and which are more productive than the old technologies were.

Technological advance arises from formal research and development programmes and from informal trial and error, and involves discovering new ways of getting more out of our resources.

To reap the benefits of technological change, capital must increase. Some of the most powerful and far-reaching fundamental technologies are embodied in human capital – for example, language, writing and mathematics. But most technologies are embodied in physical capital. For example, to reap the benefits of the internal combustion engine, millions of horse-drawn carriages had to be replaced with cars; and to reap the benefits of digital music, millions of Discmans had to be replaced by iPods, and giant server farms had to be built to operate iTunes and other online shops.

ECONOMICS IN ACTION

Intellectual Property Rights Propel Economic Growth

In 1760, when the states that 16 years later would become the United States of America were developing agricultural economies, England was on the cusp of an economic revolution, the Industrial Revolution.

For 70 dazzling years, technological advances in the use of steam power, the manufacture of cotton, wool, iron and steel, and in transport, accompanied by massive capital investment associated with these technologies, transformed the economy of England. Incomes rose and brought an explosion in an increasingly urbanised population.

By 1825, advances in steam technology had reached a level of sophistication that enabled Robert Stephenson to build the world's first steam-powered rail engine (the Rocket pictured here), and led to the birth of the world's first railway.

Why did the Industrial Revolution happen? Why did it start in 1760? And why in England?

Economic historians say that intellectual property rights – England's patent system – provides the answer.

England's patent system began with the Statute of Monopolies of 1624, which gave inventors a monopoly to use their idea for a term of 14 years. For about 100 years, the system was used to reward friends of the royal court

rather than true inventors. But from around 1720 onward, the system started to work well. To be granted a 14-year monopoly, an inventor had only to pay the required £100 fee (about £14,000 in today's money) and register his or her invention. The inventor was not required to describe the invention in too much detail, so registering and getting a patent didn't mean sharing the invention with competitors.

This patent system, which is in all essentials the same as today's, aligned the self-interest of entrepreneurial inventors with the social interest, and unleashed a flood of inventions, the most transformative of which was steam power and, by 1825, the steam locomotive.

Figure 22.11   Sources of Economic Growth

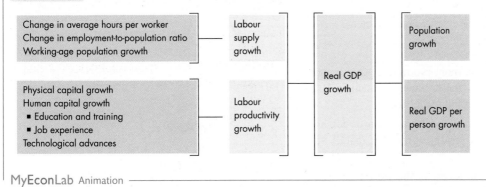

MyEconLab Animation

Figure 22.11 summarises the sources of labour productivity growth and, more broadly, of real GDP growth. The figure also emphasises that for real GDP per person to grow, real GDP must grow faster than the population.

Economics in the News on the next page provides an example of today's labour productivity growth arising from the spread of robot technologies.

<table>
<tr><td colspan="2">◆ REVIEW QUIZ</td></tr>
</table>

1 What are the preconditions for labour productivity growth?
2 Explain the influences on the pace of labour productivity growth?

Do these questions in Study Plan 22.4 and get instant feedback.   MyEconLab

ECONOMICS IN THE NEWS

Robots as Skilled Workers

Skilled Work, Without the Worker

A new wave of robots, far more adept than those now commonly used by carmakers and other heavy goods manufacturers, are replacing workers around the world in both manufacturing and distribution.

Source: *The New York Times*, 18 August 2012

Some Facts

'The Robot Report' (www.therobotreport.com) agrees with the news clip. The car industry has been the main customer for industrial robots, but the scene is changing. Robot manufacturers are creating equipment tailored to the requirements of producers of a wide range of items, just a few of which are metals, food and drink, glass, pharmaceuticals, medical devices and solar panels.

Around 200 established firms worldwide specialise in the design and production of robots, and more than 147 start-up companies entered this industry in the past year. Almost 2,000 firms have some connection with industrial robots.

The Questions

◆ How will the widespread adoption of industrial robots change employment, the real wage rate and potential GDP?

◆ Do robots kill jobs and create unemployment?

The Answers

◆ Robots make workers more productive. One person working with a robot can produce as much as 100s of workers with non-robot technology.

◆ Robots replace some workers but create a demand for other workers to design, produce, install and maintain robots.

◆ In aggregate, robots increase the productivity of labour. Figure 1 shows that the production function shifts upward in part (a) and the demand for labour curve shifts rightward in part (b).

◆ The equilibrium real wage rate rises, employment increases and potential GDP increases.

◆ As robot production technologies spread, many jobs will disappear, but many new jobs will be created.

◆ Some displaced workers will take new jobs with lower wages. Others will take jobs as skilled robot technicians and producers with higher wages. Average wages will rise.

A robot arm seals a box of Lego building toys for shipping.

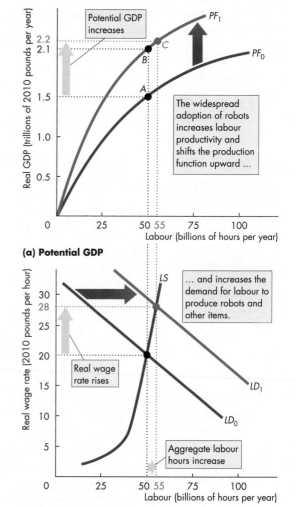

(a) Potential GDP

(b) The labour market

Figure 1 The Effects of Robots on Employment and GDP

Growth Theories, Evidence and Policies

You've seen how the growth of population and labour productivity make potential GDP grow. You've also seen that the growth of physical capital and human capital and technological advances make labour productivity grow. How do these factors interact? What is cause and what is effect? Growth theories address these questions.

Alternative theories of economic growth provide insights into the process of economic growth, but none provides a complete and definite answer to the basic questions: What causes economic growth and why do growth rates vary? Economics has some way to go before it can provide definite answers to these questions. We look at the current state of the empirical evidence. Finally, we'll look at the policies that might achieve faster growth.

Let's start by studying the three main theories of economic growth:

◆ Classical growth theory

◆ Neoclassical growth theory

◆ New growth theory

Classical Growth Theory

Classical growth theory is the view that the growth of real GDP per person is temporary, and that when it rises above the subsistence level, a population explosion eventually brings it back to the subsistence level. Adam Smith, Thomas Robert Malthus and David Ricardo – the leading economists of the late eighteenth century and early nineteenth century – proposed this theory, but the view is most closely associated with the name of Malthus and is sometimes called the *Malthusian theory*. Charles Darwin's ideas about evolution by natural selection were inspired by the insights of Malthus.

Modern-Day Malthusians

Many people today are Malthusians. They say that if today's global population of 6.9 billion explodes to 11 billion by 2050 and perhaps 35 billion by 2300, we will run out of resources, real GDP per person will decline and we will return to a primitive standard of living. We must, say Malthusians, contain population growth.

Modern-day Malthusians also point to global warming and climate change as reasons to believe that, eventually, real GDP per person will decrease.

Neoclassical Growth Theory

Neoclassical growth theory is the proposition that real GDP per person grows because technological change induces saving and investment that make physical capital grow. Diminishing returns end growth if technological change stops. Robert Solow of MIT suggested the most popular version of this growth theory in the 1950s.

Neoclassical growth theory's big break with its classical predecessor is its view about population growth.

The Neoclassical Theory of Population Growth

The population explosion of eighteenth-century Europe that created the classical theory of population eventually ended. The birth rate fell, and while the population continued to increase, its rate of increase moderated.

The opportunity cost of a woman's time is the key influence that slowed the population growth rate. As women's wage rates increase and their job opportunities expand, the opportunity cost of having children increases. Faced with a higher opportunity cost, families choose to have fewer children and the birth rate falls.

Technological advances that bring higher incomes also bring advances in healthcare that extend lives. So as incomes increase, both the birth rate and the death rate decrease. These opposing forces offset each other and result in a slowly rising population.

This modern view of population growth and the historical trends that support it contradict the views of the classical economists. They also call into question the modern doomsday view that the planet will be swamped with more people than it can support.

Technological Change and Diminishing Returns

In neoclassical growth theory, the pace of technological change influences the economic growth rate but economic growth does not influence the pace of technological change. It is assumed that technological change results from chance. When we're lucky, we have rapid technological change, and when bad luck strikes, the pace of technological advance slows.

To understand neoclassical growth theory, imagine the world of the mid-1950s, when Robert Solow is explaining his idea. Income per person is around $12,000 a year in today's money. The population is growing at about 1 per cent a year. Saving and investment are about 20 per cent of GDP, enough to keep the quantity of capital per hour of labour constant. Income per person is growing but not very fast.

Then technology begins to advance at a more rapid pace across a range of activities. The transistor revolutionises an emerging electronics industry. New plastics revolutionise the manufacture of household appliances. The interstate highway system revolutionises road transportation. Jet airliners start to replace piston-engine airplanes and speed air transportation.

These technological advances bring new profit opportunities. Businesses expand, and new businesses are created to exploit the newly available profitable technologies. Investment and saving increase. The economy enjoys new levels of prosperity and growth. But will the prosperity last? And will the growth last? Neoclassical growth theory says that the prosperity will last but the growth will not last unless technology keeps advancing.

According to neoclassical growth theory, the prosperity will persist because there is no classical population growth to induce the wage rate to fall. So the gains in income per person are permanent.

Growth Stops Without Technological Change

Growth will eventually stop if technology stops advancing because of diminishing returns to capital. The high profit rates that result from technological change bring increased saving and capital accumulation. But as more capital is accumulated, more and more projects are undertaken that have lower rates of return – diminishing returns. As the return on capital falls, the incentive to invest weakens. With weaker incentives to save and invest, saving decreases and the rate of capital accumulation slows. Eventually, the pace of capital accumulation slows so that it is only keeping up with population growth. Capital per worker remains constant.

A Problem with Neoclassical Growth Theory

All economies have access to the same technologies and capital is free to roam the globe, seeking the highest available real interest rate. Capital will flow until rates of return are equal, and rates of return will be equal when capital per hour of labour is the same around the world. Real GDP growth rates and income levels per person will converge. Figure 22.5 on p. 510 shows that while there is some sign of convergence among the rich countries in part (a), convergence is slow, and part (b) shows that it does not appear to be imminent for all countries. New growth theory overcomes this shortcoming of neoclassical growth theory. It also explains what determines the pace of technological change.

New Growth Theory

New growth theory holds that real GDP per person grows because of the choices people make in the pursuit of profit, and that growth will persist indefinitely. Paul Romer of Stanford University developed this theory during the 1980s, based on ideas of Joseph Schumpeter during the 1930s and 1940s.

According to new growth theory, the pace at which new discoveries are made – and at which technology advances – is not determined by chance. It depends on how many people are looking for a new technology and how intensively they are looking. The search for new technologies is driven by incentives.

Profit is the spur to technological change. The forces of competition squeeze profits, so to increase profit, people constantly seek either lower-cost methods of production or new and better products for which people are willing to pay a higher price. Inventors can maintain a profit for several years by taking out a patent or a copyright but, eventually, a new discovery is copied and profits disappear. So more research and development is undertaken in the hope of creating a new burst of profitable investment and growth.

A Public Good and No Diminishing Returns

Two facts about discoveries and technological knowledge play a key role in new growth theory: discoveries are (at least eventually) a public capital good; and knowledge is capital that is not subject to diminishing returns.

Economists call a good a public good when no one can be excluded from using it and when one person's use does not prevent others from using it. National defence is the classic example of a public good. The programming language used to write apps for the iPhone is another.

Because knowledge is a *public good*, as the benefits of a new discovery spread, free resources become available. Nothing is given up when they are used: they have a zero opportunity cost. When a student in York writes a new iPhone app, his use of the programming language doesn't prevent another student in Leeds from using it.

Knowledge is even more special because it is not subject to diminishing returns. But increasing the stock of knowledge makes both labour and machines more productive. Knowledge capital does not bring diminishing returns. Biotech knowledge illustrates this idea well. Biologists have spent a lot of time developing DNA-sequencing technology. As more has been discovered, the productivity of this knowledge capital has relentlessly increased. In 1990, it cost about £50 to sequence one DNA base pair. That cost had fallen to £1 by 2000 and to 1/10,000th of a penny by 2010.

The implication of this simple and appealing observation is astonishing. Unlike the other two theories, new growth theory has no growth-stopping mechanism. As physical capital accumulates, the return to capital – the real interest rate – falls. But the incentive to innovate and earn a higher profit becomes stronger. So innovation occurs, capital becomes more productive, the demand for capital increases, and the real interest rate rises again.

Labour productivity grows indefinitely as people discover new technologies that yield a higher real interest rate. The growth rate depends only on people's incentives and ability to innovate.

A Perpetual Motion Economy

New growth theory sees the economy as a perpetual motion machine, which Figure 22.12 illustrates.

No matter how rich we become, our wants exceed our ability to satisfy them. We always want a higher standard of living. In the pursuit of a higher standard of living, human societies have developed incentive systems – markets, property rights and money – that enable people to profit from innovation. Innovation leads to the development of new and better techniques of production and new and better products. To take advantage of new techniques and to produce new products, new firms start up and old firms go out of business – firms are born and die. As old firms die and new firms are born, some jobs are destroyed and others are created. The new jobs created are better than the old ones and they pay higher real wage rates. Also, with higher wage rates and more productive techniques, leisure increases. New and better jobs and new and better products lead to more consumption goods and services and, combined with increased leisure, bring a higher standard of living.

But our insatiable wants are still there, so the process continues: wants and incentives create innovation, new and better products, and a yet higher standard of living.

Figure 22.12   A Perpetual Motion Machine

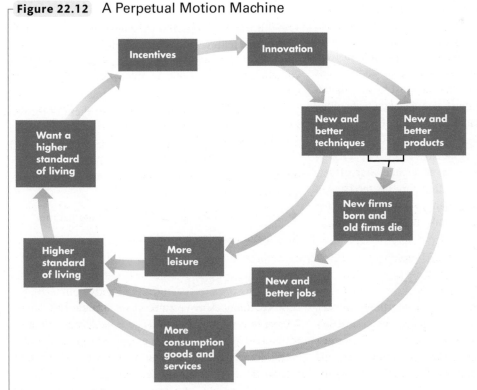

People want a higher standard of living and are spurred by profit incentives to make the innovations that lead to new and better techniques and new and better products, which in turn lead to the birth of new firms and the death of some old firms, new and better jobs, more leisure and more consumption of goods and services. The result is a higher standard of living. But people want a still higher standard of living and the growth process continues.

Source: Based on a similar figure in *These Are the Good Old Days: A Report on United States Living Standards*, Federal Reserve Bank of Dallas 1993 Annual Report.

New Growth Theory versus Malthusian Theory

The contrast between Malthusian theory and new growth theory couldn't be more sharp. Malthusians see the end of prosperity as we know it today and new growth theorists see unending plenty. The contrast becomes clearest by thinking about the differing views about population growth.

To a Malthusian, population growth is part of the problem. To a new growth theorist, population growth is part of the solution. People are the ultimate economic resource. A larger population brings forth more wants, but it also brings a greater amount of scientific discovery and technological advance. So rather than being the source of falling real GDP per person, population growth generates faster labour productivity growth and rising real GDP per person. Resources are limited, but the human imagination and ability to increase productivity are unlimited.

Sorting Out the Theories

Which theory is correct? None of them tells us the whole story, but each teaches us something of value.

Classical growth theory reminds us that our physical resources are limited and that without advances in technology, we must eventually hit diminishing returns.

Neoclassical growth theory reaches the same conclusion but not because of a population explosion. Instead, it emphasises diminishing returns to capital and reminds us that we cannot keep growth going just by accumulating physical capital. We must also advance technology and accumulate human capital. We must become more creative in our use of scarce resources.

New growth theory emphasises the capacity of human resources to innovate at a pace that offsets diminishing returns. New growth theory fits the facts of today's world more closely than do either of the other two theories, but that doesn't make it correct.

The Empirical Evidence on the Causes of Economic Growth

Economics makes progress by the interplay between theory and empirical evidence. A theory makes predictions about what we will observe if the theory is correct. Empirical evidence, the data generated by history and the natural experiments that it performs, provides the data for testing the theory.

Economists have done an enormous amount of research confronting theories of growth with the empirical evidence. The way in which this research has been conducted has changed over the years.

In 1776, when Adam Smith wrote about 'the nature and causes of the Wealth of Nations' in his celebrated book, empirical evidence took the form of carefully selected facts described in words and stories. Today, large databases, sophisticated statistical methods and fast computers provide numerical measurements of the causes of economic growth.

Economists have looked at the growth rate data for more than 100 countries for the period since 1960 and explored the correlations between the growth rate and more than 60 possible influences on it. The conclusion of this data crunching is that most of these possible influences have variable and unpredictable effects, but a few of them have strong and clear effects. Table 22.1 summarises these more robust influences. They are arranged in order of difficulty (or in the case of region, the impossibility) of changing. Political and economic systems are hard to change, but market distortions, investment and openness to international trade are features of a nation's economy that can be influenced by policy.

Let's now look at growth policies.

Policies for Achieving Faster Growth

Growth theory supported by empirical evidence tells us that to achieve faster economic growth, we must increase the growth rate of physical capital, the pace of technological advance or the growth rate of human capital and openness to international trade.

The main suggestions for achieving these objectives are:

◆ Stimulate saving

◆ Stimulate research and development

◆ Improve the quality of education

◆ Provide international aid to developing nations

◆ Encourage international trade

Stimulate Saving

Saving finances investment, so stimulating saving increases economic growth. The East Asian economies have the highest growth rates and the highest saving rates. Some African economies have the lowest growth rates and the lowest saving rates.

Tax incentives can increase saving. Economists claim that a tax on consumption rather than on income provides the best saving incentive.

Table 22.1

The Influences on Economic Growth

Influence	Good for economic growth	Bad for economic growth
Region	◆ Far from equator	◆ Sub-Saharan Africa
Politics	◆ Rule of law	◆ Revolutions
	◆ Civil liberties	◆ Military coups
		◆ Wars
Economic system	◆ Capitalist	
Market distortions		◆ Exchange rate distortions
		◆ Price controls and black markets
Investment	◆ Human capital	
	◆ Physical capital	
International trade	◆ Open to trade	

Source of information: Xavier Sala-i-Martin, 'I Just Ran Two Million Regressions', *The American Economic Review*, Vol. 87, No 2 (May 1997), pp. 178–183.

Stimulate Research and Development

Everyone can use the fruits of basic research and development efforts. For example, all biotechnology firms can use advances in gene-splicing technology. Because basic inventions can be copied, the inventor's profit is limited and the market allocates too few resources to this activity. Governments can direct public funds towards financing basic research, but this solution is not foolproof. It requires a mechanism for allocating the public funds to their highest-valued use.

Improve the Quality of Education

The free market produces too little education because it brings benefits beyond those valued by the people who receive the education. By funding basic education and by ensuring high standards in basic skills such as language, mathematics and science, governments can contribute to a nation's growth potential. Education can also be stimulated and improved by using tax incentives to encourage improved private provision.

Provide International Aid to Developing Nations

It seems obvious that if rich countries give financial aid to developing countries, investment and growth will increase in the recipient countries. Unfortunately, the obvious does not routinely happen. A large amount of data-driven research on the effects of aid on growth has turned up a zero and even a negative effect. Aid often gets diverted and spent on consumption.

Encourage International Trade

Trade, not aid, stimulates economic growth. It works by extracting the available gains from specialisation and trade. The fastest-growing nations are those most open to trade. If the rich nations truly want to aid economic development, they will lower their trade barriers against developing nations, especially in farm products. The World Trade Organisation's efforts to achieve more open trade are being resisted by the richer nations.

 REVIEW QUIZ

1 What is the central idea of classical growth theory that leads to the dismal outcome?
2 What, according to neoclassical growth theory, is the fundamental cause of economic growth?
3 What is the key proposition of new growth theory that makes growth persist?

Do these questions in Study Plan 22.5 and get instant feedback.   MyEconLab

To complete your study of economic growth, take a look at *Reading Between the Lines* on pp. 526–527 and see how two African nations have performed.

READING BETWEEN THE LINES

Making an Economy Grow

How to Make South Africa's Economy Roar

Helen Zillie

It is clear South Africa needs a radical change in direction. This weekend the opposition Democratic Alliance aims to show how this is possible, launching a strategy to accelerate annual growth to 8 percent. In particular, it proposes tough reforms to labour laws by removing the automatic extension of collective bargaining agreements across sectors; establishing 'jobs zones' featuring special exemptions from restrictive regulations; and lifting administrative requirements for small businesses. . . .

These changes will reduce barriers to entry, encourage flexibility, and stimulate productivity in . . . mining, manufacturing and agriculture. Combined with focused employment incentives such as a youth wage subsidy and market-driven skills development programmes, the plan provides a radical overhaul of the country's labour market . . . .

Our plan contains ... policies to distribute shares in state-owned companies; introduce tax deductions to incentivise employee shared-ownership schemes; promote a joint ownership model in the agricultural sector; and lower the cost barriers facing first-time homeowners.

These measures are essential for facilitating broad-based participation in the economy. . . .

South Africa falls short when it comes to the ease of doing business, and the barriers caused by excessive regulation and state inefficiency. My party's proposals in this area will cut the tax and regulatory burdens inhibiting new business growth.

Seven of the 10 fastest-growing economies in the world are in Africa. . . . With the right policies in place, South Africa can be part of this story.

FT   *Source*: The Financial Times, 27 July 2012.
© The Financial Times Limited. All Rights Reserved.

The Essence of the Story

- South Africa's opposition party wants real GDP to grow by 8 per cent per year.

- Labour market reforms would limit union agreements, establish 'jobs zones' with exemptions from restrictive regulations, subsidise youth wages and develop market-driven skills.

- Capital market reforms would ease small-business regulation, cut taxes, distribute shares in state-owned companies, provide tax incentives for employee shared ownership and make homeownership easier.

- The reforms aim to reduce barriers to entry and boost labour productivity in all parts of the economy.

Economic Analysis

◆ Since 1995, South Africa's real GDP per person has increased at a slower rate than that of the other BRICS countries and slower than its neighbour, Botswana.

◆ Figure 1 shows real GDP per person in South Africa and Botswana from 1980 to 2012.

◆ Botswana's real GDP per person has grown more rapidly than South Africa's because of its higher rate of investment in new capital.

◆ Figure 2 shows that Botswana invests double the percentage of GDP invested by South Africa.

◆ The growth of physical capital and human capital and technological change are proceeding at a rapid pace in Botswana and bringing rapid growth in real GDP per person.

◆ Figure 3 illustrates how the production function is changing: shifting upward at a more rapid pace in Botswana than in South Africa.

◆ Why is Botswana more successful than South Africa and would the policies proposed in the news article raise South Africa's growth rate to the desired 8 per cent per year?

◆ Economists Daron Acemoglu, Simon Johnson and James Robinson say that Botswana had the right institutions for growth – well-defined and widely respected private property rights.

◆ The proposals in the news article don't directly address strengthening private propery rights, but they do have that effect.

◆ The labour market reforms would increase human capital and labour productivity.

◆ The labour market and capital market reforms together would make capital accumulation and technological change more profitable and further raise labour productivity growth.

◆ A target of 8 per cent growth is probably too ambitious.

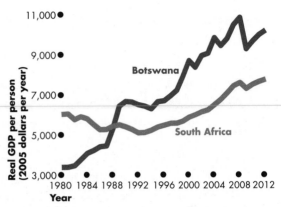

Figure 1   Real GDP in Two African Economies

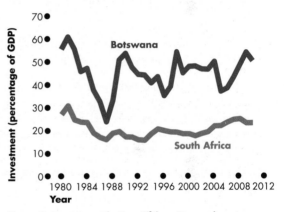

Figure 2   Investment in Two African Economies

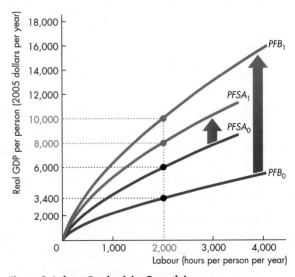

Figure 3   **Labour Productivity Growth in Two African Economies**

SUMMARY

Key Points

The Basics of Economic Growth

(pp. 506–508)

◆ Economic growth is the sustained expansion of production possibilities and is measured as the annual percentage growth rate of real GDP.

◆ The Rule of 70 tells us the number of years in which real GDP doubles – 70 divided by the annual percentage growth rate.

Do Problems 1 to 5 to get a better understanding of the basics of economic growth.

Long-Term Growth Trends (pp. 509–511)

◆ Real GDP per person in the UK has grown at an average rate of 1.6 per cent per year. Growth was more rapid during the 1960s and the 1980s.

◆ The gap in real GDP per person between the US and Central and South America has persisted. The gaps between the US and Hong Kong, Korea and China have narrowed. The gaps between the US and Africa and Central Europe have widened.

Do Problem 6 to get a better understanding of economic growth trends.

How Potential GDP Grows (pp. 512–517)

◆ The aggregate production function and equilibrium in the aggregate labour market determine potential GDP.

◆ Potential GDP grows if the labour supply grows or if labour productivity grows.

◆ Only labour productivity growth makes real GDP per person and the standard of living grow.

Do Problems 7 to 14 to get a better understanding of how potential GDP grows.

Why Labour Productivity Grows

(pp. 517–520)

◆ Labour productivity growth requires an incentive system created by firms, markets, property rights and money.

◆ The sources of labour productivity growth are growth of physical capital and human capital and advances in technology.

◆ Physical capital growth has diminishing returns, but human capital growth and advances in technology don't have diminishing returns.

Do Problems 15 and 16 to get a better understanding of why labour productivity grows.

Growth Theories, Evidence and Policies (pp. 521–525)

◆ In classical theory, real GDP per person keeps returning to the subsistence level.

◆ In neoclassical growth theory, diminishing returns to capital limit economic growth.

◆ In new growth theory, economic growth persists indefinitely at a rate determined by decisions that lead to innovation and technological change.

◆ Policies for achieving faster growth include stimulating saving and research and development, encouraging international trade and improving the quality of education.

Do Problems 17 and 18 to get a better understanding of growth theories, evidence and policies.

Key Terms

Aggregate production function, 512
Classical growth theory, 521
Economic growth, 506
Growth rate, 506
Labour productivity, 516
Neoclassical growth theory, 521
New growth theory, 522
Real GDP per person, 506
Real wage rate, 513
Rule of 70, 507

STUDY PLAN PROBLEMS AND APPLICATIONS

Do Problems 1 to 18 in MyEconLab Chapter 22 Study Plan and get instant feedback.   MyEconLab

The Basics of Economic Growth
(Study Plan 22.1)

1   Brazil's real GDP was 1,520 trillion reais in 2011 and 1,585 trillion reais in 2012. Brazil's population was 195 million in 201 and 196.5 million in 2012. Calculate:

   a   The growth rate of real GDP.

   b   The growth rate of real GDP per person.

   c   The approximate number of years it takes for real GDP per person in Brazil to double if the 2012 economic growth rate and population growth rate are maintained.

2   Japan's real GDP was 548 trillion yen in 2011 and 560 trillion yen in 2012. Japan's population was 127.2 million in 2011 and 127 million in 2012. Calculate:

   a   The growth rate of real GDP.

   b   The growth rate of real GDP per person.

   c   The approximate number of years it takes for real GDP per person in Japan to double if the real GDP growth rate returns to 3 per cent a year and the population growth rate is maintained.

Use the following data in Problems 3 and 4.

China's real GDP per person was 11,480 yuan in 2011 and 12,515 yuan in 2012. India's real GDP per person was 45,045 rupees in 2011 and 47,995 rupees in 2012.

3   By maintaining their current growth rates, which country will double its 2012 standard of living first?

4   The population of China is growing at 1 per cent a year and the population of India is growing at 1.4 per cent a year. Calculate the growth rate of real GDP in each country.

5   **China's Economy Picks Up Speed**

   China's trend growth rate of real GDP per person was 2.2 per cent a year before 1980 and 8.7 per cent a year after 1980. In the year to August 2009, China's output increased by 11.3 per cent.

            Source: World Economic Outlook and FT.com, 14 September 2009

   a   Distinguish between a rise in China's economic growth rate and a temporary cyclical expansion.

   b   How long, at the current growth rate, will it take for China to double its real GDP per person?

Long-Term Growth Trends
(Study Plan 22.2)

6   China was the largest economy for centuries because everyone had the same type of economy – subsistence – and so the country with the most people would be economically biggest. Then the Industrial Revolution sent the West on a more prosperous path. Now the world is returning to a common economy, this time technology- and information-based, so once again population triumphs.

   a   Why was China the world's largest economy until 1890?

   b   Why did the US surpass China in 1890 to become the world's largest economy?

How Potential GDP Grows
(Study Plan 22.3)

Use the following information in Problems 7 and 8.

Suppose that France cracks down on illegal immigrants and returns millions of workers to their home countries.

7   Explain what will happen to potential GDP, employment and the real wage rate in France.

8   Explain what will happen to potential GDP, employment and the real wage rate in the countries to which the immigrants return.

Use the following news clip in Problems 9 to 11.

US Workers World's Most Productive

Americans work longer hours than those in other rich nations. Americans also produce more per person, but only part of US productivity growth can be explained by the longer hours they work. Americans also create more wealth per hour of work. US employees worked an average of 1,804 hours in 2006, compared to 1,564.4 for the French, but far less than the 2,200 hours that Asians worked. But in Asian countries, average labour productivity is lower.

            Source: CBS News, 3 September 2007

9   What is the difference between productivity in this news clip and real GDP per person?

10   Identify and correct a confusion in the news clip between levels and growth rates of labour productivity.

11   If workers in developing Asian economies work more hours than Americans, why are they not the world's most productive?

Use the following tables in Problems 12 to 14.

The tables describe an economy's labour market and its production function in 2010.

Real wage rate (euros per hour)	Labour hours supplied	Labour hours demanded
80	45	5
70	40	10
60	35	15
50	30	20
40	25	25
30	20	30
20	15	35

Labour (hours)	Real GDP (2010 euros)
5	425
10	800
15	1,125
20	1,400
25	1,625
30	1,800
35	1,925
40	2,000

12 What are the equilibrium real wage rate, the quantity of labour employed in 2010, labour productivity and potential GDP in 2010?

13 In 2011, the population increases and labour hours supplied increase by 10 at each real wage rate. What are the equilibrium real wage rate, labour productivity and potential GDP in 2011?

14 In 2011, the population increases and labour hours supplied increase by 10 at each real wage rate. Does the standard of living in this economy increase in 2011? Explain why or why not.

Why Labour Productivity Grows

(Study Plan 22.4)

15 Labour Productivity on the Rise

During the year ended June 2009, US non-farm sector output fell 5.5 per cent as labour productivity increased 1.9 per cent – the largest increase since 2003. But in the manufacturing sector, output fell 9.8 per cent as labour productivity increased by 4.9 per cent – the largest increase since the first quarter of 2005.

Source: bls.gov/news.release, 11 August 2009

In both sectors, output fell while labour productivity increased. Did the quantity of labour (aggregate hours) increase or decrease? In which sector was the change in the quantity of labour larger?

16 For three years there was no technological change in Longland, but capital per hour of labour increased from €10 to €20 to €30 and real GDP per hour of labour increased from €3.80 to €5.70 to €7.13. Then, in the fourth year, capital per hour of labour remained constant, but real GDP per hour of labour increased to €10. Does Longland experience diminishing returns? Explain why or why not.

Growth Theories, Evidence and Policies (Study Plan 22.5)

17 Explain the processes that will bring the growth of real GDP per person to a stop according to:

a Classical growth theory.

b Neoclassical growth theory.

c New growth theory.

18 In the economy of Cape Despair, the subsistence real wage rate is €15 an hour. Whenever real GDP per hour rises above €15, the population grows, and whenever real GDP per hour of labour falls below this level, the population falls. The table shows Cape Despair's production function:

Labour (billions of hours per year)	Real GDP (billions of 2010 euros)
0.5	8
1.0	15
1.5	21
2.0	26
2.5	30
3.0	33
3.5	35

Initially, the population of Cape Despair is constant and real GDP per hour of labour is at the subsistence level of €15. Then a technological advance shifts the production function upward by 50 per cent at each level of labour.

a What are the initial levels of real GDP and labour productivity?

b What happens to labour productivity immediately following the technological advance?

c What happens to the population growth rate following the technological advance?

d What are the eventual levels of real GDP and real GDP per hour of labour?

ADDITIONAL PROBLEMS AND APPLICATIONS

Do these problems in MyEconLab if assigned by your lecturer.

MyEconLab

The Basics of Economic Growth

19 If in 2012 China's real GDP is growing at 9 per cent a year, its population is growing at 1 per cent a year, and these growth rates continue, in what year will China's real GDP per person be twice what it is in 2012?

20 South Africa's real GDP was 1,900 billion rand in 2011 and 1,970 billion rand in 2012. South Africa's population was 50.5 million in 2011 and 51.0 million in 2012. Calculate:

  a The growth rate of real GDP.

  b The growth rate of real GDP per person.

  c The approximate number of years it takes for real GDP per person in South Africa to double if the current growth rate of real GDP and the population growth rate are maintained.

21 Turkey's real GDP was 97.1 billion Turkish lira in 2009 and 104.7 billion Turkish lira in 2010. Turkey's population was 70.5 million in 2009 and 71.4 million in 2010. Calculate:

  a The economic growth rate.

  b The growth rate of real GDP per person.

  c The approximate number of years it takes for real GDP per person in Turkey to double if economic growth returns to its average since 2009 of 3.6 per cent a year and is maintained.

Long-Term Growth Trends

22 **The New World Order**

While gross domestic product growth is cooling a bit in emerging market economies, the results are still tremendous compared with the US and much of Western Europe. The emerging market economies posted a 6.7 per cent jump in real GDP in 2008, down from 7.5 per cent in 2007. The advanced economies grew an estimated 1.6 per cent in 2008. The difference in growth rates represents the largest spread between emerging market economies and advanced economies in the 37-year history of the survey.

Source: *Fortune*, 14 July 2008

Do growth rates over the past few decades indicate that gaps in real GDP per person around the world are shrinking, growing or staying the same? Explain.

How Potential GDP Grows

23 If a large increase in investment increases labour productivity, explain what happens to:

  a Potential GDP.

  b Employment.

  c The real wage rate.

24 If a severe drought decreases labour productivity, explain what happens to:

  a Potential GDP.

  b Employment.

  c The real wage rate.

Use the following tables in Problems 25 to 27.

The first table describes an economy's labour market and the second table describes its production function in 2010.

Real wage rate (euros per hour)	Labour hours supplied	Labour hours demanded
80	55	15
70	50	20
60	45	25
50	40	30
40	35	35
30	30	40
20	25	45

Labour (hours)	Real GDP (2010 euros)
15	1,425
20	1,800
25	2,125
30	2,400
35	2,625
40	2,800
45	2,925
50	3,000

25 What are the equilibrium real wage rate and the quantity of labour employed in 2010?

26 What are labour productivity and potential GDP in 2010?

27 Suppose that labour productivity increases in 2010. What effect does the increased labour productivity have on the demand for labour, the supply of labour, potential GDP and real GDP per person?

Why Labour Productivity Grows

28 **India's Economy Hits the Wall**

Just six months ago, India was looking good. Annual growth was 9 per cent, consumer demand was huge, and foreign investment was growing. But now most economic forecasts expect growth to slow to 7 per cent – a big drop for a country that needs to accelerate growth. India needs urgently to upgrade its infrastructure and education and healthcare facilities. Agriculture is unproductive and needs better technology. The legal system needs to be strengthened with more judges and courtrooms.

Source: *Business Week*, 1 July 2008

Explain five potential sources for faster economic growth in India suggested in this news clip.

29 **Boost Productivity or We'll be Poorer**

In 2011, UK output per hour was 16 percentage points below the average for the rest of the G7, and such a productivity gap has not been this large since 1993. The ONS reported that UK real wages have fallen.

Source: *The Sunday Times*, 17 February 2013

a How might the UK increase its labour productivity?

b Explain how an increase in UK labour productivity would influence the average real wage rate and the UK standard of living.

Growth Theories, Evidence and Policies

30 **The Productivity Watch**

According to former Federal Reserve chairman Alan Greenspan, IT investments in the 1990s boosted productivity, which boosted corporate profits, which led to more IT investments, and so on, leading to a nirvana of high growth.

Source: *Fortune*, 4 September 2006

Which of the growth theories that you've studied in this chapter best corresponds to the explanation given by Mr Greenspan?

31 Is faster economic growth always a good thing? Argue the case for faster growth and the case for slower growth. Then reach a conclusion on whether growth should be increased or slowed.

32 **Makani Power: A Mighty Wind**

Makani Power aims to generate energy from what are known as high-altitude wind-extraction technologies. And that's about all its 34-year-old Aussie founder, Saul Griffith, wants to say about it. But Makani can't hide

entirely, not when its marquee investor is Google.org, the tech company's philanthropic arm. Makani's plan is to capture that high-altitude wind with a very old tool: kites. Harnessing higher-altitude wind, at least in theory, has greater potential than the existing wind industry because at a thousand feet above the ground, the wind is stronger and more consistent.

Source: *Fortune*, 28 April 2008

Explain which growth theory best describes the news clip.

Economics in the News

33 After you have studied *Reading Between the Lines* on pp. 526–527, answer the following questions:

a How do South Africa and Botswana compare on the real GDP growth rates?

b For South Africa to go grow faster, how would the percentage of GDP invested in new capital need to change?

c If South Africa is able to achieve a growth rate of 8 per cent per year, in how many years will real GDP have doubled?

d Describe the policies proposed by the author of the news article and explain how they might change labour productivity.

e What is the source of Botswana's growth success story and what must South Africa do to replicate that success?

f Draw a *PPF* graph to show what has happened in Botswana and South Africa since 1980.

34 **Make Way for India – The Next China**

China grows at around 9 per cent a year, but its one-child policy will start to reduce the size of China's working population within the next 10 years. India, by contrast, will have an increasing working population for another generation at least.

Source: *The Independent*, 1 March 2006

a Given the expected population changes, do you think China or India will have the greater economic growth rate? Why?

b Would China's growth rate remain at 9 per cent a year without the restriction on its population growth rate?

c India's population growth rate is 1.6 per cent a year, and in 2005 its economic growth rate was 8 per cent a year. China's population growth rate is 0.6 per cent a year and in 2005 its economic growth rate was 9 per cent a year. In what year will real GDP per person double in each country?

23 Finance, Saving and Investment

After studying this chapter you will be able to:

- ◆ Describe the flows of funds in financial markets
- ◆ Explain how saving and investment decisions interact in the loanable funds market
- ◆ Explain how governments influence financial markets
- ◆ Explain how international borrowing and lending influence financial markets

During 2008, the financial centres of the world went into meltdown. Rescuing banks on the edge of collapse, European governments increased their own debts to crisis levels that threaten to destroy the euro. Behind the scenes of the drama and headlines, the world's capital markets play an unseen role funnelling funds from savers and lenders to investors and borrowers. This chapter shows how these markets work and explains their place in the economy.

In *Reading Between the Lines* at the end of the chapter, you will apply what you have learned to explain why interest rates on borrowed funds differ between countries in the euro zone.

Financial Institutions and Financial Markets

The financial institutions and markets that we study in this chapter play a crucial role in the economy. They provide the channels through which saving flows to finance the investment in new capital that makes the economy grow. In studying the economics of financial institutions and markets, we distinguish between:

◆ Finance and money
◆ Physical capital and financial capital

Finance and Money

In economics, we use the term *finance* to describe the activity of borrowing and lending. Borrowing and lending provides the funds that finance expenditures on capital that make productivity grow.

The study of finance examines how households, firms and governments obtain and use financial resources and how they cope with the risks that arise in this activity.

We use the term *money* to describe the stuff that we use to make payments for goods and services, for factors of production including expenditures on new capital and to make financial transactions – to receive and repay loans.

The study of money looks at how households and firms use it, how much money they hold, how banks create money and manage it, and how the quantity of money influences the economy.

In the economic lives of individuals, businesses and governments, finance and money are closely interrelated. Money is what you get when you borrow from a bank. Money is what you use when you finance the purchase of a new car. And banks and other financial institutions provide both financial services and monetary services. Nevertheless, by distinguishing between *finance* and *money* and studying them separately, we will better understand our financial and monetary markets and institutions.

For the rest of this chapter, we study finance. Money is the topic of the next chapter.

Physical Capital and Financial Capital

Economists distinguish between physical capital and financial capital. *Physical capital* is the tools, instruments, machines, buildings and other items that have been produced in the past and which are used today to produce goods and services. Inventories of raw materials, semifinished goods and components are part of physical capital. When economists use the term *capital*, they mean physical capital. The funds that firms use to buy physical capital are called **financial capital**.

Along the *aggregate production function* in Chapter 22 (see p. 512), the quantity of capital is fixed. An increase in the quantity of capital increases production possibilities and shifts the aggregate production function upward. You're going to see, in this chapter, how investment, saving, borrowing and lending decisions influence the quantity of capital and make it grow, and, as a consequence, make real GDP grow. We begin by describing the links between capital and investment and between wealth and saving.

Capital and Investment

The quantity of capital changes because of investment and depreciation. *Investment* increases the quantity of capital and *depreciation* decreases it (see Chapter 20, p. 462). The total amount spent on new capital is called **gross investment**. The change in the value of capital is called **net investment**. Net investment equals gross investment minus depreciation. Figure 23.1 illustrates these terms. On 1 January 2013, Ace Bottling Inc. had machines worth €30,000 – Ace's initial capital. During 2013, the market value of Ace's machines fell by 67 per cent – €20,000. After this depreciation, Ace's machines were valued at €10,000. During 2013, Ace spent €30,000 on new machines. This amount is Ace's gross investment. By 31 December 2013, Ace Bottling had capital valued at €40,000, so its capital had increased by €10,000. This amount is Ace's net investment. Ace's net investment equals its gross investment of €30,000 minus depreciation of its initial capital of €20,000.

Wealth and Saving

Wealth is the value of all the things that people own. What people own is related to what they earn, but it is not the same thing. People earn an income, which is the amount they receive during a given time period from supplying the services of the resources they own. **Saving** is the amount of income that is not paid in taxes or spent on consumption goods and services.

Saving increases wealth. Wealth also increases when the market value of assets rises – called capital gains – and decreases when the market value of assets falls – called capital losses.

Figure 23.1   Capital and Investment

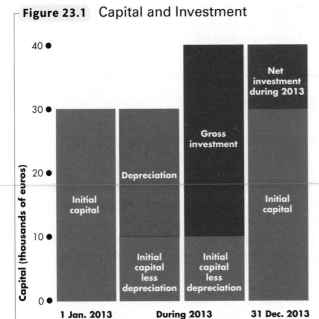

On 1 January 2013, Ace Bottling had capital worth €30,000. During the year, the value of Ace's capital fell by €20,000 – depreciation – and it spent €30,000 on new capital – gross investment. Ace's net investment was €10,000 (€30,000 gross investment minus €20,000 depreciation) so that at the end of 2013, Ace had capital worth €40,000.

MyEconLab Animation ⸺⸺⸺⸺⸺⸺◆

For example, at the end of term you have €250 in the bank and a coin collection worth €300, so your wealth is €550. During the summer, you earn €5,000 (net of taxes) and spend €1,000 on consumption goods and services, so your saving is €4,000. Your bank account increases to €4,250 and your wealth becomes €4,550. The €4,000 increase in wealth equals saving. If coins rise in value and your coin collection is now worth €500, you have a capital gain of €200, which is also added to your wealth.

National wealth and national saving work like this personal example. The wealth of a nation at the end of a year equals its wealth at the start of the year plus its saving during the year, which equals income minus consumption expenditure.

To make real GDP grow, saving and wealth must be transformed into investment and capital. This transformation takes place in the markets for financial capital and through the activities of financial institutions. We're now going to describe these markets and institutions.

Financial Capital Markets

Saving is the source of the funds that are used to finance investment, and these funds are supplied and demanded in three types of financial markets:

◆ Loan markets

◆ Bond markets

◆ Stock markets

Loan Markets

Businesses often want short-term finance to buy inventories or to extend credit to their customers. Sometimes they get this finance in the form of a loan from a bank. Households often want finance to purchase a high expenditure item, such as a car or household furnishings and appliances. They get this finance as bank loans, often in the form of outstanding credit card balances. Households also get finance to buy new homes. (Expenditure on new homes is counted as part of investment.) These funds are usually obtained as a loan that is secured by a **mortgage** – a legal contract that gives ownership of a home to the lender in the event that the borrower fails to meet the agreed loan payments (repayments and interest). Mortgage loans were at the centre of the sub-prime loans crisis of 2007–2008. All of these types of financing take place in loan markets.

Bond Markets

When Wal-Mart (the largest retailer in the world) expands its business into China, it gets the finance it needs by selling bonds. National and local governments also raise finance by issuing bonds.

A **bond** is a promise to make specified payments on specified dates. For example, you can buy a Wal-Mart bond that promises to pay $5.00 every year until 2024 and then to make a final payment of $100 in 2025.

The buyer of a bond from Wal-Mart makes a loan to the company and is entitled to the payments promised by the bond. When a person buys a newly issued bond, he or she may hold the bond until the borrower has repaid the amount borrowed or sell it to someone else. Bonds issued by firms and governments are traded in the **bond market**.

The term of a bond might be long (decades) or short (just a month or two). Firms often issue very short-term bonds as a way of getting paid for their sales before the buyer is able to pay. These short-term bonds are called commercial paper. For example, when Rolls-Royce sells £100 million of aero engines to Qantas, Rolls-Royce wants to be paid when the items are shipped. But Qantas doesn't want to pay until the engines are installed and the engines are earning an income. In this situation, Qantas might promise to pay Rolls-Royce £101 million three months in the future. A bank would be willing to buy this promise for (say) £100 million. Rolls-Royce gets £100 million immediately and the bank gets £101 million in three months when Qantas honours its promise. The UK Treasury issues promises of this type, called Treasury bills.

Another type of bond is a **mortgage-backed security**, which entitles its holder to the income from a package of mortgages. Mortgage lenders create mortgage-backed securities. They make mortgage loans to homebuyers and then create securities that they sell to obtain more funds to make more mortgage loans. The holder of a mortgage-backed security is entitled to receive payments that derive from the payments received by the mortgage lender from the homebuyer–borrower.

Mortgage-backed securities were at the centre of the storm in the financial markets in 2007–2008.

Stock Markets

When BP wants finance to expand its oil and gas explorations, it issues stock. A **stock** is a certificate of ownership and claim to the firm's profits. BP has issued about 19 billion shares of its stock. So if you owned 19,000 BP shares, you would own one millionth of BP and be entitled to receive one millionth of its profits. Unlike a stockholder, a bondholder does not own part of the firm that issued the bond.

A **stock market** is a financial market in which shares of stocks of corporations are traded. The London Stock Exchange, the Frankfurt Stock Exchange, the New York Stock Exchange and the Tokyo Stock Exchange are all examples of stock markets.

Financial Institutions

Financial markets are highly competitive because of the role played by financial institutions in those markets. A **financial institution** is a firm that operates on both sides of the markets for financial capital. The financial institution is a borrower in one market and a lender in another.

Financial institutions also stand ready to trade so that households with funds to lend and firms or households seeking funds can always find someone on the other side of the market with whom to trade.

The key financial institutions are:

- Commercial banks
- Mortgage companies
- Pension funds
- Insurance companies

Commercial Banks

Commercial banks are financial institutions that accept deposits, provide payment services and make loans to firms and households. The bank that you use for banking services and which issues your debit card is a commercial bank. These institutions play a central role in the monetary system and we study them in detail in Chapter 24.

Mortgage Companies

Mortgage companies (building societies in the UK) are financial institutions that specialise in making loans for property purchases. Loans for house purchase are packaged into mortgage-backed securities and sold to banks. These securities were at the heart of the global financial crisis of 2008 (see *Economics in Action* below).

 ECONOMICS IN ACTION

The Financial Crisis and the Fix

The 2008 financial crisis, the after-effects of which remain in place, began in the United States. Between 2002 and 2005, US mortgage lending exploded and home prices rocketed. Mortgage lenders bundled their loans into mortgage-backed securities and sold them to eager buyers around the world. UK and European banks were among the buyers.

When interest rates began to rise in 2006 and asset prices fell, financial institutions took big losses. By 2008, some losses were too big to bear and big-name institutions, among them Lloyds Group and the Royal Bank of Scotland Group (RBS), sustained enormous losses.

Faced with banks on the edge of collapse, the UK government announced a £500 billion bank rescue package to restore confidence in the banking system. This huge injection of taxpayer money included the part-nationalisation of Lloyds and RBS.

The UK government also set up an Independent Commission on Banking chaired by economist Sir John Vickers – see *At Issue* in Chapter 24, p. 563. The Commission (Vickers Commission) was to study the banking

Pension Funds

Pension funds are financial institutions that use the pension contributions of firms and workers to buy bonds and stocks. These funds also hold mortgage-backed securities issued by specialised mortgage lenders in the US and the UK. Some pension funds are very large and play an active role in the firms whose stock they hold.

Insurance Companies

Insurance companies enable households and firms to cope with risks such as accident, theft, fire, ill-health and a host of other misfortunes. They receive premiums from their customers and pay claims. Insurance companies use the funds they have received but not paid out as claims to buy bonds and stocks on which they earn interest income.

In normal times, insurance companies have a steady inflow of funds from premiums and interest and a steady, but smaller, outflow of funds paying claims. Their profit is the gap between the two flows.

In unusual times, when large and widespread losses are being incurred, insurance companies can run into difficulty in meeting their obligations.

Insolvency and Illiquidity

A financial institution's **net worth** is the market value of its assets (what it has lent) minus the market value of its liabilities (what it has borrowed). If net worth is positive, the institution is solvent. But if net worth is negative, the institution is insolvent. The owners of an insolvent financial institution – usually its stockholders – bear the loss.

A financial institution both borrows and lends, so it is exposed to the risk that its net worth might become negative. Financial regulation seeks to limit that risk by defining the maximum ratio of lending to net worth.

Sometimes, a financial institution is solvent but illiquid. A firm is *illiquid* if it has made long-term loans with borrowed funds and is faced with a sudden demand to repay more of what it has borrowed than its available cash.

In normal times, a financial institution that is illiquid can borrow from another institution. But if all the financial institutions are short of cash, the market for loans among financial institutions dries up. In such a situation, only the central bank can provide funds.

Insolvency and illiquidity were at the core of the financial meltdown of 2008.

industry and make recommendations for reforms of the UK banking market that would reduce the risk of future bank failure and avoid the need for bailouts financed by the tax payer.

The bank as a high street retailer where loans can be arranged and cash deposited and withdrawn is a tiny part of the operations of a modern bank. Its main business is conducted by its corporate and investment arms, and these are the parts of the banking industry that generate risk.

To isolate retail banking from the riskier corporate and investment banking, the Vickers Commission recommended that the two activities be separated and that each have its own governance structure: a setup called 'ring-fencing'.

The objective of ring-fencing is to allow a banking group to remain as a single entity but to separate its operations so as to avoid infection of the retail operations from the investment operations. With the two parts of a bank separated, government guarantees will apply only to retail banking.

The reforms remain to be tested by crisis. But they are being tested by persistently slow economic growth. At a time when the UK government wants banks to lend more to fuel a recovery, bank lending is growing slowly. This slow growth might be an unintended consequence of ring-fencing.

Two UK casualties of the 2008 financial meltdown

Interest Rates and Asset Prices

Stocks, bonds, short-term securities and loans are collectively called *financial assets*. The interest rate on a financial asset is the interest received expressed as a percentage of the price of the asset.

Because the interest rate is a percentage of the price of an asset, if the asset price rises, other things remaining the same, the interest rate falls. Conversely, if the asset price falls, other things remaining the same, the interest rate rises.

To see this inverse relationship between an asset price and the interest rate, let's look at an example. We'll consider a bond that promises to pay its holder €5 a year forever. What is the rate of return – the interest rate – on this bond? The answer depends on the price of the bond. If you could buy this bond for €50, the interest rate would be 10 per cent per year:

$$\text{Interest rate} = (€5 \div €50) \times 100 = 10 \text{ per cent.}$$

But if the price of this bond increased to €200, its rate of return or interest rate would be only 2.5 per cent per year. That is

$$\text{Interest rate} = (€5 \div €200) \times 100 = 2.5 \text{ per cent.}$$

This relationship means that the price of an asset and the interest rate on that asset are determined simultaneously – one implies the other.

This relationship also means that if the interest rate on the asset rises, the price of the asset falls, debts become harder to pay and the net worth of the financial institution falls. Insolvency can arise from a previously unexpected large rise in the interest rate. In the next part of this chapter, we learn how interest rates and asset prices are determined in the financial markets.

 REVIEW QUIZ

1 Distinguish between physical capital and financial capital and give two examples of each.
2 What is the distinction between gross investment and net investment?
3 What are the three main types of markets for financial capital and what makes them different?
4 What are the main types of financial institutions and how do they differ?
5 Explain the connection between the price of a financial asset and its interest rate.

Do these questions in Study Plan 23.1 and get instant feedback.   MyEconLab

The Loanable Funds Market

In macroeconomics, we group all the financial markets that we described in the previous section into a single loanable funds market. The **loanable funds market** is the aggregate of all the individual financial markets.

The circular flow model of Chapter 20 (see p. 461) can be extended to include flows in the loanable funds market that finance investment.

Funds that Finance Investment

Figure 23.2 shows the flows of funds that finance investment. They come from three sources:

1 Household saving
2 Government budget surplus
3 Borrowing from the rest of the world

Households' income, Y, is spent on consumption goods and services, C, saved, S, or paid in net taxes, T. **Net taxes** are the taxes paid to governments minus the cash transfers received from governments (such as social security and unemployment benefits). So income is equal to the sum of consumption expenditure, saving and net taxes:

$$Y = C + S + T$$

You saw in Chapter 20 (p. 462) that Y also equals the sum of the items of aggregate expenditure: consumption expenditure, C, investment, I, government expenditure, G, and exports, X, minus imports, M. That is:

$$Y = C + I + G + X - M$$

By using these two equations, you can see that

$$I + G + X = M + S + T$$

Subtract G and X from both sides of the last equation to obtain

$$I = S + (T - G) + (M - X)$$

This equation tells us that investment, I, is financed by household saving, S, the government budget balance, $(T - G)$, and borrowing from the rest of the world, $(M - X)$.

A government budget surplus, $T > G$, contributes funds to finance investment, but a government budget deficit, $T < G$, competes with investment for funds and decreases the amount available to invest.

Figure 23.2 Financial Flows and the Circular Flow of Expenditure and Income

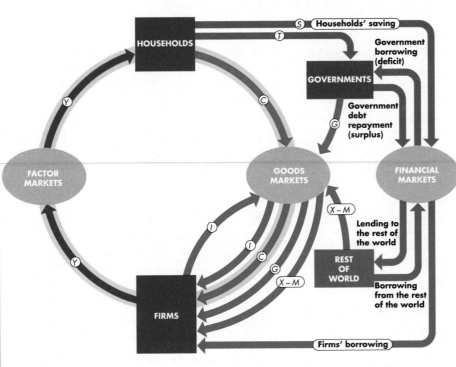

Households use their income for consumption expenditure (*C*), saving (*S*) and net taxes (*T*). Firms borrow to finance their investment expenditure.

Governments borrow to finance a budget deficit or repay debt if they have a budget surplus. The rest of the world borrows to finance its deficit or lends its surplus.

MyEconLab Animation

If we export less than we import, we borrow ($M - X$) from the rest of the world to finance some of our investment. If we export more than we import, we lend ($X - M$) to the rest of the world and part of UK saving finances investment in other countries.

The sum of private saving, *S*, and government saving, ($T - G$), is called **national saving**. National saving and foreign borrowing finance investment.

In 2012, total investment in the UK was £229 billion. The government (national and local combined) had a deficit of £98 billion. This total of £327 billion was financed by private saving of £290 billion and borrowing from the rest of the world (negative net exports) of £37 billion.

You're going to see how investment and saving and the flows of loanable funds – all measured in constant 2005 euros – are determined. The price in the loanable funds market that achieves equilibrium is an interest rate, which we also measure in real terms as the real interest rate. In the loanable funds market, there is just one interest rate, which is an average of the interest rates on all the different types of financial securities that we described earlier. Let's see what we mean by the real interest rate.

The Real Interest Rate

The **nominal interest rate** is the number of pounds or euros that a borrower pays and a lender receives in interest in a year expressed as a percentage of the number of pounds or euros borrowed and lent. For example, if the annual interest paid on a €500 loan is €25, the nominal interest rate is 5 per cent per year: €25 ÷ €500 × 100 or 5 per cent.

The **real interest rate** is the additional goods and services that the lender can buy with the interest received. It is the nominal interest rate adjusted to remove the effects of inflation on the buying power of money. The real interest rate is approximately equal to the nominal interest rate minus the inflation rate.

You can see why if you suppose that you have put €500 in a savings account that earns 5 per cent a year. At the end of a year, you have €525 in your savings account. Suppose that the inflation rate is 2 per cent per year – during the year, all prices increased by 2 per cent. Now, at the end of the year, it costs €510 to buy what €500 would have bought one year ago. Your money in the bank has really increased by only €15, from €510 to €525. That €15 is equivalent to a real interest rate of

3 per cent a year on your original €500. So the real interest rate is the 5 per cent nominal interest rate minus the 2 per cent inflation rate.[1]

The real interest rate is the opportunity cost of loanable funds. The real interest paid on borrowed funds is the opportunity cost of borrowing. And the real interest rate forgone when funds are used either to buy consumption goods and services or to invest in new capital goods is the opportunity cost of not saving or not lending those funds.

We're now going to see how the loanable funds market determines the real interest rate, the quantity of funds loaned, saving and investment. In the rest of this section, we'll ignore the government and the rest of the world and focus on households and firms in the loanable funds market. We'll study:

◆ The demand for loanable funds

◆ The supply of loanable funds

◆ Equilibrium in the loanable funds market

The Demand for Loanable Funds

The *quantity of loanable funds demanded* is the total quantity of funds demanded to finance investment, the government budget deficit and international investment or lending during a given period. Our focus here is on investment. We'll bring the other two items into the picture in later sections of this chapter.

What determines investment and the demand for loanable funds to finance it? Many details influence this decision, but we can summarise them in two factors:

1   The real interest rate

2   Expected profit

Firms invest in capital only if they expect to earn a profit, and fewer projects are profitable at a high real interest rate than at a low real interest rate, so:

Other things remaining the same, the higher the real interest rate, the smaller is the quantity of loanable funds demanded; and the lower the real interest rate, the greater is the quantity of loanable funds demanded.

---

[1] The exact real interest rate formula, which allows for the change in the purchasing power of both the interest and the loan, is:
Real interest rate = (Nominal interest rate − Inflation rate) ÷
(1 + Inflation rate/100). If the nominal interest rate is 5 per cent a year and the inflation rate is 2 per cent a year, the real interest rate is:
(5 − 2) ÷ (1 + 0.02) = 2.94 per cent a year.

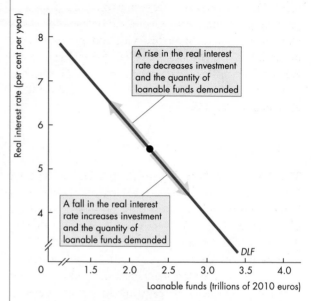

Figure 23.3   The Demand for Loanable Funds

A rise in the real interest rate decreases investment and the quantity of loanable funds demanded

A fall in the real interest rate increases investment and the quantity of loanable funds demanded

DLF

A change in the real interest rate changes the quantity of loanable funds demanded and brings a movement along the demand for loanable funds curve.

MyEconLab Animation ──────────────◆

Demand for Loanable Funds Curve

The **demand for loanable funds** is the relationship between the quantity of loanable funds demanded and the real interest rate, when all other influences on borrowing plans remain the same. The demand curve *DLF* in Figure 23.3 is a demand for loanable funds curve.

To understand the demand for loanable funds, think about Amazon.com's decision to borrow €100 million to build a new warehouse. If Amazon expects a return of €5 million a year from this investment before paying interest costs and the interest rate is less than 5 per cent a year, Amazon would make a profit, so it builds the warehouse. But if the interest rate is more than 5 per cent a year, Amazon would incur a loss, so it doesn't build the warehouse. The quantity of loanable funds demanded is greater the lower is the real interest rate.

Changes in the Demand for Loanable Funds

When the expected profit changes, the demand for loanable funds changes. Other things remaining the same, the greater the expected profit from new capital, the greater is the amount of investment and the greater the demand for loanable funds.

Expected profit rises during a business cycle expansion and falls during a recession; rises when technological change creates profitable new products; rises as a growing population brings increased demand for goods and services; and fluctuates with contagious swings of optimism and pessimism, called 'animal spirits' by Keynes and 'irrational exuberance' by Alan Greenspan.

When expected profit changes, the demand for loanable funds curve shifts.

The Supply of Loanable Funds

The *quantity of loanable funds supplied* is the total funds available from private saving, the government budget surplus and international borrowing during a given period. Our focus here is on saving. We'll bring the other two items into the picture later.

How do you decide how much of your income to save and supply in the loanable funds market? Your decision is influenced by many factors, but chief among them are:

1   The real interest rate
2   Disposable income
3   Expected future income
4   Wealth
5   Default risk

We begin by focusing on the real interest rate.

Other things remaining the same, the higher the real interest rate, the greater is the quantity of loanable funds supplied; and the lower the real interest rate, the smaller is the quantity of loanable funds supplied.

The Supply of Loanable Funds Curve

The **supply of loanable funds** is the relationship between the quantity of loanable funds supplied and the real interest rate when all other influences on lending plans remain the same. The curve *SLF* in Figure 23.4 is a supply of loanable funds curve.

Think about a student's decision to save some of what she earns from her summer job. With a real interest rate of 2 per cent a year, she decides that it is not worth saving much – better to spend the income and take a student loan if funds run out during the term. But if the real interest rate jumped to 10 per cent a year, the payoff from saving would be high enough to encourage her to cut back on spending and increase the amount she saves.

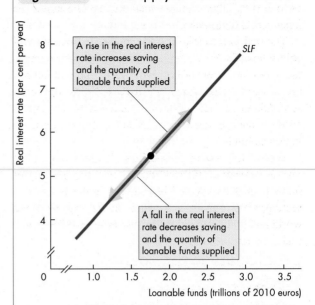

Figure 23.4   The Supply of Loanable Funds

A rise in the real interest rate increases saving and the quantity of loanable funds supplied

A fall in the real interest rate decreases saving and the quantity of loanable funds supplied

A change in the real interest rate changes the quantity of loanable funds supplied and brings a movement along the supply of loanable funds curve.

MyEconLab Animation ───────────────◆

Changes in the Supply of Loanable Funds

The supply of loanable funds changes if disposable income, expected future income, wealth or default risk changes.

Disposable Income

A household's *disposable income* is the income minus net taxes. When disposable income increases, both saving and consumption expenditure increase. So the greater a household's disposable income, other things remaining the same, the greater is its saving.

Expected Future Income

The higher a household's expected future income, the smaller is its saving today.

Wealth

The higher a household's wealth, other things remaining the same, the smaller is its saving. If a person's wealth increases because of a capital gain, the person sees less need to save.

For example, during 2007 when house prices were still rising, wealth increased despite the fact that personal saving dropped close to zero.

Default Risk

Default risk is the risk that a loan will not be repaid. The greater that risk, the higher is the interest rate needed to induce a person to lend and the smaller is the supply of loanable funds.

Shifts of the Supply of Loanable Funds Curve

When any of the four influences on the supply of loanable funds changes, the supply of loanable funds changes and the supply curve shifts. An increase in disposable income, a decrease in expected future income, a decrease in wealth, or a fall in default risk increases saving and increases the supply of loanable funds.

Equilibrium in the Loanable Funds Market

You've seen that other things remaining the same, the higher the real interest rate, the greater is the quantity of loanable funds supplied and the smaller is the quantity of loanable funds demanded. There is one real interest rate at which the quantities of loanable funds demanded and supplied are equal, and that interest rate is the equilibrium real interest rate.

Figure 23.5 shows how the demand for and supply of loanable funds determine the real interest rate. The *DLF* curve is the demand curve and the *SLF* curve is the supply curve. If the real interest rate exceeds 6 per cent a year, the quantity of loanable funds supplied exceeds the quantity demanded – a surplus of funds. Borrowers find it easy to get funds, but lenders are unable to lend all their funds. The real interest rate falls until the quantity of funds supplied equals the quantity demanded.

If the real interest rate is less than 6 per cent a year, the quantity of loanable funds supplied is less than the quantity demanded – a shortage of funds. Borrowers can't get the funds they want, but lenders are able to lend all the funds they have available. So the real interest rate rises and continues to rise until the quantity of funds supplied equals the quantity demanded.

Regardless of whether there is a surplus or a shortage of loanable funds, the real interest rate changes and is pulled towards an equilibrium level. In Figure 23.5, the equilibrium real interest rate is 6 per cent a year. At this interest rate there is neither a surplus nor a shortage of loanable funds. Borrowers can get the funds they want, and lenders can lend all the funds they have available. The investment plans of borrowers and the saving plans of lenders are consistent with each other.

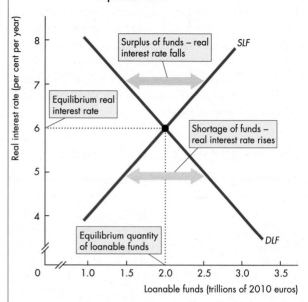

Figure 23.5 Loanable Funds Market Equilibrium

A surplus of funds lowers the real interest rate and a shortage of funds raises it. At an interest rate of 6 per cent a year, the quantity of funds demanded equals the quantity supplied and the market is in equilibrium.

MyEconLab Animation ——————————◆

Changes in Demand and Supply

Financial markets are highly volatile in the short run but remarkably stable in the long run. Volatility in the market comes from fluctuations in either the demand for loanable funds or the supply of loanable funds. These fluctuations bring fluctuations in the real interest rate and in the equilibrium quantity of funds lent and borrowed. They also bring fluctuations in asset prices.

Here we'll illustrate the effects of increases in demand and supply in the loanable funds market.

An Increase in Demand

If the profits that firms expect to earn increase, they increase their planned investment and increase their demand for loanable funds to finance that investment. With an increase in the demand for loanable funds, but no change in the supply of loanable funds, there is a shortage of funds. As borrowers compete for funds, the interest rate rises and lenders increase the quantity of funds supplied.

Figure 23.6(a) illustrates these changes. An increase in the demand for loanable funds shifts the demand curve rightward from DLF_0 to DLF_1. With no change in

Figure 23.6   Changes in Demand and Supply

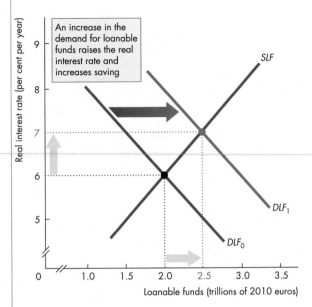

(a) An increase in demand

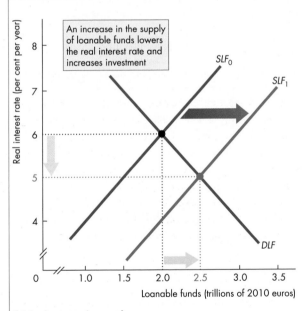

(b) An increase in supply

In part (a), the demand for loanable funds increases and supply doesn't change. The real interest rate rises (financial asset prices fall) and the quantity of funds increases.

In part (b), the supply of loanable funds increases and demand doesn't change. The real interest rate falls (financial asset prices rise) and the quantity of funds increases.

the supply of loanable funds, there is a shortage of funds at a real interest rate of 6 per cent a year. The real interest rate rises until it is 7 per cent a year. Equilibrium is restored and the equilibrium quantity of funds has increased.

An Increase in Supply

If one of the influences on saving plans changes and increases saving, the supply of loanable funds increases. With no change in the demand for loanable funds, the market is flush with loanable funds. Borrowers find bargains and lenders find themselves accepting a lower interest rate. At the lower interest rate, borrowers find additional investment projects profitable and increase the quantity of loanable funds that they borrow.

Figure 23.6(b) illustrates these changes. An increase in supply shifts the supply curve rightward from SLF_0 to SLF_1. With no change in demand, there is a surplus of funds at a real interest rate of 6 per cent a year. The real interest rate falls until it is 5 per cent a year. Equilibrium is restored and the equilibrium quantity of funds has increased.

Long-Run Growth of Demand and Supply

Over time, both demand and supply in the loanable funds market fluctuate and the real interest rate rises and falls. Both the supply of loanable funds and the demand for loanable funds tend to increase over time. On average, they increase at a similar pace, so although demand and supply trend upward, the real interest rate has no trend. It fluctuates around a constant average level.

REVIEW QUIZ

1   What is the loanable funds market?
2   Why is the real interest rate the opportunity cost of loanable funds?
3   How do firms make investment decisions?
4   What determines the demand for loanable funds and what makes it change?
5   How do households make saving decisions?
6   What determines the supply of loanable funds and what makes it change?
7   How do changes in the demand for and supply of loanable funds change the real interest rate and quantity of loanable funds?

Do these questions in Study Plan 23.2 and get instant feedback.   MyEconLab

ECONOMICS IN ACTION

Loanable Funds to Kick-Start the UK Property Market

The global financial crisis of 2008 had strong effects on the UK housing market, which in turn had effects on the UK loanable funds market.

The effect of the financial crisis on the housing market was twofold. First, it brought falling house prices. By 2012, house prices in the UK were 11 per cent below their 2007 levels. We can think of the rate of change in house prices as an indicator of the expected profit from house purchases. With house prices falling, people expect to incur losses, so the demand for houses decreases. A decrease in the demand for houses decreases the demand for loanable funds.

Second, falling house prices increases the number of defaults, which makes lending for house purchases more risky. An increase in the riskiness of loans decreases the supply of loanable funds.

Figure 1 illustrates these effects in the UK loanable funds market, starting in 2007. In that year, the demand for loanable funds was DLF_{07} and the supply of loanable funds was SLF_{07}. The equilibrium real interest rate was 3.5 per cent a year and the equilibrium quantity of loanable funds was £2.5 trillion (in 2010 pounds).

In the five years to 2012, the recession and falling house prices led to a decrease in the demand for mortgages and the demand for loanable funds curve shifted leftward to DLF_{12}. The increased riskiness from default led to a decrease in the supply of loanable funds, and the supply of loanable funds

curve shifted leftward to SLF_{12}. The real interest rate fell to 1.2 per cent and the quantity of loanable funds decreased to £2.15 trillion – a decrease of 12 per cent in five years.

In July 2012, the UK government announced a special 'funding for lending' scheme whereby the Bank of England would buy mortgage and loan assets from the commercial banks to a total of £20 billion to release funds for the banks to lend for house purchase and small business lending.

The scheme has been slow to boost business lending, but signs of the mortgage market reviving were seen in March 2013, with lending for house purchases increasing by 9 per cent over February and an increase in mortgage lending in the first quarter of £31 billion (in 2010 prices).

The object of the 'funding for lending' scheme is to get the loanable funds market growing again, in particular for growth in mortgage lending and lending to small businesses.

Figure 2 shows the effect of the 'funding for lending' scheme. The increased demand for loanable funds shifted the demand for loanable funds curve from DLF_{12} to DLF_{13} and the increased supply of loanable funds shifted the supply of loanable funds curve from SLF_{12} to SLF_{13}. The quantity of loanable funds increased from £2.15 trillion to £2.27 trillion in 2013, but the equilibrium interest rate rose above 1.2 per cent a year.

While there is little evidence that the 'funding for lending' scheme has revived lending to small businesses, house prices were rising at the beginning of 2013 and mortgage companies were offering loans in the range of 95 to 100 per cent of the value of the property purchased. Loans at this level were last seen in mid-2007.

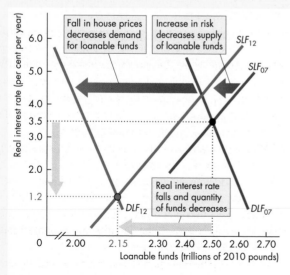

Figure 1 Loanable Funds Market: Effects of Fall in House Prices

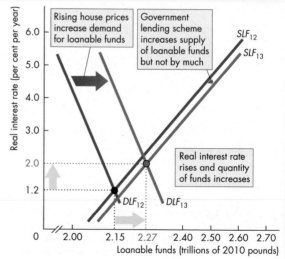

Figure 2 Loanable Funds Market: Effects of Lending Scheme

Government in the Loanable Funds Market

Government enters the loanable funds market when it has a budget surplus or budget deficit. A government budget surplus increases the supply of loanable funds and contributes to financing investment; a government budget deficit increases the demand for loanable funds and competes with businesses for funds. Let's study the effects of government on the loanable funds market.

A Government Budget Surplus

A government budget surplus increases the supply of loanable funds. The real interest rate falls, which decreases household saving and decreases the quantity of private funds supplied. The lower real interest rate increases the quantity of loanable funds demanded and increases investment.

Figure 23.7 shows these effects of a government budget surplus. The private supply of loanable funds curve is *PSLF*. The supply of loanable funds curve, *SLF*, shows the sum of private supply and the government budget surplus. Here, the government budget surplus is €1 trillion, so at each real interest rate the *SLF* curve lies €1 trillion to the right of the *PSLF* curve. That is, the horizontal distance between the *PSLF* curve and the *SLF* curve equals the government budget surplus.

With no government surplus, the real interest rate is 6 per cent a year, the quantity of loanable funds is €2 trillion a year and investment is €2 trillion a year. But with the government surplus of €1 trillion a year, the equilibrium real interest rate falls to 5 per cent a year and the equilibrium quantity of loanable funds increases to €2.5 trillion a year.

The fall in the interest rate decreases private saving to €1.5 trillion, but investment increases to €2.5 trillion, which is financed by private saving plus the government budget surplus (government saving).

Government budget surpluses are rare today. Most governments, including the UK, the US and most in the EU, have deficits and some of them very large ones.

Let's see how a government budget deficit influences the loanable funds market.

A Government Budget Deficit

A government budget deficit increases the demand for loanable funds. The real interest rate rises, which increases household saving and increases the quantity of private funds supplied. But the higher real interest rate decreases investment and the quantity of loanable funds demanded by firms to finance investment.

Figure 23.8 shows these effects of a government budget deficit. The private demand for loanable funds curve is *PDLF*. The demand for loanable funds curve, *DLF*, shows the sum of private demand and the government budget deficit. Here, the government budget deficit is €1 trillion, so at each real interest rate the *DLF* curve lies €1 trillion to the right of the *PDLF* curve. That is, the horizontal distance between the *PDLF* curve and the *DLF* curve equals the government budget deficit.

With no government deficit, the real interest rate is 6 per cent a year, the quantity of loanable funds is €2 trillion a year and investment is €2 trillion a year. But with the government budget deficit of €1 trillion a year, the equilibrium real interest rate rises to 7 per cent a year and the equilibrium quantity of loanable funds increases to €2.5 trillion a year.

The rise in the real interest rate increases private saving to €2.5 trillion, but investment decreases to €1.5 trillion because €1 trillion of private saving must finance the government budget deficit.

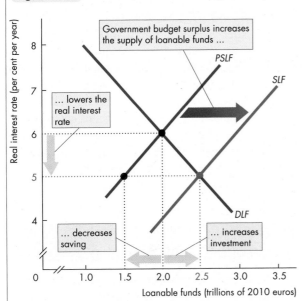

Figure 23.7 A Government Budget Surplus

A government budget surplus of €1 trillion is added to private saving and the private supply of loanable funds (*PSLF*) to determine the supply of loanable funds, *SLF*. The real interest rate falls to 5 per cent a year, private saving decreases, but investment increases to €2.5 trillion.

MyEconLab Animation ⬥

Figure 23.8   A Government Budget Deficit

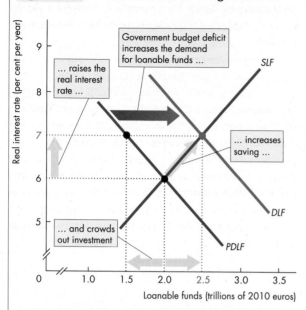

A government budget deficit adds to the private demand for loanable funds curve (*PDLF*) to determine the demand for loanable funds curve, *DLF*. The real interest rate rises, saving increases, but investment decreases – a crowding-out effect.

MyEconLab Animation ──────────────◆

Figure 23.9   The Ricardo–Barro Effect

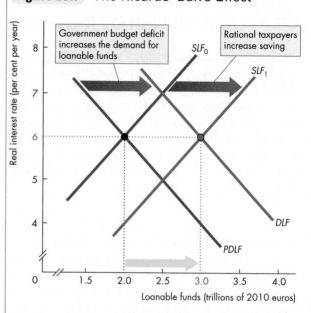

A budget deficit increases the demand for loanable funds. Rational taxpayers increase saving, which increases the supply of loanable funds curve from SLF_0 to SLF_1. Crowding out is avoided: increased saving finances the budget deficit.

MyEconLab Animation ──────────────◆

The Crowding-Out Effect

The tendency for a government budget deficit to raise the real interest rate and decrease investment is called the **crowding-out effect**. The budget deficit crowds out investment by competing with businesses for scarce financial capital.

The crowding-out effect does not decrease investment by the full amount of the government budget deficit because the higher real interest rate induces an increase in private saving that partly contributes toward financing the deficit.

The Ricardo–Barro Effect

First suggested by the English economist David Ricardo in the eighteenth century and refined by Robert J. Barro of Harvard University, the Ricardo–Barro effect holds that both of the effects we've just shown are wrong, and that the government budget, whether in surplus or deficit, has no effect on either the real interest rate or investment.

Barro says that taxpayers are rational. They can see that a budget deficit today means that future taxes will be higher and future disposable incomes will be smaller.

With smaller expected future disposable incomes, saving increases today. Private saving and the private supply of loanable funds increase to match the quantity of loanable funds demanded by the government. So the budget deficit has no effect on either the real interest rate or investment. Figure 23.9 shows this outcome.

Most economists regard the Ricardo–Barro view as extreme. But there might be some change in private saving that goes in the direction suggested by the Ricardo–Barro effect that lessens the crowding-out effect.

◆ REVIEW QUIZ

1   How does a government budget surplus or deficit influence the loanable funds market?
2   What is the crowding-out effect and how does it work?
3   What is the Ricardo–Barro effect and how does it modify the crowding-out effect?

Do these questions in Study Plan 23.3 and get instant feedback.   MyEconLab

The Global Loanable Funds Market

The loanable funds market is global, not national. Lenders on the supply side of the market want to earn the highest possible real interest rate, and they will seek it by looking everywhere in the world. Borrowers on the demand side of the market want to pay the lowest possible real interest rate, and they will seek it by looking everywhere in the world. Financial capital is mobile: it moves to the best advantage of lenders and borrowers.

International Capital Mobility

If a US supplier of loanable funds can earn a higher interest rate in Tokyo than in New York, funds supplied in Japan will increase and funds supplied in the US will decrease – funds will flow from the US to Japan.

If a US demander of loanable funds can pay a lower interest rate in Paris than in New York, the demand for funds in France will increase and the demand for funds in the US will decrease – funds will flow from France to the US.

Because lenders are free to seek the highest real interest rate and borrowers are free to seek the lowest real interest rate, the loanable funds market is a single, integrated, global market. Funds flow into the country in which the interest rate is highest and out of the country in which the interest rate is lowest.

When funds leave the country with the lowest interest rate, a shortage of funds raises the real interest rate. When funds move into the country with the highest interest rate, a surplus of funds lowers the real interest rate. The free international mobility of financial capital pulls real interest rates around the world toward equality.

Only when the real interest rates in New York, Tokyo and Paris are equal does the incentive to move funds from one country to another stop.

Equality of real interest rates does not mean that if you calculate the average real interest rate in New York, Tokyo and Paris, you'll get the same number. To compare real interest rates, we must compare financial assets of equal risk.

Lending is risky. A loan might not be repaid. Or the price of a stock or bond might fall. Interest rates include a risk premium – the riskier the loan, other things remaining the same, the higher is the interest rate. The interest rate on a risky loan minus that on a safe loan is called the *risk premium* and the gaps between interest rates are called *interest rate spreads*.

International capital mobility brings real interest rates in all parts of the world to equality except for differences that reflect differences in risk – differences in the risk premium.

International Borrowing and Lending

A country's loanable funds market connects with the global market through net exports. If a country's net exports are negative ($X < M$), the rest of the world supplies funds to that country and the quantity of loanable funds in that country is greater than national saving. If a country's net exports are positive ($X > M$), the country is a net supplier of funds to the rest of the world and the quantity of loanable funds in that country is less than national saving.

Demand and Supply in the Global and National Markets

The demand for and supply of funds in the global loanable funds market determine the world equilibrium real interest rate. This interest rate makes the quantity of loanable funds demanded equal the quantity supplied in the world economy. But it does not make the quantity of funds demanded and supplied equal in each national economy. The demand for and supply of funds in a national economy determine whether the country is a lender to or a borrower from the rest of the world.

The Global Loanable Funds Market

Figure 23.10(a) illustrates the global market. The demand for loanable funds curve, DLF_W, is the sum of the demands in all countries. Similarly, the supply of loanable funds curve, SLF_W, is the sum of the supplies in all countries. The world equilibrium real interest rate makes the quantity of funds supplied in the world as a whole equal to the quantity demanded. In this example, the equilibrium real interest rate is 5 per cent a year and the equilibrium quantity of funds is €10 trillion.

An International Borrower

Figure 23.10(b) shows the loanable funds market in a country that borrows from the rest of the world. The country's demand for loanable funds curve, DLF, is part of the world demand in Figure 23.10(a). The country's supply of loanable funds curve, SLF_D, is part of the world supply.

Figure 23.10 Borrowing and Lending in the Global Loanable Funds Market

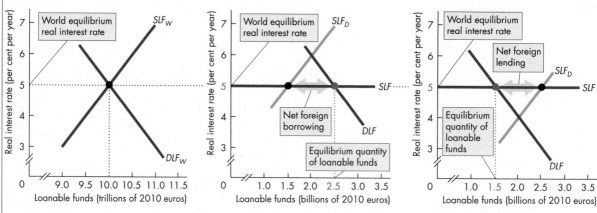

(a) The global market   **(b) An international borrower**   **(c) An international lender**

In the global loanable funds market in part (a), the demand for loanable funds curve, DLF_W, and the supply of funds curve, SLF_W, determine the world real interest rate. Each country can get funds at the world real interest rate and faces the (horizontal) supply curve SLF in parts (b) and (c).

At the world real interest rate, borrowers in part (b) want more funds than the quantity supplied by domestic lenders (SLF_D). The shortage is made up by international borrowing.

At the world real interest rate, domestic lenders in part (c) want to lend more than domestic borrowers demand. The excess quantity supplied goes to foreign borrowers.

MyEconLab Animation ————————————————————————————————◆

If this country were isolated from the global market, the real interest rate would be 6 per cent a year (where the DLF and SLF_D curves intersect). But if the country is integrated into the global economy, with an interest rate of 6 per cent a year, funds would *flood into* it. With a real interest rate of 5 per cent a year in the rest of the world, suppliers of loanable funds would seek the higher return in this country. In effect, the country faces the supply of loanable funds curve SLF, which is horizontal at the world equilibrium real interest rate.

The country's demand for loanable funds and the world interest rate determine the equilibrium quantity of loanable funds – €2.5 billion in Figure 23.10(b).

An International Lender

Figure 23.10(c) shows the situation in a country that lends to the rest of the world. As before, the country's demand for loanable funds curve, DLF, is part of the world demand, and the country's supply of loanable funds curve, SLF_D, is part of the world supply in Figure 23.10(a).

If this country were isolated from the global economy, the real interest rate would be 4 per cent a year (where the DLF and SLF_D curves intersect). But if this country is integrated into the global economy, with an interest rate of 4 per cent a year, funds would quickly

flow out of it. With a real interest rate of 5 per cent a year in the rest of the world, domestic suppliers of loanable funds would seek the higher return in other countries. Again, the country faces the supply of loanable funds curve SLF, which is horizontal at the world equilibrium real interest rate.

The country's demand for loanable funds and the world interest rate determine the equilibrium quantity of loanable funds – €1.5 billion in Figure 23.10(c).

Changes in Demand and Supply

A change in the demand or supply in the global loanable funds market changes the real interest rate in the way shown in Figure 23.6 (see p. 543). The effect of a change in demand or supply in a national market depends on the size of the country. A change in demand or supply in a small country has no significant effect on global demand or supply, so it leaves the world real interest rate unchanged and changes only the country's net exports and international borrowing or lending. A change in demand or supply in a large country has a significant effect on global demand or supply, so it changes the world real interest rate as well as the country's net exports and international borrowing or lending. Every country feels some of the effect of a large country's change in demand or supply.

ECONOMICS IN ACTION

Greenspan's Interest Rate Puzzle

The real interest rate paid by big corporations in the US fell from 5.5 per cent a year in 2001 to 2.5 per cent a year in 2005. Alan Greenspan, then the Chairman of the Federal Reserve, said he was puzzled that the real interest rate was falling at a time when the US government budget deficit was increasing.

Why did the real interest rate fall?

The answer lies in the global loanable funds market. Rapid economic growth in Asia and Europe brought a large increase in global saving, which in turn increased the global supply of loanable funds. The supply of loanable funds increased because Asian and European saving increased strongly.

The US government budget deficit increased the US and global demand for loanable funds. But this increase was very small compared with the increase in the global supply of loanable funds.

The result of a large increase in supply and a small increase in demand was a fall in the world equilibrium real interest rate and an increase in the equilibrium quantity of loanable funds.

Figure 1 illustrates these events. The supply of loanable funds increased from SLF_{01} in 2001 to SLF_{05} in 2005. (In the figure, we ignore the change in the global demand for loanable funds because it was small relative to the increase in supply.)

With the increase in supply, the real interest rate fell from 5.5 per cent to 2.5 per cent a year and the quantity of loanable funds increased.

In the US, borrowing from the rest of the world increased to finance the increased government budget deficit.

The interest rate puzzle illustrates the important fact that the loanable funds market is a global market, not a national market.

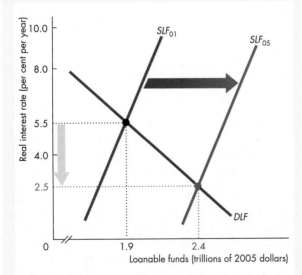

Figure 1   The Global Loanable Funds Market

REVIEW QUIZ

1. Why do loanable funds flow among countries?
2. What determines the demand for and supply of loanable funds in an individual economy?
3. What happens if a country has a shortage of loanable funds at the world real interest rate?
4. What happens if a country has a surplus of loanable funds at the world real interest rate?
5. How is a government budget deficit financed in an open economy?

Do these questions in Study Plan 23.4 and get instant feedback.   MyEconLab

To complete your study of financial markets, take a look at *Reading Between the Lines* on pp. 550–551 and see how you can use the model of the loanable funds market to understand the events in the EU financial market crisis of 2010.

READING BETWEEN THE LINES

Loanable Funds in Europe

Europe's SMEs Face Interest Rate Squeeze

Ralph Atkins

Emergency central bank action to calm the eurozone crisis has failed to prevent a surge in borrowing costs faced by small businesses in Italy and Spain this year, pushing the divergence with German interest rates back to mid-2012 levels. . . .

Reversing falls late last year, the interest rate on one- to five-year bank loans of up to €1 million rose in Spain to 5.97 per cent in January, up from 5.65 per cent in December, according to ECB data.

Italy saw a rise to 5.82 per cent from 5.55 per cent.

Even after the latest increases, interest rates paid by Spanish and Italian SMEs [small and medium entreprises] were still lower than July last year when Mario Draghi, ECB President, pledged to do 'whatever it takes' to preserve the eurozone's integrity.

The ECB has also pumped more than €1 trillion in cheap three-year loans in the eurozone financial system.

But calculations by Barclays show the spread between interest rates on Italian and Spanish business loans of less than €1m and equivalent loans in Germany was wider in January than last July – suggesting German companies were benefiting more from the ultra-loose monetary policy of the ECB and other central banks worldwide. . . .

Spreads between 10-year Spanish and Italian government bonds and their German equivalents also widened in January, although they remained far below last July's levels.

FT *Source:* FT.com, 6 March 2013.
© The Financial Times Limited. All Rights Reserved.

 The Essence of the Story

- The European Central Bank has made more than €1 trillion available to SMEs.

- The goal was to lower the interest rate faced by SMEs in Italy and Spain, but the funds have benefited mainly German small companies.

- The spread between interest rates on loans to Italian and Spanish SMEs over equivalent loans to German SMEs widened in 2013.

- The spreads between Spanish and Italian 10-year government bonds over German equivalent bonds also increased in January 2013.

Economic Analysis

◆ Interest rates in Italy and Spain (and some other euro area countries) are much higher than in Germany, whose bonds are considered to be free of default risk.

◆ The gap between the real interest rate in Italy and Spain and the real interest rate in Germany is called the interest rate spread. Figure 1 shows the interest rate spread on government bonds since 2009.

◆ The main reason why interest rates in Spain and Italy are higher than in Germany is that their governments have larger budget deficits and larger government debts.

◆ In contrast, Germany has a small budget deficit and low government debt.

◆ Figure 2 shows the government budget deficit and government debt in the three countries.

◆ A budget deficit increases the demand for loanable funds. A large government debt increases the risk of default and decreases the supply of loanable funds. Both effects raise the real interest rate.

◆ Figure 3 illustrates these effects. The demand for loanable funds with no budget deficit is *PDLF*. The supply of loanable funds with no default risk is *SLF*$_0$. The real interest rate is 5 per cent a year. This situation is similar to that in Germany.

◆ A large budget deficit increases the demand for loanable funds and shifts the demand curve rightward to *DLF*. A large debt increases default risk, which decreases the supply of loanable funds and shifts the supply curve leftward to *SLF*$_1$. The real interest rate rises to 7 per cent a year. This situation is similar to that of Italy and Spain.

◆ SMEs compete with governments and other borrowers for funds, and the interest rate they face includes a risk premium that is low for German SMEs and high for Italian and Spanish SMEs.

Figure 1   Bond Interest Rate Spreads

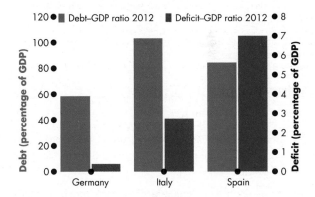

Figure 2   Budget Deficits and Debts

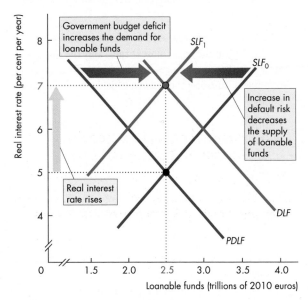

Figure 3   The Loanable Funds Market

SUMMARY

Key Points

Financial Institutions and Financial Markets (pp. 534–538)

◆ Capital (*physical capital*) is a real productive resource; financial capital is the funds used to buy capital.

◆ Gross investment increases the quantity of capital and depreciation decreases it. Saving increases wealth.

◆ The markets for financial capital are the markets for loans, bonds and stocks.

◆ Financial institutions ensure that borrowers and lenders can always find someone with whom to trade.

Do Problems 1 to 5 to get a better understanding of financial institutions and markets.

The Loanable Funds Market (pp. 538–544)

◆ Investment in capital is financed by household saving, a government budget surplus and funds from the rest of the world.

◆ The quantity of loanable funds demanded depends negatively on the real interest rate and the demand for loanable funds changes when profit expectations change.

◆ The quantity of loanable funds supplied depends positively on the real interest rate, and the supply of loanable funds changes when disposable income, expected future income, wealth and default risk change.

◆ Equilibrium in the loanable funds market determines the real interest rate and quantity of funds.

Do Problems 6 to 9 to get a better understanding of the loanable funds market.

Government in the Loanable Funds Market (pp. 545–546)

◆ A government budget surplus increases the supply of loanable funds, lowers the real interest rate and increases investment and the equilibrium quantity of loanable funds.

◆ A government budget deficit increases the demand for loanable funds, raises the real interest rate and increases the equilibrium quantity of loanable funds, but decreases investment in a crowding-out effect.

◆ The Ricardo–Barro effect is the response of rational taxpayers to a budget deficit: private saving increases to finance the budget deficit. The real interest rate remains constant and the crowding-out effect is avoided.

Do Problems 10 to 15 to get a better understanding of government in the loanable funds market.

The Global Loanable Funds Market (pp. 547–549)

◆ The loanable funds market is a global market.

◆ The equilibrium real interest rate is determined in the global loanable funds market, and national demand and supply determine the quantity of international borrowing or lending.

Do Problems 16 to 18 to get a better understanding of the global loanable funds market.

Key Terms

Bond, 535
Bond market, 535
Crowding-out effect, 546
Demand for loanable funds, 540
Financial capital, 534
Financial institution, 536
Gross investment, 534
Loanable funds market, 538
Mortgage, 535
Mortgage-backed security, 536
National saving, 539
Net investment, 534
Net taxes, 538
Net worth, 537
Nominal interest rate, 539
Real interest rate, 539
Saving, 534
Stock, 536
Stock market, 536
Supply of loanable funds, 541
Wealth, 534

STUDY PLAN PROBLEMS AND APPLICATIONS

Do Problems 1 to 18 in MyEconLab Chapter 23 Study Plan and get instant feedback. MyEconLab

Financial Institutions and Financial Markets (Study Plan 23.1)

Use the following information in Problems 1 and 2.

Michael is an Internet service provider. On 31 December 2012, he bought an existing business with servers and a building worth €400,000. During his first year of operation, his business grew and he bought new servers for €500,000. The market value of some of his older servers fell by €100,000.

1 Calculate Michael's gross investment, depreciation and net investment during 2013.

2 What is the value of Michael's capital at the end of 2013?

3 Lori is a student who teaches golf at the weekend, and in a year earns €20,000 after paying her taxes. At the beginning of 2010, Lori owned €1,000 worth of books, DVDs and golf clubs and she had €5,000 in a savings account at the bank. During 2010, the interest on her savings account was €300 and she spent a total of €15,300 on consumption goods and services. There was no change in the market values of her books, DVDs and golf clubs.

  a How much did Lori save in 2010?

  b What was her wealth at the end of 2010?

4 In a speech at the CFA Society of Nebraska in February 2007, William Poole, former Chairman of the St Louis Federal Reserve Bank said:

Over most of the post–Second World War period, the personal saving rate averaged about 6 per cent, with some higher years from the mid-1970s to mid-1980s.

The negative trend in the saving rate started in the mid-1990s, about the same time the stock market boom started. Thus it is hard to dismiss the hypothesis that the decline in the measured saving rate in the late 1990s reflected the response of consumption to large capital gains from corporate equity stock.

Evidence from panel data of households also supports the conclusion that the decline in the personal saving rate since 1984 is largely a consequence of capital gains on corporate equities.

  a Is the purchase of corporate equities part of household consumption or saving? Explain your answer.

  b Equities reap a capital gain in the same way that houses reap a capital gain. Does this mean that the purchase of equities is investment? If not, explain why it is not.

5 **Interest Rate on Government Bonds Rising**

The interest rates on UK and German government bonds have risen. For example, the interest rate on 10-year UK government bonds rose above 2.6 per cent today.

        Source: *The Financial Times*, 14 August 2013

  a What is the relationship between the price of a bond and the interest rate it earns?

  b Explain why the interest rates on UK and German bonds have risen.

The Loanable Funds Markets
(Study Plan 23.2)

Use the following information in Problems 6 and 7.

First Call plc is a mobile phone company. It plans to build an assembly plant that costs £10 million if the real interest rate is 6 per cent a year. If the real interest rate is 5 per cent a year, First Call will build a larger plant that costs £12 million. And if the real interest rate is 7 per cent a year, First Call will build a smaller plant that costs £8 million.

6 Draw a graph of First Call's demand for loanable funds curve.

7 First Call expects its profit from the sale of mobile phones to double next year. If other things remain the same, explain how this increase in expected profit influences First Call's demand for loanable funds.

8 Draw a graph to illustrate how an increase in the supply of loanable funds and a decrease in the demand for loanable funds can lower the real interest rate and leave the equilibrium quantity of loanable funds unchanged.

9 Use the information in Problem 4.

  a US household income has grown considerably since 1984. Has US saving been on a downward trend because Americans feel wealthier?

  b Explain why households preferred to buy corporate equities rather than bonds.

Government in the Loanable Funds Market (Study Plan 23.3)

Use the following table in Problems 10 to 12.

The table shows an economy's demand for loanable funds and the supply of loanable funds schedules, when the government's budget is balanced.

Real interest rate (per cent per year)	Loanable funds demanded	Loanable funds supplied
	(billions of 2010 euros)	
4	850	550
5	800	600
6	750	650
7	700	700
8	650	750
9	600	800
10	550	850

10 Suppose that the government has a budget surplus of €100 billion. What are the real interest rate, the quantity of investment and the quantity of private saving? Is there any crowding out in this situation?

11 Suppose that the government has a budget deficit of €100 billion. What are the real interest rate, the quantity of investment and the quantity of private saving? Is there any crowding out in this situation?

12 Suppose that the government has a budget deficit of €100 billion and the Ricardo–Barro effect occurs. What are the real interest rate and the quantity of investment?

Use the table in Problem 10 and the following information in Problems 13 to 15.

Suppose that the quantity of loanable funds demanded increases by €100 billion at each real interest rate and the quantity of loanable funds supplied increases by €200 billion at each interest rate.

13 If the government budget is balanced, what are the real interest rate, the quantity of loanable funds, investment and private saving? Does any crowding out occur?

14 If the government budget becomes a deficit of €100 billion, what are the real interest rate, the quantity of loanable funds, investment and private saving? Does any crowding out occur?

15 If the government wants to stimulate investment and increase it to €900 billion, what must it do?

The Global Loanable Funds Market (Study Plan 23.4)

Use the following news clip in Problems 16 and 17.

UK Savings and Current Account Deficit
The current account deficit of the UK in 2012 was 3.7 per cent of GDP. The UK was a net borrower to the tune of £54 billion. Companies and households in the UK are saving more because they borrowed too much in the boom years. The rise in savings has depressed domestic demand, but the fall in domestic demand has not been offset by a rise in foreign demand. Economic commentators say that exports will increase eventually and the current account deficit will decline as British exports increase as world growth increases.

Source: *BBC*, 2 April 2013

16 Why is the UK a net borrower in international capital markets?

17 **a** What implications do the UK current account deficit (negative net exports) and our reliance on foreign credit have for economic performance in the UK?

b What policies, if any, should be used to address this situation?

18 **IMF Says It Battled Crisis Well**

The International Monetary Fund (IMF) reported that it acted effectively in combating the global recession. Since September 2008, the IMF made $163 billion available to developing countries. While the IMF urged developed countries and China to run deficits to stimulate their economies, the IMF required developing countries with large deficits to cut spending and not increase spending.

Source: *The Wall Street Journal*, 29 September 2009

a Explain how increased government budget deficits change the loanable funds market.

b Would the global recession have been less severe had the IMF made larger loans to developing countries?

ADDITIONAL PROBLEMS AND APPLICATIONS

Do these problems in MyEconLab if assigned by your lecturer.

MyEconLab

Financial Institutions and Financial Markets

19 On 1 January 2012, Terry's Towing Service owned 4 tow trucks valued at €300,000. During 2012, Terry's bought 2 new trucks for a total of €180,000. At the end of 2012, the market value of all of the firm's trucks was €400,000. What was Terry's gross investment? Calculate Terry's depreciation and net investment.

Use the following information in Problems 20 and 21.

The Office for National Statistics reported that the UK capital stock was £5,014 billion at the end of 2011, £4,982 billion at the end of 2010 and £4,908.6 billion at the end of 2009. Depreciation in 2010 was £152 billion, and gross investment during 2011 was £198 billion (all in 2006 pounds).

20 Calculate UK net investment and gross investment during 2010.

21 Calculate UK depreciation and net investment during 2011.

22 Annie runs a fitness centre. On 31 December 2012, she bought an existing business with exercise equipment and a building worth €300,000. During 2013, business improved and she bought some new equipment for €50,000. At the end of 2013, her equipment and buildings were worth €325,000. Calculate Annie's gross investment, depreciation and net investment during 2013.

23 Karrie is a golf pro and, after she paid taxes, her income from golf and interest from financial assets was €1,500,000 in 2013. At the beginning of 2013, she owned €900,000 worth of financial assets. During 2013, the market value of her financial assets did not change. At the end of 2013, her financial assets were worth €1,900,000.

a How much did Karrie save during 2010?

b How much did she spend on consumption goods and services?

The Loanable Funds Markets

Use the following information in Problems 24 and 25.

In 2013, the Lee family had disposable income of £80,000, wealth of £140,000, and an expected future income of £80,000 a year. At a real interest rate of 4 per cent a year, the Lee family saves £15,000 a year; at a real interest rate of 6 per cent a year, they save £20,000 a year; and at a real interest rate of 8 per cent, they save £25,000 a year.

24 Draw a graph of the Lee family's supply of loanable funds curve.

25 In 2014, suppose that the stock market crashes and the default risk increases. Explain how this increase in default risk influences the Lee family's supply of loanable funds curve.

26 Draw a graph to illustrate the effect of an increase in the demand for loanable funds and an even larger increase in the supply of loanable funds on the real interest rate and the equilibrium quantity of loanable funds.

27 **Greenspan's Conundrum Spells Confusion for Us All**

In January 2005, the interest rate on bonds was 4 per cent a year and it was expected to rise to 5 per cent a year by the end of 2005. As the rate rose to 4.3 per cent a year during February, most commentators focused, not on why the interest rate rose, but on why it was so low before. Explanations of this 'conundrum' included that unusual buying and expectations for an economic slow-down were keeping the interest rate low.

Source: *The Financial Times*, 26 February 2005

a Explain how 'unusual buying' might lead to a low real interest rate.

b Explain how investors' 'expectations for an economic slowdown' might lead to a lower real interest rate.

Government in the Loanable Funds Market

Use the following news clip in Problems 28 and 29.

India's Economy Hits the Wall

At the start of 2008, India had an annual growth of 9 per cent, huge consumer demand, and increasing foreign investment. But by July 2008, India had 11.4 per cent a year inflation, large government deficits, and rising interest rates. Economic growth is expected to fall to 7 per cent a year by the end of 2008. A Goldman Sachs report suggests that India needs to lower the government's deficit, raise educational achievement, control inflation and liberalise its financial markets.

Source: *Business Week*, 1 July 2008

28 If the Indian government reduces its deficit and returns to a balanced budget, how will the demand or supply of loanable funds in India change?

29 With economic growth forecasted to slow, future incomes are expected to fall. If other things remain the same, how will the demand or supply of loanable funds in India change?

30 Return of Growth and the Deficit

While UK government borrowing is on a downward track, the recent growth rates that show a recovering economy may not be enough to reduce the government's deficit at a faster rate. Government current spending in April–July was 4.3 per cent up on a year ago, which is an odd form of austerity. Much of this is local authority spending which is bringing forward capital spending plans. Weak earnings depress tax revenues and also corporations have become adept in avoiding taxes. However, stronger growth in 2013 will feed into revenues and the deficit could come in lower than forecasted by the Office for Budget Responsibility.

Source: *The Sunday Times*, 25 August 2013

Explain how the UK government's budget deficit and the stronger economic growth influence the loanable funds market in the UK.

31 Explain how an increase in the government budget deficit influences the loanable funds market. Explain whether the demand for loanable funds or the supply of loanable funds or both change. On a graph, show how the real interest rate and the quantity of loanable funds change.

32 Explain how an increase in government debt influences the loanable funds market. Explain whether the demand for loanable funds or the supply of loanable funds or both change. On a graph, show how the real interest rate and the quantity of loanable funds change.

The Global Loanable Funds Market

33 IMF Readies Rescue Plan for Italy

The International Monetary Fund (IMF) has prepared a rescue plan worth up to 600 billion euros. The market interest rate on two-year and five-year Italian government bonds has risen above 7 per cent per year but the IMF would guarantee interest rates of 4 per cent or 5 per cent per year on its loan.

Source: ninemsn.com.au, 27 November 2011

a Explain how an IMF loan to Italy influences the global loanable funds market.

b On a graph illustrate the effects.

34 The Global Savings Glut and Its Consequences

Several developing countries are running large current account surpluses (representing an excess of savings over investment) and rapid growth has led to high saving rates as people save a large fraction of additional income. In India, the saving rate has risen from 23 per cent a decade ago to 33 per cent today. China's saving rate is 55 per cent. The glut of saving in Asia is being put into US bonds. When a poor country buys US bonds, it is in effect lending to the US.

Source: The Cato Institute, 8 June 2007

a Graphically illustrate and explain the impact of the 'glut of savings' on the real interest rate and the quantity of loanable funds.

b How do the high saving rates in Asia influence investment in the US?

Use the following news clip in Problems 35 to 38.

The UK had record trade deficits in 2006 and 2007 because it imported more manufactured goods than it sold abroad. This deficit, although large, was dwarfed by capital flows into the UK. Capital had flowed into the UK to finance new enterprises and foreign takeovers. The result is that, through foreign capital, the UK has been able to live well beyond its means for decades. Domestic interest rates have remained low as British banks borrowed funds from the global financial market.

Source: David Smith's *Sunday Times* blog,
25 February 2007

35 Explain why, for more than a decade, capital flows into the UK dwarfed the record trade deficit in goods.

36 Explain what effect the inflow of funds into the UK will have on the interest rate on foreign borrowed funds and domestic interest rates.

37 Funds had been flowing into the UK for a decade before the global banking crisis. Why might this have caused a problem during the global banking crisis of 2007–2008?

38 Could the UK government have stopped funds from flowing in from other countries? If so, how?

Economics in the News

39 After you have studied *Reading Between the Lines* on pp. 550–551, answer the following questions.

a What is the distinction between a government budget deficit and government debt?

b Explain why interest rates on Italian and Spanish government bonds are higher than the interest rate on German government bonds.

c What might be the reason for the risk premium on Italian and Spanish bonds?

d Why are the interest rates faced by the governments of Italy and Spain and the SMEs in those countries higher than those faced by government and SMEs in Germany? Illustrate your answer with a graph.

24

Money, the Price Level and Inflation

After studying this chapter you will be able to:

- ◆ Define money and describe its functions
- ◆ Explain what banks are and their economic functions
- ◆ Describe the functions of a central bank
- ◆ Explain how the banking system creates money
- ◆ Explain how the demand for and supply of money determine the nominal interest rate
- ◆ Explain how the quantity of money influences the price level and the inflation rate

Money, like fire and the wheel, has been around for a long time, and it has taken many forms. Today, we use pounds and euros, or swipe a card or, in some places, tap a mobile phone. Are all these things money?

In this chapter, we study money, its functions, how it gets created, and what happens when its quantity changes. In *Reading Between the Lines* at the end of the chapter, we see what happens when the European Central Bank changes the quantity of money in the euro area.

What Is Money?

What do cowrie shells, wampum, whales' teeth, tobacco, cattle and pennies have in common? The answer is that all of them are (or have been) forms of money. **Money** is any commodity or token that is generally acceptable as a means of payment. A **means of payment** is a method of settling a debt. When a payment has been made there is no remaining obligation between the parties to a transaction. So what cowrie shells, wampum, whales' teeth, cattle and pennies have in common is that they have served (or still do serve) as the means of payment. But money has three other functions:

◆ A medium of exchange
◆ A unit of account
◆ A store of value

Medium of Exchange

A *medium of exchange* is an object that is generally accepted in exchange for goods and services. Money acts as such a medium. Without money, it would be necessary to exchange goods and services directly for other goods and services – an exchange called *barter*. Barter requires a double coincidence of wants, a situation that rarely occurs. For example, if you want a pizza, you might offer a CD in exchange for it. But you must find someone who is selling pizza and who wants your CD.

A medium of exchange overcomes the need for a double coincidence of wants. And money acts as a medium of exchange because people with something to sell will always accept money in exchange for it. But money isn't the only medium of exchange. You can buy with a credit card. But a credit card isn't money. It doesn't make a final payment and the debt it creates must eventually be settled by using money.

Unit of Account

A *unit of account* is an agreed measure for stating the prices of goods and services. To get the most out of your budget you have to work out, among other things, whether seeing one more film is worth the price you have to pay, not in pounds and pence, but in terms of the number of ice creams, beers or cups of tea that you have to give up. It's easy to do such calculations when all these goods have prices in terms of pounds and pence (see Table 24.1). If the price of a cinema ticket is £4 and

a pint of beer in the Students' Union costs £1, you know straight away that seeing one more film costs you 4 pints of beer. If the price of a cup of tea is 50 pence, one more cinema ticket costs 8 cups of tea. You need only one calculation to work out the opportunity cost of any pair of goods and services.

But imagine how troublesome it would be if your local cinema posted its price as 4 pints of beer; and if the Students' Union announced that the price of a pint of beer was 2 ice creams; and if the corner shop posted the price of an ice cream as 1 cup of tea; and if the café priced a cup of tea as 5 rolls of mints!

Now how much running around and calculating do you have to do to work out how much that film is going to cost you in terms of the beer, ice cream, tea or mints that you must give up to see it? You get the answer for beer from the sign posted at the cinema, but for all the other goods you're going to have to visit many different shops to establish the prices you need to work out the opportunity costs you face.

Cover up the column labelled 'price in money units' in Table 24.1 and see how hard it is to work out the number of local telephone calls it costs to see one film.

It is much simpler for everyone to express their prices in terms of pounds and pence.

Table 24.1

The Unit of Account Function of Money Simplifies Price Comparisons

Good	Price in money units	Price in units of another good
Cinema ticket	£4.00 each	4 pints of beer
Beer	£1.00 per pint	2 ice creams
Ice cream	£0.50 per cone	1 cup of tea
Tea	£0.50 per cup	5 rolls of mints
Mints	£0.10 per roll	1 local phone call

Money as a unit of account. The price of a cinema ticket is £4 and the price of a cup of tea is 50 pence, so a cinema ticket costs 8 cups of tea (£4.00/£0.50 = 8).

No unit of account. You go to a cinema and learn that the price of a ticket is 4 pints of beer. You go to a café and learn that a cup of tea costs 5 rolls of mints. But how many rolls of mints does it cost you to see a film? To answer that question, you go to the Students' Union bar and find that a pint of beer costs 2 ice creams. Now you head for the ice cream shop, where an ice cream costs 1 cup of tea. Now you get out your pocket calculator: 1 cinema ticket costs 4 pints of beer, or 8 ice creams, or 8 cups of tea or 40 rolls of mints!

Store of Value

Money is a *store of value* in the sense that it can be held and exchanged later for goods and services. If money were not a store of value, it could not serve as a means of payment.

Money is not alone in acting as a store of value. A physical object such as a house, a car, a work of art or a computer can act as a store of value. The most reliable and useful stores of value are items that have a stable value. The more stable the value of a commodity or token, the better it can act as a store of value and the more useful it is as money. No store of value has a completely stable value. The value of a house, a car or a work of art fluctuates over time. The values of the commodities and tokens that are used as money also fluctuate over time. When there is inflation, their values persistently fall.

Because inflation brings a falling value of money, a low inflation rate is needed to make money as useful as possible as a store of value.

Money in the UK Today

In the UK today, money consists of:

◆ Currency
◆ Deposits at banks and building societies

Currency

The notes and coins held by the public (individuals and businesses) are known as **currency**. These notes and coins are money because the government declares them to be so. The Royal Mint maintains the inventory of coins in circulation and the Bank of England issues notes. (In Scotland and Northern Ireland, private banks also issue notes, but they must hold £1 of Bank of England notes for every £1 they issue.)

Deposits at Banks and Building Societies

Deposits at banks and building societies are also money. This type of money is an accounting entry in an electronic database in the banks' and building societies' computers. They are money because they can be converted instantly into currency and because they are used directly to settle debts. In fact, deposits at banks and building societies are the main means of settling debts in modern societies. The owner of a deposit transfers ownership to another person simply by making an electronic payment or by writing a cheque – an instruction to a bank – that tells the bank to change its database, debiting the account of one depositor and crediting the account of another.

The Official UK Measure of Money

The official measure of money in the UK today is known as M4. **M4** consists of currency held by the public plus bank deposits and building society deposits. M4 does *not* include currency held by banks and building societies and it does *not* include currency or bank deposits owned by the UK government. Figure 24.1 shows the components that make up M4.

Are All the Components of M4 Really Money?

Money is the means of payment. So the test of whether something is money is whether it serves as a means of payment. Currency passes the test.

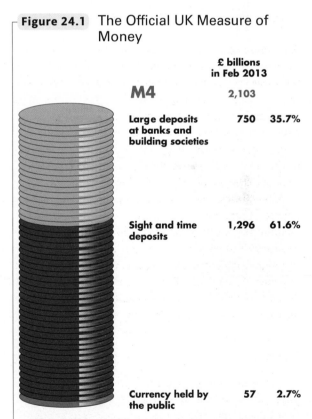

Figure 24.1   The Official UK Measure of Money

	£ billions in Feb 2013	
M4	2,103	
Large deposits at banks and building societies	750	35.7%
Sight and time deposits	1,296	61.6%
Currency held by the public	57	2.7%

M4 is the official measure of money in the UK. It is the sum of currency held by the public, bank deposits and building society deposits. Currency represents only 2.7 per cent of the money in the UK economy.

Source of data: Bank of England.

MyEconLab Animation ───────────────────◆

Deposits are divided into two types: sight deposits and time deposits. A *sight deposit* (sometimes called a chequeable deposit) can be transferred from one person to another by writing a cheque or using a debit card. So a sight deposit is clearly money. A *time deposit* is a deposit that has a fixed term to maturity. Although not usually a chequeable deposit, technological advances in the banking industry have made it easy to switch funds from a time deposit to a sight deposit. Because of the ease with which funds in a time deposit can be switched into a sight deposit, time deposits are included in the definition of money.

 ## ECONOMICS IN ACTION

Money in the Eurozone

The official Eurozone measure of money is called M3, but the items included in the Eurozone M3 are very similar to those in M4 in the UK. Figure 1 shows the numbers. The most interesting feature of euro money is the large amount of currency held by the public, 9.0 per cent of the total, compared with 2.7 per cent in the UK. Think about the reasons for this huge difference!

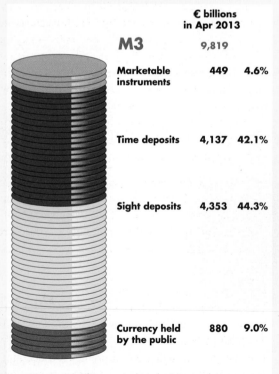

	€ billions in Apr 2013	
M3	9,819	
Marketable instruments	449	4.6%
Time deposits	4,137	42.1%
Sight deposits	4,353	44.3%
Currency held by the public	880	9.0%

Figure 1   Official Eurozone Measure of Money

Source of data: European Central Bank.

Cheques, Debit Cards and Credit Cards Are Not Money

The funds you've got in the bank are your money. When you write a cheque, you are telling your bank to move some funds from your account to the account of the person to whom you've given the cheque. Writing a cheque doesn't create more money. The money existed before you wrote the cheque. When your cheque is paid the money is still there, but it moves from you to the person to whom you wrote the cheque.

Using a debit card is just like writing a cheque except that the transaction takes place in an instant. The funds are electronically transferred from your account to that of the person you are paying the moment your card is read.

A credit card is just an ID card, but one that lets you take a loan at the instant you buy something. When you sign a credit card sales slip, you are saying: "I agree to pay for these goods when the credit card company bills me." Once you get your statement from the credit card company, you must make the minimum payment due (or clear your balance). To make that payment you need money – currency or a bank deposit. So although you use a credit card when you buy something, the credit card is not the *means of payment* and it is not money. The currency or the bank deposit that you use is money.

REVIEW QUIZ

1   What makes something money? What functions does money perform? Why do you think Polo mints don't serve as money?
2   What are the largest components of money in the UK and in the Eurozone today?
3   Are all the components of M4 really money?
4   Why are cheques, debit cards and credit cards not money?

Do these questions in Study Plan 24.1 and get instant feedback.   MyEconLab

We've seen that the main component of money is deposits at banks and building societies. These institutions play a crucial role in our economic life and we're now going to examine that role.

Monetary Financial Institutions

A **monetary financial institution** is a financial firm that gets most of its funds by taking deposits from households and firms. These deposits are components of the M4 monetary aggregate.

You're now going to learn what these institutions are, what they do, the economic benefits they bring, how they are regulated and how they have innovated to create new financial products.

Types of Monetary Financial Institutions

The deposits of two types of financial firms make up the UK's money. They are:

◆ Commercial banks
◆ Building societies

Commercial Banks

A *commercial bank* is a private firm, licensed by the Bank of England under the Banking Act 1987 to take deposits and make loans.

UK commercial banks are very large, and five firms dominate the banking markets: Barclays, HSBC, Lloyds Banking Group, Royal Bank of Scotland Group and Standard Chartered. The assets of the largest commercial banks exceed £2 trillion.

These very large firms offer a wide range of banking services and have extensive international operations. The deposits of commercial banks represent the bulk of the deposits in the M4 definition of money.

Building Societies

A *building society* is a private firm licensed under the Building Societies Act 1986 to accept deposits and make loans mostly to mortgage borrowers.

Building societies are much smaller than commercial banks and most of them serve their local communities. The largest, Nationwide, has assets of £195 billion. Size falls steeply, with the assets of the next largest, Yorkshire, at £33 billion and the third largest, Coventry, at £29 billion.

Unlike a bank, a building society is owned by its depositors, obtains its funds in the form of savings accounts and keeps its reserves not at the Bank of England but as a deposit in a commercial bank.

What Monetary Financial Institutions Do

Monetary financial institutions provide services such as cheque clearing, account management, credit cards and Internet banking, all of which provide an income from service fees. But they earn most of their income by using the funds they receive from depositors to make loans and to buy securities that earn a higher interest rate than that paid to depositors. In this activity, they must perform a balancing act, weighing return against risk. To see this balancing act, we'll focus on the commercial banks.

A commercial bank puts the funds it receives from depositors and other funds that it borrows into four types of assets:

1 A bank's **reserves** are notes and coins in the bank's vault or in a deposit account at the Bank of England. (We'll study the Bank of England later in this chapter.) These funds are used to meet depositors' currency withdrawals and to make payments to other banks. In normal times, a bank keeps about 1 per cent of deposits as reserves.

2 *Liquid assets* are overnight loans to other banks and institutions, UK government Treasury bills and commercial bills. These assets are the banks' first line of defence if they need reserves. Liquid assets can be sold and instantly converted into reserves with virtually no risk of loss. Because they have a low risk, they earn a low interest rate.

The interest rate on overnight loans is closely linked to the interest rate set by the Bank of England as its main policy interest rate (see p. 566).

3 *Investment securities* are UK government bonds and other bonds such as mortgage-backed securities. These assets can be sold and converted into reserves but at prices that fluctuate, so they are riskier than liquid assets and have a higher interest rate.

4 *Loans and advances* are funds committed for an agreed-upon period of time to corporations to finance investment and to households to finance the purchase of homes, cars and other durable goods. The outstanding balances on credit card accounts are also bank loans. Loans are a bank's riskiest and highest-earning assets: they can't be converted into reserves until they are due to be repaid, and some borrowers default and never repay.

Table 24.2 provides a snapshot of the sources and uses of funds of all the monetary financial institutions in the UK in February 2013.

Economic Benefits Provided by Monetary Financial Institutions

You've seen that a monetary financial institution earns part of its profit because it pays a lower interest rate on deposits than it earns on loans. What benefits do these institutions provide that make this outcome occur? Monetary financial institutions provide four benefits:

◆ Create liquidity
◆ Pool risk
◆ Lower the cost of borrowing
◆ Lower the cost of monitoring borrowers

Create Liquidity

Monetary financial institutions create liquidity by *borrowing short and lending long* – taking deposits and standing ready to repay them on short notice or on demand and making loan commitments that run for terms of many years.

Table 24.2

Monetary Financial Institutions: Sources and Uses of Funds

	Funds (billions of pounds)	Percentage of deposits
Total funds	3,708	117
Sources		
Deposits	3,160	100
Borrowing	123	4
Own capital and other sources	425	13
Uses		
Reserves	286	9
Liquid assets	441	14
Investment securities*	523	17
Loans and advances	2,458	78

Commercial banks get most of their funds from depositors and use most of them to make loans and advances. Before the global financial crisis, UK banks held about 1 per cent of deposits as reserves, but in 2013 they held an unusually large 9 per cent as reserves. The data relate only to the sterling business of UK banks.

Source of data: Bank of England. The data are for February 2013.
*Investment securities includes other assets.

Pool Risk

A loan might not be repaid – a default. If you lend to one person who defaults, you lose the entire amount loaned. If you lend to 1,000 people (through a bank) and one person defaults, you lose almost nothing. Monetary financial institutions pool risk.

Lower the Cost of Borrowing

Imagine there are no monetary financial institutions and a firm is looking for £1 million to buy a new factory. It hunts around for several dozen people from whom to borrow the funds. Monetary financial institutions lower the cost of this search. The firm gets its £1 million from a single institution that gets deposits from a large number of people but spreads the cost of this activity over many borrowers.

Lower the Cost of Monitoring Borrowers

By monitoring borrowers, a lender can encourage good decisions that prevent defaults. But this activity is costly. Imagine how costly it would be if each household that lent money to a firm incurred the costs of monitoring that firm directly. Monetary financial institutions can perform this task at a much lower cost.

How Monetary Financial Institutions Are Regulated

The collapse of a large bank would have damaging effects on the entire financial system and economy. Regulation seeks to lower the risk of collapse and lessen the damage if it occurs.

To lower the risk of bank failure, commercial banks are required to hold levels of reserves and owners' capital that equal or surpass ratios laid down by regulation.

The **required reserve ratio** is the minimum percentage of deposits that a bank is required to hold in reserves. This minimum is designed to ensure that a bank does not run out of cash. The *required capital ratio* is the minimum percentage of assets that must be financed by the bank's owners. This ratio is designed to ensure that a bank's assets will never be worth less than its deposits.

The Financial Services Act 2012 established today's framework for regulating UK financial services. The Financial Policy Committee monitors financial stability. The Prudential Regulation Authority ensures the prudential regulation of financial institutions, and the Financial Conduct Authority supervises financial business conduct and consumer protection.

AT ISSUE

No More Too Big to Fail?

The final report on the reform of banking in the United Kingdom, the Independent Commission on Banking led by economist Sir John Vickers – the Vickers Report – made three recommendations:

1. Retain deposit insurance guarantees for high street banks but separate them from the investment banking activities of a banking group – "ring-fencing".
2. Increase the percentage of a bank's funds coming from its own capital – increased capital requirements
3. Increase competition by creating a major new bank and making it easier to switch banks and understand bank charges.

The goal of the Vickers Report is to ensure there are no banks that are "too big to fail".

For the Vickers Report Recommendations

Sir John Vickers,
Chairman of the Independent Commission on Banking

George Osborne, Chancellor of the Exchequer, who supports the Vickers recommendatons

The supporters of the Vickers report include George Osborne, Chancellor of the Exchequer, and much of the financial media. Supporters argue that:

◆ Changes are needed to protect the taxpayer from another bank failure.
◆ Ring-fencing is necessary to avoid greed overcoming good governance.
◆ If a bank flouts the rules, it will be broken up, not just a ring-fenced bank.
◆ Increasing banks' own capital is necessary to increase the loss absorption capacity of the banks.
◆ Competition is vital for the health of the banking system.

Against the Recommendations

Professor Patrick Minford is a prominent opponent of the Vickers recommendations. He says:

◆ Increasing the banks' capital requirements in the current state of the UK economy will delay a return to the normal pace of economic growth by restricting the flow of credit to small and medium-sized firms.
◆ Even delaying an increase in banks' capital requirements will influence banks' expectations and reduce their lending to firms.
◆ Banks will switch their lending from firms to investing in government bonds, thereby financing the government deficit.

Another critic, Professor Charles Goodhart, argues that:

◆ Higher capital ratios may protect the taxpayer from a future bailout, but they will not make the banking sector safer.
◆ A ring-fenced bank will not be able to diversify its risks like a universal bank, and will be exposed to the risks coming from the UK property cycle.
◆ The separation of the retail banks from investment banks will make the supply of banking services more costly to the customer.

Patrick Minford
Two of the critics of Vickers

Charles Goodhart

ECONOMICS IN ACTION

Northern Rock and the Sub-Prime Loans Crisis

Northern Rock plc is a UK bank that was taken into public ownership at the height of the financial crisis caused by the problems created by US sub-prime loans.

Formerly a building society that converted to a bank in 1997, Northern Rock continued to specialise in mortgage lending. During the 2000s, the bank expanded its deposits and borrowing from £22 billion in 2000 to £109 billion in 2007. Its profit rose from £149 million in 1997 to a peak of £557 million in 2006.

Northern Rock's business model was 'originate' and 'distribute'. The bank borrowed on the interbank loans market and used the funds to make mortgage loans to its customers (originate). By 2006, some of its lending was in the form of sub-prime (high-risk) mortgages. It then created mortgage-backed securities, which it sold on the global capital market (distribute).

The interest the bank received on its mortgage loans was paid to the holders of the mortgage-backed securities and the funds raised by selling these securities were used to pay back lenders in the interbank loans market.

This part of Northern Rock's business was kept separate from its normal banking business and no required capital ratio applied to it, so the bank was able to expand its borrowing and lending without having to use any of its own funds.

Figure 1 shows how the bank's balance sheet expanded and the bank's growing dependence on borrowing (the red bars) rather than on customers' deposits (the blue bars).

When the sub-prime loans crisis hit the world economy, Northern Rock was unable to raise funds in the interbank market. The bank faced a liquidity crisis as customers queued to withdraw their deposits. In February 2008, the bank was taken into public ownership. In 2010, Northern Rock was split into an asset management company (bad bank) that remained under public ownership (managing £50 billion of assets) and a banking business (good bank) that was sold to Virgin Money in 2012 as a going concern.

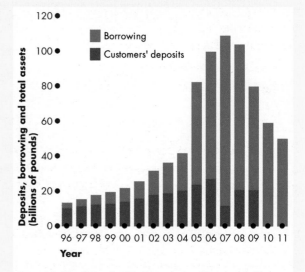

Figure 1 Northern Rock's Spectacular Rise and Fall

Source of data: Bureau van dijk Bankscope.

Financial Innovation

In the pursuit of larger profit, banks and building societies are constantly seeking ways to improve their products in a process called *financial innovation*. The major financial innovations included the introduction of credit cards, debit cards, automatic teller machines, interest-bearing sight deposits and automatic transfers between sight and time deposits. These innovations occurred because the development of computing power lowered the cost of calculations and record keeping.

During the 2000s, when interest rates were low and banks were flush with funds, sub-prime mortgages were developed in the US. To avoid the risk of carrying these mortgages, mortgage-backed securities were developed. The original lending institution sold these securities, lowered their own exposure to risk and obtained funds to make more loans. The model of originating mortgage loans and selling them as mortgage-backed securities to other financial institutions was copied by a number of UK banks – the most notorious being Northern Rock.

REVIEW QUIZ

1 What is a monetary financial institution?
2 What are the main economic functions of a monetary financial institution?
3 What are the four types of assets held by banks?
4 How do monetary financial institutions create liquidity, pool risk and lower borrowing costs?

Do these questions in Study Plan 24.2 and get instant feedback.   MyEconLab

You now know what money is. Your next task is to learn about central banking and the ways in which a central bank can influence the quantity of money.

Central Banking

A central bank is a public authority that provides banking services to governments and commercial banks, supervises and regulates financial institutions and markets and conducts monetary policy. *Monetary policy* is the attempt to control inflation, moderate the business cycle and provide the foundation for sustained economic growth by influencing the quantity of money, interest rates and the exchange rate. We study monetary policy in Chapter 30. Our aim in this chapter is to learn about the role of a central bank in the process of creating and influencing the quantity of money and the interest rate. We'll briefly describe two central banks:

◆ The European Central Bank
◆ The Bank of England

The European Central Bank

The **European Central Bank (ECB)** is the central bank of the Eurozone – the members of the European Union that use the euro as their currency. The ECB was established on 1 June 1998.

National central banks, the largest of which are the Banque de France, Deutsche Bundesbank and Banca d'Italia, provide banking services to their governments and commercial banks and supervise and regulate their national financial institutions and markets. The Executive Board of the ECB together with the governors of the national central banks of the Eurozone constitute the Governing Council, which is the highest decision-making body in the ECB. Through this membership of the Governing Council, national central banks play a role in setting Eurozone monetary policy.

The Bank of England

The **Bank of England** is the central bank of the UK. It was established by Parliament in 1694 in a deal between a syndicate of wealthy individuals and the government of King William and Queen Mary. The syndicate lent the government £1.2 million in return for the right to issue bank notes. And so the Bank of England notes we use today were born.

The Bank of England was first formally recognised as the central bank with the passage of the Bank of England Act of 1946, which took the Bank into public ownership.

For the next 50 years, the Bank of England was under the firm day-to-day control of the Treasury (the government) and its role was to implement the government's decisions. But in 1997, a major change occurred. The Bank is now independent, and its Monetary Policy Committee makes the monetary policy decisions, subject to objectives set by the government.

Monetary Policy Committee

The Bank of England's **Monetary Policy Committee (MPC)** formulates the UK's monetary policy. Its members are the Governor and two Deputy Governors of the Bank, two members appointed by the Governor of the Bank after consultation with the Chancellor of the Exchequer, and four members appointed by the Chancellor of the Exchequer. The persons appointed by the Chancellor must have 'knowledge or experience which is likely to be relevant to the Committee's functions' – which in practice means that they are academic economists.

To appreciate the monetary policy tools available to a central bank, we must first learn about its financial structure, summarised in its balance sheet. We'll focus here on the Bank of England, but the principles apply to all central banks.

The Bank of England's Balance Sheet

The Bank of England influences the economy through the size and composition of it balance sheet – the assets that it owns and the liabilities that it owes.

The Bank's Assets

The Bank of England has two main assets:

1 UK government securities
2 Loans to monetary financial institutions

The Bank holds UK government securities – Treasury bills and longer term government bonds – that it buys in the bond market. When the Bank buys or sells bonds, it participates in the *loanable funds market* (see Chapter 23, pp. 538–543).

The Bank makes loans to monetary financial institutions. These loans are made using *repurchase agreements*. Under a repurchase agreement – called a **repo** – a commercial bank sells a government bond to the Bank of England and simultaneously agrees to *repurchase* it (buy it back) usually two weeks later. In normal times this item is small, but during the global financial crisis the Bank provided loans on an unprecedented scale.

The Bank's Liabilities

The Bank has two liabilities:

1 Notes in circulation
2 Deposits of commercial banks

Bank of England notes are the £5, £10, £20 and £50 notes that we use in our cash transactions. Some of these notes are part of *currency* – a component of the M4 definition of money (see p. 559). And some of them are in the tills and vaults of the commercial banks – part of the banks' reserves.

The Bank of England's other liability is the deposits of commercial banks, which are part of these institutions' reserves. In normal times the banks' reserves are very small, but since the global financial crisis of 2008 this item has swollen to match the extraordinarily large volume of loans to banks on the assets side of the Bank of England's balance sheet.

The Monetary Base

The Bank of England's liabilities plus the coins issued by the Royal Mint make up the **monetary base**. Coins are part of the monetary base but do not appear in the Bank of England balance sheet because the Royal Mint, which issues coins, is a branch of the government and not a part of the Bank of England.

The Bank's assets are the sources of the monetary base. They are also called the backing for the monetary base. The Bank's liabilities are the uses of the monetary base as currency held by the public and bank reserves (notes and coins in the bank's vault or in a deposit account at the Bank of England).

Table 24.3 provides a snapshot of the sources and uses of the monetary base in April 2013.

We'll next look at the Bank's tool kit.

Table 24.3

The Sources and Uses of the Monetary Base

Sources (billions of pounds)		Uses (billions of pounds)	
Government bonds	13	Notes held by the public	58
Loans to banks	331	Bank reserves	286
Monetary base	**344**	**Monetary base**	**344**

Source of data: Bank of England. The data are for 17 April 2013.

The Bank of England's Policy Tools

The Bank of England has four policy tools to influence the quantity of money and the interest rate. They are:

◆ Bank Rate
◆ Open market operations
◆ Lender of last resort
◆ Required reserve ratio

Bank Rate

Bank Rate is the interest rate that the Bank of England charges on secured overnight loans to commercial banks. It is the official policy interest rate to which many other interest rates are linked. Among them are the interest rate that the Bank pays to commercial banks on their reserve deposits and the interest rates the commercial banks pay on deposits and charge on loans.

Open Market Operations

An **open market operation** is the purchase or sale of securities by the central bank in the *loanable funds market*. The term 'open market' refers to commercial banks and the general public but not the government. The Bank of England does not transact with the government.

When the Bank buys government bonds, it pays for them with newly created bank reserves. When the Bank sells government bonds, the Bank is paid with reserves held by the commercial banks. So open market operations directly influence the reserves of banks. By changing the quantity of bank reserves, the Bank of England changes the amount of bank lending, which influences the quantity of money and the economy more broadly.

An Open Market Purchase

To see how an open market operation changes bank reserves, suppose the Bank of England buys £100 million of government securities from HSBC. When the Bank of England makes this transaction, two things happen:

1 HSBC has £100 million less securities, and the Bank has £100 million more securities.

2 The Bank places £100 million in HSBC's deposit account at the Bank of England (bank reserves in Table 24.3) to pay for the securities.

Figure 24.2 shows the effects of these actions on the balance sheets of the Bank and HSBC. Ownership of the securities passes from HSBC to the Bank of England, so

Figure 24.2 The Bank of England Buys Securities in the Open Market

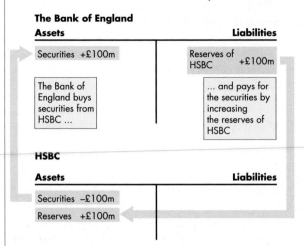

When the Bank of England buys securities in the open market, it increases bank reserves. The Bank of England's assets and liabilities increase and the selling bank's reserves increase and securities decrease.

MyEconLab Animation ─────────────────◆

HSBC's assets decrease by £100 million and the Bank's assets increase by £100 million, as shown by the blue arrow running from HSBC to the Bank. The Bank pays for the securities by placing £100 million in HSBC's reserve account at the Bank, as shown by the green arrow running from the Bank to HSBC. The Bank's assets and liabilities increase by £100 million. HSBC's total assets are unchanged: it sold securities to increase its reserves.

An Open Market Sale
If the Bank of England sells £100 million of government securities to HSBC in the open market:

1 HSBC has £100 million more securities, and the Bank has £100 million less securities.

2 HSBC pays for the securities by using £100 million of its reserve deposit at the Bank.

You can follow the effects of these actions by reversing the arrows and the plus and minus signs in Figure 24.2. Ownership of the securities passes from the Bank to HSBC, so the Bank's assets decrease by £100 million and HSBC's assets increase by £100 million. HSBC uses £100 million of its reserves to pay for the securities. Both the Bank's assets and liabilities decrease by £100 million. HSBC's total assets are unchanged: it has used reserves to buy securities.

 ECONOMICS IN ACTION

The Bank of England's Balance Sheet Explodes

The Bank of England's balance sheet has seen remarkable change since the financial crisis of 2007–2008 and the recession that it triggered.

The figure shows the changes in the size and composition of the monetary base by comparing the situation in December 2010 and April 2013 with that before the financial crisis began in January 2007.

In 2007, a normal year, the monetary base was £61 billion and two-thirds of it was currency. But the Bank of England made huge repo loans to commercial banks that more than doubled the monetary base by 2010 and increased it by 460 per cent by 2013. Almost all of this increase is in bank reserves, not currency.

Left unchecked, this huge volume of bank reserves would eventually be loaned by the banks and create an explosion in the quantity of money.

When, and how quickly, to unwind the large increase in the monetary base and bank reserves is a source of disagreement and debate.

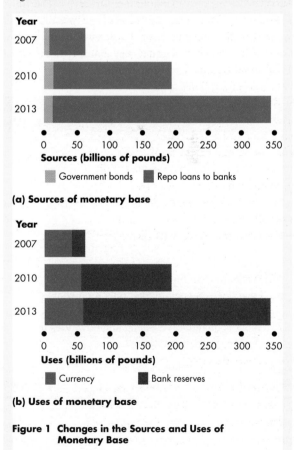

(a) Sources of monetary base

(b) Uses of monetary base

Figure 1 Changes in the Sources and Uses of Monetary Base

Source of data: Bank of England.

Lender of Last Resort

The Bank of England is the **lender of last resort**, which means that if all the banks are short of reserves, they can borrow from the central bank. Normally, last-resort loans are made overnight and secured with a repurchase agreement (a *repo*).

In recent years the Bank of England has lent on repurchase agreements for longer periods and boosted the reserves of the commercial banks massively. This form of injection of reserves is called **quantitative easing**. The reserves made available by quantitative easing are indicated in Table 24.3 as 'Loans to banks'.

In September 2007 the Bank of England made a large last-resort loan facility available to the bank Northern Rock when it was unable to obtain funds from the wholesale interbank market.

Required Reserve Ratio

The *required reserve ratio* (the minimum percentage of deposits that a bank is required to hold as reserves) can be varied to make banks hold more reserves. The Bank of England doesn't vary this percentage very often. But some central banks (the People's Bank of China is one) frequently use this tool, and it is available to the Bank of England if it should choose to use it.

REVIEW QUIZ

1. What is a central bank?
2. What are the central banks of the Eurozone and the UK and what functions do they perform?
3. What are the main items in the balance sheet of a central bank?
4. What is the monetary base and how does it relate to the items in the Bank of England's balance sheet?
5. What are a central bank's policy tools?
6. How does an open market operation change the monetary base?
7. What is quantitative easing and how does it change the monetary base?

Do these questions in Study Plan 24.3 and get instant feedback.　　MyEconLab

Next, we're going to see how the banking system – the commercial banks and the Bank of England – creates money and how the quantity of money changes when the Bank of England changes the monetary base.

How Banks Create Money

Banks[2] create money. But this doesn't mean that they have smoke-filled back rooms in which counterfeiters are busily working. Remember that most money is in the form of deposits, not currency. What banks create is deposits and they do so by making loans.

Creating Deposits by Making Loans

The easiest way to see that banks create deposits is to think about what happens when Helen fills up her car with petrol at a BP service station and pays using her Visa credit card issued by Barclays. When Helen keys in her PIN, she takes a loan from Barclays and obligates herself to repay the loan at a later date. The electronic transfer of funds from Helen's Barclays Visa account to BP's bank is instantaneous. Barclays credits BP's bank account with the value of the sale (less the commission).

You can see that these transactions have created a bank deposit and a loan. Helen has increased the size of her loan (her credit card balance), and BP has increased the size of its bank deposit (minus the bank's commission). And because deposits are money, this transaction has created money.

If Helen and BP use the same bank, no further transactions take place. But the outcome is essentially the same when two banks are involved. If BP's bank is the Royal Bank of Scotland, then Barclays uses its reserves to pay the Royal Bank.

Barclays still has an increase in loans, but now it has a decrease in its reserves at the Bank of England; the Royal Bank of Scotland has an increase in its reserves at the Bank of England and an increase in deposits.

The banking system as a whole has an increase in loans and deposits and no change in reserves.

You know that the interest rate that banks pay on deposits is much less than what they receive on loans. So creating deposits by making loans is a profitable business. What keeps this business in check?

The quantity of loans and deposits that the banking system can create is limited by three factors:

◆ The monetary base

◆ Desired reserves

◆ Desired currency holding

---

[2] In this section, we'll use the term 'banks' to refer to commercial banks and building societies – the monetary financial institutions whose deposits are money.

The Monetary Base

You've seen that the *monetary base* is the sum of Bank of England notes and banks' deposits at the Bank of England – the Bank of England's liabilities – plus coins issued by the Royal Mint. The size of the monetary base limits the total quantity of money that the banking system can create because banks have a desired level of reserves, households and firms have a desired level of currency holding, and both of these desired holdings of the monetary base depend on the quantity of deposits.

Desired Reserves

A bank's *desired reserves* – the reserves that it *plans* to hold – contrast with its *required reserves*, which are the minimum quantity of reserves that a bank must hold.

The quantity of desired reserves depends on the level of deposits and is determined by the **desired reserve ratio** – the ratio of reserves to deposits that the banks plan to hold. The desired reserve ratio exceeds the required reserve ratio by an amount that the banks determine to be prudent on the basis of their daily requirements and in the light of the current situation.

Desired Currency Holding

The ratio of money held as currency to money held as bank deposits depends on how households and firms choose to make payments: whether they plan to use currency or debit cards and cheques. These plans change slowly so the desired ratio of currency to deposits also changes slowly. If bank deposits increase, desired currency holding also increases. For this reason, when banks make loans that increase deposits, some currency leaves the banks – the banking system leaks reserves. We call the leakage of reserves into currency the *currency drain* and we call the ratio of currency to deposits the **currency drain ratio**.

We've sketched the way that a loan creates a deposit and described the three factors that limit the amount of loans and deposits that can be created. We're now going to examine the money creation process more closely and discover a money multiplier.

The Money Creation Process

The money creation process begins with an increase in the monetary base, which occurs if the Bank of England buys securities. The Bank pays for the securities it buys with newly created bank reserves.

When the Bank of England buys securities from a bank, the bank's reserves increase. Deposits at the bank don't change, so the bank has excess reserves. A bank's **excess reserves** are its actual reserves minus its desired reserves.

When a bank has excess reserves, it makes loans and creates deposits and money in a process like the one we described on the previous page when Helen buys petrol with her credit card.

When the entire banking system has excess reserves, total loans and deposits increase. One bank can make a loan and get rid of excess reserves. But the banking system as a whole can't get rid of excess reserves so easily. When the banks make loans and create deposits, the extra deposits lower excess reserves for two reasons:

◆ The increase in deposits increases desired reserves.

◆ A currency drain decreases total reserves.

But excess reserves don't completely disappear, so the banks lend some more and the process repeats.

As the process of making loans and increasing deposits repeats, desired reserves increase, total reserves decrease through the currency drain and, eventually, enough new deposits have been created to use all the new monetary base.

Figure 24.3 on p. 571 summarises one round in the process we've just described. The sequence, which repeats until excess reserves are eliminated, has the following eight steps:

1 Banks have excess reserves.

2 Banks lend excess reserves.

3 The quantity of money increases.

4 New money is used to make payments.

5 Some of the new money remains on deposit.

6 Some of the new money is a *currency drain*.

7 Desired reserves increase because deposits have increased.

8 Excess reserves decrease.

If the Bank of England sells securities, then banks have negative excess reserves – they are short of reserves. When the banks are short of reserves, loans and deposits decrease and the process we've described above works in a downward direction until desired reserves plus desired currency holdings have decreased by an amount equal to the decrease in the monetary base.

A money multiplier determines the change in the quantity of money that results from a change in the monetary base.

ECONOMICS IN THE NEWS

A Massive Open Market Operation

The Overrated Impact of QE

The Bank of England has been conducting a policy of quantitative easing (QE) – buying long-term government bonds – but this policy is not working. By April 2013, the monetary base had expanded but M4 had fallen from its peak in January 2010.

Source: *The Financial Times*, 26 April 2013

Some Data

Year	Currency	Reserves	Deposits
2006	£45 billion	£18 billion	£1,423 billion
2013	£63 billion	£277 billion	£2,030 billion

The Questions

◆ What is *quantitative easing* and how is it done?

◆ Calculate the monetary base in each year.

◆ Calculate the quantity of money in each year.

◆ Calculate the money muliplier in each year.

◆ Why has the money multiplier fallen?

The Answers

◆ *Quantitative easing* or QE is an open market operation similar to that described in Figure 24.2 on p. 567 but with one more step, because when the Bank of England buys securities, not only banks sell the bonds.

◆ In Figure 1, when the Bank of England buys securities, its assets increase. Its liabilities also increase because it creates monetary base to pay for the securities. For the businesses that sell bonds, their assets change – securities decrease and bank deposits increase. For the commercial banks, deposit liabilities increase and reserves, an asset, also increase.

◆ The monetary base is currency plus reserves, which was £64 billion in 2006 and £340 billion in 2013.

◆ The quantity of money is currency plus deposits, which was £1,469 billion in 2006 and £2,093 billion in 2013.

◆ The money multiplier is the quantity of money divided by the monetary base, which was 22.9 in 2006 and 6.1 in 2013.

◆ The money multiplier fell from 22.9 in 2006 and 6.1 in 2013 because the commercial banks' desired

Bond traders in London.

The Bank of England

Assets (billions)		Liabilities (billions)	
Securities	+£600	Reserves of banks	+£600

The Bank of England buys securities

Businesses, Pension Funds, and other Bond Holders

Assets (billions)		Liabilities (billions)
Securities	−£600	
Bank deposits	+£600	

The Bank of England pays with electronic funds transfer

Commercial Banks

Assets (billions)		Liabilities (billions)	
Reserves	+£600	Bank deposits	+£600

Commercial banks credit customers' deposit accounts and collect payment from the Bank of England

Figure 1 The QE Transactions

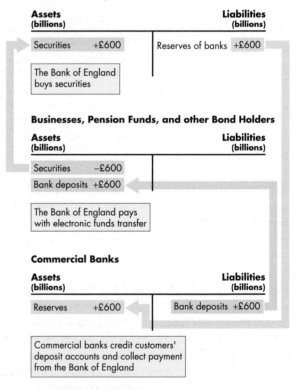

reserve ratio increased from 0.013 to 0.137, a tenfold increase.

◆ The currency drain ratio had almost no effect on the money multiplier: it decreased slightly from 0.32 in 2006 to 0.31 in 2013.

Figure 24.3 How the Banking System Creates Money by Making Loans

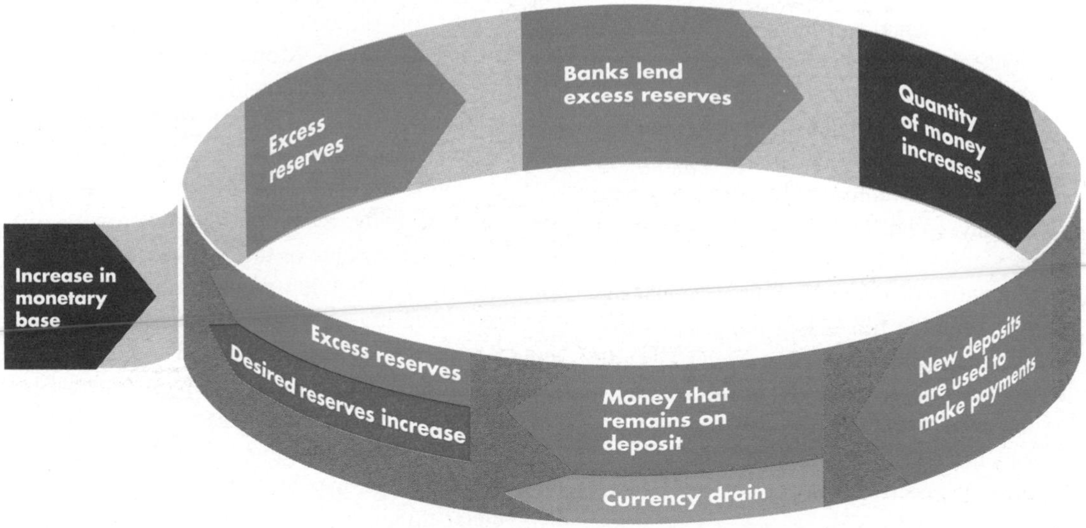

The Bank of England increases the monetary base, which increases bank reserves and creates excess reserves. Banks lend the excess reserves, new bank deposits are created and the quantity of money increases. New money is used to make payments. Some of the new money remains on deposit at banks and some leaves the banks in a currency drain. The increase in bank deposits increases banks' desired reserves. But the banks still have excess reserves, though less than before. The process repeats until excess reserves have been eliminated.

MyEconLab Animation ◆

ECONOMICS IN ACTION

The Variable Money Multiplier

We can measure the money multiplier, other things remaining the same, as the ratio of the quantity of money to the monetary base.

In the UK in 2007, the monetary base (in round numbers) was £60 billion and M4 was £1,500 billion, so M4 was 25 times the monetary base. The money multiplier was 25: a £1 million change in the monetary base would bring a £25 million change in M4.

The situation in 2013 was very different from that in 2007. In 2013, the monetary base was £344 billion and M4 was £2,103 billion, so M4 was only 6 times the monetary base. The money multiplier was 6: a £1 million change in the monetary base would bring a £6 million change in M4.

What happened to make the money multiplier fall so much? The answer is a global financial crisis and a very large increase in the commercial banks' desired reserve ratio. The currency drain ratio increased slightly.

The Money Multiplier

The **money multiplier** is the ratio of the change in the quantity of money to the change in monetary base. For example, if a £1 million increase in the monetary base increases the quantity of money by £2.5 million, then the money multiplier is 2.5.

The smaller the banks' desired reserve ratio and the smaller the currency drain ratio, the larger is the money multiplier. (See the Mathematical Note on pp. 580–581 for details on the money multiplier.)

REVIEW QUIZ

1 How do banks create money?
2 What factors limit the quantity of money that the banking system can create?
3 A bank manager tells you that she doesn't create money. She just lends the money that people deposit in the bank. Explain to her why she's wrong.

Do these questions in Study Plan 24.4 and get instant feedback. MyEconLab

The Money Market

There is no limit to the amount of money we would like to *receive* in payment for our labour or as interest on our savings. But there is a limit to how big an inventory of money we would like to *hold* and neither spend nor use to buy assets that generate an income. The *quantity of money demanded* is the inventory of money that people plan to hold on any given day. It is the quantity of money in our wallets and in our deposit accounts at banks. The quantity of money held must equal the quantity supplied, and the forces that bring about this equality in the money market have powerful effects on the economy, as you will see in the rest of this chapter.

But first, we need to explain what determines the amount of money that people plan to hold.

The Influences on Money Holding

The quantity of money that people choose to hold depends on four main factors. They are:

♦ The price level

♦ The *nominal* interest rate

♦ Real GDP

♦ Financial innovation

Let's look at each of them.

The Price Level

The quantity of money measured in pounds is *nominal money*. The quantity of nominal money demanded is proportional to the price level, other things remaining the same: if the price level rises by 10 per cent, people hold 10 per cent more nominal money. If you hold £20 to buy your weekly movies and coffee, you will increase your money holding to £22 if the prices of movies and coffee – and your wage rate – increase by 10 per cent.

The quantity of money measured in constant pounds (for example, in 2010 pounds) is real money. *Real money* is equal to nominal money divided by the price level and is the quantity of money measured in terms of what it will buy.

In the above example, when the price level rises by 10 per cent and you increase your money holding by 10 per cent, your real money holding is constant. Your £22 at the new price level buys the same quantity of goods and is the same quantity of real money as your £20 at the original price level. *The quantity of real money demanded is independent of the price level.*

The Nominal Interest Rate

A fundamental principle of economics is that as the opportunity cost of something increases, people try to find substitutes for it. Money is no exception. The higher the opportunity cost of holding money, other things remaining the same, the smaller is the quantity of real money demanded.

The interest rate is the opportunity cost of holding money. To see why, recall that the opportunity cost of any activity is the value of the best alternative forgone. The alternative to holding money is holding a savings bond or a Treasury bill that earns interest. By holding money instead, you forgo the interest that you otherwise would have received. This forgone interest is the opportunity cost of holding money.

Money loses value because of inflation. Shouldn't the inflation rate be part of the cost of holding money? It is. Other things remaining the same, the higher the expected inflation rate, the higher is the interest rate and so the higher is the opportunity cost of holding money.

Real GDP

The quantity of money that households and firms plan to hold depends on the amount they spend, and the quantity of money demanded in the economy as a whole depends on aggregate expenditure – real GDP.

Again, suppose that you hold an average of £50 to finance your weekly purchases of goods. Now imagine that the prices of these goods and of all other goods remain constant, but that your income increases. As a consequence, you now spend more and you also keep a larger amount of money on hand to finance your higher volume of expenditure.

Financial Innovation

Technological change and the arrival of new financial products – called *financial innovation* – change the quantity of money held. The major financial innovations are the widespread use of:

♦ Interest-bearing sight deposits

♦ Automatic transfers between sight and time deposits

♦ Automatic teller machines

♦ Credit cards and debit cards

These innovations have occurred because of the development of computing power that has lowered the cost of calculations and record keeping.

The Demand for Money Curve

We summarise the effects of the influences on money holding by using the demand for money curve. The **demand for money** is the relationship between the quantity of real money demanded and the interest rate – the opportunity cost of holding money – all other influences on the amount of money that people wish to hold remaining the same.

Figure 24.4 shows a demand for money curve, *MD*. When the interest rate rises, everything else remaining the same, the opportunity cost of holding money rises and the quantity of money demanded decreases – there is a movement along the demand for money curve. Similarly, when the interest rate falls, the opportunity cost of holding money falls and the quantity of money demanded increases – there is a downward movement along the demand for money curve.

When any influence on the amount of money that people plan to hold changes, there is a change in the demand for money and the demand for money curve shifts. Let's look at these shifts.

Shifts in the Demand for Money Curve

A change in real GDP or a financial innovation changes the demand for money and shifts the demand for money curve.

Figure 24.5 illustrates the changes in the demand for money. A decrease in real GDP decreases the demand for money and shifts the demand for money curve leftward from MD_0 to MD_1. An increase in real GDP has the opposite effect: it increases the demand for money and shifts the demand for money curve rightward from MD_0 to MD_2.

The influence of financial innovation on the demand for money curve is more complicated. Financial innovation decreases the demand for currency and might increase the demand for some types of deposits and decrease the demand for others. But generally financial innovation decreases the demand for money.

Changes in real GDP and financial innovation have brought large shifts in the UK demand for money curve.

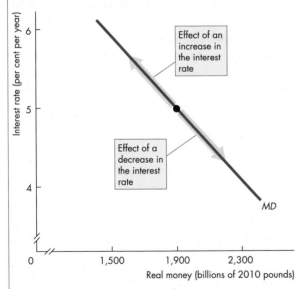

Figure 24.4 The Demand for Money

The demand for money curve, *MD*, shows the relationship between the quantity of real money that people plan to hold and the interest rate, other things remaining the same. The interest rate is the opportunity cost of holding money. A change in the interest rate leads to a movement along the demand for money curve.

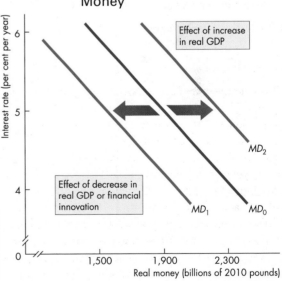

Figure 24.5 Changes in the Demand for Money

A decrease in real GDP decreases the demand for money and shifts the demand curve leftward from MD_0 to MD_1. An increase in real GDP increases the demand for money and shifts the demand curve rightward from MD_0 to MD_2. Financial innovation can either increase or decrease the demand for money depending on the specific innovation.

Money Market Equilibrium

You now know what determines the demand for money, and you've seen how the banking system creates money. Let's now see how the money market reaches equilibrium.

Money market equilibrium occurs when the quantity of money demanded equals the quantity of money supplied. The adjustments that occur to bring money market equilibrium are fundamentally different in the short run and the long run.

Short-Run Equilibrium

The quantity of money supplied is determined by the actions of the banks and the Bank of England. A change in the quantity of money brings a change in the interest rate.

In Figure 24.6, the Bank uses open market operations to make the quantity of real money supplied £1,900 billion and the supply of money curve *MS*. With the demand for money curve *MD*, the equilibrium interest rate is 5 per cent a year.

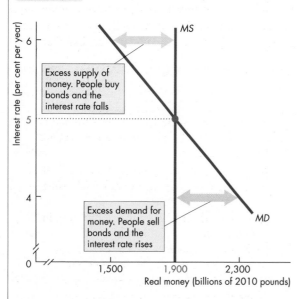

Figure 24.6 Money Market Equilibrium

Money market equilibrium occurs when the quantity of money demanded equals the quantity supplied. In the short run, real GDP determines the demand for money curve, *MD*, and the Bank of England determines the quantity of real money supplied and the supply of money curve, *MS*. The interest rate adjusts to achieve equilibrium, here 5 per cent a year.

If the interest rate were 4 per cent a year, people would want to hold more money than is available. They would sell bonds, bid down their price and the interest rate would rise. If the interest rate were 6 per cent a year, people would want to hold less money than is available. They would buy bonds, bid up their price and the interest rate would fall.

The Short-Run Effect of a Change in the Supply of Money

Starting from a short-run equilibrium, if the Bank of England increases the quantity of money, people find themselves holding more money than the quantity demanded. With a surplus of money holding, people enter the loanable funds market and buy bonds. The increase in demand for bonds raises the price of a bond and lowers the interest rate (refresh your memory by looking at Chapter 23, p. 538).

If the Bank of England decreases the quantity of money, people find themselves holding less money than the quantity demanded. They enter the loanable funds market and sell bonds. The increase in the supply of bonds lowers the price of a bond and raises the interest rate.

Figure 24.7 illustrates the effects of the changes in the quantity of money that we've just described. When the supply of money curve shifts rightward from MS_0 to MS_1, the interest rate falls to 4 per cent a year; when the supply of money curve shifts leftward to MS_2, the interest rate rises to 6 per cent a year.

Long-Run Equilibrium

You've just seen how the nominal interest rate is determined in the money market at the level that makes the quantity of money demanded equal the quantity supplied. You learned in Chapter 23 (on p. 542) that the real interest rate is determined in the loanable funds market at the level that makes the quantity of loanable funds demanded equal the quantity of loanable funds supplied. You also learned in Chapter 23 (on p. 539) that the real interest rate equals the nominal interest rate minus the inflation rate.

When the inflation rate equals the expected (or forecast) inflation rate and when real GDP equals potential GDP, the money market, the loanable funds market, the goods market and the labour market are in long-run equilibrium – the economy is in long-run equilibrium.

If, in long-run equilibrium, the quantity of money increases, eventually a new long-run equilibrium is

Figure 24.7 A Change in the Supply of Money

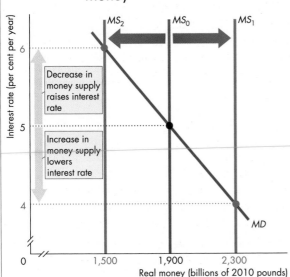

An increase in the supply of money shifts the supply of money curve from MS_0 to MS_1 and the interest rate falls. A decrease in the supply of money shifts the supply of money curve from MS_0 to MS_2 and the interest rate rises.

MyEconLab Animation ————————◆

reached in which nothing real has changed. Real GDP, employment, the real quantity of money and the real interest rate all return to their original levels. But something does change: the price level. The price level rises by the same percentage as the rise in the quantity of money. Why does this outcome occur in the long run?

The reason is that real GDP and employment are determined by the demand for labour, the supply of labour and the production function – the real forces described in Chapter 22 (pp. 512–514); and the real interest rate is determined by the demand for and supply of (real) loanable funds – the real forces described in Chapter 23 (pp. 540–542). The only variable that is free to respond to a change in the supply of money in the long run is the price level. The price level adjusts to make the quantity of real money supplied equal to the quantity demanded.

So when the nominal quantity of money changes, in the long run the price level changes by a percentage equal to the percentage change in the quantity of nominal money. In the long run, the change in the price level is proportional to the change in the quantity of money.

The Transition from the Short Run to the Long Run

How does the economy move from the first short-run response to an increase in the quantity of money to the long-run response?

The adjustment process is lengthy and complex. Here, we'll only provide a sketch of the process. A more thorough account must wait until you get to Chapter 26.

We start out in long-run equilibrium and the Bank of England increases the quantity of money by 10 per cent. There is an excess demand for money and the nominal interest rate falls (just like you saw in Figure 24.6). The real interest rate falls too.

With a lower real interest rate, people want to borrow and spend more. Firms want to borrow to invest and households want to borrow to invest in bigger homes or to buy more consumer goods.

The increase in the demand for goods cannot be met by an increase in supply because the economy is already at full employment. So there is a general shortage of all kinds of goods and services, which makes the price level rise. As the price level rises, the real quantity of money decreases. The decrease in the quantity of real money raises the nominal interest rate and the real interest rate. As the interest rate rises, spending plans are cut back, and, eventually, the original full-employment equilibrium is restored. At the new long-run equilibrium, the price level has risen by 10 per cent and nothing real has changed.

REVIEW QUIZ

1 What are the main influences on the quantity of real money that people and businesses plan to hold?
2 Show the effects of a change in the nominal interest rate and a change in real GDP using the demand for money curve.
3 How is money market equilibrium determined in the short run?
4 How does a change in the supply of money change the interest rate in the short run?
5 How does a change in the supply of money change the interest rate in the long run?

Do these questions in Study Plan 24.5 and get instant feedback.   MyEconLab

We explore the long-run link between money and the price level on the next two pages, where we study the quantity theory of money.

The Quantity Theory of Money

In the long run, the price level adjusts to make the quantity of real money demanded equal the quantity supplied. A special theory of the price level and inflation – the quantity theory of money – explains this long-run adjustment of the price level.

The **quantity theory of money** is the proposition that in the long run, an increase in the quantity of money brings an equal percentage increase in the price level. To explain the quantity theory of money, we first need to define the velocity of circulation.

The **velocity of circulation** is the average number of times a pound of money is used annually to buy the goods and services that make up GDP. But GDP equals the price level (P) multiplied by real GDP (Y). That is:

$$\text{GDP} = PY$$

Call the quantity of money M. The velocity of circulation, V, is determined by the equation:

$$V = PY/M$$

For example, if GDP is £1,000 billion ($PY = £1,000$ billion) and the quantity of money is £250 billion, then the velocity of circulation is 4.

From the definition of the velocity of circulation, the *equation of exchange* tells us how M, V, P and Y are connected. This equation is:

$$MV = PY$$

Given the definition of the velocity of circulation, the equation of exchange is always true – it is true by definition. It becomes the quantity theory of money if the quantity of money does not influence the velocity of circulation or real GDP. In this case, the equation of exchange tells us that the price level in the long run is determined by the quantity of money. That is:

$$P = M(V/Y)$$

where (V/Y) is independent of M. So a change in M brings a proportional change in P.

We can also express the equation of exchange in growth rates,[3] in which form it states that:

$$\begin{matrix} \text{Money} \\ \text{growth rate} \end{matrix} + \begin{matrix} \text{Rate of} \\ \text{velocity} \\ \text{change} \end{matrix} = \begin{matrix} \text{Inflation} \\ \text{rate} \end{matrix} + \begin{matrix} \text{Real GDP} \\ \text{growth rate} \end{matrix}$$

Solving this equation for the inflation rate gives:

$$\begin{matrix} \text{Inflation} \\ \text{rate} \end{matrix} = \begin{matrix} \text{Money} \\ \text{growth rate} \end{matrix} + \begin{matrix} \text{Rate of} \\ \text{velocity} \\ \text{change} \end{matrix} - \begin{matrix} \text{Real GDP} \\ \text{growth rate} \end{matrix}$$

ECONOMICS IN ACTION

Does the Quantity Theory Work?

On average, as predicted by the quantity theory of money, the inflation rate fluctuates in line with fluctuations in the money growth rate plus the velocity growth rate minus the real GDP growth rate. Figure 1 shows the relationship between money growth (M4 definition) and inflation in the UK. You can see a clear relationship between the two variables.

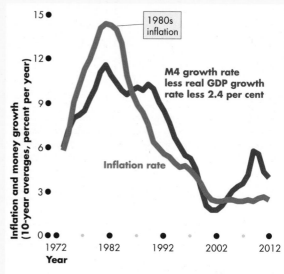

Figure 1 UK Money Growth and Inflation

Source of data: Bank of England.

In the long run, the rate of velocity change is not influenced by the money growth rate. More strongly, in the long run, the rate of velocity change is approximately zero. With this assumption, the inflation rate in the long run is determined as

---

[3] To obtain this equation, begin with

$$MV = PY$$

and then changes in these variables are related by the equation

$$\Delta MV + M\Delta V = \Delta PY + P\Delta Y$$

Divide this equation by the equation of exchange to obtain

$$\Delta M/M + \Delta V/V = \Delta P/P + \Delta Y/Y$$

The term $\Delta M/M$ is the money growth rate, $\Delta V/V$ is the rate of velocity change, $\Delta P/P$ is the inflation rate and $\Delta Y/Y$ is the real GDP growth rate.

Over the period since 1973, velocity has steadily decreased at an average annual rate of 2.5 per cent and we have subtracted that constant from the growth rate of M4 minus the growth rate of real GDP. These data are 10-year averages to reflect the long-run nature of the quantity theory.

International data also support the quantity theory. Figure 2 shows a scatter diagram of the inflation rate and the money growth rate in 134 countries and Figure 3 shows the inflation rate and money growth rate in countries with inflation rates below 20 per cent a year. You can see

a general tendency for money growth and inflation to be correlated, but the quantity theory (the red line) does not predict inflation precisely.

The correlation between money growth and inflation isn't perfect, and the correlation does *not* tell us that money growth *causes* inflation.

Money growth might cause inflation; inflation might cause money growth; or some third variable might cause both inflation and money growth. Other evidence does confirm, though, that *causation runs from money growth to inflation*.

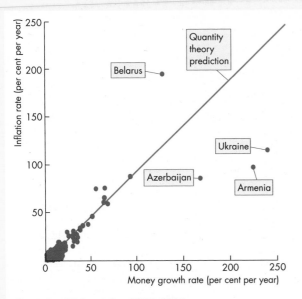

Figure 2 134 Countries: 1990–2005

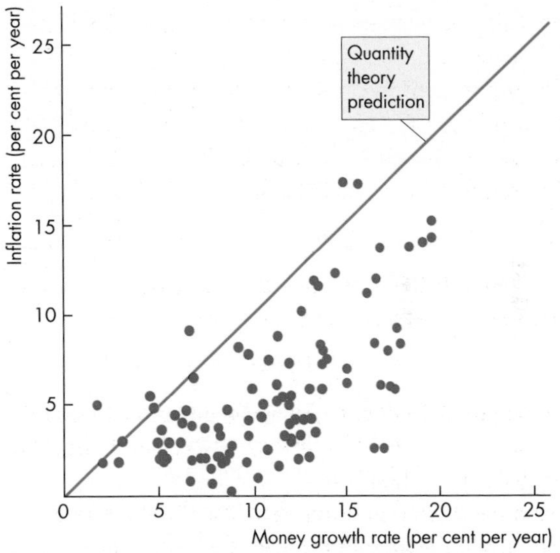

Figure 3 Lower-inflation Countries: 1990–2005

Sources of data: *International Financial Statistics Yearbook*, 2008, and International Monetary Fund, *World Economic Outlook*, October 2008.

$$\text{Inflation rate} = \text{Money growth rate} - \text{Real GDP growth rate}$$

In the long run, fluctuations in the money growth rate minus the real GDP growth rate bring equal fluctuations in the inflation rate.

Also, in the long run, with the economy at full employment, real GDP equals potential GDP, so the real GDP growth rate equals the potential GDP growth rate. This growth rate might be influenced by inflation, but the influence is most likely small and the quantity theory assumes that it is zero. So the real GDP growth rate is given and doesn't change when the money growth rate changes – inflation is correlated with money growth.

REVIEW QUIZ

1 What is the quantity theory of money?
2 How is the velocity of circulation calculated?
3 What is the equation of exchange?
4 Does the quantity theory accurately predict the effects of money growth on inflation?

Do these questions in Study Plan 24.6 and get instant feedback.

MyEconLab

You now know what money is, how the banks create it and how the quantity of money influences the nominal interest rate in the short run and the price level in the long run. *Reading Between the Lines* on pp. 578–579 looks at the actions taken by the ECB to increase the quantity of money and lower interest rates.

Interest Rate Cut in Eurozone

All Eyes on ECB as Markets Expect Rate Cut

Michael Steen

The European Central Bank's governing council was discussing a possible interest rate cut for the eurozone on Thursday, with a growing number of economists predicting action despite doubts over the effectiveness of loosening. . . .

Of those predicting a cut, most expect the bank to shave a quarter percentage point off its main refinancing rate, which has stood at 0.75 per cent since last July. . . .

Those advocating a cut were given further ammunition on Thursday when the eurozone's manufacturing purchasing managers' index compiled by Market fell to 46.7, a four month low. Any reading below 50 indicates a contraction in activity.

A rate cut has however also become widely regarded as a mostly symbolic move since the ECB has for months acknowledged that its low interest rates do not get sufficiently passed through to companies and households in countries worst affected by the sovereign debt crisis, such as Spain, Portugal and Greece. . . .

. . . Francois Hollande, the French president, made clear which way he wanted the independent central bank to move. "We need the lowest possible interest rates," Mr Hollande said. "It's already the case in many countries, notably in France. At the same time many small companies are having a hard time getting funding. And there are countries with interest rates that are too high."

France is likely to be the biggest beneficiary of any interest rate move since it has been seeing the benefit of ECB rate moves. For the countries where in ECB jargon the interest rate transmission mechanism is impaired, the bank has said it is thinking about ways it can help ensure its interest rates are passed on to small and medium businesses, who have been worst hit by an effective credit crunch.

FT   *Source*: FT.com, 2 May 2013.
© The Financial Times Limited. All Rights Reserved.

The Essence of the Story

- In April 2013, a survey of manufacturers' purchasing managers indicated that an already weak economy would see further contraction.

- With a deteriorating economic outlook, many economists expected the ECB to cut its policy interest rate from 0.75 per cent to 0.5 per cent.

- France has benefitted from low interest rates and wants that benefit strengthened with an even lower rate.

- Spain, Portugal and Greece have not benefitted and it was expected that a further rate cut would not feed through to lower interest rates in those countries.

Economic Analysis

◆ In the weak eurozone economy of April 2013, the ECB was expected to cut its key policy interest rate (called the main refinancing operations or MRO rate) from 0.75 per cent to 0.50 per cent.

◆ To achieve this lower interest rate, the ECB conducts an open market operation to increase the monetary base and increase the supply of money.

◆ Figure 1 illustrates what the ECB does. The demand for money in the eurozone economy is MD_{EZ}. Initially, the supply of money in the eurozone economy is MS_0. The equilibrium interest rate is 0.75 per cent. To lower the interest rate, the ECB increases the supply of money to MS_1, which lowers the equilibrium interest rate to 0.5 per cent.

◆ The interest rates faced by firms and governments in the eurozone are higher than the policy interest rate set by the ECB. Figure 2 shows the interest rates in six eurozone countries in April 2013. The rates vary across the countries because the risk of default by firms and governments varies.

◆ The average of these interest rates is determined in the loanable funds market (explained in Chapter 23).

◆ In Figure 3, the demand for loanable funds is DLF. When the ECB increases the money supply, the banks increase loans, the supply of loanable funds increases from SLF_0 to SLF_1, and the interest rate faced by firms and governments in that market falls.

◆ But the average interest rate falls by a small amount, and the interest rates in the high-risk, high-rate countries usually fall least.

◆ That is the problem of the impaired transmission mentioned in the news article and the reason why the rate cut might be "seen as a mostly symbolic move".

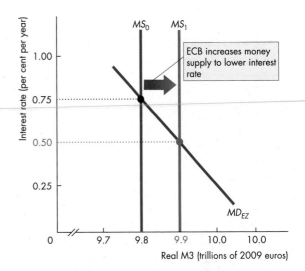

Figure 1 The Money Market in the Eurozone

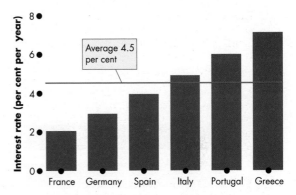

Figure 2 Interest Rates in Six Eurozone Countries in 2013

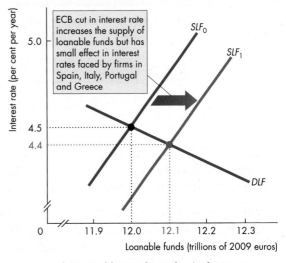

Figure 3 The Loanable Funds Market in the Eurozone

The Money Multiplier

This note explains the basic maths of the money multiplier and shows how the value of the multiplier depends on the banks' desired reserve ratio and the currency drain ratio.

To make the process of money creation concrete, we work through an example for a banking system in which each bank has a desired reserve ratio of 10 per cent of deposits and the currency drain ratio is 50 per cent of deposits. (Although these ratios are larger than the ones in the UK economy, they make the process end more quickly and enable you to see more clearly the principles at work.)

Figure 1 keeps track of the numbers. Before the process begins, all the banks have no excess reserves. Then the monetary base increases by £100,000 and one bank has excess reserves of this amount.

The bank lends the £100,000 of excess reserves. When this loan is made, new money increases by £100,000.

Some of the new money will be held as currency and some as deposits. With a currency drain ratio of 50 per cent of deposits, one-third of the new money will be held as currency and two-thirds will be held as deposits. That is, £33,333 drains out of the banks as currency and £66,667 remains in the banks as deposits. The increase in the quantity of money of £100,000 equals the increase in deposits plus the increase in currency holdings.

The increased bank deposits of £66,667 generate an increase in desired reserves of 10 per cent of that amount, which is £6,667. Actual reserves have increased by the same amount as the increase in deposits: £66,667. So the banks now have excess reserves of £60,000.

The process we've just described repeats but begins with excess reserves of £60,000. The figure shows the next two rounds. At the end of the process, the quantity of money has increased by a multiple of the increase in the monetary base. In this case, the increase is £250,000, which is 2.5 times the increase in the monetary base.

The sequence in the figure shows the first stages of the process that finally reaches the total shown in the final row of the 'money' column.

To calculate what happens at the later stages in the process and the final increase in the quantity of money,

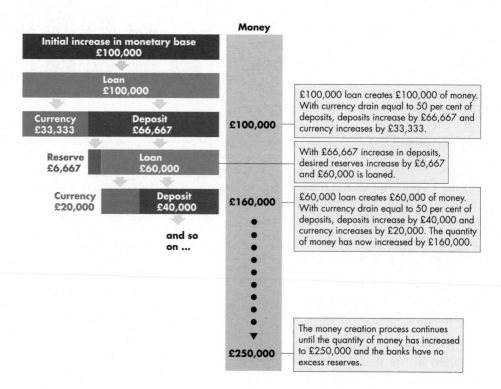

Figure 1 The Money Creation Process

look closely at the numbers in the figure. The initial increase in reserves is £100,000 (call it *A*). At each stage, the loan is 60 per cent (0.6) of the previous loan and the quantity of money increases by 0.6 of the previous increase. Call that proportion *L* (*L* = 0.6). We can write down the complete sequence for the increase in the quantity of money as:

$$A + AL + AL^2 + AL^3 + AL^4 + AL^5 + \ldots$$

Remember, *L* is a fraction, so at each stage in this sequence, the amount of new loans and new money gets smaller. The total value of loans made and money created at the end of the process is the sum of the sequence,[4] which is:

$$A/(1 - L)$$

If we use the numbers from the example, the total increase in the quantity of money is:

£100,000 + 60,000 + 36,000 + . . .

$$= £100,000 \, (1 + 0.6 + 0.36 + \ldots)$$

$$= £100,000 \, (1 + 0.6 + 0.6^2 + \ldots)$$

$$= £100,000 \times 1/(1 - 0.6)$$

$$= £100,000 \times 1/(0.4)$$

$$= £100,000 \times 2.5$$

$$= £250,000$$

The magnitude of the money multiplier depends on the banks' desired reserve ratio and the currency drain ratio. Let's explore this relationship.

The money multiplier is the ratio of money to the monetary base. Call the money multiplier *mm*, the quantity of money *M*, and the monetary base *MB*. Then:

$$mm = M/MB$$

Next recall that money, *M*, is the sum of deposits and currency. Call deposits *D* and currency *C*. Then:

$$M = D + C$$

Finally, recall that the monetary base, *MB*, is the sum of banks' reserves and currency. Call banks' reserves *R*. Then:

$$MB = R + C$$

Use the equations for *M* and *MB* in the *mm* equation to give:

$$mm = M/MB = (D + C)/(R + C)$$

Now divide all the variables on the right-hand side of the equation by *D* to give:

$$mm = M/MB = (1 + C/D)/(R/D + C/D)$$

In this equation, *C/D* is the *currency drain ratio* and *R/D* is the banks' reserve ratio. If we use the values of the example on the previous page, *C/D* = 0.5 and *R/D* = 0.1, and:

$$mm = (1 + 0.5)/(0.1 + 0.5)$$

$$= 1.5/0.6 = 2.5$$

The UK Money Multiplier

The money multiplier in the UK can be found by using the formula above along with the values of *C/D* and *R/D* in the UK economy.

Using the M4 definition of money to measure deposits, *D*, the numbers for March 2013 are:

$$C = £64 \text{ billion}$$
$$R = £280 \text{ billion}$$
$$MB = £344 \text{ billion}$$
$$D = £2{,}037 \text{ billion}$$
$$C/D = 0.0314$$
$$R/D = 0.1375$$

So

$$mm = (1 + 0.0314)/(0.1375 + 0.0314) = 6.11$$

---

[4] The sequence of values is called a convergent geometric series. To find the sum of a series such as this, begin by calling the sum *S*. Then write the sum as

$$S = A + AL + AL^2 + AL^3 + AL^4 + AL^5 + \ldots$$

Multiply by *L* to get

$$LS = AL + AL^2 + AL^3 + AL^4 + AL^5 + AL^6 + \ldots$$

and then subtract the second equation from the first to get

$$S(1 - L) = A$$

or

$$S = A/(1 - L)$$

SUMMARY

Key Points

What is Money? (pp. 558–560)

◆ Money is the means of payment and it functions as a medium of exchange, unit of account and store of value.

◆ M4 – currency held by the public and bank and building society deposits – is the main measure of money in the UK today.

Do Problems 1 to 4 to get a better understanding of what money is.

Monetary Financial Institutions (pp. 561–564)

◆ Commercial banks and building societies are monetary financial institutions: their liabilities are money.

◆ Monetary financial institutions create liquidity, minimise the cost of borrowing, minimise the cost of monitoring borrowers and pool risk.

Do Problems 5 and 6 to get a better understanding of monetary financial institutions.

Central Banking (pp. 565–568)

◆ A central bank is a public authority that provides banking services to banks and governments and manages the nation's financial system.

◆ The liabilities of the central bank are bank notes and bank reserves. These items plus coins are the monetary base.

Do Problems 7 to 9 to get a better understanding of central banks.

How Banks Create Money (pp. 568–571)

◆ Banks create money by making loans.

◆ The total quantity of money that can be created is limited by the monetary base, the banks' desired reserve ratio and the currency drain ratio.

Do Problems 10 to 14 to get a better understanding of how banks create money.

The Money Market (pp. 572–575)

◆ The quantity of money demanded is the amount of money that people plan to hold.

◆ The quantity of real money equals the quantity of nominal money divided by the price level.

◆ The quantity of real money demanded depends on the nominal interest rate, real GDP and financial innovation.

◆ The nominal interest rate makes the quantity of money demanded equal the quantity supplied.

◆ When the quantity of money increases, the nominal interest rate falls (the short-run effect).

◆ In the long run, when the quantity of money increases, the price level rises and the nominal interest rate returns to its initial level.

Do Problems 15 and 16 to get a better understanding of the money market.

The Quantity Theory of Money (pp. 576–577)

◆ The quantity theory of money is the proposition that money growth and inflation move up and down together in the long run.

Do Problem 17 to get a better understanding of the quantity theory of money.

Key Terms

STUDY PLAN PROBLEMS AND APPLICATIONS

Do Problems 1 to 19 in MyEconLab Chapter 24 Study Plan and get instant feedback.   MyEconLab

What is Money? (Study Plan 24.1)

1 In the UK today, money includes which of the following items?

   a Bank of England bank notes in Barclay's cash machines

   b Your bank debit card

   c Coins inside a vending machine

   d A £10 bank note in your wallet

   e The cheque you've just written to pay for your rent

   f The loan you took out last August to pay for your university fees

2 Suppose that in June, currency held by individuals and businesses was £400 billion; sight deposits were £4,800 billion; time deposits were £2,000 billion; M4 was £9,000 billion. What is the other item that makes up M4 and what is its value?

3 Suppose that in July, the public held £1,500 billion in currency, £5,000 billion in bank deposits and £7,000 billion in building societies. Banks held £10,000 billion in currency and building societies held £2,000 billion in currency. Calculate M4.

4 **One More Thing Mobile Phones Could Do: Replace Wallets**

Soon you'll be able to pull out your mobile phone and wave it over a scanner to make a payment. The convenience of whipping out your phone as a payment mechanism is driving the transition.

        Source: *USA Today*, 21 November 2007

If people can use their mobile phones to make payments, will currency disappear? How will the components of M4 change?

Monetary Financial Institutions

(Study Plan 24.2)

Use the following news clip in Problems 5 and 6.

Basel Committee Unveils Bank Capital Buffer Plan

Regulators want banks to hold a 'counter-cyclical capital buffer' – a required capital ratio that fluctuates with the state of the economy. The idea is to strengthen the global banking industry by putting the brakes on lending when a bubble emerges and provide a cushion to protect the banks from falling into financial difficulty.

        Source: *The Financial Times*, 17 July 2010

5 Explain a bank's 'balancing act' and how the required capital ratio makes bank failure less likely.

6 During the time of an emerging credit bubble, why might it be beneficial for the banks to be required to have a larger capital ratio?

Central Banking (Study Plan 24.3)

7 Suppose that at the end of December 2009, the monetary base was €700 billion, euro bank notes were €650 billion and banks' reserves at the ECB were €20 billion. Calculate the quantity of coins.

8 **Fast Growth in 'Broad' Money**

The Bank of England's quantitative easing programme may be having an increasing effect. Holdings of M4 'broad' money were up from 6.2 per cent in the three months to April. The Bank of England pumped £200bn in newly created cash into the economy between February 2009 and early 2010.

        Source: *The Financial Times*, 30 June 2010

What are the Bank of England's policy tools and which policy tool did it use when it 'pumped £200bn in newly created cash into the economy'?

9 The Bank of England sells £20 million of securities to HSBC. Enter the transactions that take place to show the changes in the following balance sheets.

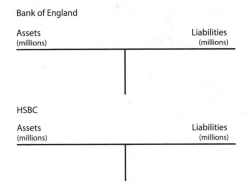

How Banks Create Money

(Study Plan 24.4)

10 The commercial banks in Zap have

   Reserves €250 million

   Loans €1,000 million

   Deposits €2,000 million

   Total assets €2,500 million

If the banks hold no excess reserves, calculate their desired reserve ratio.

Use the following information in Problems 11 and 12.

In the economy of Nocoin, banks have deposits of €300 billion. Their reserves are €15 billion, two-thirds of which is in deposits with the central bank. Households and businesses hold €30 billion in bank notes. There are no coins!

11 Calculate the monetary base and the quantity of money.

12 Calculate the banks' desired reserve ratio and the currency drain ratio (as percentages).

Use the following news clip in Problems 13 and 14.

People's Bank of China Reduces Reserve Requirement

The People's Bank of China cut the required reserve ratio by 50 basis points to 20.5 per cent of deposits, which is expected to free up Rmb 400 billion for new bank lending. The economy is still growing fast, but it has slowed down significantly from the previous year.

Source: *The Financial Times*, 20 February 2012

13 Explain how a decrease in the reserve ratio influences the commerical banks' money creation process.

14 Why might a lower reserve ratio stimulate the economy to grow faster?

The Money Market (Study Plan 24.5)

15 The spreadsheet provides information about the demand for and supply of money in Minland. Column A is the nominal interest rate, r. Columns B and C show the quantity of money demanded at two different levels of real GDP: Y_0 is £10 billion and Y_1 is £20 billion. The quantity of money supplied is £3 billion and initially real GDP is £20 billion.

	A	B	C
1	r	Y_0	Y_1
2	7	1.0	1.5
3	6	1.5	2.0
4	5	2.0	2.5
5	4	2.5	3.0
6	3	3.0	3.5
7	2	3.5	4.0
8	1	4.0	4.5

What happens in Minland if the interest rate:

a Exceeds 4 per cent a year?

b Is less than 4 per cent a year?

16 The figure shows the demand for money curve.

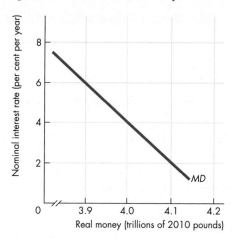

If the central bank decreases the quantity of real money supplied from £4 trillion to £3.9 trillion, explain how the price of a bond will change.

The Quantity Theory of Money
(Study Plan 24.6)

17 Quantecon is a country in which the quantity theory of money operates. In year 1, the economy is at full employment and real GDP is £400 million, the price level is 200 and the velocity of circulation is 20. In year 2, the quantity of money increases by 20 per cent. Calculate the quantity of money, the price level, real GDP, and the velocity of circulation in year 2.

Mathematical Note (Study Plan 24.MN)

18 In Problem 11, the banks have no excess reserves. Suppose that the Bank of Nocoin, the central bank, increases bank reserves by €0.5 billion.

   a What happens to the quantity of money?

   b Explain why the change in the quantity of money is not equal to the change in the monetary base.

   c Calculate the money multiplier.

19 In Problem 11, the banks have no excess reserves. Suppose that the Bank of Nocoin, the central bank, decreases bank reserves by €0.5 billion.

   a Calculate the money multiplier.

   b What happens to the quantity of money, deposits and currency?

ADDITIONAL PROBLEMS AND APPLICATIONS

What is Money?

20 Sara withdraws £1,000 from her savings account at the Lucky Building Society, keeps £50 in cash, and deposits the balance in her chequing account at HSBC. What is the immediate change in currency and in M4?

21 Rapid inflation in Brazil in the early 1990s caused the cruzeiro to lose its ability to function as money. Which of the following commodities would most likely have taken the place of the cruzeiro in the Brazilian economy? Explain why.

a Tractor parts

b Packs of cigarettes

c Loaves of bread

d Impressionist paintings

22 From Paper-Clip to House, in 14 Trades

A 26-year-old Montreal man appears to have succeeded in his quest to barter a single, red paperclip all the way up to a house. It took almost a year and 14 trades on eBay.

Source: CBC News, 7 July 2006

Is barter a means of payment? Is it just as efficient as money when trading on eBay? Explain.

Monetary Financial Institutions

Use the following news clip in Problems 23 and 24.

The War on Moral Hazard Begins at Home

Northern Rock was a narrow bank, with only retail customers, and Northern Rock failed; Lehman Brothers was a pure investment bank, but Lehman too failed. The issues in financial reform are to do with the behaviour of businesses, not the structure of their industry. Wrong. The point of structural reform of the banking system is not to prevent banks from failing. It is to allow them to fail without imposing large costs on taxpayers, their customers and the global economy.

Source: *The Financial Times*, 26 January 2011

23 Explain why attempts by banks to maximise profits can sometimes lead to bank failures.

24 Explain the effects of higher required capital ratios, higher required reserve ratios and restrictions on the types of investments banks are permitted to make. What types of structural reforms might allow banks to fail without imposing large costs on taxpayers and bank customers?

Central Banking

25 Explain the distinction between a central bank and a commercial bank.

26 If the Bank of England makes an open market sale of £1 million of securities to a bank, what initial changes occur in the economy?

27 Set out the transactions that the Bank of England undertakes to increase the quantity of money.

28 Describe the Bank of England's assets and liabilities. What is the monetary base and how does it relate to the Bank of England's balance sheet?

29 Eurozone Banks Reluctant to Return ECB's Funds

The European Central Bank (ECB) injected €73.5 billion into the region's banks to combat the Irish debt crisis by buying government bonds. The banks are reluctant to return these funds and offered the ECB just over €60 billion. They want to keep the extra liquidity.

Source: *The Financial Times*, 29 December 2010

What is the rationale behind the ECB injecting funds into the region's banks and why might the banks be reluctant to repay the funds?

How Banks Create Money

30 Banks in New Transylvania have a desired reserve ratio of 10 per cent and no excess reserves. The currency drain ratio is 50 per cent. Then the central bank increases the monetary base by €1,200 billion.

a How much do the banks lend in the first round of the money creation process?

b How much of the initial amount lent flows back to the banking system as new deposits?

c How much of the initial amount lent does not return to the banks but is held as currency?

d Why does a second round of lending occur?

The Money Market

31 Explain the change in the nominal interest rate in the short run if

  a Real GDP increases.

  b The money supply increases.

  c The price level rises.

32 In Minland in Problem 15, the interest rate is 4 per cent a year. Suppose that real GDP decreases to $10 billion and the quantity of money supplied remains unchanged. Do people buy bonds or sell bonds? Explain how the interest rate changes.

The Quantity Theory of Money

33 The table provides some data for the US in the first decade following the Civil War.

Item	1869	1879
Quantity of money	$1.3 billion	$1.7 billion
Real GDP (1929 dollars)	$7.4 billion	Z
Price level (1929 = 100)	X	54
Velocity of circulation	4.50	4.61

Source of data: Milton Friedman and Anna J. Schwartz, *A Monetary History of the United States 1867–1960*

  a Calculate the value of X in 1869.

  b Calculate the value of Z in 1879.

  c Are the data consistent with the quantity theory of money? Explain your answer.

Mathematical Note

34 In the UK, the currency drain ratio is 0.38 of deposits and the reserve ratio is 0.002. In Australia, the quantity of money is $150 billion, the currency drain ratio is 33 per cent of deposits and the reserve ratio is 8 per cent.

  a Calculate the UK money multiplier.

  b Calculate the monetary base in Australia.

Economics in the News

35 After you have studied *Reading Between the Lines* on pp. 578–579, answer the following questions.

  a How does the ECB change the interest rate in the eurozone?

  b What is the difference between the interest rate set by the ECB and that paid by firms and governments in the eurozone?

  c How is the interest rate paid by firms and governments determined and how can the ECB influence that rate?

  d Why are interest rates higher in Greece than in Germany?

  e What is meant by an 'impaired transmission mechanism'?

36 **Europe's Banks Must Be Forced to Recapitalise**

In addition to specifying higher prudential capital ratios, European governments must now bully banks to act immediately. Where private funding is not forthcoming, recapitalisation must be imposed, in return for fundamental changes in the way financial institutions operate and burdens are shared.

    Source: *The Financial Times*, 24 November 2011

  a Why do European banks need to hold more capital?

  b What exactly is the "capital" referred to in the news clip?

  c How might the requirement to hold more capital make banks safer?

37 **US Federal Reserve at Odds with ECB over Value of Policy Tool**

Many central banks use monetary aggregates as a guide to policy decision, but Bernanke believes US reliance on monetary aggregates would be unwise because the empirical relationship between US money growth, inflation and output growth is unstable. Bernanke said that the Federal Reserve had 'philosophical' and economic differences with the ECB and the Bank of England regarding the role of money and that debate between institutions is healthy. 'Unfortunately, forecast errors for money growth are often significant,' reducing their effectiveness as a tool for policy, Bernanke said. 'There are differences between the US and Europe in terms of the stability of money demand.' Ultimately, the risk of bad policy arising from a devoted following of money growth led the Federal Reserve to downgrade the importance of money measures.

    Source: *International Herald Tribune*, 10 November 2006

  a Explain how the debate surrounding the quantity theory of money could make monetary aggregates a less useful tool for policy makers.

  b What do Bernanke's statements reveal about his stance on the accuracy of the quantity theory of money?

25 International Finance

After studying this chapter you will be able to:

- ◆ Explain how the foreign exchange rate is determined
- ◆ Explain why the exchange rate fluctuates
- ◆ Describe the alternative exchange rate regimes
- ◆ Explain the benefits and costs of the euro
- ◆ Describe the balance of payments accounts and explain what causes international deficits and surpluses

The pound (£), the euro (€), the yen (¥) and the US dollar ($) are the world's most widely used currencies, but their values fluctuate every day. What causes the value of one country's money to fluctuate in value against the money of other countries?

If a country buys more from other countries than it sells to them, how does it settle the account?

You'll find the answers in this chapter. And in *Reading Between the Lines* at the end of the chapter, you will see how Japan is lowering the value of the yen and stirring fears of a currency war.

The Foreign Exchange Market

When Tesco imports DVD players from Japan, it pays for them using Japanese yen. And when China Airlines buys aircraft engines from Rolls Royce, it pays using pounds sterling. Whenever people buy things from another country, they use the currency of that country to make the transaction. It doesn't make any difference what the item is that is being traded internationally. It might be a DVD player, a jet engine, insurance or banking services, property, the stocks and bonds of a government or corporation, or even an entire business.

Foreign Currencies

Foreign money is just like money in the UK. It consists of notes and coins issued by a central bank and mint and deposits in banks and other monetary financial institutions. When we described UK and EU money in Chapter 24, we distinguished between currency (notes and coins) and deposits. But when we talk about foreign money, we refer to it as foreign currency. **Foreign currency** is the money of other countries, regardless of whether that money is in the form of notes, coins or bank deposits.

UK pounds are called *pounds sterling*. We buy foreign currencies in exchange for pounds sterling and foreigners buy pounds sterling in exchange for their own currencies in the foreign exchange market.

Trading Currencies

The currency of one country is exchanged for the currency of another in the **foreign exchange market**. The foreign exchange market consists of thousands of buyers and sellers. Some of these people are importers and exporters of goods and services; some are banks and other financial institutions; and some are specialist traders called *foreign exchange brokers*.

The foreign exchange market opens on Monday morning in Hong Kong. As the day advances, the foreign exchange markets in Singapore, Tokyo, Bahrain, Frankfurt, London, New York, Chicago and San Francisco open for trade. As the US West Coast markets close, Hong Kong is only an hour away from opening for the next day of business. The sun barely sets on the foreign exchange market. Dealers around the world are continually in contact by telephone, and on a typical day in 2013 around $3 trillion (of all currencies) were traded in the foreign exchange market – or more than $600 trillion in a year.

Exchange Rates

An **exchange rate** is the price at which one currency exchanges for another currency in the foreign exchange market. For example, on 14 May 2013, £1 would buy 1.53 US dollars, 156 Japanese yen or 1.18 euros. So the exchange rate was 1.53 dollars per pound or, equivalently, 156 yen or 118 euros per pound.

The exchange rate fluctuates. Sometimes it rises and sometimes it falls. A rise in the exchange rate is called an *appreciation* of the pound, and a fall in the exchange rate is called a *depreciation* of the pound. For example, when the exchange rate rises from 1.60 dollars to 2.00 dollars per pound, the pound appreciates, and when the exchange rate falls from 2.00 dollars to 1.50 dollars per pound, the pound depreciates.

Economics in Action on the next page shows the fluctuations in the pound sterling against three currencies since 2000. Two important questions arise from an examination of the movements of the exchange rate. First, how is the exchange rate determined? Second, how do exchange rate fluctuations influence our international trade and international payments? We begin by learning how trading in the foreign exchange market determines the exchange rate.

An Exchange Rate is a Price

An exchange rate is a price, and like all prices an exchange rate is determined in a market – the *foreign exchange market*.

The pound sterling trades in the foreign exchange market and is supplied and demanded by tens of thousands of traders every hour of every business day.

Because it has many traders and no restrictions on who may trade, the foreign exchange market is a *competitive market*.

In a competitive market, demand and supply determine the price. So to understand the forces that determine the exchange rate, we need to study the factors that influence demand and supply in the foreign exchange market. But there is a feature of the foreign exchange market that makes it special.

The Demand for One Money Is the Supply of Another Money

When people who are holding the money of some other country want to exchange it for pounds sterling, they demand pounds sterling and supply that other country's money. And when people who are holding pounds

ECONOMICS IN ACTION

The Pound Sterling Against the Euro, the Dollar and the Yen

Figure 1 shows the pound sterling exchange rate against the three big currencies – the euro, the US dollar and the Japanese yen – since January 2000.

Against the euro, the pound has been on a one-way track – downward. In January 2000 you would have needed €1.65 to buy £1.00. In April 2013 €1.18 would buy £1.00. This fall has come in two stages: a drop of about 20 euro cents in 2003 and an additional drop of 25 euro cents in 2008 and 2009. Since 2009 the pound has increased in value as the Eurozone sovereign debt crisis weakened the euro.

Against the dollar and the yen, the pound has moved in both directions. From January 2000 to 2007, the pound appreciated. It rose from $1.65 US to more than $2.00 and from ¥173 to ¥248. But through the global financial crisis and the following recession, the pound crashed against these two big currencies.

The fall was most spectacular against the yen – a depreciation of almost 50 per cent from ¥248 per pound to ¥120 yen per pound by the end of May 2012. The pound appreciated a little to ¥151 during April 2013.

The fall against the US dollar was from $2.08 down to $1.56 per pound, a depreciation of 25 per cent – about the same as the appreciation from 2000 to 2007.

Notice that the exchange rates display high-frequency fluctuations (rapid brief up and down movements) around the broad trends that we've just described.

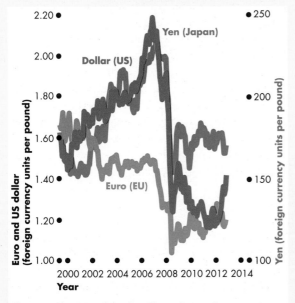

Figure 1 The Pound Against Three Currencies

sterling want to exchange them for the money of some other country, they supply pounds sterling and demand that other country's money.

So the factors that influence the demand for pounds sterling also influence the supply of US dollars, or EU euros, or Japanese yen. And the factors that influence the demand for that other country's money also influence the supply of pounds sterling.

We'll first look at the influences on the demand for pounds sterling in the foreign exchange market.

Demand in the Foreign Exchange Market

People buy pounds sterling in the foreign exchange market so that they can buy UK-produced goods and services – UK exports. They also buy pounds sterling so that they can buy UK assets such as bonds, stocks, businesses and property or so that they can keep part of their money holding in a UK bank account.

The quantity of pounds demanded in the foreign exchange market is the amount that traders plan to buy during a given time period at a given exchange rate. This quantity depends on many factors, but the main ones are:

◆ The exchange rate

◆ World demand for UK exports

◆ Interest rates in the UK and other countries

◆ The expected future exchange rate

We look first at the relationship between the quantity of pounds sterling demanded in the foreign exchange market and the exchange rate when the other three influences remain the same.

Law of Demand for Foreign Exchange

The law of demand applies to pounds sterling just as it does to anything else that people value. Other things remaining the same, the higher the exchange rate, the smaller is the quantity of pounds demanded in the foreign exchange market. The exchange rate influences the quantity of pounds demanded for two reasons:

◆ Exports effect
◆ Expected profit effect

Exports Effect

The larger the value of UK exports, the larger is the quantity of pounds demanded in the foreign exchange market. But the value of UK exports depends on the prices of UK-produced goods and services *expressed in the currency of the foreign buyer*. And these prices depend on the exchange rate. The lower the exchange rate, other things remaining the same, the lower are the prices of UK-produced goods and services to foreigners and the greater is the volume of UK exports. So if the exchange rate falls (and other influences remain the same), the quantity of pounds demanded in the foreign exchange market increases.

To see the exports effect at work, think about orders for the Rolls-Royce Adour turbine engine by the US navy. If the price of an engine is £300,000 and the exchange rate is $2.00 per pound, the price of the engine to the US Navy is $600,000. The navy decides that this price is too high. But if the exchange rate falls to $1.50 per pound and other things remain the same, the price of an engine falls to $450,000. The US Navy now decides to buy the engine and buys pounds in the foreign exchange market to pay for it.

Expected Profit Effect

The larger the expected profit from holding pounds, the greater is the quantity of pounds demanded in the foreign exchange market. But expected profit depends on the exchange rate. For a given expected future exchange rate, the lower the exchange rate today, the larger is the expected profit from buying pounds today and holding them, so the greater is the quantity of pounds demanded in the foreign exchange market today. Let's look at an example. Suppose that the Bank of New York Mellon expects the exchange rate to be $1.50 per pound at the end of the year. If today's exchange rate is also $1.50 per pound, BNY Mellon expects no profit from buying pounds sterling and holding them until the end of the year. But if today's exchange rate is $1.40 per pound and BNY Mellon buys pounds, it expects to sell those pounds at the end of the year for $1.50 per pound and make a profit of 10 cents per pound sterling.

The lower the exchange rate today, other things remaining the same, the greater is the expected profit from holding pounds and the greater is the quantity of pounds sterling demanded in the foreign exchange market today.

Demand Curve for Pounds Sterling

Figure 25.1 shows the demand curve for pounds sterling in the foreign exchange market. A change in the exchange rate, other things remaining the same, brings a change in the quantity of pounds demanded and a movement along the demand curve. The arrows show such movements.

We will look at the factors that change demand in the next section of this chapter. Before doing that, let's see what determines the supply of pounds.

Figure 25.1 The Demand for Pounds

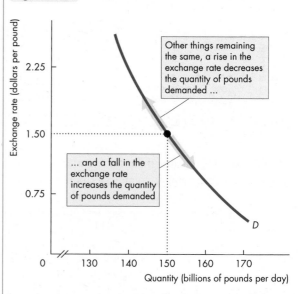

The quantity of pounds that people plan to buy depends on the exchange rate. Other things remaining the same, if the exchange rate rises, the quantity of pounds demanded decreases and there is a movement up along the demand curve for pounds. If the exchange rate falls, the quantity of pounds demanded increases and there is a movement down along the demand curve for pounds.

MyEconLab Animation ——————————————◆

Supply in the Foreign Exchange Market

People sell pounds and buy other currencies so that they can buy foreign-produced goods and services – UK imports. People also sell pounds and buy foreign currencies so that they can buy foreign assets such as bonds, stocks, businesses and real estate or so that they can hold part of their money in bank deposits denominated in a foreign currency. The quantity of pounds supplied in the foreign exchange market is the amount that traders plan to sell during a given time period at a given exchange rate. This quantity depends on many factors, but the main ones are:

◆ The exchange rate

◆ UK demand for imports

◆ Interest rates in the UK and other countries

◆ The expected future exchange rate

Let's look at the law of supply in the foreign exchange market – the relationship between the quantity of pounds supplied in the foreign exchange market and the exchange rate when the other three influences remain the same.

Law of Supply of Foreign Exchange

Other things remaining the same, the higher the exchange rate, the greater is the quantity of pounds supplied in the foreign exchange market. The exchange rate influences the quantity of pounds supplied for two reasons:

◆ Imports effect

◆ Expected profit effect

Imports Effect

The larger the value of UK imports, the larger is the quantity of pounds sterling supplied in the foreign exchange market. But the value of UK imports depends on the prices of foreign-produced goods and services *expressed in pounds*. These prices depend on the exchange rate.

The higher the exchange rate, other things remaining the same, the lower are the prices of foreign-produced goods and services to residents in the UK and the greater is the volume of imports. So if the exchange rate rises (and other influences remain the same), the

quantity of pounds supplied in the foreign exchange market increases.

Expected Profit Effect

This effect works just like that on the demand for pounds but in the opposite direction. For given expected future exchange rates, the higher the exchange rate of the pound today, other things remaining the same, the larger is the expected profit from selling pounds today and holding foreign currencies, so the greater is the quantity of pounds supplied.

Supply Curve of Pounds Sterling

Figure 25.2 shows the supply curve of pounds in the foreign exchange market. A change in the exchange rate, other things remaining the same, brings a change in the quantity of pounds supplied and a movement along the supply curve. The arrows show such movements.

Figure 25.2 The Supply of Pounds

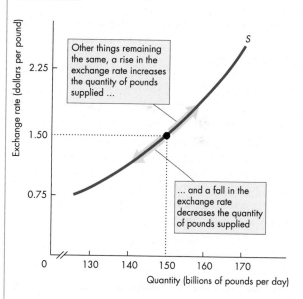

The quantity of pounds that people plan to sell depends on the exchange rate. Other things remaining the same, if the exchange rate rises, the quantity of pounds supplied increases and there is a movement up along the supply curve of pounds. If the exchange rate falls, the quantity of pounds supplied decreases and there is a movement down along the supply curve of pounds.

MyEconLab Animation ───────────────────◆

Next we bring demand and supply together and determine equilibrium in the foreign exchange market.

Market Equilibrium

Equilibrium in the foreign exchange market depends on how the Bank of England, the ECB and other central banks operate. Here, we will study equilibrium when central banks keep out of this market. In a later section (on pp. 598–599), we examine the effects of alternative actions that the Bank of England or another central bank might take in the foreign exchange market.

Figure 25.3 shows the demand curve for pounds, *D*, from Figure 25.1 and the supply curve of pounds, *S*, from Figure 25.2, and the equilibrium exchange rate.

The exchange rate acts as a regulator of the quantities demanded and supplied. If the exchange rate is too high, there is a surplus of pounds – the quantity supplied exceeds the quantity demanded – and the exchange rate falls. For example, in Figure 25.3, if the exchange rate is $2.25 per pound, there is a surplus of pounds.

If the exchange rate is too low, there is a shortage of pounds – the quantity supplied is less than the quantity demanded – and the exchange rate rises. For example, if the exchange rate is $0.75 per pound, there is a shortage of pounds.

At the equilibrium exchange rate, there is neither a shortage nor a surplus – the quantity supplied equals the quantity demanded. In Figure 25.3, the equilibrium exchange rate is $1.50 per pound. At this exchange rate, the quantity demanded and the quantity supplied are each £150 billion a day.

The Powerful Pull of Equilibrium

The foreign exchange market is constantly pulled to its equilibrium by the forces of supply and demand. Foreign exchange traders around the world are constantly looking for the best price they can get. If they are selling, they want the highest price available. If they are buying, they want the lowest price available.

Information flows from trader to trader through the worldwide computer network, and the price adjusts minute by minute to keep buying plans and selling plans in balance. That is, the price adjusts minute by minute to keep the exchange rate at its equilibrium.

Figure 25.3 shows how the exchange rate between the pound sterling and the US dollar is determined. The exchange rates between the pound and all other currencies are determined in a similar way. So are the exchange rates among the other currencies. But the exchange rates are tied together so that no profit can be made by buying one currency, selling it for a second one, and then buying back the first one. If such a profit

Figure 25.3 Equilibrium Exchange Rate

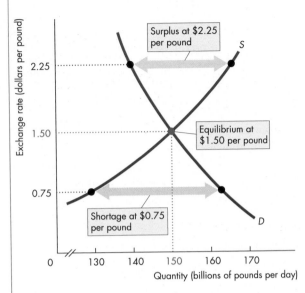

The demand curve for pounds is *D* and the supply curve is *S*. If the exchange rate is $2.25 per pound, there is a surplus of pounds and the exchange rate falls. If the exchange rate is $0.75 per pound, there is a shortage of pounds and the exchange rate rises. If the exchange rate is $1.50 per pound, there is neither a shortage nor a surplus of pounds and the exchange rate remains constant. The market is in equilibrium.

MyEconLab Animation ━━━━━━━━━━━━━━━◆

were available, traders would spot it, demand and supply would change, and the exchange rates would snap into alignment.

◆ REVIEW QUIZ

1 What are the influences on the demand for pounds in the foreign exchange market?
2 Provide an example of the exports effect on the demand for pounds.
3 What are the influences on the supply of pounds in the foreign exchange market?
4 Provide an example of the imports effect on the supply of pounds.
5 How is the equilibrium exchange rate determined?
6 What happens if there is a shortage or a surplus of pounds in the foreign exchange market?

Do these questions in Study Plan 25.1 and get instant feedback.   MyEconLab

Exchange Rate Fluctuations

You've seen (in *Economics in Action* on p. 589) that the pound fluctuates a lot against the euro, the dollar and the yen. Changes in the demand for pounds or the supply of pounds bring these exchange rate fluctuations. We'll now look at the factors that make demand and supply change, starting with the demand side of the market.

Changes in the Demand for Pounds

The demand for pounds in the foreign exchange market changes when there is a change in:

◆ World demand for UK exports

◆ UK interest rate relative to the foreign interest rate

◆ The expected future exchange rate

World Demand for UK Exports

An increase in world demand for UK exports increases the demand for pounds. To see this effect, think about the sale of commercial air engines by Rolls Royce. An increase in demand for air travel in Australia sends Qantas on a global shopping spree to buy the Rolls Royce Trent 900 to power its expanding fleet of Super Airbuses. The demand for pounds now increases.

UK Interest Rate Relative to the Foreign Interest Rate

People and businesses buy financial assets to make a return. The higher the interest rate that people can make on UK assets compared with foreign assets, the more UK assets they buy.

What matters is not the level of the UK interest rate but the UK rate minus the foreign rate – a gap that is called the **UK interest rate differential**. If the UK interest rate rises and the foreign interest rate remains constant, the UK interest rate differential increases. The larger the UK interest rate differential, the greater is the demand for UK assets and the greater is the demand for pounds in the foreign exchange market.

The Expected Future Exchange Rate

For a given current exchange rate, other things remaining the same, a rise in the expected future exchange rate increases the profit that people expect to make by holding pounds, and the demand for pounds increases today.

Figure 25.4 summarises the influences on the demand for pounds. An increase in the demand for UK exports, a rise in the UK interest rate differential, or a rise in the expected future exchange rate increases the demand for pounds today and shifts the demand curve rightward from D_0 to D_1. A decrease in the demand for UK exports, a fall in the UK interest rate differential, or a fall in the expected future exchange rate decreases the demand for pounds today and shifts the demand curve leftward from D_0 to D_2.

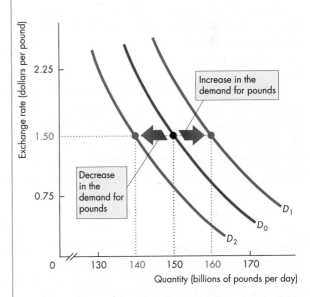

Figure 25.4 Changes in the Demand for Pounds

A change in any influence on the quantity of pounds that people plan to buy, other than the exchange rate, brings a change in the demand for pounds.

The demand for pounds

Increases if	*Decreases if*
◆ World demand for UK exports increases	◆ World demand for UK exports decreases
◆ The UK interest rate differential rises	◆ The UK interest rate differential falls
◆ The expected future exchange rate rises	◆ The expected future exchange rate falls

MyEconLab Animation ——————————◆

Changes in the Supply of Pounds

The supply of pounds in the foreign exchange market changes when there is a change in:

◆ UK demand for imports
◆ UK interest rate differential
◆ The expected future exchange rate

UK Demand for Imports

An increase in the UK demand for imports increases the supply of pounds in the foreign exchange market. To see why, think about Tesco's purchase of DVD players. An increase in the demand for DVD players sends Tesco out on a global shopping spree. Tesco decides that Panasonic DVD players produced in Japan are the best buy, so it increases its purchases of these players. The supply of pounds now increases as Tesco goes to the foreign exchange market for Japanese yen to pay Panasonic.

UK Interest Rate Differential

The effect of the UK interest rate differential on the supply of pounds is the opposite of its effect on the demand for pounds. The larger the UK interest rate differential, the smaller is the supply of pounds in the foreign exchange market. With a higher UK interest rate differential, people decide to keep more of their funds in sterling assets and less in foreign currency assets. They buy a smaller quantity of foreign currency and sell a smaller quantity of pounds in the foreign exchange market. So, a rise in the UK interest rate, other things remaining the same, decreases the supply of pounds in the foreign exchange market.

The Expected Future Exchange Rate

For a given current exchange rate, other things remaining the same, a fall in the expected future exchange rate decreases the profit that can be made by holding pounds and decreases the quantity of pounds that people want to hold. To reduce their holdings of sterling assets, people must sell pounds. When they do so, the supply of pounds in the foreign exchange market increases.

Figure 25.5 summarises the influences on the supply of pounds. If the supply of pounds decreases, the supply curve shifts leftward from S_0 to S_1. And if the supply of pounds increases, the supply curve shifts rightward from S_0 to S_2.

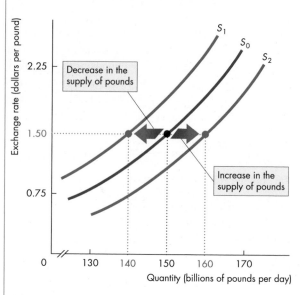

Figure 25.5   Changes in the Supply of Pounds

A change in any influence on the quantity of pounds that people plan to sell, other than the exchange rate, brings a change in the supply of pounds.

The supply of pounds

Increases if	*Decreases if*
◆ UK demand for imports increases	◆ UK demand for imports decreases
◆ The UK interest rate differential falls	◆ The UK interest rate differential rises
◆ The expected future exchange rate falls	◆ The expected future exchange rate rises

MyEconLab Animation ━━━━━━━━━━━━━━━━━━◆

Changes in the Exchange Rate

If the demand for pounds increases and the supply does not change, the exchange rate rises. If the demand for pounds decreases and the supply does not change, the exchange rate falls. Similarly, if the supply of pounds decreases and the demand does not change, the exchange rate rises. If the supply of pounds increases and the demand does not change, the exchange rate falls.

These predictions are exactly the same as those for any other market. Two episodes in the life of the pound illustrate these predictions.

ECONOMICS IN ACTION

The Rise and Fall of the Pound

The foreign exchange market is a striking example of a competitive market. The expectations of thousands of traders around the world influence this market minute by minute throughout the 24-hour global trading day.

Demand and supply rarely stand still and their fluctuations bring a fluctuating exchange rate. Two episodes in the life of the pound and the yen illustrate these fluctuations: 2001–2007, when the pound appreciated, and 2007–2011, when the pound depreciated.

An Appreciating Pound: 2001–2007

Between January 2001 and July 2007, the pound appreciated against the yen: it rose from 173 to 248 yen per pound. Part (a) of Figure 1 provides an explanation for this appreciation.

In 2001, the demand and supply curves were those labelled D_{01} and S_{01}. The exchange rate was 173 yen per pound. During this period, the UK was a good place to invest. Property prices were rising and banks in the UK increasingly borrowed from foreign banks, particularly Japanese banks, in the global market for mortgage-backed securities. The Bank of England raised the *bank rate* from 3.5 per cent in 2003 to 5.75 per cent in July 2007, but interest rates in Japan barely changed. With the rise in the UK interest rate differential, funds flowed into the UK. Also, currency traders, anticipating this increased flow of funds into the UK, expected the pound to appreciate against the

yen. The demand for pounds increased, and the supply of pounds decreased.

In the figure, the demand curve shifted rightward from D_{01} to D_{07} and the supply curve shifted leftward from S_{01} to S_{07}. The exchange rate rose to 248 yen per pound. In the figure, the equilibrium quantity remained unchanged – an assumption.

A Depreciating Pound: 2007–2011

Between July 2007 and December 2011, the pound depreciated against the yen: it fell from 248 to 120 yen per pound. Part (b) of Figure 1 provides a possible explanation for this depreciation. The demand and supply curves D_{07} and S_{07} are the same as in part (a).

From the third quarter of 2007 to the fourth quarter of 2011, the UK economy, along with the US and other developed economies, entered a severe financial crisis. Investment returns and property values fell sharply. The Bank of England cut the *bank rate*, but the Bank of Japan kept the interest rate in Japan unchanged. With a narrowing of the UK interest rate differential and a reversal of investment returns, funds flowed out of the UK. Also, currency traders expected the pound to depreciate against the yen. The demand for pounds decreased and the supply of pounds increased.

In part (b) of the figure, the demand curve shifted leftward from D_{07} to D_{11}, the supply curve shifted rightward from S_{07} to S_{11}, and the exchange rate fell to 120 yen per pound.

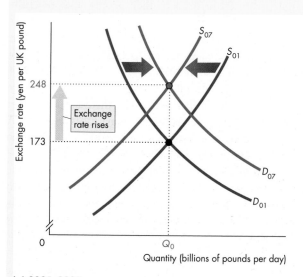

(a) 2001–2007

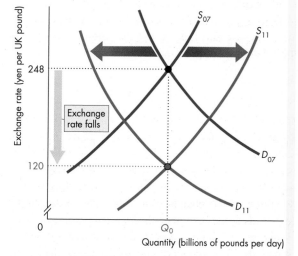

(b) 2007–2011

Figure 1 The Rising and Falling UK Pound

Fundamentals, Expectations and Arbitrage

Changes in the expected exchange rate change the actual exchange rate. But what makes the expected exchange rate change? The answer is new information about the *fundamental influences* on the exchange rate – the world demand for UK exports, UK demand for imports, and the UK interest rate relative to the foreign interest rate. Expectations about these variables change the exchange rate through their influence on the expected exchange rate, and the effect is instant.

To see why, suppose news breaks that the Bank of England will raise the interest rate next week. Traders now expect the demand for pounds to increase, the supply of pounds to decrease, and the pound to appreciate. They expect to profit by buying pounds today and selling them next week for a higher price than they paid. The rise in the expected future value of the pound increases the demand for pounds today, decreases the supply of pounds today, and raises the exchange rate. The exchange rate changes as soon as the news about a fundamental influence is received.

Profiting by trading in the foreign exchange market often involves arbitrage – the practice of buying in one market and selling for a higher price in another related market. Arbitrage ensures that the exchange rate is the same in New York, Tokyo, London and all other trading centres. It isn't possible to buy at a low price in London and sell for a higher price in New York. If it were possible, demand would increase in London and decrease in New York to make the prices equal.

Arbitrage also removes profit from borrowing in one currency and lending in another and buying goods in one currency and selling them in another. These arbitrage activities bring about:

◆ Interest rate parity
◆ Purchasing power parity

Interest Rate Parity

Suppose that the interest rate on a bank deposit in pounds in London is 5 per cent a year and on a US dollar bank deposit in New York is 3 per cent a year. In this situation, why does anyone deposit money in New York? Why doesn't all the money flow to London? The answer is because of exchange rate expectations.

Suppose people expect the pound to depreciate by 2 per cent a year. This 2 per cent depreciation must be subtracted from the 5 per cent interest to obtain the net return of 3 per cent a year that an American can earn by depositing funds in London. The two returns are equal. This situation is one of **interest rate parity**, which means *equal rates of return*.

Adjusted for risk, interest rate parity always prevails. Funds move to get the highest return available. If for a few seconds a higher return is available in London than in New York, the demand for pounds increases and the pound appreciates until interest rate parity is restored.

Purchasing Power Parity

Suppose the price of a pair of Levi's jeans is £20 in London and $30 in New York. If the exchange rate is $1.50 per pound, the two monies have the same value. You can buy the jeans in London or New York for either £20 or $30 – the same price in the two currencies.

The situation we've just described is called **purchasing power parity**, which *means equal value of money*. If purchasing power parity does not prevail, powerful arbitrage forces go to work.

Arbitrage Forces

To see these forces, suppose that the price of Levi's jeans in London rises to £30, but in New York they remain at $30. The exchange rate remains at $1.50 per pound. In this case, a pair of jeans in New York still costs $30 or £20, but in London it costs £30 or $45. Money buys more in the US than in the UK. Money is not of equal value in the two countries.

If all (or most) prices have increased in the UK and not increased in the US, then people will generally expect that the value of the pound in the foreign exchange market must fall. In this situation, the exchange rate is expected to fall. The demand for pounds decreases, and the supply of pounds increases. The exchange rate falls, as expected. If the exchange rate falls to $1.00 per pound and there are no further price changes, purchasing power parity is restored. A pair of jeans that costs £30 in London also costs the equivalent of £30 ($30) in New York.

If prices rise in the US and other countries but remain constant in the UK, people will expect the pound to appreciate. The demand for pounds increases and the supply of pounds decreases. The exchange rate rises, as expected.

So far we've been looking at the forces that determine the *nominal* exchange rate – the amount of one money that another money buys. We're now going to study the *real* exchange rate.

The Real Exchange Rate

The **real exchange rate** is the relative price of UK-produced goods and services to foreign-produced goods and services. It is a measure of the quantity of the real GDP of other countries that a unit of UK real GDP buys.

The real US dollar exchange rate, *RER*, is

$$RER = (E \times P)/P*$$

where *E* is the exchange rate ($ per £), *P* is the UK price level and *P** is the US price level.

To understand the real exchange rate, suppose that each country produces only one good and that the exchange rate *E* is $1.50 per pound. The UK produces only bagpipes priced at £300 each, so *P* equals £300 and *E* × *P* equals $450. The US produces only Stetson hats priced at $100, so *P** equals $100. Then the real pound exchange rate is

$$RER = (1.5 \times 300)/100 = 4.5 \text{ Stetson hats per bagpipe}$$

The Short Run

In the short run, if the nominal exchange rate changes, the real exchange rate also changes. The reason is that prices and the price levels in the UK and US don't change every time the exchange rate changes. Sticking with the bagpipes and Stetson hats example, if the pound appreciates to $2.00 per pound and prices don't change, the real exchange rate rises to 6 Stetson hats per bagpipe. The price of a Stetson hat in the UK falls to £50 ($100 ÷ $2.00 per pound = £50).

Changes in the real exchange rate bring short-run changes in the quantity of imports demanded and the quantity of exports supplied.

The Long Run

In the long run, the situation is radically different: the nominal exchange rate and the price level are determined together and the real exchange rate does not change when the nominal exchange rate changes.

In the long run, demand and supply in the markets for goods and services determine prices. In the bagpipes and Stetson hats example, the world markets for bagpipes (they make them in Pakistan, India and Canada as well!) and Stetson hats determine their relative price. In our example the relative price is 4.5 hats per bagpipe. The same forces determine all relative prices and so determine nations' relative price levels. The quantity of money determines the price level and the exchange rate.

The Quantity Theory of Money Again

In the long run, if the pound appreciates prices do change. To see why, recall the quantity theory of money that you met in Chapter 24 (pp. 576–577).

In the long run, the quantity of money determines the price level. But the quantity theory of money applies to all countries, so the US quantity of money determines the US price level and the UK quantity of money determines the UK price level.

For a given real exchange rate, a change in the quantity of money brings a change in the price level *and* a change in the exchange rate.

Suppose that the quantity of money in the US doubles. The pound appreciates (the dollar depreciates) from $1.50 per pound to $3.00 per pound and all US prices double, so the price of a Stetson hat rises from $100 to $200. At the new US price and the new exchange rate, a Stetson hat in the UK still costs £66.67 ($200 ÷ $3.00 per pound or £66.67); and the real exchange rate remains at 4.5 Stetson hats per bagpipe.

If the US and the UK produced identical goods (if GDP in both countries consisted only of bagpipes), the real exchange rate in the long run would equal 1.

In reality, although there is overlap in what each country produces, UK real GDP is a different bundle of goods and services from US real GDP. So the relative price of US and UK real GDP – the real exchange rate – is not 1, and it changes over time.

The forces of demand and supply in the markets for the millions of goods and services that make up real GDP determine the relative price of US and UK real GDP, and changes in these forces change the real exchange rate.

◆ REVIEW QUIZ

1 Why does the demand for pounds change?
2 Why does the supply of pounds change?
3 What makes the pound exchange rate change?
4 What is interest parity and what happens when this condition does not hold?
5 What is purchasing power parity and what happens when this condition does not hold?
6 What determines the real exchange rate and the nominal exchange rate in the short run?
7 What determines the real exchange rate and the nominal exchange rate in the long run?

Do these questions in Study Plan 25.2 and get instant feedback.   MyEconLab

Exchange Rate Policy

Because the exchange rate is the price of a country's money in terms of another country's money, governments and central banks must have a policy towards the exchange rate. Three possible exchange rate policies are:

♦ Flexible exchange rate
♦ Fixed exchange rate
♦ Crawling peg

Flexible Exchange Rate

A **flexible exchange rate** is an exchange rate that is determined by demand and supply in the foreign exchange market with no direct intervention by the central bank.

Today, most countries, including the UK, operate a flexible exchange rate, and the foreign exchange market that we have studied so far in this chapter is an example of a flexible exchange rate regime.

But even a flexible exchange rate is influenced by central bank actions. If the Bank of England raises the UK interest rate and other countries keep their interest rates unchanged, the demand for pounds increases, the supply of pounds decreases, and the exchange rate rises. (Similarly, if the Bank of England lowers the UK interest rate, the demand for pounds decreases, the supply increases, and the exchange rate falls.)

In a flexible exchange rate regime, when the central bank changes the interest rate, its purpose is not usually to influence the exchange rate, but to achieve some other monetary policy objective. (We return to this topic at length in Chapter 30.)

Fixed Exchange Rate

A **fixed exchange rate** is an exchange rate that is determined by a decision of the government or the central bank and is achieved by central bank intervention in the foreign exchange market to block the unregulated forces of demand and supply.

The world economy operated a fixed exchange rate regime from the end of the Second World War to the early 1970s. China had a fixed exchange rate until recently. Hong Kong has had a fixed exchange rate for many years and continues with that policy today.

Active intervention in the foreign exchange market is required to achieve a fixed exchange rate. If the Bank of England wanted to fix the pound sterling exchange rate against the US dollar, it would have to sell pounds to prevent the exchange rate from rising above the target value and buy pounds to prevent the exchange rate from falling below the target value.

There is no limit to the quantity of pounds that the Bank of England can *sell*. The Bank of England creates pounds and can create any quantity it chooses. But there is a limit to the quantity of pounds the Bank of England can *buy*. That limit is set by the foreign currency reserves held at the Bank of England because to buy pounds the Bank of England must sell foreign currency. Intervention to buy pounds stops when the foreign currency reserves run out.

Let's look at the foreign exchange interventions that the Bank of England can make.

Suppose the Bank of England wants the exchange rate to be steady at $1.50. If the exchange rate rises above $1.50, the Bank of England sells pounds. If the exchange rate falls below $1.50, the Bank of England buys pounds. By these actions, the Bank of England keeps the exchange rate close to its target rate of $1.50 per pound.

Figure 25.6 shows the Bank of England's intervention in the foreign exchange market. The supply of pounds is S and initially the demand for pounds is D_0. The equilibrium exchange rate is $1.50 per pound. This exchange rate is also the Bank of England's target exchange rate, shown by the horizontal red line.

When the demand for pounds increases and the demand curve shifts rightward to D_1, the Bank of England sells £10 billion. This action prevents the exchange rate from rising. When the demand for pounds decreases and the demand curve shifts leftward to D_2, the Bank of England buys £10 billion. This action prevents the exchange rate from falling.

If the demand for pounds fluctuates between D_1 and D_2 and on average is D_0, the Bank of England can repeatedly intervene in the way we've just seen. Sometimes the Bank of England buys and sometimes it sells but, on average, it neither buys nor sells.

But suppose the demand for the pound *increases permanently* from D_0 to D_1. To maintain the exchange rate at $1.50, the Bank of England must sell pounds and buy dollars, so foreign currency reserves would be increasing. At some point, the Bank of England would abandon the exchange rate of $1.50 per pound and stop piling up foreign currency reserves.

Now suppose the demand for pounds *decreases permanently* from D_0 to D_2. In this situation, the Bank of England cannot maintain the exchange rate at $1.50 per pound indefinitely. To hold the exchange rate at $1.50,

Figure 25.6 Foreign Exchange Market Intervention

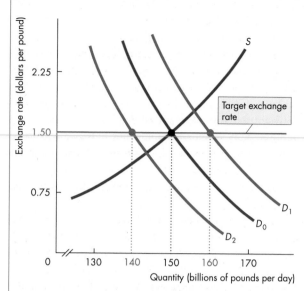

Initially, the demand for pounds is D_0, the supply of pounds is S, and the exchange rate is $1.50 per pound. The Bank of England can intervene in the foreign exchange market to keep the exchange rate close to target ($1.50 per pound in this example). If the demand for pounds increases and the demand curve shifts to D_1, the Bank of England sells pounds. If the demand for pounds decreases and the demand curve shifts to D_2, the Bank of England buys pounds. Persistent intervention on one side of the market cannot be sustained.

MyEconLab Animation ◆

the Bank of England must buy pounds. When the Bank of England buys pounds in the foreign exchange market, it uses its foreign currency reserves. So the Bank of England's action decreases its foreign currency reserves. Eventually, the Bank of England would run out of foreign currency and would then have to abandon the target exchange rate of $1.50.

Crawling Peg

A **crawling peg** is an exchange rate that follows a path determined by a decision of the government or the central bank and is achieved in a similar way to a fixed exchange rate by central bank intervention in the foreign exchange market. A crawling peg works like a fixed exchange rate except that the target value might change at fixed intervals or at random intervals. The peg seeks only to prevent large swings in the expected future

ECONOMICS IN ACTION

Currency Wars

Brazil, Chile and China are three countries accused of manipulating their exchange rates to undervalue their currencies and make their exports cheap so they are able to take market share from other countries.

A country that manipulates its exchange rate in this way is using a fixed exchange rate or crawling peg policy and is buying foreign currency and selling its own currency to keep its price down.

A *currency war* breaks out when countries retaliate against exchange rate manipulators. So far, the world has avoided a currency war, and it would take a retaliation from the US, the EU or Japan to start a big one. *Reading Between the Lines* on pp. 606–607 looks at Japan's recent monetary and exchange rate policy actions that might trigger a currency war.

What you've learned in this chapter tells you that currency manipulation is a short-run policy. Keeping the exchange rate low to lower export prices works as long as the low exchange rate doesn't bring higher import prices and a rise in wages and the overall price level. In the long run, that is exactly what happens. A policy of exchange rate manipulation can bring short-run gains at the expense of a higher price level in the long run.

A currency war is a self-defeating exercise that results in competitive depreciation and a general outbreak of inflation among the participating nations.

exchange rate that change demand and supply and make the exchange rate fluctuate too wildly.

A crawling peg departs from the ideal if, as often happens with a fixed exchange rate, the target rate departs from the equilibrium exchange rate for too long. When this happens, the country either runs out of reserves or piles up reserves.

REVIEW QUIZ

1 What is a flexible exchange rate and how does it work?
2 What is a fixed exchange rate and how is its value fixed?
3 What is a crawling peg and how does it work?

Do these questions in Study Plan 25.3 and get instant feedback.   MyEconLab

European Monetary Union

The European Monetary Union (EMU), formed on 1 January 1999, now consists of 17 member states of the EU that use the euro as their national currency. The UK is the only major member state to have remained outside the euro area. What is the UK missing and what is it gaining? Let's review the benefits and costs of the euro.

The Benefits of the Euro

A single currency in Europe has three benefits. It:

◆ Improves transparency and competition

◆ Decreases transactions costs

◆ Eliminates foreign exchange risk

Improves Transparency and Competition

A single currency provides a single unit of account so that prices are easily compared across the entire Eurozone. A country might gain a competitive advantage by becoming more efficient, but it cannot gain an advantage by artificially lowering the prices of its exports through a depreciation of its currency.

Decreases Transactions Costs

A single currency eliminates foreign exchange transactions costs – the costs of exchanging pesetas for francs at a bank or travel agent, such as commission charges or the margin between the buy and sell exchange rates we see posted in banks and currency exchanges. The removal of these costs benefits the consumer, who knows that a euro in France buys the same as a euro in Germany.

The total benefit from eliminating the transactions costs of currency exchange has been estimated at 0.3 to 0.4 per cent of EU GDP a year. For a country with an advanced banking system as in the UK, the EU Commission estimates that the benefits would be 0.1 per cent of GDP a year.

Eliminates Foreign Exchange Risk

With a single currency, exporters and importers no longer face foreign exchange risk. For example, Alpine Gardens, an Austrian garden company, has ordered a consignment of garden gnomes to be supplied by Britannia Gnomes Ltd, a Gloucester company, in three months' time. The contract and the price are set today, but payment will take place in three months' time.

Alpine Gardens has to pay £50,000 in three months' time. To protect itself against an adverse change in the exchange rate, it buys £50,000 today in the forward market at today's exchange rate.

The reduction in exchange rate risk improves trade between EU countries. Cacharel, the French clothing designer, can source its material from Rome or Paris. On a strict exchange rate comparison, the Italian product is cheaper. But in the pre-euro days, the exchange rate between the French franc and Italian lira fluctuated unpredictably. Cacharel would not have wanted to be tied into a contract with the Italian supplier if the price in francs fluctuated with the exchange rate. Cacharel would have sourced the material from the more expensive French supplier because the price was guaranteed, but Cacharel had to charge its customers a higher price. Now, with the euro, a single currency eliminates this exchange rate risk. Cacharel can source its material from Rome, pay a lower price and pass the benefits of the lower price on to its customers. The lower price increases the quantity demanded of Cacharel clothing, which in turn increases the orders from Rome.

The removal of exchange risk means that many large companies are able to reduce their administration and financial management costs. They also no longer need to diversify their operations across borders and can consolidate them in one location.

If the euro had only benefits, a nation's choice would be simple, but the euro has costs too.

The Economic Costs of the Euro

A single currency in Europe has two costs:

◆ Loss of sovereignty

◆ Inability to respond to national shocks

Loss of Sovereignty

The pursuit of national economic goals requires policy instruments under the control of a national government. The EMU places all the instruments of monetary policy beyond the reach of national governments and a Stability and Growth Pact places strict limits on the use of fiscal policy and regional policy.

Common regional policy enables transfers to be made from Germany and France to Italy and Spain. But a political consensus must be found to sustain such transfers. In effect, a single currency implies a political union. A loss of monetary sovereignty implies a loss of political sovereignty.

Inability to Respond to National Shocks

Many, perhaps most, economic shocks that call for a monetary policy response are country-specific shocks or shocks that affect different countries in different ways.

For example, the dismantling of the Berlin Wall had a major impact on the German economy but barely any effect on the economies of Ireland and Portugal. Also, the shock had different effects on the two parts of Germany. East German workers were less productive and earned lower wage rates than their West German counterparts. Productivity and earnings differences induced a massive reallocation and relocation of jobs and people. A common monetary policy might stimulate the economy in the East and bring inflation to the West or keep inflation in check in the West and bring prolonged recession in the East.

Another example is the Greek sovereign debt crisis of 2012. The Greek government has run a large budget deficit and built up a huge debt, which creates a fear that the Greek government might default – might fail to repay its debts. Greek government bond interest rates have risen sharply in recent years to reflect the risk of default, making it difficult for the Greek government to raise funds in the international bond market. There is a further risk that the Greek government might exit the euro and return to using its own currency, the drachma. A common monetary policy cannot deal with the results of this type of country-specific shock.

The Optimum Currency Area

When there are benefits and costs, they must be weighed against each other and an optimum outcome found. Imagine a world in which the Welsh leek and Scottish thistle exchange for each other and for the English pound at exchange rates that fluctuate every day. The UK is almost certainly better off using one currency rather than three. Is Europe better off using the euro than 17 national currencies? And why stop at Europe? Would the world be better off with one currency rather than its 200-plus currencies?

To answer these questions, we need the concept of an **optimal currency area**, a geographical area that is better served by a single currency than by several currencies. Robert Mundell, an economics professor at Columbia University in New York City, won the Nobel Prize in 1999 for his work on this topic. Mundell claimed that the key factor required for an optimal currency area is free labour mobility either across regions or between jobs.

On this criterion, Scotland, Wales and England are better off with a single currency than they would be with an English pound, a 'Welsh leek' and a 'Scottish thistle'. No cultural or language barriers hamper the movement of labour. If a factory closes down in Merseyside and another opens in Clwyd, workers from Merseyside can travel to Wales to seek employment.

Lack of regional mobility is not a problem if there is mobility between jobs. For example, if Volkswagen closes a Polo production plant in Pamplona, Spain, and opens a new plant in Wolfsburg, Germany, we would not expect former Spanish car workers to migrate to Germany – although by current EU labour laws there is nothing stopping them from doing just that. If jobless car workers in Pamplona can easily retrain and find a new job in Spain, the absence of regional labour mobility doesn't weaken the case for a single currency.

A second criterion for an optimal currency area is that regions within the area face common economic shocks. It is claimed by some economists that economies with similar industrial structures and extensive trade with each other satisfy this criterion. And it is further claimed that the Eurozone countries have sufficiently similar industrial structures and sufficiently extensive trade links to meet this criterion.

Unlike the country-specific shocks that we've just considered, common shocks can be dealt with by a common monetary policy run by a common central bank. For example, if a rise in the price of oil affected all the countries in a monetary union in the same way, the central bank could react in a way that is appropriate for all the countries in the union.

Even if a country does not share a similar industrial structure and have extensive trade links with its neighbours, some argue that a single currency area will bring convergence to a common industrial structure and stimulate trade flows. For example, each major Canadian city is closer to a major US city than to other Canadian cities. But there is significantly more trade among Canadian cities (using one currency) than between the closer Canadian and US cities (using two currencies).

◆ REVIEW QUIZ

1   What is the EMU?
2   What are the benefits of a single currency for Europe?
3   What are the costs of a single currency for Europe?
4   What is an optimal currency area?

Do these questions in Study Plan 25.4 and get instant feedback.   MyEconLab

Financing International Trade

You now know how the exchange rate is determined, but what is the effect of the exchange rate? How does currency depreciation or currency appreciation influence our international trade and payments? We're going to lay the foundation for addressing these questions by looking at the scale of international trading, borrowing and lending, and at the way in which we keep our records of international transactions. These records are called the *balance of payments accounts*.

Balance of Payments Accounts

A country's **balance of payments accounts** record its international trading and its borrowing and lending. There are three balance of payments accounts:

◆ Current account
◆ Capital and financial account
◆ Reserve assets account

Current Account

The **current account** records the receipts from the sale of goods and services to foreigners, the payments for goods and services bought from foreigners, and income and other transfers (such as foreign aid payments) received from and paid to foreigners. The large items in the current account are the receipts from the sale of goods and services to foreigners (exports) and the payments made for goods and services bought from foreigners (imports). Net income is the earnings from foreign financial assets such as bonds and shares, and net earnings of UK workers abroad and foreign workers in the UK. Net transfers – gifts to foreigners minus gifts from foreigners – are relatively small items.

Capital and Financial Account

The **capital and financial account** records all UK investments abroad and foreigners' investments in the UK. This account balance equals the amount that a country borrows from the rest of the world minus the amount that it lends to it.

Reserve Assets Account

The **reserve assets account** shows the net increase or decrease in a country's holdings of foreign currency reserves that comes about from the official financing of

the sum of the current account and the capital and financial account balances. The Office for National Statistics shows the change in reserve assets as an item in the capital and financial account. We show it separately because it represents a policy choice, not the outcome of private transactions. It records how government has influenced the foreign exchange market.

The Data in 2012

Table 25.1 shows the UK balance of payments accounts in 2012. Items in the current and capital and financial accounts with a positive sign provide the UK with foreign currency and items that have a minus sign cost the UK foreign currency. The table shows that UK imports of goods and services exceeded UK exports of goods and services in 2012 and that the current account balance was –£58 billion. How do we pay for our current account deficit? We pay by borrowing from abroad. The capital and financial account tells us by how much. We borrowed £127 billion but made loans of £66 billion, so our net foreign borrowing was £61 billion. Another £5 billion represents unidentified capital flows and trade. Adding the balancing item to the capital and financial account gives a total of £66 billion.

Table 25.1	
UK Balance of Payments Accounts in 2012	
	(billions of pounds)
Current account	
Exports of goods and services	+488
Imports of goods and services	–525
Net income	+2
Net transfers	–23
Current account balance	–58
Capital and financial account	
Foreign investment in the UK	+127
UK investment abroad	–66
Balancing item*	+5
Capital and financial account balance	66
Reserve assets account	
Increase(–)/Decrease(+) in the UK's official foreign currency reserves	–8

Source of data: Office for National Statistics, Statistical Bulletin, Balance of Payments Q4, March 2013.
*In the ONS accounts, the balancing item is a separate item.

◈ ECONOMICS IN ACTION

Persistent Current Account Deficits

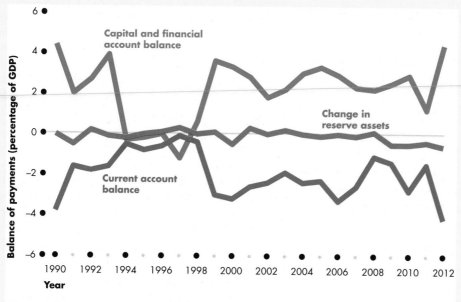

Figure 1 The UK Balance of Payments

Source of data: Office for National Statistics.

The numbers in Table 25.1 give a snapshot of the balance of payments accounts in 2012. Figure 1 puts that snapshot into a longer perspective by showing the balances over the period 1990 to 2012.

The UK has had a current account deficit every year. In 1997, the current account deficit got close to zero but not quite.

The capital and financial account balance is almost a mirror image of the current account deficit.

The £66 billion balance plus –£58 billion, the current account balance, is the change in official UK reserves – the government's holdings of foreign currency. In 2012, those reserves increased by £8 billion. An increase in reserves is like lending to the rest of the world, so it appears in the balance of payments accounts as a negative item. The sum of the balances on the three balance of payments accounts equals zero.

To see more clearly what the nation's balance of payments accounts mean, think about your own balance of payments accounts. They are similar to the nation's accounts.

Individual Balance of Payments Accounts

An individual's current account records the income from supplying the services of factors of production and the expenditure on goods and services. Consider, for example, Joanne. She earned an income in 2013 of £25,000. Joanne has £10,000 worth of investments that earned her an income of £1,000. Joanne's current account shows an income of £26,000. Joanne spent £18,000 buying goods and services for consumption.

She also bought a new studio apartment, which cost her £60,000. So Joanne's total expenditure was £78,000. The difference between her expenditure and income is £52,000 (£78,000 minus £26,000). This amount is Joanne's current account deficit.

To pay for expenditure of £52,000 in excess of her income, Joanne has either to use the money that she has in the bank or to take out a loan. In fact Joanne took a mortgage of £50,000 to help buy her house. This mortgage was the only borrowing that Joanne did, so her capital account surplus was £50,000. With a current account deficit of £52,000 and a capital account surplus of £50,000, Joanne was still £2,000 short. She got that £2,000 from her own bank account. Her cash holdings decreased by £2,000.

Joanne's income from her work and investments is analogous to a country's income from its exports. Her purchases of goods and services, including her purchase of a house, are analogous to a country's imports. Joanne's mortgage – borrowing from someone else – is analogous to a country's foreign borrowing. The change in her bank account is analogous to the change in the country's reserve assets.

Borrowers and Lenders, Debtors and Creditors

A country that is borrowing more from the rest of the world than it is lending to it is called a **net borrower**. Similarly, a **net lender** is a country that is lending more to the rest of the world than it is borrowing from it. A net borrower might be going deeper into debt or might simply be reducing its net assets held in the rest of the world. The total stock of foreign investment determines whether a country is a debtor or a creditor.

A **debtor nation** is a country that during its entire history has borrowed more from the rest of the world than it has lent to it. It has a stock of outstanding debt to the rest of the world that exceeds the stock of its own claims on the rest of the world. The UK is currently a debtor nation, but for a long time it was a creditor. A **creditor nation** is a country that has invested more in the rest of the world than other countries have invested in it. The largest creditor nation today is Japan.

Flows and Stocks

At the heart of the distinction between a net borrower and a debtor nation or a net lender and a creditor nation is the distinction between flows and stocks, which you have encountered many times in your study of macroeconomics.

Borrowing and lending are *flows* – amounts borrowed or lent per unit of time. Debts are *stocks* – amounts owed at a point in time. The flow of borrowing and lending changes the stock of debt. But the outstanding stock of debt depends mainly on past flows of borrowing and lending, not on the current period's flows. The current period's flows determine the change in the stock of debt outstanding.

During the 1960s and the 1970s, the UK current account periodically swung from surplus to deficit. When the current account was a surplus, the capital account was a deficit. On the whole the UK was a net lender to the rest of the world. It was not until the late 1980s that it became a significant net borrower.

The UK today is a small net debtor. But there are many countries that are debtor nations. The US is one. But the largest debtor nations are the capital-hungry developing countries. The international debt of these countries grew from less than one-third to more than one-half of their gross domestic product during the 1980s and created what was called the 'Third World debt crisis'.

Is Borrowing and Debt a Problem?

Does it matter if a country is a net borrower rather than a net lender? The answer to this question depends mainly on what the net borrower is doing with the borrowed money. If borrowed money is used to finance investment that in turn is generating economic growth and higher income, borrowing is not a problem. If the borrowed money is being used to finance consumption, then higher interest payments are being incurred and, as a consequence, consumption will eventually have to be reduced. In this case, the more the borrowing and the longer it goes on, the greater is the reduction in consumption that will eventually be necessary.

Current Account Balance

What determines the current account balance and the scale of a country's net foreign borrowing or lending? You've seen in Table 25.1 that the current account balance equals net exports plus two small items, net interest and net transfers. So net exports drives the current account balance. But what determines net exports?

To answer this question, we need to use the national income accounts. Table 25.2 will refresh your memory and summarise the necessary calculations for you. Part (a) lists the national income variables that are needed, with their symbols. Their values in the UK in 2012 are also shown.

Part (b) presents two key national income equations. First, equation (1) reminds us that GDP, Y, equals aggregate expenditure, which is the sum of consumption expenditure, C, investment, I, government expenditure on goods and services, G, and net exports (exports, X, minus imports, M). Equation (2) reminds us that aggregate income is used in three different ways. It can be consumed, saved, or paid to the government in net taxes (taxes net of transfer payments). Equation (1) tells us how our expenditure generates our income. Equation (2) tells us how we dispose of that income.

Part (c) of the table looks at three balances – net exports, the government budget and the private sector. To get these balances, first subtract equation (2) from equation (1) in Table 25.2. The result is equation (3). By rearranging equation (3), we obtain a relationship for net exports that appears as equation (4) in the table.

Net exports, in equation (4), is made up of two components. The first is net taxes minus government expenditure and the second is saving minus investment. These items are the balances of the government and private

Table 25.2

Sector Balances in 2012

	Symbols and equations	Billions of pounds
(a) Variables		
Gross domestic product (GDP)	Y	1,562
Consumption expenditure	C	1,029
Investment	I	229
Government expenditure on goods and services	G	341
Exports	X	490
Imports	M	527
Saving	S	290
Net taxes	T	243

(b) Domestic income and expenditure

(1) $Y = C + I + G + X - M$

(2) $Y = C + S + T$

(3) $0 = I - S + G - T + X - M$

Aggregate expenditure (1)
Uses of income (2)
(1) minus (2) (3)

(c) Surpluses and deficits

Net exports (4) $X - M = (T - G) + (S - I)$

Government budget (5) $T - G = 243 - 341 = -98$

Private sector (6) $S - I = 290 - 229 = 61$

Net export (7) $X - M = (T - G) + (S - I)$
$= -98 + 61 = -37$

(d) Financing investment

Investment is financed by the sum of:

Private saving, $S = 290$

Net government saving and $T - G = -98$

Net foreign saving $M - X = 37$

That is: (7) $I = S + (T - G) + (M - X)$
$= 290 - 98 + 37$
$= 229$

Source of data: Office for National Statistics, Quarterly Bulletin March 2013, and authors' calculations.

sectors. Net taxes minus government expenditure on goods and services is the *government's budget balance*. If that number is positive, the government's budget is a surplus, and if the number is negative, it is a deficit.

The *private sector balance* is saving minus investment. If saving exceeds investment, the private sector has a surplus to lend to other sectors. If investment exceeds saving, the private sector has a deficit that has to be financed by borrowing from other sectors. As you can see from our calculations, the net exports deficit is equal to the sum of the government's budget deficit and

the private sector surplus. In the UK in 2012, the private sector had a balance of £61 billion and the government sector had a balance of –£98 billion. The private sector balance plus the government sector balance equals net exports of –£37 billion.

Part (d) of Table 25.2 shows how investment is financed. To increase investment, either private saving must increase, or the government deficit or net exports must decrease.

Where Is the Exchange Rate?

We haven't mentioned the exchange rate while discussing the balance of payments. Doesn't it play a role? The answer is that in the short run it does but in the long run it doesn't.

In the short run, a fall in the pound lowers the real exchange rate, which makes imports into the UK more costly and UK exports more competitive. A higher price of imported consumption goods and services might induce a decrease in consumption expenditure and an increase in saving. A higher price of imported capital goods might induce a decrease in investment. Other things remaining the same, an increase in saving or a decrease in investment decreases the private sector deficit and decreases the current account deficit.

But in the long run, a change in the nominal exchange rate leaves the real exchange rate unchanged and plays no role in influencing the current account balance.

REVIEW QUIZ

1 What are the transactions that we record in the balance of payments accounts?
2 Is the UK a net borrower or a net lender? Is it a debtor nation or a creditor nation?
3 How are the current account balance, the government sector balance and the private sector balance related?

Do these questions in Study Plan 25.5 and get instant feedback. MyEconLab

You can complete your study of international finance in *Reading Between the Lines* on pp. 606–607, which looks at the effect of Japan's monetary policy on the yen exchange rate and the fears it is creating among Japan's international competitors.

Monetary Policy Affects the Exchange Rate

Abenomics Propels Yen Weakness

Alice Ross, Michael Mackenzie and Jonathan Soble

Japan's currency has tumbled through ¥100 against the dollar to hit its weakest level in more than four years. Abenomics is working – for Japan at least.

Other countries though, are less thrilled at the effects of the aggressive programme of monetary easing unveiled by the Bank of Japan in April. Tokyo's action to revive its economy and pull out of its deflationary quagmire is making them less competitive in the global export race. A new episode of the currency wars may have begun.

The yen's latest fall caps a slide of nearly 30 per cent against the dollar since November, matched by a similar slide versus the euro to ¥131. Investors have been waiting weeks for this moment. The ¥100 barrier against the US dollar is not merely symbolic. Analysts and traders believe the yen will now weaken further.

If so, Tokyo can claim some measure of success. Weakening the currency has been central to Japan's renewed efforts since the election of Shinzo Abe as prime minister to arrest two decades of falling prices and stimulate the economy. . . .

Officials in Japan have stated that their policies are not aimed at targeting the exchange rate, in line with an agreement signed by the Group of 20 nations. That was a message the governor of the Bank of Japan, Haruhiko Kuroda, repeated at the start of the Group of Seven nations meeting near London on Friday. Yet Japan could still face criticism.

'Trading partners may start complaining,' says Alan Ruskin, currency strategist at Deutsche Bank, who has a ¥110 year-end target for the yen.

The Essence of the Story

- Japan's Prime Minister, Shinzo Abe, wants to stimulate the economy by raising the inflation rate and lowering the value of the yen.

- Between November 2012 and May 2013, the Japanese yen fell by almost 30 per cent against the US dollar to below 100 yen per dollar – its lowest level in more than four years.

- The yen also fell against other currencies and is expected to fall further.

- Other countries are concerned that they will not be competitive in global export markets.

- Bank of Japan governor, Haruhiko Kuroda, says the Bank's policies are not aimed at targeting the exchange rate.

Economic Analysis

◆ Under pressure from the Japanese government, the Bank of Japan (the central bank of Japan) is trying to stimulate the Japanese economy.

◆ In pursuit of this goal, the Bank of Japan has dramatically increased the monetary base by using open market operations like those described in Chapter 24.

◆ Figure 1 shows effects of the Bank's actions. In May 2013, Japan's monetary base had increased by more than 30 per cent over the same month in 2012.

◆ The rapid growth rate of the monetary base fuelled expectations that the yen would depreciate, which increased the supply of yen, decreased the demand for yen and lowered the exchange rate as expected.

◆ Figure 2 illustrates the market for yen between November 2012 and May 2013. In November, demand was D_0, supply was S_0, and the exchange rate $1.30 per 100 yen.

◆ By May 2013, demand was D_1, supply was S_1, and the exchange rate had fallen to $0.98 per 100 yen.

◆ The decrease in demand and increase in supply was directly caused by an expected fall in the yen exchange rate, but this expectation was caused by the Bank of Japan's increase in the monetary base.

◆ The yen fell against all currencies, and Figure 3 shows this fall against both the US dollar and the UK pound.

◆ The fall in the value of the yen has made Japanese goods cheaper in the world market and made competitor countries worried about their own exports. South Korea, Australia and New Zealand have attempted to prevent their currencies being too strong against the yen.

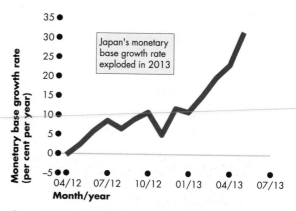

Figure 1 **Japan's Monetary Base Growth Rate**

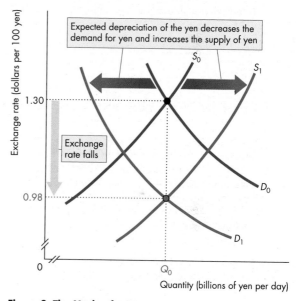

Figure 2 **The Market for Yen**

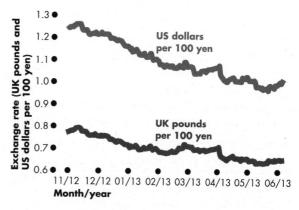

Figure 3 **The Japanese Yen Against the Pound and the US Dollar**

SUMMARY

Key Points

The Foreign Exchange Market

(pp. 588–592)

◆ Foreign currency is obtained in exchange for domestic currency in the foreign exchange market.

◆ Demand and supply in the foreign exchange market determine the exchange rate.

◆ The higher the exchange rate, the smaller is the quantity of pounds demanded and the greater is the quantity of pounds supplied.

◆ The equilibrium exchange rate makes the quantity of pounds demanded equal the quantity of pounds supplied.

Do Problems 1 to 6 to get a better understanding of the foreign exchange market.

Exchange Rate Fluctuations

(pp. 593–597)

◆ Changes in the world demand for UK exports, the UK interest rate differential and the expected future exchange rate change the demand for pounds.

◆ Changes in UK demand for imports, the UK interest rate differential and the expected future exchange rate change the supply of pounds.

◆ Exchange rate expectations are influenced by purchasing power parity and interest rate parity.

◆ In the long run, the nominal exchange rate is a monetary phenomenon and the real exchange rate is independent of the nominal exchange rate.

Do Problems 7 to 15 to get a better understanding of exchange rate fluctuations.

Exchange Rate Policy (pp. 598–599)

◆ An exchange rate can be flexible, fixed or on a crawling peg.

◆ To achieve a fixed or crawling exchange rate, a central bank must intervene in the foreign exchange market and either buy or sell foreign currency.

Do Problems 16 and 17 to get a better understanding of exchange rate policy.

European Monetary Union (pp. 600–601)

◆ The EMU is a group of 17 EU member states that use the euro as their national currency.

◆ The benefits of a single currency are improved transparency and competition, lower transactions costs and the elimination of exchange risk.

◆ The costs of a single currency are the loss of the ability to respond to a national economic shock and the loss of sovereignty.

◆ An optimal currency area is one for which the benefits outweigh the costs.

Do Problems 18 and 19 to get a better understanding of the European Monetary Union.

Financing International Trade

(pp. 602–605)

◆ International trade, borrowing and lending are financed using foreign currency.

◆ A country's balance of payments accounts record its international transactions.

◆ The current account balance is similar to net exports and is determined by the government sector balance and the private sector balance.

Do Problems 20 and 21 to get a better understanding of financing international trade.

Key Terms

Balance of payments accounts, 602
Capital and financial account, 602
Crawling peg, 599
Creditor nation, 604
Current account, 602
Debtor nation, 604
Exchange rate, 588
Fixed exchange rate, 598
Flexible exchange rate, 598
Foreign currency, 588
Foreign exchange market, 588
Interest rate parity, 596
Net borrower, 604
Net lender, 604
Optimal currency area, 601
Purchasing power parity, 596
Real exchange rate, 597
Reserve assets account, 602
UK interest rate differential, 593

STUDY PLAN PROBLEMS AND APPLICATIONS

Do Problems 1 to 21 in MyEconLab Chapter 25 Study Plan and get instant feedback.

MyEconLab

The Foreign Exchange Market

(Study Plan 25.1)

Use the following data in Problems 1 to 3.

The US dollar exchange rate decreased from 83.8 euro cents in January 2009 to 76.9 euro cents in January 2010, and it increased from $0.89 Canadian in June 2009 to $0.96 Canadian in June 2010.

1 Did the US dollar appreciate or depreciate against the euro? Did the US dollar appreciate or depreciate against the Canadian dollar?

2 What was the value of the Canadian dollar in terms of US dollars in June 2009 and June 2010? Did the Canadian dollar appreciate or depreciate against the US dollar over the year June 2009 to June 2010?

3 What was the value of 1 euro (100 euro cents) in terms of US dollars in January 2009 and January 2010? Did the euro appreciate or depreciate against the US dollar in 2009?

Use the following data in Problems 4 to 6.

In January 2010, the exchange rate was 91 yen per US dollar. By September 2010, the exchange rate had fallen to 84 yen per US dollar.

4 Explain the exports effect of this change in the exchange rate.

5 Explain the imports effect of this change in the exchange rate.

6 Explain the expected profit effect of this change in the exchange rate.

Exchange Rate Fluctuations

(Study Plan 25.2)

7 On 3 August 2010, the US dollar was trading at 86 yen per US dollar on the foreign exchange market. On 13 September 2010, the US dollar was trading at 83 yen per US dollar.

  a What events in the foreign exchange market might have brought this fall in the value of the US dollar?

  b Did the events change the demand for US dollars, the supply of US dollars, or both demand and supply in the foreign exchange market?

8 Colombia is the world's biggest producer of roses. The global demand for roses increases and, at the same time, the central bank in Colombia increases the interest rate. In the foreign exchange market for Columbian pesos, what happens to:

  a The demand for pesos?

  b The supply of pesos?

  c The quantity of pesos demanded?

  d The quantity of pesos supplied?

  e The exchange rate of the peso against the US dollar?

9 If a euro deposit in a bank in Paris, France, earns interest of 4 per cent a year and a yen deposit in Tokyo, Japan, earns 0.5 per cent a year, other things remaining the same and adjusted for risk, what is the exchange rate expectation of the Japanese yen?

10 The UK pound is trading at 1.54 US dollars per UK pound. There is purchasing power parity at this exchange rate. The interest rate in the US is 2 per cent a year and the interest rate in the UK is 4 per cent a year.

  a Calculate the UK interest rate differential.

  b What is the UK pound expected to be worth in terms of US dollars one year from now?

  c Which country more likely has the lower inflation rate? How can you tell?

11 Suppose that you can purchase a particular laptop from an online computer store for 827.12 euros or 477.25 pounds. The exchange rate is 1.4831 euros per pound. Does purchasing power parity prevail?

12 **When the Chips Are Down**

  The Economist uses the price of a Big Mac to determine whether a currency is undervalued or overvalued. In July 2010, the price of a Big Mac was $3.73 in New York, 13.2 yuan in Beijing and 6.50 Swiss francs in Geneva. The exchange rates were 6.78 yuan per US dollar and 1.05 Swiss francs per US dollar.

  Source: *The Economist*, 22 July 2010

  a Was the yuan undervalued or overvalued relative to purchasing power parity?

  b Was the Swiss franc undervalued or overvalued relative to purchasing power parity?

  c Do you think the price of a Big Mac in different countries provides a valid test of purchasing power parity?

13 **The Lesson: Buy Ruffles in Myanmar**

  A small bag of cheese-flavoured Ruffles potato chips is $1.69 in Japan and only 8 cents in Myanmar. One hour at an Internet cafe costs $0.62 in Vietnam, $1.48 in China and $3.40 in South Africa.

  Source: *Los Angeles Times*, 23 April 2006

  Do these prices indicate that purchasing power parity does not prevail? Why or why not?

14 The price level in the Eurozone is 112.4, the price level in the US is 109.1, and the nominal exchange rate is 80 euro cents per US dollar. What is the real exchange rate expressed as Eurozone real GDP per unit of US real GDP?

15 The US price level is 106.3, the Japanese price level is 95.4, and the real exchange rate is 103.6 Japanese real GDP per unit of US real GDP. What is the nominal exchange rate?

Exchange Rate Policy (Study Plan 25.3)

16 With the strengthening of the yen against the US dollar in 2010, Japan's central bank did not take any action. A leading Japanese politician has called on the central bank to take actions to weaken the yen, saying it will help exporters in the short run and have no long-run effects.

   a What is Japan's current exchange rate policy?

   b What does the politician want the exchange rate policy to be in the short run? Why would such a policy have no effect on the exchange rate in the long run?

17 **Firefighting**

   In 1992, European currencies were linked to the German currency the D-Mark. The system started to come apart when Italy exited. On 16 September 1992, after an interest rate rise of 3 percentage points and the expenditure of £27 billion in foreign currency reserves in defending sterling, the UK exited the system. Spain, Portugal and, eventually, France were forced to follow. Politicians felt that financial markets failed to understand their commitment to maintain the exchange rate parities with the D-Mark and the primacy of politics over markets. But markets often send useful signals about the sustainability of economic policies.

   Source: *The Economist*, 14 July 2011

   a When the UK joined the European exchange rate system at a parity of DM 2.965 in 1990, the current account deficit was £20 billion and the economy was sliding into recession. Why might this situation pose a problem for the fixed exchange rate with the DM?

   b Explain why currency intervention by the Bank of England failed to maintain the exchange rate parity with the DM.

   c Explain why a currency can experience short-run fluctuations that seem to have little to do with the economy's fundamentals. Illustrate with a graph.

European Monetary Union
(Study Plan 25.4)

18 In the coalition accord following the 2010 General Election, the Conservative and Liberal Democrat parties agreed that 'Britain will not join or prepare to join the euro in this parliament'.

   What are the costs of membership of the EMU that the UK avoids by retaining the pound sterling as its national currency? What are the benefits of membership that the UK is missing?

19 What are the benefits and costs that would arise if Wales left the pound sterling and established the 'Welsh leek' as its currency? Why might the balance of costs and benefits go against such a move?

Financing International Trade
(Study Plan 25.5)

20 The table gives some information about UK international transactions in 2011.

Item	Billions of pounds
Imports of goods and services	516
Foreign investment in the UK	359
Exports of goods and services	492
UK investment abroad	378
Net interest income	26
Net transfers	−22

   a Calculate the current account balance.

   b Calculate the capital and financial account balance (assume a zero balancing item).

   c Did UK reserves assets increase or decrease?

   d Was the UK a net borrower or a net lender in 2011? Explain your answer.

21 **Net Foreign Borrower**

   The US has a persistent balance of trade and current account deficit and uses foreign capital to finance the difference between domestic investment and domestic saving. When a country has a persistent current account deficit it is building up liabilities to foreigners that are financed by capital inflows. Eventually these have to be paid back. Solvency of a country requires that the deficits of a country be paid for through future surpluses.

   Source: IMF, 28 March 2012

   a Explain why a current account deficit 'must be financed by capital inflows'.

   b Under what circumstances should the the persistent current account deficit of the US be a concern?

ADDITIONAL PROBLEMS AND APPLICATIONS

Do these problems in MyEconLab if assigned by your lecturer.

MyEconLab

The Foreign Exchange Market

22 Suppose that yesterday the euro was trading on the foreign exchange market at 0.75 euros per US dollar and today the euro is trading at 0.78 euros per US dollar. Which of the two currencies (the euro or the US dollar) appreciated and which depreciated today?

23 Suppose that the exchange rate fell from 1.20 euros per pound to 1.16 euros per pound. What is the effect of this change on the quantity of euros that people plan to buy in the foreign exchange market?

24 Suppose that the exchange rate rose from 71 yen per US dollar to 100 yen per US dollar. What is the effect of this change on the quantity of US dollars that people plan to sell in the foreign exchange market?

25 Today's exchange rate between the yuan and the US dollar is 6.78 yuan per dollar and the central bank of China is buying US dollars in the foreign exchange market. If the central bank of China did not purchase US dollars would there be excess demand or excess supply of US dollars in the foreign exchange market? Would the exchange rate remain at 6.78 yuan per US dollar? If not, which currency would appreciate?

Exchange Rate Fluctuations

26 Yesterday, the current exchange rate was 0.95 US dollars per Canadian dollar and traders expected the exchange rate to remain unchanged for the next month. Today, with new information, traders now expect the exchange rate next month to rise to 1 US dollar per Canadian dollar. Explain how the revised expected future exchange rate influences the demand for Canadian dollars, or the supply of Canadian dollars, or both in the foreign exchange market.

27 On 1 January 2010 the exchange rate was 91 yen per US dollar. Over the year the supply of US dollars increased and by January 2011 the exchange rate fell to 84 yen per US dollar. What happened to the quantity of US dollars that people planned to buy in the foreign exchange market?

Use the following news clip in Problems 28 and 29.

Speculative Capital Inflows and the Korean Won

South Korea has introduced a series of capital controls in recent months to try and stem speculative capital inflows. Foreign speculators have been buying won-denominated assets in anticipation of an appreciation against the US dollar. However, analysts say that it would be difficult to use capital controls and other measures to reverse the strengthening of the won because the Korean currency has been boosted by the country's relatively strong economic fundamentals and widening trade surplus.

Source: *The Financial Times*, 30 January 2013

28 Explain why foreign speculators have been buying won-denominated assets.

29 Explain what the outcome is on the won–dollar exchange rate as more speculators buy won assets. Would expectations become self-fulfilling?

Use the following information in Problems 30 and 31.

Brazil's Overvalued Real

The Brazilian real has appreciated 33 per cent against the US dollar and has pushed up the price of a Big Mac in Sao Paulo to $4.60, higher than the New York price of $3.99. Despite Brazil's interest rate being at 8.75 per cent a year compared to the US interest rate at near zero, foreign funds flowing into Brazil surged in October.

Source: Bloomberg News, 27 October 2009

30 Does purchasing power parity hold? If not, does PPP predict that the Brazilian real will appreciate or depreciate against the US dollar? Explain.

31 Does interest rate parity hold? Will the Brazilian real appreciate further or depreciate against the US dollar if the US central bank raises the interest rate while the Brazilian interest rate remains at 8.75 per cent a year?

Exchange Rate Policy

Use the following news clip in Problems 32 to 35.

US Declines to Cite China as Currency Manipulator

The US has declined to cite China for manipulating its currency to gain unfair trade advantages against the US. America's growing trade deficit with China, which last year hit an all-time high of $256.3 billion, is the largest deficit ever recorded with a single country. Chinese currency, the yuan, has risen in value by 18.4 per cent against the US dollar since the Chinese government loosened its currency system in July 2005. However, US manufacturers contend the yuan is still undervalued by as much as 40 per cent, making Chinese products more competitive in the US and US goods more expensive in China. China buys US dollar-denominated securities to maintain the value of the yuan in terms of the US dollar.

Source: MSN, 15 May 2008

32 What was the exchange rate policy adopted by China until July 2005? Explain how it worked. Draw a graph to illustrate your answer.

33 What was the exchange rate policy adopted by China after July 2005? Explain how it works.

34 Explain how fixed and crawling peg exchange rates can be used to manipulate trade balances in the short run, but not in the long run.

35 Explain the long-run effect of China's current exchange rate policy.

36 **Aussie Dollar Hit by Interest Rate Talk**

The Australian dollar fell against the US dollar to its lowest value in the past two weeks. The CPI inflation rate was reported to be generally as expected but not high enough to justify previous expectations for an aggressive interest rate rise by Australia's central bank next week.

Source: Reuters, 28 October 2009

a What is Australia's exchange rate policy? Explain why expectations about the Australian interest rate lowered the value of the Australian dollar against the US dollar.

b To avoid the fall in the value of the Australian dollar against the US dollar, what action could the central bank of Australia have taken? Would such an action signal a change in Australia's exchange rate policy?

37 Japan's foreign exchange reserves have grown from $0.25 trillion in 2001 to $1.1 trillion in 2010. What has been Japan's exchange rate policy through these years?

European Monetary Union

38 The unemployment rate is much higher in Spain than in Germany. Does this fact mean that Spain would be better off leaving the euro and re-establishing the peseta as its national currency?

39 If the euro is a good idea, why isn't a single currency for the entire global economy an even better idea?

Financing International Trade

Use the following data in Problems 40 to 42. The table gives some data about the UK economy in 2006.

Item	Billions of pounds
Consumption expenditure	976
Exports of goods and services	492
Government expenditure	336
Net taxes	249
Investment	229
Saving	291

40 Calculate the private sector balance.

41 Calculate the government sector balance.

42 Calculate net exports and show the relationship between the government sector balance and net exports.

Economics in the News

43 After you have studied *Reading Between the Lines* on pp. 606–607, answer the following questions.

a What does the Bank of Japan hope to achieve with its expansionary monetary stimulus?

b What is the effect of the monetary stimulus in the foreign exchange market?

c Why are other countries concerned about the fall in the value of the yen?

d What will happen in the foreign exchange markets for yen, pounds, dollars and euros if other countries respond to the Japanese actions with similar actions of their own?

44 **Gulf Countries Must Opt for Basket of Currencies**

Before 2008, the six countries of the Gulf Cooperation Council (GCC) had fixed exchange rates against the US dollar. Faced with a surge in inflation, they decided to establish the Gulf Monetary Union and common currency pegged to a basket of currencies, comprising the US dollar, the euro, the Japanese yen and the British pound. The exchange rate would be managed to tailor monetary policy to domestic conditions and withstand external shocks.

Source: *The Gulf Daily News*, 18 December 2008

a Explain why the GCC countries lacked independent monetary policy when their currencies were fixed to the US dollar.

b If the GCC countries had pursued an independent monetary policy and held their inflation steady, what would have happened to their exchange rates? Explain and illustrate.

c Why might a new common currency for the GCC countries linked to the US dollar, euro, yen and pound provide better insulation from US monetary policy?

d What would be the benefits arising from Gulf Monetary Union? What would be the costs of monetary union?

26 Aggregate Supply and Aggregate Demand

After studying this chapter you will be able to:

◆ Explain what determines aggregate supply

◆ Explain what determines aggregate demand

◆ Explain how real GDP and the price level are determined and what brings economic growth, inflation and the business cycle

◆ Describe the main schools of thought in macroeconomics

Real GDP grew by 3.6 per cent in 2007 and shrank by 4.0 per cent in 2009. The inflation rate swung between a low of 1.2 per cent in 2001 and a high of 4.5 per cent in 2011. Why does our economy fluctuate?

This chapter explains the economic fluctuations that we call the business cycle. You will study the aggregate supply–aggregate demand model or *AS-AD* model – a model of real GDP and the price level. And in *Reading Between the Lines* at the end of the chapter, you will use that model to interpret and explain the state of the Eurozone economy in 2012–2013.

Aggregate Supply

The purpose of the aggregate supply–aggregate demand model that you study in this chapter is to explain how real GDP and the price level are determined and how they interact. The model uses ideas similar to those that you encountered in Chapter 3 when you learned how the quantity and price in a competitive market are determined. But the *aggregate* supply–*aggregate* demand model (*AS–AD* model) isn't just an application of the competitive market model. Some differences arise because the *AS–AD* model is a model of an imaginary market for the total of all the final goods and services. The quantity in this 'market' is real GDP and the price is the price level measured by the GDP deflator.

One thing that the *AS–AD* model shares with the competitive market model is that both distinguish between *supply* and the *quantity supplied*. We begin by explaining what we mean by the quantity of real GDP supplied.

Quantity Supplied and Supply

The *quantity of real GDP supplied* is the total quantity of goods and services, valued in constant base year (2009) pounds, that firms plan to produce during a given period. This quantity depends on the quantity of labour employed, the quantity of physical and human capital and the state of technology.

At any given time, the quantity of capital and the state of technology are fixed. They depend on decisions that were made in the past. The population is also fixed. But the quantity of labour is not fixed. It depends on decisions made by households and firms about the supply of and demand for labour.

The labour market can be in any one of three states: at full employment, above full employment, or below full employment. At full employment the quantity of real GDP supplied is *potential GDP*, which depends on the full-employment quantity of labour (see Chapter 22, pp. 512–514). Over the business cycle, employment fluctuates around full employment and the quantity of real GDP supplied fluctuates around potential GDP.

Aggregate Supply Time Frames

Aggregate supply is the relationship between the quantity of real GDP supplied and the price level. This relationship is different in the long run and the short run, and to study aggregate supply we distinguish between two time frames:

◆ Long-run aggregate supply
◆ Short-run aggregate supply

Long-Run Aggregate Supply

Long-run aggregate supply is the relationship between the quantity of real GDP supplied and the price level when the money wage rate changes in step with the price level to maintain full employment. The quantity of real GDP supplied at full employment equals potential GDP, and this quantity is the same regardless of the price level.

The *long-run aggregate supply curve* in Figure 26.1 illustrates long-run aggregate supply as the vertical line at potential GDP labelled *LAS*. Along the long-run aggregate supply curve, as the price level changes, the money wage rate also changes so the real wage rate remains at the full-employment equilibrium level and real GDP remains at potential GDP. The long-run aggregate supply curve is always vertical and is always located at potential GDP.

The long-run aggregate supply curve is vertical because potential GDP is independent of the price level. The reason for this independence is that a movement along the *LAS* curve is accompanied by a change in two sets of prices: the prices of goods and services – the price level – and the prices of the factors of production, most notably the money wage rate. A 10 per cent increase in the prices of goods and services is matched by a 10 per cent increase in the money wage rate. Because the price level and the money wage rate change by the same percentage, the real wage rate remains unchanged at its full-employment equilibrium level. So when the price level changes and the real wage rate remains constant, employment remains constant and real GDP remains constant at potential GDP.

Production at a Pepsi Plant

You can see more clearly why real GDP is unchanged when all prices change by the same percentage by thinking about production decisions at a Pepsi bottling plant. How does the quantity of Pepsi supplied change if the price of Pepsi changes and the wage rate of the workers and prices of all the other resources used vary by the same percentage? The answer is that the quantity supplied doesn't change. The firm produces the quantity that maximises profit. That quantity depends on the price of Pepsi relative to the cost of producing it. With no change in price relative to cost, production doesn't change.

Short-Run Aggregate Supply

Short-run aggregate supply is the relationship between the quantity of real GDP supplied and the price level when the money wage rate, the prices of other resources and potential GDP remain constant. Figure 26.1 illustrates this relationship as the short-run aggregate supply curve *SAS* and the short-run aggregate supply schedule. Each point on the *SAS* curve corresponds to a row of the short-run aggregate supply schedule. For example, point *A* on the *SAS* curve and row *A* of the schedule tell us that if the price level is 95, the quantity of real GDP supplied is £1,400 billion. In the short run, a rise in the price level brings an increase in the quantity of real GDP supplied. The short-run aggregate supply curve slopes upward.

With a given money wage rate, there is one price level at which the real wage rate is at its full-employment equilibrium level. At this price level, the quantity of real GDP supplied equals potential GDP and the *SAS* curve intersects the *LAS* curve. In this example, that price level is 105. If the price level rises above 105, the quantity of real GDP supplied increases along the *SAS* curve and exceeds potential GDP; if the price level falls below 105, the quantity of real GDP supplied decreases along the *SAS* curve and is less than potential GDP.

Back at the Pepsi Plant

You can see why the short-run aggregate supply curve slopes upward by returning to the Pepsi bottling plant. If production increases, marginal cost rises and if production decreases, marginal cost falls (see Chapter 2, p. 35).

If the price of Pepsi rises with no change in the money wage rate and other costs, Pepsi can increase profit by increasing production. Pepsi is in business to maximise its profit, so it increases production.

Similarly, if the price of Pepsi falls while the money wage rate and other costs remain constant, Pepsi can avoid a loss by decreasing production. The lower price weakens the incentive to produce, so Pepsi decreases production.

And for the Economy

What's true for Pepsi bottlers is true for the producers of all goods and services. When all prices rise, the *price level* rises. If the price level rises and the money wage rate and other factor prices remain constant, all firms increase production and the quantity of real GDP supplied increases. A fall in the price level has the opposite effect and decreases the quantity of real GDP supplied.

Figure 26.1 Long-Run and Short-Run Aggregate Supply

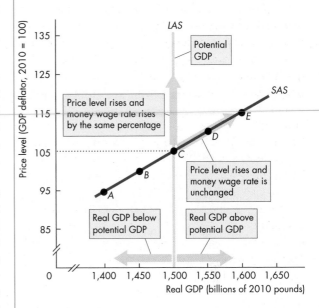

	Price level (GDP deflator)	Real GDP (billions of 2010 pounds)
A	95	1,400
B	100	1,450
C	105	1,500
D	110	1,550
E	115	1,600

In the long run, the quantity of real GDP supplied is potential GDP and the *LAS* curve is vertical at potential GDP. In the short run, the quantity of real GDP supplied increases if the price level rises, while all other influences on supply plans remain the same.

The short-run aggregate supply curve, *SAS*, slopes upward. The short-run aggregate supply curve is based on the aggregate supply schedule in the table. Each point *A* to *E* on the curve corresponds to the row in the table identified by the same letter.

When the price level is 105, real GDP equals potential GDP (£1,500 billion). If the price level is greater than 105, real GDP exceeds potential GDP; if the price level is below 105, real GDP is less than potential GDP.

MyEconLab Animation

Changes in Aggregate Supply

A change in the price level brings a change in the quantity of real GDP supplied, which is illustrated by a movement along the short-run aggregate supply curve. It does not change aggregate supply. Aggregate supply changes when an influence on production plans other than the price level changes. These other influences are changes in potential GDP and changes in the money wage rate. Let's begin by looking at a change in potential GDP.

Changes in Potential GDP

An increase in potential GDP increases both long-run aggregate supply and short-run aggregate supply. Figure 26.2 shows these effects.

Initially, the long-run aggregate supply curve is LAS_0 and the short-run aggregate supply curve is SAS_0. If potential GDP increases to £1,600 billion, long-run aggregate supply increases and the long-run aggregate supply curve shifts rightward to LAS_1. Short-run aggregate supply also increases, and the short-run aggregate supply curve shifts rightward to SAS_1. The two supply curves shift by the same amount only if the full-employment price level remains constant, which we will assume to be the case.

Potential GDP can increase for any of three reasons:

◆ An increase in the full-employment quantity of labour

◆ An increase in the quantity of capital

◆ An advance in technology

Let's look at these influences on potential GDP and the aggregate supply curves.

An Increase in the Full-Employment Quantity of Labour

A Pepsi bottling plant that employs 100 workers bottles more Pepsi than an otherwise identical plant that employs 10 workers. The same is true for the economy as a whole. The larger the quantity of labour employed, the greater is real GDP.

Over time, real GDP increases because the labour force increases. But (with constant capital and technology) *potential* GDP increases only if the full-employment quantity of labour increases. Fluctuations in employment over the business cycle bring fluctuations in real GDP. But these changes in real GDP are fluctuations around potential GDP and long-run aggregate supply.

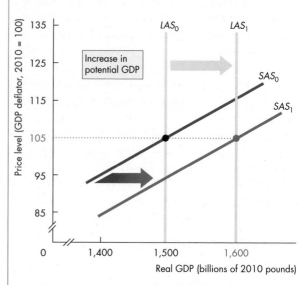

Figure 26.2 A Change in Potential GDP

An increase in potential GDP increases both long-run aggregate supply and short-run aggregate supply. The long-run aggregate supply curve shifts rightward from LAS_0 to LAS_1 and the short-run aggregate supply curve shifts from SAS_0 to SAS_1.

MyEconLab Animation ──────────────◆

An Increase in the Quantity of Capital

A Pepsi bottling plant that has two production lines has more capital and produces more output than an otherwise identical plant that has one production line. For the economy, the larger the quantity of capital, the more productive is the workforce and the greater is its potential GDP. Potential GDP per person in capital-rich EU economies is vastly greater than that in capital-poor China and Russia.

Capital includes *human capital*. One bottling plant is managed by an economics graduate with an MBA and has a workforce with an average of 10 years of experience. This plant produces a much larger output than an otherwise identical plant that is managed by someone with no business training or experience and which has a young workforce that is new to bottling. The first plant has a greater amount of human capital than the second. For the economy as a whole, the larger the quantity of *human capital* – the skills that people have acquired in school and through on-the-job-training – the greater is potential GDP.

An Advance in Technology

A Pepsi bottling plant that has pre-computer age machines produces less than one that uses the latest robot technology. Technological change enables firms to produce more from any given amount of inputs. So even with fixed quantities of labour and capital, improvements in technology increase potential GDP.

Technological advances are by far the most important source of increased production over the past two centuries. Because of technological advances, one farmer in the UK today can feed 100 people and one auto worker can produce almost 14 cars and lorries in a year.

Let's now look at the effects of changes in the money wage rate and other resource prices.

Changes in the Money Wage Rate and Other Resource Prices

When the money wage rate or the money price of another resource (such as the price of oil) changes, short-run aggregate supply changes but long-run aggregate supply does not change.

Figure 26.3 shows the effect on aggregate supply of an increase in the money wage rate. Initially, the short-run aggregate supply curve is SAS_0. A rise in the money wage rate *decreases* short-run aggregate supply and shifts the short-run aggregate supply curve leftward to SAS_2.

The money wage rate (and other resource prices) affect short-run aggregate supply because they influence firms' costs. The higher the money wage rate, the higher are firms' costs and the smaller is the quantity that firms are willing to supply at each price level. So an increase in the money wage rate decreases short-run aggregate supply.

A change in the money wage rate does not change long-run aggregate supply because on the *LAS* curve a change in the money wage rate is accompanied by an equal percentage change in the price level. With no change in *relative* prices, firms have no incentive to change production and real GDP remains constant at potential GDP. With no change in potential GDP, the long-run aggregate supply curve remains at *LAS*.

What Makes the Money Wage Rate Change?

The money wage rate can change for two reasons: departures from full employment and expectations about inflation. Unemployment above the natural rate puts downward pressure on the money wage rate, and unemployment below the natural rate puts upward pressure on the money wage rate. An expected increase in the inflation rate makes the money wage rate rise faster, the inflation rate makes the money wage rate rise faster,

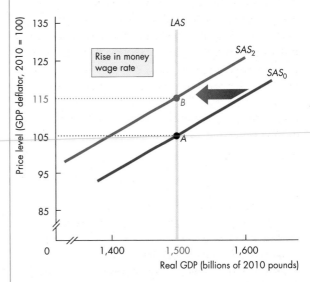

Figure 26.3   A Change in the Money Wage Rate

A rise in the money wage rate decreases short-run aggregate supply and shifts the short-run aggregate supply curve leftward from SAS_0 to SAS_2. A rise in the money wage rate does not change potential GDP, so the long-run aggregate supply curve does not shift.

MyEconLab Animation ─────────────────◆

and an expected decrease in the inflation rate slows the rate at which the money wage rate rises.

REVIEW QUIZ

1   If the price level and the money wage rate rise by the same percentage, what happens to the quantity of real GDP supplied? Along which aggregate supply curve does the economy move?

2   If the price level rises and the money wage rate remains constant, what happens to the quantity of real GDP supplied? Along which aggregate supply curve does the economy move?

3   If potential GDP increases, what happens to aggregate supply? Is there a shift of or a movement along the *LAS* curve? Does the *SAS* curve shift or is there a movenment along the *SAS* curve?

4   If the money wage rate rises and potential GDP remains the same, does the *LAS* curve or the *SAS* curve shift or is there a movement along the *LAS* curve or the *SAS* curve?

Do these questions in Study Plan 26.1 and get instant feedback.   MyEconLab

Aggregate Demand

The quantity of real GDP demanded is the sum of real consumption expenditure (C), investment (I), government expenditure (G) and exports (X) minus imports (M). That is:

$$Y = C + I + G + X - M$$

The *quantity of real GDP demanded* is the total amount of final goods and services produced in the UK that people, businesses, governments and foreigners plan to buy.

These buying plans depend on many factors. The four main ones are:

1   The price level
2   Expectations
3   Fiscal policy and monetary policy
4   The world economy

We first focus on the relationship between the quantity of real GDP demanded and the price level. To study this relationship, we keep all other influences on buying plans the same and ask: How does the quantity of real GDP demanded vary as the price level varies?

The Aggregate Demand Curve

Other things remaining the same, the higher the price level, the smaller is the quantity of real GDP demanded. This relationship between the quantity of real GDP demanded and the price level is called **aggregate demand**. Aggregate demand is described by an aggregate demand schedule and an aggregate demand curve.

Figure 26.4 shows an aggregate demand curve (AD) and an aggregate demand schedule. Each point on the AD curve corresponds to a row of the schedule. For example, point C' on the AD curve and row C' of the schedule tell us that if the price level is 105, the quantity of real GDP demanded is £1,500 billion.

The aggregate demand curve slopes downward for two reasons:

◆   Wealth effect
◆   Substitution effects

Wealth Effect

When the price level rises but other things remain the same, *real* wealth decreases. Real wealth is the amount

Figure 26.4   Aggregate Demand

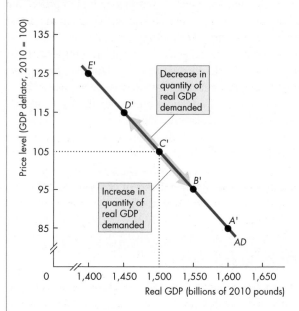

	Price level (GDP deflator)	**Real GDP** (billions of 2010 pounds)
A'	85	1,600
B'	95	1,550
C'	105	1,500
D'	115	1,450
E'	125	1,400

The aggregate demand curve (AD) shows the relationship between the quantity of real GDP demanded and the price level. The aggregate demand curve is based on the aggregate demand schedule in the table. Each point A' to E' on the curve corresponds to the row in the table identified by the same letter. For example, when the price level is 105, the quantity of real GDP demanded is £1,500 billion, shown by point C' in the figure.

A change in the price level with all other influences on aggregate buying plans remaining the same brings a change in the quantity of real GDP demanded and a movement along the AD curve.

MyEconLab Animation ——————————————◆

of money in the bank, bonds, shares and other assets that people own, measured not in pounds but in terms of the goods and services that this money, bonds and shares will buy.

People save and hold money, bonds, shares and other assets for many reasons. One reason is to build up funds for education expenses. Another reason is to build up enough funds to meet possible medical or other big bills. But the biggest reason is to build up enough funds to provide a retirement income.

If the price level rises, real wealth decreases. People then try to restore their wealth. To do so, they must increase saving and, equivalently, decrease current consumption. Such a decrease in consumption is a decrease in aggregate demand.

Maria's Wealth Effect

You can see how the wealth effect works by thinking about Maria's buying plans. Maria lives in Moscow, Russia. She has worked hard all summer and saved 20,000 rubles (the ruble is the currency of Russia), which she plans to spend attending graduate school when she has finished her economics degree. So Maria's wealth is 20,000 rubles. Maria has a part-time job, and her income from this job pays her current expenses. The price level in Russia rises by 100 per cent, and now Maria needs 40,000 rubles to buy what 20,000 rubles once bought. To try to make up some of the fall in value of her savings, Maria saves even more and cuts her current spending to the bare minimum.

Substitution Effects

When the price level rises and other things remain the same, interest rates rise. The reason is related to the wealth effect that you've just studied. A rise in the price level decreases the real value of the money in people's pockets and bank accounts. With a smaller amount of real money around, banks can get a higher interest rate on loans. But faced with higher interest rates, people and businesses delay plans to buy new capital and consumer durable goods and cut back on spending.

This substitution effect involves changing the timing of capital consumer durable goods purchases and is called an *intertemporal* substitution effect – a substitution across time. Saving increases to increase future consumption.

To see this intertemporal substitution effect more clearly, think about your own plan to buy a new computer. At an interest rate of 5 per cent a year, you might borrow £1,000 and buy the new machine you've been researching. But at an interest rate of 10 per cent a year, you might decide that the payments would be too high. You don't abandon your plan to buy the computer, but you decide to delay your purchase.

A second substitution effect works through international prices. When the UK price level rises and other

things remain the same, UK-made goods and services become more expensive relative to foreign-made goods and services. This change in *relative prices* encourages people to spend less on UK-made items and more on foreign-made items. For example, if the UK price level rises relative to the price level in France, fewer Vauxhall Insignias are sold in France and more Renaults are sold in the UK. Exports from the UK decrease, imports into the UK increase and the quantity of UK real GDP demanded decreases.

Maria's Substitution Effects

In Moscow, Maria makes some substitutions. She was planning to trade in her old motor scooter and get a new one. But with a higher price level and faced with higher interest rates, she decides to make her old scooter last one more year. Also, with the prices of Russian goods sharply increasing, Maria substitutes a low-cost dress made in Malaysia for the Russian-made dress she had originally planned to buy.

Changes in the Quantity of Real GDP Demanded

When the price level rises and other things remain the same, the quantity of real GDP demanded decreases – a movement up along the *AD* curve as shown by the arrow in Figure 26.4. When the price level falls and other things remain the same, the quantity of real GDP demanded increases – a movement down along the *AD* curve.

We've now seen how the quantity of real GDP demanded changes when the price level changes. How do other influences on buying plans affect aggregate demand?

Changes in Aggregate Demand

A change in any factor that influences buying plans other than the price level brings a change in aggregate demand. The main factors are:

◆ Expectations
◆ Fiscal policy and monetary policy
◆ The world economy

Expectations

An increase in expected future disposable income, other things remaining the same, increases the amount of consumption goods (especially items such as cars) that people plan to buy today and increases aggregate demand today.

An increase in the expected future inflation rate increases aggregate demand today because people decide to buy more goods and services at today's relatively lower prices. An increase in expected future profit increases the investment that firms plan to undertake today and increases aggregate demand today.

Fiscal Policy and Monetary Policy

The government's attempt to influence the economy by setting and changing taxes, making transfer payments and purchasing goods and services is called **fiscal policy**. A tax cut or an increase in transfer payments – for example, unemployment benefits or welfare payments – increases aggregate demand. Both of these influences operate by increasing households' *disposable* income. **Disposable income** is aggregate income minus taxes plus transfer payments. The greater the disposable income, the greater is the quantity of consumption goods and services that households plan to buy and the greater is aggregate demand.

Government expenditure on goods and services is one component of aggregate demand. So if the government spends more on hospitals, schools and motorways, aggregate demand increases.

Monetary policy consists of changes in interest rates and in the quantity of money in the economy. The quantity of money in the UK is determined by the Bank of England and the banks (in a process described in Chapter 24). An increase in the quantity of money increases aggregate demand.

To see why money affects aggregate demand, imagine that the Bank of England borrows the army's helicopters, loads them with millions of new £5 notes and sprinkles these notes like confetti across the nation. People gather the newly available money and plan to spend some of it. So the quantity of goods and services demanded increases. But people don't plan to spend all the new money. They save some of it and lend it to others through the banks. The interest rate falls. With a lower interest rate, people plan to buy more consumer durables and firms plan to increase their investment.

The World Economy

Aggregate demand in each individual country is influenced by events in the world economy. The two main influences are changes in the foreign exchange rate and changes in world income. The *foreign exchange rate* is the amount of a foreign currency that you can buy

 ECONOMICS IN ACTION

Fiscal Policy to Fight Recession

In 2008, as recession deepened, the world's two largest economies embarked on a massive fiscal stimulus. The US Congress cut taxes by $300 billion and increased government expenditure by $540 billion, totalling 6 per cent of US GDP. In China, government spending was increased by $200 billion or 5 per cent of GDP. The UK stimulus was 1.5 per cent of GDP.

The idea of these fiscal measures was to stimulate business investment and consumption expenditure and increase aggregate demand.

Monetary Policy to Fight Recession

In October 2008 and the months that followed, the central banks of the major Western economies, the US Federal Reserve, the European Central Bank, the Bank of Canada and the Bank of England, together cut their interest rates and took other measures to ease credit and encourage banks and other financial institutions to increase their lending.

Like the accompanying fiscal stimulus packages, the idea of these interest rate cuts and easier credit was to stimulate business investment and consumption expenditure and increase aggregate demand.

 0.20%

**Ben Bernanke
Federal Reserve**

 1.75%

**Jean-Claude Trichet
ECB**

0.50%

**Mervyn King
Bank of England**

 0.25%

**Mark Carney
Bank of Canada**

with a unit of domestic currency. Other things remaining the same, a rise in a country's foreign exchange rate decreases aggregate demand.

To see how the UK's foreign exchange rate influences aggregate demand in the UK, suppose that £1 is worth €1.10. A pair of Gucci shoes made in Italy costs €220 and an equivalent pair of Church's shoes made in England costs £190. In pounds, the Gucci shoes cost £200, so people around the world buy the cheaper Church's shoes from the UK.

Now suppose the exchange rate rises to €1.40 per pound. The Gucci shoes now cost £157.14 and are cheaper than the Church's shoes. People switch from Church's to Gucci shoes. As they make this switch, UK exports decrease, UK imports increase and aggregate demand in the UK decreases.

An increase in foreign income increases UK exports and increases UK aggregate demand – the aggregate demand for UK-produced goods and services. For example, an increase in income in the US, Japan and Germany increases American, Japanese and German consumers' and producers' planned expenditures on UK-produced consumption goods and capital goods.

Shifts of the Aggregate Demand Curve

When aggregate demand changes, the aggregate demand curve shifts. Figure 26.5 shows two changes in aggregate demand and summarises the factors that bring about such changes.

Aggregate demand increases and the aggregate demand curve shifts rightward from AD_0 to AD_1 when expected future disposable income, inflation or profit increases; government expenditure on goods and services increases; taxes are cut; transfer payments increase; the quantity of money increases and interest rates fall; the foreign exchange rate falls; or foreign income increases.

Aggregate demand decreases and the aggregate demand curve shifts leftward from AD_0 to AD_2 when expected future disposable income, inflation or profit decreases; government expenditure on goods and services decreases; taxes increase; transfer payments decrease; the quantity of money decreases and interest rates rise; the foreign exchange rate rises; or foreign income decreases.

Figure 26.5   Changes in Aggregate Demand

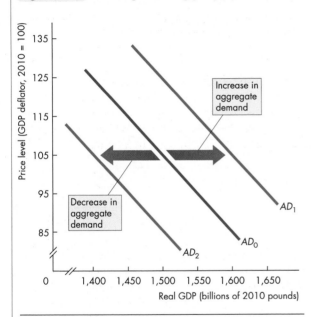

Aggregate demand

Decreases if:

◆ Expected future disposable income, inflation or profit decreases

◆ Fiscal policy decreases government expenditure on goods and services, increases taxes or decreases transfer payments

◆ Monetary policy increases interest rates and decreases the quantity of money

◆ The foreign exchange rate increases or foreign income decreases

Increases if:

◆ Expected future disposable income, inflation or profit increases

◆ Fiscal policy increases government expenditure on goods and services, decreases taxes or increases transfer payments

◆ Monetary policy decreases interest rates and increases the quantity of money

◆ The foreign exchange rate decreases or foreign income increases

MyEconLab Animation ——————————————◆

Explaining Macroeconomic Trends and Fluctuations

The purpose of the *AS–AD* model is to explain changes in real GDP and the price level. The model's main purpose is to explain business cycle fluctuations in these variables. But the model also aids our understanding of economic growth and inflation trends. We begin by combining aggregate supply and aggregate demand to determine real GDP and the price level in equilibrium. Just as there are two time frames for aggregate supply, there are also two time frames for macroeconomic equilibrium: a long-run equilibrium and a short-run equilibrium. We'll first look at short-run equilibrium.

Short-Run Macroeconomic Equilibrium

The aggregate demand curve tells us the quantity of real GDP demanded at each price level, and the short-run aggregate supply curve tells us the quantity of real GDP supplied at each price level. **Short-run macroeconomic equilibrium** occurs when the quantity of real GDP demanded equals the quantity of real GDP supplied. That is, short-run macroeconomic equilibrium occurs at the intersection point of the *AD* curve and the *SAS* curve.

Figure 26.6 illustrates such an equilibrium at a price level of 105 and real GDP of £1,500 billion (points *C* and *C'*).

To see why this position is the equilibrium, think about what happens if the price level is something other than 105. Suppose, for example, that the price level is 115 and that real GDP is £1,600 billion (at point *E* on the *SAS* curve). The quantity of real GDP demanded is less than £1,600 billion, so firms are unable to sell all their output. Unwanted inventories (stocks) pile up, and firms cut both production and prices. Production and prices are cut until firms can sell all their output. This situation occurs only when real GDP is £1,500 billion and the price level is 105.

Now suppose that the price level is 95 and real GDP is £1,400 billion (at point *A* on the *SAS* curve). The quantity of real GDP demanded exceeds £1,400 billion, so firms are unable to meet demand for their output. Inventories (stocks of finished but unsold items) decrease and customers clamour for more goods and services than firms are producing. So firms increase production and raise prices. Production and prices increase until firms can meet demand. This situation occurs only

Figure 26.6 Short-Run Macroeconomic Equilibrium

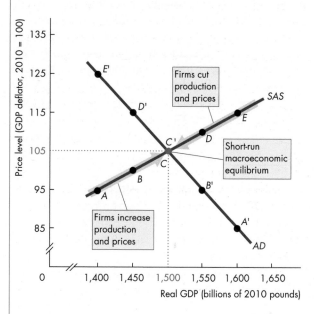

Short-run macroeconomic equilibrium occurs when the quantity of real GDP demanded equals the quantity of real GDP supplied – at the intersection of the aggregate demand curve (*AD*) and the short-run aggregate supply curve (*SAS*).

MyEconLab Animation ⬥

when real GDP is £1,500 billion and the price level is 105.

In short-run macroeconomic equilibrium, the money wage rate is fixed. It does not adjust to bring full employment. So in the short run, real GDP can be greater than or less than potential GDP. But in the long run, the money wage rate does adjust and real GDP moves towards potential GDP. Let's look at the long-run equilibrium and see how we get there.

Long-Run Macroeconomic Equilibrium

Long-run macroeconomic equilibrium occurs when real GDP equals potential GDP – equivalently, when the economy is on its *LAS* curve.

When the economy is away from long-run equilibrium, the money wage rate adjusts. If the money wage rate is too high, short-run equilibrium is below potential GDP and the unemployment rate is above the natural rate. With an excess supply of labour, the money wage rate falls. If the money wage rate is too low, short-run equilibrium is above potential GDP and the unemployment rate is below the natural rate. With an excess demand for labour, the money wage rate rises.

Figure 26.7 shows the long-run equilibrium and how it comes about. If the short-run aggregate supply curve is SAS_1, the money wage rate is too high to achieve full employment. A fall in the money wage rate shifts the SAS curve to SAS^* and brings full employment. If the short-run aggregate supply curve is SAS_2, the money wage rate is too low to achieve full employment. Now, a rise in the money wage rate shifts the SAS curve to SAS^* and brings full employment.

In long-run equilibrium, potential GDP determines real GDP, and potential GDP and aggregate demand together determine the price level. The money wage rate adjusts to put the SAS curve through the long-run equilibrium point.

Let's now see how the $AS–AD$ model helps us to understand economic growth and inflation.

Figure 26.7 Long-Run Macroeconomic Equilibrium

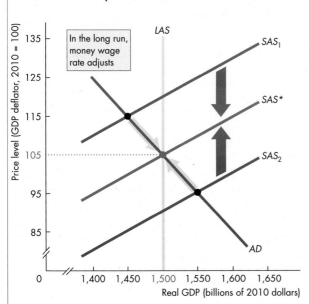

In long-run macroeconomic equilibrium, real GDP equals potential GDP. So long-run equilibrium occurs where the aggregate demand curve AD intersects the long-run aggregate supply curve LAS. In the long run, aggregate demand determines the price level and has no effect on real GDP. The money wage rate adjusts in the long run, so the SAS curve intersects the LAS curve at the long-run equilibrium price level.

Economic Growth and Inflation in the $AS–AD$ Model

Economic growth results from a growing workforce and increasing labour productivity, which together make potential GDP grow (Chapter 22, pp. 514–517). Inflation results from a growing quantity of money that outpaces the growth of potential GDP (Chapter 24, pp. 576–577).

The $AS–AD$ model explains and illustrates economic growth and inflation. It explains economic growth as increasing long-run aggregate supply and it explains inflation as a persistent increase in aggregate demand at a faster pace than that of the increase in potential GDP.

 ECONOMICS IN ACTION

UK Economic Growth and Inflation

Figure 1 is a scatter diagram of UK real GDP and the price level. The graph has the same axes as those of the $AS–AD$ model. Each dot represents a year between 1960 and 2012. The red dots are recession years. The pattern formed by the dots shows the combination of economic growth and inflation. Economic growth was fastest during the 1960s; inflation was fastest during the 1970s.

The $AS–AD$ model interprets each dot as being at the intersection of the SAS and AD curves.

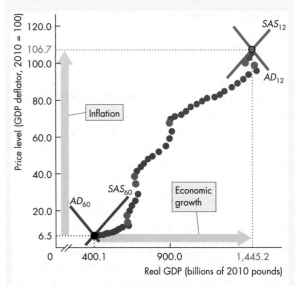

Figure 1 The Path of Real GDP and the Price Level

Source of data: Office for National Statistics.

Figure 26.8 illustrates this explanation in terms of the shifting *LAS* and *AD* curves.

When the *LAS* curve shifts rightward from LAS_0 to LAS_1, potential GDP grows from £1,500 billion to £1,600 billion, and in long-run equilibrium real GDP also grows to £1,600 billion.

When the *AD* curve shifts rightward from AD_0 to AD_1, which is a growth of aggregate demand that outpaces the growth of potential GDP, the price level rises from 105 to 115.

If aggregate demand were to increase at the same pace as long-run aggregate supply, real GDP would grow with no inflation.

Our economy experiences periods of growth and inflation, like those shown in Figure 26.8, but it does not experience steady growth and steady inflation. Real GDP fluctuates around potential GDP in a business cycle. When we study the business cycle, we ignore economic growth and focus on the fluctuations around the trend. By doing so, we see the business cycle more clearly. Let's now see how the *AS–AD* model explains the business cycle.

The Business Cycle in the AS–AD Model

The business cycle occurs because aggregate demand and short-run aggregate supply fluctuate, but the money wage rate does not adjust quickly enough to keep real GDP at potential GDP. Figure 26.9 shows three types of short-run equilibrium.

Figure 26.9(a) shows an above full-employment equilibrium. An **above full-employment equilibrium** is an equilibrium in which real GDP exceeds potential GDP. The gap between real GDP and potential GDP is the **output gap**. When real GDP exceeds potential GDP, the output gap is called an **inflationary gap**.

The above full-employment equilibrium shown in Figure 26.9(a) occurs where the aggregate demand curve AD_0 intersects the short-run aggregate supply

ECONOMICS IN ACTION

The UK Business Cycle

The UK economy had an inflationary gap in 2007 (at *A* in Fgure 1), full employment in 2008 (at *B*) and a recessionary gap in 2009 (at *C*). The fluctuating output gap in the figure is the real-world version of Figure 26.9(d) and is generated by fluctuations in aggregate demand and short-run aggregate supply.

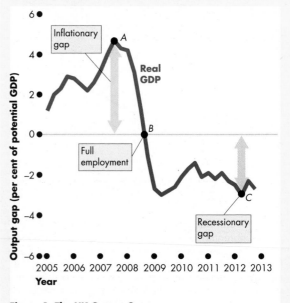

Figure 1 The UK Output Gap

Sources of data: see Figure 20.6.

Figure 26.8 Economic Growth and Inflation

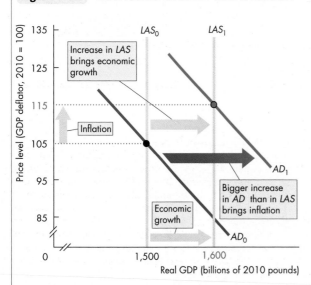

Economic growth is the persistent increase in potential GDP. Economic growth is shown as an ongoing rightward shift of the *LAS* curve. Inflation is the persistent rise in the price level. Inflation occurs when aggregate demand increases by more than the increase in long-run aggregate supply.

MyEconLab Animation ─────────────── ◆

curve SAS_0 at a real GDP of £1,520 billion. There is an inflationary gap of £20 billion.

Figure 26.9(b) is an example of **full-employment equilibrium**, in which real GDP equals potential GDP. In this example, the equilibrium occurs where the aggregate demand curve AD_1 intersects the short-run aggregate supply curve SAS_1 at an actual and potential GDP of £1,500 billion.

In part (c), there is a below full-employment equilibrium. A **below full-employment equilibrium** is an equilibrium in which potential GDP exceeds real GDP. When potential GDP exceeds real GDP, the output gap is called a **recessionary gap**.

The below full-employment equilibrium shown in Figure 26.9(c) occurs where the aggregate demand curve AD_2 intersects the short-run aggregate supply curve SAS_2 at a real GDP of £1,480 billion with a recessionary gap of £20 billion.

The economy moves from one type of macroeconomic equilibrium to another as a result of fluctuations in aggregate demand and in short-run aggregate supply. These fluctuations produce fluctuations in real GDP. Figure 26.9(d) shows how real GDP fluctuates around potential GDP.

Let's now look at some of the sources of these fluctuations around potential GDP.

Figure 26.9 The Business Cycle

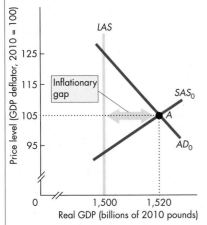

(a) Above full-employment equilibrium

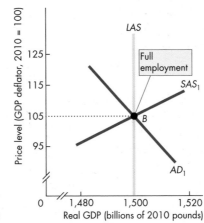

(b) Full-employment equilibrium

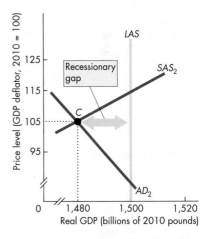

(c) Below full-employment equilibrium

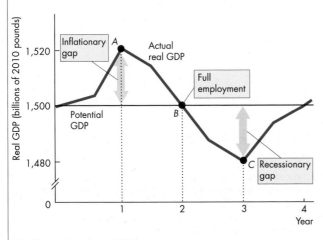

(d) Fluctuations in real GDP

Part (a) shows an above full-employment equilibrium in year 1, part (b) shows a full-employment equilibrium in year 2, and part (c) shows a below full-employment equilibrium in year 3. Part (d) shows how real GDP fluctuates around potential GDP in a business cycle.

In year 1, an inflationary gap exists and the economy is at point A, in parts (a) and (d). In year 2, the economy is in full-employment equilibrium and the economy is at point B in parts (b) and (d). In year 3, a recessionary gap exists and the economy is at point C in parts (c) and (d).

MyEconLab Animation

Fluctuations in Aggregate Demand

One reason why real GDP fluctuates around potential GDP is that aggregate demand fluctuates. Let's see what happens when aggregate demand increases.

Figure 26.10(a) shows an economy at full employment. The aggregate demand curve is AD_0, the short-run aggregate supply curve is SAS_0 and the long-run aggregate supply curve is LAS. Real GDP equals potential GDP at £1,500 billion and the price level is 105.

Now suppose that the world economy expands and that the demand for UK-made goods increases in Japan, Canada and the US. The increase in UK exports increases aggregate demand and the aggregate demand curve shifts rightward from AD_0 to AD_1 in Figure 26.10(a).

Faced with an increase in demand, firms increase production and raise prices. Real GDP increases to £1,550 billion and the price level rises to 110. The economy is now in an above full-employment equilibrium.

Real GDP exceeds potential GDP and there is an inflationary gap.

The increase in aggregate demand has increased the prices of all goods and services. Faced with higher prices, firms have increased their output rates. At this stage the prices of goods and services have increased, but the money wage rate has not changed. (Recall that as we move along a short-run aggregate supply curve, the money wage rate is constant.)

Because the price level has increased and the money wage rate is unchanged, workers have experienced a fall in the buying power of their wages and firms' profits have increased. In these circumstances, workers demand higher wages, and firms, anxious to maintain their employment and output levels, meet those demands. If firms do not raise the money wage rate, they will either lose workers or have to hire less productive ones.

As the money wage rate rises, the short-run aggregate supply curve begins to shift leftward. In Figure 26.10(b),

Figure 26.10 An Increase in Aggregate Demand

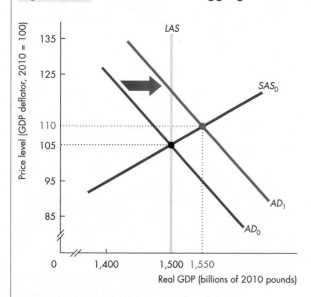

(a) Short-run effect

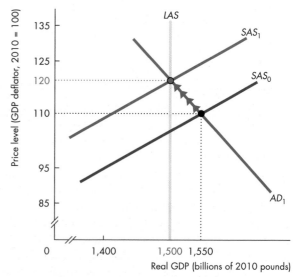

(b) Long-run effect

An increase in aggregate demand shifts the aggregate demand curve from AD_0 to AD_1. In the short run (part a), real GDP increases from £1,500 billion to £1,550 billion and the price level rises from 105 to 110. The economy has moved up along the SAS curve. In this situation, an inflationary gap exists.

In the long run (part b), with an inflationary gap, the money wage rate starts to rise. The short-run aggregate supply curve starts to shift leftward from SAS_0 to SAS_1. As the SAS curve shifts leftward, it intersects the aggregate demand curve AD_1 at higher price levels and real GDP decreases. Eventually, the price level rises to 120 and real GDP decreases to £1,500 billion – potential GDP.

the short-run aggregate supply curve shifts from SAS_0 towards SAS_1. The rise in the money wage rate and the shift in the SAS curve produce a sequence of new equilibrium positions. Along the adjustment path, real GDP decreases and the price level rises. The economy moves up along its aggregate demand curve, as the arrow heads show.

Eventually, the money wage rate rises by the same percentage as the price level. At this time, the aggregate demand curve AD_1 intersects SAS_1 at a new long-run equilibrium. The price level has risen to 120, and real GDP is back where it started, at potential GDP.

A decrease in aggregate demand has similar but opposite effects to those of an increase in aggregate demand. That is, a decrease in aggregate demand shifts the aggregate demand curve leftward. Real GDP decreases to less than potential GDP and a recessionary gap emerges. Firms cut prices. The lower price level increases the purchasing power of wages and increases firms' costs relative to their output prices because the money wage rate remains unchanged. Eventually, the money wage rate falls and the short-run aggregate supply curve shifts rightward. But the money wage rate changes slowly, so real GDP slowly returns to potential GDP and the price level falls slowly.

Let's now work out how real GDP and the price level change when aggregate supply changes.

Fluctuations in Aggregate Supply

Fluctuations in short-run aggregate supply can bring fluctuations in real GDP around potential GDP. Suppose that, initially, real GDP equals potential GDP. Then there is a large but temporary rise in the price of oil. What happens to real GDP and the price level?

Figure 26.11 answers this question. The aggregate demand curve is AD_0, the short-run aggregate supply curve is SAS_0 and the long-run aggregate supply curve is LAS. Equilibrium real GDP is £1,500 billion, which equals potential GDP, and the price level is 105. Then the price of oil rises. Faced with higher energy and transportation costs, firms decrease production. Short-run aggregate supply decreases and the short-run aggregate supply curve shifts leftward to SAS_1. The price level rises to 115 and real GDP decreases to £1,450 billion.

Because real GDP decreases, the economy experiences recession. Because the price level increases, the economy experiences inflation. A combination of recession and inflation, called **stagflation**, actually occurred in the UK in the mid-1970s.

Figure 26.11 A Decrease in Aggregate Supply

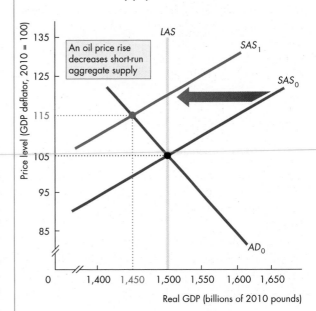

An oil price rise decreases short-run aggregate supply

An increase in the price of oil decreases short-run aggregate supply and shifts the short-run aggregate supply curve leftward from SAS_0 to SAS_1. Real GDP decreases from £1,500 billion to £1,450 billion, and the price level increases from 105 to 115. The economy experiences both recession and inflation – a situation known as stagflation.

MyEconLab Animation ————————————◆

We can use the AS–AD model to explain and illustrate the views of the alternative schools of thought in macroeconomics. That is your next task.

Macroeconomic Schools of Thought

Macroeconomics is an active field of research, and much remains to be learned about the forces that make our economy grow, bring inflation and generate business cycles. There is a greater degree of consensus and certainty about economic growth and inflation trends – the longer-term changes in real GDP and the price level – than there is about the business cycle – the short-term fluctuations in these variables. Here, we'll look only at differences of view about short-term fluctuations.

The *AS–AD* model that you've studied in this chapter provides a good foundation for understanding the range of views that macroeconomists hold about this topic. But what you will learn here is just a first glimpse at the scientific controversy and debate. We'll return to these issues at various later points in the text and deepen your appreciation of the alternative views.

Classification usually requires simplification. And classifying macroeconomists is no exception to this general rule. The classification that we'll use here is simple, but it is not misleading. We identify three macroeconomic schools of thought and examine the views of each group in turn. We examine:

◆ The classical view
◆ The Keynesian view
◆ The monetarist view

The Classical View

A **classical** macroeconomist believes that the economy is self-regulating and that it is always at full employment. The term 'classical' derives from the name of the founding school of economics, which includes Adam Smith, David Ricardo and John Stuart Mill.

The **new classical** view is that business cycle fluctuations are the efficient responses of a well-functioning market economy that is bombarded by shocks that arise from the uneven pace of technological change.

The classical view can be understood in terms of beliefs about aggregate demand and aggregate supply.

Aggregate Demand Fluctuations

In the classical view, technological change is the most significant influence on both aggregate demand and aggregate supply. For this reason, classical macroeconomists don't use the *AS–AD* framework. But their

views can be interpreted in this framework. A technological change that increases the productivity of capital brings an increase in aggregate demand because firms increase their expenditure on new plant and equipment. A technological change that lengthens the useful life of existing capital decreases the demand for new capital, which decreases aggregate demand.

Aggregate Supply Response

In the classical view, the money wage rate that lies behind the short-run aggregate supply curve is instantly and completely flexible. The money wage rate adjusts so quickly to maintain equilibrium in the labour market that real GDP always adjusts to equal potential GDP.

Potential GDP itself fluctuates for the same reason that aggregate demand fluctuates: technological change. When the pace of technological change is rapid, potential GDP increases quickly and so does real GDP. When the pace of technological change slows, so does the growth rate of potential GDP.

Classical Policy

The classical view of policy emphasises the potential for taxes to stunt incentives and create inefficiency. By minimising the disincentive effects that taxes have, employment, investment and technological advance are at their efficient levels and the economy expands at an appropriate and rapid pace.

The Keynesian View

A **Keynesian** macroeconomist believes that, left alone, the economy would rarely operate at full employment and that to achieve and maintain full employment active help from fiscal policy and monetary policy is required. The term 'Keynesian' derives from the name of one of the twentieth century's most famous economists, John Maynard Keynes.

The Keynesian view is based on beliefs about the forces that determine aggregate demand and short-run aggregate supply.

Aggregate Demand Fluctuations

In the Keynesian view, *expectations* are the most significant influence on aggregate demand. And expectations are based on herd instinct, or on what Keynes himself called 'animal spirits'. A wave of pessimism about future profit prospects can lead to a fall in aggregate demand and plunge the economy into recession.

Aggregate Supply Response

In the Keynesian view, the money wage rate that lies behind the short-run aggregate supply curve is extremely sticky downward. Basically, the money wage rate doesn't fall. So if there is a recessionary gap, there is no automatic mechanism for getting rid of it. If it were to happen, a fall in the money wage rate would increase short-run aggregate supply and restore full employment. But the money wage rate doesn't fall, so the economy remains stuck in recession.

A modern version of the Keynesian view known as the **new Keynesian** view holds that not only is the money wage rate sticky but prices of goods and services are also sticky. With a sticky price level, the short-run aggregate supply curve is horizontal at a fixed price level.

Policy Response Needed

The Keynesian view calls for fiscal policy and monetary policy to actively offset the changes in aggregate demand that bring recession. By stimulating aggregate demand in a recession, full employment can be restored.

The Monetarist View

A **monetarist** is a macroeconomist who believes that the economy is self-regulating and that it will normally operate at full employment, provided that monetary policy is not erratic and that the pace of money growth is kept steady. The term 'monetarist' was coined by an outstanding twentieth-century economist, Karl Brunner, to describe his own and Milton Friedman's views.

The monetarist view can be interpreted in terms of beliefs about the forces that determine aggregate demand and short-run aggregate supply.

Aggregate Demand Fluctuations

In the monetarist view, the *quantity of money* is the most significant influence on aggregate demand. And the quantity of money is determined by the Bank of England. If the Bank of England keeps money growing at a steady pace, aggregate demand fluctuations will be minimised and the economy will operate close to full employment. But if the Bank of England decreases the quantity of money or even just slows its growth rate too

abruptly, the economy will go into recession. In the monetarist view, all recessions result from inappropriate monetary policy.

Aggregate Supply Response

The monetarist view of short-run aggregate supply is the same as the Keynesian view – the money wage rate is sticky. If the economy is in recession, it will take an unnecessarily long time for it to return unaided to full employment.

Monetarist Policy

The monetarist view of policy is the same as the classical view on fiscal policy. Taxes should be kept low to avoid disincentive effects that decrease potential GDP. Provided that the quantity of money is kept on a steady growth path, no active stabilisation is needed to offset changes in aggregate demand.

The Way Ahead

You will encounter classical, Keynesian and monetarist views in the chapters that follow. In the next chapter, we study the classical model. Then we study the Keynesian model. From there, we study money and inflation and lay the foundation for a deeper look at the sources of macroeconomic fluctuations and economic growth. We finish with a close look at the fiscal policy and monetary policy that try to achieve faster growth, stable prices and a smoother cycle.

 REVIEW QUIZ

1 What are the defining features of classical macroeconomics and what policies do classical macroeconomists recommend?
2 What are the defining features of Keynesian macroeconomics and what policies do Keynesian macroeconomists recommend?
3 What are the defining features of monetarist macroeconomics and what policies do monetarist macroeconomists recommend?

Do these questions in Study Plan 26.4 and get instant feedback.   MyEconLab

To complete your study of the *AS–AD* model, take a look at the Eurozone economy in 2012–2013 through the eyes of this model in *Reading Between the Lines* on pp. 630–631.

Aggregate Supply and Aggregate Demand in Action

Eurozone Sets Bleak Record of Longest Term in Recession

Michael Steen

Hopes for a Eurozone recovery suffered a blow on Wednesday as the recession afflicting the 17-nation bloc became the longest since the single currency was born at the turn of the century. This latest dismal record came after unemployment hit 12.1 per cent, its highest level.

France fell back into a recession, Italian output continued to contract and even Germany, the strongest and biggest Eurozone economy, only managed a weak swing back to growth.

Gross domestic product in the Eurozone as a whole shrank 0.2 per cent in the first quarter compared with the last quarter of 2012, when it shrank 0.6 per cent, Eurostat, the EU's statistical office, said. The Italian economy shrank 0.5 per cent, matching Spain which reported its GDP figures last month,

while France contracted 0.2 per cent. The German economy grew 0.1 per cent.

The sixth consecutive quarter of decline is the longest on record for the Eurozone, beating the post-Lehman recession of 2008 and 2009 in its duration, albeit not in its severity.

'All hopes remain pinned on a revival of external demand,' Peter Vanden Houte, an economist at ING said. 'But with fiscal tightening in the US and the recovery in China still in doubt, the stimulus from net exports is not going to be large.'

The only glimmers of hope were that the pace of contraction had slowed and Germany, long criticised for failing to stimulate its domestic economy, actually offset declining investment in the first quarter with strong private consumption. . . .

 The Essence of the Story

- The Eurozone economy remains in a long recession.

- Eurozone real GDP fell by 0.6 per cent in the last quarter of 2012 and by 0.2 per cent in the first quarter of 2013.

- In the first quarter of 2013, real GDP fell by 0.5 per cent in both Italy and Spain and by

0.2 per cent in France. German real GDP grew but at only a 0.1 per cent rate.

- Expansion is not expected until external demand increases but weak growth in the US and China makes such help unlikely in the near term.

Economic Analysis

◆ The Eurozone economies have been in recession for six quarters – the longest recession since the global crisis of 2008–2009.

◆ Figure 1 shows the depth of the recession for the four large economies and the Eurozone.

◆ Like the Eurozone in aggregate, Italy and Spain have been in recession for six quarters. France has been in recession since the last quarter of 2012. Only Germany has not been in recession, but GDP in Germany fell by 0.7 per cent in the last quarter of 2012.

◆ The strongest economy in the Eurozone is Germany and it depends heavily on external demand for its exports.

◆ The quantity of real GDP demanded is given by the equation $Y = C + I + G + X - M$.

◆ Figure 2 shows the growth of consumption, investment and exports for Germany from the first quarter of 2011 to the first quarter of 2013. You can see that consumption and investment have grown slowly or fallen over this period. Exports grew until the two most recent quarters.

◆ Germany's export growth depends on the growth of the world economy, and the two largest economies in the world, the US and China, have grown at a slower than normal rate, which has hit German exports.

◆ Figure 3 shows aggregate demand and aggregate supply in the Eurozone economy in 2012 and 2013. The long-run aggregate supply curve is *LAS*, which is at 9.8 trillion euros in 2012 prices. In 2012, the short-run aggregate supply curve was SAS_0 and the aggregate demand curve was AD_0.

◆ A fall in world demand decreased aggregate demand and the *AD* curve shifted leftward to AD_1. A rise in the money wage rate and other input prices decreased short-run aggregate supply and the *SAS* curve shifted leftward to SAS_1.

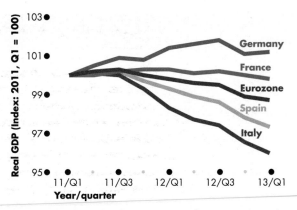

Figure 1 Real GDP in the Eurozone and 4 Large Economies

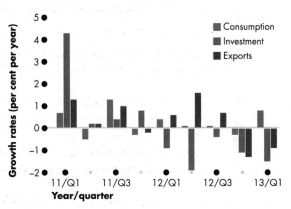

Figure 2 Germany's Consumption, Investment and Exports

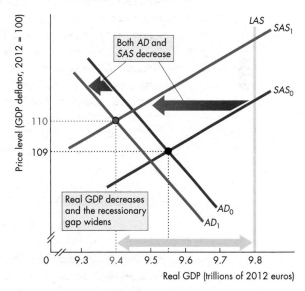

Figure 3 Eurozone Aggregate Demand and Aggregate Supply

◆ in 2013, the short-run equilibrium is at a price level of 101 and GDP of 9.4 trillion euros in 2012 prices.

SUMMARY

Key Points

Aggregate Supply (pp. 614–617)

◆ In the long run, the quantity of real GDP supplied is potential GDP.

◆ In the short run, a rise in the price level increases the quantity of real GDP supplied.

◆ A change in potential GDP changes both long-run and short-run aggregate supply. A change in the money wage rate or other resource prices changes only short-run aggregate supply.

Do Problems 1 to 3 to get a better understanding of aggregate supply.

Aggregate Demand (pp. 618–621)

◆ A rise in the price level decreases the quantity of real GDP demanded because of wealth and substitution effects.

◆ Changes in expectations, fiscal policy, monetary policy and the world economy change aggregate demand.

Do Problems 4 to 7 to get a better understanding of aggregate demand.

Explaining Macroeconomic Trends and Fluctuations (pp. 622–627)

◆ Aggregate demand and short-run aggregate supply determine real GDP and the price level.

◆ In the long run, real GDP equals potential GDP and aggregate demand determines the price level.

◆ Economic growth occurs because potential GDP increases and inflation occurs because aggregate demand grows more quickly than potential GDP.

◆ Business cycles occur because aggregate demand and aggregate supply fluctuate.

Do Problems 8 to 17 to get a better understanding of macroeconomic trends and fluctuations

Macroeconomic Schools of Thought (pp. 628–629)

◆ Classical economists believe that the economy is self-regulating and always at full employment.

◆ Keynesian economists believe that full employment can be achieved only with active policy.

◆ Monetarist economists believe that recessions result from inappropriate monetary policy.

Do Problems 18 and 19 to get a better understanding of macroeconomic schools of thought.

Key Terms

Above full-employment equilibrium, 624
Aggregate demand, 618
Below full-employment equilibrium, 625
Classical, 628
Disposable income, 620
Fiscal policy, 620
Full-employment equilibrium, 625
Inflationary gap, 624
Keynesian, 628
Long-run aggregate supply, 614
Long-run macroeconomic equilibrium, 622
Monetarist, 629
Monetary policy, 620
New classical, 628
New Keynesian, 629
Output gap, 624
Recessionary gap, 625
Short-run aggregate supply, 615
Short-run macroeconomic equilibrium, 622
Stagflation, 627

STUDY PLAN PROBLEMS AND APPLICATIONS

Do Problems 1 to 19 in MyEconLab Chapter 26 Study Plan and get instant feedback.   MyEconLab

Aggregate Supply (Study Plan 26.1)

1 Explain the influence of each of the following events on the quantity of real GDP supplied and aggregate supply in India and use a graph to illustrate.

   ◆ UK firms move their call handling, IT and data functions to India.

   ◆ Petrol prices rise.

   ◆ Walmart and Starbucks open in India.

   ◆ Universities in India increase the number of engineering graduates.

   ◆ The money wage rate rises.

   ◆ The price level in India increases.

2 **Wages Could Hit Steepest Plunge in 18 Years**

   A bad economy is starting to drag down wages for millions of workers. The average weekly wage has fallen 1.4% this year through September. Colorado will become the first state to lower its minimum wage since the federal minimum wage law was passed in 1938, when the state cuts its rate by 4 cents an hour.

   Source: *USA Today*, 16 October 2009

   Explain how the fall in the average weekly wage and the minimum wage will influence aggregate supply.

3 Chinese Premier Wen Jiabao has warned Japan that its companies operating in China should raise pay for their workers. Explain how a rise in wages in China will influence the quantity of real GDP supplied and aggregate supply in China.

Aggregate Demand (Study Plan 26.2)

4 South Africa trades with the UK. Explain the effect of each of the following events on South Africa's aggregate demand.

   ◆ The government of South Africa cuts income taxes.

   ◆ The UK experiences strong economic growth.

   ◆ South Africa sets new environmental standards that require power utilities to upgrade their production facilities.

5 The Bank of England cuts the quantity of money and all other things remain the same. Explain the effect of the cut in the quantity of money on aggregate demand in the short run.

6 Kenya trades with the UK. Explain the effect of each of the following events on the quantity of real GDP demanded and aggregate demand in Kenya.

   ◆ The UK goes into a recession.

   ◆ The price level in Kenya rises.

   ◆ Kenya increases the quantity of money.

7 **Italy Tries to Revive Its Economy**

   The Italian government has approved a new package of urgent measures aimed at restarting the country's economy, including a €3 billion investment in infrastructure works across the Italian regions – mainly focusing on improving the country's rail and highway networks – and aim to create some 30,000 new jobs in the sector.

   Source: *The Wall Street Journal*, 16 June 2013

   Explain how the items in the news clip influence Italy's aggregate demand.

Explaining Macroeconomic Trends and Fluctuations (Study Plan 26.3)

Use the following graph in Problems 8 to 10.

Initially, the short-run aggregate supply curve is SAS_0 and the aggregate demand curve is AD_0.

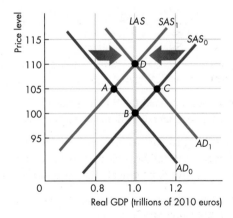

8 Some events change aggregate demand from AD_0 to AD_1. Describe two events that could have created this change in aggregate demand. What is the equilibrium after aggregate demand changed? If potential GDP is €1 trillion, the economy is at what type of macroeconomic equilibrium?

9 Some events change aggregate supply from SAS_0 to SAS_1. Describe two events that could have created this change in aggregate supply. What is the equilibrium after aggregate supply changed? If potential GDP is €1 trillion, does the economy have an inflationary gap, a recessionary gap or no output gap?

10 Some events change aggregate demand from AD_0 to AD_1 and aggregate supply from SAS_0 to SAS_1. What is the new macroeconomic equilibrium?

Use the following data in Problems 11 to 13.

The following events have occurred in UK history:

◆ A deep recession hits the world economy.

◆ The world oil price rises sharply.

◆ UK businesses expect future profits to fall.

11 Explain for each event whether it changes short-run aggregate supply, long-run aggregate supply, aggregate demand or some combination of them.

12 Explain the separate effects of each event on UK real GDP and the price level, starting from a position of long-run equilibrium.

13 Explain the combined effects of these events on UK real GDP and the price level, starting from a position of long-run equilibrium.

Use the following data in Problems 14 and 15.

The table shows the aggregate demand and short-run aggregate supply schedules of Mainland, a country in which potential GDP is €1,050 billion.

Price level	Real GDP demanded	Real GDP supplied in the short run
	(billions of 2010 euros)	
100	1,150	1,050
110	1,100	1,100
120	1,050	1,150
130	1,000	1,200
140	950	1,250
150	900	1,300
160	850	1,350

14 What is the short-run macroeconomic equilibrium real GDP and price level?

15 Does the country have an inflationary gap or a recessionary gap and what is its magnitude?

16 **Italy Tries to Revive Its Economy**

The government will lower electricity costs, which will increase consumer spending. The government will spend millions of euros upgrading infrastructure and renovating school buildings.

Source: *The Wall Street Journal*, 16 June 2013

a Explain the effects of an increase in consumer spending on the short-run macroeconomic equilibrium.

b Explain the effects of an increase in government investment on the short-run macroeconomic equilibrium.

17 If as Italy's economy grows its exports increase, explain the effect of the increase in exports on the short-run macroeconomic equilibrium.

Macroeconomic Schools of Thought

(Study Plan 26.4)

18 Describe what a classical macroeconomist, a Keynesian and a monetarist would want to do in response to each of the events listed in Problem 11.

19 **Krugman on Monetary and Fiscal Policy**

New York Times columnist and Nobel Laureate economist Paul Krugman has launched an all-out attack on the monetary policy actions and inactions of Fed Chairman Ben Bernanke. Bernanke has increased the quantity of money by historically large amounts and in mid-2012 was cautiously trying to determine whether more stimulation was needed. Krugman says Bernanke is too cautious and should print money faster and move the inflation rate upward.

Krugman also wants Congress to cut taxes and increase spending. And his advice to boost government spending isn't limited to the US. He says European governments should boost their spending too.

Sources: *The New York Times*, *Washington Post*, and other papers and blogs, April 2012

a Explain which macroeconomic school of thought Paul Krugman most likely represents in the views described above.

b Explain which macroeconomic school of thought supports Ben Bernanke's actions described above.

ADDITIONAL PROBLEMS AND APPLICATIONS

Do these problems in MyEconLab if assigned by your lecturer.

MyEconLab

Aggregate Supply

20 Explain for each event whether it changes the quantity of real GDP supplied, short-run aggregate supply, long-run aggregate supply or a combination of them.

- ◆ UK car producers switch to a new technology that raises productivity.
- ◆ Toyota and Honda build additional plants in the UK.
- ◆ The prices of car parts imported from China rise.
- ◆ Workers in UK car plants agree to a cut in the money wage rate.
- ◆ The UK price level rises.

Aggregate Demand

21 Explain for each event whether it changes the quantity of real GDP demanded or aggregate demand.

- ◆ UK car producers switch to a new technology that raises productivity.
- ◆ Toyota and Honda build new plants in the UK.
- ◆ The prices of car parts imported from China rise.
- ◆ Workers in UK car plants agree to a lower money wage rate.
- ◆ The UK price level rises.

22 Inventories Surge

The US Commerce Department reported that wholesale inventories rose 1.3 per cent in July, the best performance since July 2008. A major driver of the economy since late last year has been the restocking of depleted store shelves.

Source: Associated Press, 13 September 2010

Explain how a surge in inventories influences current aggregate demand.

23 Consumer Caution Hits US Retail Sales

Struggling US retailers reported falling sales. Top retailers JC Penney, Barnes and Noble and Best Buy report like-for-like sales down between 9 and 12 per cent. Walmart and Macy's also report a downturn in sales. 'Consumers are spending later and spending less' said Walter Loeb, a specialist retail analyst.

Source: *The Financial Times*, 20 August 2013

Explain how a fall in consumer expenditure influences the quantity of real GDP demanded and aggregate demand.

Explaining Macroeconomic Trends and Fluctuations

Use the following information in Problems 24 to 26.

The following events have occurred in UK history:

- ◆ The world economy goes into an expansion.
- ◆ UK businesses expect future profits to rise.
- ◆ The government increases its expenditure on goods and services in a time of war or increased international tension.

24 Explain for each event whether it changes short-run aggregate supply, long-run aggregate supply, aggregate demand or some combination of them.

25 Explain the separate effects of each event on UK real GDP and the price level, starting from a position of long-run equilibrium.

26 Explain the combined effects of these events on UK real GDP and the price level, starting from a position of long-run equilibrium.

Use the following data in Problems 27 and 28.

In Japan, potential GDP is 600 trillion yen and the table shows the aggregate demand and short-run aggregate supply schedules.

Price level	Real GDP demanded	Real GDP supplied in the short run
	(billions of 2010 yen)	
75	600	400
85	550	450
95	500	500
105	450	550
115	400	600
125	350	650
135	300	700

27 a Draw a graph of the aggregate demand curve and the short-run aggregate supply curve.

 b What is the short-run equilibrium real GDP and price level?

28 Does Japan have an inflationary gap or a recessionary gap and what is its magnitude?

Use the following news clip in Problems 29 to 31.

Spending by Women Jumps

The magazine *Women of China* reported that Chinese women in big cities spent 63% of their income on consumer goods last year, up from a meager 26% in 2007. Clothing accounted for the biggest chunk of that spending, at nearly 30%, followed by digital products such as mobile phones and cameras (11%) and travel (10%). Chinese consumption as a whole grew faster than the overall economy in the first half of the year and is expected to reach 42% of GDP by 2020, up from the current 36%.

Source: *The Wall Street Journal*, 27 August 2010

29 Explain the effect of a rise in consumption expenditure on real GDP and the price level in the short run.

30 If the economy had been operating at a full-employment equilibrium:

  a Describe the macroeconomic equilibrium after the rise in consumer spending.

  b Explain and draw a graph to illustrate how the economy can adjust in the long run to restore a full-employment equilibrium.

31 Why do changes in consumer spending play a large role in the business cycle?

32 **Foreign Investment**

The ability of the UK to win investment has been a crucial source of growth over many years. Last year, the UK had 697 foreign-backed investment projects, which created a more than 30,000 new jobs. The UK had the biggest foreign investment of any European country, followed by Germany and Spain.

Source: BBC News, 5 June 2013

Explain and draw a graph to illustrate the effect of foreign direct investment on an economy operating with a recessionary gap.

Macroeconomic Schools of Thought

33 **Cut Taxes and Boost Spending? Raise Taxes and Cut Spending? Cut Taxes and Cut Spending?**

This headline expresses three views about what to do to get the American economy growing more rapidly and contribute to closing a large recessionary gap.

Economists from which macroeconomic school of thought would recommend a second spending stimulus and which a permanent tax cut?

Economics in the News

34 After you have studied *Reading Between the Lines* on pp. 630–631, answer the following questions.

  a Describe the growth of the Eurozone economy during 2011 and 2012.

  b Overall, does the Eurozone economy in the first quarter of 2013 have a recessionary gap, an inflationary gap, or is it at full employment?

  c Describe the growth of the German economy during 2011 and 2012. Which components of German GDP contributed most to German growth?

  d Use the *AS–AD* model to illustrate the Eurozone economy in 2013.

  e Suppose that the world economy growth increases in 2014 and German exports increase. Explain the effect of this increase in German exports on the Eurozone economy.

  f Use the *AS–AD* model to illustrate the effect of an increase in German exports on the Eurozone economy in 2014.

27 Expenditure Multipliers

After studying this chapter you will be able to:

◆ Explain how expenditure plans are determined when the price level is fixed

◆ Explain how real GDP is determined when the price level is fixed

◆ Explain the expenditure multiplier

◆ Explain the relationship between aggregate expenditure and aggregate demand, and explain the multiplier when the price level changes

Exports and investment fluctuate like the volume of a rock singer's voice and the uneven surface of a potholed road. How does the economy react to those fluctuations? Does it amplify them and spread them out to affect the many millions of participants in an economic rock concert? Or does it absorb the shocks like a limousine and provide a smooth ride for the economy's passengers?

You will explore these questions in this chapter. In *Reading Between the Lines* at the end of the chapter, you will see how a fall in investment put the economy of France into recession in 2013.

Fixed Prices and Expenditure Plans

In the Keynesian model that we study in this chapter, all the firms are like your grocery store: they set their prices and sell the quantities their customers are willing to buy. If they persistently sell a greater quantity than they plan to and are constantly running out of inventory, they eventually raise their prices. And if they persistently sell a smaller quantity than they plan to and have inventories piling up, they eventually cut their prices. But on any given day their prices are fixed and the quantities they sell depend on demand, not supply.

Because each firm's prices are fixed, for the economy as a whole:

◆ The *price level* is fixed and

◆ *Aggregate demand* determines real GDP.

The Keynesian model explains fluctuations in aggregate demand at a fixed price level by identifying the forces that determine expenditure plans.

Expenditure Plans

Aggregate expenditure has four components: consumption expenditure, investment, government expenditure on goods and services and net exports (exports minus imports). These four components of aggregate expenditure sum to real GDP (see Chapter 20, pp. 461–462).

Aggregate planned expenditure is equal to the sum of the *planned* levels of consumption expenditure, investment, government expenditure on goods and services and exports minus imports. Two of these components of planned expenditure, consumption expenditure and imports, change when income changes and so they depend on real GDP.

A Two-Way Link Between Aggregate Expenditure and Real GDP

There is a two-way link between aggregate expenditure and real GDP. Other things remaining the same,

◆ An increase in real GDP increases aggregate expenditure and

◆ An increase in aggregate expenditure increases real GDP.

You are now going to study this two-way link, starting with a review of the influences on consumption plans and saving plans.

Consumption and Saving Plans

Several factors influence consumption expenditure and saving plans. The more important ones are

◆ Disposable income

◆ Real interest rate

◆ Wealth

◆ Expected future income

Disposable income is aggregate income minus taxes plus transfer payments. Aggregate income equals real GDP, so disposable income depends on real GDP. To explore the two-way link between real GDP and planned consumption expenditure, we focus on the relationship between consumption expenditure and disposable income when the other three factors listed above are constant.

Consumption Expenditure and Saving

The table in Figure 27.1 lists the consumption expenditure and the saving that people plan at each level of disposable income. Households can only spend their disposable income on consumption or save it, so planned consumption expenditure plus planned saving always equals disposable income.

The relationship between consumption expenditure and disposable income, other things remaining the same, is called the **consumption function**. The relationship between saving and disposable income, other things remaining the same, is called the **saving function**.

Consumption Function

Figure 27.1(a) shows a consumption function. The *y*-axis measures consumption expenditure and the *x*-axis measures disposable income. Along the consumption function, the points labelled *A* to *F* correspond to the rows of the table. For example, point *E* shows that when disposable income is £800 billion, consumption expenditure is £750 billion. As disposable income increases, consumption expenditure also increases.

At point *A* on the consumption function, consumption expenditure is £150 billion even though disposable income is zero. This consumption expenditure is called *autonomous consumption*, and it is the amount of consumption expenditure that would take place in the short run even if people had no current income. Consumption expenditure in excess of this amount is called *induced consumption*, which is the consumption expenditure that is induced by an increase in disposable income.

45° Line

Figure 27.1(a) contains a 45° line, the height of which measures disposble income. At each point on this line, consumption expenditure equals disposable income. Between points A and D, consumption expenditure exceeds disposable income; between points D and F consumption expenditure is less than disposable income; and at point D, consumption expenditure equals disposable income.

Saving Function

Figure 27.1(b) shows a saving function. Again, the points A to F correspond to the rows of the table. For example, point E shows that when disposable income is £800 billion, saving is £50 billion. As disposable income increases, saving increases. Notice that when consumption expenditure exceeds disposable income in part (a), saving is negative in part (b). Negative saving is called *dissaving*.

Figure 27.1 Consumption Function and Saving Function

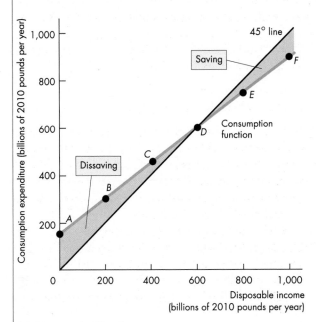

(a) Consumption function

	Disposable income	Planned consumption expenditure	Planned saving
	(billions of 2010 pounds per year)		
A	0	150	−150
B	200	300	−100
C	400	450	−50
D	600	600	0
E	800	750	50
F	1,000	900	100

The table shows consumption expenditure and saving plans at various levels of disposable income. When disposable income is £800 (row E) planned consumption expenditure is £750 and planned saving is £50.

Part (a) of the figure shows the consumption function (the relationship between consumption expenditure and disposable income). The height of the consumption function measures consumption expenditure at each level of disposable income.

Part (b) shows the saving function (the relationship between saving and disposable income). The height of the saving function measures saving at each level of disposable income. Points A to F on the consumption and saving functions correspond to the rows in the table.

The height of the 45° line in part (a) measures disposable income. So along the 45° line, consumption expenditure equals disposable income. Consumption expenditure plus saving equals disposable income.

When the consumption function is above the 45° line, saving is negative (dissaving occurs). When the consumption function is below the 45° line, saving is positive. At the point where the consumption function intersects the 45° line, all disposable income is consumed and saving is zero.

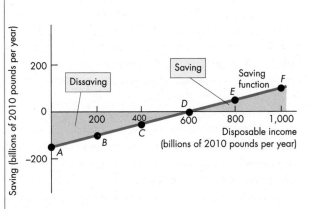

(b) Saving function

MyEconLab Animation

Marginal Propensities

The **marginal propensity to consume** (*MPC*) is the fraction of a *change* in disposable income that is consumed. It is calculated as the *change* in consumption expenditure (ΔC) divided by the *change* in disposable income (ΔYD) that brought it about. That is:

$$MPC = \frac{\Delta C}{\Delta YD}$$

In the table in Figure 27.1, when disposable income increases from £600 billion to £800 billion, consumption expenditure increases from £600 billion to £750 billion. The *MPC* is £150 billion divided by £200 billion, which equals 0.75.

The **marginal propensity to save** (*MPS*) is the fraction of a *change* in disposable income that is saved. It is calculated as the *change* in saving (ΔS) divided by the *change* in disposable income (ΔYD) that brought it about. That is:

$$MPS = \frac{\Delta S}{\Delta YD}$$

In the table in Figure 27.1, when disposable income increases by £200 billion, saving increases by £50 billion. The *MPS* is £50 billion divided by £200 billion, which equals 0.25.

Because an increase in disposable income is either spent on consumption or saved, the marginal propensity to consume plus the marginal propensity to save equals 1. You can see why by using the following equation:

$$\Delta C + \Delta S = \Delta YD$$

Divide both sides of the equation by the change in disposable income to obtain:

$$\frac{\Delta C}{\Delta YD} + \frac{\Delta S}{\Delta YD} = 1$$

$\Delta C/\Delta YD$ is the *marginal propensity to consume* (*MPC*) and $\Delta S/\Delta YD$ is the *marginal propensity to save* (*MPS*), so:

$$MPC + MPS = 1$$

Slopes and Marginal Propensities

The slope of the consumption function is the marginal propensity to consume and the slope of the saving function is the marginal propensity to save.

Figure 27.2(a) shows the *MPC* as the slope of the consumption function. A £200 billion increase in disposable income, shown as the base of the red triangle, brings a £150 billion increase in consumption expenditure, shown as the height of the red triangle. The slope of the consumption function is given by the formula 'slope equals rise over run' and is £150 billion divided by £200 billion, which equals 0.75 – the *MPC* is 0.75.

Figure 27.2(b) shows the *MPS* as the slope of the saving function. A £200 billion increase in disposable income, the base of the red triangle, increases saving by £50 billion, the height of the triangle. The slope of the saving function is £50 billion divided by £200 billion, which equals 0.25 – the *MPS* is 0.25.

Figure 27.2   Marginal Propensities to Consume and Save

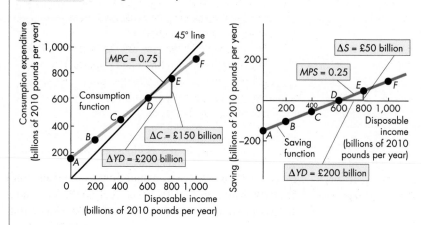

(a) Consumption function

(b) Saving function

The *MPC* is equal to the change in consumption expenditure divided by the change in disposable income. It is measured by the slope of the consumption function. In part (a), the *MPC* is 0.75.

The marginal propensity to save, *MPS*, is equal to the change in saving divided by the change in disposable income. It is measured by the slope of the saving function. In part (b), the *MPS* is 0.25.

MyEconLab Animation ◆

ECONOMICS IN ACTION

The UK Consumption Function

Figure 1 shows the UK consumption function. Each blue dot represents consumption expenditure and disposable income for a particular year. (The dots are for the years 1970 to 2012 and the dots of nine of the years are identified.)

The line CF_{70} is an estimate of the UK consumption function in 1970, and the line CF_{12} is an estimate of the UK consumption function in 2012.

The slope of the consumption function in the figure is 0.8, which means that a £100 billion increase in disposable income brings an £80 billion increase in consumption expenditure. This slope is an estimate of the marginal propensity to consume and it is the middle of the range of values that economists have estimated for the marginal propensity to consume.

The consumption function shifts upward over time as other influences on consumption expenditure change. Of these other influences, the real interest rate and wealth fluctuate and so bring upward *and* downward shifts in the consumption function.

But rising expected future disposable income brings a steady upward shift in the consumption function. As the consumption function shifts upward, autonomous consumption expenditure increases.

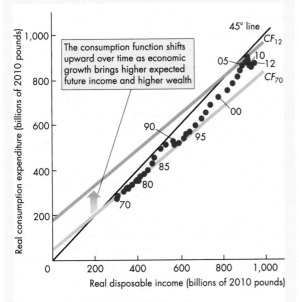

Figure 1 The UK Consumption Function

Source of data: Office for National Statistics.

Consumption and Real GDP

Consumption expenditure changes when disposable income changes, and disposable income changes when real GDP changes. So consumption expenditure is a function of real GDP. An increase in real GDP increases disposable income, which increases consumption expenditure. We use this link between consumption expenditure and real GDP to determine equilibrium expenditure. But before we do so, we need to look at one other component of aggregate expenditure: imports. Like consumption expenditure, imports are influenced by real GDP.

Import Function

UK imports are determined by a number of factors, but in the short run with fixed prices, one factor dominates: UK real GDP. Other things remaining the same, the greater the UK real GDP, the larger is the quantity of UK imports. So an increase in UK real GDP brings an increase in UK imports.

The relationship between imports and real GDP is determined by the **marginal propensity to import** – the fraction of an increase in real GDP that is spent on imports. It is calculated as the change in imports divided by the change in real GDP that brought it about, other things remaining the same. For example, if a £100 billion increase in real GDP increases imports by £20 billion, the marginal propensity to import is 0.2.

REVIEW QUIZ

1   Which components of aggregate planned expenditure are influenced by real GDP?
2   Define and explain how we calculate the marginal propensity to consume and the marginal propensity to save.
3   How do we calculate the effects of real GDP on consumption expenditure and imports by using the marginal propensity to consume and the marginal propensity to import?

Do these questions in Study Plan 27.1 and get instant feedback.   MyEconLab

Real GDP influences consumption expenditure and imports, which in turn influence real GDP. Your next task is to study the second piece of the two-way link between aggregate expenditure and real GDP and see how all the components of aggregate planned expenditure interact to determine real GDP.

Real GDP with a Fixed Price Level

You are now going to learn how expenditure plans determine real GDP when the price level is fixed. We begin by studying the relationship between aggregate planned expenditure and real GDP. We describe this relationship either by an aggregate expenditure schedule or by an aggregate expenditure curve. The *aggregate expenditure schedule* lists aggregate planned expenditure generated at each level of real GDP. The *aggregate expenditure curve* is a graph of the aggregate expenditure schedule.

Then we'll learn about the key distinction between *planned* expenditure and *actual* expenditure. And finally, we'll define and learn what determines equilibrium expenditure and real GDP.

Aggregate Planned Expenditure

The table in Figure 27.3 sets out an aggregate expenditure schedule together with the components of aggregate planned expenditure. To calculate aggregate planned expenditure at a given real GDP, we add the various components together. The first column of the table shows real GDP and the second column shows the consumption expenditure generated by each level of real GDP. An increase in real GDP of £1,000 billion from row A to row B of the table generates an increase in consumption expenditure of £700 billion – the *MPC* is 0.7.

The next two columns show investment and government expenditure on goods and services. Investment depends on factors such as the real interest rate and the expected future profit. But at a given point in time, these factors generate a particular level of investment. Suppose this level of investment is £225 billion. Also, suppose that government expenditure on goods and services is £350 billion.

The next two columns show exports and imports. Exports are influenced by income in the rest of the world, prices of foreign-produced goods and services relative to the prices of similar UK-produced goods and services, and foreign exchange rates. But exports are not directly affected by UK real GDP. In the table, exports appear as a constant £175 billion. In contrast, imports increase as real GDP increases. A £100 billion increase in real GDP generates a £20 billion increase in imports – the marginal propensity to import is 0.2.

The final column of the table shows aggregate planned expenditure – the sum of planned consumption expenditure, investment, government expenditure and exports minus imports.

Figure 27.3 plots an aggregate expenditure curve. Real GDP is shown on the *x*-axis and aggregate planned expenditure on the *y*-axis. The aggregate expenditure curve is the red line *AE*. Points *A* to *F* on this curve correspond to the rows of the table. The *AE* curve is a graph of aggregate planned expenditure (the last column) plotted against real GDP (the first column).

Figure 27.3 also shows the components of aggregate expenditure. The constant components – investment (*I*), government expenditure (*G*) and exports (*X*) – are shown by the vertical gaps between the horizontal lines. Consumption expenditure (*C*) is the vertical gap between the lines labelled $I + G + X + C$ and $I + G + X$.

To construct the *AE* curve, subtract imports (*M*) from the $I + G + X + C$ line. Aggregate expenditure is expenditure on UK-produced goods and services. But the components of aggregate expenditure, *C*, *I* and *G*, include expenditure on imported goods and services. For example, if you buy a new mobile phone, your expenditure is part of consumption expenditure. But if the mobile phone is a Nokia made in Finland, your expenditure on it must be subtracted from consumption expenditure to find out how much is spent on goods and services produced in the UK – on UK real GDP. Money paid to Nokia for mobile phone imports from Finland does not add to aggregate expenditure in the UK.

Because imports are only a part of aggregate expenditure, when we subtract imports from the other components of aggregate expenditure, aggregate planned expenditure still increases as real GDP increases, as you can see in Figure 27.3.

Consumption expenditure minus imports, which varies with real GDP, is called **induced expenditure**. The sum of investment, government expenditure and exports, which does not vary with real GDP, is called **autonomous expenditure**. Consumption expenditure and imports can also have an autonomous component – a component that does not vary with real GDP. Another way of thinking about autonomous expenditure is that it would be the level of aggregate planned expenditure if real GDP were zero.

In Figure 27.3, autonomous expenditure is £750 billion – aggregate planned expenditure when real GDP is zero. For each £100 billion increase in real GDP, induced expenditure increases by £50 billion.

The aggregate expenditure curve summarises the relationship between aggregate planned expenditure and real GDP. But what determines the point on the aggregate expenditure curve at which the economy operates? What determines *actual* aggregate expenditure?

Figure 27.3 Aggregate Expenditure

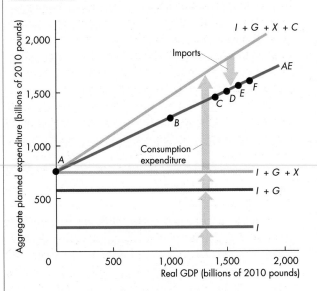

Aggregate planned expenditure is the sum of planned consumption expenditure, investment, government expenditure and exports minus imports. When real GDP is zero (row *A* of the table), aggregate planned expenditure is £750 billion. When real GDP is £1,000 billion (row *B* of the table), planned consumption expenditure is £700 billion, planned investment is £225 billion, planned government expenditure is £350 billion, planned exports are £175 billion and planned imports are £200 billion, so aggregate planned expenditure is £1,250 billion (£700 billion + £225 billion + £350 billion + £175 billion – £200 billion).

The graph shows the relationship between the components of aggregate expenditure and real GDP. The green, blue and orange arrows show investment, government expenditure and exports – the expenditures that do not vary with real GDP. The red and purple arrows show consumption expenditure and imports – the expenditures that vary with real GDP. The red curve *AE* is the aggregate planned expenditure curve.

| | Real GDP (Y) | Planned expenditure | | | | | Aggregate planned expenditure (AE = C + I + G + X − M) |
		Consumption expenditure (C)	Investment (I)	Government expenditure (G)	Exports (X)	Imports (M)	
				(billions of 2010 pounds)			
A	0	0	225	350	175	0	750
B	1,000	700	225	350	175	200	1,250
C	1,400	980	225	350	175	280	1,450
D	1,500	1,050	225	350	175	300	1,500
E	1,600	1,120	225	350	175	320	1,550
F	1,700	1,190	225	350	175	340	1,600

Actual Expenditure, Planned Expenditure and Real GDP

Actual aggregate expenditure is always equal to real GDP, as we saw in Chapter 20 (p. 462). But aggregate *planned* expenditure does not necessarily equal actual aggregate expenditure and real GDP. How can actual expenditure and planned expenditure differ from each other? Why don't expenditure plans get implemented? The main reason is that firms might end up with greater inventories or with smaller inventories than planned. People carry out their consumption expenditure plans,

the government implements its planned expenditure on goods and services, and net exports are as planned. Firms carry out their plans to purchase new buildings, plant and equipment. But one component of investment is the increase in firms' inventories of goods. If aggregate planned expenditure is less than real GDP, firms don't sell all the goods and services they produce and they end up with more inventories than they had planned. They have unplanned inventories. If aggregate planned expenditure is greater than real GDP, firms sell more goods and services than they produce and inventories fall to below the level that firms had planned.

Equilibrium Expenditure

Equilibrium expenditure is the level of aggregate expenditure that occurs when aggregate *planned* expenditure equals real GDP. Equilibrium expenditure is a level of aggregate expenditure and real GDP at which everyone's spending plans are fulfilled. When the price level is fixed, equilibrium expenditure determines real GDP. When aggregate planned expenditure and actual aggregate expenditure are unequal, a process of conver-

gence towards equilibrium expenditure occurs. And throughout this convergence process real GDP adjusts. Let's examine equilibrium expenditure and the process that brings it about.

Figure 27.4(a) illustrates equilibrium expenditure. The table sets out aggregate planned expenditure at various levels of real GDP. These values are plotted as points A to F along the AE curve. The 45° line shows all the points at which aggregate planned expenditure equals real GDP. So where the AE curve lies above the

---

Figure 27.4   Equilibrium Expenditure

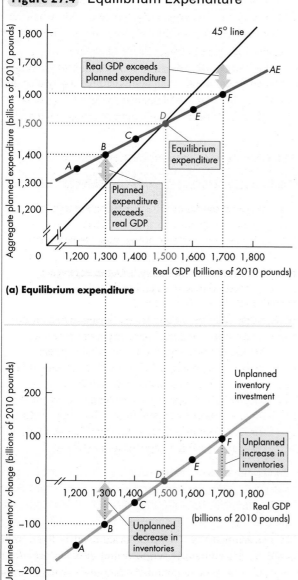

(a) Equilibrium expenditure

(b) Unplanned inventory change

	Real GDP (Y)	**Aggregate planned expenditure** (AE)	**Unplanned inventory change** $(Y - AE)$
	(billions of 2010 pounds)		
A	1,200	1,350	−150
B	1,300	1,400	−100
C	1,400	1,450	−50
D	**1,500**	**1,500**	**0**
E	1,600	1,650	50
F	1,700	1,600	100

The table shows expenditure plans at different levels of real GDP. When real GDP is £1,500 billion, aggregate planned expenditure equals real GDP.

Part (a) of the figure illustrates equilibrium expenditure, which occurs when aggregate planned expenditure equals real GDP at the intersection of the 45° line and the AE curve.

Part (b) of the figure shows the forces that bring about equilibrium expenditure.

When aggregate planned expenditure *exceeds* real GDP, firms' inventories decrease – for example, point B in both parts of the figure. Firms have an unplanned decrease in inventories, so they increase production. Real GDP increases.

When aggregate planned expenditure is *less than* real GDP, firms' inventories increase – for example, point F in both parts of the figure. Firms have an unplanned increase in inventories, so they decrease production. Real GDP decreases.

When aggregate planned expenditure *equals* real GDP, there are no unplanned inventory changes and real GDP remains constant at equilibrium expenditure.

45° line, aggregate planned expenditure exceeds real GDP; where the *AE* curve lies below the 45° line, aggregate planned expenditure is less than real GDP; and where the *AE* curve intersects the 45° line, aggregate planned expenditure equals real GDP. Point *D* illustrates equilibrium expenditure. At this point, real GDP is £1,500 billion.

Convergence to Equilibrium

What are the forces that move aggregate expenditure towards its equilibrium level? To answer this question, we must look at a situation in which aggregate expenditure is away from its equilibrium level.

From Below Equilibrium

Suppose that in Figure 27.4, actual aggregate expenditure is £1,300 billion. But aggregate *planned* expenditure is £1,400 billion, point *B* in Figure 27.4(a). Aggregate planned expenditure exceeds *actual* expenditure. When people spend £1,400 billion and firms produce goods and services worth £1,300 billion, firms' inventories fall by £100 billion, point *B* in Figure 27.4(b). Because the change in inventories is part of investment, *actual* investment is £100 billion less than *planned* investment.

Real GDP doesn't remain at £1,300 billion for very long. Firms have inventory targets based on their sales. When inventories fall below target, firms increase production to restore inventories to their target levels. To increase inventories, firms hire additional labour and increase production.

Suppose that firms increase production in the next period by £100 billion. Real GDP increases by £100 billion to £1,400 billion. But again, aggregate planned expenditure exceeds real GDP. When real GDP is £1,400 billion, aggregate planned expenditure is £1,450 billion, point *C* in Figure 27.4(a). Again, inventories decrease, but this time by less than before. With real GDP of £1,400 billion and aggregate planned expenditure of £1,450 billion, inventories decrease by £50 billion, point *C* in Figure 27.4(b). Again, to restore inventories, firms hire additional labour and production increases; real GDP increases yet further.

The process that we have just described – planned expenditure exceeds real GDP, inventories decrease and production increases to restore the inventories – ends when real GDP has reached £1,500 billion. At this real GDP, there is equilibrium. Unplanned inventory changes are zero. Firms do not change their production.

From Above Equilibrium

If in Figure 27.4, actual aggregate expenditure is £1,700 billion, the process that we've just described works in reverse. With real GDP at £1,700 billion, actual aggregate expenditure is also £1,700 billion, but aggregate planned expenditure is £1,600 billion at point *F* in part (a). Actual expenditure exceeds planned expenditure. When people spend £1,600 billion and firms produce goods and services worth £1,700 billion, firms' inventories rise by £100 billion, point *F* in part (b). Now, real GDP begins to fall. As long as actual expenditure exceeds planned expenditure, inventories rise, and production decreases. Again, the process ends when real GDP has reached £1,500 billion, the equilibrium at which firms do not change their production.

This process of convergence to equilibrium is driven by changes in production and real GDP, not by changes in prices. Throughout the entire process the price level (and the price of every firm's output) remains fixed.

 REVIEW QUIZ

1 Explain the relationship between aggregate planned expenditure and real GDP.
2 Distinguish between autonomous expenditure and induced expenditure.
3 What is the relationship between aggregate planned expenditure and real GDP at equilibrium expenditure?
4 What adjusts to achieve equilibrium expenditure?
5 If real GDP and aggregate expenditure are less than equilibrium expenditure, what happens to firms' inventories? How do firms change their production? What happens to real GDP?
6 If real GDP and aggregate expenditure are greater than equilibrium expenditure, what happens to firms' inventories? How do firms change their production? What happens to real GDP?

Do these questions in Study Plan 27.2 and get instant feedback.

MyEconLab

We've learned that when the price level is fixed, real GDP is determined by equilibrium expenditure. And we've seen how unplanned changes in inventories and the production response they generate bring a convergence towards equilibrium expenditure. We're now going to study *changes* in equilibrium expenditure and discover an economic amplifier called the *multiplier*.

The Multiplier

Investment and exports can change for many reasons. A fall in the real interest rate might induce firms to increase their planned investment. A wave of innovation, such as occurred with the spread of multimedia computers in the 1990s, might increase expected future profits and lead firms to increase their planned investment. An economic boom in the US and Canada might lead to a large increase in their expenditure on UK-produced goods and services – UK exports. These are all examples of increases in autonomous expenditure in the UK.

When autonomous expenditure increases, aggregate expenditure increases and so do equilibrium expenditure and real GDP. But the increase in equilibrium expenditure and real GDP is *larger* than the change in autonomous expenditure. The **multiplier** is the amount by which a change in autonomous expenditure is magnified or multiplied to determine the change in equilibrium expenditure and real GDP.

To understand the basic idea of the multiplier, we'll work with an example economy in which there are no income taxes and no imports. So we'll first assume that these factors are absent. Then, when you understand the basic idea, we'll bring these factors back into play and see what difference they make to the multiplier.

The Basic Idea of the Multiplier

Suppose that investment increases. The additional expenditure by businesses means that aggregate expenditure and real GDP increase. The increase in real GDP increases disposable income, and with no income taxes, real GDP and disposable income increase by the same amount. The increase in disposable income brings an increase in consumption expenditure. And the increased consumption expenditure adds even more to aggregate expenditure. Real GDP and disposable income increase further, and so does consumption expenditure. The initial increase in investment brings an even bigger increase in aggregate expenditure because it induces an increase in consumption expenditure. The magnitude of the increase in aggregate expenditure that results from an increase in autonomous expenditure is determined by the *multiplier*.

The table in Figure 27.5 sets out aggregate planned expenditure. When real GDP is £1,400 billion, aggregate planned expenditure is £1,425 billion. For each £100 billion increase in real GDP, aggregate planned expenditure increases by £75 billion. This aggregate expenditure schedule is shown in the graph as the aggregate expenditure curve AE_0.

Initially, equilibrium expenditure is £1,500 billion. You can see this equilibrium in row B of the table, and in the graph where the curve AE_0 intersects the 45° line at the point marked B.

Now suppose that autonomous expenditure increases by £50 billion. What happens to equilibrium expenditure? You can see the answer in Figure 27.5. When this increase in autonomous expenditure is added to the original aggregate planned expenditure, aggregate planned expenditure increases by £50 billion at each level of real GDP. The new aggregate expenditure curve is AE_1. The new equilibrium expenditure, highlighted in the table (row D'), occurs where AE_1 intersects the 45° line and is £1,700 billion (point D'). At this point, aggregate planned expenditure equals real GDP. Equilibrium expenditure is £1,700 billion.

The Multiplier Effect

In Figure 27.5, the increase in autonomous expenditure of £50 billion increases equilibrium expenditure from £1,500 billion to £1,700 billion – an increase of £200 billion. That is, the change in autonomous expenditure leads, like the rock singer's electronic equipment, to an amplified change in equilibrium expenditure. This amplified change is the multiplier effect – equilibrium expenditure increases by more than the increase in autonomous expenditure. The multiplier is greater than 1.

Initially, when autonomous expenditure increases, aggregate planned expenditure exceeds real GDP. As a result, firm's inventories decrease. Firms respond by increasing production to restore their inventories to their target levels. As production increases, so does real GDP. With a higher level of real GDP, *induced expenditure* increases. So equilibrium expenditure increases by the sum of the initial increase in autonomous expenditure and the increase in induced expenditure. In this example, the initial increase in autonomous expenditure is £50 billion and induced expenditure increases by £150 billion, so equilibrium expenditure increases by £200 billion.

Although we have just analysed the effects of an *increase* in autonomous expenditure, the same analysis applies to a decrease in autonomous expenditure. If initially the aggregate expenditure curve is AE_1, equilibrium expenditure and real GDP are £1,700 billion. A decrease in autonomous expenditure of £50 billion shifts the aggregate expenditure curve downward by

Figure 27.5 The Multiplier

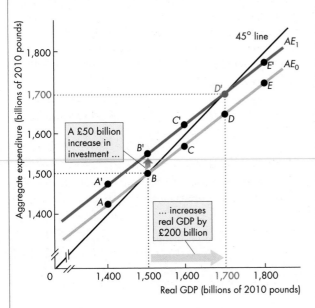

Real GDP (Y)	Aggregate planned expenditure			
	Original (AE₀)		New (AE₁)	
	(billions of 2010 pounds)			
1,400	A	1,425	A'	1,475
1,500	**B**	**1,500**	**B'**	**1,550**
1,600	C	1,575	C'	1,625
1,700	**D**	**1,650**	**D'**	**1,700**
1,800	E	1,725	E'	1,775

A £50 billion increase in autonomous expenditure shifts the AE curve upward by £50 billion from AE₀ to AE₁. Equilibrium expenditure increases by £200 billion from £1,500 billion to £1,700 billion. The increase in equilibrium expenditure is 4 times the increase in autonomous expenditure, so the multiplier is 4.

MyEconLab Animation ━━━━━━━━━━━━━━━━◆

£50 billion to AE₀. Equilibrium expenditure decreases from £1,700 billion to £1,500 billion. The decrease in equilibrium expenditure (£200 billion) is larger than the decrease in autonomous expenditure that brought it about (£50 billion).

Why Is the Multiplier Greater Than 1?

We've seen that equilibrium expenditure increases by more than the increase in autonomous expenditure. This makes the multiplier greater than 1. How come? Why does equilibrium expenditure increase by more than the increase in autonomous expenditure?

The multiplier is greater than 1 because of induced expenditure – an increase in autonomous expenditure *induces* further increases in expenditure. If Vodafone spends £10 million on a new telephone-video system, aggregate expenditure and real GDP immediately increase by £10 million. But that is not the end of the story. Electrical engineers and video-system designers now have more income and they spend part of the extra income on consumption goods and services.

Real GDP now increases by the initial £10 million plus the extra consumption expenditure induced by the £10 million increase in income. The producers of consumption goods and services now have increased incomes and they, in turn, spend part of the increase in their incomes on consumption goods and services. Additional income induces additional expenditure, which creates additional income.

The Size of the Multiplier

The economy is in a recession and now profit prospects start to look better. Firms are making plans for large increases in investment. The world economy is also heading towards expansion and exports are increasing. The question on everyone's lips is: how strong will the expansion be? This is a hard question to answer. But an important ingredient in the answer is working out the size of the multiplier.

The *multiplier* is the amount by which a change in autonomous expenditure is multiplied to determine the change in equilibrium expenditure that it generates. To calculate the multiplier, we divide the change in equilibrium expenditure by the change in autonomous expenditure. Let's calculate the multiplier for the example in Figure 27.5. Initially, equilibrium expenditure is £1,500 billion. Then autonomous expenditure increases by £50 billion and equilibrium expenditure increases by £200 billion to £1,700 billion. So:

$$\text{Multiplier} = \frac{\text{Change in equilibrium expenditure}}{\text{Change in autonomous expenditure}}$$

$$= \frac{£200 \text{ billion}}{£50 \text{ billion}} = 4$$

The Multiplier and the Slope of the *AE* Curve

The magnitude of the multiplier depends on the slope of the *AE* curve. In Figure 27.6, the *AE* curve in part (a) is steeper than the *AE* curve in part (b), and the multiplier is larger in part (a) than in part (b). To see why, let's do a calculation.

Aggregate expenditure and real GDP change because induced expenditure and autonomous expenditure change. The change in real GDP (ΔY) equals the change in induced expenditure (ΔN) plus the change in autonomous expenditure (ΔA). That is:

$$\Delta Y = \Delta N + \Delta A$$

But the change in induced expenditure is determined by the change in real GDP and the slope of the *AE* curve. To see why, begin with the fact that the slope of the *AE* curve equals the 'rise', ΔN, divided by the 'run', ΔY. That is:

$$\text{Slope of the } AE \text{ curve} = \Delta N \div \Delta Y$$

So:

$$\Delta N = \text{Slope of the } AE \text{ curve} \times \Delta Y$$

Now use this equation to replace ΔN in the first equation above to give:

$$\Delta Y = (\text{Slope of the } AE \text{ curve} \times \Delta Y) + \Delta A$$

Now, solve for ΔY as:

$$(1 - \text{Slope of the } AE \text{ curve}) \times \Delta Y = \Delta A$$

and rearrange to give:

$$\Delta Y = \frac{\Delta A}{1 - \text{Slope of the } AE \text{ curve}}$$

Finally, divide both sides of this equation by ΔA:

$$\text{Multiplier} = \frac{\Delta Y}{\Delta A} = \frac{1}{1 - \text{Slope of the } AE \text{ curve}}$$

Using the numbers for Figure 27.5, the slope of the *AE* curve is 0.75, so:

$$\text{Multiplier} = \frac{1}{1 - 0.75} = \frac{1}{0.25} = 4$$

When there are no income taxes and no imports, the slope of the *AE* curve equals the marginal propensity to consume (*MPC*). So the multiplier is:

$$\text{Multiplier} = \frac{1}{(1 - MPC)}$$

But $(1 - MPC)$ equals *MPS*. So another formula for the multiplier is:

$$\text{Multiplier} = \frac{1}{MPS}$$

Because the marginal propensity to save (*MPS*) is a fraction – a number between 0 and 1 – the multiplier is greater than 1.

Figure 27.6 The Multiplier and the Slope of the AE Curve

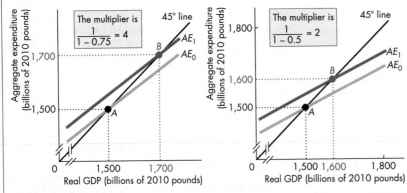

Imports and income taxes make the *AE* curve less steep and reduce the value of the multiplier. In part (a), with no imports and income taxes, the slope of the *AE* curve is 0.75 (the marginal propensity to consume) and the multiplier is 4.

But with imports and income taxes, the slope of the *AE* curve is less than the marginal propensity to consume. In part (b), the slope of the *AE* curve is 0.5. In this case, the multiplier is 2.

(a) Multiplier is 4

(b) Multiplier is 2

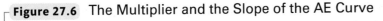

MyEconLab Animation

Imports and Income Taxes

Imports and income taxes influence the size of the multiplier and make it smaller than it otherwise would be.

To see why, think about what happens following an increase in UK investment. An increase in investment increases real GDP, which in turn increases consumption expenditure in the UK. But part of this increase in consumption expenditure is expenditure on imported goods and services, not expenditure on UK-produced goods and services. Only expenditure on goods and services produced in the UK increases UK real GDP. The larger the marginal propensity to import, the smaller is the change in UK real GDP.

Income taxes also make the multiplier smaller than it otherwise would be. Again, think about what happens following an increase in investment. An increase in investment increases real GDP. But because income taxes increase, disposable income increases by less than the increase in real GDP. Consequently, consumption expenditure increases by less than it would if taxes had not changed. The larger the income tax rate, the smaller is the change in disposable income and real GDP.

The marginal propensity to import and the marginal tax rate together with the marginal propensity to consume determine the multiplier. And their combined influence determines the slope of the *AE* curve.

Over time, changes in the marginal propensity to consume, the marginal propensity to import and the income tax rate change the value of the multiplier. These changes make the multiplier hard to predict. But they do not alter the fundamental fact that an initial change in autonomous expenditure leads to a magnified change in aggregate expenditure and real GDP.

The Mathematical Note on pp. 658–661 shows the effects of taxes, imports and the *MPC* on the multiplier.

The Multiplier Process

The multiplier effect isn't a one-shot, overnight event. It is a process that plays out over a few months. Figure 27.7 illustrates the multiplier process. In round 1, autonomous expenditure increases by £50 billion. At this time, real GDP increases by £50 billion (the green bar in round 1). This increase in real GDP increases induced expenditure in round 2. With the slope of the *AE* curve equal to 0.75, induced expenditure increases by 0.75 times the increase in real GDP, so the increase in real GDP of £50 billion induces a further increase in

expenditure of £37.5 billion. This change in induced expenditure (the green bar in round 2), when added to the previous increase in expenditure (the blue bar in round 2), increases aggregate expenditure and real GDP by £87.5 billion. The round 2 increase in real GDP induces a round 3 increase in expenditure. The process repeats through successive rounds. Each increase in real GDP is 0.75 times the previous increase. The cumulative increase in real GDP gradually approaches £200 billion.

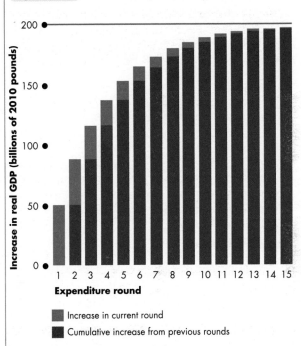

Figure 27.7 The Multiplier Process

Autonomous expenditure increases by £50 billion. In round 1, real GDP increases by the same amount. With the slope of the *AE* curve equal to 0.75, each additional pound of real GDP induces an additional 0.75 of a pound of induced expenditure.

The round 1 increase in real GDP brings an increase in induced expenditure of £37.5 billion in round 2. At the end of round 2, real GDP has increased by £87.5 billion.

The extra £37.5 billion of real GDP in round 2 brings a further increase in induced expenditure of £28.1 billion in round 3. At the end of round 3, real GDP has increased to £115.6 billion.

This process continues with real GDP increasing by ever smaller amounts. When the process comes to an end, real GDP has increased by a total of £200 billion.

MyEconLab Animation ◆

ECONOMICS IN ACTION

The Multiplier in the Great Depression

The aggregate expenditure model and its multiplier were developed during the 1930s by John Maynard Keynes to understand the most traumatic event in economic history, the *Great Depression*.

In 1929, the global economies were booming. Real GDP had never been higher. By 1933, real GDP had fallen to 94 per cent of its 1929 level and unemployment had doubled from 1.25 million to 2.5 million.

Table 1 shows the GDP numbers and components of aggregate expenditure (in 1929 pounds) in 1929 and 1933.

Autonomous investment and exports fell sharply but autonomous consumption rose because a 14 per cent fall in the price level increased the real value of wealth.

Government expenditure held steady. In all, however, autonomous expenditure fell from $10.7 billion to $10.1 billion.

Figure 1 uses the *AE* model to illustrate the Great Depression. In 1929, with autonomous expenditure of £10.7 billion, the *AE* curve was AE_{29}. Equilibrium expenditure and real GDP were £15.1 billion. By 1933, autonomous expenditure had fallen to £10.1 billion – a fall of £0.6 billion – and the *AE* curve had shifted downward to AE_{33}. Equilibrium expenditure and real GDP had fallen to £14.2 billion.

The decrease in autonomous expenditure of £0.6 billion brought a decrease in real GDP of £0.9 billion. The multiplier was £0.9/£0.6 = 1.5. The slope of the *AE* curve is 0.33 – the fall in induced expenditure, £0.3 billion, divided by the fall in real GDP, £0.9 billion. The multiplier formula, 1/(1 – Slope of the *AE* curve), delivers a multiplier of 1.5.

Table 1

Components of Expenditure

	1929	1933
	(billions of 1929 pounds)	
Induced consumption	8.4	7.9
Induced imports	−4.0	−3.8
Induced expenditure	4.4	4.1
Autonomous consumption	3.2	4.6
Investment	1.9	1.1
Government expenditure	1.8	1.9
Exports	3.8	2.5
Autonomous expenditure	10.7	10.1
GDP	15.1	14.2

Source of data: London & Cambridge Economic Service 1970.

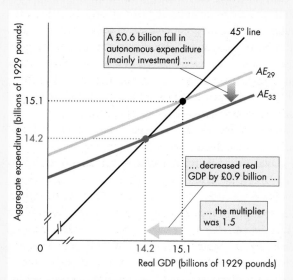

Figure 1 Aggregate Expenditure in the Great Depression

Business Cycle Turning Points

At business cycle turning points, the economy moves from expansion to recession or from recession to expansion. Economists understand these business cycle turning points the way seismologists understand earthquakes. They know quite a lot about the forces and mechanisms that produce them, but they can't predict them. The forces that bring business cycle turning points are the swings in investment and exports. The multiplier is the mechanism that gives momentum to the economy's new direction.

 REVIEW QUIZ

1 What is the multiplier? What does it determine? Why does it matter?
2 How do the marginal propensity to consume, the marginal propensity to import and the income tax rate influence the multiplier?
3 How do fluctuations in autonomous expenditure influence real GDP?

Do these questions in Study Plan 27.3 and get instant feedback. *MyEconLab*

The Multiplier and the Price Level

We have just considered adjustments in spending that occur in the very short run when the price level is fixed. In this time frame, the economy's potholes, which are changes in investment and exports, are not smoothed by shock absorbers like those on the car travelling along a country road. Instead, they are amplified like a rock singer's voice. But these outcomes occur only when the price level is fixed. We now investigate what happens after a long enough time lapse for the price level to change.

Adjusting Quantities and Prices

When firms can't keep up with sales and their inventories fall below target, they increase production, but at some point they raise their prices. Similarly, when firms find unwanted inventories piling up, they decrease production, but eventually they cut their prices.

So far, we've studied the macroeconomic consequences of firms changing their production levels when their sales change, but we've not looked at the effects of price changes. When individual firms change their prices, the economy's price level changes.

To study the simultaneous determination of real GDP and the price level, we use the *aggregate supply–aggregate demand model*, which is explained in Chapter 26. But to understand how aggregate demand adjusts, we need to work out the connection between the aggregate supply–aggregate demand model and the equilibrium expenditure model that we've used in this chapter. The key to understanding the relationship between these two models is the distinction between aggregate *expenditure* and aggregate *demand* and the related distinction between the *aggregate expenditure curve* and the *aggregate demand curve*.

Aggregate Expenditure and Aggregate Demand

The aggregate expenditure curve is the relationship between aggregate planned expenditure and real GDP, when all other influences on aggregate planned expenditure remain the same. The aggregate demand curve is the relationship between the aggregate quantity of goods and services demanded and the price level, when all other influences on aggregate demand remain the same. Let's explore the links between these two relationships.

Deriving the Aggregate Demand Curve

When the price level changes, aggregate planned expenditure changes and the quantity of real GDP demanded changes. The aggregate demand curve slopes downward. Why?

There are two main reasons:

◆ Wealth effect

◆ Substitution effects

Wealth Effect

Other things remaining the same, the higher the price level, the smaller is the purchasing power of people's real wealth. For example, suppose you have £100 in the bank and the price level is 105. If the price level rises to 125, your £100 will buy fewer goods and services. You are less wealthy. With less wealth, you will probably want to spend a bit less and save a bit more. The higher the price level, other things remaining the same, the higher is saving and the lower are consumption expenditure and aggregate planned expenditure.

Substitution Effects

For a given expected future price level, a rise in the price level today makes current goods and services more expensive relative to future goods and services, and results in a delay in purchases – an *intertemporal substitution*. A rise in the UK price level, other things remaining the same, makes UK-produced goods and services more expensive relative to foreign-produced goods and services. As a result, UK imports increase and UK exports decrease – an *international substitution*.

When the price level rises, each of these effects reduces aggregate planned expenditure at each level of real GDP. As a result, when the price level *rises*, the aggregate expenditure curve shifts *downward*. A fall in the price level has the opposite effect. When the price level *falls*, the aggregate expenditure curve shifts *upward*.

Figure 27.8(a) shows the shifts of the *AE* curve. When the price level is 105, the aggregate expenditure curve is AE_0, which intersects the 45° line at point *B*. Equilibrium expenditure is £1,500 billion. If the price level increases to 125, the aggregate expenditure curve shifts downward to AE_1, which intersects the 45° line at point *A*. Equilibrium expenditure decreases to £1,400 billion. If the price level decreases to 85, the aggregate expenditure curve shifts upward to AE_2, which intersects the 45° line at point C. Equilibrium expenditure increases to £1,600 billion.

We've just seen that when the price level changes, other things remaining the same, the aggregate expenditure curve shifts and the equilibrium expenditure changes. But when the price level changes, other things remaining the same, there is a movement along the aggregate demand curve.

Figure 27.8(b) shows the movements along the aggregate demand curve. At a price level of 105, the aggregate quantity of goods and services demanded is £1,500 billion – point B on the AD curve. If the price level rises to 125, the aggregate quantity of goods and services demanded decreases to £1,400 billion. There is a movement up along the aggregate demand curve to point A. If the price level falls to 85, the aggregate quantity of goods and services demanded increases to £1,600 billion. There is a movement down along the aggregate demand curve to point C.

Each point on the aggregate demand curve corresponds to a point of equilibrium expenditure. The equilibrium expenditure points A, B and C in Figure 27.8(a) correspond to the points A, B and C on the aggregate demand curve in Figure 27.8(b).

Changes in Aggregate Expenditure and Aggregate Demand

When any influence on aggregate planned expenditure other than the price level changes, both the aggregate expenditure curve and the aggregate demand curve shift. For example, an increase in investment or exports increases both aggregate planned expenditure and aggregate demand and shifts both the AE curve and the AD curve. Figure 27.9 illustrates the effect of such an increase.

Initially, the aggregate expenditure curve is AE_0 in part (a) and the aggregate demand curve is AD_0 in part (b). The price level is 105, real GDP is £1,500 billion and the economy is at point A in both parts of Figure 27.9.

Now suppose that investment increases by £100 billion. At a constant price level of 105, the aggregate expenditure curve shifts upward to AE_1. This curve intersects the 45° line at an equilibrium expenditure of £1,700 billion (point B). This equilibrium expenditure of £1,700 billion is the aggregate quantity of goods and services demanded at a price level of 105, as shown by point B in part (b). Point B lies on a new aggregate

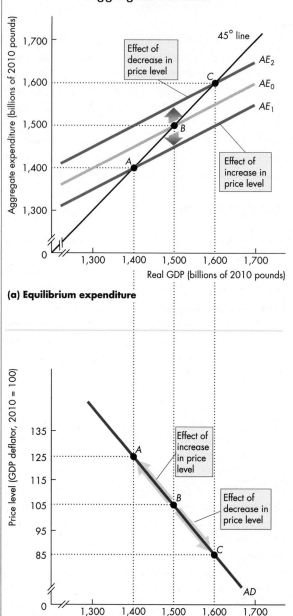

Figure 27.8 Equilibrium Expenditure and Aggregate Demand

(a) Equilibrium expenditure

(b) Aggregate demand

When the price level is 105, the AE curve is AE_0 and equilibrium expenditure is £1,500 billion at point B. When the price level rises to 125, the AE curve shifts downward to AE_1 and equilibrium expenditure is £1,400 billion at point A. When the price level falls to 85, the AE curve shifts upward to AE_2 and equilibrium expenditure is £1,600 billion at point C. Points A, B and C on the AD curve correspond to the equilibrium expenditure points A, B and C.

MyEconLab Animation ──────────────◆

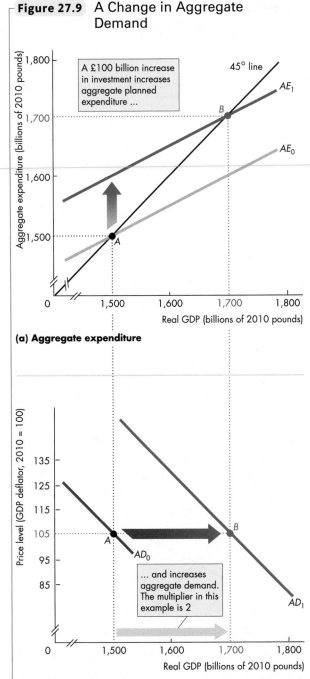

Figure 27.9 A Change in Aggregate Demand

(a) Aggregate expenditure

(b) Aggregate demand

The price level is 105. When the aggregate expenditure curve is AE_0 in part (a), the aggregate demand curve is AD_0 in part (b). An increase in autonomous expenditure shifts the AE curve upward to AE_1. In the new equilibrium, real GDP is £1,700 billion (at point B). Because the quantity of real GDP demanded at a price level of 105 increases to £1,700 billion, the AD curve shifts rightward to AD_1.

demand curve. The aggregate demand curve has shifted rightward to AD_1.

But how do we know by how much the AD curve shifts? The multiplier determines the answer. The larger the multiplier, the larger is the shift in the aggregate demand curve that results from a given change in autonomous expenditure. In this example, the multiplier is 2. A £100 billion increase in investment produces a £200 billion increase in the aggregate quantity of goods and services demanded at each price level. That is, a £100 billion increase in autonomous expenditure shifts the aggregate demand curve rightward by £200 billion.

A decrease in autonomous expenditure shifts the aggregate expenditure curve downward and shifts the aggregate demand curve leftward. You can see these effects by reversing the change that we've just described. If the economy is initially at point B on the aggregate expenditure curve AE_1 and on the aggregate demand curve AD_1, a decrease in autonomous expenditure shifts the aggregate expenditure curve downward to AE_0. The aggregate quantity of goods and services demanded decreases from £1,700 billion to £1,500 billion, and the aggregate demand curve shifts leftward to AD_0.

Let's summarise what we've just discovered:

> **If some factor other than a change in the price level increases autonomous expenditure, the AE curve shifts upward and the AD curve shifts rightward. The size of the AD curve shift equals the change in autonomous expenditure multiplied by the multiplier.**

Equilibrium Real GDP and the Price Level

In Chapter 26, we learned that aggregate demand and short-run aggregate supply determine equilibrium real GDP and the price level. We've now put aggregate demand under a more powerful microscope and have discovered that a change in investment (or in any component of autonomous expenditure) changes aggregate demand and shifts the aggregate demand curve. The magnitude of the shift depends on the multiplier.

But whether a change in autonomous expenditure results ultimately in a change in real GDP, a change in the price level, or a combination of the two depends on aggregate supply. There are two time frames to consider: the short run and the long run. First we'll see what happens in the short run.

An Increase in Aggregate Demand in the Short Run

Figure 27.10 describes the economy. In part (a), the aggregate expenditure curve is AE_0 and equilibrium expenditure is £1,500 billion – point A. In part (b), aggregate demand is AD_0 and the short-run aggregate supply curve is SAS. (Chapter 26, pp. 615–617 explains the SAS curve.) Equilibrium is at point A, where the aggregate demand and short-run aggregate supply curves intersect. The price level is 105 and real GDP is £1,500 billion.

Now suppose that investment increases by £100 billion. With the price level fixed at 105, the aggregate expenditure curve shifts upward to AE_1. Equilibrium expenditure increases to £1,700 billion – point B in part (a). In part (b), the aggregate demand curve shifts rightward by £200 billion, from AD_0 to AD_1. How far the AD curve shifts is determined by the multiplier when the price level is fixed.

But with this new AD curve, the price level does not remain fixed. The price level rises and, as it does so, the AE curve shifts downward. Short-run equilibrium occurs when the aggregate expenditure curve has shifted downward to AE_2 and the new aggregate demand curve, AD_1, intersects the short-run aggregate supply curve at point C. Real GDP is £1,630 billion and the price level is 118.

When the price level effects are taken into account, the increase in investment still has a multiplier effect on real GDP, but the multiplier effect is smaller than it would be if the price level were fixed. The steeper the slope of the SAS curve, the larger is the increase in the price level and the smaller is the multiplier effect on real GDP.

An Increase in Aggregate Demand in the Long Run

Figure 27.11 illustrates the effect of an increase in aggregate demand starting at full employment. Real GDP equals potential GDP, which is £1,500 billion. The long-run aggregate supply curve is LAS. Initially, the economy is at point A in part (a) and part (b).

Investment increases by £100 billion. The aggregate expenditure curve shifts upward to AE_1 and the aggregate demand curve shifts rightward to AD_1. With no change in the price level, the economy would move to point B and real GDP would increase to £1,700 billion. But in the short run, the price level rises to 118 and real GDP increases to £1,630 billion. With the higher price

Figure 27.10   The Multiplier in the Short Run

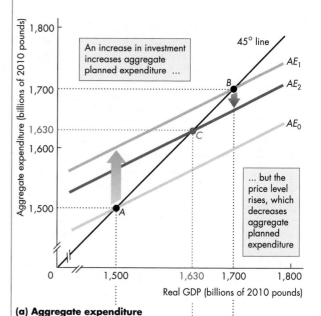

(a) Aggregate expenditure

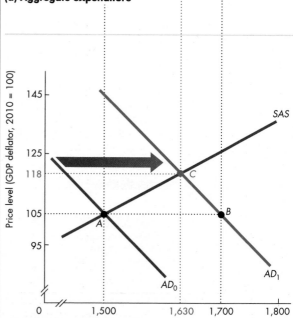

(b) Aggregate demand

An increase in investment shifts the AE curve from AE_0 to AE_1 in part (a) and shifts the AD curve from AD_0 to AD_1 in part (b). The price level does not remain at 105 but rises, and the higher price level shifts the AE curve downward from AE_1 to AE_2. The economy moves to point C. In the short run, when prices are flexible, the multiplier is smaller than when the price level is fixed.

MyEconLab Animation ⬥

Figure 27.11 The Multiplier in the Long Run

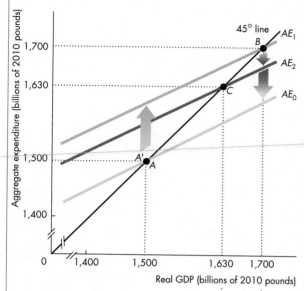

(a) Aggregate expenditure

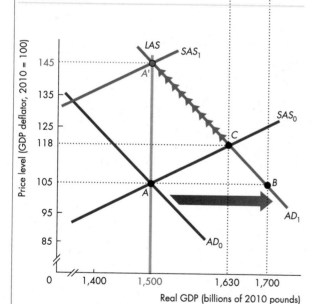

(b) Aggregate demand

Starting from point *A*, an increase in investment shifts the *AE* curve upward to AE_1 and shifts the *AD* curve rightward to AD_1. In the short run, the economy moves to point *C*. In the long run, the money wage rate rises, the *SAS* curve shifts to SAS_1, the price level rises, the *AE* curve shifts back to AE_0 and real GDP decreases. The economy moves to point *A'* and in the long run the multiplier is zero.

MyEconLab Animation ———————◆

level, the aggregate expenditure curve shifts from AE_1 to AE_2. The economy is now in a short-run equilibrium at point *C*.

But real GDP now exceeds potential GDP. The workforce is more than fully employed, and in the long run shortages of labour increase the money wage rate.

The higher money wage rate increases costs, which decreases short-run aggregate supply. The *SAS* curve begins to shift leftward towards SAS_1. The price level rises further and real GDP decreases. There is a movement along AD_1, and the *AE* curve shifts downward from AE_2 towards AE_0.

When the money wage rate and the price level have increased by the same percentage, real GDP again equals potential GDP and the economy is at point *A'*. In the long run, the multiplier is zero.

REVIEW QUIZ

1 How does a change in the price level influence the *AE* curve and the *AD* curve?

2 If autonomous expenditure increases with no change in the price level, what happens to the *AE* curve and the *AD* curve? Which curve shifts by an amount determined by the multiplier? Explain why.

3 How does an increase in autonomous expenditure change real GDP in the short run? Does real GDP change by the same amount as the change in aggregate demand? Why or why not?

4 How does real GDP change in the long run when autonomous expenditure increases? Does real GDP change by the same amount as the change in aggregate demand? Why or why not?

Do these questions in Study Plan 27.4 and get instant feedback. MyEconLab

You're now ready to build on what you've learned about aggregate expenditure fluctuations. We'll study the business cycle and the roles of fiscal policy and monetary policy in smoothing the cycle while achieving price stability and sustained economic growth. In Chapter 28 we study the UK business cycle and inflation, and in Chapters 29 and 30 we study fiscal policy and monetary policy, respectively. But before you leave the current topic, *Reading Between the Lines* on pp. 656–657 looks at the effects of expectations on consumption expenditure and investment in France.

France in Recession

Struggling France Strives to Shake off Economic Gloom

James Fontanella-Khan

Eric Hémar has a privileged bird's eye view of the French economy as he observes what kind of products enter and exit one of his many warehouses across the country.

'Mobiles are down, textiles are down, computers are down . . . in fact all the non-necessary stuff is down,' he says referring to the stockpiles of goods stored in his depots. 'Food is stable . . . the French are still eating but not more than usual.' . . .

France's biggest problem appears to be the generalised gloom infecting businesses and households.

. . . With household consumption of goods down 0.4 per cent in the first three months of this year, companies are also being forced to restrain their investment plans, chocking growth. According to the European Commission, corporate investment will continue to decline in 2013. . . .

Among Europeans, the French are the most pessimistic about the future, according to a poll conducted by the Pew Research Centre think-tank.

'Only 11 per cent of the French think their economy will improve over the next 12 months . . . and just 9 per cent think their children will be better off financially than their parents, by far the gloomiest forecast for the next generation,' Pew Research said. . . .

President Francois Hollande is under mounting pressure from business to revive French competitiveness through a series of tax cuts.

Pierre Gattaz, a French entrepreneur running to become the next head of Medef, the employers' federation, says that unless M. Hollande lowers corporate taxes and cuts social security spending – stated to be 469bn euro in 2013 – companies will be in no position to invest and create jobs.

The Essence of the Story

◆ The French economy is in a recession.

◆ Consumer spending and business investment have decreased.

◆ Pessimism and expectations of continued slow economic growth are holding back investment and consumer spending.

◆ French business leaders are calling for a cut in the rate of corporate tax to boost confidence and increase investment.

Economic Analysis

- France's real GDP was the same in 2012 as in 2011. But in the final quarter of 2012 and first quarter of 2013, real GDP decreased, putting France into a recession.

- Figure 1 shows the quarterly changes in real GDP in 2012 and the first quarter of 2013.

- Figure 2 shows the contributions of changes in consumption, investment and exports to the change in real GDP for the same five quarters.

- In the second quarter of 2012, a big fall in consumer spending lowered real GDP.

- French households decreased *autonomous* consumption expenditure and increased saving because they were pessimistic about future growth prospects and expected higher unemployment.

- In the fourth quarter of 2012 and first quarter of 2013, it was lower investment and exports that decreased real GDP.

- French businesses cut investment because they were pessimistic about being able to earn a profit. Exports fell because the rest of the EU was going into a recession.

- With a fall in autonomous expenditure, the *AE* curve shifted downward and a multiplier decreased real GDP by more than the fall in autonomous expenditure.

- Figure 3 shows the multiplier in the French economy in 2012–2013. In the first quarter of 2012, the *AE* curve was AE_0 and the equilibrium real GDP was €453 billion (2005 euros).

- In the first quarter of 2013, a fall in autonomous expenditure of €1.2 billion shifted the *AE* curve downward to AE_1. Equilibrium real GDP decreased by €2 billion to €451 billion.

- The tax cut called for by French business leaders would have shifted the *AE* curve upward and helped bring an expansion of real GDP.

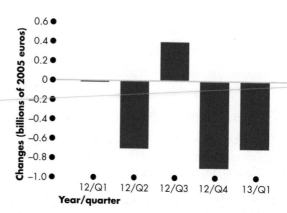

Figure 1 Changes in Real GDP

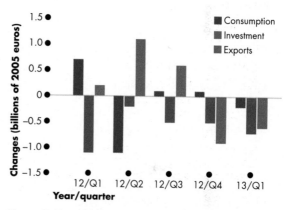

Figure 2 Changes in the Expenditure Items

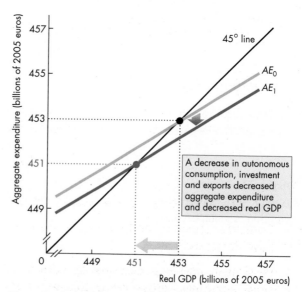

A decrease in autonomous consumption, investment and exports decreased aggregate expenditure and decreased real GDP

Figure 3 The Multiplier in France in 2012–2013

The Algebra of the Multiplier

This note explains the multiplier in greater detail. We begin by defining the symbols we need:

◆ Aggregate planned expenditure, AE

◆ Real GDP, Y

◆ Consumption expenditure, C

◆ Investment, I

◆ Government expenditure, G

◆ Exports, X

◆ Imports, M

◆ Net taxes, T

◆ Disposable income, YD

◆ Autonomous expenditure, A

◆ Autonomous consumption expenditure, a

◆ Autonomous taxes, T_a

◆ Marginal propensity to consume, b

◆ Marginal propensity to import, m

◆ Marginal tax rate, t

Aggregate Expenditure

Aggregate planned expenditure (AE) is the sum of planned consumption expenditure (C), investment (I), government expenditure (G) and exports (X) minus the planned amount of imports (M). That is:

$$AE = C + I + G + X - M$$

Consumption Function

Consumption expenditure (C) depends on disposable income (YD) and we write the consumption function as:

$$C = a + bYD$$

Disposable income (YD) equals real GDP minus net taxes ($Y - T$). So replacing YD with ($Y - T$), the consumption function becomes:

$$C = a + b(Y - T)$$

Net taxes equal autonomous taxes (that are independent of income), T_a, plus induced taxes (that vary with income), tY.

So we can write net taxes as

$$T = T_a + tY$$

Use this equation in the previous one to obtain:

$$C = a - bT_a + b(1 - t)Y$$

This equation describes consumption expenditure as a function of real GDP.

Import Function

Imports depend on real GDP and the import function is:

$$M = mY$$

Aggregate Expenditure Curve

Use the consumption function and the import function to replace C and M in the aggregate planned expenditure equation. That is:

$$AE = a - bT_a + b(1 - t)Y + I + G + X - mY$$

Collect the terms on the right-side of the equation that involve Y to obtain:

$$AE = [a - bT_a + I + G + X] + [b(1 - t) - m]Y$$

Autonomous expenditure (A) is $[a - bT_a + I + G + X]$ and the slope of the AE curve is $[b(1 - t) - m]$. So the equation for the AE curve, which is shown in Figure 1, is:

$$AE = A + [b(1 - t) - m]Y$$

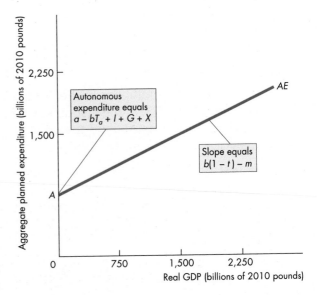

Figure 1 The AE Curve

Equilibrium Expenditure

Equilibrium expenditure occurs when aggregate planned expenditure (*AE*) equals real GDP (*Y*). That is:

$$AE = Y$$

In Figure 2, the scales of the *x*-axis (real GDP) and the *y*-axis (aggregate planned expenditure) are identical, so the 45° line shows the points at which aggregate planned expenditure equals real GDP. That is, along the 45° line, *AE* equals *Y*.

Figure 2 shows the point of equilibrium expenditure at the intersection of the *AE* curve and the 45° line.

To calculate equilibrium expenditure and real GDP, we solve the equations for the *AE* curve and the 45° line for the two unknown quantities *AE* and *Y*. So, starting with:

$$AE = A + [b(1 - t) - m]Y$$

$$AE = Y$$

replace *AE* with *Y* in the *AE* equation to obtain:

$$Y = A + [b(1 - t) - m]Y$$

The solution for *Y* is:

$$Y = \frac{1}{1 - [b(1 - t) - m]} A$$

The Multiplier

The *multiplier* equals the change in equilibrium expenditure and real GDP (*Y*) that results from a change in autonomous expenditure (*A*) divided by the change in autonomous expenditure. A change in autonomous expenditure (Δ*A*) changes equilibrium expenditure and real GDP (Δ*Y*) by:

$$\Delta Y = \frac{1}{1 - [b(1 - t) - m]} \Delta A$$

$$\text{Multiplier} = \frac{1}{1 - [b(1 - t) - m]}$$

The size of the multiplier depends on the slope of the *AE* curve, and the larger the slope, the larger is the multiplier. So the multiplier is larger:

1   The greater the marginal propensity to consume (*b*)

2   The smaller the marginal tax rate (*t*)

3   The smaller the marginal propensity to import (*m*)

An economy with no imports and no marginal taxes has *m* = 0 and *t* = 0. In this special case, the multiplier equals 1/(1 − *b*). If *b* is 0.75, the multiplier is 4, as shown in Figure 3.

In an economy with *b* = 0.75, *t* = 0.2 and *m* = 0.1, the multiplier is 1/[1 − 0.75(1 − 0.2) + 0.1], which equals 2.

Make up some more examples to show the effects of different values of *b*, *t* and *m* on the multiplier.

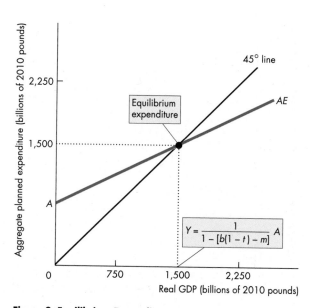

Figure 2 Equilibrium Expenditure

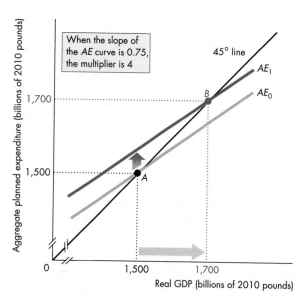

Figure 3 The Multiplier

Government Expenditure Multiplier

The **government expenditure multiplier** equals the change in equilibrium real GDP (Y) that results from a change in government expenditure (G) divided by the change in government expenditure. Because autonomous expenditure is equal to

$$A = a - bT_a + I + G + X$$

the change in autonomous expenditure equals the change in government expenditure. That is,

$$\Delta A = \Delta G$$

You can see from the solution for equilibrium expenditure Y that

$$\Delta Y = \frac{1}{1 - [b(1 - t) - m]} \Delta G$$

The government expenditure multiplier equals

$$\frac{1}{1 - [b(1 - t) - m]}$$

In an economy in which $t = 0$ and $m = 0$, the government expenditure multiplier is $1/(1 - b)$. With $b = 0.75$, the government expenditure multiplier is 4, as Figure 4 shows.

Make up some examples and use the above formula to show how b, m and t influence the government expenditure multiplier.

Autonomous Tax Multiplier

The **autonomous tax multiplier** equals the change in equilibrium expenditure (Y) that results from a change in autonomous taxes (T_a) divided by the change in autonomous taxes. Because autonomous expenditure is equal to

$$A = a - bT_a + I + G + X$$

the change in autonomous expenditure equals $-b$ multiplied by the change in autonomous taxes. That is,

$$\Delta A = -b\Delta T_a$$

You can see from the solution for equilibrium expenditure Y that

$$\Delta Y = \frac{-b}{1 - [b(1 - t) - m]} \Delta T_a$$

The autonomous tax multiplier equals

$$\frac{-b}{1 - [b(1 - t) - m]}$$

In an economy in which $t = 0$ and $m = 0$, the autonomous tax multiplier is $-b/(1 - b)$. In this special case, with $b = 0.75$, the autonomous tax multiplier equals -3, as Figure 5 shows.

Make up some examples and use the above formula to show how b, m and t influence the autonomous tax multiplier.

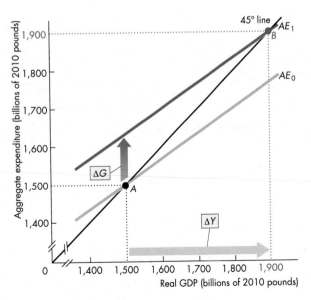

Figure 4   Government Expenditure Multiplier

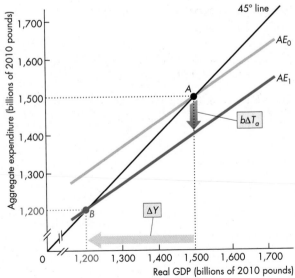

Figure 5   Autonomous Tax Multiplier

Balanced Budget Multiplier

The **balanced budget multiplier** equals the change in equilibrium expenditure (Y) that results from equal changes in government expenditure and autonomous taxes divided by the change in government expenditure. Because government expenditure and autonomous taxes change by the same amount, the budget balance does not change.

The change in equilibrium expenditure that results from the change in government expenditure is

$$\Delta Y = \frac{1}{1 - [b(1 - t) - m]} \Delta G$$

And the change in equilibrium expenditure that results from the change in autonomous taxes is

$$\Delta Y = \frac{-b}{1 - [b(1 - t) - m]} \Delta T_a$$

So the change in equilibrium expenditure resulting from the changes in government expenditure and autonomous taxes is

$$\Delta Y = \frac{1}{1 - [b(1 - t) - m]} \Delta G$$

$$+ \frac{-b}{1 - [b(1 - t) - m]} \Delta T_a$$

Notice that

$$\frac{1}{1 - [b(1 - t) - m]}$$

is common to both terms on the right side. So we can rewrite the equation as

$$\Delta Y = \frac{-b}{1 - [b(1 - t) - m]} (\Delta G - \Delta T_a)$$

The AE curve shifts upward by $\Delta G - b\Delta T_a$, as shown in Figure 6.

But the change in government expenditure equals the change in autonomous taxes. That is,

$$\Delta G = \Delta T_a$$

So we can write the equation as

$$\Delta Y = \frac{1 - b}{1 - [b(1 - t) - m]} \Delta G$$

The balanced budget multiplier equals

$$\frac{1 - b}{1 - [b(1 - t) - m]}$$

In an economy in which $t = 0$ and $m = 0$, the balanced budget multiplier is $(1 - b)/(1 - b)$, which equals 1, as Figure 6 shows.

Make up some examples and use the above formula to show how b, m and t influence the balanced budget multiplier.

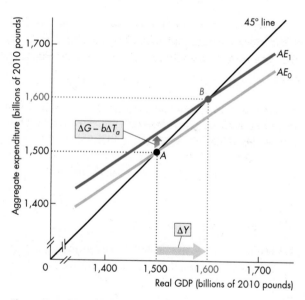

Figure 6 Balanced Budget Multiplier

SUMMARY

Key Points

Fixed Prices and Expenditure Plans

(pp. 638–641)

◆ When the price level is fixed, expenditure plans determine real GDP.

◆ Consumption expenditure is determined by disposable income, and the marginal propensity to consume (*MPC*) determines the change in consumption expenditure brought about by a change in disposable income. Real GDP is the main influence on disposable income.

◆ Imports are determined by real GDP, and the marginal propensity to import determines the change in imports brought about by a change in real GDP.

Do Problems 1 to 3 to get a better understanding of fixed prices and expenditure plans.

Real GDP with a Fixed Price Level

(pp. 642–645)

◆ Aggregate *planned* expenditure depends on real GDP.

◆ Equilibrium expenditure occurs when aggregate planned expenditure equals actual expenditure and real GDP.

Do Problems 4 to 7 to get a better understanding of real GDP with a fixed price level.

The Multiplier (pp. 646–650)

◆ The multiplier is the magnified effect of a change in autonomous expenditure on equilibrium expenditure and real GDP.

◆ The multiplier is determined by the slope of the *AE* curve.

◆ The slope of the *AE* curve is influenced by the marginal propensity to consume, the marginal propensity to import and the income tax rate.

Do Problems 8 to 11 to get a better understanding of the multiplier.

The Multiplier and the Price Level

(pp. 651–655)

◆ The aggregate demand curve is the relationship between the quantity of real GDP demanded and the price level, other things remaining the same.

◆ The aggregate expenditure curve is the relationship between aggregate planned expenditure and real GDP, other things remaining the same.

◆ At a given price level, there is a given aggregate expenditure curve. A change in the price level changes aggregate planned expenditure and shifts the aggregate expenditure curve. A change in the price level also creates a movement along the aggregate demand curve.

◆ A change in autonomous expenditure that is not caused by a change in the price level shifts the aggregate expenditure curve and shifts the aggregate demand curve. The magnitude of the shift of the aggregate demand curve depends on the multiplier and the change in autonomous expenditure.

◆ The multiplier decreases as the price level changes. The multiplier in the long run is zero.

Do Problems 12 to 24 to get a better understanding of the multiplier and the price level.

Key Terms

Aggregate planned expenditure, 638
Autonomous expenditure, 642
Autonomous tax multiplier, 660
Balanced budget multiplier, 661
Consumption function, 638
Disposable income, 638
Equilibrium expenditure, 644
Government expenditure multiplier, 660
Induced expenditure, 642
Marginal propensity to consume, 640
Marginal propensity to import, 641
Marginal propensity to save, 640
Multiplier, 646
Saving function, 638

STUDY PLAN PROBLEMS AND APPLICATIONS

Do Problems 1 to 25 in MyEconLab Chapter 27 Study Plan and get instant feedback.   MyEconLab

Fixed Prices and Expenditure Plans

(Study Plan 27.1)

Use the following data in Problems 1 and 2.

You are given the following information about the US economy.

Disposable income	Consumption expenditure
(trillions of dollars per year)	
3	3.4
4	4.2
5	5.0
6	5.8
7	6.6

1 Calculate the marginal propensity to consume.

2 Calculate saving at each level of disposable income and calculate the marginal propensity to save.

3 Collapsing Saving Rate

Before 1984, the US saving rate held steady for decades, though it dipped during the Great Depression and rose sharply during WWII, when there was little to buy besides war bonds. The rate dipped briefly again after WWII, and then rose steadily until 1984, when saving was 10.2 per cent of income. Since 1984, saving has fallen to between 2 per cent and 3 per cent of income.

Source: *Deseret*, 18 August 2012

Compare the *MPC* and *MPS* in the US at different dates. Why might they differ?

Real GDP with a Fixed Price Level

(Study Plan 27.2)

Use the figure in the next column in Problems 4 and 5.

The figure illustrates the components of aggregate planned expenditure on Turtle Island. Turtle Island has no imports or exports, no income taxes and the price level is fixed.

4 Calculate autonomous expenditure and the marginal propensity to consume.

5 a What is aggregate planned expenditure when real GDP is €6 billion?

   b If real GDP is €4 billion, what is happening to inventories?

   c If real GDP is €6 billion, what is happening to inventories?

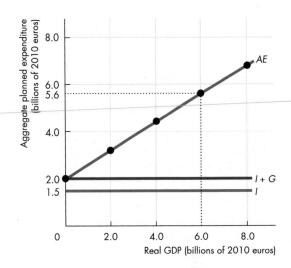

6 Explain the difference between induced consumption expenditure and autonomous consumption expenditure. Why isn't all consumption expenditure induced expenditure?

7 US Recovery?

In the second quarter, US businesses increased spending on equipment and software by 21.9 per cent, while a category that includes home building grew amid a rush by consumers to take advantage of tax credits for homes.

Source: *The Wall Street Journal*, 31 July 2010

Explain how an increase in business investment at a constant price level changes equilibrium expenditure.

The Multiplier (Study Plan 27.3)

Use the following data in Problems 8 and 9.

An economy has a fixed price level, no imports and no income taxes. *MPC* is 0.80 and real GDP is £150 billion. Businesses increase investment by £5 billion.

8 Calculate the multiplier and the change in real GDP.

9 Calculate the new real GDP and explain why real GDP increases by more than £5 billion.

Use the following data in Problems 10 and 11.

An economy has no imports and no income taxes. An increase in autonomous expenditure of £200 billion increases equilibrium expenditure by £800 billion.

10 Calculate the multiplier and the marginal propensity to consume.

11 What happens to the multiplier if an income tax is introduced?

The Multiplier and the Price Level

(Study Plan 27.4)

Use the following data in Problems 12 to 16.

Suppose that the economy is at full employment, the price level is 100 and the multiplier is 2. Investment increases by £100 billion.

12 What is the change in equilibrium expenditure if the price level remains at 100?

13 a What is the immediate change in the quantity of real GDP demanded?

b In the short run, does real GDP increase by more than, less than or the same amount as the immediate change in the quantity of real GDP demanded?

14 In the short run, does the price level remain at 100? Explain why or why not.

15 a In the long run, does real GDP increase by more than, less than or the same amount as the immediate increase in the quantity of real GDP demanded?

b Explain how the price level changes in the long run.

16 Are the values of the multipliers in the short run and the long run larger or smaller than 2?

Use the following news clip in Problems 17 and 18.

Vladimir Putin Unveils $14bn Plan to Revive Russian Economy

Russia will spend billions of dollars on investment in infrastructure as a means of countering a slowing economy. Roads and high speed rail including the trans-Siberian express figure in the increase in government investment.

Source: *The Financial Times*, 21 June 2013

17 Will a $1 billion increase in Russian investment increase aggregate expenditure in Russia by more than, less than or exactly $1 billion? Explain.

18 Explain and draw a graph to illustrate how an increase in investment will influence aggregate expenditure and aggregate demand in both the short run and the long run.

Use the following news clip in Problems 19 to 21.

Consumer Growth Could Buoy China's Economy

Annual double-digit wage growth since 2000 has created a Chinese middle class ready to spend. And spend they have. Spending by China's consumers has grown at double-digit rates for a decade. Digital Luxury Group, a Geneva-based market researcher, reports that Chinese travellers made 70 million overseas trips in 2011 to places that include Bali, Dubai, Paris, London, Singapore and Hong Kong. To cope with all this extra travel, China plans to build 56 new airports before the end of 2016. China's wealthy consumers in aggregate are poised to spend more on luxury goods than consumers in Japan and the United States.

Source: *The New York Times*, 13 August 2012

19 Explain and draw a graph to illustrate the changes in autonomous expenditure and induced expenditure and the multiplier process at work in the news clip.

20 Explain how China's real GDP is influenced by an increase in overseas travel and vacations.

21 Explain how China's consumption expenditure influences real GDP in the countries to which Chinese tourists travel in the short run and the long run.

Use the following news clip in Problems 22 to 24.

Weak Exports Hinder Recovery

With the pound weakening, UK exports should be booming. Why has this not happened as predicted by standard economic theory? Danny Gabay from Fathom economic consultancy says that almost half of British exports go the EU. 'No matter what the price it is hard to sell to a customer that has shut up shop.' Also, one of Britain's most successful exports, its banking services, is in low demand.

Source: *The Financial Times*, 21 August 2013

22 Explain and draw a graph to illustrate the process by which a fall in exports results in a fall in real GDP demanded.

23 Explain and draw a graph to illustrate how real GDP will be driven back to potential GDP in the long run.

24 Explain why the multiplier is only a short-run influence on real GDP.

Mathematical Note (Study Plan 27.MN)

25 You are given the following information about an economy: autonomous consumption expenditure is €50 billion, investment is €200 billion and government expenditure is €250 billion. The marginal propensity to consume is 0.7 and net taxes are €250 billion. Exports are €500 billion and imports are €450 billion. Assume that net taxes and imports are autonomous and the price level is fixed.

a What is the consumption function?

b What is the equation of the *AE* curve?

c Calculate equilibrium expenditure.

d Calculate the multiplier.

e If investment decreases to €150 billion, what is the change in equilibrium expenditure?

f Describe the process in part (e) that moves the economy to its new equilibrium expenditure.

ADDITIONAL PROBLEMS AND APPLICATIONS

Do these problems in MyEconLab if assigned by your lecturer.

MyEconLab

Fixed Prices and Expenditure Plans

Use the following data about the economy of Australia in Problems 26 and 27.

Disposable income	Saving
(billions of dollars per year)	
0	–5
100	20
200	45
300	70
400	95

26 Calculate the marginal propensity to save.

27 Calculate consumption at each level of disposable income. Calculate the marginal propensity to consume.

Use the following news clip in Problems 28 to 30.

Rising Household Wealth Hides Widening Wealth Gap

UK household wealth increased from £4.34 trillion in 2003 to £7.05 trillion in 2012, a 62 per cent increase. During the same period, the CPI rose 29 per cent. Average household wealth in 2012 was £255,000, but the wealth gap between the rich and poor has increased. The richest 10 per cent had 22 times more wealth than the poorest 50 per cent. Consumer spending increased in 2012 at the time of the London Olympics.

Source: *The Independent*, 8 April 2013

Additional information: between 2003 and 2012, real consumption expenditure increased by 7 per cent and real disposable income increased by 9 per cent.

28 How did the consumption function and saving function change between 2003 and 2012? Draw graphs to illustrate the changes.

29 How would the change in real wealth be expected to influence the consumption function and saving function between 2003 and 2012? Draw graphs to illustrate the changes.

30 Explain and reconcile the actual and predicted changes in the consumption function and saving function between 2003 and 2012.

Real GDP with a Fixed Price Level

Use the following spreadsheet in Problems 31 and 32.

	A	B	C	D	E	F	G
1		Y	C	I	G	X	M
2	A	100	110	50	60	60	15
3	B	200	170	50	60	60	30
4	C	300	230	50	60	60	45
5	D	400	290	50	60	60	60
6	E	500	350	50	60	60	75
7	F	600	410	50	60	60	90

The spreadsheet lists real GDP (*Y*) and the components of aggregate planned expenditure in billions of pounds.

31 Calculate autonomous expenditure and the marginal propensity to consume.

32 a What is aggregate planned expenditure when real GDP is £200 billion?

b If real GDP is £200 billion, explain the process that moves the economy towards equilibrium expenditure.

c If real GDP is £500 billion, explain the process that moves the economy towards equilibrium expenditure.

33 UK Recovery Fears Remain Despite Growth

Second quarter 2010 growth of the UK economy was at the fastest pace in 11 years. Despite this momentum, doubts remain over whether a strong recovery can be sustained. The two key components of demand that grew fastest were consumption expenditure and inventory investment. Inventory investment added 1 percentage point to growth and is at its highest since 1994.

With the effect of inventory investment likely to be short-lived and no other sources of stimulus, growth may slow.

Source: *The Financial Times*, 28 August 2010

Explain why a rise in inventories is associated with recovery and why the contribution of inventory investment to aggregate expenditure is likely to be short-lived.

The Multiplier

34 EU Leaders Eye Balanced Budget Pact

EU leaders meeting Monday in Brussels are expected to agree on a balanced budget pact amid persistent concern over the Greek economy.

Source: france24.com, 30 January 2012

If the government decision is to increase taxes and cut government expenditure by equal amounts, which of the two actions would have the larger effect on equilibrium expenditure if the price level remained the same?

35 Cameron Bets On Northern Recipe For Growth

David Cameron has claimed that his 'northern alliance' with Nordic and Baltic states will become a driving force in 'the greenest region in the world' and 'avant-garde in delivering jobs and growth'. Mr Cameron announced that energy ministers would work on plans for an 'electricity super grid' to take green energy from one country to another and from offshore wind farms through sub-sea cables.

Source: *The Financial Times*, 21 January 2011

If the UK along with the Nordic and Baltic states spent £100 billion on green energy projects, how would equilibrium expenditure change if the price level remained unchanged?

The Multiplier and the Price Level

36 Stimulating Debate

Should the government hire people to bury banknotes down disused mineshafts, so that private firms can hire yet more people to dig them up again? Keynes said that there are circumstances in which government spending as wasteful as this could nevertheless be beneficial.

Source: *The Financial Times*, 30 October 2010

Explain and draw a graph to illustrate the effect of the activities described in the news clip on equilibrium expenditure, real GDP and the price level and contrast the outcomes for (a) an economy with considerable unemployment and (b) an economy that is close to full employment.

Use the following news clip in Problems 37 to 39.

Where Americans Will (and Won't) Cut Back

As consumer confidence tumbled consumers have cut back on spending, but not all spending. Americans are reluctant to give up on everyday pleasures, but many are forced to prioritise and scale back some of their spending. Spending on dining out, out-of-the-home entertainment, clothes, vacations and buying lunch tend to be the first to be cut and many Americans are driving less and staying at home more. A whopping 50 per cent of Americans plan to buy an HD or flat-panel TV in the next year. Cable and satellite TV subscriptions are also way down the list on cutbacks. Despite the expense, another thing consumers refuse to go without completely is travel. Even in these tough times, 59 per cent of Americans plan to take a trip in the next six months.

Source: CNN, 16 July 2008

37 Which of the expenditures listed in the news clip are part of induced consumption expenditure and which are part of autonomous consumption expenditure? Explain why not all consumption expenditure is induced expenditure.

38 Explain and draw a graph to illustrate how declining consumer confidence influences aggregate expenditure and aggregate demand in the short run.

39 Explain and draw a graph to illustrate the long-run effect on aggregate expenditure and aggregate demand of the decline in consumer confidence.

Economics in the News

40 After you have studied *Reading Between the Lines* on pp. 656–657, answer the following questions.

 a What happened to GDP growth in France in the fourth quarter of 2012?

 b Which components of GDP contributed most to the growth outcome in the fourth quarter of 2012?

 c What happened to GDP growth in France in the first quarter of 2013?

 d Which components of GDP contributed most to the growth outcome in the first quarter of 2013?

 e What is the explanation in the article for the downturn in the French economy?

 f What 'other things' could have happened in the French economy that might have led to a different outcome?

41 The Biggest Risk to Growth

The biggest risk to growth in the UK is that the economies of its trading partners suffer badly, slowing demand for UK exports.

Source: *The Financial Times*, 11 November 2010

 a Does the decrease in UK exports bring a movement along the *AE* curve or a shift of the *AE* curve?

 b Suppose that UK exports decrease by £120 billion in 2011 and the multiplier is 1.5. If other things remain the same, what is the decrease in real GDP?

 c Suppose that the UK economy is at full employment in 2011 and exports increase by £120 billion. Will there still be a multiplier effect?

Mathematical Note

42 In an economy, autonomous spending is £20 billion and the slope of the *AE* curve is 0.6.

 a What is the equation of the *AE* curve?

 b Calculate equilibrium expenditure.

 c Calculate the multiplier if the price level is fixed.

28 Inflation and Output Cycles

After studying this chapter you will be able to:

- ◆ Explain how demand-pull and cost-push forces bring cycles in inflation and output
- ◆ Explain the short-run trade-off between inflation and unemployment
- ◆ Explain the mainstream business cycle theory and real business cycle theory

We care about inflation because it raises our cost of living. And we care about unemployment because it takes our jobs. We want low inflation, low unemployment and rapid income growth. But can we have all these things at the same time? Or do we face a trade-off among them? As this chapter explains, we face a trade-off in the short run but not in the long run.

At the end of the chapter, in *Reading Between the Lines*, you'll see how the UK short-run trade-off has been changing in the past few years.

Inflation Cycles

In the long run, inflation is a monetary phenomenon. It occurs if the quantity of money grows faster than potential GDP. But in the short run, many factors can start an inflation, and real GDP and the price level interact. To study these interactions, we distinguish between two sources of inflation:

◆ Demand-pull inflation
◆ Cost-push inflation

Demand-Pull Inflation

An inflation that results from an initial increase in aggregate demand is called **demand-pull inflation**. Demand-pull inflation can be kicked off by any of the factors that change aggregate demand. Examples are a cut in the interest rate, an increase in the quantity of money, an increase in government expenditure, a tax cut, an increase in exports or an increase in investment stimulated by an increase in expected future profits.

Initial Effect of an Increase in Aggregate Demand

Suppose that last year the price level was 105 and both real GDP and potential GDP were £1,500 billion. Figure 28.1(a) illustrates this situation. The aggregate demand curve is AD_0, the short-run aggregate supply curve is SAS_0 and the long-run aggregate supply curve is LAS.

Now aggregate demand increases and the aggregate demand curve shifts rightward to AD_1. Such a situation arises if, for example, the Bank of England lowers the interest rate or exports increase.

With no change in potential GDP and with no change in the money wage rate, the long-run aggregate supply curve and the short-run aggregate supply curve remain at LAS and SAS_0, respectively.

The price level rises to 108 and real GDP increases above potential GDP to £1,550 billion. The economy experiences a 2.9 per cent rise in the price level (a price level of 108 compared with 105 in the previous year) and a rapid expansion of real GDP. Unemployment falls below its natural rate. The next step in the unfolding story is a rise in the money wage rate.

Figure 28.1 A Demand-Pull Rise in the Price Level

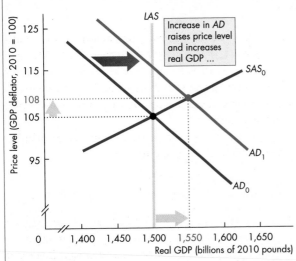

(a) Initial effect

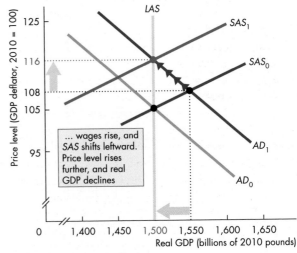

(b) The money wage adjusts

In part (a), the aggregate demand curve is AD_0, the short-run aggregate supply curve is SAS_0 and the long-run aggregate supply curve is LAS. The price level is 105 and real GDP is £1,500 billion, which equals potential GDP. Aggregate demand increases to AD_1. The price level rises to 108 and real GDP increases to £1,550 billion.

In part (b), starting from above full employment, the money wage rate begins to rise and the short-run aggregate supply curve shifts leftward towards SAS_1. The price level rises further and real GDP returns to potential GDP.

MyEconLab Animation ──────────────────────────────── ◆

Money Wage Response

Real GDP cannot remain above potential GDP for ever. With unemployment below its natural rate, there is a shortage of labour. In this situation, the money wage rate begins to rise. As the money wage rate rises, short-run aggregate supply starts to decrease and the *SAS* curve starts to shift leftward. The price level rises further and real GDP begins to decrease.

With no further change in aggregate demand – the aggregate demand curve remains at AD_1 – this process comes to an end when the short-run aggregate supply curve has shifted to SAS_1 in Figure 28.1(b). At this time, the price level has increased to 116 and real GDP has returned to potential GDP of £1,500 billion, the level from which it started.

A Demand-Pull Inflation Process

The events that we've just studied bring *a one-time rise in the price level*, not inflation. For inflation to occur, aggregate demand must persistently increase.

The only way in which aggregate demand can persistently increase is if the quantity of money persistently increases. Suppose the government has a budget deficit that it finances by selling bonds. Also suppose that the Bank of England buys these bonds. When the Bank of England buys bonds, it creates more money. If the Bank of England responds continually to the budget deficit, aggregate demand increases year after year. The aggregate demand curve keeps shifting rightward. This persistent increase in aggregate demand puts continual upward pressure on the price level. The economy now experiences demand-pull inflation.

Figure 28.2 illustrates the process of demand-pull inflation. The starting point is the same as that shown in Figure 28.1. The aggregate demand curve is AD_0 and the short-run aggregate supply curve is SAS_0. Real GDP is £1,500 billion and the price level is 105. Aggregate demand increases, shifting the aggregate demand curve to AD_1. Real GDP increases to £1,550 billion and the price level rises to 108. The economy is at an above full-employment equilibrium. There is a shortage of labour and the money wage rate rises. The short-run aggregate supply curve shifts leftward to SAS_1. The price level rises to 116 and real GDP returns to potential GDP.

But the Bank of England increases the quantity of money again and aggregate demand continues to increase. The aggregate demand curve shifts rightward to AD_2. The price level rises further to 120 and real GDP again exceeds potential GDP at £1,550 billion. Yet

Figure 28.2 A Demand-Pull Inflation Spiral

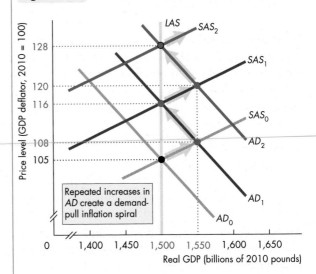

Each time the quantity of money increases, aggregate demand increases and the aggregate demand curve shifts rightward from AD_0 to AD_1 to AD_2 and so on.

Each time real GDP goes above potential GDP, the money wage rate rises and the short-run aggregate supply curve shifts leftward from SAS_0 to SAS_1 to SAS_2 and so on.

The price level rises from 105 to 108, 116, 120, 128 and so on. There is a perpetual demand-pull inflation. Real GDP fluctuates between £1,500 billion and £1,550 billion.

MyEconLab Animation ────────────────◆

again, the money wage rate rises and decreases short-run aggregate supply. The *SAS* curve shifts to SAS_2 and the price level rises further to 128. As the quantity of money continues to grow, aggregate demand increases and the price level rises in an ongoing demand-pull inflation process.

The process you have just studied generates inflation – a persistently rising price level.

Demand-Pull Inflation in Liverpool

You may better understand the inflation process that we've just described by considering what is going on in an individual part of the economy, such as a Liverpool soft drinks factory.

Initial Increase in Demand

Initially, when aggregate demand increases, the demand for soft drinks increases and the price of soft drinks rises. Faced with a higher price, the soft drinks factory works overtime and increases production. Conditions are good for workers in Liverpool, and the soft drinks factory finds it hard to hang on to its best people. To do so it has to offer higher money wages. As money wages increase, so do the soft drinks factory's costs.

Aggregate Demand

What happens next depends on what happens to aggregate demand. If aggregate demand remains unchanged, the firm's costs are increasing, but the price of soft drinks is not increasing as quickly as the factory's costs. Production is scaled back. Eventually, the money wage rate and costs increase by the same percentage as the price of soft drinks. In real terms, the soft drinks factory is in the same situation as it was initially – before the increase in aggregate demand. The soft drinks factory produces the same quantity of soft drinks and employs the same amount of labour as before the increase in aggregate demand.

But if aggregate demand continues to increase, so does the demand for soft drinks, and the price of lemonade rises at the same rate as the money wage rate. The soft drinks factory continues to operate above full employment and there is a persistent shortage of labour. Prices and wages chase each other upward in an unending spiral.

Demand-Pull Inflation in the UK

A demand-pull inflation like the one you've just studied occurred in the UK during the 1970s.

In 1972–1973, the government pursued an expansionary monetary and fiscal policy. Its goal was to lower the unemployment rate and boost the rate of economic growth. The aggregate demand curve shifted rightward, the price level increased quickly and real GDP moved above potential GDP. The money wage rate started to rise more quickly and the short-run aggregate supply curve shifted leftward.

The Bank of England responded with a further increase in the growth rate of the quantity of money. Aggregate demand increased even more quickly and a demand-pull inflation spiral unfolded.

By the mid-1970s, the inflation rate had reached more than 20 per cent a year. Contrary to the government's goal, the growth rate of real GDP didn't increase and the unemployment rate didn't decrease. On the contrary, the late 1970s were years of extremely high unemployment and slow real GDP growth.

You've seen how demand-pull inflation arises. Let's now see how an aggregate supply shock brings cost-push inflation.

Cost-Push Inflation

An inflation that is kicked off by an increase in costs is called **cost-push inflation**. The two main sources of increases in costs are:

1 An increase in the money wage rate
2 An increase in the money prices of raw materials

At a given price level, the higher the cost of production, the smaller is the amount that firms are willing to produce. So if the money wage rate rises or if the prices of raw materials (for example, oil) rise, firms decrease their supply of goods and services. Aggregate supply decreases, and the short-run aggregate supply curve shifts leftward.[1]

Let's trace the effects of such a decrease in short-run aggregate supply on the price level and real GDP.

Initial Effect of a Decrease in Aggregate Supply

Suppose that last year the price level was 105 and real GDP was £1,500 billion. Potential real GDP was also £1,500 billion. Figure 28.3(a) illustrates this situation. The aggregate demand curve was AD_0, the short-run aggregate supply curve was SAS_0 and the long-run aggregate supply curve was LAS.

Now the world's oil producers form a price-fixing organisation that strengthens their market power and increases the relative price of oil. They raise the price of oil, and this action decreases short-run aggregate supply. The short-run aggregate supply curve shifts leftward to SAS_1. The price level rises to 112 and real GDP decreases to £1,450 billion. The economy is at a below full-employment equilibrium and there is a recessionary gap.

The event that we've just described is a *one-time rise in the price level*. It is not inflation. In fact, a supply shock on its own cannot cause inflation. Something more must happen to enable a one-time supply shock, which causes a one-time rise in the price level, to be converted into a process of ongoing inflation. The quantity of money must persistently increase. Sometimes it does increase, as you'll now see.

---

[1] Some cost-push forces, such as an increase in the price of oil accompanied by a decrease in the availability of oil, can also decrease long-run aggregate supply. We'll ignore such effects here and examine cost-push factors that change only short-run aggregate supply.

Figure 28.3 A Cost-Push Rise in the Price Level

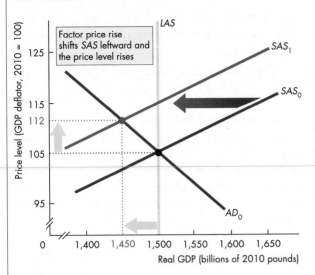

(a) Initial cost push

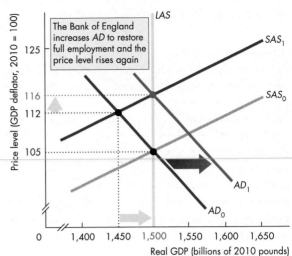

(b) The Bank of England responds

Initially, the aggregate demand curve is AD_0, the short-run aggregate supply curve is SAS_0 and the long-run aggregate supply curve is LAS. A decrease in aggregate supply shifts the short-run aggregate supply curve to SAS_1. The price level rises to 112 and real GDP decreases to £1,450 billion. The economy experiences a one-time rise in the price level.

In part (b), if the Bank responds by increasing aggregate demand to restore full employment, the aggregate demand curve shifts rightward to AD_1. The economy returns to full employment but the price level rises further to 116.

MyEconLab Animation ———————————————————————————◆

Aggregate Demand Response

When real GDP decreases, unemployment rises above its natural rate. In such a situation, there is often an outcry of concern and a call for action to restore full employment. Suppose that the Bank of England cuts the interest rate and increases the quantity of money. Aggregate demand increases. In Figure 28.3(b), the aggregate demand curve shifts rightward to AD_1 and full employment is restored. But the price level rises further to 116.

A Cost-Push Inflation Process

The oil producers now see the prices of everything they buy increasing, so they increase the price of oil again to restore its new high relative price. Figure 28.4 continues the story. The short-run aggregate supply curve now shifts to SAS_2. The price level rises and real GDP decreases.

The price level rises further, to 124, and real GDP decreases to £1,450 billion. Unemployment increases above its natural rate.

If the Bank of England responds yet again with an increase in the quantity of money, aggregate demand increases and the aggregate demand curve shifts to AD_2. The price level rises even higher – to 128 – and full employment is again restored. A cost-push inflation spiral results. The combination of a rising price level and falling real GDP is called **stagflation**.

You can see that the Bank of England has a dilemma. If it does not respond when producers raise the oil price, the economy remains below full employment. If it lowers the interest rate and increases the quantity of money to restore full employment, it invites another oil price hike that will call forth yet a further increase in the quantity of money.

If the Bank of England responds to each oil price hike by increasing the quantity of money, inflation will rage along at a rate decided by oil producers. But if it keeps the lid on money growth, the economy remains below full employment.

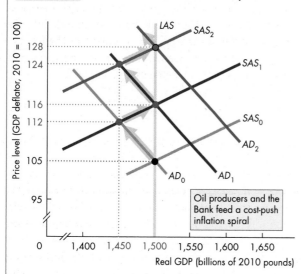

Figure 28.4   A Cost-Push Inflation Spiral

When a cost increase (for example, an increase in the world oil price) decreases short-run aggregate supply from SAS_0 to SAS_1, the price level rises to 112 and real GDP decreases to £1,450 billion. The Bank of England responds with an increase in the quantity of money that shifts the aggregate demand curve from AD_0 to AD_1. The price level rises again to 116 and real GDP returns to £1,500 billion. A further cost increase occurs, which shifts the short-run aggregate supply curve again, this time to SAS_2. Real GDP decreases again and the price level now rises to 124. The Bank responds again and the cost-push inflation spiral continues.

MyEconLab Animation ──────────────────◆

Cost-Push Inflation in Liverpool

What is going on in the Liverpool soft drinks factory when the economy is experiencing cost-push inflation?

When the oil price increases, so do the costs of producing soft drinks. These higher costs decrease the supply of soft drinks, increase the price and decrease the quantity produced. The factory lays off some workers.

This situation persists until either the Bank of England increases aggregate demand or the price of oil falls. If the Bank increases aggregate demand, the demand for soft drinks increases and so does the price. The higher price of soft drinks brings higher profits and the factory increases its production. It rehires the laid-off workers.

Cost-Push Inflation in the UK

A cost-push inflation like the one you've just studied occurred in the UK during the 1970s. In 1974 the Organisation of the Petroleum Exporting Countries

(OPEC) raised the price of oil fourfold. The higher oil price decreased aggregate supply, which caused the price level to rise more quickly and real GDP to shrink. The Bank of England then faced a dilemma: would it increase the quantity of money and accommodate the cost-push forces or would it keep aggregate demand growth in check by limiting money growth?

In 1975, 1976 and 1977, the Bank of England repeatedly allowed the quantity of money to grow and inflation proceeded rapidly. In 1979 and 1980, OPEC was again able to push oil prices higher. On that occasion, the Bank of England decided not to respond to the oil price hike with an increase in the quantity of money. The result was a recession but also, eventually, a fall in inflation.

Expected Inflation

If inflation is expected, the fluctuations in real GDP that accompany demand-pull and cost-push inflation that you've just studied don't occur. Instead, inflation proceeds as it does in the long run, with real GDP equal to potential GDP and unemployment at its natural rate. Figure 28.5 explains why.

Suppose that last year the aggregate demand curve was AD_0, the aggregate supply curve was SAS_0 and the long-run aggregate supply curve was LAS. The price level was 105 and real GDP was £1,500 billion, which is also potential GDP.

To keep things as simple as possible, suppose that potential GDP does not change, so the LAS curve does not shift. Also suppose that aggregate demand *is expected to increase* to AD_1.

In anticipation of this increase in aggregate demand, the money wage rate rises and the short-run aggregate supply curve shifts leftward. If the money wage rate rises by the same percentage as the price level is expected to rise, the short-run aggregate supply curve for next year is SAS_1.

If aggregate demand turns out to be the same as expected, the aggregate demand curve is AD_1. The short-run aggregate supply curve, SAS_1, and AD_1 determine the actual price level at 116. Between last year and this year, the price level increased from 105 to 116 and the economy experienced an inflation rate equal to that expected. If this inflation is ongoing, aggregate demand increases (as expected) in the following year and the aggregate demand curve shifts to AD_2. The money wage rate rises to reflect the expected inflation and the short-run aggregate supply curve shifts to SAS_2. The price level rises, as expected, to 128.

Figure 28.5   Expected Inflation

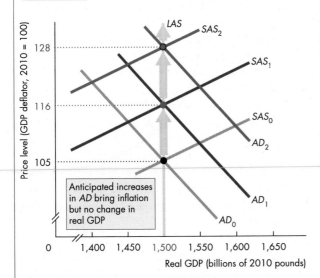

Potential real GDP is £1,500 billion. Last year, the aggregate demand curve was AD_0 and the short-run aggregate supply curve was SAS_0. The actual price level was the same as the expected price level – 105.

This year, aggregate demand is expected to increase to AD_1. The rational expectation of the price level changes from 105 to 116. As a result, the money wage rate rises and the short-run aggregate supply curve shifts to SAS_1.

If aggregate demand actually increases as expected, the actual aggregate demand curve AD_1 is the same as the expected aggregate demand curve. Real GDP is £1,500 billion and the actual price level is 116. The inflation is correctly expected.

Next year, the process continues with aggregate demand increasing as expected to AD_2 and the money wage rate rising to shift the short-run aggregate supply curve to SAS_2. Again, real GDP remains at £1,500 billion and the price level rises, as expected, to 128.

MyEconLab Animation ——————————————◆

What caused this inflation? The immediate answer is that because people expected inflation, the money wage rate increased and the price level increased. But the expectation was correct. Aggregate demand was expected to increase and it did increase. It is the actual and expected increase in aggregate demand that caused the inflation.

An expected inflation at full employment is exactly the process that the quantity theory of money predicts. To review the quantity theory of money, see Chapter 24, pp. 576–577.

This broader account of the inflation process and its short-run effects shows why the quantity theory of money doesn't explain the fluctuations in inflation. The economy follows the course described in Figure 28.5 but, as predicted by the quantity theory, only if aggregate demand growth is forecasted correctly.

Forecasting Inflation

To anticipate inflation, people must forecast it. Some economists who work for macroeconomic forecasting agencies, banks, insurance companies, trades unions and large companies specialise in inflation forecasting. The best forecast available is one that is based on all the relevant information and is called a **rational expectation**. A rational expectation is not necessarily a correct forecast. It is simply the best forecast with the information available. It will often turn out to be wrong, but no other forecast that could have been made with the information available could do better.

Inflation and the Business Cycle

When the inflation forecast is correct, the economy operates at full employment. If aggregate demand grows faster than expected, real GDP rises above potential GDP, the inflation rate exceeds its expected rate and the economy behaves as it does in a demand-pull inflation. If aggregate demand grows more slowly than expected, real GDP falls below potential GDP and the inflation rate slows.

◆ REVIEW QUIZ

1   How does demand-pull inflation begin?
2   What must happen to create a demand-pull inflation spiral?
3   How does cost-push inflation begin?
4   What must happen to create a cost-push inflation spiral?
5   What is stagflation and why does cost-push inflation cause stagflation?
6   How does expected inflation occur?
7   How do the price level and real GDP change if the forecast of inflation is incorrect?

Do these questions in Study Plan 28.1 and get instant feedback.   MyEconLab

Inflation and Unemployment: The Phillips Curve

Another way of studying inflation cycles focuses on the relationship and the short-run trade-off between inflation and unemployment, a relationship called the **Phillips curve** – so named because it was first suggested by New Zealand economist A.W. Phillips.

Why do we need another way of studying inflation? What is wrong with the *AS–AD* explanation of the fluctuations in inflation and real GDP? The first answer to both questions is that we often want to study changes in both the expected and actual inflation rates, and for this purpose the Phillips curve provides a simpler tool and clearer insights than the *AS–AD* model provides. The second answer to both questions is that we often want to study changes in the short-run trade-off between inflation and real economic activity (real GDP and unemployment), and again the Phillips curve serves this purpose well.

To begin our explanation of the Phillips curve, we distinguish between two time frames (similar to the two aggregate supply time frames). We study:

◆ The short-run Phillips curve

◆ The long-run Phillips curve

The Short-Run Phillips Curve

The **short-run Phillips curve** shows the relationship between inflation and unemployment, holding constant:

1 The expected inflation rate

2 The natural unemployment rate

You've just seen in the previous section what determines the expected inflation rate. You learned about the natural unemployment rate and the factors that influence it in Chapter 21, pp. 489–490.

Figure 28.6 shows a short-run Phillips curve, *SRPC*. Suppose that the expected inflation rate is 10 per cent a year and the natural unemployment rate is 6 per cent, point *A*. A short-run Phillips curve passes through this point.

If inflation rises above its expected rate, the unemployment rate falls below its natural rate. This joint movement in the inflation rate and the unemployment rate is illustrated as a movement up the short-run Phillips curve from point *A* to point *B*. Similarly, if

Figure 28.6 A Short-Run Phillips Curve

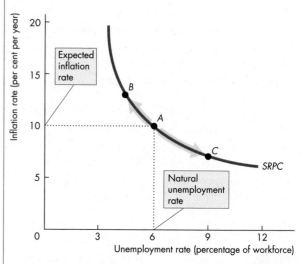

The short-run Phillips curve, *SRPC*, shows the relationship between the inflation rate and the unemployment rate at a given expected inflation rate and given natural unemployment rate. With an expected inflation rate of 10 per cent a year and a natural unemployment rate of 6 per cent, the short-run Phillips curve passes through point *A*.

An unexpected increase in aggregate demand lowers the unemployment rate and increases the inflation rate – a movement up the short-run Phillips curve to point *B*. An unexpected decrease in aggregate demand increases the unemployment rate and lowers the inflation rate – a movement down the short-run Phillips curve to point *C*.

MyEconLab Animation ————————◆

inflation falls below its expected rate, unemployment rises above the natural rate. In this case, there is movement down the short-run Phillips curve from point *A* to point *C*.

The Short-Run Phillips Curve and the Short-Run Aggregate Supply Curve

The short-run Phillips curve is like the short-run aggregate supply curve. A movement along the *SAS* curve that brings a higher price level and an increase in real GDP is equivalent to a movement along the short-run Phillips curve from *A* to *B* that brings an increase in the inflation rate and a decrease in the unemployment rate.

Similarly, a movement along the *SAS* curve that brings a lower price level and a decrease in real GDP is equivalent to a movement along the short-run Phillips curve from *A* to *C* that brings a decrease in the inflation rate and an increase in the unemployment rate.

The Long-Run Phillips Curve

The **long-run Phillips curve** is a curve that shows the relationship between inflation and unemployment, when the actual inflation rate equals the expected inflation rate. The long-run Phillips curve is vertical at the natural unemployment rate. It is shown in Figure 28.7 as the vertical line *LRPC*.

The long-run Phillips curve tells us that any expected inflation rate is possible at the natural unemployment rate. This proposition is the same as the one you discovered in the *AS–AD* model, which predicts that when inflation is expected, real GDP equals potential GDP and unemployment is at its natural rate.

Changes in the Expected Inflation Rate

The short-run Phillips curve intersects the long-run Phillips curve at the expected inflation rate. A change in the expected inflation rate shifts the short-run Phillips curve but it does not shift the long-run Phillips curve.

In Figure 28.7, if the expected inflation rate is 10 per cent a year, the short-run Phillips curve is $SRPC_0$. If the expected inflation rate falls to 7 per cent a year, the short-run Phillips curve shifts downward to $SRPC_1$. The vertical distance by which the short-run Phillips curve shifts from point *A* to point *D* is equal to the change in the expected inflation rate. If the actual inflation rate also falls from 10 per cent to 7 per cent, there is a movement down the long-run Phillips curve from *A* to *D*. An increase in the expected inflation rate has the opposite effect to that shown in Figure 28.7.

The other source of a shift in the Phillips curve is a change in the natural unemployment rate.

Changes in the Natural Unemployment Rate

The natural unemployment rate changes for many reasons that are explained in Chapter 21, pp. 489–490. A change in the natural unemployment rate shifts both the short-run and the long-run Phillips curves. Figure 28.8 illustrates such effects. If the natural unemployment rate

Figure 28.7 Short-Run and Long-Run Phillips Curves

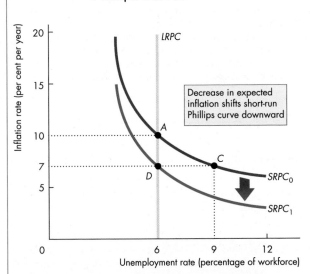

The long-run Phillips curve is *LRPC*, a vertical line at the natural unemployment rate. A fall in expected inflation shifts the short-run Phillips curve downward by the amount of the fall in the expected inflation rate.

For example, if the expected inflation rate falls from 10 per cent to 7 per cent a year, the short-run Phillips curve shifts downward from $SRPC_0$ to $SRPC_1$. The new short-run Phillips curve intersects the long-run Phillips curve at the new expected inflation rate – point *D*.

With the original expected inflation rate (10 per cent a year), an actual inflation rate of 7 per cent a year would occur at an unemployment rate of 9 per cent, at point *C*.

Figure 28.8 A Change in the Natural Unemployment Rate

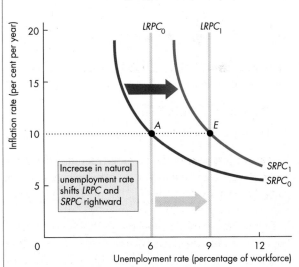

A change in the natural unemployment rate shifts both the short-run and long-run Phillips curves. Here the natural unemployment rate increases from 6 per cent to 9 per cent and the two Phillips curves shift rightward to $SRPC_1$ and $LRPC_1$. The new Phillips curves intersect at the expected inflation rate – point *E*.

ECONOMICS IN ACTION

The Shifting Short-Run Trade-Off

When A.W. (Bill) Phillips first discovered the curve that bears his name, he was looking at data on wage inflation and unemployment between 1861 and 1957. It was hard to see the Phillips curve in the data. The scatter diagram of data covering almost 100 years was more like a snowstorm than a neat inverse relationship.

Figure 1(a) continues the story that Phillips began by showing a scatter diagram of the UK inflation rate and the unemployment rate from 1960 to 2012. Each dot represents the inflation rate and unemployment rate in a particular year. We certainly cannot see a Phillips curve similar to that shown in Figure 28.6.

But we can interpret the data in terms of a shifting short-run Phillips curve like those in Figures 28.7 and 28.8. Three short-run Phillips curves appear in Figure 1(b). During the 1960s the expected inflation rate was 2 per cent a year and the natural unemployment rate was 2 per cent at point A, so the short-run Phillips curve was $SRPC_0$. From the mid-1970s to the mid-1980s the expected inflation rate averaged 12.5 per cent a year and the natural unemployment rate averaged 8 per cent at point B, so the short-run Phillips curve was $SRPC_1$. During the 1990s the expected inflation rate was 2.5 per cent a year and the natural unemployment rate was 5 per cent at point C, so the short-run Phillips curve was $SRPC_2$.

All the points in the graph are on short-run Phillips curves that lie between those shown.

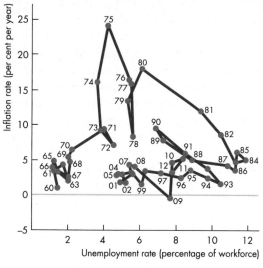

(a) Time sequence

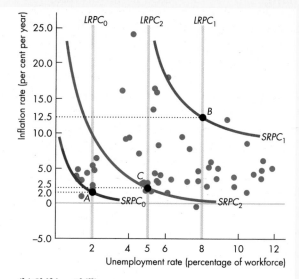

(b) Shifting Phillips curves

Figure 1   Phillips Curves in the UK

Source of data: Office for National Statistics.

increases from 6 per cent to 9 per cent, the long-run Phillips curve shifts from $LRPC_0$ to $LRPC_1$. If expected inflation is constant at 10 per cent a year, the short-run Phillips curve shifts from $SRPC_0$ to $SRPC_1$. Because the expected inflation rate is constant, the short-run Phillips curve $SRPC_1$ intersects the long-run curve $LRPC_1$ (point E) at the same inflation rate as that at which the short-run Phillips curve $SRPC_0$ intersects the long-run curve $LRPC_0$ (point A).

Changes in both the expected inflation rate and the natural unemployment rate have shifted the UK Phillips curve, but the expected inflation rate has had the greater effect.

REVIEW QUIZ

1   How would you use the Phillips curve to illustrate an unexpected change in the inflation rate?
2   If the expected inflation rate increases by 10 percentage points, how would the short-run Phillips curve and long-run Phillips curve change?
3   If the natural unemployment rate increases, what happens to the short-run Phillips curve and the long-run Phillips curve?
4   Does the UK have a stable short-run Phillips curve? Explain why or why not.

Do these questions in Study Plan 28.2 and get instant feedback.   MyEconLab

The Business Cycle

The business cycle is easy to describe but hard to explain, and business cycle theory remains unsettled and a source of controversy. We'll look at two approaches to understanding the business cycle:

◆ Mainstream business cycle theory
◆ Real business cycle theory

Mainstream Business Cycle Theory

The mainstream business cycle theory is that potential GDP grows at a steady rate while aggregate demand grows at a fluctuating rate. Because the money wage rate is sticky, if aggregate demand grows faster than potential GDP, real GDP moves above potential GDP and an inflationary gap emerges. And if aggregate demand grows more slowly than potential GDP, real GDP moves below potential GDP and a recessionary gap emerges. If aggregate demand decreases, real GDP also decreases in a recession.

Figure 28.9 illustrates this business cycle theory. Initially, actual and potential GDP are £1,200 billion. The long-run aggregate supply curve is LAS_0, the aggregate demand curve is AD_0 and the price level is 100. The economy is at full employment at point A.

An expansion occurs when potential GDP increases and the LAS curve shifts rightward to LAS_1. During an expansion, aggregate demand also increases, and usually by more than potential GDP, so the price level rises. Assume that in the current expansion the price level is expected to rise to 105 and the money wage rate has been set based on that expectation. The short-run aggregate supply curve is SAS_1.

If aggregate demand increases to AD_1, real GDP increases to £1,500 billion, the new level of potential GDP, and the price level rises, as expected, to 105. The economy remains at full employment but now at point B.

If aggregate demand increases more slowly to AD_2, real GDP grows by less than potential GDP and the economy moves to point C, with real GDP at £1,450 billion and the price level at 102. Real GDP growth is slower and inflation is lower than expected.

If aggregate demand increases more quickly to AD_3, real GDP grows by more than potential GDP and the economy moves to point D, with real GDP at £1,550 billion and the price level at 108. Real GDP growth is faster and inflation is higher than expected.

Growth, inflation and the business cycle arise from the relentless increases in potential GDP, faster (on average) increases in aggregate demand and fluctuations in the pace of aggregate demand growth.

Figure 28.9 The Mainstream Business Cycle Theory

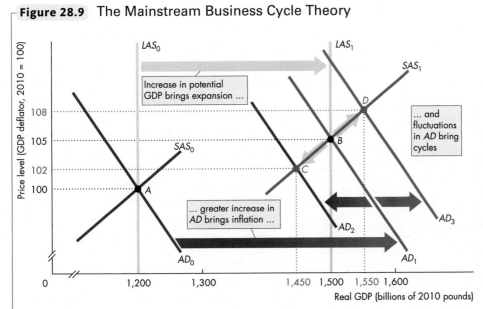

In a business cycle expansion, potential GDP increases and the LAS curve shifts rightward from LAS_0 to LAS_1. A greater than expected increase in aggregate demand brings inflation.

If the aggregate demand curve shifts to AD_1, the economy remains at full employment. If the aggregate demand curve shifts to AD_2, a recessionary gap arises. If the aggregate demand curve shifts to AD_3, an inflationary gap arises.

This mainstream theory comes in a number of special forms that differ regarding the source of fluctuations in aggregate demand growth and the source of money wage stickiness.

Keynesian Cycle Theory

In **Keynesian cycle theory**, fluctuations in investment driven by fluctuations in business confidence – summarised by the phrase 'animal spirits' – are the main source of fluctuations in aggregate demand.

Monetarist Cycle Theory

In **monetarist cycle theory**, fluctuations in both investment and consumption expenditure, driven by fluctuations in the growth rate of the quantity of money, are the main source of fluctuations in aggregate demand.

Both the Keynesian and monetarist cycle theories simply assume that the money wage rate is rigid, and don't explain that rigidity.

Two newer theories seek to explain money wage rate rigidity and to be more careful about working out its consequences.

New Classical Cycle Theory

In **new classical cycle theory**, the rational expectation of the price level, which is determined by potential GDP and *expected* aggregate demand, determines the money wage rate and the position of the *SAS* curve. In this theory, only unexpected fluctuations in aggregate demand bring fluctuations in real GDP around potential GDP.

New Keynesian Cycle Theory

The **new Keynesian cycle theory** emphasises the fact that today's money wage rates were negotiated at many past dates, which means that *past* rational expectations of the current price level influence the money wage rate and the position of the *SAS* curve. In this theory, both unexpected and currently expected fluctuations in aggregate demand bring fluctuations in real GDP around potential GDP.

The mainstream cycle theories don't rule out the possibility that occasionally an aggregate supply shock might occur. An oil price rise, a widespread drought or another natural disaster could, for example, bring a recession, but supply shocks are not the normal source of fluctuations in mainstream theories. In contrast, real business cycle theory puts supply shocks at centre stage.

Real Business Cycle Theory

The newest theory of the business cycle, known as **real business cycle theory** (or RBC theory), regards random fluctuations in productivity as the main source of economic fluctuations. These productivity fluctuations are assumed to result mainly from fluctuations in the pace of technological change, but they might also have other sources, such as international disturbances, climate fluctuations, or natural disasters. The origins of RBC theory can be traced to the rational expectations revolution set off by Robert E. Lucas, Jr, but the first demonstrations of the power of this theory were given by Edward Prescott and Finn Kydland and by John Long and Charles Plosser. Today, RBC theory is part of a broad research agenda called *dynamic general equilibrium analysis*, and hundreds of young macroeconomists do research on this topic.

We'll explore RBC theory by looking first at its impulse and then at the mechanism that converts that impulse into a cycle in real GDP.

The RBC Impulse

The impulse in RBC theory is the growth rate of productivity that results from technological change. RBC theorists believe this impulse to be generated mainly by the process of research and development that leads to the creation and use of new technologies (see *Economics in Action* opposite).

The pace of technological change and productivity growth is not constant. Sometimes productivity growth speeds up, sometimes it slows and occasionally it even *falls* – labour and capital become less productive, on average. A period of rapid productivity growth brings a business cycle expansion, and a slowdown or fall in productivity triggers a recession (as it did in 2009).

It is easy to understand why technological change brings productivity growth. But how does it *decrease* productivity? All technological change eventually increases productivity. But if, initially, technological change makes a sufficient amount of existing capital – especially human capital – obsolete, productivity can temporarily fall. At such a time, more jobs are destroyed than are created and more businesses fail than start up.

The RBC Mechanism

Two effects follow from a change in productivity that sparks an expansion or a contraction. Investment demand changes and the demand for labour changes.

ECONOMICS IN ACTION

The Real Business Cycle Impulse

To isolate the RBC impulse, economists measure the change in the growth rate of the combined productivity of capital and labour. Figure 1 shows the RBC impulse for the UK from 1972 to 2012.

You can see that fluctuations in productivity growth are correlated with real GDP fluctuations. You can also see that most recessions are associated with a slowdown in productivity growth. The 2008–2009 recession is an example. Productivity growth was slowing before the recession and became negative in 2008 and 2009 when real GDP growth crashed.

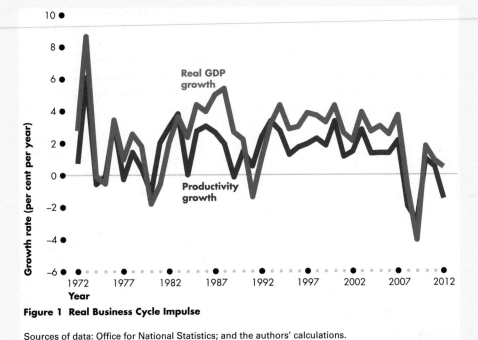

Figure 1 Real Business Cycle Impulse

Sources of data: Office for National Statistics; and the authors' calculations.

We'll study these effects and their consequences during a recession. In an expansion, they work in the direction opposite to what is described here.

Technological change makes some existing capital obsolete and temporarily decreases productivity. Firms expect future profits to fall and see their labour productivity falling. With lower profit expectations, they cut back their purchases of new capital, and with lower labour productivity, they plan to lay off some workers. So the initial effect of a temporary fall in productivity is a decrease in investment demand and a decrease in the demand for labour.

Figure 28.10 illustrates these two initial effects of a decrease in productivity. Part (a) shows the effects of a decrease in investment demand in the loanable funds market. The demand for loanable funds curve is DLF and the supply of loanable funds curve is SLF (both of which are explained in Chapter 23, pp. 540–544). Initially, the demand for loanable funds curve is DLF_0

and the equilibrium quantity of funds is £150 billion at a real interest rate of 6 per cent a year. A decrease in productivity decreases investment demand, and the demand for loanable funds curve shifts leftward from DLF_0 to DLF_1. The real interest rate falls to 4 per cent a year, and the equilibrium quantity of loanable funds decreases to £120 billion.

Figure 28.10(b) illustrates the effect of a decrease in productivity in the aggregate labour market (which is explained in Chapter 22, pp. 512–514).

Initially, the demand for labour curve is LD_0, the supply of labour curve is LS_0 and equilibrium employment is 50 billion hours a year at a real wage rate of £17.50 an hour. The decrease in productivity decreases the demand for labour, and the demand for labour curve shifts leftward from LD_0 to LD_1.

Before we can determine the new level of employment and real wage rate, we need to take a ripple effect into account – the key effect in RBC theory.

Figure 28.10 The Loanable Funds and Labour Markets in a Real Business Cycle

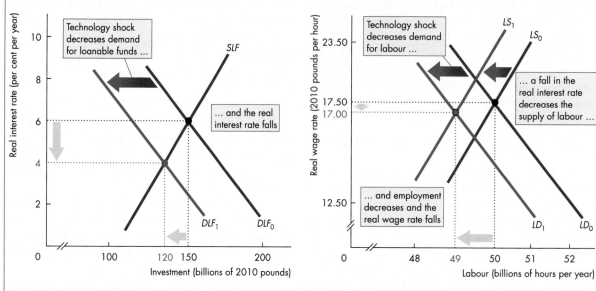

(a) Loanable funds and interest rate

(b) Labour and wage rate

In part (a), the supply of loanable funds, *SLF*, and initial demand for loanable funds, DLF_0, determine the real interest rate at 6 per cent a year. In part (b), the initial demand for labour, LD_0, and supply of labour, LS_0, determine the real wage rate at £17.50 an hour and employment at 50 billion hours a year.

A technological change temporarily decreases productivity, which decreases both the demand for loanable funds and the demand for labour. The demand curves shift leftward to DLF_1 and LD_1 respectively.

In part (a), the real interest rate falls to 4 per cent a year. In part (b), the fall in the real interest rate decreases the supply of labour (the when-to-work decision) and the supply curve shifts leftward to LS_1. Employment decreases to 49 billion hours and the real wage rate falls to £17 an hour. A recession is under way.

MyEconLab Animation ————————————————————————◆

The Key Decision: When to Work?

According to RBC theory, people decide when to work by doing a cost–benefit calculation. They compare the return from working in the current period with the expected return from working in a later period. You make such a comparison every day at university. Suppose your goal in this course is to get an A. To achieve this goal, you work hard most of the time. But during the few days before the midterm and final exams, you work especially hard. Why? Because you believe that the return from studying close to the exam is greater than the return from studying when the exam is a long time away. So during the term, you take time off for the movies and other leisure pursuits, but at exam time, you study every evening and weekend.

RBC theory says that workers behave like you. They work fewer hours, sometimes zero hours, when the real wage rate is temporarily low, and they work more hours when the real wage rate is temporarily high. But to properly compare the current wage rate with the expected future wage rate, workers must use the real interest rate.

If the real interest rate is 6 per cent a year, a real wage of £1 an hour earned this week will become £1.06 a year from now. If the real wage rate is expected to be £1.05 an hour next year, today's real wage of £1 looks good. By working longer hours now and shorter hours a year from now, a person can get a 1 per cent higher real wage. But suppose the real interest rate is 4 per cent a year. In this case, £1 earned now is worth £1.04 next year. Working fewer hours now and more next year is the way to get a 1 per cent higher real wage.

So the when-to-work decision depends on the real interest rate. The lower the real interest rate, other things remaining the same, the smaller is the supply of labour today. Many economists believe this *intertemporal substitution effect* to be of negligible size. RBC theorists believe that the effect is large, and it is the key feature of the RBC mechanism.

You saw in Figure 28.10(a) that the decrease in the demand for loanable funds lowers the real interest rate. This fall in the real interest rate lowers the return to current work and decreases the supply of labour.

In Figure 28.10(b), the labour supply curve shifts leftward to LS_1. The effect of the decrease in productivity on the demand for labour is larger than the effect of the fall in the real interest rate on the supply of labour. That is, the demand curve shifts farther leftward than does the supply curve. As a result, the real wage rate falls to £17 an hour and employment decreases to 49 billion hours. A recession has begun and is intensifying.

What Happened to Money?

The name *real* business cycle theory is no accident. It reflects the central prediction of the theory. Real things, not nominal or monetary things, cause the business cycle. If the quantity of money changes, aggregate demand changes. But if there is no real change – with no change in the use of resources and no change in potential GDP – the change in the quantity of money changes only the price level. In RBC theory, this outcome occurs because the aggregate supply curve is the *LAS* curve, which pins real GDP down at potential GDP, so when aggregate demand changes, only the price level changes.

Cycles and Growth

The shock that drives the business cycle of RBC theory is the same as the force that generates economic growth: technological change. On average, as technology advances, productivity grows; but as you saw in *Economics in Action* on p. 679, it grows at an uneven pace. Economic growth arises from the upward trend in productivity growth and, according to RBC theory, the mostly positive but occasionally negative higher frequency shocks to productivity bring the business cycle.

Criticisms of RBC Theory

The three main criticisms of RBC theory are that: (1) the money wage rate *is* sticky, and to assume otherwise is at odds with a clear fact; (2) intertemporal substitution is too weak a force to account for large fluctuations in labour supply and employment with small real wage rate changes; and (3) productivity shocks are as likely to be caused by *changes in aggregate demand* as by technological change.

If aggregate demand fluctuations cause the fluctuations in productivity, then the traditional aggregate demand theories are needed to explain them. Fluctuations in productivity do not cause the business cycle but are caused by it!

Building on this theme, the critics of RBC theory point out that the measured productivity fluctuations are correlated with changes in the growth rate of money and other indicators of changes in aggregate demand, and could be caused entirely by demand-side shocks.

In Defence of RBC Theory

The defenders of RBC theory claim that the theory explains the macroeconomic facts about the business cycle and is consistent with the facts about economic growth. In effect, a single theory explains *both growth and the business cycle*.

Its defenders also claim that RBC theory is consistent with a wide range of *micro*economic evidence about labour supply decisions, labour demand and investment demand decisions, and information on the distribution of income between labour and capital.

The strongest defence of RBC theory is not its detailed explanation of the cycle and growth but its method, the *dynamic general equilibrium* approach to studying the aggregate economy that is employed today by new classical and new Keynesian researchers as they continue to gain a better understanding of the economy.

◆ REVIEW QUIZ

1 Explain the mainstream theory of the business cycle.
2 What are the four special forms of the mainstream theory of the business cycle and how do they differ?
3 According to RBC theory, what is the source of the business cycle? What is the role of fluctuations in the rate of technological change?
4 According to RBC theory, how does a fall in productivity growth influence investment demand, the market for loanable funds, the real interest rate, the demand for labour, the supply of labour, employment and the real wage rate?
5 What are the main criticisms of RBC theory and how do its supporters defend it?

Do these questions in Study Plan 28.3 and get instant feedback.   MyEconLab

You can complete your study of inflation and economic fluctuations in *Reading Between the Lines* on pp. 682–683, which looks at the shifting trade-off between inflation and unemployment in the UK and the link, if any, with the popularity of the government.

READING BETWEEN THE LINES

UK Inflation–Unemployment Trade-Off

Has Misery Peaked?

Keith Fray

Amid talk of how governments should measure 'happiness', we should perhaps note that 'misery' – at least economic misery – may have recently peaked.

This week's releases of inflation data in the UK and US and labour market numbers for the UK should see the 'misery index' continue to fall in both countries.

This index – simply the unemployment rate plus the annual rate of inflation – has seen a modest revival of interest among economists in recent years.

Originally proposed by Arthur Okun, economic adviser to President Lyndon Johnson, the measure came to prominence in the 1979s, when the inflationary effects of the Vietnam war and two oil price shocks combined with the first major recessions since the Second World War to give the word 'stagflation' to the English language.

It has been given a new lease of life in the fallout from the 2008 crisis.

The index is a crude measure but is useful in conceptualising the pressures of the crisis on the population, with those not hit by redundancies subject to falling living standards as wage rises fail to keep up with prices.

In the UK, the index was at its highest last September, at 13.5 per cent (unemployment at 8.3 per cent; annual inflation at 5.2 per cent), the highest since mid-1992. Inflation is now forecast to fall and the unemployment rate to stabilise in the first half of the year. . . .

 The Essence of the Story

- The Misery Index, first proposed by Arthur Okun, is the sum of the unemployment rate and inflation rate.

- The index is crude but useful.

- The index reflects falling living standards for those with jobs if wage rises fail to keep up with inflation.

- The UK Misery Index peaked at 13.5 per cent in September 2011.

Economic Analysis

◆ Figure 1 shows the unemployment rate, the assumed natural unemployment rate and the inflation rate from 2010 to early 2013.

◆ Figure 2 shows a scatter diagram of the inflation and unemployment data graphed in Figure 1 and interprets the data using the short-run and long-run Phillips curves.

◆ The long-run Phillips curve is vertical at the natural unemployment rate.

◆ Rising inflation in 2010 and 2011 and falling inflation in 2011 and 2012 influenced expected inflation, which shifted the short-run Phillips curve.

◆ At the beginning of 2010, the expected inflation rate was 4.5 per cent and the short-run Phillips curve was $SRPC_{10}$.

◆ During 2010, the rise in inflation increased the expected inflation rate to 6 per cent a year (our assumption) and the short-run Phillips curve shifted upward to $SRPC_{11}$ by the beginning of 2011.

◆ During 2011, the fall in inflation decreased the expected inflation rate to 3 per cent a year (our assumption) and the short-run Phillips curve shifted downward to $SRPC_{12}$ by the beginning of 2012.

◆ The fall in the Misery Index is mainly a fall in the inflation rate with little change in the unemployment rate.

◆ Figure 3 shows that despite the fall in the Misery Index, the popularity of the government has fallen.

◆ The fall in government popularity has two possible interpretations: either the state of the economy is not the main influence on popularity or the Misery Index isn't a good measure of 'misery'.

◆ The cost of persistently high unemployment is greater than the benefit of falling inflation.

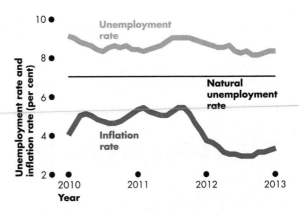

Figure 1 **Inflation and Unemployment: 2010–2013**

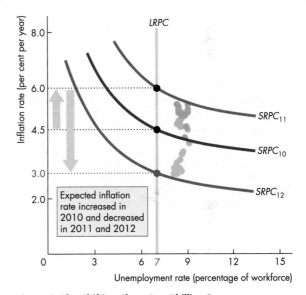

Figure 2 **The Shifting Short-Run Phillips Curve**

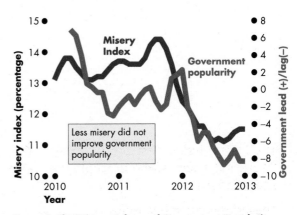

Figure 3 **The Misery Index and Government Popularity**

SUMMARY

Key Points

Inflation Cycles (pp. 668–673)

◆ Demand-pull inflation is triggered by an increase in aggregate demand and fuelled by ongoing money growth. Real GDP cycles above full employment.

◆ Cost-push inflation is triggered by an increase in the money wage rate or raw material prices and is fuelled by ongoing money growth. Real GDP cycles below full employment in a stagflation.

◆ When the forecast of inflation is correct, real GDP remains at potential GDP.

Do Problems 1 to 11 to get a better understanding of inflation cycles.

Inflation and Unemployment: The Phillips Curve (pp. 674–676)

◆ The short-run Phillips curve shows the trade-off between inflation and unemployment when the expected inflation rate and the natural unemployment rate are constant.

◆ The long-run Phillips curve, which is vertical, shows that when the actual inflation rate equals the expected inflation rate, the unemployment rate equals the natural unemployment rate.

Do Problems 12 to 14 to get a better understanding of inflation and unemployment: the Phillips curve.

The Business Cycle (pp. 677–681)

◆ The mainstream business cycle theory explains the business cycle as fluctuations of real GDP around potential GDP and as arising from a steady expansion of potential GDP combined with an expansion of aggregate demand at a fluctuating rate.

◆ Real business cycle theory explains the business cycle as fluctuations of potential GDP, which arise from fluctuations in the influence of technological change on productivity growth.

Do Problem 15 to get a better understanding of the business cycle.

Key Terms

Cost-push inflation, 670
Demand-pull inflation, 668
Keynesian cycle theory, 678
Long-run Phillips curve, 675
Monetarist cycle theory, 678
New classical cycle theory, 678
New Keynesian cycle theory, 678
Phillips curve, 674
Rational expectation, 673
Real business cycle theory, 678
Short-run Phillips curve, 674
Stagflation, 671

Do Problems 1 to 18 in MyEconLab Chapter 28 Study Plan and get instant feedback.

MyEconLab

Inflation Cycles (Study Plan 28.1)

1 **Best to Get Used to High Food and Energy Prices – They're Here to Stay**

Rising energy and food costs are slowing the economy at a time when it is already facing severe headwinds. Just as Western Europe and North America are showing a bit of sparkle, along comes another oil price shock or food price shock to put out the light.

On top of rising energy prices, a severe US drought, a poor monsoon season in Asia, and a bad harvest in Russia and Ukraine have sent grain prices soaring. Globally, this is the third major food price shock in five years.

Source: *The Telegraph,* 29 August 2012

Explain what type of inflation the news clip is describing and provide a graphical analysis of it.

Use the following figure in Problems 2, 3, 4 and 5. In each question, the economy starts out on the curves labelled AD_0 and SAS_0.

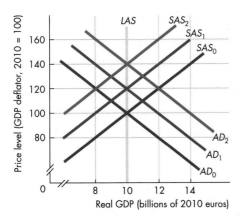

2 Some events occur and the economy experiences demand-pull inflation.

a List the events that might cause demand-pull inflation.

b Describe the initial effects of demand-pull inflation.

c Describe what happens as demand-pull inflation spiral proceeds.

3 Some events occur and the economy experiences cost-push inflation.

a List the events that might cause cost-push inflation.

b Describe the initial effects of cost-push inflation.

c Describe what happens as a cost-push inflation spiral proceeds.

4 Some events occur and the economy is expected to experience inflation.

a List the events that might cause an expected inflation.

b Describe the initial effects of an expected inflation.

c Describe what happens as an expected inflation proceeds.

5 Suppose that people expect deflation (a falling price level), but aggregate demand remains at AD_0.

a What happens to the short-run and long-run aggregate supply curves? (Draw some new curves if you need to.)

b Describe the initial effects of an expected deflation.

c Describe what happens as it becomes obvious to everyone that the expected deflation is not going to occur.

Use the following news clip in Problems 6 to 8.

Official: China May Face Heavy Inflation Pressure

China is expected to face great inflationary pressure in the future due to higher costs and an abundant global money supply, a senior Chinese official said in an article published Tuesday.

He said inflation in China is also the result of excessive global liquidity from loose monetary policies adopted by developed nations, China's lending expansion, and a pile-up of outstanding foreign exchange funds.

China's consumer price index (CPI), a main gauge of inflation, rose 4.9 percent year on year in February, the same level as in January. The CPI data for March is scheduled to be released this week and is estimated to show a rise above 5 percent.

Source: *China Daily,* 12 April 2011

6 Is China experiencing demand-pull or cost-push inflation? Explain.

7 Draw a graph to illustrate the initial rise in the price level and the money wage rate response to a one-time rise in the price level.

8 Draw a graph to illustrate and explain how China might experience an inflation spiral.

Use the following news clip in Problems 9 to 11.

Money's Too Loose to Mention

UK inflation at 3.7 per cent is above target and above forecasts. This inflation can't be blamed on temporary factors such as a rise in commodity prices or a tax increase, although these events did occur and will make inflation worse before it gets better. Rather, embedded inflation and inflation expectations seem to be rising and the UK now has higher inflation than any other developed economy.

Source: *The Financial Times*, 19 January 2011

9 Does the news clip describe a situation in which the UK is experiencing demand-pull inflation, cost-push inflation or an expected inflation spiral? Explain.

10 Draw a graph to illustrate the effects of the temporary factors noted in the news clip.

11 Draw a graph to illustrate and explain how the UK might be experiencing an expected inflation spiral.

Use the following news clip in Problems 12 to 14.

Energy Prices Drive Inflation to Nine-month High
Energy and fuel price rises pushed inflation up to its highest in the nine months to February 2013. The annual inflation rate in February was 2.8 per cent per year. Higher energy costs also led to higher transport and heating costs. Higher oil prices are expected to add to inflation in the coming months. Inflation continues to outstrip wage growth and the latest inflation figures indicate little room for the Bank of England to pump money into a flat lining economy.

Source: Sky News, 19 March 2013

12 Explain the type of inflation described in the news clip.

13 Use a graph to demonstrate the effect of the rise in energy prices.

14 **a** Use a graph to demonstrate the effect of the Bank of England pumping more money into the economy.

b Why do you think wages have not kept up with the rise in prices?

c On your graph show the effect on the economy if wages had kept up with rising prices.

Inflation and Unemployment: The Phillips Curve (Study Plan 28.2)

15 **Iran Postpones Cutting Petrol Subsidies**
Inflation is about 10 per cent and the unemployment rate is about 14 per cent. Earlier this month Iran's main audit body slammed the government's plan to scrap petrol subsidies, warning that implementing such a reform might result in unrest. The government also intends to scrap subsidies on natural gas, which most Iranians use for cooking and heating, as well as electricity, but the new prices are still not known. However, in recent weeks some households have received electricity bills with nearly sevenfold price increases.

Source: AFP, 15 September 2010

a If Iran unexpectedly removes the subsidies and consumers don't know what the higher prices will be, draw a graph to show the most likely path of inflation and unemployment.

b If Iran removes the subsidies and announces the new prices so that consumers know what they are, draw a graph to show the most likely path of inflation and unemployment.

16 **Eurozone Unemployment Hits Record High As Inflation Rises Unexpectedly**
Spain is suffering mass unemployment with a 25 per cent unemployment rate and half of those out of work under 25. Eurozone unemployment as a whole rose to 10.7 per cent. At the same time, eurozone inflation unexpectedly rose to 2.7 per cent a year, up from the previous month's 2.6 per cent a year.

Source: *Huffington Post*, 1 March 2012

a How does the Phillips curve model account for a very high unemployment rate?

b Explain the change in unemployment and inflation in the eurozone in terms of what is happening to the short-run and long-run Phillips curves.

17 **Inflation Report Press Conference**
Despite weak demand, inflation is above the 2 per cent target. The slack in the economy is likely to reduce inflationary pressure, but it is possible that rising import prices and commodity prices will push up inflation and inflation expectations.

Source: Bank of England, 10 November 2010

Explain this report in terms of shifts and movements along a short-run and long-run Phillips curve.

The Business Cycle (Study Plan 28.3)

18 **Debate on Causes of Joblessness Grows**
What is the cause of the high unemployment rate? One side says more government spending can reduce joblessness. The other says it's a structural problem – people who can't move to take new jobs because they are tied down to burdensome mortgages or firms that can't find workers with the requisite skills to fill job openings.

Source: *The Wall Street Journal*, 4 September 2010

Which business cycle theory would say that the rise in unemployment is cyclical? Which would say it is an increase in the natural rate? Why?

ADDITIONAL PROBLEMS AND APPLICATIONS

Do these problems in MyEconLab if assigned by your lecturer.

MyEconLab

Inflation Cycles

Use the following news clip in Problems 19 and 20.

Inflation Should Be Feared

The US Federal Reserve is trying as hard as it can to spur growth, and to create some inflation, but it must be careful. Inflation remains a danger because US debt is skyrocketing, with no visible plan to pay it back. For the moment, foreigners are buying that debt. But they are buying out of fear that their governments are worse. They are short-term investors, waiting out the storm, not long-term investors confident that the US will pay back its debts. If their fear passes, or they decide some other haven is safer, watch out. Inflation will come with a vengeance. It's not happening yet: interest rates are low now. But so were mortgage-backed security rates and Greek government debt rates just a few years ago. But if it happens, it will happen with little warning, the Federal Reserve will be powerless to stop it, and it will bring stagnation rather than prosperity.

Source: John H. Cochrane, *The New York Times*,
22 August 2012

19 What type of inflation process does John Cochrane warn could happen? Explain the role that inflation expectations would play if the outbreak of inflation were to 'happen with little warning'.

20 Explain why the inflation that John Cochrane fears would 'bring stagnation rather than prosperity'.

Use the following news clip in Problems 21 to 23.

Inflation in Brazil

Dilma Rouseff, Brazil's incoming president, will face the challenge of consumer price inflation running well above the government's target of 4.5 per cent a year. Prices rose by 5.6 per cent in the 12 months to November and the rate is expected to reach 6 per cent by the year end. Price rises have spread to other sectors as the fast growth in Brazil's economy, expected to be about 7.5 per cent this year, puts pressure on supply.

Source: *The Financial Times*, 22 December 2010

21 Is Brazil experiencing demand-pull or cost-push inflation? Explain.

22 Draw a graph to illustrate the initial rise in the price level and the money wage rate response to a one-time rise in the price level.

23 Draw a graph to illustrate and explain how Brazil might experience an inflation spiral

Inflation and Unemployment: The Phillips Curve

Use the following information in Problems 24 and 25.

The Reserve Bank of New Zealand (the central bank) signed an agreement with the New Zealand government in which the Bank agreed to maintain inflation inside a low target range. Failure to achieve the target would result in the governor of the Bank losing his job.

24 Explain how this arrangement might have influenced New Zealand's short-run Phillips curve.

25 Explain how this arrangement might have influenced New Zealand's long-run Phillips curve.

Use the following information and the figure in Problems 26 and 27.

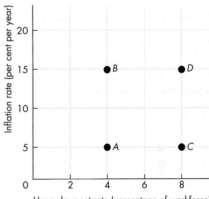

An economy has an unemployment rate of 4 per cent and an inflation rate of 5 per cent a year at point *A* in the figure. Some events occur that move the economy in a clockwise loop from *A* to *B* to *D* to *C* and back to *A*.

26 Describe the events that could create this sequence. Has the economy experienced demand-pull inflation, cost-push inflation, expected inflation, or none of these?

27 Draw in the figure the sequence of the economy's short-run and long-run Phillips curves.

Use the following news clip in Problems 28 and 29.

Inflation Risks and Monetary Policy

The Bank of England is taking risks with inflation. Its policy has increased the monetary base and this will eventually feed into increased money growth as the economy recovers. Interest rate doves believe that the UK can grow without inflation because there is a sizeable output gap, but as the the output gap shrinks banks will increase lending and drive up inflation. The soft patch in growth in 2011–12 has not changed the dynamics off inflation, just simply delayed it.

Source: *Daily Telegraph*, 27 August 2013

28 Explain how the increase in the monetary base might influence (a) the short-run unemployment–inflation trade-off and (b) the long-run unemployment–inflation trade-off. Will the influence come from changes in the expected inflation rate, the natural unemployment rate or both?

29 Explain what the news clip means when it states that the 'soft patch' in growth has only delayed the dynamics of inflation.

The Business Cycle

Use the following information in Problems 30 to 32.

Suppose that the business cycle in the UK is best described by RBC theory and that a new technology increases productivity.

30 Draw a graph to show the effect of the new technology in the market for loanable funds.

31 Draw a graph to show the effect of the new technology in the labour market.

32 Explain the when-to-work decision when technology advances.

33 **Productivity and Real Wages**

Technological progress increases the economic pie but not everyone benefits from that gain. Labour productivity increased by 80 per cent from 1973 to 2011 while average hourly wage rates rose by 10 per cent. Since 2000 productivity has risen 23 per cent while real wage rates have stagnated.

Source: *The New York Times*, 12 January 2013

Explain the relationship between wages and productivity in this news clip in terms of real business cycle theory.

Economics in the News

34 After you have studied *Reading Between the Lines* on pp. 682–683, answer the following questions.

  a What has happened to the UK inflation rate since the beginning of 2010?

  b What do you think has happened to inflation expectations and why?

  c How do you explain the fall in inflation and the fall in unemployment in the UK since the beginning of 2010?

  d What is the Misery Index? Explain what has happened to it in 2012 in the UK.

  e Why might the Misery Index be a predictor of voting intentions?

35 **Germany Leads Slowdown in Eurozone**

The pace of German economic growth has weakened 'markedly', but the reason is the weaker global prospects. Although German policymakers worry about the country's exposure to a fall in demand for its export goods, evidence is growing that the recovery is broadening with real wage rates rising and unemployment falling, which will lead into stronger consumer spending.

Source: *The Financial Times*, 23 September 2010

  a How does 'exposure to a fall in demand for its export goods' influence Germany's aggregate demand, aggregate supply, unemployment and inflation?

  b Use the *AS–AD* model to illustrate your answer to part (a).

  c Use the Phillips curve model to illustrate your answer to part (a).

  d What do you think the news clip means by 'the recovery is broadening with real wage rates rising and unemployment falling, which will lead into stronger consumer spending'?

  e Use the *AS–AD* model to illustrate your answer to part (d).

  f Use the Phillips curve model to illustrate your answer to part (d).

29 Fiscal Policy

After studying this chapter you will be able to:

◆ Describe the UK government's recent budget and recent history of receipts, outlays, deficit and debt

◆ Explain the supply-side effects of fiscal policy

◆ Explain how fiscal policy redistributes benefits and costs across generations

◆ Understand and explain fiscal stimulus in recession

Does it matter if a government runs a large budget deficit and accumulates debt? Do deficits boost demand and create jobs? Or do they raise interest rates, kill investment and slow economic growth?

How do taxes and government spending influence the economy? Does a pound spent by the government have the same effect as a pound spent by someone else? Does it create jobs, or does it destroy them?

This chapter studies these fiscal policy questions. And in *Reading Between the Lines* at the end of the chapter, we look at the UK government's idea to create jobs and speed income growth by planning a future increase in its investment spending.

Government Budgets

A government's **budget** is an annual statement of projected outlays and receipts during the next year together with the laws and regulations that will support those outlays and receipts. The finance minister – the Chancellor of the Exchequer in the UK – presents the budget to Parliament in what is often a piece of political theatre and always a major media event.

A government's budget has three major purposes:

1   To state the scale and allocation of the government's outlays and its plans to finance its activities

2   To stabilise the economy

3   To encourage the economy's long-term growth and balanced regional development

Before the Second World War, the budget had only the first of these goals – to plan and finance the business of government.

But during the late 1940s and early 1950s, the budget began to assume its second purpose – stabilisation of the economy.

In more recent years, the budget has assumed its third goal of helping to secure faster sustained economic growth and to seek balance across regions.

Today, the budget is the tool used by a government in pursuit of its fiscal policy. **Fiscal policy** is a government's use of its budget to achieve macroeconomic objectives such as full employment, sustained economic growth and price-level stability. It is the fiscal policy aspects of the budget that we focus on in this chapter.

Government budgets differ in size and detail, but they all have the same components. Here, we'll illustrate a government budget by looking at the UK.

Highlights of the UK Budget in 2013

Table 29.1 shows the main items in the UK government's budget. The numbers are projections for the fiscal year beginning in April 2013. The three main items in the budget are:

◆   Receipts

◆   Outlays

◆   Budget balance

Table 29.1

The Government Budget in 2013/14

Item	Projections (billions of pounds)
Receipts	**612**
Taxes on income and wealth	212
Taxes on expenditure	249
National Insurance contributions	107
Other receipts and royalties	44
Outlays	**720**
Expenditure on goods and services	449
Health	137
Education	97
Law and order	31
Defence	40
Other[1]	144
Transfer payments	220
Debt interest	51
Budget balance (surplus +/deficit –)	**–108**

Source of data: HM Treasury, *Budget 2013*.

[1] Other outlays include personal social services (£31 billion), housing and the environment (£23 billion), transport (£21 billion), and industry, agriculture and employment (£16 billion).

Receipts

Receipts come from four sources:

1   Taxes on income and wealth

2   Taxes on expenditure

3   National Insurance contributions

4   Other receipts and royalties

In 2013/14, *taxes on income and wealth* were projected at £212 billion. These taxes are paid by individuals on their incomes and wealth and by businesses on their profits. These taxes were the second largest source of revenue in 2013/14.

The largest revenue source is *taxes on expenditure*, which in 2013/14 were projected to be £249 billion. These taxes include VAT and special taxes on gambling, alcoholic drinks, petrol, luxury items and imports.

Third in size are *National Insurance contributions*, projected in 2013/14 to be £107 billion. This revenue comes from contributions paid by workers and employers to fund the welfare and healthcare programmes.

The *other receipts and royalties* include oil royalties, stamp duties, car taxes, miscellaneous rents, dividends from abroad and profits from nationalised industries.

Outlays

Outlays are classified in three broad categories:

1 Expenditure on goods and services
2 Transfer payments
3 Debt interest

Expenditure on goods and services are by far the largest item at £449 billion in 2013/14.

Table 29.1 lists some of the larger components of these expenditures. Health (expenditure on the National Health Service) took £137 billion and education took another £97 billion. The provision of law and order and defence, the two traditional roles of government, took only £71 billion between them.

Transfer payments – £220 billion in 2013/14 – are payments to individuals, businesses, other levels of government and the rest of the world. These payments include National Insurance benefits, healthcare benefits, unemployment benefits, welfare supplements, grants to local authorities and aid to developing countries.

Debt interest, which in 2013/14 is projected to be £51 billion, is the interest on the government debt minus interest received by the government on its own investments.

The bottom line of the government budget is the balance – the surplus or deficit.

Budget Balance

The government's budget balance is equal to its receipts minus its outlays. That is:

Budget balance = Receipts – Outlays

If receipts exceed outlays, the government has a **budget surplus**. If outlays exceed receipts, the government has a **budget deficit**. If receipts equal outlays, the government has a **balanced budget**. In fiscal year 2013/14, with projected receipts of £612 billion and outlays of £720 billion, the projected government deficit is £108 billion.

How typical is the budget of 2013/14? Let's look at its recent history.

The Budget in Historical Perspective

Figure 29.1 shows the government's receipts, outlays and budget balance since 1988. The figure expresses the receipts, outlays and budget balance as percentages of GDP. Expressing them in this way lets us see how large government is relative to the size of the economy, and it helps us to study *changes* in the scale of government over time. You may think of these percentages of GDP as telling you how many pence of each pound that we earn get paid to and spent by the government.

Figure 29.1 UK Government Receipts, Outlays and Budget Balance

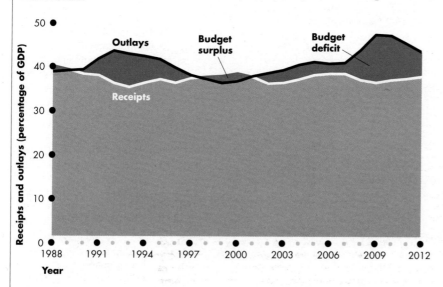

The figure records the UK government's receipts, outlays and budget deficit as percentages of GDP.

In 1988, the government had a small budget surplus, but income tax cuts and an increase in outlays turned the budget into a deficit during most of the 1990s.

The budget returned to a small surplus at the end of the 1990s and in 2000, but for the rest of the 2000s, a large and growing deficit emerged. In recent years, the government has been reducing its deficit.

Source of data: HM Treasury, *Budget 2013*.

Throughout most of this period there was a budget deficit. The deficit increases in recessions and decreases in expansions. The budget was in surplus only in 1988 and 1989 and again from 1998 to 2000. The deficit was large during the recession of the early 1990s, but even larger during 2009 and 2010 when it reached almost 11 per cent of GDP – the largest deficit ever recorded.

Why does the government budget deficit fluctuate? And why did it grow so sharply in recent years? The immediate answer is that receipts and outlays fluctuate, and in recent years as the deficit climbed to a record high, receipts decreased and outlays increased.

Which components of receipts and outlays fluctuate most? And which components of receipts decreased in recent years and which components of outlays increased? To answer these questions, we must look at receipts and outlays in a bit more detail.

Receipts

Figure 29.2 shows the components of government receipts as a percentage of GDP, from 1988 to 2012. Relative to the size of the economy, these receipts have been remarkably steady at 37.5 per cent of GDP. But receipts decreased from 1988 to 1993, during the early 2000s and in 2008 and 2009; and they increased from 1993 to 2000 and from 2002 to 2007.

Fluctuations in receipts result from fluctuations in income tax receipts and expenditure tax receipts. In the recessions of 1990–1992 and 2008–2010 and the slowdown of the early 2000s, firms' profits fell, which lowered the taxes on business profits. Also, as the unemployment rate increased, personal incomes shrank and government receipts from personal income taxes decreased.

Receipts from expenditure taxes fluctuate because people spend less on higher-taxed items in recessions.

Even the small receipts from National Insurance contributions are cyclical, but they fluctuate less than the two larger components of government receipts.

Outlays

Figure 29.3 shows the components of government outlays as percentages of GDP, between 1988 and 2012. Like receipts, outlays fluctuate over the business cycle. But unlike receipts, outlays have trended upwards. Expenditure on goods and services increased from 21 per cent of GDP in 1988 to 24 percent in 2012, but peaked at 26 per cent in 2009. Transfer payments increased too, from 14 per cent of GDP in 1988 to 17 per cent in 2012, with a peak of 20 per cent in 2009.

Interest payments on government debt is a small component of government outlays and its amount depends on the level of debt and the level of interest rates. In recent years, the ratio of debt to GDP has increased but interest rates have decreased, and the effects of lower interest rates have decreased this outlay.

Figure 29.2 UK Government Receipts

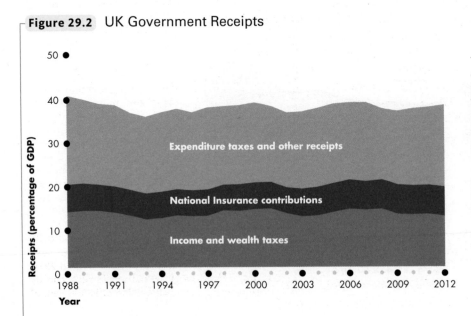

The figure shows the three components of government receipts: income and wealth taxes (including taxes on business profits), National Insurance contributions and expenditure taxes (including VAT).

Receipts from income and wealth fell during the recession of the early 1990s and 2008–2009.

Receipts increased during the strong expansion years from 1994 to 2001.

Source of data: HM Treasury, *Budget 2013*.

MyEconLab Animation

Figure 29.3 UK Government Outlays

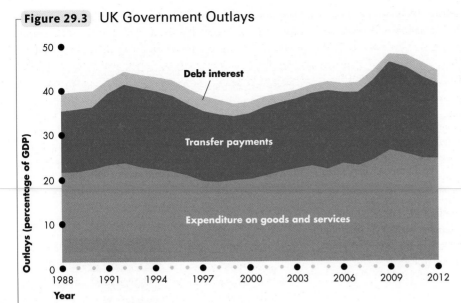

The figure shows three components of government outlays: expenditure on goods and services, transfer payments and debt interest.

Expenditure on goods and services has trended upward.

Transfer payments have also trended upward, but they are dominated by their cyclical changes.

Debt interest fell from 1996 to 2009 but then jumped in 2010.

Source of data: HM Treasury, *Budget 2013*.

MyEconLab Animation ————————————————————————◆

Deficit, Debt and Capital

Government debt is the total amount of borrowing by the government. It is the sum of past deficits minus the sum of past surpluses plus payments to buy assets minus receipts from the sale of assets.

A budget deficit or the purchase of assets increases government debt and a budget surplus or the sale of state-owned assets reduces government debt.

Figure 29.4 shows the history of UK government debt from 1988 to 2012. In 1988, the debt–GDP ratio was 30 per cent. The debt–GDP ratio fell slightly during the next 3 years but increased during the recession of the early 1990s. It decreased again through the rest of the 1990s but then started to rise again. Debt increased sharply following the recession of 2008–2009 and rose to an all-time peace time high of 90 per cent in 2012.

Like individual and business debt, government debt is incurred to buy assets. Governments own public assets such as roads, bridges, schools and universities, public libraries and defence equipment. But the value of UK government assets is only £400 billion, which falls well short of its total debt.

How do the UK deficit and debt compare with deficits and debts in other major economies and the EU?

Figure 29.4 UK Government Debt

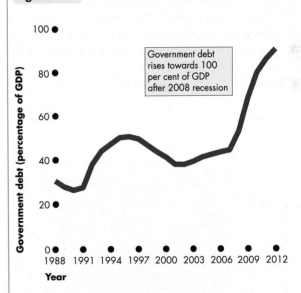

Government debt rises towards 100 per cent of GDP after 2008 recession

In 1988, UK government debt was 30 per cent of GDP. Government debt increased sharply during the 1990–1992 recession but decreased from 1997 to 2002. Through the rest of the 2000s debt increased, and by 2012 it had reached a peace time high of 90 per cent of GDP.

Source of data: Office for National Statistics.

MyEconLab Animation ————————————————————————◆

ECONOMICS IN ACTION

EU Government Budget Balances and Debts

The budget of each member state of the EU has similar categories of receipts and outlays to the UK budget. In addition to the national budgets, the Council of the EU draws up the EU budget, which the European Parliament approves.

The EU receives 85 per cent of its receipts from the member states and 15 per cent from EU tariffs on imports from non-member countries. Member states' contributions are based on VAT, which provides 15 per cent of revenue, and on gross national product, which produces 73 per cent of receipts. (A country's gross national product is equal to its gross domestic product plus net property income from the rest of the world.)

The total EU budget in 2012 was €147.2 billion – equivalent to less than 1 per cent of EU GDP. Figure 1 shows how the EU spends its receipts. Structural growth measures – grants to weaker economic regions and expenditure on measures to improve competitiveness – take the largest slice at 46 per cent of total EU outlays. Management of natural resources – support for the Common Agricultural Policy (CAP) and the environment – take the next largest slice at 42 per cent of total EU outlays.

Despite its small size relative to GDP, the EU budget is hotly debated and contributes to economic life in many EU countries. For example, Ireland in the past has benefited from both the CAP and the EU structural programmes.

Most government revenue and outlays in the EU remain with the member states. The 27 members of the EU span a huge range of budgetary outcomes. Two aspects of these budgets are budget balances and government debt.

Figure 2 shows the budget balances of the 27 EU members in 2012. They range from a deficit of 11 per cent of GDP in Spain to a surplus of 4 per cent in Slovakia.. The EU average is a deficit at 4 per cent of GDP. The UK has the fifth largest deficit.

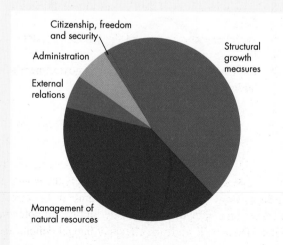

Figure 1 EU Budget Outlays 2012

Source of data for Figures 1, 2 and 3: Eurostat.

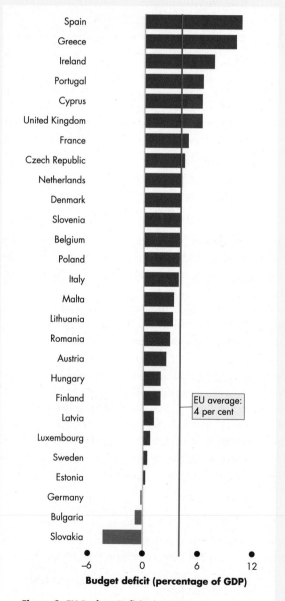

Figure 2 EU Budget Deficits in 2012

Figure 3 shows the EU government debt in 2012. It ranges from a high of 157 per cent of GDP in Greece to a low of 10 per cent of GDP in Estonia. The EU average debt is 91 per cent of GDP.

In the recession, government receipts fall, as we saw in Figure 29.2, but outlays on welfare and transfer payments rise, as in Figure 29.3. The budget deficit increases in the recession and governments borrow to finance the deficit, which adds to the existing stock of debt.

There is a correlation between the size of a country's deficit and the total amount of its debt (as percentages of GDP). But the correlation isn't perfect because debt depends on how long a government has been in deficit.

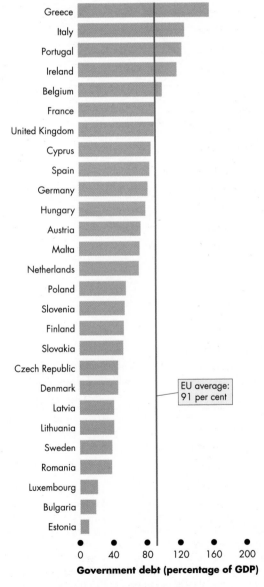

Figure 3 EU Government Debt in 2012

UK and EU Budget Balances and Debt in a Global Perspective

In *Economics in Action* (opposite), you can see that in 2012 the UK had a budget deficit of 6 per cent of GDP and the EU nations on average had a budget deficit of 4 per cent of EU GDP. How do these deficits compare with those in other advanced economies?

The answer is that the UK has one of the largest deficits and the EU average is in the middle of the pack. Of the advanced economies outside the EU, only the US and Japan have budget deficits greater than the EU average deficit.

Among the countries that have smaller deficits than the EU average are the newly industrialised Asian economies (Hong Kong, Singapore, South Korea and Taiwan), Australia and Canada.

There is nothing inherently wrong with a government running a deficit, provided the resources are being used to add to the stock of social capital. There is also a case for a temporary government deficit to try to lift an economy from recession. We look more closely at using a deficit to stimulate the economy later in this chapter.

REVIEW QUIZ

1 What are the functions of a government's budget?
2 What are the goals of fiscal policy?
3 Describe the main sources of receipts and outlays in the budget of the UK government.
4 Under what circumstances does a government have a budget surplus?
5 Which members of the EU ran a budget deficit in 2012?
6 Which members of the EU had the largest debt levels in 2012?
7 Explain the connection between a government's budget deficit and its debt.

Do these questions in Study Plan 29.1 and get instant feedback.   MyEconLab

Now that you know what the main components of the government's budget are, it is time to study the *effects* of fiscal policy. We'll begin by learning about the effects of taxes on employment, aggregate supply and potential GDP. Then we'll study the effects of budget deficits and see how fiscal policy brings redistribution across generations. Finally, we'll look at fiscal stimulus and see how it might be used to speed recovery from recession and stabilise the business cycle.

Supply-Side Effects of Fiscal Policy

How do taxes on personal and corporate income affect real GDP and employment? The answer to these questions is controversial. Some economists, known as supply-siders, believe these effects to be large, and an accumulating body of evidence suggests that they are correct. To see why these effects might be large, we'll begin with a refresher on how full employment and potential GDP are determined in the absence of taxes. Then we'll introduce an income tax and see how it changes the economic outcome.

Full Employment and Potential GDP

You learned in Chapter 22 (pp. 512–514) how the full-employment quantity of labour and potential GDP are determined. At full employment, the real wage rate adjusts to make the quantity of labour demanded equal to the quantity supplied. Potential GDP is the real GDP that the full-employment quantity of labour produces.

Figure 29.5 illustrates a full-employment situation. In part (a), the demand for labour curve is *LD*, and the supply of labour curve is *LS*. At a real wage rate of £15 an hour and 50 billion hours of labour a year employed, the economy is at full employment.

In Figure 29.5(b), the production function is *PF*. When 50 billion hours of labour are employed, real GDP – which is also potential GDP – is £1,600 billion.

Let's now see how an income tax changes potential GDP.

The Effects of the Income Tax

The tax on labour income influences potential GDP and aggregate supply by changing the full-employment quantity of labour. The income tax weakens the incentive to work and drives a wedge between the take-home wage of workers and the cost of labour to firms. The result is a smaller quantity of labour and a lower potential GDP.

Graphical Analysis and Illustration

Figure 29.5 shows the outcome we've just described. In the labour market, the income tax has no effect on the demand for labour, which remains at *LD*. The reason is that the quantity of labour that firms plan to hire depends only on how productive labour is and what it costs – its real wage rate.

Figure 29.5   The Effects of the Income Tax on Aggregate Supply

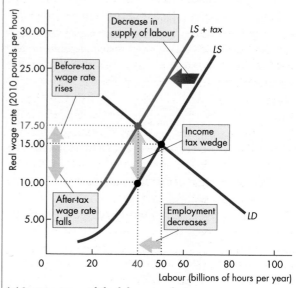

(a) Income tax and the labour market

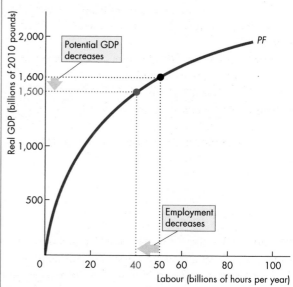

(b) Income tax and potential GDP

In part (a), with no income tax, the real wage rate is £15 an hour and employment is 50 billion hours. In part (b), potential GDP is £1,600 billion. An income tax shifts the supply of labour curve leftward to *LS + tax*. The before-tax wage rate rises to £17.50 an hour, the after-tax wage rate falls to £10 an hour, and the quantity of labour employed decreases to 40 billion hours. With less labour, potential GDP decreases to £1,500 billion.

MyEconLab Animation ────────────────◆

But the supply of labour does change. With no income tax, the real wage rate is £15 an hour and 50 billion hours of labour a year are employed. An income tax weakens the incentive to work and decreases the supply of labour. The reason is that for each pound of before-tax earnings, workers must pay the government an amount determined by the income tax code. So workers look at the after-tax wage rate when they decide how much labour to supply. An income tax shifts the supply curve leftward to *LS + tax*. The vertical distance between the *LS* curve and the *LS + tax* curve measures the amount of income tax. With the smaller supply of labour, the before-tax wage rate rises to £17.50 an hour but the after-tax wage rate falls to £10 an hour. The gap created between the before-tax and after-tax wage rates is called the **tax wedge**.

The new equilibrium quantity of labour employed is 40 billion hours a year – less than in the no-tax case. Because the full-employment quantity of labour decreases, so does potential GDP. And a decrease in potential GDP decreases aggregate supply.

In this example, the tax rate is high – £7.50 tax on a £17.50 wage rate is a tax rate of about 43 per cent. A lower tax rate would have a smaller effect on employment, which in turn would have a smaller effect on potential GDP.

An increase in the tax rate to above 43 per cent would decrease the supply of labour by more than the decrease shown in Figure 29.5. Equilibrium employment and potential GDP would also decrease still further. A tax cut would increase the supply of labour, increase equilibrium employment and increase potential GDP.

Taxes on Expenditure and the Tax Wedge

The tax wedge that we've just considered is only a part of the wedge that affects labour-supply decisions. Taxes on consumption expenditure add to the wedge. The reason is that a tax on consumption raises the prices paid for consumption goods and services and is equivalent to a cut in the real wage rate.

The incentive to supply labour depends on the goods and services that an hour of labour can buy. The higher the taxes on goods and services and the lower the after-tax wage rate, the less is the incentive to supply labour. If the income tax rate is 25 per cent and the tax rate on consumption expenditure is 10 per cent, a pound earned buys only 65 pence worth of goods and services. The tax wedge is 35 per cent.

ECONOMICS IN ACTION

Some Real-World Tax Wedges

Edward C. Prescott of Arizona State University, who shared the 2004 Nobel Prize in Economic Sciences, has estimated the tax wedges for a number of countries, among them the US, the UK and France.

The US Tax Wedge

The US tax wedge is a combination of 13 per cent tax on consumption and 32 per cent tax on incomes. The income tax component of the US tax wedge includes social security taxes and is the marginal tax rate – the tax rate paid on the marginal dollar earned.

France's Tax Wedge

Prescott estimates that in France, taxes on consumption are 33 per cent and taxes on incomes are 49 per cent.

The UK Tax Wedge

The estimates for the UK fall between those for the US and France. Figure 1 shows these components of the tax wedges in the three countries.

Does the Tax Wedge Matter?

According to Prescott's estimates, the tax wedge has a powerful effect on employment and potential GDP. Potential GDP in France is 14 per cent below that of the US (per person), and the entire difference can be attributed to the difference in the tax wedge in the two countries.

Potential GDP in the UK is 41 per cent below that of the US (per person), and about a third of the difference arises from the different tax wedges. (The rest is due to different productivities.)

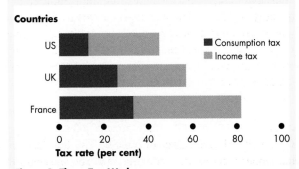

Figure 1 Three Tax Wedges

Source of data: Edward C. Prescott, *American Economic Review*, 2003.

Taxes and the Incentive to Save and Invest

A tax on interest income weakens the incentive to save and drives a wedge between the after-tax interest rate earned by savers and the interest rate paid by firms. These effects are analogous to those of a tax on labour income. But they are more serious for two reasons.

First, a tax on labour income lowers the quantity of labour employed and lowers potential GDP, while a tax on capital income lowers the quantity of saving and investment and slows the growth rate of real GDP.

Second, the true tax rate on interest income is much higher than that on labour income because of the way in which inflation and taxes on interest income interact. Let's examine this interaction.

Effect of Tax Rate on Real Interest Rate

The interest rate that influences investment and saving plans is the real after-tax interest rate. The real after-tax interest rate subtracts the income tax rate paid on interest income from the real interest rate. But the taxes depend on the nominal interest rate, not the real interest rate. So the higher the inflation rate, the higher is the true tax rate on interest income. Here is an example. Suppose the real interest rate is 4 per cent a year and the tax rate is 40 per cent.

If there is no inflation, the nominal interest rate equals the real interest rate. The tax on 4 per cent interest is 1.6 per cent (40 per cent of 4 per cent), so the real after-tax interest rate is 4 per cent minus 1.6 per cent, which equals 2.4 per cent.

If the inflation rate is 6 per cent a year, the nominal interest rate is 10 per cent. The tax on 10 per cent interest is 4 per cent (40 per cent of 10 per cent), so the real after-tax interest rate is 4 per cent minus 4 per cent, which equals zero. The true tax rate in this case is not 40 per cent but 100 per cent!

Effect of Income Tax on Saving and Investment

In Figure 29.6, initially there are no taxes. Also, the government has a balanced budget. The demand for loanable funds curve, which is also the investment demand curve, is *DLF*. The supply of loanable funds curve, which is also the saving supply curve, is *SLF*. The interest rate is 3 per cent a year, and the quantity of funds borrowed and lent is £200 billion a year.

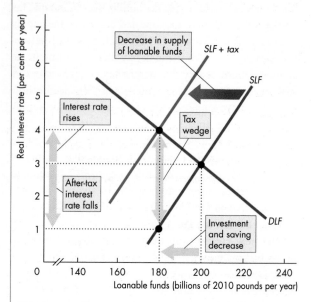

Figure 29.6 The Effects of a Tax on Capital Income

The demand for loanable funds and investment demand curve is *DLF*, and the supply of loanable funds and saving supply curve is *SLF*. With no income tax, the real interest rate is 3 per cent a year and investment is £200 billion. An income tax shifts the supply curve leftward to *SLF* + *tax*. The interest rate rises to 4 per cent a year, the after-tax interest rate falls to 1 per cent a year, and investment decreases to £180 billion. With less investment, the real GDP growth rate decreases.

MyEconLab Animation ————————◆

A tax on interest income has no effect on the demand for loanable funds. The quantity of investment and borrowing that firms plan to undertake depends only on how productive capital is and what it costs – its real interest rate. But a tax on interest income weakens the incentive to save and lend and decreases the supply of loanable funds. For each pound of before-tax interest, savers must pay the government an amount determined by the tax code. So savers look at the after-tax real interest rate when they decide how much to save.

When a tax is imposed, saving decreases and the supply of loanable funds curve shifts leftward to *SLF* + *tax*. The amount of tax payable is measured by the vertical distance between the *SLF* curve and the *SLF* + *tax* curve. With this smaller supply of loanable funds, the interest rate rises to 4 per cent a year, but the after-tax interest rate falls to 1 per cent a year. A tax wedge is driven between the interest rate and the after-tax interest rate, and the equilibrium quantity of loanable funds decreases. Saving and investment also decrease.

ECONOMICS IN THE NEWS

Taxes and the Global Location of Business

US Firms Move Abroad to Cut Taxes

More big US companies are moving abroad. Tax bills are their main reason and some are moving because they worry that US taxes will rise in the future as the tax code changes to shrink the federal budget deficit.

Source: *The Wall Street Journal*, 28 August 2012

Some Facts about Corporate Income Taxes

◆ The US corporate income tax rate is among the world's highest.

◆ Figure 1 shows the corporation income tax rates in a selection of countries.

The Questions

◆ On which factor incomes does the corporate income tax fall?

◆ How does the corporate income tax influence investment, potential GDP and its growth rate?

◆ How does the corporate income tax rate influence employment?

The Answers

◆ The corporate income tax is a tax on interest earned by capital and on profit earned by entrepreneurs.

◆ The corporate income tax rate influences investment and the level and growth rate of potential GDP by driving a wedge between the interest paid by borrowers and the interest earned by lenders.

◆ Figure 2 illustrates the corporate income tax wedge in the market for loanable funds.

◆ The demand for loanable funds is *DLF*, and with no corporate income tax the supply of loanable funds is *SLF*. The equilibrium real interest rate is 3.4 per cent a year and the quantity of loanable funds finances saving and investment of $2.5 trillion. (The numbers are assumed but realistic.)

◆ With the tax wedge from the US 40 per cent corporate tax rate, the supply of loanable funds curve is *SLF + US tax*. The real interest rate is 4 per cent a year and investment and saving are only $2 trillion.

◆ With the smaller tax wedge from the UK 24 per cent corporate tax rate, the supply of loanable funds curve is *SLF + UK tax*. The real interest rate is lower at 3.8 per cent a year and investment and saving are higher at $2.2 trillion.

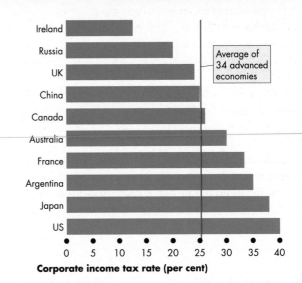

Figure 1   International Comparison of Corporate Income Tax Rates

◆ A smaller amount of saving and investment means a smaller capital stock, smaller potential GDP and a slower growth rate of potential GDP.

◆ A smaller capital stock means that labour is less productive, the demand for labour is lower and the quantity of labour employed is smaller.

◆ The high US corporate income tax rate lowers US incomes and costs US jobs but creates jobs in lower-tax countries.

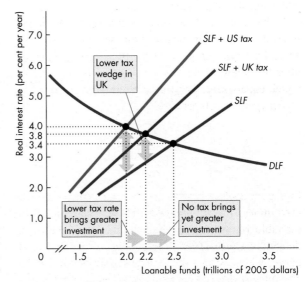

Figure 2   How the Corporate Tax Rate Changes Saving and Investment

AT ISSUE

How, Whether and When to Balance the Government's Budget

The details change from year to year but the central issue remains: should fiscal policy focus on stimulating demand to achieve full-employment and redistribute income from the richest to the rest? Or should the focus be on strengthening the incentives to invest, save and work and on lowering the ratio of government debt to GDP to increase potential GDP and speed economic growth?

Both sides argue that their approach is better. Let's look at the competing proposals.

The IMF and Keynesians

◆ In 2013, the UK economy was expanding slowly and the International Monetary Fund (IMF) believed that low and slow-growing aggregate demand was the reason.

◆ In its April 2013 *World Economic Outlook*, the IMF expressed the view that UK fiscal policy was a source of weak aggregate demand and that a different policy was needed.

◆ The IMF argued that fiscal policy should be more flexible and used to stimulate aggregate demand by undertaking government investment projects at an earlier date than planned.

◆ The IMF predicted that this approach would stimulate private investment and speed real GDP growth.

◆ Shadow Chancellor Ed Balls agreed with the IMF and said more bluntly that the government's fiscal policy was a drag on economic growth.

◆ Some Keynesian economists agreed with this line of reasoning and argued that with interest rates near zero, a rise in government spending will increase the expected inflation rate, lower the real interest rate and boost investment.

Osborne's Budget Strategy

◆ Chancellor of the Exchequer George Osborne recognised that subdued growth is making the recovery from recession more uneven and slower than expected but was unmoved by the IMF report and reasserted that there is 'no plan B'.

◆ The government's strategy of fiscal consolidation and austerity is built on two principles: (1) contain public debt and pursue a credible deficit-reduction plan, and (2) implement supply-side reforms that create jobs and increase productivity and incomes.

◆ Osborne proposes to increase government capital spending by £3 billion a year in 2015, paid for by cutting government consumption spending and public sector pay.

◆ The budget plan maintains spending on education and health services, which represent investments in human capital.

◆ The main supply-side part of the fiscal strategy is to cut the corporation income tax rate to 20 per cent, which would equal the lowest rate in the G20 countries (but be higher than Ireland's rate).

" . . . planned fiscal tightening . . . will be a drag on the economy [and] with unemployment high and interest rates low, the government should take the opportunity to bring forward "high value" spending that has big long-term payoffs."
IMF Survey, 22 May 2013

Christine Lagarde,
IMF Managing Director

" . . . a stark reminder of the debt problems facing our country – and the clearest possible warning to anyone who thinks we can run away from dealing with those problems."
George Osborne on news that UK downgraded by debt rating agency Moody's, 23 February 2013

George Osborne,
Chancellor of the Exchequer

Tax Revenues and the Laffer Curve

An interesting consequence of the effect of taxes on employment and saving is that a higher tax rate does not always bring greater tax revenue. A higher tax rate brings in more revenue per pound earned. But because a higher tax rate decreases the number of pounds earned, two forces operate in opposite directions on the tax revenue collected.

The relationship between the tax rate and the amount of tax revenue collected is called the **Laffer curve**. The curve is so named because Arthur B. Laffer, a member of US President Ronald Reagan's Economic Policy Advisory Board, drew such a curve on a table napkin and launched the idea that tax cuts could increase tax revenue.

Figure 29.7 shows a Laffer curve. The tax rate is on the x-axis, and total tax revenue is on the y-axis. For tax rates below T^*, an increase in the tax rate increases tax revenue; at T^*, tax revenue is maximised; and a tax rate increase above T^* decreases tax revenue.

Most people think that the UK is on the upward-sloping part of the Laffer curve; so is the US. But France might be close to the maximum point or perhaps even beyond it.

The Supply-Side Debate

Before 1980, few economists paid attention to the supply-side effects of taxes on employment and potential GDP. Then, when Ronald Reagan took office as president, a group of supply-siders began to argue the virtues of cutting taxes. Arthur Laffer was one of them. Laffer and his supporters were not held in high esteem among mainstream economists, but they were influential for a period. They correctly argued that tax cuts would increase employment and increase output. But they incorrectly argued that tax cuts would increase tax revenues and decrease the budget deficit. For this prediction to be correct, the US would have had to be on the 'wrong' side of the Laffer curve. Given that US tax rates are among the lowest in the industrial world, it is unlikely that this condition was met. And when the Reagan administration did cut taxes, the budget deficit increased, a fact that reinforces this view.

Supply-side economics became tarnished because of its association with Laffer and came to be called 'voodoo economics'. But mainstream economists, including Martin Feldstein, a Harvard professor who was Reagan's chief economic advisor, recognised the power of tax cuts as incentives but took the standard

Figure 29.7 A Laffer Curve

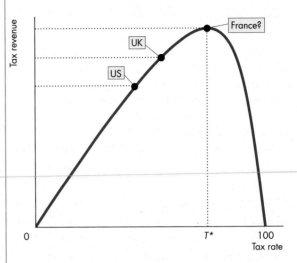

A Laffer curve shows the relationship between the tax rate and tax revenues. For tax rates below T^*, an increase in the tax rate increases tax revenue. At the tax rate T^*, tax revenue is maximised. For tax rates above T^*, an increase in the tax rate decreases tax revenue.

MyEconLab Animation ————————◆

view that tax cuts without spending cuts would swell the budget deficit and bring serious further problems. This view is now widely accepted by economists of all political persuasions.

 REVIEW QUIZ

1   How does a tax on labour income influence the equilibrium quantity of employment?
2   How does the tax wedge influence potential GDP?
3   Why are consumption taxes relevant for measuring the tax wedge?
4   Why are income taxes on capital income more powerful than those on labour income?
5   What is the Laffer curve, and why is it unlikely that the UK is on the 'wrong' side of it?

Do these questions in Study Plan 29.2 and get instant feedback.   MyEconLab

You now know how taxes influence potential GDP and saving and investment. Next we look at the generational effects of fiscal policy.

Generational Effects of Fiscal Policy

Is a budget deficit a burden on future generations? If it is, how will the burden be borne? And is the budget deficit the only burden on future generations? What about the deficit in the state pension fund? Does it matter who owns the bonds that the government sells to finance its deficit? What about the bonds owned by foreigners? Won't repaying those bonds impose a bigger burden than repaying bonds owned by UK residents?

To answer questions like these, we use a tool called **generational accounting** – an accounting system that measures the lifetime tax burden and benefits of each generation. This accounting system was developed by Alan Auerbach of the University of Pennsylvania and Laurence Kotlikoff of Boston University. Generational accounts for the UK have been prepared by Roberto Cardarelli and James Sefton of the National Institute of Economic and Social Research in London and Laurence Kotlikoff (reported in the *Economic Journal*, November 2000).

Generational Accounting and Present Value

Income taxes and National Insurance contributions are paid by people who have jobs. Pensions are paid to people after they retire. Healthcare benefits are also provided on a larger scale to older retired people. So to compare taxes and benefits, we must compare the value of taxes paid by people during their working years with the benefits received in their retirement years. To compare the value of an amount of money at one date with that at a later date, we use the concept of present value. A **present value** is an amount of money that, if invested today, will grow to equal a given future amount when the interest that it earns is taken into account. We can compare pounds today with pounds in 2030 or any other future year by using present values.

For example, if the interest rate is 5 per cent a year, £1,000 invested today will grow, with interest, to £11,467 after 50 years. So the present value (in 2010) of £11,467 in 2060 is £1,000.

By using present values, we can assess the magnitude of the government's debts to older citizens in the form of state pensions and medical benefits.

But the assumed interest rate and growth rate of taxes and benefits critically influence the answers we get. For example, at an interest rate of 3 per cent a year, the

present value (in 2010) of £11,467 in 2060 is £2,616. The lower the interest rate, the greater is the present value of a given future amount.

Because there is uncertainty about the proper interest rate to use to calculate present values, plausible alternative numbers are used to estimate a range of present values.

Using generational accounting and present values, economists have studied the situation facing the governments arising from their pension and healthcare obligations, and they have found some time bombs!

The UK Welfare State and the Pensions Time Bomb

In 1942, as the Second World War was raging, William Beveridge (an economist and Director of the London School of Economics) envisaged a world in which the state provided social insurance that protected everyone from the five evils of 'want, disease, ignorance, squalor and idleness'. The *Beveridge Report* became the blueprint for the creation of the post-war welfare state, which provided universal pensions and health services as well as education and housing.

When state pensions and the National Health Service (NHS) were introduced, today's demographic situation was not foreseen. The age distribution of the UK population is dominated by a surge in the birth rate after the Second World War that created what is called the 'baby boom generation'. More than 12 million 'baby boomers' (almost 20 per cent of the population) are now retired or of retirement age. By 2033, more than 20 per cent of the population will have reached retirement age. Under today's arrangements, outlays on pensions and operating the NHS in 2033 will vastly exceed today's outlays. The obligation to make these outlays is a debt owed by the government and is just as real as the bonds that the government has issued to finance its budget deficits.

Fiscal Imbalance

To assess the government's obligations, economists use the concept of fiscal imbalance. **Fiscal imbalance** is the present value of the government's commitments to pay benefits minus the present value of its tax revenues. Fiscal imbalance is an attempt to measure the scale of the government's true liabilities – its true debt. The production of these accounts requires assumptions about future population trends, taxes, transfers and government expenditure, the initial value of government debt and the real rate of interest used in the present value discounting. The calculation of the fiscal imbalance is highly sensitive to these assumptions. For example, it matters very much whether pensions and unemployment benefits are linked to inflation or to earnings growth.

Estimates of UK and Other Fiscal Imbalances

On the assumption of strict control of government spending, Cardelli, Sefton and Kotlikoff reckon that the fiscal imbalance is 20 per cent of GDP. This figure is large but not an impossible one for the government to plan for. A more recent estimate is much less optimistic. Four economists at Freiburg University[1] estimate the UK's fiscal imbalance at a staggering 510 per cent of GDP. If this figure is correct, when added to the government's market debt in 2010, the total debt obligation of the UK government is 575 per cent of GDP – or £8.3 trillion (in 2010 prices).

Figure 29.8 shows the Freiburg economists' estimates of international fiscal imbalances for eight countries. The UK has the largest fiscal imbalance, but the US, France and Germany also have sizeable fiscal imbalances.

Fiscal imbalance is an enormous obligation for many countries and it points to a catastrophic future. How can the UK government meet its pension and NHS obligations?

Coping With Fiscal Imbalances

There are five possible ways of coping with the fiscal imbalances:

1 Raise income taxes

2 Raise National Insurance contributions

3 Cut government discretionary spending

4 Cut unemployment and other welfare state benefits

5 Raise the state pension age

None of these measures is painless or free from political controversy. By combining the five measures, the pain from each could be lessened, but it would still be severe.

Raising income taxes or raising National Insurance contributions would have damaging supply-side effects.

[1] Christian Hagist, Stefan Moog, Bernd Raffelhüschen and Johannes Vatter, *Public Debt and Demography – An International Comparison Using Generational Accounting*, Cesifo DICE Report 4 2009.

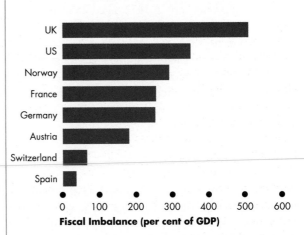

Figure 29.8 Fiscal Imbalances in Eight Economies

Fiscal imbalance is an enormous problem for many countries. On current tax and benefit rates, the UK government has a true debt of more than 5 years' GDP. The US government isn't far behind at almost 4 years' GDP. Even Norway and Germany, normally considered to have sound fiscal policies, owe almost 3 years' GDP to future citizens. Spain is at the other extreme with a fiscal imbalance of only a few months' GDP.

Source of data: Hagist, Moog, Raffelhüschen and Vatter (see footnote 1).

MyEconLab Animation ──────────────────▶

Either action would lower potential GDP and the growth rate of real GDP and lower the well-being of future generations. Government discretionary spending is just about impossible to cut, and doing so presents challenges for national security and public health and safety. This leaves cutting benefits as the only viable option.

There is one further way of meeting these obligations and that is to pay for them by printing money. But the consequence of this solution is a seriously high inflation rate (see Chapter 24, pp. 576–577).

Generational Imbalance

A fiscal imbalance must eventually be corrected, and when it is, people either pay higher taxes or receive lower benefits. The concept of generational imbalance tells us who will pay. **Generational imbalance** is the division of the fiscal imbalance between the current and future generations, assuming that the current generation will enjoy the existing levels of taxes and benefits.

The numbers produced by Cardarelli, Sefton and Kotlikoff (at the low end of the range of estimates) suggest that people born in 1972 (aged 25 in 1997) will pay 65 per cent more in taxes over their lifetime than those born in 1997.

Because the estimated fiscal imbalance is so large, it is not possible to predict how it will be resolved. But we can predict that the outcome will involve both lower benefits and higher taxes or paying bills with new money and creating inflation.

International Debt

You've seen that borrowing from the rest of the world is one source of loanable funds. What value of UK bonds are held abroad? Research by Adam Chester and Hann-Ju Ho of Lloyds TSB suggests that 30 per cent or £284 billion of UK government bonds are held by foreign investors. This amount is well short of total UK foreign indebtedness because foreign investors own corporate bonds, shares and bank deposits.

The international debt of the UK is important because, when that debt is repaid, the UK will transfer real resources to the rest of the world. Instead of running a large net trade deficit, the UK will need a surplus of exports over imports. To make a surplus possible, UK saving must increase and consumption must decrease. Some tough choices lie ahead.

REVIEW QUIZ

1   What is a present value?
2   Distinguish between fiscal imbalance and generational imbalance.
3   How large was the estimated UK fiscal imbalance in 2010 and what is an indicator of how it divides between current and future generations?
4   What is the source of the UK fiscal imbalance and what are the painful choices that we face?
5   How much of UK government debt is held by the rest of the world?

Do these questions in Study Plan 29.3 and get instant feedback.   MyEconLab

You now know how the supply-side effects of fiscal policy work and you've seen the shocking scale of fiscal imbalance. We conclude this chapter by looking at fiscal policy as a tool for fighting a recession.

 Fiscal Stimulus

The 2008–2009 recession brought Keynesian macroeconomic ideas back into fashion and put a spotlight on **fiscal stimulus** – the use of fiscal policy to increase production and employment. But whether fiscal policy is truly stimulating and, if so, how stimulating, are questions that generate much discussion and disagreement. You're now going to explore these questions.

Fiscal stimulus can be either automatic or discretionary. A fiscal policy action that is triggered by the state of the economy with no action by government is called **automatic fiscal policy**. The increase in total unemployment benefits triggered by the massive rise in the unemployment rate through 2009 is an example of automatic fiscal policy.

A fiscal policy action initiated by government is called **discretionary fiscal policy**. It requires a change in a spending programme or in a tax law. A fiscal stimulus initiated by the Obama administration in the US in 2009 as a means of dealing with the recession is an example of discretionary fiscal policy.

Whether automatic or discretionary, an increase in government outlays or a decrease in government receipts can stimulate production and jobs. An increase in expenditure on goods and services directly increases aggregate expenditure. And an increase in transfer payments (such as unemployment benefits) or a decrease in tax revenues increases disposable income, which enables people to increase consumption expenditure. Lower taxes also strengthen the incentives to work and invest.

We'll begin by looking at automatic fiscal policy and the interaction between the business cycle and the budget balance.

Automatic Fiscal Policy and Cyclical and Structural Budget Balances

Two items in the government budget change automatically in response to the state of the economy. They are *tax revenues* and *means-tested spending*.

Automatic Changes in Tax Revenues

The tax laws that Parliament enacts don't legislate the number of pounds the government will raise. Rather they define the tax rates that people must pay. The number of pounds paid depends on tax rates and incomes. But incomes vary with real GDP, so tax revenues depend on real GDP. When real GDP increases in a business cycle expansion, wages and profits rise, so tax revenues from these incomes rise. When real GDP decreases in a recession, wages and profits fall, so tax revenues fall.

Means-tested Spending

The government creates programmes that pay benefits to qualified people and businesses. The spending on these programmes results in transfer payments that depend on the economic state of individual citizens and businesses. When the economy expands, unemployment falls and the number of people experiencing economic hardship decreases, so means-tested spending decreases. When the economy is in a recession, unemployment is high and the number of people experiencing economic hardship increases, so means-tested spending on unemployment benefits and food stamps increases.

Automatic Stimulus

Because government receipts fall and outlays increase in a recession, the budget provides automatic stimulus that helps to shrink the recessionary gap. Similarly, because receipts rise and outlays decrease in a boom, the budget provides automatic restraint to shrink an inflationary gap.

Cyclical and Structural Budget Balances

To identify the government budget deficit that arises from the business cycle, we distinguish between the **structural surplus or deficit**, which is the budget balance that would occur if the economy were at full employment, and the **cyclical surplus or deficit**, which is the actual budget balance *minus* the structural surplus or deficit.

Figure 29.9 illustrates these concepts. Outlays *decrease* as real GDP increases, so the outlays curve slopes downward; and receipts *increase* as real GDP increases, so the receipts curve slopes upward.

In Figure 29.9(a), potential GDP is £1,600 billion, and if real GDP equals potential GDP, the government has a *balanced budget*. There is no structural surplus or deficit. But there might be a cyclical surplus or deficit. If real GDP is less than potential GDP at £1,500 billion, outlays exceed receipts and there is a *cyclical deficit*. If real GDP is greater than potential GDP at £1,700 billion, outlays are less than receipts and there is a *cyclical surplus*.

Figure 29.9 Cyclical and Structural Surpluses and Deficits

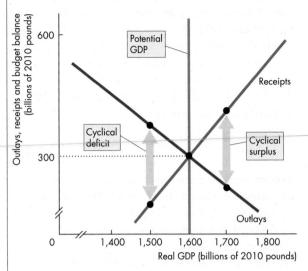

(a) Cyclical deficit and cyclical surplus

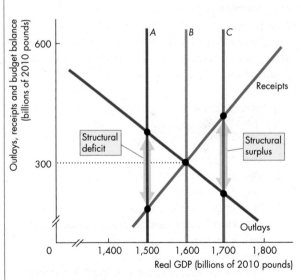

(b) Structural deficit and structural surplus

In part (a), potential GDP is £1,600 billion. When real GDP is less than potential GDP, the budget is in a cyclical deficit. When real GDP exceeds potential GDP, the budget is in a cyclical surplus. The government has a balanced budget when real GDP equals potential GDP.

In part (b), if potential GDP is £1,500 billion, there is a structural deficit, and if potential GDP is £1,700 billion, there is a structural surplus. If potential GDP is £1,600 billion, the budget is in structural balance.

MyEconLab Animation

In Figure 29.9(b), if potential GDP equals £1,600 billion (line *B*), the structural balance is zero. But if potential GDP is £1,500 billion (line *A*), the government budget has a *structural deficit*. And if potential GDP is £1,700 billion (line *C*), the government budget has a *structural surplus*.

UK Structural Budget Balance

The UK budget deficit in 2012 was £121 billion. The recessionary gap (the gap between real GDP and potential GDP) was about 2.5 to 3 per cent of potential GDP. With such a significant recessionary gap, you would expect some of the deficit to be cyclical. But how much of the 2012 deficit was cyclical and how much was structural?

The Office for Budget Responsibility of HM Government estimates that the UK had a structural deficit of 5.9 per cent of potential GDP in 2012.

Figure 29.10 shows the UK actual and structural deficits. The gap between the two shows the cyclical deficit. You can see that the cyclical deficit was small from 2004 to 2008, but that it exploded in 2009. When full employment returns to the UK, the cyclical deficit will vanish.

Figure 29.10 UK Cyclical and Structural Budget Balance

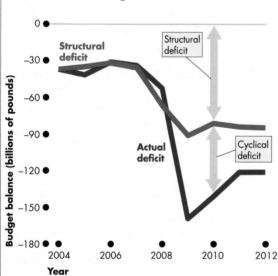

As real GDP shrank during the 2008–2009 recession, government receipts fell, outlays increased and the budget deficit increased. The cyclical deficit was small compared with the actual deficit and most of the 2012 deficit was structural.

Source of data: HM Treasury, *Budget 2010*.

MyEconLab Animation ───────────────◆

ECONOMICS IN ACTION

The Largest Fiscal Stimulus Ever

Back in 2008, when Gordon Brown was the UK Prime Minister, he called on all governments to cut taxes and increase spending to stimulate a flagging global economy. The world's largest economy came to Brown's party in grand style when, in February 2009, Barack Obama signed into law his third and most ambitious in a series of stimulus packages aimed at increasing investment and consumer expenditure and creating jobs.

The total package added $862 billion to the US government's budget deficit: $288 billion from tax cuts and the rest from increased spending. The spending increases included payments to state and local governments ($144 billion), spending on infrastructure and science projects ($111 billion), and programmes in healthcare ($59 billion), education and training ($53 billion) and energy ($43 billion).

Despite this massive fiscal policy action, US unemployment barely moved for a further four years.

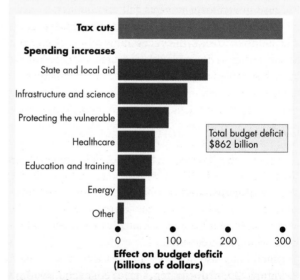

Figure 1 The Components of the 2009 Fiscal Stimulus Act

Obama signs the 2009 Fiscal Stimulus Act.

Discretionary Fiscal Stimulus

Most discussion of discretionary fiscal stimulus focuses on its effects on aggregate demand. But you've seen (on pp. 696–698) that taxes influence aggregate supply and that the balance of taxes and spending – the government budget deficit – can crowd out investment and slow the pace of economic growth. So discretionary fiscal stimulus has both supply-side and demand-side effects that end up determining its overall effectiveness.

We're going to begin our examination of discretionary fiscal stimulus by looking at its effects on aggregate demand.

Fiscal Stimulus and Aggregate Demand

An increase in government expenditure has a direct effect on aggregate demand. A tax cut influences aggregate demand by increasing disposable income and consumption expenditure. Both forms of fiscal stimulus have multiplier effects.

Let's look at the two main fiscal policy multipliers: the government expenditure and tax multipliers.

The **government expenditure multiplier** is the quantitative effect of a change in government expenditure on real GDP. Because government expenditure is a component of aggregate expenditure, an increase in government spending increases aggregate expenditure and real GDP. But does a £1 billion increase in government expenditure increase real GDP by £1 billion, or more than £1 billion, or less than £1 billion?

When an increase in government expenditure increases real GDP, incomes rise and the higher incomes bring an increase in consumption expenditure. If this were the only consequence of increased government expenditure, the government expenditure multiplier would be greater than 1.

But an increase in government expenditure increases government borrowing (or decreases government lending if there is a budget surplus) and raises the real interest rate. With a higher cost of borrowing, investment decreases, which partly offsets the increase in government spending. If this were the only consequence of increased government expenditure, the multiplier would be less than 1.

The actual multiplier depends on which of the above effects is stronger, and the consensus is that the crowding-out effect is strong enough to make the government expenditure multiplier less than 1.

The **tax multiplier** is the quantitative effect of a change in taxes on real GDP. The demand-side effects of a tax cut are likely to be smaller than an equivalent increase in government expenditure. The reason is that a tax cut influences aggregate demand by increasing disposable income, only part of which gets spent. So the initial injection of expenditure from a £1 billion tax cut is less than £1 billion.

A tax cut has similar crowding-out consequences to a spending increase. It increases government borrowing (or decreases government lending), raises the real interest rate and cuts investment.

The tax multiplier effect on aggregate demand depends on these two opposing effects and is probably quite small.

Figure 29.11 shows how fiscal stimulus is supposed to work if it is perfectly executed and has its desired effects.

Potential GDP is £1,600 billion and real GDP is below potential at £1,500 billion so the economy has a recessionary gap of £100 billion.

To restore full employment, the government passes a fiscal stimulus package. An increase in government

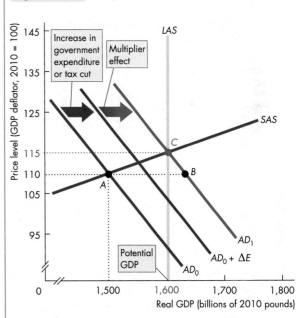

Figure 29.11 Expansionary Fiscal Policy

Potential GDP is £1,600 billion, real GDP is £1,500 billion, and there is a £100 billion recessionary gap. An increase in government expenditure and a tax cut increase aggregate expenditure by ΔE. The multiplier increases consumption expenditure. The *AD* curve shifts rightward to AD_1, the price level rises to 115, real GDP increases to £1,600 billion and the recessionary gap is eliminated.

MyEconLab Animation ─────────────◆

expenditure and a tax cut increase aggregate expenditure by ΔE. If this were the only change in spending plans, the AD curve would shift rightward to become the curve labelled $AD_0 + \Delta E$ in Figure 29.11. But if fiscal stimulus sets off a multiplier process that increases consumption expenditure, and does not crowd out much investment expenditure, aggregate demand increases further and the AD curve shifts to AD_1.

With no change in the price level, the economy would move from point A to point B on AD_1. But the increase in aggregate demand brings a rise in the price level along the upward-sloping SAS curve and the economy moves to point C.

At point C, the economy returns to full employment and the recessionary gap is eliminated.

Fiscal Stimulus and Aggregate Supply

You've seen earlier in this chapter that taxes influence aggregate supply. A tax on labour income (on wages) drives a wedge between the cost of labour and the take-home pay of workers and lowers employment and output (p. 696). A tax on capital income (on interest) drives a wedge between the cost of borrowing and the return to lending and lowers saving and investment (p. 698). With less saving and investment, the real GDP growth rate slows.

These negative effects of taxes on real GDP and its growth rate and on employment mean that tax cuts increase real GDP and its growth rate and increase employment.

These supply-side effects of tax cuts occur along with the demand-side effects and are probably much larger than the demand-side effects and make the overall tax multiplier much larger than the government expenditure multiplier – see *Economics in Action*.

An increase in government expenditure financed by borrowing increases the demand for loanable funds. The real interest rate rises, which decreases investment and private saving. This cut in investment is the main reason why the government expenditure multiplier is so small and why a deficit-financed increase in government spending ends up making only a small contribution to job creation. And because government expenditure crowds out investment, it lowers future real GDP.

So a fiscal stimulus package that is heavy on tax cuts and light on government spending works. But an increase in government expenditure alone is not an effective way to stimulate production and create jobs.

The description of the effects of discretionary fiscal stimulus and its graphical illustration in Figure 29.11

makes it look easy: calculate the recessionary gap and the multipliers, change government expenditure and taxes, and eliminate the gap. In reality, getting the magnitude and the timing right is difficult.

Magnitude of Stimulus

Economists have diverging views about the size of the government expenditure and tax multipliers. This fact makes it impossible for government to determine the amount of stimulus needed to close a given output gap. Further, the actual output gap is not known and can only be estimated with error. For these two reasons, discretionary fiscal policy is risky.

 ECONOMICS IN ACTION

How Big Are the Fiscal Multipliers?

When the government cuts taxes by £1 billion or increases its expenditure by £1 billion, by how much do aggregate expenditure and real GDP change? How big are the fiscal policy multipliers? Is the government expenditure multiplier larger than the tax multiplier? And is the multiplier bigger for a change in government capital expenditure than for a change in current consumption expenditure? These questions are about the multiplier effects on equilibrium real GDP, not just on aggregate demand.

Two American economists have different answers to these questions. Obama's former economic adviser Christina Romer, a University of California, Berkeley, professor, says the government expenditure multiplier is about 1.5. She agrees that the biggest fiscal stimulus in history (see *Economics in Action* on p. 706) didn't deliver in line with a multiplier of 1.5, but says other factors deteriorated and without the fiscal stimulus the outcome would have been even worse. Robert Barro, a professor at Harvard University, says Romer's multiplier number is not in line with previous experience and that the multiplier is 0.5.

Patrick Minford, a professor at Cardiff University, says that the government expenditure multiplier on real GDP is even smaller and is 0.35. He arrives at this number based on 30 years of research on the UK economy. Harald Uhlig, a professor at the University of Chicago, agrees with Minford's assessment of the multiplier and says this number also applies to the US.

There is greater agreement about tax multipliers. Because tax cuts strengthen the incentive to work and to invest, they increase aggregate supply as well as aggregate demand. These multipliers get bigger as more time elapses. Harald

Time Lags

Discretionary fiscal stimulus actions are also seriously hampered by three time lags:

◆ Recognition lag
◆ Law-making lag
◆ Impact lag

Recognition Lag

The recognition lag is the time it takes to figure out that fiscal policy actions are needed. This process involves assessing the current state of the economy and forecasting its future state.

Law-making Lag

The law-making lag is the time it takes to pass the laws needed to change taxes or spending. This process takes time because each MP has a different idea about what is the best tax or spending programme to change, so long debates and committee meetings are needed to reconcile conflicting views. The economy might benefit from fiscal stimulation today, but by the time the law has been passed a different fiscal medicine might be needed.

Impact Lag

The impact lag is the time it takes from passing a tax or spending change to its effects on real GDP being felt. This lag depends partly on the speed with which government agencies can act and partly on the timing of changes in spending plans by households and businesses. These changes are spread out over a number of quarters and possibly a number of years.

Economic forecasting is steadily improving, but it remains inexact and subject to error. The range of uncertainty about the magnitudes of the government expenditure and tax multipliers make discretionary fiscal stimulus an imprecise tool for boosting production and jobs. Also the crowding-out consequences of fiscal stimulus raise serious questions about its effects on long-term economic growth.

Uhlig says that after one year the tax multiplier is 0.5, so a £1 billion tax cut would increase real GDP by about £500 million after a year. But with two years to respond, real GDP would be £2 billion higher – a multiplier of 2. And after three years, the tax multiplier builds up to more than 6. Patrick Minford's research on the UK economy supports the findings of Uhlig.

The implications of the work of Barro, Uhlig and Minford are that tax cuts are a powerful way to stimulate real GDP and employment but spending increases are not effective.

The fiscal multipliers assumed by the UK Treasury don't fit well with the general consensus and the assumed tax multipliers are the smallest, not the largest. The Treasury's multipliers are 0.35 for a change in the VAT rate, 0.3 for a change in personal taxes, 0.6 for a change in government current expenditure, and 1.0 for a change in government capital expenditure.

Christina Romer 1.5

Robert Barro 0.50

Patrick Minford 0.35

REVIEW QUIZ

1 What is the distinction between automatic and discretionary fiscal policy?
2 How do taxes and means-tested spending programmes work as automatic stabilisers to dampen the business cycle?
3 How do we tell whether a budget deficit needs discretionary action to remove it?
4 How can the government use discretionary fiscal policy to stimulate the economy?
5 Why might fiscal stimulus crowd out investment?

Do these questions in Study Plan 29.4 and get instant feedback.   MyEconLab

You've now seen the effects of fiscal policy, and *Reading Between the Lines* on pp. 710–711 applies what you've learned to the fiscal policy actions of the UK government in using contractionary fiscal policy alongside an announced future increase in government expenditure on infrastructure projects.

Fiscal Policy in the UK

Danny Alexander Puts Flesh on Chancellor's Spending Plans

George Parker, Political Editor

Britain's transport, energy, housing and communications are set for the biggest investment in a generation, the Treasury claimed on Thursday, in the latest attempt to re-launch its much-criticised infrastructure programme.

Danny Alexander, Treasury chief secretary, committed £100bn to new projects stretching to the end of the decade, partly funded by the sale of government assets and delivered with the aid of commercial sector expertise.

The Lib Dem minister promised "the biggest public housing programme for over 20 years, the largest rail investment since Victorian times and the greatest investment in our roads since the 1970s and fast online access for the whole country".

The announcement put flesh on plans for capital spending announced by George Osborne, the chancellor, in his spending review on Wednesday, in which he committed £300bn to capital spending, of which £100bn would be allocated to specific projects. The statement ranged from new roads and bridges to nuclear power stations and flood defences, along with a promise to build 165,000 new low cost homes – a priority for the Lib Dems. . . .

Ed Miliband, Labour leader, may still offer to outspend the coalition's proposed £300bn in the next parliament, but he would probably have to fund it through higher borrowing – a risky step for the opposition party.

Labour was dismissive of his statement, saying ministers should follow the advice of the International Monetary Fund by bringing forward capital projects now, instead of making promises far into the future.

The Essence of the Story

- The UK government announced plans to spend £300 billion on infrastructure projects over the rest of the decade.

- The £100 billion will be financed from the sale of government assets.

- The Opposition Labour party says these projects should be done now instead of promised far into the future

- The Opposition may propose even higher spending financed by higher borrowing.

Economic Analysis

◆ The UK government plans to cut its budget deficit to less than 3 per cent of GDP by 2017, but the debt to GDP ratio will rise to exceed 100 per cent before starting to fall. Figure 1 shows this plan and projection.

◆ The government expects real GDP growth to remain low so that even by 2017 it expects a recessionary gap of 2.1 per cent of potential GDP. Figure 2 shows these forecasts.

◆ The IMF has suggested that the UK government seek to boost economic growth by bringing forward spending on planned infrastructure projects.

◆ But it takes time to identify projects and then to organise their implementation.

◆ The government has announced plans for infrastructure spending on road, rail and housing projects to begin in 2015.

◆ But the government does not intend this increase in spending to increase its deficit. Instead, the government plans to cut spending on current consumption items, including public sector pay.

◆ The government believes that by announcing the projects now, it will influence expectations and help stimulate private investment.

◆ Figure 3 illustrates the government's hoped-for outcome. With aggregate demand curve AD_0, real GDP is £1.50 trillion, below potential GDP of £1.60 trillion.

◆ On its own, a cut in government expenditure would decrease aggregate demand and the AD curve would shift leftward to AD_1. Real GDP would decrease.

◆ But firms anticipating future government infrastructure projects, gear up now for an expected increase in aggregate demand, and an increase in investment increases aggregate demand. The AD curve shifts rightward to AD_2 and real GDP increases to £1.53 trillion. It remains below potential GDP, but the output gap shrinks.

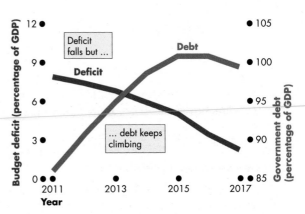

Figure 1 Projected Government Debt and Budget Deficit

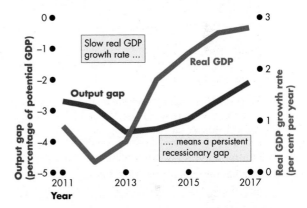

Figure 2 Projected Output Gap and Real GDP Growth Rate

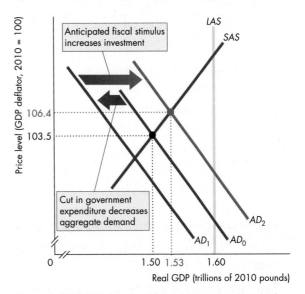

Figure 3 UK Aggregate Supply and Aggregate Demand

SUMMARY

Key Points

Government Budgets (pp. 690–695)

◆ The government budget finances the activities of the government and is used to conduct fiscal policy.

◆ Government receipts come from taxes on income and wealth, taxes on expenditure and National Insurance contributions.

◆ When government outlays exceed receipts, the government has a budget deficit.

Do Problems 1 to 3 to get a better understanding of government budgets.

Supply-Side Effects of Fiscal Policy
(pp. 696–701)

◆ Fiscal policy has supply-side effects because taxes weaken the incentive to work and decrease employment and potential GDP.

◆ Fiscal policy has supply-side effects because taxes weaken the incentive to save and invest, which lowers the growth rate of real GDP.

◆ The Laffer curve shows the relationship between the tax rate and the amount of tax revenue collected.

Do Problems 4 to 7 to get a better understanding of the supply-side effects of fiscal policy.

Generational Effects of Fiscal Policy
(pp. 702–704)

◆ Generational accounting measures the lifetime tax burden and benefits of each generation.

◆ One study estimates the UK fiscal imbalance to be 510 per cent of the value of one year's production.

◆ Future generations will pay for 65 per cent of the benefits of the current generation.

◆ About 30 per cent of UK government debt is held by the rest of the world.

Do Problems 8 and 9 to get a better understanding of the generational effects of fiscal policy.

Fiscal Stimulus (pp. 704–709)

◆ Fiscal policy can be automatic or discretionary.

◆ Automatic fiscal policy might moderate the business cycle by stimulating demand in recession and restraining demand in a boom.

◆ Discretionary fiscal stimulus influences aggregate demand and aggregate supply.

◆ Discretionary changes in government expenditure or taxes have multiplier effects of uncertain magnitude, but the tax multiplier is likely to be the larger one.

◆ Fiscal stimulus policies are hampered by uncertainty about multipliers and by time lags (law-making lags and the difficulty of correctly diagnosing and forecasting the state of the economy).

Do Problems 10 to 21 to get a better understanding of fiscal stimulus.

Key Terms

Automatic fiscal policy, 704
Balanced budget, 691
Budget, 690
Budget deficit, 691
Budget surplus, 691
Cyclical surplus or deficit, 705
Discretionary fiscal policy, 704
Fiscal imbalance, 702
Fiscal policy, 690
Fiscal stimulus, 704
Generational accounting, 702
Generational imbalance, 703
Government debt, 693
Government expenditure multiplier, 707
Laffer curve, 701
Present value, 702
Structural surplus or deficit, 705
Tax multiplier, 707
Tax wedge, 697

STUDY PLAN PROBLEMS AND APPLICATIONS

Do Problems 1 to 22 in MyEconLab Chapter 29 Study Plan and get instant feedback.

MyEconLab

Government Budgets (Study Plan 29.1)

Use the following news clip in Problems 1 and 2.

The Budget

George Osborne says he has little option but to push on with the harshest public spending cuts in living memory because a reversal would alarm the bond markets and plunge Britain into 'financial turmoil'. Responding to growing clamour for him to explore a 'plan B' for recovery, the chancellor insisted that there would be no weakening of the government's resolve in implementing austerity measures.

Source: *The Financial Times*, 30 January 2011

1 What is the UK government's plan for fiscal policy in the budget 2010?

2 What would be a 'plan B' for the government to adopt?

3 At the end of 2008, the government of China's debt was ¥4,700 billion. (¥ is yuan, the currency of China.) In 2009, the government spent ¥6,000 billion and ended the year with a debt of ¥5,300 billion. How much did the government receive in tax revenue in 2009? How can you tell?

Supply-Side Effects of Fiscal Policy

(Study Plan 29.2)

4 The government is considering raising the tax rate on labour income and asks you to report on the supply-side effects of such an action. Answer the following questions using appropriate graphs. You are being asked about *directions* of change, not exact magnitudes. What will happen to

  a The supply of labour and why?

  b The demand for labour and why?

  c The equilibrium level of employment and why?

  d The equilibrium before-tax wage rate and why?

  e The equilibrium after-tax wage rate and why?

  f Potential GDP?

5 What fiscal policy action might increase investment and speed economic growth? Explain how the policy action would work.

6 Suppose that instead of taxing *nominal* capital income, the government taxed real capital income. Use appropriate graphs to explain and illustrate the effect that this change would have on

  a The tax rate on capital income.

  b The supply of and demand for loanable funds.

  c Investment and the real interest rate.

7 Suppose that in Sinoland, investment is £400 billion, saving is £400 billion, taxes are £500 billion, exports are £300 billion and imports are £200 billion.

  a Calculate government expenditure and the government budget balance.

  b Explain the impact the government is exerting on investment: is the impact positive or negative?

Generational Effects of Fiscal Policy

(Study Plan 29.3)

8 The Office for Budget Responsibility projects that, under current policies, government debt will reach 233 per cent of GDP in 30 years and nearly 500 per cent in 50 years.

  a What is a fiscal imbalance? How might the government reduce the fiscal imbalance?

  b How would your answer to part (a) influence the generational imbalance?

9 **Increase in US Payroll Taxes Needed for Social Security**

US Social Security faces a $5.3 trillion shortfall over the next 75 years, but a congressional report says the massive gap could be erased by increasing payroll taxes paid by both employees and employers from 6.2 per cent to 7.3 per cent and by raising the retirement age to 70.

Source: *USA Today*, 21 May 2010

  a Why is US Social Security facing a $5.3 trillion shortfall over the next 75 years?

  b Explain how the suggestions in the news clip would reduce the shortfall.

  c Would the suggestions in the news clip change the generational imbalance?

Fiscal Stimulus (Study Plan 29.4)

10 The economy is in a recession, and the recessionary gap is large.

  a Describe the discretionary and automatic fiscal policy actions that might occur.

  b Describe a discretionary fiscal stimulus package that could be used that would not bring an increase in the budget deficit.

  c Explain the risks of discretionary fiscal policy in this situation.

Use the following news clip in Problems 11 to 13.

Obama's Economic Recovery Plan

If the president is serious about focusing on jobs, a good start would be to freeze all tax rates and cut government expenditure on goods and services back to where it was before all the recent bailouts and stimulus spending.

Source: *USA Today*, 9 September 2010

11 What would be the effect on the budget deficit and real GDP of freezing tax rates and cutting government expenditure?

12 What would be the effect on jobs of freezing tax rates and cutting government spending?

13 If the government froze its current expenditure on goods and services and instead cut taxes, what would be the effect on investment and jobs?

14 The economy is in a recession, the recessionary gap is large, and the government has a budget deficit.

  a Do we know whether the budget deficit is structural or cyclical? Explain your answer.

  b Do we know whether automatic stabilisers are increasing or decreasing the output gap? Explain your answer.

  c If a discretionary increase in government expenditure occurs, what happens to the structural deficit or surplus? Explain.

15 The research of economists Patrick Minford and Harald Uhlig suggests that tax cuts to stimulate the economy would pay for themselves in the long run.

  a Explain what is meant by tax cuts paying for themselves. What does this statement imply about the tax multiplier?

  b Why would tax cuts not pay for themselves?

Use the following news clip in Problems 16 and 17.

Shadow Chancellor urges increased borrowing to finance infrastructure spending

Ed Balls, the Shadow Chancellor, announced that a future labour government would be prepared to borrow more to finance infrastructure spending. He urged the Chancellor to increase capital spending in this year and the next to get the economy growing again. With interest rates low and the economy still weak it would be foolish to deny a case for increased capital spending on roads and our infrastructure.

Source: *Daily Mail*, 24 June 2013

16 Is this expenditure on infrastructure a fiscal stimulus? Would such expenditure be a discretionary or an automatic fiscal policy?

17 Explain how the rebuilding of roads and other infrastructure would drive the economic recovery.

Use the following news clip in Problems 18 to 20.

Stimulus Debate Turns on Rebates

In 2008, as pressure built up on Washington to juice the economy, a one-time consumer rebate emerged as the likely centrepiece of a \$150-billion stimulus programme. But who should actually get rebates? Everyone who pays income taxes? Or only lower- and middle-income households because they are more likely to spend more of their rebate than are higher-income households, spend it quickly, and every dollar spent on stimulus could generate a dollar in GDP?

Source: *CNN*, 22 January 2008

18 **a** Explain the intended effect of the \$150 billion fiscal stimulus package. Draw a graph to illustrate the effect.

  b Explain why the effect of this fiscal policy depends on who receives the tax rebates.

19 What would have a larger effect on aggregate demand: \$150 billion worth of tax rebates or \$150 billion worth of government spending?

20 Explain whether a stimulus package centred around a one-time consumer tax rebate is likely to have a small or a large supply-side effect.

21 Compare the impact on equilibrium real GDP of a same-sized decrease in taxes and increase in government expenditure.

Economics in the News (Study Plan 29.N)

22 Pubs in budget VAT cut demand

Struggling pubs want the VAT on food and accommodation to be cut from 20 per cent to just 5 per cent for pubs, restaurants and hotels to give members much-needed relief. An independent report found the move would create 78,000 jobs and raise £2.6 billion for the Treasury over ten years.

Source: *The Sun*, 8 March 2013

  a Explain how a cut in the tax rate affects the equilibrium wage rate and the employment level of hospitality workers.

  b Explain how a cut in the tax rate might, as predicted in the news clip, increase the tax revenue received by government.

  c Explain how a cut in the tax rate on food and accommodation would change consumption expenditure. Would it have a multiplier effect?

ADDITIONAL PROBLEMS AND APPLICATIONS

Do these problems in MyEconLab if assigned by your lecturer.

MyEconLab

Government Budgets

23 UK public sector net debt as a percentage of GDP in 2009/10 was 154.7, but excluding 'financial interventions' by the Bank of England the net debt was 53.6 per cent of GDP.

Explain what accounts for this big difference in the two figures. What did the UK government do in 2008 to inflate the budget deficit and increase the debt–GDP ratio?

Supply-Side Effects of Fiscal Policy

Use the following information in Problems 24 and 25.

Suppose that in the UK investment is £160 billion, saving is £140 billion, government expenditure on goods and services is £150 billion, exports are £200 billion and imports are £250 billion.

24 What is the amount of tax revenue? What is the government budget balance?

25 **a** Is the government's budget exerting a positive or negative impact on investment?

b What fiscal policy action might increase investment and speed economic growth? Explain how the policy action would work.

26 Suppose that capital income taxes are based (as they are in the UK and most countries) on nominal interest rates. And suppose that the inflation rate increases by 5 per cent. Use appropriate diagrams to explain and illustrate the effect that this change would have on

a The tax rate on capital income.

b The supply of loanable funds.

c The demand for loanable funds.

d Equilibrium investment.

e The equilibrium real interest rate.

Use the following news clip in Problems 27 and 28.

Sir Richard Lambert, the outgoing head of the CBI, accused the government of failing to articulate a clear vision for economic growth. Commenting on the 50 per cent tax rate, he said that business investment in the UK will suffer if high paid individuals drifted elsewhere for tax reasons.

Source: *The Financial Times*, 25 January 2011

27 Why has the UK government raised the top rate of tax to 50 per cent?

28 What are the possible long-term consequences of such a tax rise on the supply-side of the economy, for tax revenues and the budget deficit?

Use the following news clip in Problems 29 to 31.

Tax Hikes for Top Earners

750,000 more people will start to pay the 40% rate of tax as a result of forthcoming tax rises. However, 500,000 people will no longer be paying income tax because the point at which income tax starts to be paid will rise. The government has made the tax changes revenue neutral. The main gainers from the tax changes are lone parents and low income households.

Source: BBC, 31 January 2011

29 What do you think the term 'revenue neutral' means?

30 Explain the potential demand-side effect of the tax changes.

31 Explain the potential supply-side effects of the tax changes.

Generational Effects of Fiscal Policy

32 **Push to Cut Deficit Collides With Politics as Usual**

So it goes in Campaign 2010 where cutting the deficit is a big issue but where support for doing some of the hard things to achieve that is running into politics as usual. Nowhere is that more apparent than in the debate – or lack thereof – on the nation's spending on big entitlement programs. According to the latest projections from the Congressional Budget Office, spending on the big three entitlement programs – Social Security, Medicare and Medicaid – is to rise by 70 per cent, 79 per cent, and 99 per cent, respectively, over the next 10 years.

Source: *The Wall Street Journal*, 5 October 2010

If politicians continue to avoid debating the projected increases in these three entitlement programmes, how do you think the fiscal imbalance will change? If Congress holds the budget deficit at $3.1 trillion, who will pay for the projected increases in expenditure?

Fiscal Stimulus

33 The economy is in a boom and the inflationary gap is large.

  a Describe the discretionary and automatic fiscal policy actions that might occur.

  b Describe a discretionary fiscal restraint package that could be used that would not produce serious negative supply-side effects.

  c Explain the risks of discretionary fiscal policy in this situation.

34 The economy is growing slowly, the inflationary gap is large and there is a budget deficit.

  a Do we know whether the budget deficit is structural or cyclical? Explain your answer.

  b Do we know whether automatic stabilisers are increasing or decreasing aggregate demand? Explain your answer.

  c If a discretionary decrease in government expenditure occurs, what happens to the structural budget balance? Explain your answer.

Use the following news clip in Problems 35 to 37.

Juicing the Economy Will Come at a Cost

The $150-billion stimulus plan will bump up the deficit, but not necessarily dollar for dollar. Here's why: if the stimulus works, the increased economic activity will generate federal tax revenue. But it isn't clear what the cost to the economy will be if a stimulus package comes too late – a real concern since legislation could get bogged down by politics.

Source: CNN, 23 January 2008

35 Explain why $150 billion of stimulus won't increase the budget deficit by $150 billion.

36 Is the budget deficit arising from the action described in the news clip structural or cyclical or a combination of the two? Explain.

37 Why might the stimulus package come 'too late'? What are the potential consequences of the stimulus package coming 'too late'?

Economics in the News

38 After you have studied *Reading Between the Lines* on pp. 710–711, answer the following questions.

  a What is the policy the IMF has suggested that the UK government implement regarding fiscal policy?

  b What is the policy the UK government has announced in its budget in 2013?

  c What is the UK budget deficit and debt expected to be in 2014 and 2015?

  d What is the policy that the government announced in the Spending Review in June 2013?

  e Is the policy in part (d) included in the budget projections of 2013?

  f What does the government hope to achieve by announcing increased infrastructure spending in the future?

39 **US Financial Crisis Over? Not Really**

Economist Deepak Lal says the US financial crisis is not solved and contains the seeds of a more serious future crisis. For India and China, with no structural deficit, a temporary budget deficit above that resulting from automatic stabilisers makes sense. But it doesn't make sense for the US with its large structural deficit.

Source: rediff.com, 18 October 2010

More Fiscal Stimulus Needed

Economist Laura Tyson says there is a strong argument for more fiscal stimulus combined with a multi-year deficit reduction plan.

Source: marketwatch.com, 15 October 2010

  a How has the business cycle influenced the US federal budget in the 2008–2009 recession?

  b With which news clip opinion do you agree and why?

  c Why might Laura Tyson favour a multi-year deficit reduction plan and would that address the concerns of Deepak Lal?

30 Monetary Policy

After studying this chapter you will be able to:

- Describe the objectives of UK monetary policy and the framework for achieving them
- Explain how the Bank of England influences interest rates
- Explain the transmission channels through which the Bank of England influences real GDP, jobs and inflation
- Explain the Bank of England's extraordinary policy actions since 2008

Every month, six eminent economists join the Governor and Deputy Governors of the Bank of England to analyse and deliberate on the state of the UK economy and to decide whether to change the interest rate. How does the Bank of England make its interest rate decisions? How does it get the interest rate to change? And how do its decisions influence the economy?

This chapter explains monetary policy. And in *Reading Between the Lines* at the end of the chapter, we look at the Bank of England's policy challenge in mid-2013.

Monetary Policy Objectives and Framework

A nation's monetary policy objectives and the framework for setting and achieving them stem from the relationship between the central bank and government. Monetary policy making involves two activities:

1 Setting the policy objectives
2 Achieving the policy objectives

In a few countries, the central bank sets the objectives and decides how to achieve them. And in some countries, the government makes all the monetary policy decisions and tells the central bank what actions to take. But in most countries, including the UK, the government sets the monetary policy objectives and the central bank decides how to achieve them.

Here, we'll describe the objectives of UK monetary policy and the framework and assignment of responsibility for achieving those objectives.

Monetary Policy Objectives

The objectives of monetary policy are ultimately political and are determined by government. But they are pursued by the actions of the central bank. The Bank of England Act of 1998 sets out the objectives of UK monetary policy.

Bank of England Act 1998

The 1998 Bank of England Act sets out the Bank's monetary policy objectives as being:

(a) to maintain price stability, and

(b) subject to that, to support the economic policy of Her Majesty's Government, including its objectives for growth and employment.[1]

The Act also requires the Chancellor of the Exchequer to specify annually in writing:

(a) what price stability is to be taken to consist of, and

(b) what the economic policy of Her Majesty's Government is to be taken to be.[2]

One of the most important innovations in the 1998 Act is its establishment of the Monetary Policy Committee

[1] Bank of England Act (1998) section 11.
[2] Bank of England Act (1998) section 12.

or MPC, an independent group of six experts who with the Governor and two Deputy Governors make the monetary policy decisions. (See Chapter 24, p. 565 for more details on the composition of the MPC.)

Remit for the Monetary Policy Committee

The Chancellor renews and if necessary modifies the remit for the Monetary Policy Committee at roughly annual intervals. This remit is stated in two parts corresponding to the two monetary policy objectives.

Price Stability Objective

The first part of the remit for the Monetary Policy Committee is an operational definition of 'price stability'. Since the beginning of 2004, this objective has been specified as a target inflation rate of 2 per cent a year as measured by the 12-month increase in the Consumer Prices Index (CPI).

Although the inflation target is renewed annually, the intention is that inflation be locked in at a low and stable rate over the long term. To achieve long-term price stability, deviations from the inflation target in either direction that exceed 1 percentage point require the Governor of the Bank to write an open letter to the Chancellor explaining why the target has been missed and what steps will be taken to bring the inflation rate back to its target. And for every three months that the inflation rate misses its target by more than 1 percentage point, a further explanation must be provided.

Government Economic Policy Objectives

The government's economic policy objectives as they relate to monetary policy are to achieve high and stable levels of economic growth and employment.

Price stability is the key goal and a major contributor to achieving the other goals of government economic policy. Price stability provides the best available environment for households and firms to make the saving and investment decisions that bring economic growth. So price stability encourages the maximum sustainable growth rate of potential GDP.

But in the short run, the Bank of England faces a trade-off between inflation and economic growth and employment. Taking an action that is designed to lower the inflation rate and achieve stable prices might mean slowing the economic growth rate and lowering employment.

In both the primary objective of price stability and the consequential goal of high and stable growth and employment, monetary policy in the UK is similar to that in the rest of the EU (see *Economics in Action* on p. 720).

Actual Inflation and the Inflation Target

Figure 30.1 compares the CPI measure and the target of 2 per cent a year since the beginning of 2004. January 2004 was the date the Bank of England was charged by the Chancellor of the Exchequer to switch from a target of 2.5 per cent a year inflation measured by the Retail Prices Index less mortgage interest payments (RPIX) to a target of 2 per cent a year measured by the Consumer Prices Index (CPI). During this period, the average rate of increase of the CPI was above the target at 2.7 per cent a year.

The Bank of England was successful in keeping inflation within the target range of 1 per cent to 3 per cent a year for three years from the beginning of 2004. But during those years, the inflation rate moved from the bottom to the top of the target range. Inflation burst through the upper limit of the target range in March 2007. This event triggered an open letter from the Governor to the Chancellor as required by the Chancellor's remit for the Monetary Policy Committee. The 3 per cent a year upper bound was breached again from May 2008 to February 2009 and during 2012.

Rationale for an Inflation Target

Two main benefits flow from adopting an inflation target. The first is that the purpose of the Bank of England's policy actions is more clearly understood by financial market traders. A clearer understanding leads to fewer surprises and mistakes on the part of savers and investors.

The second benefit is that the target provides an anchor for expectations about future inflation. Firmly held expectations of low inflation make the short-run output–inflation (or unemployment–inflation) trade-off as favourable as possible – see Chapter 28, pp. 674–676. Also, firmly held (and correct) inflation expectations help individuals and firms to make better economic decisions, which in turn help to achieve a more efficient allocation of resources and a more stable economic growth rate.

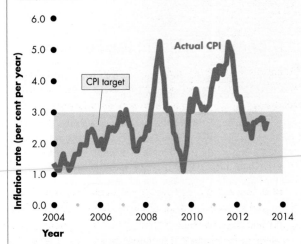

Figure 30.1 Inflation Target and Outcomes

The MPC's inflation target is 2 per cent a year with a range of 1 per cent to 3 per cent a year. Inflation was inside the target range from 2004 till March 2007. From May 2008 to February 2009 and from January 2010 to April 2012, inflation was above the top of the target range.

Source of data: Office for National Statistics.

MyEconLab Animation ————————————◆

Controversy About Inflation Targeting

Not everyone agrees that inflation targeting brings benefits. Critics argue that by focusing on inflation, the Bank of England sometimes permits the unemployment rate or real GDP growth rate to suffer.

The fear of these critics is that if the inflation rate begins to edge upward towards and perhaps beyond a full percentage point above target, the Bank of England might reign in aggregate demand and push the economy into recession. At the same time, the Bank might end up permitting the pound to rise on the foreign exchange market and making exports suffer.

One response of supporters of inflation targeting is that by keeping inflation low and stable, monetary policy makes its maximum possible contribution towards achieving full employment and sustained economic growth.

Another response is 'look at the growth and unemployment record'. From May 1997, when the Bank of England was made operationally independent and given the goal of price stability, until 2008, the UK economy was free from recession and had falling unemployment. Only when the entire global economy was reeling from financial crisis did the UK real GDP fall and unemployment begin to rise.

ECONOMICS IN ACTION

Monetary Policy in the Eurozone

The Eurozone is the 17 member states of the EU whose currency is the euro. The European Central Bank (ECB), established in 1998, is the Eurozone's central bank.

The objectives of Eurozone monetary policy are laid out in Article 105 of the Treaty Establishing the European Community (the Treaty of Rome), which assigns overriding importance to price stability as the ECB's monetary policy goal. The Treaty also requires the ECB to support broader EU economic policies, which means supporting policies aimed at achieving sustained growth and high employment.

While the conduct of monetary policy by the ECB is very similar to that by the Bank of England and the central banks of most industrial countries – using similar objectives, tools and decision-making frameworks – the ECB uses a twin-pillar approach. The first pillar is based on identifying the short-term influences on inflation arising from shocks to the goods market (commodity prices, exchange rate fluctuations, cost pressure). The second pillar examines the medium- to long-term pressures that derive from the long-run link between money and prices. The two-pillar approach is designed to ensure that no relevant information is lost in the assessment of the risks to price stability.

The ECB defines price stability as a year-on-year increase in the Harmonised Index of Consumer Prices (HICP) of below, but close to, 2 per cent a year over the medium term.

Like the Bank of England, the ECB recognises that ensuring price stability is the most important contribution that monetary policy can make to achieving sustained growth and high employment. In other words, price stability is the goal of monetary policy *because it contributes to the achievement of other economic objectives.*

REVIEW QUIZ

1   What are the objectives of monetary policy?
2   What is the rationale for setting an inflation target?
3   What is the Bank of England's record in achieving the inflation target?

Do these questions in Study Plan 30.1 and get instant feedback.   MyEconLab

---

You now know the objective of monetary policy and the Bank of England's record in achieving it. You're now going to see how the Bank conducts monetary policy.

The Conduct of Monetary Policy

How does the Bank of England conduct its monetary policy? This question has two parts:

◆   What is the monetary policy instrument?
◆   How does the Bank make its monetary policy decisions?

The Monetary Policy Instrument

A **monetary policy instrument** is a variable that a central bank can directly control or closely target. The Bank of England must choose between two possible instruments: the monetary base or an interest rate.

The Bank's choice of monetary policy instrument is an interest rate. The Bank sets Bank Rate (also known as the Bank of England Base Rate), which is linked to the interest rate that banks earn on reserves and pay on borrowed reserves. The Bank then trades in the repo market to make the **repo rate** – the interest rate in the repo market – equal to Bank Rate. Banks can borrow and lend reserves in the repo market. A bank that is short of reserves and a bank that has excess reserves can use a repo to move the reserves from one bank to the other. The Bank of England also trades in the repo market.

Figure 30.2 shows Bank Rate since January 2004. Bank Rate is normally changed in steps of a quarter of a percentage point.[3] The rate reached a peak of 5.75 per cent a year in 2007 and then fell in rapid succession in much greater steps than a quarter of a per cent to a low of 0.5 per cent a year in April 2009. The sharp fall in the Bank Rate was a coordinated attempt by the central banks of the developed world to deal with the credit crunch and the global financial crisis.

Between 2004 and 2007, Bank Rate was on a rising trend. The reason is that the inflation rate had moved up from below target to above target, and by 2007 the inflation rate was pushing against the upper limit of a 3 per cent a year rate of increase of the CPI.

Since 2007, the Bank Rate has been lowered, first in short steps and then in rapid steps as the full scale of the economic crisis became apparent. The last cut, to 0.5 per cent, occurred in March 2009. Since then the interest rate has remained at that historically low rate. During 2010, the inflation rate moved above the upper bound of

---

[3] When you read about interest changes in the press, you might encounter the term 25 basis points. A basis point is 100th of 1 per cent, so 25 basis points is 0.25 percentage points.

Figure 30.2 Bank Rate

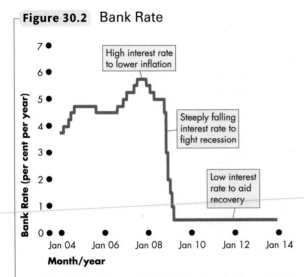

The Bank of England sets Bank Rate and then takes actions to ensure that the banking system is supplied with its desired level of reserves. When the inflation rate is above 2 per cent a year and the Bank wants to avoid going above target, it raises Bank Rate. When the inflation rate is below 2 per cent a year and the Bank wants to avoid going below target, it lowers Bank Rate.

Source of data: Bank of England.

MyEconLab Animation ━━━━━━━━━━━━━◆

Figure 30.3 The Market for Bank Reserves

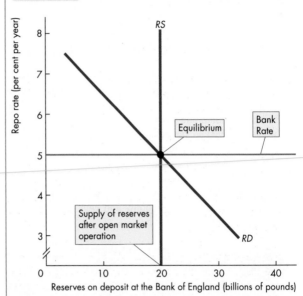

The demand curve for bank reserves is *RD*. The quantity of bank reserves demanded decreases as the repo rate rises because the repo rate is the opportunity cost of holding bank reserves. The supply curve of bank reserves is *RS*. The Bank of England uses open market operations to make the supply of reserves (£20 billion in this case) equal the quantity of reserves demanded at a repo rate equal to Bank Rate (5 per cent a year in this case).

MyEconLab Animation ━━━━━━━━━━━━━━━━━━━━━━━◆

3 per cent a year, but the Bank of England was more concerned about slow growth than inflation, so it chose to keep the interest rate at 0.5 per cent.

Having decided the appropriate level for Bank Rate, how does the Bank of England move the repo rate to its target level? The answer is by using open market operations (see Chapter 24, pp. 566–567) to adjust the quantity of monetary base.

To see how an open market operation changes the repo rate, we need to examine the repo market. The higher the repo rate, the greater is the quantity of overnight loans supplied on repurchase agreements and the smaller is the quantity of overnight loans demanded in the repo market. The equilibrium repo rate balances the quantities demanded and supplied.

An equivalent way of looking at the forces that determine the repo rate is to consider the demand for and supply of bank reserves. Banks hold reserves to meet their desired reserve ratio so that they can always make payments. But reserves are costly to hold. The alternative to holding reserves is to lend them in the repo market and earn the repo rate. The higher the repo rate, the higher is the opportunity cost of holding reserves and the greater is the incentive for banks to economise on the quantity of reserves held.

So the quantity of reserves demanded by banks depends on the repo rate. The higher the repo rate, other things remaining the same, the smaller is the quantity of reserves demanded.

Figure 30.3 illustrates the demand for bank reserves. The *x*-axis measures the quantity of reserves that banks hold on deposit at the Bank of England, and the *y*-axis measures the repo rate. The demand for reserves is the curve labelled *RD*.

The Bank's open market operations determine the supply of reserves shown by the supply curve *RS*. To decrease reserves, the Bank conducts an open market sale. To increase reserves, the Bank conducts an open market purchase.

Equilibrium in the market for bank reserves determines the repo rate where the quantity of reserves demanded by the commercial banks equals the quantity of reserves supplied by the Bank of England. By using open market operations, the Bank adjusts the supply of reserves to keep the repo rate equal to Bank Rate.

Next, we see how the Bank makes its policy decision.

ECONOMICS IN ACTION

Bank of England Decision Making

The MPC meets monthly to set Bank Rate, and throughout the month the committee gets an extensive briefing by the economists of the Bank of England where all the available industry, national and international data on economic performance, financial markets and inflation expectations are reviewed, discussed and weighed in a careful deliberative process.

The MPC meeting lasts two days and on the second day members explain their views as to what they think are the important factors in the economy and what they think the interest rate decision should be.

The Governor of the Bank then puts to the meeting the decision that he thinks will command a majority. Any member in a minority is asked to record what the interest rate should be and justify that decision formally in the minutes.

The interest rate decision is announced at 12 noon on the second day of the deliberations. After announcing a Bank Rate decision, the Bank engages in public communication to explain the reasons for the MPC's decision. The Bank of England's communication exercise is extremely thorough and includes a detailed and carefully researched *Inflation Report* and press conference with the Governor.

The Governor's press conference is recorded and a video placed on the Bank's website. (Take a look!)

The Bank of England's Decision-Making Strategy

The Bank of England (along with most other central banks) follows a process that uses an *inflation targeting rule*. To implement its inflation targeting rule, the Bank must gather and process a large amount of information about the economy, the way it responds to shocks and the way it responds to policy. The Bank must then process all this data and come to a judgement about the best level at which to set Bank Rate.

The process begins with an exercise that uses a model of the UK economy that you can think of as a sophisticated version of the *AS–AD* model (see Chapter 26). The Bank's economists provide the MPC with a variety of forecasts and scenarios running two years into the future. Crucially the inflation rate is forecasted with

probabilities assigned to each scenario so that the MPC is aware of the uncertainty and risks that surround any particular forecast.

REVIEW QUIZ

1 What is the Bank of England's monetary policy instrument?
2 What is the main influence on the MPC's interest rate decision?
3 What happens when the Bank of England buys or sells securities in the open market?
4 How is the repo rate determined?

Do these questions in Study Plan 30.2 and get instant feedback.   MyEconLab

Monetary Policy Transmission

You've seen that the Bank of England's goal is to keep the price level stable (keep the CPI inflation rate at 2 per cent a year) and to achieve maximum growth and employment (keep the output gap close to zero). And you've seen how the Bank can use its power to set Bank Rate at its desired level. We're now going to trace the events that follow a change in Bank Rate and see how those events lead to the ultimate policy goal. We'll begin with a quick overview of the transmission process and then look at each step a bit more closely.

Quick Overview

When the Bank of England lowers Bank Rate, other short-term interest rates and the exchange rate also fall. The quantity of money and the supply of loanable funds increase. The long-term real interest rate falls. The lower real interest rate increases consumption expenditure and investment. And the lower exchange rate makes UK exports cheaper and imports more costly. So net exports increase. Easier bank loans reinforce the effect of lower interest rates on aggregate expenditure. Aggregate demand increases, which increases real GDP and the price level relative to what they would have been. Real GDP growth and inflation speed up.

When the Bank raises Bank Rate, the sequence of events that we've just reviewed plays out, but the effects are in the opposite directions.

Figure 30.4 provides a schematic summary of these ripple effects for both a cut (on the left) and a rise (on the right) in Bank Rate.

The ripple effects summarised in Figure 30.4 stretch out over a period of between one and two years, but the time lags involved and the strength of each of the effects are never quite the same and are unpredictable.

The interest rate and exchange rate effects are immediate. They occur on the same day that the MPC announces its decision. Sometimes they even anticipate the decision. The effects on money and bank loans follow in a few weeks and run for a few months. Real long-term interest rates change quickly and often in anticipation of the short-term rate changes. Spending plans change and real GDP growth changes after about one year. And the inflation rate changes between one year and two years after the change in Bank Rate. But these time lags are especially hard to predict and can be longer or shorter.

We're going to look at each stage in the transmission process, starting with the interest rate effects.

Figure 30.4 The Ripple Effects of a Change in Bank Rate

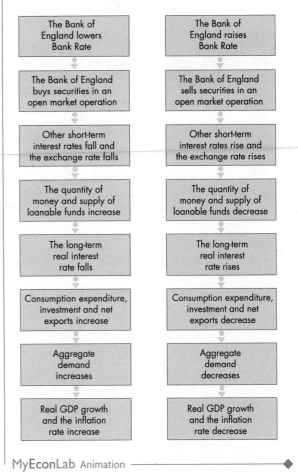

MyEconLab Animation ⟶

Interest Rate Changes

The first effect of a monetary policy decision by the MPC is a change in Bank Rate. Other interest rates then change. Short-term interest rate effects occur quickly and predictably. Long-term interest rate effects occur more slowly and less predictably. Figure 30.5 shows the fluctuations in three interest rates: the repo rate, a short-term bill rate and a long-term bond rate.

Repo Rate

As soon as the MPC announces a new setting for Bank Rate, the Bank of England's bond dealers undertake the necessary open market operations to adjust reserves. There is little doubt about how the interest rate changes shown in Figure 30.5 are generated. They are driven by the Bank of England's monetary policy.

Figure 30.5 Three Interest Rates

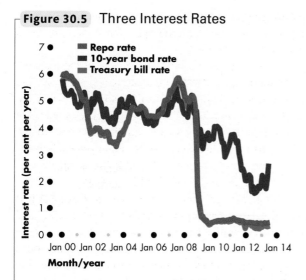

The short-term interest rates – repo rate and the Treasury bill rate – move closely together. The long-term bond rate fluctuates less than the short-term rates, but long-term and short-term interest rates move in the same general direction.

Source of data: Bank of England.

MyEconLab Animation ————————◆

The Short-Term Bill Rate

The *short-term bill rate* is the interest rate paid by the UK government on 3-month Treasury bills. It is similar to the interest rate paid by UK businesses on short-term loans. Notice how closely the short-term bill rate follows the repo rate. The two rates are almost identical.

A powerful substitution effect keeps the 3-month Treasury bill rate and the repo rate close. Commercial banks have a choice about how to hold their short-term liquid assets. And an overnight loan to another bank is a close substitute for short-term securities such as 3-month Treasury bills. If the interest rate on the Treasury bill is higher than the repo rate, the quantity of overnight loans supplied decreases and the demand for Treasury bills increases. The price of a Treasury bill rises and the interest rate falls.

Similarly, if the interest rate on a Treasury bill is lower than the repo rate, the quantity of overnight loans supplied increases and the demand for Treasury bills decreases. The price of a Treasury bill falls, and the interest rate on Treasury bills rises.

When the interest rate on Treasury bills is close to the repo rate, there is no incentive for a bank to switch between making an overnight loan and buying Treasury bills. Both the Treasury bill market and the repo market are in equilibrium.

The Long-Term Bond Rate

The *long-term bond rate* is the interest rate paid on bonds issued by large corporations. It is this interest rate that businesses pay on the loans that finance their purchase of new capital and which influences their investment decisions.

Two features of the long-term bond rate stand out: it does not track closely with the short-term rates, and it fluctuates less than the short-term rates so that in some years the long-term rate exceeds the short-term rate and in other years the gap is reversed.

A dominant effect on the long-term interest rate is the long-term expected inflation rate. In 1997, just before the Bank of England began inflation targeting, the expected inflation rate was high, so the long-term bond rate was also high, and much higher than the short-term rate. In an environment of uncertain long-term inflation, long-term loans are riskier than short-term loans. To provide the incentive that brings forth a supply of long-term loans, lenders must be compensated for the additional risk. Without compensation for the additional risk, only short-term loans would be supplied.

The long-term interest rate fluctuates less than the short-term rates because it is influenced by expectations about future short-term interest rates as well as current short-term interest rates. The alternative to borrowing or lending long term is to borrow or lend using a sequence of short-term securities. If the long-term interest rate exceeds the expected average of future short-term interest rates, people will lend long term and borrow short term. The long-term interest rate will fall. If the long-term interest rate is below the expected average of future short-term interest rates, people will borrow long term and lend short term. The long-term interest rate will rise.

These market forces keep the long-term interest rate close to the expected average of future short-term interest rates. And the expected average future short-term interest rate fluctuates less than the current short-term interest rate.

Exchange Rate Fluctuations

The exchange rate responds to changes in the interest rate in the UK relative to the interest rates in other countries – *the UK interest rate differential*. We explain this influence in Chapter 25 (see pp. 593–594).

When the Bank of England raises Bank Rate, the UK interest rate differential rises and, other things remaining the same, the pound appreciates. And when the Bank lowers Bank Rate, the UK interest rate differential falls and, other things remaining the same, the pound depreciates.

Many factors other than the UK interest rate differential influence the exchange rate, so when the Bank changes Bank Rate, the exchange rate does not usually change in exactly the way it would with other things remaining the same. So while monetary policy influences the exchange rate, many other factors also make the exchange rate change.

Money and Bank Loans

The quantity of money and bank loans changes when the Bank of England changes Bank Rate. A rise in Bank Rate decreases the quantity of money and bank loans and a fall in Bank Rate increases the quantity of money and bank loans. These changes occur for two reasons: the quantity of money supplied by the banking system changes, and the quantity of money demanded by households and firms changes.

You've seen that the Bank changes the quantity of bank reserves to keep the repo rate equal to Bank Rate. A change in the quantity of bank reserves changes the monetary base, which in turn changes the quantity of deposits and loans that the banking system can create. A rise in Bank Rate decreases reserves and decreases the quantity of deposits and bank loans created; and a fall in Bank Rate increases reserves and increases the quantity of deposits and bank loans created.

The quantity of money created by the banking system must be held by households and firms. The change in the interest rate changes the quantity of money demanded. A fall in the interest rate increases the quantity of money demanded and a rise in the interest rate decreases the quantity of money demanded.

A change in the quantity of money and the supply of bank loans directly affects consumption and investment plans. With more money and easier access to loans, consumers and firms spend more. With less money and loans harder to get, consumers and firms spend less.

The Long-Term Real Interest Rate

Demand and supply in the market for loanable funds determine the long-term real interest rate, which equals the long-term nominal interest rate minus the expected inflation rate. The long-term real interest rate influences expenditure decisions.

In the long run, demand and supply in the loanable funds market depend only on real forces – on saving and investment decisions. But in the short run, when the price level is not fully flexible, the supply of loanable funds is influenced by the supply of bank loans. Changes in Bank Rate change the supply of bank loans, which changes the supply of loanable funds and changes the interest rate in the loanable funds market.

A fall in Bank Rate that increases the supply of bank loans increases the supply of loanable funds and lowers the equilibrium real interest rate. A rise in Bank Rate that decreases the supply of bank loans decreases the supply of loanable funds and raises the equilibrium real interest rate.

These changes in the real interest rate, along with the other factors we've just described, change expenditure plans.

Expenditure Plans

The ripple effects that follow a change in Bank Rate change three components of aggregate expenditure:

◆ Consumption expenditure
◆ Investment
◆ Net exports

Consumption Expenditure

Other things remaining the same, the lower the real interest rate, the greater is the amount of consumption expenditure and the smaller is the amount of saving.

Investment

Other things remaining the same, the lower the real interest rate, the greater is the amount of investment.

Net Exports

Other things remaining the same, the lower the interest rate, the lower is the exchange rate and the greater are exports and the smaller are imports.

So eventually, a cut in Bank Rate increases aggregate expenditure and a rise in Bank Rate curtails aggregate expenditure. These changes in aggregate expenditure plans change aggregate demand, real GDP and the price level.

Change in Aggregate Demand, Real GDP and the Price Level

The final link in the transmission chain is a change in aggregate demand and a resulting change in real GDP and the price level. By changing real GDP and the price level relative to what they would have been without a change in Bank Rate, the Bank influences its ultimate goals: the inflation rate and full employment.

The Bank Fights Recession

If inflation is low and real GDP is below potential GDP, the Bank takes actions that are designed to restore full employment. Figure 30.6 shows the effects of the Bank of England's actions, starting in the market for bank reserves and ending in the market for real GDP.

Market for Bank Reserves

In Figure 30.6(a), which shows the market for bank reserves, the MPC lowers Bank Rate from 5 per cent to

4 per cent a year. To keep the repo rate close to Bank Rate, the Bank of England buys securities and increases the supply of bank reserves from RS_0 to RS_1.

Money Market

With increased reserves, the banks create deposits by making loans and the supply of money increases. The short-term interest rate falls and the quantity of money demanded increases. In Figure 30.6(b), the increase in the supply of money shifts the supply of money curve from MS_0 to MS_1. The interest rate falls from 5 per cent to 4 per cent a year and the quantity of money increases from £1,400 billion to £1,500 billion. The interest rate in the money market and the repo rate are kept close to each other by the powerful substitution effect described on p. 724.

Loanable Funds Market

Banks create money by making loans. In the long run, an increase in the supply of bank loans is matched by a rise in the price level, and the quantity of real loans is

Figure 30.6   The Bank of England Fights Recession

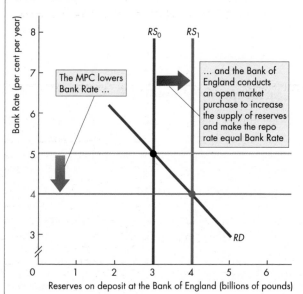

(a) The market for bank reserves

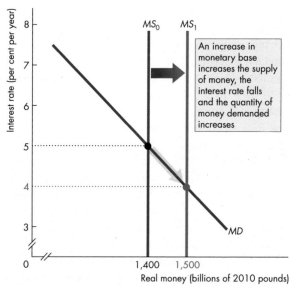

(b) Money market

In part (a), the MPC lowers the Bank Rate target from 5 per cent to 4 per cent a year. To make the repo rate equal to Bank Rate, the Bank of England buys securities in an open market operation and increases the supply of reserves from RS_0 to RS_1.

In part (b), the increase in monetary base increases the supply of money from MS_0 to MS_1. The short-term interest rate falls and the quantity of money demanded increases. The short-term interest rate and Bank Rate change by similar amounts.

MyEconLab Animation

unchanged. But in the short run, with a sticky price level, an increase in the supply of bank loans increases the supply of (real) loanable funds.

In Figure 30.6(c), the supply of loanable funds increases and the supply of loanable funds curve shifts rightward from SLF_0 to SLF_1. With the demand for loanable funds at DLF, the real interest rate falls from 6 per cent to 5.5 per cent a year. (Here, we assume a zero inflation rate so that the real interest rate equals the nominal interest rate.) The long-term interest rate changes by a smaller amount than the change in the short-term interest rate as described on p. 724.

The Market for Real GDP

Figure 30.6(d) shows aggregate demand and aggregate supply. Potential GDP is £1,600 billion, where LAS is located. The short-run aggregate supply curve is SAS and, initially, the aggregate demand curve is AD_0. Real GDP is £1,500 billion, which is less than potential GDP, so there is a recessionary gap. The Bank is reacting to this recessionary gap.

The increase in the supply of loans and the decrease in the real interest rate increase aggregate planned expenditure. (Not shown in the figure, a fall in the interest rate lowers the exchange rate, which increases net exports and also aggregate planned expenditure.) The increase in aggregate expenditure, ΔE, increases aggregate demand and also shifts the aggregate demand curve rightward to $AD_0 + \Delta E$. A multiplier process begins. The increase in expenditure increases income, which induces an increase in consumption expenditure. Aggregate demand increases further, and the aggregate demand curve eventually shifts rightward to AD_1.

The new equilibrium is at full employment. Real GDP is equal to potential GDP. The price level rises to 105 and then becomes stable at that level, so after a one-time adjustment, there is price stability.

In this example, we have given the Bank a perfect hit at achieving full employment and keeping the price level stable. It is unlikely that the Bank would be able to achieve the precision of this example. A Bank Rate cut that is too little or too late leaves the economy in a recession, and too big a cut sends inflation above target.

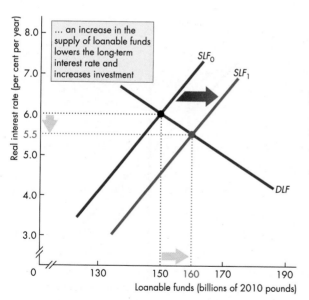

(c) The market for loanable funds

In part (c), an increase in the supply of bank loans increases the supply of loanable funds and shifts the supply of loanable funds curve from SLF_0 to SLF_1. The real interest rate falls and investment increases.

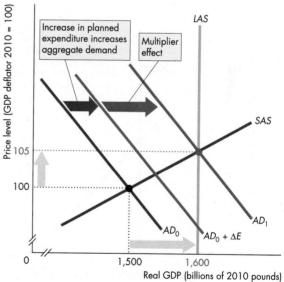

(d) Real GDP and the price level

In part (d), the increase in investment increases aggregate planned expenditure. The aggregate demand curve shifts to $AD_0 + \Delta E$ and eventually shifts rightward to AD_1. Real GDP increases to potential GDP and the price level rises.

The Bank Fights Inflation

If the inflation rate is too high and real GDP is above potential GDP, the Bank of England takes actions that are designed to lower the inflation rate and restore price stability. Figure 30.7 shows the effects of the Bank's actions starting in the market for reserves and ending in the market for real GDP.

Market for Bank Reserves

In Figure 30.7(a), which shows the market for bank reserves, the MPC raises Bank Rate from 5 per cent to 6 per cent a year. To keep the repo rate close to Bank Rate, the Bank sells securities and decreases the supply of reserves of the banking system from RS_0 to RS_1.

Money Market

With decreased reserves, the banks shrink deposits by decreasing loans and the supply of money decreases. The short-term interest rate rises and the quantity of money demanded decreases. In Figure 30.7(b), the supply of money decreases from MS_0 to MS_1, the interest rate rises from 5 per cent to 6 per cent a year and the quantity of money decreases from £1,400 billion to £1,300 billion.

Loanable Funds Market

With a decrease in reserves, banks must decrease the supply of loans. The supply of (real) loanable funds decreases, and the supply of loanable funds curve shifts leftward in Figure 30.7(c) from SLF_0 to SLF_1. With the demand for loanable funds at DLF, the real interest rate rises from 6 per cent to 6.5 per cent a year. (Again, we're assuming a zero inflation rate so that the real interest rate equals the nominal interest rate.)

The Market for Real GDP

Figure 30.7(d) shows aggregate demand and aggregate supply in the market for real GDP. Potential GDP and LAS are £1,600 billion. The short-run aggregate supply curve is SAS and, initially, the aggregate demand is AD_0. Now, real GDP is £1,700 billion, which is greater than potential GDP, so there is an inflationary gap. The Bank is reacting to this inflationary gap.

Figure 30.7 The Bank of England Fights Inflation

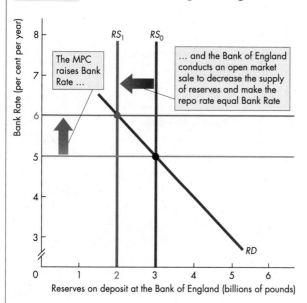

(a) The market for bank reserves

In part (a), the MPC raises Bank Rate from 5 per cent to 6 per cent. To make the repo rate equal to Bank Rate the Bank of England sells securities in an open market operation to decrease the supply of reserves from RS_0 to RS_1.

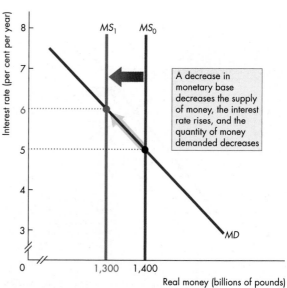

(b) Money market

In part (b), the supply of money decreases from MS_0 to MS_1, the short-term interest rate rises and the quantity of money demanded decreases. The short-term interest rate and Bank Rate change by similar amounts.

The decrease in the supply of bank loans, and the increase in the real interest rate decrease aggregate planned expenditure. (Not shown in the figures, a rise in the interest rate raises the exchange rate, which decreases net exports and also aggregate planned expenditure.)

The decrease in aggregate expenditure, ΔE, decreases aggregate demand and the aggregate demand curve shifts to $AD_0 - \Delta E$. A multiplier process begins. The decrease in expenditure decreases income, which induces a decrease in consumption expenditure. Aggregate demand decreases further, and the aggregate demand curve eventually shifts leftward to AD_1.

The economy returns to full employment. Real GDP is equal to potential GDP. The price level falls to 105 and then becomes stable at that level, so after a one-time adjustment, there is price stability.

Again, in this example, we have given the Bank a perfect hit at achieving full employment and keeping the price level stable. If the Bank raised Bank Rate by too little or too late, the economy would have remained with an inflationary gap and the inflation rate would have moved above the target. And if the Bank raised Bank

Rate by too much it would push the economy from inflation to recession.

Loose Links and Long and Variable Lags

The ripple effects of monetary policy that we've just analysed with the precision of an economic model are, in reality, very hard to predict and anticipate.

To achieve its inflation target and its additional mandate to support the government's economic policy of keeping real GDP growing at the maximum sustainable rate and maintaining full employment, the Bank needs a combination of good judgement and good luck.

Too large an interest rate cut can bring inflation, as it did during the 1970s. And too large an interest rate rise in an inflationary economy can create unemployment, as it did in 1981 and 1991.

Loose links in the chain that runs from Bank Rate to the ultimate policy goals make unwanted policy outcomes inevitable. And time lags that are both long and variable add to the Bank of England's challenges.

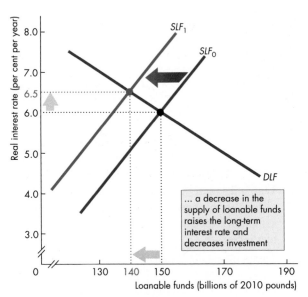

(c) The market for loanable funds

In part (c), a decrease in the supply of bank loans decreases the supply of loanable funds and shifts the supply of loanable funds curve from SLF_0 to SLF_1. The real interest rate rises and investment decreases.

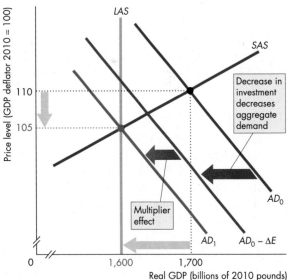

(d) Real GDP and the price level

In part (d), the decrease in investment decreases aggregate planned expenditure. The aggregate demand curve shifts to $AD_0 - \Delta E$ and eventually shifts leftward to AD_1. Real GDP decreases to potential GDP and the price level falls.

ECONOMICS IN THE NEWS

Monetary Stimulus Not Stimulating

Bank of England Should Stimulate Lending

Years of conventional monetary stimulus has failed to bring a sustained and balanced recovery. To get the economy moving, Bank of England Governor Mark Carney's priority should be to ensure that Britain's banks start lending to small businesses.

Source: *The Financial Times*, 4 July 2013

Some Facts

◆ Figure 30.2 (p. 721) shows how Bank Rate changed.

◆ Figure 1 shows the effects of the Bank of England's open market operations on the monetary base and Figure 2 shows how M4 changed.

◆ Figure 30.5 (p. 724) shows how interest rates changed.

◆ Between 2008 and 2012, the pound depreciated, exports increased slightly and consumption expenditure and investment decreased.

The Questions

◆ What are the ripple effects of a change in Bank Rate?

◆ At which stage in the ripple effects that began in 2008 did conventional monetary stimulus *not* work?

The Answers

◆ Figure 30.4 (p. 723) shows the eight stages in the transmission of monetary stimulus.

◆ The first three steps unfolded as expected: Bank Rate was lowered to the floor of 0.5 per cent a year; open market operations brought a massive increase in the monetary base; all short-term interest rates fell; and in the foreign exchange market, the pound depreciated against the US dollar and the euro.

◆ The ripple effects came to an end when the quantity of money and the supply of loanable funds stopped growing. Figure 2 shows that after growing, quickly to a peak in February 2010, M4 stopped growing, and for the next two and a quarter years, M4 shrank.

◆ Bank loans create bank deposits and increase the quantity of money. Shrinking M4 is a sign that the banks were not renewing loans and not entering into new loans.

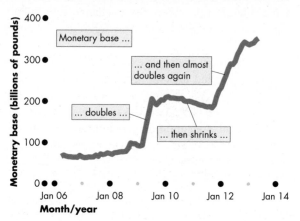

Figure 1 The Monetary Base

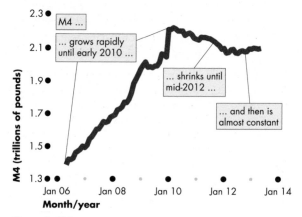

Figure 2 M4

◆ With no increase in the supply of loanable funds, the long-term real interest rate did not fall by much. (It eventually did fall, but not until late 2011.)

◆ With a decrease in bank loans and not much change in long-term interest rates, no ripples reached consumption expenditure and investment plans, so neither increased.

◆ The depreciated pound brought a small increase in exports, but not by enough to outweigh the decrease in planned consumption expenditure and investment.

◆ With no increase in aggregate planned expenditure, real GDP growth did not increase.

◆ Inflation increased, most likely because the lower foreign exchange value of the pound increased import prices, which decreased short-run aggregate supply.

ECONOMICS IN ACTION

A Look at the Long and Variable Lag

You've studied the theory of monetary policy. Does it really work in the way we've described? It does, and Figure 1 provides some evidence to support this conclusion.

The Bank of England targets Bank Rate, and the blue line in Figure 1 shows the long-term bond rate minus Bank Rate.

You saw in Figure 30.5 (p. 724) that short-term interest rates fluctuate more than long-term rate. We can view the gap between the long-term bond rate and Bank Rate as a measure of how hard the Bank is trying to steer a change in course. When the Bank of England is attempting to boost aggregate demand and stimulate real GDP growth, the Bank lowers Bank Rate. The long-term bond rate minus Bank Rate rises and the blue line slopes upward. And when the Bank raises Bank Rate, it is attempting to decrease aggregate demand, restrain inflation and slow real GDP growth. The long-term bond rate minus Bank Rate falls and the blue line slopes downward.

The red line in Figure 1 shows the real GDP growth rate two years later.

You can see that when the Bank of England raises Bank Rate, the real GDP growth rate slows two years later. And when the Bank of England lowers Bank Rate, the real GDP growth rate speeds up two years later.

Not shown in this figure, and with other things remaining the same, the inflation rate increases and decreases in line with the fluctuations in the real GDP growth rate. But

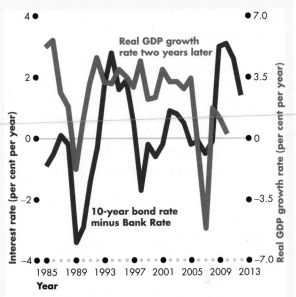

Figure 1 Interest Rates and Real GDP Growth

Sources of data: Bank of England and Office for National Statistics.

the effects of an interest rate change on the inflation rate take even longer. In addition, other influences on the inflation rate break the link between inflation and real GDP fluctuations.

Loose Link from Bank Rate to Spending

The real long-term interest rate that influences spending plans is linked only loosely to Bank Rate. Also, the response of the real long-term interest rate to a change in the nominal rate depends on how inflation expectations change. And the response of expenditure plans to changes in the real interest rate depends on many factors that make the response hard to predict.

Time Lags in the Adjustment Process

The Bank is especially handicapped by the fact that the monetary policy transmission process is long and drawn out. Also, the economy does not always respond in exactly the same way to a policy change. Further, many factors other than policy are constantly changing and bringing new situations to which policy must respond.

 REVIEW QUIZ

1 Describe the channels by which monetary policy ripples through the economy and explain how each channel operates.
2 Do interest rates fluctuate in response to the Bank of England's actions?
3 How do the Bank of England's actions change the exchange rate?
4 How do the Bank of England's actions influence real GDP and how long does it take for real GDP to respond to the Bank's policy changes?
5 How do the Bank's actions influence the inflation rate and how long does it take for the inflation rate to respond to the Bank's policy changes?

Do these questions in Study Plan 30.3 and get instant feedback.

MyEconLab

Extraordinary Monetary Stimulus

During the financial crisis and recession of 2007–2009, the Bank of England lowered the Bank Rate to 0.5 per cent a year. Bank Rate cannot fall much further, so what can the Bank do to stimulate the economy? The Bank of England has answered this question with some extraordinary policy actions. To understand those actions, we need to dig a bit into the anatomy of the financial crisis to which the Bank is responding. That's what we'll now do. We'll look at the key elements in the financial crisis and then look at the Bank's response.

The Key Elements of the Crisis

We can describe the crisis by identifying the events that changed the values of the assets and liabilities of banks and other financial institutions. Figure 30.8 shows the stylised balance sheet of a bank: deposits plus own capital equals reserves plus loans and securities (see Chapter 24, p. 562). Deposits and own capital are the banks' sources of funds (other borrowing is ignored here).

Deposits are the funds loaned to the bank by households and firms. A bank's *own capital* is the funds provided by its shareholders and includes the bank's undistributed profits (and losses). A bank's reserves are currency and its deposit at the Bank of England. A bank's loans and securities are the loans made by the bank and government bonds, private bonds, asset-backed bonds and other securities that the bank holds.

Three main events can put a bank under stress:

◆ A widespread fall in asset prices

◆ A significant currency drain

◆ A run on the bank

Figure 30.8 summarises the problems that each event presents to a bank. A widespread fall in asset prices means that the bank suffers a capital loss. It must write down the value of its assets, and the value of the bank's own capital decreases by the same amount as the fall in the value of its securities. If the fall in asset prices is large enough, the value of a bank's own capital might fall to zero, in which case the bank is insolvent. It fails.

A significant currency drain means that depositors withdraw funds and the bank loses reserves. This event puts the bank in a liquidity crisis. It is short of cash reserves.

A run on the bank occurs when depositors lose confidence in the bank and massive withdrawals of deposits occur. The bank loses reserves and must call in loans and sell off securities at unfavourable prices. Its own capital shrinks.

The red arrows in Figure 30.8 summarise the effects of these events and the problems they brought in the 2007–2009 financial crisis. A widespread fall in asset prices was triggered by the bursting of a house-price bubble in the US that saw house prices switch from rapidly rising to falling. With falling house prices, subprime mortgage defaults occurred and the prices of mortgage-backed securities and derivatives whose values were based on these securities began to fall. Many of these mortgage-backed securities were being held by banks and financial institutions around the world.

People with money market mutual fund deposits began to withdraw them, which created a fear of a massive withdrawal of these funds analagous to a bank run like the one experienced by Northern Rock.

With low reserves and even lower own capital, banks, in turn, called in loans. A lot of these loans were to other banks in the money market. The loanable funds market and money market dried up.

Because the loanable funds market is global, the same problems quickly spread to other economies, and foreign exchange markets became highly volatile.

Hard-to-get loans, market volatility and increased uncertainty transmitted the financial and monetary crisis to real expenditure decisions.

Figure 30.8 The Ingredients of a Financial and Banking Crisis

Event	Deposits	+ Own capital	= Reserves	+ Loans and securities	Problem
Widespread fall in asset prices		▼		▼	Solvency
Currency drain	▼		▼		Liquidity
Run on bank	▼	▼	▼	▼	Liquidity and solvency

The Policy Actions

Policy actions in response to the financial crisis on both sides of the Atlantic dribbled out over a period of more than a year. Here, we'll focus on the UK policy actions, which may be placed under four broad headings:

◆ Interest rate cuts

◆ Bank bailouts

◆ Quantitative easing

◆ Macro-prudential regulation

Interest Rate Cuts

The Bank of England's first and natural response to the 2007 financial crisis was to lower Bank Rate. But it acted slowly at first. In August 2007 when the initial shocks were felt, Bank Rate was at a relatively high 5.75 per cent. The Bank was more concerned about the risk that inflation would burst through the 3 per cent upper bound of its target than it was about the risk of recession so the Bank Rate cuts were timid: down to 5.5 per cent in December, 5.25 per cent in February 2008, and 5 per cent in April 2008.

It wasn't until the crisis deepened with massive bank failures in the US and tottering UK banks that interest rates fell steeply. But starting in October 2008, the fall was steep, down to 0.5 per cent by March 2009.

Bank Bailouts

The first sign that the financial crisis might be serious and need an extraordinary policy response was the run on Northern Rock. At first, the Bank of England hesitated to act. But in September 2007, it extended a deposit insurance guarantee to Northern Rock's depositors and provided emergency loans to the bank.

The serious risk of bank failure and massive bailouts didn't come until a year later, in October 2008, when the biggest banks – RBS, Lloyds TSB and HBOS – were on the brink of collapse.

The policy response to this situation blurs the distinction between monetary policy and fiscal policy, for it was the UK government, not the Bank of England, that made the bold moves. The government forced a merger between Lloyds and HBOS and injected £37 billion into RBS and the enlarged Lloyds TSB. These banks were now partly owned by the taxpayer – 81 per cent in the case of RBS and 40 per cent in the case of Lloyds.

The other two large commercial banks, Barclays and HSBC, raised additional capital without government help. The bailed-out RBS and Lloyds turned out to need a further injection of public funds in November 2009 when they received a further £31 billion. This injection of funds took the taxpayer stake in RBS to 84 per cent, making it virtually a nationalised firm.

The goal of these massive and unusual injections of public funds into large commercial banks was designed to ensure that the banks didn't fail. Failure would have had a ripple effect (a tsunami effect is perhaps a better metaphor) through the entire national and global financial system and would have brought an enormous crash in the quantity of money in the UK economy.

Quantitative Easing

The Bank of England launched a programme of quantitative easing in March 2009. **Quantitative easing (QE)** occurs when the Bank of England creates an increase in the monetary base by buying government bonds and high-grade corporate bonds in the open market. The sellers of these bonds might be commercial banks but they also are pension funds and insurance companies. The Bank conducted £200 billion of QE purchases during March and November 2009 and launched QE2 of a further £75 billion in October 2011 and a further £100 billion in 2012. The total QE operation was £375 billion.

You can see that QE is a type of *open market operation*. In normal times, the Bank of England performs open market operations by buying repurchase agreements, *repos*, and UK Treasury Bills. These open market operations (see p. 721) supply the quantity of reserves that enable the Bank of England to keep short-term interest rates close to Bank Rate.

With the large interest rate cuts after October 2008, open market operations were used on a massive scale to keep the banks well supplied with reserves. This action lowered bank holdings of securities and increased their reserves.

The Bank of England's QE open market operations take place in the market for loanable funds. With short-term interest rates as low as they can go, the goal of QE is to increase the monetary base and lower long-term interest rates.

The idea is that QE would make the banks flush with excess reserves, which they would lend to firms and households. The quantity of money would increase and asset prices would rise. With easier access to credit and greater wealth from higher asset prices,

AT ISSUE

Is the Bank of England's Monetary Stimulus Just Right, Too Tight or Too Loose?

In mid-2013, the inflation rate was 3 per cent per year, the unemployment rate was 7.8 per cent, and real GDP was growing very slowly at less than 1 per cent per year. Bank rate was 0.5 per cent and QE stood at £375 billion.

The remit for the Bank of England's Monetary Policy Committee (MPC), renewed in March 2013, was to return the inflation rate to 2 per cent per year, but to do so mindful of the short-run trade-off between inflation and real activity at a pace expected to restore full employment and achieve sustained economic growth.

Not everyone agreed that the MPC had made the best decisions. And perhaps not surprisingly, the MPC's critics were divided on whether the economy needed more stimulus or less.

Let's look at the three views on this issue in July 2013.

Just Right

- Deputy Governors Charles Bean and Paul Tucker, along with most other members of the MPC, regarded the monetary policy setting as appropriate.
- They argued that, although there were signs of an improving economy, monetary stimulus must not be withdrawn too early.
- They believed that additional stimulus would keep inflation above target for too long and withdrawing stimulus risked stopping the recovery and raising unemployment.
- Charles Bean thought that more stimulus might delay recovery by slowing the process of structural change.

Too Tight

- Some MPC members thought that further stimulus was required.
- Some MPC members favoured extending QE asset purchases to £400 billion or higher.
- New Governor Mark Carney favoured forward guidance – committing to keep Bank Rate at 0.5 per cent for a specified time or, more likely, until the output gap or unemployment rate reached a specified level.
- More stimulation carries the risk that inflation expectations become unanchored and inflation takes off, a risk accentuated by the impossibility of observing the output gap or natural unemployment rate.

Too Loose

- The Shadow Monetary Policy Committee* (SMPC) thought Bank Rate should be raised from 0.5 per cent and there should be no further QE asset purchases.
- Some SMPC members thought that a Bank Rate as low as 0.5 per cent made the price of risk too low and induced a misallocation of capital resources.
- SMPC member Peter Warburton argued that the economy was improving and that forward guidance needed to advise markets that Bank Rate would rise to 2.5 per cent in the next 2 years.
- The risk from reducing stimulus is that the recovery stalls and the unemployment rate rises.

Bank of England Deputy Governor **Charlie Bean** warned that very loose monetary policy can delay the return to growth if it "inhibits the process of creative destruction as unprofitable firms are closed and the liberated resources shifted to the expanding sectors".

Bank of England Governor **Mark Carney** thought forward guidance that Bank Rate will remain at 0.5 per cent until some recovery targets are achieved could provide stimulus to growth and employment without undue inflation risk.

SMPC member **Peter Warburton** says forward guidance, if needed, should prepare markets for a rise in Bank Rate to 2.5 per cent in the next two years.

*http://www.iea.org.uk/smpc

consumption expenditure and investment would increase aggregate demand and real GDP would grow more quickly.

Did QE succeed in achieving its goals? The final verdict is not yet in, but a first look at the effects of QE is not encouraging. QE may not have lowered long-term interest rates (although it might have prevented them from rising) and it did not bring a large increase in either bank lending or the quantity of money.

Interest rates on long-term bonds had fallen from around 5 per cent in mid-2008 to around 3.25 per cent in March 2009 when QE began. From March 2009 to the end of 2010, interest rates on long-term bonds had no visible trend or change. But from mid-2011 to the end of 2012, long-term interest rates fell.

The commercial banks' reserves swelled but, rather than increasing loans to firms and households, the banks have sat on their excess reserves. Consumers have used any spare cash to pay off debt (repay loans to the banks).

The overall outcome is that the monetary base has risen, but the quantity of money has not. Figure 30.9 shows the growth of the M4 definition of money and the money multiplier. Both fell dramatically during 2009 and remained low during 2011–2012.

Supporters of QE say that without it the recession would be even worse, and if there is a fault it is that the Bank of England has been too timid and should have employed QE on a larger scale.

Macro-Prudential Regulation

Macro-prudential regulation is regulation of the monetary financial institutions and other financial institutions and financial markets to lower the risk of crisis and failure of these institutions and markets.

We briefly described how monetary financial institutions are regulated in Chapter 24 (see p. 562). The key components of this regulation are the assignment of responsibility for oversight and monitoring of financial institutions and markets, and rules governing the liquidity and scale of own funds for financial institutions.

UK macro-prudential regulation is evolving and will change over the next few years as the Bank of England plays an enhanced role along with the Treasury, the Prudential Regulation Authority and the Financial Conduct Authority (see Chapter 24, p. 562).

A debate will be ongoing about what it means for a bank to be 'too big to fail' and whether large banks should be broken up. A further debate will consider the appropriate scale and cyclical characteristics of commercial banks' own funds and the appropriate composition of a bank's assets and liabilities.

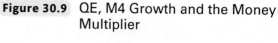

Figure 30.9 QE, M4 Growth and the Money Multiplier

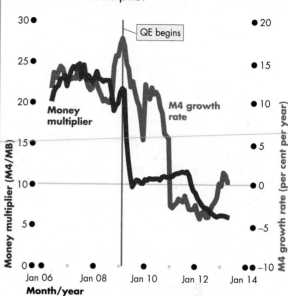

Before the Bank of England embarked on its QE policy, the money multiplier was falling and the growth rate of M4 was slowing. After QE began, the money multiplier crashed as commercial banks sat on their excess reserves, and M4 growth slowed even further as people paid off existing bank loans.

Source of data: Bank of England.

MyEconLab Animation ————————————————◆

While all the extraordinary measures evolve and respond to the changing situation, the Bank of England will need to keep a firm grip on its main policy objective: its inflation target.

◆ REVIEW QUIZ

1 What are the three main ingredients of a financial and banking crisis?
2 What policy actions have the Bank of England and the UK government taken in response to the financial and banking crisis?
3 What is QE and what is the key idea in using it?
4 Did QE work?

Do these questions in Study Plan 30.3 and get instant feedback.   MyEconLab

To complete your study of monetary policy, take a look at *Reading Between the Lines* on pp. 736–737 and see how the Bank of England faced a monetary policy dilemma in 2013.

Another New Monetary Policy

What Works at the Fed Might not be Quite Right for Britain

Chris Giles

Mark Carney's first interest rate decision as Bank Governor comes on Thursday amid stronger data that are unlikely to warrant dramatic immediate monetary easing. So the real impact of the Canadian import will come a month later when the BoE will introduce his big idea: forward guidance.

Telling companies, households and markets how long monetary policy will remain ultra-stimulative is all the rage in central banks, including the US Federal Reserve and the Bank of Japan. It is coming to Britain.

The new BoE Governor can muster strong arguments for a change. Guidance can ensure that markets know policy will remain loose for longer than the current expectation that rates will rise in 2015, providing useful monetary activism and stimulus for a chronically weak economy. . . . The simplest form of guidance is time-contingent, committing

the BoE to keep policy ultra-loose for a certain time. Even though Mr Carney is certain this idea saved Canada in 2009, such pre-commitment is risky: the central bank really has little idea today how long it needs to keep its foot on the accelerator. So the BoE will follow the Fed and plump for state-contingent guidance, linking . . . a future tightening of policy to the moment spare capacity is judged to have fallen sufficiently as the recovery progresses.

Sadly, measures of UK slack are erratic at the moment. There is no possible way to be polite: all are useless for the task of guidance. . . .

The lack of a reliable measure of UK slack should not spell the end of Mr Carney's ambitions. He just needs to go back to first principles and provide some certainty on policy related to the variables that matter for Britain's economic health.

 The Essence of the Story

- ◆ The new Bank of England Governor, Mark Carney, thinks forward guidance – providing information about the conditions on which interest rates will start to rise – can stimulate the economy.

- ◆ The simplest forward guidance commits to keeping interest rates low for a specified time, but this approach is too risky because the

central bank can't predict when it will need to start raising interest rates.

- ◆ State-contingent forward guidance links future interest rate increases to when enough spare capacity is eliminated, but this approach is difficult because there are no reliable measures of spare capacity.

Economic Analysis

◆ The Bank of England projects that the inflation rate will remain above 2 per cent a year until the second quarter of 2015, by which time inflation will have returned to target.

◆ There is much uncertainty around this projection. Figure 1 shows the Bank of England's projection and uncertainty in mid-2013.

◆ The Bank says that the inflation rate is very unlikely to exceed 4.5 per cent a year or fall below minus 0.5 per cent a year.

◆ This enormous range of uncertainly arises partly because no one knows the size of the output gap.

◆ As the news article suggests, because the size of the output gap is unknown, forward guidance conditional on the output gap may not be appropriate.

◆ Figures 2 and 3 illustrate the problem. Both figures show the state of the UK economy in the first quarter of 2013. The aggregate demand curve AD_0 and the short-run aggregate supply curve SAS_0 determine equilibrium real GDP at £1.51 trillion and a price level of 105.

◆ In Figure 2, potential GDP (and LAS) is £1.54 trillion. Forward guidance increases aggregate demand to AD_1. Real GDP rises above potential GDP, the money wage rate rises, and the SAS curve shifts leftward to SAS_1. The price level rises to 109 in a demand-pull inflation of 4 per cent.

◆ In Figure 3, potential GDP (and LAS) is £1.57 trillion. When forward guidance increases aggregate demand to AD_1, real GDP increases to potential GDP and the price level rises to 107 in an anticipated 2 per cent inflation.

◆ A large recessionary gap (Figure 3) looks at odds with an inflation rate that has been above target since 2009 and is expected to remain above target until 2015. The risk is that Figure 2 is closer than Figure 3 to the actual situation.

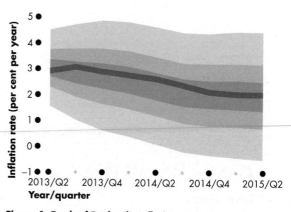

Figure 1 Bank of England's Inflation Projection

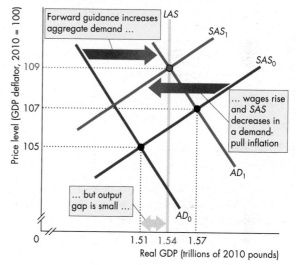

Figure 2 If the Output Gap is Small

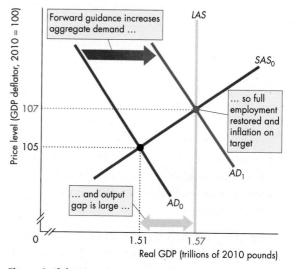

Figure 3 If the Output Gap is Large

SUMMARY

Key Points

Monetary Policy Objectives and Framework (pp. 718–720)

◆ The Bank of England Act 1998 requires the Bank to use monetary policy to achieve stable prices and to support the government's economic policies of high and stable economic growth and employment.

◆ Each year, the Chancellor of the Exchequer specifies the Bank's remit in terms of a numerical target for the inflation rate.

◆ Since 2004, the Bank has been required to achieve an inflation rate measured by the CPI of 2 per cent a year.

Do Problems 1 to 5 to get a better understanding of monetary policy objectives and framework.

The Conduct of Monetary Policy (pp. 720–722)

◆ The Bank's monetary policy instrument is Bank Rate.

◆ The Bank's Monetary Policy Committee (MPC) sets Bank Rate and announces any change at roughly monthly intervals.

◆ The Bank pushes the repo rate close to Bank Rate by using open market operations.

◆ By buying or selling securities in the open market, the Bank is able to change bank reserves and change the repo rate.

Do Problems 6 to 10 to get a better understanding of the conduct of monetary policy.

Monetary Policy Transmission (pp. 723–731)

◆ A change in Bank Rate changes other interest rates, the exchange rate, the quantity of money and loans, aggregate demand and eventually real GDP and the price level.

◆ A change in Bank Rate changes real GDP a year to 18 months later and changes the inflation rate with an even longer time lag.

Do Problems 11 to 20 to get a better understanding of monetary policy transmission.

Extraordinary Monetary Stimulus (pp. 732–735)

◆ A financial crisis has three ingredients: a widespread fall in asset prices, a currency drain and a run on banks.

◆ The Bank of England and Treasury responded to the financial crisis with four groups of measures: steep interest rate cuts, bank bailouts, quantitative easing and macro-prudential regulation.

Do Problems 21 to 26 to get a better understanding of extraordinary monetary stimulus.

Key Terms

Macro-prudential regulation, 735
Monetary policy instrument, 720
Quantitative easing (QE), 733
Repo rate, 720

STUDY PLAN PROBLEMS AND APPLICATIONS

Do Problems 1 to 26 in MyEconLab Chapter 30 Study Plan and get instant feedback.

MyEconLab

Monetary Policy Objectives and Framework (Study Plan 30.1)

1 'Unemployment is a more serious economic problem than inflation and it should be the focus of the Bank of England's monetary policy.' Evaluate this statement and explain why the Bank's primary policy goal is price stability and not full employment.

2 'Because the CPI inflation rate includes the prices of food and fuel, which are volatile and influenced by global demand and supply, the Bank of England should strip these items from the index that it targets.' Explain why the Bank of England is required to target the CPI inflation rate.

3 'Monetary policy is too important to be left to the MPC. The government should be responsible for it.' How is responsibility for monetary policy allocated among the MPC, Parliament and the government?

4 **Mervyn King Gives Warning over UK Public Deficit**

Mervyn King says the government must cut the public deficit.

Source: BBC, 20 January 2010

a Does the Governor of the Bank of England have either authority or responsibility for the UK government budget deficit?

b How might a government budget deficit complicate the Bank's monetary policy? [Hint: Think about the effects of a deficit on interest rates.]

c How might the Bank's monetary policy complicate Parliament's deficit cutting? [Hint: Think about the effects of monetary policy on interest rates.]

5 **Inflation: Surging Fuel Costs Push CPI to 3.4 per cent**

At 3.4 per cent, consumer price inflation (CPI) is now way above the Bank of England's government-set target of 2 per cent, the highest since January and one of the steepest rates in Europe.

Source: The Guardian, 20 April 2010

a What does this news clip imply about the MPC's interest rate decisions?

b How can the 3.4 per cent inflation rate be reconciled with the Bank of England's obligations under the 1998 Bank of England Act?

The Conduct of Monetary Policy (Study Plan 30.2)

6 What are the two possible monetary policy instruments? Which one does the Bank of England use and how has its value behaved since 2004?

7 How does the Bank of England hit its repo rate target? Illustrate your answer with an appropriate graph.

8 What does the Bank of England do to determine whether Bank Rate should be raised, lowered or left unchanged?

Use the following news clip in Problems 9 and 10.

Bank of England's Trade-Off

When the Bank of England's MPC meets on Thursday, it will be shaping up for its first three-way vote, amid an intensifying debate on the trade-off between apparent signs of inflation and indications that the economy is sinking into stagnation.

Source: The Financial Times, 6 October 2010

9 Explain the dilemma faced by the Bank of England in October 2010.

10 a Why might the MPC have decided to cut Bank Rate in the months following the October 2010 meeting?

b Why might the MPC have decided to raise Bank Rate in the months following the October 2010 meeting?

Monetary Policy Transmission (Study Plan 30.3)

11 What are the roles of Bank Rate and the long-term interest rate in the monetary policy transmission process?

12 a Is it the long-term nominal interest rate or the long-term real interest rate that influences spending decisions? Explain why.

b How does the market determine the long-term nominal interest rate and why doesn't it move as much as the short-term rates?

Use the following news clip in Problems 13 and 14.

The Pound's Sharp Fall

Masahiro Sakane, chairman of Komatsu, the Japanese maker of construction and mining equipment, says the company's plant in north-east England will benefit from the pound's sharp fall against the euro.

Source: *The Financial Times*, 5 March 2010

13 How does a lower sterling exchange rate influence monetary policy transmission?

14 Would a fall in the exchange rate mainly influence unemployment or inflation?

Use the following news clip in Problems 15 to 17.

Economists Growth Forecasts

Economic recovery and job creation in the UK over the next few years will depend on growth in business investment.

Source: *The Financial Times*, 29 December 2010

15 Explain the effects of the Bank of England's low interest rates on business investment. Draw a graph to illustrate your explanation.

16 Explain the effects of business investment on aggregate demand. Would you expect it to have a multiplier effect? Why or why not?

17 What actions might the Bank of England take to stimulate business investment further?

Use the following news clip in Problems 18 to 20.

Growth Revision Fuels Recovery Hopes

The UK economy grew faster in the second quarter of 2013, with manufacturing and construction growing better than expected and exports growing at its fastest pace since the end of 2011. Despite the Bank of England providing 'forward guidance' on interest rates, the markets will take some convincing that interest rates will remain on hold for the next two years.

Source: *The Financial Times*, 23 August 2013

18 If real GDP grows faster than potential GDP, what will happen to the output gap and unemployment in 2014?

19 **a** What actions that the Bank of England had taken in 2012 and 2013 would you expect to influence UK real GDP growth in 2014? Explain how those policy actions would transmit to real GDP.

b Draw a graph of aggregate demand and aggregate supply to illustrate your answer to part (a).

20 What further actions might the Bank of England take in 2014 to influence the real GDP growth rate in 2014? [Remember the time lags in the operation of monetary policy.]

Extraordinary Monetary Stimulus

(Study Plan 30.4)

Use the following news clip in Problems 21 to 23.

UK Pound Weakens on QE Bets

The pound fell to the weakest level in almost seven months against the euro as mortgage approvals dropped to the least since March 2009, heightening speculation that the Bank of England may soon be pressed into quantitative easing.

Source: fxnonstop.com, 25 October 2010

21 What is the connection between actions that the Bank of England might take and the foreign exchange value of the pound?

22 What is the significance of falling mortgage approvals? How does that suggest further QE?

23 Why might the Bank contemplate further QE? What are the arguments for and against further quantitative easing at the beginning of 2011?

24 Suppose that the UK government had not bailed out RBS and Lloyds and instead had allowed them to fail.

a How would the failure have changed the quantity of money and interest rates?

b How would real GDP and the inflation rate have been different?

25 Suppose that the Bank of England had raised Bank Rate in 2010 as the inflation rate moved above the 3 per cent upper bound.

a How would the repo rate have differed from its actual path?

b How would real GDP and the inflation rate have been different?

26 **Prospects Rise for US Federal Reserve Easing Policy**

William Dudley, president of the New York Fed, raised the prospect of the Fed becoming more explicit about its inflation goal to 'help anchor inflation expectations at the desired rate'.

Source: ft.com, 1 October 2010

a Why might inflation targeting be especially important in a financial crisis?

b How does 'anchor[ing] inflation expectations at the desired rate' help to make QE work better?

ADDITIONAL PROBLEMS AND APPLICATIONS

Do these problems in MyEconLab if assigned by your lecturer.

MyEconLab

Monetary Policy Objectives and Framework

Use the following information in Problems 27 to 29.

The statutory role of the Bank of England is to maintain price stability and, subject to that, to support the economic policy of Her Majesty's Government, including its objectives for growth and employment.

27 Explain the harmony among these goals in the long run.

28 Explain the conflict among these goals in the short run.

29 Based on the performance of UK inflation and unemployment in 2010, which of the Bank's goals appears to have taken priority?

30 The deep 2008–2009 recession and the overshoot of inflation above the upper bound of the target suggests that the inflation target should be raised. Do you agree? Why or why not?

31 Suppose the Chancellor of the Exchequer decided to strip the Bank of England of its operational independence to meet a government-specified inflation target and gave Cabinet the task of deciding interest rate changes. How would you expect the policy choices to change? Which arrangement would most likely provide price stability?

32 The European Central Bank (ECB) targets the Eurozone inflation rate to make it remain below but close to 2 per cent a year. To pursue this goal, the ECB sets the official ECB interest rate but pays close attention to the growth rate of the quantity of money.

  a Compare and contrast the policy objectives of the ECB and the Bank of England.

  b Compare and contrast the policy strategies of the ECB and the Bank of England.

Use the following news clip in Problems 33 and 34.

The budget deficit is £1.6 billion higher in the period April–July 2013 than in the same period of 2012. The deterioration in the public finances is caused by strong growth in central government spending which is now 4.3 per cent higher than at the same point last year.

Source: *The Financial Times*, 21 August 2013

33 How would the government deficit change in 2014 and 2015 if the Bank of England raised interest rates?

34 How would the government deficit change in 2014 and 2015 if the Bank of England did not raise the rate of interest and the value of sterling depreciated sharply?

The Conduct of Monetary Policy

35 Looking at Bank Rate since 2000, identify periods during which, with the benefit of hindsight, the rate might have been kept too low. Identify periods during which it might have been too high.

36 Explain the dilemma that rising inflation and weakening growth poses for the Bank of England.

37 Why might the Bank of England decide to lower interest rates when inflation is rising and growth is weakening?

38 Why might the Bank of England decide to raise interest rates when inflation is rising and growth is weakening?

Monetary Policy Transmission

Use the following information in Problems 39 to 41.

From 2008 to 2010 the rate of interest on UK 10-year maturity bonds fell from 4.6 per cent a year to 3.6 per cent a year. During the same period, Bank Rate fell from 4.7 per cent a year to 0.5 per cent a year.

39 What role does the long-term real interest rate play in the monetary policy transmission process?

40 How does Bank Rate influence the long-term real interest rate?

41 What do you think happened to inflation expectations between 2008 and 2010 and why?

Use the following information in problems 42 and 43.

Financial markets predict a 95 per cent or more certainty that rates will rise by a quarter of a percentage point in June, October and January over 2011 and 2012, leaping from 0.5 per cent to 1.25 per cent.

Source: *The Financial Times*, 24 January 2011

42 How do expectations of the future of the interest rate influence the exchange rate?

43 How does monetary policy influence the exchange rate?

44 **Dollar Tumbles to 15-Year Low Against Yen**

The dollar tumbled to a fresh 15-year low on persistent fears over the US economic outlook.

Source: yahoo.com, 7 October 2010

  a How do 'fears over the US economic outlook' influence the exchange rate between the US dollar and the UK pound?

  b How does US monetary policy influence the exchange rate between the US dollar and the UK pound?

  c How does US monetary policy influence the UK economy?

Use the following news clip in Problems 45 and 46.

Top Economist says America Could Plunge into Recession

Robert Shiller, Professor of Economics at Yale University, predicted that there was a very real possibility that the US would be plunged into a Japan-style slump, with house prices declining for years.

Source: timesonline.co.uk, 31 December 2007

45 What challenge do falling house prices pose for the conduct of monetary policy? How could monetary policy prevent house prices from falling?

46 Describe the time lags in the response of output and inflation to monetary policy actions designed to respond to falling house prices.

Use the following news clip in Problems 47 and 48.

Greenspan Says Economy Strong

The US central bank chairman, Alan Greenspan, said inflation was low, consumer spending had held up well through the downturn, housing-market strength was likely to continue, and businesses appeared to have unloaded their glut of inventories, setting the stage for a rebound in production.

Source: cnn.com, 16 July 2002

47 What monetary policy actions would you expect to have created the situation described by Alan Greenspan?

48 What monetary policy actions would you expect a central bank to take in the situation described by Alan Greenspan?

Extraordinary Monetary Stimulus

49 Between August 2007 when the global financial crisis started and April 2008, Bank Rate was cut from 5.75 per cent to 5 per cent. Only when the shockwaves intensified in October 2008 did the Bank of England respond with extraordinary rate cuts, dropping Bank Rate to 0.5 per cent by March 2009.

   a Why was the Bank of England so timid in its initial interest rate cuts in the first year of the global financial crisis?

   b How would you expect the massive rate cuts between October 2008 and March 2009 to influence real GDP and the inflation rate in 2009, 2010 and 2011? Describe the transmission mechanisms and the time lags.

50 Explain how bailing out troubled banks and taking them into public ownership avoids the risk of a serious collapse of aggregate demand. Does the government borrowing to buy the troubled banks have any effect on aggregate demand?

51 Explain the key differences between QE and normal open market operations.

52 What are the three ingredients of a financial and banking crisis and how do the four extraordinary monetary policy actions address each of them?

53 The UK economy suffered a shock contraction in real GDP in the fourth quarter of 2010. Shadow chancellor Ed Balls said the figures were a matter of 'great concern' and due largely to the speed and scope of the coalition government's deficit reduction programme.

Source: BBC, 24 January 2011

   a If the Bank of England had expected the economy to weaken in the fourth quarter, what policy actions might it have taken differently from what it did take?

   b Describe the time lags in the response of output to the policy actions you have prescribed.

Economics in the News

54 After you have studied *Reading Between the Lines* on pp. 736–737, answer the following questions.

   a What is meant by forward guidance and how is it likely to be applied to monetary policy in the UK?

   b What is forward guidance meant to achieve?

   c How does the policy forward guidance work through the economic system?

   d What are the dangers of such a policy? Use the AS–AD model to explain your answer?

55 In a poll of economists, 50 per cent of those interviewed said that forward guidance by the Bank of England would be conditioned on the unemployment rate.

Source: Reuters, 11 July 2013

   a What does such forward guidance mean for UK interest rates during 2013 and 2014? Explain your answer.

   b What change will have occur in the UK economy before interest rates start to rise?

   c What are the dangers of using the unemployment rate to determine monetary policy?

Glossary

Abatement technology A production technology that reduces pollution. (p. 371)

Above full-employment equilibrium A macroeconomic equilibrium in which real GDP exceeds potential GDP. (p. 624)

Absolute advantage A person has an absolute advantage if that person more is productive than others. (p. 41)

Adverse selection The tendency for people to enter into agreements in which they can use their private information to their own advantage and to the disadvantage of the less-informed party. (p. 446)

Aggregate demand The relationship between the quantity of real GDP demanded and the price level. (p. 618)

Aggregate planned expenditure The expenditure that households, firms, governments and foreigners plan to undertake in given circumstances. It is the sum of planned consumption expenditure, planned investment, planned government expenditure on goods and services and planned exports minus planned imports. (p. 638)

Aggregate production function The relationship between real GDP and the quantity of labour when all other influences on production remain the same. (p. 512)

Allocative efficiency A situation in which goods and services are produced at the lowest possible cost and in quantities that provide the greatest benefit. We cannot produce more of any good without giving up some of another good that we value more highly. (p. 35)

Antitrust law A law that regulates oligopolies and prevents them from becoming monopolies or behaving like monopolies. (p. 334)

Asymmetric information The situation in a market in which buyers and sellers have private information. (p. 446)

Automatic fiscal policy A fiscal policy action that is triggered by the state of the economy with no action by the government. (p. 704)

Autonomous expenditure The sum of those components of aggregate planned expenditure that do not vary with real GDP. Autonomous expenditure equals the sum of investment, government expenditure, exports and the autonomous parts of consumption expenditure and imports. (p. 642)

Autonomous tax multiplier The magnification effect of a change in autonomous taxes on equilibrium expenditure and real GDP. (p. 660)

Average cost pricing rule A rule that sets price to cover cost including normal profit, which means setting the price equal to average total cost. (p. 292)

Average fixed cost Total fixed cost per unit of output. (p. 226)

Average product The average product of a factor of production. It equals total product divided by the quantity of the resource employed. (p. 221)

Average total cost Total cost per unit of output. (p. 226)

Average variable cost Total variable cost per unit of output. (p. 226)

Balanced budget A government budget in which revenues and outlays are equal. (p. 691)

Balanced budget multiplier The multiplier that arises from a fiscal policy action that changes both government expenditure and taxes by the same amount so that the government's budget balance remains unchanged. (p. 661)

Balance of payments accounts A country's record of international trading and its borrowing and lending. (p. 602)

Bank of England The central bank of the UK. (p. 565)

Bank Rate The Bank of England's official interest rate. The interest rate that the Bank of England charges on secured overnight loans to the commercial banks. (p. 566)

Barrier to entry A legal or natural constraint that protects a firm from potential competitors. (p. 276)

Below full-employment equilibrium A macroeconomic equilibrium in which potential GDP exceeds real GDP. (p. 625)

Benefit The benefit of something is the gain or pleasure that it brings and is determined by preferences. (p. 10)

Big trade-off A trade-off between equity and efficiency. (pp. 115, 431)

Bilateral monopoly A situation in which a monopoly seller faces a monopsony buyer. (p. 399)

Black market An illegal trading arrangement in which the price exceeds the legally imposed price ceiling. (p. 126)

Bond A promise to make specified payments on specified dates. (p. 535)

Bond market The market in which bonds issued by firms and governments are traded. (p. 535)

Budget An annual statement of the government's projected outlays and receipts during the next year together with the laws and regulations that support those outlays and receipts. (p. 690)

Budget deficit A government's budget balance that is negative – outlays exceed receipts. (p. 691)

Budget line The limits to a household's consumption choices. (p. 174)

Budget surplus A government's budget balance that is positive – receipts exceed outlays. (p. 691)

Business cycle The periodic but irregular up-and-down movement of total production and other measures of economic activity. (p. 467)

Capital The tools, equipment, buildings and other constructions that have been produced in the past and which businesses now use to produce goods and services. (p. 4)

Capital accumulation The growth of capital resources. (p. 38)

Capital and financial account A record of all UK investments abroad and foreigners' investments in the UK. (p. 602)

Capture theory A theory of regulation that states that the regulation is in the self-interest of producers. (p. 291)

Cartel A group of firms that has entered into a collusive agreement to limit output and increase prices and profits. (p. 321)

Ceteris paribus Other things being equal – all other relevant things remaining the same. (p. 24)

Chain volume measure A measure that uses the prices of two adjacent years to calculate the real GDP growth rate. (p. 474)

Change in demand A change in buyers' plans that occurs when some influence on those plans other than the price of the good changes. It is illustrated by a shift of the demand curve. (p. 56)

Change in supply A change in sellers' plans that occurs when some influence on those plans other than the price of the good changes. It is illustrated by a shift of the supply curve. (p. 61)

Change in the quantity demanded A change in buyers' plans that occurs when the price of a good changes, but all other influences on buyers' plans remain unchanged. It is illustrated by a movement along the demand curve. (p. 59)

Change in the quantity supplied A change in sellers' plans that occurs when the price of a good changes, but all other influences on sellers' plans remain unchanged. It is illustrated by a movement along the supply curve. (p. 63)

Classical A macroeconomist who believes that the economy is self-regulating and that it is always at full employment. (p. 628)

Classical growth theory A view that the growth of real GDP per person is temporary, and that when it rises above the subsistence level, a population explosion brings it back to the subsistence level. (p. 521)

Coase theorem The proposition that if property rights exist, only a small number of parties are involved and transactions costs are low, then private transactions are efficient. (p. 372)

Collusive agreement An agreement between two (or more) producers to restrict output, raise the price and increase profits. (p. 324)

Command system A method of organising production that uses a managerial hierarchy. (pp. 104, 201)

Common resource A resource that is rival and non-excludable. (p. 348)

Comparative advantage A person or country has a comparative advantage in an activity if that person or country can perform the activity at a lower opportunity cost than anyone else or any other country. (p. 41)

Competitive market A market that has many buyers and many sellers, so no single buyer or seller can influence the price. (p. 54)

Complement A good that is used in conjunction with another good. (p. 57)

Compound interest The interest on an initial investment plus the interest on the interest that the investment has previously earned. (p. 408)

Constant returns to scale Features of a firm's technology that lead to constant long-run average cost as output increases. When constant returns to scale are present, the *LRAC* curve is horizontal. (p. 234)

Consumer Prices Index (CPI) An index that measures the average of the prices paid by consumers for a fixed 'basket' of consumer goods and services. (p. 493)

Consumer surplus The value of a good minus the price paid for it, summed over the quantity bought. (p. 107)

Consumption expenditure The total payment for consumer goods and services. (p. 461)

Consumption function The relationship between consumption expenditure and disposable income, other things remaining the same. (p. 638)

Contestable market A market in which firms can enter and leave so easily that firms in the market face competition from potential entrants. (p. 332)

Cooperative equilibrium The outcome of a game in which the players make and share the monopoly profit. (p. 330)

Cost-push inflation An inflation that results from an initial increase in costs. (p. 670)

Crawling peg An exchange rate that follows a path determined by a decision of the government or the central bank and is achieved in a similar way to a fixed exchange rate by central bank intervention in the foreign exchange market. (p. 599)

Creditor nation A country that during its entire history has invested more in the rest of the world than other countries have invested in it. (p. 604)

Credit risk The risk that a borrower, also known as a creditor, might not repay a loan. (p. 449)

Cross elasticity of demand The responsiveness of the demand for a good to a change in the price of a substitute or complement, other things remaining the same. It is calculated as the percentage change in the quantity demanded of the good divided by the percentage change in the price of the substitute or complement. (p. 90)

Crowding-out effect The tendency for the government budget deficit to raise the real interest rate and decrease investment. (p. 546)

Currency The notes and coins held by households and firms. (p. 559)

Currency drain ratio The ratio of currency to deposits. (p. 569)

Current account A record of the receipts from the sales of goods and services to foreigners, the payments for goods and services bought from foreigners, income and other transfers received from and paid to foreigners. (p. 602)

Cycle A tendency for a variable to alternate between upward and downward movements. (p. 482)

Cyclical surplus or deficit The actual budget balance minus the structural surplus or deficit. (p. 705)

Cyclical unemployment The fluctuations in unemployment over the business cycle. (p. 489)

Deadweight loss A measure of inefficiency. It is equal to the decrease in consumer surplus and producer surplus that results from an inefficient level of production. (p. 111)

Debtor nation A country that during its entire history has borrowed more from the rest of the world than it has lent to it. (p. 604)

Default risk The risk that a borrower, also known as a creditor, might not repay a loan. (p. 449)

Deflation A process in which the price level persistently falls – a negative inflation. (p. 492)

Demand The relationship between the quantity of a good that consumers plan to buy and the price of the good when all other influences on buyers' plans remain the same. It is described by a demand schedule and illustrated by a demand curve. (p. 55)

Demand curve A curve that shows the relationship between the quantity

demanded of a good and its price when all other influences on consumers' planned purchases remain the same. (p. 56)

Demand for loanable funds The relationship between the quantity of loanable funds demanded and the real interest rate when all other influences on borrowing plans remain the same. (p. 540)

Demand for money The relationship between the quantity of real money demanded and the interest rate – the opportunity cost of holding money – when all other influences on the amount of money that people plan to hold remain the same. (p. 573)

Demand-pull inflation An inflation that results from an initial increase in aggregate demand. (p. 668)

Depreciation The decrease in the value of a firm's capital that results from wear and tear and obsolescence. (p. 462)

Deregulation The process of removing a previously imposed regulation. (p. 291)

Derived demand The demand for a factor of production, which is derived from the demand for the goods and services produced by the factor. (p. 391)

Desired reserve ratio The ratio of reserves to deposits that banks consider prudent to hold. (p. 569)

Diminishing marginal rate of substitution The general tendency for the marginal rate of substitution to diminish as the consumer moves along an indifference curve, increasing consumption of the good on the x-axis and decreasing consumption of the good on the y-axis. (p. 178)

Diminishing marginal returns The tendency for the marginal product of an additional unit of a factor of production to be less than the marginal product of the previous unit of the factor. (p. 223)

Direct relationship A relationship between two variables that move in the same direction. (p. 18)

Discounting The conversion of a future amount of money to its present value. (p. 408)

Discouraged workers People who are available and willing to work but have stopped actively looking for jobs because they believe that no jobs are available. (p. 487)

Discretionary fiscal policy A fiscal policy action that is initiated by the government (Chancellor of the Exchequer in the UK). (p. 704)

Diseconomies of scale Features of a firm's technology that lead to rising long-run average cost as output increases. (p. 234)

Disposable income Aggregate income minus taxes plus transfer payments. (pp. 416, 620, 638)

Doha Development Agenda (Doha Round) Negotiations held in Doha, Qatar, to lower tariff barriers and quotas that restrict international trade in farm products and services. (p. 161)

Dominant-strategy equilibrium An equilibrium in which the best strategy of each player is to cheat, regardless of the strategy of the other player. (p. 323)

Dumping The sale by a foreign firm of exports at a lower price than the cost of production. (p. 162)

Duopoly A market structure in which two producers of a good or service compete. (p. 320)

Economic activity rate The percentage of the working-age population who are economically active. (p. 487)

Economically active The people who have a job or are willing and able to take a job. (p. 485)

Economically inactive The people who do not want a job. (p. 485)

Economic depreciation The change in the market value of capital over a given period. (p. 197)

Economic efficiency A situation that occurs when the firm produces a given output at the least cost. (p. 199)

Economic growth The expansion of production possibilities that results from capital accumulation and technological change. (pp. 38, 506)

Economic model A description of some aspect of the economic world that includes only those features of the world that are needed for the purpose at hand. (p. 12)

Economic profit A firm's total revenue minus total cost. (p. 196)

Economic rent Any surplus – consumer surplus, producer surplus or economic profit. It is also the income received by the owner of a factor of production over and above the amount required to induce that owner to offer the factor for use. (p. 284)

Economics The social science that studies the choices that individuals, businesses, governments and entire societies make and how they cope with scarcity and the incentives that influence and reconcile those choices. (p. 2)

Economies of scale Features of a firm's technology that lead to a falling long-run average cost as output increases. (pp. 210, 234)

Economies of scope Decreases in average total cost that occur when a firm uses specialised resources to produce a range of goods and services. (p. 211)

Efficiency A situation in which the available resources are used to produce goods and services at the lowest possible cost and in quantities that give the greatest value or benefit. (p. 5)

Efficient scale The quantity at which average total cost is a minimum – the quantity at the bottom of the U-shaped *ATC* curve. (p. 306)

Elastic demand Demand with a price elasticity greater than 1; other things remaining the same, the percentage change in the quantity demanded exceeds the percentage change in price. (p. 84)

Elasticity of supply The responsiveness of the quantity supplied of a good to a change in its price, other things remaining the same. (p. 92)

Employment rate The percentage of people of working age who have jobs. (p. 486)

Entrepreneurship The human resource that organises the other three factors of production: labour, land and capital. (p. 4)

Equilibrium expenditure The level of aggregate expenditure that occurs when aggregate planned expenditure equals real GDP. (p. 644)

Equilibrium price The price at which the quantity demanded equals the quantity supplied. (p. 64)

Equilibrium quantity The quantity bought and sold at the equilibrium price. (p. 64)

European Central Bank (ECB) The central bank of the Eurozone – the members of the EU that use the euro as their currency. (p. 565)

Excess capacity A firm has excess capacity if it produces below its efficient scale. (p. 306)

Excess reserves A bank's actual reserves minus its desired reserves. (p. 569)

Exchange rate The price at which one currency exchanges for another currency in the foreign exchange market. (p. 588)

Excludable A good is excludable if it is possible to prevent someone from enjoying its benefits. (p. 348)

Expansion A business cycle phase between a trough and a peak – the phase in which real GDP increases. (p. 467)

Expected utility The utility value of what a person expects to own at a given point in time. (p. 441)

Expected wealth The money value of what a person expects to own at a given point in time. (p. 440)

Exports The goods and services that we sell to people in other countries. (pp. 150, 462)

Export subsidy A payment made by a government to a domestic producer of an exported good. (p. 160)

Externality A cost or a benefit that arises from production or consumption of a private good and which falls on someone other than the producer or the consumer. (p. 348)

Factors of production The productive resources that businesses use to produce goods and services. (p. 3)

Final good An item that is bought by its final user during a specified time period. (p. 460)

Financial capital The funds that firms use to buy physical capital. (p. 534)

Financial institution A firm that operates on both sides of the market for financial capital. It is a borrower in one market and a lender in another. (p. 536)

Firm An economic unit that hires factors of production and organises those factors to produce and sell goods and services. (pp. 44, 196)

Fiscal imbalance The present value of the government's commitments to pay benefits minus the present value of its tax revenues. (p. 702)

Fiscal policy The government's attempt to influence the economy by setting and changing taxes, making transfer payments and purchasing goods and services. (pp. 620, 690)

Fiscal stimulus The use of fiscal policy to increase production and employment. (p. 704)

Five-firm concentration ratio A measure of market power that is calculated as the percentage of total revenue (the value of sales) in an industry accounted for by the five firms with the largest value of sales. (p. 206)

Fixed exchange rate A foreign exchange rate that is pegged at a value determined by the central bank and is achieved by central bank intervention in the foreign exchange market. (p. 598)

Flexible exchange rate A foreign exchange rate that is determined by market forces in the absence of central bank intervention. (p. 598)

Foreign currency The money of other countries, regardless of whether that money is in the form of coins, notes or bank deposits. (p. 588)

Foreign exchange market The market in which the currency of one country is exchanged for the currency of another. (p. 588)

Free-rider problem The absence of an incentive for people to pay for what they consume. (p. 351)

Frictional unemployment The unemployment that arises from normal labour turnover – from people entering and leaving the workforce and from the ongoing creation and destruction of jobs. (p. 489)

Full employment A situation in which the unemployment rate equals the natural unemployment rate. At full employment, there is no cyclical unemployment – all unemployment is frictional and structural. (p. 489)

Full-employment equilibrium A macroeconomic equilibrium in which real GDP equals potential GDP. (p. 625)

Game theory A tool that economists use to analyse strategic behaviour – behaviour that takes into account the expected behaviour of others and the recognition of mutual interdependence. (p. 322)

GDP deflator One measure of the price level, which is an index of the prices of all the goods and services in GDP. It is calculated as nominal GDP divided by real GDP, multiplied by 100. (p. 496)

Generational accounting An accounting system that measures the lifetime tax burden and benefits of each generation. (p. 702)

Generational imbalance The division of the fiscal imbalance between the current and future generations, assuming that the current generation will enjoy the existing levels of taxes and benefits. (p. 703)

Gini coefficient The area between the line of equality and the Lorenz curve as a percentage of the entire area beneath the line of equality. (p. 419)

Goods and services The objects that people value and produce to satisfy their wants. (p. 3)

Government debt The total amount of borrowing by the government. It equals the sum of past budget deficits minus the sum of past budget surpluses plus payments to buy assets minus receipts from the sale of assets. (p. 693)

Government expenditure Goods and services bought by the government. (p. 462)

Government expenditure multiplier The magnification effect of a change in government expenditure on goods and services on equilibrium expenditure and real GDP. (pp. 660, 707)

Government failure A situation in which government actions lead to inefficiency – to either underprovision or overprovision. (p. 346)

Gross domestic product (GDP) The market value of all the final goods and services produced within a country during a given time period – usually a year. (p. 460)

Gross investment The total amount spent on purchases of new capital and on replacing depreciated capital. (pp. 462, 534)

Growth rate The annual percentage change in real GDP. (p. 506)

Hotelling Principle The proposition that the price of a non-renewable natural resource is expected to rise at a rate equal to the interest rate. (p. 404)

Human capital The knowledge and skill that people obtain from education, on-the-job training and work experience. (p. 3)

Hyperinflation An inflation rate that exceeds 50 per cent a month. (p. 492)

Implicit rental rate The firm's opportunity cost of using its own capital. (p. 196)

Import quota A restriction that limits the maximum quantity of a good that may be imported in a given period. (p. 158)

Imports The goods and services that we buy from people in other countries. (pp. 150, 462)

Incentive A reward that encourages an action or a penalty that discourages one. (p. 2)

Incentive system A method of organising production that uses a market-like mechanism inside the firm. (p. 201)

Income effect The effect of a change in income on consumption, other things remaining the same. (p. 183)

Income elasticity of demand The responsiveness of demand to a change in income, other things remaining the same. It is calculated as the percentage change in the quantity demanded divided by the percentage change in income. (p. 89)

Indifference curve A line that shows combinations of goods among which a consumer is indifferent. (p. 177)

Individual transferable quota (ITQ) A production limit that is assigned to an individual who is free to transfer the quota to someone else. (p. 380)

Induced expenditure The sum of the components of aggregate planned expenditure that vary with real GDP. Induced expenditure equals consumption expenditure minus imports. (p. 642)

Inelastic demand A demand with a price elasticity between 0 and 1; the percentage change in the quantity demanded is less than the percentage change in price. (p. 83)

Inferior good A good for which demand decreases as income increases. (p. 58)

Inflation A process in which the price level is persistently rising and money is losing value. (p. 492)

Inflationary gap The amount by which real GDP exceeds potential GDP. (p. 624)

Inflation rate The annual percentage change in the price level. (p. 495)

Interest The income that capital earns. (p. 4)

Interest rate parity A situation in which the rates of return on assets in different currencies are equal. (p. 596)

Intermediate good An item that is produced by one firm, bought by another firm and used as a component of a final good or service. (p. 460)

Inverse relationship A relationship between variables that move in opposite directions. (p. 19)

Investment The purchase of new plant, equipment and buildings and additions to inventories. (p. 461)

Isocost line A line that shows the combinations of labour and capital that can be bought for a given total cost and given factor prices. (p. 245)

Isocost map A series of isocost lines, each one of which represents a different total cost but for given prices of labour and capital. (p. 245)

Isoquant A curve that shows the different combinations of labour and capital required to produce a given quantity of output. (p. 243)

Isoquant map A series of isoquants, one for each different output level. (p. 243)

Job A contract for the trade of labour services. (p. 390)

Keynesian A macroeconomist who believes that, left alone, the economy would rarely operate at full employment, and that to achieve and maintain full employment, active help from fiscal policy and monetary policy is required. (p. 628)

Keynesian cycle theory The theory that fluctuations in investment driven by fluctuations in business confidence – summarised in the phrase 'animal spirits' – are the main source of fluctuations in aggregate demand. (p. 678)

Labour The work time and work effort that people devote to producing goods and services. (p. 3)

Labour productivity The quantity of real GDP produced per hour of labour. (p. 516)

Laffer curve The relationship between the tax rate and the amount of tax revenue collected. (p. 701)

Land The gifts of nature that we use to produce goods and services. (p. 3)

Law of demand Other things remaining the same, the higher the price of a good, the smaller is the quantity demanded; the lower the price of a good, the larger is the quantity demanded. (p. 55)

Law of diminishing marginal rate of substitution The marginal rate of substitution of labour for capital diminishes as the amount of labour increases and the amount of capital decreases. (p. 244)

Law of diminishing returns As a firm uses more of a variable input, with a given quantity of other inputs (fixed inputs), the marginal product of the variable input eventually diminishes. (p. 223)

Law of supply Other things remaining the same, the higher the price of a good, the greater is the quantity supplied; the lower the price of a good, the smaller is the quantity supplied. (p. 60)

Least-cost technique The combination of labour and capital that minimises the total cost of producing a given level of output. (p. 246)

Legal monopoly A market structure in which there is one firm and entry is restricted by the granting of a monopoly franchise, government licence, patent or copyright. (p. 276)

Lemons problem The problem that in a market in which it is not possible to distinguish reliable products from lemons, there are too many lemons and too few reliable products traded. (p. 446)

Lender of last resort The Bank of England is the lender of last resort in the UK – if all the banks are short of reserves they can borrow from the Bank of England. (p. 568)

Limit pricing The practice of setting the price at the highest level that inflicts a loss on an entrant. (p. 333)

Linear relationship A relationship between two variables that is illustrated by a straight line. (p. 18)

Loanable funds market The aggregate of all the individual markets in which

households, firms, governments, banks and other financial institutions borrow and lend. (p. 538)

Long run A period of time in which the quantities of all factors of production can be varied. (p. 220)

Long-run aggregate supply The relationship between the quantity of real GDP supplied and the price level when the money wage rate changes in step with the price level to maintain full employment; real GDP equals potential GDP. (p. 614)

Long-run average cost curve The relationship between the lowest attainable average total cost and output when both capital and labour are varied. (p. 233)

Long-run macroeconomic equilibrium A situation that occurs when real GDP equals potential GDP – the economy is on its long-run aggregate supply curve. (p. 622)

Long-run Phillips curve A curve that shows the relationship between inflation and unemployment when the actual inflation rate equals the expected inflation rate. (p. 675)

Lorenz curve A curve that graphs the cumulative percentage of income or wealth against the cumulative percentage of households or population. (p. 417)

M4 A measure of money that consists of currency held by the public plus bank deposits and building society deposits. (p. 559)

Macroeconomics The study of the performance of the national economy and the global economy. (p. 2)

Macro-prudential regulation Regulation of the monetary financial institutions and other financial institutions and financial markets to lower the risk of crisis and failure of these institutions and markets. (p. 735)

Margin When a choice is changed by a small amount or by a little at a time, the choice is made at the margin. (p. 11)

Marginal benefit The benefit that a person receives from consuming one more unit of a good or service. It is measured as the maximum amount that a person is willing to pay for one more unit of the good or service. (pp. 11, 36)

Marginal benefit curve A curve that shows the relationship between the marginal benefit of a good and the quantity of that good consumed. (p. 36)

Marginal cost The opportunity cost of producing one more unit of a good or service. It is the best alternative forgone. It is calculated as the increase in total cost divided by the increase in output. (pp. 11, 35, 226)

Marginal cost pricing rule A rule that sets the price of a good or service equal to the marginal cost of producing it. (p. 291)

Marginal external benefit The benefit from an additional unit of a good or service that people other than the consumer enjoy. (p. 355)

Marginal external cost The cost of producing an additional unit of a good or service that falls on people other than the producer. (p. 369)

Marginal private benefit The benefit from an additional unit of a good or service that the consumer of that good or service receives. (p. 355)

Marginal private cost The cost of producing an additional unit of a good or service that is borne by the producer of that good or service. (p. 369)

Marginal product The increase in total product that results from a one-unit increase in the variable input, with all other inputs remaining the same. It is calculated as the increase in total product divided by the increase in the variable input employed, when the quantities of all other inputs are constant. (p. 221)

Marginal propensity to consume The fraction of a change in disposable income that is consumed. It is calculated as the change in consumption expenditure divided by the change in disposable income that brought it about. (p. 640)

Marginal propensity to import The fraction of an increase in real GDP that is spent on imports. (p. 641)

Marginal propensity to save The fraction of a change in disposable income that is saved. It is calculated as the change in saving divided by the change in disposable income that brought it about. (p. 640)

Marginal rate of substitution The rate at which a person will give up good y (the good measured on the y-axis) to get an additional unit of good x (the good measured on the x-axis) and at the same time remain indifferent (remain on the same indifference curve). (p. 178)

Marginal rate of substitution of labour for capital The increase in labour needed per unit decrease in capital to allow output to remain constant. (p. 243)

Marginal revenue The change in total revenue that results from a one-unit increase in the quantity sold. It is calculated as the change in total revenue divided by the change in quantity sold. (p. 250)

Marginal social benefit The marginal benefit enjoyed by society – by the consumer of a good or service (marginal private benefit) plus the marginal benefit enjoyed by others (marginal external benefit). (p. 355)

Marginal social cost The marginal cost incurred by the entire society – by the producer and by everyone else on whom the cost falls. It is calculated as the sum of marginal private cost and the marginal external cost. (p. 369)

Market Any arrangement that enables buyers and sellers to get information and to do business with each other. (p. 44)

Market failure A situation in which the market does not allocate resources efficiently. (p. 111)

Markup The amount by which the firm's price exceeds its marginal cost. (p. 307)

Means of payment A method of settling a debt. (p. 558)

Microeconomics The study of the choices that individuals and businesses make, the way those choices interact in markets and the influence governments exert on them. (p. 2)

Minimum efficient scale The smallest quantity of output at which the long-run average cost curve reaches its lowest level. (p. 235)

Minimum wage A regulation that makes the hiring of labour below a specified wage rate illegal. The lowest wage rate at which a firm may legally hire labour. (p. 129)

Mixed good A private good the production or consumption of which creates an externality. (p. 348)

Monetarist A macroeconomist who believes that the economy is self-regulating and that it will normally operate at full employment, provided that monetary policy is not erratic and that the pace of money growth is kept steady. (p. 629)

Monetarist cycle theory A theory that regards fluctuations in both investment and consumption expenditure, driven by fluctuations in the growth rate of the quantity of money, as the main source of fluctuations in aggregate demand. (p. 678)

Monetary base The sum of the liabilities of the Bank of England plus coins issued by the Royal Mint. (p. 566)

Monetary financial institution A financial firm that takes deposits from households and firms. (p. 561)

Monetary policy The central bank conducts a nation's monetary policy by changing interest rates and adjusting the quantity of money. (p. 620)

Monetary Policy Committee (MPC) The committee in the Bank of England that has the responsibility for formulating monetary policy. (p. 565)

Monetary policy instrument A variable that the central bank can directly control or closely target. (p. 720)

Money Any commodity or token that is generally acceptable as a means of payment. (pp. 44, 558)

Money multiplier The ratio of the change in the quantity of money to the change in monetary base. (p. 571)

Money price The number of pounds or euros that must be given up in exchange for a good or service. (p. 54)

Monopolistic competition A market structure in which a large number of firms compete by making similar but slightly different products and compete on product quality, price and marketing, and are free to enter and exit the industry. (pp. 205, 302)

Monopoly A market structure in which there is one firm, that produces a good or service that has no close substitute, and in which the firm is protected from competition by a barrier preventing the entry of new firms. (pp. 206, 276)

Monopsony A market in which there is a single buyer. (p. 399)

Moral hazard A situation in which one of the parties to an agreement has an incentive after the agreement is made to act in a manner that brings additional benefits to himself or herself at the expense of the other party. (p. 446)

Mortgage A legal contract that gives ownership of a home to the lender in the event that the borrower fails to meet the agreed loan payments (repayments and interest). (p. 535)

Mortgage-backed security A type of bond that entitles its holder to the income from a package of mortgages. (p. 536)

Multiplier The amount by which a change in autonomous expenditure is magnified or multiplied to determine the change in equilibrium expenditure and real GDP. (p. 646)

Nash equilibrium The outcome of a game that occurs when player A takes the best possible action given the action of player B and player B takes the best possible action given the action of player A. (p. 323)

National saving The sum of private saving (saving by households and businesses) and government saving (budget surplus). (p. 539)

Natural monopoly A market in which economies of scale enable one firm to supply the entire market at the lowest possible cost. (p. 276)

Natural monopoly good A good that is non-rival and excludable. When buyers can be excluded if they don't pay but the good is non-rival, marginal cost is zero. (p. 348)

Natural unemployment rate Natural unemployment as a percentage of the labour force. The unemployment rate when the economy is at full employment – all unemployment is frictional and structural. (p. 489)

Negative externality A cost that arises when the social cost of production exceeds the private cost. (p. 369)

Negative relationship A relationship between variables that move in opposite directions. (p. 19)

Neoclassical growth theory The proposition that real GDP grows because technological change induces saving and investment that make physical capital grow. (p. 521)

Net borrower A country that is borrowing more from the rest of the world than it is lending to it. (p. 604)

Net exports The value of exports minus the value of imports. (p. 462)

Net investment Net increase in the capital stock – gross investment minus depreciation. (pp. 462, 534)

Net lender A country that is lending more to the rest of the world than it is borrowing from it. (p. 604)

Net taxes Taxes paid to governments minus cash transfers received from governments. (p. 538)

Net worth The market value of what a financial institution has lent minus the market value of what it has borrowed. (p. 537)

New classical A macroeconomist who holds the view that business cycle fluctuations are the efficient responses of a well-functioning market economy bombarded by shocks that arise from the uneven pace of technological change. (p. 628)

New classical cycle theory A rational expectations theory of the business cycle in which the rational expectation of the price level, which is determined by potential GDP and expected aggregate demand, determines the money wage rate and the position of the *SAS* curve. (p. 678)

New growth theory A theory of economic growth based on the idea that real GDP per person grows because of the choices that people make in the pursuit of ever greater profit, and that growth can persist indefinitely. (p. 522)

New Keynesian A Keynesian who holds the view that not only is the money wage rate sticky but prices of goods and services are also sticky. (p. 629)

New Keynesian cycle theory A rational expectations theory of the business cycle that emphasises the fact that today's money wage rates were negotiated at many past dates, which means that past rational expectations of the current price level influence the money wage rate and the position of the *SAS* curve. (p. 678)

Nominal GDP The value of the final goods and services produced in a given year valued at the prices that prevailed in that same year. It is a more precise name for GDP. (p. 465)

Nominal interest rate The number of pounds (or euros) that a. (p. 539)

Non-excludable A good is non-excludable if everyone benefits from it regardless of whether they pay for it. (p. 348)

Non-renewable natural resource A natural resource that can be used only once and which cannot be replaced once it has been used. (p. 390)

Non-rival A good is non-rival if one person's use does not decrease the quantity available for someone else. (p. 348)

Normal good A good for which demand increases as income increases. (p. 58)

Normal profit The return that an entrepreneur can expect to receive on average. (p. 197)

Offshore outsourcing Buying goods, components or services from firms in other countries. (p. 163)

Oligopoly A market structure in which a small number of firms compete and natural or legal barriers prevent the entry of new firms. (pp. 205, 320)

Open market operation The purchase or sale of securities by the central bank in the loanable funds market. (p. 566)

Opportunity cost The highest-valued alternative that we give up to get something. (pp. 10, 33)

Optimal currency area A geographical area that is better served by a single currency than by several currencies. (p. 601)

Original income The wages, interest, rent and profit earned in factor markets and before paying income taxes. (p. 416)

Output gap Real GDP minus potential GDP. (pp. 490, 624)

Payoff matrix A table that shows the payoffs for every possible action by each player in a game for every possible action by each other player. (p. 322)

Perfect competition A market in which there are many firms each selling an identical product; there are many buyers; there are no restrictions on entry into the industry; firms in the industry have no advantage over potential new entrants; and firms and buyers are well informed about the price of each firm's product. (pp. 205, 250)

Perfectly elastic demand Demand with an infinite price elasticity; the quantity demanded changes by an infinitely large percentage in response to a tiny price change. (p. 84)

Perfectly inelastic demand Demand with a price elasticity of zero; the quantity demanded remains constant when the price changes. (p. 83)

Perfect price discrimination Price discrimination that extracts the entire consumer surplus. (p. 288)

Phillips curve A curve that shows a relationship between inflation and unemployment. (p. 674)

Pigovian taxes Taxes that are used as an incentive for producers to cut back on an activity that creates an external cost. (p. 372)

Political equilibrium The situation in which the choices of voters, firms, politicians and civil servants are all compatible and no group can see a way of improving its position by making a different choice. (p. 347)

Pooling equilibrium The equilibrium in a market when only one message is available and an uninformed person cannot determine quality. (p. 449)

Positive externality A benefit that arises when the social benefit exceeds the private benefit. (p. 355)

Positive relationship A relationship between two variables that move in the same direction. (p. 18)

Potential GDP The quantity of real GDP at full employment – when all the economy's labour, capital, land and entrepreneurial ability are fully employed. (p. 466)

Poverty A situation in which a household's income is too low to be able to buy the quantities of food, shelter and clothing that are deemed necessary. (p. 421)

Predatory pricing Setting a low price to drive competitors out of business with the intention of setting a monopoly price when the competition has gone. (p. 336)

Preferences A description of a person's likes and dislikes and the intensity of those feelings. (pp. 10, 36)

Present value The amount of money that, if invested today, will grow to be as large as a given future amount when the interest that it will earn is taken into account. (pp. 408, 702)

Price cap A government regulation that sets the maximum price that may legally be charged. (p. 126)

Price cap regulation A regulation that specifies the highest price that the firm is permitted to set. (p. 293)

Price ceiling A government regulation that sets the maximum price that may legally be charged. (p. 126)

Price discrimination The practice of selling different units of a good or service for different prices or of charging one customer different prices for different quantities bought. (p. 277)

Price effect The effect of a change in the price of a good on the quantity of the good consumed, other things remaining the same. (p. 181)

Price elasticity of demand A units-free measure of the responsiveness of the quantity demanded of a good to a change in its price, when all other influences on buyers' plans remain the same. (p. 82)

Price floor A regulation that makes it illegal to charge a price lower than a specified level. (p. 129)

Price level The average level of prices. (p. 492)

Price support A government-guaranteed minimum price of a good. (p. 139)

Price taker A firm that cannot influence the price of the good or service it produces. (p. 250)

Principal–agent problem The problem of devising compensation rules that induce an agent to act in the best interest of a principal. (p. 201)

Principle of minimum differentiation The tendency for competitors to make themselves similar as they try to appeal to the maximum number of clients or voters. (p. 353)

Private good A good or service that is both rival and excludable. (p. 348)

Private information Information that is available to one person but is too costly for anyone else to obtain. (p. 446)

Producer surplus The price received for a good minus its minimum supply-price (or marginal cost) summed over the quantity sold. (p. 109)

Product differentiation Making a product slightly different from the product of a competing firm. (pp. 205, 302)

Production efficiency A situation in which the economy cannot produce more of one good without producing less of some other good. (p. 33)

Production possibilities frontier The boundary between the combinations of goods and services that can be produced and the combinations that cannot. (p. 32)

Production quota An upper limit to the quantity of a good that may be produced in a specified period. (p. 137)

Production subsidy A payment made by the government to a producer for each unit produced. (p. 138)

Profit The income earned by entrepreneurship. (p. 4)

Progressive income tax A tax on income at an average rate that increases with the level of income. (p. 429)

Property rights Legally established titles to the ownership, use and disposal of anything that people value, and which are enforceable in the courts. (pp. 44, 371)

Proportional income tax A tax on income at a constant average rate, regardless of the level of income. (p. 429)

Public choice A decision that has consequences for many people and perhaps for the entire society. (p. 346)

Public good A good or service that is both non-rival and non-excludable. It can be consumed simultaneously by everyone and no one can be excluded from enjoying its benefits. (p. 348)

Public production The production of a good or service by a public authority that receives its revenue from the government. (p. 357)

Purchasing power parity A situation in which the prices in two countries are equal when converted at the exchange rate. (p. 596)

Quantitative easing (QE) Lending on repurchase agreements to inject reserves into commercial banks. (pp. 568, 733)

Quantity demanded The amount of a good or service that consumers plan to buy during a given time period at a particular price. (p. 55)

Quantity supplied The amount of a good or service that producers plan to sell during a given time period at a particular price. (p. 60)

Quantity theory of money The proposition that in the long run, an increase in the quantity of money brings an equal percentage increase in the price level. (p. 576)

Rate of return regulation A regulation that requires the firm to justify its price by showing that the price enables it to earn a specified target per cent return on its capital. (p. 292)

Rational choice A choice that compares costs and benefits and achieves the greatest benefit over cost for the person making the choice. (p. 10)

Rational expectation The most accurate forecast possible – a forecast that uses all the available relevant information. (p. 673)

Real business cycle theory A theory that regards random fluctuations in productivity as the main source of economic fluctuations. (p. 678)

Real exchange rate The price of UK-produced goods and services relative to foreign-produced goods and services. (p. 597)

Real GDP The value of final goods and services produced in a given year when valued at the prices of a reference base year. (p. 465)

Real GDP per person Real GDP divided by the population. (pp. 466, 506)

Real income A household's income expressed as a quantity of goods that the household can afford to buy. (p. 175)

Real interest rate The quantity of goods and services that a unit of capital earns. It is the nominal interest rate adjusted for inflation and is approximately equal to the nominal interest rate minus the inflation rate. (p. 539)

Real wage rate The quantity of goods and services that an hour's work can buy. It is equal to the money wage rate divided by the price level. (p. 513)

Recession A business cycle phase in which real GDP decreases for at least two successive quarters. (p. 467)

Recessionary gap The amount by which potential GDP exceeds real GDP. (p. 625)

Reference base period The period in which the CPI or RPI is defined to be 100. (p. 493)

Regressive income tax A tax on income at an average rate that decreases with the level of income. (p. 429)

Regulation Rules administered by a government agency to influence prices, quantities, entry and other aspects of economic activity in a firm or industry. (p. 291)

Relative price The ratio of the price of one good or service to the price of another good or service. A relative price is an opportunity cost. (pp. 54, 175)

Rent The income that land earns. (p. 4)

Rent ceiling A regulation that makes it illegal to charge a rent higher than a specified level. (p. 126)

Rent seeking Lobbying for special treatment by the government to create economic profit or to divert consumer surplus or producer surplus away from others. (p. 165)

Repo A repurchase agreement in which a commercial bank sells a government bond to the Bank of England and simultaneously agrees to *repurchase* it (buy it back) usually two weeks later. (p. 565)

Repo rate The interest rate in the repo market. (p. 720)

Required reserve ratio The ratio of reserves to deposits that banks are required, by regulation, to hold. (p. 562)

Resale price maintenance A distributor's agreement with a manufacturer to resell a product *at or above a specified minimum price*. (p. 335)

Reserve assets account The record of the net increase or decrease in a country's holdings of foreign currency reserves that comes about from the official financing of the difference between the current account and capital and financial account balances. (p. 602)

Reserves Cash in a bank's vault plus its deposit at the central bank. (p. 561)

Retail Prices Index (RPI) An index that measures the average of the prices paid by consumers for a fixed 'basket' of consumer goods and services. (p. 493)

Risk aversion The dislike of risk. (p. 440)

Rival A good is rival if one person's use decreases the quantity available for someone else. (p. 348)

Rule of 70 A rule that states that the number of years it takes for the level of a variable to double is approximately 70 divided by the annual percentage growth rate of the variable. (p. 507)

Saving The amount of income that households have left after they have paid their taxes and bought their consumption goods and services. (p. 534)

Saving function The relationship between saving and disposable income, other things remaining the same. (p. 638)

Scarcity Our inability to satisfy all our wants. (p. 2)

Scatter diagram A diagram that plots the value of one economic variable against the value of another for a number of different values of each variable. (p. 16)

Screening Inducing an informed party to reveal private information. (p. 449)

Search activity The time spent looking for someone with whom to do business. (p. 126)

Self-interest The choices that you think are the best for you. (p. 5)

Separating equilibrium The equilibrium in a market when signalling provides full information

to a previously uninformed person. (p. 449)

Short run The period of time in which the quantity of at least one factor of production is fixed and the quantities of the other factors can be varied. The fixed factor is usually capital – that is, the firm has a given plant size. (p. 220)

Short-run aggregate supply The relationship between the quantity of real GDP supplied and the price level when the money wage rate, the prices of other factors of production and potential GDP remain constant. (p. 615)

Short-run macroeconomic equilibrium A situation that occurs when the quantity of real GDP demanded equals the short-run quantity of real GDP supplied – at the point of intersection of the *AD* curve and the *SAS* curve. (p. 622)

Short-run market supply curve A curve that shows how the quantity supplied in a market varies as the market price varies when each firm's plant and the number of firms remain the same. (p. 256)

Short-run Phillips curve A curve that shows the trade-off between inflation and unemployment, holding constant the expected inflation rate and the natural unemployment rate. (p. 674)

Shutdown point The output and price at which the firm just covers its total variable cost. In the short run, the firm is indifferent between producing the profit-maximising output and shutting down temporarily. (p. 254)

Signal An action taken by an informed person (or firm) to send a message to uninformed people or an action taken outside a market that conveys information that can be used by that market. (p. 310)

Signalling A situation in which an informed person takes actions that send information to uninformed persons. (p. 448)

Single-price monopoly A monopoly that must sell each unit of its output for the same price to all its customers. (p. 277)

Slope The change in the value of a variable measured on the *y*-axis divided by the change in the value of the variable measured on the *x*-axis. (p. 22)

Social interest Choices that are the best for society as a whole. (p. 5)

Social interest theory A theory that politicians supply the regulation that achieves an efficient allocation of resources. (p. 291)

Stagflation The combination of inflation and recession. (pp. 627, 671)

Stock A certificate of ownership and claim to the firm's profits. (p. 536)

Stock market A financial market in which shares of stocks of corporations are traded. (p. 536)

Strategies All the possible actions of each player in a game. (p. 322)

Structural surplus or deficit The budget balance that would occur if the economy were at full employment and real GDP were equal to potential GDP. (p. 705)

Structural unemployment The unemployment that arises when changes in technology or international competition change the skills needed to perform jobs or change the locations of jobs. (p. 489)

Subsidy A payment made by the government to a domestic producer based on the quantity produced. (p. 357)

Substitute A good that can be used in place of another good. (p. 57)

Substitution effect The effect of a change in price of a good or service on the quantity bought when the consumer (hypothetically) remains indifferent between the original and the new consumption situations – that is, the consumer remains on the same indifference curve. (p. 184)

Sunk cost The past expenditure on a plant that has no resale value. (p. 220)

Supply The relationship between the quantity of a good that producers plan to sell and the price of the good when all other influences on sellers' plans remain the same. It is described by a supply schedule and illustrated by a supply curve. (p. 60)

Supply curve A curve that shows the relationship between the quantity supplied and the price of a good when all other influences on producers' planned sales remain the same. (p. 60)

Supply of loanable funds The relationship between the quantity of loanable funds supplied and the real interest rate when all other influences on lending plans remain the same. (p. 541)

Symmetry principle A requirement that people in similar situations be treated similarly. (p. 116)

Tariff A tax that is imposed by the importing country when an imported good crosses its international boundary. (p. 155)

Tax incidence The division of the burden of a tax between the buyer and the seller. (p. 131)

Tax multiplier The quantitative effect of a change in taxes on real GDP. (p. 707)

Tax wedge The gap between the before-tax and after-tax wage rates. (p. 697)

Technological change The development of new goods and better ways of producing goods and services. (p. 38)

Technological efficiency A situation that occurs when the firm produces a given output by using the least amount of inputs. (p. 199)

Technology Any method of producing a good or service. (p. 198)

Time-series graph A graph that measures time (for example, months or years) on the x-axis and the variable or variables in which we are interested on the y-axis. (p. 481)

Total cost The cost of all the factors of production that a firm uses. (p. 225)

Total fixed cost The cost of the firm's fixed inputs. (p. 225)

Total product The maximum output that a given quantity of factors of production can produce. (p. 221)

Total revenue The value of a firm's sales. It is calculated as the price of the good multiplied by the quantity sold. (pp. 86, 250)

Total revenue test A method of estimating the price elasticity of demand by observing the change in total revenue that results from a change in the price, when all other influences on the quantity sold remain the same. (p. 86)

Total surplus The sum of consumer surplus and producer surplus. (p. 110)

Total variable cost The cost of all the firm's variable inputs. (p. 225)

Trade-off An exchange – giving up one thing to get something else. (p. 10)

Trades union An organised group of workers whose purpose is to increase wages and to influence other job conditions. (p. 398)

Tragedy of the commons The absence of incentives to prevent the overuse and depletion of a common resource. (p. 376)

Transactions costs The costs that arise from finding someone with whom to do business, of reaching an agreement about the price and other aspects of the exchange, and of ensuring that the terms of the agreement are fulfilled. The opportunity costs of conducting a transaction. (pp. 113, 210, 372)

Trend The general tendency for a variable to move in one direction. (p. 482)

Tying arrangement An agreement to sell one product only if the buyer agrees to buy another, different product. (p. 335)

UK interest rate differential A gap equal to the UK interest rate minus the foreign interest rate. (p. 593)

Unemployment rate The percentage of the people in the labour force who are unemployed. (p. 486)

Unit elastic demand Demand with a price elasticity of 1; the percentage change in the quantity demanded equals the percentage change in price. (p. 83)

Utilitarianism A principle that states that we should strive to achieve 'the greatest happiness for the greatest number of people'. (p. 114)

Value of marginal product The value to the firm of hiring one more unit of a factor of production. (p. 391)

Velocity of circulation The average number of times a pound (or euro) of money is used annually to buy the goods and services that make up GDP. (p. 576)

Voucher A token that the government provides to households, which they can use to buy specified goods and services. (p. 357)

Wages The income that labour earns. (p. 4)

Wealth The market value of all the things that people own. (pp. 418, 534)

Workforce The sum of the people who are employed and who are unemployed. (p. 485)

Working-age population The total number of people aged 16 to 64 who are not in prison, hospital or some other form of institutional care. (p. 485)

World Trade Organisation (WTO) An international body established by the world's major trading nations for the purpose of supervising international trade and lowering the barriers to trade. (p. 161)

Index

Note: key terms and pages on which they are defined appear in **bold**.

Publisher's Acknowledgements

We are grateful to the following for permission to reproduce copyright material:

Cartoons

Cartoon on page 2 from © Frank Modell/The New Yorker Collection/www.cartoonbank.com; Cartoon on page 111 from © Mike Twohy/The New Yorker Collection/www.cartoonbank.com; Cartoon on page 180 from © Robert Weber/The New Yorker Collection/www.cartoonbank.com; Cartoon on page 289 from *Voodoo Economics*, Chronicle Books (Hamilton, W. 1992) p.3, reprinted with permission from William Hamilton.

Photographs

(Key: b-bottom; c-centre; l-left; r-right; t-top)

1 Alamy Images: Juice Images. 6 Getty Images: Adek Berry/AFP (t). Reuters: STR new (b). 7 Alamy Images: imagebroker (l). Shutterstock.com: Francey (r). 8 Alamy Images: Pictorial Press Ltd (r). Getty Images: Peter Macdiarmid (l). 9 Newscom: Alberto Martin/EFE Photos. 31 Alamy Images: David R. Frazier Photolibrary, Inc. (l). Getty Images: Si Barber/Bloomberg via Getty Images (r). 39 Getty Images: Matthew Lloyd. 53 Alamy Images: Jim Wileman. 67 Getty Images: Akio Kon/Bloomberg via Getty Images. 69 Getty Images: Alexey Sazonov/AFP. 81 Alamy Images: Pete Titmuss. 103 Domino's Pizza Group UK: (l). Shutterstock.com: Lisa F. Young (r). 117 Corbis: Luke MacGregor/Reuters. 119 Getty Images: Munshi Ahmed/

Bloomberg via Getty Images. 125 Alamy Images: Patricia Phillips. 149 Alamy Images: Caro. 160 Reuters: Pillar Lee. 164 Alamy Images: Joerg Boethling. 173 Alamy Images: Mar Photographics. 182 Alamy Images: Keith Morris. 195 Alamy Images: Magictorch. 202 Shutterstock.com: Andrey_Popov. 205 Alamy Images: Philip Quirk (tl); Kevin Britland (br); David Pearson (bl). Getty Images: Alastair Miller/Bloomberg via Getty Images (tr). 211 Alamy Images: Oliver Leedham. 219 Alamy Images: Jim West. 229 Alamy Images: Kumar Sriskandan (tl); British Retail Photography (tr). 235 Alamy Images: vario images GmbH & Co. KG. 249 Alamy Images: Cyberstock. 259 Alamy Images: Mark Fagelson. 261 Alamy Images: Imagestate Media Partners Ltd – Impact Photos (r). Fotolia.com: Fotolia/terex (l). 263 Getty Images: UIG via Getty Images. 275 Getty Images: Simon Dawson/Bloomberg via Getty Images. 290 Juien Gong Min: used under Creative Commons Licence Attribution 2.0 Generic http:// creativecommons.org/licenses/by/2.0/deed.en_GB. 301 Alamy Images: Shopping Mall. 319 Alamy Images: chrisstockphoto. 331 © Airbus S.A.S. 2012 – photo by ExM company/A. Doumenjou (t). Copyright © Boeing. All Rights Reserved: (b). 337 Alamy Images: Peter Cavanagh. 345 Alamy Images: pf. 349 Fotolia.com: Mike Shannon. 353 Alamy Images: 67photo. 359 Alamy Images: Justin Kase z12z. 367 Alamy Images: Francisco Martinez. 368 Alamy Images: Caro (r). Getty Images: Mike Hewitt/Getty Images News (l). 375 Alamy Images: david pearson (l). Getty Images:

Patrick Jube (r). 377 Bridgeman Art Library Ltd: A river valley with a swineherd resting under a tree in the foreground, a hamlet beyond (oil on panel), Ryckaert, Marten (1587–1631)/Private Collection/Photo © Christie's Images/The Bridgeman Art Library. 389 Alamy Images: Richard Smith. 397 Shutterstock.com: alphaspirit. 400 Alamy Images: Loop Images Ltd. 415 Alamy Images: Kumar Sriskandan. 439 Getty Images: MyLoupe/UIG via Getty Images. 447 Alamy Images: Big Pants productions. 459 Science Photo Library Ltd: Ria Novosti. 468 Alamy Images: Caro (r); Ace Stock Limited (l). 469 Alamy Images: Juice Images (l); Catchlight Visual (r). 470 Alamy Images: Friedrich Stark (r). Getty Images: Jerome Favre/Bloomberg via Getty Images (l). 483 Alamy Images: Caro. 484 Getty Images: Fox Photos. 505 Getty Images: Alexander Joe/AFP. 518 Press Association Images: AP Photo/Jose Silva Pinto. 519 Science & Society Picture Library: National Railway Museum. 520 Photo Researchers, Inc: Philippe Psaila. 533 Getty Images: Simon Dawson/Bloomberg via Getty Images. 537 Getty Images: Shaun Curry/AFP (b); Peter Macdiarmid/Getty Images News (t). 549 Reuters: Kevin Lamarque. 557 Alamy Images: Mark Richardson. 563 Corbis: Andrew Winning/Reuters (bl). Getty Images: Simon Dawson/Bloomberg via Getty Images (tl); Mark H Milstein/Bloomberg via Getty Images (br). Patrick Minford: (bc). 570 Getty Images: Ramin Talaie/Bloomberg via Getty Images. 587 Alamy Images: IMAGE_/Alamy. 589 Getty Images: Tomohiro Ohsumi/Bloomberg via Getty Images. 613 Getty Images: Jochen Eckel/Bloomberg via

Getty Images. **620 Press Association Images:** Sean Kilpatrick/The Canadian Press (br); Johnny Green/PA Archive (bc); J. Scott Applewhite/AP (tc); Christian Lutz/AP (tr); Charles Dharapak/AP (l). **637 Getty Images:** Chris Ratcliffe/Bloomberg via Getty Images. **667 Alamy Images:** Juice Images. **689 Getty Images:** Lefteris Pitarakis – WPA Pool. **700 Alamy Images:** Gautier Stephane/ Sagaphoto.com (l); Allstar Picture Library (r). **706 Getty Images:** Charles Ommanney/Getty Images News. **709 Getty Images:** Tom Williams/ Roll Call (t). **Robert Barro, Harvard University:** (c). **Patrick Minford:** (b). **717 Alamy Images:** epa european pressphoto agency b.v. **722 Getty Images:** Jason Alden/AFP. **734 Getty Images:** Chris Ratcliffe/Bloomberg via Getty Images (l); Chris Ratcliffe/ Bloomberg via Getty Images(c). **Dr Peter Warburton:** (r).

Cover images: *Front:* **Getty Images**

All other images © Pearson Education

Figures

Figure 22.10 after *These Are the Good Old Days: A Report on US Living Standards*, Federal Reserve Bank of Dallas 1993 Annual Report. Reproduced with permission.

Text

Extract on page 46 adapted from Biofuels and the food that's going up in smoke, *The Telegraph*, 5 October 2012 (Lean, G.), © Geoffrey Lean/ The Daily Telegraph; Extract on page 96 adapted from Minimum alcohol pricing will not deter abuse, *The Telegraph*, 16 December 2012 (Martin, B.), © Ben Martin/The Daily Telegraph; Extract on page 118 adapted from Charge Motorists Per Mile, says IFS, *The Independent*, 15 May 2012 (Morris, N.), Copyright The Independent; Extract on page 188 adapted from Blow for families as Supermarket Own Brand Product Prices 'Rise by Nearly Half', *Telegraph*, 17 December 2012 (Hough,

A.), © Telegraph Media Group Limited 2012; Extract on page 212 adapted from Facebook Launches Real-time Bidding for Advertisers, *Telegraph*, 13 September 2012 (Rushton, K.), © Telegraph Media Group Limited 2012; Extract on page 268 adapted from Because of the iPhone, There is an App for That, by Ryan Kim 29 June 2012, http://gigaom.com/2012/06/29/because-of-the-iphone-there-is-an-app-for-that/. Used with permission of GigaOM.com Copyright © 2013. All rights reserved; Extract on page 294 after EU: Google Antitrust Case Not Affected by US FTC Ruling, *Telegraph*, 4 January 2013 (Warman, M.), © Telegraph Media Group Limited 2013; Extract on page 338 republished with permission of Dow Jones, from Dirty secrets in soap prices by M. Colchester and C. Passariello, *Wall Street Journal*, 9 December 2011, http://online.wsj.com/article/SB10001424052970203413304577086251676539124.html; permission conveyed through Copyright Clearance Center, Inc; Extract on page 360 adapted from US Government spends more on health than the NHS by Edmund Conway, 30 June 2010, http://blogs.telegraph.co.uk/finance/edmundconway/100006775/us-government-spends-more-on-health-than-the-nhs/, © Telegraph Media Group Limited 2010; Extract on page 406 adapted from Salaries 'Rise 10pc' for Scarce Nuclear Clean-up Engineers, *The Telegraph*, 21 April 2013 (Gosden, E.), © Telegraph Media Group Limited 2013; Extract on page 432 after Rise in household wealth masks huge inequalities by Simon Read, *The Independent*, 8 April 2013, Copyright The Independent; Extract on page 452 after Warning over 'grade inflation' as first-class degrees double by Graeme Paton, 12 January 2012, http://www.telegraph.co.uk/education/universityeducation/9011098/Warning-over-grade-inflation-as-first-class-degrees-double.html, © Telegraph Media Group Limited 2012; Extract on page 526 after How to make South Africa's economy roar by Helen Zillie,

27 July 2012, FT.com, http://www.ft.com/cms/s/0/1bc1beec-d67c-11e1-ba60-00144feabdc0.html#axzz2fzzXGOFe, with permission from Democratic Alliance; Extract on page 687 adapted from Inflation should be feared by John H. Cochrane, http://www.nytimes.com/roomfordebate/2012/08/21/should-the-fed-risk-inflation-to-spur-growth/inflation-should-be-feared, 22 August 2012, with permission from John H. Cochrane.

Financial Times

Articles sourced from the Financial Times have been referenced with the FT logo. These articles remain the Copyright of the Financial Times Limited and were originally published between 2011 and 2013. All Rights Reserved. FT and 'Financial Times' are trademarks of The Financial Times Ltd. Pearson Education Ltd. is responsible for providing any adaptation of the original articles:

Extract on page 72 adapted from Bread to cost more dough, *The Financial Times*, 10 September 2012 (Blas, J.); Extract on page 142 adapted from Farm subsidies cropped to a 30-year low, *The Financial Times*, 22 September 2011 (Blas, J); Extract on page 166 after Koreans Question Benefit of EU Trade Deal, FT.com, 12 September 2012 (Mundy, S. and Jung-a, S.), http://www.ft.com/cms/s/5ab8d5f8-fcc0-11e1-9dd2-00144feabdc0,s01=1.html; Extract on page 236 adapted from Jaguar Land Rover to Create 700 Jobs, FT.com, 5 March 2013 (Marsh, P.), http://www.ft.com/cms/s/3e9ae13c-85a4-11e2-9ee3-00144feabdc0,s01=1.html; Extract on page 312 adapted from Samsung unveils challenger to iPhone in smartphone battle, *Financial Times*, 2 May 2012 (Nuttall, C. and Thomas, D); Extract on page 382 adapted from UK businesses warn on emissions tax, FT.com, 31 March 2013 (Clark, P. and Environment Correspondent), http://www.ft.com/cms/s/

852306da-9700-11e2-8950-00144feabdc0,s01=1.html; Extract on page 472 adapted from Squeezed households are happier, says ONS, FT.com, 20 November 2012 (Jones, C. and Allen, K.), http://www.ft.com/cms/s/128fo694-3339-11e2-8e44-00144feabdc0,s01=1.html; Extract on page 498 after Eurozone joblessness stays at record high, FT.com, 2 April 2013 (Fontanella-Khan, J.), http://www.ft.com/cms/s/4do97a56-9b7c-11e2-a820-00144feabdc0,s01=1.html; Extract on page 550 adapted from Europe's SMEs face interest rate squeeze, FT.com, 6 March 2013 (Atkins, R.), http://www.ft.com/cms/s/506e9228-8676-11e2-ad73-00144feabdc0,s01=1.html; Extract on page 578 adapted from All eyes on ECB as markets expect rate cut, FT.com, 2 May 2013 (Steen, M.), http://www.ft.com/cms/s/1e8dde7a-b2ff-11e2-b5a5-00144feabdc0,s01=1.html; Extract on page 606 after Abenomics propels Yen weakness, FT.com, 9 May 2013 (Ross, A., Mackenzie, M. and Soble, J.), http://www.ft.com/cms/s/dbdc8d5c-b8d9-11e2-869f-00144feabdc0,s01=1.html; Extract on page 630 after Eurozone sets bleak record of longest term in recession, FT.com, 15 May 2013 (Steen, M.), http://www.ft.com/cms/s/2c5024d2-bd27-11e2-890a-00144feab7de,s01=1.html; Extract on page 656 adapted from Struggling France Strives to Shake off Economic Gloom, FT.com, 14 May 2013 (Fontanella-Khan, J.), http://www.ft.com/cms/s/2c57c28e-bc76-11e2-9519-00144feab7de, s01=1.html; Extract on page 682 after Has misery peaked?, FT Blogs, 14 February 2012 (Fray, K.), http://blogs.ft.com/ftdata/2012/02/14/has-misery-peaked; Extract on page 710 after Danny Alexander puts flesh on chancellor's spending plans, FT.com, 27 June 2013 (Parker, G. and Political Editor), http://www.ft.com/cms/s/24ee4d5a-df3b-11e2-a9f4-00144feab7de,s01=1.html; Extract on page 736 adapted from What works at the Fed might not be quite right for Britain, FT.com, 3 July 2013 (Giles, C.).

In some instances we have been unable to trace the owners of copyright material, and we would appreciate any information that would enable us to do so.